ADOBE FLASH EXPOSED

TOR LOWRY

ADOBE FLASH EXPOSED

ISBN 1453745130

Foreword

Welcome to the incredible world of Flash! This book is **unlike any other Flash book on the market**! Finally a book that takes you through the steps of creating extraordinary Flash projects **without** writing one line of ActionScript! That's right; you can **unlock the power of Flash** just by using a series of simple steps! In the past decade, I have taught hundreds of students how to unlock the power of Flash **without writing any code.** For instance, did you know you can create a Shooting Game; Hangman game; Drag 'n' Drop game; and a Roulette game that keeps track of your winnings and many other sophisticated projects — all without writing any ActionScript?

If you are like the majority of Flash users who can't wrap their brains around ActionScript (*especially the new ActionScript 3.0*), then this is the **best book you will ever own!** By the time you finish this book you will be able to create incredible Flash files you never thought were possible! Even if you are in the process of learning ActionScript, you **MUST KNOW** the valuable lessons contained in this book. You can literally create dynamic games and projects in a quarter of the time it takes to write code. And when it comes to working with clients — **TIME IS MONEY**!

In ten years of working with Flash, I have never turned away a Flash project because it was too *"difficult"* or because *"there wasn't enough time."* In my mind I can create anything; and **FAST!** You can create high quality Flash files in record time that will **really impress** your clients! That's what I'm known for and that's what this book will do for you! Just one Flash project will more than pay for this book.

Here is a typical example. I created an interactive psychic game for a popular psychic website that allows the user to predict cards and even measures the user's psychic ability at the end of the game. The game became a user favorite on this website and to say the client was happy is an understatement. Here's the kicker: This is a game that only took a few hours to create! Even if you are skilled in ActionScript, this game would take up to five days of writing code. Then you have to debug the code which could take several more hours! And if there is a problem with the Flash file, you have to start digging through hundreds of lines of ActionScript to find the error! Using my technique you will literally save hundreds of hours! The name of the game is finishing the project and moving on to the next one! Oh, and one more thing: my method works with **ALL** versions of Flash (from Flash 4 to Flash CS4/CS5)!

Here is another example. A client wanted a roulette game that allows users to put dollar chips on symbols, a roulette wheel that randomly stops on symbols, and a counter that tallies the user's money total. And here's the best part: the Flash designer they had hired previously needed two weeks to write the ActionScript. I told the client I could have the same game ready by the **next day**; and it was! Even more exciting is that it was better than they had ever imagined! Their previous Flash designer called me soon after and asked what version of ActionScript I used. When I told him that I don't write any code at all, he did not believe me! When I explained my technique, he was **first in line to order** my book!

In ten years of working in Flash, my clients have ranged from movie studios all the way to famous sculptors and TV Reality stars. I create simple to complex Flash files every week and they all have the same thing in common: **They're above and beyond what the client is expecting.** When you work fast you can afford to give the clients a little extra; that's what keeps them coming back, and what makes them refer you to others! Providing the files quickly is an extra bonus for **every** client! The bottom line in this business is profit based on speed and quality.

So you can either spend months, or even years, learning ActionScript 3.0 or you can read this book and jumpstart your Flash career **NOW**! I am **positive** you will be creating **interactive**, **dynamic projects** by the time you finish this book! So even if you are learning ActionScript, take a couple days and go through this book; that way you'll be taking Flash jobs while you're learning ActionScript! **How cool is that?**

Like I said; time is money. Don't pass up good paying jobs because *"there isn't enough time."* Begin making $1,000 and more for simple projects such as my Roulette Game **NOW!** You paid a lot of money for your Flash program - now put it to work the **FAST**, **EASY** way!!

T. R. Lowry

CONTENTS

Chapter One: Flash Introduction

Chapter Two: Buttons & Movie clips

Chapter Three: Scenes & Labels

Chapter Four: Load Movie

Chapter Five: **Odds 'n Ends**

Chapter Six: **Flash Projects**

Chapter Seven: Publish Movies

Chapter Eight: Flash Code Diagram

Chapter Nine: Quick Banner

Chapter One:
Flash Introduction

FLASH INTERFACE:

If you are new to Flash you'll need to familiarize yourself with the Flash layout. As with all software programs (especially Adobe programs) they tend to be overburdened with all sorts of tools, panels and other goodies you'll rarely use. Since my goal is to get you up and running as quickly as possible, I'm going to focus on those panels and tools you'll use **most often** in your Flash projects. All Flash files are available at **www.adobe-flash-tutorials.info/chapters.htm**.

Open up Flash and you'll see this window:

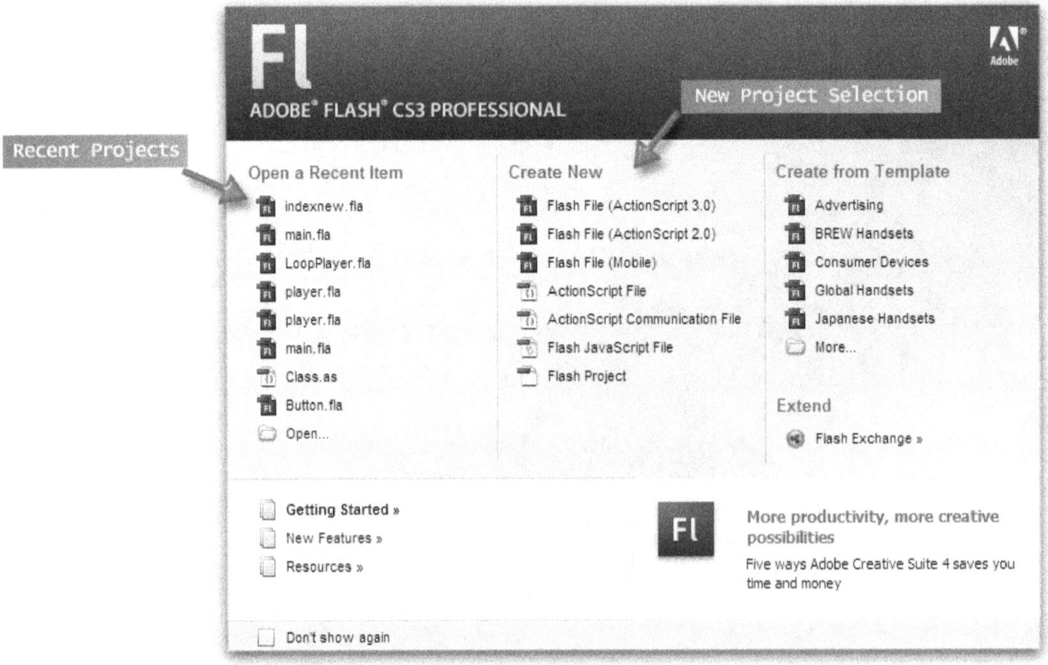

Note: I've updated this book to reflect any changes that have been implemented by CS4/CS5/CS5.

When you first open up Flash CS3/CS4/CS5/CS5 you will see this screen. On the left you will see any recent projects that you have been working on. The last project I was working on was **indexnew.fla**. The file before that was **main.fla**. And so on. In the middle are the selections you can choose from for starting your new Flash file. On newer versions of Flash it will ask you if you want to open up **Flash File (ActionScript 3.0)** or **Flash file (ActionScript 2.0)**. If you are learning ActionScript then you'll need to select **Flash File (ActionScript 3.0)**.

Since we're not writing code select **Flash File (ActionScript 2.0)**:

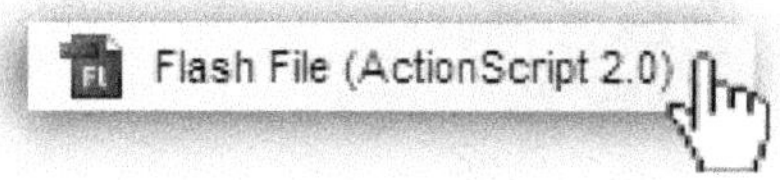

If you are working on an earlier version of Flash you won't see the selection for **Flash file (ActionScript 3.0)**. You will want to click the selection called **Flash Document**.

Flash has upgraded its programming language from ActionScript 2.0 to ActionScript 3.0. Creating Flash files in version 3.0 means they will only work with the latest Flash plugins. Selecting version 2.0 means your projects will be backward compatible to Flash player 6.

The next screen you will see is the Flash Interface:

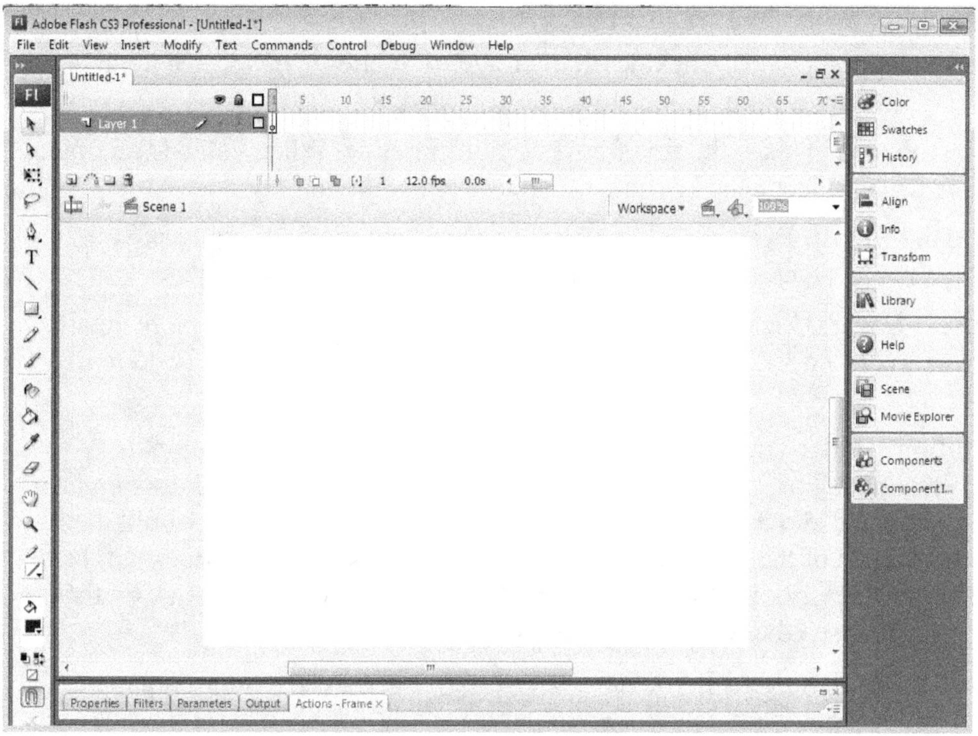

You'll notice several things. First, there is a timeline at the top of the screen. This is where you'll be doing all of your animating:

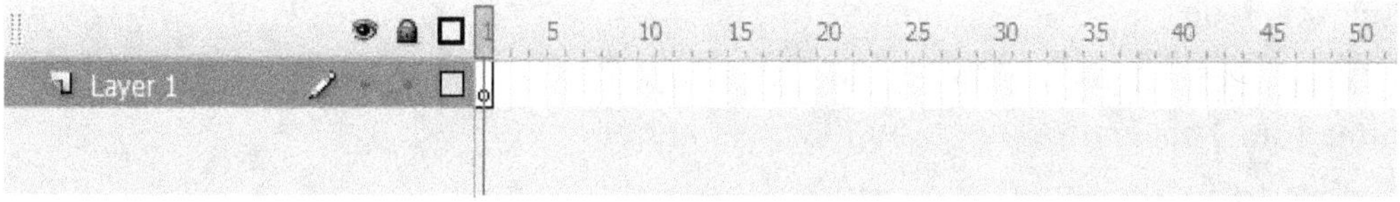

If you examine the Timeline closer you'll notice several interesting icons:

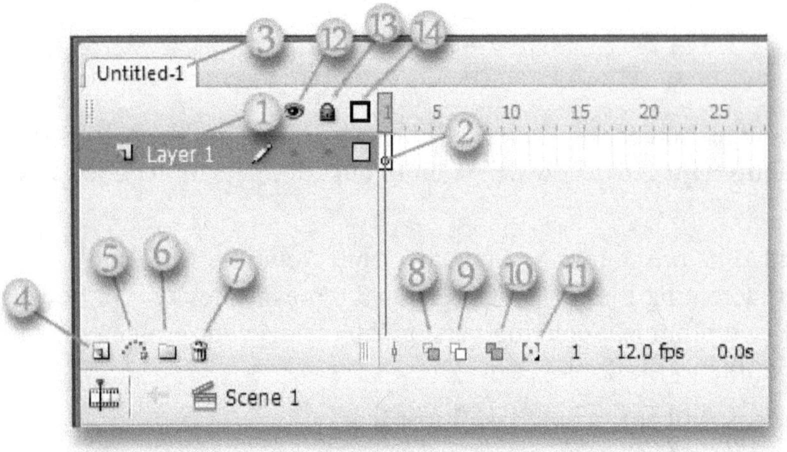

1. Layer Name. Double-clicking on the Layer will allow you to give it a unique name. It's always a good idea to name your layers.

2. First Frame. This is the first frame of your timeline. When you add an object to your flash project the keyframe will go from white to grey.

3. Name of Flash Project. When you save your new project it will ask you to give it a name. Once you do that name is reflected on the timeline.

4. Insert Layer. Clicking this icon will add a layer. We'll get into more detail later on layers but I usually create a new layer for every object I add to my project.

5. Motion Guide. The Motion Guide is used if you have an animation that involves a path. For instance, if you want a ball to animate in a figure eight then you would add a Motion Guide to the ball's layer. The ball would then follow the path of the Motion Guide. **Note:** Flash CS4/CS5/CS5 does not have an icon for the Motion Guide (**5**). In CS4/CS5/CS5 you can right-click on the layer and choose **Classic Motion Guide**.

6. Insert Layer Folder. If you have several layers and you want to organize them, you can put them into a folder. I usually do this when I have several layers that are part of the same animation. You'll be using this option quite a bit.

7. Garbage Can. If you no longer need a layer you can simply highlight it and click this icon.

8. Onion Skin. This enables you to simultaneously see multiple frames of animation. This is used by Flash animators.

9. Onion Skin Outlines. This allows you to see the Onion-skinned frames as outlines.

10. Edit Multiple Frames. This allows you to edit several layers at one time. We'll be examining this option later in an exercise.

11. Modify Onion Markers. When you're dealing with Onion-skinned frames 2 markers will indicate beginning and end of the sequence. This allows you to modify that

12. Layer Eye. Anyone familiar with Photoshop will recognize this icon. It's the ubiquitous eye. Click this icon will render the highlighted layer invisible. This is great if you're working on a layer and you have several other layers that are getting in your way; you can simply click their Eye icon and they'll be invisible. Although when you text and publish your movie they'll become visible once again.

13. Layer Lock. Click this if you don't a layer's object moved, or if you don't want elements accidentally dropped into a certain layer.

14. Show All Layers as Outlines. This is great if you don't need to see certain objects, but you need to see their outlines for positioning other elements. You'll be using this option quite a bit.

The next part of the interface we'll discuss is the **Toolbar**. Note: **Flash CS4/CS5/CS5** has added new Tools: **3D Rotation Tool**, **Deco Tool** and the **Bone Tool**:

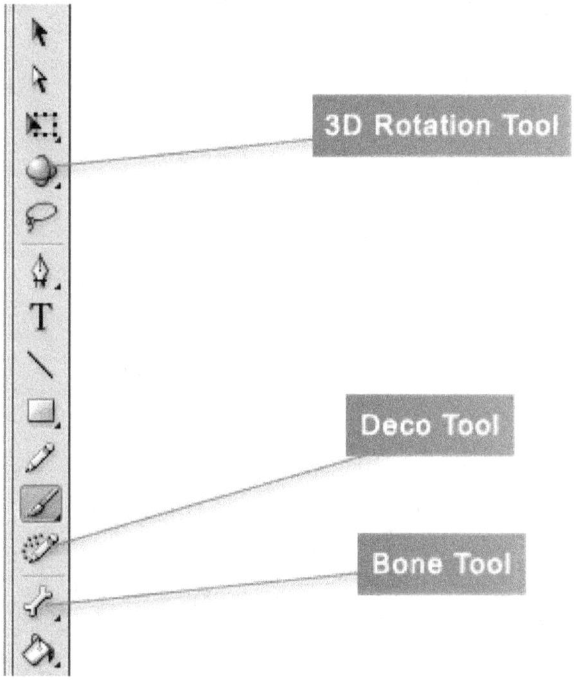

FLASH CS4/CS5/CS5:

Deco Tool: This tool is used for spraying a pattern across the stage like vines or flowers. You can even create your own images to create patterns.

Bone Tool: The bone tool creates human like movement by creating hinges within objects.

3D Rotation Tool: This tool allows you to rotate a Movie clip in a 3D space.

Users of earlier versions of Flash will see the more common **Toolbar** as pictured here:

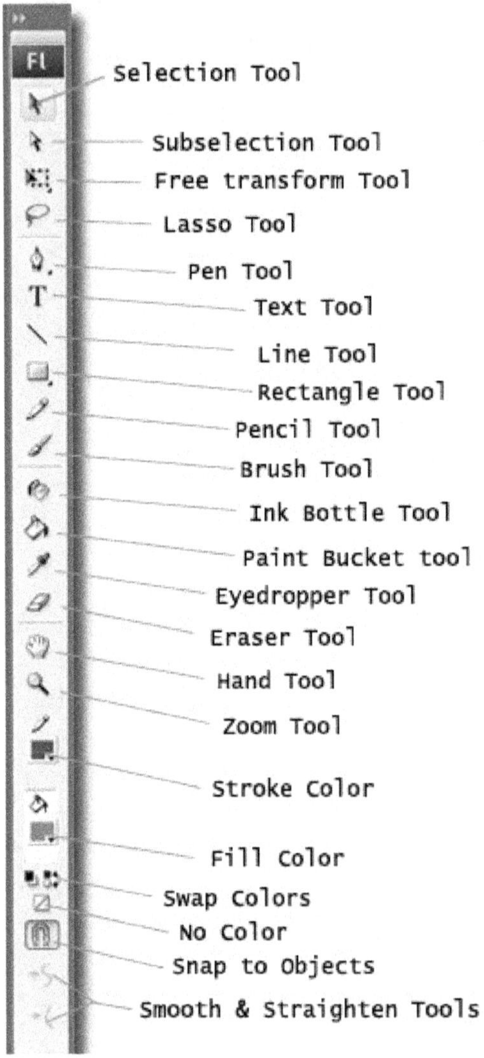

Selection Tool. This is the tool you'll be using the most. This tool is mainly used for selecting and moving objects.

Subselection Tool. This tool is used mainly to manipulate points of a path.

Free Transform Tool. This Tool is used for changing the dimensions of an object.

Lasso Tool. The Lasso tool is mainly used for selecting areas.

Pen Tool. The pen tool is used for creating complex paths.

Text Tool. Just as you might expect, the Text Tool adds text to your Flash project.

Line Tool. A tool that creates a vector line that can have color applied to it.

Rectangle Tool. Creates a rectangle or square.

Pencil Tool. Works in conjunction with the Smooth & Straighten Tools. Used mainly for drawing organic shapes.

Brush Tool. A tool that draws strokes as if you were painting. When selected, you will receive two options on the bottom of the tool bar for size and shape of brush.

Ink Bottle Tool. Applies strokes to shapes.

Paint Bucket Tool. Fills shapes with a specified color.

Eyedropper Tool. This tool is used for sampling a color.

Eraser Tool. Just as you would assume, this tool will erase shapes.

Hand Tool. When selected you can grab the canvas and move it around.

Zoom Tool. Just as the name suggests, clicking on this allows you to zoom in and out of your project.

Stroke color. This is the color selector for your stroke.

Fill color. This is the color selector for the brush and paint bucket tools, along with other tools.

Swap Color. Clicking this swaps the colors between the Stroke and Fill. Clicking the little icon to the left of **Swap Color** resets the **Stroke color** and **Fill color** to the default black and white.

No Color. Clicking this means that no color will be added.

Snap to Objects. Selecting this will allow your objects to snap together when close together allowing for easier alignment.

Smooth & Straighten Tools. These tools are used to smooth and straighten lines.

In the next section we'll be going through the tools as we create the first project. All of the files can be found at www.adobe-flash-tutorials.info/chapters.htm.

As you start working in Flash you'll want to arrange your workspace so that's easier to work. On the right of the Interface you'll notice several panel shortcuts:

Click on the **Expand Dock** button at the top of the panels:

Your panels should now be expanded:

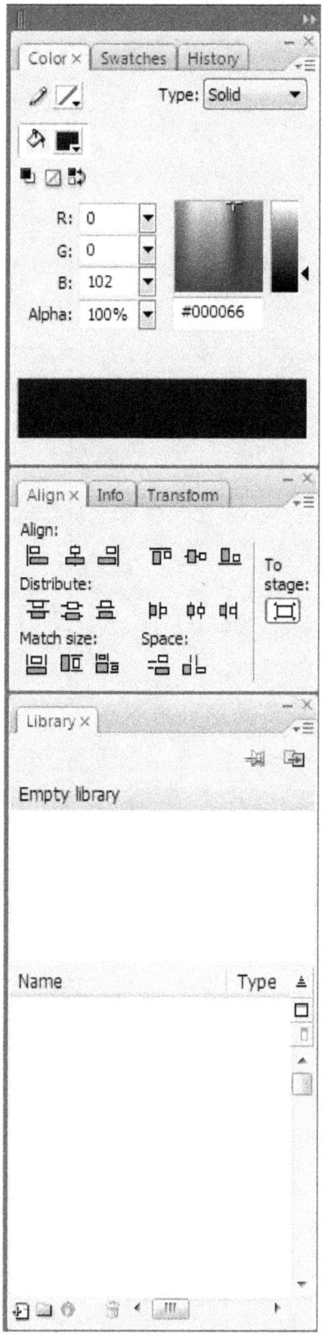

You can rearrange the panels any way you would like. It's entirely up to you. To move a panel you simple click-and-hold on the name of the panel:

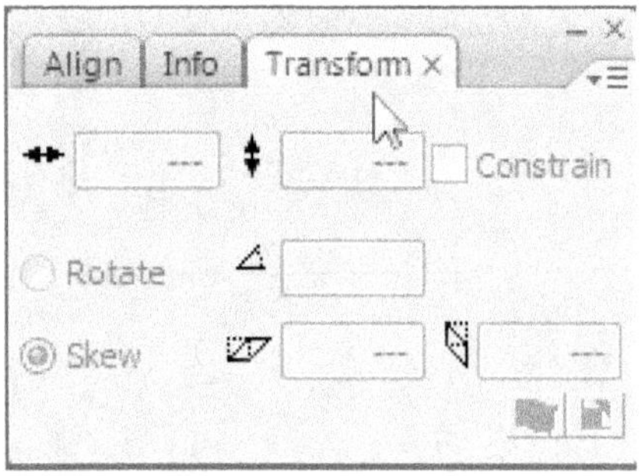

Then you can drag it wherever you like:

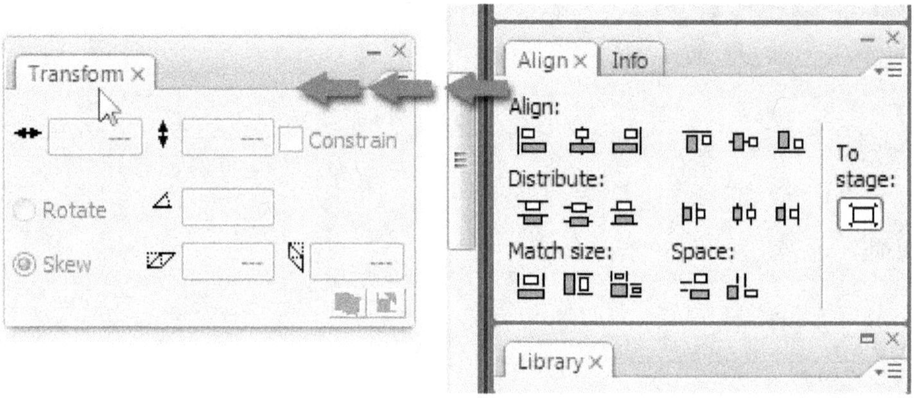

You can even add the panel to another set of panels:

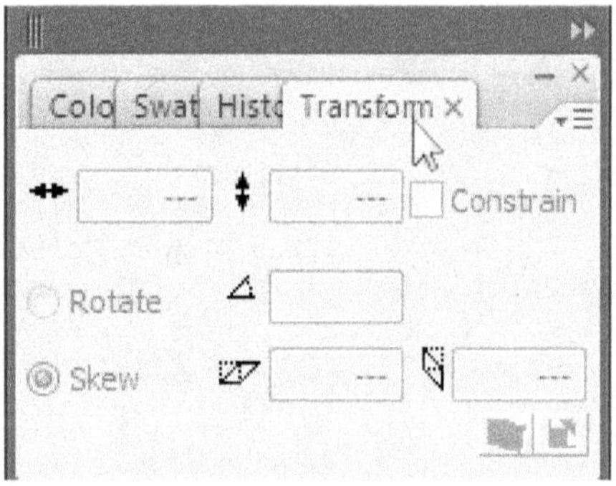

To close the panels simply click the **Collapse to Icons** button:

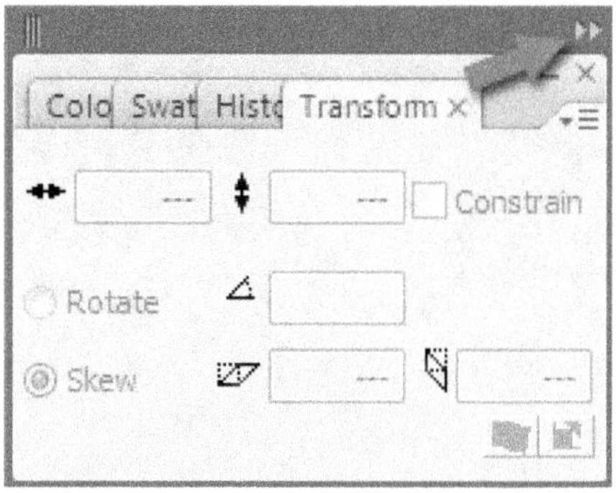

Flash also allows you to save your customized workspace. Once you become familiar with Flash it's a good idea to arrange the workspace so only the panels you use most often are visible. You can save this custom workspace by clicking on the Workspace button:

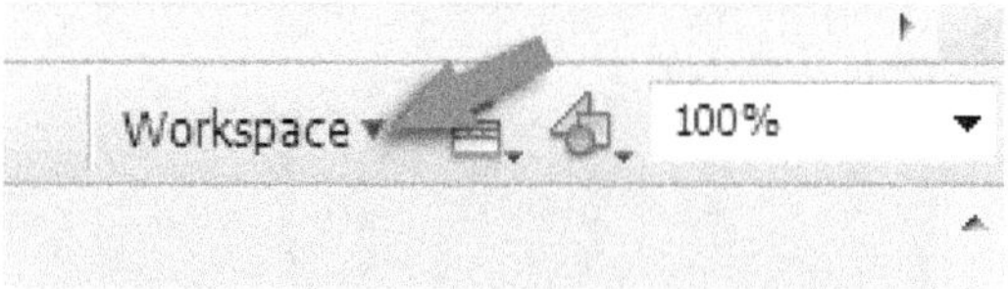

Then select **Save Current**. Name this new layout. Of course, the best way to learn is by creating a project. This next exercise will incorporate tools and panels so you have a better idea of how to use them.

Simple Animations

Open up the file called **SimpleAnimations.fla**. This file can be found in the Chapter One folder at www. adobe-flash-tutorials.info /chapters.htm. Click on the button called **Chapter One** and you'll be asked to download a file named **chapterone.zip**. We'll be creating a simple animation project which uses many of the panels and tools. The first thing we want to do is select the **Rectangle Tool** in the **Toolbar**:

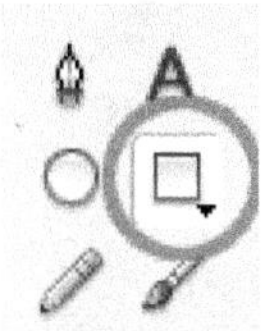

Next, we'll create a color for the rectangle shape. We do this by clicking on the **Fill color** icon near the bottom of the **Toolbar**. A color palette will open. Select the color **red**:

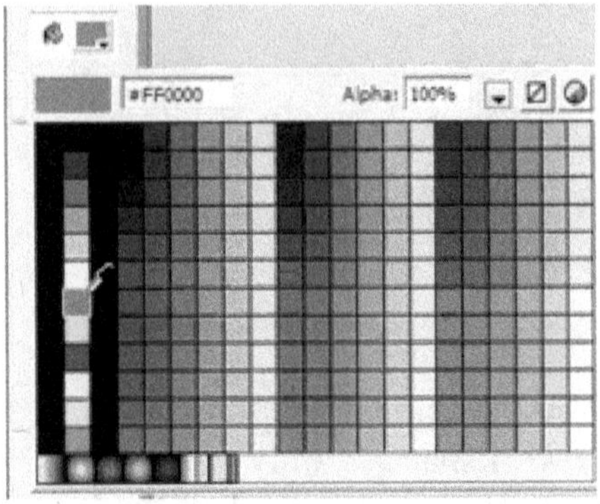

Notice that the **Stroke color** box has a line through it:

This means that we won't be adding a stroke color to the shape yet (a stroke creates a colored line that surrounds the shape). Next, we'll draw a small square on the canvas. We do this by clicking and dragging the **Rectangle Tool** on the stage. Hold down **SHIFT** to constrain the dimensions:

Once you finish creating the square you'll want to center it in the middle of the canvas. We center objects in Flash using the Align panel.

Before you do this you'll want to select your **Selection Tool** in the **Toolbar**:

Next, click on the square:

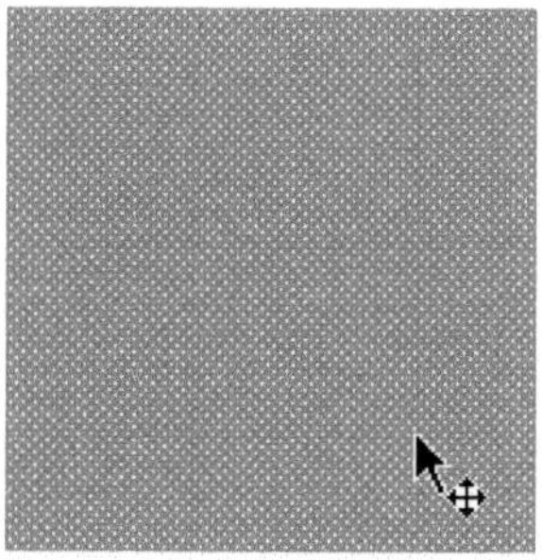

Notice how the box changes into a series of dots? This lets you know the shape is selected. Now that your square is selected we'll put it dead center in the canvas. We do this by finding your **Align** panel shortcut and clicking it once (If you don't see the **Align** panel go to **Window** then select **Align**):

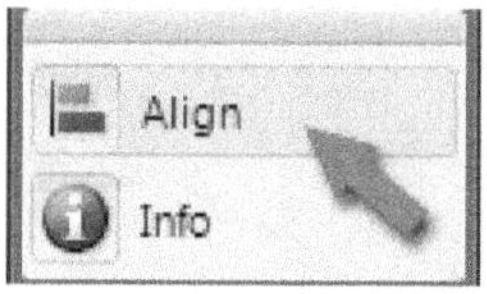

When the Align panel opens, click the **Stage Align** button. This tells Flash that you want the shape aligned in the canvas as opposed to being aligned with other objects. Next click on the **Align Vertical Center**, and then the **Align Horizontal Center** button:

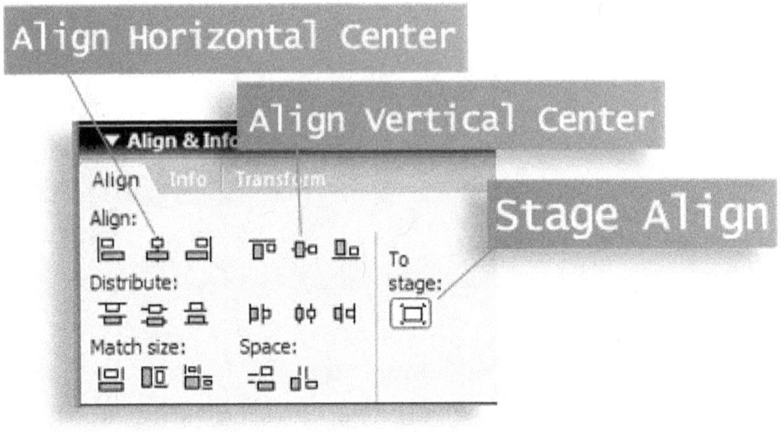

You should now see your square centered in your canvas:

Next, we'll change the color of the square to blue. De-select your square by clicking anywhere on the white around the square. The tiny dots will go away. Go to your **Color Swatches** panel and select **blue** (if you don't see the **Color Swatches** panel go to **Window, Swatches**):

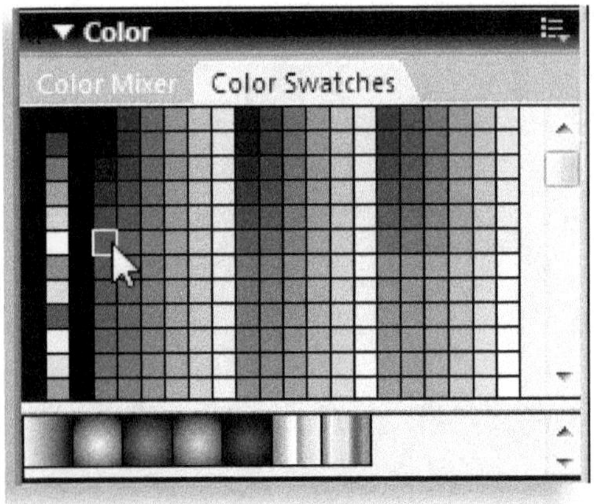

Click on the **Paint Bucket Tool**:

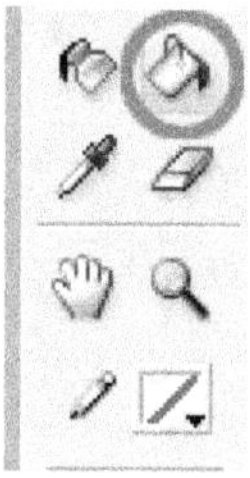

Using the **Paint Bucket Tool** click anywhere in the square to change its color to **blue**:

We're now going to add a stroke color to the square. Select your **Ink Bottle Tool**:

CS4/CS5/CS5 users - The **Ink Bottle Tool** is a sub-selection of the **Paint Bucket Tool**.

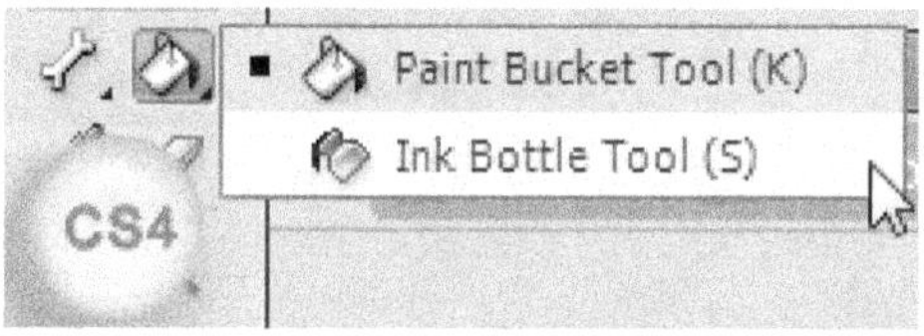

Next, we'll add a color to the stroke. Select **Stroke color** and choose the color **red**:

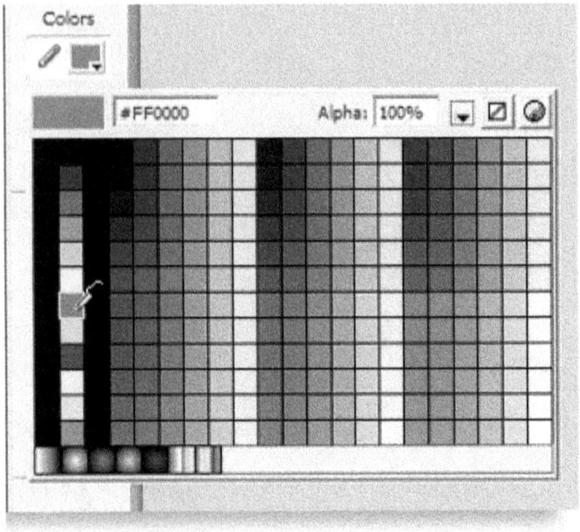

The next attribute we'll change is the size of the stroke. At the bottom of the Flash window you'll see the stroke settings in the **Properties** panel:

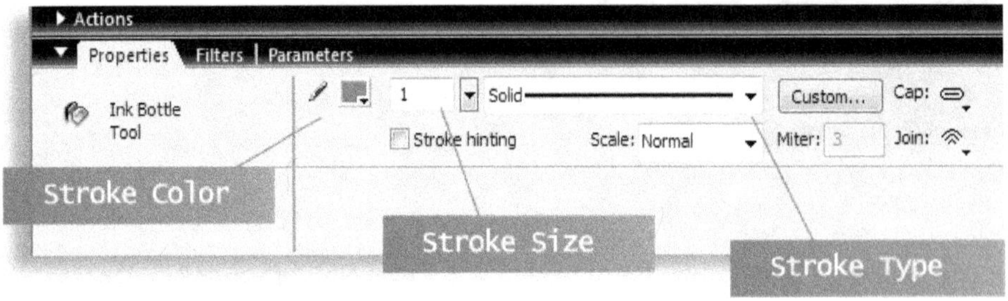

Note: In **CS4/CS5/CS5** the Properties and Stroke panels may look slightly different than previous versions:

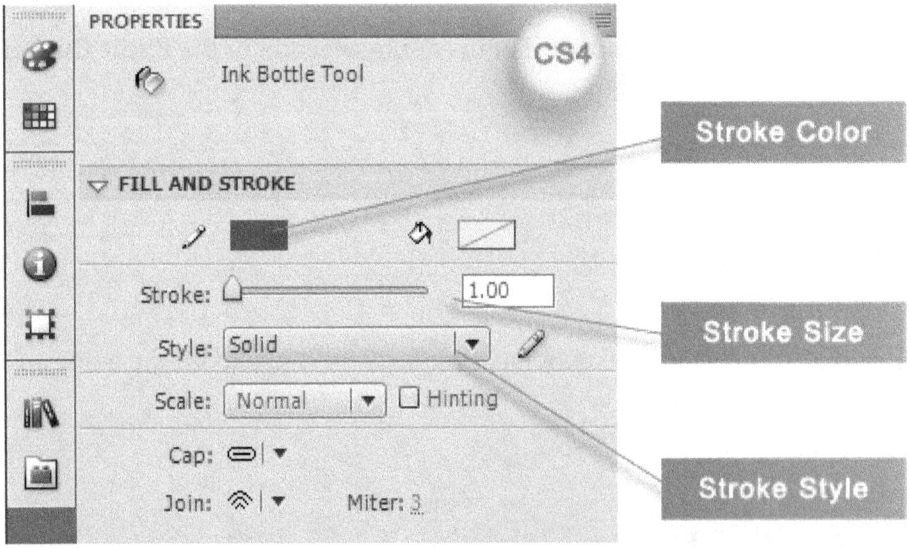

Click on the **Stroke color** icon and change the color to **red**. The **Stroke Size** controls the size of the stroke line that surrounds your shape. The **Style Selector** has several options including **Solid**, **Ragged**, and **Dotted** as well as a few others. Keep this setting at **Solid** for now.

Remember! If you don't see the panel you're looking for, click on the Window button. You'll see a list of all the panels.

You'll see several settings in the **Properties** panel. The only settings we'll worry about now are **Stroke color**, **Stroke Size** and **Stroke Type** (**CS4/CS5/CS5 - Style**). The **Stroke color** is red, since we selected that earlier. The **Stroke Size** is at **1**, but you can increase or decrease this number. Let's increase this number to **2**. The stroke type is set at **Solid**; if you click in this window you'll see several selections to choose from; for now, however, **Solid** is fine. Click on the square with your **Ink Bottle Tool** and you should now see a red stroke surrounding the square:

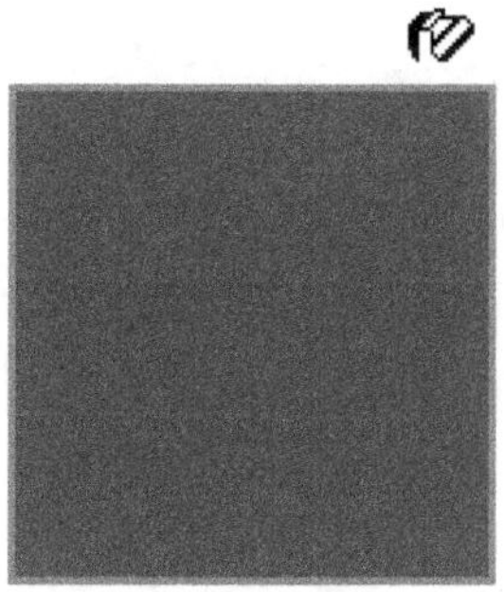

Let's make the square a little bit bigger. We'll do this by using the **Free Transform Tool**. Before we can enlarge the square, though, we need to select it. Click once on your blue square:

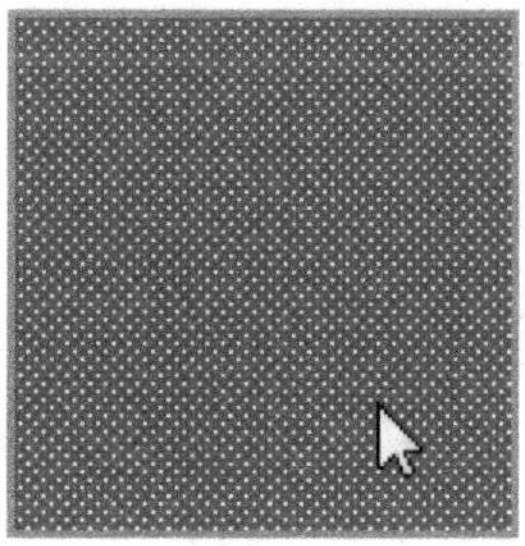

You'll notice that the blue square is highlighted (the blue square is now made up of many dots). But we also have to select the stroke (the stroke is seen as a separate element by Flash).

Double-click on the square and now the stroke is also selected:

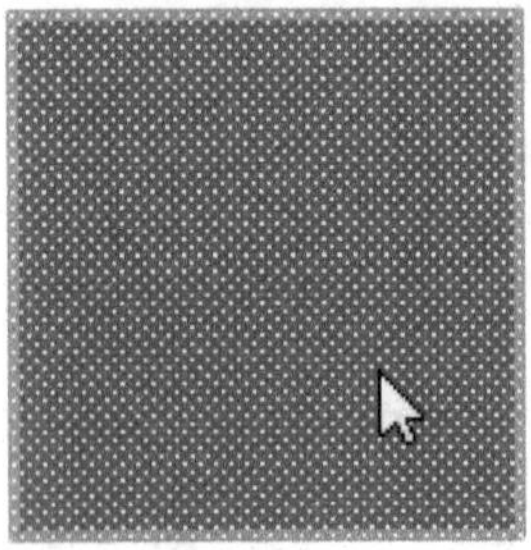

Next, select the **Free Transform Tool**:

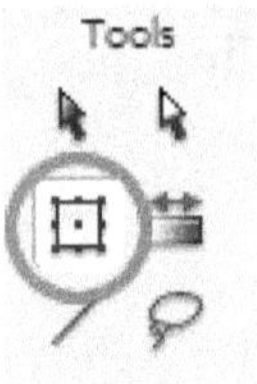

Once you click on the **Free Transform Tool** the square will look like this:

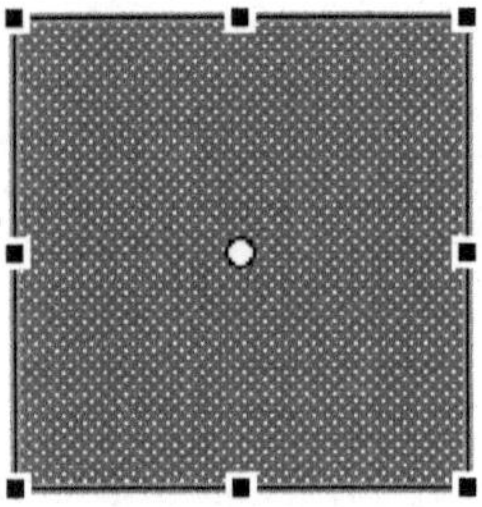

Put your cursor over one of the corner transform boxes that surround your blue square. The cursor will then change to a double arrow:

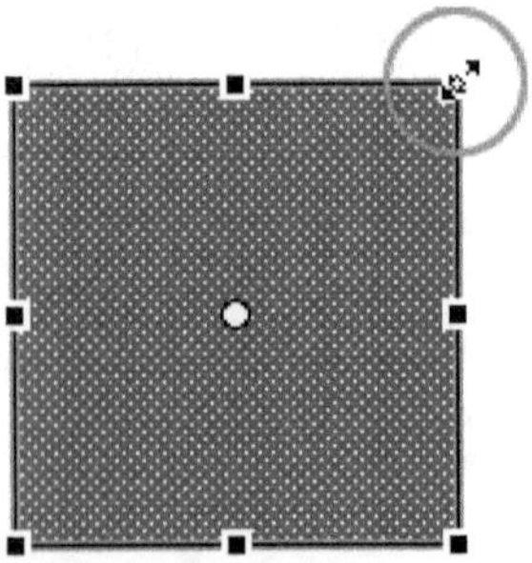

Click-and-drag this corner upward to increase the square's size. We want to keep the shape as a square so make sure you hold down the SHIFT key while dragging. Increase the square by about 10%.

Now we're going to erase part of the blue square. We'll do this by selecting the **Eraser Tool**:

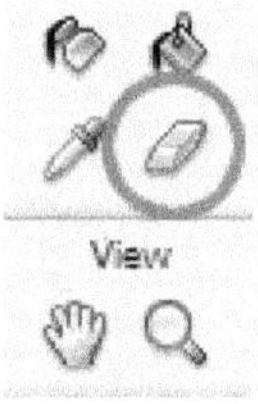

Once you have the **Eraser Tool** selected, you'll see the **Eraser Tool** options at the bottom of the **Toolbar**. These options allow you to choose the shape and size of the **Eraser Tool**. Choose the third round brush from the top:

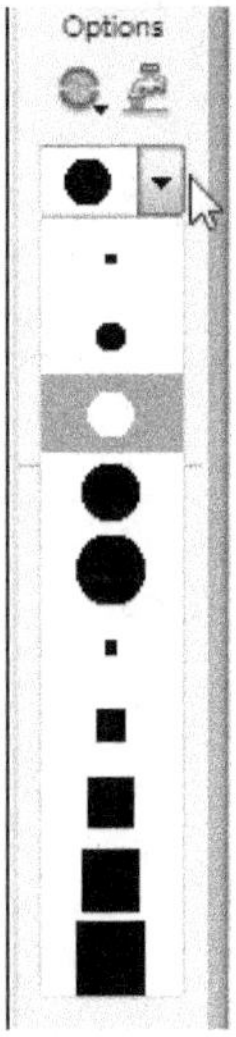

Next, we'll make a hole in the middle of the square with the **Eraser Tool**. Using the **Eraser Tool**, click once in the middle of your square.

You should now see the white background through the hole. Next, we'll use the **Info panel** to get some information regarding the square. Click the **Info** shortcut so you can see the panel:

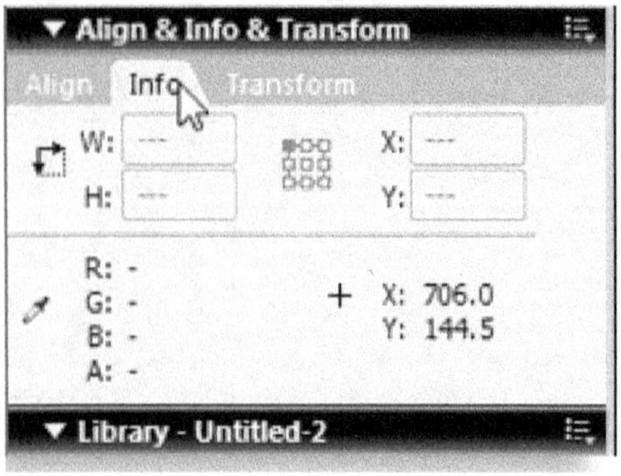

Click once on your square and the **Info** panel will instantly give you information regarding the square; you'll see the width and height of the square along with its coordinates.

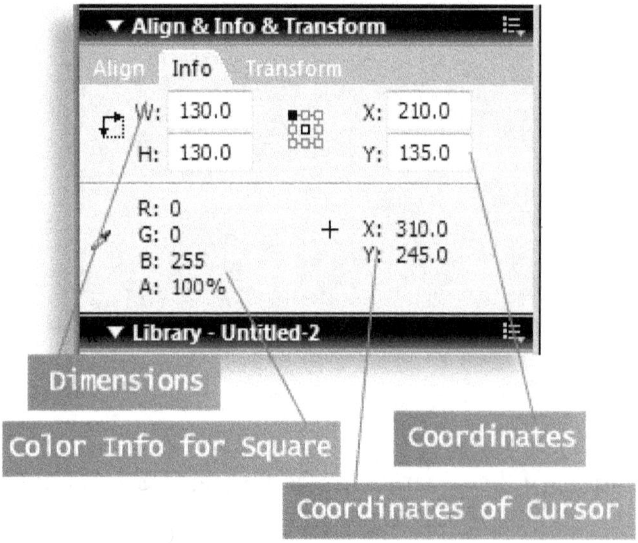

You'll notice that the square I created has a width of 130 pixels. The height is the same 130 pixels. The X coordinate of the square is 210 (X coordinate is basically the square's horizontal or left to right position). The Y coordinate is 135 (Y coordinate is basically the square's vertical or up and down position). The RGB information for the square is Red: 0 (no red color in the square), Green: 0 (no green color in the square), and Blue: 255 (255 is the highest number. That means the square is 100% blue.

If you move your cursor from left to right across the screen you will notice that the cursor's coordinates reflect instantly the position of the cursor. If you place your cursor over the left edge of the Flash canvas (where the white meets the gray), the X coordinate should read 0.

Double-click the square again to select both the square and the stroke. We're going to convert this shape to a symbol. What is a symbol? A symbol is a graphic, button, or Movie clip that we can use over and over again without increasing download time; also, once we convert a shape or picture to a symbol, we can add effects to it. To get a better idea of how this works let's convert this square to a symbol by clicking on **Modify**, then **Convert to Symbol (F8)**:

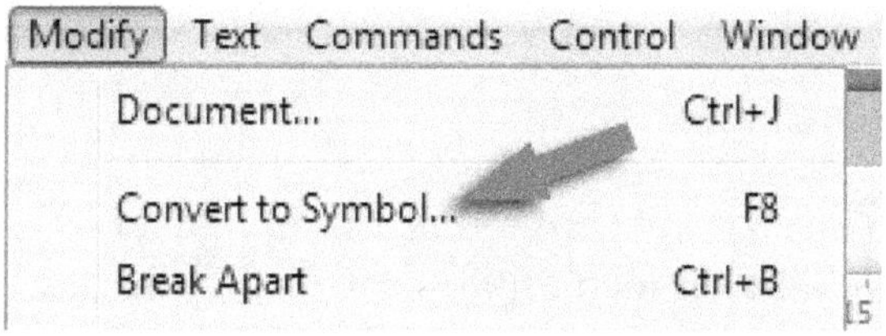

You should now see the **Convert to Symbol** window with these options:

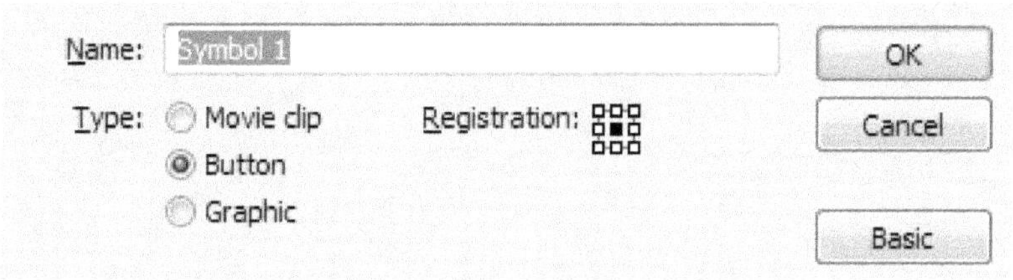

We'll learn more about Buttons and Movie clips later, but for now select **Graphic** and name the symbol **Square**. The **Convert to Symbol** box should now look like this:

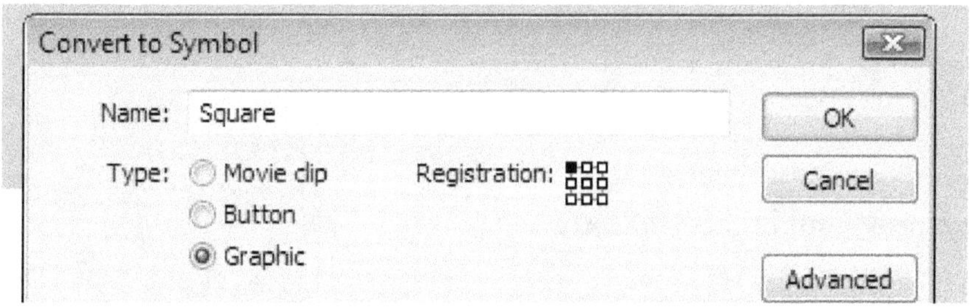

Hit **OK** to close the **Convert to Symbol** window. Your square will no longer have the tiny dots when you select it. In fact, when you select it, the square and the stroke are now one element. If you look in your **Library panel** you'll see this new graphic:

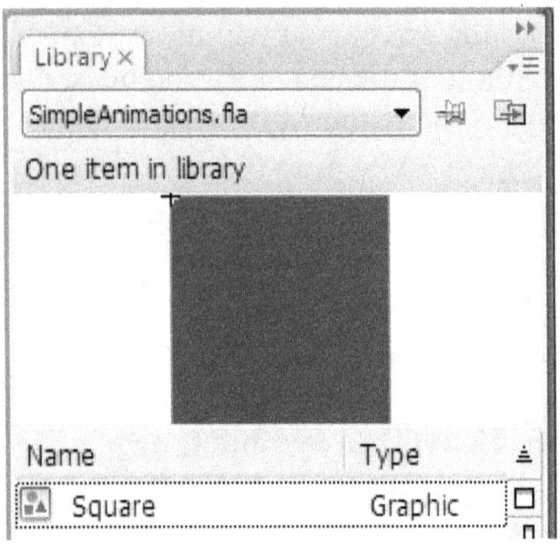

Whenever you create a new symbol you'll see it appear in your Library panel. Let's create the animation and you'll have a better idea of why converting shapes to symbols is important.

Before we begin, let's briefly go over the **Hand Tool** and the **Zoom Tool**. Click on the **Zoom Tool**:

With your **Zoom Tool** selected, keep clicking on your square until the Zoom Percentage window says **400%**:

Next, select the **Hand Tool** in the **Toolbar**:

Using the **Hand Tool**, click anywhere on the stage and move it around. You'll be using this tool quite a bit when working on projects in which you have to zoom in to the stage.

Let's bring the stage back to 100%. You can either select the **Reduce Tool** and click on the stage until it is back where you want it:

Or you can type **100** into the percentage window and hit ENTER:

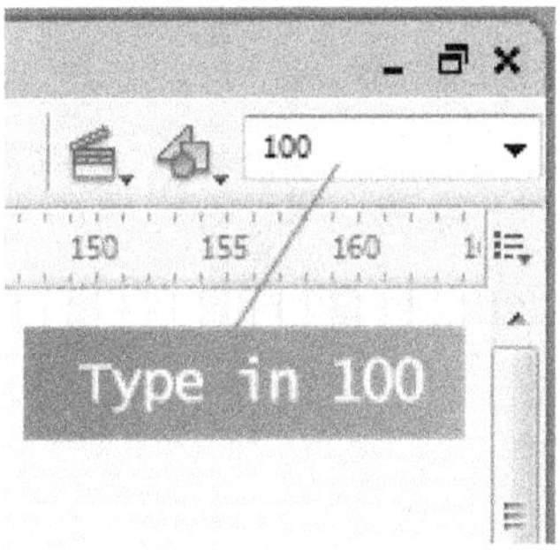

The stage should be back to normal.

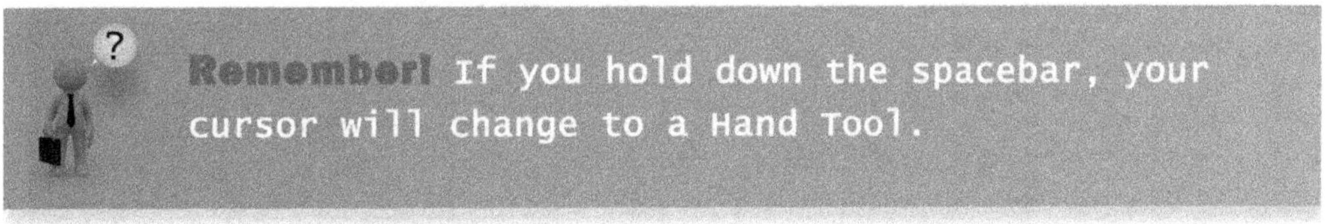
?
Remember! If you hold down the spacebar, your cursor will change to a Hand Tool.

Next, we'll create a simple animation. Go to your timeline and click on frame **30**:

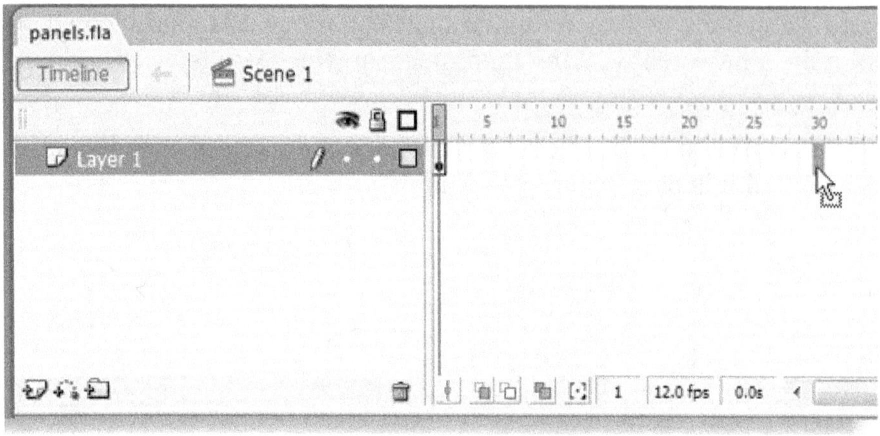

We'll now insert a keyframe. Go to **Insert**, **Timeline**, and **Keyframe**:

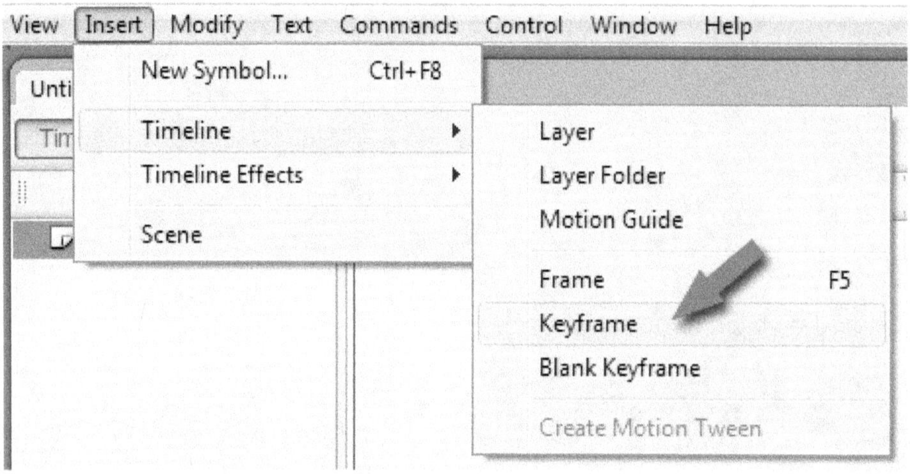

Your timeline should now look like this:

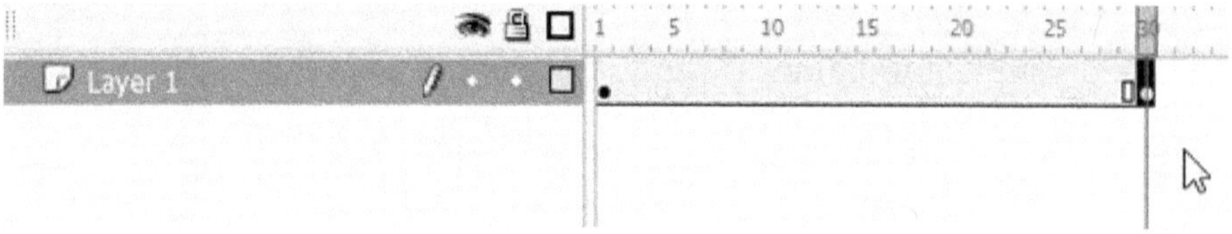

Select the square and move it to the top right of the stage:

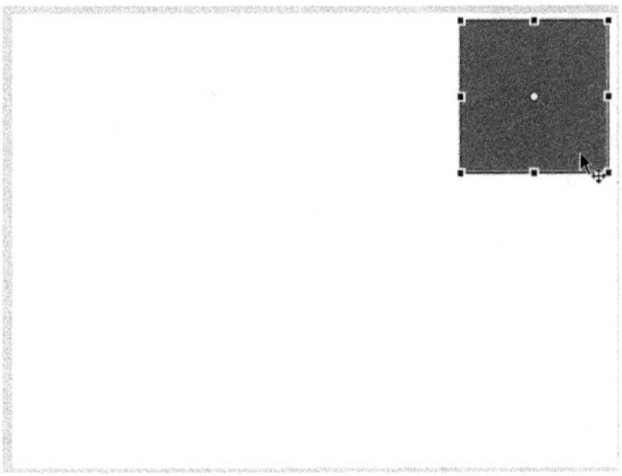

Now for the fun part! Click on any frame between the keyframes:

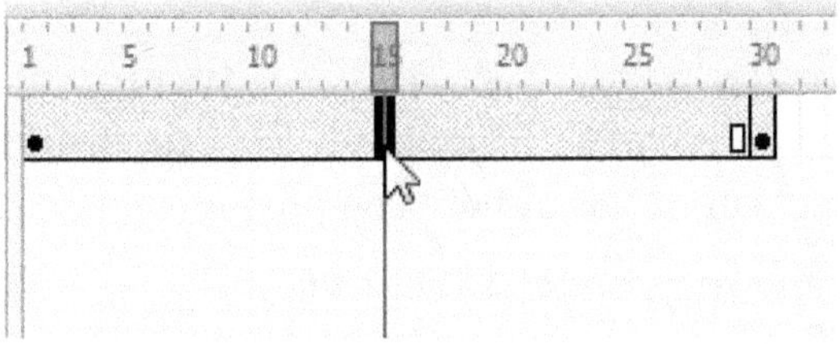

Go to **Insert**, **Timeline**, **Create Motion Tween**:

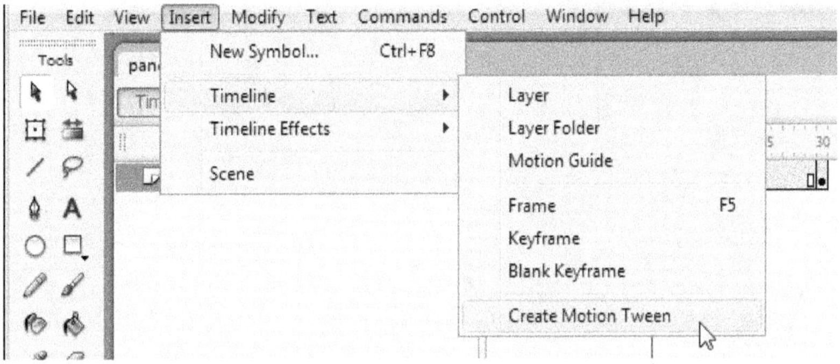

CS4/CS5/CS5 Users: Go to **Insert**, **Classic Tween**:

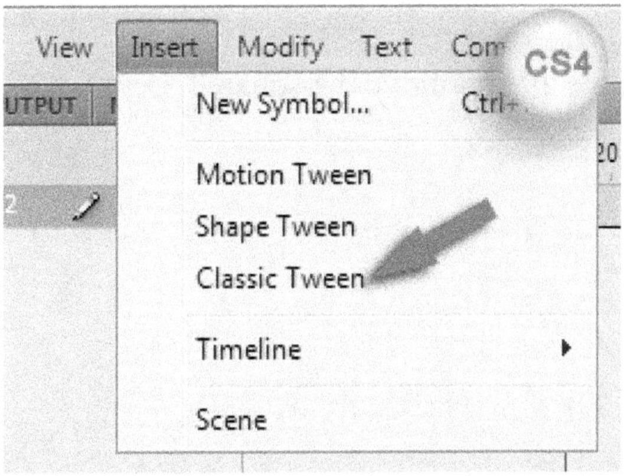

The timeline should now look like this:

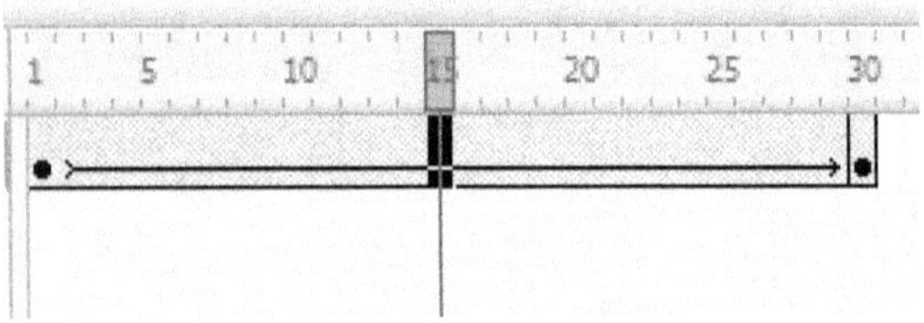

Congratulations! You just created your first animation! To see your animation play, simply hit the ENTER key, or go to **Control**, **Play**. Your square should now travel from the middle of the stage to the top right of the stage.

What is a Motion Tween? Simply put, tween is short for *in between.* If you define the starting and ending positions for your square using keyframes (in the case frame **1** and frame **30**), Flash calculates all of the in-between positions.

As you can tell by looking at the timeline the square travels between the keyframes. For instance, click on frame **30** where the second keyframe is:

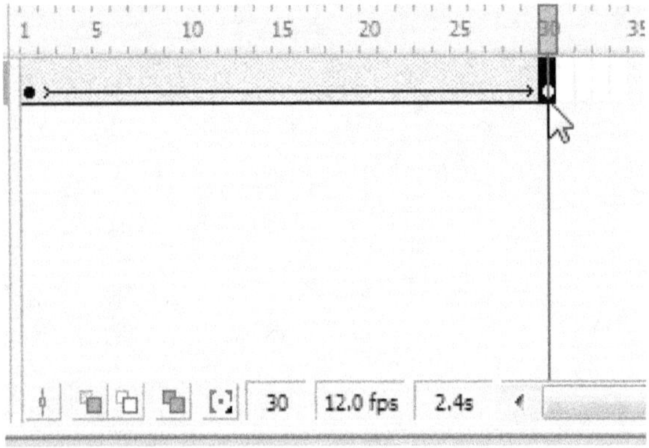

With frame 30 selected, select the square and move it to the top left of the stage. Hit ENTER again and watch as your square animates from the center to the top left of the stage.

Now, what would happen if we select frame **20** and move the square? Let's try it. Click on frame **20**:

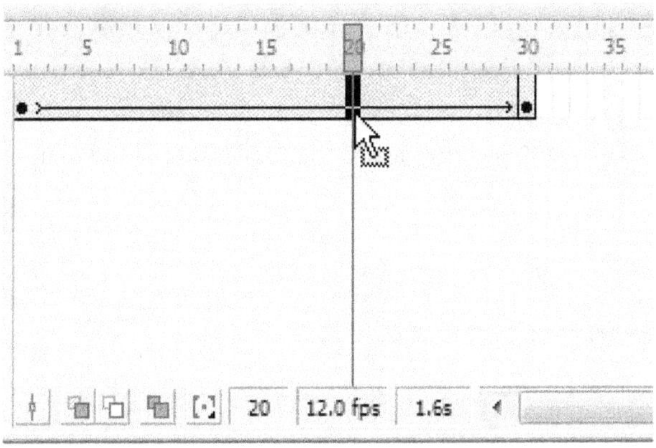

With frame **20** selected, move the square to the bottom left. Hit ENTER and watch as your square goes from the center, to the bottom left, then the top left. You'll notice that when we moved the square to the bottom left a keyframe was automatically inserted at frame 20. Each keyframe represents a destination point. So, by looking at the timeline, we have three destination points. The square starts off in the center, then moves to the bottom left, then travels to the top left.

What if we wanted to create a loop making the animation seamless? First, we'll click on frame **50**:

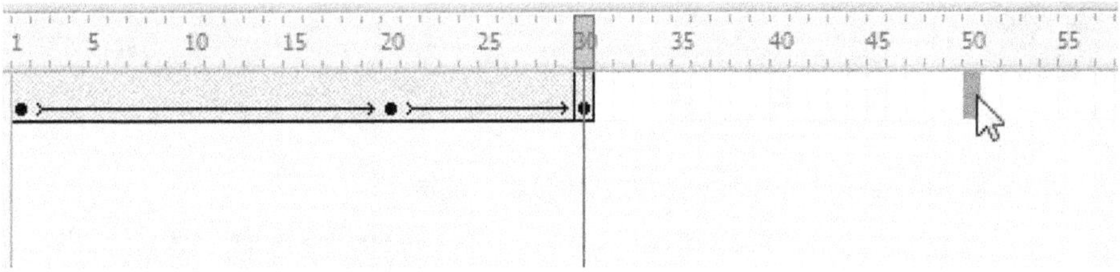

Insert a keyframe on frame 50 (**Insert**, **Timeline**, **Keyframe**). The timeline should now look like this:

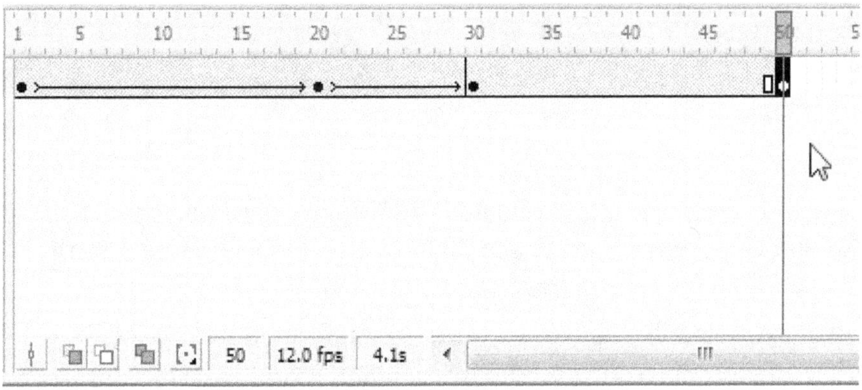

We would like the square to be in the same position on frame **50** as it is in frame **1** (an animation will play until it gets to the final frame then it will go back to frame 1 and repeat). To ensure that the frame **50** square will be in the same position as the square in frame **1** we need them both to have the same coordinates. Select frame **1**:

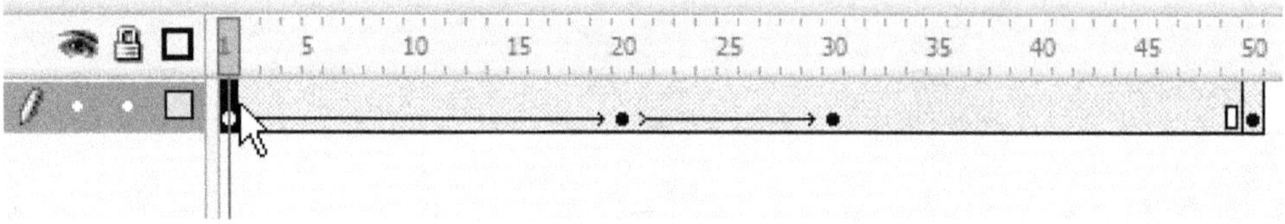

Next, select the square on the stage. You should now see the coordinates in the Properties panel. If you don't see the Properties panel, click on the Properties panel shortcut:

You should now see the coordinates of the square:

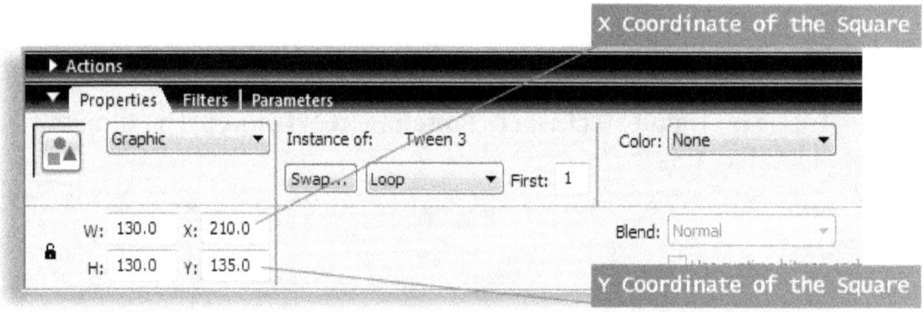

The X coordinate is **210** and the Y coordinate is **135** (your coordinates will differ slightly). We want the coordinates on frame **50** to be the same as frame **1** so the squares will be exactly in the same area.

Select frame **50**. Next, select the square on the stage. You should now see the coordinates of the square. Enter the coordinate numbers from the square on frame **1** into the coordinate fields. Here is what my updated Properties panel looks like after entering the X and Y coordinates:

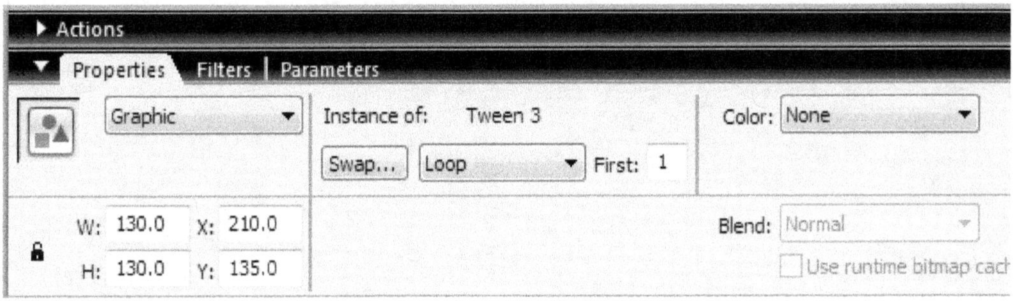

The square on frame **50** will now be in the center of the stage since we added the same coordinates as the square from frame **1**.

Just as we did before, we're going to add a motion tween to frame **50**. We do this the same way we did the previous motion tween. Click on any frame between frame **30** and frame **50**:

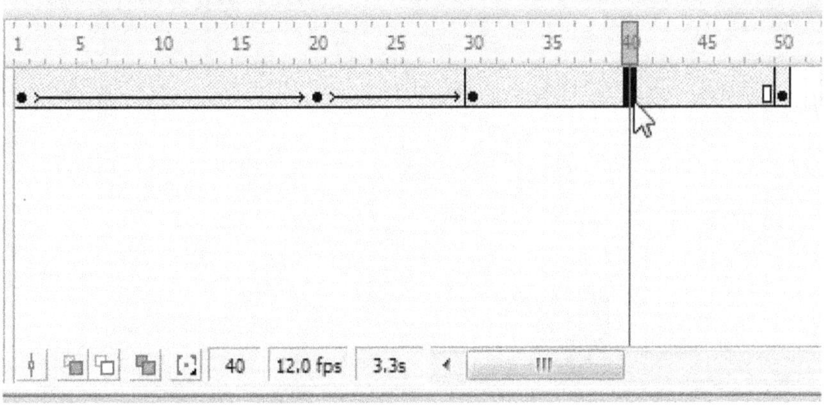

Go to **Insert, Timeline, Create Motion Tween** (**CS4/CS5/CS5 - Insert, Classic Tween**) . You should now see the motion tween between frames **30** and **50**:

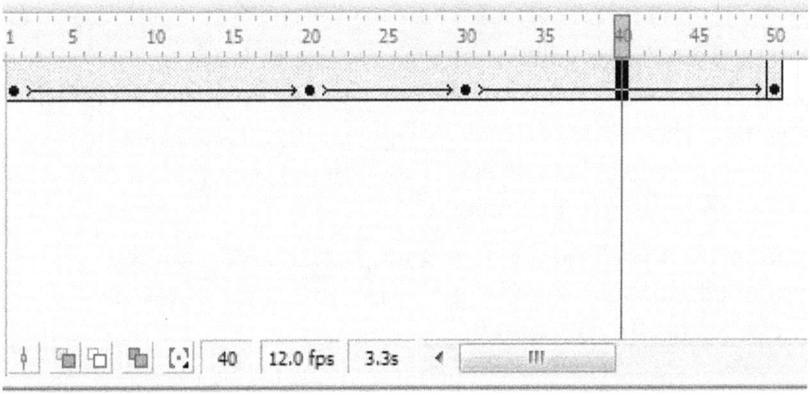

Test this movie by going to **Control**, **Test Movie** (CTRL + ENTER):

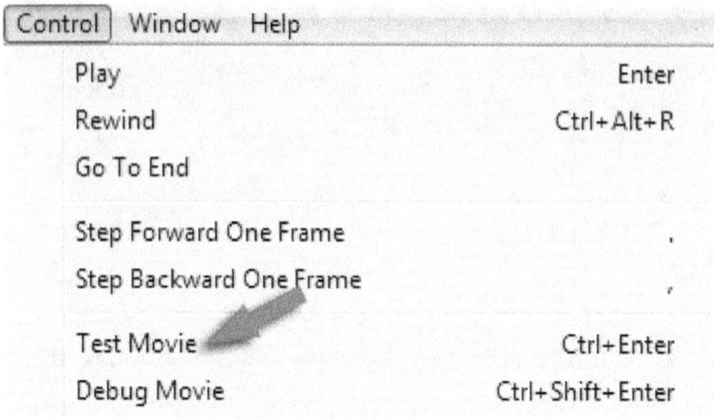

You should see a pop-up window which displays your animation. This is how the animation will play once it's uploaded to the internet:

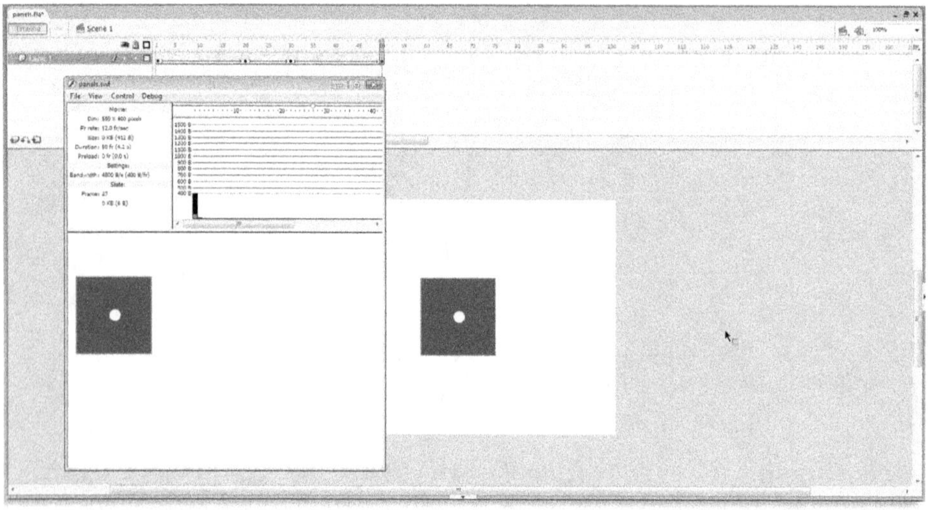

If you open the Chapter Two folder you'll notice a new file called SimpleAnimation.swf. This file is created whenever you test your movie (CTRL + ENTER) as we just did. This is the file that will eventually be uploaded to the web server. As you work on your Flash projects, each time you test your movie (CTRL + ENTER) the SWF file will be updated.

As you watch your animation you'll notice that it loops seamlessly but the animation is a bit stuttered, not very smooth at all. Let's fix that. Close the Test Movie window. Click on **Modify**, **Document**:

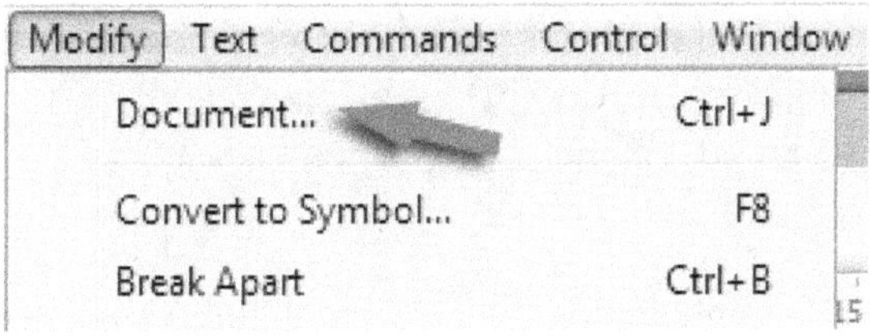

You should now see your **Document Properties** window:

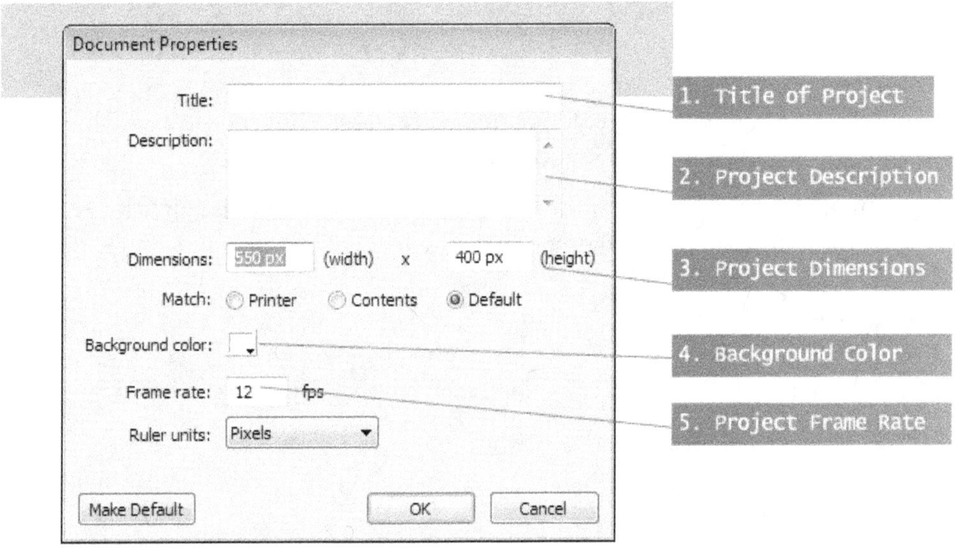

This window displays several pieces of information regarding your Flash project (the new **CS4/CS5 Document Properties** looks slightly different than the above image):

1. **Title of Project**. This is where you can display the title of your project. This information will be embedded and is strictly for search engines.

2. **Project Description**. Write the description of your project here. This information, like the title, is embedded in the flash file and is for search engines.

3. **Project Dimensions**. You can place your dimensions here. If you're creating a website your dimensions may be 900px (width) and 600px (height). If you're doing a banner your dimensions may only be 220px (width) and 50px (height).

4. **Background color**. This simply changes the background color of your project. The default is white.

5. **Frame rate.** This is the frame rate for your project. The two settings you'll be changing the most in the Document Properties window are the dimensions and the frame rate. The frame rate controls how smooth your animations are

going to be. A slower frame rate downloads faster on the web but produces a stuttered type effect. Increasing the frame rate to around 30 creates a much smoother animation. I usually use 30 for all of my animations.

In the **Frame Rate** window enter **30**:

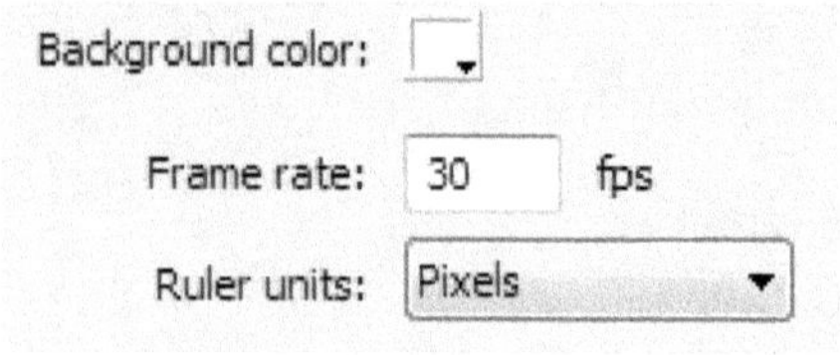

Hit **OK** and the window will close. Once again let's test your movie (CTRL + ENTER). You should see a much smoother animation.

Next, we'll create a second animation. First, though, let's name the first layer. Double-click on the layer where the name is:

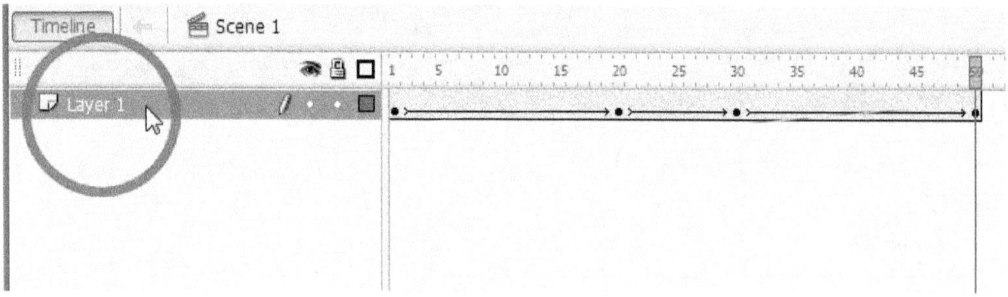

Type **Animation 1** and hit ENTER. It should now look like this:

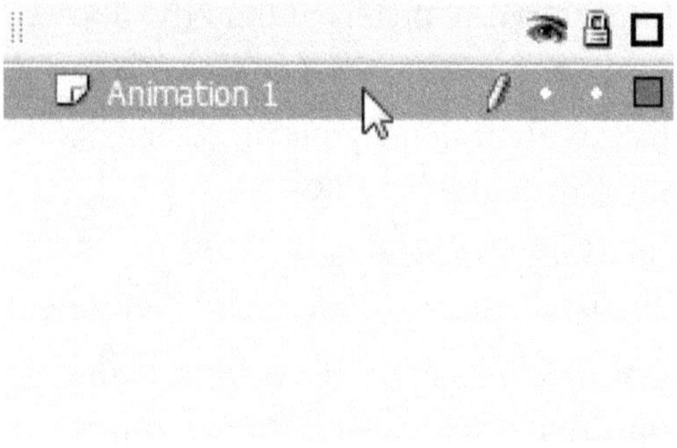

Click on the **Insert Layer** icon:

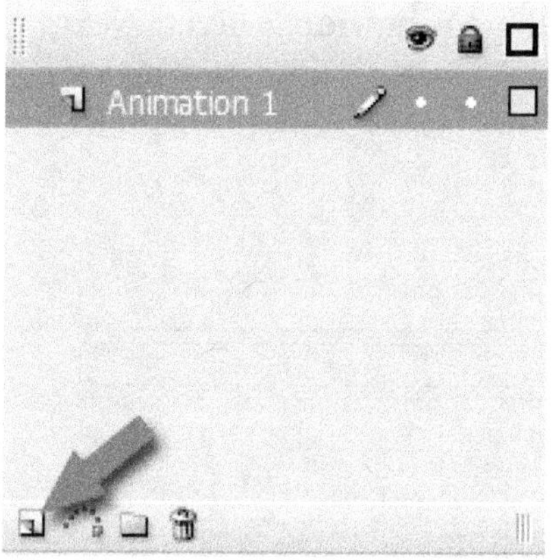

You'll now see a second layer called **Layer 2**. Double-click on this layer and change the name to **Animation 2**. Here is what it should look like when you're done:

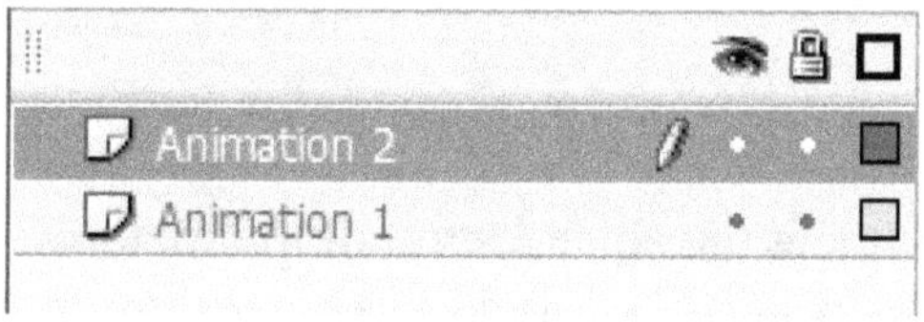

We'll next add the square symbol to the second animation. Click-and-drag the Square symbol from the library onto the stage:

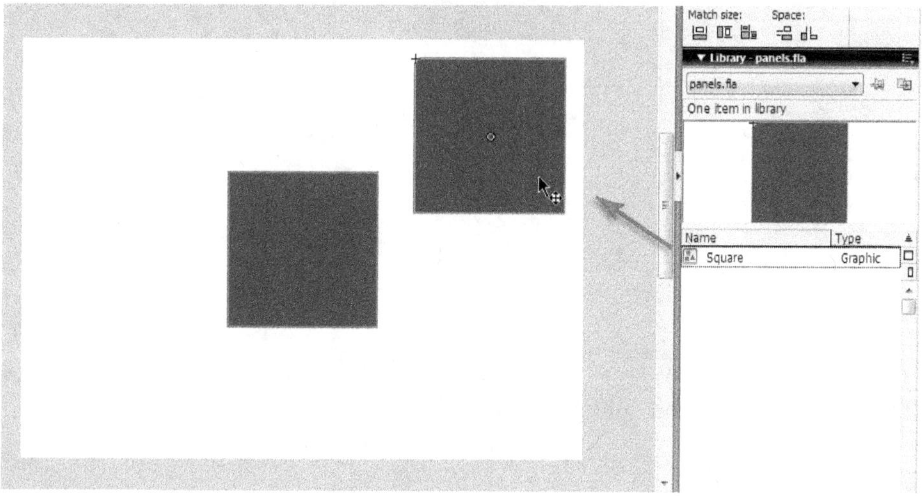

The new layer, **Animation 2**, now contains the square symbol. So now we'll create the animation. But this time we're not going to be moving the square around the stage; instead, we're going to animate the transparency of the square.

We'll start by inserting a keyframe on frame **50** of the **Animation 2** layer. Next, select any frame between 1 and 50 and go to **Insert**, **Timeline**, **Create Motion Tween** (**CS4/CS5 - Insert, Classic Tween**). Your second layer should now look like this:

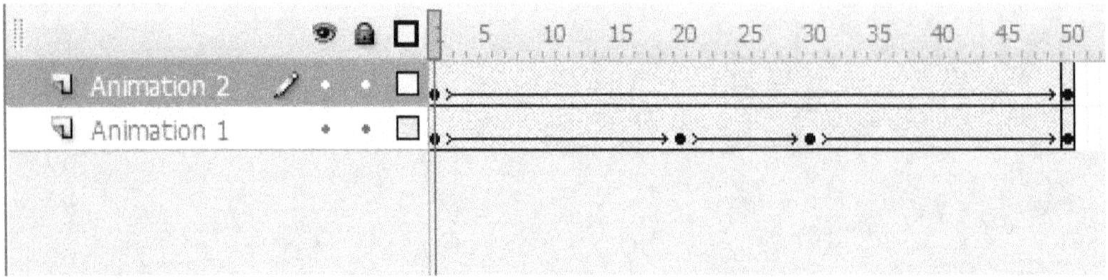

Insert a keyframe on frame **25** of the **Animation 2** layer.

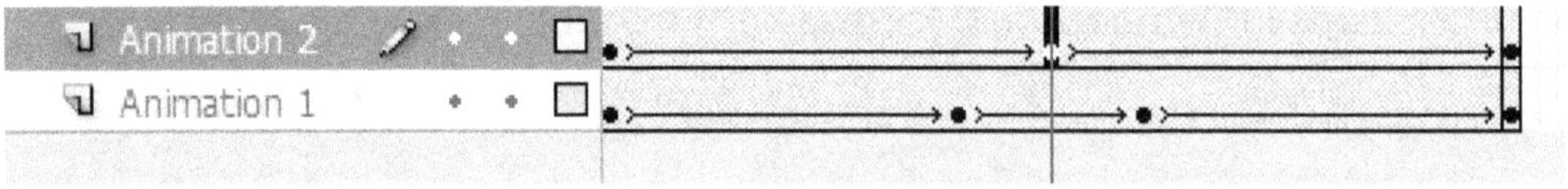

Select frame **25** where the keyframe is, then select the square symbol that belongs to the **Animation 2** layer. Open the Properties panel. You should see an option for **Color**:

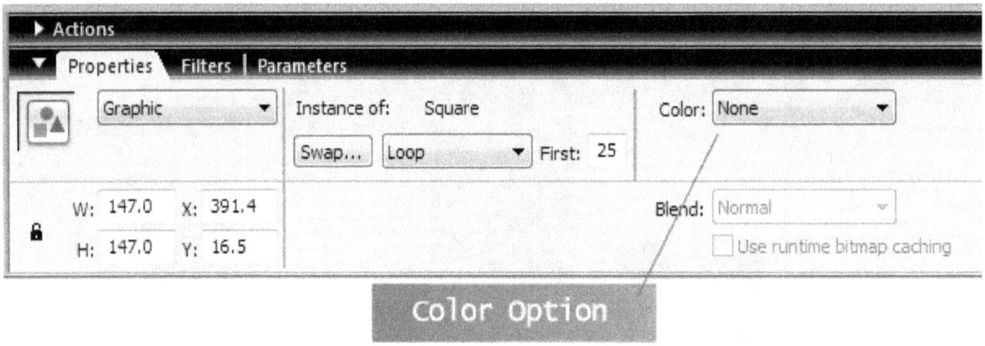

Click on the drop-down arrow next to **Color** (**CS4/CS5 Users** will click the drop-down arrow next to **Style**) and select **Alpha**:

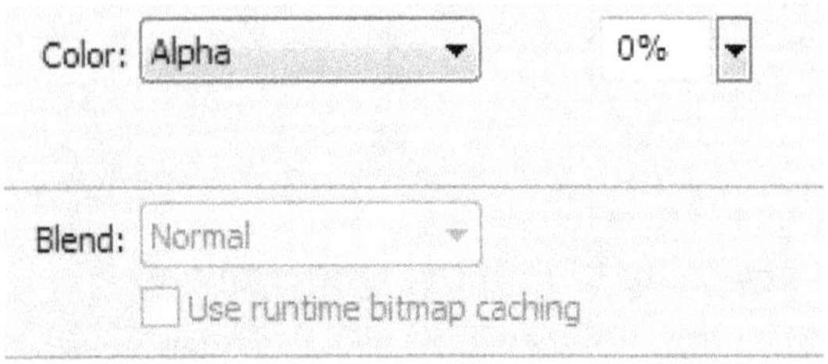

You should see a percentage window appear next to it. If it's not already at 0% then go ahead and change it to 0%.

Test your movie (CTRL + ENTER) to view the new animation. You now have two animations. The first animation where the square travels around the stage. And the second animation where the square becomes transparent then visible.

We'll now find out why *converting the original square into a symbol was so important*. Let's say your client calls and now he wants the square to be yellow, and the stroke to be blue. You already have two animations that use this square symbol and you're almost ready to panic. But wait! We wisely converted the square to a symbol before we created the two animations. Which means all we have to do is edit the square symbol in the library and both of the animations will instantly be updated.

The first thing we need to do is double-click the **Square** symbol in the library:

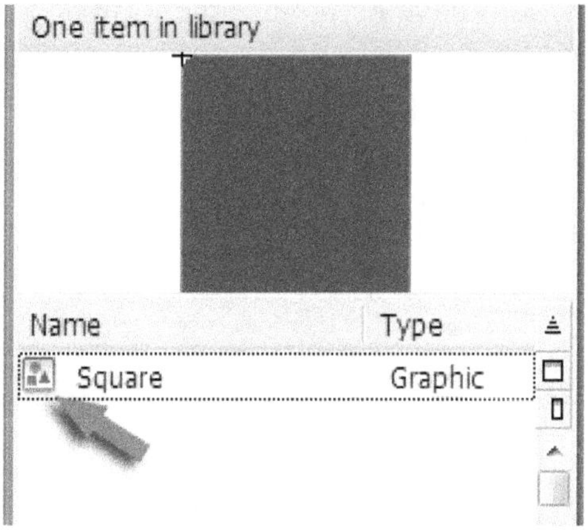

You should now be in the **Square** symbol editing stage. The names of the stages should now say **Scene 1** and **Square**:

Since we are no longer in the main timeline (**Scene 1**) the timeline only has one layer with the default name of **Layer 1**. So now let's change the color of the square. Click on the square and you'll see those familiar dots again. Since we are in the editing stage for the square it is back to its original state. This time, with the square still selected, click on **Fill color** and select **yellow**:

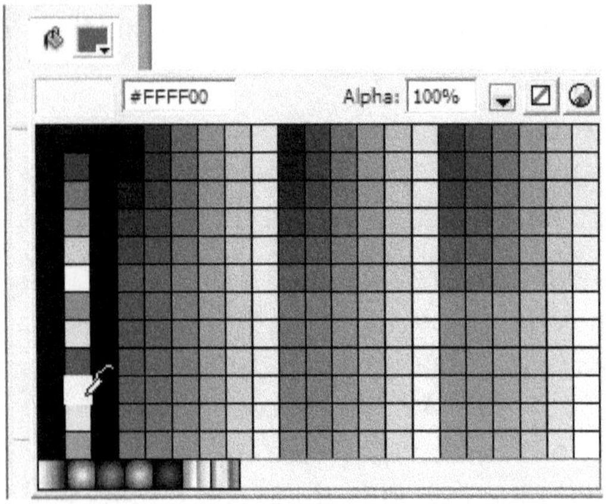

Since the square was already selected it will instantly change to yellow. If the square wasn't selected (no tiny dots) then we would have had to use the **Paint Bucket Tool** as we did earlier in this chapter.

Using the **Zoom Tool**, click once on your square. Your percentage window should show 200%.

Select the **Selection Tool** and click on the stroke:

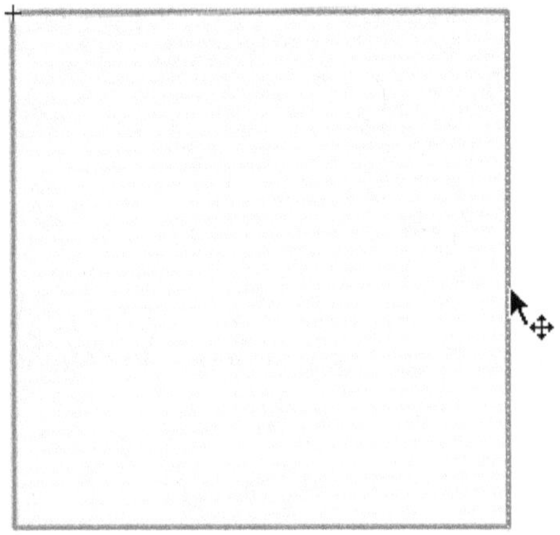

Notice how when you clicked on the stroke only one side of the stroke was selected? Flash considers every angle of a stroke a separate element. To make sure that the entire stroke is selected, *double-click* on any part of the stroke. The entire stroke should now be a series of tiny dots:

Open the Properties panel if it isn't already open and look at the **Stroke** information:

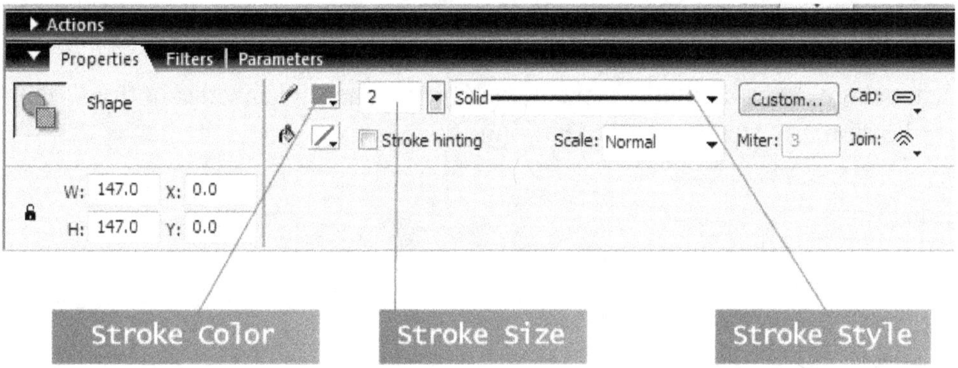

We'll be keeping the stroke size the same and also the style. The stroke color needs to change to **blue**, so click the **Stroke color** box and select **blue**:

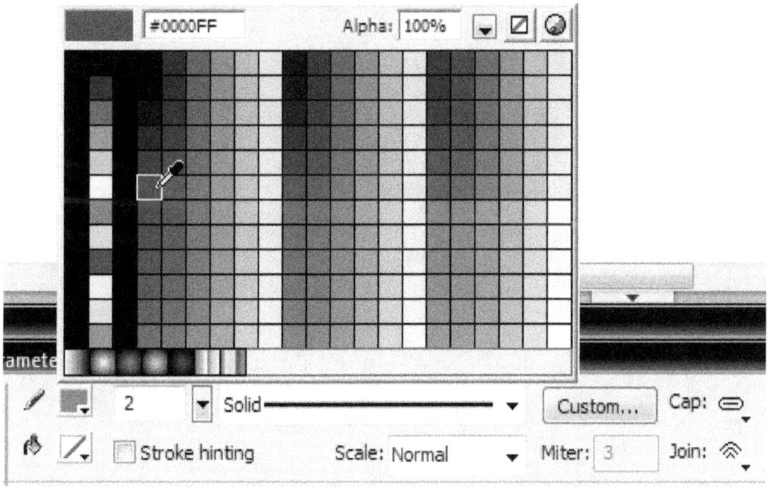

The Stroke color should now be blue:

Test your movie (CTRL + ENTER) to watch the animation. Both of the animations now have yellow squares. So even if you had a hundred animations using the square symbol, they would all be updated once we changed the color of the square to yellow.

We'll learn more about symbols in the next chapter when we discuss buttons. This is where Flash really starts to get interesting.

Chapter Two:
Buttons & Movie clips

Buttons and Movie clips. Mastering buttons and Movie clips is the key to unlocking the power of Flash. Once you understand how they both work you'll never look at Flash the same way again.

We'll first discuss buttons then jump right into Movie clips.

Simple Buttons

Open the **Chapter Two** folder and select the Flash file named Buttons.fla:

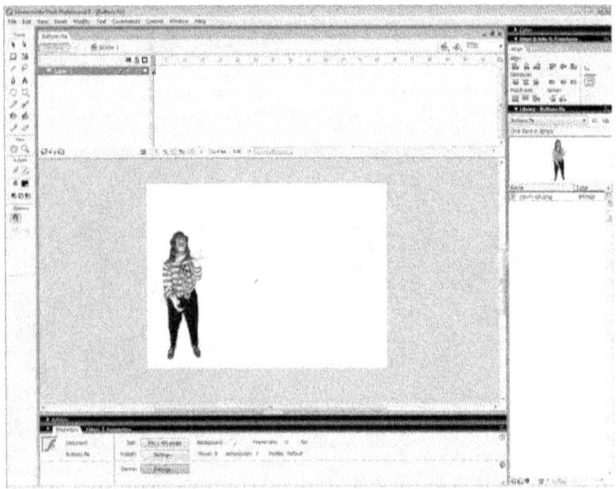

What we would like to do in this chapter is have the juggler throw a ball in the air and have two buttons that control the action.

Let's get started. You'll notice that in the library there is an object named **clown-69.png.** Whenever you import a picture (a jpeg, png, gif, etc.) it will show up in your library:

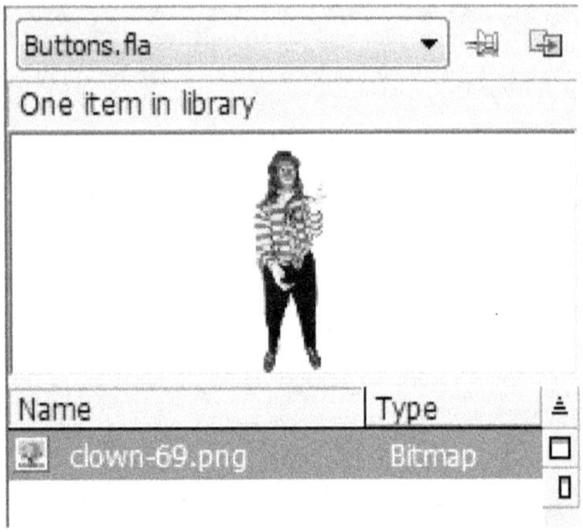

A good way to keep your files organized in Flash is to put library objects into folders. Let's put the **clown-69.png** image into a folder. Click on the **New Folder** icon at the bottom of the Library panel:

You should now see a new folder in the Library:

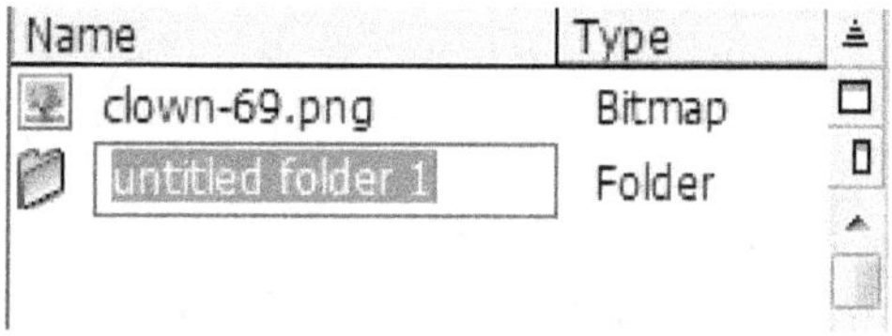

Go ahead and type **Pictures** into the text area of the folder and hit ENTER. When you're done it should look like this:

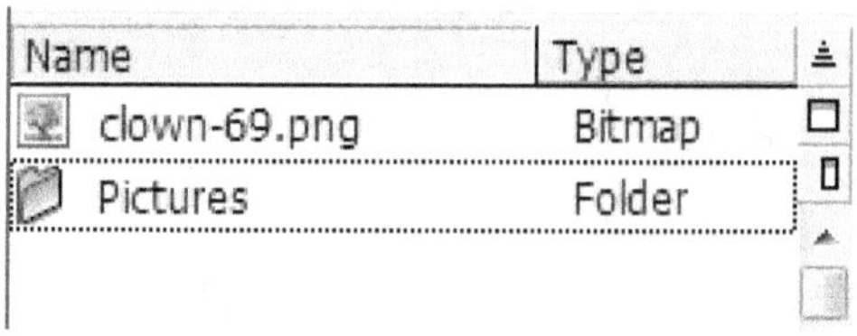

Drag **clown-69.png** into the Pictures folder:

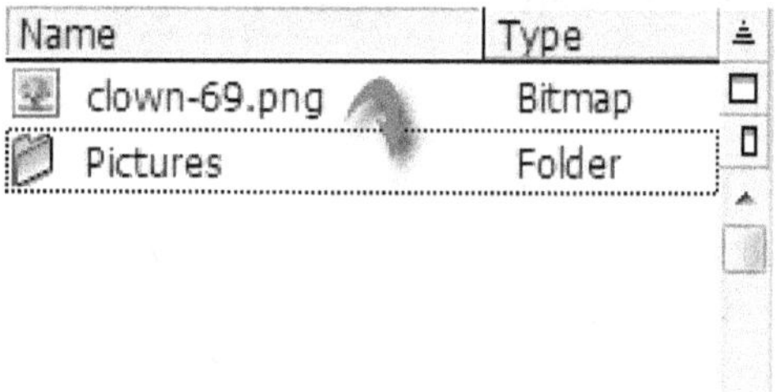

You should now only see the Pictures folder in the library:

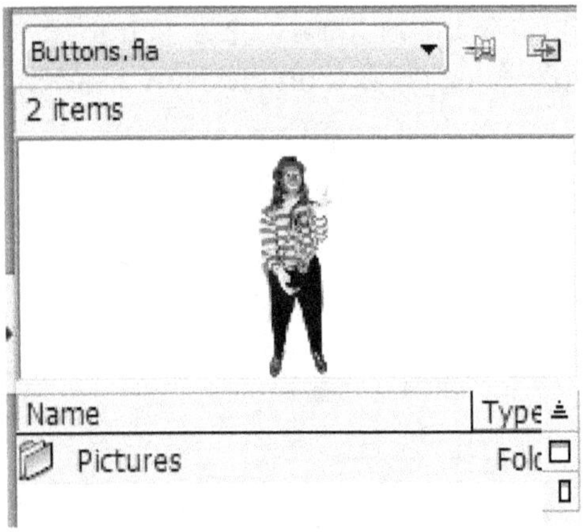

Every time you import a picture you can drag it into a folder. When you're doing more complex Flash projects, you'll have a variety of different objects in your library such as: jpegs, gif files, audio files, videos, etc. It's a good idea to create a folder for every type of object so you can stay organized.

Let's get back to the animation. Since the character will be juggling, we'll need to create a ball. Click on the **Oval Tool**:

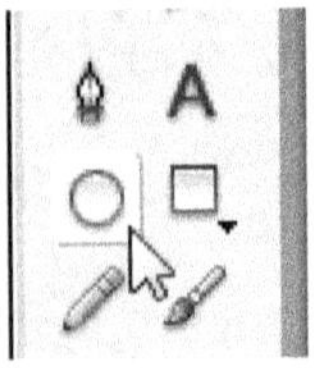

In CS4/CS5 the **Oval Tool** is a sub-selection of the **Rectangle Tool**:

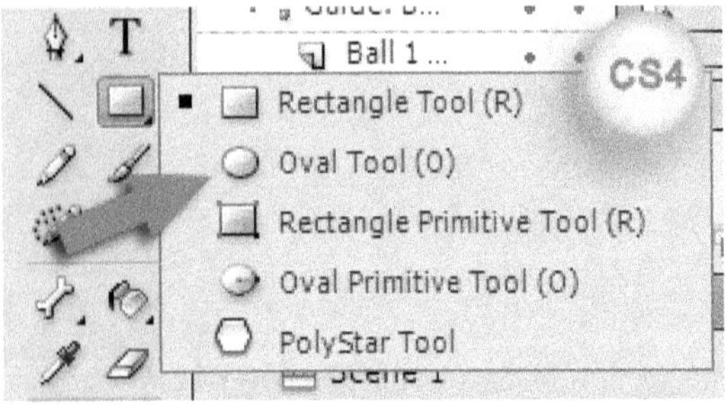

Click on **Fill color** and select the red gradient:

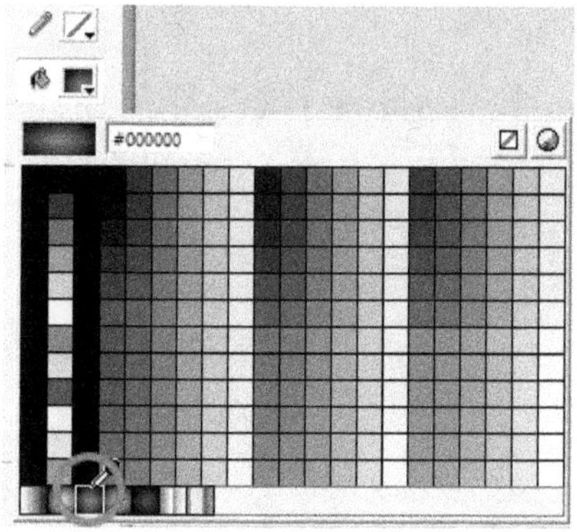

A gradient has two or more colors in it. The red gradient we chose has red and black. Let's adjust the color slightly of the gradient. We do that by clicking on the Color panel shortcut to open it up (if you don't see it go to **Window**, **Color**):

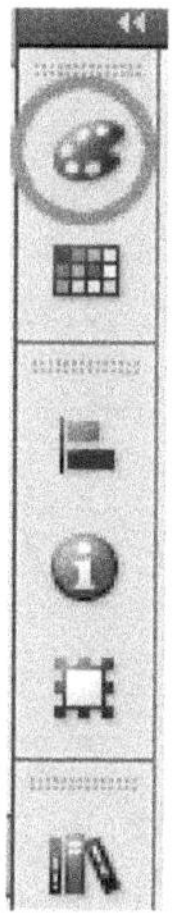

Once the Color panel is open, click on the **Color Mixer** tab:

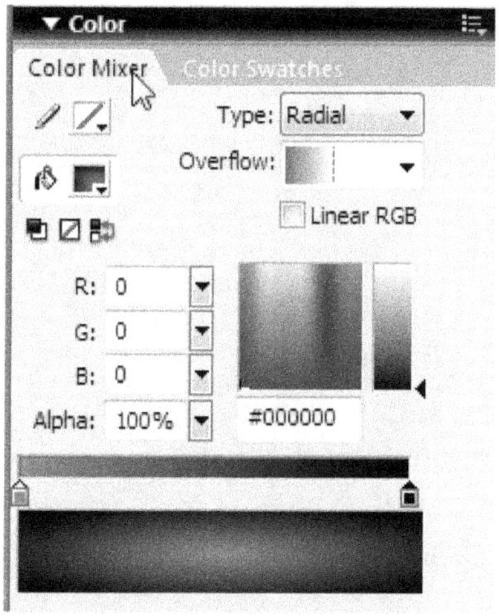

Color Mixer is where you can modify solid and gradient colors. If you look at the bottom of the panel you'll see the gradient colors: red and black. We'll change the black color and make it more of a gray color. So first, click on the black icon:

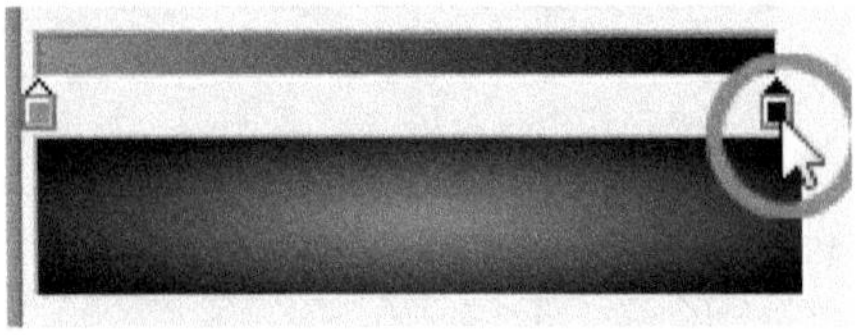

Once you click on it you can modify its color. We do that by moving the **Color Slider** slightly upward:

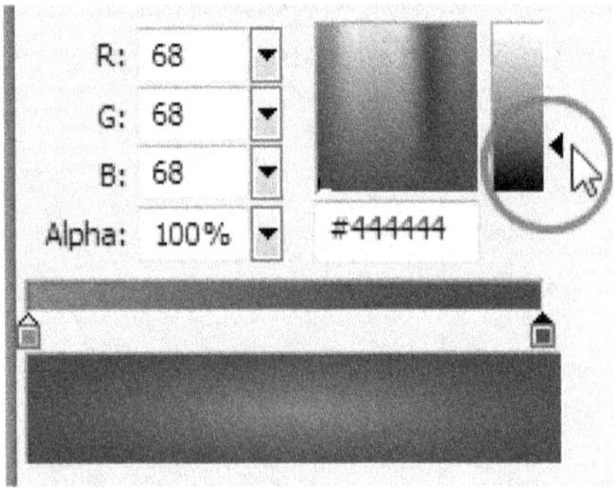

You should now notice that the color gradient is red and gray, instead of red and black.

Before we make a ball on the stage, we need to create a new layer to hold the ball. Click on the **New Layer** icon and name the new layer **Ball 1 Animation**:

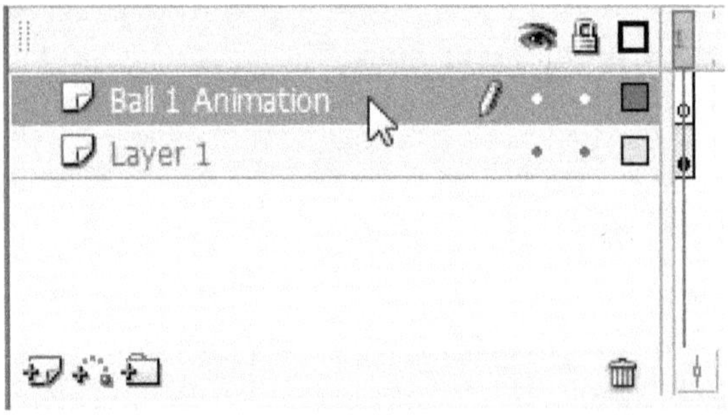

Since we just named the ball layer, let's also name the Juggler layer (Layer 1). Give this layer the name: **Juggler**. After you name it, click on the padlock icon:

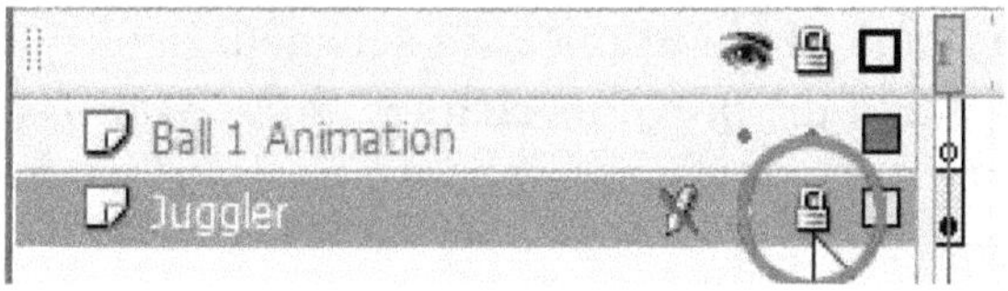

We lock the layer so we don't accidentally move the juggler image. We also lock layers so objects won't accidentally be added to them. This option isn't 100% necessary but it's a good practice to get into. If you need to unlock the layer simply click on the padlock icon.

Let's make the juggling ball. With the **Oval Tool** still selected, click-and-drag to create a circle above the juggler's left hand (remember to hold down SHIFT to make a perfect circle):

We now have the first ball. We want the ball to start where it's at, continue to the top of its arc, and then fall into the juggler's right hand. First, we need to make the ball a symbol. Since we'll be using the same ball for all three animations then it makes sense to convert it to a symbol in case we have to modify it later.

Click on the ball to select it:

You'll notice that the ball is made up of many tiny dots once it's selected. Let's convert the ball to a symbol. Just as we did in the previous chapter go to **Modify**, **Convert to Symbol**:

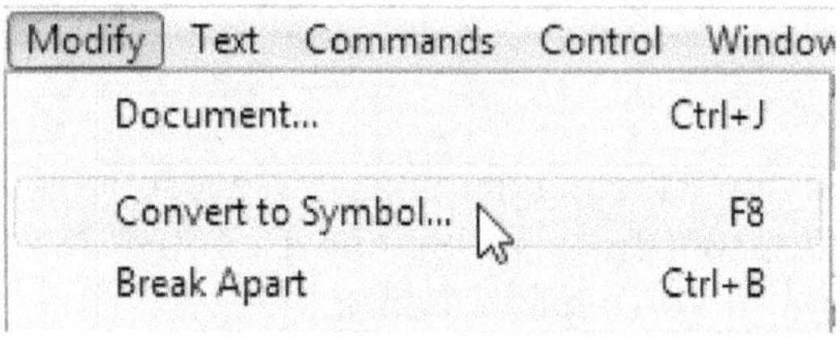

You'll now see the **Convert to Symbol** window. Make sure **Graphic** is selected and give it a name of **Ball**:

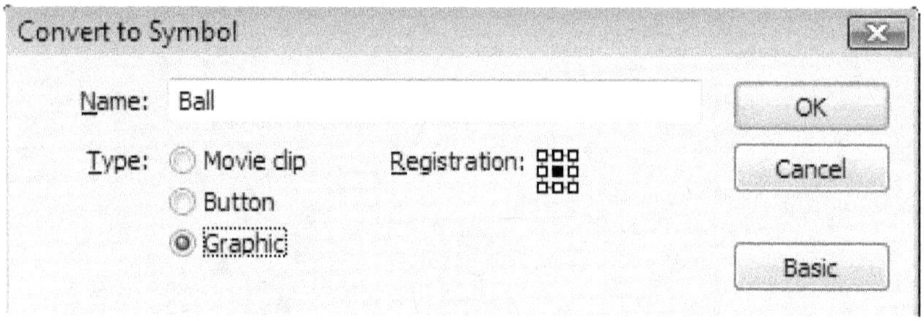

Hit **OK** and your new Ball symbol will be in your library:

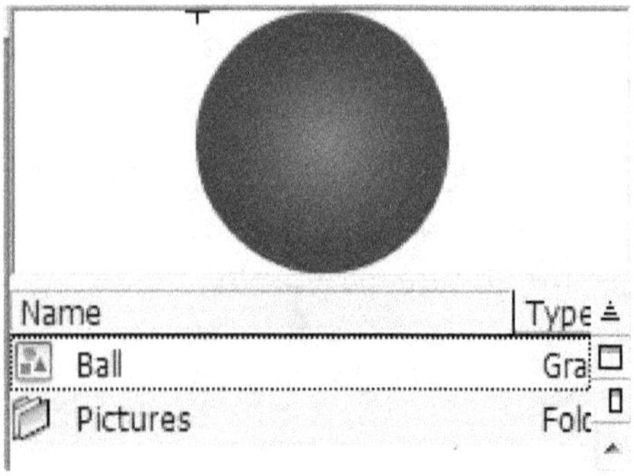

We need the ball to fly up in the air and land in the Juggler's right hand. We'll do this by using a **Motion Guide**. A **Motion Guide** is simply a path that you can attach to your object. Click on the **Motion Guide** icon:

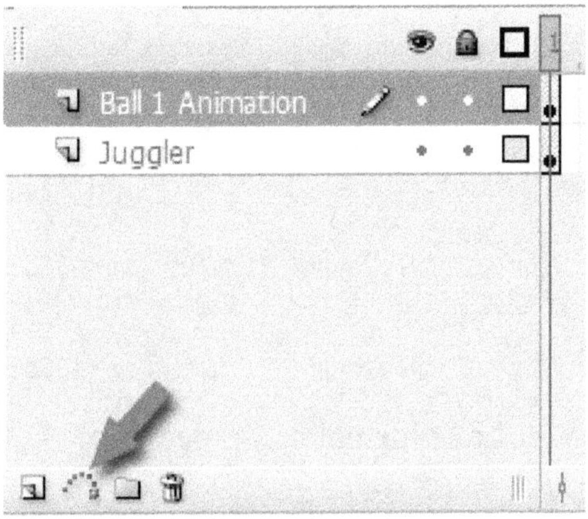

CS4/CS5 users will have to **right-click** on the **Ball 1 Animation** layer and select **Add Classic Motion Guide**:

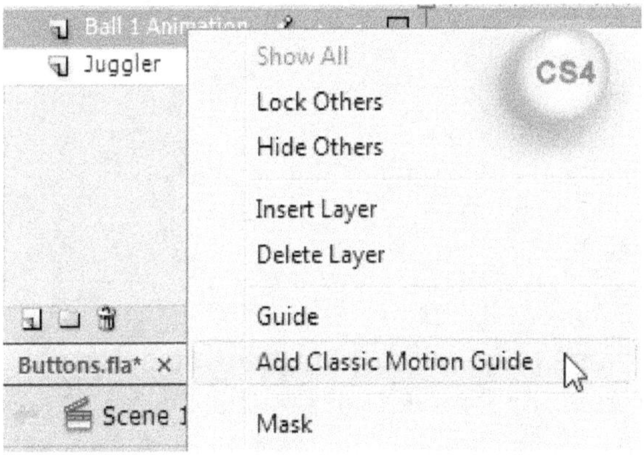

You should now see a **Motion Guide** layer:

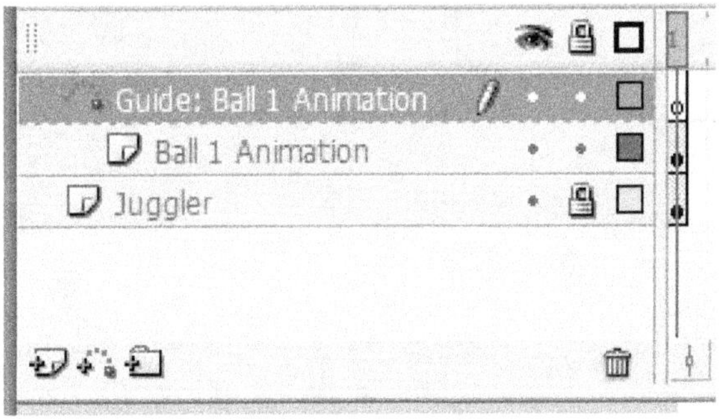

When a layer is using a **Motion Guide** layer it will be indented. We'll now draw a path for the ball to follow. Grab your **Pencil Tool**:

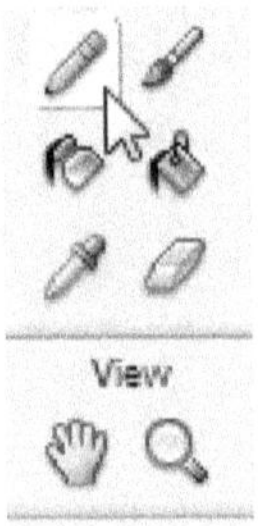

Select a color for your **Pencil Tool** using the **Stroke color** palette. Select the color **blue**:

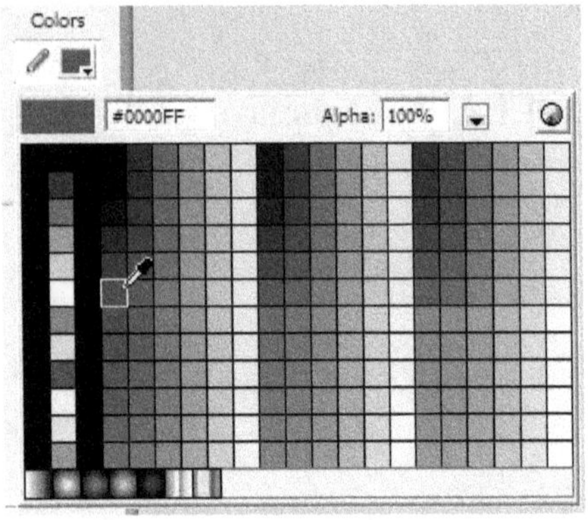

Once you've selected your color you'll want to ensure that the path you draw with your pencil is smooth. Select **Smooth** from the **Pencil Tool** options:

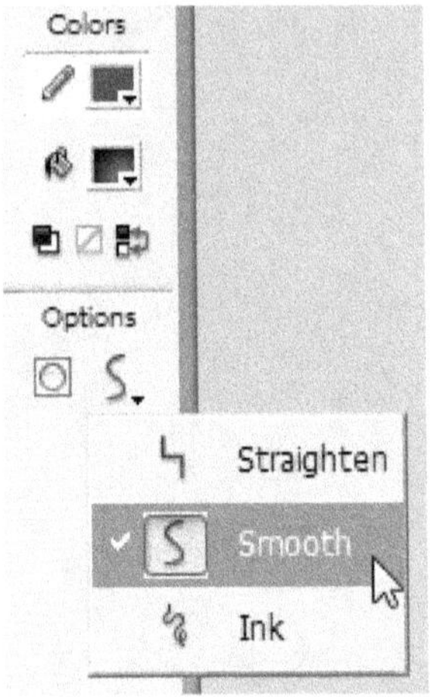

Draw your ball path. We want the ball to travel upward then drop into the opposite hand. You can make it similar to mine (zoom into the stage if you're having trouble drawing the path):

The actual path is only visible when editing. When the Flash file is published, the path will be invisible.

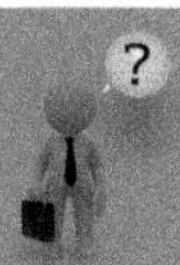

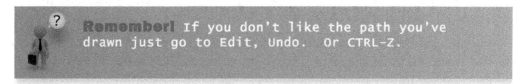

Remember! If you don't like the path you've drawn just go to Edit, Undo. Or CTRL-Z.

So now we have the path for the ball. The next step before we start on the animation is to change the frame rate setting. As we did in the previous chapter, go to **Modify**, **Document**:

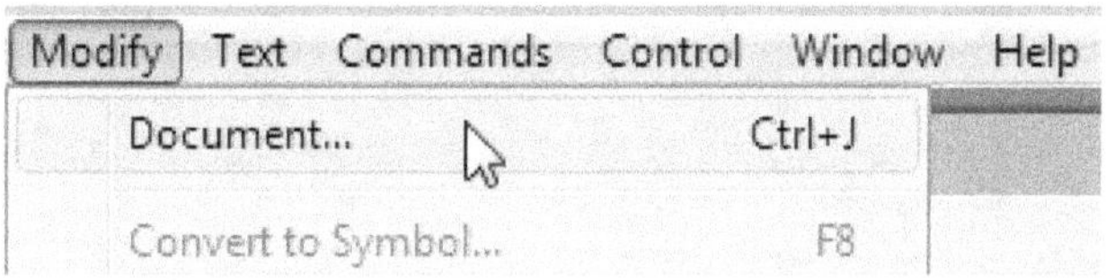

The **Document Properties** window will open. Insert the number **30** into the **Frame Rate** field:

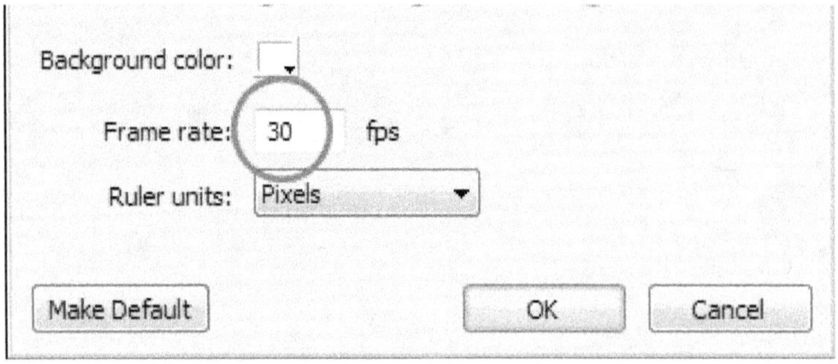

Click on **OK**. The next step is to determine how many frames the animation is going to contain. The way I determine that is by trying to figure out how much time the ball is going to be in the air. So, for this exercise, I tossed a ball in the air and caught it with my right hand. The total time the ball was in the air was about 1 second.

Since the frame rate is 30 frames per second, and the animation is going to be 1 second, then the total animation will be 30 frames. Insert a keyframe at frame 30 of your **Ball 1 Animation** layer:

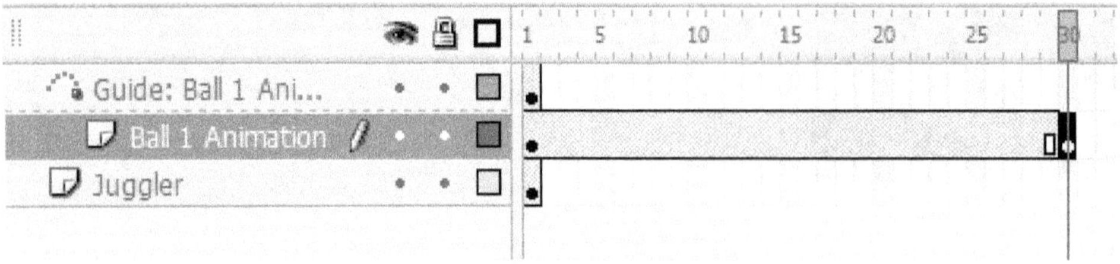

If you've forgotten how to insert keyframes, remember to click on frame **30** then go to **Insert**, **Timeline**, and **Keyframe**.

You'll notice that **Ball 1 Animation** has 30 frames, but the other two layers still have one frame. Also, on the stage the only thing we can see is the ball. So we'll need to add more frames to the other layers so they equal the frames of the **Ball 1 Animation** layer.

Click on frame 30 of the **Motion Guide** layer:

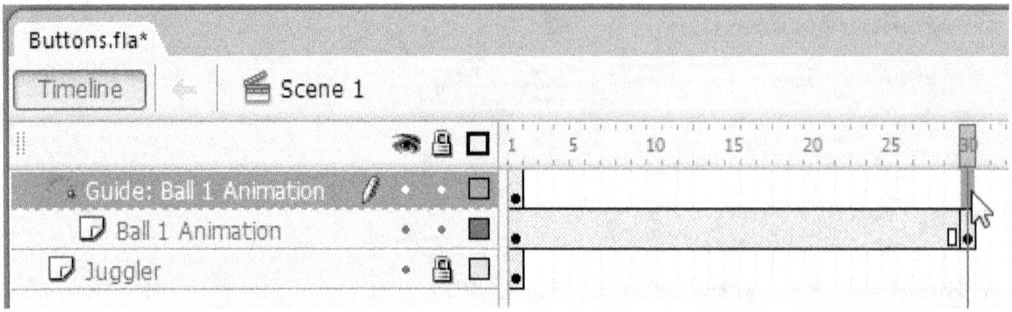

Next, go to **Insert, Timeline,** and **Frame:**

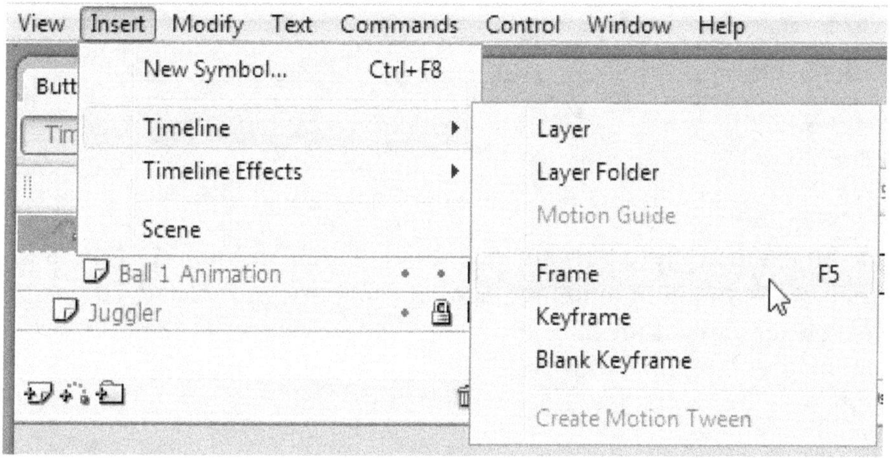

The timeline should now look like this:

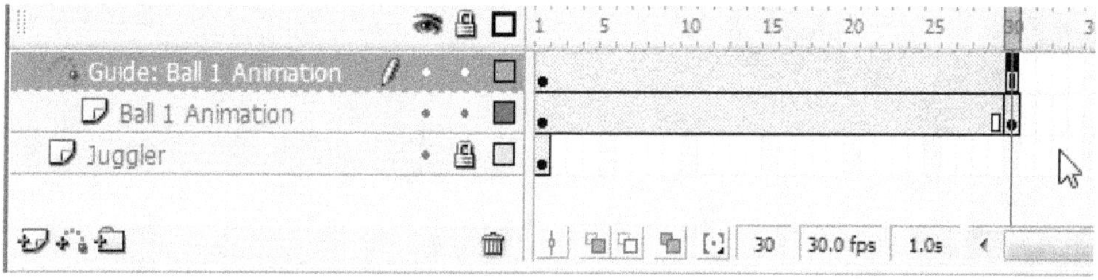

Now, add a frame to frame **30** of the **Juggler** layer. You should now have an equal amount of frames in all three layers:

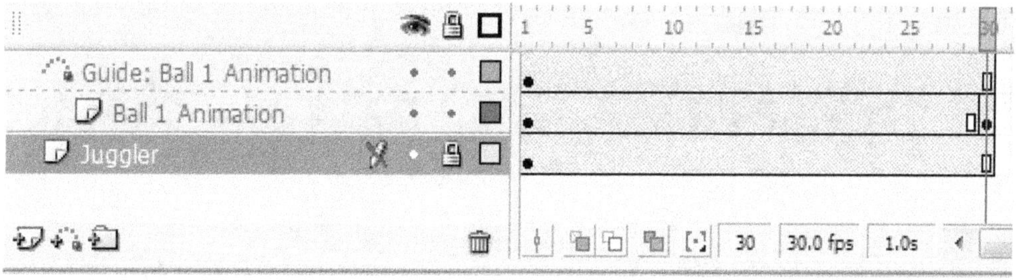

Next, we need to create a Motion Tween for the **Ball 1 Animation** layer.

Select any frame between **1** and **30** of the **Ball 1 Animation** layer, then go to **Insert, Timeline,** and **Create Motion Tween** (**CS4/CS5 - Insert, Classic Tween**).

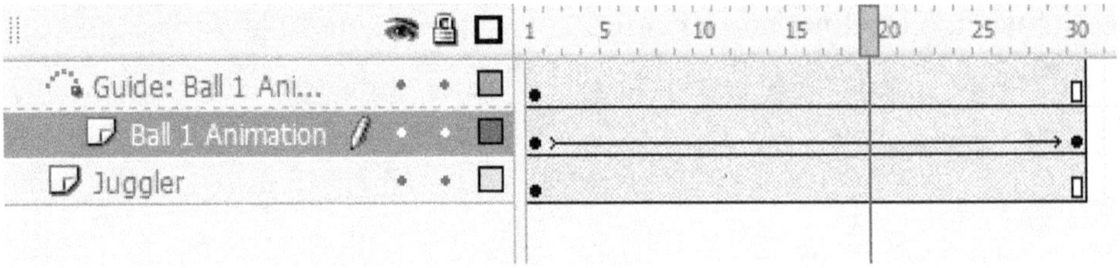

We're going to attach the Ball to the path we created. Click on frame **1** of the **Ball 1 Animation** layer. Next, zoom in to the stage (400%). Use your **Hand Tool** so that you have a closer view of the ball:

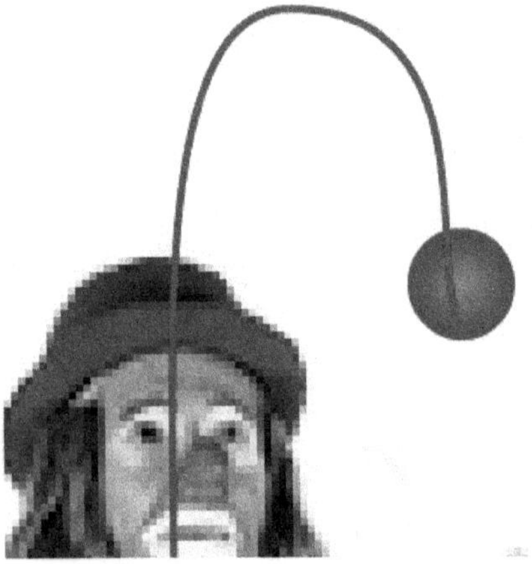

We want the ball to *snap* to the beginning of the line. With frame 1 of the **Ball 1 Animation** layer still selected, open the Properties panel. In the Properties panel make sure **Snap** is selected:

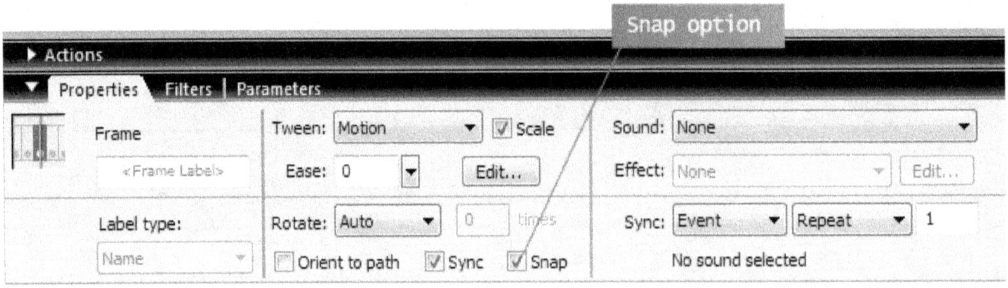

Selecting **Snap** ensures that the Ball symbol snaps to the beginning and end of the blue path. The ball has to snap into place before it will follow the path of the Motion Guide.

We want the ball to start at the beginning of the blue line. Drag the ball so the center of the Ball is over the start of the line; you should feel it slightly snap into place once the center of the ball gets near the line:

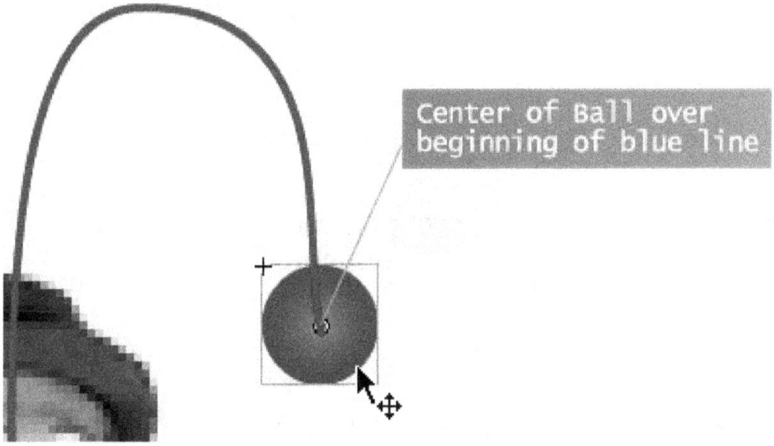

Next we'll attach the ball to the end of the blue path. Click on frame **30** of the **Ball 1 Animation** layer. Drag the ball to the end of the blue path:

Remember! If your animation isn't working, make sure the center of the ball is precisely over the ends of the blue path!

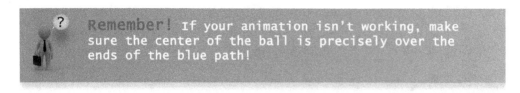

Make sure the center of the ball (indicated by a little circle) is lined up with the end of the Blue path.

On frame **1** the ball is at the beginning of the blue path, and at frame **30** the ball is at the end of the blue path. Hit ENTER so you can see the animation. Looking good! The ball should be following the blue path.

Of course, if this were a real ball it would have to adhere to the laws of physics. Which means the speed of the ball going up would be slower than the speed of the ball going down. How do we do this? We do this by using Motion Tween's Ease controls. Let's try it out.

Click on frame **1** of the **Ball 1 Animation** layer. Open the Properties panel so you can see the options:

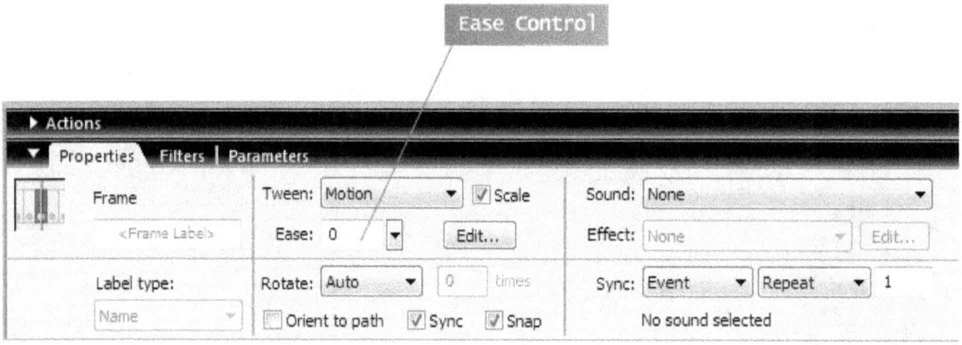

Don't worry about all the other options on the Properties panel. We'll get to those later. Next to **Ease** enter **100** (or use the slider):

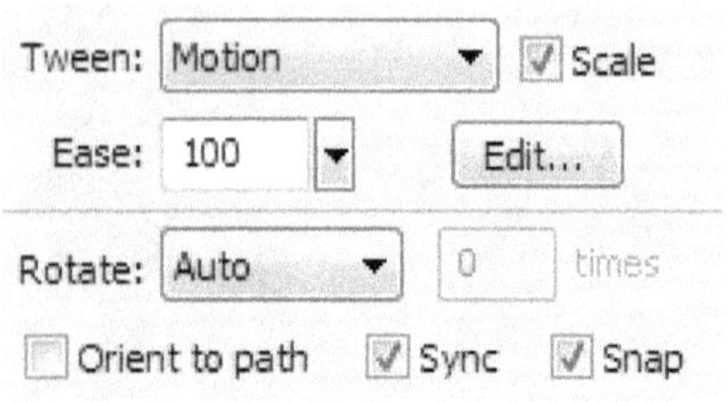

CS4/CS5 users - The Ease control is within the Tweening panel:

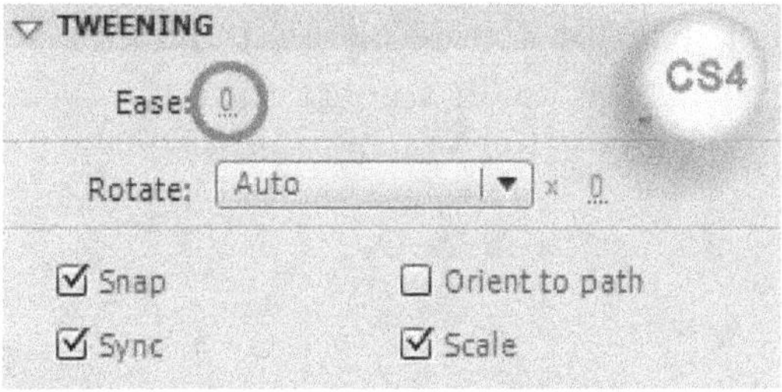

Test your movie (CTRL + ENTER). Notice how the ball starts off really fast then slows down by the end of its animation? That's not quite what we want. Change the Ease to **-100** (or use the slider):

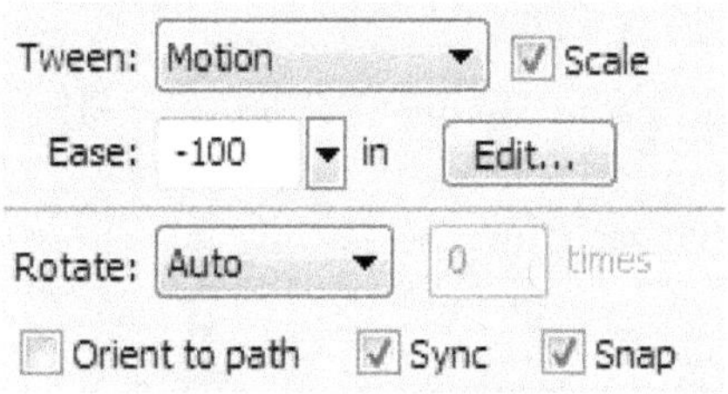

Test the movie again. That's a little better. The ball starts off slower then builds up speed. It's not quite perfect though, so take down the number a bit. Type **-50** into the **Ease** field:

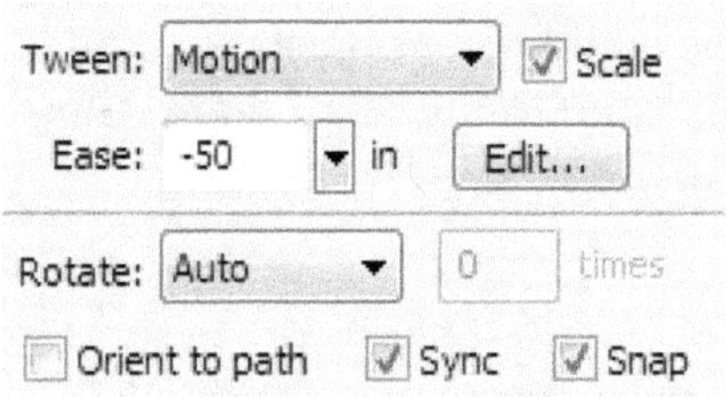

Test your movie (CTRL + ENTER). The animation should now be more realistic. Now we need to stop the ball once it gets to the Juggler's right hand. How do we do that? Easy! We use Script Assist. Add a fourth layer to the timeline by clicking the **New Layer** icon:

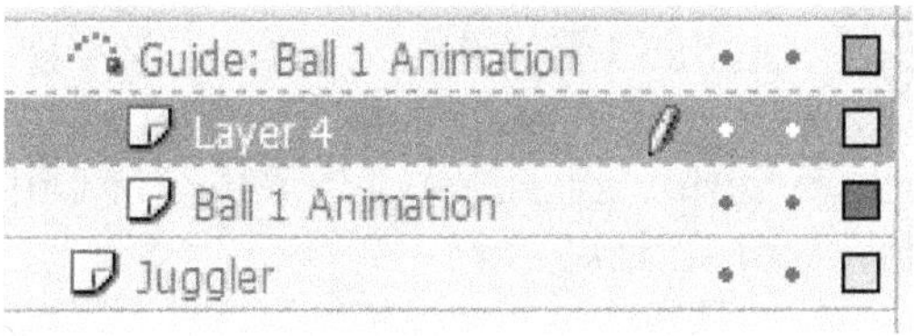

Notice how Flash put the new layer under the **Motion Guide** layer? It did this because Flash will insert a new layer above whatever layer you are currently working on. Click and drag **Layer 4** so that it's above the **Motion Guide** layer:

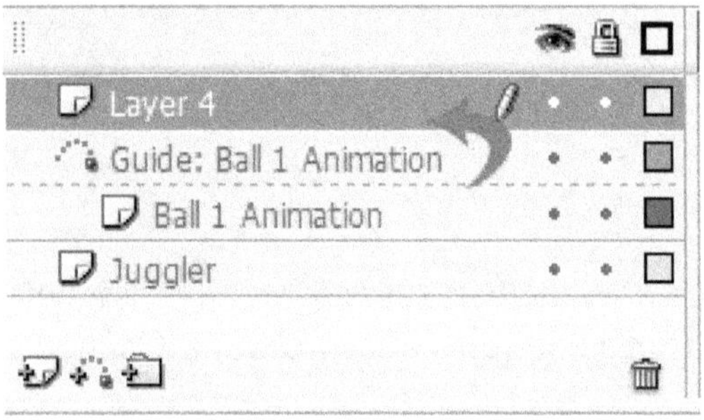

Name this layer **Actions**. Next, select frame **30** and go to **Insert**, **Timeline**, and **Keyframe**. Your timeline should now look like this:

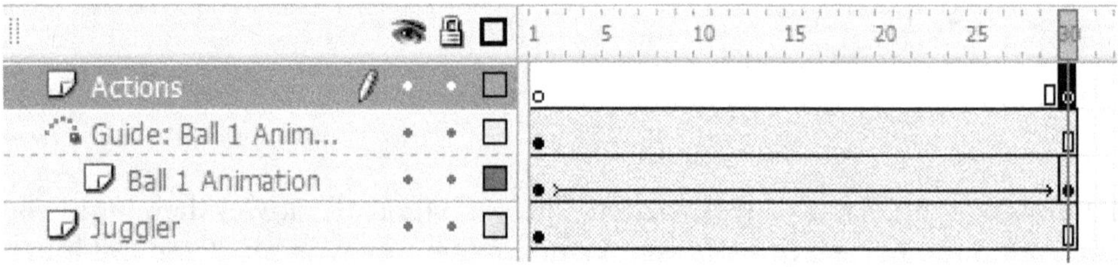

Since this is the **Actions** layer we're not going to be adding any objects to it, but we are going to be adding some ActionScript. Make sure frame **30** of the **Actions layer** is selected and click on your Actions panel shortcut:

Your Actions panel should now be open. Click on the Script Assist button (in CS5 click on the Menu Selector at the top right of the panel to see the Script Assist setting **CTRL + SHIFT + E**). When you are in Script Assist mode the button will have a 'pressed' look and the Actions window will shrink:

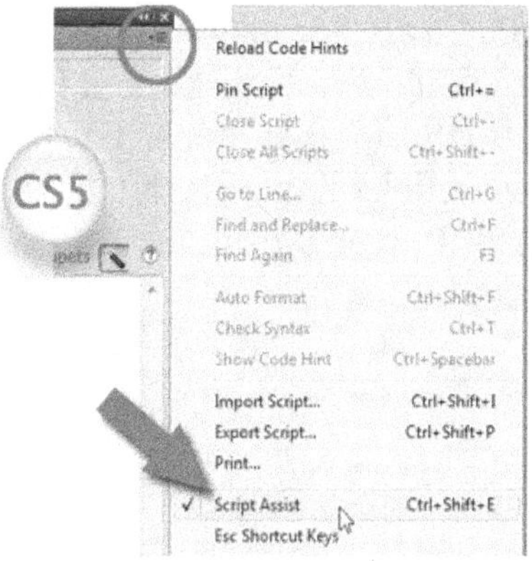

In Script Assist mode you may want to open the window more so you can see the code. You do that by putting your cursor between the Actions panel and the stage; your cursor should change to a double-arrow. Drag upward to open the Actions window:

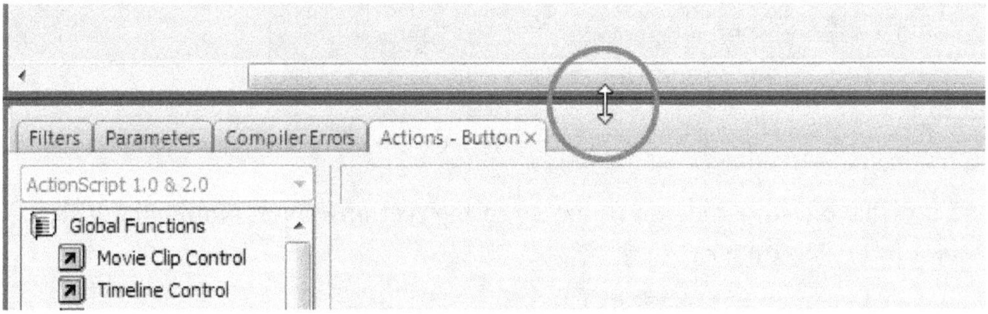

On the left side of the Actions panel click on **Global Functions, Timeline Control** and double-click **stop**:

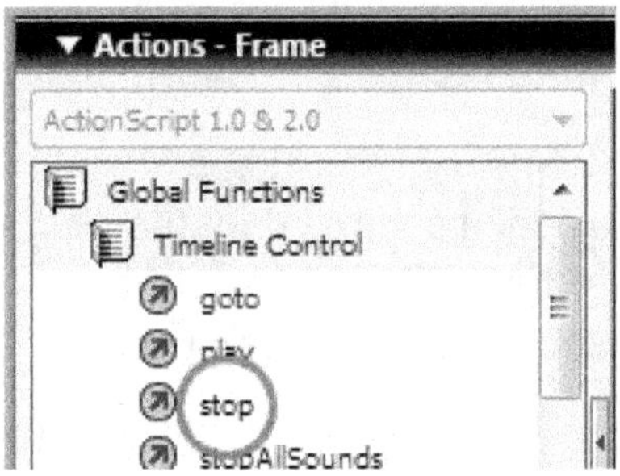

Flash will instantly create the ActionScript code for **stop**:

```
1 stop();
2
```

CS3/CS4/CS5/ users: in order to add ActionScript to buttons you have to make sure you are not working in Flash 10. Flash 10 uses a different approach to adding ActionScript to buttons. To change the setting go to **File**, **Publish Settings**.... Next, click on the **Flash** tab. Next to **Player** click on the drop-down arrow; select **Flash Player 8** from the list. Next to **Script** select **ActionScript 2.0**.

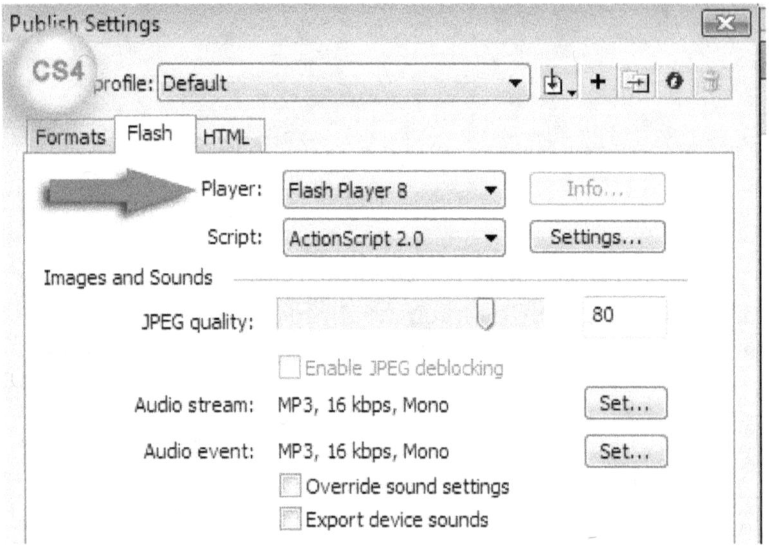

So we now have a **stop** code on frame 30 of the **Actions** layer. Notice the little symbol **a** in the keyframe:

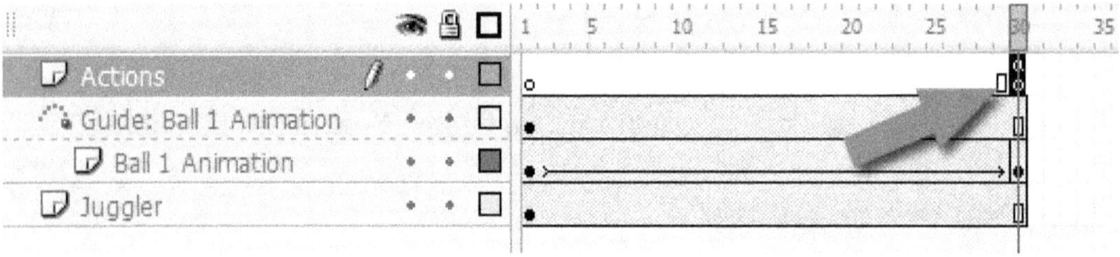

This **a** in the frame stands for ActionScript. Since we added a **stop** code, the keyframe now reflects that. Test your movie (CTRL + ENTER) and watch the animation. It should stop at frame 30 when the ball reaches the Juggler's right hand.

What if we wanted to create two buttons that controlled the action of the animation? One button would play the animation and the other button would stop it. Let's create the first button; select the **Rectangle Tool**:

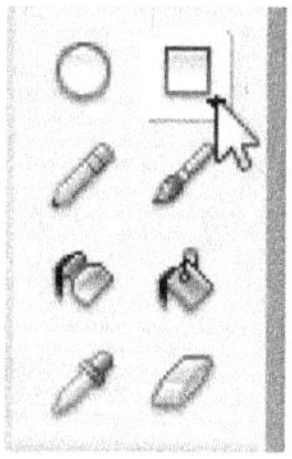

Make sure there is no stroke color selected. We do this by clicking on the **Stroke color** icon then selecting the icon that has the red line through it:

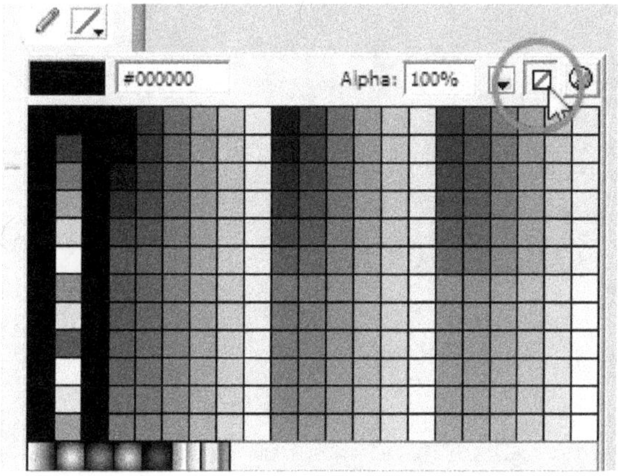

Next, select the color **green** for the **Fill color**:

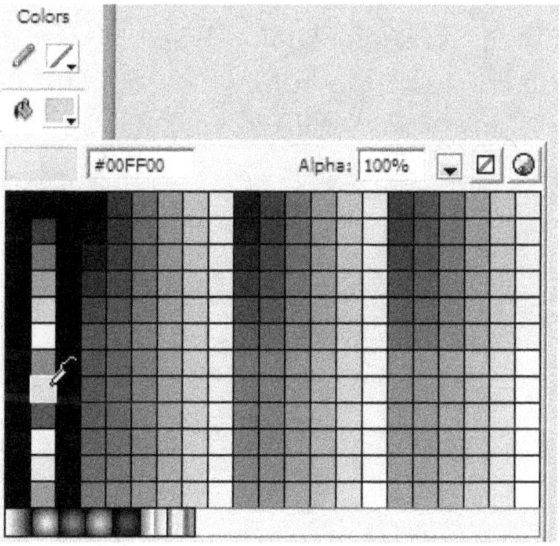

Now that you have your **Fill color** selected, we're almost ready to make a button. First, though, remember to make a new layer for your button. Since we want the new layer above the **Guide** Layer we need to highlight the **Guide Layer** by selecting it:

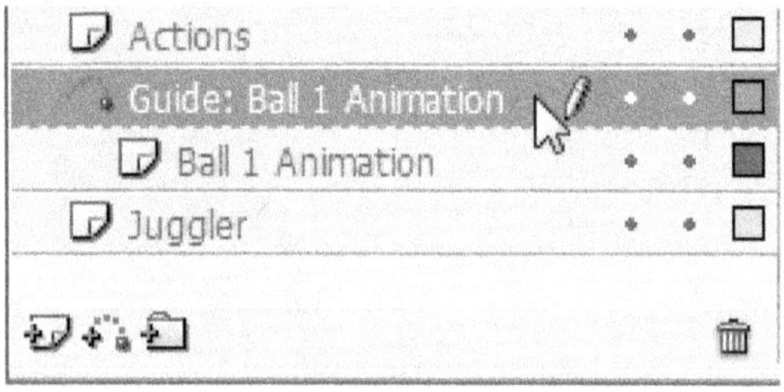

When we now click the **New Layer** icon, it will create a new layer above the **Guide Layer**:

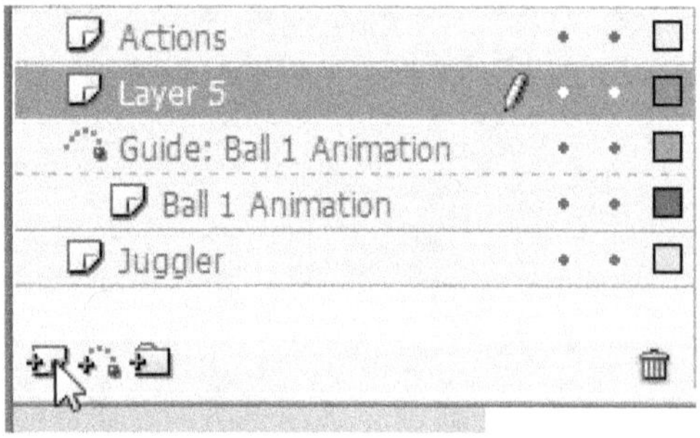

The new layer is now above the **Guide** layer. It's a good practice to keep the **Actions** layer as the topmost layer. It's not absolutely necessary that you do this, but it will make this layer easier to find when you're working on Flash projects that have several layers.

Name this new layer: **Button 1**. Next, with the **Rectangle Tool** still selected, draw out your button shape on the stage (you don't need to hold down the Shift key since we're not making a square):

As we did in the first chapter, we need to convert the shape to a symbol. Select this button shape and go to **Modify**, **Convert to Symbol** (F8). When the **Convert to Symbol** window appears, type **ButtonPlay** for the name, and select **Button** for **Type**:

When you're done, hit **OK**. Your shape should now be a symbol:

This will be the **Play** button. When the animation gets to frame 30 and stops (due to the **stop** code) clicking this button plays the animation again. So now we need to add the ActionScript to this button.

First, select this new Button Symbol. Next, open the Actions panel and make sure Script Assist is turned on.

The first thing we need to do is tell the new button what to control. We would like the button to control the timeline since that is where the animation is. On the left part of the Actions panel you'll see several selections. Scroll down to **Deprecated** and click once:

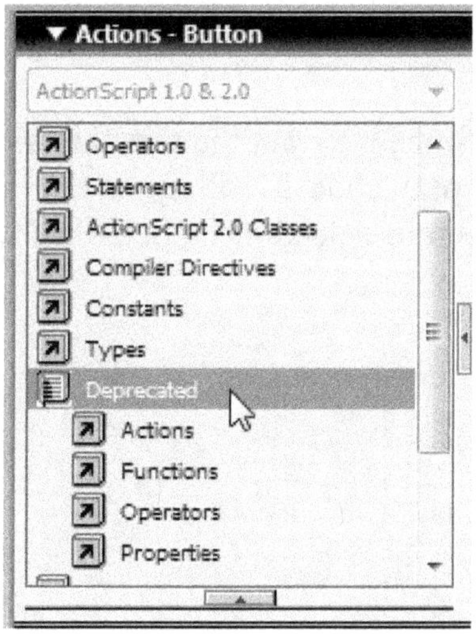

Next, click on **Actions**. You'll then see a selection called **tellTarget**. Double-click **tellTarget**:

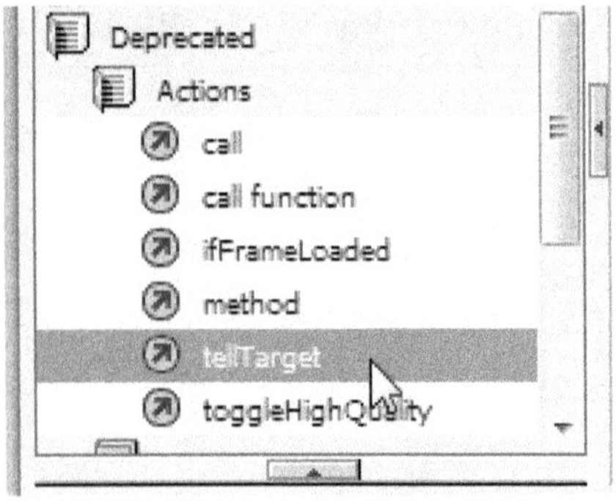

As soon as you double-click **tellTarget** your Actions panel will update with a new **Target** Window:

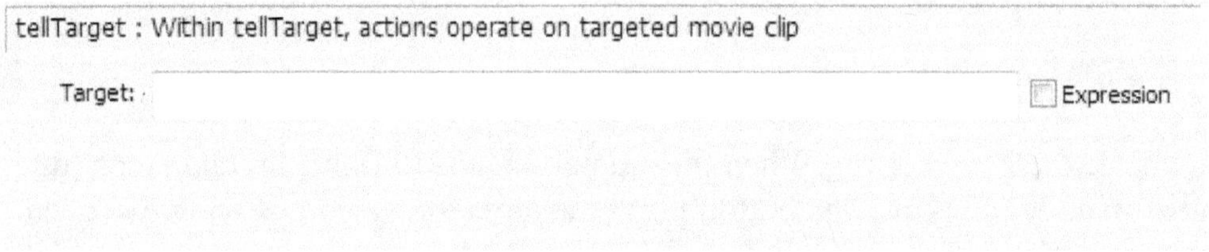

In the **Target** window type **_level0/**:

_level0/ is code which means *main timeline*. This code controls the main timeline: **Scene 1**.

We need to add one more bit of code to this button. Since we want the timeline to begin playing once the button is clicked, we'll add a **play** code. Scroll up on the selections and click once on **Global Functions** to open its selections. Click once on **Timeline Control** then double-click **play**:

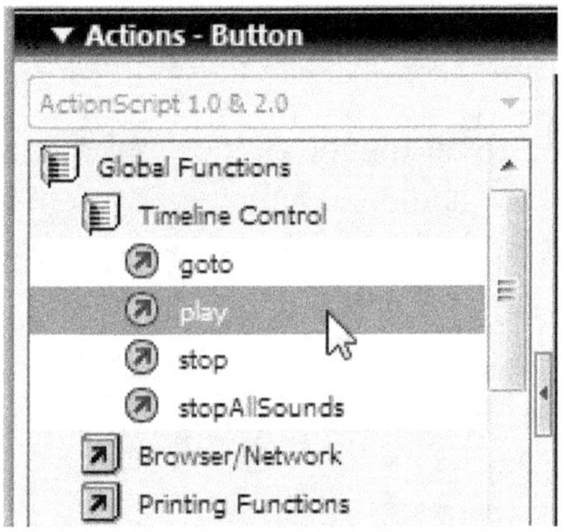

That's it! When you use Script Assist Flash will write the code for you! Test your movie (**CTRL + ENTER**). When your animation comes to an end click your button; your animation should start over again.

The button is a little boring so let's make it do something when the cursor rolls over the top of it. To modify the button go to the library, and then double-click the **ButtonPlay** button:

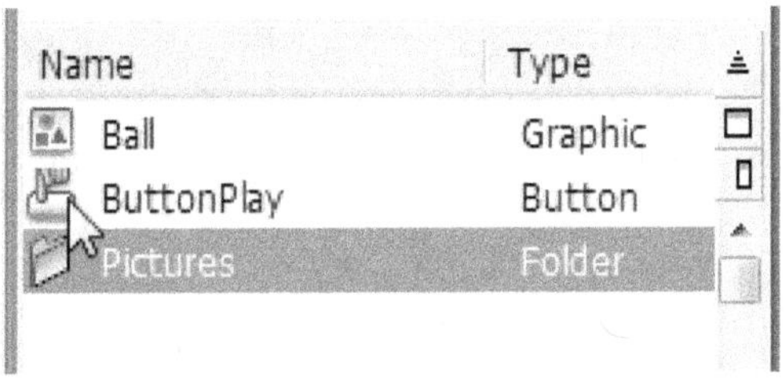

Remember to *double-click the icon* and not the text (ButtonPlay). You should now be in the editing stage for the button:

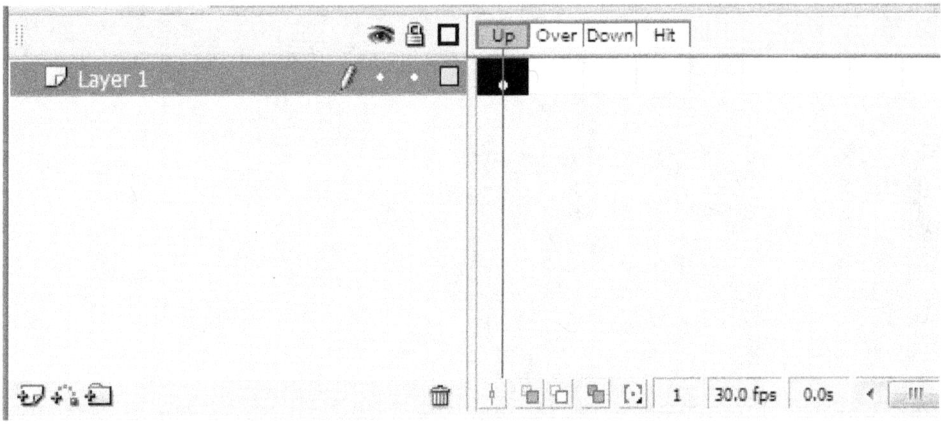

You should see the four states of the button: **Up, Over, Down** and **Hit**.

Up basically refers to what the button looks like. For instance, if you look at your stage, the **Up** state refers to the green rectangle.

Over refers to what happens when your cursor goes over the top of your button. If you want your button to change to the color red when someone puts their cursor over your button, this is where you add that color. Let's do that now so you have a better understanding.

Click on the frame right below **Over**. Then, insert a keyframe (**Insert, Timeline, Keyframe**). You'll notice that Flash automatically inserted a copy of the Green button on the stage:

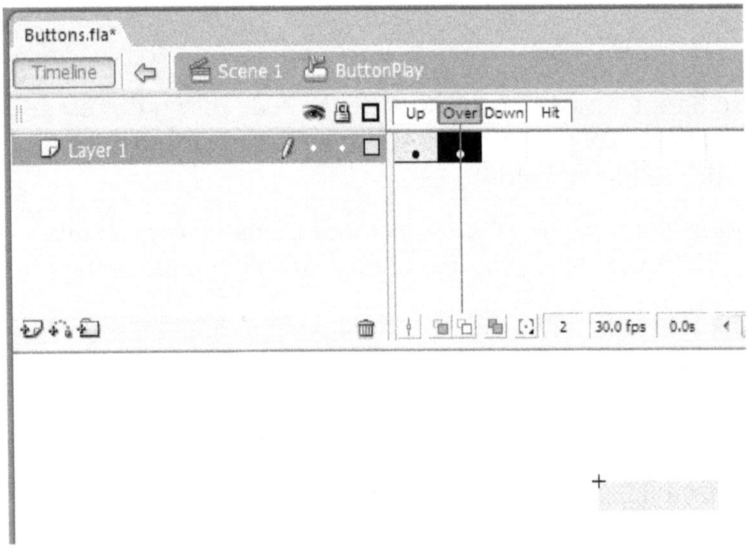

With the Green Button still selected, change its color to red. Click on **Fill color** and select **red**:

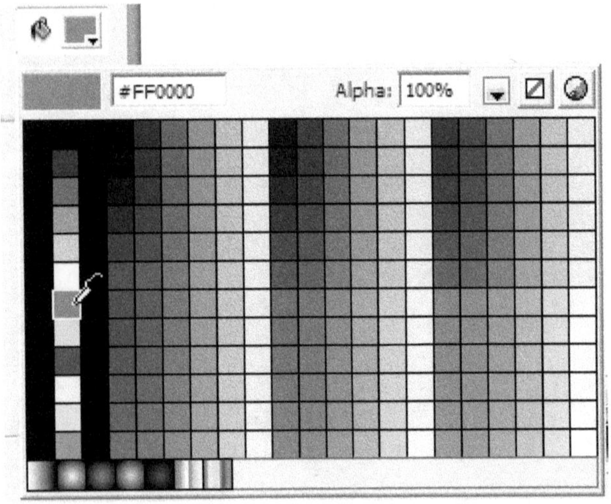

The button should now be red. When a user rolls over this button, the button will turn red. Try it out by testing your movie (CTRL + ENTER) and roll over the button. We'll now add a different color for the **Down** state. Insert a keyframe under **Down**:

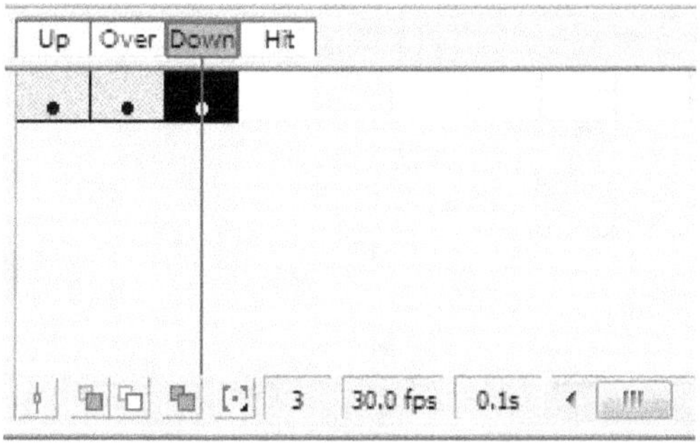

You should now have a copy of the red rectangle shape on the stage. Change the color of this new shape to **blue**:

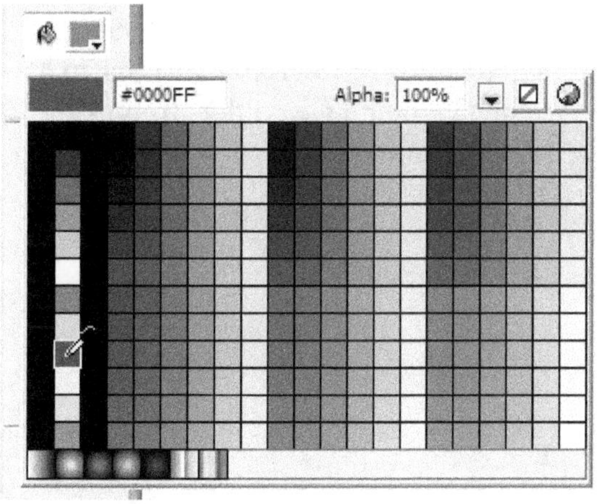

Test your movie (CTRL + ENTER). Watch what happens when you **press down** on this button:

See how the color is blue only on the **Down** state? We now have three colors on this button: green for **Up**, red for **Over**, and blue for **Down**.

Next we'll add a sound effect to this button to give it some life. First, name the first layer **Button.** Then, add a new layer by clicking on the **Insert Layer** button and name it **Sound**:

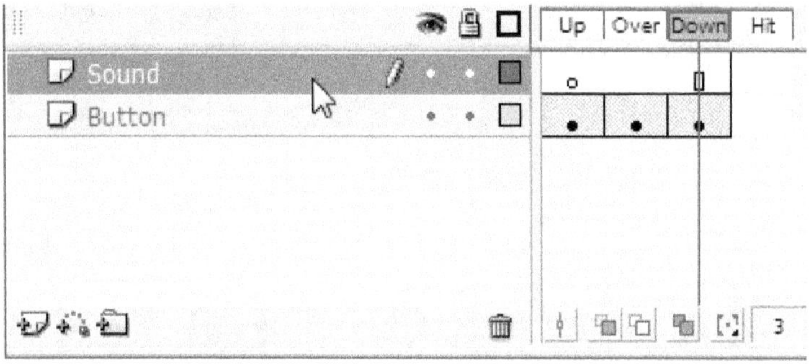

We only want the sound to occur when the cursor goes over the button. So when the button turns red, we want the sound. Add a keyframe under **Over** in the **Sound** layer. We'll now add the sound file. Go to **File**, **Import** and **Import to Library**. Open the **Sounds** folder located in the Chapter Two folder. Import the file called **beep.mp3.** You should now see it in your library:

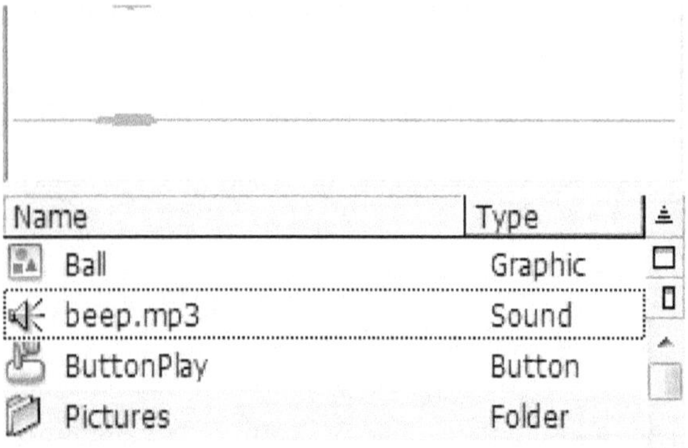

Click on the keyframe you just made under **Over**:

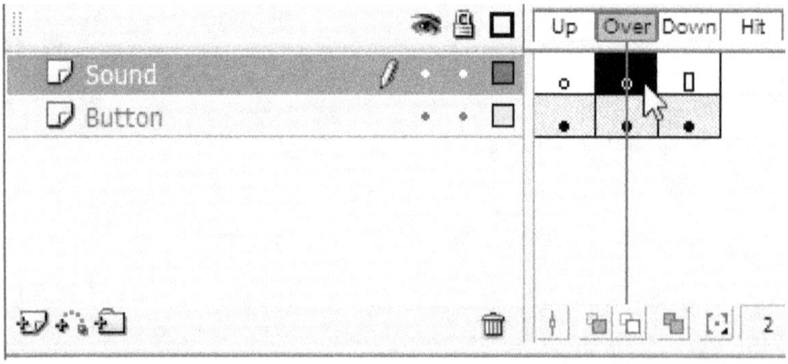

Open Properties panel. You'll see an option for Sound on the far right. Click the arrow next to **None** and select **Beep.mp3**:

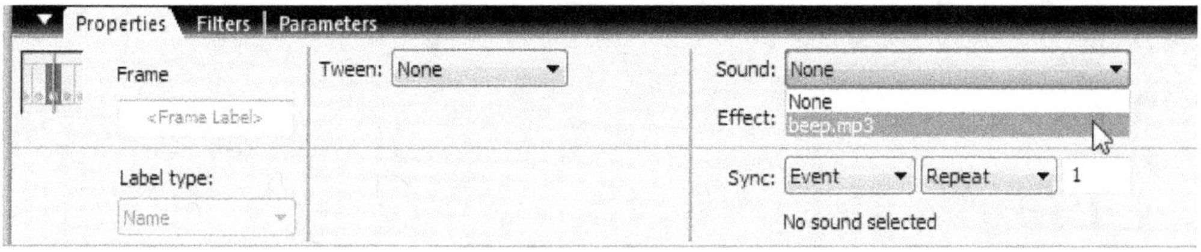

It should look like this when you're done:

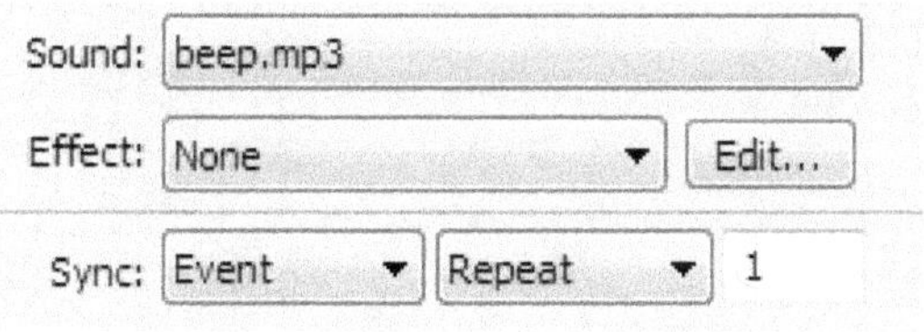

Test your movie (CTRL + ENTER). When you roll over the button it should make a beep noise. So now you're probably wondering what the **Hit** state means. The **Hit** state refers to the shape and active area of the button; also, whatever shape is placed in the **Hit** state will be transparent when you publish your movie.

To better understand how the **Hit** state works, select the frame under **Hit**:

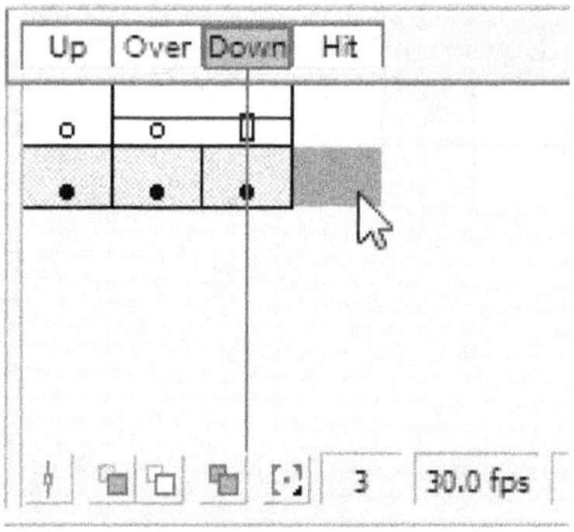

Go to **Insert**, **Timeline**, and **Blank Keyframe**:

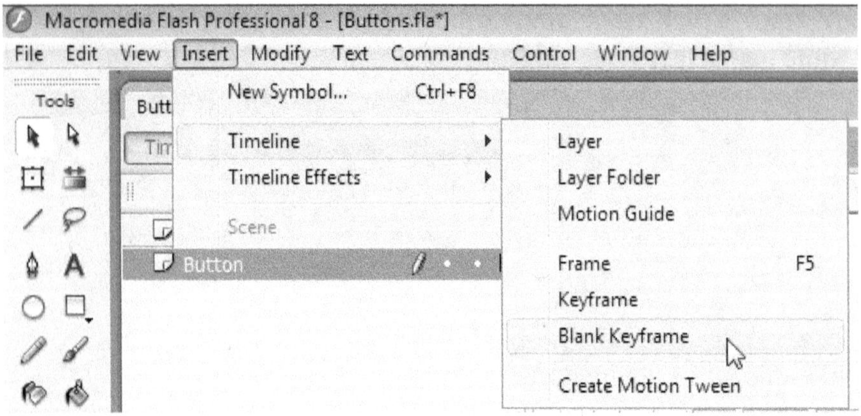

The Hit frame should now look like this:

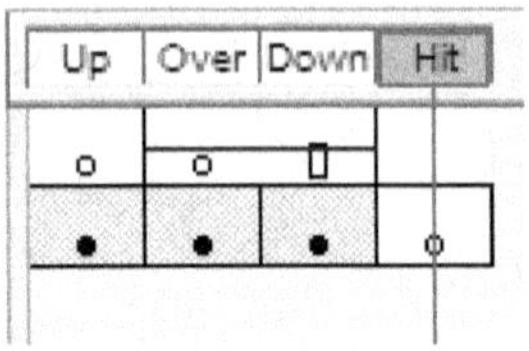

Test your movie (**CTRL + ENTER**) and try your button. You'll soon notice that your button is no longer working. There is no Hit area since we added a blank keyframe under **Hit**. So you can understand this better, click on **Scene 1** next to **ButtonPlay** (**CS3/CS4/CS5** - these links are located above the stage):

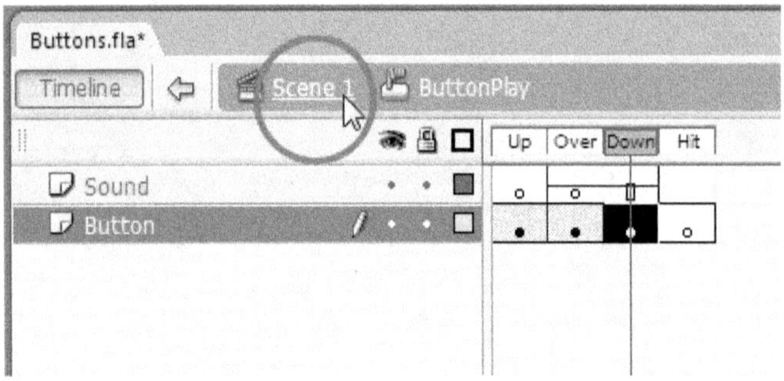

You should now be back on your main scene. This time, instead of selecting the button in the library to edit it, double-click your button on the stage to enter its editing stage:

Notice that when we double-click this button you're able to edit it while still viewing the Juggler? This is a great way to edit symbols since you're able to still see elements on the main timeline.

Select the blank keyframe under **Hit**. Next, draw a circle on the stage above the Juggler's head using the **Oval Tool** (use any Fill color you like):

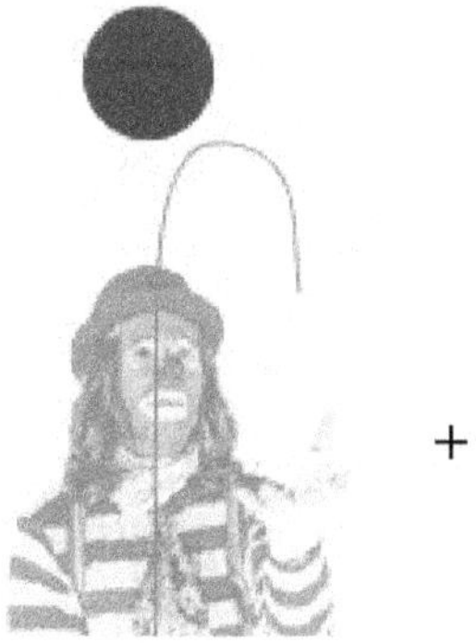

Test your movie (CTRL + ENTER). You'll now notice that your button only works when you roll over the circle you just created:

So, wherever you place your object under **Hit** is where your active area is. Go back to the Button's editing stage. Click on the keyframe under **Hit**. What we're going to do now is remove that keyframe. Go to **Modify**, **Timeline**, and **Clear Keyframe**.

Since you cleared the keyframe under **Hit**, Flash put a frame in its place. Test your movie (CTRL + ENTER). The button should be back to normal.

We'll make another button that will stop the animation. We can either make another button from scratch, or, we can make a copy of the button we just created. Let's do that. First, go back to Scene 1 by clicking the **Scene 1** link above the timeline/stage:

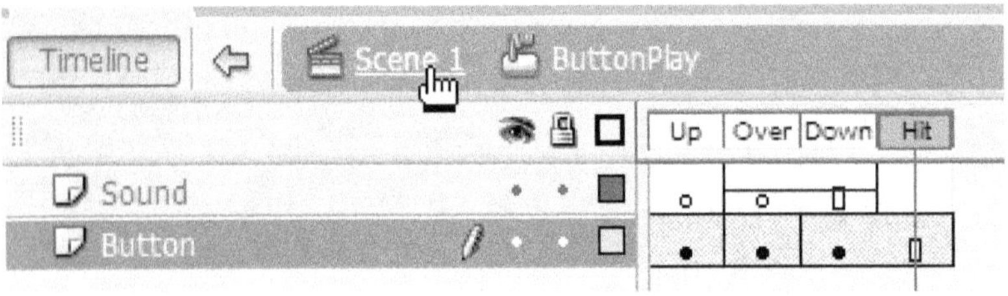

Next, we need to copy the button. We do that by first selecting the button, then going to **Edit**, and **Copy**:

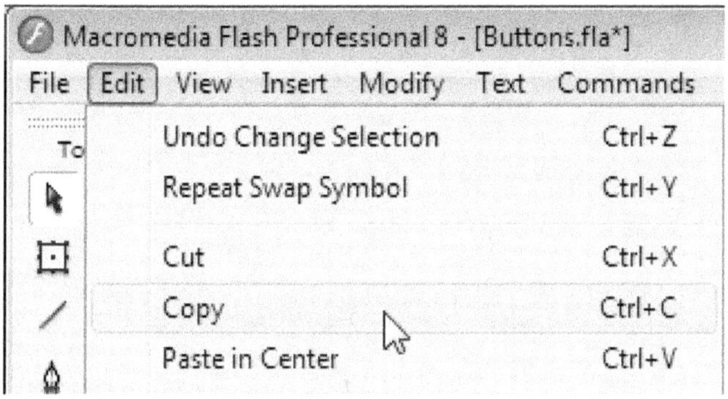

Before we paste the copied button on the stage, we need to create a new layer for it. Highlight the **Button 1** layer:

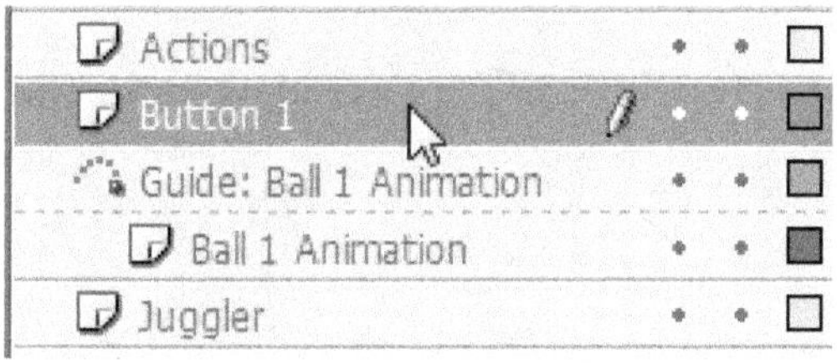

Next, click on the **New Layer** icon and name this new layer **Button 2**. Click once on the first frame of this new layer:

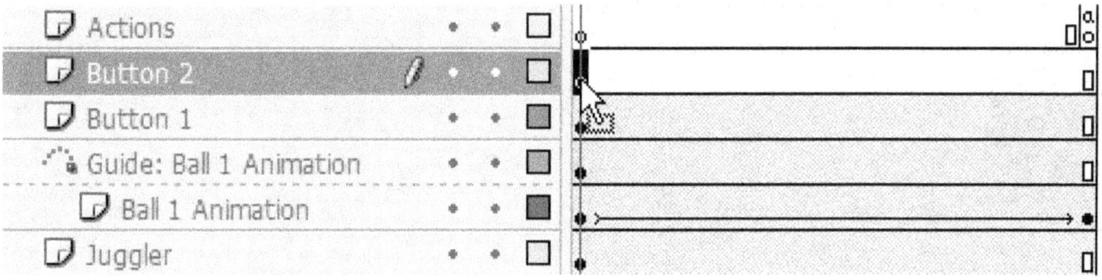

Go to **Edit**, **Paste in Place** (this will paste the copied button in the exact same spot as the first button):

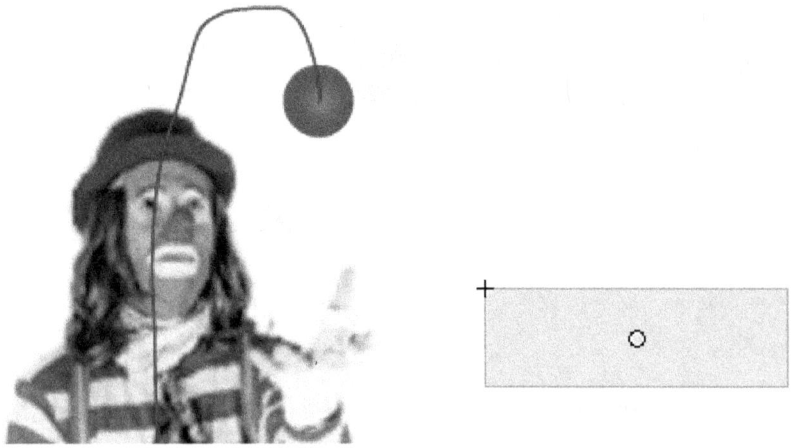

This new button is now in frame 1 of the **Button 2** layer. Drag this new button so that it's below the first button:

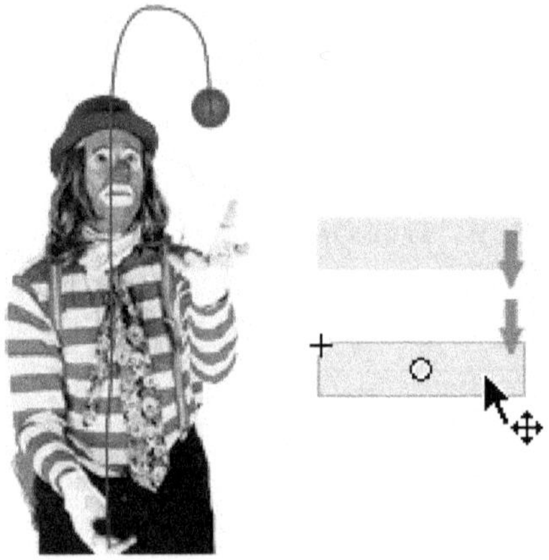

Now we have two identical buttons. If you look in your Actions panel you'll see that it has the same ActionScript as the first button (buttons that are copied will also copy over their ActionScript):

```
on (release) {
    tellTarget ("_level0/") {
        play();
    }
}
```

Since we want this button to tell the timeline to stop we need to add that code now. Click on the line that has the tellTarget code. It should turn blue:

```
on (release) {
    tellTarget ("_level0/") {
        play();
    }
}
```

Next, go to **Global Functions**, **Timeline Control** and double-click **stop**. This **stop** code will be placed below the tellTarget code:

```
on (release) {
    tellTarget ("_level0/") {
        stop();
        play();
    }
}
```

Click on the word **play**. It should turn blue which means it's selected. Hit DELETE and your final code should now look like this:

```
on (release) {
    tellTarget ("_level0/") {
        stop();
    }
}
```

Go ahead and test your movie (CTRL + ENTER). When the ball is in the air click on the second button. It should stop the animation. To continue the animation select the first button. Basically both buttons are controlling the timeline. One stops it and the other one plays it.

Next, we'll change the color of the second button. Double-click on the second button to enter its editing stage. Select the first frame:

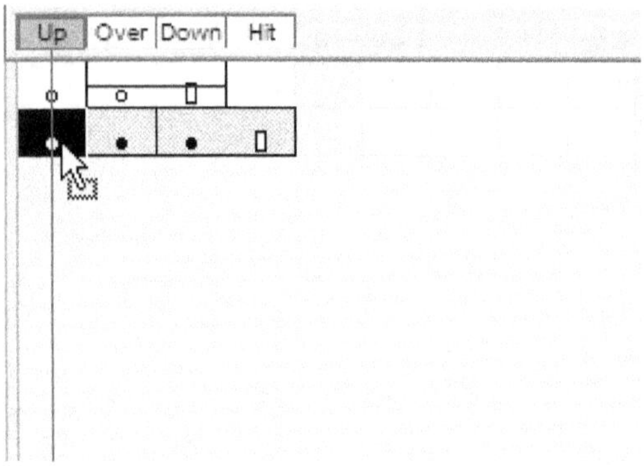

Clicking this frame will highlight the green shape on the stage. Change the **Fill color** to **red**:

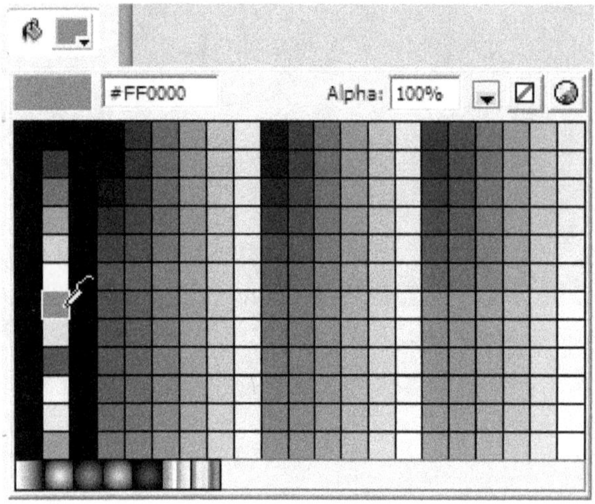

The green shape should now be red. Test your movie (CTRL + ENTER). Your second button is red, but so is the first one now! That's not quite what we wanted. Why did the first button also change color? Well, whenever you duplicate a symbol (as we did with the first button) any edit changes you make to your duplicated symbol will also happen to the original symbol.

So we need to make the second button an entirely separate symbol. Before we do this, let's change the button color back to green by going to **Edit**, **Undo Fill color** (CTRL + Z). Once you're done, click on the **Scene 1** link and return to Scene 1.

We need to make the second button a separate symbol so you can edit it without affecting the first button. Select the second button then look at the Properties panel; you'll see a button named **Swap**:

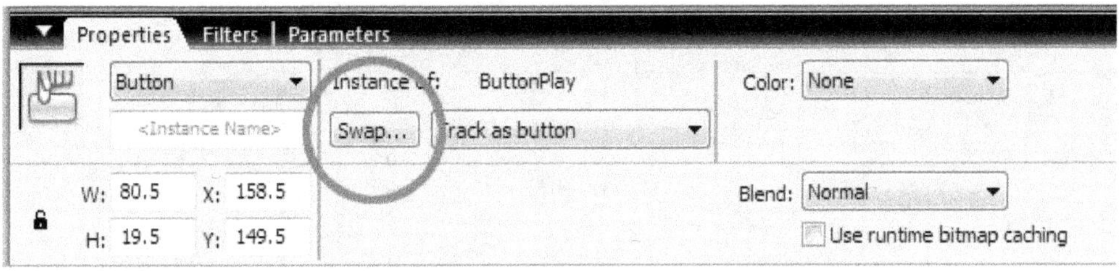

Click the **Swap** button and the **Swap Symbol** window will appear:

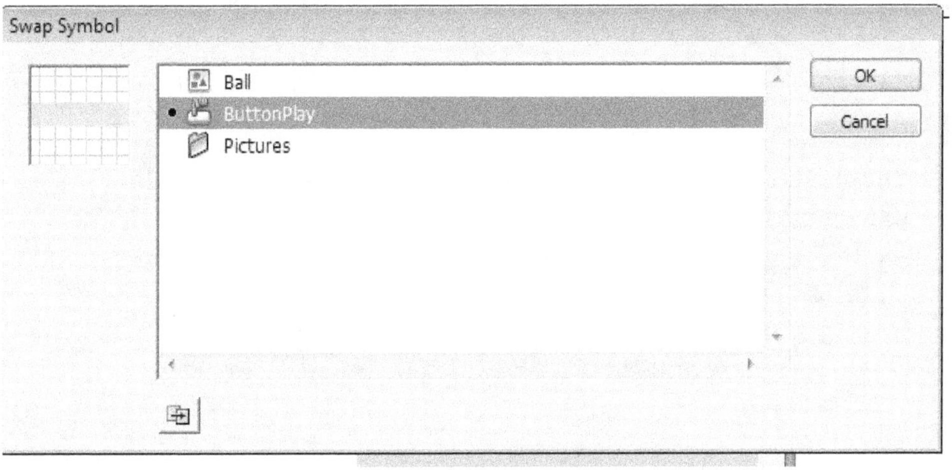

Highlight **ButtonPlay** (if it isn't already highlighted) and then click the **Duplicate Symbol** button:

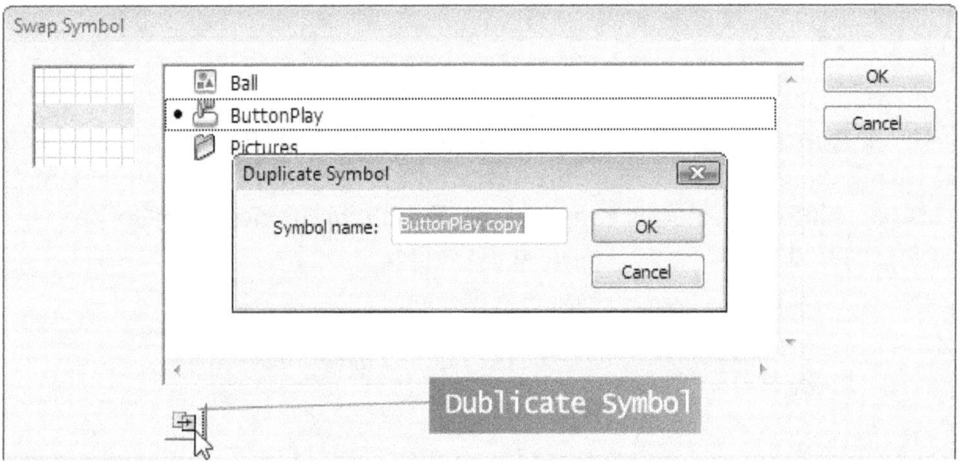

You'll then see a box pop up asking you to name the new button symbol. Type **ButtonStop**:

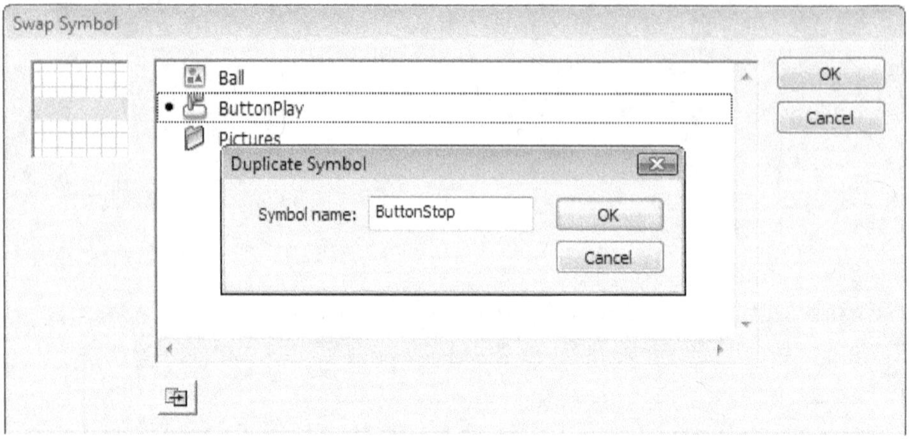

Hit **OK**. You should now see the new button (The **Swap Symbol** window displays all the items in your library):

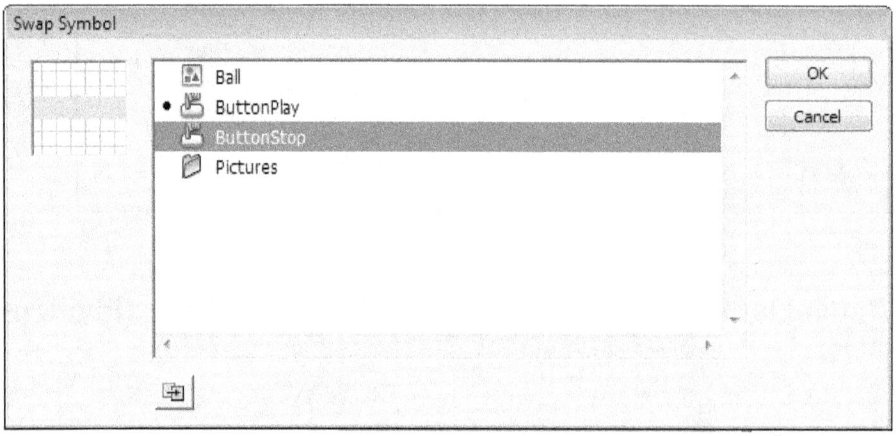

Double-click **ButtonStop** and the pop-up window will close. The second button is now its own button and any editing changes won't affect the first button. Double-click this new button to enter its editing stage. Highlight the first frame of the **Button** layer to select the green shape on the stage:

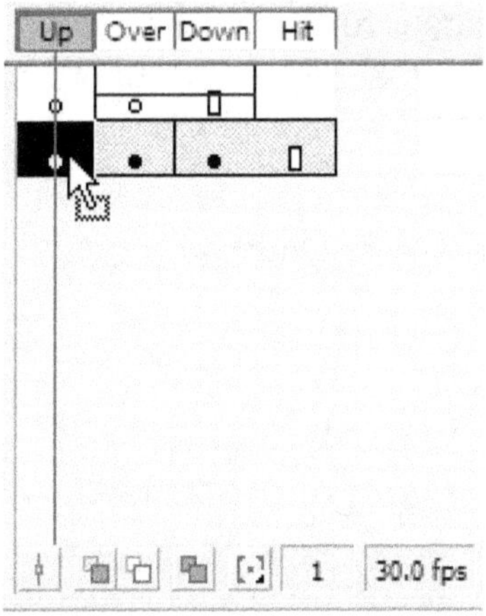

Change the **Fill color** to **red**. The green shape should now be red:

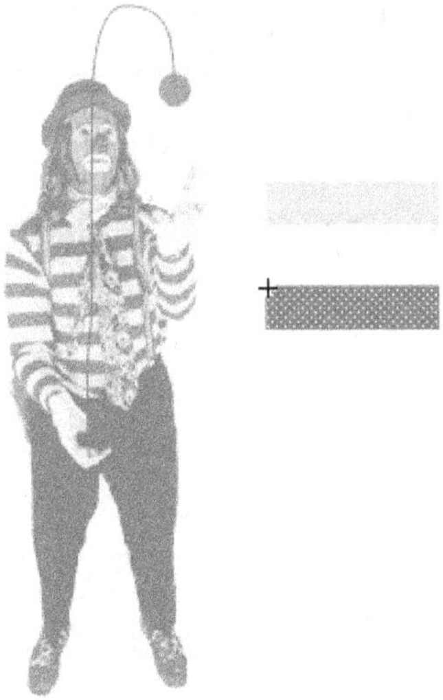

Since the **Over** color is red we'll have to change that to a different color. Select the second keyframe of the **Button** layer:

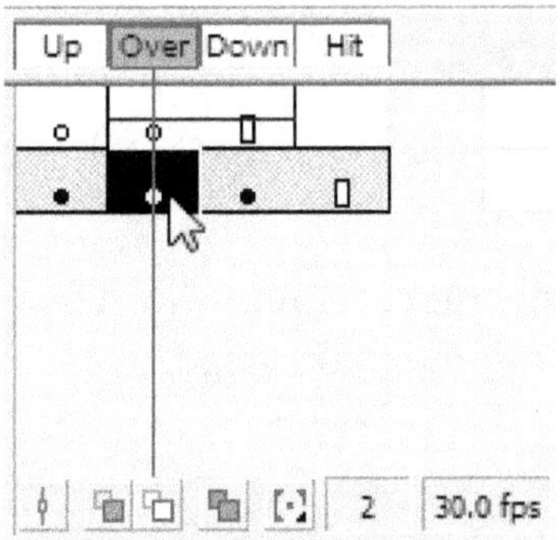

Next, change the **Fill color** to **green**. When the user's cursor rolls over the second button it will change to green. Test your movie (CTRL + ENTER) and test both buttons.

You should have a better understanding of how buttons work. In the next project we'll create a fancier button that utilizes a Movie clip. If you're ready, let's get started.

Animated Button

In this section we'll be discussing a more advanced type of button. Instead of just changing color when the user rolls over the button, an animation will play. In this exercise when the user rolls over a fireplace button, a fire begins animating. In this project you'll be using Buttons, a Movie clip, and a Mask.

Go to the Chapter 2 folder and open the file called **Button_Movie.fla**. You'll notice in the library that there are three elements:

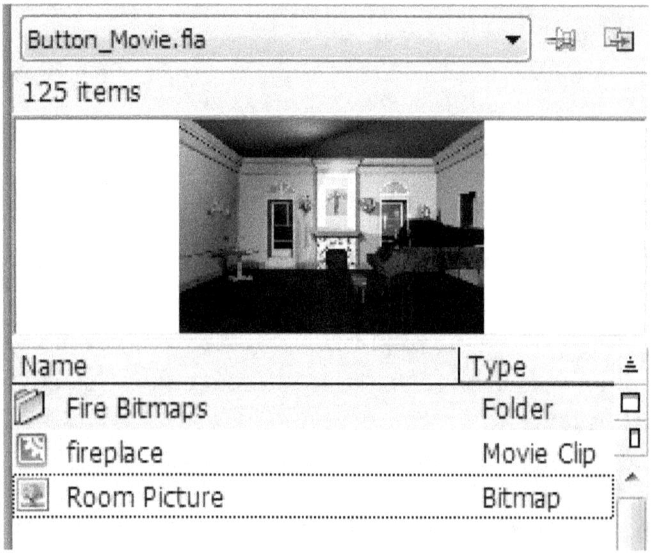

A folder with the Fire bitmaps, Room Picture, and the **fireplace** Movie clip. The first thing we want to do is drag the **Room Picture** over to the main stage:

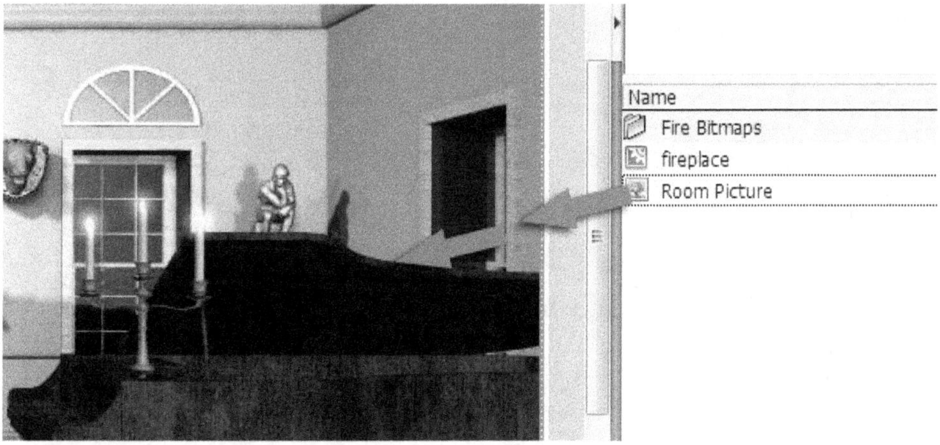

We want the picture to be exactly in the center of the stage so you'll need to use the **Align Tools**. Select the **Room Picture** and open the Align panel. Select **To Stage**, **Align Vertical Center** and **Align Horizontal Center**:

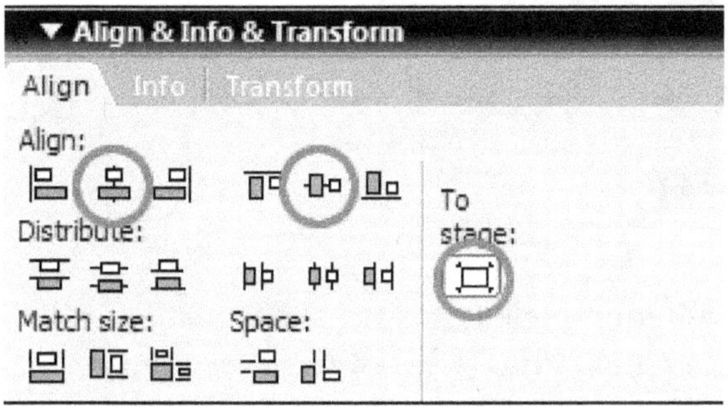

The picture will now be perfectly centered on the stage. Rename Layer 1 **Background**:

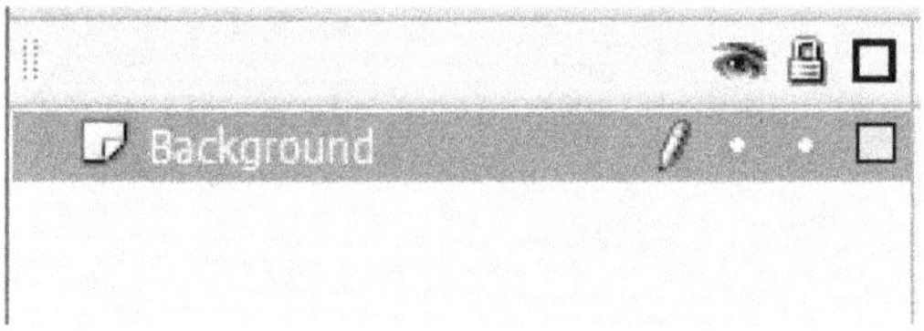

Create a new layer and name it **Fireplace Button**:

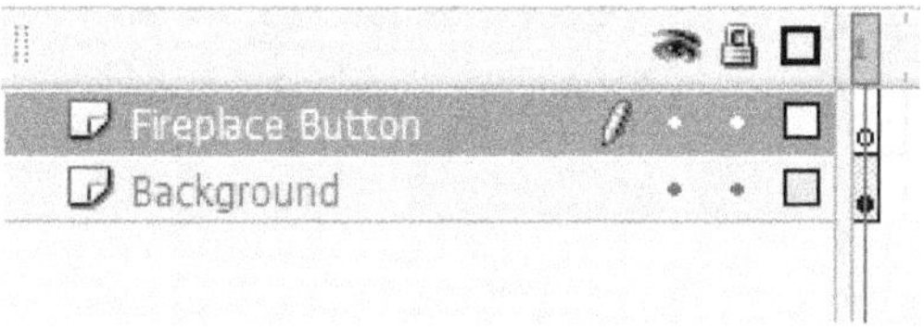

The next thing we'll do is create the button. Select the **Rectangle Tool**:

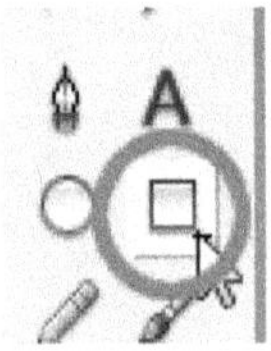

Use **red** as the **Fill color**. Zoom into the stage 200% and create a square shape over the fireplace:

We now need to convert this shape to a button. Select this red shape and go to **Modify**, **Convert to Symbol**. When the **Convert to Symbol** window appears, type **Fireplace** for the name and select **Button** for **Type**:

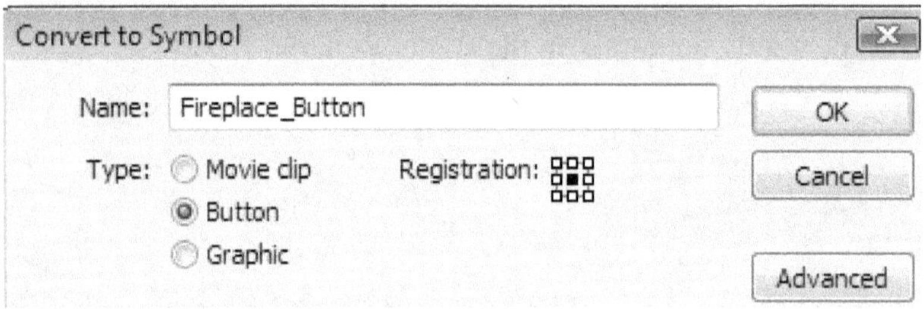

Hit **OK**. Your red shape is now a button. Double-click this new button to enter its editing stage:

The background image should still be visible. We don't want the red shape to show up when we publish the Flash file, so we need to make this shape transparent. We do this by first selecting the red shape, then clicking on **Fill color**. Next, take the **Alpha** down to **0**:

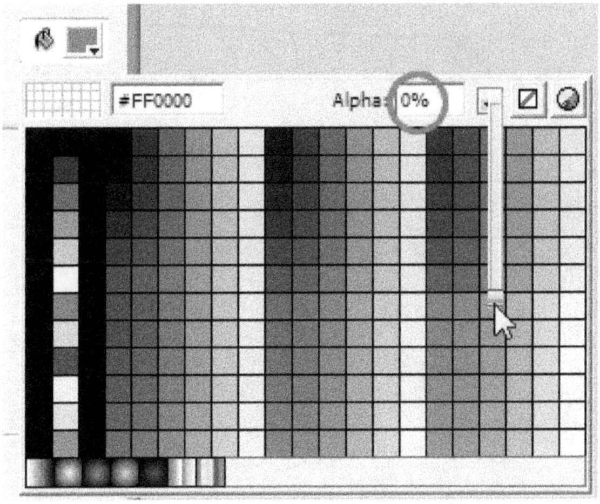

Test your movie (CTRL + ENTER). This button should now be transparent:

Insert a keyframe into the frame under the **Over** state (**Insert, Timeline,** and **Keyframe**).

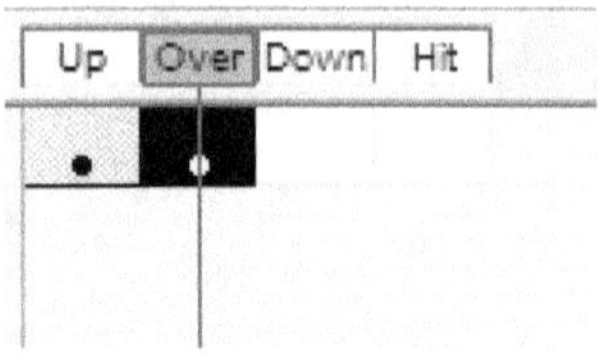

You'll notice that Flash duplicated what was in the first frame and placed it in the **Over** state. Since we don't want this shape under the **Over** state we need to delete it. Select it on the stage and go to **Edit**, **Cut** (or hit DELETE).

Drag the **fireplace** Movie clip onto the stage; position it so that it's directly over the fireplace:

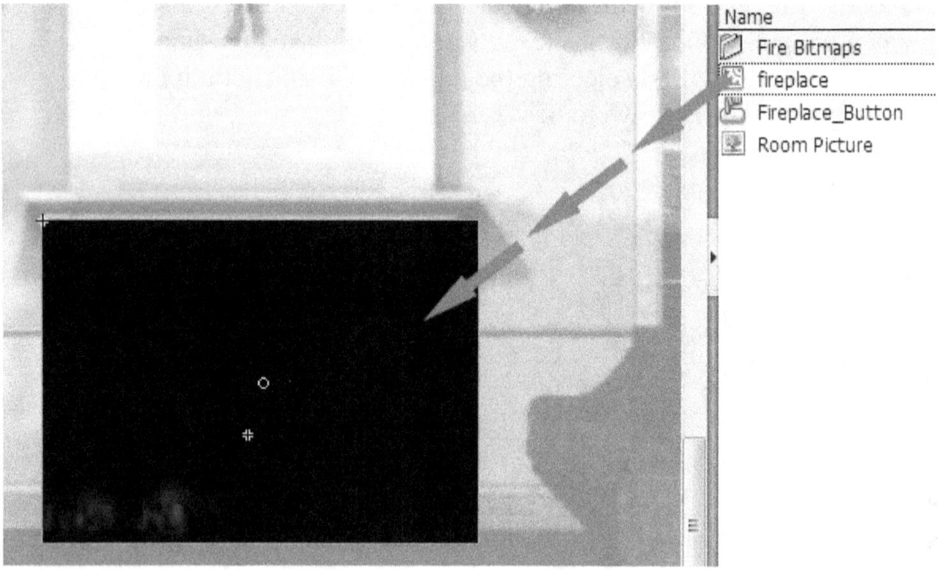

Test your movie (CTRL + ENTER). When you roll over the button area you should see the fire begin animating:

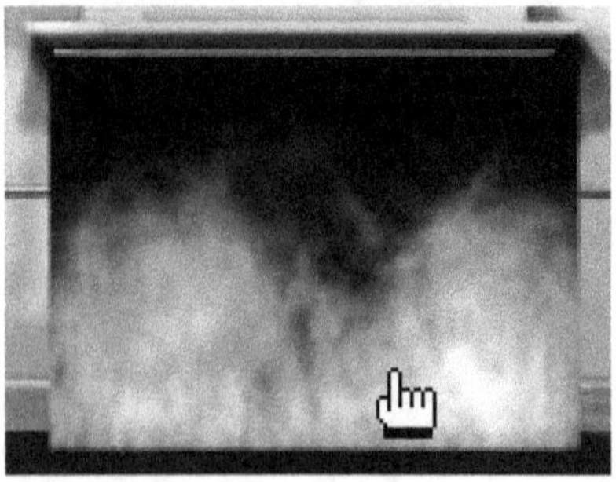

You'll notice right away that there are two problems. Number one, the animation isn't that smooth. Number two, the fire should be inside the fireplace not outside of it. Let's tackle the first problem. As we learned earlier, when an animation isn't smooth it's usually because the frame rate is too low. Click on **Modify**, and **Document**. The **Document Properties** window will appear. Change the **Frame Rate** to **30**:

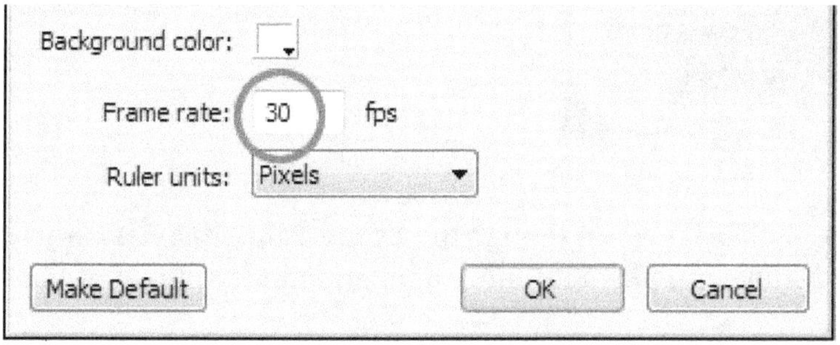

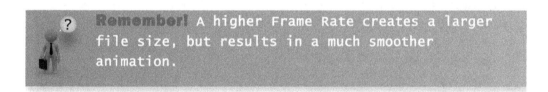

> **Remember!** A higher Frame Rate creates a larger file size, but results in a much smoother animation.

Hit **OK**. Test your movie (CTRL + ENTER) again. Roll over the button area. You'll notice that the fire is much smoother now. Very realistic. But now we need to tackle the second problem: how do we put the fire inside the fireplace?

To understand this you need to understand how a Movie clip works. A Movie clip is basically a symbol that *has its own timeline*. A Movie clip can have an animation that runs several seconds or minutes. You can then place this Movie clip into your main timeline and this Movie clip will play its entire animation even if the main timeline has only one frame.

So you have a better idea of how Movie Clips work, go back to **Scene 1** by clicking its link above the timeline/stage:

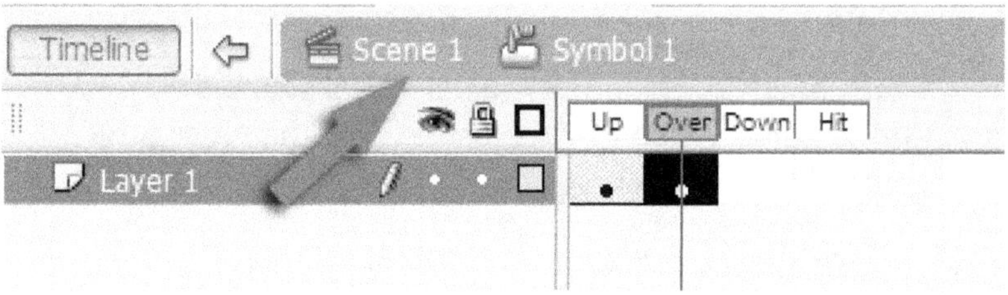

Drag the **fireplace** Movie clip onto the main stage anywhere you like:

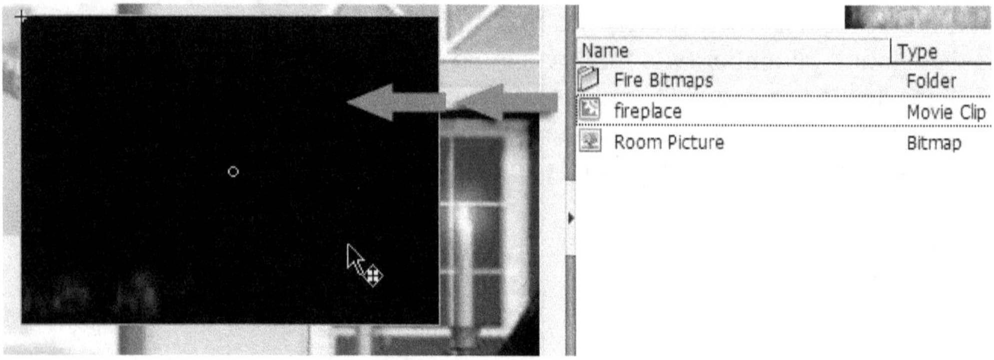

Test your movie (CTRL + ENTER). Even though the **Scene 1** timeline has only one frame, the **fireplace** Movie clip plays its entire animation independent of the main timeline.

Go ahead and delete this Movie Clip. **Double-click** on the **Fireplace Button** to enter its editing stage. What we want to do now is make the fire look like it's really in the fireplace. Select the keyframe under **Over**. Next, double-click the **fireplace** Movie clip to enter its editing stage. You should see the keyframes of the fire animation:

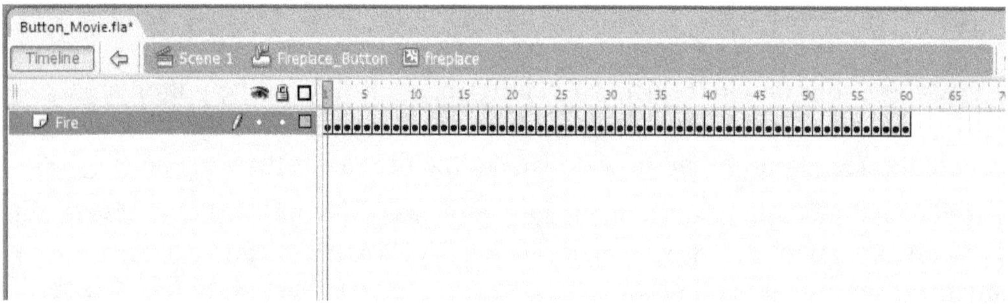

In the timeline you'll notice that the fire animation has 60 frames. Since we changed the frame rate to 30 frames per second, this animation will be 2 seconds long (30 x 2). Hit ENTER and watch the animation. The fire looks good but we'll need to place it inside the fireplace.

To do this we need to create a **mask**. Very simply, a mask is a shape that determines what part of your symbol is seen by the user. Click the **New Layer** icon and name this new layer **Mask**:

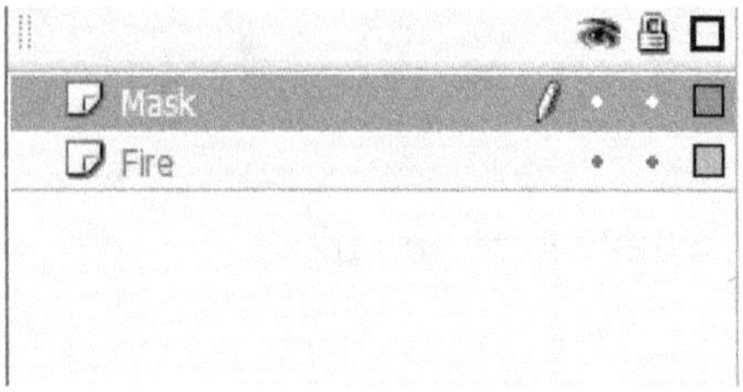

Whenever you create a new shape always make sure the frame you want to place it on is selected; otherwise, the new shape may end up on another layer. Before we create this new shape, we'll select the first frame of the **Mask** layer:

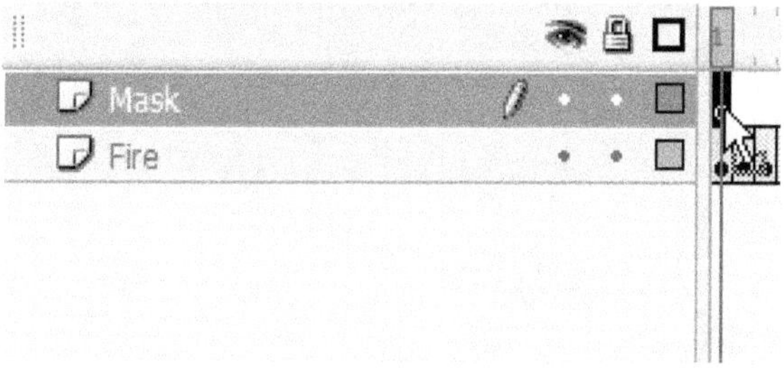

Next, click on the **Outline** button for the **Fire** layer:

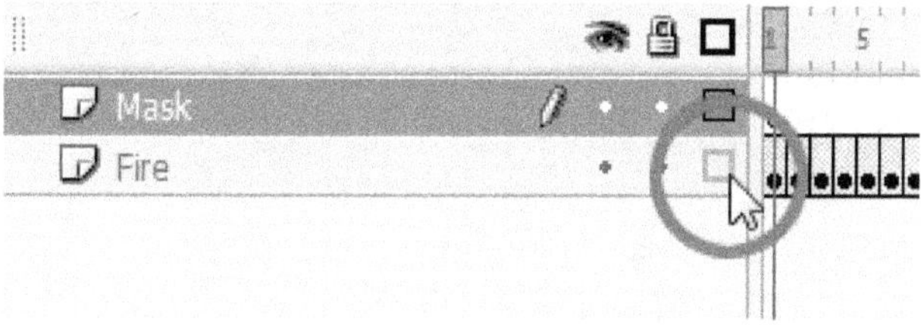

What the **Outline** option does is make your Movie clip transparent except for a colored outline:

Select the **Brush Tool** and change the **Fill color** to **red**. Select the third from the largest brush size:

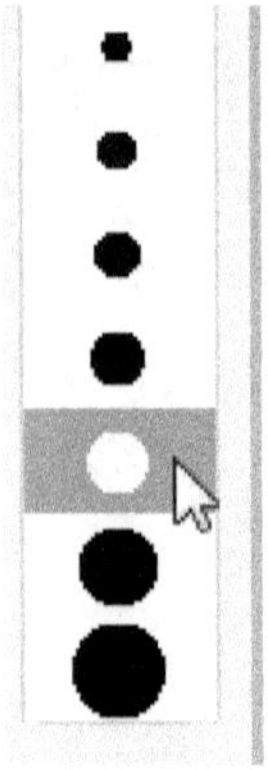

Make sure the stage is zoomed in at 200%:

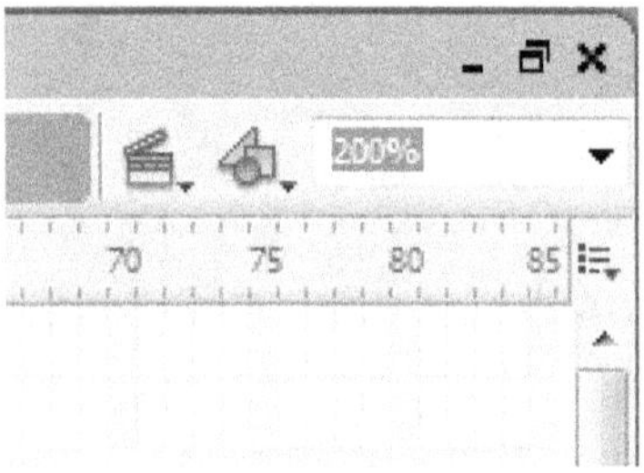

Color in the area of just the fireplace using the **Brush Tool**:

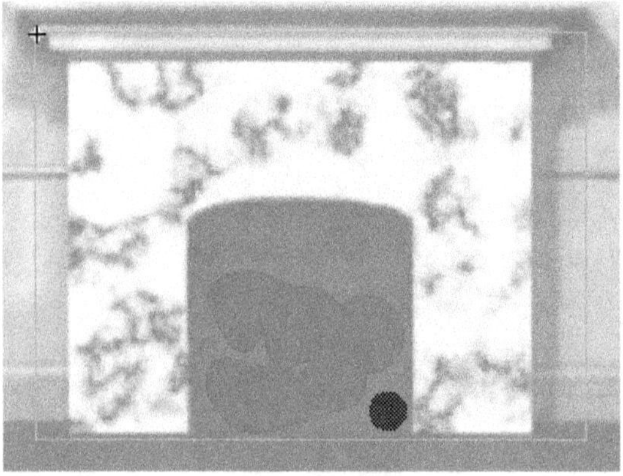

Keep going until the entire fireplace area is red:

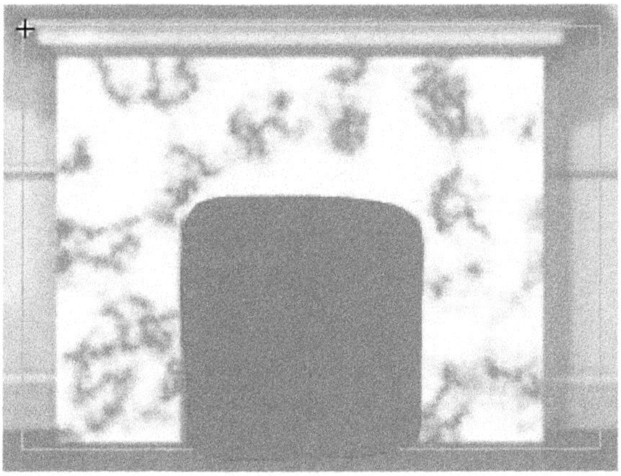

Don't worry if it's not perfect, we can always adjust it later. Test your movie (CTRL + ENTER) and roll over the fireplace button. Problem! Your fire isn't masked and now we have a large red shape in the middle of it. That's because we have one final step to make the new shape a mask. Close the Test Movie window. *Right-click* on the **Mask** layer. You should see several selections; choose **Mask**:

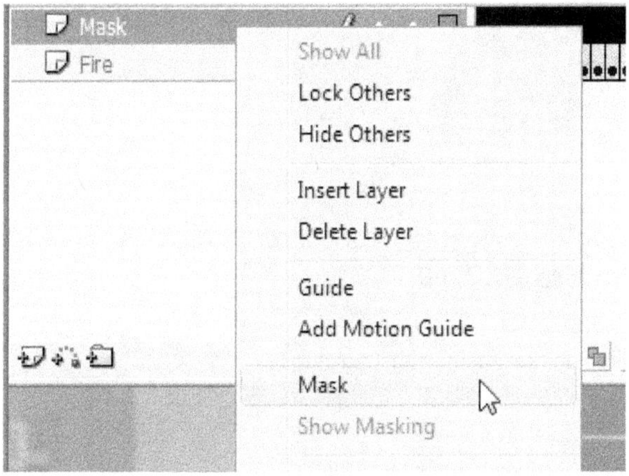

The **Fire** layer will now be indented under the Mask layer indicating that it's being masked:

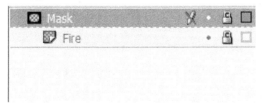

Also, you'll see that both layers are now locked. Test your movie (CTRL + ENTER). The fire is now inside the fireplace! If you notice that your fire animation isn't perfectly inside the fireplace, you can modify the mask shape with the **Eraser** tool. Let's do that now. The first thing we need to do is unlock both layers by clicking the padlock icons on both layers:

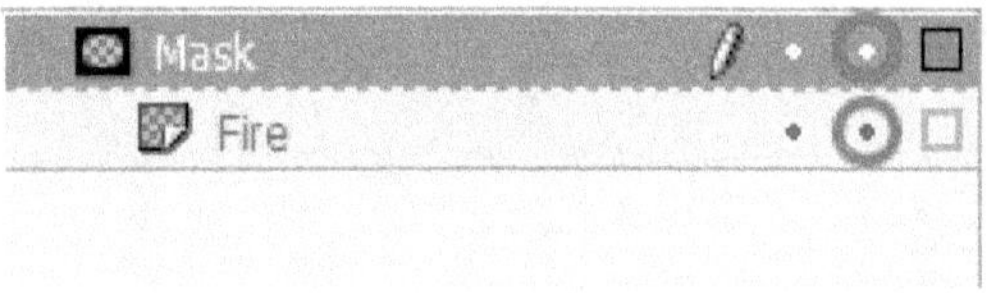

The fireplace area should now look like this:

When you use a mask, Flash automatically locks the mask layer and any layers that are being masked. Next, select the **Eraser Tool**:

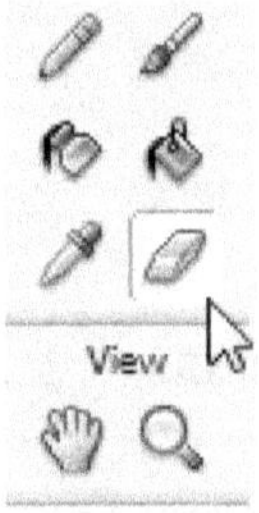

Zoom into the stage 400%. Use the **Hand Tool** to position the fireplace in the center of the window. Using the **Eraser Tool**, erase any areas of the red mask that go outside the fireplace:

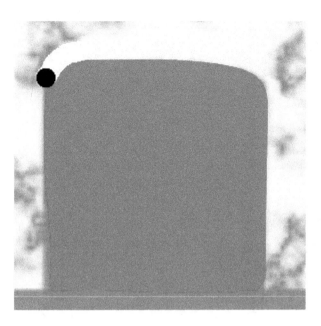

Once you finish erasing any areas of the red that are outside the fireplace area, the next step is to paint in any areas that need to be filled in. On my mask there is a small area that needs to be filled in with red paint:

Selecting the **Brush Tool**, and choosing the color red (any color will work though), I'll start painting in the area that needs to be filled in:

My mask looks better now. If you have finished tweaking your mask, go ahead and test your movie (CTRL + ENTER). It should now look similar to mine:

Before we wrap on this project, let's do a couple more things. What if we want the eyes of the animals on the wall to turn red when we roll over the fireplace button? And let's say that we want an animal noise to occur when this happens. Not sure why we would want this but why not. First, click the Fireplace Button link above the timeline (**CS3/CS4/CS5**: stage links are above the stage area):

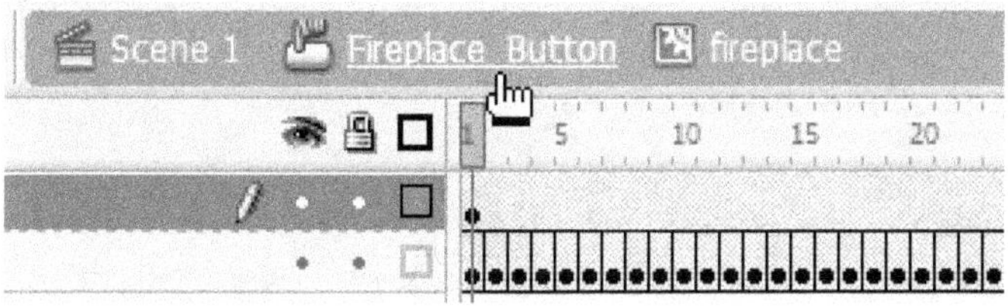

This will take you back to the button's editing stage. Next, name the first layer **Fireplace** and then make a new layer and name it **Eyes**. Insert a keyframe under the **Over** state on the **Eyes** layer:

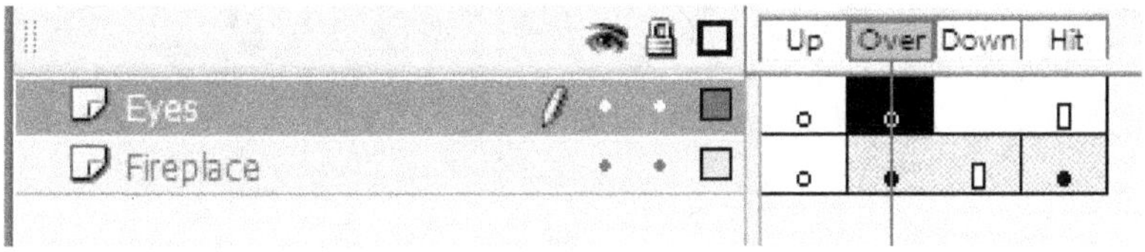

Make sure the stage is zoomed in at 400%. Using the **Hand** Tool, move the stage so that you have a good view of the animals on the wall:

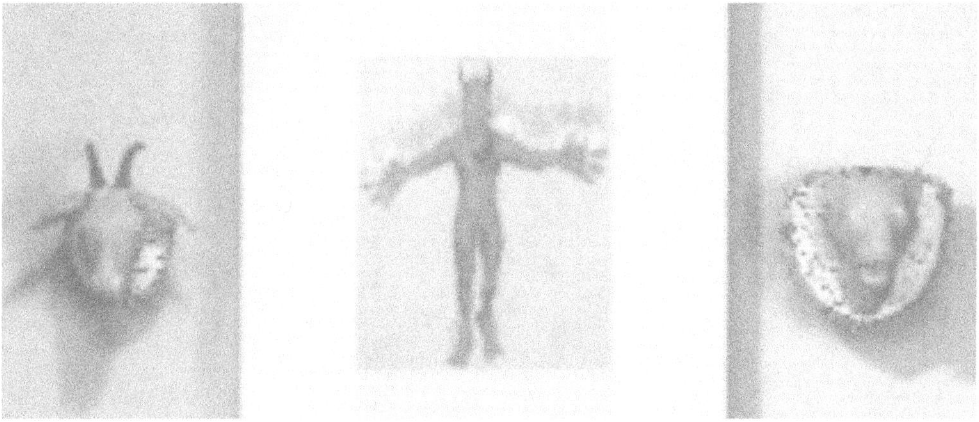

What we would like to do now is use the **Brush Tool** to paint red in their eyes. Grab the **Brush Tool**, select **red** for the **Fill color**, and make sure you use a small brush size:

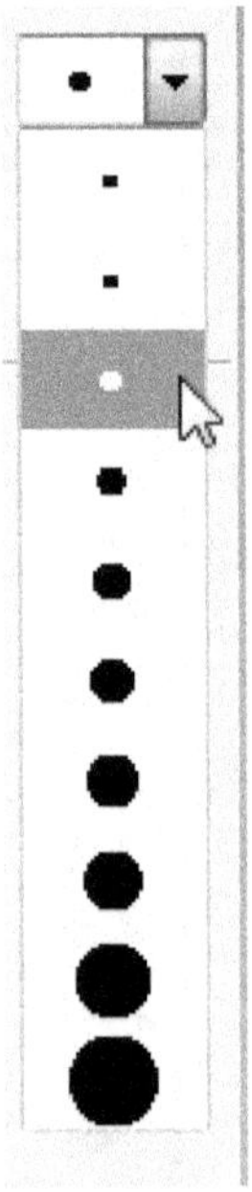

Paint over the eyes of the animals:

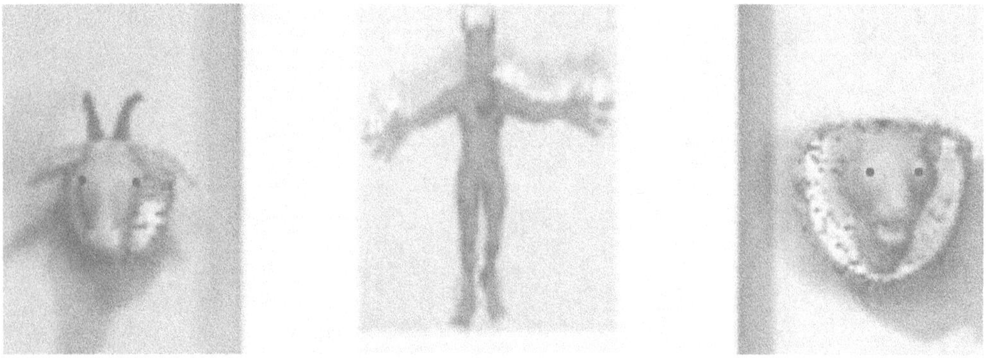

Once you're done test your movie (CTRL + ENTER). When you roll over the fireplace button the animals' eyes turn red. But now we need an animal sound. Make a new layer and name it **Sound**. Next, insert a keyframe under the **Over** state on the **Sound** layer:

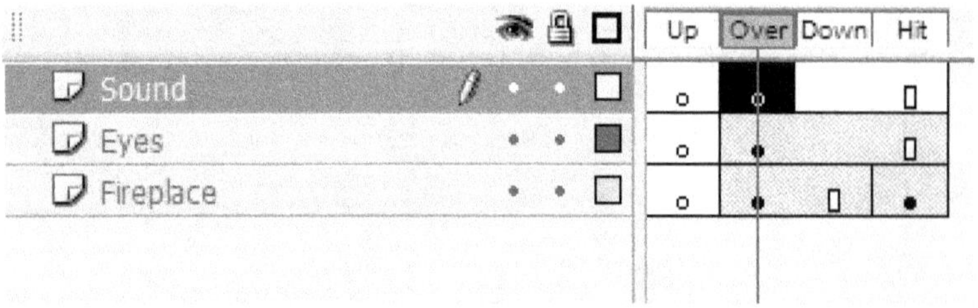

Go to **File, Import,** and **Import to Library**. Open the **Sounds** folder located in the Chapter Two folder. Import the file named **lion growls.wav.** You should now see it in your library:

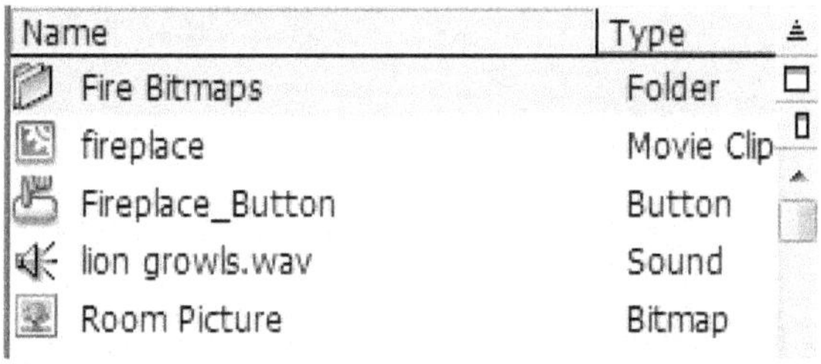

Select the keyframe under **Over**:

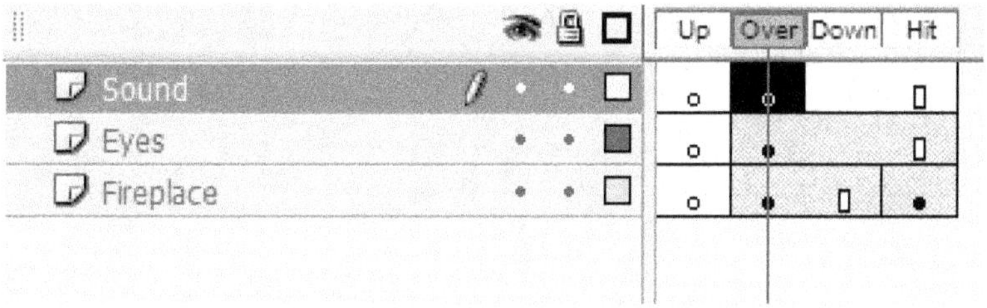

Open the Properties panel. Just as before, we're going to add a sound to a frame. Select the drop-down arrow next to **Sound** and select **lion growls.wav**:

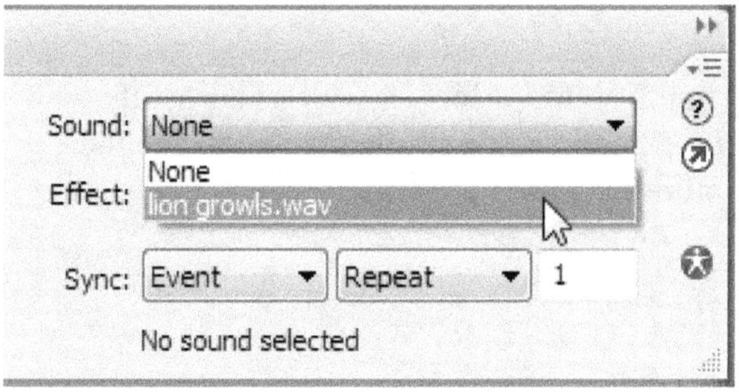

Test your movie (CTRL + ENTER). Roll over the fireplace button and you should hear a lion growl. The problem is that it doesn't start right away and it's too long; also, when we roll off the fireplace button the sound effect should stop and this sound effect continues playing. Let's fix these problems.

First, click on the **Edit** button:

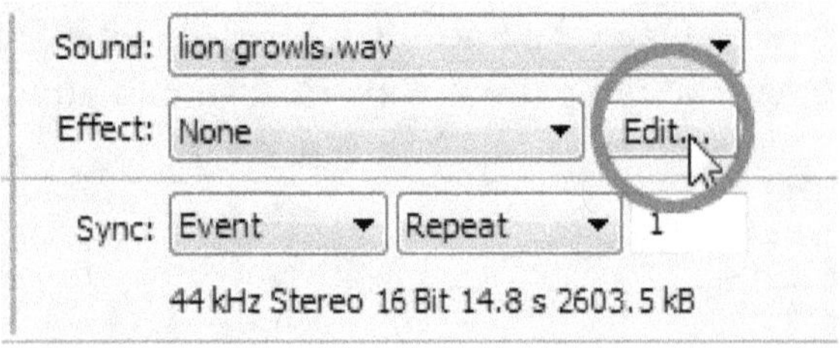

You should then see the **Edit Envelope** window:

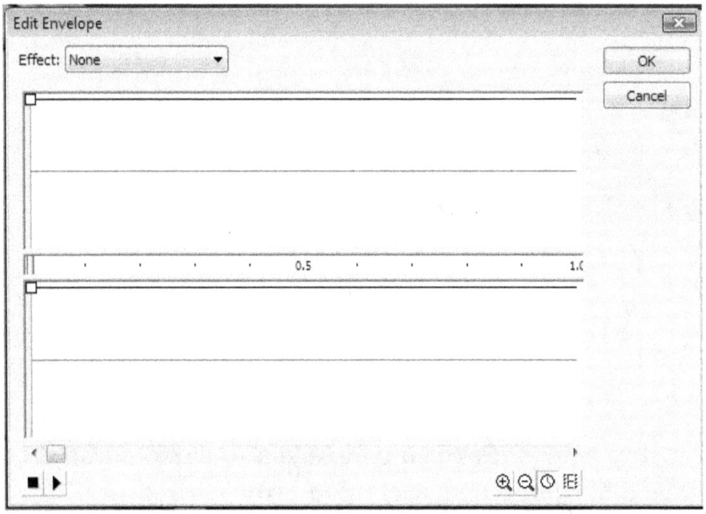

In this window you'll be able to shorten the sound effect as well as adjust its volume. Before we can edit the sound we need to Zoom out so we can see the waveform. Click the **Zoom out** button until you see the waveform:

The **Edit Envelope** window should look similar to this:

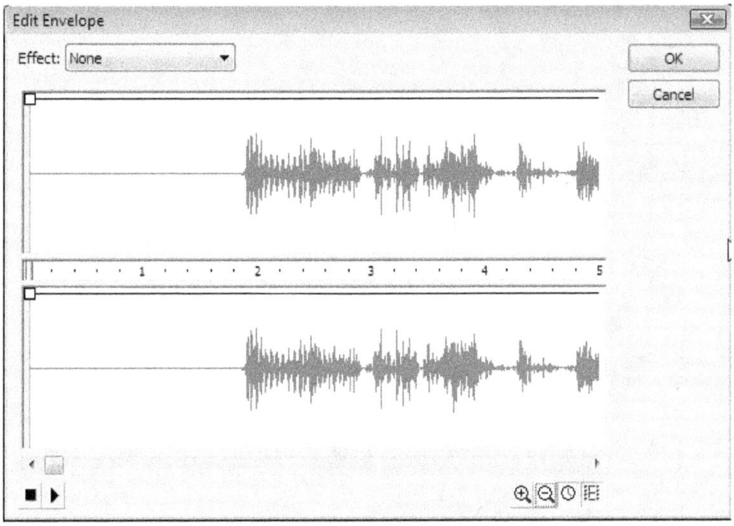

You'll notice that there are two waveforms. The top waveform is the left channel, and the bottom waveform is the right channel. Between the waveforms you'll see the Edit Envelope timeline. This timeline will either be displayed in seconds, or in frames. You can toggle between frames and seconds by clicking the buttons next to the Zoom buttons:

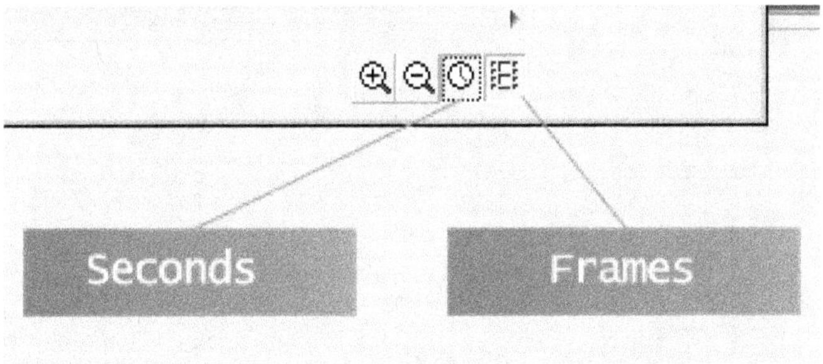

For now, make sure **Seconds** is selected. In the timeline you'll notice that the audio doesn't begin until the two second mark. So we need to remove the first two seconds of silence. We do that by moving the **Time In** slider over to the very beginning of the audio; we do this by clicking and holding the **Time In** slider:

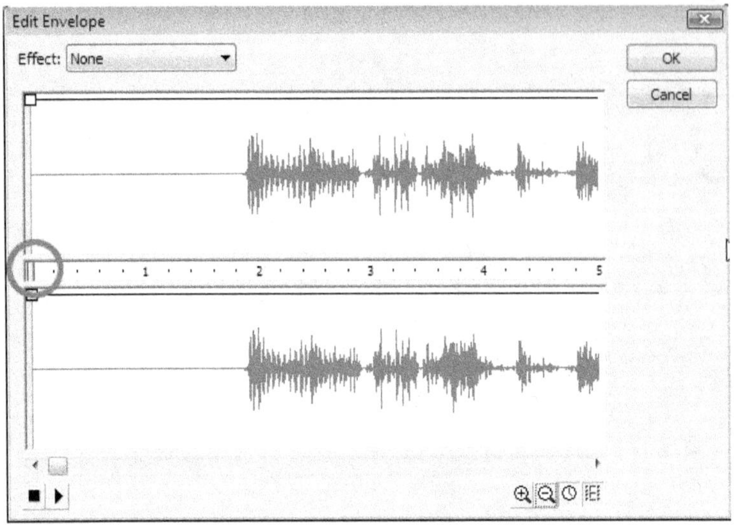

Move it to the right until it reaches the beginning of the audio:

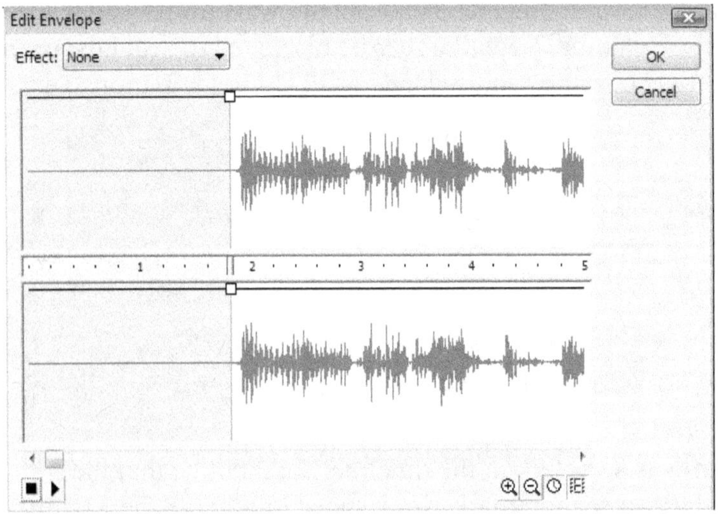

The first two seconds will now be grayed out indicating that they won't be used. Click your **Play** button to hear your new shortened audio:

The growl should start playing right away. Much better. But now we need to stop the sound as soon as the user rolls off the button; to do this we need to select the keyframe under the **Up** stage on the **Sound** layer:

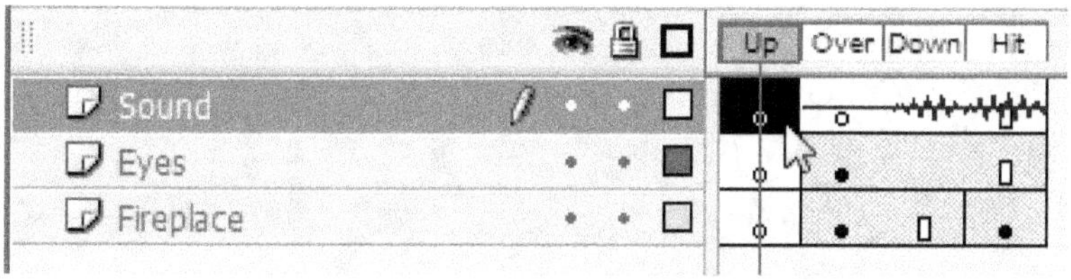

Next, with the Properties panel open, select **lion growls.wav** from the sound drop-down selections:

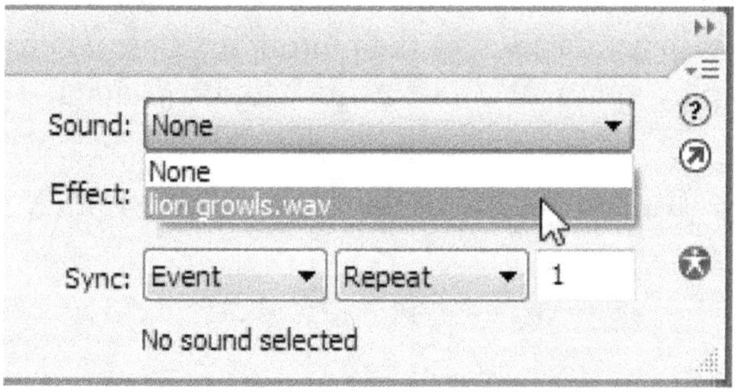

Now we need to tell this frame to stop the sound. We do that by selecting **Stop** from the **Sync** list:

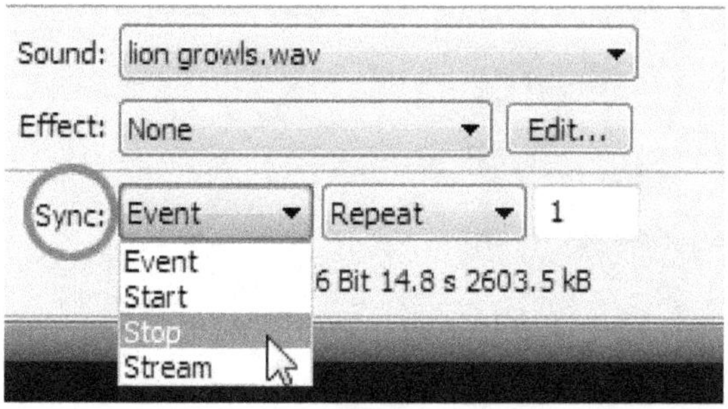

Now test your movie (CTRL + ENTER). Roll over the button and you should hear the lion sound effect. Roll off the button and the sound should stop immediately. That's it! You completed another project!

By now you should have a basic understanding of how buttons work, and how you can add movies and sound to them. Of course, there's a lot more you can do with buttons as you'll soon find out! If you're ready, let's go to the next project.

Traveling Button

In the last project you learned how to create a button that utilizes a fire Movie clip when the user rolls over the button. This time we're going to create a balloon button that travels around the stage. When we roll over the button, it stops; when we roll off the button it continues to play again. We'll be using Motion Guides again in this exercise.

So let's get started. Open the **Balloon_Button.fla** file in the Chapter Two folder. It should look like this:

So here we have the scene. A nice picture of an ocean with a balloon hovering above it. What we would like to do is have the balloon fly around the stage and when we roll over it, it should stop; when we roll off the balloon button, it should continue to float around the stage.

The first thing we need to do is convert the balloon to a button. Click on the balloon then go to **Modify**, and **Convert to Symbol**. Select **Button** as **Type**, and type **Balloon Button** next to **Name**:

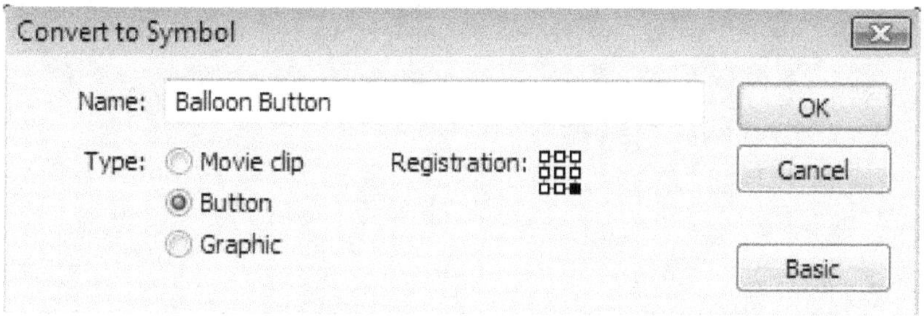

Hit **OK** when you're finished. The balloon is now a button. Let's add some ActionScript to this new button. The first thing we have to do is tell the button what to control. Since we want the timeline animation to stop when we roll over the button, then we need to target the timeline. Make sure the Balloon Button is still selected, then open the Actions panel. Make sure you are in Script Assist mode:

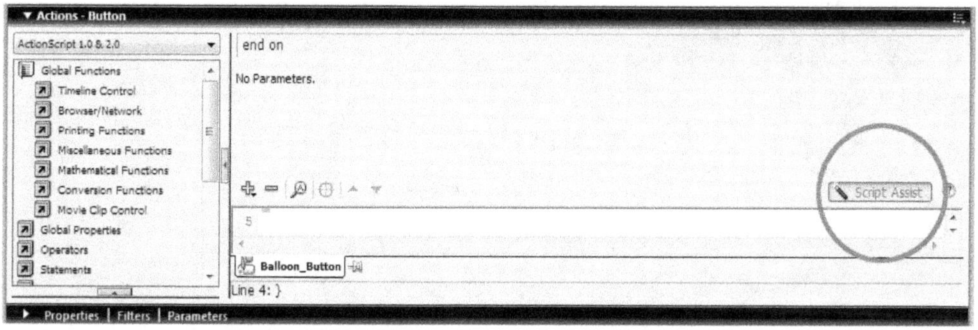

Next, scroll down your list of selections on the left and click on **Deprecated**:

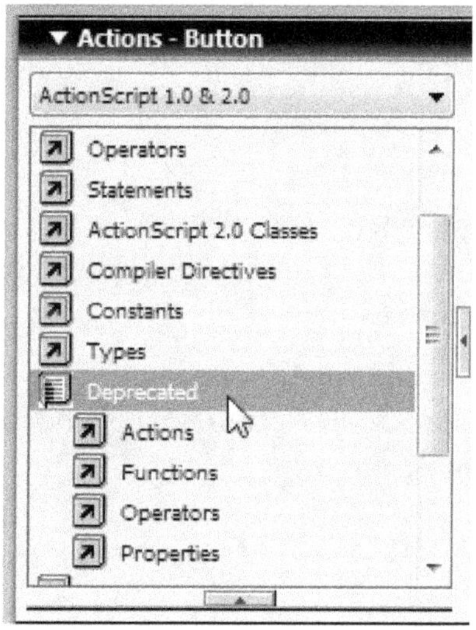

Next, click on **Actions** then double-click **tellTarget**. Type **_level0/** next to Target:

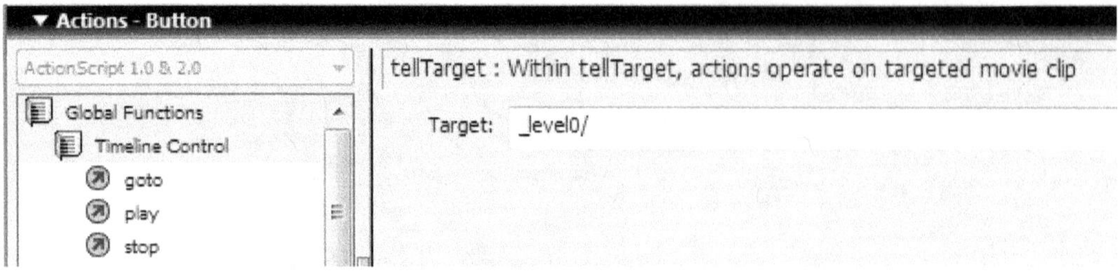

_level0/ is ActionScript meaning **Main Timeline**. You'll be using this code over and over again as you continue your Flash career.

We've now targeted the main timeline. But now we have to tell **_level0/** (main timeline) what to do when we roll over the button. We want the balloon to stop, so we need to add that code now. On the left side of the Actions panel, click on **Global Functions** to reveal its selections. Next, select **Timeline Control** and double-click **stop**:

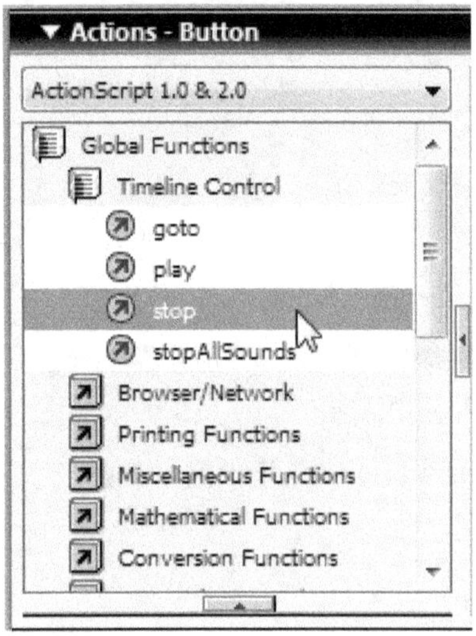

So now we have the code that will perform its actions when the user releases their mouse button. But we want the actions to be performed when the user rolls their mouse *over the button.* So we need to change the mouse event setting.

Remember, when using Script Assist you may have to enlarge the Actions window so you can see the code. Place your cursor above the **Actions** panel and right below the stage; the cursor will change to a double arrow:

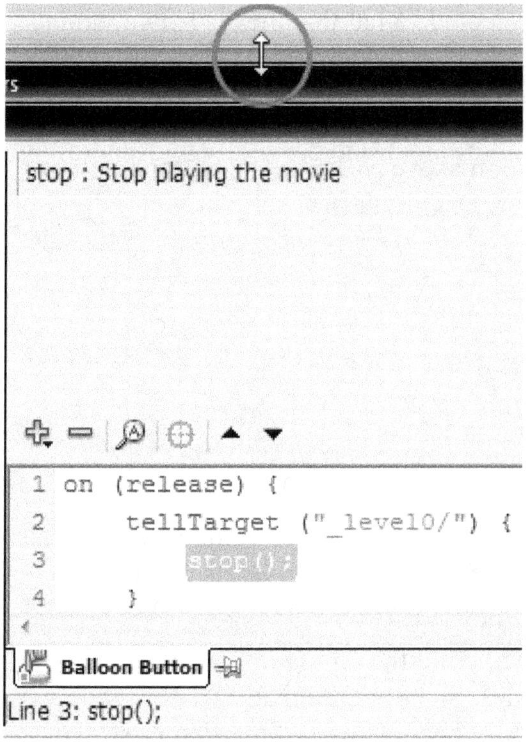

Drag upward until the Actions window is larger. This will make it easier to work in the Actions window. Click on the word **release** in the ActionScript:

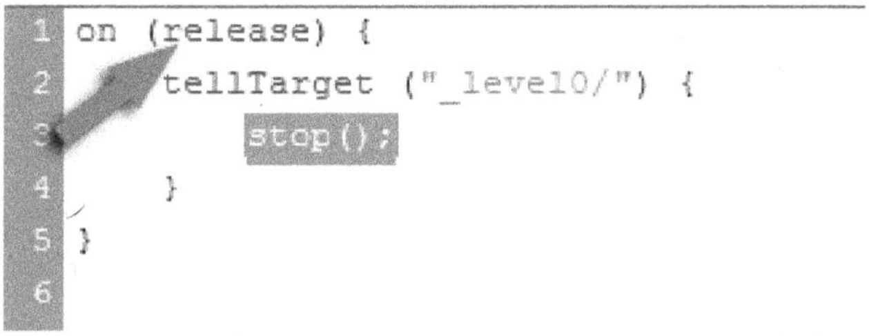

You should now be in the **mouse event** window. This is the window that will determine which mouse events will trigger the actions:

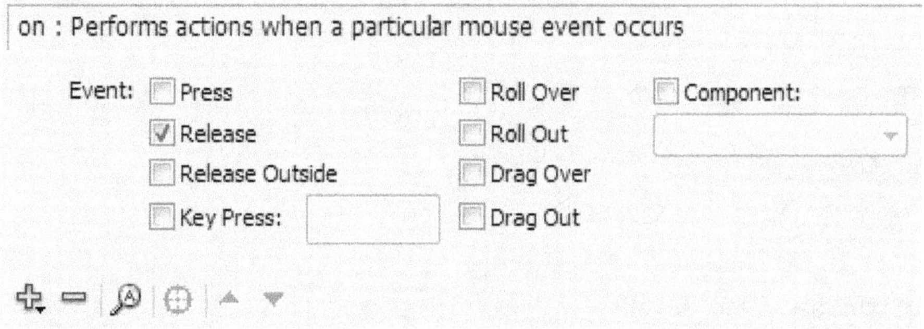

Next to **Event** you'll see that **Release** is selected. What that means is that when the button on the mouse is released, the actions in the window will be triggered. So, basically, when you roll over the floating balloon and click and release the mouse button, the action **stop** will happen. That's not quite what we want. We want this button to perform its action as soon as we *roll over* the balloon button. Uncheck **Release** and select **Roll Over** and **Drag Over**:

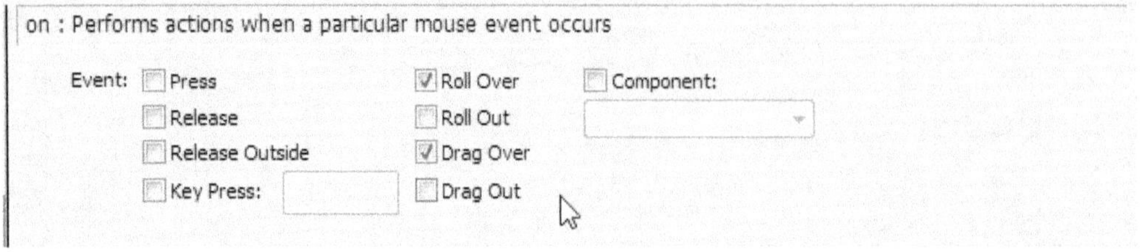

Now when the cursor rolls over the button it will stop. You'll notice that we also selected **Drag Over**; **Drag Over** is when the user clicks and holds the mouse button *before* rolling over the button.

Now we need to add the ActionScript for playing the animation once we roll off the button. The opposite of what we just did. Since we're creating a new code we want to make sure that it doesn't accidentally become part of the first code. To start a new code we need to click on the closing bracket of the first set of code:

```
on (release) {
    tellTarget ("_level0/") {
        stop();
    }
}
```

Just as before, go to **Deprecated, Actions**, and double-click **tellTarget**:

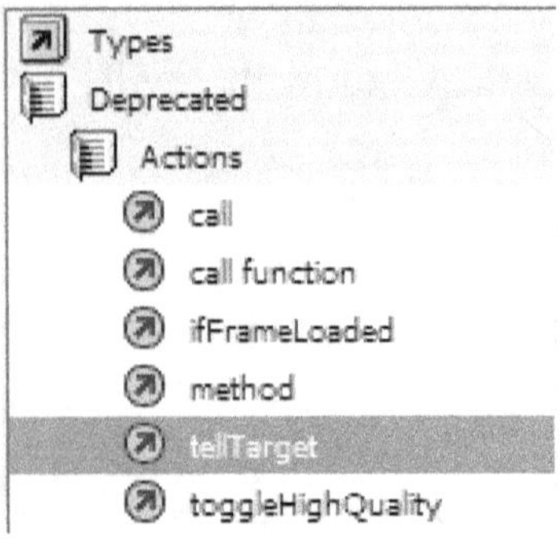

In the Target window enter **_level0/**:

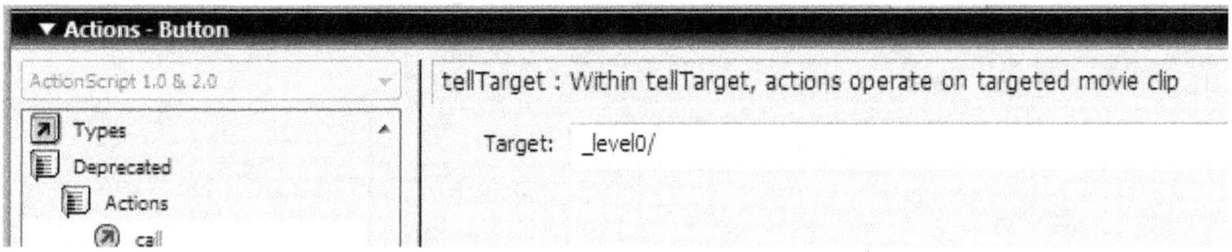

On the left, scroll up and click on **Global Functions**. Select **Timeline Control** and double-click **play**:

Once again, click on the word **release** in the Actions window; you should then see the **mouse event** settings window:

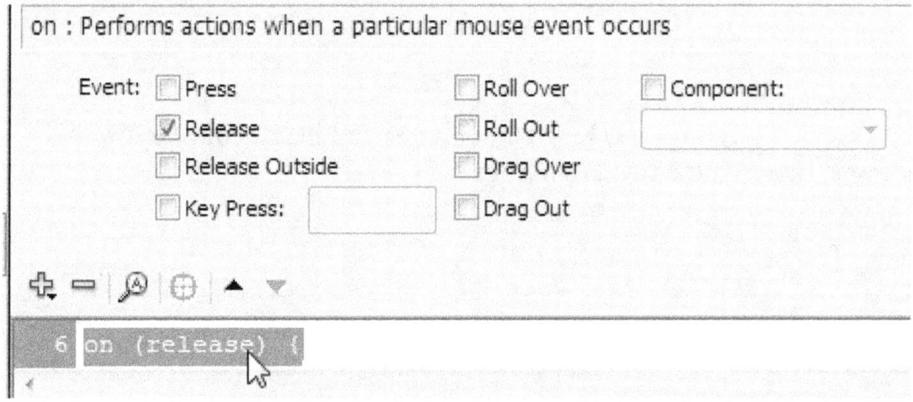

Just as before, uncheck **Release**, but this time select **Roll Out** and **Drag Out**:

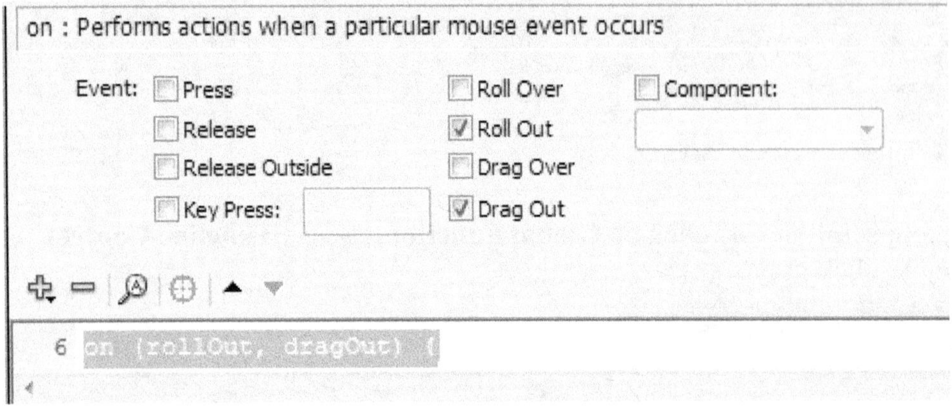

Now, when the cursor rolls off the button the **play** action will be triggered.

We now have the ActionScript in place. Next, we'll add the animation so we can test this button. Select frame **60** of the **Balloon** layer:

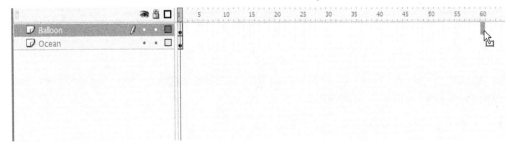

Next, go to **Insert, Timeline,** and **Keyframe**. After you insert your keyframe select any frame between the two keyframes:

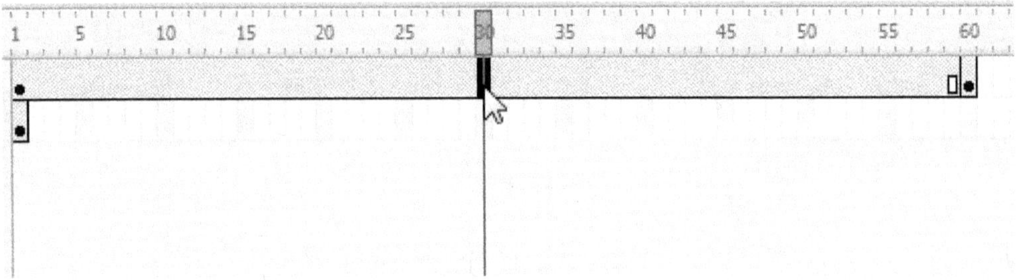

Then go to **Insert, Timeline,** and **Create Motion Tween (CS4/CS5 - Insert, Classic Tween)**:

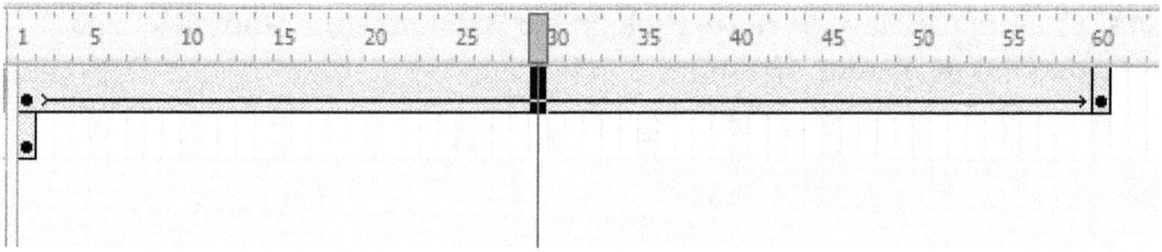

The **Balloon Button** is ready for animation. But you'll notice that the background has disappeared. If you look at the timeline the **Button Layer** has 60 frames while the **Ocean** layer has one frame. Let's add more frames to this layer.

Select frame **60** of the **Ocean** layer:

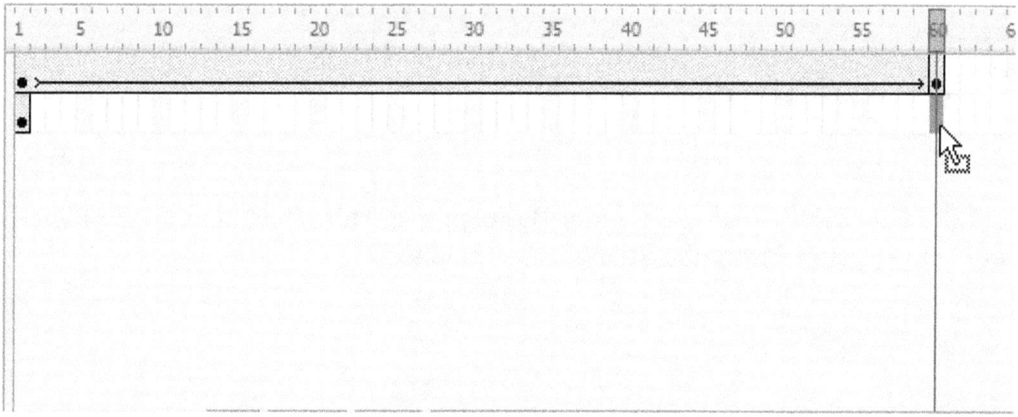

Next, go to **Insert, Timeline,** and **Frame**:

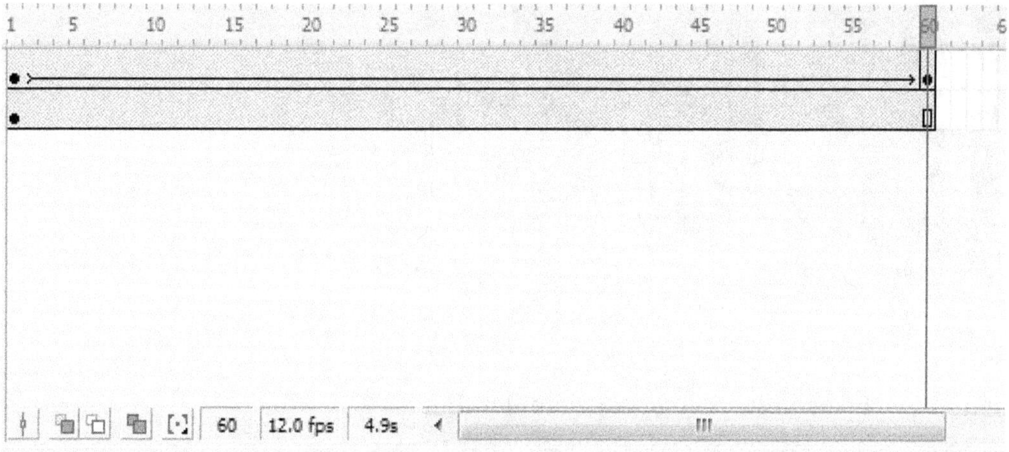

The ocean background is now back. We'll next create a path for the balloon. Select **frame 1** of the **Balloon** Layer and click on the **Add Motion Guide** button

(**CS4/CS5** users will have to **right-click** on the **Balloon Animation** layer and select **Add Classic Motion Guide**):

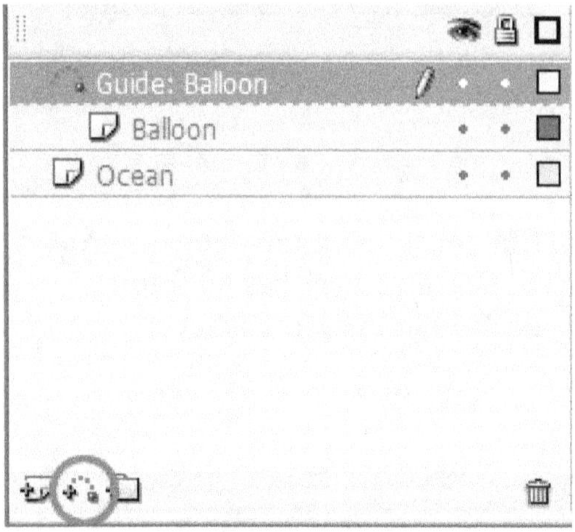

Let's draw the path! With the **Guide: Balloon** layer still selected, grab the **Pencil Tool**, and select **red** from the **Stroke color** palette:

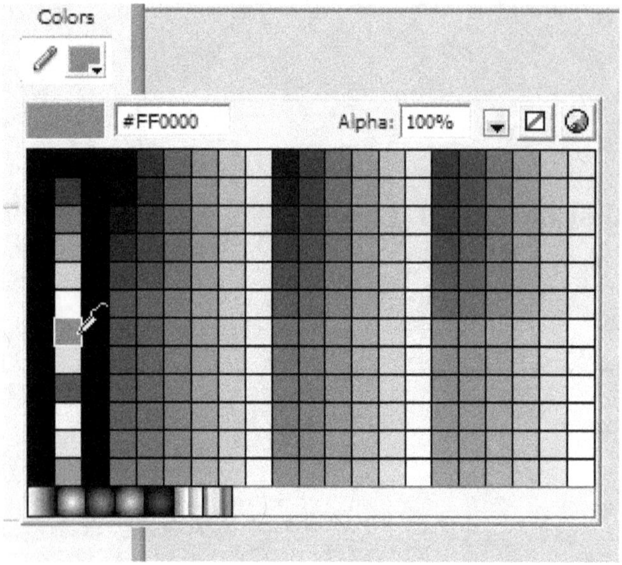

Next, draw a path around your stage similar to this:

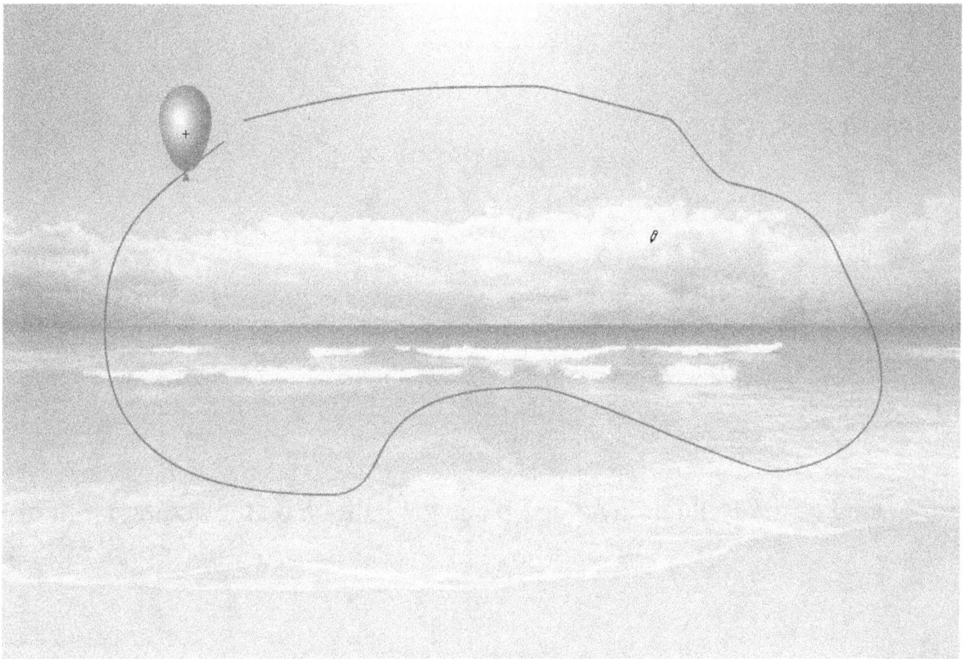

Don't worry if your path doesn't look exactly like mine. When creating a path you can be as creative as you like!

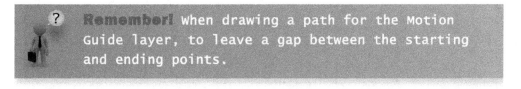

Remember! When drawing a path for the Motion Guide layer, to leave a gap between the starting and ending points.

Next, attach the balloon to the starting point. Select the balloon and place the center of it on the beginning of the path (it may slightly snap into place):

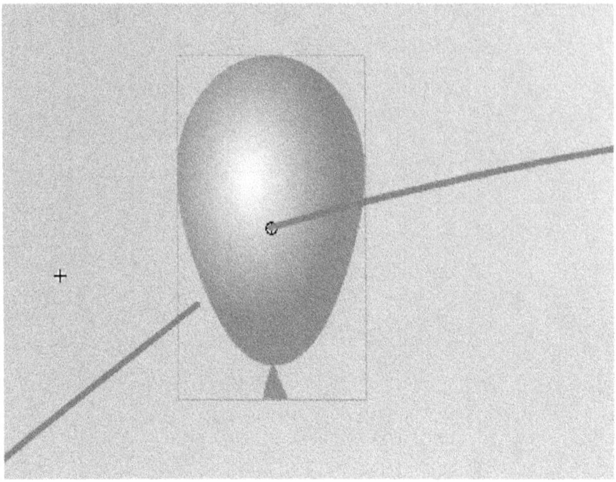

Select frame **60** of the **Balloon** layer and place the balloon on the ending point of the path:

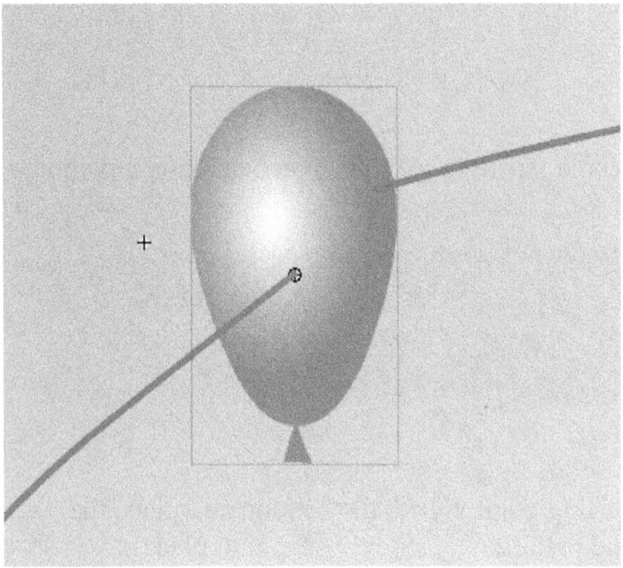

Test your movie (CTRL + ENTER). The balloon should be floating around the stage. When you roll your mouse over the balloon it should stop. When you roll off the balloon it should start floating around the stage again.

Note: if your balloon isn't animating, check to make sure that the center of the balloon is exactly positioned on the path (above).

The balloon's animation is a bit stuttered. So, as in earlier projects, we'll increase the frame rate. Click on **Modify**, and **Document**. Type **30** next to **Frame Rate**:

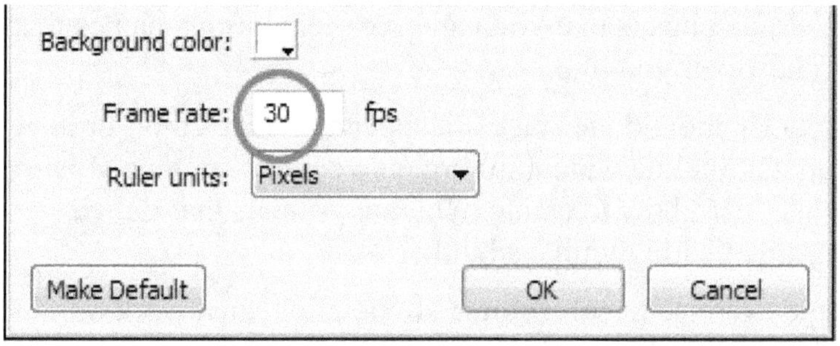

Hit **OK**. Test your movie (CTRL + ENTER) again. Much smoother, but the balloon is going way too fast! Let's slow it down. The easiest way to slow down an animation is to extend the amount of frames.

Select keyframe **60** of the **Balloon** layer, and *click-and-drag* the keyframe to frame **200**:

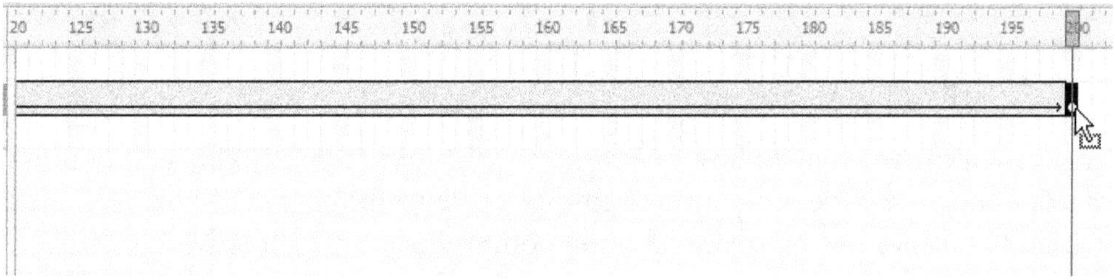

By adding more frames to the animation it will take longer to complete the path which will slow down the animation.

You'll notice that, just as before, the background is gone. Click on frame **200** of the **Ocean** layer and insert a frame. Do the same thing for the **Guide Layer**:

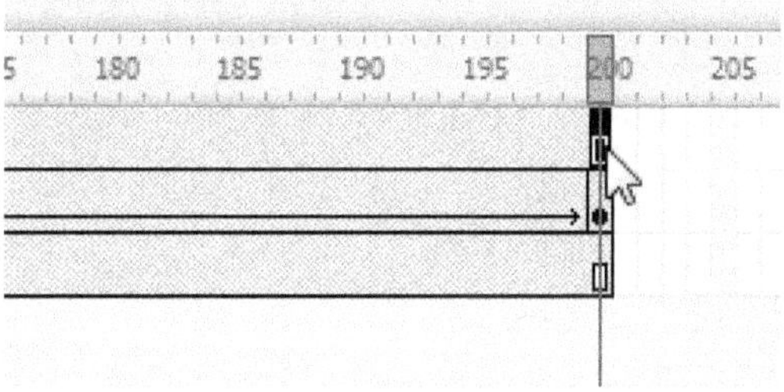

Test your movie (CTRL + ENTER). It should play much slower now. More like a real balloon. Roll over your balloon and it should stop. Roll off the balloon and it should continue to play. If the button isn't working correctly go over the steps again until you get it to work.

In the next exercise we'll be controlling a Movie clip. As you learned earlier, Movie clips are portable timelines that you can place anywhere you like. What you may not know about Movie clips is that you can give them unique names that allow you to control them however you like.

You can tell a Movie clip to fly around the stage, disappear, change color, or have it go to a specific frame on its timeline which, in turn, can control another Movie clip. In future chapters you'll learn how to create dynamic projects that utilize several Movie clips all communicating with each other.

We'll start off with a simple exercise in controlling Movie clips, then work our way up to more complex projects in future chapters. So if you're ready let's get started!

Controlling a Movie clip

This exercise introduces us to how we can control Movie clips either with buttons or frames. Take your time and go through this exercise making sure you understand the principles involved. A good comprehension of how Movie clips work is needed before we tackle the more sophisticated projects coming up. The exciting

Open up the **Car_Animation.fla** file in **the Chapter Two** folder. The file should look like this:

You'll notice in the library there is a file called **toy-car-15.png**. This is the car that will be traveling across the screen. Before we can add this car image to the stage we'll need to create a new layer on the timeline. Click on the **Insert Layer** button and name the new layer **Car**:

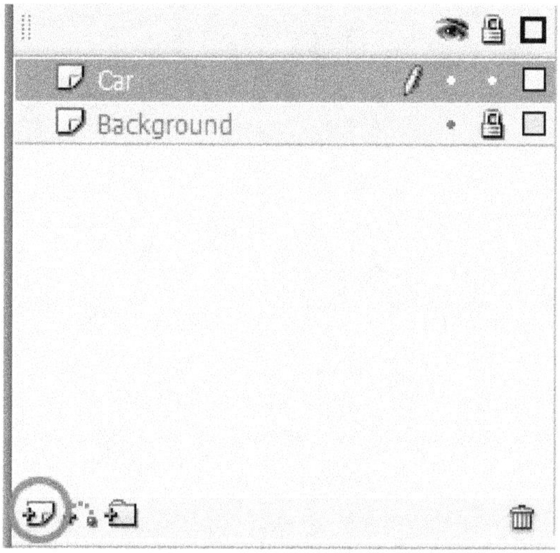

Drag **toy-car-15.png** from the library onto the stage. Place it on the right side of the stage so that the wheels are below the bottom of the stage:

Ok, now we have the car and some really big sunflowers. When we did animations in the earlier exercises, all the animation was done within the main timeline. This time, we're going to have all the animation take place in a Movie clip.

Select your car and go to **Modify**, and **Convert to Symbol** (**F8**). Select **Movie clip** for **Type** and enter **Car** for the **Name**:

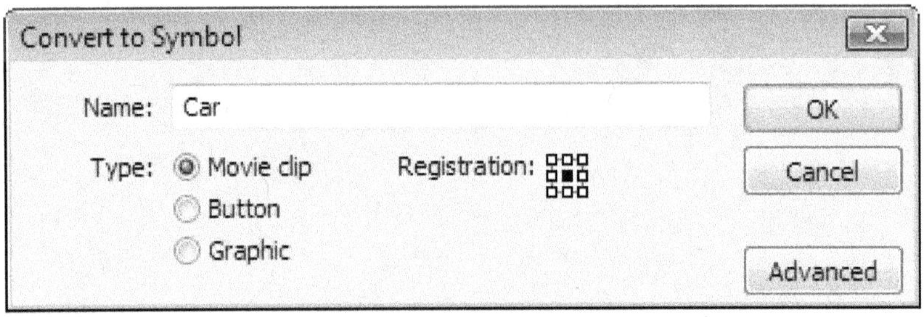

Hit **OK**. The car image is now a Movie clip. As I explained earlier, Movie clips have their own timelines. Also, Movie clips can be controlled by buttons and frames. But, *to control a Movie clip we must give it an Instance Name*. An Instance Name is a unique name that we give Movie clips so we can control them with ActionScript.

Think of it as doing a circus act with several dogs. If none of the dogs have names it would be hard to control them individually; but, once you give them all names, you can single out which dog you want to control by calling their name. The **Instance Name** is basically the Movie clip's name.

Select the **Car** Movie clip and open the Properties panel. In the Instance Name window type **car**:

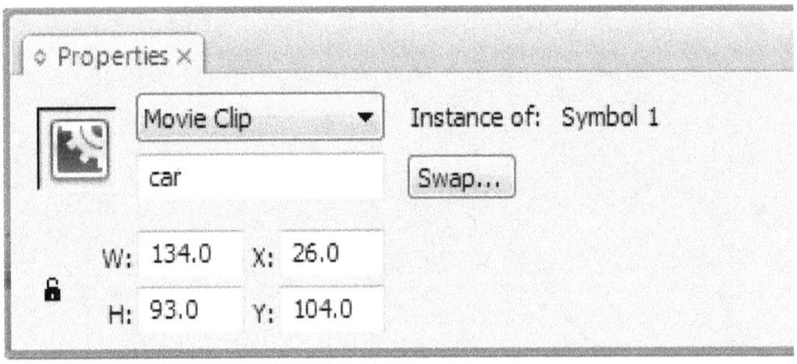

This new Movie clip is ready to be controlled! Note, Instance Names don't have to be capitalized. If you do capitalize the Instance Name, just remember to capitalize the name when creating the ActionScript, since the code is case-sensitive. Double-click the **Car** Movie clip to enter its editing stage:

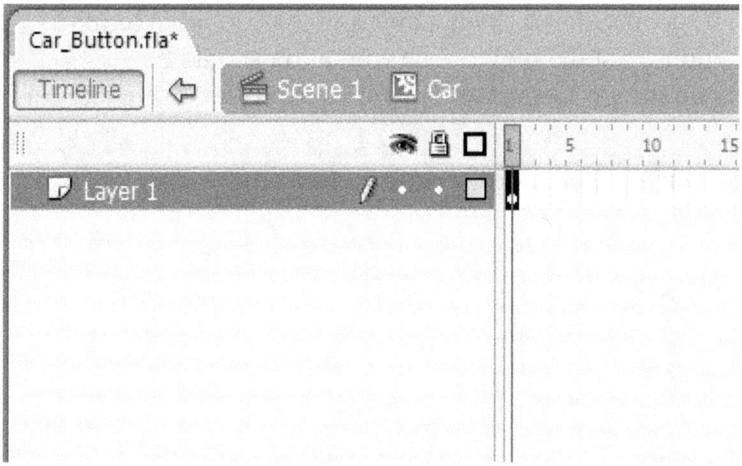

Insert a keyframe on frame **120** of **Layer 1**:

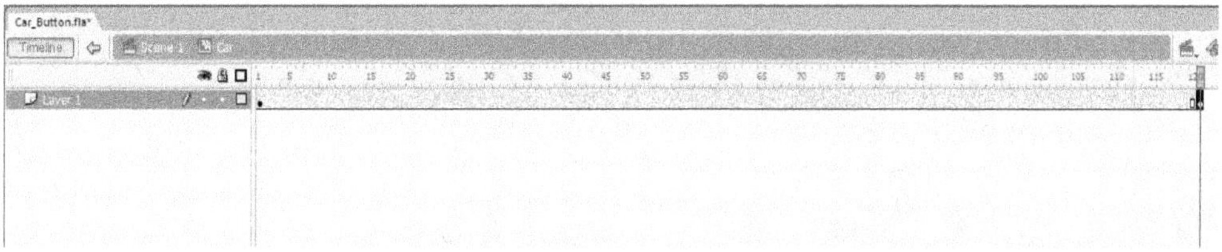

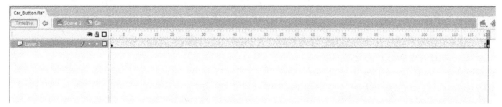

Click on any frame between the keyframes and insert a Motion Tween (**CS4/CS5 - Insert, Classic Tween**); also, change the name of the layer to **Car**:

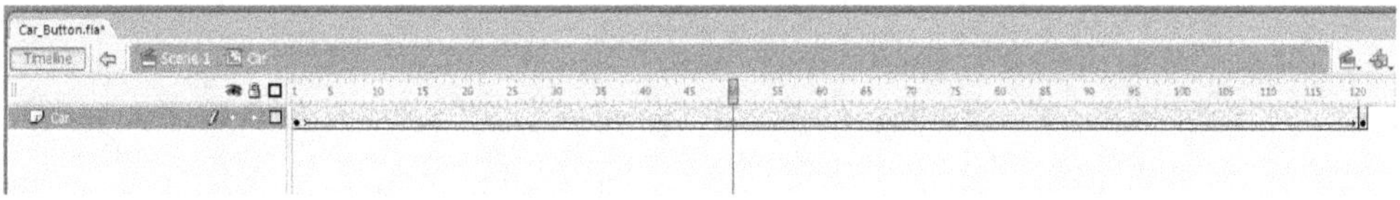

Click on frame **120** then select the car symbol on the stage. Drag the car to the left side of the stage so that it's completely off the background picture:

Before we test this movie, go ahead and change the frame rate to **30** (**Modify**, **Document**). Once that's done, test the movie. The animation should be very smooth. We may even want the car to start off slow then speed up, like a real car. Let's do that now.

Select frame **1** and type **-100** (or use the slider) next to **Ease** in the Properties panel:

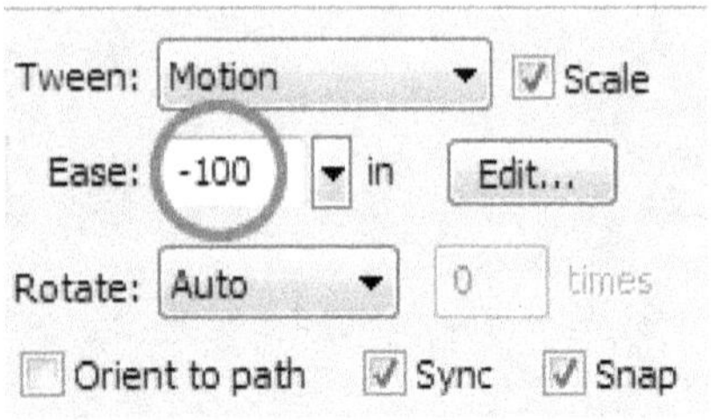

Test your movie (CTRL + ENTER) again. See how the car starts off slow then speeds up? Pretty cool. But what if you want a little more control over the speed? That's where the **Custom Ease In /Ease Out** comes into play. Click on the **Edit...** button next to **Ease**:

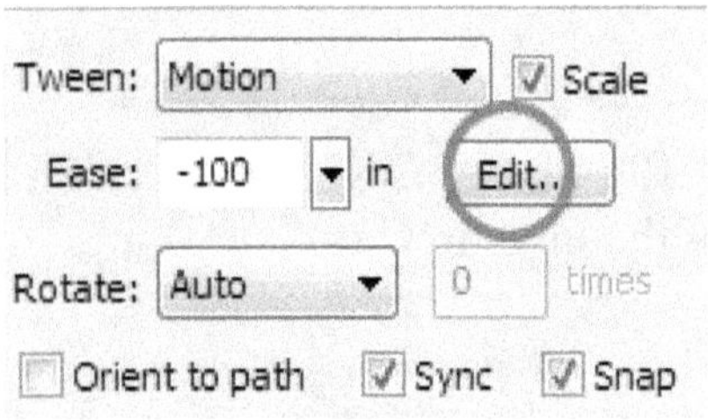

CS4/CS5 - The **Edit Button** is the Pencil icon:

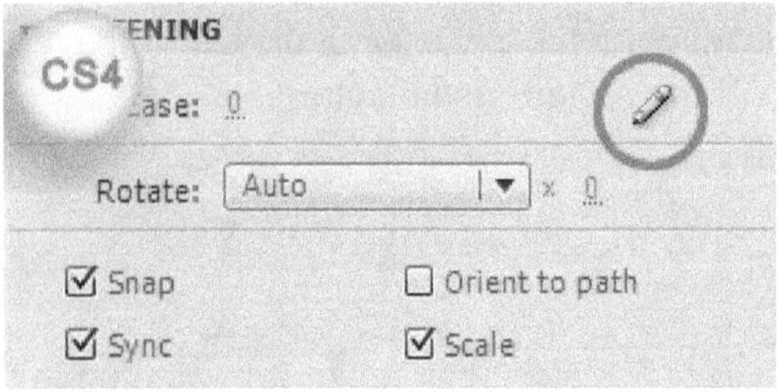

You should now be in the **Custom Ease In / Ease Out box**:

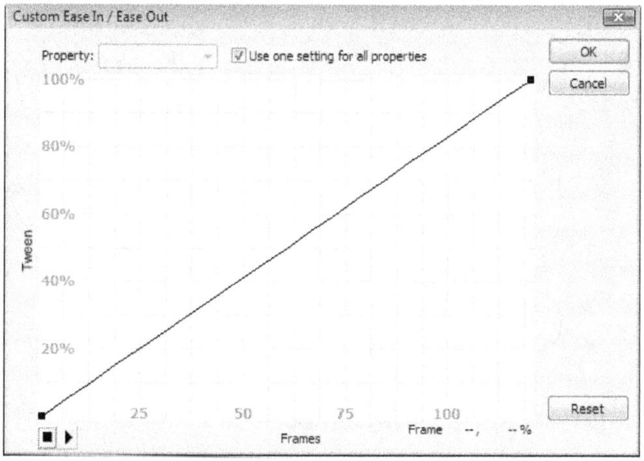

This is where you can really customize the speed of objects in Flash. We changed the Ease to -100 which tells the car to start off slow then speed up. But now we want the car to start off a bit slower, then really take off. Before we begin adjusting the controls, move the **Custom Ease In / Ease Out** window so that you can see the car on the stage. When we make a change in this window we can hit the **play** button on the bottom left to see the animation:

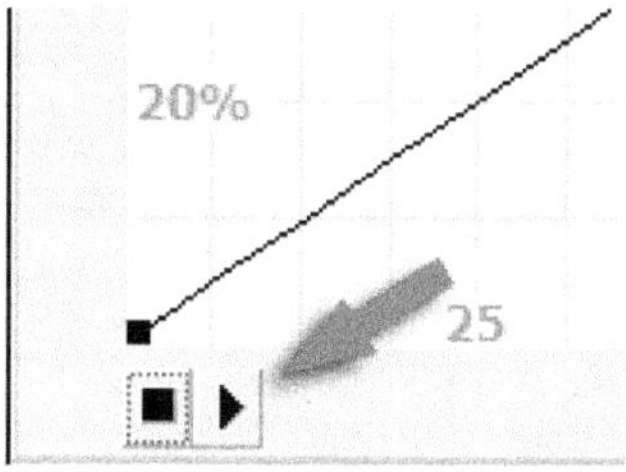

If you look at the bottom of the **Custom Ease In / Ease Out** window you'll see the word **Frames**. The numbers that run across the bottom of the grid represent the amount of frames in the car animation. On the side of the box we see **Tween**. This represents the percentage of speed. Let's first adjust the speed of the car taking off. Click the small black box at the bottom of the diagonal line:

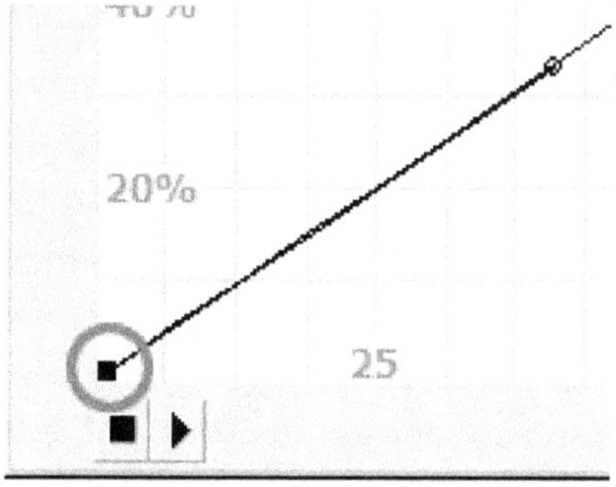

As soon as you click this black box a second line will appear over the diagonal line. This is a handle that you'll be using to control the speed. Click the top of this new handle where the small circle is:

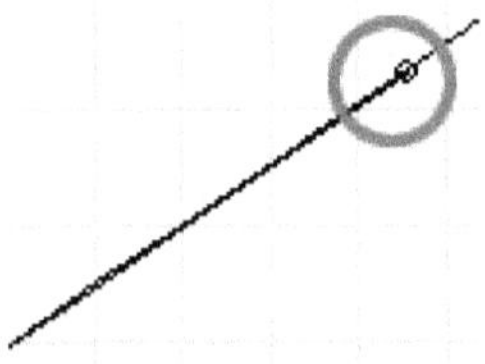

Click-and-drag this handle so that it rests against the number 100:

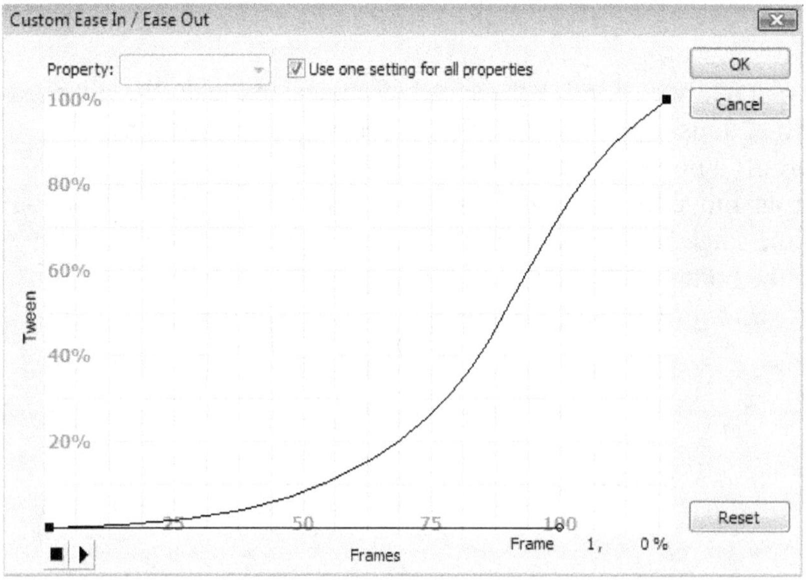

If you look at the line, it starts off flat then gradually starts to go up at frame 25. Which means the car will barely be moving until it gets to frame 25.

Hit the **play** button and watch the car's animation. Nice. Let's do one more tweak. Click on the black box at the top of the diagonal line; you should see another handle appear:

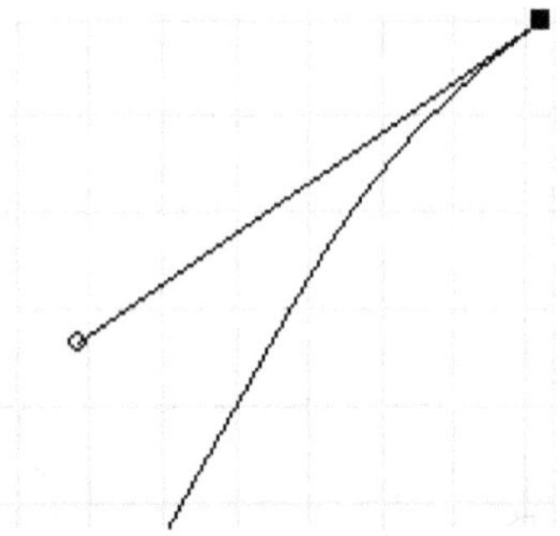

Click the circle at the end of the handle and drag it straight down until it's even with **60%**:

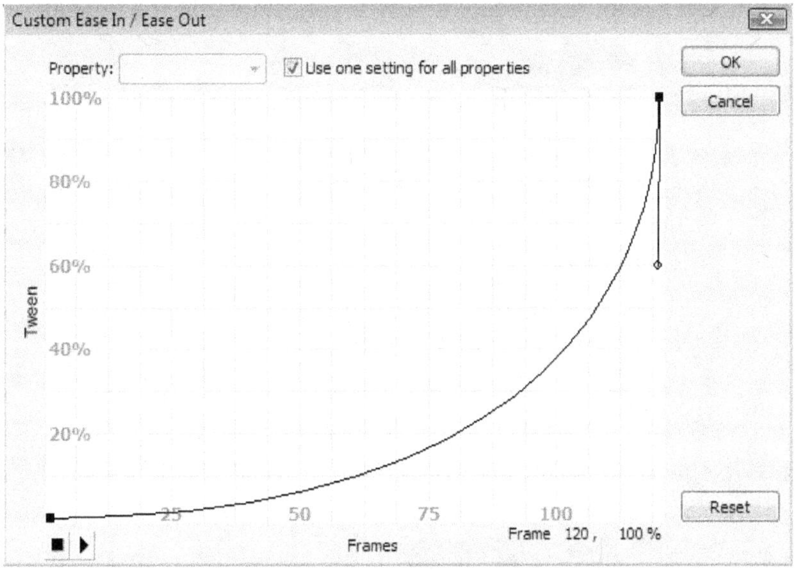

If you look at the line, you'll see that the car will start to pick up speed by frame 100, and then it reaches its fastest speed by frame 120. Hit the **play** button again and watch as the car starts off slowly then takes off by frame 100. Hit **OK** to close out.

We now need to go back to **Scene 1**. In previous projects we clicked on the Scene 1 link above the timeline/stage. This time, we're going to click the **Clapboard** icon to the right of the timeline; once you click on it, you'll see **Scene 1**. Go ahead and select it:

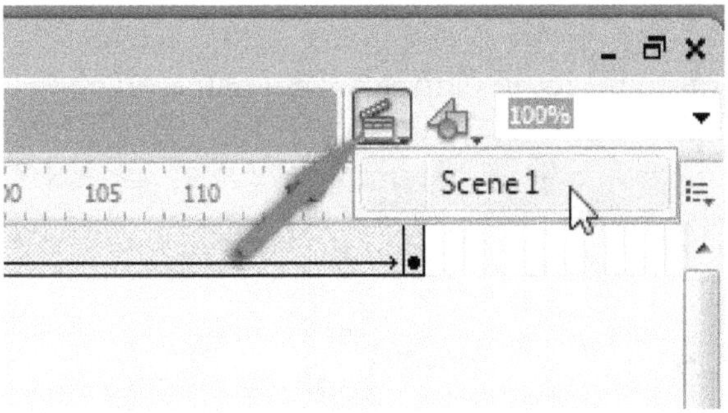

You should be back in **Scene 1**. Test the movie again (CTRL + ENTER). Even though Scene 1 has only one frame, the car plays through its entire animation because it's a Movie Clip.

Next, we're going to add a stoplight that will control the car's animation. Go to **File**, **Import**, **Import to Library**. Select stoplight.png which is located in the Chapter Two folder. Once it's imported create a new layer and name it **Stoplight**:

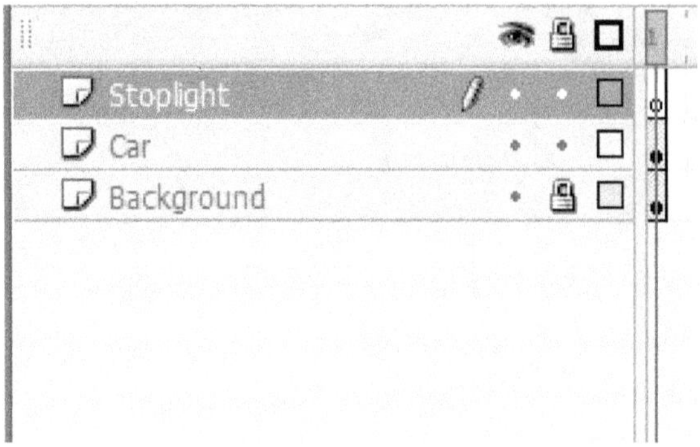

Drag **stoplight.png** from the library onto the stage and place it in the top left of the stage:

Select the stoplight image and convert it to a Movie Clip; give it a name of **Stoplight**:

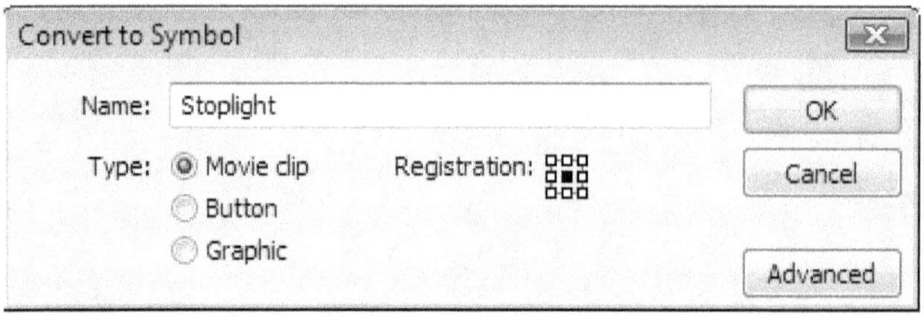

Hit **OK**. Just like the **Car** Movie clip, we need to give this Movie clip an Instance Name so we can control it. In the Properties panel type **stoplight** in the **Instance Name** window:

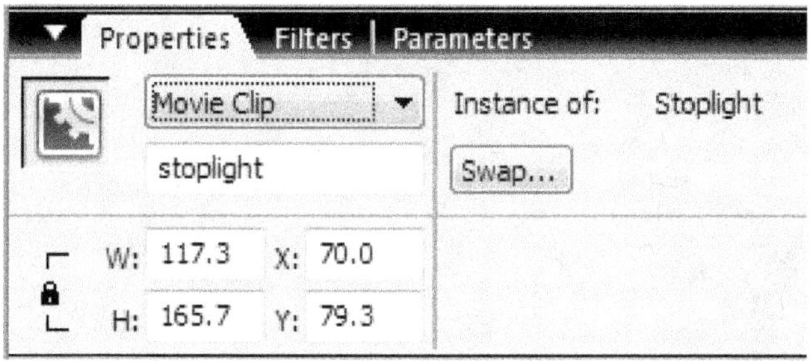

Double-click the **Stoplight** Movie clip to enter its editing stage. Rename the existing layer **Stoplight**. Create two new layers and name them **GO** and **STOP**:

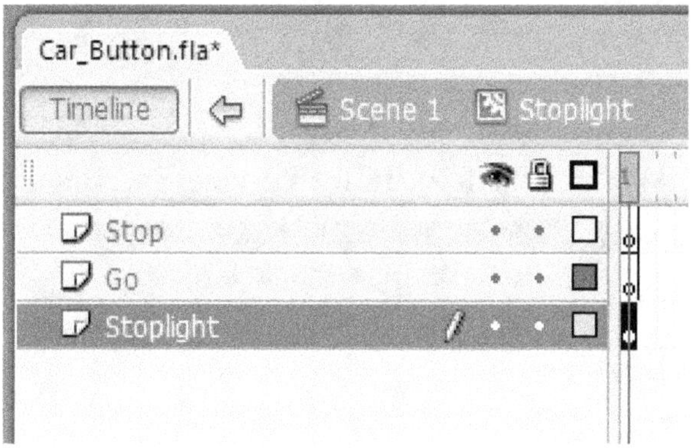

Select the first frame of the **GO** layer and select the **Text Tool**:

Next, select the color **green**:

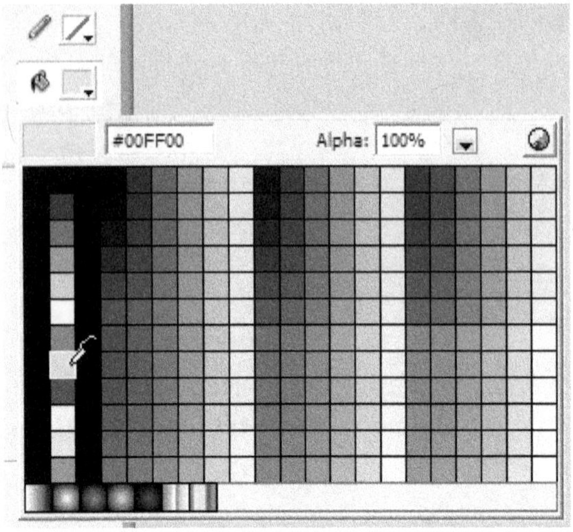

Open the properties panel and select **Arial** for the font, **16** for the size, and **Bold**:

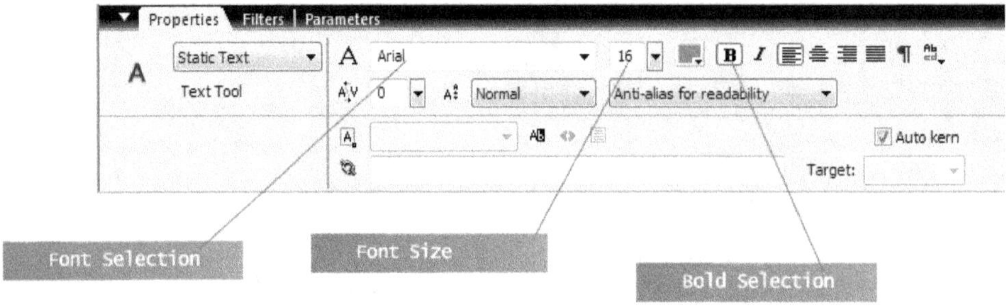

Type the word GO under the Stoplight image:

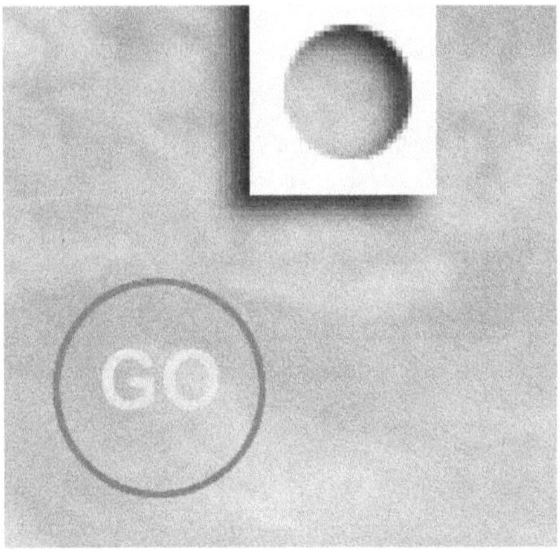

Next, click on the first frame of the **Stop** layer. Type the word **STOP** and change the text color to red:

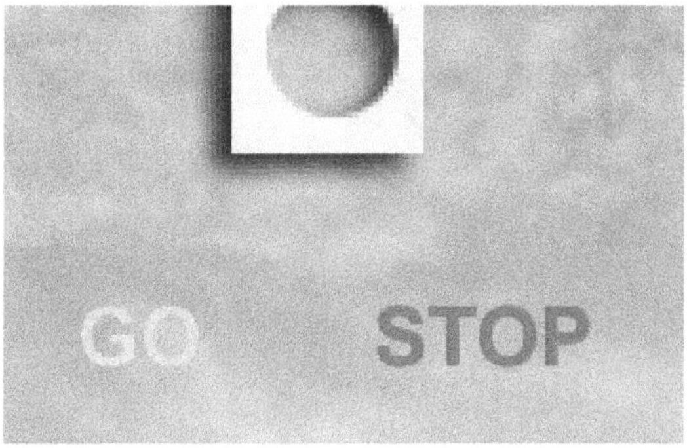

This project will have two parts. In the first part of the this project we'll convert **GO** and **STOP** to buttons which will control the car. In the second part of this project we'll use the **GO** and **STOP** buttons to control the stoplight which will then control the car.

Let's finish the first part of this project. Click on **GO** and convert it to a button (**Modify**, and **Convert to Symbol**); name it **Go Button**:

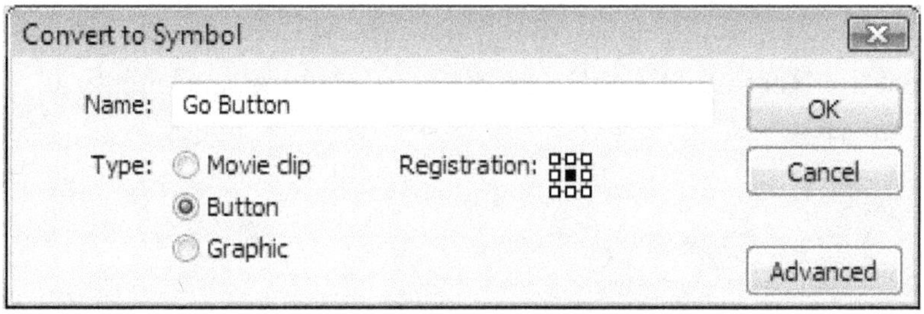

Hit **OK**. Double-click on the **Go Button** symbol so that you are in the **Go Button** editing stage:

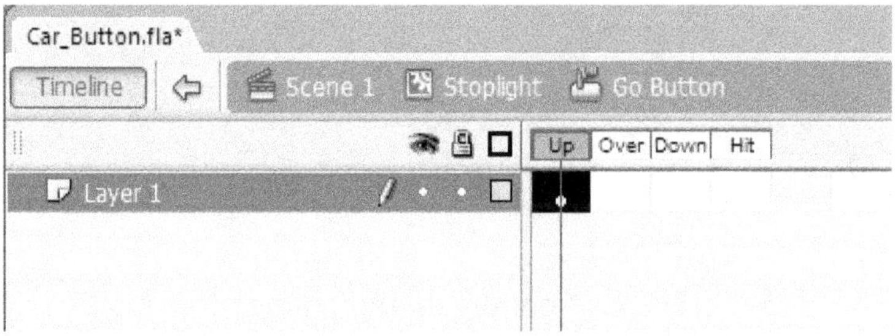

We'll have the word **GO** change to white when a user rolls over the button. Under the **Over** state insert a keyframe. You should now have a copy of the word **GO** in your **Over** state. Select the text **GO** on your stage and change the color to white (click inside the word GO, and go to **Edit**, **Select All** to highlight the text. Then, change the color to white):

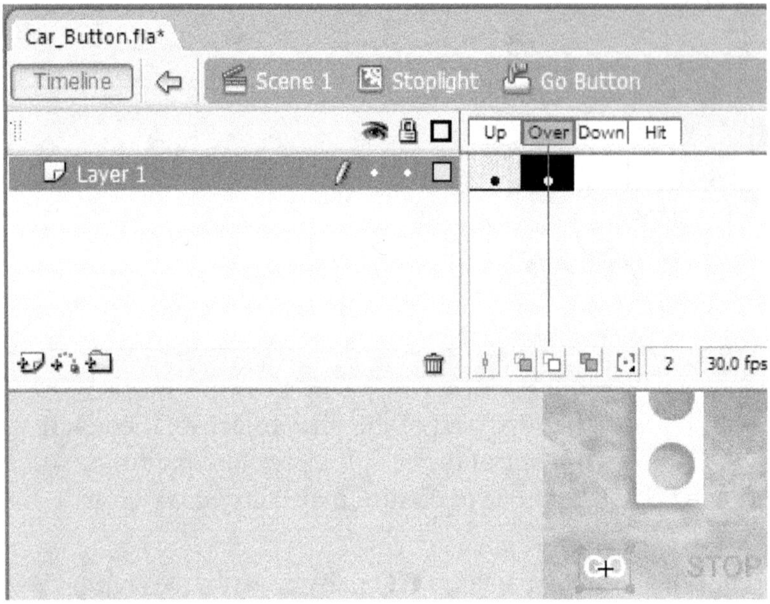

To finish this button we need to add a shape under the **Hit** state. Insert a keyframe under **Hit**. Next, select the **Rectangle Tool**, turn off **Stroke color**, and create a shape that covers the GO text:

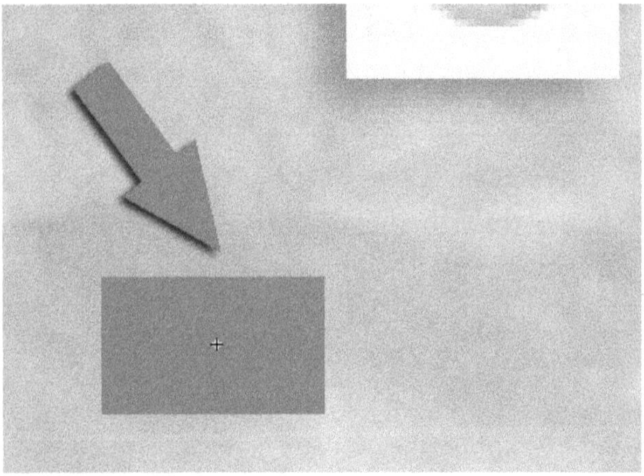

Test your movie (CTRL + ENTER). The **GO** button should change to white when you roll over it. Perfect. Next, we'll add the ActionScript. Go back to the Stoplight stage by clicking its link above the timeline/stage:

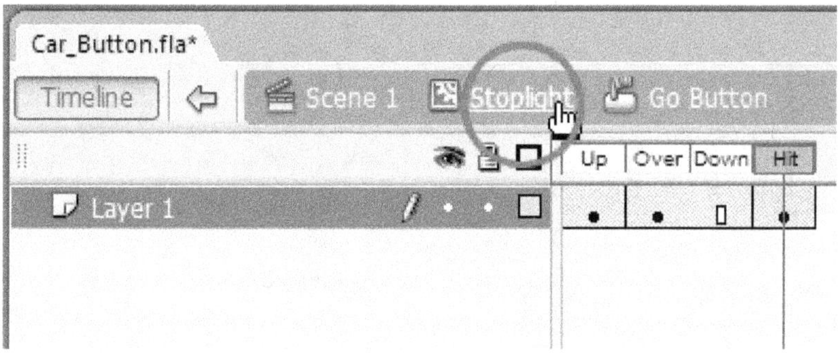

You should now be in the Stoplight editing stage. Select the **GO Button** and open the Actions panel. Make sure you are still in Script Assist mode. Just as we did before, go to **Deprecated**, **Actions**, and double-click **tellTarget**:

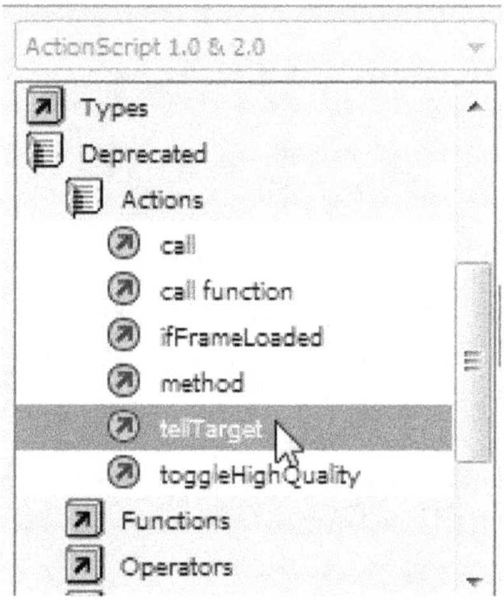

Since we want to control the car, type **/car** next to **Target**:

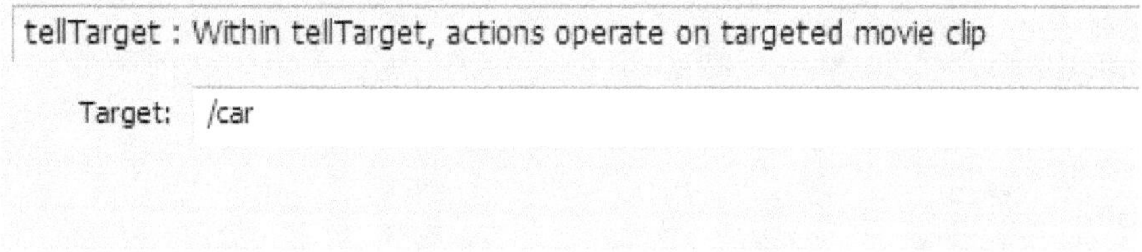

Whenever you use the tellTarget command always remember to put a slash (/) before the Instance Name of the Movie clip. In this case, the Instance Name of the **Car** Movie clip is **car**. So the Target name will be **/car**.

Next, we'll add the rest of the ActionScript that will make the car take off when the **Go** button is clicked. Scroll up to **Global Functions**, **Timeline Control**, and double-click **play**:

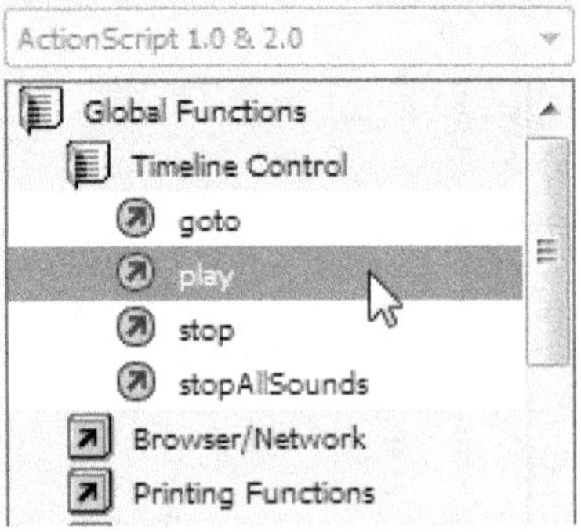

Your final code should look like this:

```
on (release) {
    tellTarget ("/car") {
        play();
    }
}
```

That's it! Test your movie (CTRL + ENTER). Notice the problem? The car is taking off on its own rather than waiting for us to click the **Go** button. We need the car animation to wait for this command.

Go back to **Scene 1**. Double-click the **Car** Movie clip so that you are in its editing stage. Add a new layer and name it **Actions**; select its first frame:

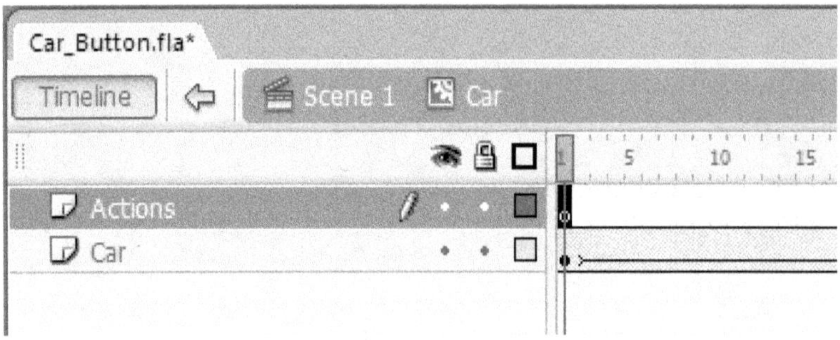

Open the Actions panel and go to **Global Functions**, **Timeline Control**, and double-click **stop.** This will add a simple **stop code** to the timeline preventing the animation from playing:

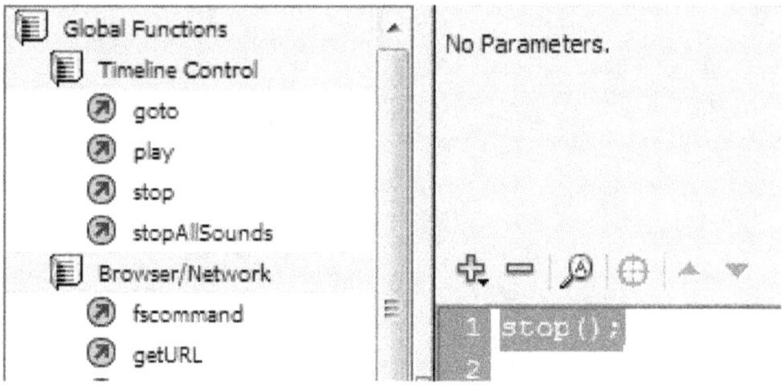

Test your movie again (CTRL + ENTER). Aha! When you click the **GO** button the car takes off! Nice. You'll notice that when the car finishes its animation it goes back to its first frame. A Movie clip will loop its animation indefinitely unless a **stop** code is place in one of its frames. In this case, we placed a **stop** code in the first frame preventing the animation from playing.

Let's add the ActionScript to the **Stop** button. Double-click on the Stoplight symbol so that you are in the Stoplight editing stage. Select the **STOP** text and convert it to a button; give it the name **Stop Button**:

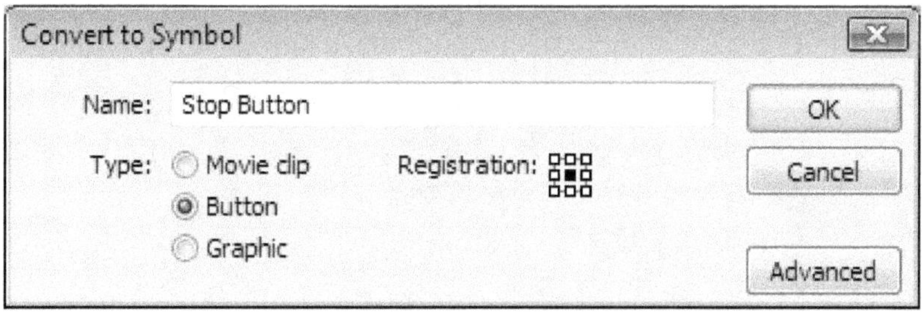

Hit **OK**. Double-click on the **Stop Button** to enter its editing stage. Just as you did with the **GO** button, add a keyframe under **Over**; next, change the color of **STOP** to white.

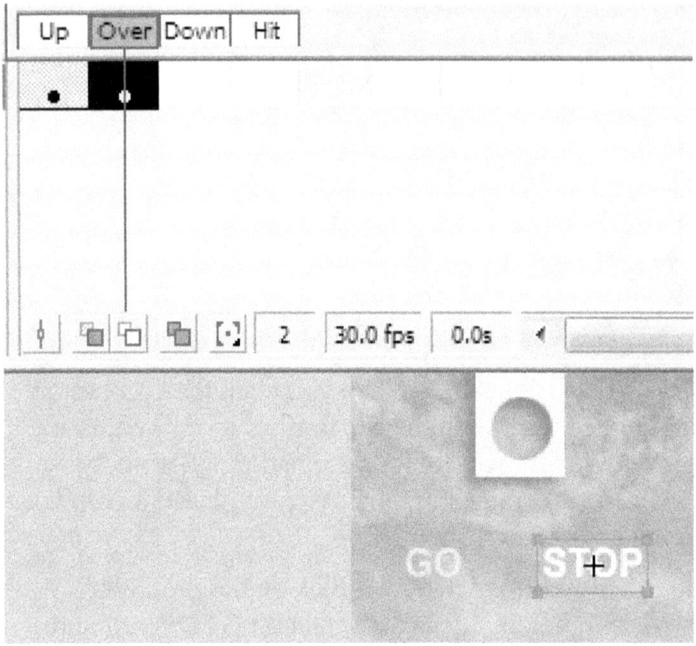

Add a keyframe under the **Hit** state and create a shape that's similar in size to the **STOP** text:

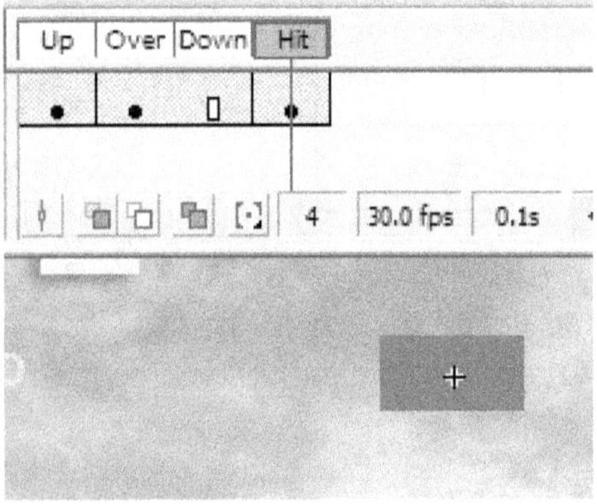

The **STOP** button is now done. Let's add the ActionScript. Go back to the **Stoplight** stage. Select the **Stop Button** and open the Actions panel. We will now repeat the steps we did for the GO button except for the last step. First, make sure you're in Script Assist mode, then go to **Deprecated**, **Actions**, and double-click **tellTarget**:

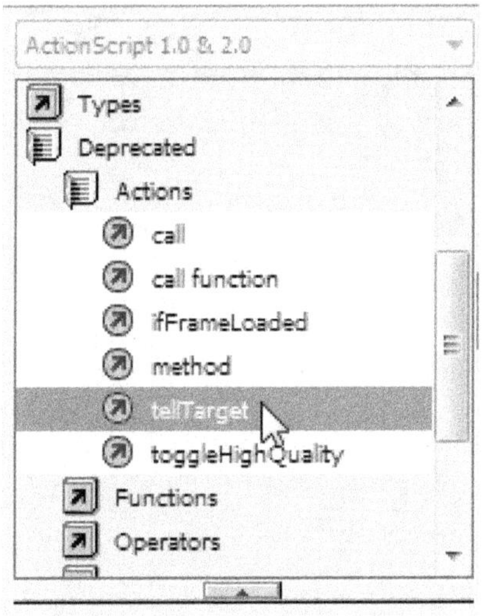

Type **/car** next to **Target**:

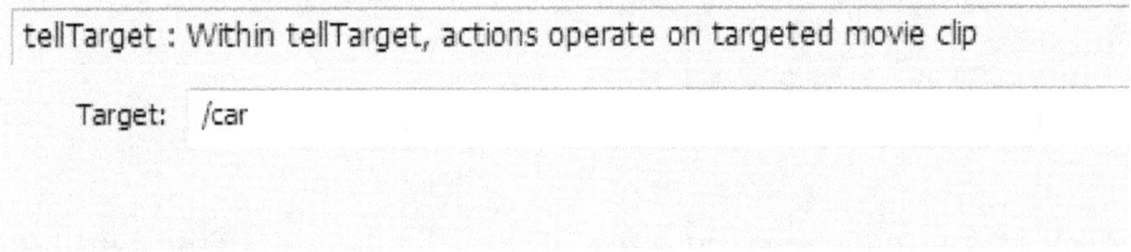

Here is where the ActionScript will differ from the **GO** button. Since we want the car to stop when we click the **Stop Button**, then we need to select the code **stop** instead of **play** (as we did for the **GO** button). Go to **Global Functions**, **Timeline Control**, and double-click **stop**:

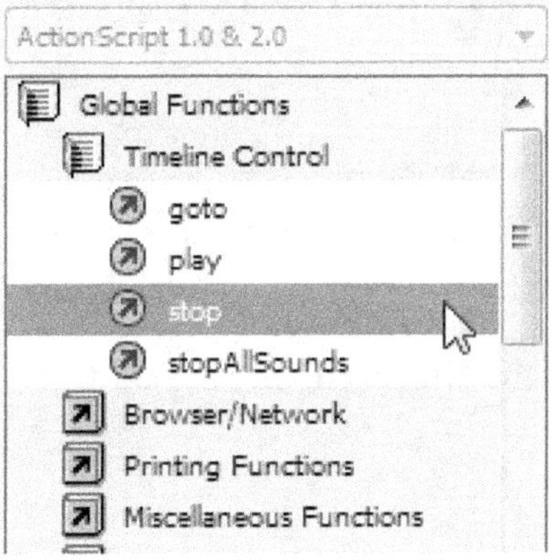

Test the movie (CTRL + ENTER). Great! Your Stop Button is stopping the car's animation. Your **GO** button makes the car take off again. Very cool!

In the next part of the project we're going to do something really exciting. The **GO** and **STOP** buttons are going to control the stoplight, which, in turn, will control the car. Make sure you understand the first part of this project before continuing.

One thing you'll notice is that when you use Script Assist you'll be repeating a lot of the same steps for most of your Flash projects. The most common commands we'll be using are: **play**, **stop**, and **tellTarget**.

Let's get started on the second part of the project. First, make sure you are still in the **Stoplight** editing stage. You can check that by looking at the links above the timeline/stage; they should look like this:

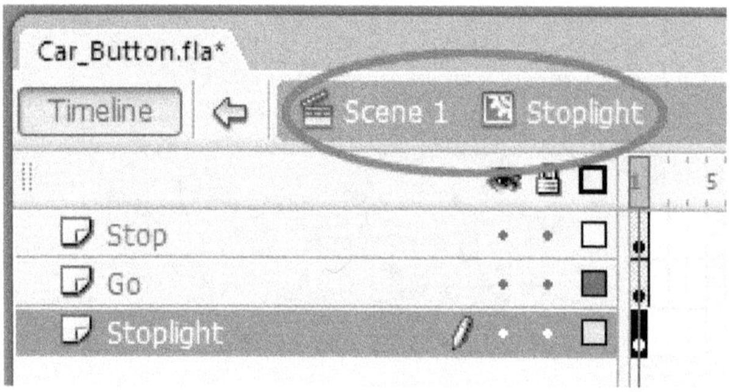

Select your Stoplight image and convert it to a Movie clip. Name it **Stoplight Lights**:

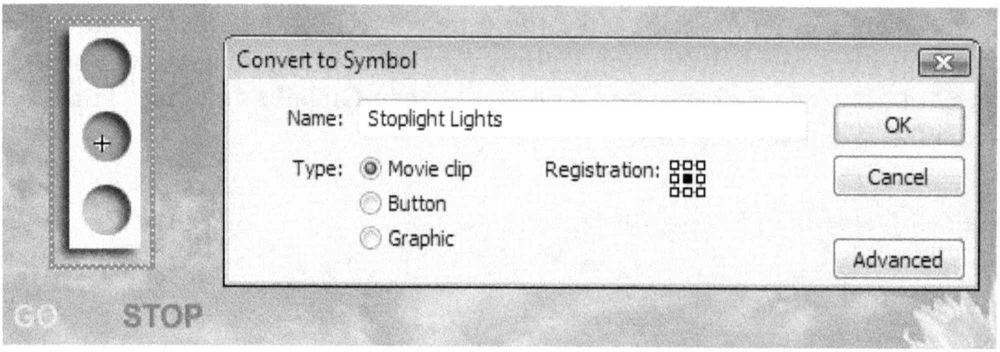

Double-click this new Movie clip so that you are in the **Stoplight Lights** editing stage. The hierarchy of stages should look like this:

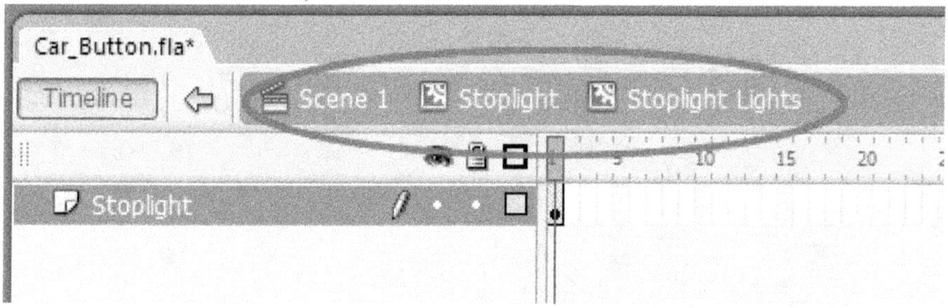

Name the layer **Stoplight**:

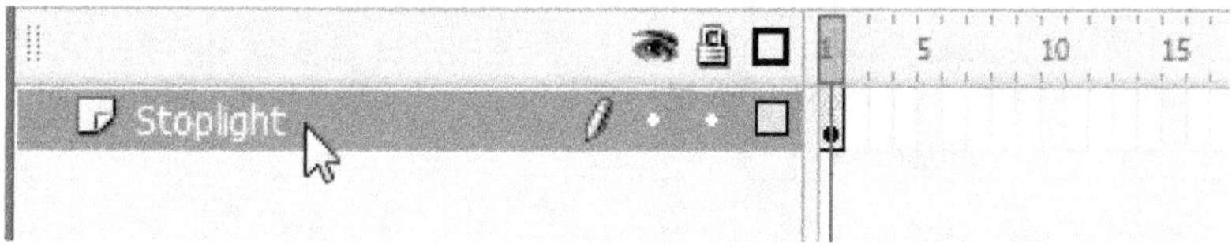

Create one more layer and name it **Green**:

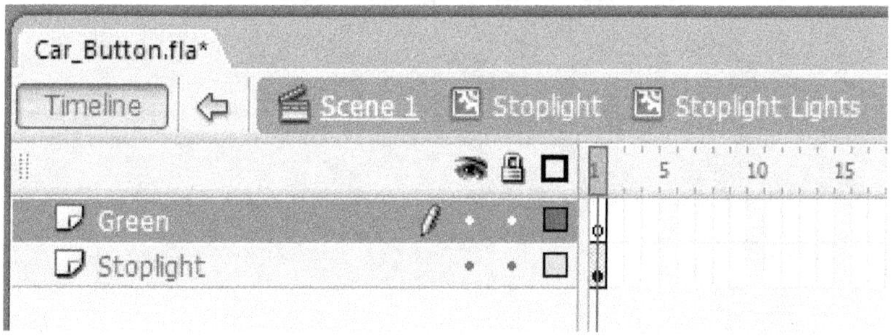

Select the **Rectangle Tool**:

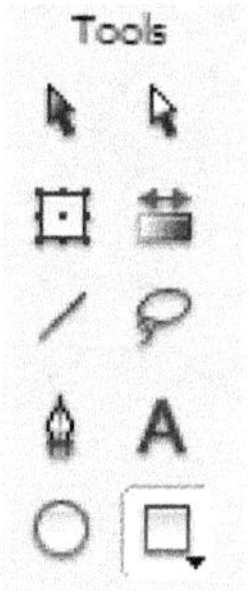

Select the color **red** for the **Fill color**:

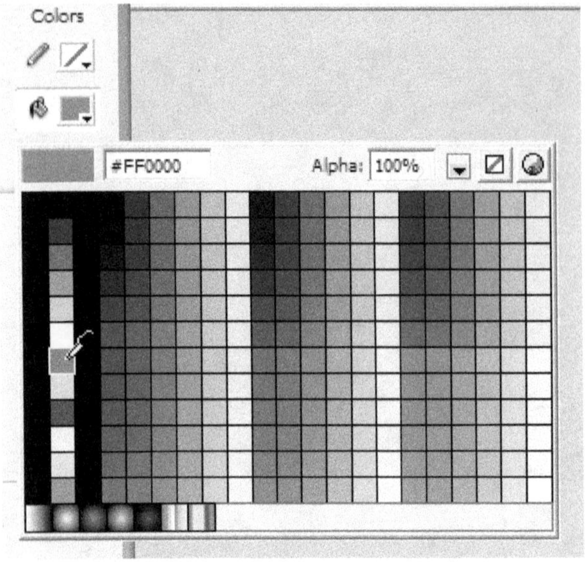

Create a red square over the bottom circle of the stoplight image:

Next, insert a keyframe on frame **20** of the **Green** layer:

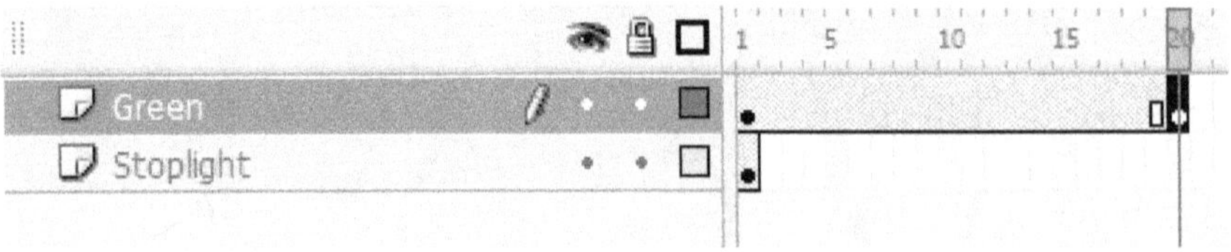

You'll notice that we can no longer see the stoplight image. Select frame **20** of the **Stoplight** layer and go to **Insert**, **Timeline**, and **Frame**.

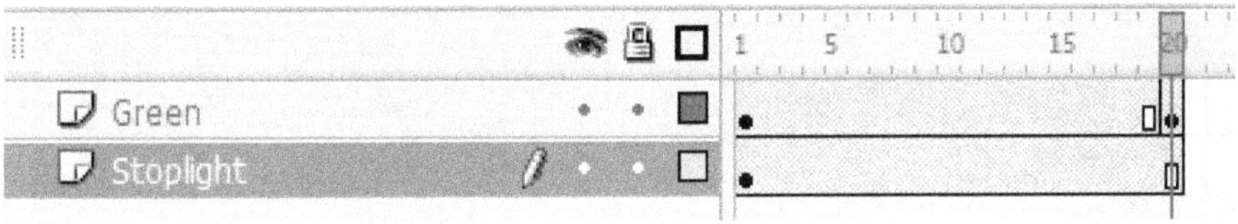

Next, select the **Paint Bucket Tool**:

Select the color **green**:

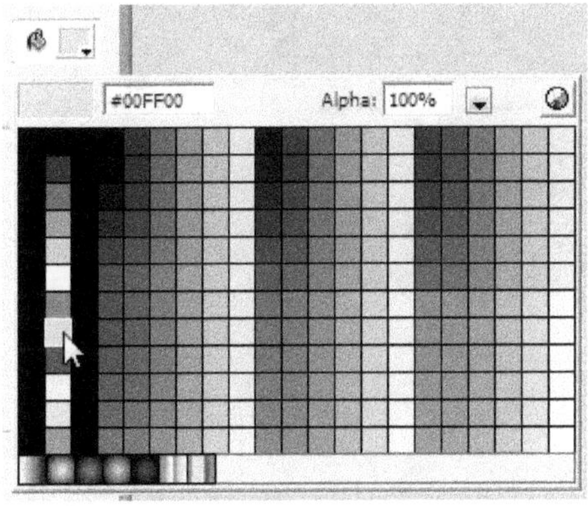

Click on the red shape using the **Paint Bucket Tool**. The shape should now be green:

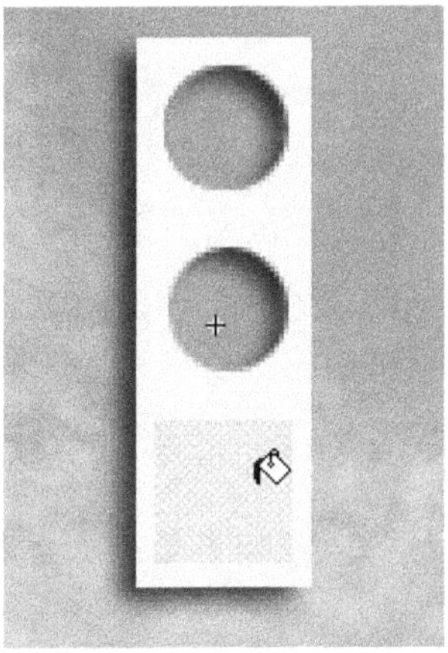

Click-and-drag the green shape so that it's over the top circle:

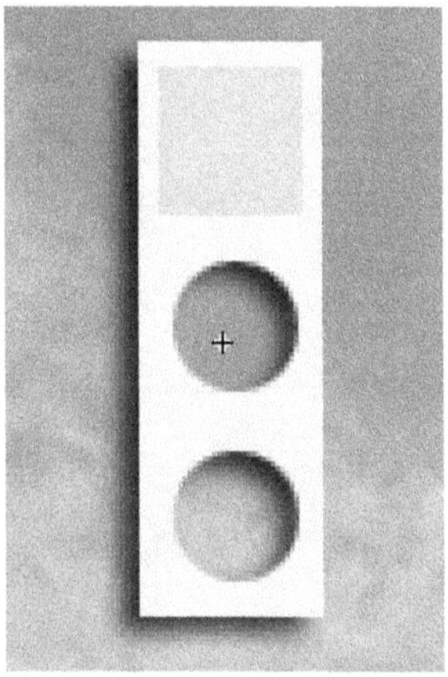

Next, insert a keyframe at frame **10** of the **Green** layer:

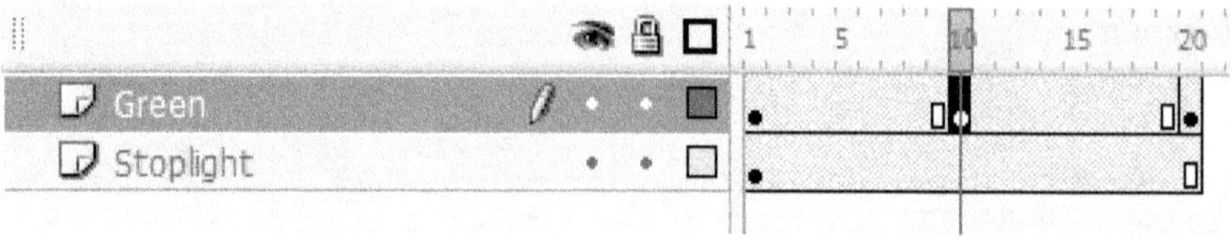

Change the **Fill color** to **yellow** and the shape will now be yellow:

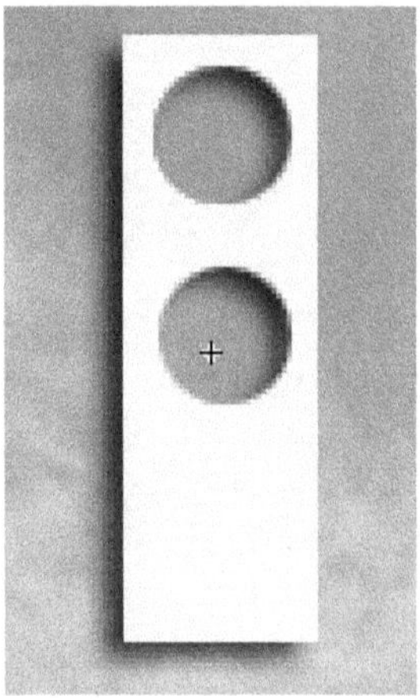

Click-and-drag the shape so that it's over the middle hole:

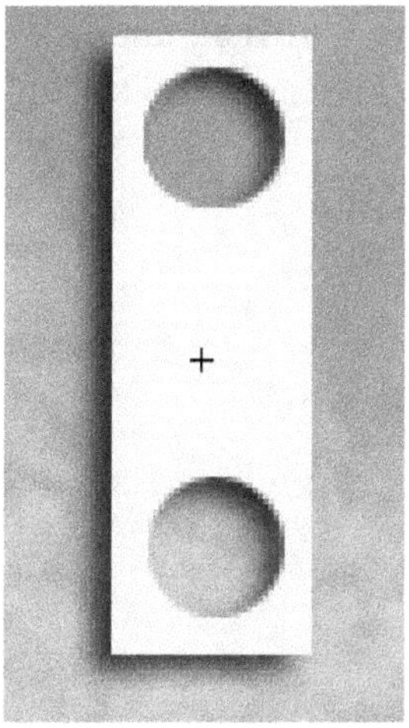

The colors are now done. But it doesn't look quite right. What we need to do now is put the colored shapes *under the Stoplight layer*. Let's do that now. Click on the **Green** layer (anywhere in the gray to the right of the name) and click-and-drag it so that it's below the **Stoplight** layer:

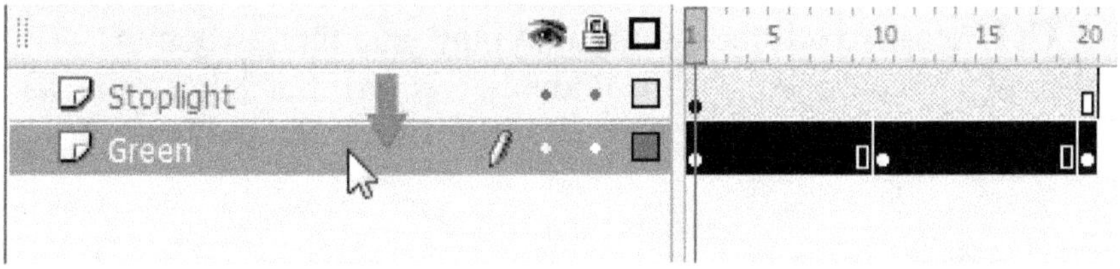

Once you're done test your movie (CTRL + ENTER). The colored shapes are now only visible through the holes of the stoplight image, but we don't want them to animate. We need to add a **stop** code to this timeline just as we did with the car animation. Create a new layer and name it **Actions**. Next, select the first frame of this layer:

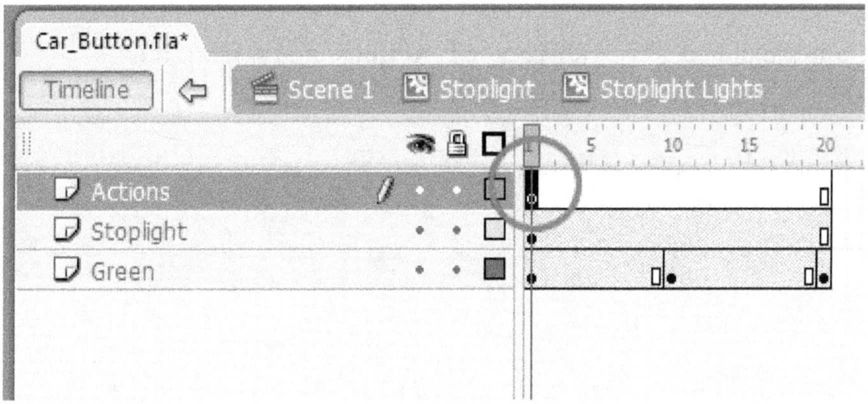

Open the Actions panel and go to **Global Functions**, **Timeline Control**, and double-click **stop**. Test your movie (CTRL + ENTER) again. The stoplight should now just show the red color:

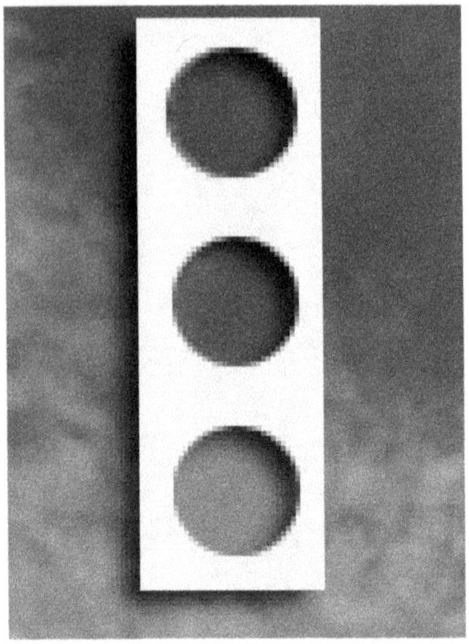

Next, we want the **GO** button to tell the stoplight to play, and then, when the stoplight gets to the color green, the car will suddenly take off. Let's do that now. Go to frame **20** of the **Actions** layer and insert a keyframe:

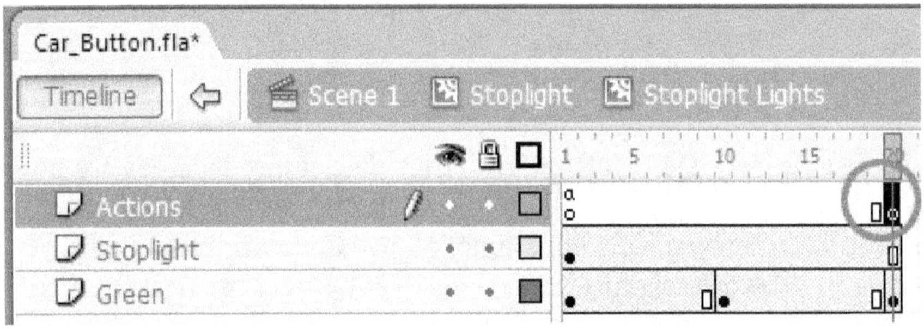

Open the **Actions** panel and go to **Deprecated**, **Actions**, and double-click **tellTarget**:

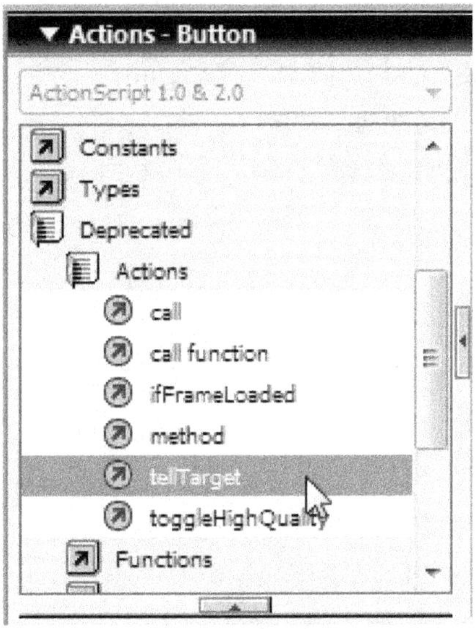

Enter **/car** in the **Target** window:

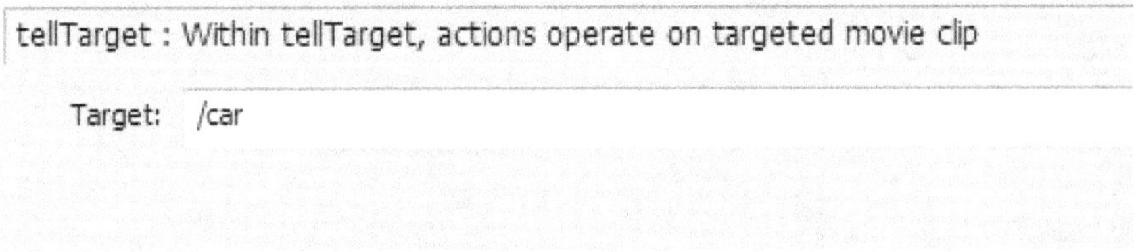

Since we want this car to animate when it gets to this frame, we need to add a **play** code. Go to **Global Functions**, **Timeline Control**, and double-click **play**:

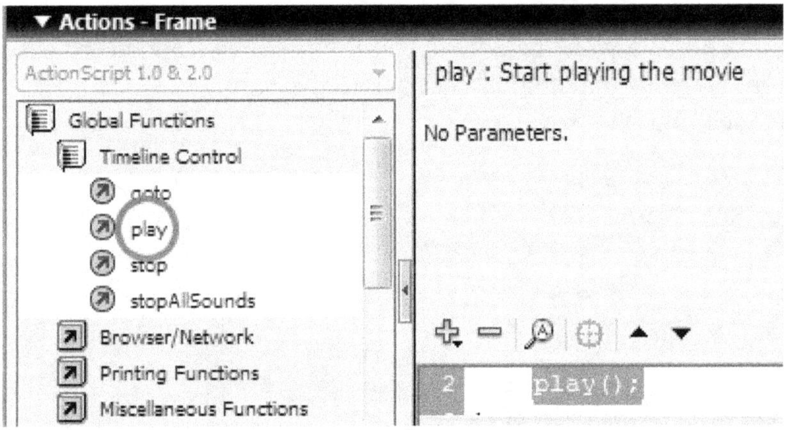

When the stoplight animation gets to frame 20 the ActionScript will tell the car to start playing. We have one more ActionScript to add. When the stoplight animation gets to frame 20 we want the animation to stop on frame 20 since that is where the green light is. If we don't add a **stop** code on this frame then the stoplight animation will return to frame 1 where the red light is. Movie clip timelines always return to frame 1 unless you insert a **stop** code.

First, so the new code doesn't become part of the first set of code, we need to click on the closing bracket of the first code:

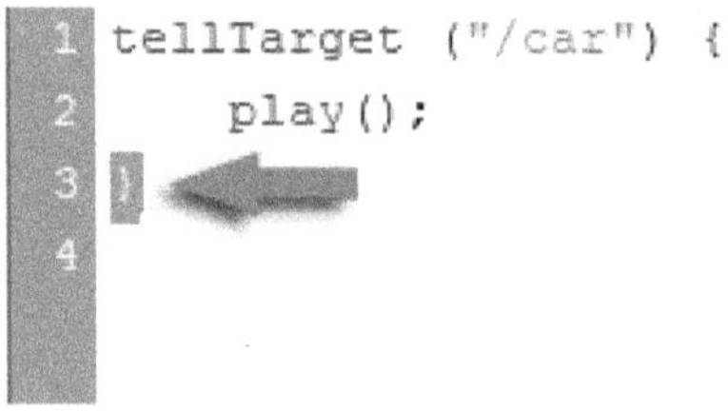

Go to **Global Functions**, **Timeline Control**, and double-click **stop**:

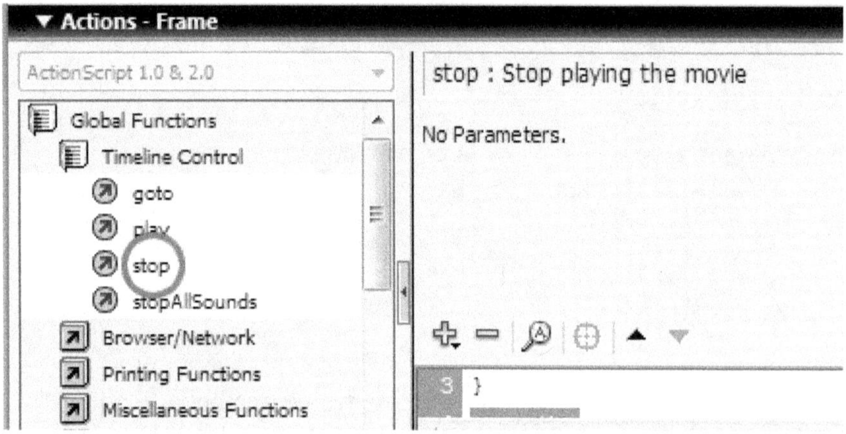

The stoplight is ready to go. We won't be able to test it until you've added the new code to the **GO** button. So let's do that now. Go back to the Stoplight stage by clicking its link above the timeline/stage:

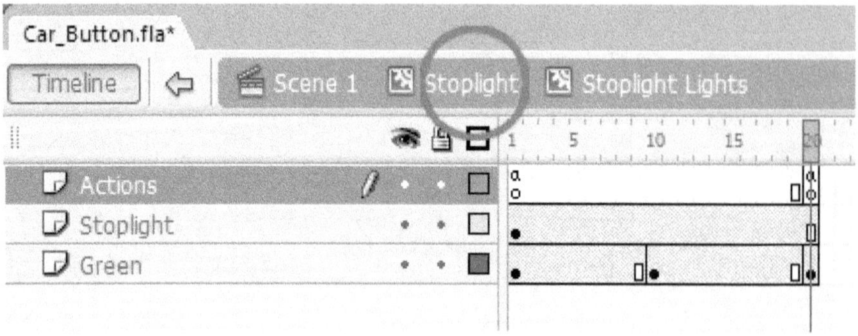

You should now be back in the Stoplight editing stage. Since we need to control the Stoplight *we need to give it a Instance Name*. Select the Stoplight symbol and open the Properties panel. Type **stoplight2** in the **Instance Name** window:

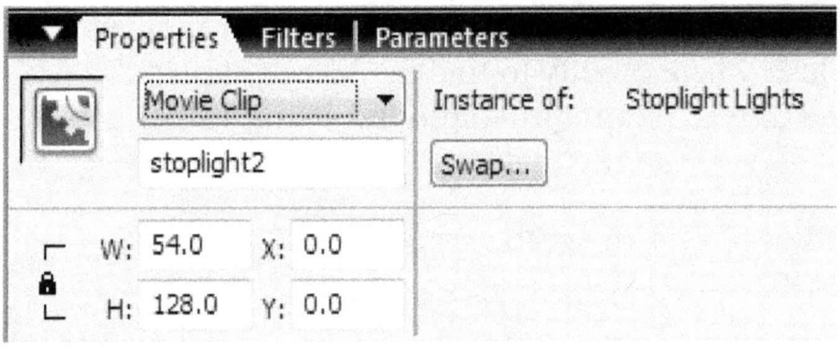

The reason we named it **stoplight2** is because this Movie clip is *within* the main **Stoplight** Movie clip which is named **stoplight**.

Now that we have the Stoplight symbol named, we need to add the ActionScript to the **GO** button. Let's do that now. Click the **GO** button and open the Actions panel so we can see its ActionScript:

```
on (release) {
    tellTarget ("/car") {
        play();
    }
}
```

We want the **GO** button to control the stoplight and not the car. So you'll need to change **/car** to **/stoplight2**. We do this by clicking on the word **car** in the code. That will bring up the Target window again. Type **/stoplight2**:

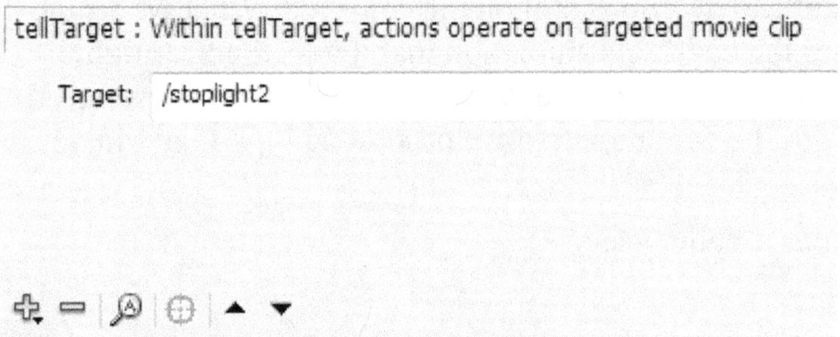


```
on (release) {
    tellTarget ("/stoplight2") {
        play();
    }
}
```

Test your movie (CTRL + ENTER). You'll notice that even though the **GO** button is targeting the **Stoplight** Movie clip, the Stoplight animation isn't playing.

Here is why it's not working. The Movie clip we're trying to control is *within* another Movie clip. If you want to control a Movie clip that's within another Movie clip you have to tell Flash where exactly to find the Movie clip you're trying to control. So we'll need to type **/stoplight/stoplight2** in the Target window:

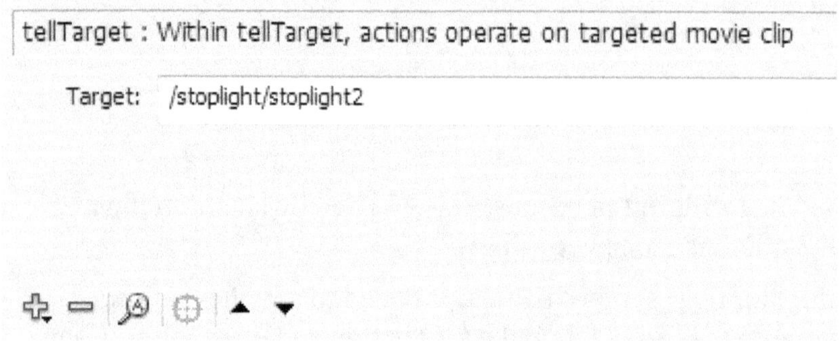

So the first part of this Target code, **/stoplight**, targets the main Movie clip on Scene 1. The second part, **stoplight2,** tells Flash to find the Movie clip named **stoplight2** within the main Movie clip.

Test your movie again (CTRL + ENTER). It works! When you click the **GO** button the stoplight begins animating, and then when it gets to the green light the car takes off!

This is the real key to the power of Flash. Once you create Movie clips and name them, you can create all sorts of amazing animations. You can even have Movie Clips control other Movie Clips as we did with the stoplight animation.

Let's do one more thing. When the car finishes its animation it returns to frame 1 and stops. But the **Stoplight** Movie clip is still on the color red. What we would like is when the car reaches the end of its animation that it tells the **Stoplight** Movie clip to return to frame 1 so that the red color shows again. Since we need to add this code to the end of the car animation we need to edit the **Car** Movie clip.

Click on **Scene 1** above your timeline/stage:

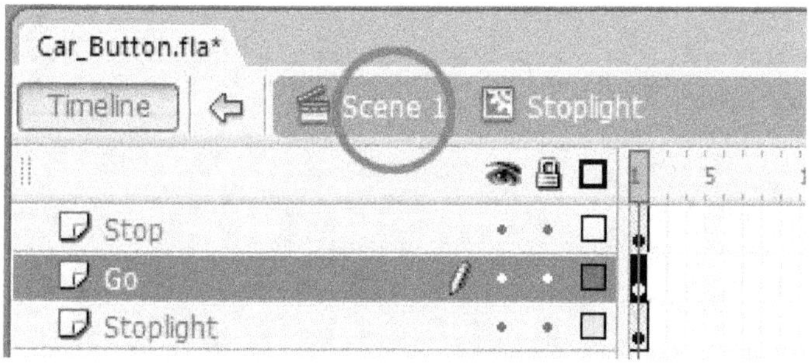

Double-click the **Car** Movie clip so that you are in its editing stage. Next, insert a keyframe on frame **120** of the **Actions** layer:

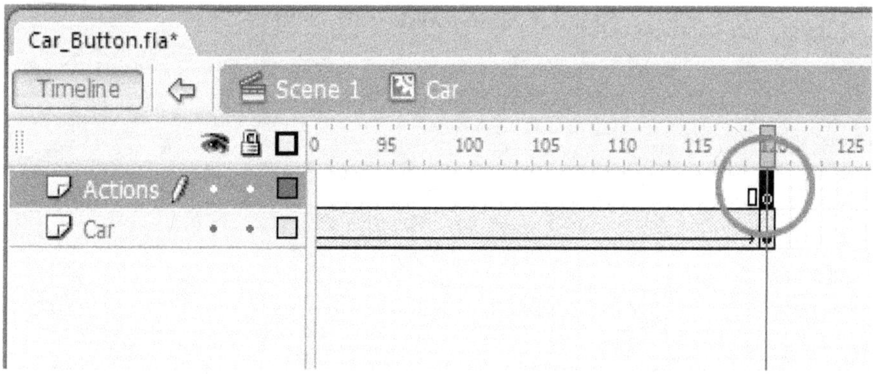

Next, open the Actions panel and make sure that Script Assist Mode is on. Go to **Deprecated**, **Actions**, and double-click on **tellTarget**:

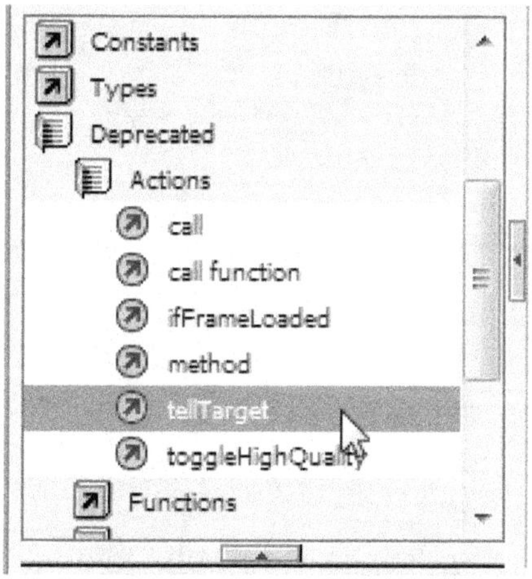

Type **/stoplight/stoplight2** in the **Target** window:

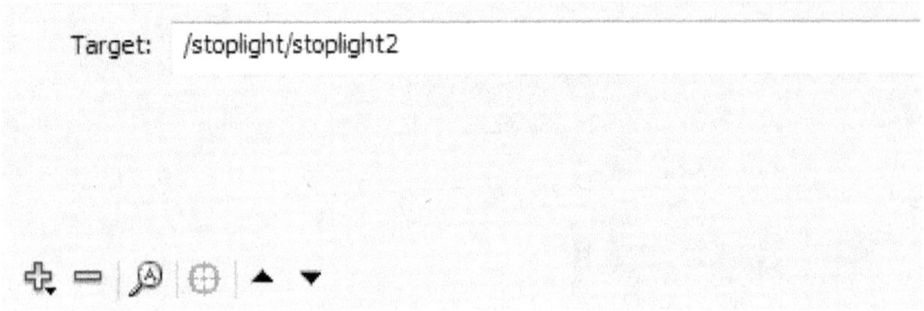

Since we want the **Stoplight** Movie clip to go to frame 1, we need to add that code now. Select **Global Functions, Timeline Control**, and double-click **goto**:

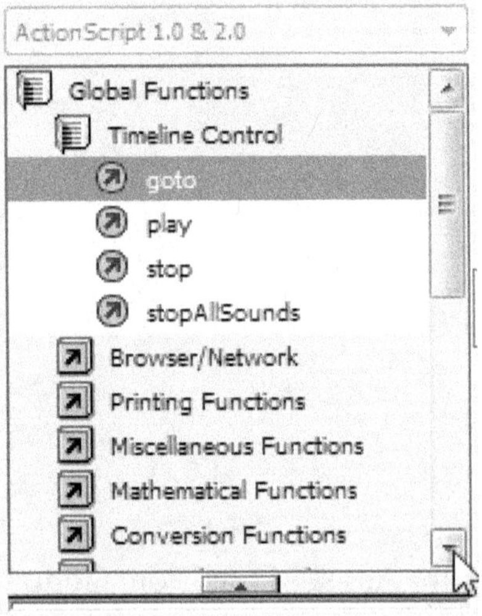

You should now be in the **goto** settings window:

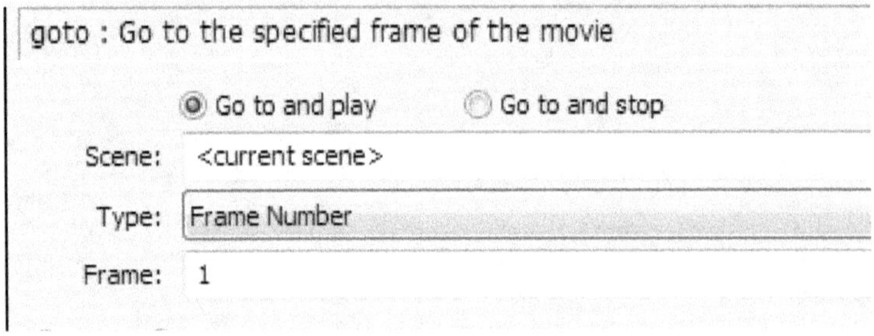

The settings here are self-explanatory. We want the **Spotlight** Movie clip to go to frame 1 and stop so we need to select **Go to and stop**:

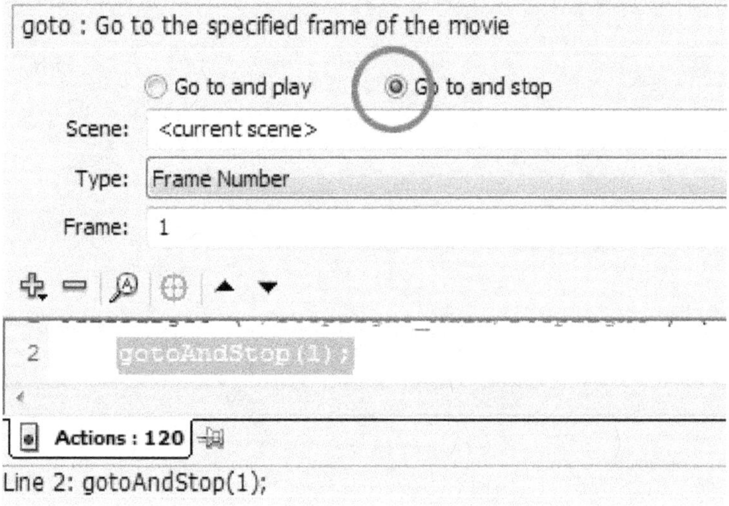

Test your movie (CTRL + ENTER) again. When the car reaches the end of its animation the **Stoplight** Movie clip should go back to frame 1 and stop. You should now see the red color in the stoplight. Pretty cool huh? By now you should have a better understanding of how powerful Movie Clips can be. Once you name your Movie Clips you can create all sorts of amazing animations!

Chapter Three:
Scenes & Labels

Once you start creating your own Flash websites or headers, you'll soon come across a time when you'll have to use scenes. You may have noticed that in the previous projects the main timeline has been called Scene 1. In Flash you can have as many Scenes as you like. What is a Scene? Well, let's say you have a Flash website and it has 5 pages. With Scenes you can place each page into its own scene. I have found that it's easier to organize your Flash website when the pages are on their own scene since it cuts down on the amount of layers if you only had one scene. We'll be going through several exercises that will teach you everything you need to know about scenes.

Also, we'll be using Labels. What's a Label? Well, just as we named Movie clips, a Label is a way of naming a frame. Let's say that on frame 30 of your main timeline you have a bird image. And, let's say that you have a button that, when clicked, will take the user to the frame with the bird. That's where a Label comes in handy. All you have to do is name the frame **bird** and tell the button to go to the Label **bird**. That's it! We'll be going through examples but you should get the hang of it after the first project is finished. So let's get started!

Download the chapter three folder from www.adobe-flash-tutorials.info/chapters.htm. Open the Flash file called Scenes.fla. You'll notice that we have four images in the library along with a blank canvas. In this project we're going to put each picture into its own scene and then have buttons direct the user to the scenes.

Drag **Deer.jpg** onto the canvas:

Don't worry about centering the picture on the canvas when you drag it over. We'll do that with the Align tools. Select the deer picture and open the Align panel. Select **To Stage**, **Align vertical center** and **Align horizontal center**:

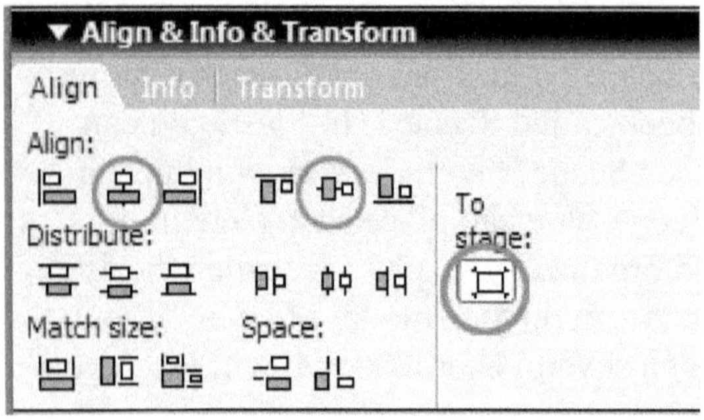

The deer picture should now be centered correctly on the stage. Name the layer **Deer** and add a new layer called **Buttons**:

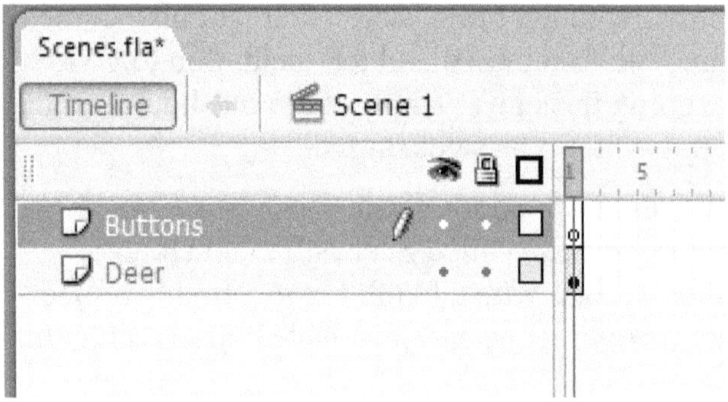

We're going to add four buttons to this scene. Grab the **Rectangle Tool** and select the color **white** for the **Fill color**. Turn off the **Stroke color**. Create a rectangle shape on the left side of the canvas:

Once we finish creating this button we can duplicate it for the other three buttons. Select the rectangle shape then go to **Modify**, and **Convert to Symbol**. Next, select **Button** and name this symbol **Deer**:

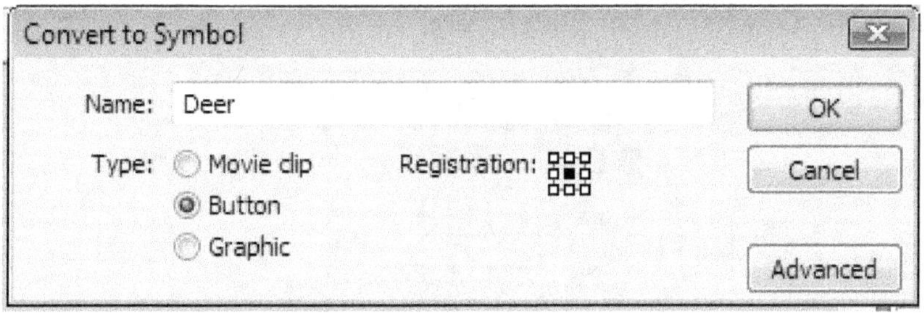

Hit **OK**. Double-click on this new button to enter its editing stage. Add a new layer and name it **Text**:

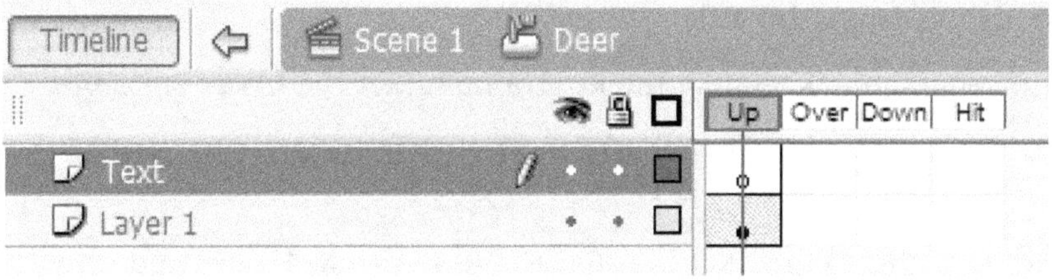

Select the **Text Tool**. Open the Properties panel and select **Verdana**, size **12**, **Bold**, **black** for the color, and click on **Align Center**:

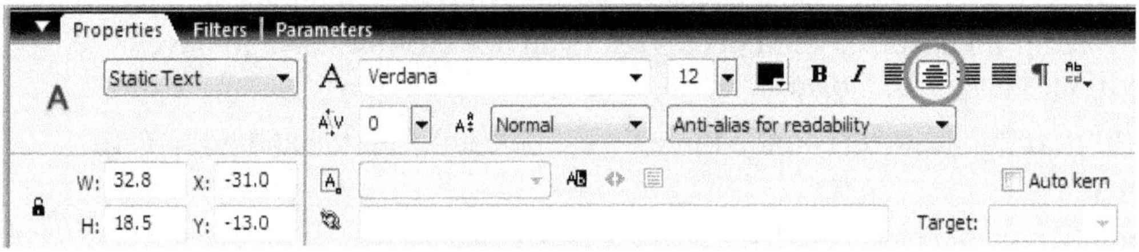

Using the **Text Tool**, click the area over the white shape and type **Deer**. You can position it when you're done so that it's centered:

Add a keyframe under the **Over** state for both layers:

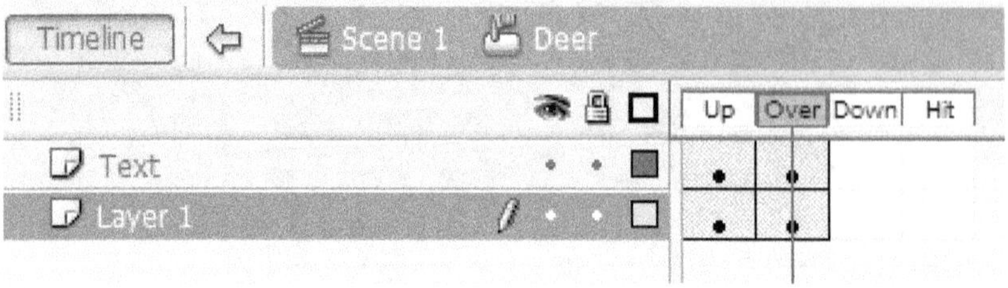

Select the **Text Tool** again and highlight the word **Deer** (click inside the word then go to **Edit**, **Select All**). Next, with the Properties still open, select the color **red**. The word Deer should now be red.

Let's make the white shape black. Select the keyframe under the **Over** state of **Layer 1**.

This will highlight the white shape. Next, grab the **Paint Bucket Tool** and select black for a **Fill color**. Your white shape should now be black. Test your movie (**CTRL + ENTER**) and check your new button. When you roll over it both the text and background should change color.

Remember, if you don't add a shape under the Hit state of buttons, it will pull the 'Hit' area from the other keyframes. Also, you don't always have to have keyframes under the Down state.

We'll next duplicate this button three times. Select the button and go to **Edit**, **Copy**:

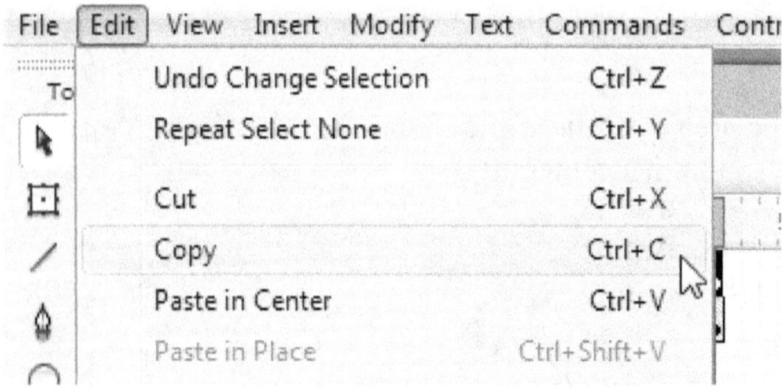

Go to **Edit**, **Paste in Place**:

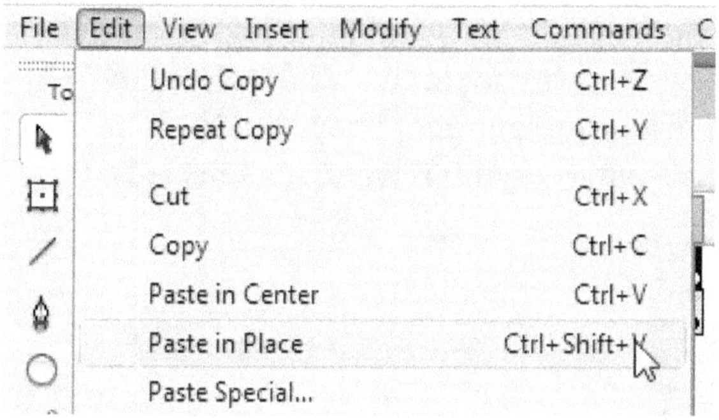

You now have an exact copy of the button. The reason you can't see it, is because when you Paste in Place it will place the new copy in the exact same location as your first button. Select this new button and drag it down below your other button:

Do these steps two more times so that we have four buttons on the side of the Canvas:

You may notice that the buttons are a little offset. We would like all the buttons aligned perfectly with each other. The easiest way to do this, is to select the first button, hold down Shift and select the rest of the buttons. They should all be highlighted now (a thin blue line will surround a symbol when it's selected):

Next, open the Align panel and select **Distribute left edge** and **Distribute vertical center**. Make sure that **To stage** is *not selected*:

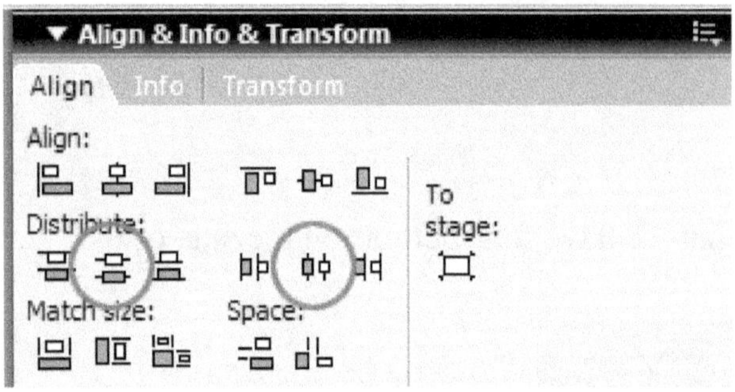

Your buttons should now be perfectly aligned with each other. Double-click the second from the top button so that you are in its editing stage. Change the word **Deer** to the word **Flowers**:

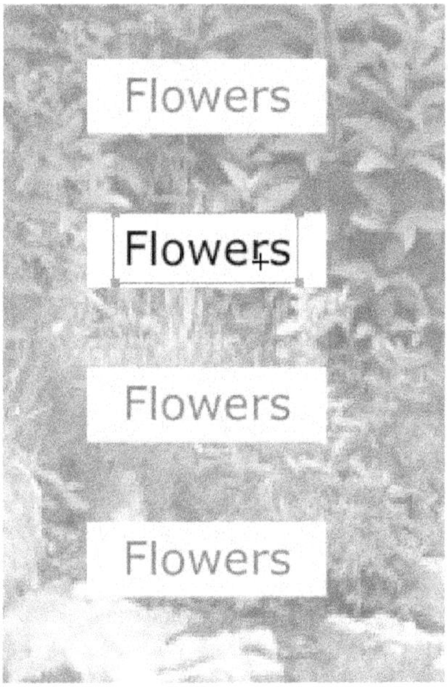

Notice anything peculiar? Since we're editing a direct copy of the original button, whenever we make an edit in this button it will affect all instances of the same button. You may now notice that all the buttons now say Flowers. Since this isn't what we wanted, undo your text edit so that it says Deer again, and go back to **Scene 1**.

This time, select the second button and open your Properties panel if it isn't already open. Click on **Swap**:

The **Swap Symbol** box should now be open. Click on the **Duplicate Symbol** button:

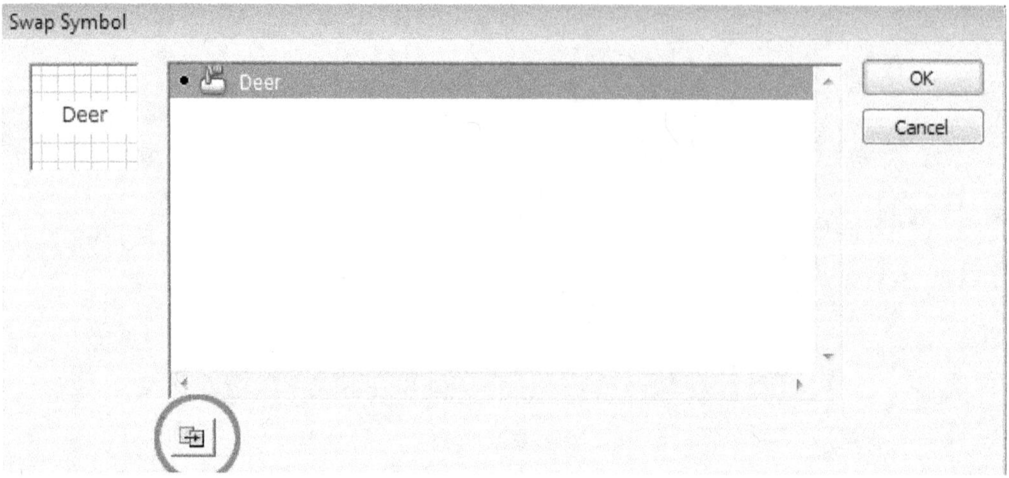

The **Duplicate Symbol** window should appear. Type **Flowers** next to **Symbol name**:

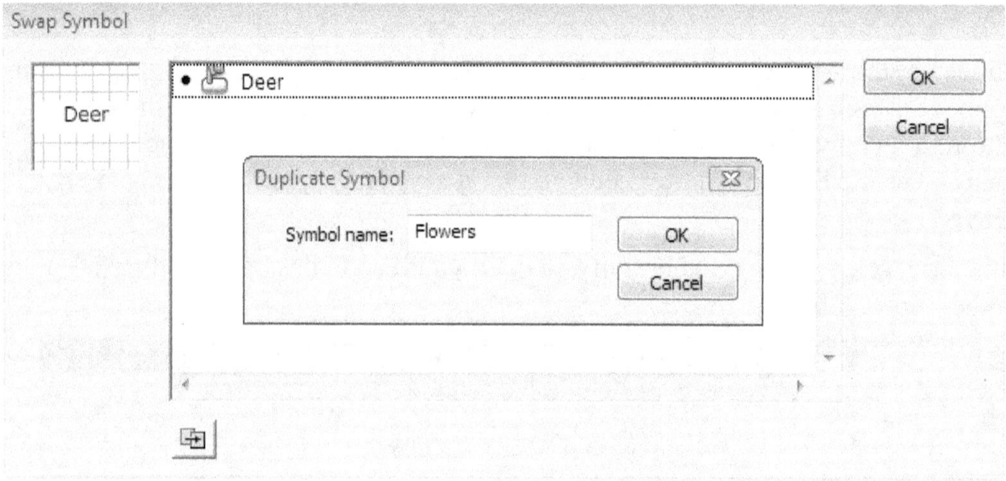

Hit **OK**. You should now see this new button in the **Swap Symbol** window:

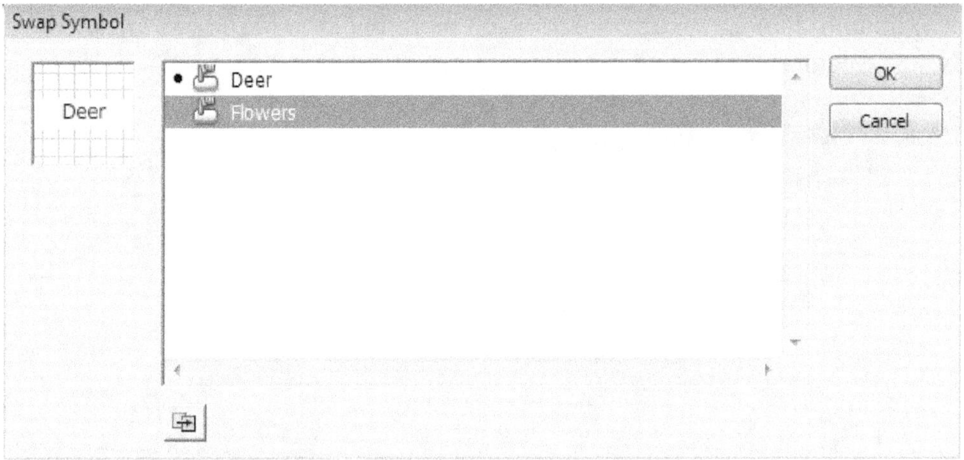

Double-click the **Flowers** button and the **Swap Symbol** window will close. You can now edit this button without affecting the other buttons.

Repeat these steps for the last two buttons. Select the third button, click on **Swap**, **Duplicate Symbol** and name it **Golf**. Remember to *always double-click your new selection* in the **Swap Symbol** window. Do these steps for the last button and name the final button **Motorcycle**.

You should now have four separate buttons. We're going to double-click the **Flowers** button and change the text to Flowers. Remember to do that for the **Over** state also. Do these steps for the final two buttons changing their text to Golf and Motorcycle. When you are finished the buttons should look like this:

You'll notice that on my last button the word Motorcycle barely fits within my button. We'll adjust this test size in a moment.

For now, though, let's create a scene for each picture. Go to **Window**, **Other panels**, and **Scene**:

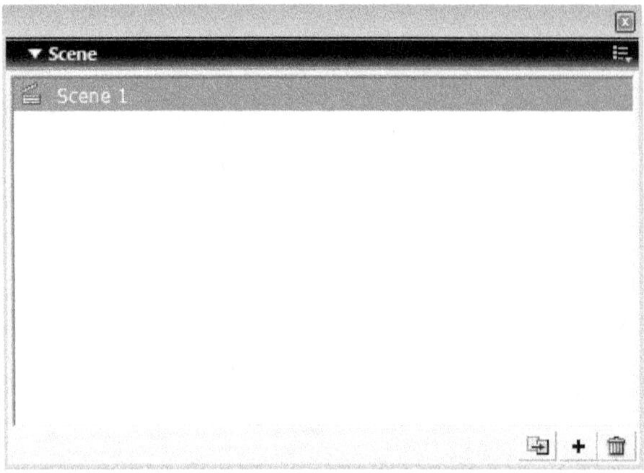

You only have one scene so far: **Scene 1**. Rename this scene **Deer**:

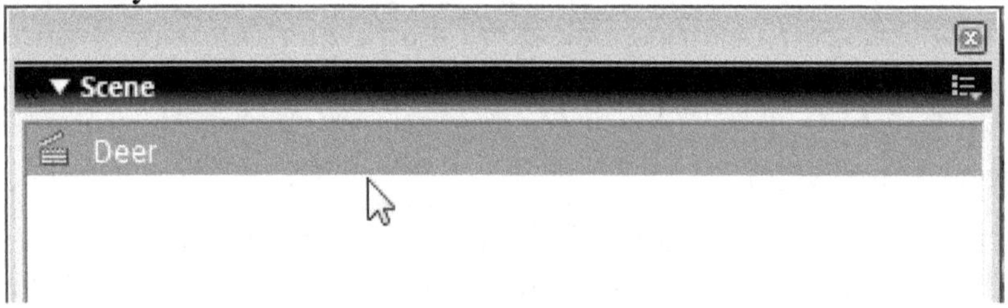

Next, we'll create a new scene. On the bottom of this panel you'll see three buttons. A **Duplicate symbol** button, **Add scene** button, and a **Delete Scene** button. For now we'll focus on the first two buttons:

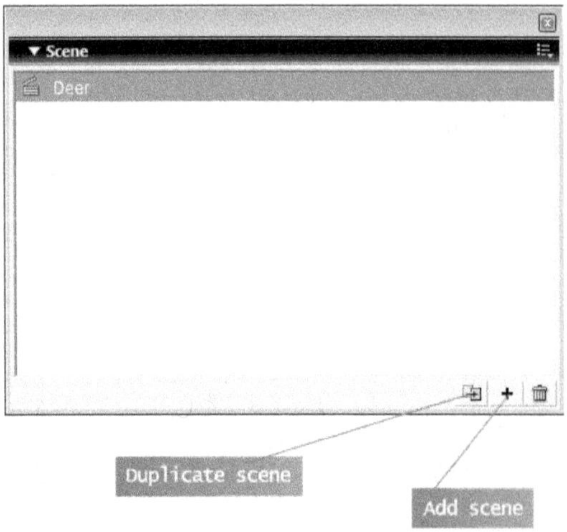

If you click the **Add scene** button you'll be creating a new scene with no elements. When you select **Duplicate scene**, Flash will duplicate whichever scene is selected (in the case, the Deer scene). Let's crate a scene from scratch. Click the **Add scene** button. You'll now see a scene called Scene 2. Also, the main canvas has changed to show you the new scene's stage. Double-click Scene 2 in the Scene panel; change the name to **Flowers**:

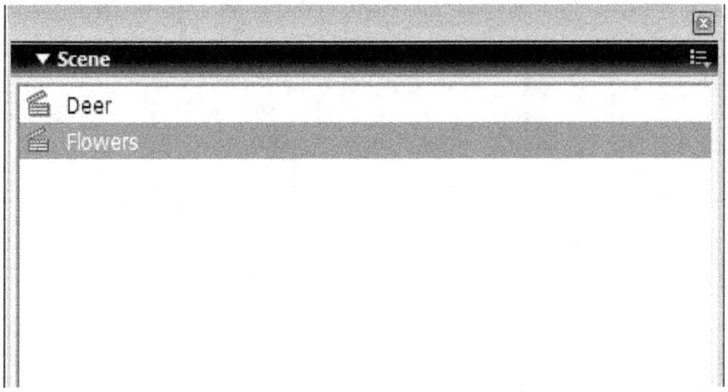

Add two more scenes and name them **Golf** and **Motorcycle**:

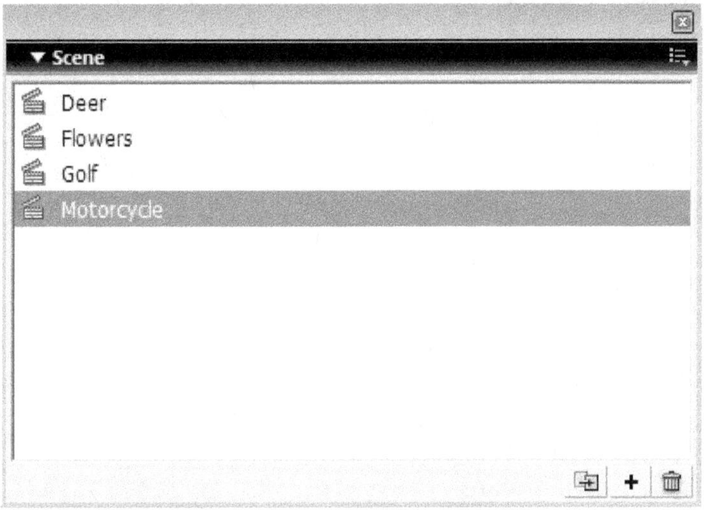

Select **Flowers** in the Scene panel and the stage will change to the new Flowers scene. We're now going to drag **Flowers.jpg** from the library over to the stage:

So now, just as we did with the Deer picture, we'll center this picture within the stage. Open the Align panel and select **To Stage**, **Align vertical center**, and **Align horizontal center**:

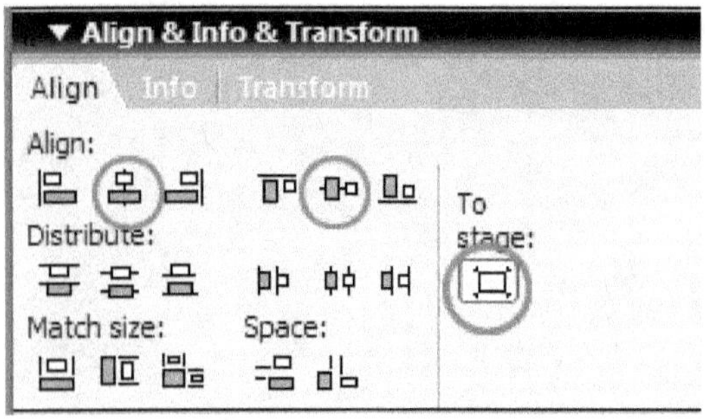

Go to the Scene panel again and select the **Golf** scene. Drag **Golf.jpg** over to the stage. Align it with the stage the same way you just did it for the Flowers picture. Repeat these steps for the final scene **Motorcycle**. When you're done you should have four scenes, each with their own picture.

Test the movie (CTRL + ENTER). You should be seeing a very fast slideshow of all the scenes. That would probably be annoying to the user. The reason this happens is because when you have more than one Scene, Flash will play through all the scenes looping them indefinitely. Whenever you have more than one Scene always add a **stop** code to your project if you don't want the scenes to loop.

In this case, we'll add a **stop** code to the first frame of the Deer Scene. In your Scene panel select the scene Deer. Create a new layer and name it **Actions**. Select the first frame of the **Actions** layer:

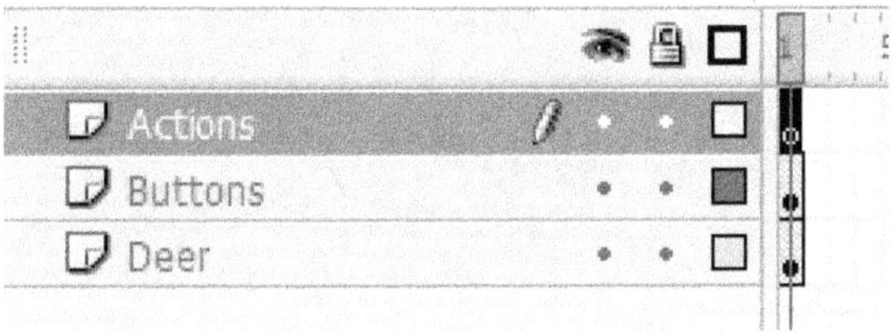

Open the Actions panel. Go to **Global Functions**, **Timeline Control**, and double-click **stop**:

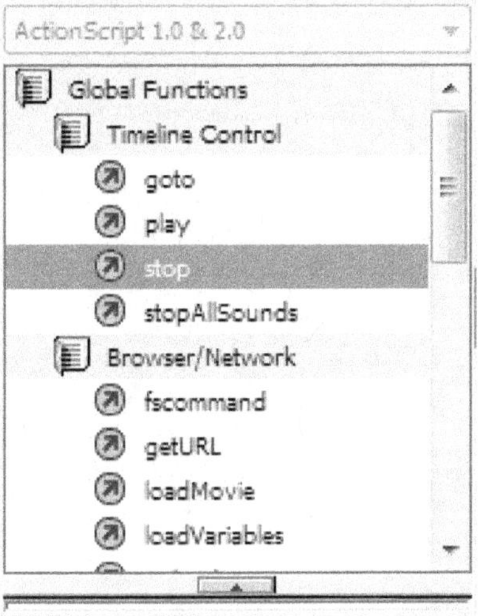

That's it. You now have a **stop** code in your frame. The frame of the **Actions** layer should have a small **a** symbol within the frame:

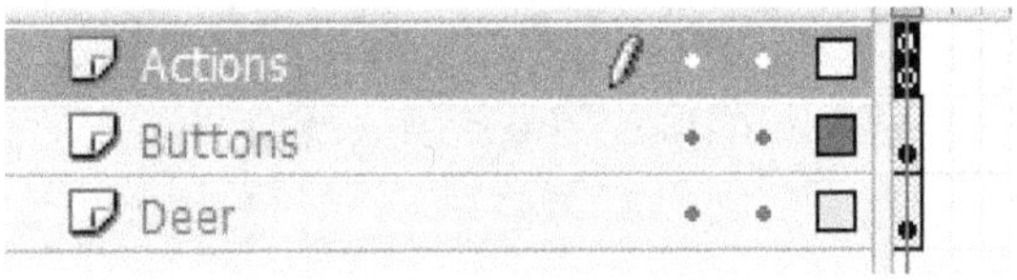

Test this movie again (CTRL + ENTER). This Flash file now stops at the Flower scene. Next, we'll add ActionScript to the buttons.

Select the **Deer** button and open the Actions panel. Make sure you are still in Script Assist mode. Next, go to **Global Functions**, **Timeline Control**, and double-click **goto**:

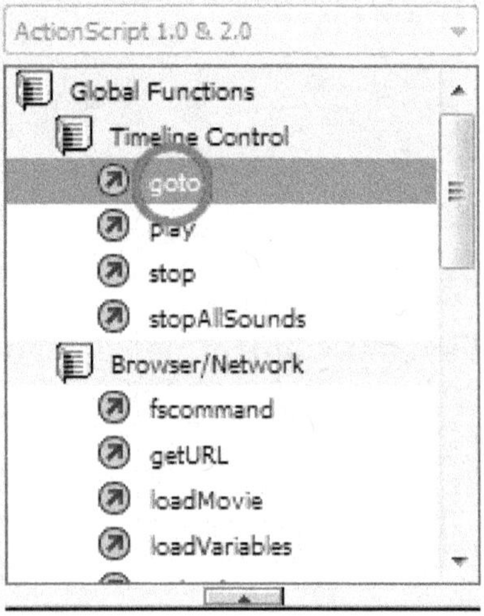

You should now see the **goto** settings in the Actions window:

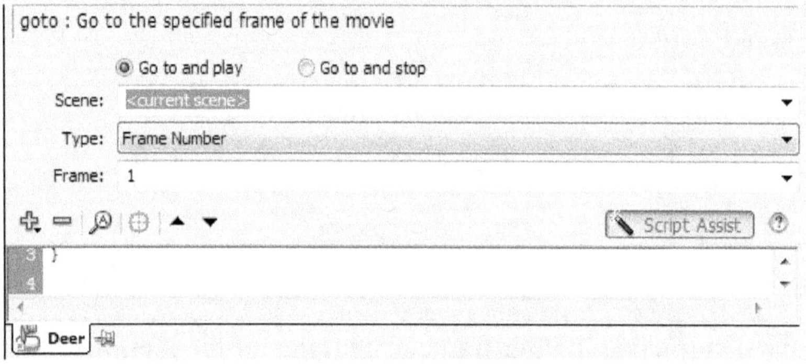

We want the user to go to the Deer scene when the **Deer** button is clicked. Click the drop-down arrow in the Scene window, and you'll see the scene choices:

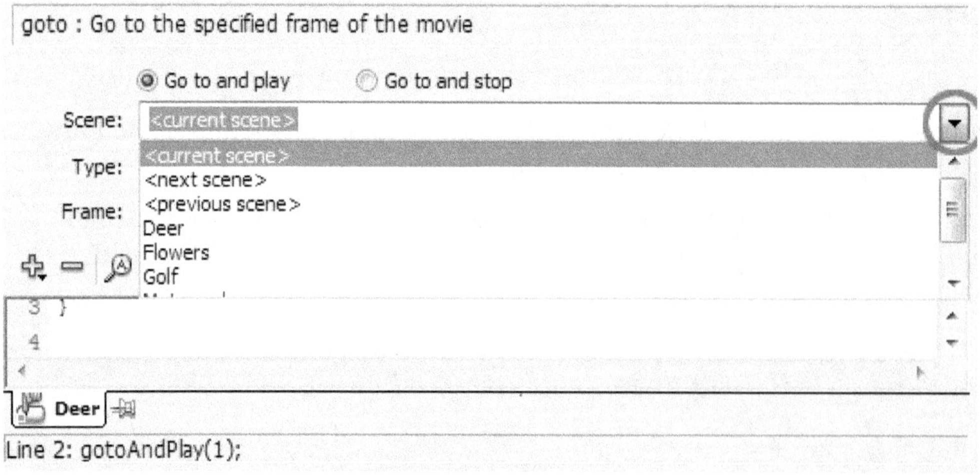

Select **Deer** from the choices. Next select **Go to and stop**:

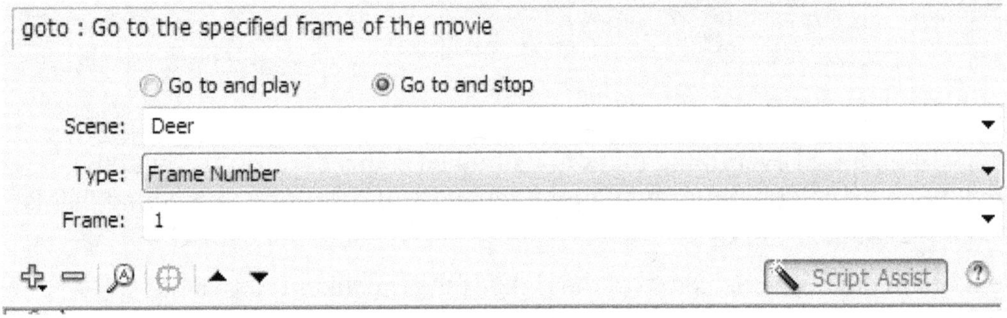

Keep **Frame** at **1** since each Scene only has one frame. When the user clicks the Deer button it will take them to the **Deer** Scene. Next, we'll repeat these steps for the Flowers button.

Select the Flowers button first, then open the Actions panel. Select **Global Functions**, **Timeline Control**, and double-click **goto**. This time, though, we're going to select the scene **Flowers**. Make sure **Go to and stop** is selected:

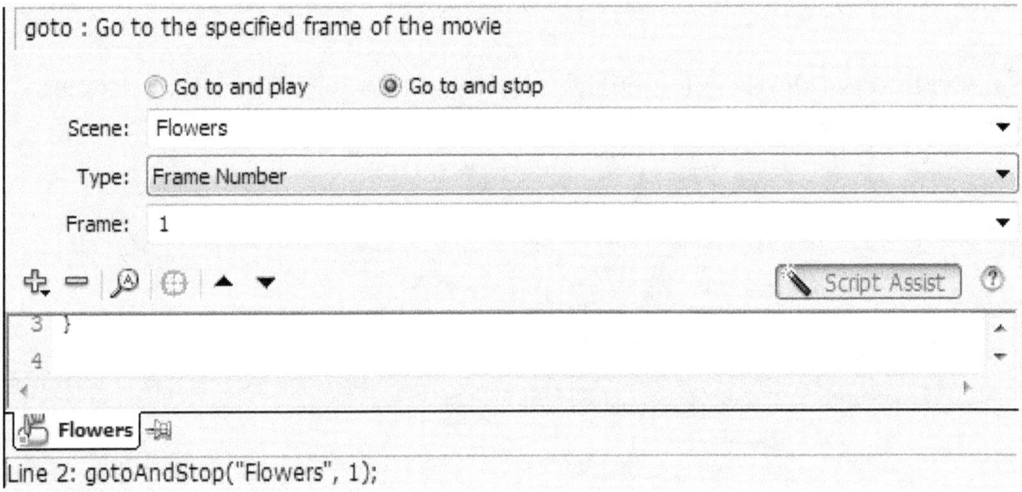

Repeat these steps for the final two buttons. Remember to select the correct scene for each button in your Actions panel; also, remember to select **Go to and stop** (if you select Go to and Play then Flash will go to the correct Scene but continue playing through the scenes until it hits a **stop** code).

When you're finished test your movie (CTRL + ENTER). The buttons should all work taking the user to the correct Scene. The only problem is that only the Deer Scene has buttons. We'll have to add those buttons to all the Scenes. Since all the buttons are on the same layer I'll show you a new way to copy over items. Go to the Deer Scene. Select the **Buttons** layer:

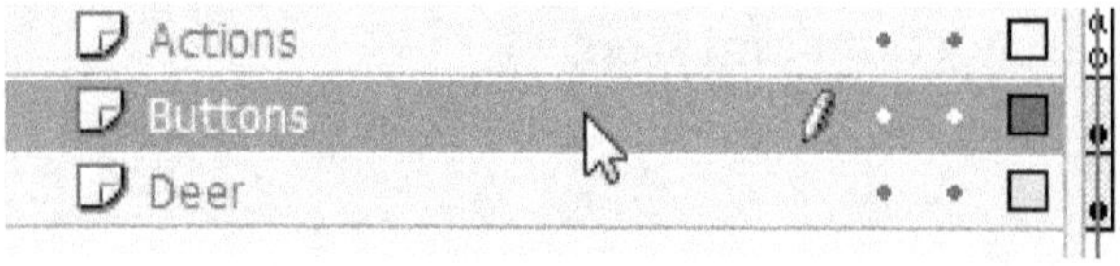

This will highlight everything that's in its frame (in this case, all the buttons). Next, go to **Edit**, **Timeline**, and **Copy Frames**. This will copy everything that is within the frame.

Next, go to the Scene Selector (to the right of the timeline. It looks like a clapboard):

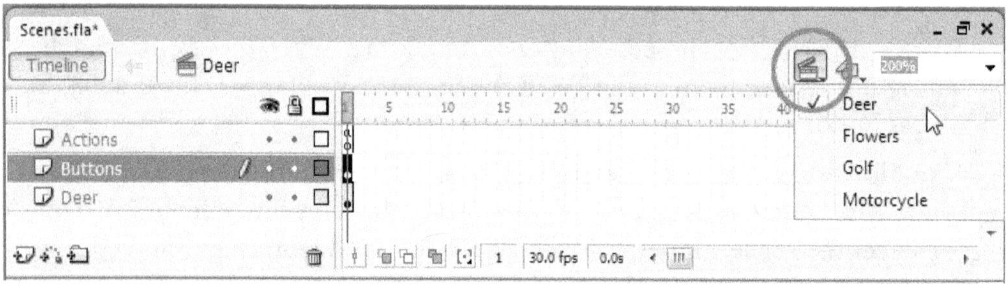

Select **Flowers** from the scene choices. You should now be in the Flowers scene. Create a new layer and name it Buttons:

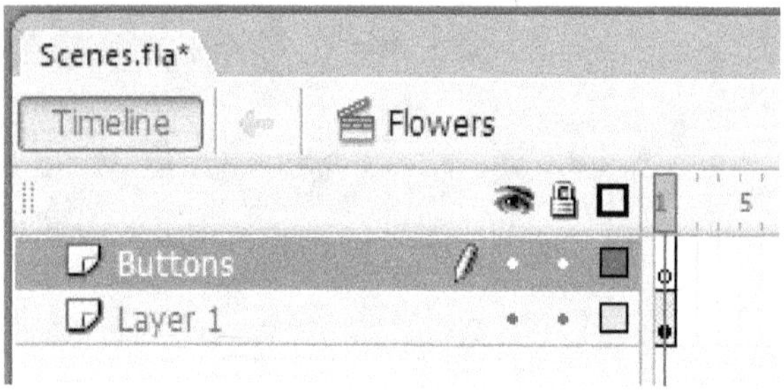

Select the first frame of the **Buttons** layer and go to **Edit**, **Timeline**, and **Paste Frames**. The buttons will be placed on the stage in the same position as the buttons in the Deer Scene:

Repeat these same steps for the **Golf** and **Motorcycle** Scenes. When you are done all four scenes should have a set of buttons. Test your movie (CTRL + ENTER) again. If you did everything correctly then you should be able to click your away around the scenes using the buttons.

We'll now adjust the text of the Motorcycle button. Double-click the Motorcycle button to enter its editing stage. Next, highlight the word Motorcycle:

In the Properties panel type **-1** in the **Letter Spacing** window:

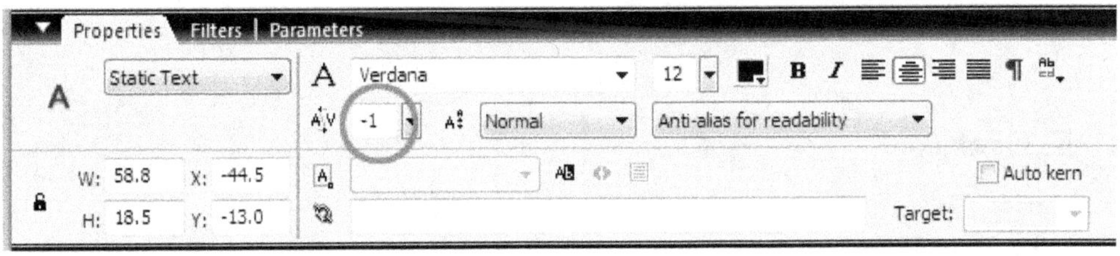

This will decrease the spacing between the letters. Select the **Over** keyframe of the **Text** layer:

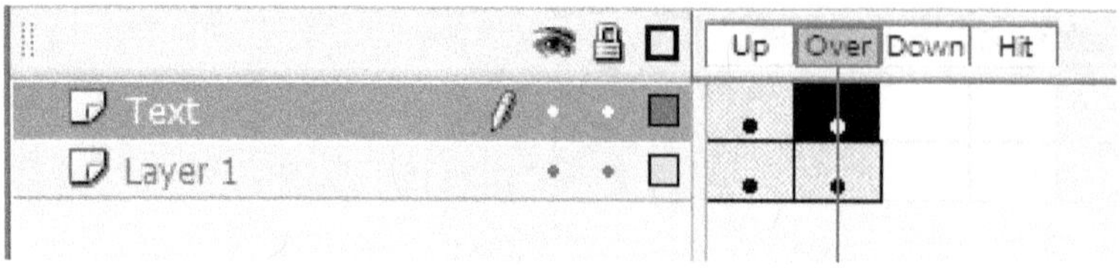

Highlight the word Motorcycle and once again change the Letter Spacing to -1. Test your movie (CTRL + ENTER) again. You'll notice that the changes you made to the Motorcycle Button are now showing up in every Scene. Since each scene is using the same Instance of the Motorcycle symbol, any change you make to the Motorcycle button will be reflected in all the scenes.

Next, we'll create a animation on one of the timelines. Go to the **Golf** Scene. The canvas should look like this:

Create a new layer and name it **Ball**:

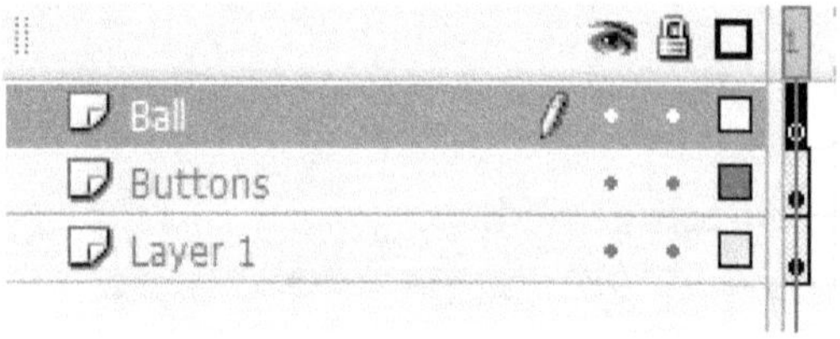

Select the **Oval Tool**:

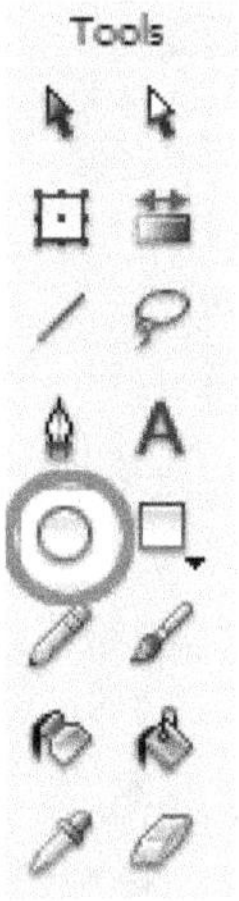

Select **white** for the **Fill color** and turn the **Stroke color** off:

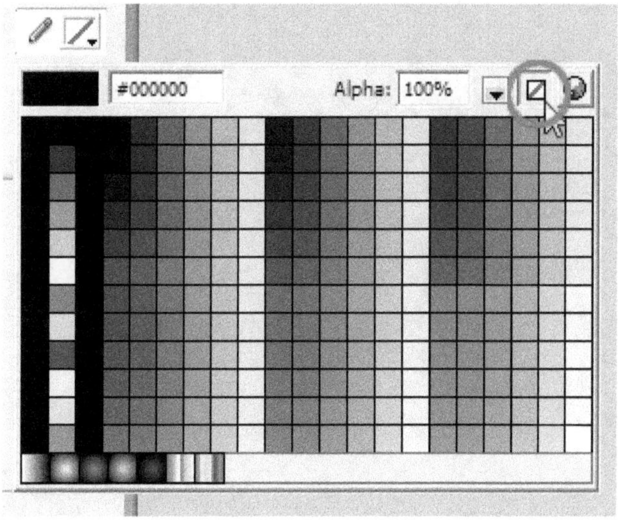

Create a circle shape on the right side of the canvas. Hold down SHIFT to create a perfect circle:

Next, add a **Motion Guide** Layer (**CS4/CS5** - Right click on the Ball layer and select **Add Classic Motion Guide**):

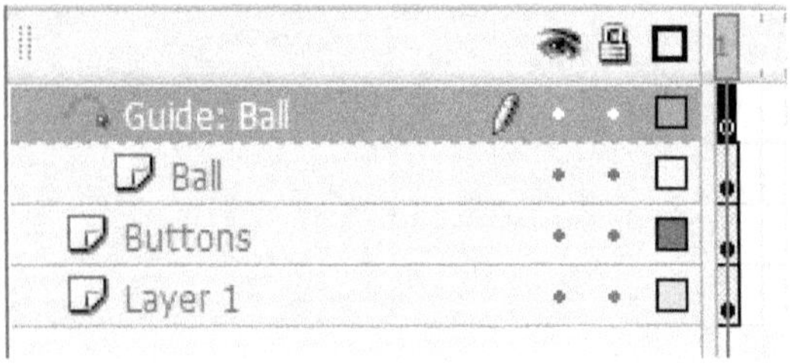

Select the **Pencil Tool**, and change the **Stroke color** to **red**. Next, draw a path line from the golf ball to the hole:

Next, add a keyframe on frame **90** of the **Ball** layer:

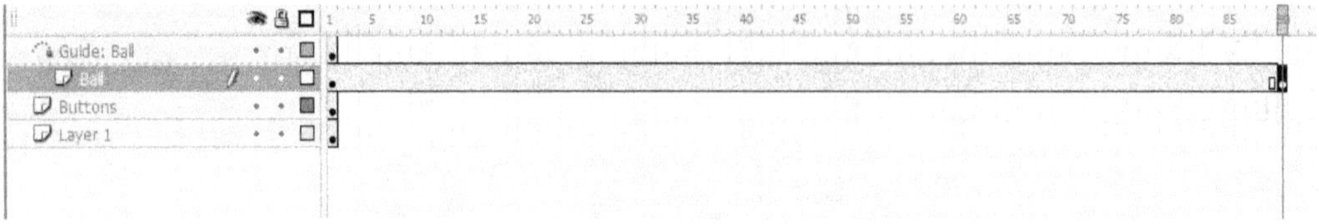

You'll notice that you can no longer see anything else on the canvas. So, to correct this, we'll add frames to the other layers on frame 90. Click on frame **90** of each layer and go to **Insert**, and **Frame**:

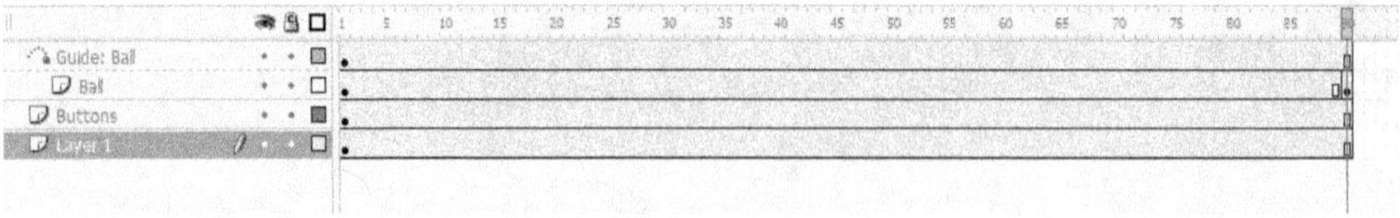

Next, add a Motion Tween to the Ball layer (**CS4/CS5 - Insert**, **Classic Tween**):

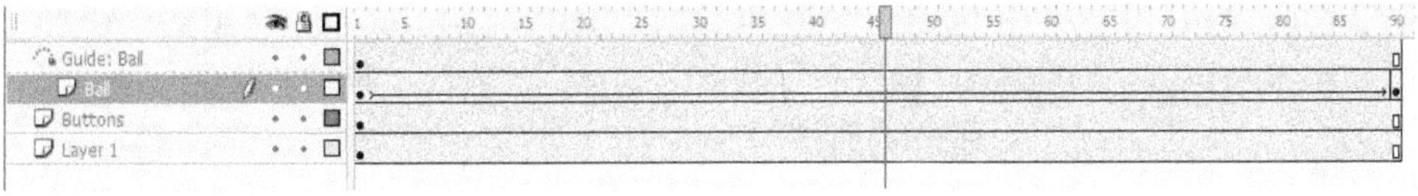

Select frame **90** of the **Ball** layer and move the Ball symbol to the end of the Motion Guide path:

Make sure the center of the ball lines up with the end of the path:

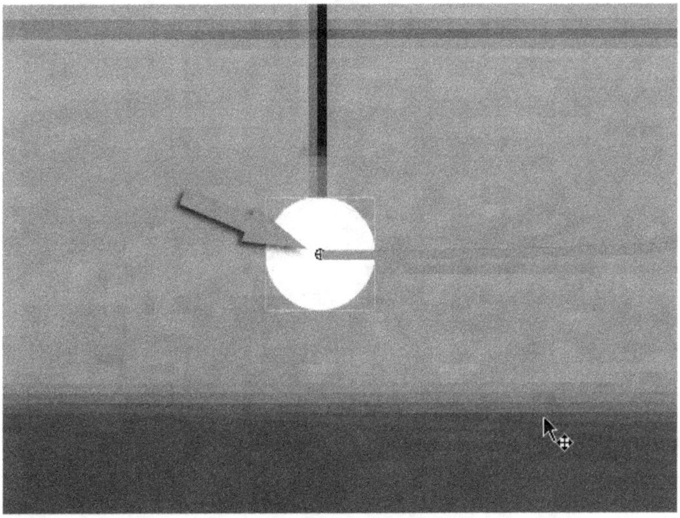

Hit ENTER on the keyboard and your ball should now be following the path. If it isn't following the path make sure that the ball on frame **1** is precisely positioned on the beginning of the path.

In earlier exercises we tested the movies by going to **Control**, and **Test Movie**. Since we don't want to test the entire movie, just this particular scene, then we're going to do something different. Go to **Control**, and **Test Scene**:

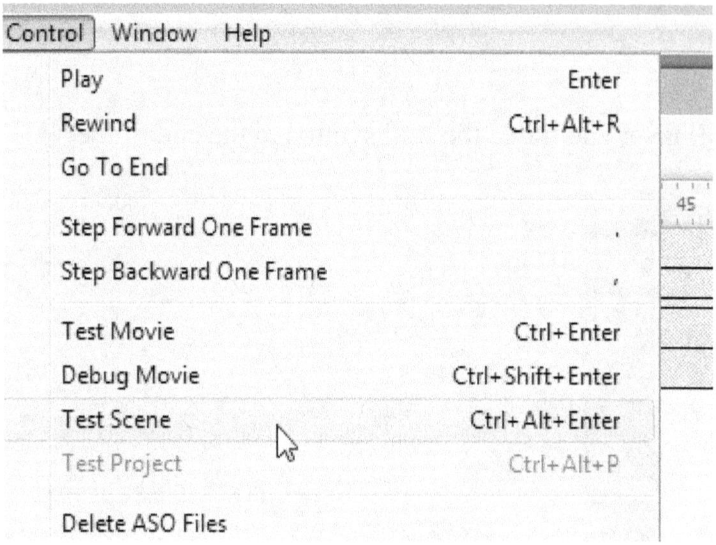

You should be able to see the scene animation play. The animation at this point doesn't look too realistic. Let's fix that. The ball should be picking up speed when it first starts heading down to the green. Select the first frame of the **Ball** layer. Next, in the Properties panel change the **Ease** number to **100**:

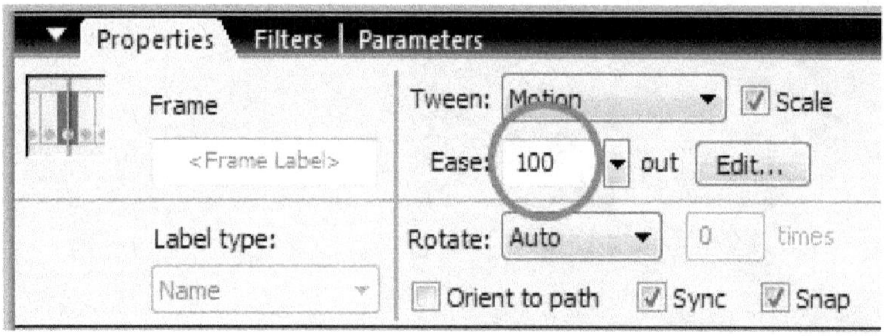

Test your Scene again (**Control**, and **Test Scene**). The animation should play nicely. If you want to tweak the speed even more, adjust the settings in the **Custom Ease In / Ease Out** window.

But you'll notice that it loops when it reaches the end of the animation. We would like the ball to stop when it reaches the hole. Add a new layer and name it **Actions**. Next, add a keyframe to frame **90** of the **Actions** layer:

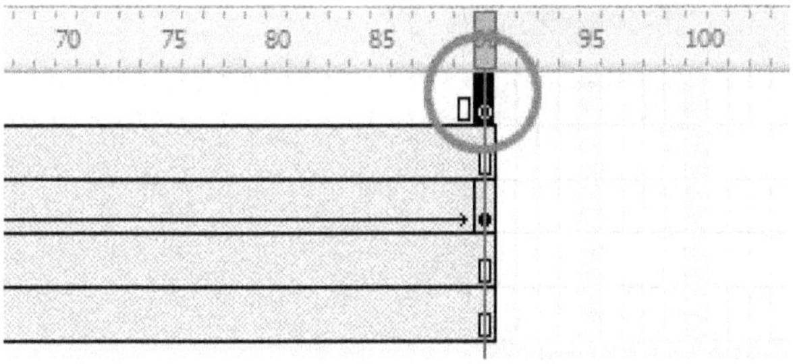

In the Actions panel go to **Global Functions**, **Timeline Control**, and double-click **stop**. Test your scene again. This time the animation will stop when the ball reaches the hole.

Open the Scenes panel. You'll notice that the order of scenes starts with **Deer**, **Flowers**, **Golf**, then **Motorcycle**:

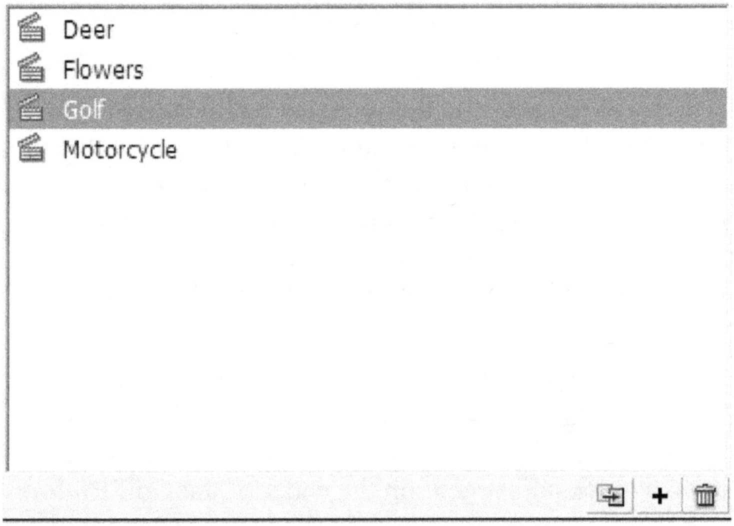

The first scene, **Deer**, will be what the user sees first since it's at the top of the list. Test your movie (CTRL + ENTER) and the first scene you will see is the Deer scene. In the Scene panel you can drag any scene to the top of the list. Let's say you want the Motorcycle scene to be the first scene a user sees. You would then *click-and-drag* the Motorcycle scene to the top of the list:

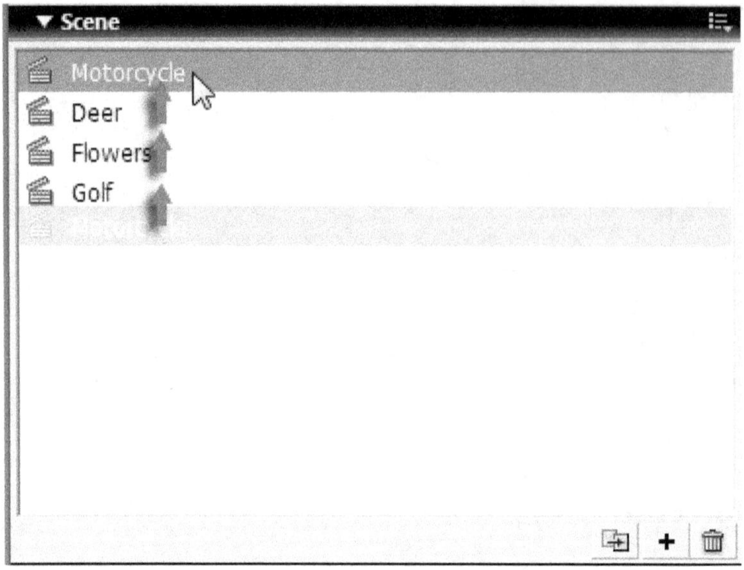

Test your movie (CTRL + ENTER) again. You'll notice that it still shows the Deer scene. The reason for this is unless you have a **stop** code in your scene, Flash will fly past that scene until it reaches a scene that does have a **stop** code. In this case that would be the Deer scene. Go to the **Motorcycle** scene and add a new layer called **Action**. Insert a keyframe on frame **1** of the **Action** layer; next, in the **Actions** panel go to **Global Functions**, **Timeline Control**, then double-click **stop**.

Test your movie (CTRL + ENTER) again. This time the first Scene that comes up is the Motorcycle Scene. Try clicking the Golf Button while you're testing the movie. You'll notice that it goes to the Golf Scene but the animation doesn't play. That's because we need to do a quick adjustment on the code for the Golf Button. Let's do that now.

In the Motorcycle scene, select the Golf button. In the Actions window click on the code **gotoAndStop**:

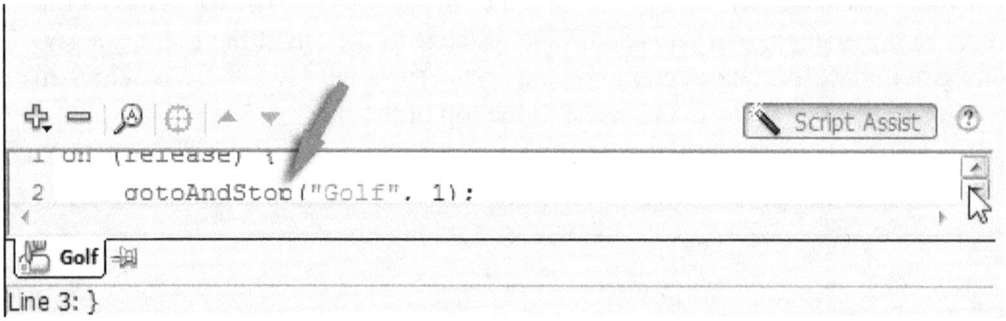

You should now see the **goto** options at the top of the panel:

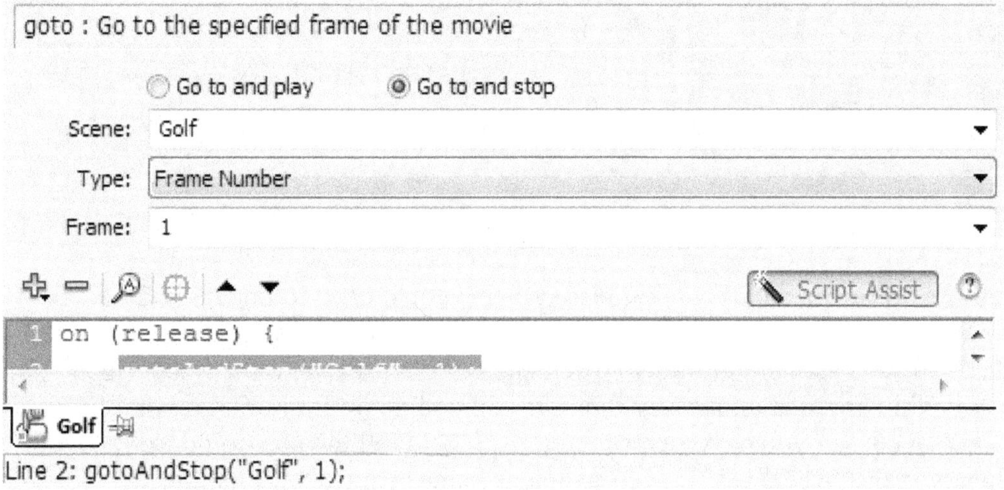

This time instead of selecting **Go to and stop**, select **Go to and play**:

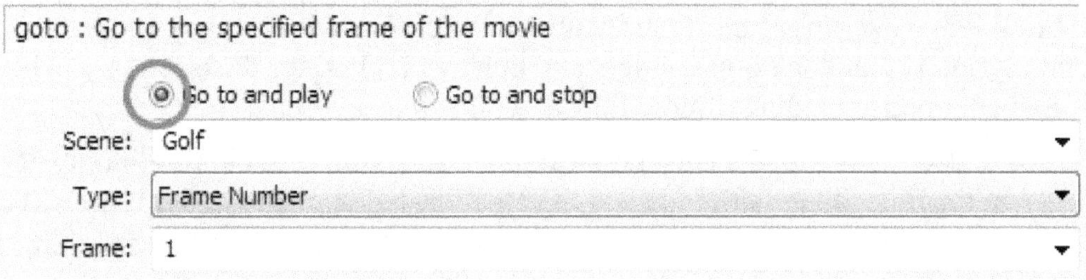

Test your movie (CTRL + ENTER) again. Click the Golf button and this time the animation should start playing immediately. That is the difference between **Go to and stop** and **Go to and play**. Pretty simple. You'll be using both codes quite frequently as you move along in your Flash career.

We changed the ActionScript for the Golf button in the Motorcycle scene, but if you test your movie (CTRL + ENTER) again, go to a different scene and you'll notice that the other buttons still have the old code: **Go to and stop**. Even though we have identical copies of the Golf button in each scene, changing ActionScript won't update the code on all the other buttons. Only changes that are made in the *Golf button editing stage* will affect all other copies of it.

So that concludes this exercise on Scenes. We'll be working more with scenes in later chapters, but hopefully now you have a better idea of how scenes are used.

Calling Labels

Before you can create dynamic Flash projects you'll need to understand Labels. Quite simply, it's a way of naming frames. Instead of a button directing a user to frame 90, we can name frame 90 **duck** and tell the user to go the Label **duck**. You may be thinking that either way the user will end up on frame 90 so what's the point? Well, say you have several buttons that all tell the user to go to frame 90. Then, you discover that you need to delete frames from your timeline. We now need the user to go to frame 75 instead. You would then have to go through the ActionScript on all the buttons and update the code to say frame 75. Or, if the code had told the user to go to the Label **duck**, all you would have to do is slide the **duck** Label over to frame 75 and you wouldn't have to update any ActionScript. If you don't quite understand don't worry! After this section you'll have a better understanding of how Labels work.

In this exercise we'll create a site similar to the last example, except we'll only be using one timeline along with Labels. Open the Flash document called **Labels.fla** in the Chapter 3 folder. You should be seeing an empty canvas. So the first thing we need to do is import the same four pictures we used in the last exercise. Go to **File**, **Import**, **Import to Library**. Go to the Pictures folder in the Chapter Three folder, select all the pictures and hit Open.

You should now have all four pictures in your Library:

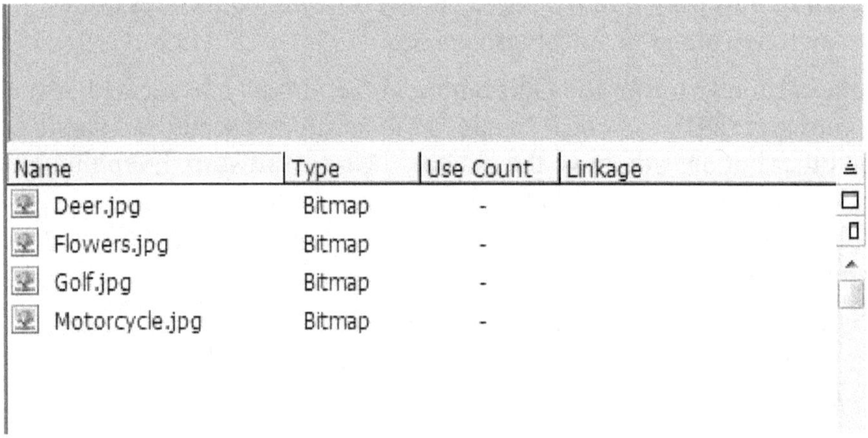

Create three new layers (you'll have four total) and name them **Deer**, **Flowers**, **Golf**, and **Motorcycle**:

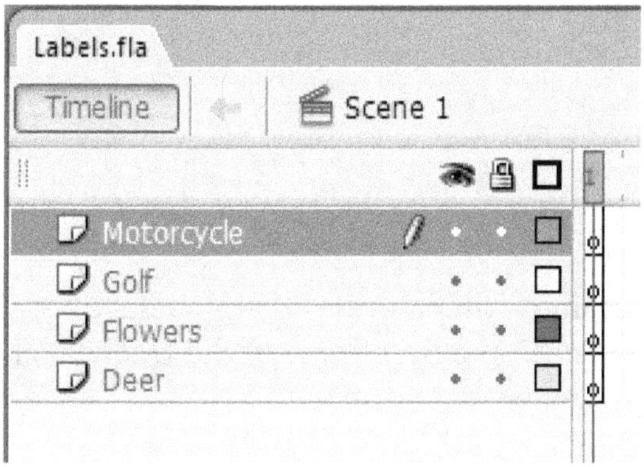

Add two more layers. Name them **Actions** and **Labels**:

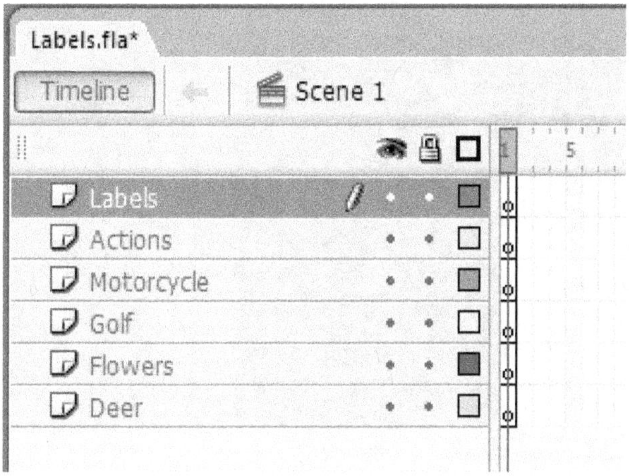

This timeline is going to have several frames so we need to insert a **stop** code into frame 1. Select the first frame of **Actions**. In the Actions panel go to **Global Functions**, **Timeline Control**, and double-click **stop**.

Next, we'll add the first Label to the **Labels** layer. Select the first frame of the **Labels** layer. In the Properties panel type **Deer** in the **Frame Label** window:

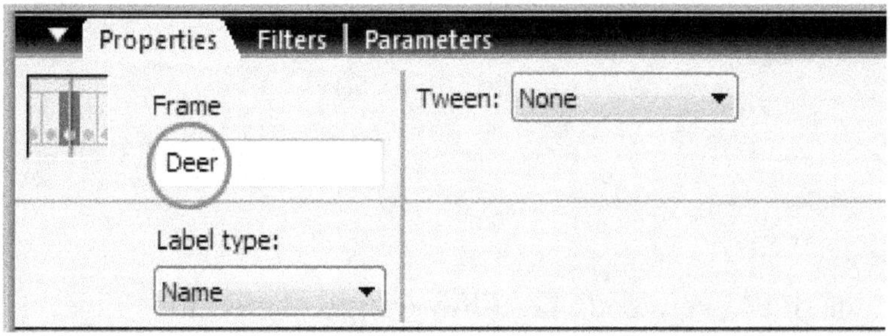

CS4/CS5 Users:

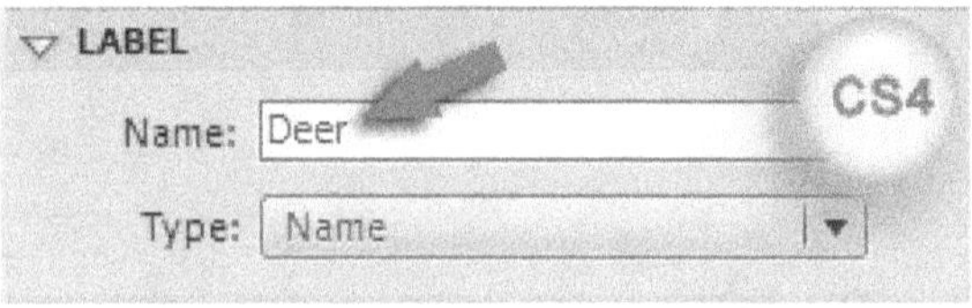

You should now see a Label Flag in your frame. This indicates that you have added a Label. We'll now add the pictures. Select the first frame of the **Deer** layer and drag **Deer.jpg** from the library onto the stage:

As we did in earlier exercises, align the picture to the stage. In the Align panel select **Align Horizontal Center**, **Align Vertical Center**, and **To Stage**:

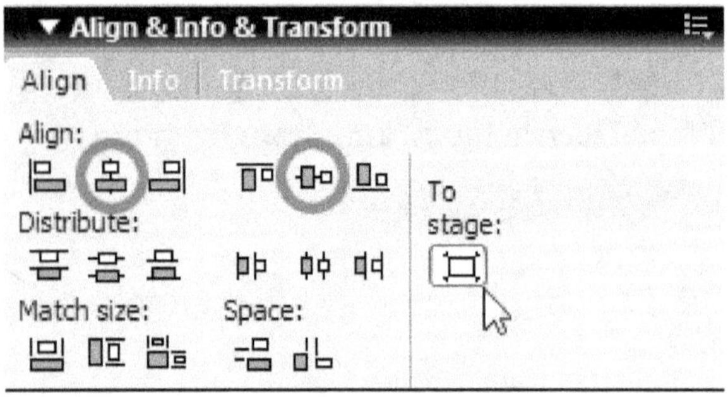

Next, select the first frame of **Flowers** and drag **Flowers.jpg** over to the Stage. Repeat the same aligning steps we used for the Deer Picture. Repeat these steps for the **Golf** and **Motorcycle** layer (remember to *select the first frame of each layer* before dragging the picture over). The timeline should now look like this:

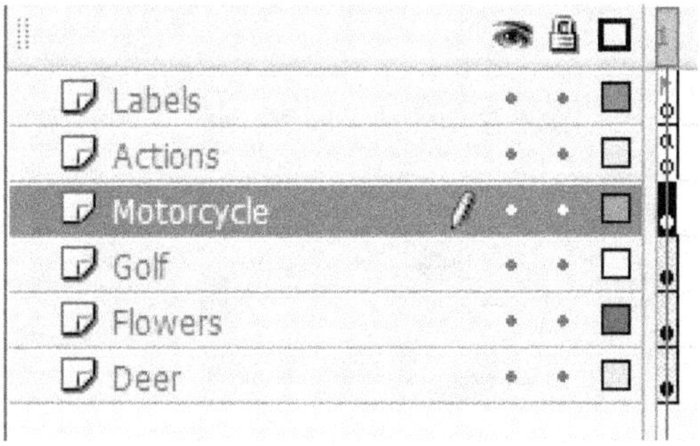

Select the first frame of the **Flowers** layer. Select the frame again but this time don't let go of the mouse button; click-and-drag this frame to frame **10**:

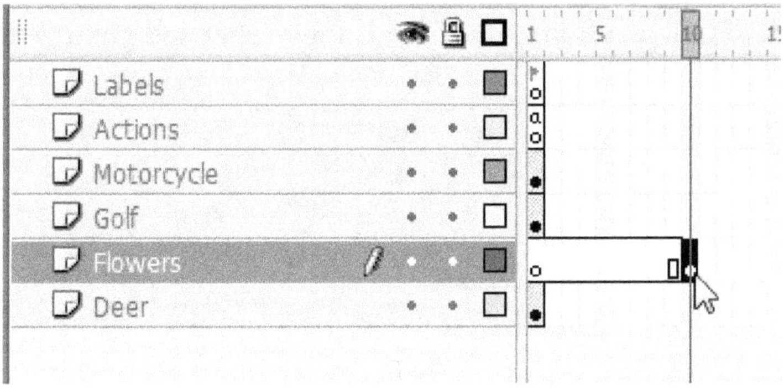

Do the same thing for the **Golf** layer. Select the first frame of the **Golf** layer, then select the frame again but don't release your mouse button; drag the frame to frame **20**:

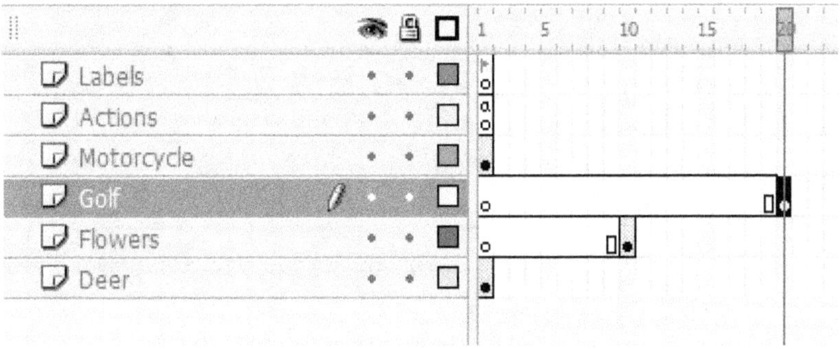

Lastly, we'll do the same steps for the **Motorcycle** frame. Drag this frame to frame **30**:

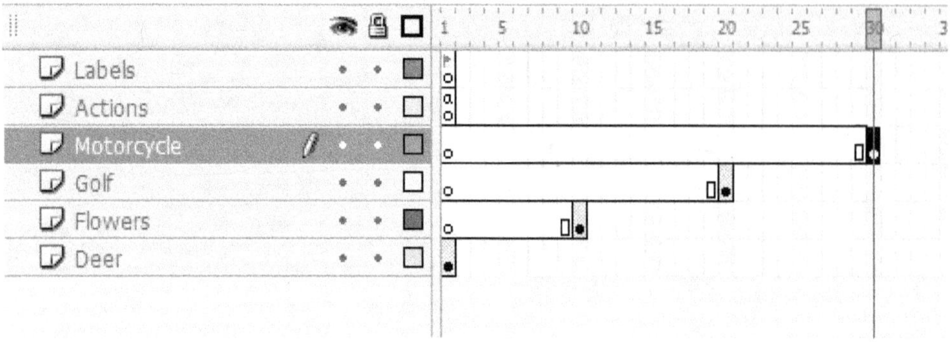

So now we have the Deer picture on frame 1, the Flowers picture on frame 10, the Golf picture on frame 20, and the Motorcycle picture on frame 30. Next, we'll add a Label to each of these frames. Select frame **10** of the **Labels** layer and go to **Insert**, **Timeline**, and **Blank Keyframe**:

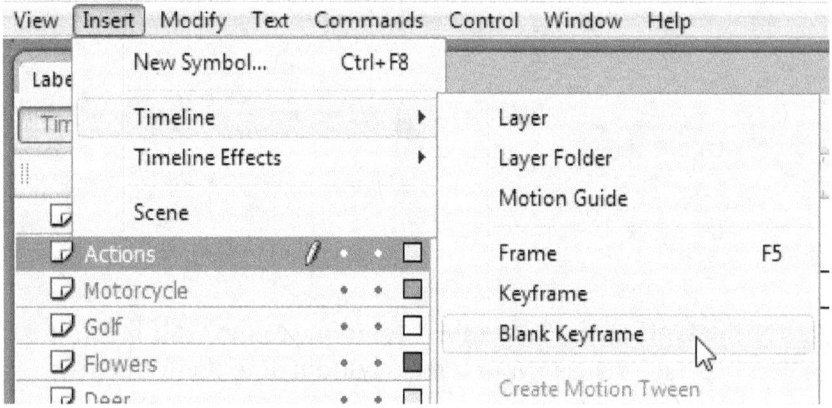

The frame should now look like this:

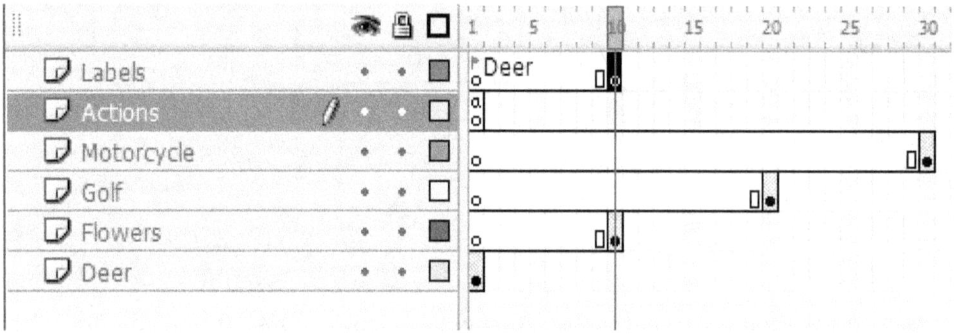

You'll now notice that since we added more frames to the Labels layer we can now read the **Deer** label we added to the first frame. With frame 10 still selected, type **Flowers** into the **Frame Labels** window in the Properties panel:

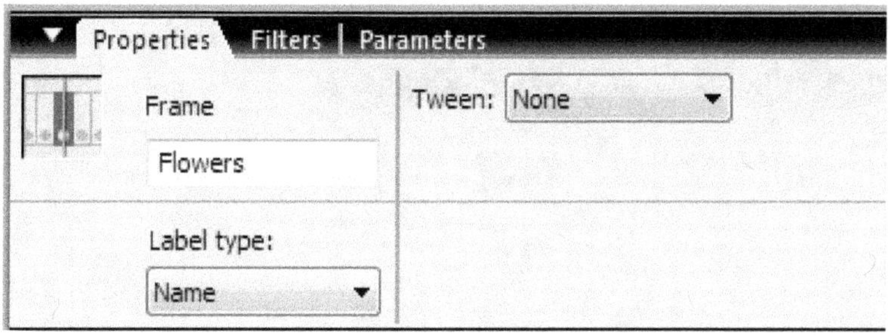

Next, insert a Blank Keyframe on frame **20** of the **Labels** layer:

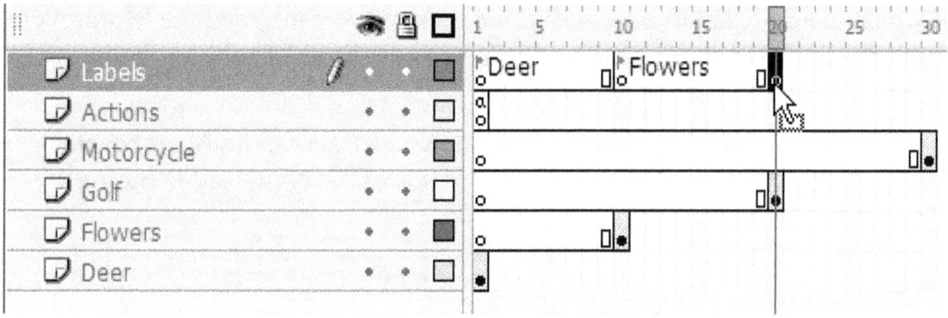

Type **Golf** into the **Frame Labels** windows in the Properties panel:

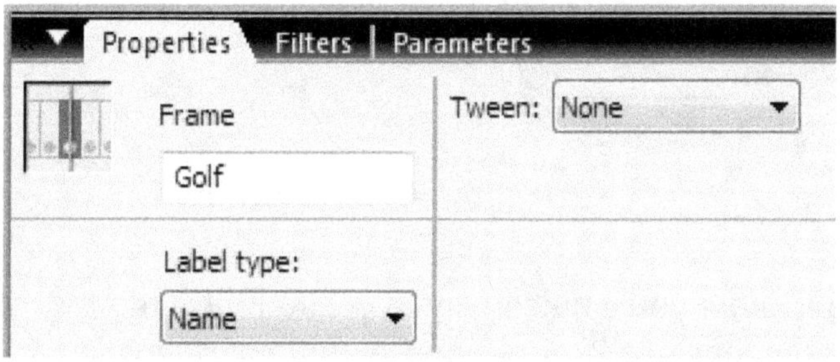

Finally, insert a Blank Keyframe on frame **30** of the **Labels** layer:

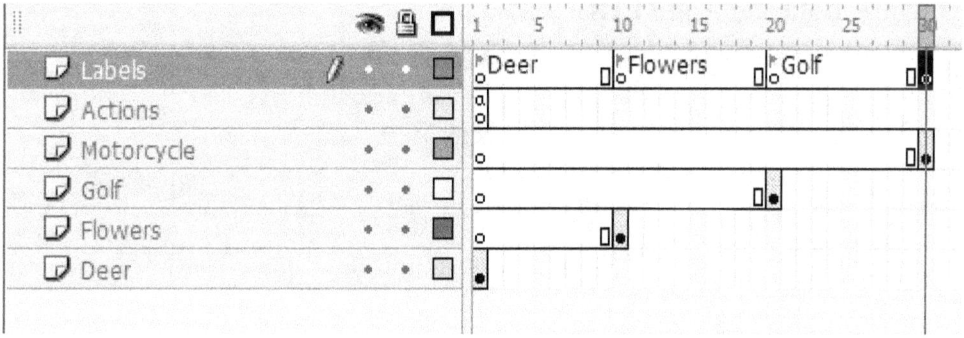

Type **Motorcycle** into the **Frame Labels** window in the Properties panel:

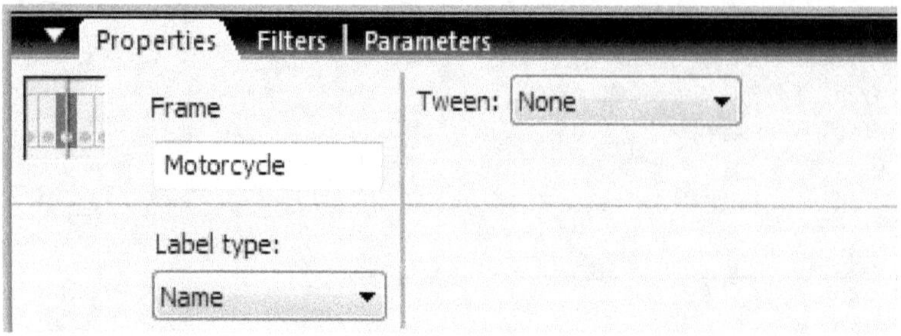

So now we have a Label above each of the pictures. We can't read the Motorcycle Label since it's the last frame. But you should see the little Label Flag in the frame.

Add a new layer and call it **Buttons**. Put the new layer above the **Motorcycle** layer (highlight the **Motorcycle** layer first then select the **New Layer** button):

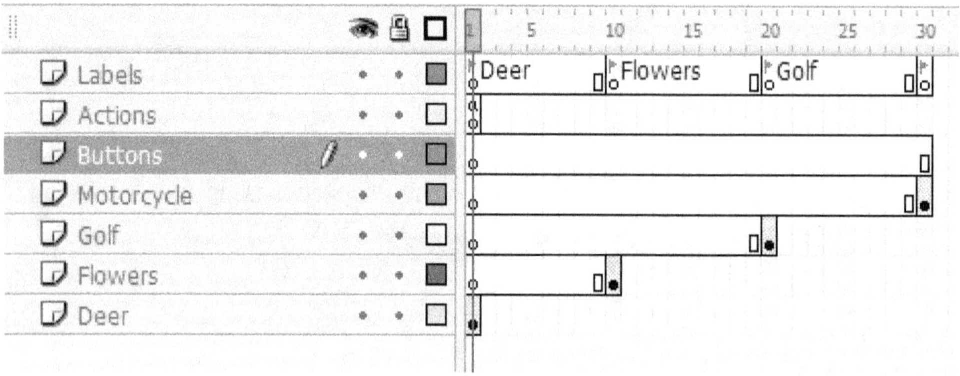

Next, we'll create the buttons. I'll show you a quick way to create four buttons. You can do this method when you don't need your buttons to animate, or when you need to create several buttons quickly.

Grab the **Text Tool** and open the Properties panel. Select **Verdana**, **Size 22**, **Color: white**, **Bold** and **Align Left**:

We need to change the line spacing. That's the amount of space between each line of text. Click on the button **Edit format options**:

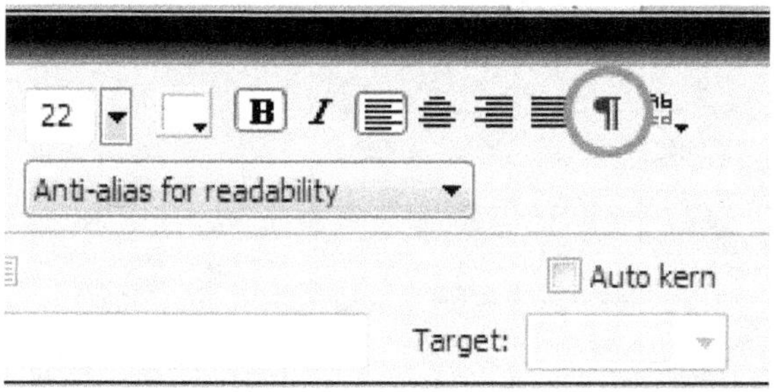

You should now see the **Format Options** box. Change the **Line spacing** to 4pt:

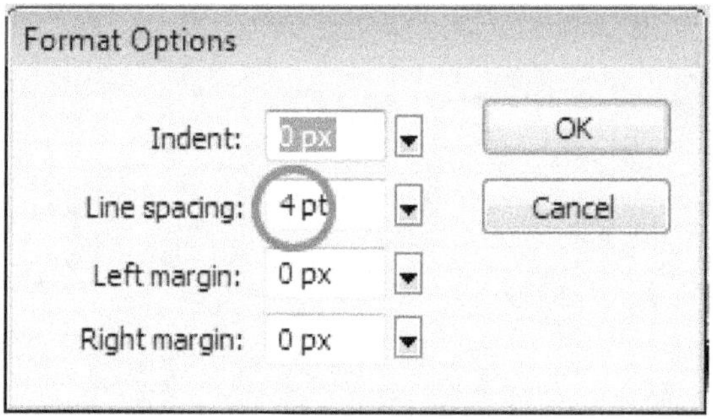

Hit **OK**. Type all the page names at the top left of the stage. Hit RETURN after every name:

We're now going to create a button that will be placed over each word. The button will be transparent, so it doesn't hide the text below it. Create a new layer and call it **Button Main**:

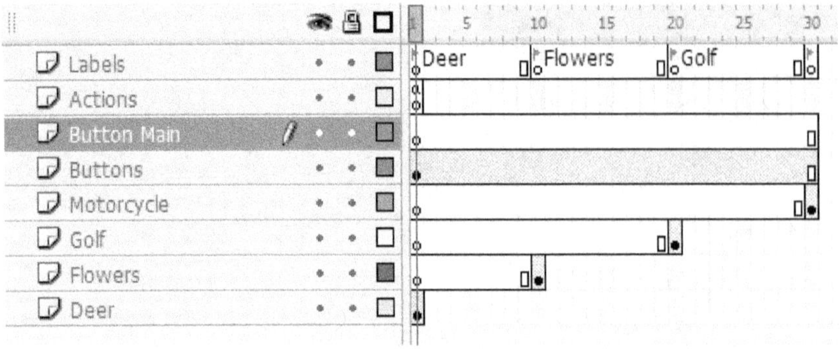

Next, select the **Rectangle Tool**:

Make sure there is no color selected for **Stroke color**:

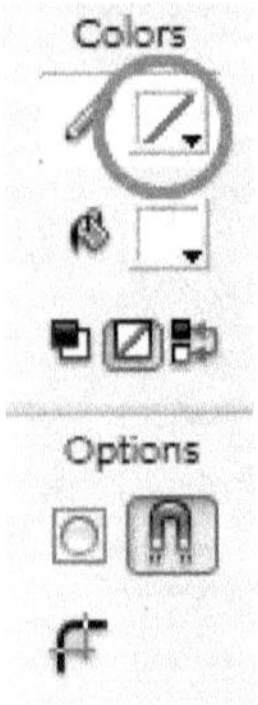

Create a rectangle shape over the word **Deer**:

Select this new shape and go to **Modify**, and **Convert to Symbol**. Convert this new shape to a **Button** and name it **Invisible Button**:

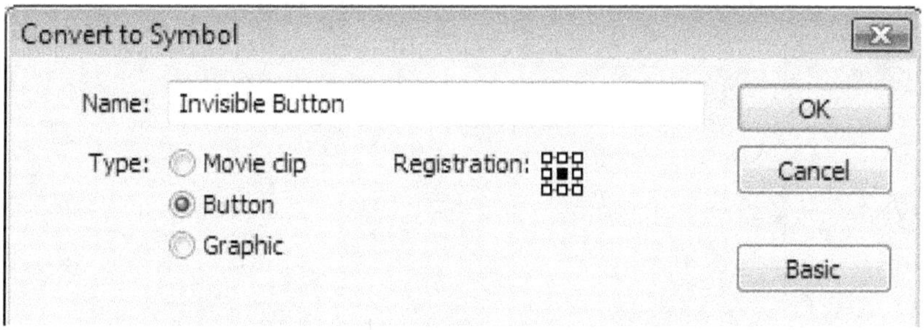

Hit **OK**. Make sure this new button is still selected and open the Properties panel. Click the drop-down arrow next to **Color**:

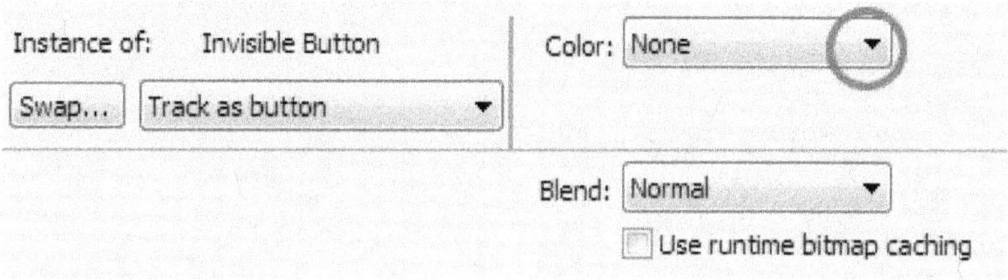

Select **Alpha** and change the percentage to **0**:

You should now be able to see through the button on the stage:

Let's add the ActionScript to this button. In the Actions panel go to **Global Functions**, **Timeline Control**, and double-click **goto**:

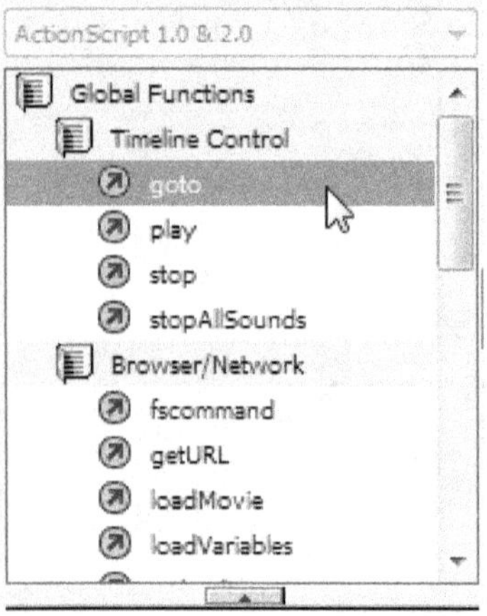

The **goto** options should now be open:

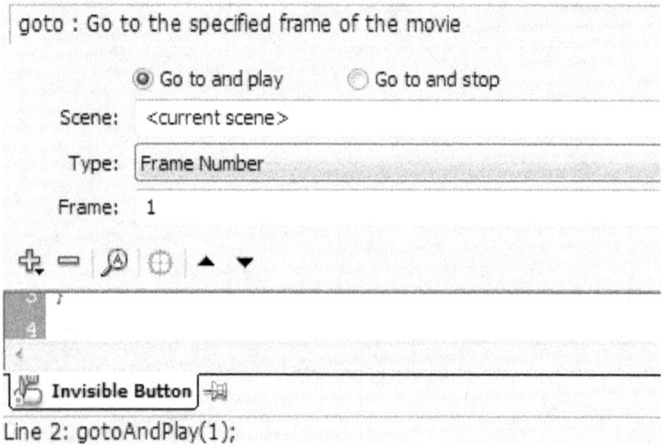

When we click the Deer button we want the user to be taken to the frame with the Label **Deer**. Change **Type** to **Frame Label**, type **Deer** in the **Frame** window , and select **Go to and stop**:

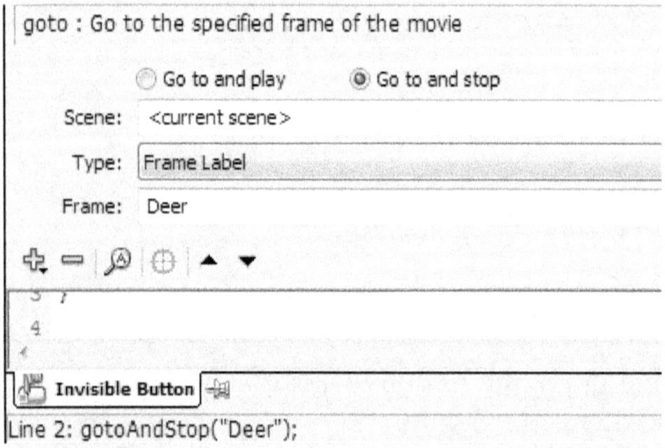

The first button is now done! Let's copy and paste this button over the Flowers text. Select this button and go to **Edit**, **Copy**. Now go to **Edit**, and **Paste in Place**. You should see the outline of this new button in the same spot as the original button. Click-and-drag this button so that it covers the **Flowers** text:

Depending on the size you made the button, it may not cover the entire area of the Flowers text. If it's a bit small you can change the size by clicking on the **Free Transform Tool**:

You should now see resize handles around this button:

Select the middle resize handle on the right side, and stretch the button to the right:

The Flowers button is now sized correctly. Since this button is an exact copy of the Deer button then it also has a copy of the Deer button's ActionScript. We need to slightly adjust the ActionScript for this new button. Open the Actions panel and click on the word **Deer** in the Actions window. This will bring up the **goto** settings window. In the **Frame** window type **Flowers**:

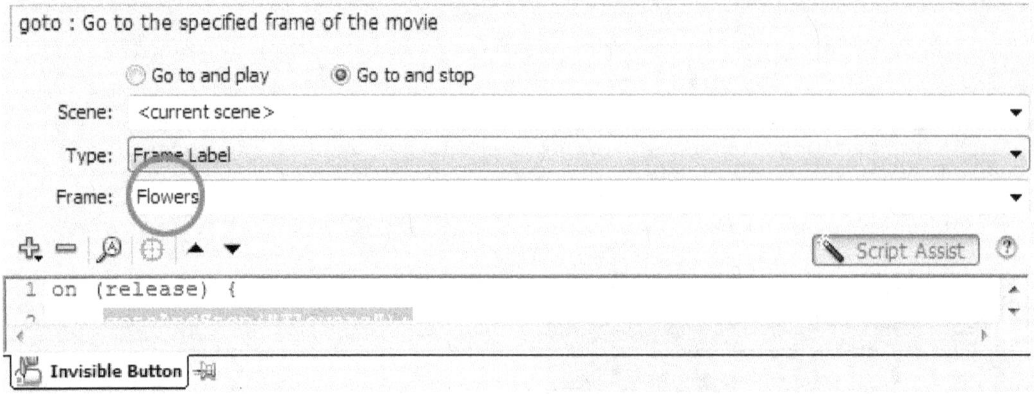

Test your movie (CTRL + ENTER). Click on the Flowers and Deer buttons going back and forth. The buttons should take you to the proper frames on the timeline. Copy the Flowers button and go to **Edit**, **Paste in Place**. Drag this new button so it covers the Golf text. As we did with the Flowers button, we need to tweak the ActionScript. Click on the word Flowers in the ActionScript, and change the Frame to **Golf**:

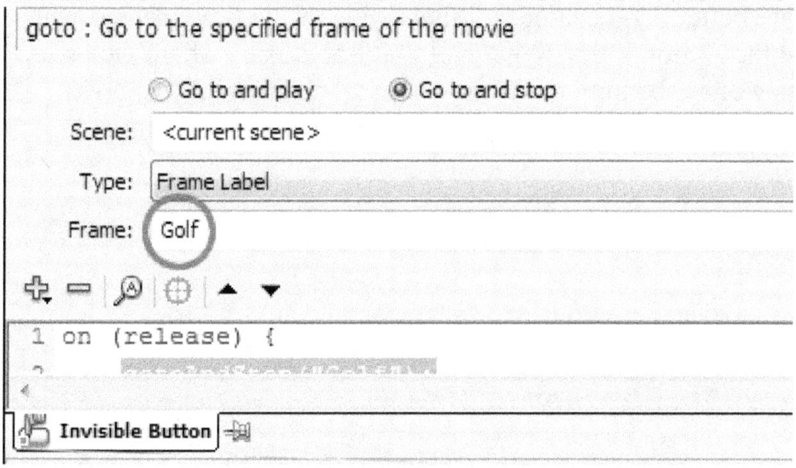

Copy this button and go to **Edit**, **Paste in Place**. Drag this new button so that it covers the Motorcycle text. Resize this new button if it doesn't cover the Motorcycle text entirely. Click on the word Golf in the ActionScript and change Frame to **Motorcycle**:

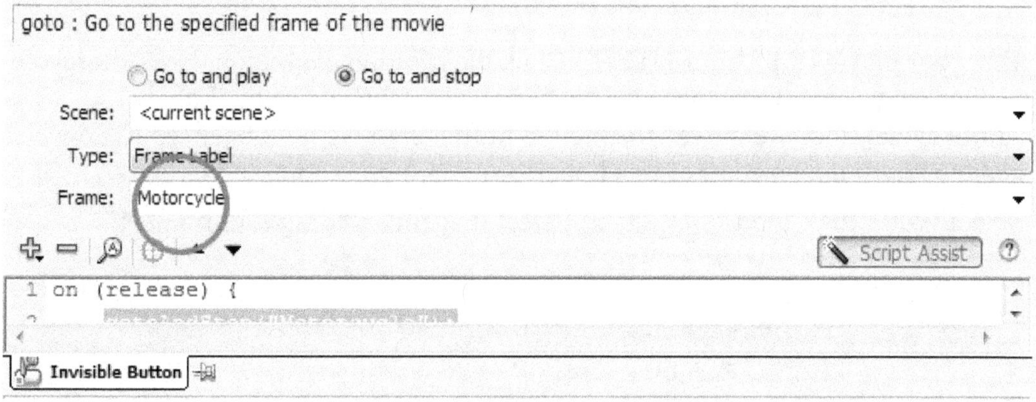

Test your movie (CTRL + ENTER). Click all the buttons to test them out. They should all take you to their respective frame. Now, we could have just as easily had the buttons go to specific frames. For example, we could have had the Deer button direct the user to frame 1 instead of the Label **Deer**. Or the Motorcycle button could have taken the user to frame 30 instead of the Label **Motorcycle**. Either one would have worked.

The reason most Flash Designers prefer Labels is that sometimes while working on a Flash project you'll come across an instance where you'll have to add some frames to your timeline. This of course would push frames farther down the timeline. And that means any button that sends the user to a specific frame would have to be updated.

That's why Labels are better. You can push Labels all over the timeline and you'll never have to adjust the ActionScript. Wherever that Label is, is where the user will end up when they click the button. I'll show you an example of that now. Select frame **30** of the Motorcycle layer. Select this frame again and drag it to frame **45**:

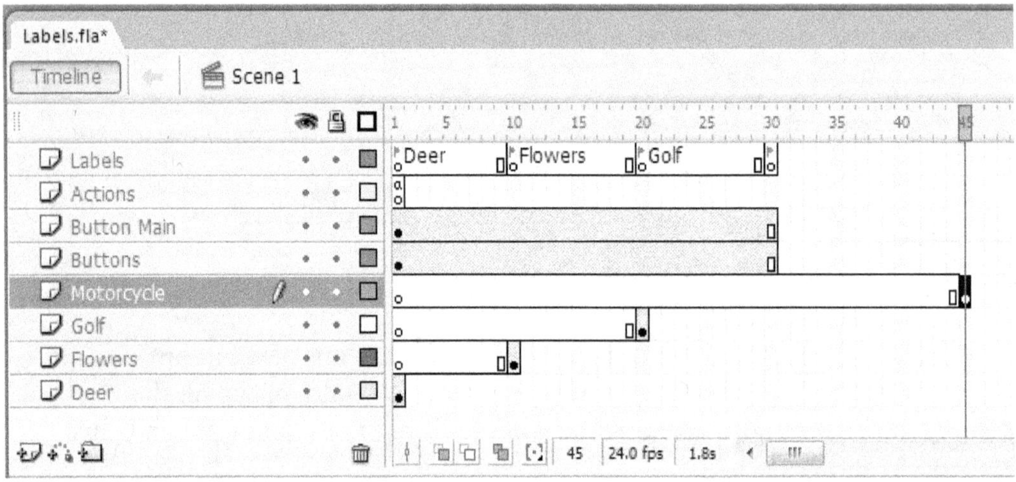

Test your movie (CTRL + ENTER). Click the Motorcycle button. No Motorcycle picture, just white. That's because the button will take you to the Label **Motorcycle**; since we moved the picture to frame 45 we no longer see it. So we need to adjust the position of this Label.

Select frame **30** of the **Labels** layer. Select it again and drag it to frame **45**:

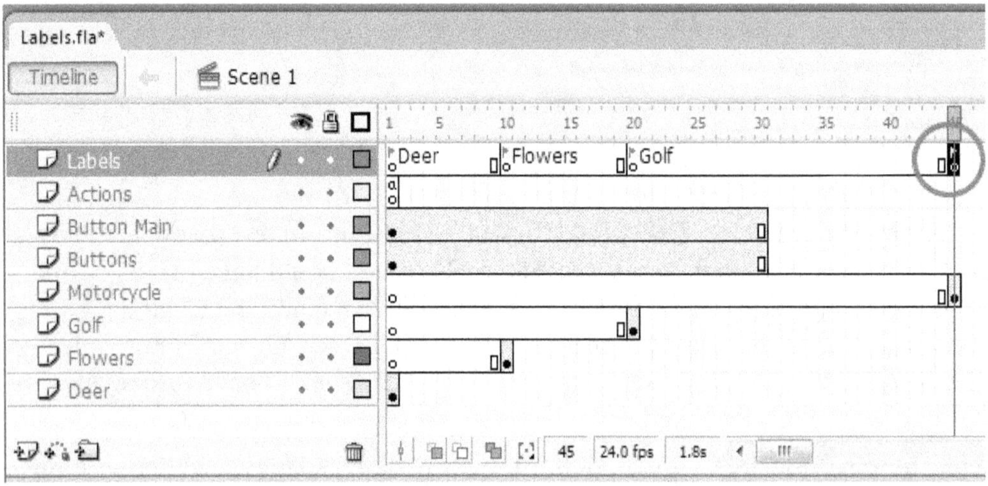

Test your movie (CTRL + ENTER) again. This time click the Motorcycle button and you should now see the Motorcycle picture. But now we can't see the buttons.

If you notice on the timeline, the button layers only go to frame 30. Let's fix that. Select frame **45** of each of the button layers and go to **Insert**, and **Frame**:

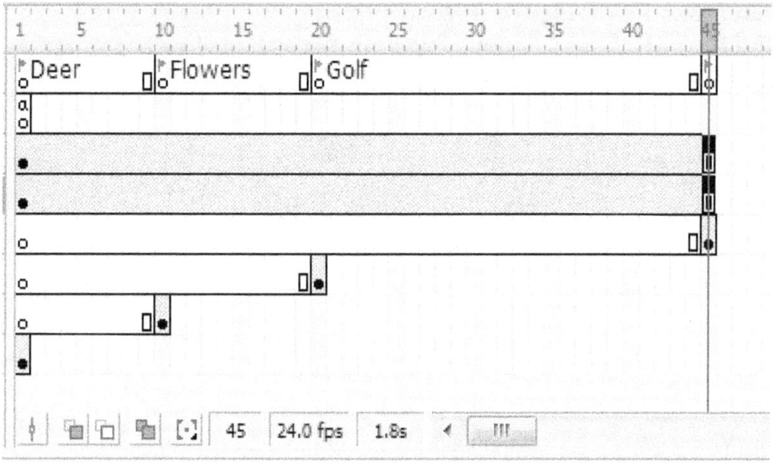

Test your movie (CTRL + ENTER) Everything should now work perfectly.

You should now have a better understanding of Labels. Also, you've probably noticed that we've repeated a lot of the Script Assist commands such as **tellTarget**, **goto**, **play**, and **stop**. Using Script Assist and just a few simple commands I'm going to show you how to bring out the beast in Flash. When you're not bogged down writing lines of code it frees you up to be as creative as you want to be. Keep going! Each section gets a little more challenging and fun!

The final exercise in this chapter combines Labels, Scenes, Buttons and Movies.

Movie clip Buttons

In this exercise we're going to be pushing your skills a bit. We'll be creating buttons that take the user to a specific Label in a specific Scene. We'll also create a Movie clip that tells the Scenes to play or stop. If you don't think you're ready for the next exercise then it might be a good idea to review the last two projects.

Also, at any time you can email questions to: torlowry@yahoo.com.

Ok, let's get started. Open the file called **Scenes_Labels.fla**. In the library you'll see two folders. One is the Pictures folder and the other one is Thumbnails. Open the thumbnails folder by double-clicking the folder icon. You should see five thumbnails.

Before we drag the thumbnails over to the stage, rename Layer 1 **Thumbnails**. Next, drag the thumbnails over to the Stage. Start with **buddhaThumb.jpg** and put it on the bottom left side of the stage. The next one, **clockThumb**, goes just to the right of the **buddhaThumb**. Don't worry about aligning them, we'll do that later. Drag fireflies **Thumb.jpg** next, then **morano Thumb.jpg**, and finally **raja Thumb.jpg**:

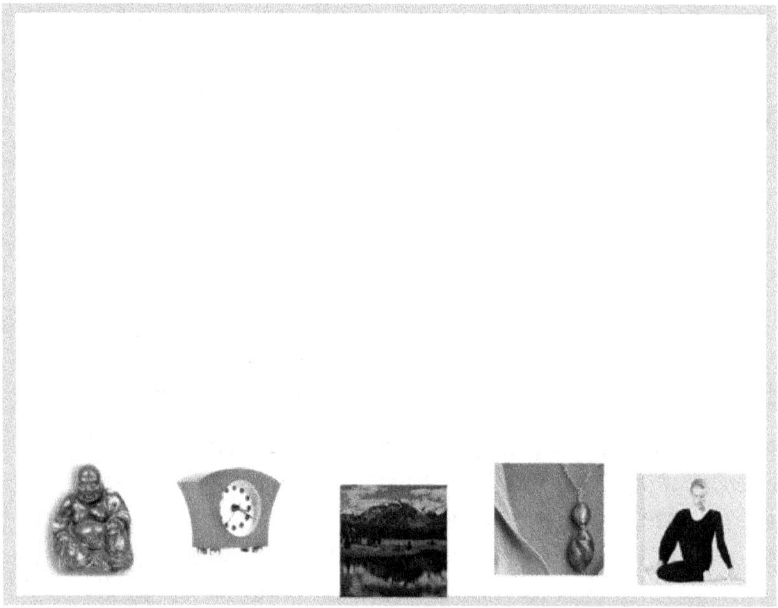

You'll notice that my row of thumbnails is very uneven. Let's correct that. Select the first frame of the **Thumbnails** layer (when you select a frame, every object in that frame will be selected). Next, go to the Align panel and select **Align top edge, Distribute horizontal center** and make sure **To stage** is not activated:

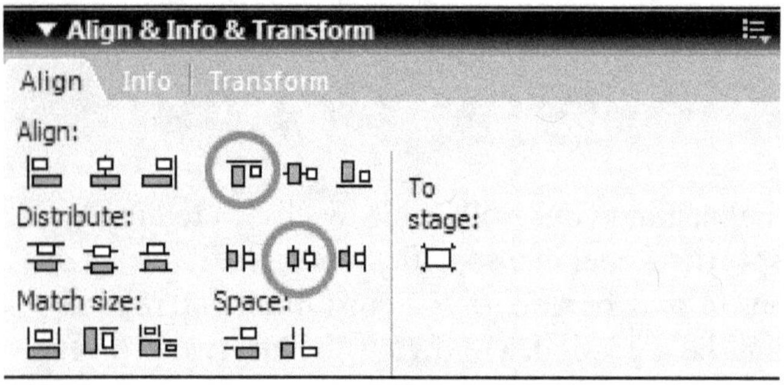

The thumbnails should now be perfectly aligned with each other. Let's change the name of the Scene. Open the Scene panel and change the name from **Scene 1** to **Home**:

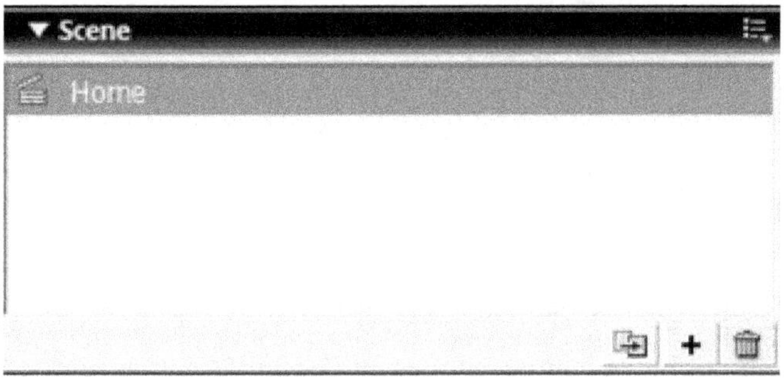

Next, we're going to create a bar that goes over all the buttons. When a user rolls over a button a colored shape will slide across the bar and stop right above the button. Create a new layer and name it **Bar**. Next, select the **Rectangle Tool**, choose **red** for **Stroke color** and **white** for the **Fill color**:

In the Properties panel make sure **1** is selected for the **Stroke Size**:

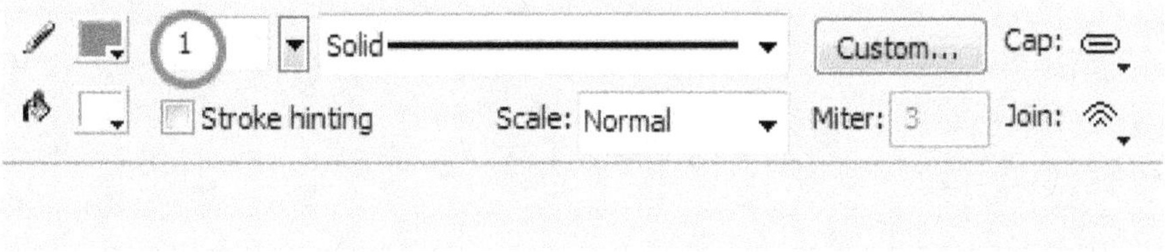

Create a long rectangle across the top of all the buttons like this:

Let's tweak the bar just a bit. Select the **Fill color** button and type the color number **#66A7DD** into the color window:

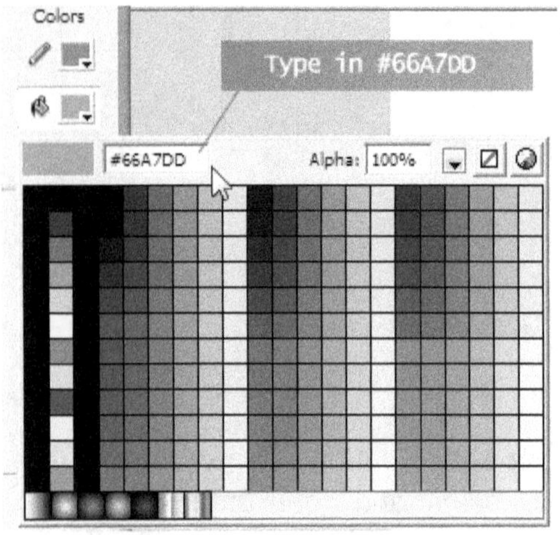

Hit ENTER. Select the **Paint Bucket Tool**:

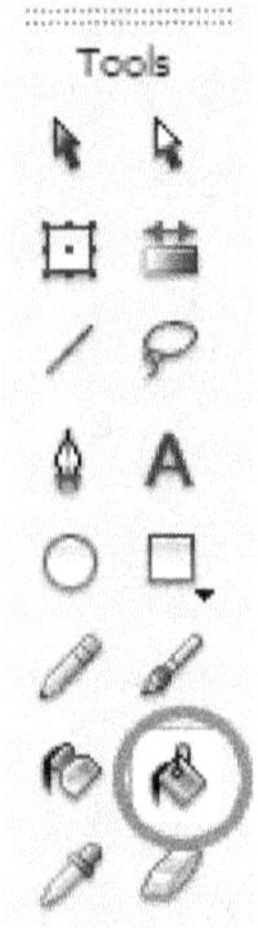

Click anywhere inside the bar:

The bar should look nicer now. Since we'll be adding an animation to this bar, we need to make it a Movie clip. Select the bar (remember to double-click the bar so the stroke is also selected) and go to **Modify**, and **Convert to Symbol**. Name it **Bar** and select Movie clip as the Type:

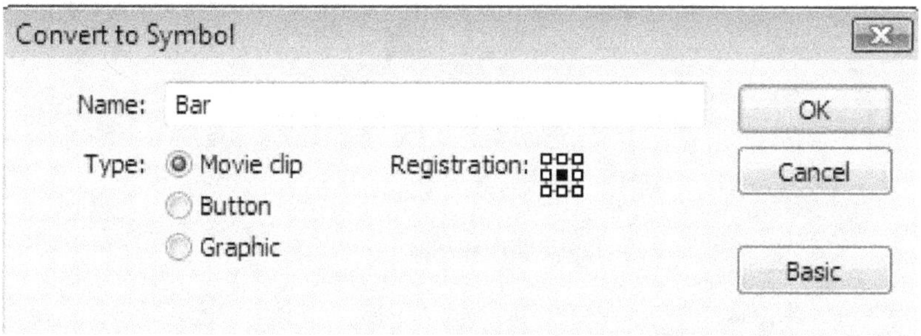

Hi **OK**. We're now going to give this new Movie clip an Instance Name since we'll be controlling the bar's animation with buttons.

Type **bar** in the **Instance Name** window of the Properties panel:

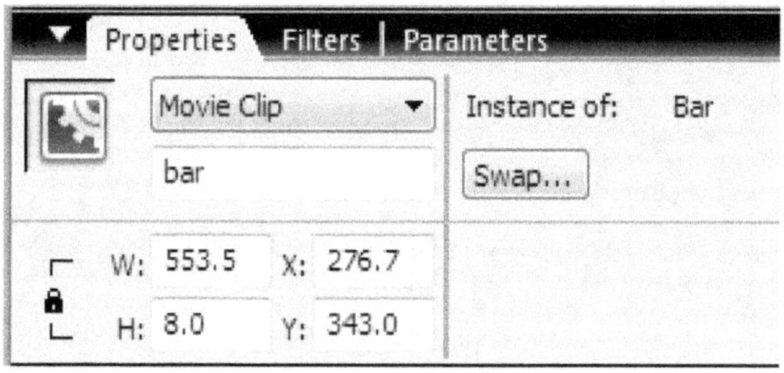

Before we work on the buttons, we need to create the animation for the bar. Double-click the **Bar** Movie clip so that you are in its editing stage. When a user rolls over a button we want a thin shape to slide in from stage left and hover above the button; then, when the user rolls off the button, we want this thin shape to return to stage left. Let's create this animation for the first button.

Name Layer 1 **Bar** and lock it. Then, create a new layer and call it **Bar Hover**:

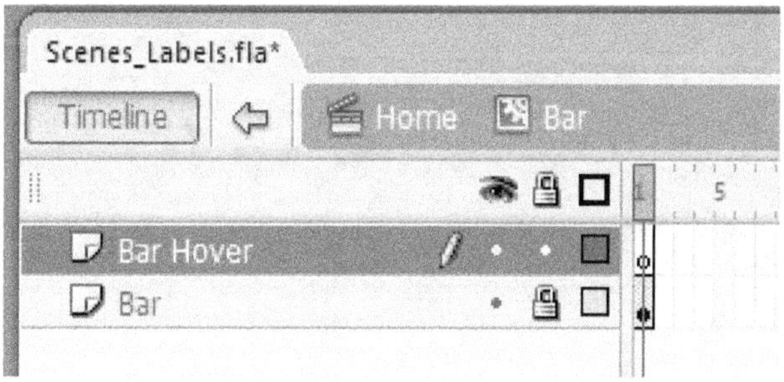

Select the **Rectangle Tool** and choose **white** for the **Fill color**; make sure that **Stroke color** is turned off. Next, create a rectangle shape above the Buddha picture (inside the bar) and make it about the same width as the picture:

Add a keyframe to the **Bar Hover** layer on frame **15**. Select any frame between **1** and **15** and insert a Motion Tween (**CS4/CS5 - Insert, Classic Tween**). Next, create a keyframe on frame **30**. Select any frame between 15 and 30 and insert a **Motion Tween**:

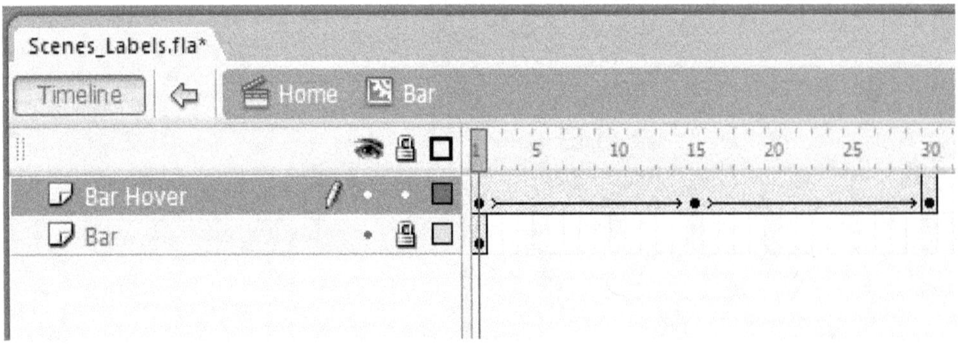

Select frame **1** of the **Bar Hover** layer and open the Properties panel. Change **Ease** to **100**:

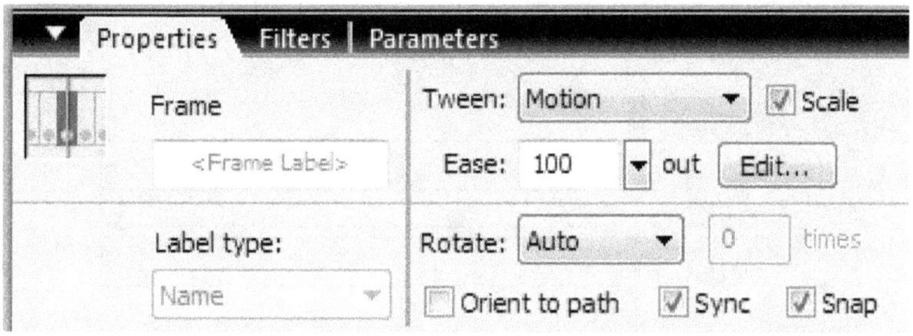

We want the **Bar Hover** layer to start on stage left and come to a rest right above the Buddha image. Select the first frame of the **Bar Hover** layer, then click-and-drag the **Bar Hover** symbol left until it's off the stage:

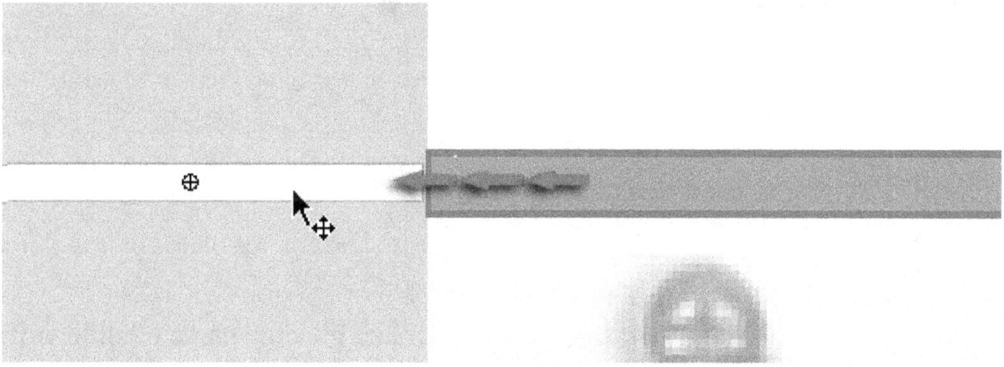

Anything that is off the stage in the gray area will not be seen by the user. Before we test this animation go to frame **30** of the **Bar** layer and insert a frame. Next, we want the bar to stop at frame 15 so we need to add a **stop** code. Next, we'll add a new layer and call it **Actions**. Insert a keyframe on frame **1** of this new layer. In the **Actions** panel go to **Global Functions**, **Timeline Control**, then double-click **stop**. We're adding this **stop** code on frame 1 since we don't want the bar symbol hovering over the Buddha image until it's commanded to do so.

Insert a keyframe on frame **15** of the **Actions** layer; put a **stop** code in that frame also.

If you go to **Control**, **Play** (ENTER) the animation no longer plays due to the **stop** code in frame **1**. Create a new layer and name it **Labels**. Create a keyframe on frame **2** of this new layer:

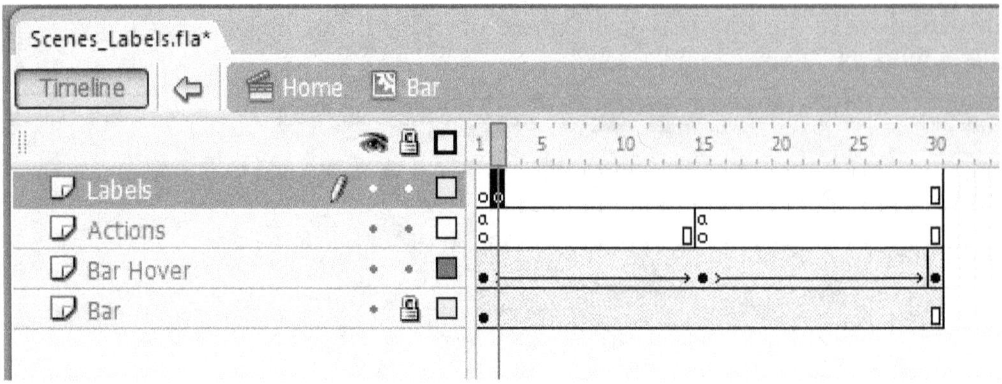

Open the Properties panel and name this frame **slide_in** (Flash doesn't allow spaces so always add the underscore between words):

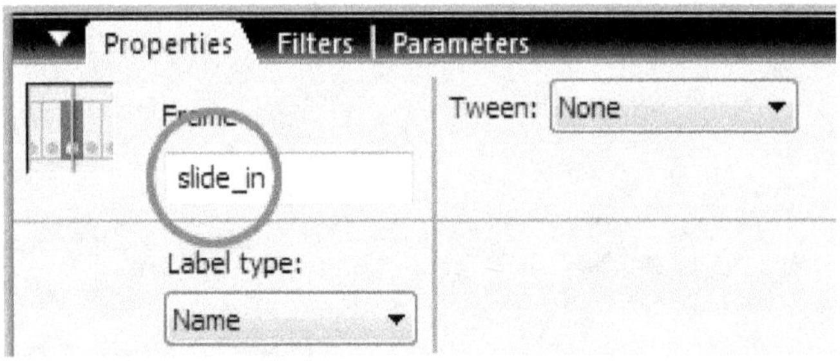

Insert a keyframe on frame **16** of the **Labels** layer and give it a name of **slide_out**. The timeline should now look like this:

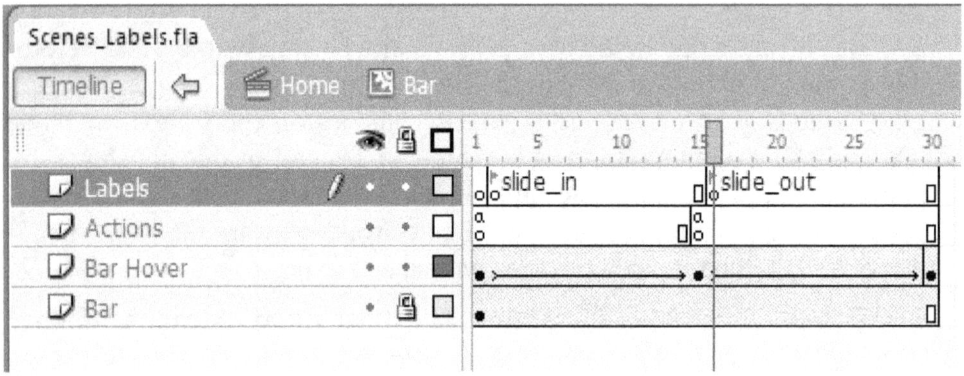

When the user rolls over the Buddha button we want it to tell the **Bar** Movie clip to go to the Label **slide_in** and **play**. When the user rolls off the button we want the button to tell the **Bar** Movie clip to go to **slide_out** and **play**.

We now want the bar symbol to return to stage left by frame 30. So let's do that now. Select frame **30** of the **Bar Hover** layer; next, select the bar symbol and drag it left until it's off the stage.

As I mentioned earlier, when a Movie clip's animation reaches its final frame, it returns to frame 1 and keeps playing, creating a continuous loop. But if you have a **stop** code in the last frame of the animation, it will stop the animation at this frame. If you have a **stop** code in the first frame, then when the animation reaches the final frame it goes to frame 1 where it stops due to this **stop** code.

We'll now add the ActionScript to the Buddha button so you can see how the animation is going to work. Select the **Home** button above the timeline (or above the stage in **CS3/CS4/CS5**):

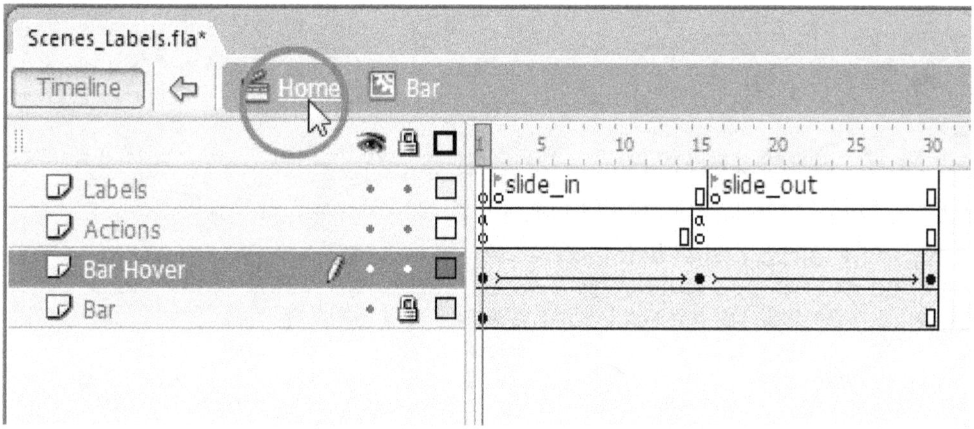

Next, select the Buddha image and go to **Modify**, and **Convert to Symbol**. Type **Buddha Button** for the **Name** and select **Button** for **Type**:

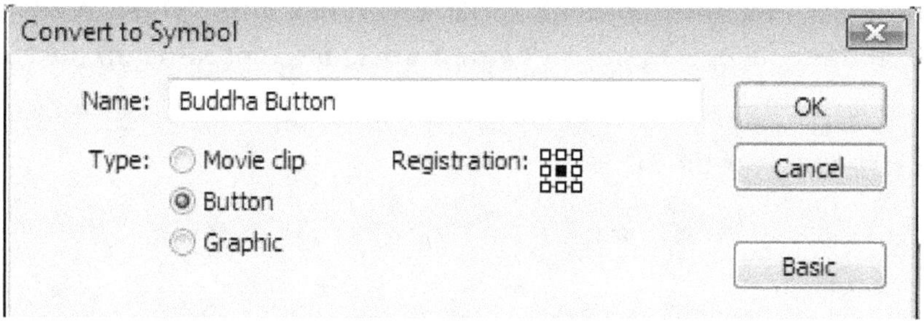

Hit **OK**. Let's add the ActionScript to this new button so we can test the animation. In the Actions panel, go to **Deprecated**, **Actions**, and double-click **tellTarget**:

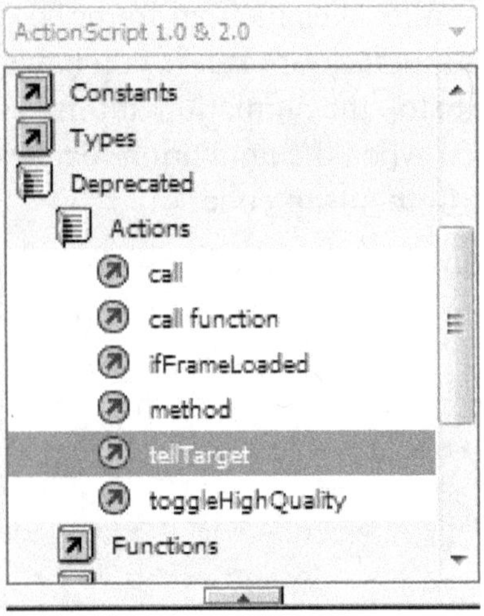

Next, type **bar** in the Target window:

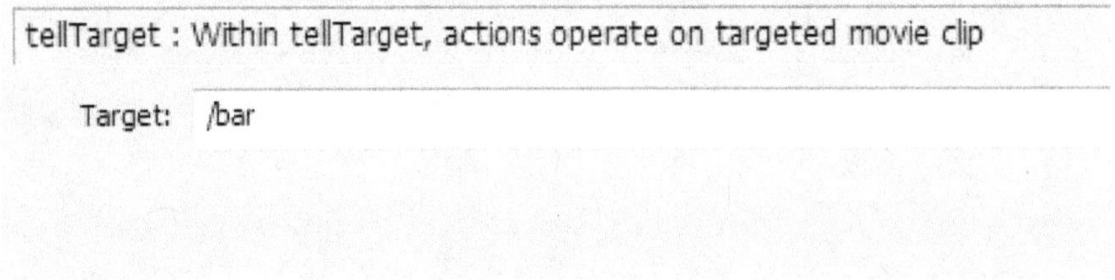

Go to **Global Functions**, **Timeline Control**, and double-click **goto**. You should now see the **goto** settings. Change **Type** to **Frame Label**, and type **slide_in** next to **Frame**:

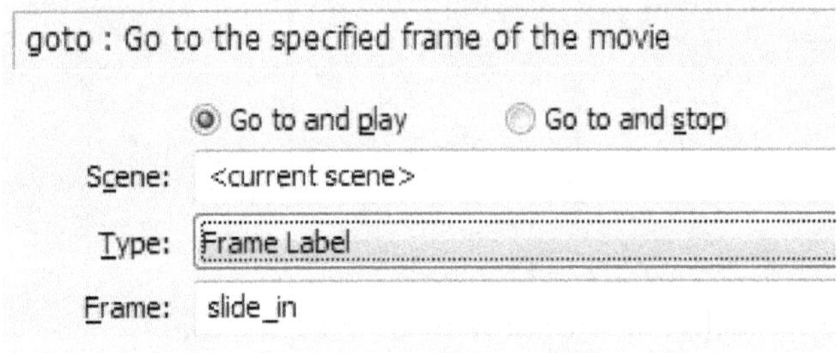

Test your movie (CTRL + ENTER). You'll notice that when you roll over the button the bar animation doesn't start. If you click your Buddha button, though, it triggers the animation. So we just need to change the mouse event setting. In the Actions window select the word **release**:

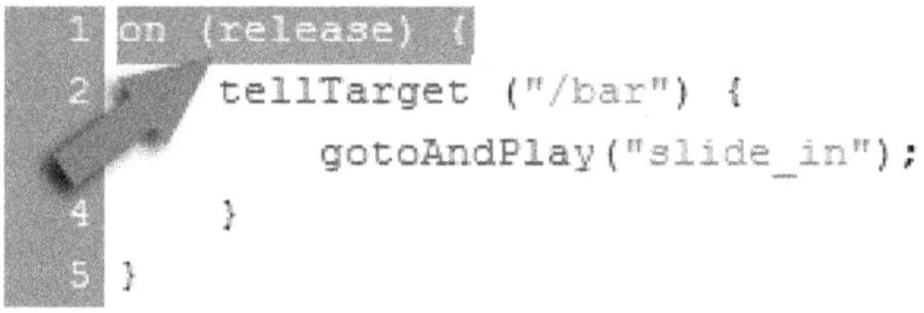
on (release) {
tellTarget ("/bar") {
gotoAndPlay("slide_in");
}
}

You should now be in the mouse event settings window. Change the setting from **Release**, to **Roll Over** and **Drag Over**:

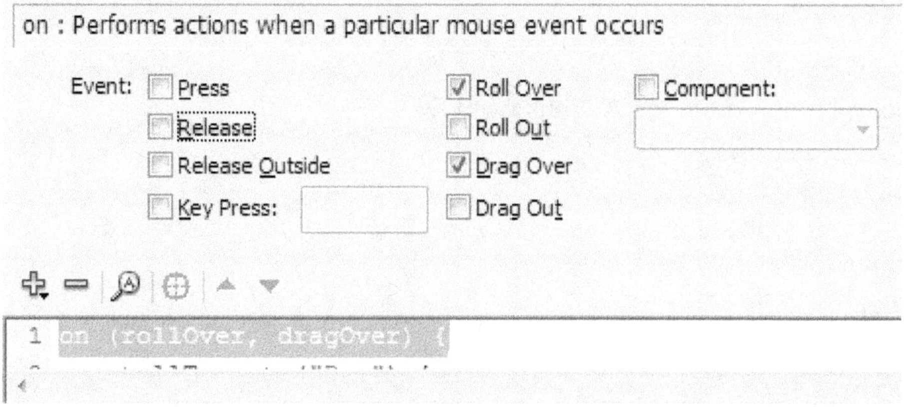
on : Performs actions when a particular mouse event occurs
Event:
Press
Release
Release Outside
Key Press:
Roll Over
Roll Out
Drag Over
Drag Out
Component:
on (rollOver, dragOver) {

Test your movie (CTRL + ENTER) again. Success! When you roll over the button the bar symbol should slide in on cue. But, when we roll off the button the bar symbol doesn't move. Let's change that. I'll show you a quick way to do this. In the Actions panel highlight the entire code:

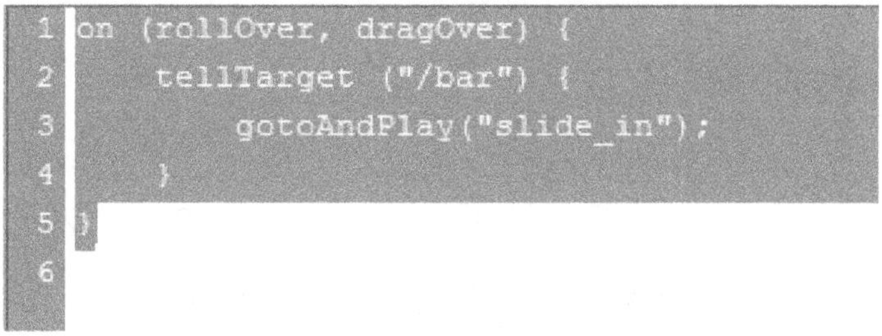
on (rollOver, dragOver) {
tellTarget ("/bar") {
gotoAndPlay("slide_in");
}
}

Go to **Edit**, and **Copy**:

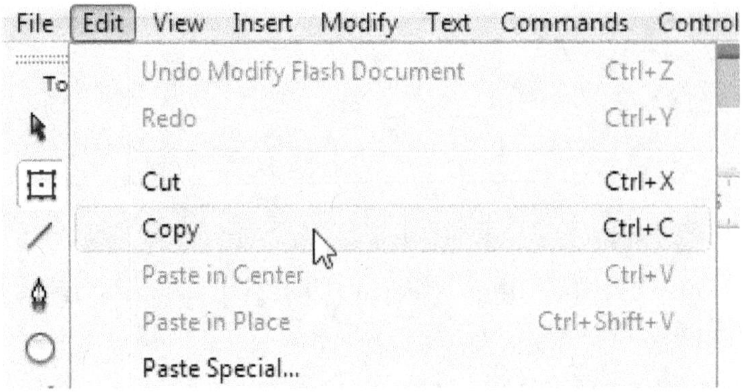

Select the closing bracket in the Actions window:

```
on (rollOver, dragOver) {
    tellTarget ("/bar") {
        gotoAndPlay("slide_in");
    }
}
```

Next, paste in the copied code (**CTRL V**, or right-click and select **Paste**). You should now have two copies of this code. On the second copy of the code click on the word **slide-in**.

```
on (rollOver, dragOver) {
    tellTarget ("/bar") {
        gotoAndPlay("slide_in");
    }
}
```

This will bring up the **goto** settings window. Change the Frame to **slide_out**:

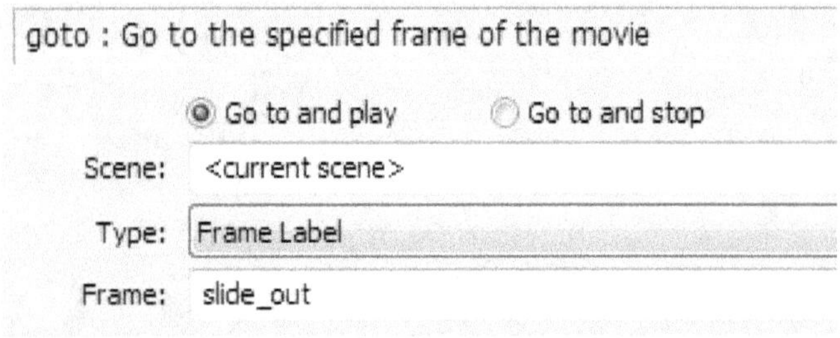

Next, click on the word **rollOver** of the second code. You should now see the mouse event settings at the top of the panel. Since this Action is for when the user *rolls off the button*, then we need to change the settings from **Roll Over** and **Drag Over**, to **Roll Out** and **Drag Out**:

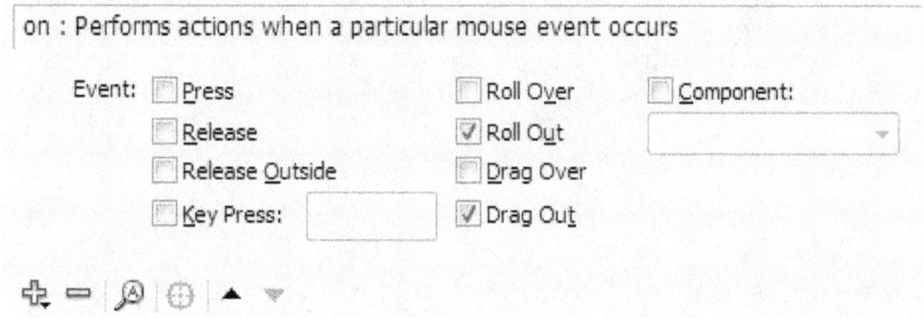

Test your movie (CTRL + ENTER). Success! When you roll over the button the animation should begin, and when you roll off the button the bar symbol should exit stage left.

Now it's probably a good idea to get a full understanding of how all of this works before we continue. Stretch open the Actions panel so you can see both codes:

```
on (rollOver, dragOver) {
    tellTarget ("/bar") {
        gotoAndPlay("slide_in");
    }
}
on (rollOut, dragOut) {
    tellTarget ("/bar") {
        gotoAndPlay("slide_out");
    }
}
```

When a user rolls over the button with his cursor it triggers the first set of code. This code commands the bar symbol to go to the Label **slide_in** and **play**. If a user rolls off the button then it tells the Target **bar** to go to the Label **slide_out** and **play**. If you double-click on the **Bar** Movie clip you can look at the labels again to refresh your memory. We can also tell Targets to go to specific frames and play without using Labels, but most Flash Designers prefer Labels.

In the last section we had a button control the **Bar** Movie clip. In this section we're going to put the Hover Bar animation inside the button itself; so the button will be controlling itself! This may sound confusing but it's actually a little simpler than the previous section. It's also something that you'll be doing quite a bit as you continue your Flash career.

Select the **Clock** image and go to **Modify**, **Convert to Symbol**. Change the name to **Clock** and the **Type** to Movie clip:

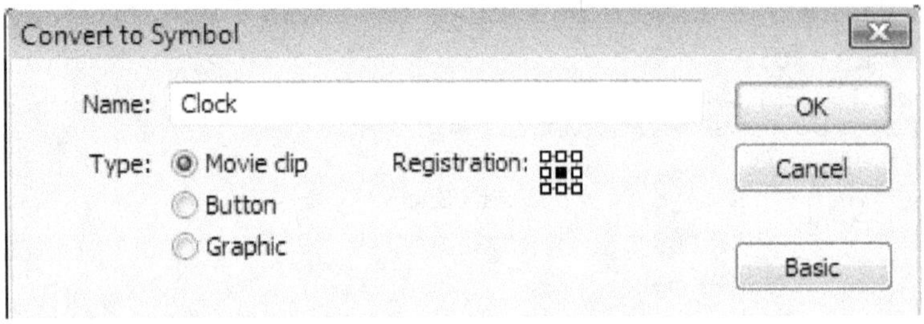

Hit **OK**. Open the Properties panel and give the new Movie clip an Instance Name of **clock**:

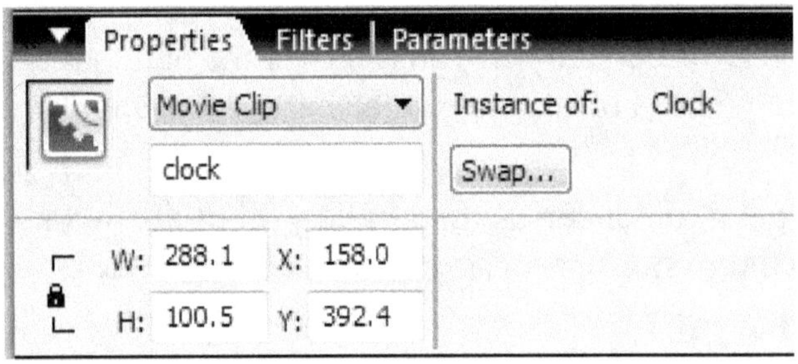

Next, double-click on this **Clock** Movie clip to enter its editing stage. Go ahead and name Layer 1 **Clock**. Then lock it. Add three more layers naming them **Bar Hover**, **Actions**, and **Labels**:

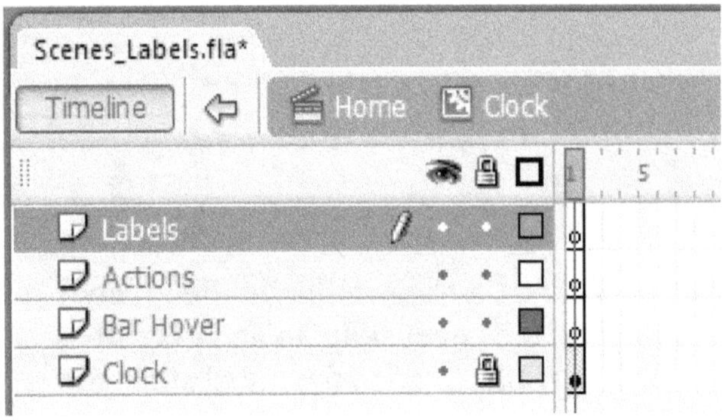

Next, select the **Bar Hover** layer and, just as we did in the previous section, create a white rectangle about the width of the Clock; make sure that **Stroke color** is turned off:

Next, click on the first frame of the **Actions** layer and add a **stop** code (**Global Functions - Timeline Control** - double-click **stop**).

Select frame **50** of each of the layers and insert a frame:

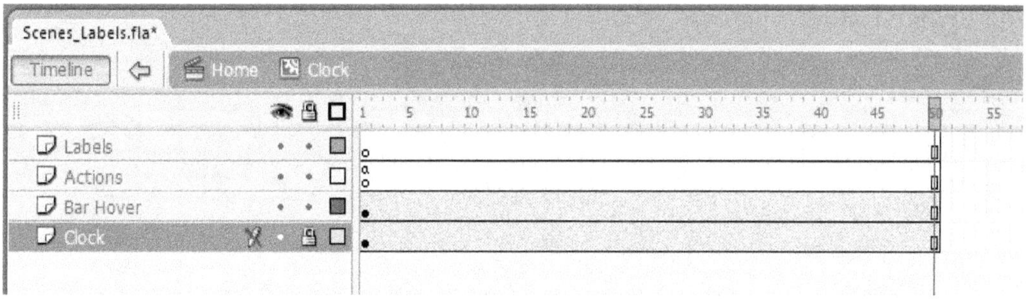

On frame **50** of the **Bar Hover** layer insert a keyframe; then, insert a **Motion Tween**:

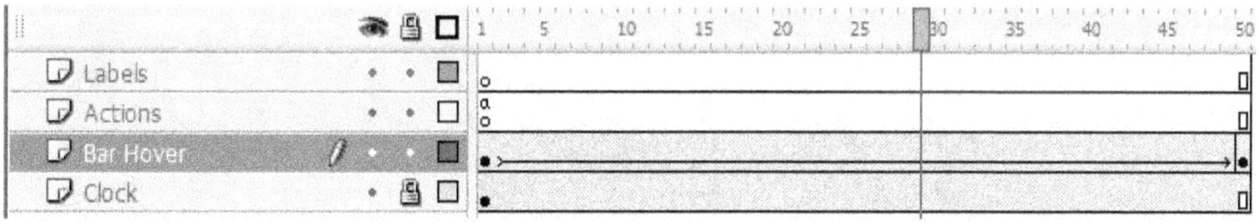

Select the first frame of the **Bar Hover** layer. Next, open the Properties panel and change the **Ease** to 100 (this forces the animation to gradually come to a stop):

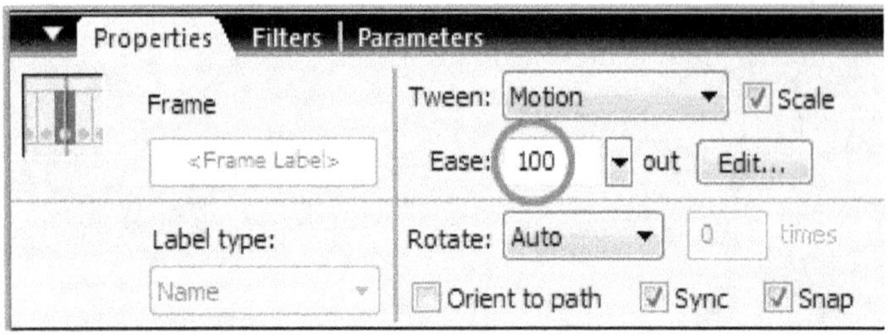

On frame 25 of the **Bar Hover** layer add a keyframe. This layer should now have three keyframes. Next, add a keyframe on frame 25 of the **Actions** layer; then, add a **stop** code to that keyframe:

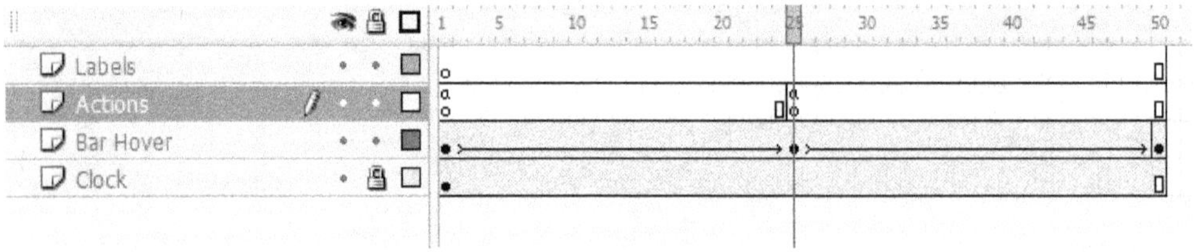

Next, we'll add the Labels. Select frame **2** of the **Labels** layer and insert a keyframe; select this new keyframe and in the Properties panel type **slide_in** in the **Frame Label** window:

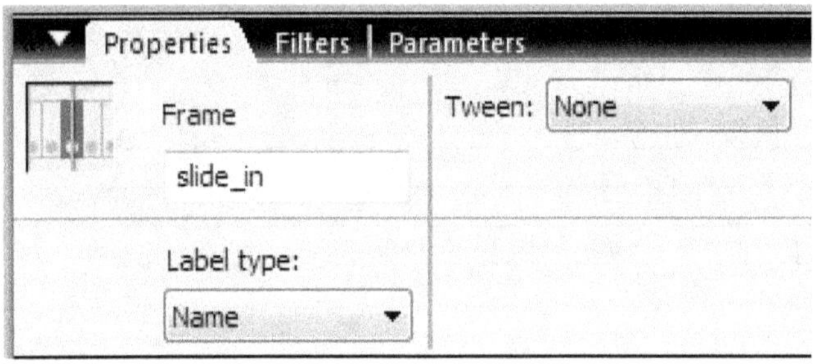

Next, create a keyframe on frame **26** and give that a Label name of **slide_out**. The timeline should now look like this:

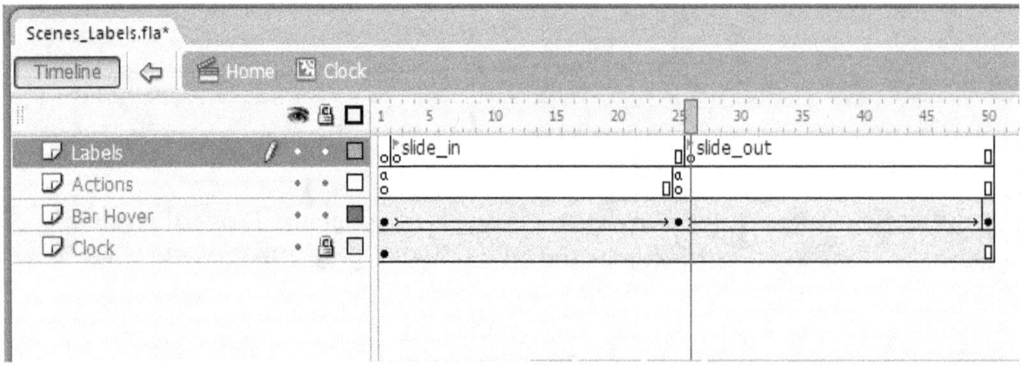

Select the first keyframe of the **Bar Hover** layer; next, select the bar symbol on the stage and drag it stage left. If you hold down the SHIFT key you can drag the symbol in a straight line. Select frame **50** of the **Bar Hover** layer and drag the bar symbol stage left.

We made the **Clock** symbol a Movie clip since it has its own animation. But we also want the Clock symbol to act as a button. That's what we'll do next. Select the **Bar Hover** layer; next, create a new layer and name it **Button**:

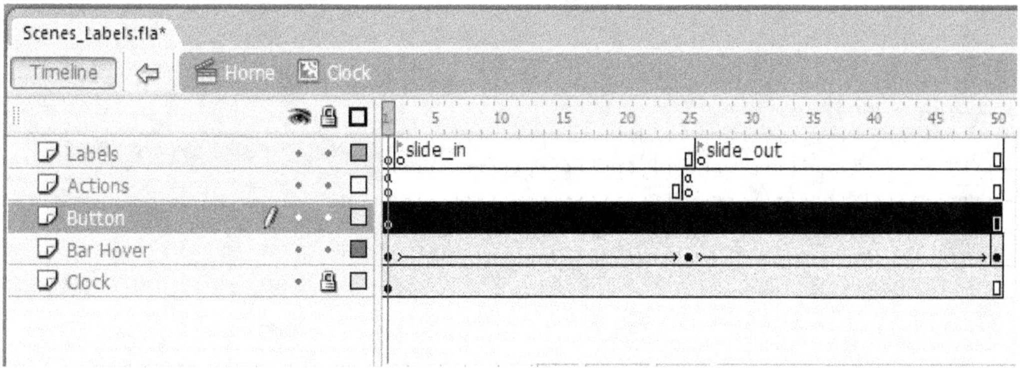

Click on the first frame of the **Button** layer and select the **Rectangle Tool**. Turn the **Stroke color** off and select any **Fill color**. Next draw a shape that covers the entire clock:

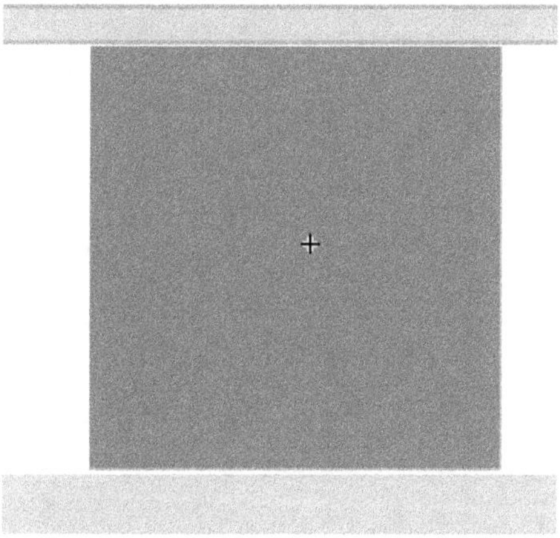

Select this new shape and go to **Modify**, and **Convert to Symbol**. Change the name to **Invisible Button** and the **Type** to **Button**:

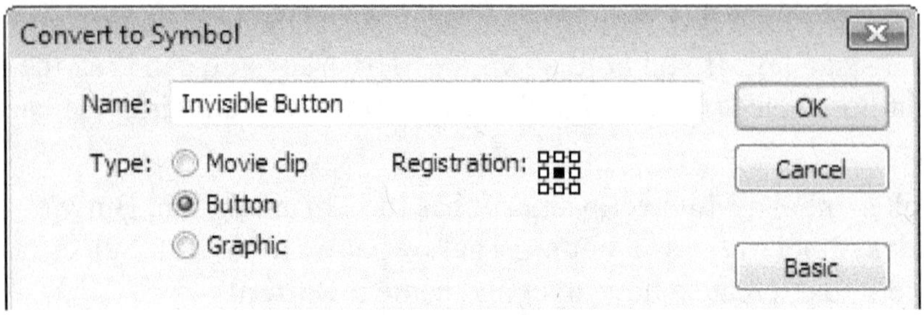

Hit **OK**. Next, in the Properties panel change **Color** to **Alpha**, and the Alpha percentage to **0**:

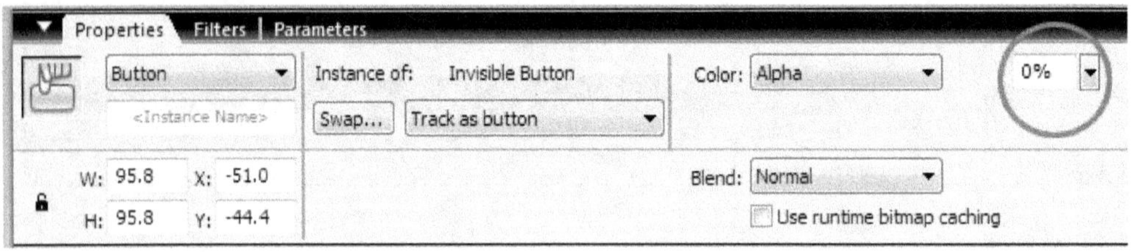

You should now see the clock again. There should be a blue outline showing where the Invisible Button is:

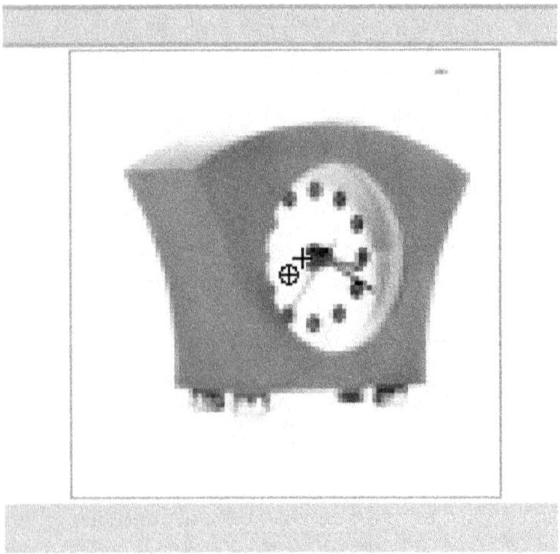

Next we'll add the ActionScript to this button. With the button still selected, open the Actions panel and go to **Deprecated**, **Actions**, and double-click **tellTarget**:

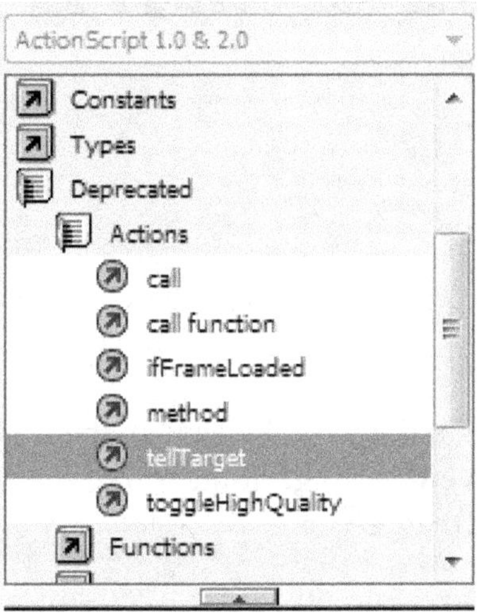

You should now see the **Target** window. Type **/clock** in the **Target** window:

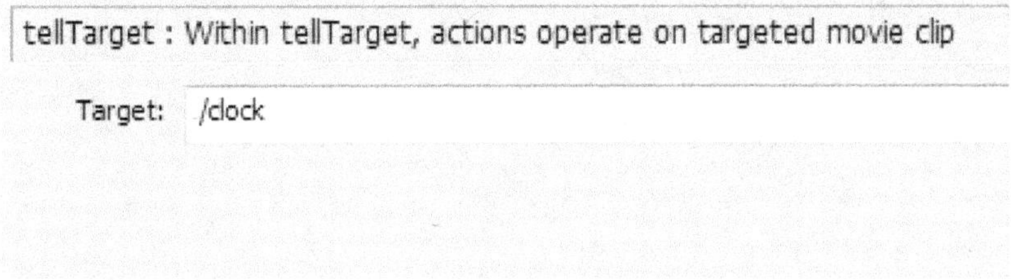

Next, select **Global Functions**, **Timeline Control**, and double-click **goto**:

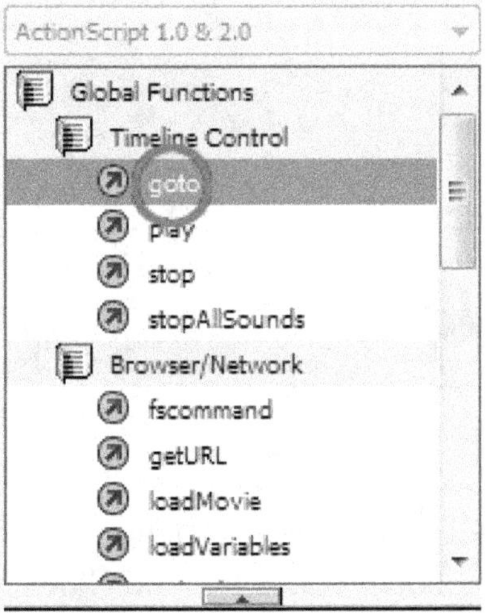

In the next set of options select **Frame label** and type **slide_in** next to **Frame**:

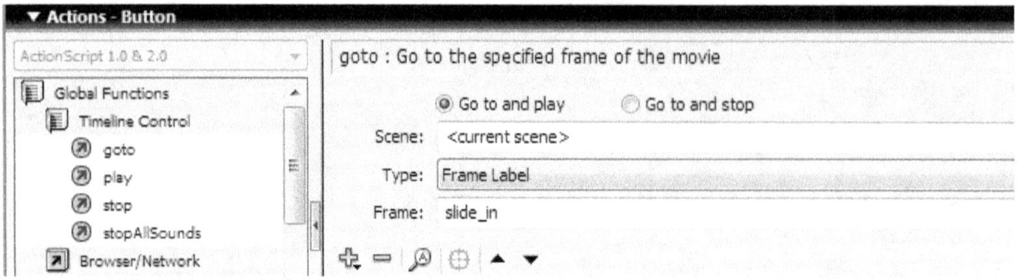

We need to change the mouse event settings. Click on the word **release** in the Actions window. You should now see the **mouse event** settings at the top of the panel. Uncheck **Release** and select **Roll Over** and **Drag Over**:

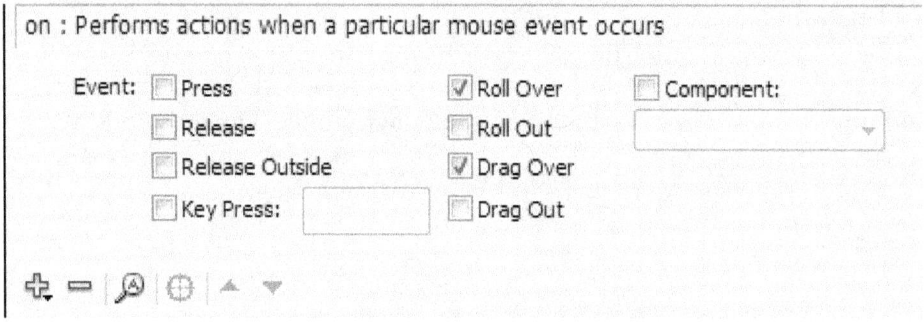

Test your movie (CTRL + ENTER). You may be wondering why it's not working. Let's go back to the Home scene and I'll explain why you can't see the animation. Click on the Home button above the timeline (**CS3/CS4/CS5** above the stage):

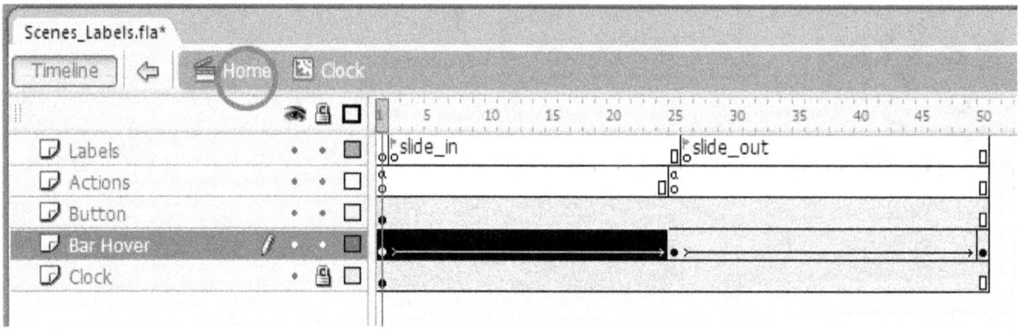

You should now be back on the Home scene. Here is why you can't see the animation when you roll over the **Clock** Movie clip. You'll notice that the **Clock** Movie clip is on the **Thumbnails** layer, which is below the **Bar** layer. As I explained earlier, layers are like stacks of books. The first book will cover up the rest of the books. So in this case, the **Bar** layer is covering up the clock animation. To fix this, click-and-drag the **Thumbnails** layer so it's above the **Bar** layer:

Test your movie (CTRL + ENTER). When you roll over the clock symbol you should see the animation on the bar. We need to create the ActionScript so that the bar exits stage left when the user rolls off the clock symbol.

Double-click the clock symbol to enter its editing stage. Select the **Invisible Button** and open the Actions panel. Since we already added code to this button we want the next set of code to go right below the first set of code. To accomplish this, click on the *closing bracket* of the first set of code:

```
on (rollOver, dragOver) {
    tellTarget ("/clock") {
        gotoAndPlay("slide_in");
    }
}
```

It's now safe to add the next set of code. Go to **Deprecated**, **Actions**, and double-**click tellTarget**:

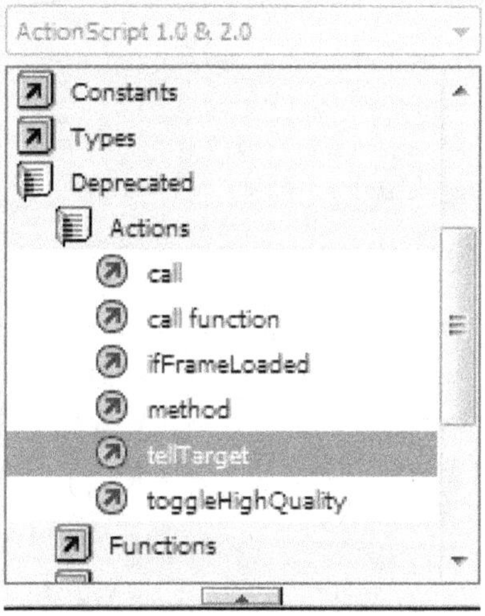

In the **Target** window type **/clock**:

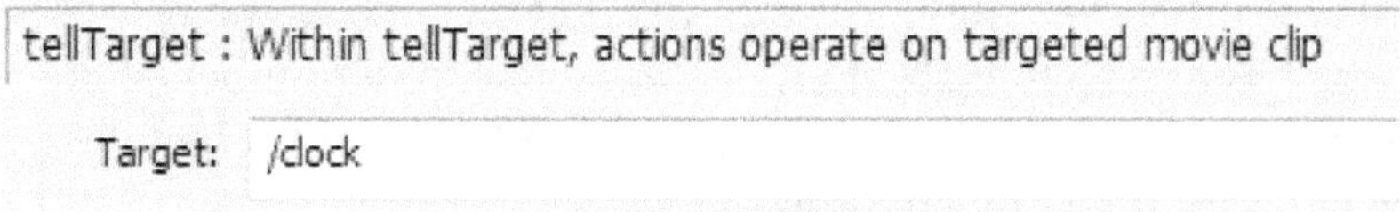

Next, go to **Global Functions**, **Timeline Control**, and double-click **goto**:

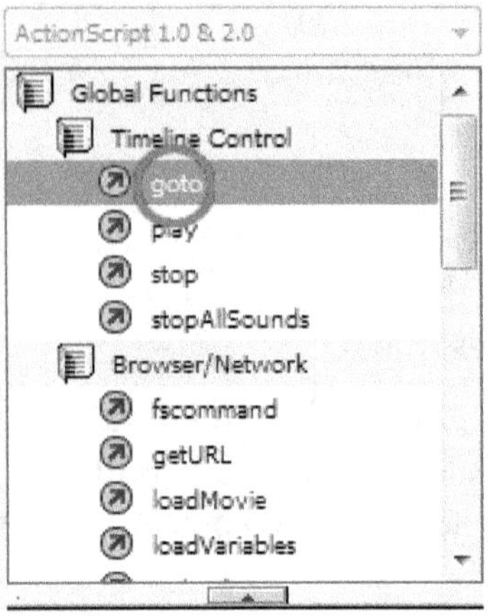

In the next set of options choose **Frame Label** for **Type** and type **slide_out** in the **Frame** window:

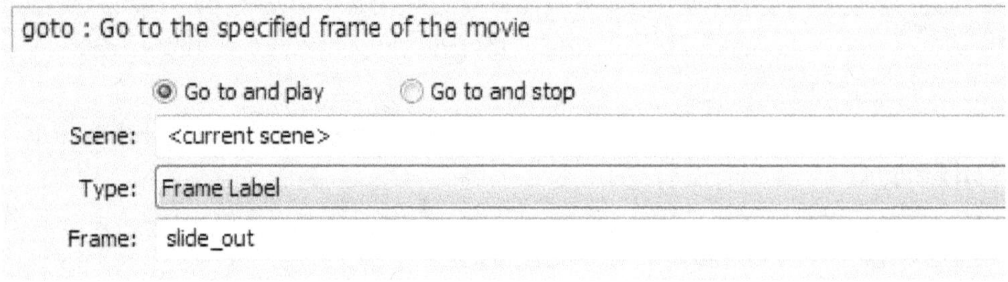

Next, uncheck **Release** and select **Roll Out** and **Drag Out**:

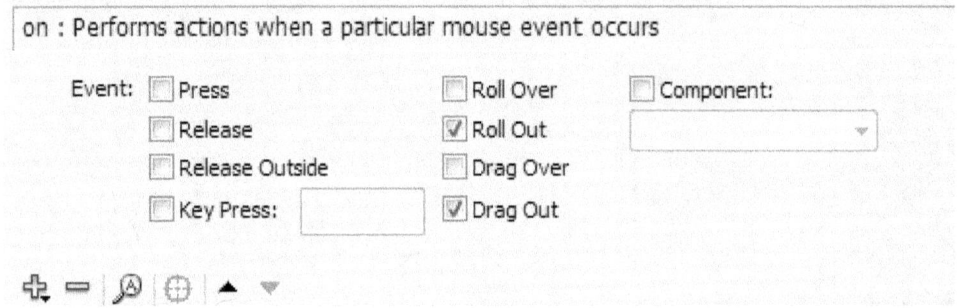

Test your movie (CTRL + ENTER). The animation should work perfectly when you roll over the clock symbol. We now just need to add this code to the rest of the thumbnails. I'll show you a couple shortcuts so you can skip a number of the steps we just did. Select the **Clock** layer, then hold down SHIFT and select the rest of the layers (they'll turn black when highlighted):

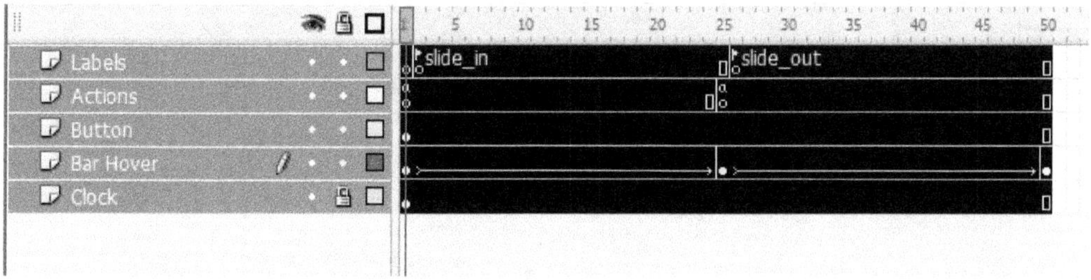

Once they're all highlighted right-click anywhere within the highlighted frames and select **Copy Frames**:

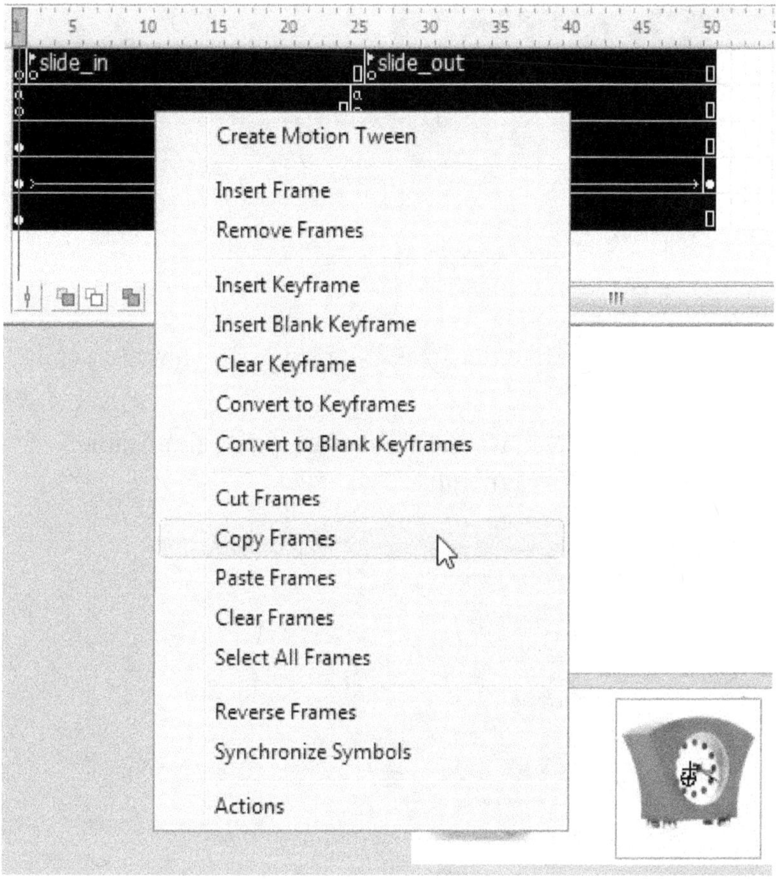

Go back to the Home scene. Select the **firefliesThumb** thumbnail; go to **Modify**, and **Convert to Symbol**. Name this new symbol **Fireflies**, and change the **Type** to Movie clip:

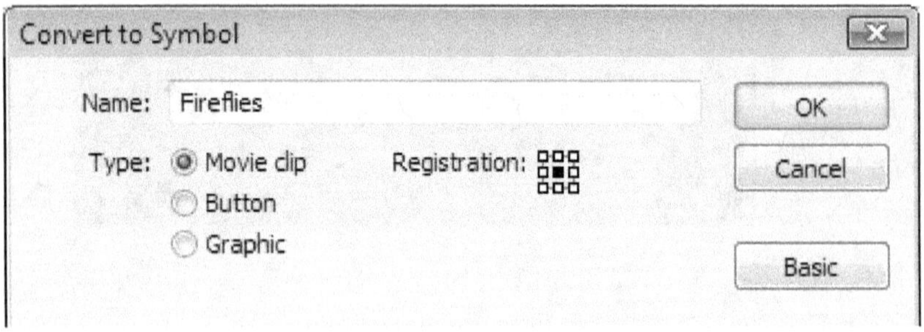

Hit **OK**. In the Properties panel, give this symbol an Instance Name of **fireflies**:

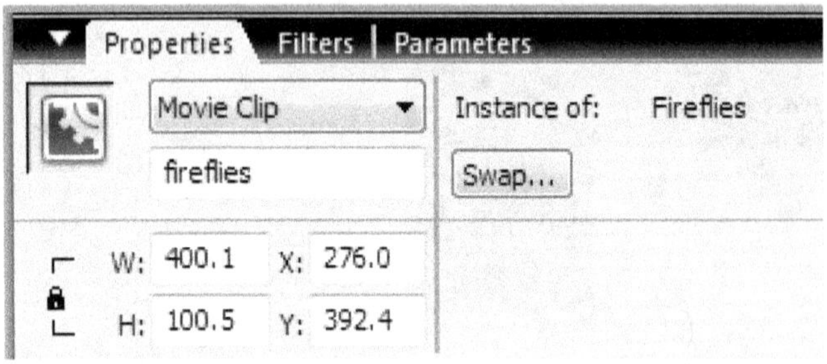

Double-click the **Fireflies** Movie clip to enter its editing stage. Rename Layer 1 **Fireflies**.

Add a new layer (you don't need to name it) and right-click on its first frame; select **Paste Frames** from the drop down menu:

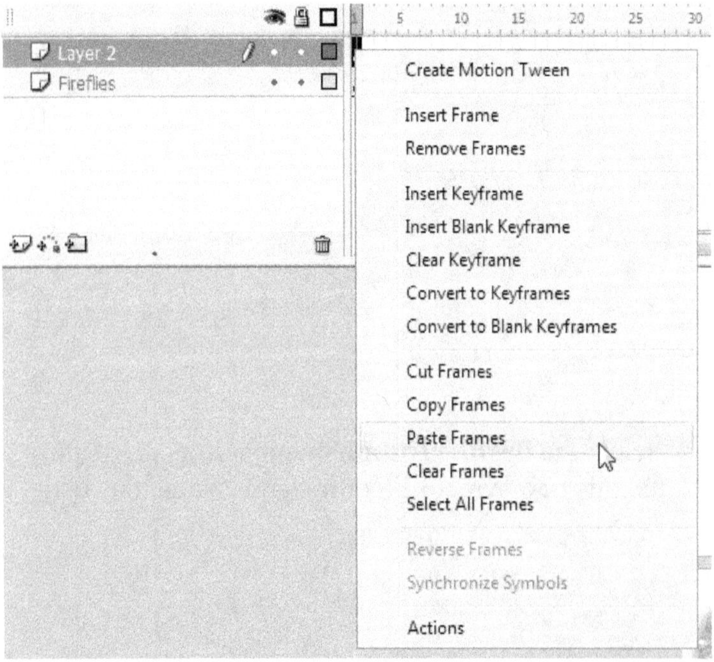

Flash will now paste in all the frames from the **Clock** Movie clip that we copied. The timeline should now look like this:

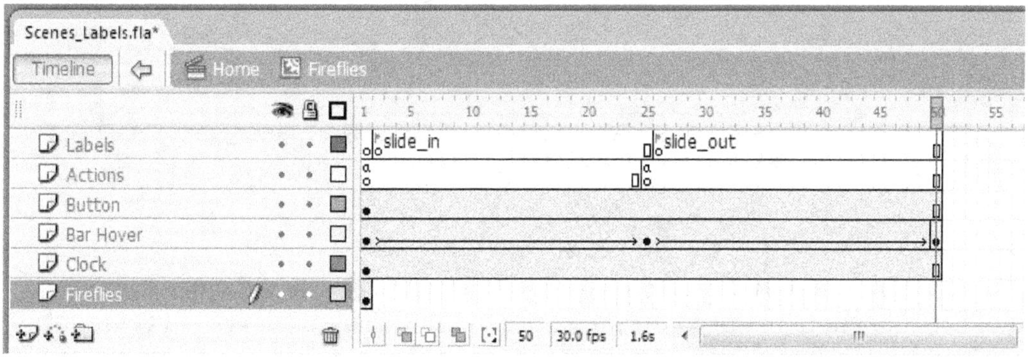

See how doing this shortcut can save time? We still have to tweak it, though, but we've saved ourselves a few steps. Since we don't need the **Clock** layer we can delete it; select this layer and click on the **Delete Layer** button:

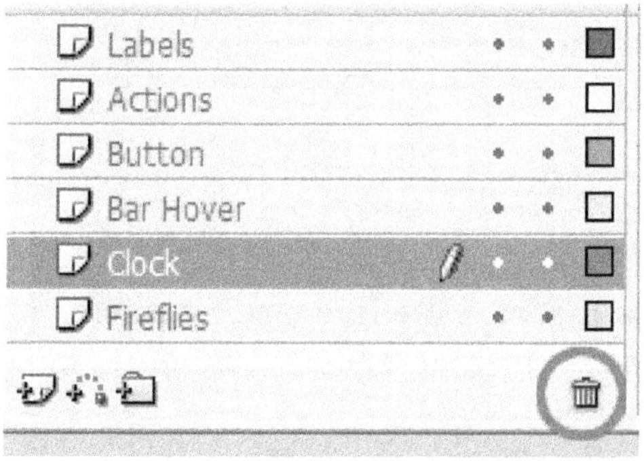

This will delete the **Clock** layer. Next, since the fireflies image is farther away from stage left than the clock image, we need to extend the animation a bit. We'll add 20 frames to the animation. Select the keyframe on frame 50 of the **Bar Hover** layer; select this keyframe again and drag it to frame **70**:

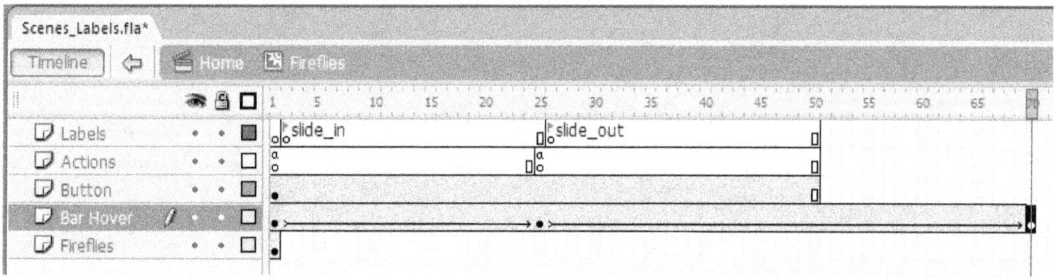

Select the keyframe on frame **25** of this layer. Select it again and drag it to frame **35**. Next, drag the keyframe at frame **25** of the **Actions** layer, and drag it to frame

35. Finally, drag the **slide_out** keyframe of the **Labels** layer to frame **36**. The timeline should now look like this:

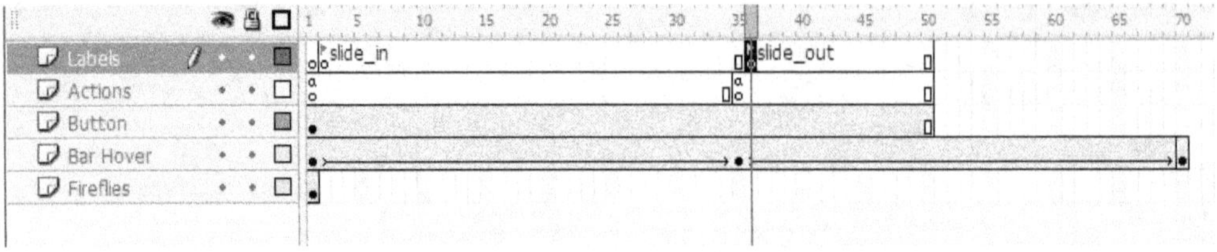

You may have noticed that we need to add frames to a few of the layers. Here's another shortcut if you need to add frames to more than one layer. Select frame **70** of the **Labels** layer and without letting go of your mouse button, drag downward selecting frame **70** of the **Actions** and **Button** layers:

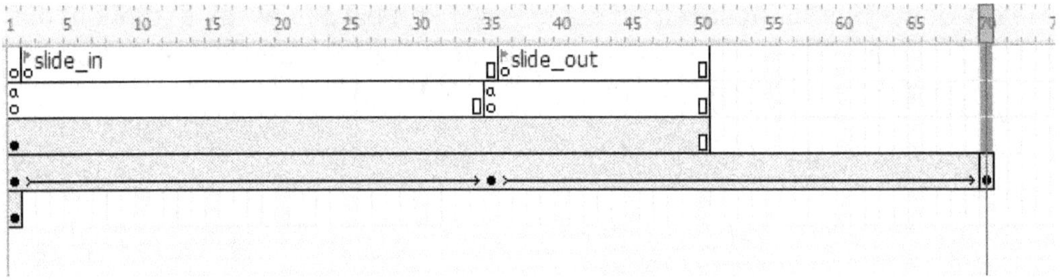

The frames should be highlighted. Next, go to **Insert**, **Timeline**, and **Frame**. Select frame **70** of the **Fireflies** layer and once again go to **Insert**, **Timeline**, and **Frame**. The timeline should now look like this:

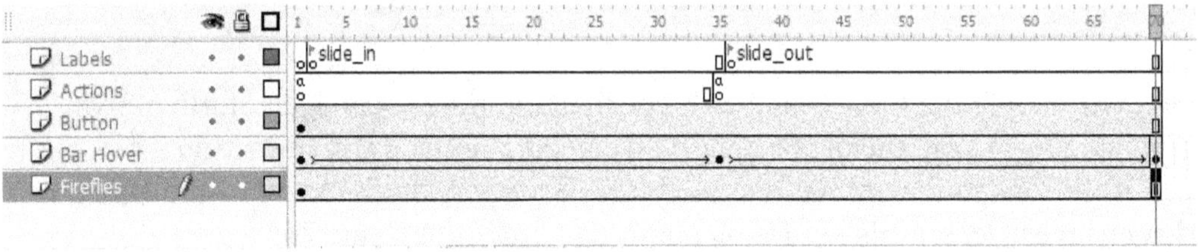

Select the Button. Open the Actions panel so you can see the code :

```
on (rollOver, dragOver) {
    tellTarget ("/clock") {
        gotoAndPlay("slide_in");
    }
}
on (rollOut, dragOut) {
    tellTarget ("/clock") {
        gotoAndPlay("slide_out");
    }
}
```

Click on the word **/clock** in the first code. You should see the **Target** window appear at the top. Change **/clock** to **/fireflies**:

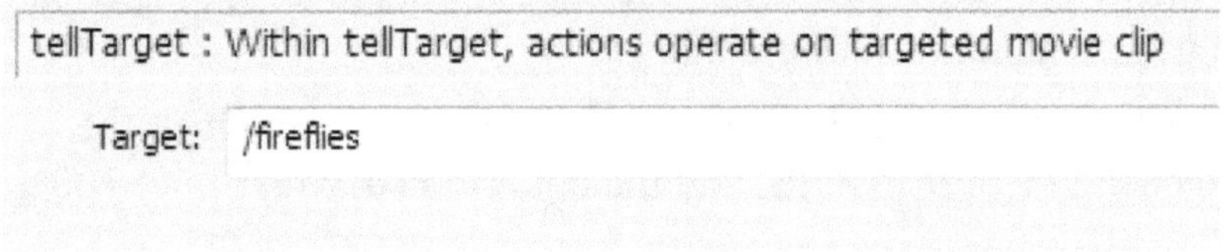

Click on the word **/clock** in the second code and change that to **/fireflies** also. The final code should now look like this:

```
on (rollOver, dragOver) {
    tellTarget ("/fireflies") {
        gotoAndPlay("slide_in");
    }
}
on (rollOut, dragOut) {
    tellTarget ("/fireflies") {
        gotoAndPlay("slide_out");
    }
}
```

That is all the code we need to change. Test your movie (CTRL + ENTER) and try out the **Fireflies** Movie clip by rolling over it. The bar should hover perfectly over the fireflies image, but when you roll off the button the bar doesn't quite make it all the way off the stage.

Since we copied the animation from the **Clock** Movie Clip, the animation will be shorter than what we need for the **Fireflies** Movie clip. We need to adjust this animation. Select frame **1** of the **Bar Hover** layer, and drag the bar symbol off the stage (hold down SHIFT to keep it on a straight line):

Select frame **70** of the **Bar Hover** layer and drag the bar symbol straight left off the stage. Test your movie (CTRL + ENTER). The animation should work perfectly now. Before we finish this Movie clip let's do one more thing. What if the bar turns from white to red by the time it hovers over the top of the thumbnail? Then, when we roll off the button, the bar exits stage left going back to the color white. I'll show you how simple this is.

Select frame **35** of the **Bar Hover** layer. Next, select the bar symbol. Open the Properties panel and change **Color** to **Tint**, and the color to **red**. Make sure 100% is selected:

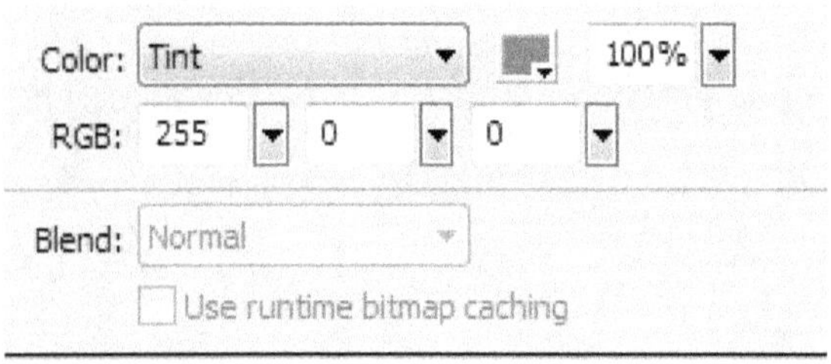

That's it, we're done. Test your movie (CTRL + ENTER). The bar should go from white to red when you roll over the **Fireflies** Movie clip. Next, we'll change the clock symbol's **Bar Hover** symbol to yellow on Rollover. Go back to the Home scene. Double-click the **Clock** Movie clip to enter its editing stage. Select frame **25** of the **Bar Hover** layer; next, select the bar symbol. Open the Properties panel and change the **Color** to **Tint**, and the color to **yellow**. Make sure 100% is selected:

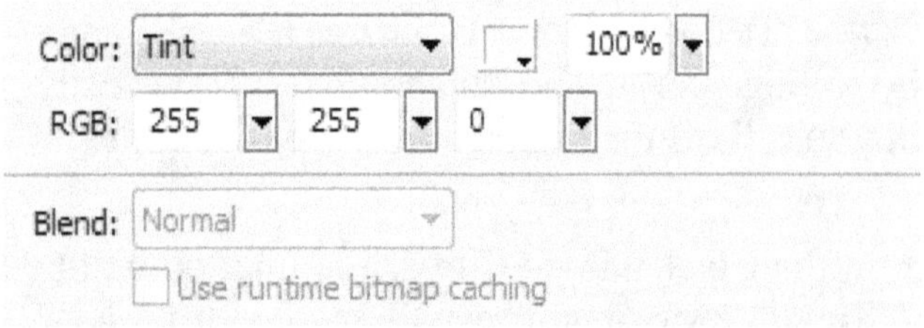

Test your movie (CTRL + ENTER). Your first three buttons should work perfectly. Let's finish the last two buttons. Go back to the Home scene.

Select the **Morano** thumbnail and go to **Modify**, and **Convert to Symbol**. Change the name to **Morano**, and the **Type** to **Movie clip**:

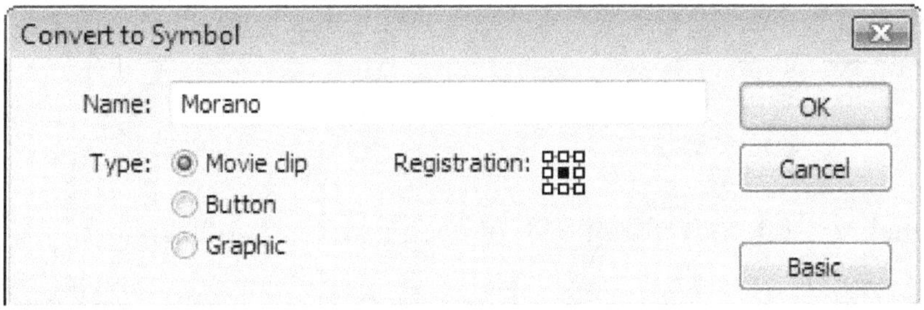

Hit **OK**. Select this new Movie clip and open the Properties panel. In the **Instance Name** window type **morano**:

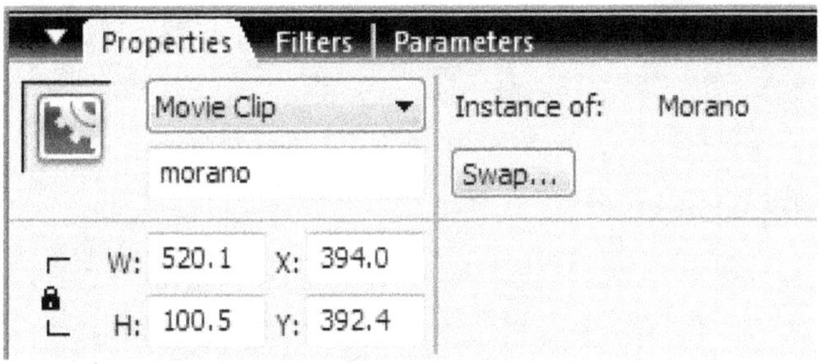

Double-click on the fireflies symbol to enter its editing stage. Just as we did previously, we're going to copy the frames of the fireflies editing stage and paste them into the next Movie clip.

Select the first layer, hold down SHIFT**,** then select the rest of the layers:

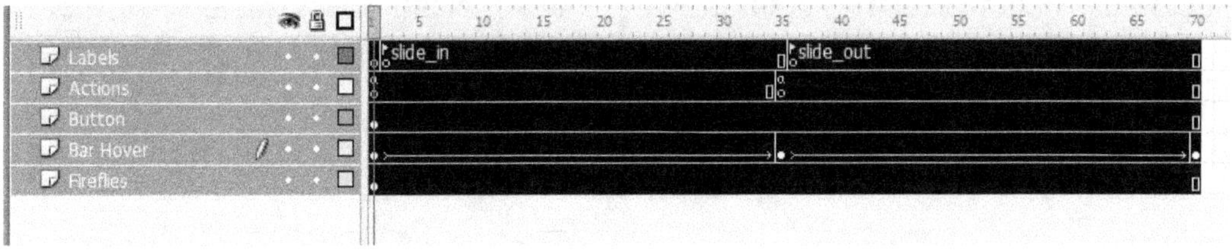

Go to **Edit**, **Timeline**, and **Copy Frames**. Go back to the Home scene.

Double-click on the **Morano** Movie clip to enter its editing stage. Create a new layer and select its first frame; next, go to **Edit**, **Timeline**, and **Paste Frames**. The timeline should now look like this:

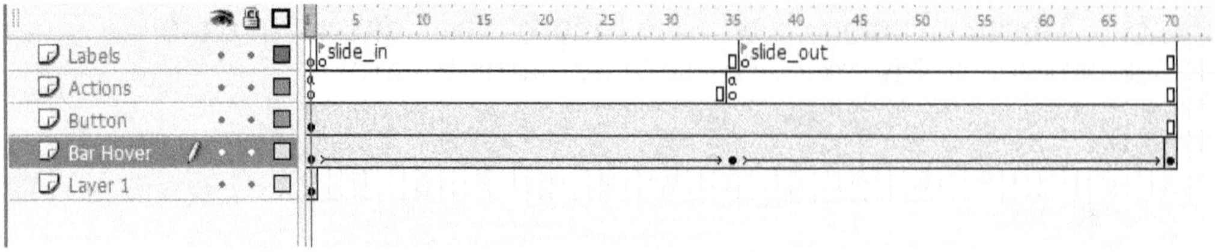

Let's tweak this timeline a bit. Select frame **90** of each layer and go to **Insert**, **Timeline**, and **Frame**:

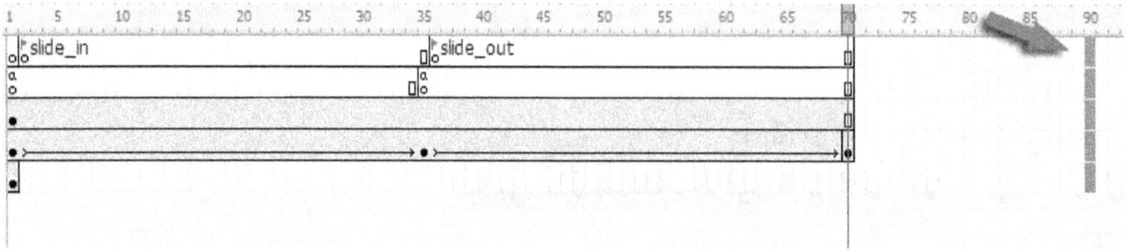

You should now have 90 frames on each layer:

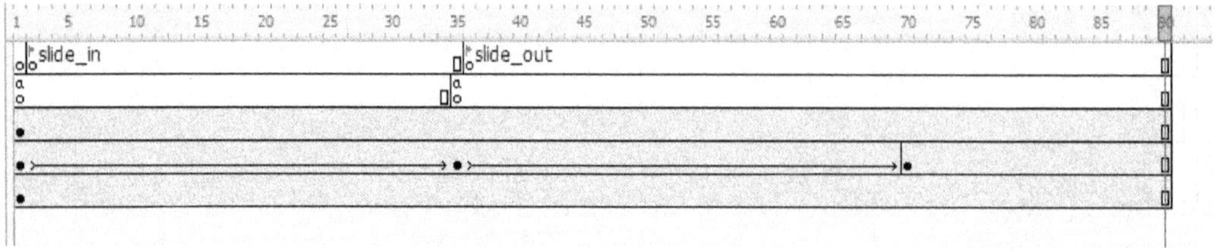

Select frame **70** of the **Bar Hover** layer. Select it again and this time don't release the mouse button; drag this keyframe to frame **90**. Next, select frame **35** of the same layer. Select the keyframe again and drag this keyframe to frame **45**. Your timeline should now look like this:

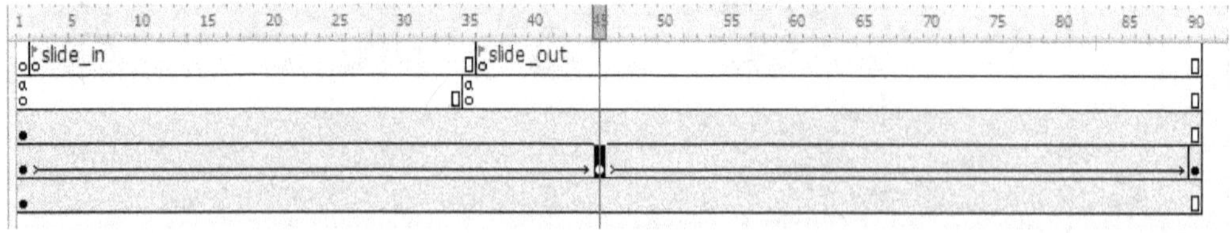

Select frame **35** of the **Actions** layer; select it again and drag it to frame **45**. Select frame **36** of the **Labels** layer; select it again and drag it to frame **46**:

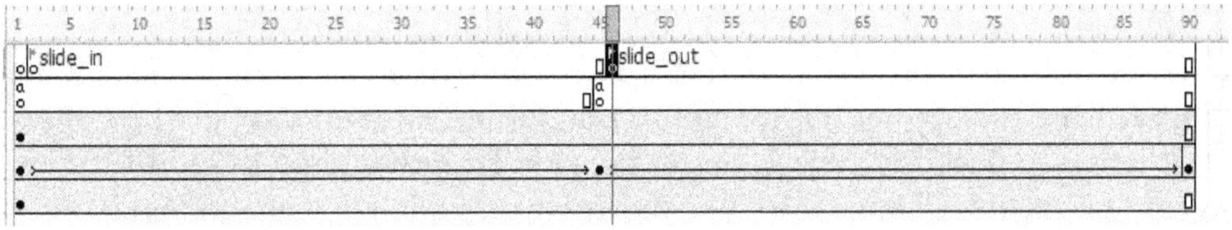

We're almost done now. We now have to slightly adjust this animation. Go to **Control**, **Play** (ENTER), and you'll notice that the Bar doesn't quite make it all the way off the stage. Select frame **1** of the **Bar Hover** layer; next, select the Bar symbol and drag it straight left off the stage (hold down SHIFT to keep a straight line).

Do the same thing with the bar symbol on frame 90. Select frame **90**, then select the bar symbol on the stage and drag it left until it's completely off the stage.

Next, select frame **45** of the **Bar Hover** layer and select the bar symbol. Open the Properties panel and change **Color** to **Tint**, and the color to **blue**:

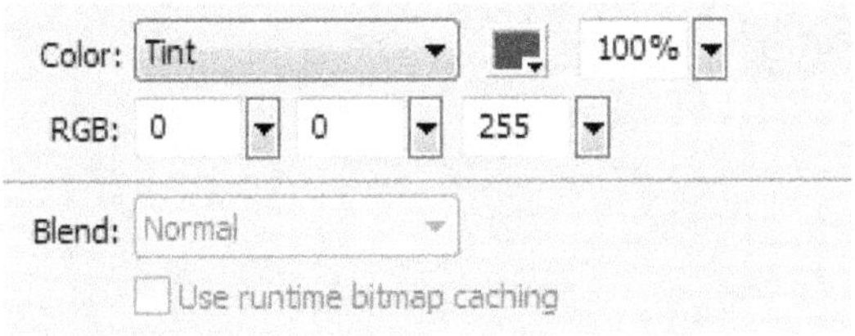

The bar will now change to the color blue when it hovers over the top of the morano thumbnail. If you test your movie you'll notice that the **Morano** Movie clip controls the fireflies animation. That's because we haven't changed the ActionScript of the morano Movie clip. Let's do that now.

Select the first frame of the **Button** layer. Next, select the button symbol on the stage. Open the Actions panel so you can see the code. Click on the word: **/fireflies** in both sets of codes and change this word to **/morano**. The ActionScript should now look like this:

```
on (rollOver, dragOver) {
    tellTarget ("/morano") {
        gotoAndPlay("slide_in");
    }
}
on (rollOut, dragOut) {
    tellTarget ("/morano") {
        gotoAndPlay("slide_out");
    }
}
```

Test your movie again (CTRL + ENTER). The buttons should work perfectly. You should only have one thumbnail left, the **rajaThumb**. By now you should be getting the hang of copying frames and ActionScript. We'll go through the steps one last time. Go back to Scene 1. Select the **rajaThumb** and go to **Modify**, and **Convert to Symbol**. Change the **Type** to **Movie clip** and the name to **Raja**:

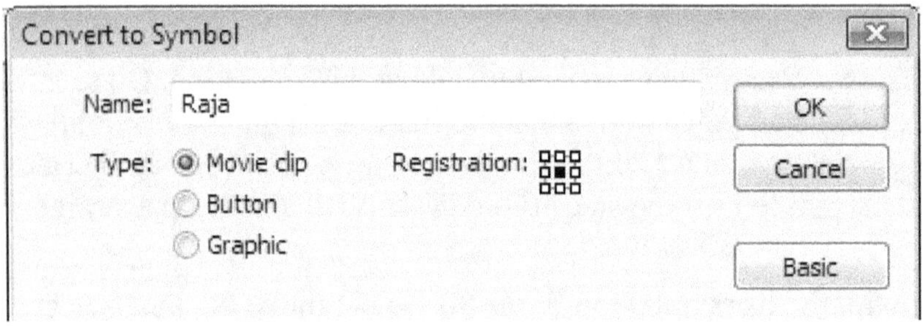

Hit **OK**. Give this new Movie clip a name. Open the Properties panel and type **raja** in the **Instance Name** window:

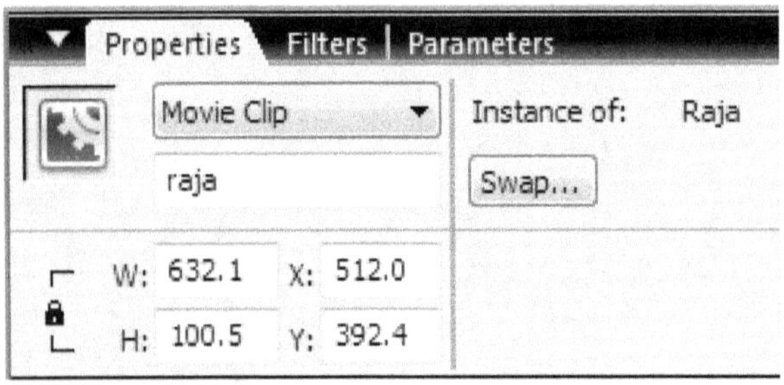

Double-click on the **Morano** Movie clip to enter its editing stage. Select all the layers except for **Layer 1**:

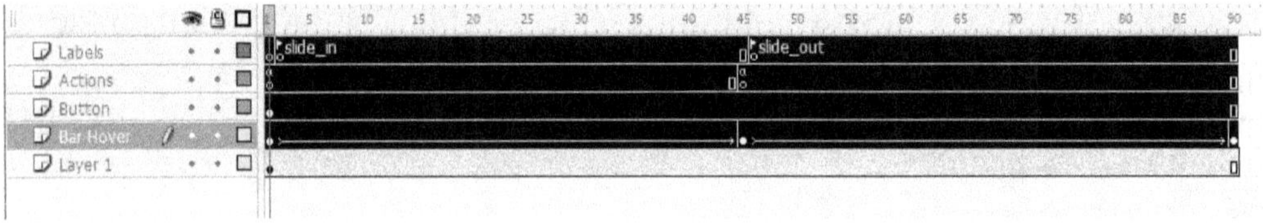

Go to **Edit**, **Timeline**, and **Copy Frames**. Return to the Home scene. Double-click on the raja symbol to enter its editing stage. Create a new layer and select its frame; next, go to **Edit**, **Timeline**, and **Paste Frames**. The timeline should now look like this:

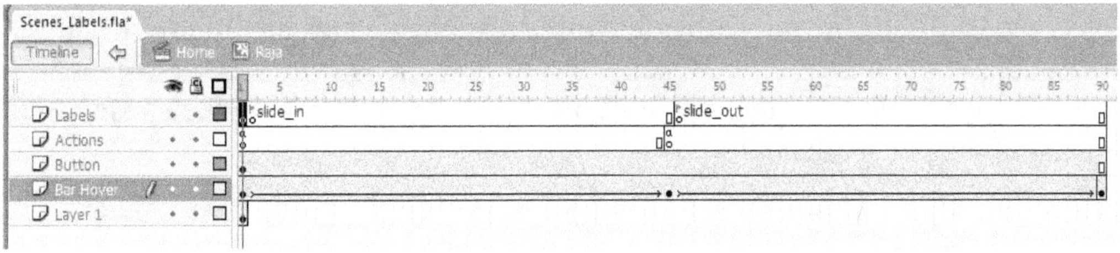

We'll now modify these frames. Click on frame **45** of the **Bar Hover** layer and move it to frame **55** (remember that to move a frame you *must select it first*, *then select it again* and drag it). Select frame **45** of the **Actions** layer and move that to frame **55**. Select frame **46** of the **Labels** layer and move it to frame **56**. Your timeline should now look like this:

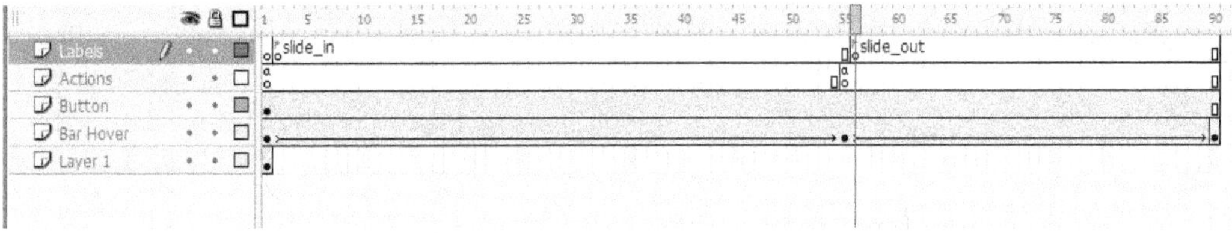

Move the keyframe of the **Bar Hover** layer to frame **110**. Select frame **110** of the other layers and go to **Insert**, **Timeline**, and **Frame**. The timeline should now look like this:

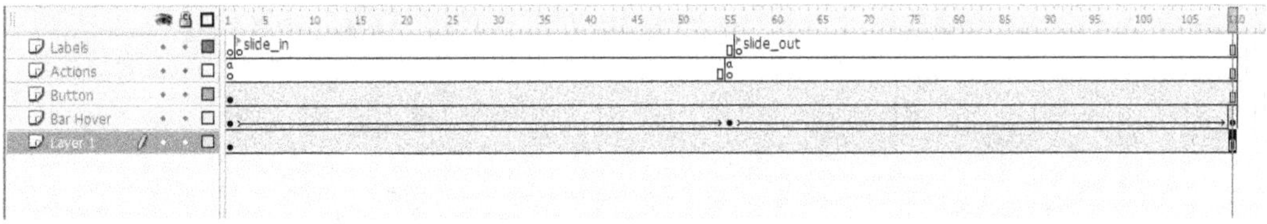

Ok, we're almost done. Select frame **110** of the **Bar Hover** layer and move the bar symbol all the way off the stage. Do that with the bar symbol on frame **1** of **the Bar Hover** layer. Next, select frame **1** of the **Button** layer. Select the button symbol on the stage and open the Actions panel. Click on the word **/morano** to open the Target window; change **/morano** to **/raja**. When you're done test the movie.

It should work perfectly! Let's change the color of the bar to green. Select frame **55** of the **Bar Hover** layer then select the bar symbol. Open the Properties panel and change **Color** to **Tint**, and the color to **green**.

Test your movie again. All your buttons should work perfectly. Next we're going to add the Scenes and link up all the buttons to the Scenes. Before we create the scenes, though, let's add some ActionScript to the Buddha Button. Go back to the Home scene.

Select the **Buddha Button**. Unlike the other symbols, which are all Movie Clips, the Buddha symbol is a button. Open the Actions panel so you can see the ActionScript. Since we're adding new code to this button click on the closing bracket of the last set of code:

```
1  on (release) {
2      tellTarget ("/bar") {
3          gotoAndPlay("slide_in");
4      }
5  }
6  on (rollOut, dragOut) {
7      tellTarget ("/bar") {
8          gotoAndPlay("slide_out");
9      }
10 }
```

We do this so the new ActionScript can start on line 11, otherwise the new code may be inserted within the previous code causing problems.

When the button is clicked we need the user to go to the Buddha scene (which we'll create next). Select **Global Functions**, **Timeline Control**, and double-click **goto**. In the **goto** settings window type **Buddha** next to **Scene**, **Type** should be **Frame Number**, and type **1** next to **Frame**; make sure **Go to and stop** is selected:

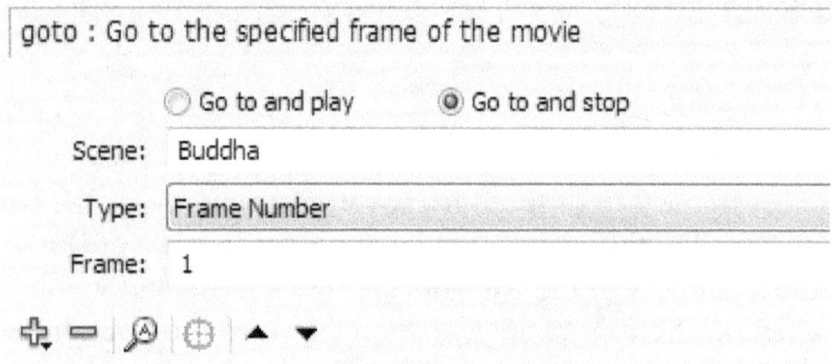

So even though we haven't created the Buddha scene yet, the code will function normally once the scene is created.

Next, we'll create the scenes. Since all of the scenes are going to have the same set of buttons as the Home scene it will save time if we just duplicate this scene; open the Scene panel and click on **Duplicate Scene**:

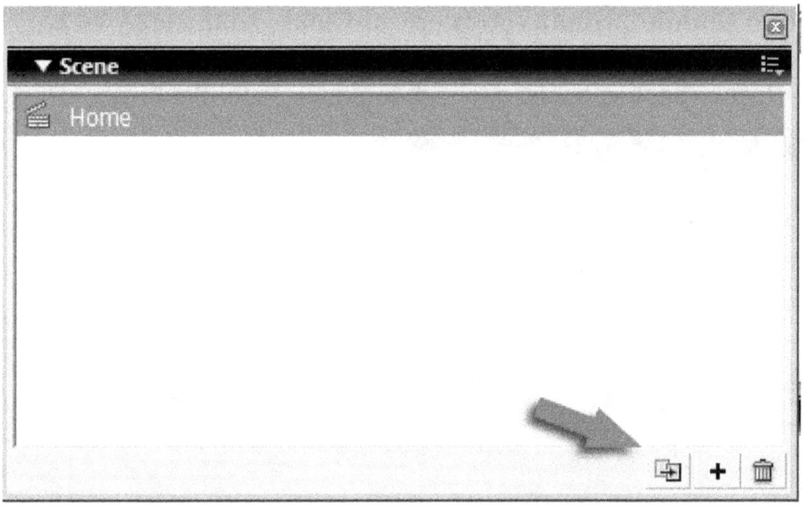

This will create an exact copy of the Home Scene. Now, we don't necessarily have to do this. We can also create a brand new scene and copy and paste the buttons into it, but using Duplicate scene saves a couple steps. You should now see the name **Home copy** at the top of the timeline:

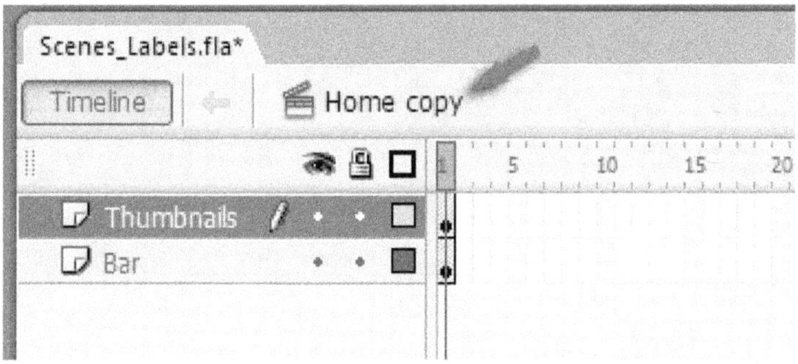

This tells you that you are now in the new duplicated scene you just created. Click the **Duplicate scene** button four more times so you have six scenes total:

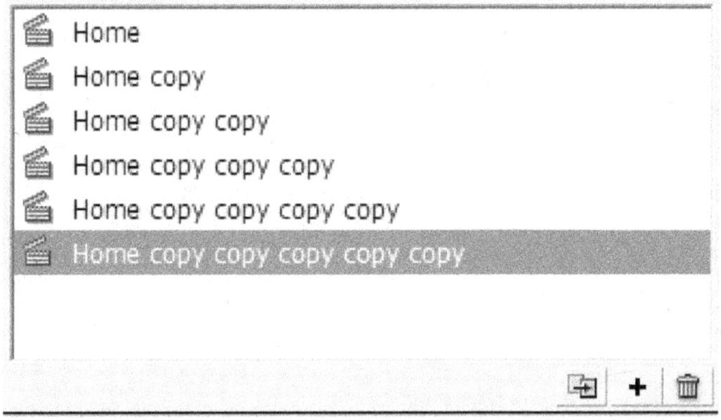

Change **Home copy** to **Buddha**, **Home copy copy** to **Clock**, **Home copy copy copy** to **Fireflies**, **Home copy copy copy copy** to **Morano**, and **Home copy copy copy copy copy** to **Raja**. The new Scene panel should now look like this:

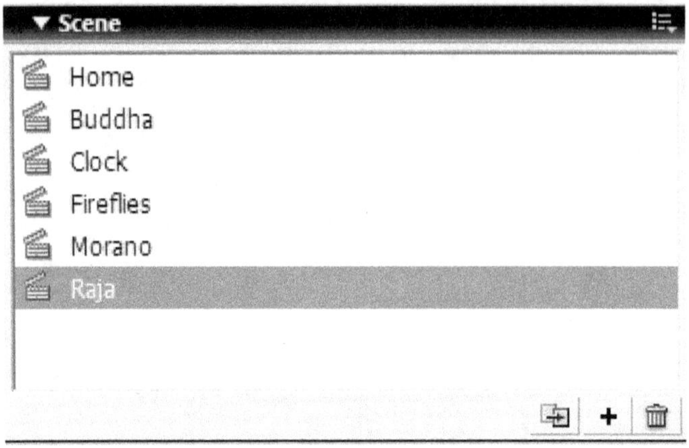

Next, we'll add pictures to each scene. Make sure **Raja** is still selected in the Scene panel. Create a new layer and call it **Picture**:

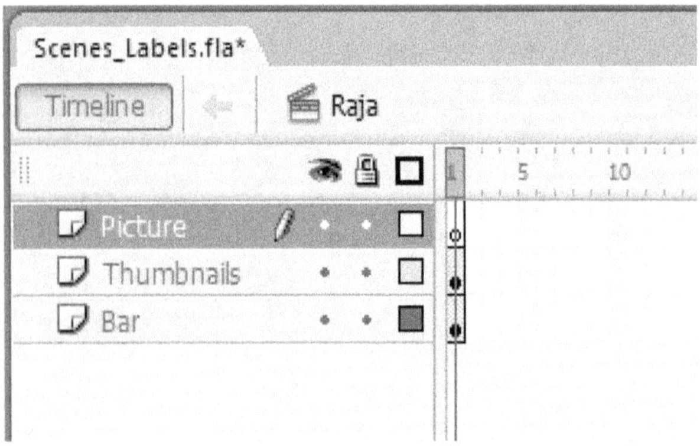

Next, go to the Library, Pictures folder, and drag **meditation.jpg** over to the stage. Center the picture using the Align panel. Select **Align horizontal center**, **Align top edge**, and make sure **To stage is selected**:

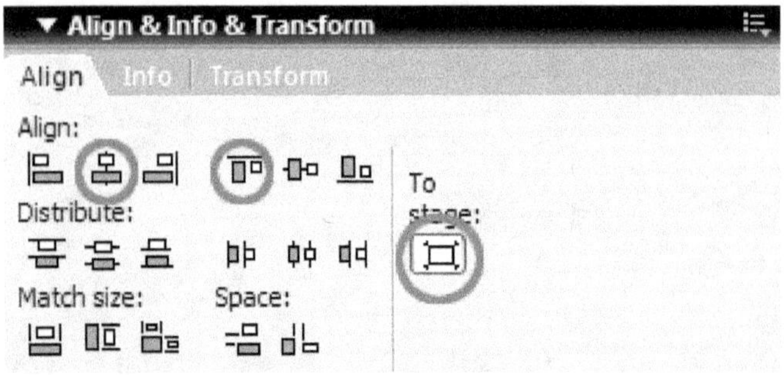

The stage should now look like this:

Repeat these steps for all the scenes. In the Scene panel select the scene **Morano**. The stage should now change to reflect the new scene. Create a new layer and name it **Picture**. Next, drag **morano.jpg** from the Pictures folder in the Library, over to the stage. Use the Align panel to center the picture:

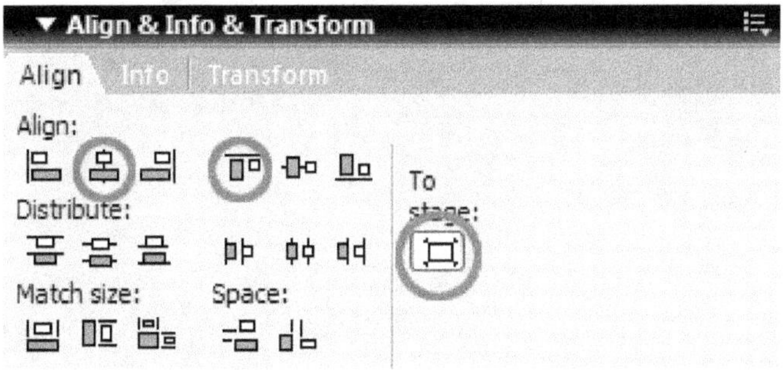

This picture should now be positioned correctly. Go ahead and test your movie. Pretty crazy huh? As we learned earlier, when we are using scenes, Flash will play all the scenes until it hits a **stop** code. Usually when you have several scenes, the first scene needs to have a **stop** code. We'll add that **stop** code in a bit. First, let's finish the rest of the scenes.

Drag the appropriate pictures to each scene using the steps we outlined above.

When you're finished adding all the pictures to the scenes, go to the **Home** scene. Remember, you can also go to a specific scene by clicking on the **Edit Scene** button at the top right of the timeline:

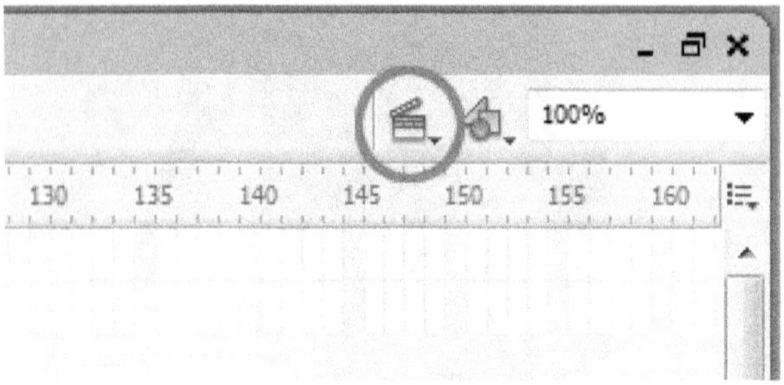

In the Home scene, create a new layer and name it **Actions**. Select its frame and open the Actions panel. Go to **Global Functions**, **Timeline**, and double-click **stop**.

If you test the movie again you'll notice that instead of playing through all the scenes, Flash stops at the Home scene which has a **stop** code. We'll add some ActionScript to the buttons so they can direct the user to the appropriate scenes. Double-click on the **Clock** Symbol so you can enter its editing stage. Select the first frame of the **Button** layer, and then select the button symbol on the stage.

Open the Actions panel, make sure Script Assist is on, and click on the closing bracket of the final set of code:

```
on (rollOver, dragOver) {
    tellTarget ("/clock") {
        gotoAndPlay("slide_in");
    }
}
on (rollOut, dragOut) {
    tellTarget ("/clock") {
        gotoAndPlay("slide_out");
    }
}
```

We're now ready to add the new ActionScript. Go to **Deprecated**, **Timeline**, and double-click **tellTarget**:

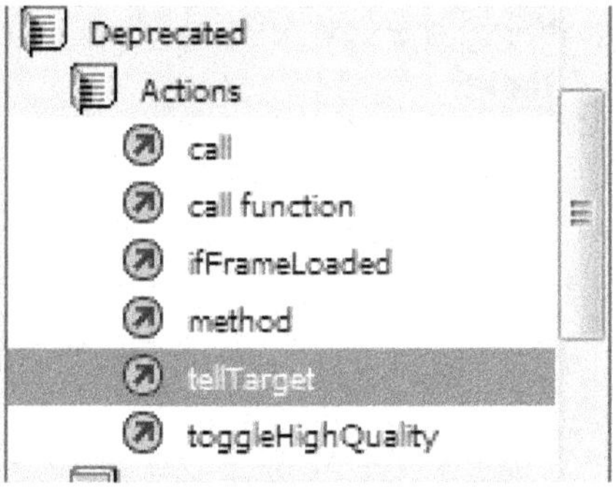

In the **tellTarget** setting window type **_level0/:**

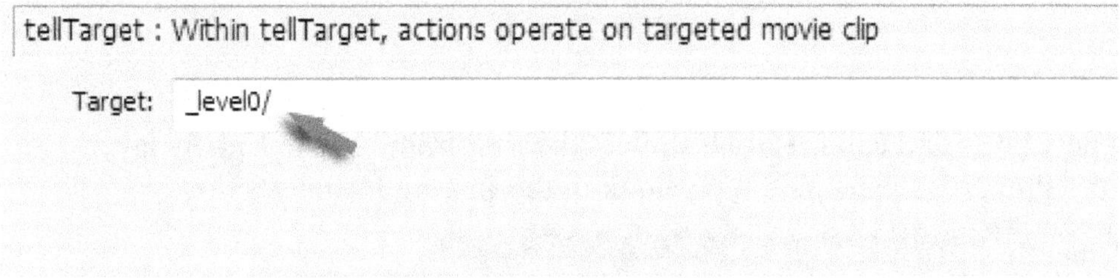

Go to **Global Functions**, **Timeline Control**, and double-click **goto**. In the **goto** settings window, change **Type** to **Frame Label**, type **clock** next to **Frame**. Also, select **Go to and stop**:

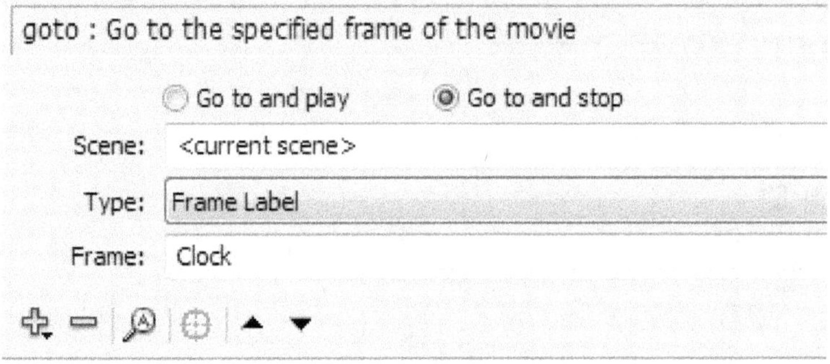

You may have noticed that the ActionScript we used for the button in the clock symbol is different than the ActionScript we used for the **Buddha** Button. If you have a button that is on a Scene timeline, like the **Buddha** Button, then you don't have to use the tellTarget code.

If you have a button that is *within* a Movie Clip, like this button is, then you have to use the *tellTarget* code. So any button that is within a Movie clip has to use the *tellTarget* code when going to a scene.

I've included a diagram at the end of the book which will help you if you get confused.

Before we can test this movie, we need to add a Label to the Clock scene. Let's do that now. Go to the **Edit Scene** button and select **Clock**:

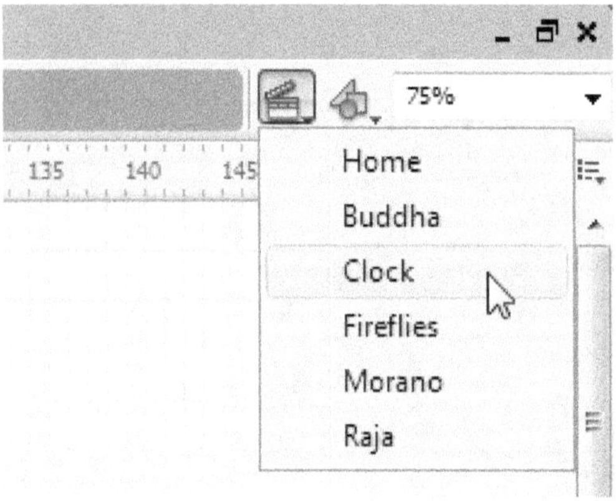

Add a new layer and call it **Labels**. Select the first frame of the **Labels** layer. Open the Properties panel and type **clock** in the **Frame Label** window:

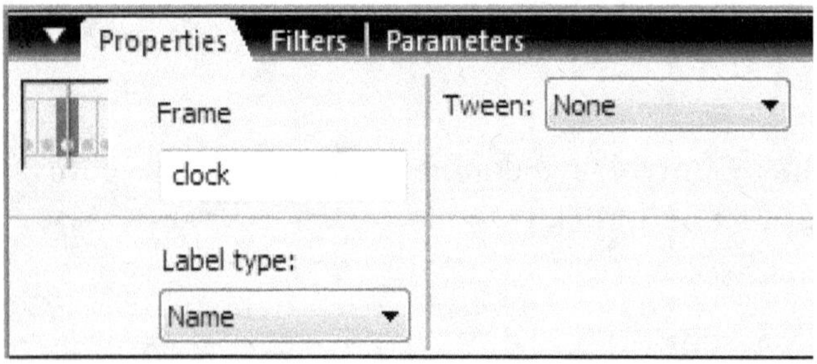

The timeline should now look like this:

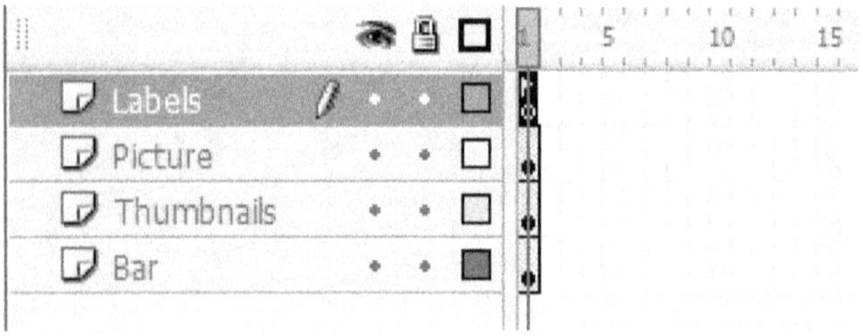

Go ahead and test your movie. When you click on the clock button it should take you to the Clock scene. Next, we'll add the ActionScript to the **Fireflies** Movie clip. Double-click on the fireflies symbol so that you are in its editing stage. Select the first frame of the **Button** layer and then select the button symbol on the stage. Next, click on the closing bracket of the last set of code:

```
on (rollOver, dragOver) {
    tellTarget ("/fireflies") {
        gotoAndPlay("slide_in");
    }
}
on (rollOut, dragOut) {
    tellTarget ("/fireflies") {
        gotoAndPlay("slide_out");
    }
}
```

Go to **Deprecated**, **Actions**, and double-click **tellTarget**. In the **tellTarget** window type **_level0/**:

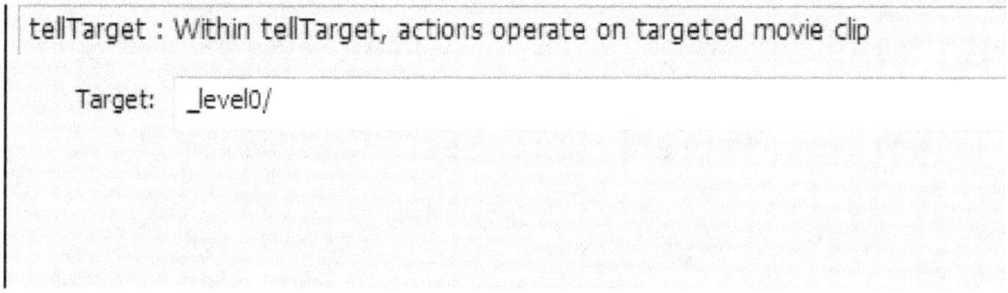

Next, go to **Global Functions**, **Timeline Control**, and double-click **goto**. In the **goto** settings window select **Frame Label** for **Type**, type **fireflies** in the **Frame** window, and make sure **Go to and stop** is selected:

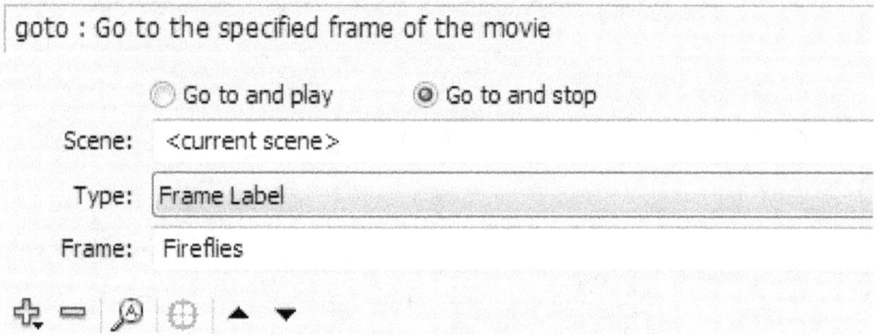

Before we can test this button we need to add a Label to the Fireflies scene. Go to the **Edit Scene** button and select **Fireflies**. Add a new layer in this scene and name it **Labels**. Select the first frame, and in the **Frame Label** window of the Properties panel type **fireflies**:

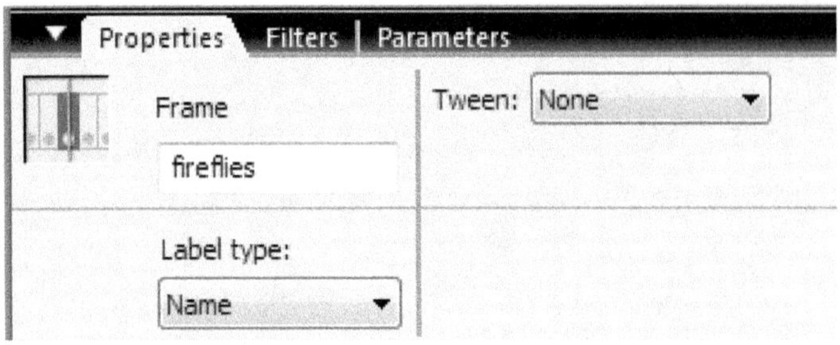

Test your movie (CTRL + ENTER). Click on the fireflies symbol and it should take you to the Fireflies scene. Now, repeat the above steps for the final two buttons. See if you can do it from memory. If you have problems remembering some of the steps, go through the previous examples to refresh your memory.

When you're done, all of the thumbnail symbols should take the users to the appropriate scenes. Let's do a couple cool things before we wrap on this chapter.

Go to the **Raja** scene. Add a new layer and call it **Actions**. Select the first frame of the **Actions** layer and add a **stop** code to it.

Next, select frame **30** of each layer and add a frame. The timeline should now look like this:

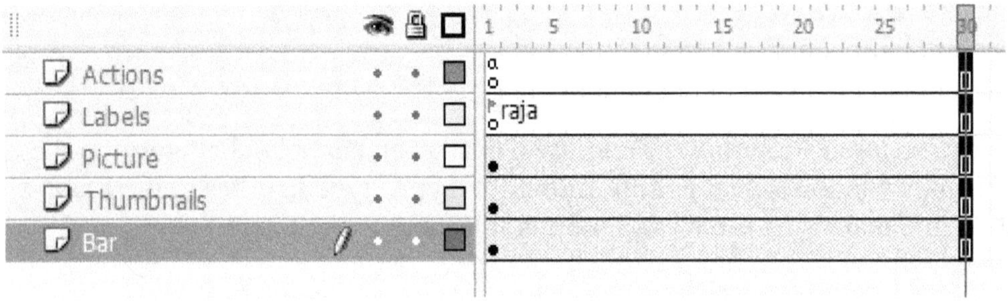

We'll next add a animation to this timeline. Add a keyframe to frame **15**, and **30** of the **Picture** layer:

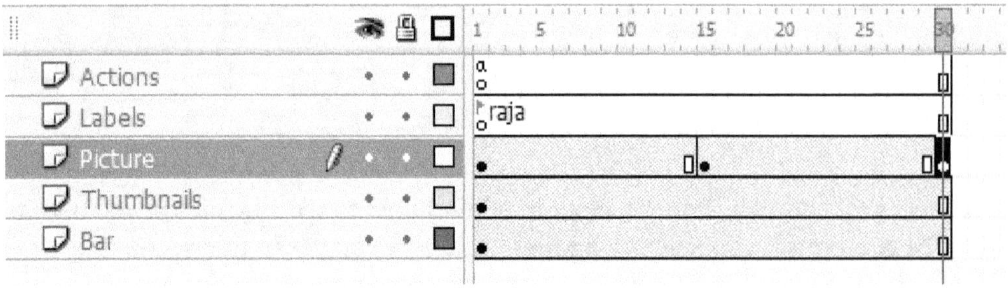

Select any frame between **1** and **15** of the **Picture** layer and insert a Motion Tween. Next, select any frame between **15** and **30** and insert a **Motion Tween (CS4/CS5 - Insert, Classic Tween)**:

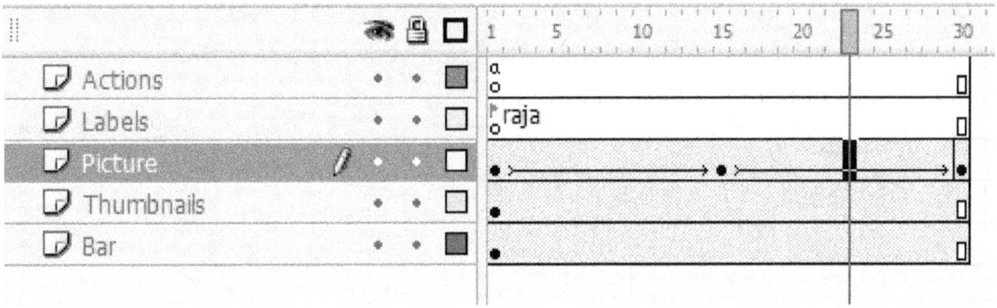

Insert a keyframe on frame 2 of the **Picture** layer. Select the **Picture** Symbol on the stage. Open the Properties panel and change the **Color** to **Alpha**, and the percentage to **0**:

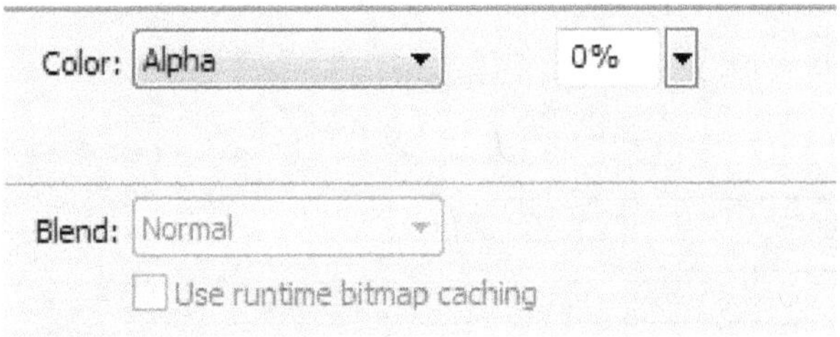

Select frame **30** of the **Picture** layer, then select the Picture symbol on the stage. Use the same settings for this symbol also: **Color**: **Alpha** and percentage: **0**.

Almost done now. Create a keyframe on frame **15** of the **Actions** layer. Next, add a **stop** code. Let's add another Label to this timeline. Insert a keyframe on frame **2** of the **Labels** layer. Select the keyframe and open the Properties panel. Type **raja_play** in the **Frame Label** window:

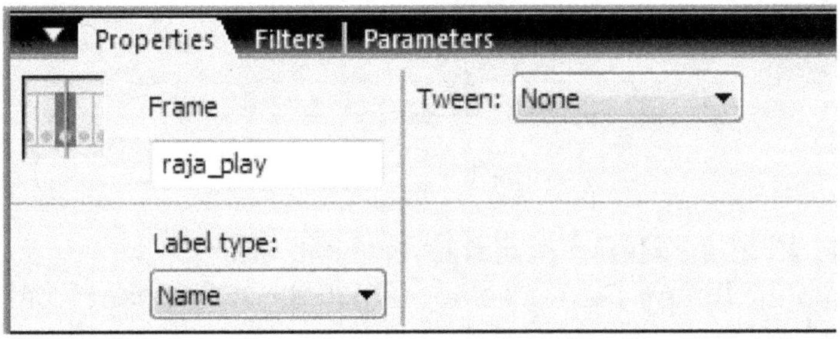

Double-click the **Raja** symbol to enter its editing stage. Select the button and open the Actions panel so you can see the ActionScript. Find the **tellTarget** code and click on the word **raja**. The **tellTarget** settings should now be visible. Next to **Frame** type **raja_play** and select **Go to and play**:

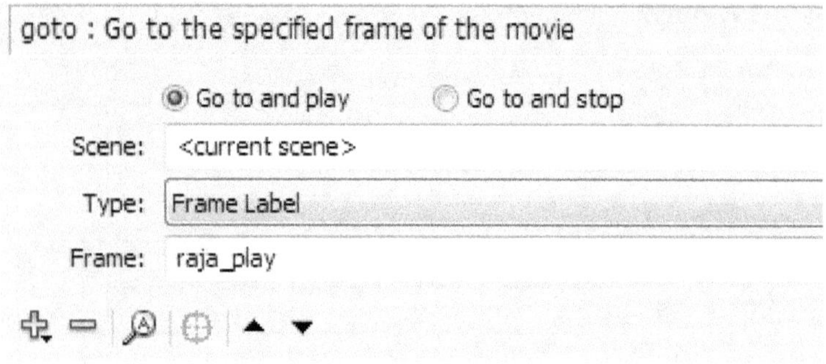

Test the movie (CTRL + ENTER). When you click the Raja button it should play the animation on your Raja scene. The picture should fade in from white and stop. If you notice on the Raja picture, it has the words *see more*. Let's make that a hyperlink that will take the user to another animation on the same timeline.

Add a frame to frame **60** for all the layers:

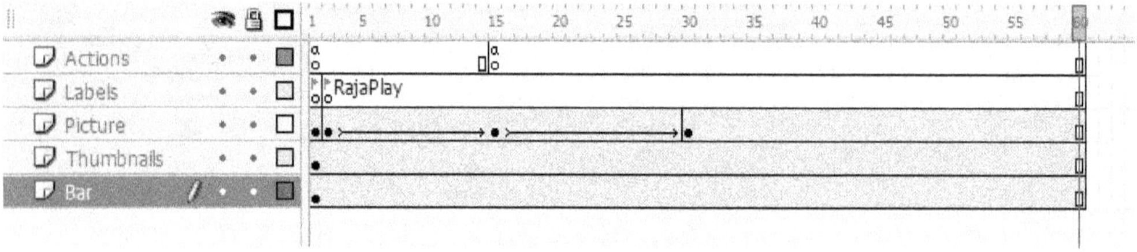

Select the **Picture** layer and click on the **New Layer** button; name this new layer **Raja Special**:

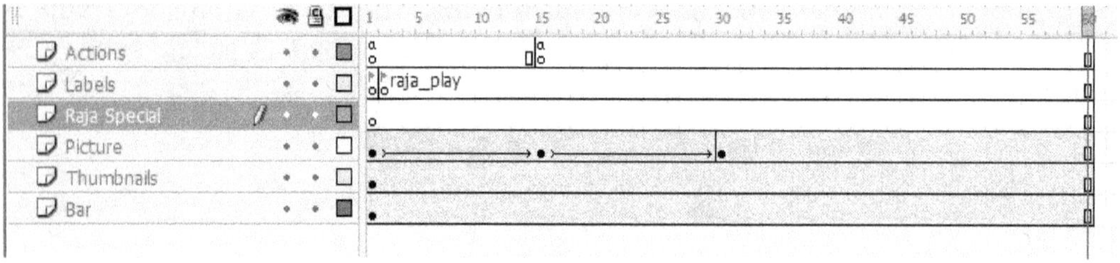

Create a keyframe on frame **45** of the **Raja Special** layer; next, drag **RajaSpecial.jpg** image from the library onto the stage. Open the **Align panel** and align the image to the top of the stage and center it:

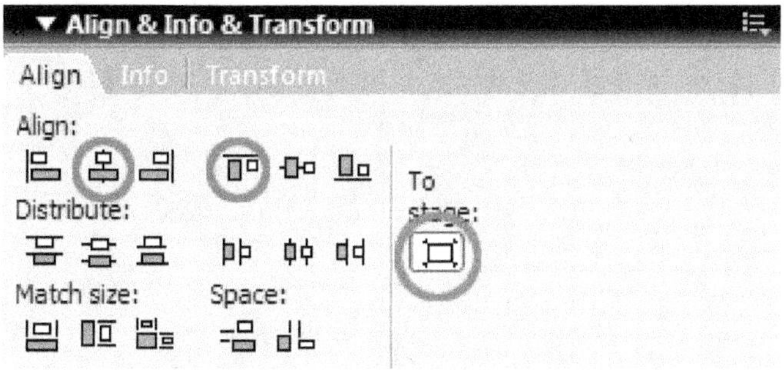

The picture should look like this on the stage:

Add a keyframe on frame **60** of the **Raja Special** layer. Click anywhere between frame **45** and **60** and go to **Insert**, **Timeline**, and **Create Motion Tween**:

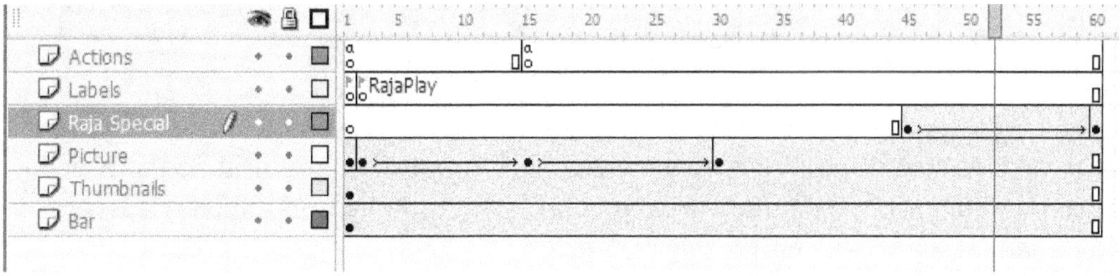

Next, select the keyframe on frame **45**. Select the **RajaSpecial** image on the stage. Open the Properties panel and change **Color** to **Tint**, and the **Color** to **white**:

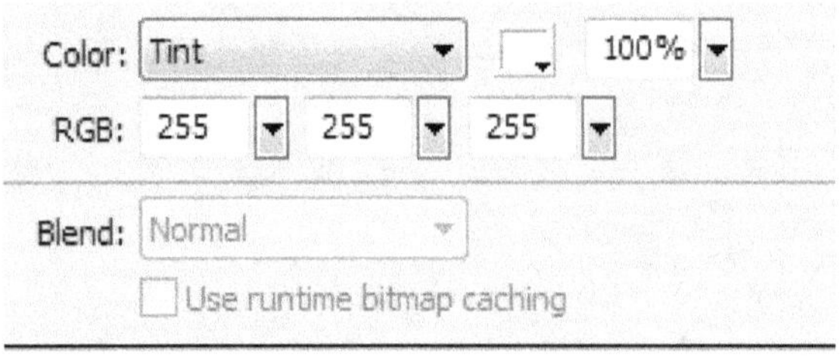

This picture will now fade in from white. But we need to add a **stop** code to frame **60** otherwise Flash will go back to frame **1**. Create a keyframe on frame **60** of the **Actions** layer and insert a **stop** code (**Global Functions - Timeline Control**, double-click **stop**).

Select frame **45** of the **Labels** layer and insert a keyframe. Open the Properties panel and type **raja_special** in the **Frame Label** window:

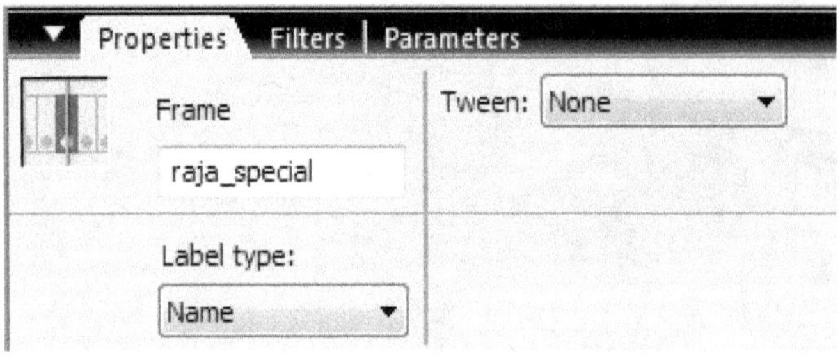

So now the timeline should look like this:

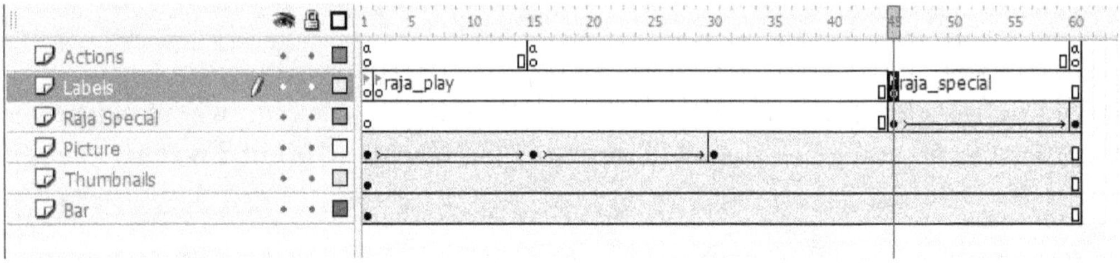

OK, we're almost done. We now want to create a button that will take the user to the new animation. Select the **Raja Special** layer and click on the **New Layer** icon. Name this new layer S**ee More Button**:

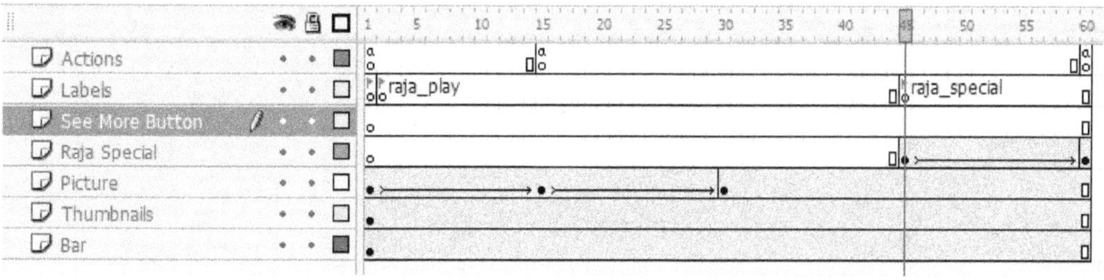

Create a keyframe on frame **15** of the **See More Button** layer. We'll create a button for this layer next. Grab the **Rectangle Tool**, turn off the **Stroke color**, and use any color for the **Fill color**. Create a shape over the **see more** text of the image:

Select this new shape and go to **Modify**, and **Convert to Symbol**. Name this new Symbol **See More Button** and change the **Type** to **Button**:

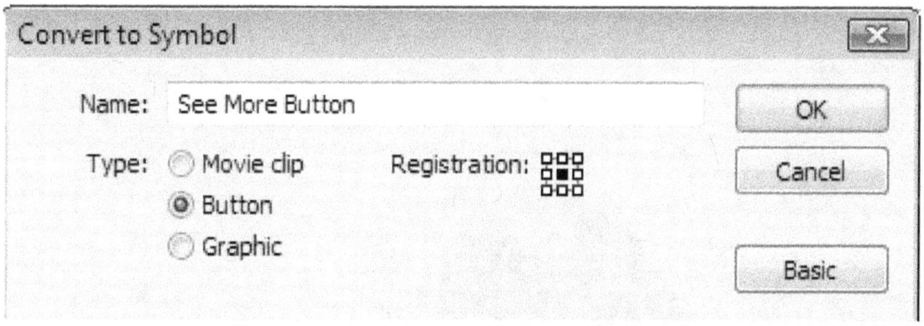

So now we have the button. We'll add the ActionScript to it now. Open the Actions panel and go to **Global Functions**, **Timeline Control**, and double-click **goto**. You should now see the **goto** settings. Change **Type** to **Frame Label**, type **raja_special** next to **Frame**, and make sure **Go to and play** is selected:

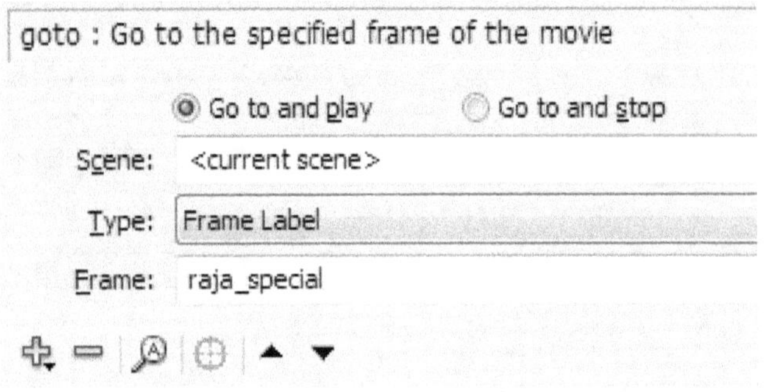

You may have noticed that the ActionScript for this button was pretty simple compared to the other buttons where we used a **tellTarget** code along with targeting the main timeline **_level0/**.

The reason for this is because you'll notice this new button is on the same timeline as the Label it is targeting. If the Label your button is targeting is on a different timeline then you have to use the **tellTarget** code as we did earlier in this chapter.

Go ahead and test the movie. Click on the **Raja** button, then click on the new **See More** button. It should take you to the new animation. The problem, of course, is that the new button covers up the See More text. Also, you'll notice that the **See More** Button is still active on the Raja Special Picture (roll your mouse over the area left of the woman's hands; your cursor should change to a hand icon showing that your button is still active). Let's fix these problems now.

Select the **See More Button** and go to the Properties panel. Change the **Color** to **Alpha**, and the percentage to **0**:

This button should now be transparent:

Next, go to frame **16** of the **See More Button** layer. Go to **Insert**, **Timeline**, and **Blank Keyframe**:

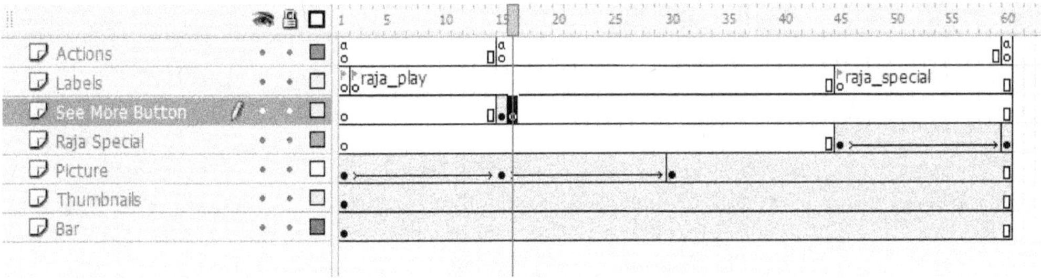

This blank keyframe stops your **See More Button** from being active on any frame but 15.

You'll notice that the **RajaSpecial** picture has a web address on it. Let's create a button that will take the user to this website. There really isn't a rajaspaspecial.com website, so we'll have the hyperlink take the user to www.yahoo.com.

Select the **Raja Special** layer and create a new layer. Name this new layer **Website Button**:

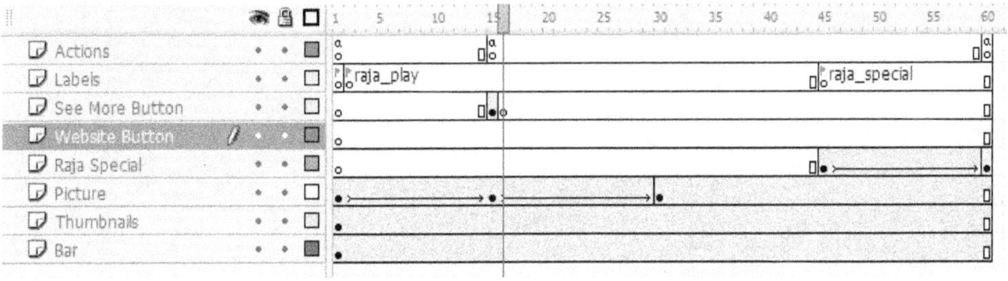

Create a keyframe on frame **60** of the **Website Button** layer. Next, grab the **Rectangle Tool**, and turn the **Stroke color** off. Use any **Fill color**, and create a shape covering the website address:

Select this new shape and go to **Modify**, and **Convert to Symbol**. Change the **Type** to **Button** and name it **Website Button**. In the Properties panel change the **Color** to **Alpha**, and the percentage to **0**:

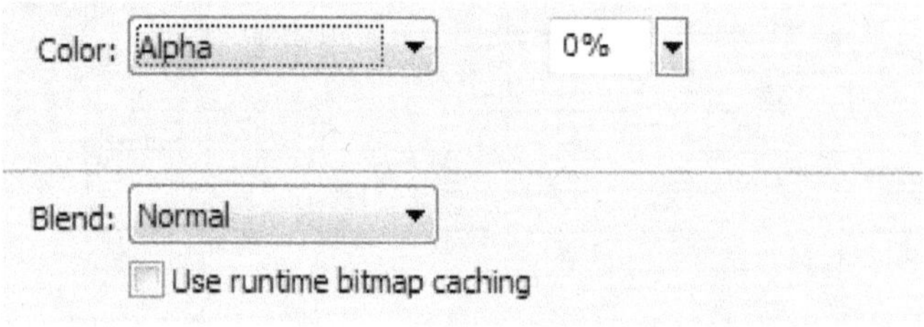

Next, open the Actions and go to **Global Functions**, **Browser/Network** and double-click **getURL**:

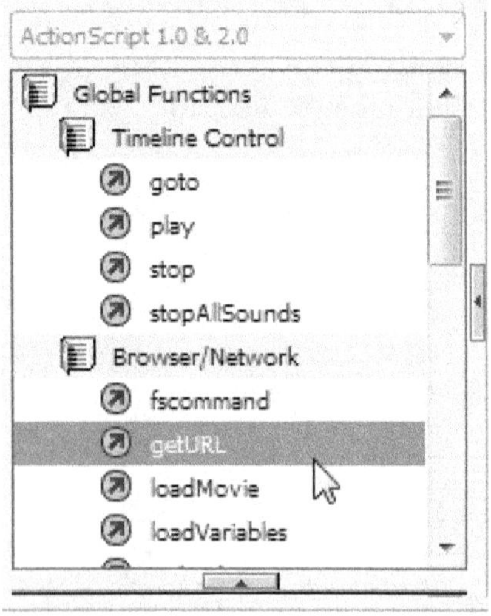

Next to **URL** type **http://www.yahoo.com**. Select **_blank** from the drop-down list:

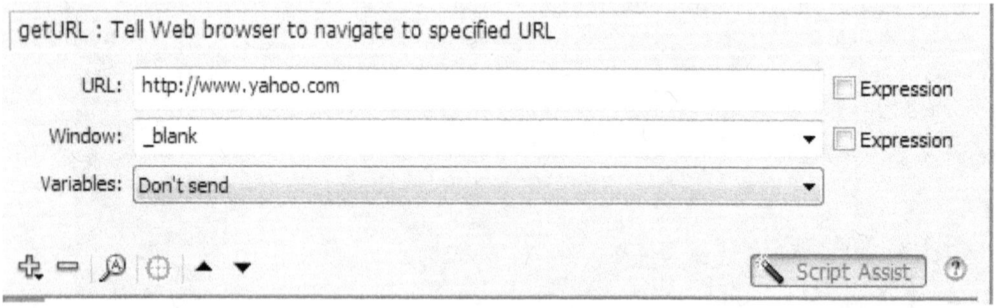

_blank simply means that the webpage you are targeting opens in its own browser window. If we don't select **_blank** then the website you're targeting will replace your website in the browser. I almost always use **_blank** whenever I use the **getURL** function. You'll notice that there are other options in the drop-down list, but the only one I've ever used is **_blank**.

Test this movie. The buttons should work fine now. When you click on the **See More** button of the **Raja** scene it should take you to the new animation with the new website button. When you click on the website button a browser should open to www.yahoo.com.

One more thing before we wrap on this chapter. What if we wanted the user to go back to the Home Scene from the Raja Scene (or any Scene for that matter)?

Let's do that now. Create a new layer in the Raja Scene and name it **Home Button**:

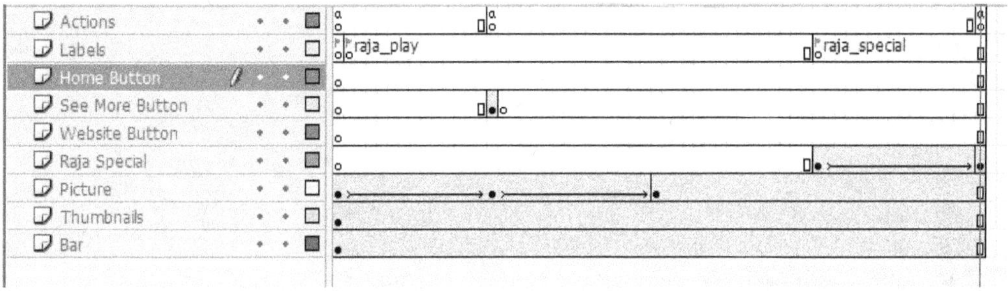

Select the keyframe on frame **1** of this new layer. Next, drag **HouseIcon.jpg** from the Library over to the stage. Position it so that it's on the top right of the stage:

While this image is still selected go to **Modify**, and **Convert to Symbol**. Change the **Type** to **Button** and name this new button **Home**:

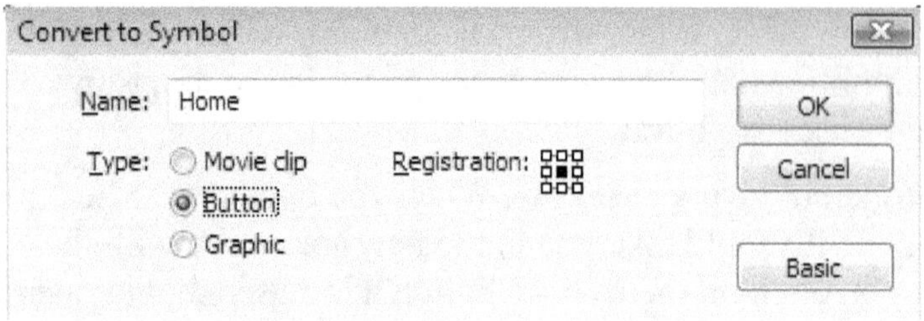

Hit **OK**. Let's add the ActionScript now. Open the Actions panel and go to **Deprecated**, **Actions**, and double-click **tellTarget**:

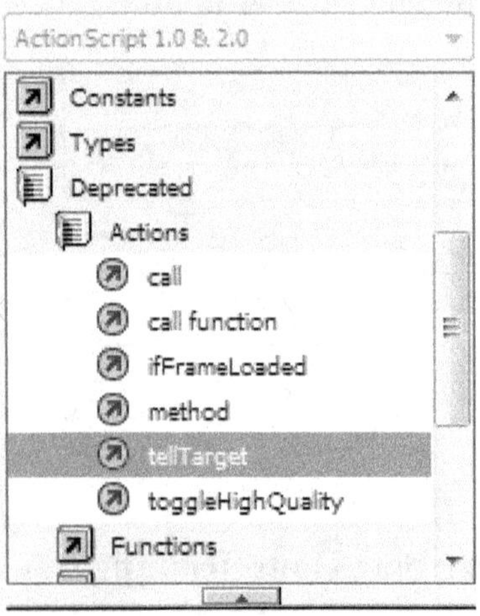

Remember what I mentioned earlier about targeting Labels? Since we're targeting a Label that's on a different timeline then we have to use the **tellTarget** code. If the Label is on the same timeline then it's a simple **goto** code. There is a Diagram at the back of the book that will help you if you get confused.

Next, type **_level0/** in the **Target** window. Next, go to **Global Functions**, **Timeline Control**, and double-click on **goto**. In the **goto** settings window change **Type** to **Frame Label**, type **home** next to **Frame**, and make sure **Go to and stop** is selected (since the Home Scene has no animation there's no need for **Go to and Play**):

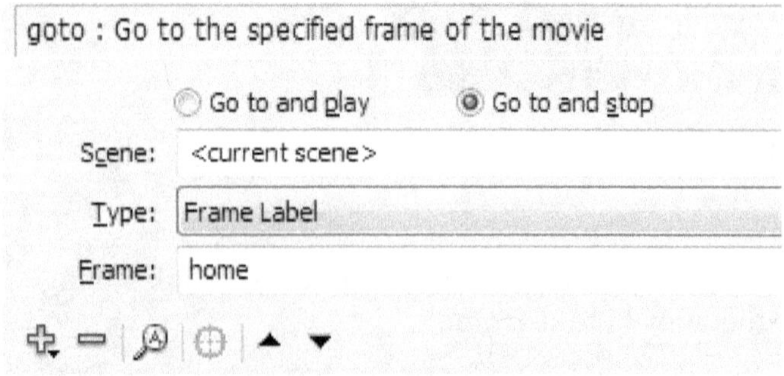

So the **Home Button** will take the user to the Label **home**. Flash will then search all the Scenes for the Label **home** (always make sure you don't have more than one Label with the same name). When Flash finds the Label **home** it will go there and stop. Next, we'll add a Label to the Home scene.

Go to the Home scene. Create a new layer and name it **Labels**. Select the first frame and open the Properties panel. In the Frame Label window type **home**:

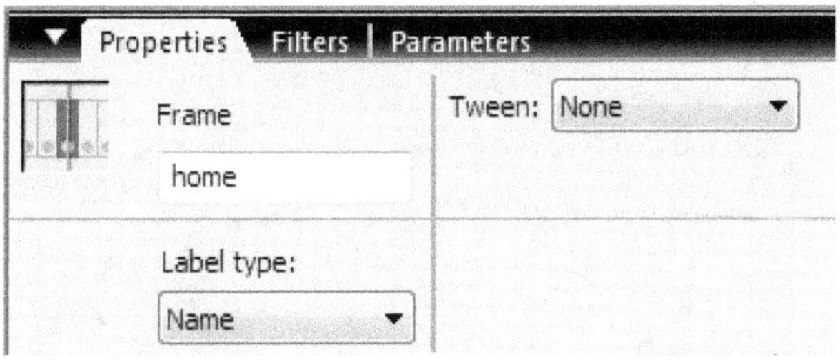

Test the movie. Select the Raja button and test the Home Button. It should take you to the Home scene.

If you would like to place this button in all the other scenes you can do that now. First, select the Home Button, then go to **Edit**, **Copy**. Open another Scene, create a new layer (make sure it's above all the other layers except for **Labels** and **Actions**) and name it **Home Button**. Next, go to **Edit**, and **Paste in Place**. Do that for every scene except for the Home Scene.

That's it! I hope by now that you have a better understanding of Labels and Scenes. The next chapter deals with the **Load Movie** function.

Chapter Four: Load Movie

Have you ever been on a website that had a lot of fancy stuff going on? Like videos, music, and exciting animations. But the website, even with all these bells and whistles, loaded almost right away. How did it load so quickly when it has video, music, and other Flash elements? The answer: the loadMovie function.

This is one of the most exciting functions of Flash. It is used in almost every high-end Flash website and I use it almost every time I develop a website. To see a website that uses the Load Movie function go to www.alicelwalker.com. This is a site that I created for the actress Alice Walker. When you reach the home page after loading this is what you should see:

If you click on the magazine button on the couch you'll see an example of a **loadMovie** function; when pressed, a Magazine Cover loads into the website. The cats on the chair is another example of a **loadMovie** function. The cats are actually a separate video file which is loaded into the web page using the **loadMovie** code. The fire in the fireplace is also loaded in separately.

If you click on the picture above the fireplace it will take you to the theater. Choose any of the selections that are on the remote. The remote will then go away and the video should start playing. Another example of **loadMovie**.

Basically, if we embed all these videos and other elements within the website it will take forever to load up. But, using **loadMovie**, we can load many of the heavier elements separately.

One last example. Go to www.jerryandersonsculptures.com. This is a website I created for Jerry Anderson, a world famous sculptor. After it loads, click on the Gallery button:

You should see four sculptures. These are all loading up using **loadMovie**. If you click on the American West sculpture you'll see more examples of the **loadMovie** function. This is a website that uses Scenes, Labels and a lot of **loadMovie** codes. This website loads up quickly since it loads all of the sculpture images separately.

So now you should understand why we need to use **loadMovie**. In the first project we'll be loading Movies into levels, then we'll be loading Movies into Targets.

Loading Levels

Open the project called **loadMovie.fla** located in the Chapter Four folder. You should see two buttons on the stage:

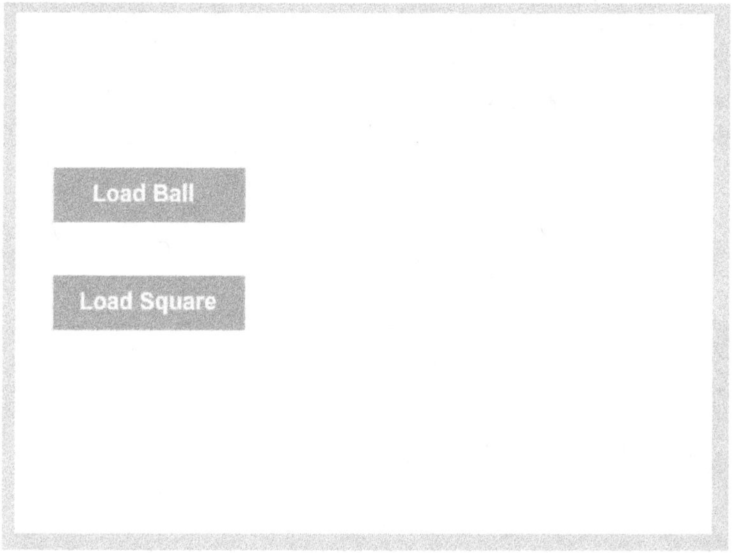

The first button will load in a ball file and the second button will load in a square file. We'll make those files now. Go to **File**, **New**:

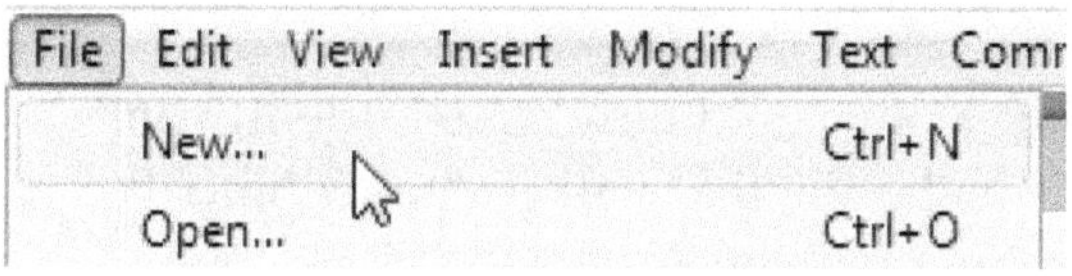

Select **Flash File (ActionScript 2.0)**:

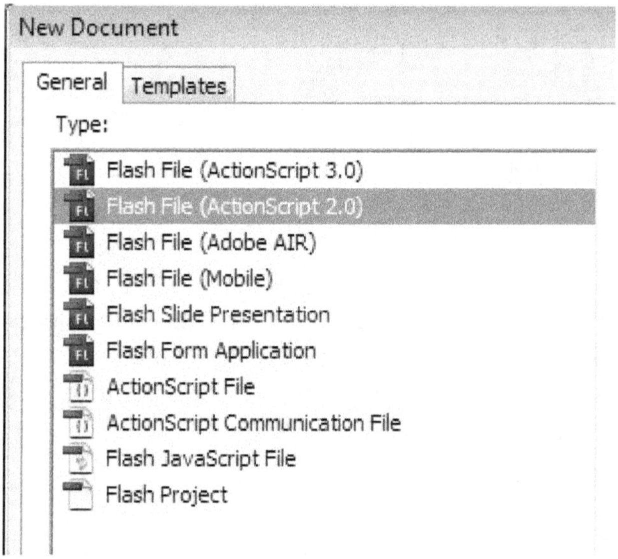

Next, go to **File**, **Save** and make sure you save it in the Chapter Four folder. Name this file **Ball**. Select the **Layer 1** layer and rename it **Ball**. Next, select the first frame of this layer and grab the **Oval Tool**. Turn the **Stroke color** off and select **red** for the **Fill color**. Create a large circle in the middle of the stage similar to this:

Let's publish this file. Go to **File**, **Publish**. You should now have a file in your Chapter Four folder called **Ball.swf**. This is the file that will be loaded into the **loadMovie.fla** project. Save this file by going to **File**, **Save**.

Go to **File**, **Save As**. Save this file as **Square.fla**. The tab above the timeline should now reflect this new name:

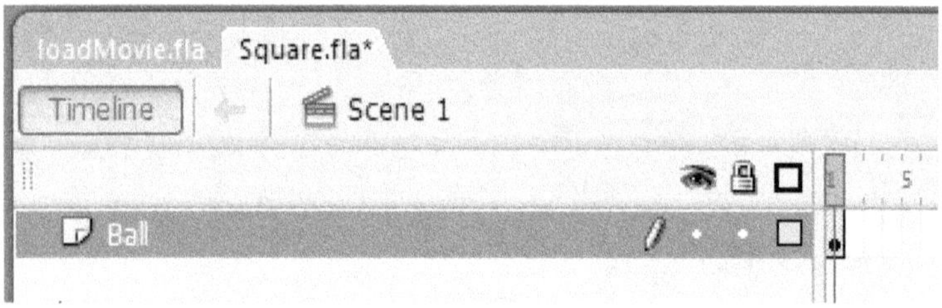

Change the name of the layer to **Square**. Delete the circle on the stage and select the **Rectangle Tool**; turn **Stroke color** off, and select **blue** for the **Fill color**. Next, create a large square in the middle of the stage like this (remember to hold down SHIFT to make a perfect square):

Just as with the Ball file, go to **File**, **Publish**. You should now have a **Square.swf** file in your Chapter Four folder. You can close this file now.

Go back to the **loadMovie.fla** file. Select the **Load Ball** Button. We're now going to add the ActionScript that loads in the **Ball** file. Open the Actions panel and make sure Script Assist is still turned on. Go to **Global Functions**, **Browser/Network**, and double-click **loadMovie**:

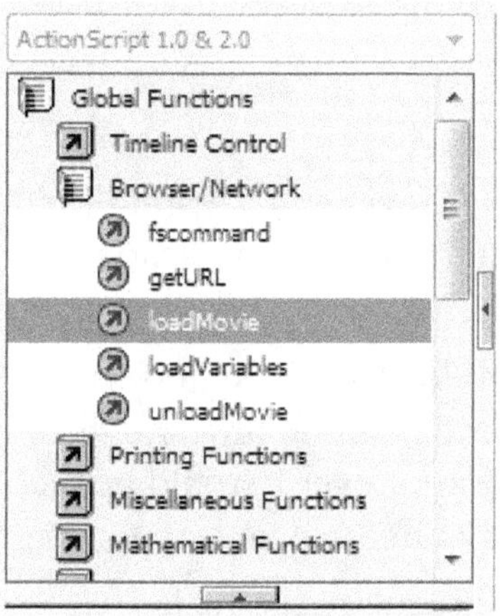

You should now see the **loadMovie** settings window. Type **Ball.swf** next to **URL** and make sure the **Location** is **Level 1**:

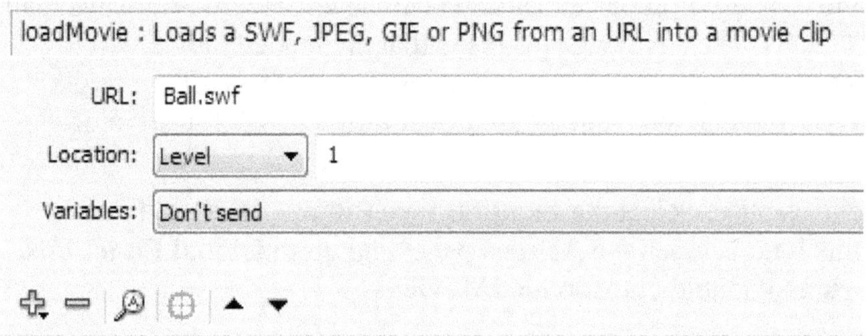

Test your movie. Click on the **Load Ball** button and the circle you created should now show up. If you made it large enough it may even cover part of the buttons like this:

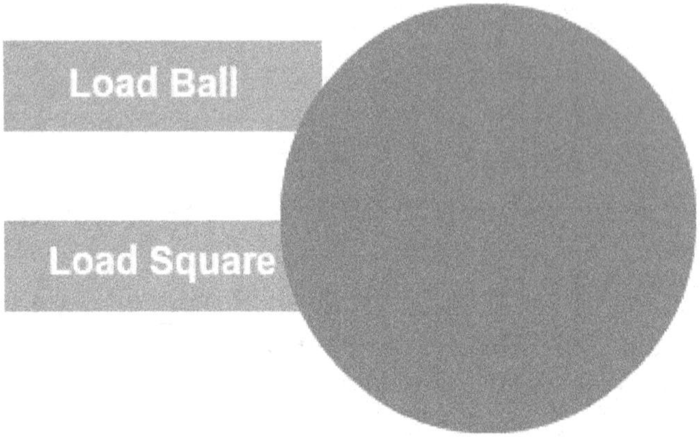

When you use loadMovie you can load a file either on a **Level** or a **Target**. We'll be working with Levels in this exercise and the next exercise we'll use Targets. Here is the difference between the two:

Levels: When you select Levels you have the option to load a Movie into any Level from 1-99. Think of levels like stories of a house. The Main timeline, the one we've been working on, is Level 0 (or the foundation). Level 1 would be the next story on the house, Level 2 would be the next story after that and so on.

So if we were to load the **Ball.swf** into Level 0, it would replace the main timeline. If you want to try it, change 1 to 0 in the Location window.

Targets: Loading movies into a Target is my favorite way of loading in movies. If you have a Movie clip on your stage you can tell the button to load the **Ball.swf** file into this Movie clip; it will replace the target Movie clip. I almost always load my movies into Targets. The advantage of this is that the loaded movie will acquire the attributes of the Movie clip it's replacing. For instance, if the target Movie clip has a red tint then the loaded movie will turn red. We'll learn more about this in the next exercise.

Back to the Levels exercise. Select the **Load Square** Button. We'll add the ActionScript to this button. Open the Actions panel and go to **Global Functions, Browser/Network** and double-click on **loadMovie**:

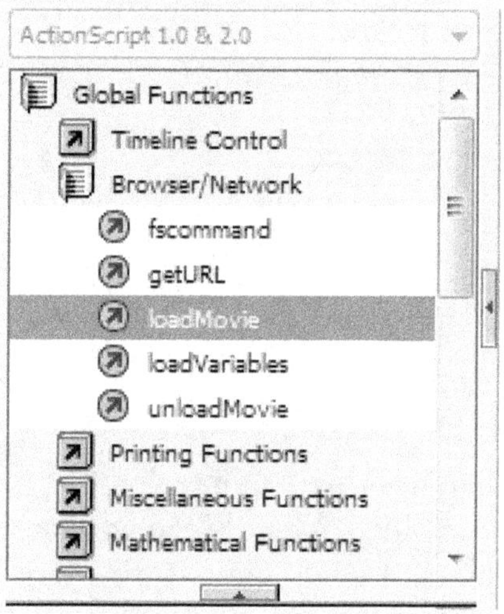

In the **loadMovie** settings window type **Square.swf** next to **URL** and change Location to **Level 2**:

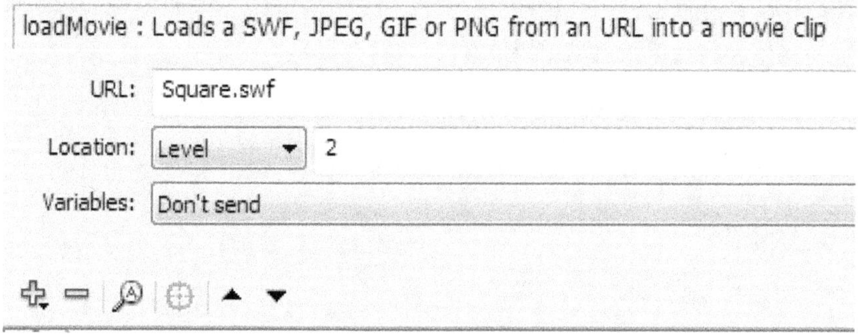

Test the movie. This time click on the **Load Ball** button first, then click on the **Load Square** button. You'll notice that since we loaded the **Square.swf** file into Level 2 that it covers the red circle which is at Level 1. In fact when you click on the **Load Square** button you may not even see the circle any more.

Let's try this. Select the **Load Ball** button and open the Actions panel. Click on the word **Ball.swf** in the Actions window; you should now see the **loadMovie** settings window. Change the **Level** from **1** to **3**:

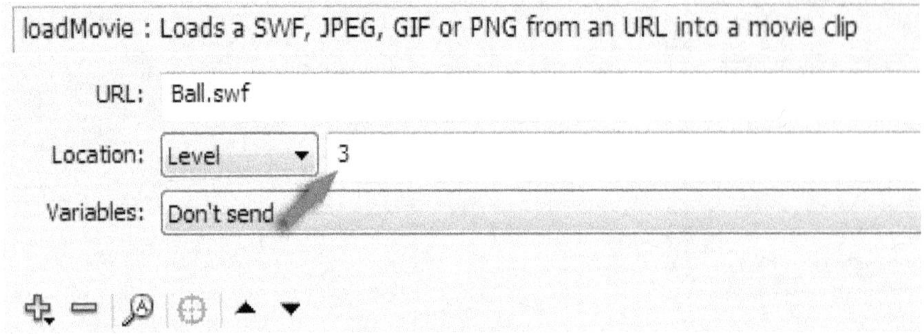

Test your movie. Click on the **Load Ball** button then the **Load Square** button. You'll now notice that the red circle is now above the blue square. Since we loaded the **Ball.swf** into Level 3 it becomes the topmost Level. Now, if we were to load the **Square.swf** file into Level 4 it would then, once again, cover the red circle.

So what would happen if you loaded **Ball.swf** and the **Square.swf** into the same Level? Let's do that now. Select the **Load Square** button. In the Actions window click on the word **Square.swf**. You should now see the settings window. Change the **Level** to **3**, the same as the **Load Ball** button:

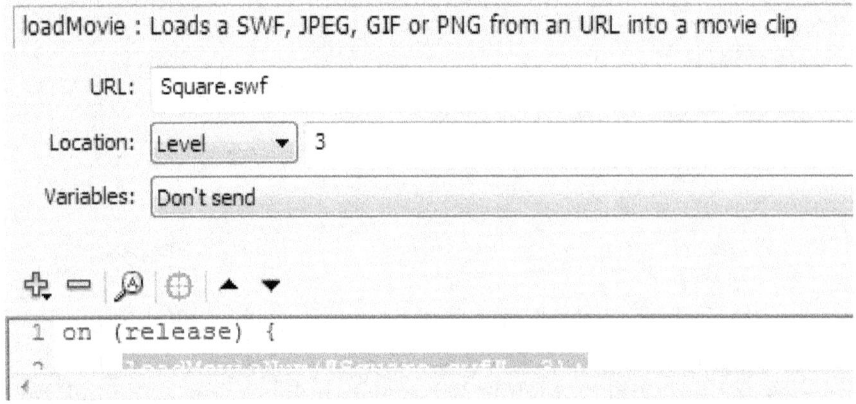

Test your movie. When you click on the buttons the loaded files will replace each other. If you click on the **Load Ball** button the red circle will appear; if you click on the **Load Square** button the blue square will replace the red circle and so on. I use this quite often. If you look at the website: www.jerryandersonsculptures.com again and go to Gallery. Select any one of the categories and go through the different pieces. All of the Gallery pieces are loading into Level 1 so they all replace each other.

What if we want to get rid of a movie that loads into a Level? For instance, if we load in the movie **Ball.swf** into a Level how do we get rid of it? That's where the **unloadMovie** function comes into play. I'll show you how it works. Drag the

Unload Button from the library over to the stage. Position it under the other two buttons:

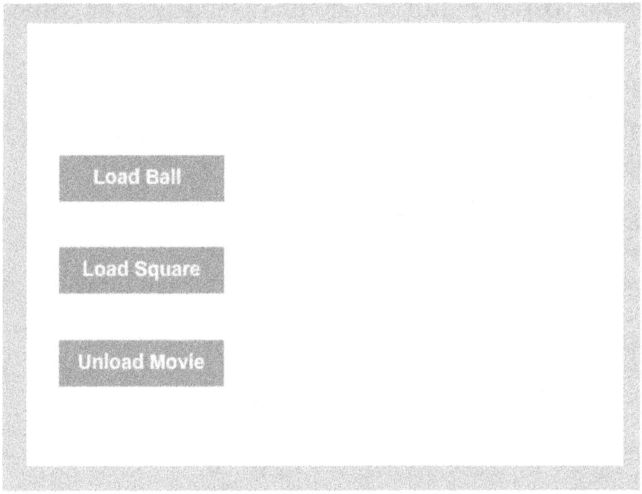

Select the **Unload Movie** button and open the Actions panel; go to **Global Functions**, **Browser/Network** and double-click **unloadMovie**:

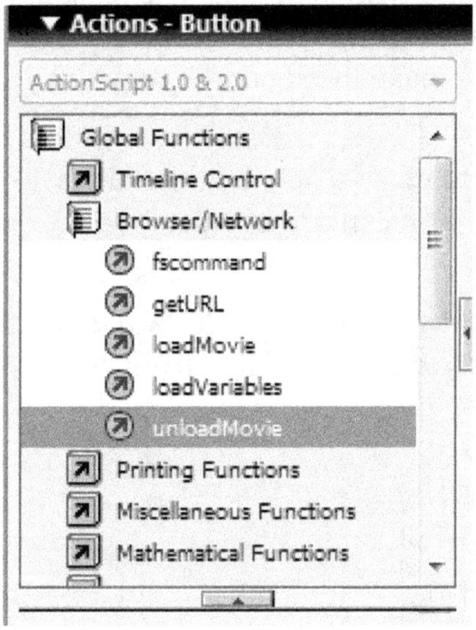

You will now see the **unloadMovie** settings window. Type **3** next to **Level**:

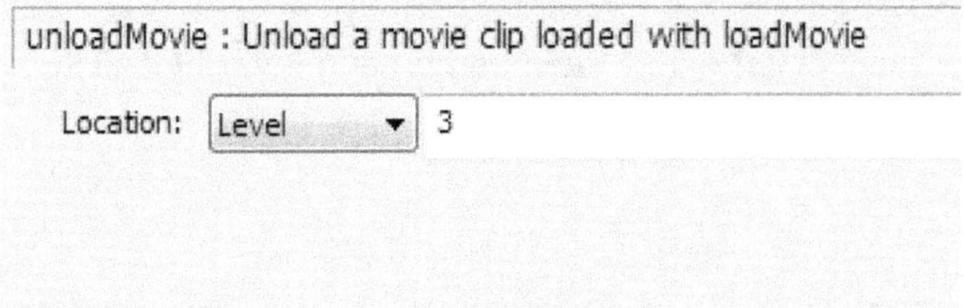

Whenever we press this button it will *unload* whatever movie is on Level 3. In this case the ball and square movies. Try it out. Test your movie and click the **Load Ball** button. Click the **Unload Movie** button. It should disappear. The same should be true of the square.

Select the **Load Ball** button and open the Actions panel. Let's have the **Ball.swf** load into Level **2** again. Click the word **Ball.swf** in the ActionScript and that will open the **loadMovie** settings window. Change the Level to 2:

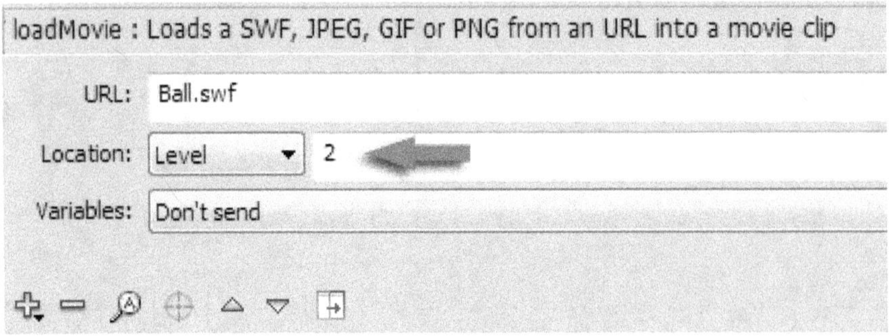

Test your movie again. When you click the **Load Ball** button and the red circle appears, you can't get rid of it by clicking the **Unload Movie** button. The reason, of course, is that the **Unload Movie** button only unloads movies on Level 3. So if you were to click the **Load Square** button you can make the square disappear by clicking on the **Unload Movie** button.

To make the red circle disappear you would have to make a new button that has ActionScript which unloads movies on Level 2, or you can add another unloadMovie action to the Unload Button.

We can also get rid of the loaded movies another way. Open the **Ball.fla** file located in the Chapter Four folder. Create a new layer and name it **Button**:

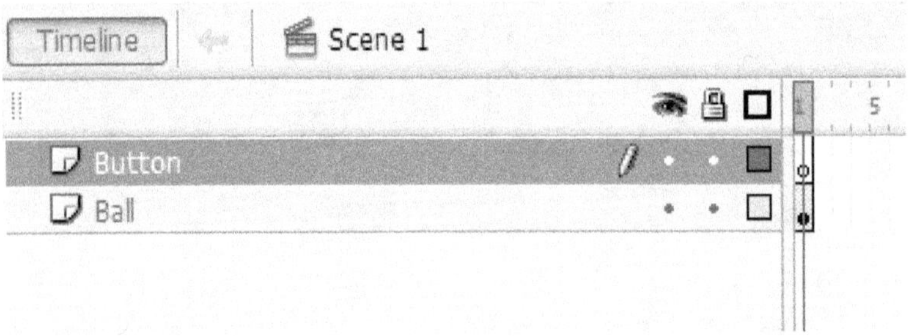

Select the **Text Tool**, change the **Fill color** to **black**, and type the word **CLOSE** at the top right of the red circle:

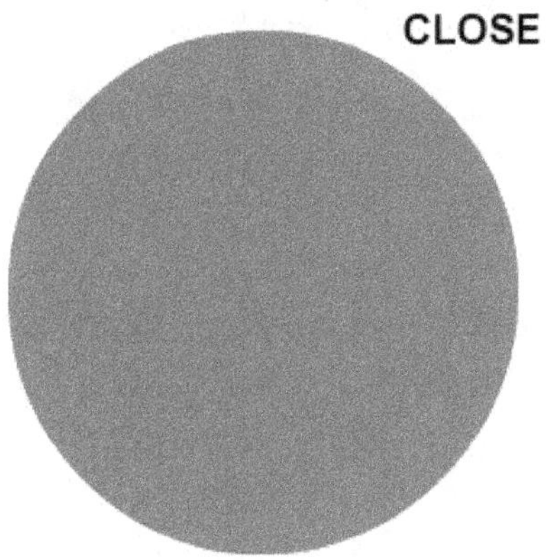

Select the word **Close** (you'll have to switch your tool to the **Selection Tool**) and go to **Modify**, **Convert to Symbol**. Change the **Type** to **Button** and name it **Close Button**:

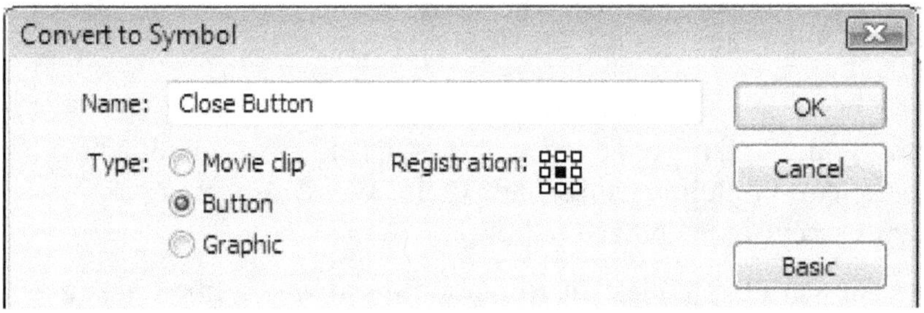

Hit **OK**. Let's add the ActionScript to this new button. Open the Actions panel and make sure Script Assist is turned on. Go to **Global Function**, **Browser/Network**, and double-click **unloadMovie**. You should now see the **unloadMovie** settings window. Type **2** next to **Level**:

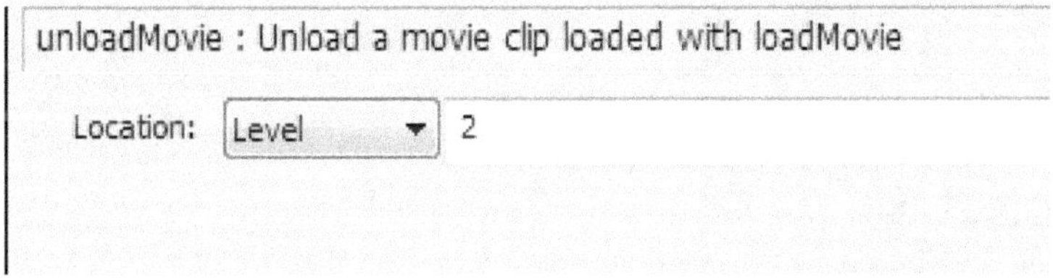

Go to **File**, **Publish**. This will update Ball.swf in your folder. Go back to the main file: **loadMovie.fla**. Test this movie. Click the **Load Ball** button and you should see the new updated red circle with the **Close** button. If you click the **Close** button the movie will disappear.

loadMovie Animation

Let's try a more advanced project using the **loadMovie** function. Open **LoadLevel.fla** in the Chapter Four folder. You should see a picture of Kolob Mountains:

In this exercise we're going to have a plane fly across the sky. We'll be loading this animation into the main timeline using loadMovie. We're also going to control the plane with a keyframe and also a button.

When you load in a file with the loadLevel command it's always a good idea to make the dimensions of the loaded file the same size as the main file. It helps with animating objects so you know exactly where the borders of the main file are.

Go to **Modify**, **Document**. Write down or remember the dimensions of this file:

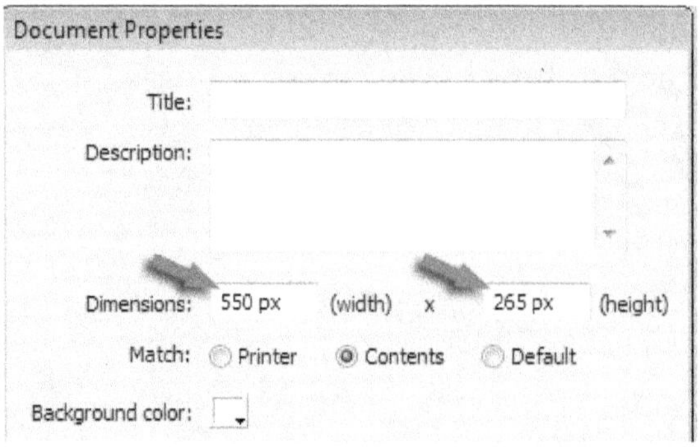

Next, go to **File**, **New**. Select **Flash File (ActionScript 2.0)**:

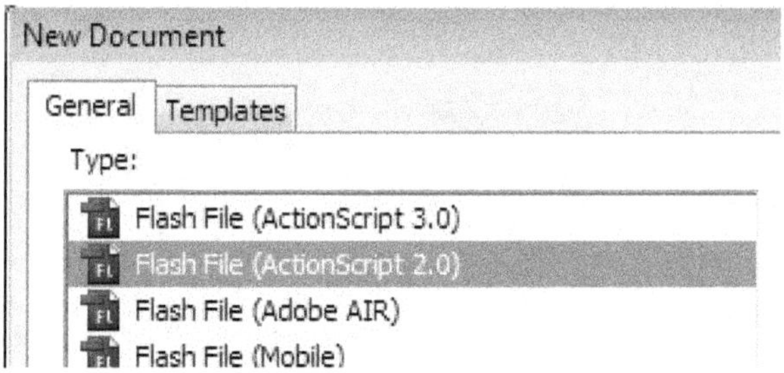

Next, go to **Modify**, **Document** and type the same dimensions as the main file. Also, change the **Frame rate** to **30**:

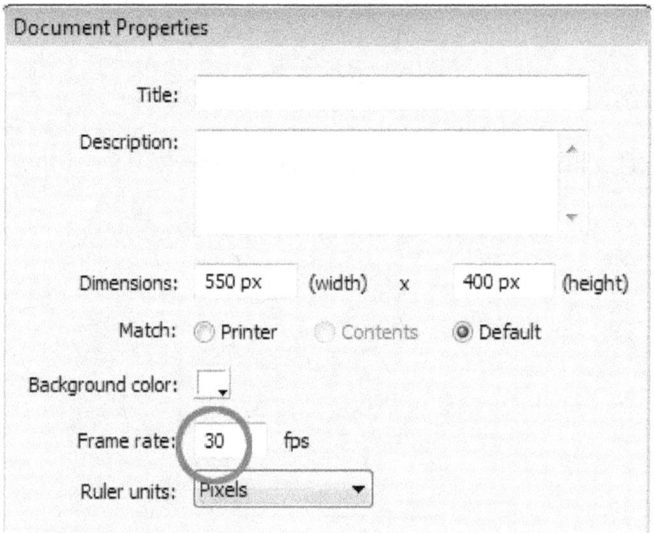

Hit **OK** when you are done. Go to **File**, **Save** and save your file as **plane.fla** in the Chapter Four folder.

Next, we'll import the plane image. Go to **File**, **Import**, and **Import to Stage**. Select **plane.png** file from the Chapter Four Pictures folder. Drag the plane image so it's off the stage at the top right:

Next, select frame **150** and insert a keyframe. Drag the plane image so it's off the stage at the top left:

Click on any frame between **1** and **150** and go to **Insert**, **Timeline**, **Create Motion Tween** (**CS4/CS5 - Insert, Classic Tween**). The timeline should now look like this:

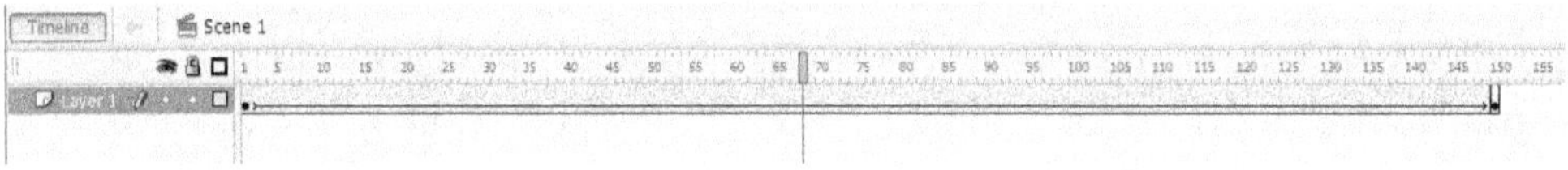

Test your movie. The plane should fly from right to left. It should then loop when it gets to the end of the animation.

Let's tweak the animation just a bit so the path isn't perfectly straight. On frame **75** insert a keyframe; then, click-and-drag the plane down slightly. Test your movie again and the plane should travel across the stage in a more realistic path.

Go back to LoadLevel.fla. We're now going to load in the plane.swf file using ActionScript.

Select frame **40** of the **Kolob** layer and insert a keyframe. Next, select any frame between **1** and **40** and insert a Motion Tween. The timeline should now look like this:

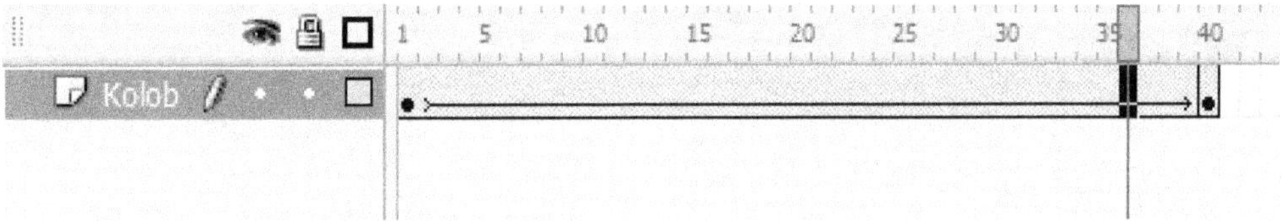

We're adding a Motion Tween because we'll be animating the Tint of this image. Create a new layer and name it **Actions**. Insert a keyframe on frame **40** of the **Actions** layer:

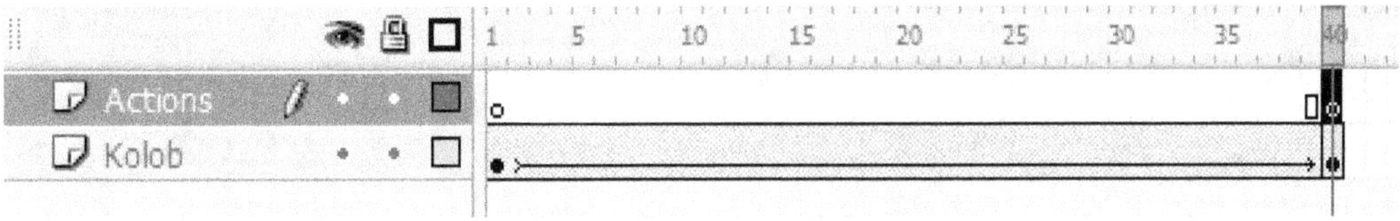

Open the Actions panel and make sure Script Assist is turned on. Go to **Global Functions**, **Timeline Control**, and double-click **stop**. This **stop** code will prevent the animation from looping.

Next, go to **Global Functions**, **Browser/Network**, and double-click **loadMovie**:

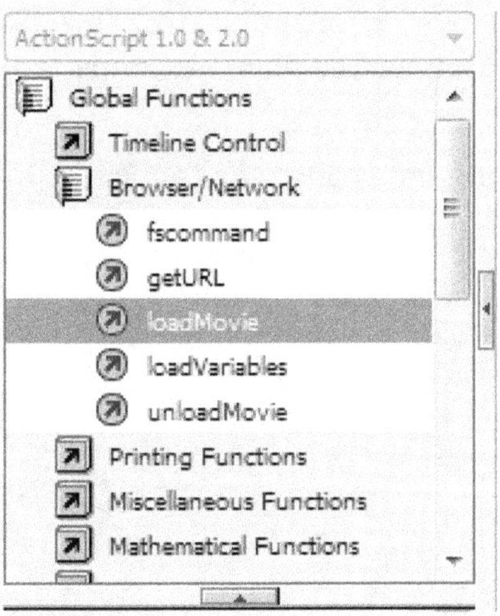

In the **loadMovie** settings window type **plane.swf** in the URL window. Make the **Location Level 1** (I never change the Variables setting):

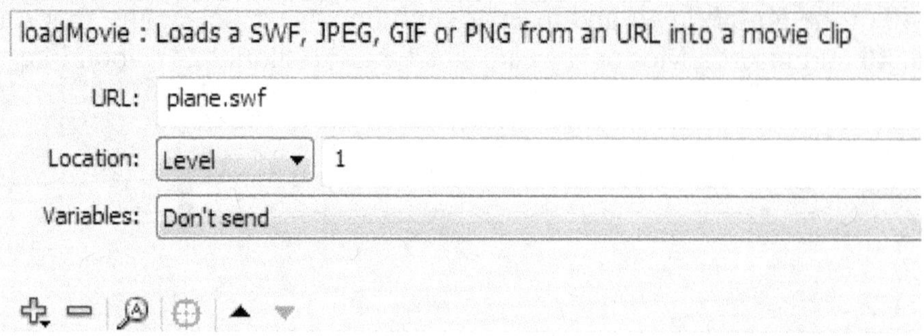

Before we test the movie let's select the first frame of the **Kolob** layer; next, select the **Kolob** image on the stage. Open the Properties panel and change the **Color** to **Tint**, and the **Color** to **white**:

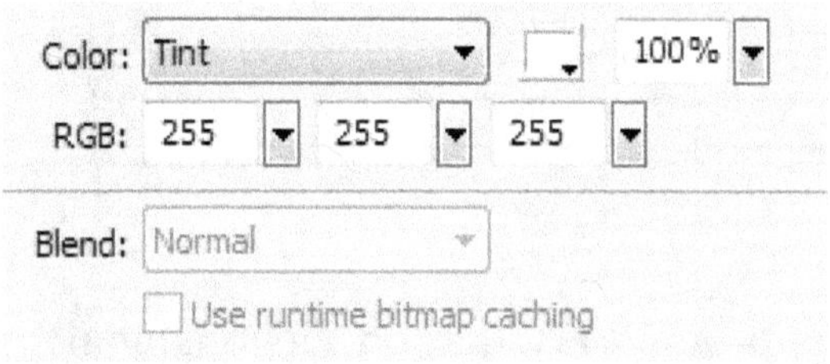

Test your movie. The picture should fade in from white. Then the plane will travel across the sky. Notice anything funny? The animation is a bit slow and stuttered. Even if the plane file that we're loading in is 30 frames per second, if we drop it into a main timeline like this one where the fps is 12, then the plane will only go 12 frames per second.

Let's quickly change that. Go to **Modify**, **Document** and change the frame rate to **30**:

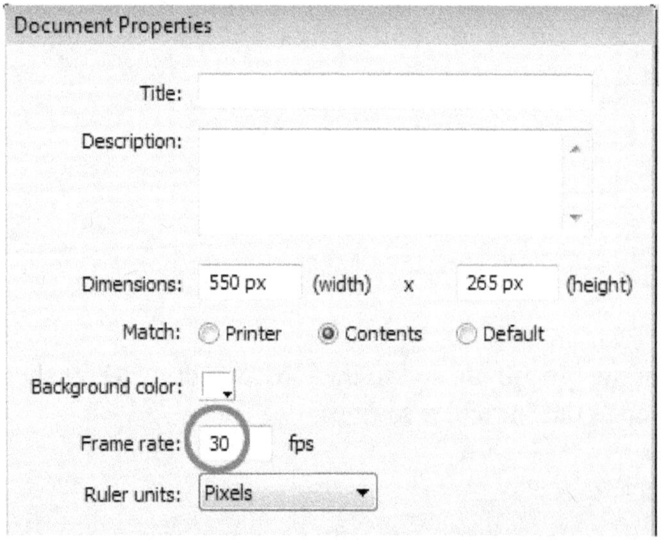

Test the movie again. The animations should be much smoother now. It's not much of a plane without sound though. So let's add a sound effect to the plane. Open the **plane.fla** file again. Create a new layer and name it **Sound**:

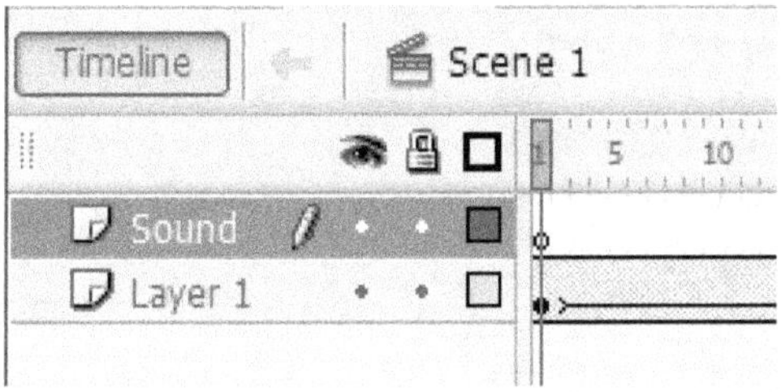

Go to **File**, **Import**, **Import to Library**. Select **cessna2.wav** from the Chapter Four folder. Click **Open** after you select it.

Select the first frame of the **Sound** layer, open the Properties panel, and select **cessna2.wav** from the **Sound** drop-down list:

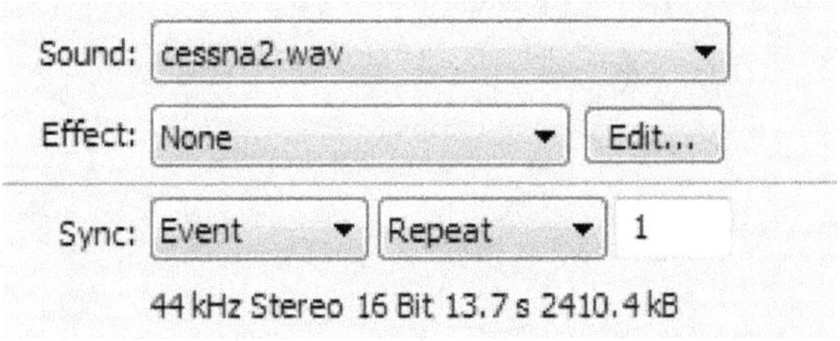

Test your movie. It seems a bit loud. Let's turn it down a bit. Click on the **Edit** button in the Properties panel:

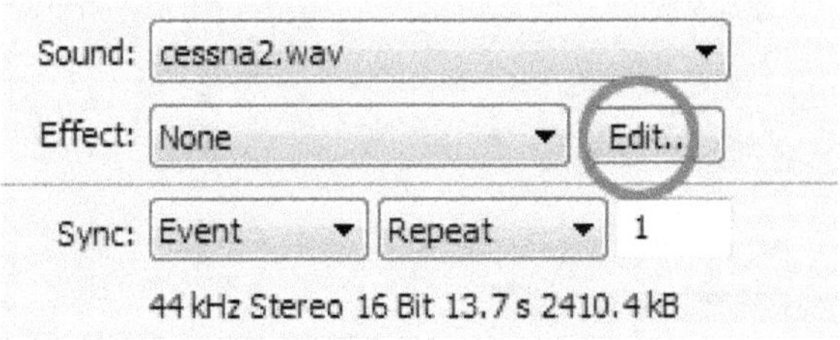

Next, select the Audio Handles at the top left of the audio graph:

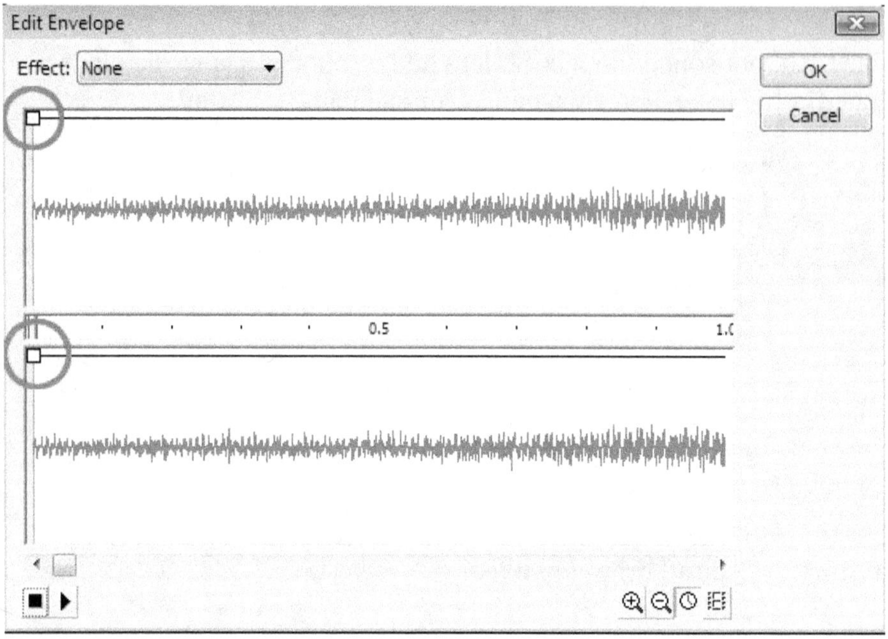

Drag both handles down about 50%:

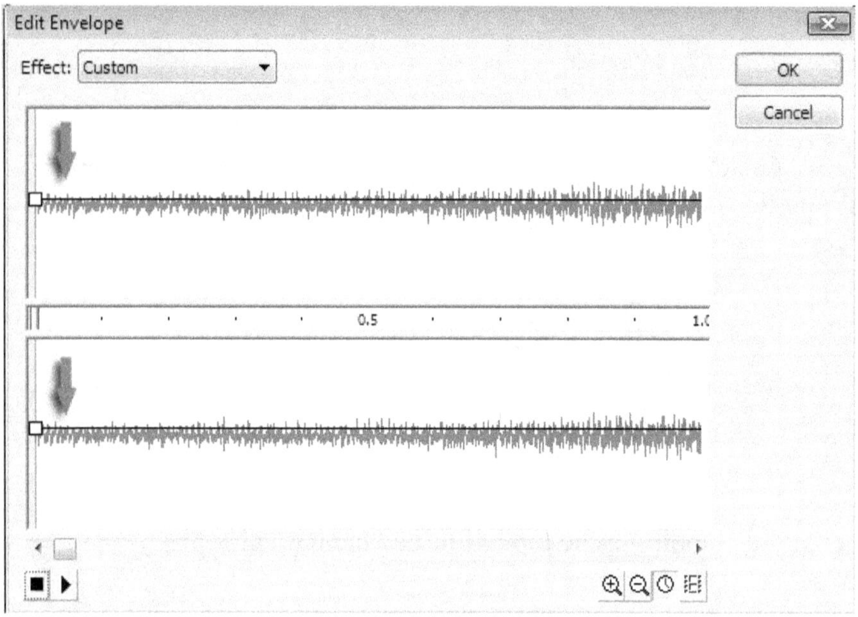

Hit **OK**. Test your movie again. The volume should be much better now. Save your project and go back to **LoadLevel.fla**. Test your movie. The plane should have the sound effect now. Let's create a button that will stop the plane mid-flight. Create a new layer and name it **Button**:

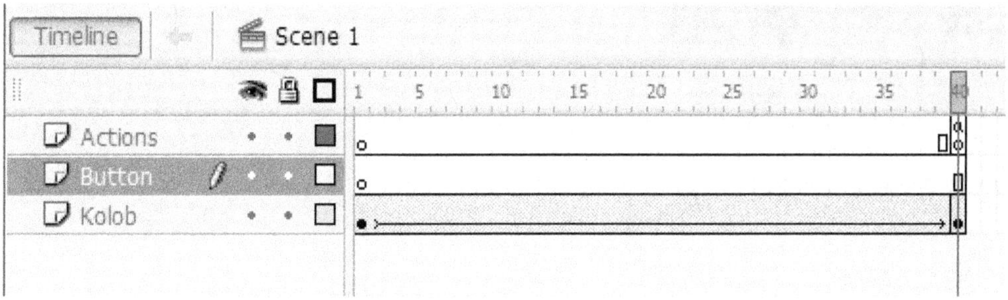

Select the first frame of the **Button** layer. Grab the **Text Tool**, change the **Fill color** to **black**, and type the word **Stop** on the left side of the stage:

Switch your tool to the **Selection Tool** and select the word **Stop** (you can lock the Kolob layer so you don't accidentally select it). Go to **Modify**, and **Convert to Symbol**. Change the **Type** to **Button** and type the **Stop Button** for the name:

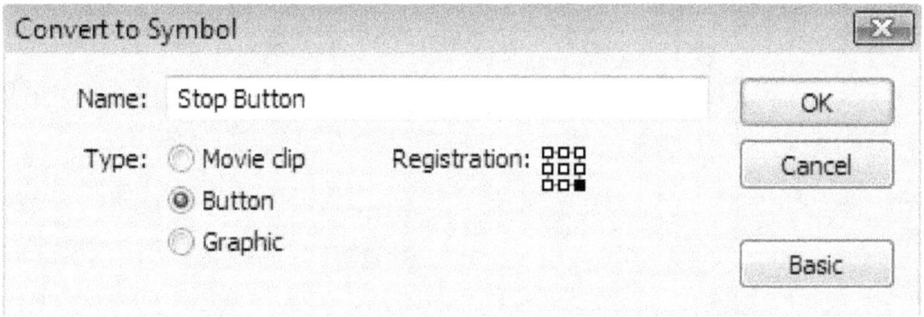

Hit **OK**. In the Actions panel go to **Deprecated**, **Actions**, and double-click **tellTarget**:

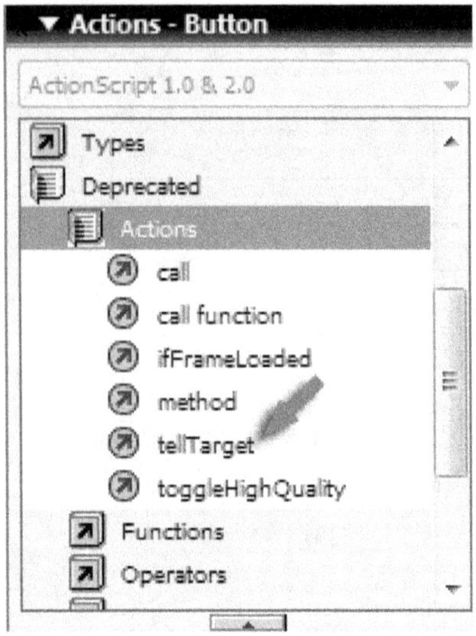

In the **tellTarget** settings window type **_level1/**:

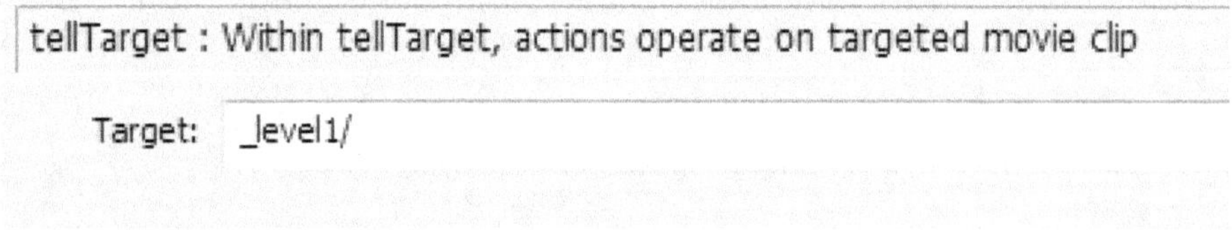

Next, go to **Global Functions**, **Timeline Control**, and double-click **stop**:

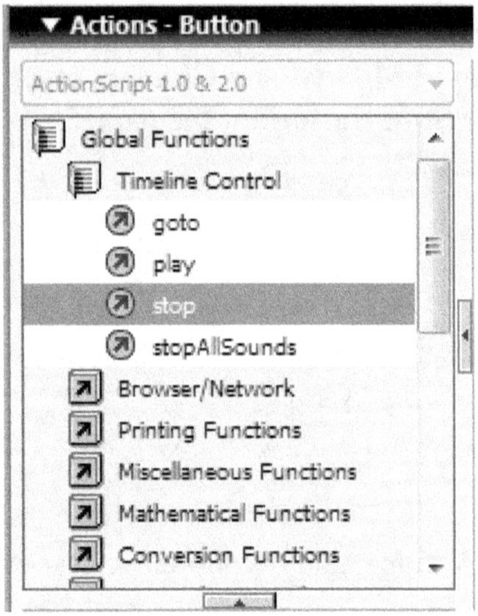

Test your movie. When the plane gets about halfway across the sky hit the **Stop** button. The plane should stop immediately. But, the sound effect keeps going. We need to fix that but first let's create the Play button.

Select the **Stop** button. Go to **Edit**, **Copy**. Next, go to **Edit**, **Paste in Place**. Flash will paste a copied button on top of the original button. Click-and-drag this new button so it's above the original:

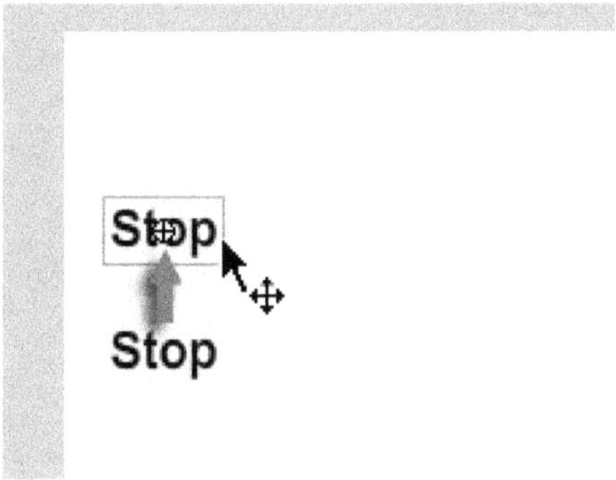

Select the new **Stop** button and go to the Properties panel. Click on the **Swap...** Button:

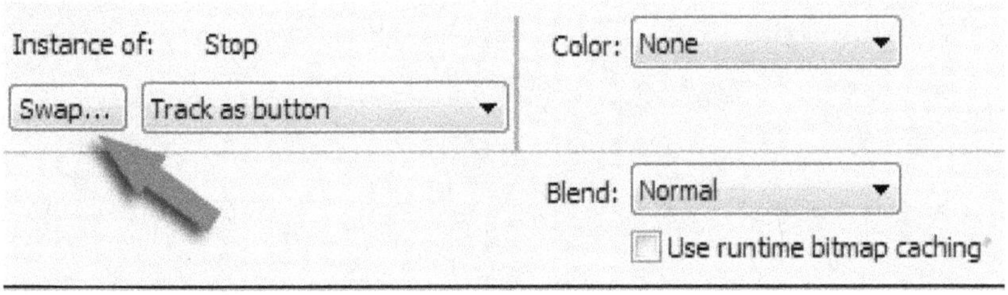

Next, click on the **Duplicate Symbol** button:

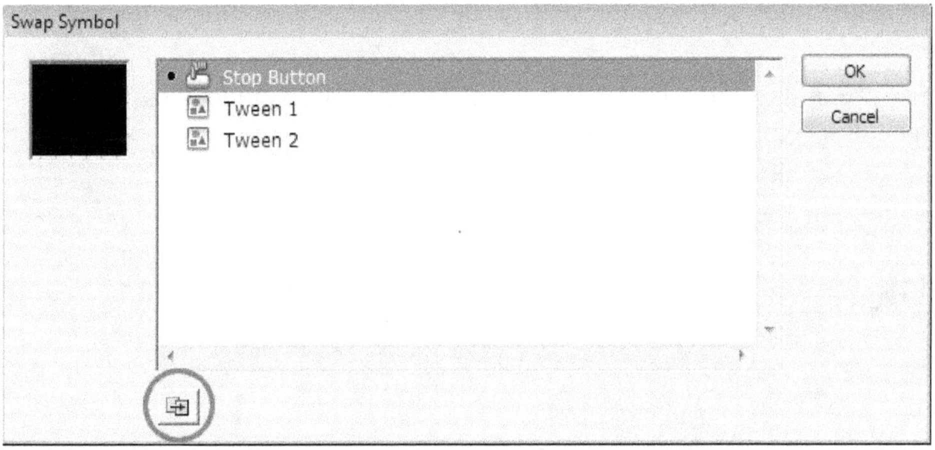

Type **Play Button** in the **Duplicate Symbol** window:

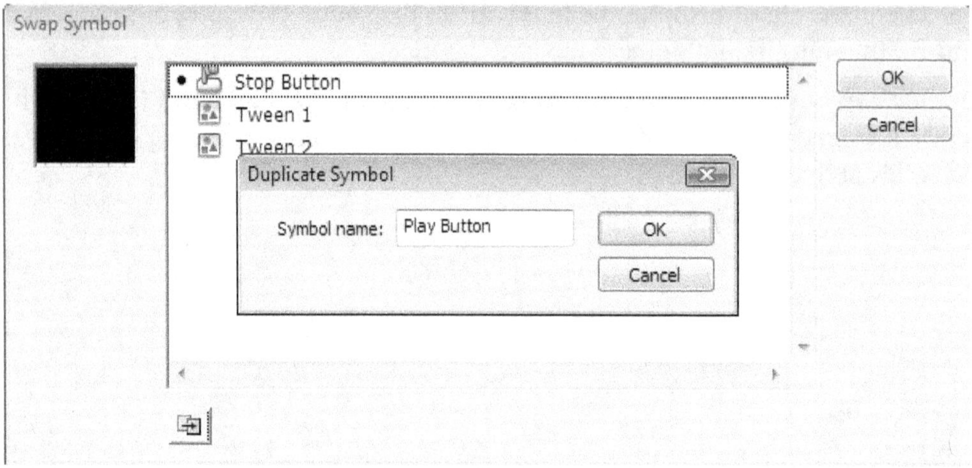

Hit **OK**. Double-click the **Play Button**:

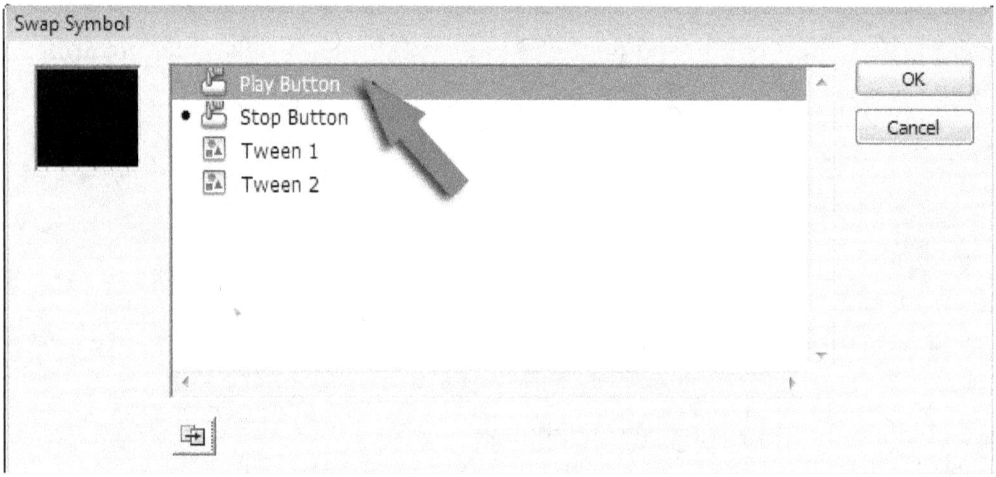

You can now edit this copy without affecting the original. Double click this new button to enter its editing stage. Change the text **Stop** to **Play**:

Go back to Scene 1. Select the **Play Button** and open the Actions panel. Since the code on this button is the same as the **Stop Button** we need to slightly tweak it. We want this button to tell the plane file (**_level1**) to play. So instead of creating a new **tellTarget** code we'll use the existing code but change the word **stop** to **play**. In the Actions window click on the word **stop** and hit DELETE. Click on the word **tellTarget** and go to **Global Functions**, **Timeline Control**, and double-click **play.** This **play** code will be inserted below the **tellTarget** code:

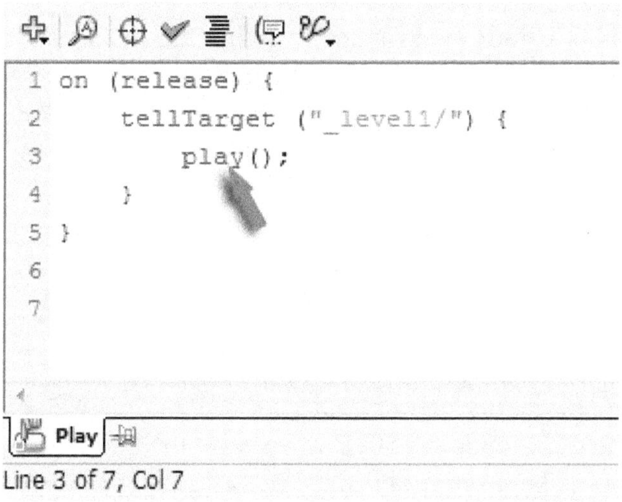

When the plane starts traveling across the sky hit the **Stop** button to halt the plane's voyage. Now, hit the **Play** button; the plane should continue on its path. But the problem is that the sound effect continues even after the plane stops. We need to fix that.

One thing you'll learn about working in Flash is that some of your time will be spent on figuring out why things aren't working, then figuring out ways to make them work. I've included a diagram at the end of the book which should solve most problems you run into. But for now, let's fix the audio.

Open the **plane.fla** file again. Select the first frame of the **Sound** layer. Next, open the Properties panel and change the **Sync** from **Event** to **Stream**:

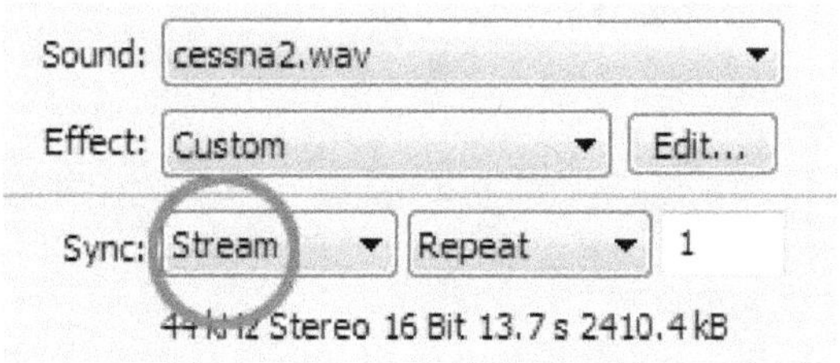

What is the difference between the two? **Event** means that the audio file will have to download completely before playing. Also, when you use Event it will be independent of your timeline which is why when we stopped the plane the sound effect kept playing.

Streamed audio doesn't download completely before it starts playing; it will start playing as soon as part of it downloads, similar to Youtube videos. One advantage of Streamed Audio is that it is in sync with the timeline. Meaning, when the timeline stops, the audio stops. When the timeline starts again, the audio starts again.

Go to **File**, **Publish**. Next, go back to **LoadLevel.fla** and test your movie. This time when you hit the **Stop** button not only does the plane stop but so does the sound effect. Much better! Hit the **Play** button and watch the plane continue on its journey. We need to make the animation a little more realistic; what if we had the audio slowly fade out as the plane ends its animation? Let's do that now.

Open the plane.fla file. Go to frame **250** and add a frame to both layers:

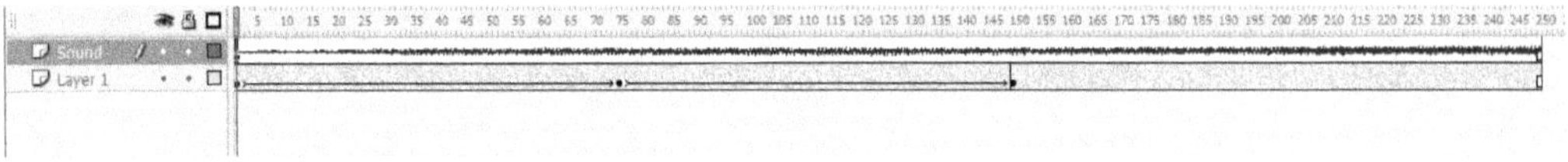

So, basically, the animation for the plane ends at 150. But we want the audio to slowly fade out from 150 to 250 to make it seem as if the plane is getting farther and farther away. To do this we need to edit the sound effect.

Select the first frame of the **Sound** layer. Open the Properties panel and click on the **Edit** button:

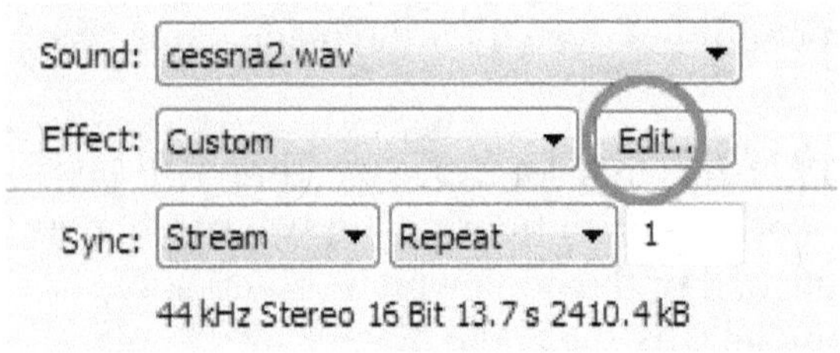

When the **Edit Envelope** window opens, select the **Frame** button:

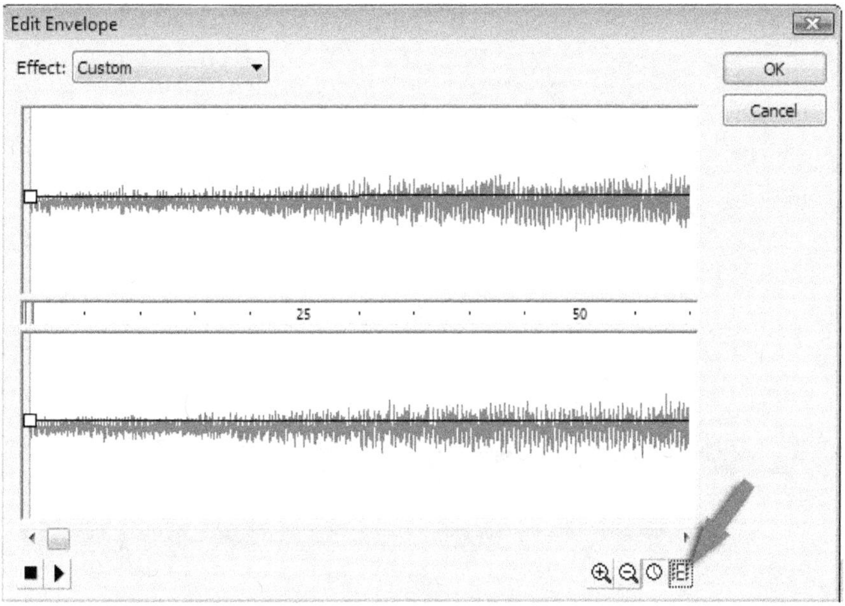

This will change the time display to frames. Click the right arrow of the horizontal scroller until you see 150 on the timeline:

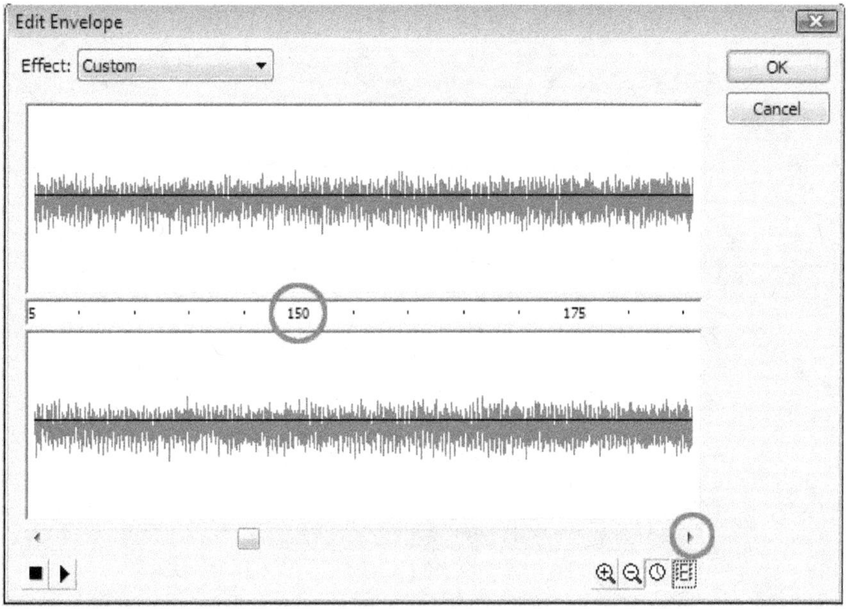

Next, click once on the line that runs through the top waveform; do the same thing for the bottom waveform. After you click the lines you should get handle boxes:

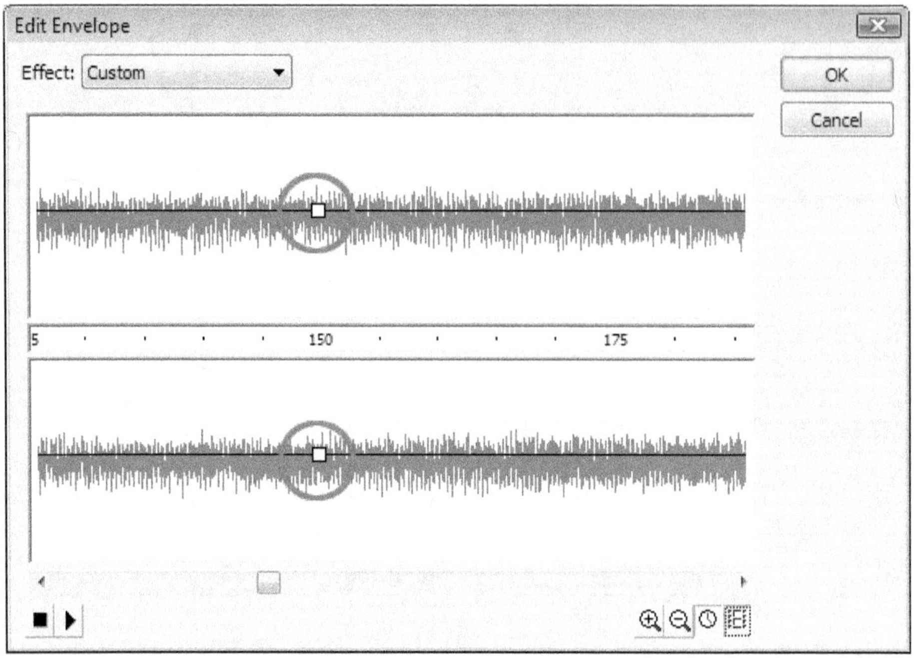

Next, click the right arrow until you get to frame 250. Click on the lines again creating the handle boxes; drag both handle boxes all the way down:

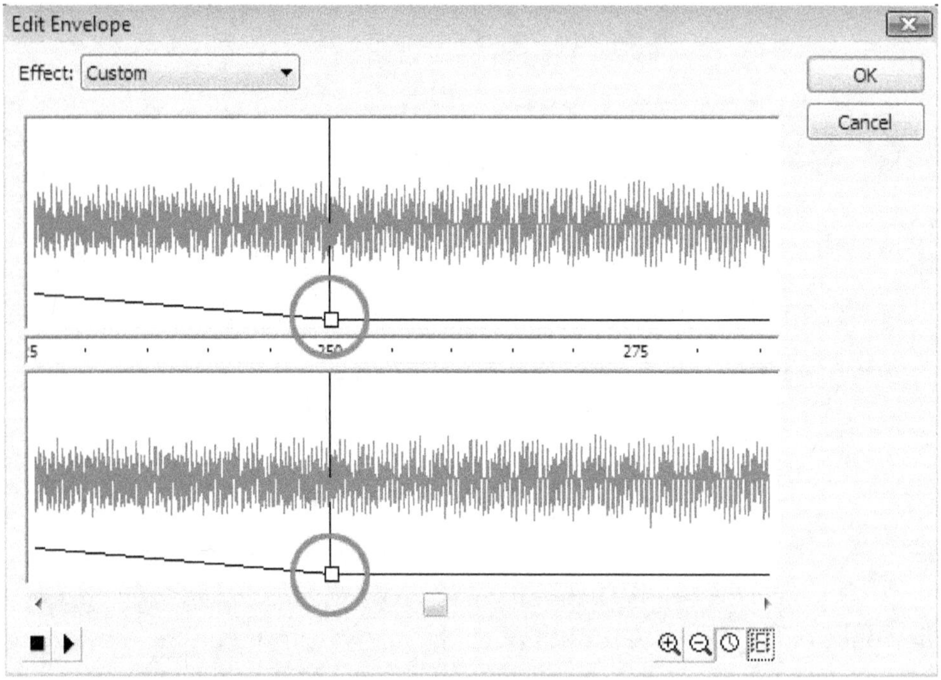

Test your movie. After the plane reaches the end of its animation the audio continues and slowly fades out by frame 250. Much more realistic. But now what if we were to put a ActionScript trigger on frame 250 that told the main timeline (LoadLevel.fla) to go to a specific frame? That would be interesting. In fact, let's add a new animation to the main timeline now before we add the ActionScript.

Open the LoadLevel.fla file. Create a new layer and name it **Lake** (make sure this layer is *beneath the Button layer*). Next, insert a frame at frame **80** for the **Actions**, **Button**, and **Lake** layers:

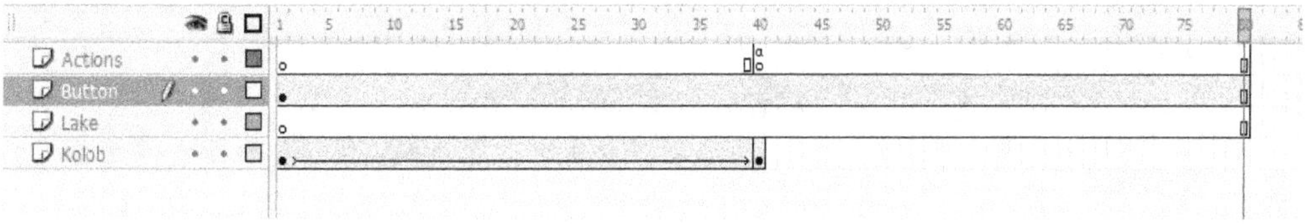

Insert a keyframe at frame **41** of the **Lake** layer. Drag the **lake.jpg** image from the Library over to the stage. Align the picture with the **Align tools**:

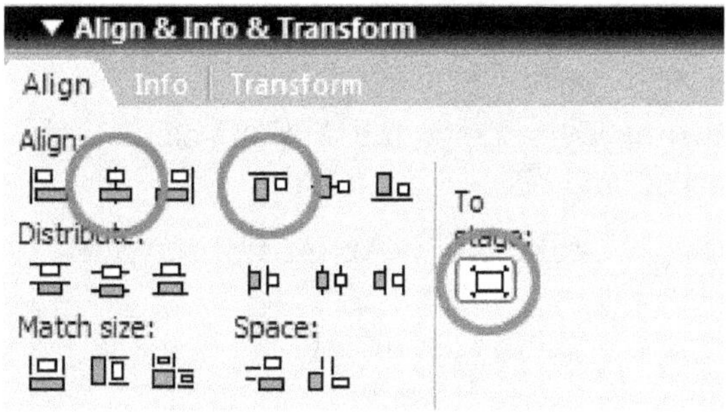

Next, insert a keyframe on frame **80** of the **Lake** layer. Select any frame between **41** and **80** and go to **Insert**, **Timeline**, **Create Motion Tween (CS4/CS5 - Insert**, **Classic Tween)**. Select frame **41** of the **Lake** layer and select the lake image on the stage; open the Properties panel and change **Color** to **Tint**, and the **Color** to **white**:

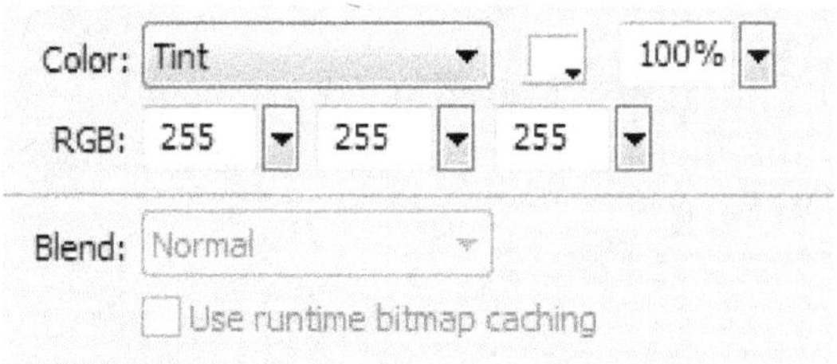

Since we're going to have **plane.fla** controlling the main timeline, we need to add a Label to this timeline. Create a new layer and name it **Labels**:

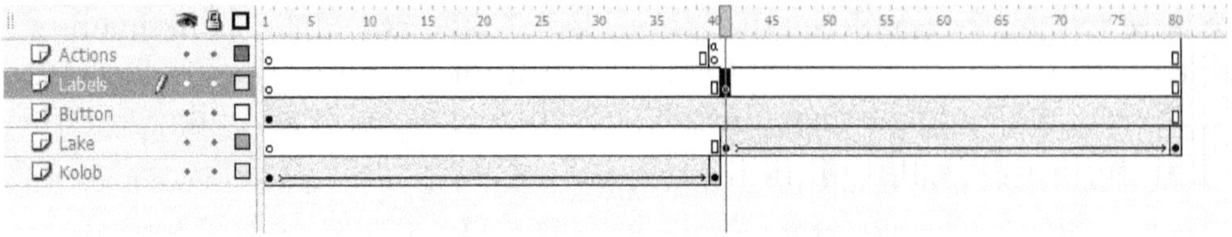

Open the Properties panel and type **lake** in the **Frame Label** window:

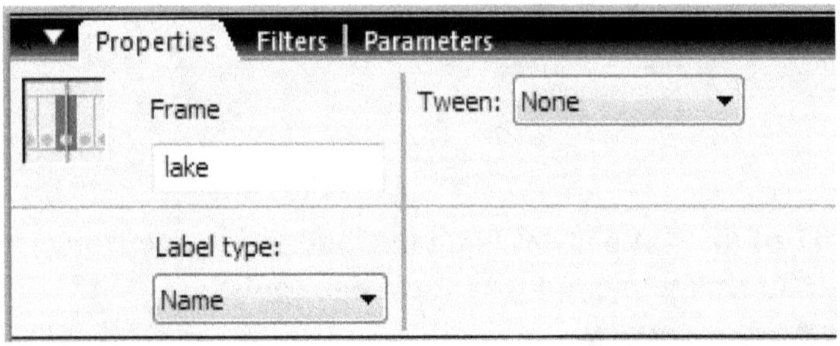

Insert a keyframe on frame **80** of the **Actions** layer. Open the Actions panel and go to **Global Functions**, **Timeline Control**, and double-click **stop**.

Go back to the plane.fla file. Create a new layer and call it **Actions**. Insert a keyframe on frame **250**:

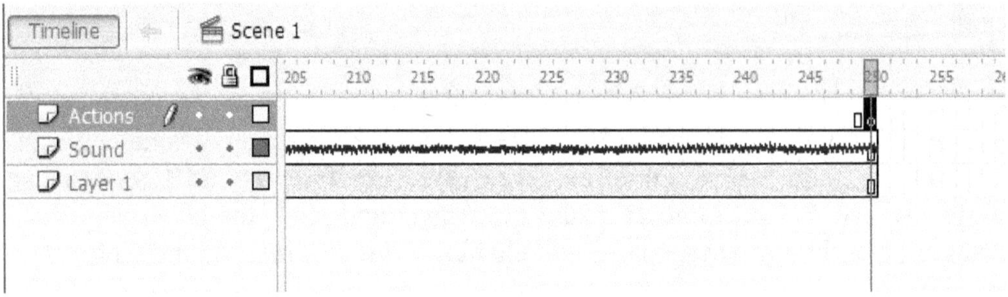

Open the Actions panel and go to **Global Functions**, **Timeline Control** and double-click **stop**. This ensures that this timeline won't loop. Next, go to **Deprecated**, **Actions**, and double-click **tellTarget**:

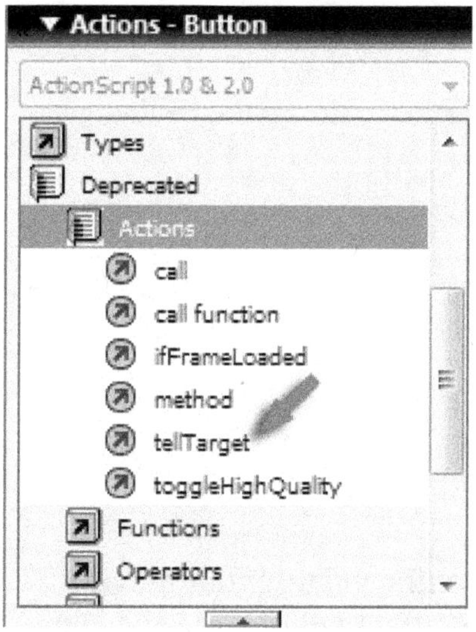

In the **tellTarget** settings window type **_level0/** next to **Target**:

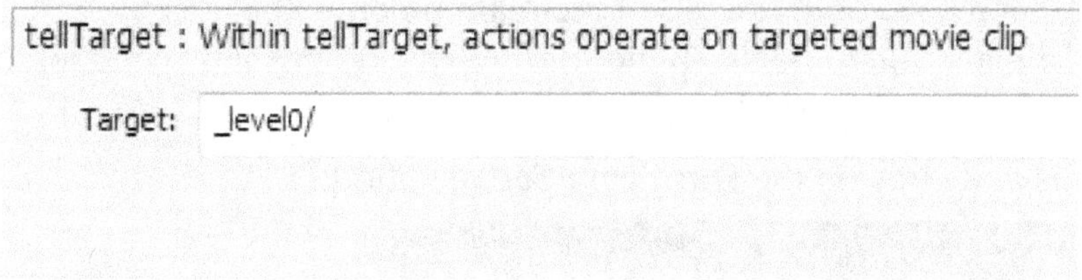

This code will target the main timeline. Go to **Global Functions**, **Timeline Control**, and double-click **goto**:

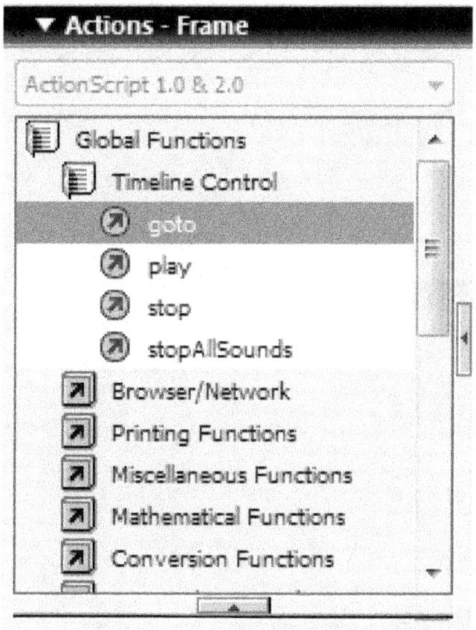

In the **goto** settings window we only need to change two settings. Change **Type** to **Frame Label** and type **lake** next to **Frame**:

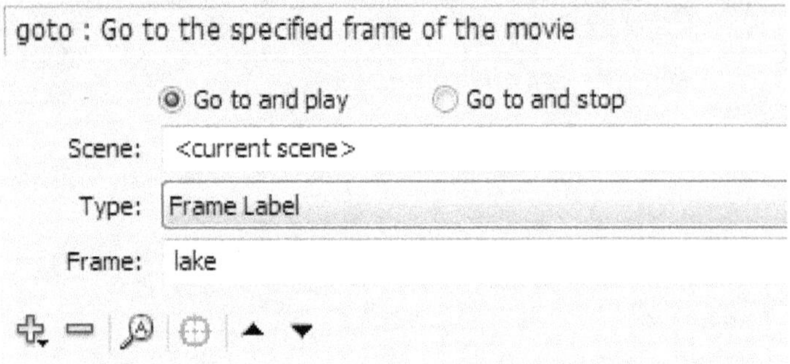

That's it. Go to **File**, **Publish**. Go back to **LoadLevel.fla** and test your movie. When the plane finishes its animation and the sound effect fades away, the main timeline should go to the **Lake** scene. But what if we want the plane to return when the lake scene appears? That's easy!

All we have to do is put a code on frame 80 of the main timeline that has commands telling the plane file to begin flying. Before we add this new code let's create this new animation in the plane file. Go back to **plane.fla**.

Open the Scene panel and click on the **Duplicate Scene** button:

Name this new scene **Plane Reverse**:

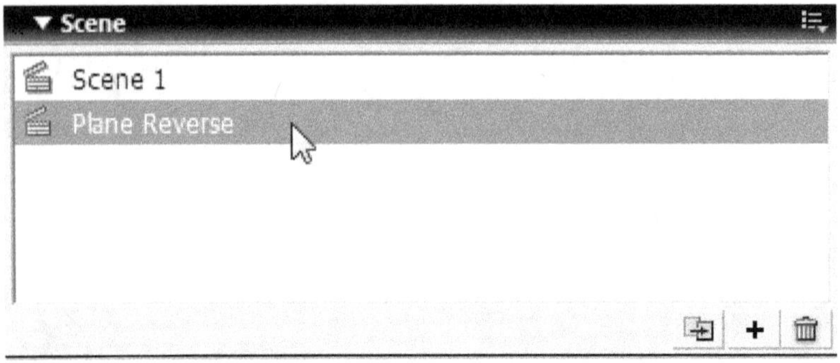

When you create a new scene Flash will automatically open that new scene for you. You can tell what scene you're on by looking above the timeline/stage:

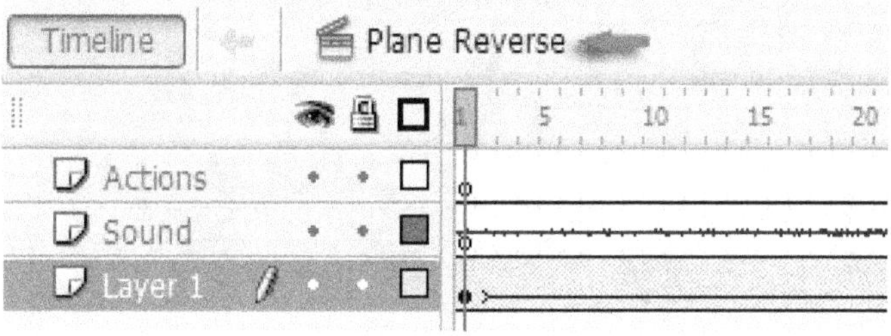

So now we want the plane to reverse direction. Also, what if we have the plane pulling a banner? And, what if we created a button on the main timeline that controlled only the banner? This is where you can start to see the power of Flash. Although this is a basic Flash project, you are learning the tools necessary to complete some of the great Flash projects that are coming up. Almost there!

Since this is a copy of Scene 1 we need to *delete the tellTarget ActionScript on frame 250*. Select frame **250** of the **Actions** layer and open the Actions panel. We don't need the code that instructs the main timeline to go to the lake Label. Highlight the code:

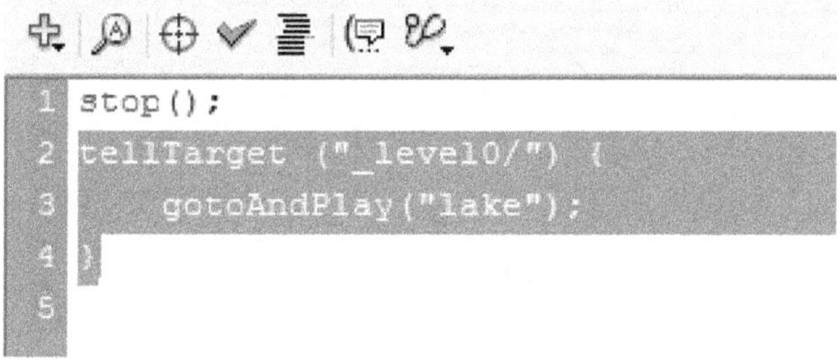

Delete this code. Now let's create the new animation. Select the first frame of **Layer 1**. Next, select the plane image on the stage. Go to **Modify**, **Transform**, **Flip Horizontal**:

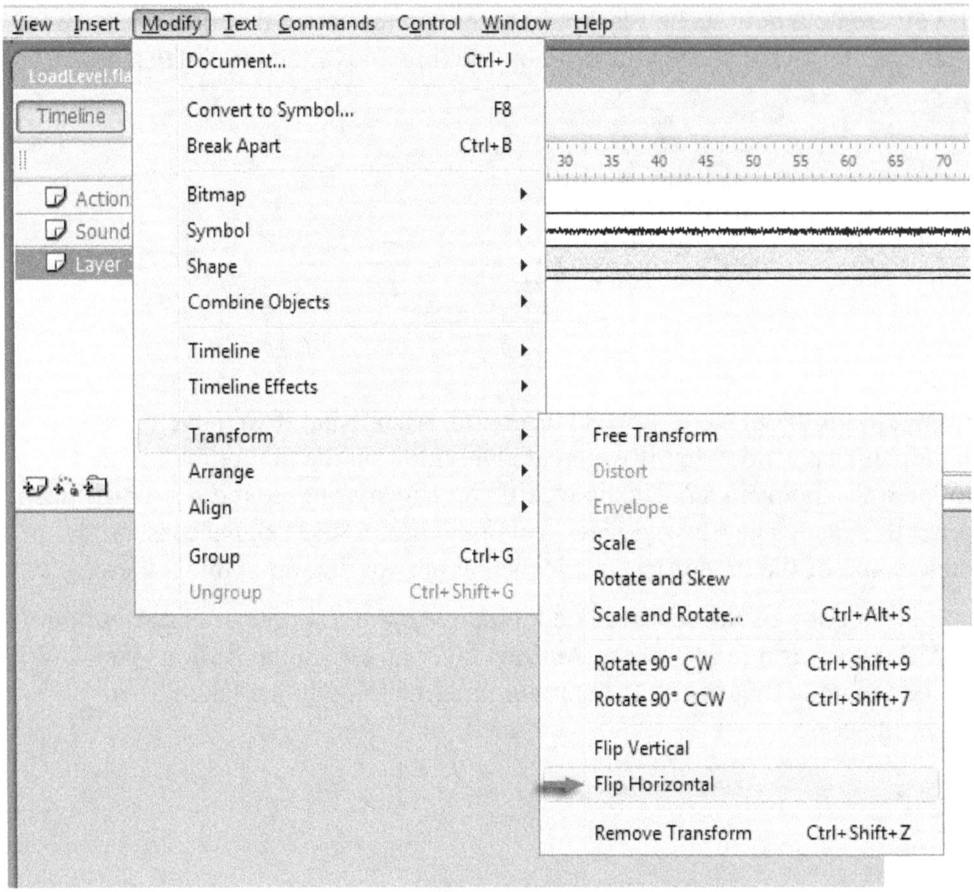

This will flip your plane so it's heading in the opposite direction. Next, click-and-drag the plane so it's offstage on the left side:

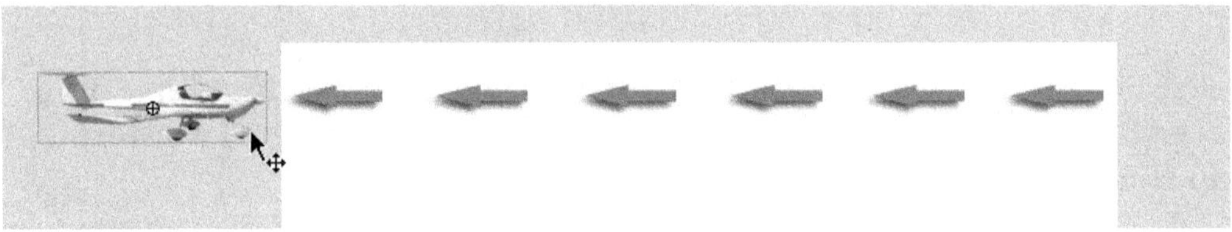

Next, we're going to clear the keyframe on frame 75 and 150. Select frame **75** and go to **Modify**, **Timeline**, and **Clear Keyframe**:

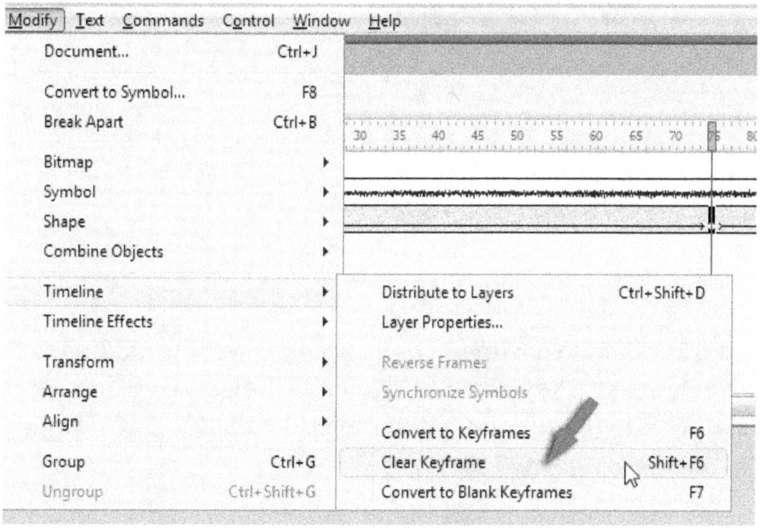

Select the keyframe on **150** and clear that keyframe also. You should now see a dotted line that goes through the timeline. This means that you'll need to add a second keyframe for any animation to happen:

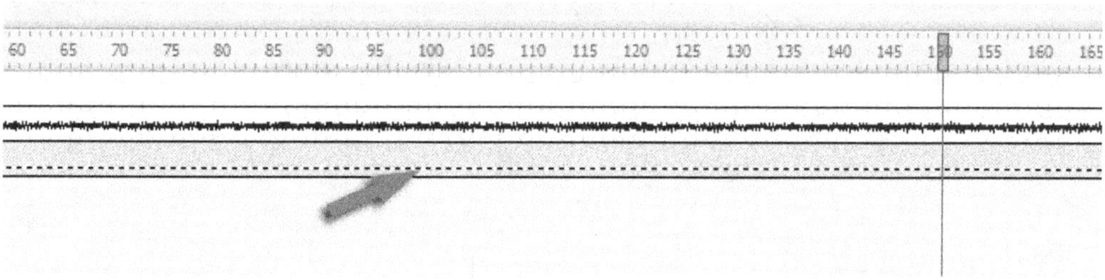

Select the first frame and then select the plane image on the stage; next, go to **Modify**, **Convert to Symbol**. Change the **Type** to **Movie** and name this new symbol **Plane**:

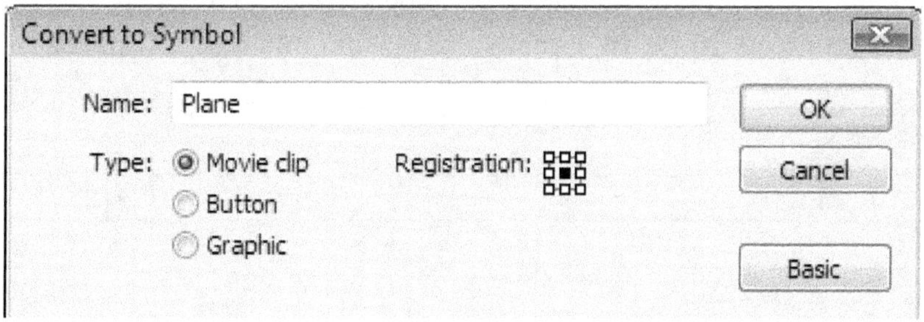

Hit **OK**. Open the Properties panel and type **plane** in the Instance Name window:

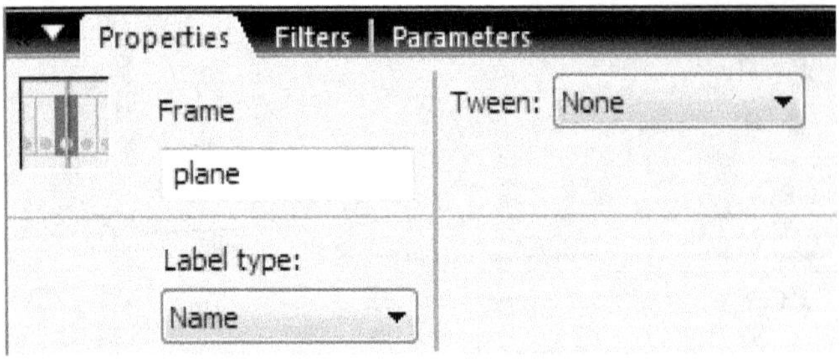

The reason we converted this plane to a Movie clip is because we'll be adding a banner animation to it. Next, insert a keyframe on frame **75**. Select the plane symbol on the stage and drag it to the middle of the stage like this:

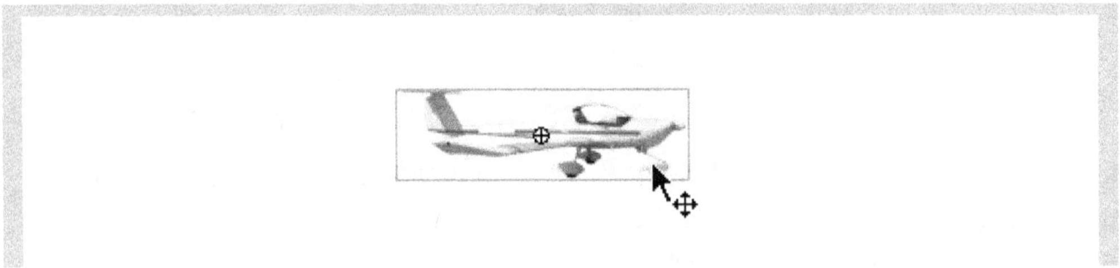

Inset a keyframe on frame **150** and drag the plane symbol offstage to the right:

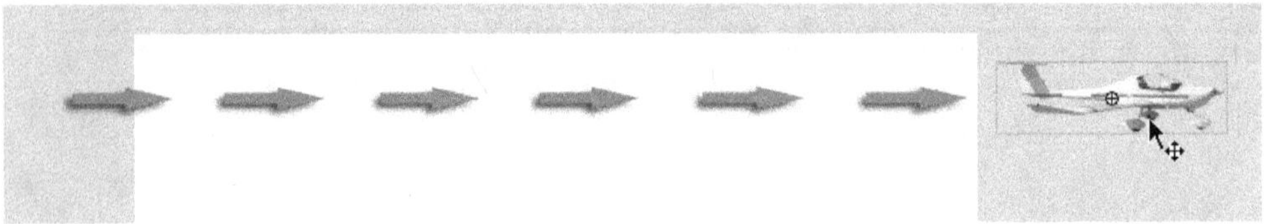

Go to **Control**, **Test Scene**. Your plane should fly in from the left and exit stage right.

Next, we'll add the banner! Double-click the new plane symbol to enter its editing stage. Insert a frame on frame **40**. Create a new layer and call it **Banner**:

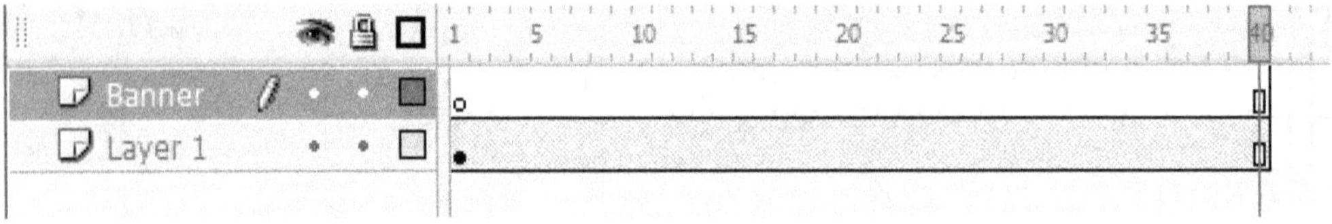

Select the **Rectangle Tool** and choose **black** for the **Stroke color** and **white** for the **Fill color**:

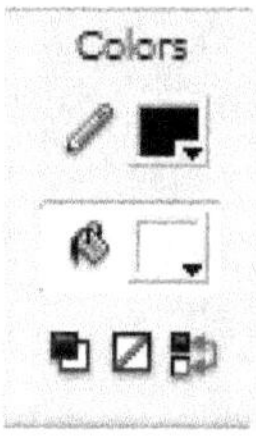

Open the Properties panel. Make the Stroke style **Solid** with a width of **1**:

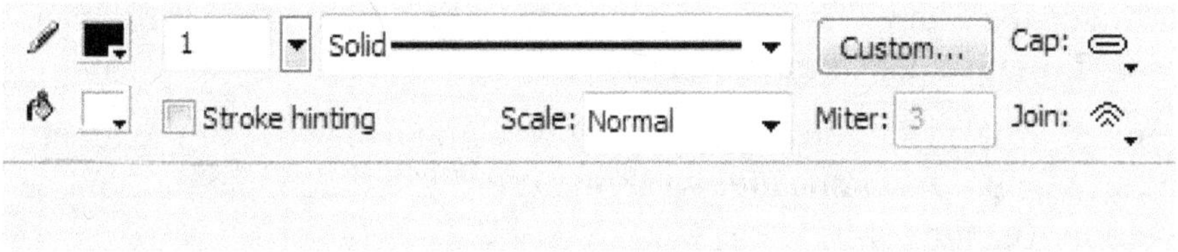

Create a rectangle shape behind the plane:

We're now going to learn about Shape Tweening. Shape Tweening is great for creating fluid, animating shapes. We want the banner to appear to be blowing in the wind so the best way to do this is through Shape Tweening. Select the first frame of the **Banner** layer; in the Properties panel change the **Tween** to **Shape**:

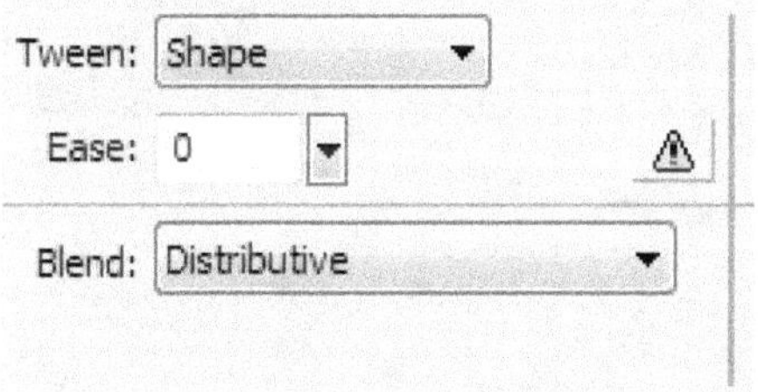

You'll notice a little warning icon with an exclamation point. This is just trying to tell you that you'll need to add another keyframe for the shape tween to work. Go to frame **40** of the **Banner** layer and insert a keyframe:

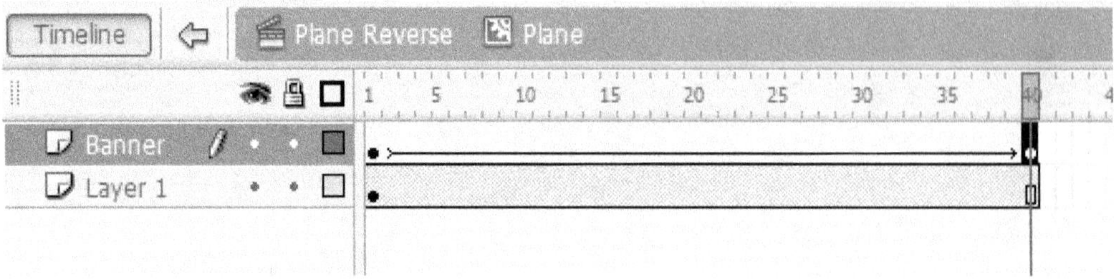

You should now see the Shape Tween. You may be asking what is the difference between **Motion Tweens** and **Shape Tweens**?

Motion Tween: A Motion Tween is what you'll be using over 90% of the time. It basically moves a symbol from one area to another; or, it will animate the Tint or Alpha of a symbol over time.

Shape Tween: A Shape Tween will actually change the shape of the symbol. So you could animate a circle morphing into a square, or vice versa.

Since we want to create the illusion of the banner blowing in the wind, we need to change the shape over time. Which is why we're using Shape tween. So let's do that now.

Insert a keyframe on frame **20** of the **Banner** layer. Next, zoom into the banner shape on the stage. You'll notice that the banner is highlighted; click anywhere outside the Banner to deselect it. Next, move your cursor over the bottom line (you'll notice a little curly symbol) and push it upward:

Grab the top of the banner and gently pull it downward:

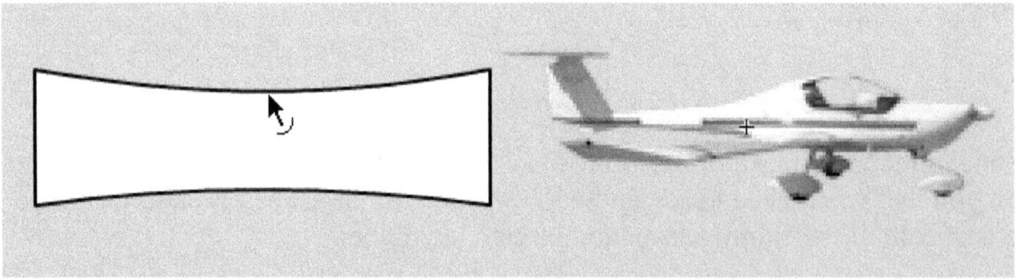

If you grab the timeline needle you can scrub the timeline to see how the animation is going to play. Next, we're going to add some text to this banner.

Create a new layer and name it **Text**. Make the **Color red**; in the Properties panel change the **Font** to **Arial**, **Size 14**, and **Bold**:

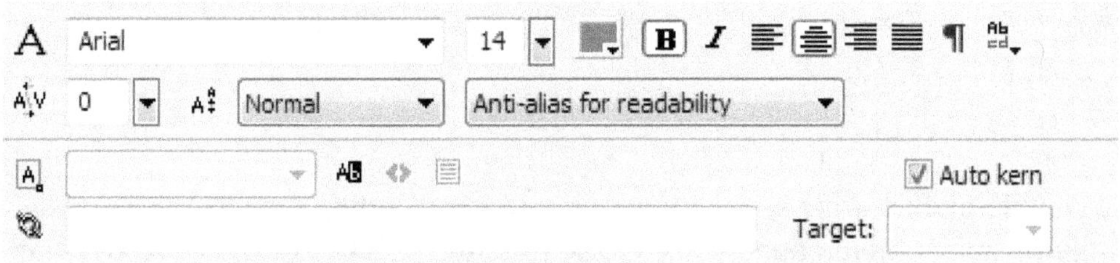

Type **Landon Travel** in the middle of the Banner:

Note: if you made your banner too small for your text to fit, simply change the Font Size to 12 or 10.

We're going to have the main timeline control the banner. Which means we have to make the banner a Movie Clip. Grab the **Selection Tool** and select the text (make sure you select the text and not the white background); then, go to **Modify**, **Convert to Symbol**. Change the **Type** to Movie clip and give it a name of **Banner**:

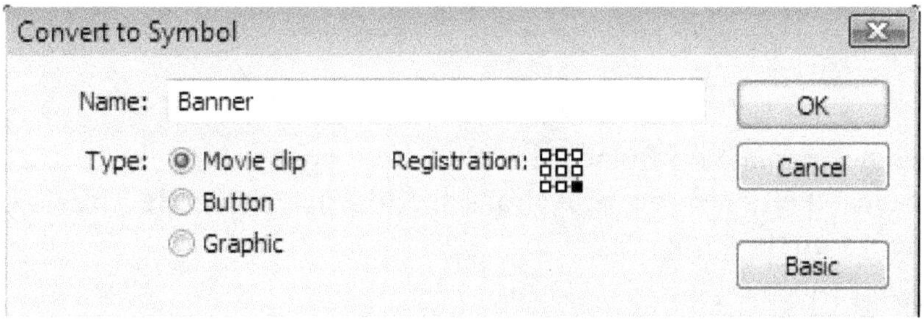

Hit **OK**. Since the main timeline is going to be controlling this Movie clip, we need to give it a name. Open the Properties panel. Type **banner** in the **Instance Name** window:

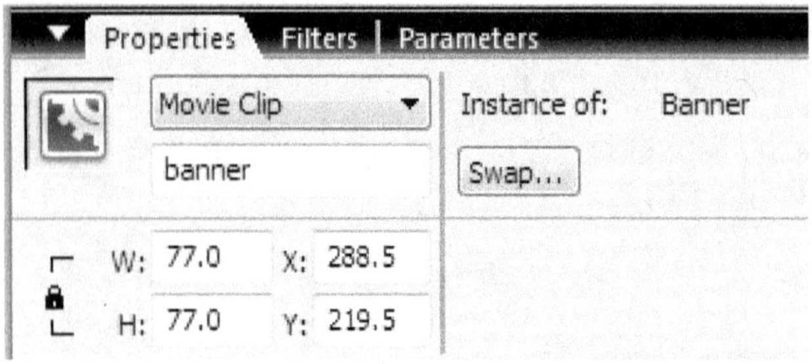

Great. Double-click on this new Movie clip to enter its editing stage. The hierarchy of stages should appear above the timeline (**CS3/CS4/CS5** - Above the stage):

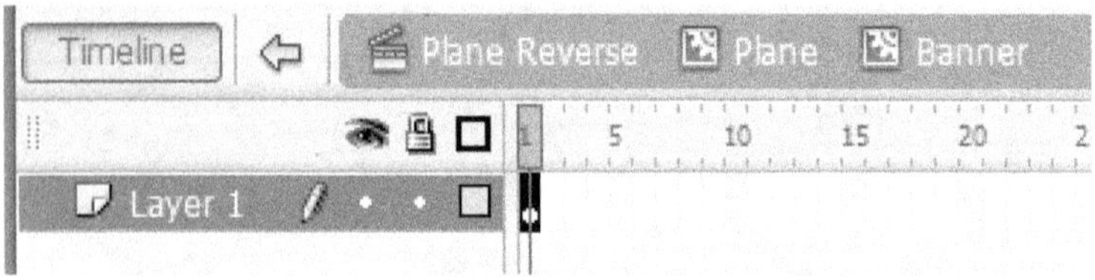

So what the hierarchy tells us is that we are now in the Banner editing stage. The **Banne**r Movie clip is within the **Plane** Movie clip, which is within the **Plane Reverse** scene.

We're now going to add a keyframe on frame 2. Select the Landon text so it's highlighted (click anywhere in the word and go to **Edit**, **Select All**). Next, open the Properties panel and change the **Color** to **blue**:

So on frame 1 the text is red and on frame 2 it's blue. Let's create a new layer and name it **Actions**. Select the first frame of Actions and insert a **stop code**. Create a new layer and name it **Labels**:

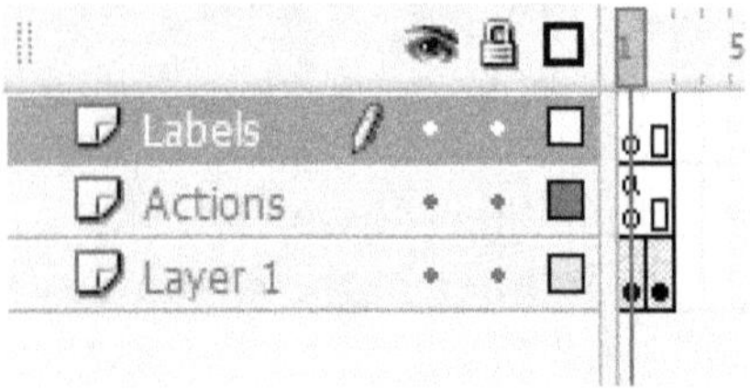

Select the first frame of **Labels**; in the Properties panel type **red** in the **Frame Label** window:

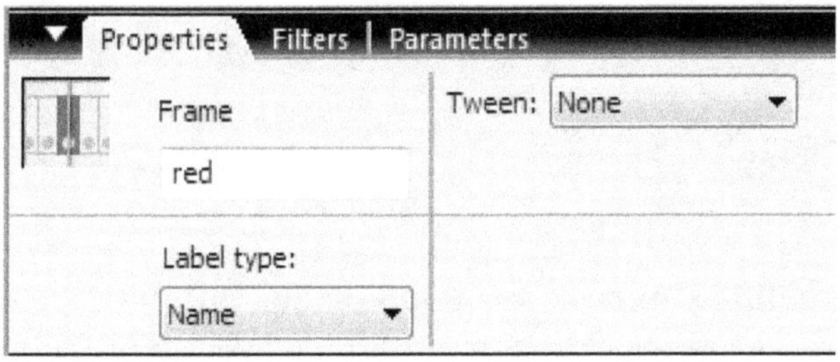

Insert a keyframe on frame **2** of the **Labels layer**. Select this new keyframe and type **blue** in the **Frame Label** window. Almost done!

One last thing. Let's add a **Labels** layer to the Plane Reverse Scene. Go back to the Plane Reverse Scene. Create a new layer and name it **Labels**. Select the first frame and type **plane_reverse** in the **Frame Label** window. Your timeline should now look like this:

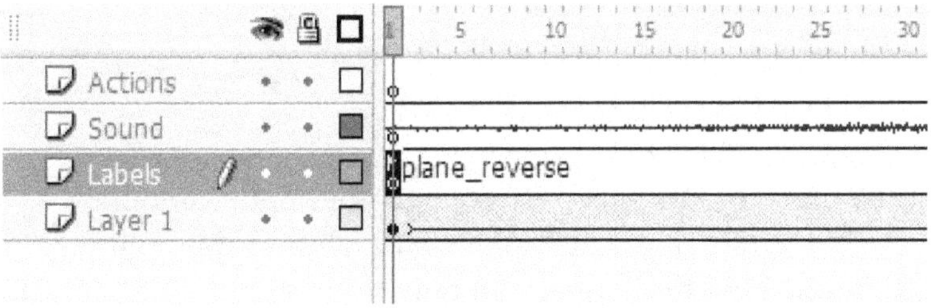

Great! We finished the animation. Go to **File**, **Publish**. Go back to the **LoadLevel.fla** file. Select frame **80** of the **Actions** layer. Open the Actions panel and make sure Script Assist is turned on. Go to **Deprecated**, **Actions**, and double-click **tellTarget**:

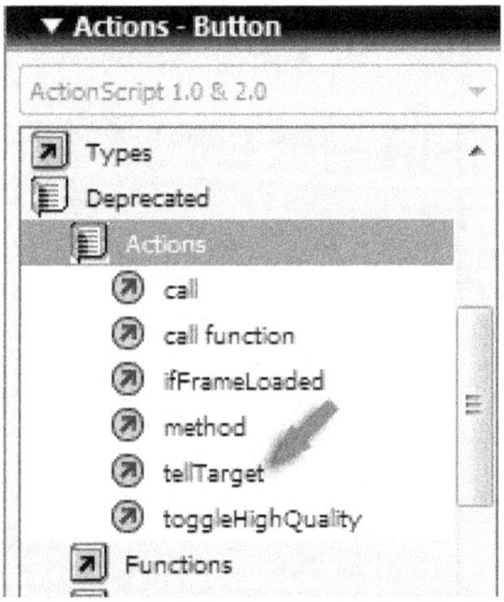

Type **_level1/** in the Target window:

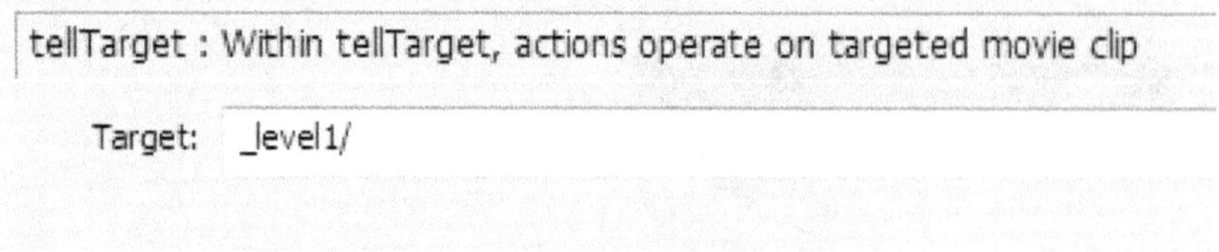

Next, go to **Global Functions**, **Timeline Control**, and double-click **goto**. In the **goto** settings window select **Frame Label** for **Type**; type **plane_reversal** in the **Frame** window:

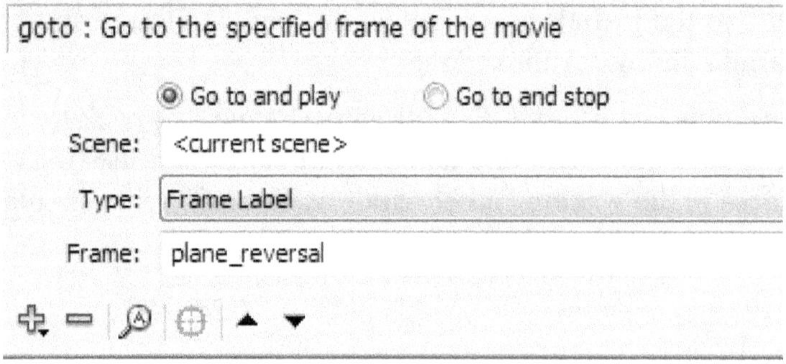

Test your movie. When the plane finishes its first voyage your main timeline should fade into the lake picture. When the lake picture finishes fading in it tells the plane file to go to the **plane_reversal** Label and play.

Next, we'll create a button that controls the **Banner**.

Select the **Play** Button. Go to **Edit, Copy**. Then go to **Edit**, **Paste in Place**. This will paste the copied button in the exact spot the original is in. Drag this new button below the **Stop** button:

With this button still selected, open the Properties panel. Click on **Swap** to bring up the **Swap Symbol** box. Click the **Duplicate Symbol** button and type **Banner**:

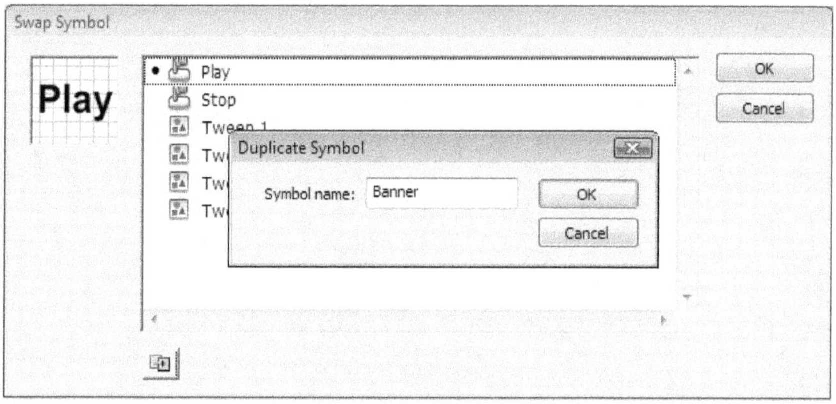

Hit **OK**. Double-click the **Banner** button to select it:

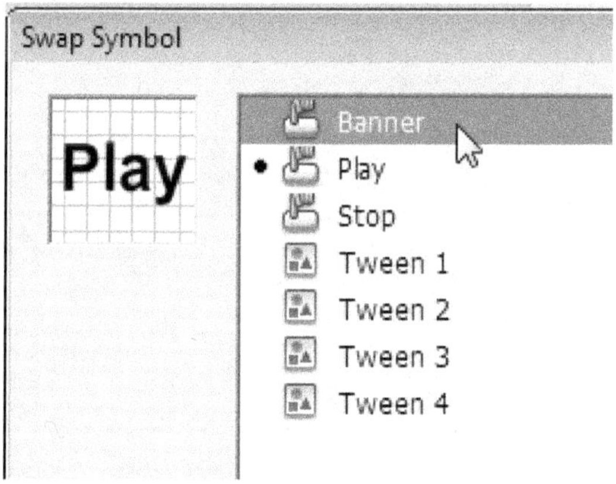

You can edit this new button without affecting the original. Double-click this button to enter its editing stage. Change the word **Play** to **Banner**. Go back to Scene 1 now. Open the Actions panel. Highlight all the code and delete it. We'll be creating the new code from scratch.

Go to **Deprecated**, **Actions**, and double-click **tellTarget**:

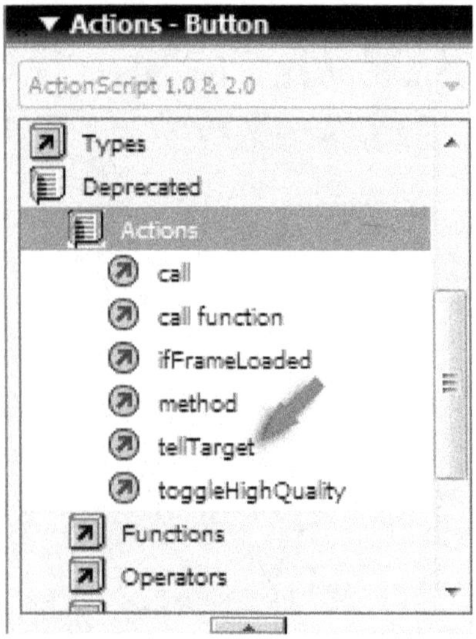

In the Target window type **_level1/plane/banner**:

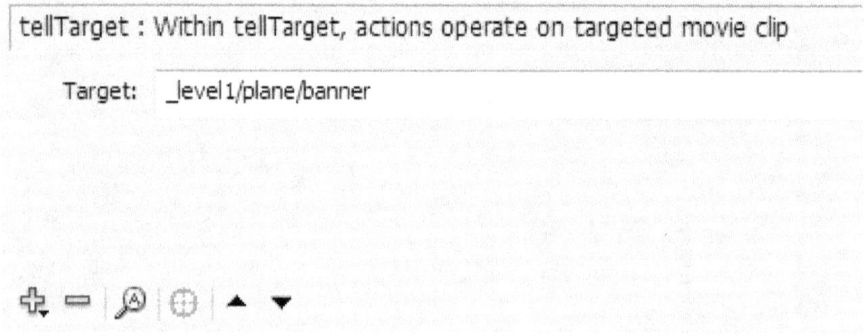

So we are targeting the **Banner** Movie clip that we named **banner**; it's inside the Movie clip that we named **plane**. And that is in the file we're loading into **Level 1**.

Next, go to **Global Functions**, **Timeline Control**, and double-click **goto**. In the **goto** settings window change the **Type** to **Frame Label**, type **blue** in the **Frame** window, and select **Go to and stop**:

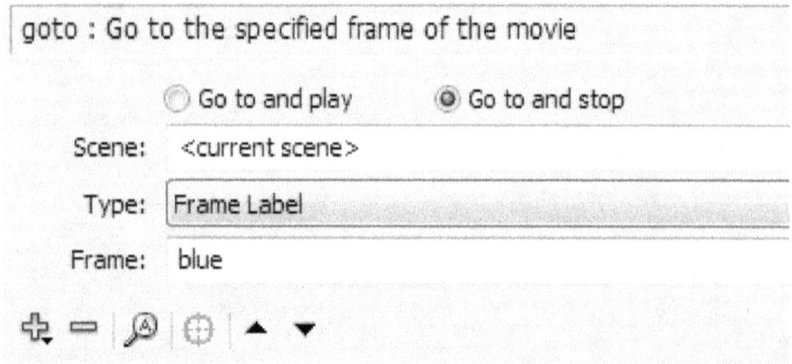

Test your movie. This time when the plane makes its return trip, hit the Stop button. Then hit the Banner button. The Banner should turn blue! Hit the Play button and the plane should take off again. Congratulations! If you didn't understand any part of this exercise you may want to go through it again until you have a better understanding of some of the steps we did. This exercise should give you a better idea of how loading levels works.

Loading Targets

In the last exercise we loaded a movie (plane movie) into Level 1 on the main timeline. This time we're going to load movies into Targets. I use this all the time and I think once you get the hang of it you'll start thinking of all sorts of cool things you'll be able to do! When you load a movie into a Target you can animate it across the screen, change the color of the movie file, or even mask the loaded movie. For instance, in a upcoming exercise we're going to load a video into a Target which is then masked to look like the video is inside a TV screen!

Open **Target.fla** located in the Chapter Four folder. You should see three buttons, **Load Picture**, **Load Television**, and **Unload Movie**:

We're going to first load in the Television image. Then, we'll load in the eagle image. Finally, we'll unload the Targets. So let's get started.

Go to **File**, **New**. Select **Flash Document** and hit **OK**. Next, go to **File**, **Import**, **Import to Stage** and go to the Pictures folder in the Chapter Four folder; select **television.jpg**:

Go to **File**, **Save**, and save the file in the Chapter Four folder. Call it **television.fla**. Go to **File**, **Publish**.

Next, go to **File**, **New** and select **Flash Document**. Select **File**, **Import**, **Import to Stage**; click on **eagle.jpg** from the Pictures folder inside the Chapter Four folder:

Go to **File**, **Save**, and save the file as **eagle.fla** in the Chapter Four folder. Select **File**, and **Publish**. You should now have a **eagle.swf** file, and a **television.swf** file in your Chapter Four folder. These are the files you will be loading in.

Go back to **Target.fla**. Since we're loading these movies into Targets instead of Levels, as we did in the previous example, we need to create the Target that the movies will load into. Create a new layer and call it **Target**:

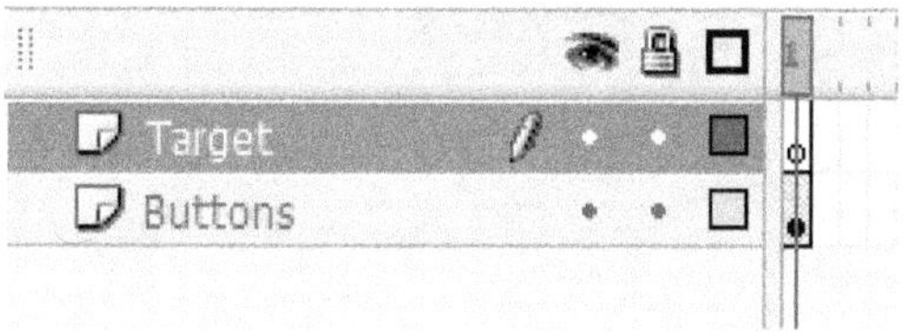

Next, grab the **Rectangle Tool**, turn off **Stroke color**, and select **red** for the **Fill color**:

Create a shape, any size or dimension, in the middle of the stage:

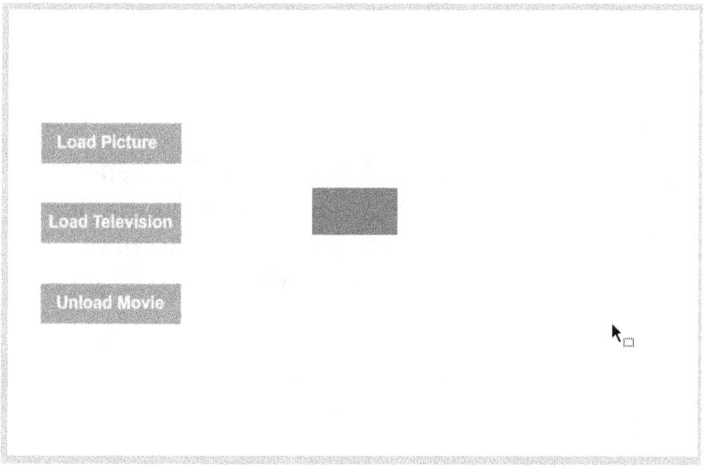

If your shape is larger or smaller than the above square don't worry. When you load movies into targets the dimensions of the Target are irrelevant. Note: a *Target must be a Movie clip*. We'll need to convert this red shape to a Movie clip. Select the shape then go to **Modify**, **Convert to Symbol**. Change the **Type** to Movie clip and name it **Target**:

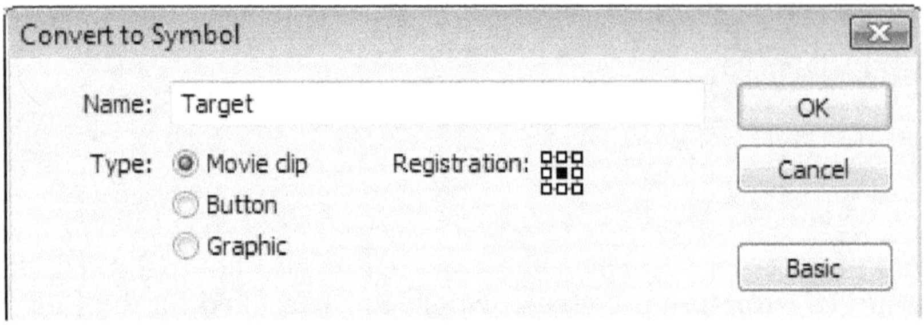

Hit **OK**. As always, whenever we create a Movie clip we need to give it an Instance Name. Open the Properties panel and type **target_television** in the **Instance Name** window:

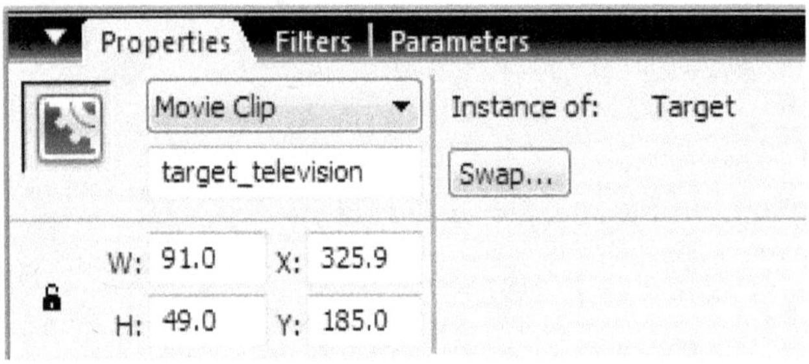

Now we're ready to add the ActionScript. Select the **Load Television** Button; open the Actions panel and turn Script Assist on. Next, go to **Global Function**, **Browser/Network**, and double-click **loadMovie**. You should now see the **loadMovie** settings window. In the **URL** window type **television.swf**. Change **Location** to **Target** and type **/target_television**:

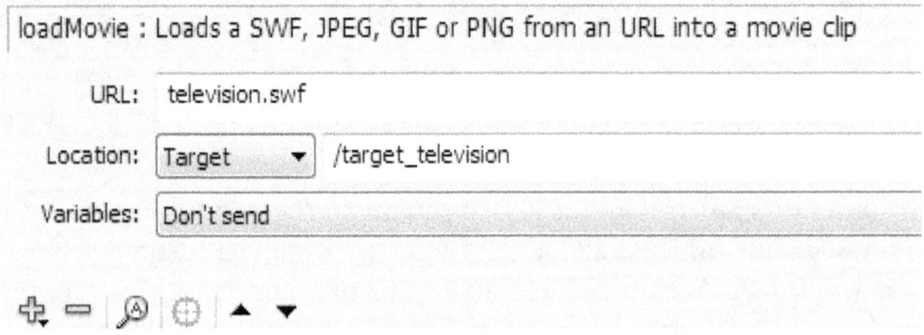

Now when we click the button it will load in the television file that we just created into the Target. Sometimes you may have more than one Target on the stage which is why we have to give unique Instance Names to each Target.

Test your movie. Click the **Load Television** button. You'll briefly see the red shape then the television image will appear. The file that is being loaded in *will* *not always load in at the exact spot of the Target.* Here is where my television image appears on my stage:

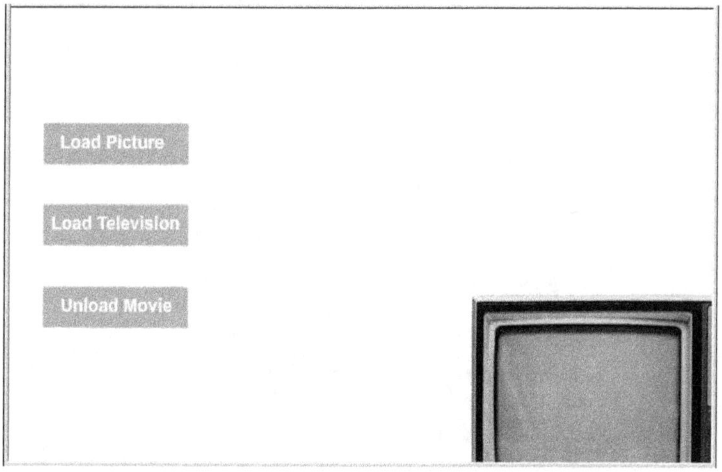

You can see that my television image is slightly off the stage so we can only see about 80% of it. The way to fix this is by *moving the Target.* Since my television file is too far to the bottom right, I need to move the Target to the top left like this:

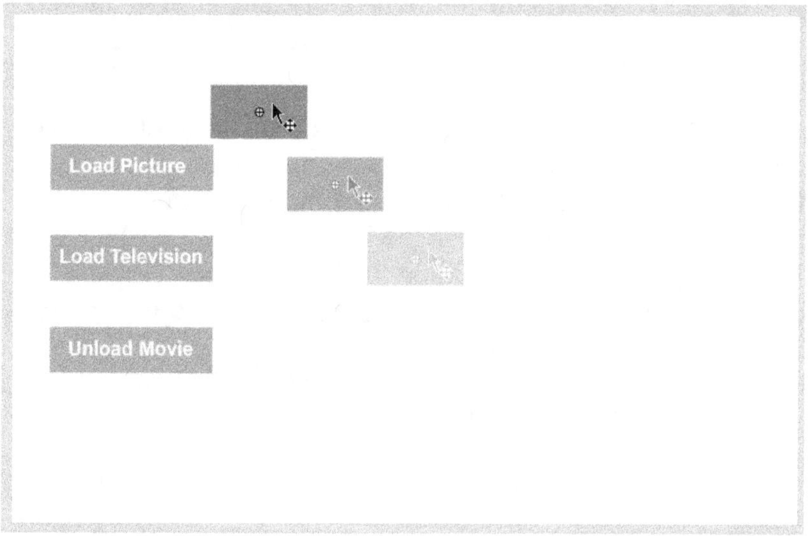

If I test my movie again the television is now positioned better on the stage:

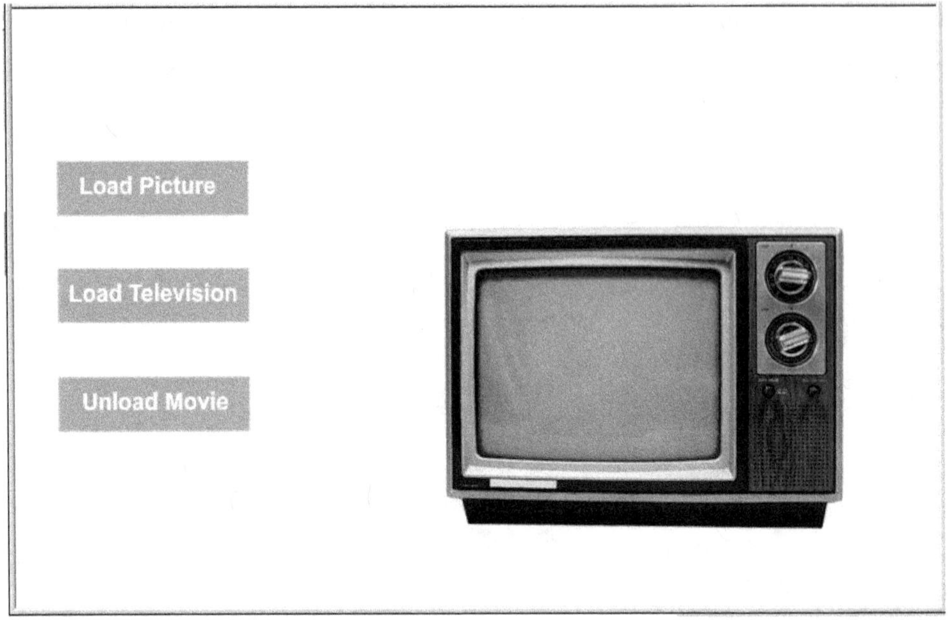

For this exercise the position of the television is fine. You can practice moving your Target around to see how it affects the positioning of the television image. When you finish, try to get the television image somewhere around the center of the stage.

Let's add the ActionScript to the **Load Picture** Button. Select the **Load Picture** Button, and then open the Actions panel. Go to **Global Functions**, **Browser/Network** and double-click **loadMovie**. You should now see the **loadMovie** settings window. Type **eagle.swf** in the **URL** window and change the **Location** to **Target**. We're going to load the eagle file into the same Target as the television so you can see what happens. Next to **Target** type **/target_television**:

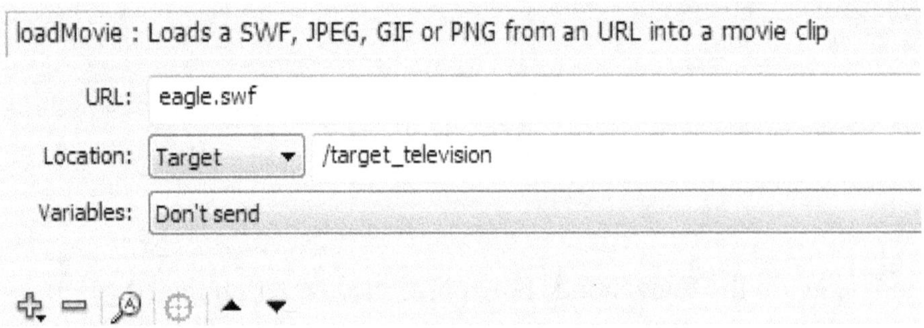

Test your movie. Click on the **Load Picture** button. You should see the eagle image appear on the stage. Click on the **Load Television** button. The television image should replace the eagle picture on the stage. You can go back and forth with each picture replacing each other. This is similar to what we did in the previous exercise with the red circle and the blue square, when we loaded them into the same level and they replaced each other.

Let's add code to the **Unload Movie** button. Select the **Unload Movie** button and open the Actions panel. Go to **Global Functions, Browser/Network** and double-click **unloadMovie**. You should now see the **unloadMovie** settings window. Change the **Location** to **Target** and type **/target_television** in the **Location** window:

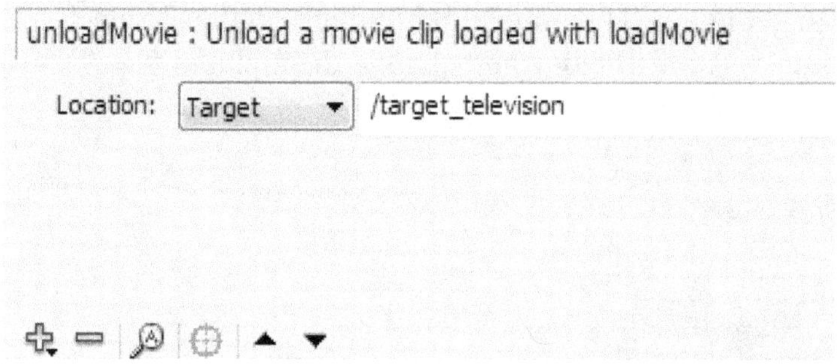

Test your movie. Click the **Load Picture** button so you can see the eagle image. Click on the **Unload Movie** button. The eagle image should disappear. Do the same thing by clicking on the **Load Television** button then clicking on the **Unload Movie** button. The television image should disappear.

You'll notice that whenever we click on one of the load buttons we see the red target very briefly. We don't want to see it at all. What is the solution? The obvious first choice would be to take down the alpha on the Target Movie clip to 0. Let's try that now so you can see what happens. Select the Target symbol; next, open the Properties panel and change the **Color** to **Alpha** and the percentage to **0**:

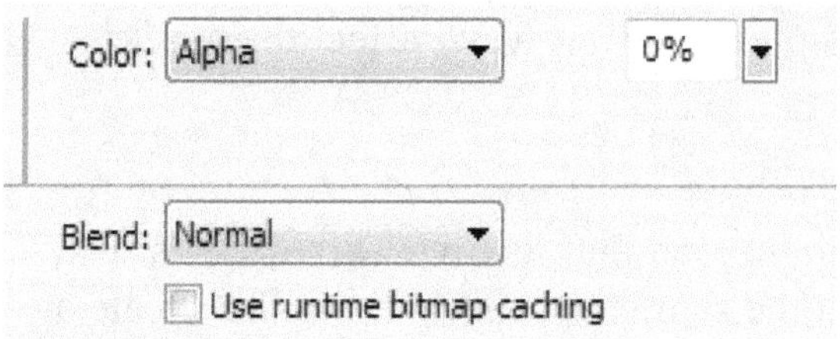

The Target should now be transparent. Let's test the movie. Click on both of the load buttons. The movies are loading in but we're unable to see them. Here is the cool part of loading movies into Targets. The loaded movie is *taking on the attributes of the Target*. Since the **Target** Movie clip has 0% Alpha, then the movie loading into it also has 0% Alpha.

So changing the Alpha isn't going to work since we want to be able to see the images. Select the Target symbol and change **Color** to **None**:

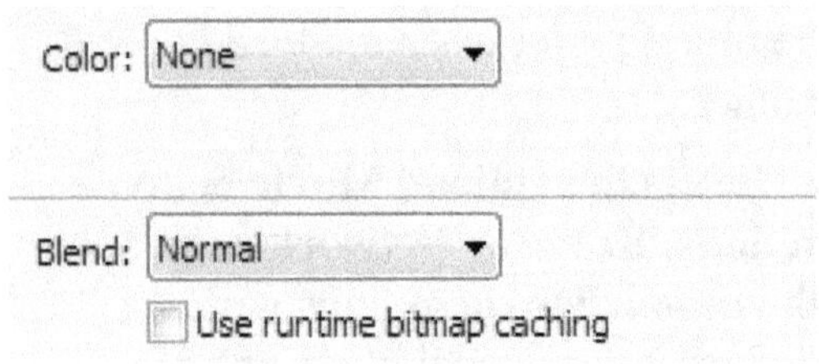

You should now see the **Target** again. This time, double-click on the Target so we can enter its editing stage. Select **Fill color** and change the alpha to **0**:

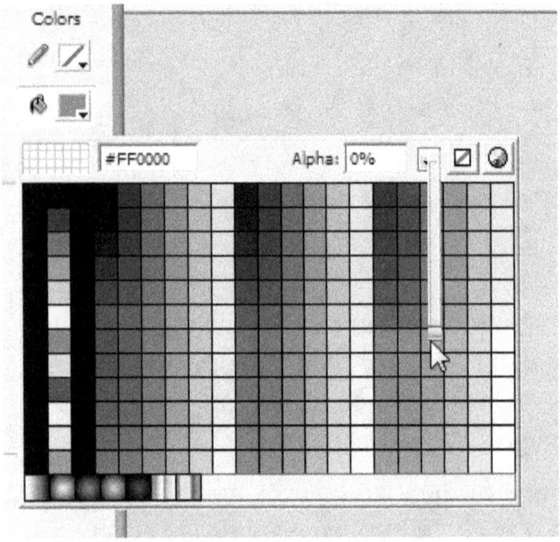

Click anywhere on the stage to de-select the red shape; it should now be transparent. Exactly what we want. Since we changed the alpha of the actual shape and not the Movie clip (as we did previously) it won't affect the movie's alpha when it gets loaded.

Go back to Scene 1. Test your movie again.

So now what if we want the eagle picture to load into its own Target? That way we can have both images on the stage at the same time. Simple, we just create a new Target symbol and give it a new Instance Name. Let's do that now.

Select the Target Symbol on the stage. If you can't find it (since it is now transparent) click on the keyframe of the **Target** layer; it should now highlight the transparent Movie clip. Select the **Target** Movie clip on the stage. Go to **Edit**, **Copy**. Create a new layer and call it **Target 2**. Select the first frame of the new layer and go to **Edit**, **Paste in Place**; there should now be a copy of the Target Symbol in your **Target 2** layer:

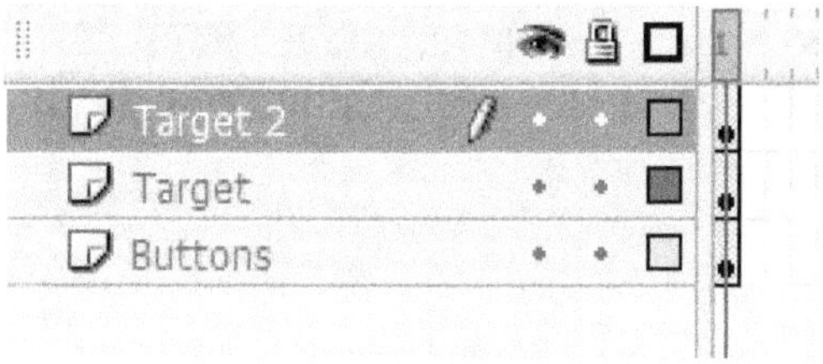

Select the new Target Symbol on the stage. It's sometimes a good idea to lock layers that you're not using so you don't accidentally select the wrong symbol. Let's **lock the Target layer**:

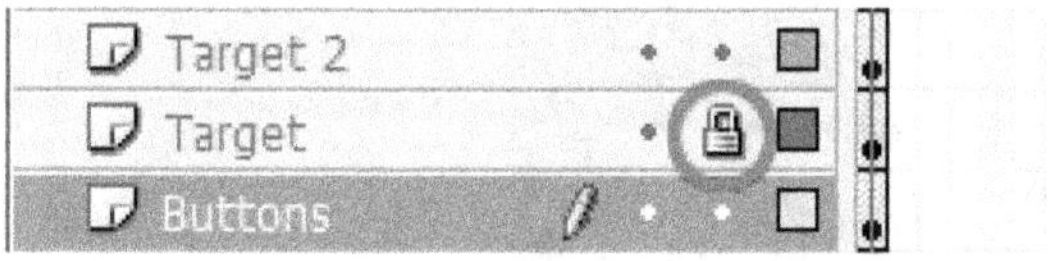

Once you select the new Target open the Properties panel. Since this is a copy of your original Target it will retain the same Instance Name: **target_television**. We need to change that to **target_eagle**:

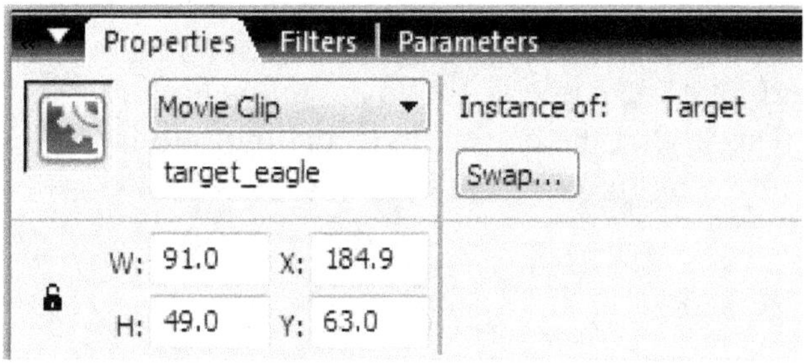

So now we have a second Target which has a unique Instance Name. Select the **Load Picture** button and open the Actions panel. Click anywhere in the word **target_television**; you should now see the **loadMovie** settings window. Change the **Target** name to **/target_eagle**:

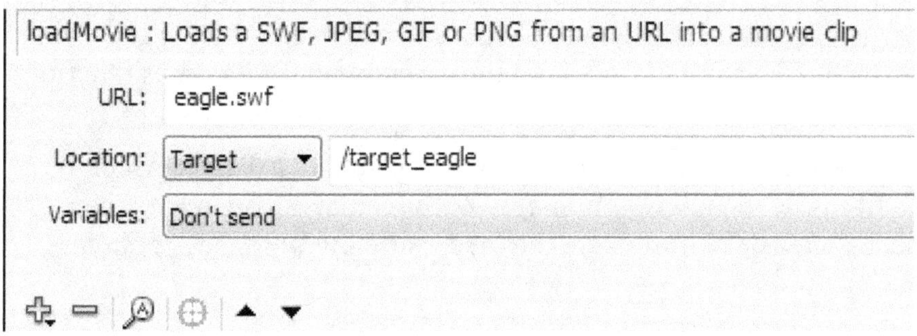

So now when you click on the **Load Picture** button it will load the eagle image into the new Target. Test your movie again and click on both Load buttons. Both images should now be on the stage:

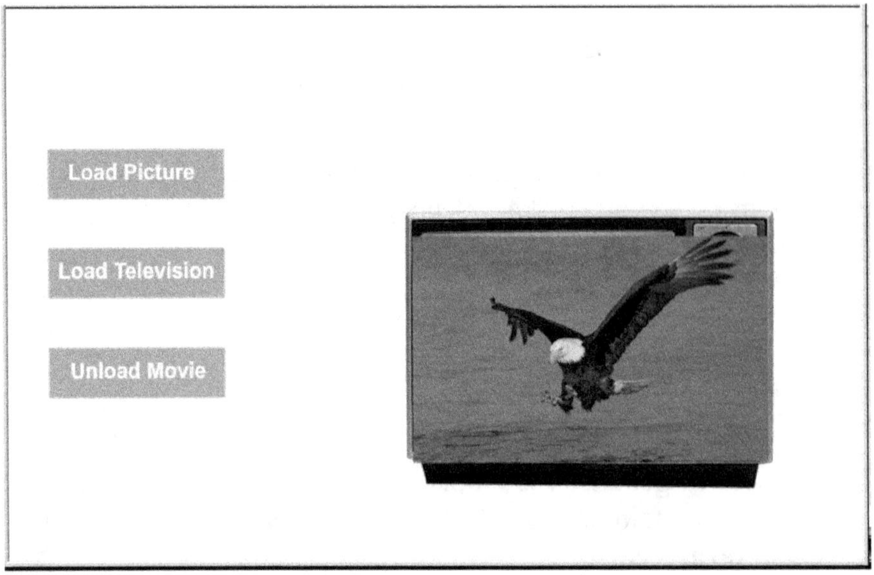

You may notice in the above picture that the eagle is above the television image. The reason for this is because the Target that the eagle file is loading into is the topmost layer. We can change this by dragging the **Target 2** layer below the **Target** layer:

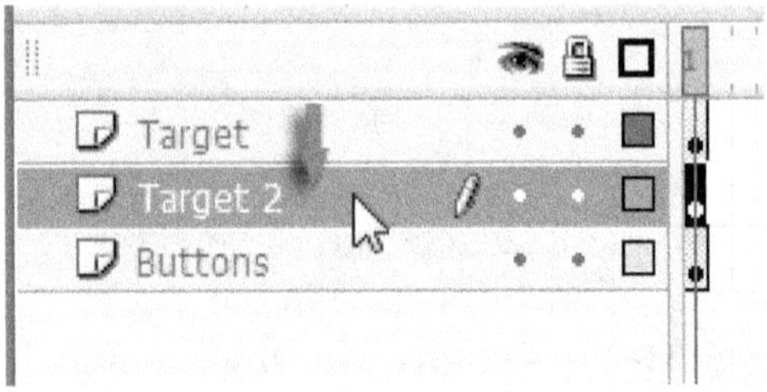

Test your movie again and the eagle image will now be covered by the television picture. So let's put the layers back to where they were with **Target 2** as the top layer.

In this next exercise we're going to load the eagle image into a Target which is then masked to fit inside the television image. Let's do that now. Create a new layer and name it **Television** (make sure the layer is **below both Target layers**):

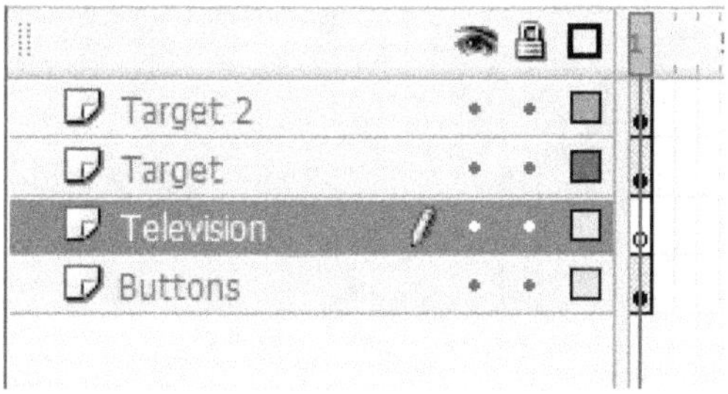

Go to **File**, **Import to Stage**; select **television.jpg** which is in the Pictures folder of the Chapter Four folder. Your stage should now look like this:

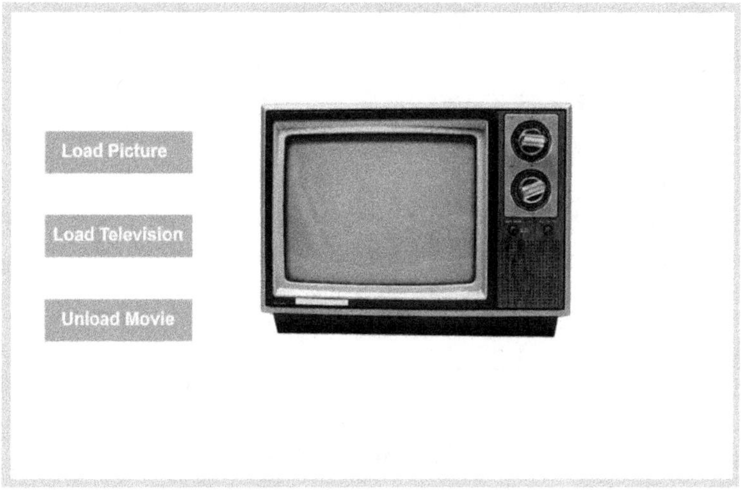

Let's create a mask for the eagle image so it fits in the television. Create a new layer above the **Target 2** layer and name it **Mask**:

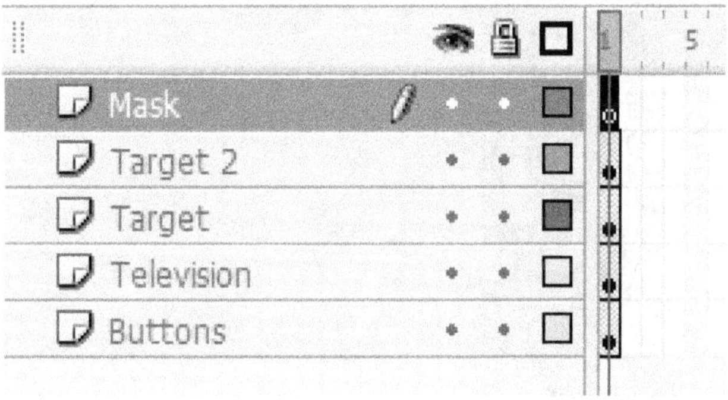

Select the **Rectangle Tool**. Change the **Fill color** to **red** and turn the **Stroke color** off. Click on the **Set Corner Radius** button at the bottom of the Toolbar:

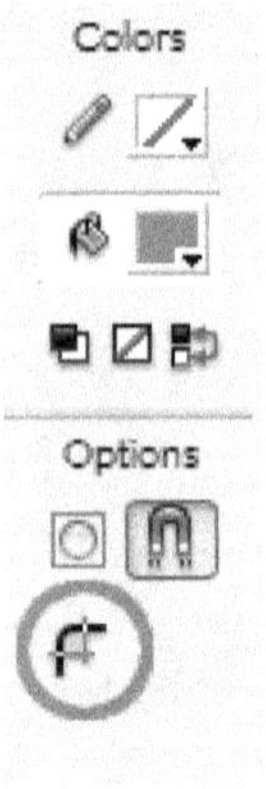

Change the **Corner Radius** to **14**:

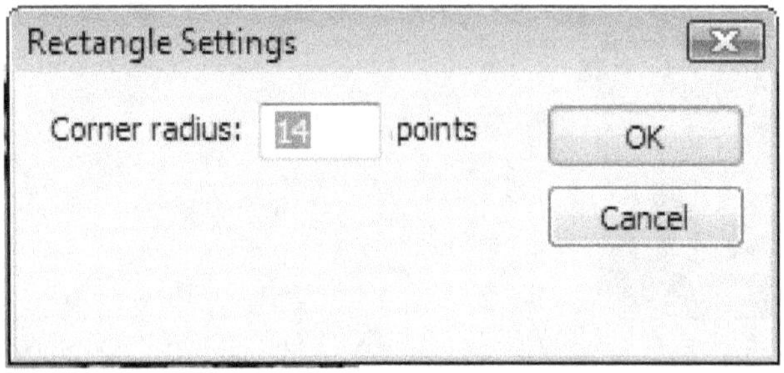

This will round the corners of your rectangle. Hit **OK** to close. Draw your shape over the television screen; try to recreate the same shape as the television screen like this (you can keep the inner shadow of the screen if you like):

The Mask shape is now done. Test your movie and click the Load Picture button to check the location of the eagle image:

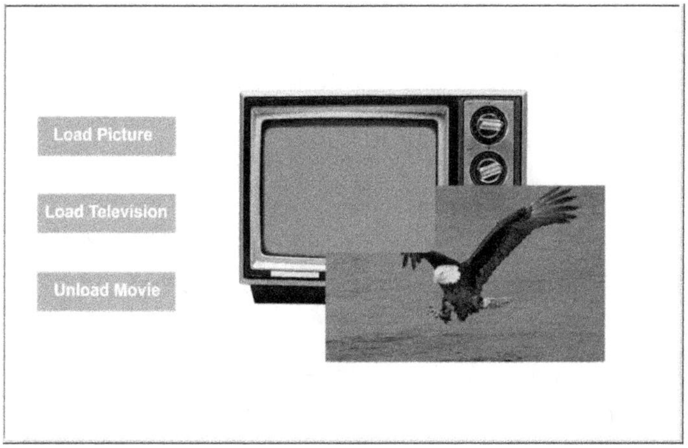

On my test my eagle image is below and to the right of where I need it to be. Your image may be in a different location. To tweak the location of the eagle image select the **Target 2** Symbol and reposition it on the stage. If you can't find your Target 2 symbol (since it's transparent) select the keyframe of the **Target 2** layer. The symbol on the stage should now be highlighted. Test your movie whenever you move your **Target 2** Symbol; keep tweaking the position until the eagle image is directly under the mask shape like this:

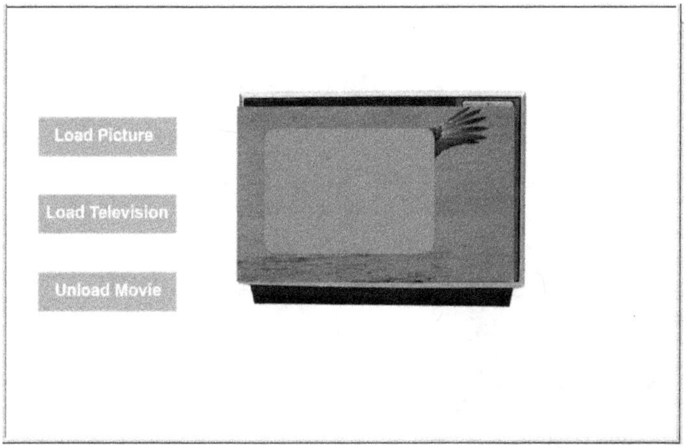

Almost done. Select your **Mask** layer and right-click on it; you should now see several selections to choose from. Select **Mask**:

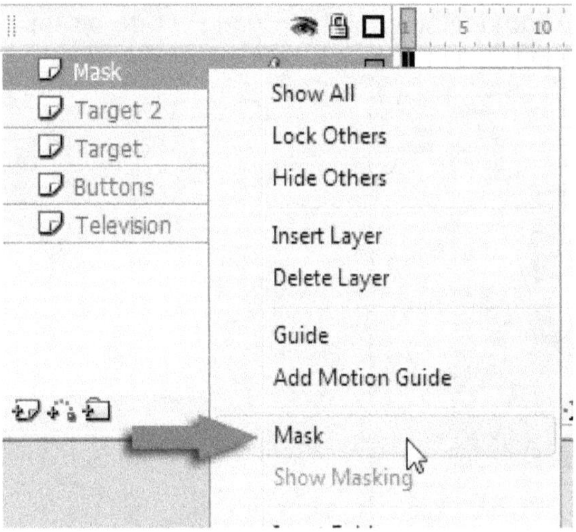

Your **Target 2** layer should now be indented under the **Mask** layer:

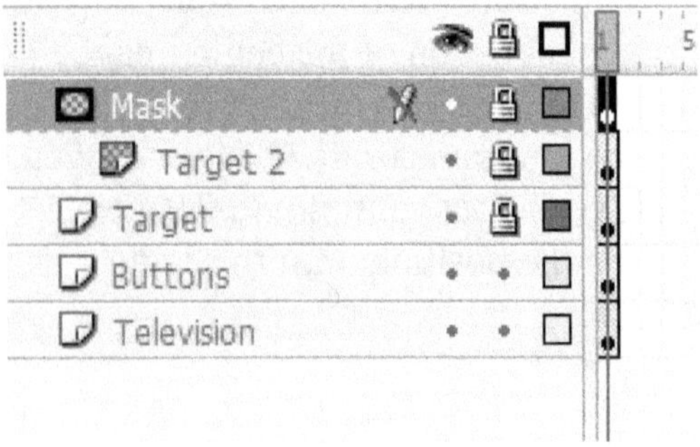

Test your movie:

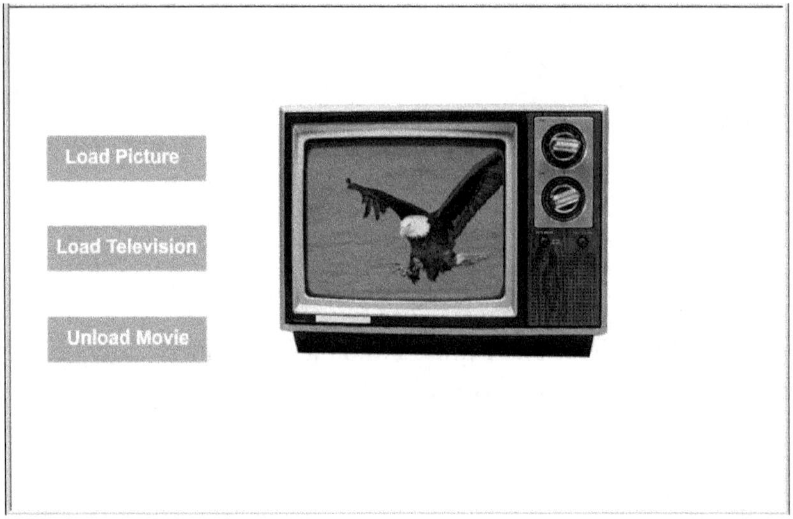

The eagle image should now be masked within the television screen. Click on the **Unload Movie** button. You'll notice that it doesn't work. Let's fix that.

Select the **Unload Movie** button. Open the Actions panel and click anywhere within the word **/target_television**. You should now see the **Target** settings window. Change **/target_television** to **/target_eagle**. Test your movie again. Click on the **Load Picture** button and you should now see the eagle picture. Click on the **Unload Movie** button. The eagle picture should disappear.

Ok. So now we'll try some cool stuff using Targets. In the next exercise we'll be loading in all sorts of movies like videos and pictures. We'll also be creating a remote control for the TV, a preloader, and a nice little slideshow.

Loading Movies

In this project we'll be creating an animated scene using the loadMovie function. We'll be loading pictures and a video into Targets, then masking them.

In the Chapter Four folder open up **Room.fla**. You should see the room image I used for the website www.alicelwalker.com:

The first thing we're going to do is load in the magazine picture. When a user clicks the magazine on the couch, a poster picture will slowly fade in . We'll also create a pre-loader for this poster picture.

Open the file called **Poster.fla** in the Chapter Four folder. You should see the poster for my movie: Destination Mars!:

First, let's animate the poster so it fades in. Create a keyframe on frame **60** of the **Poster** layer; next, click on any frame between **1** and **60** and insert a Motion Tween:

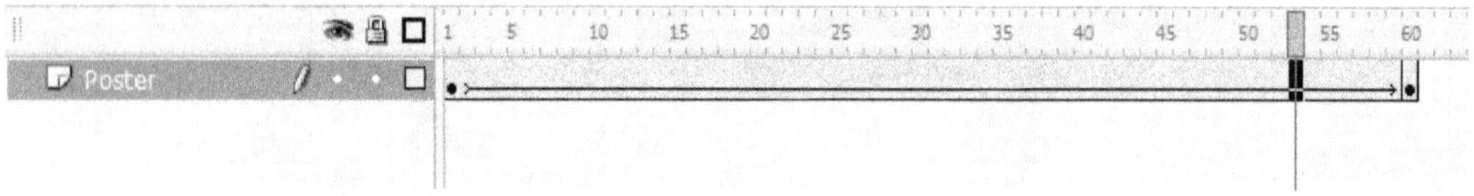

Create a new layer and name it **Actions**. On frame **60** of the **Actions** layer insert a keyframe. Select this new keyframe and open the Actions panel. Insert a **stop** code. Select the first frame of the **Poster** layer and select the Poster image on the stage. Open the Properties panel and change **Color** to **Tint** and the **Color** to **white**.

Test your movie. The Poster should now fade in from white. Whenever you test your movie you have the option to view the **Bandwidth Profiler**. Let's open that now. Go to **View, Bandwidth Profiler**:

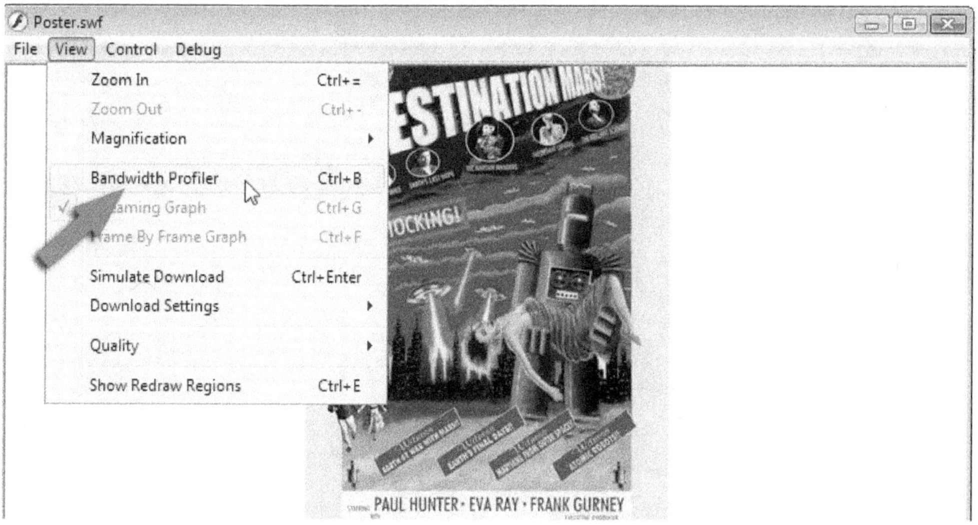

The **Bandwidth Profiler** gives you information regarding your published file, in this case **Poster.swf**:

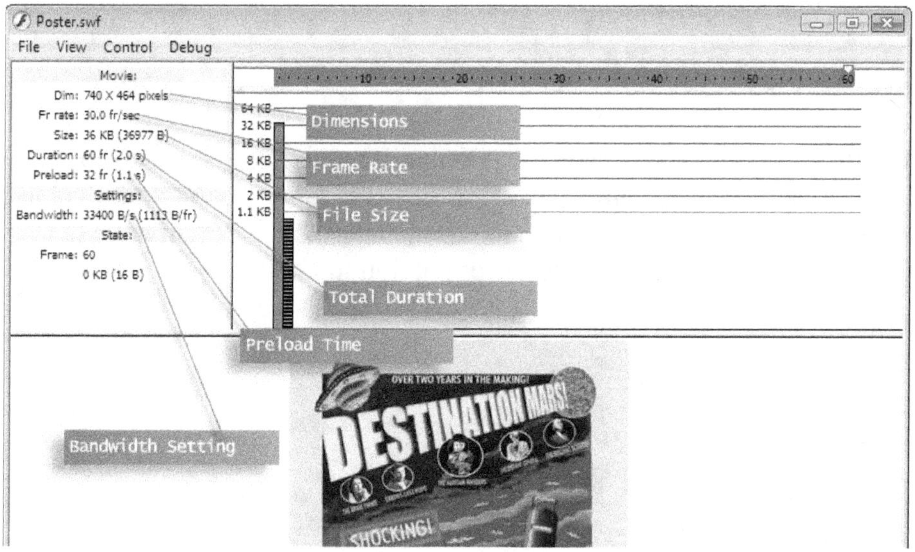

Most of the information is self-explanatory. The main thing you want to look at when using the Bandwidth Profiler is the **Preload** Time and the **Bandwidth** setting. The Preload time is simply the amount of time needed to load the published file. The Bandwidth setting is set at 33400 B/s which is DSL speed; so at this speed the Preload time will be 1.1 seconds, which means the user will see your flash file in about one second. If you want to check your published file on a dial-up modem go to **View**, **Download Settings**, and **56K**:

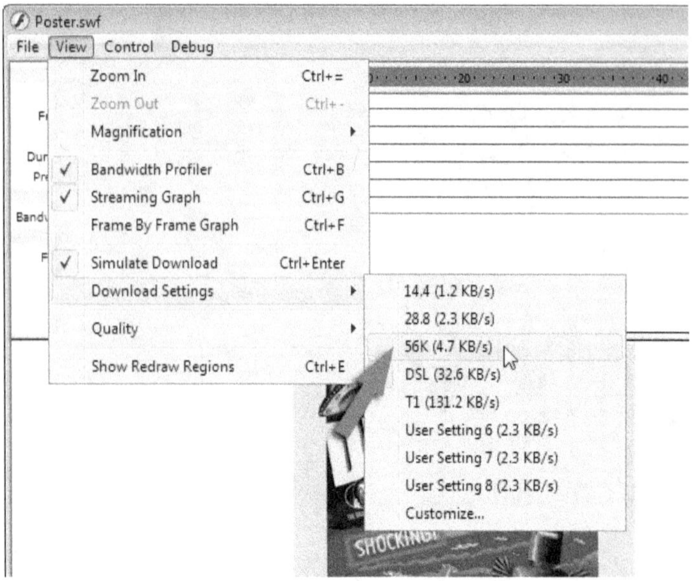

Remember! Always check the Bandwidth Profiler when creating your Flash projects. A large file size may send users packing!

Your **Bandwidth Profiler** will now show you the Preload time for a dial-up modem. If you look next to **Preload** you'll see 7.5s, and next to Bandwidth you'll see 4800 (dial-up speed). If a user has a dial-up modem then they will have to wait 7.5 seconds for the file to load and the animation to begin.

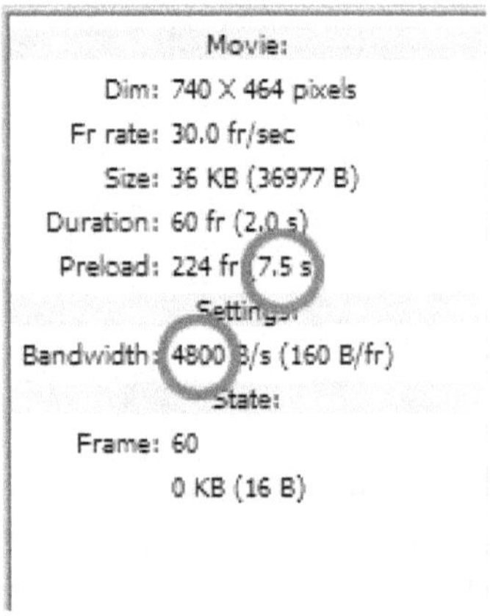

Next to the **Bandwidth Profiler** you'll see the Bandwidth timeline:

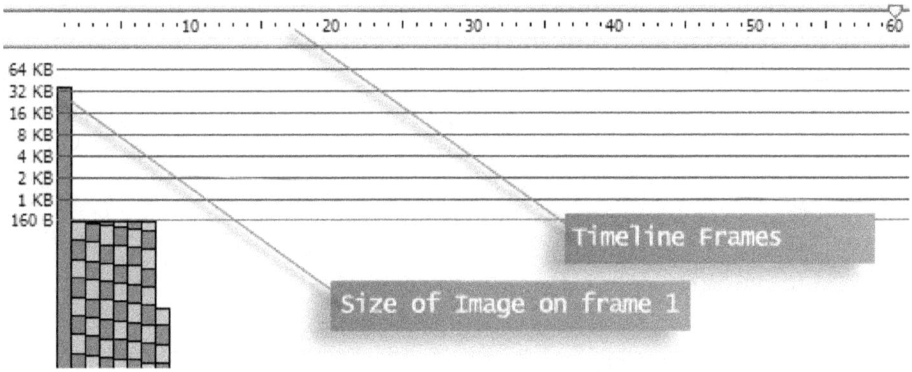

This simply shows the timeline of your main timeline broken down into how much information is downloaded in each frame. You'll notice that on frame 1 we have 32 KB of information that needs to download before continuing.

Let's go back to the editing stage. Create a keyframe on frame **30** of the **Actions** layer. Next, go to **File**, **Import**, **Import to Stage**. Select the image **lake.jpg** from the Pictures folder inside the Chapter Four Pictures folder. Test your movie again. This time you'll notice on the Bandwidth Profiler, a spike at frame **30**:

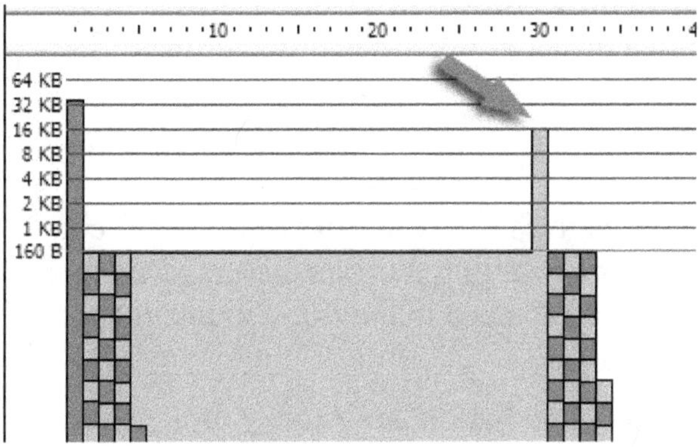

This is where the lake image is located. Go back to the editing stage and delete the lake.jpg image. Test your movie again.

If you want to simulate how a person on dial-up will view your Flash file, then go to **View**, **Simulate Download**:

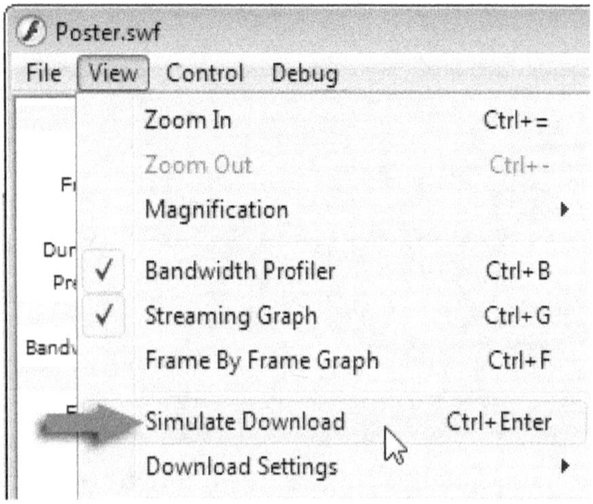

At the bottom of the **Bandwidth Profiler** the loading information will begin.

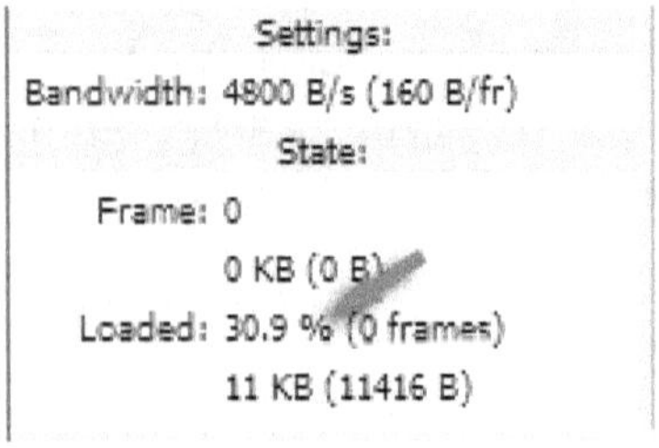

This will simulate the amount of time a visitor has to wait for your Flash file to load up. You'll notice that while the visitor is waiting they are staring at a white stage. That's where the preloader comes in. We need to have text indicating that the movie is loading. Let's do that now.

Open the Scene panel. Click on the **Add Scene** button and name your new scene **Preloader**:

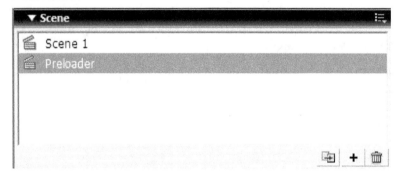

As we learned in previous exercises the Scene panel will show you the order of the scenes as they will appear for the user. For instance, in this project the first scene that will appear is Scene 1, then Preloader. Whenever you create a Preloader scene, you always want it to be the first Scene to load up. So drag the Preloader scene above Scene 1:

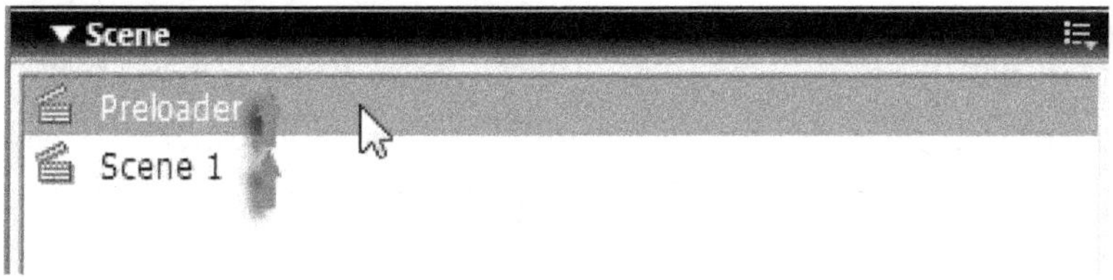

The Preloader scene will now load up first. Let's add the loading text. In the Preloader scene change the name of **Layer 1** to **Actions**. Next, add a new layer and name it **Text**:

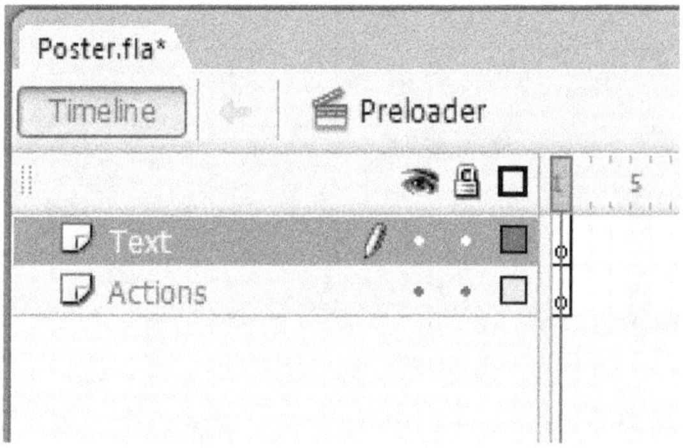

Select the **Text Tool** and type the word **Loading...** in the middle of the stage. In the Properties panel change the Text attributes to **Arial**, **Size 24**, **Color black**. Next, go to the **Align panel** and center the text in the stage:

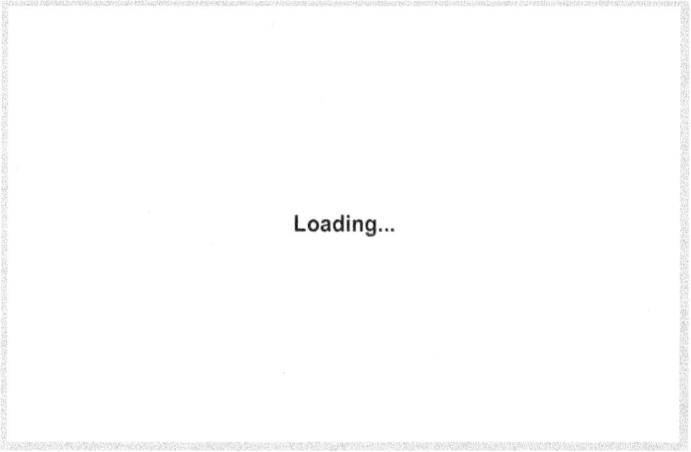

Next, we'll add the ActionScript. Select the first frame of the **Actions** Layer. Open the Actions panel and turn on Script Assist. Go to **Deprecated**, **Actions**, and double-click **ifFrameLoaded**:

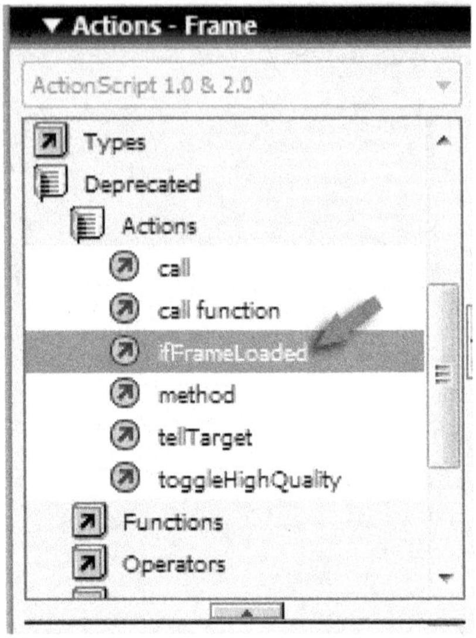

The **ifFrameLoaded** settings window should now be open. **ifFrameLoaded** is code for "if the frame is loaded." So we're telling Flash to check to see if a frame is loaded, usually the last frame of the main timeline (in this case frame 60).

Next to Scene choose **Scene 1** from the drop down selections. Make sure the **Type** is **Frame Number** and type **60** next to **Frame**:

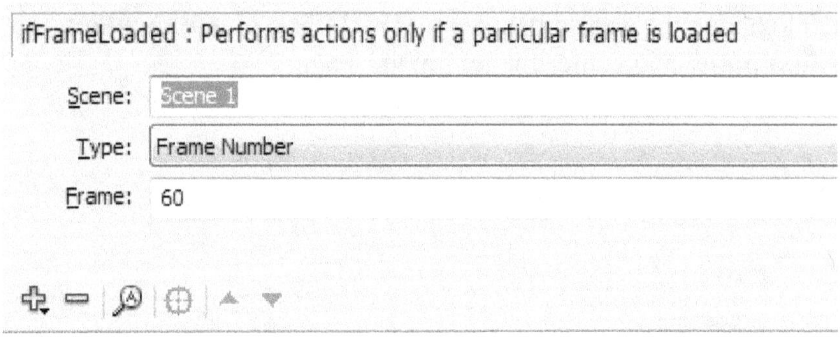

So now Flash is going to check frame 60 of the main timeline to see if it has loaded. Go to **Global Functions**, **Timeline Control**, and double-click **goto**:

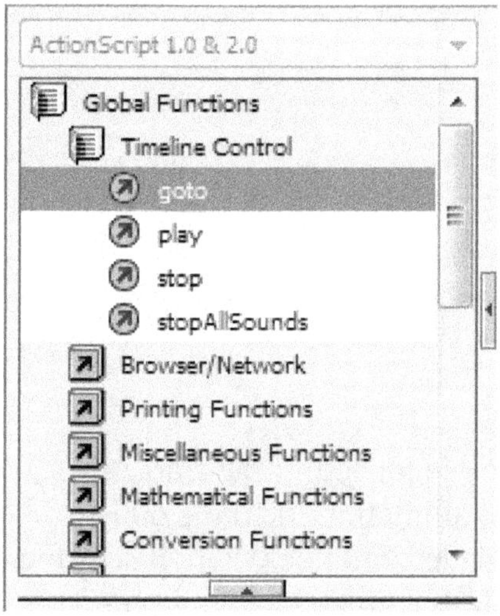

You should now see the **goto** settings window. Select **Scene 1** from the Scene drop down list. Change the **Type** to **Frame Number** and the **Frame** to **1**:

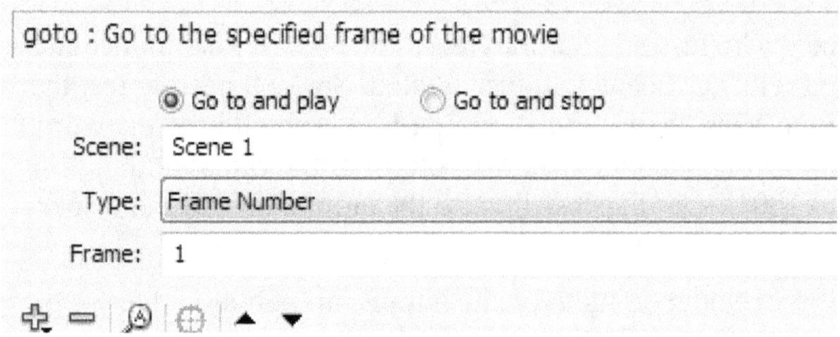

So if Flash determines that frame 60 has loaded for the visitor it will go to frame 1 of Scene 1 and play. So what happens if the visitor is on dial-up or a slow connection and frame 60 hasn't loaded for them yet? That's where the next step comes in.

Create a keyframe on frame **2** of the **Actions** layer. Select the keyframe and open the Actions panel. Go to **Global Functions**, **Timeline Control** and double-click **goto**. You should now see the **goto** settings window. Select **Current Scene** or **Preloader** from the Scene drop-down list, **Frame Number** for **Type**, and the **Frame** should be at **1**:

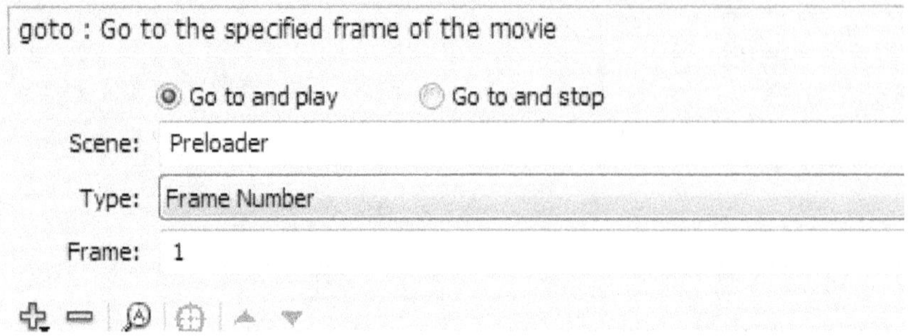

So on the first frame Flash checks to see if frame 60 is loaded; if the frame is loaded Flash goes to Scene 1 and starts playing the animation. If frame 60 isn't loaded then Flash continues to frame 2 of the Preloader timeline where it sees the code we just created above. What this code tells Flash is to go back to frame 1 (where the **ifFrameLoaded** code is). When Flash goes back to frame 1 it once again checks to see if frame 60 is loaded for the visitor. If it isn't loaded, this timeline continues to frame 2 and repeats. This loop continues until frame 60 is loaded and Flash goes to Scene 1.

Test your movie. Since you're testing your movie, frame 60 will load immediately so you'll never see the Preloader Scene you just created. So we'll need to test the movie another way; go to **View**, **Simulate Download**. You should see the word **Loading....** Watch the loading percentage at the bottom of the Bandwidth Profiler; once it gets to 100% then Flash will go to the animation and the Poster will fade in.

Go back to **Room.fla**. We're now going to create a transparent button that we'll place over the magazine on the couch. Create a new layer and name it **Button**. Next, grab **the Rectangle Tool**, turn the **Stroke color** off, and use any **Fill color** you like; create a shape over the magazine on the couch:

Select the shape and go to **Modify**, **Convert to Symbol**. Name this symbol **Magazine Button**, and change the **Type** to **Button**:

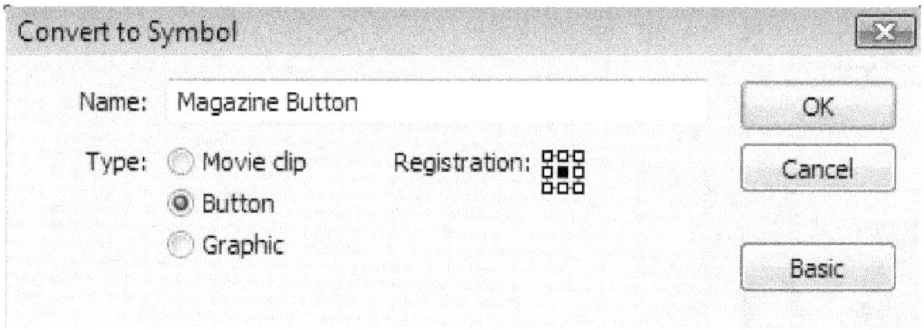

Hit **OK**. With the new button still selected, open the Properties panel. Change **Color** to **Alpha**, and the percentage to **0**:

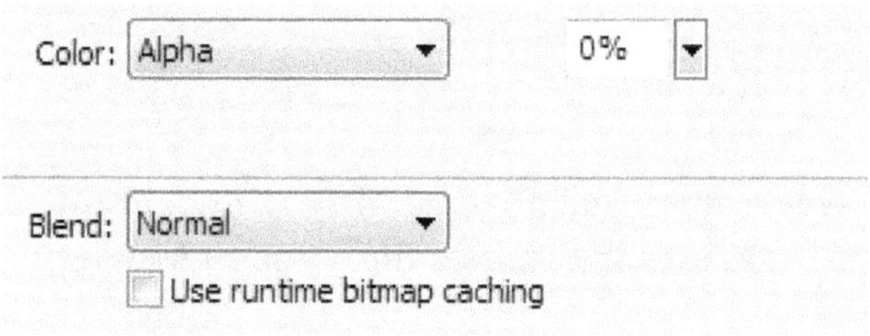

The **Magazine Button** should now be transparent. Let's create the **Target** that the Poster will load into. Create a new layer and name it **Target Magazine**:

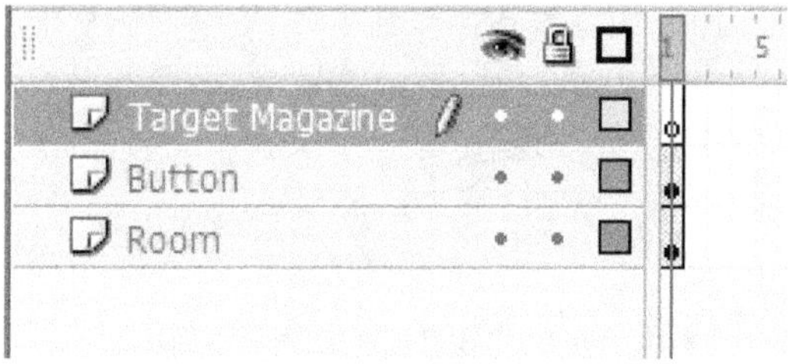

Next, grab the **Rectangle Tool**, turn off **Stroke color**, and use any **Fill color**. Create a shape and place it at the top left of the stage:

Grab the **Selection Tool** and select this new shape. Click on the **Fill color** button and take the **Alpha** down to **0**:

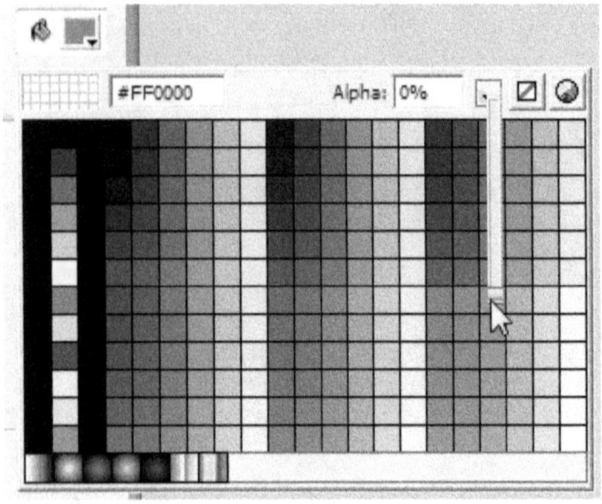

So now this shape is transparent. Select it again and go to **Modify**, **Convert to Symbol**. Name this symbol **Target Magazine**, and change the **Type** to **Movie clip**:

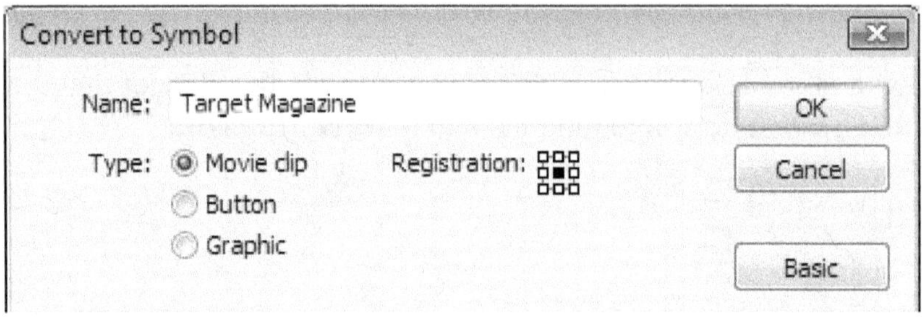

Hit **OK**. Open the Properties panel and in the **Instance Name** window type **target_magazine** (the Instance Name can't have spaces which is why we use the underscore between the words):

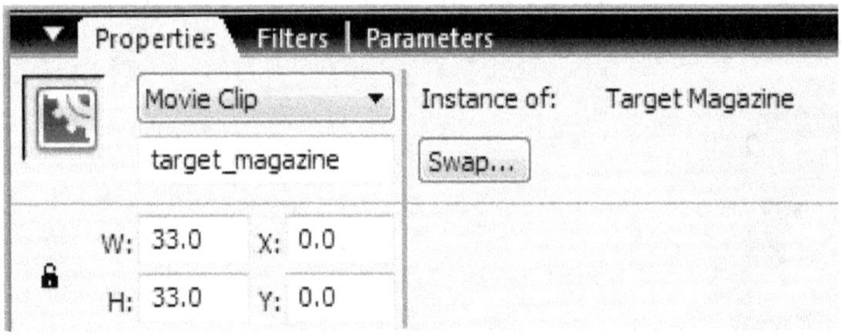

Remember! When you give your Movie clips Instance Names or when you name your Labels, you can use either upper or lowercase names. Just remember which one you use since all code is case sensitive!

So now that we have the Movie symbol done, we can add the ActionScript to the **Magazine Button**. Let's do that now. Select the **Magazine Button** and open the Actions panel; remember to turn on Script Assist. Go to **Global Functions, Browser/Network** and double-click **loadMovie**. You should now be in the **loadMovie** settings window. Type **Poster.swf** in the **URL** window. Change the **Location** to **Target** and type **/target_magazine** :

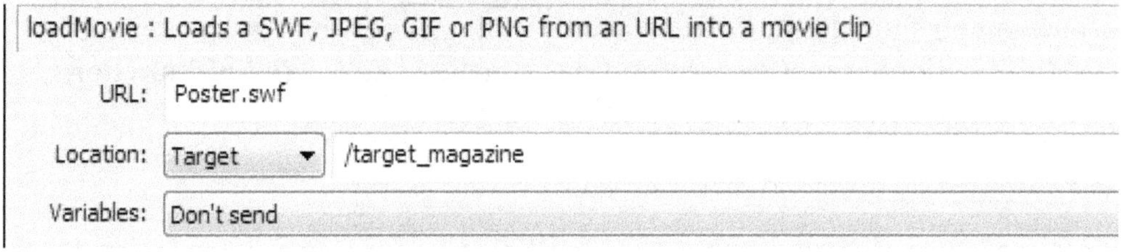

So now when the user clicks on the **Magazine Button** it will load the poster file into the **Target Magazine** Movie clip. Let's test it out. Test your movie now and click on the Magazine button. The poster file should fade in from white. Remember, if you don't like the location of the poster on the stage just *move the Target Magazine Movie clip.*

Now, the problem is that we can't close this poster file. To fix this problem, we can either add a Close button to the poster file or we can add a button to the main file. The easiest solution is to just create a Close button inside the poster file. Let's do that now.

Open **Poster.fla** once again. Go to **Scene 1** and create a new layer called **Button**. create a keyframe on frame 60 of the **Button** layer. Next, grab the **Rectangle Tool**, turn off the **Stroke color**, and use any color for the **Fill color**. Create a shape over the entire Poster:

Select this shape and go to **Modify**, **Convert to Symbol**. Name this **Poster Button** and change the **Type** to **Button.**

Next, open the Properties panel and change **Color** to **Alpha** and the percentage to **0**:

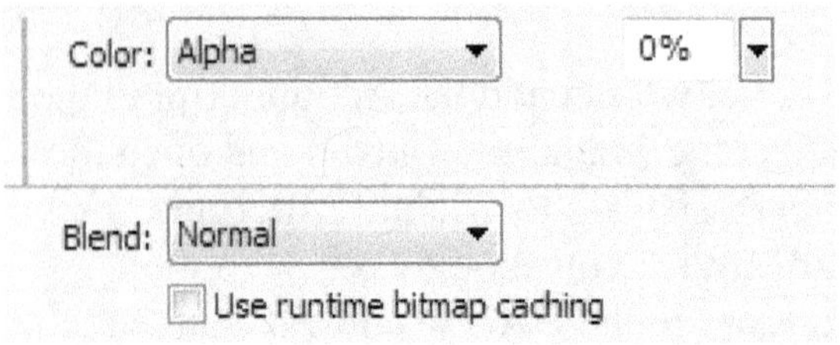

This new button should now be transparent. With this new button still selected let's add the ActionScript. Open the Actions panel and go to **Global Functions, Browser/Network** and double-click **unloadMovie**:

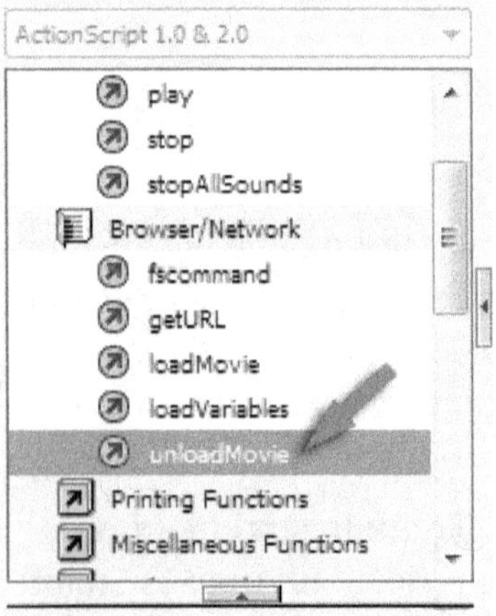

You should now see the **unloadMovie** settings window. Change the **Location** to **Target** and type **/target_magazine** in the **Location** window:

Go to **File**, **Publish**. Go back to **Room.fla**. Test your movie again and click on the **Magazine Button**. Your Poster should fade in nicely. When it finishes its animation it should become clickable due to the large transparent button we just made. Click anywhere on the Poster and it should close.

So the next thing we want to do is load the video into the TV. Then, using a remote, we'll control the video. Let's do that now.

Create a new layer and name it **Target TV**. Select frame **1** of the **Target Magazine** layer and select the **Target** Movie clip on the stage. Go to **Edit**, **Copy**. Then, select the first frame of the **Target TV** layer and go to **Edit**, **Paste in Place**.

You should now have a copy of the **Target Magazine** Movie clip in the **Target TV** layer. Select this Movie clip and open the Properties panel. Change the **Instance Name** from **target_magazine** to **target_tv**:

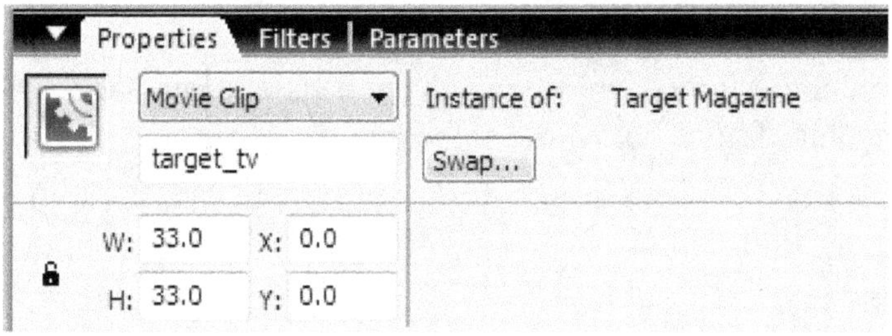

Next, we'll create a remote control that will control the TV. Create a new layer and name it **Remote**:

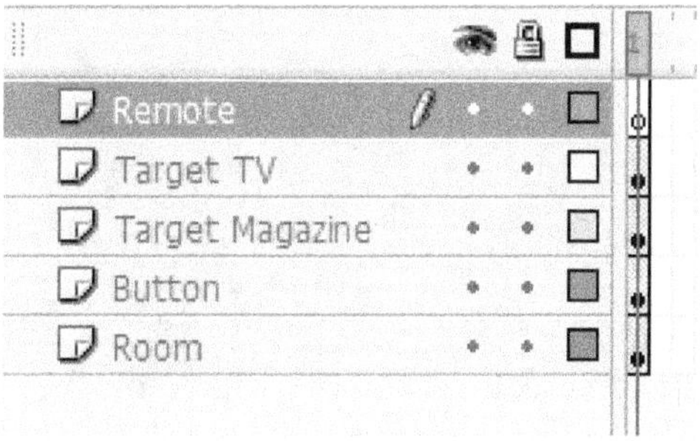

Go to **File**, **Import**, **Import to Stage**. Select **remote.png** from the Pictures folder in the Chapter Four folder. Select the remote image on the stage and go to **Modify**, **Convert to Symbol**. Change **Type** to Movie clip and type **Remote** for the Name:

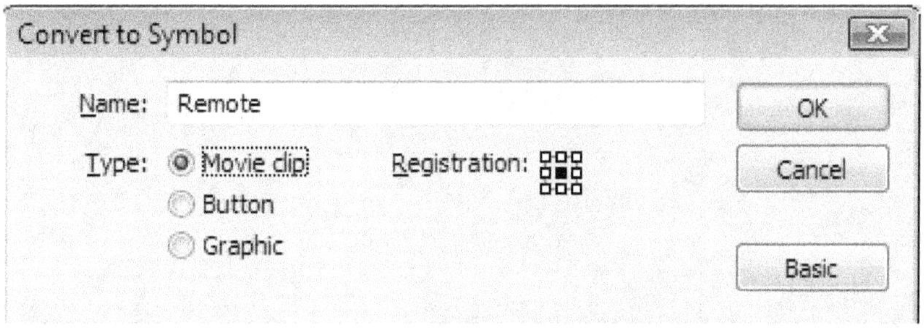

Since we'll be controlling this Movie clip we need to give it an Instance Name. In the Properties panel type **remote** in the **Instance Name** window:

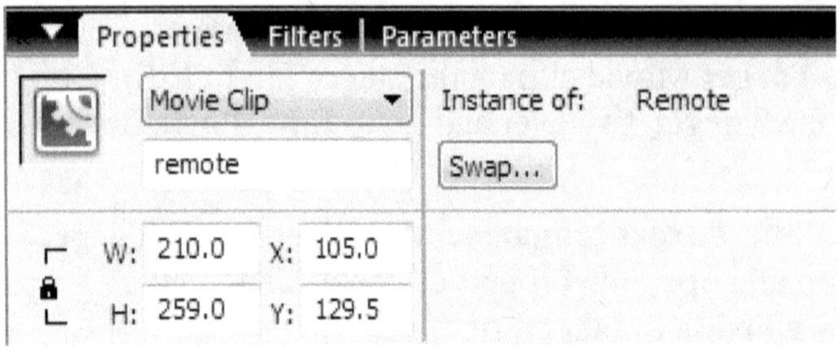

Hit **OK**. Double-click on this new Movie clip so we can enter its editing stage. Select the image on the stage and drag it below the stage and to the right:

Select frame **40** of this layer and add a keyframe. Select the remote image on the stage and drag it straight up so the bottom of the remote lines up with the bottom of the stage:

Next, select any frame between 1 and 40 and insert a Motion Tween. We want the remote to gradually come to a stop so let's tweak the animation. Select frame **1** and open the Properties panel. Change **Ease** to **100**:

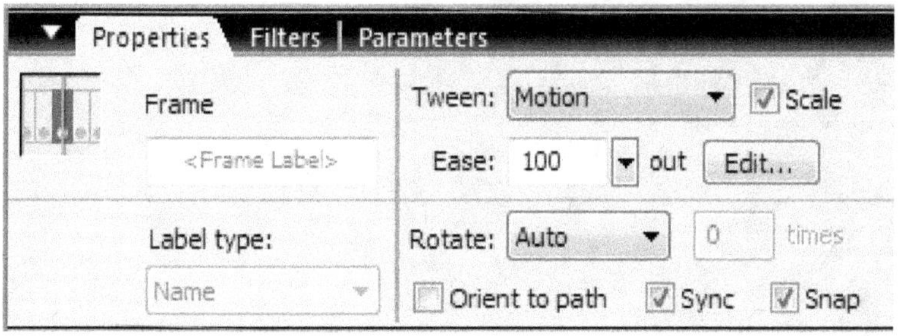

Test the movie. The animation looks good but it loops. Let's have the remote stop at the end of the animation. Create a new layer and name it **Actions**. Create a keyframe on frame **40** of the **Actions** layer and insert a **stop** code:

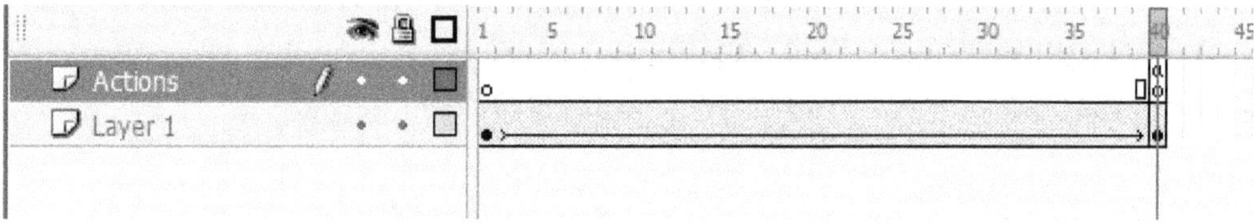

Let's add the link to the remote. Create a new layer and name it **Mars**. Create a keyframe on frame **40**. Next, grab the **Text Tool**. Open the Properties panel and select **Arial**, **Size 13**, **black**, and **Bold**:

Type the name **Destination Mars!** on the face of the remote:

With this new text still selected, go to **Modify**, **Convert to Symbol**, and change the **Type** to **Movie clip** and type **Destination Mars** for the Name:

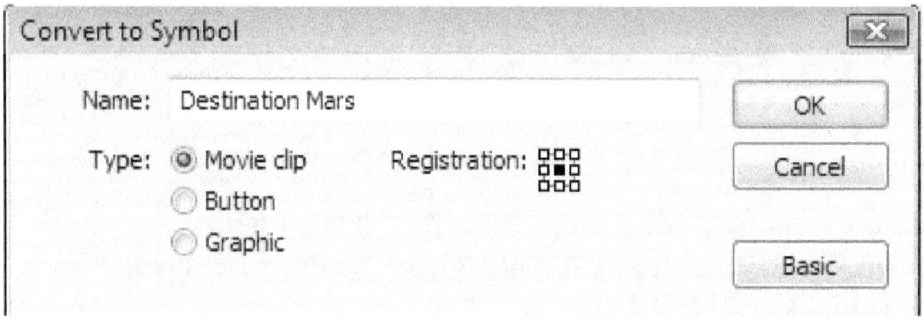

Double-click this new Movie clip to enter its editing stage. Create a keyframe on frame **20**, then insert a Motion Tween:

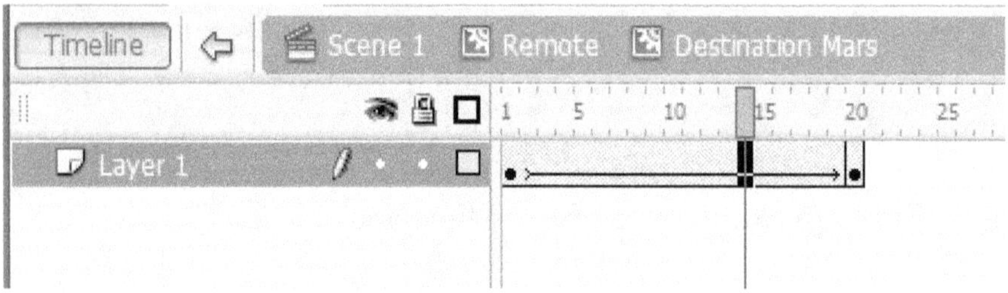

Select frame **1** of this layer then select the text symbol on the stage. Open the Properties panel and change **Color** to **Alpha**, and the percentage to **0**:

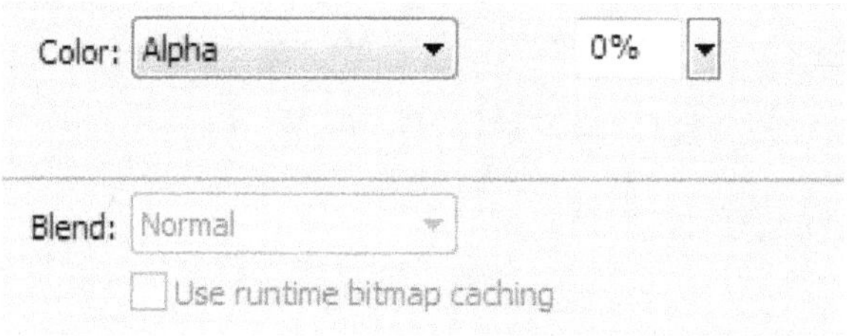

So now the text will fade in. Add a new layer and name it **Button**. Create a keyframe on frame **20**. Select the **Rectangle Tool**, turn off the **Stroke color** and create a shape over the text:

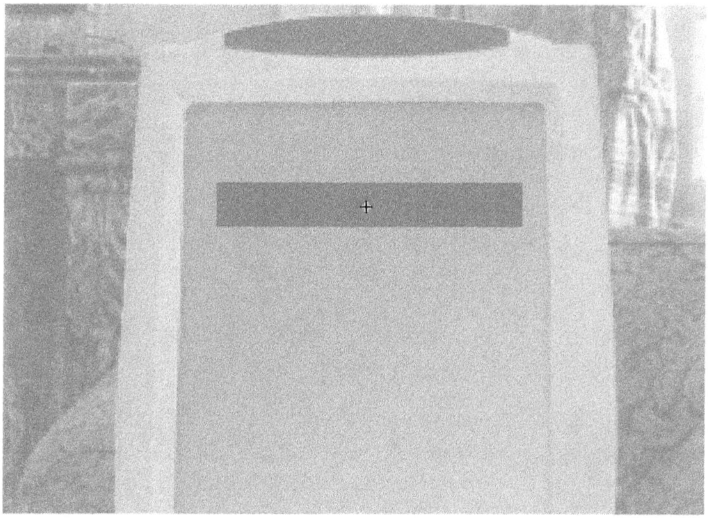

Select this shape and go to **Modify**, **Convert to Symbol**. Change the **Type** to **Button** and type **Remote Button** for the **Name**:

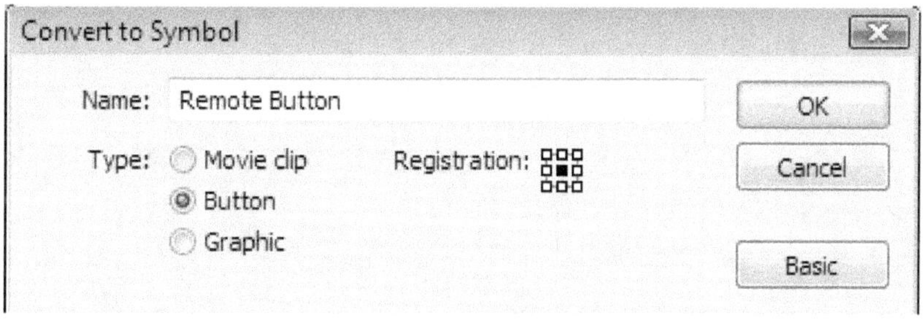

Hit **OK**. Open the Properties panel and change the **Color** to **Alpha**, and the percentage to **0**:

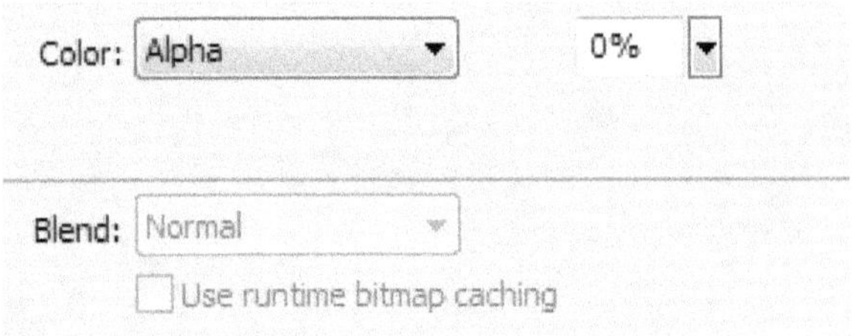

The button should now be transparent. Let's add the ActionScript. Open the Actions panel. Go to **Global Functions, Browser/Network** and double-click **loadMovie**:

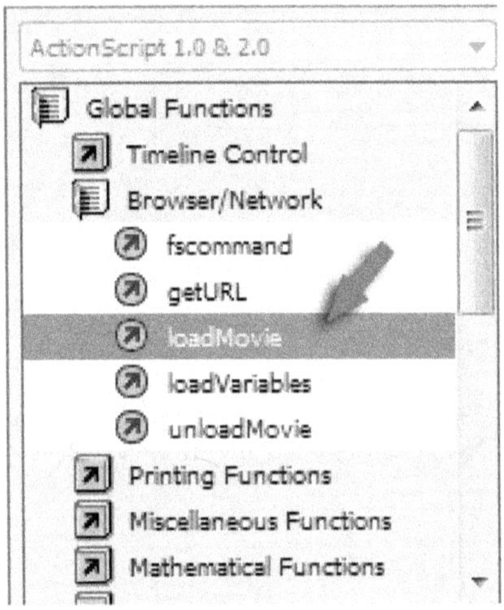

You should now see the **loadMovie** settings window. Type **mars.swf** in the **URL** window, change the **Location** to **Target** and type **/target_tv** in the **Location** window.

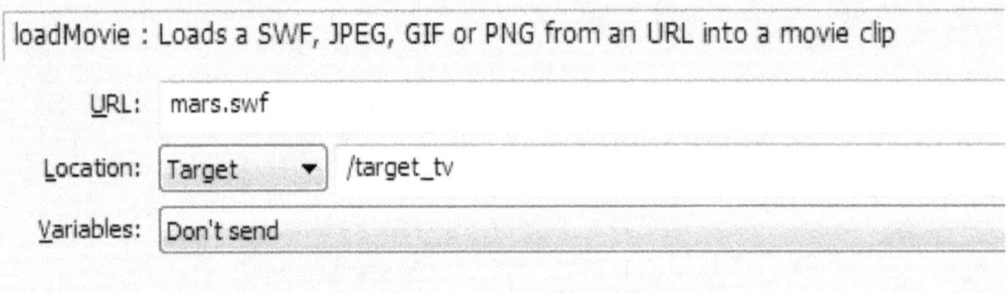

So now when we click this button, it will load in the video **mars.swf** into the Movie clip we named **target_tv**. Before we test this movie we need to add a **stop** code so the text animation doesn't loop. Create a new layer and name it **Actions**. Create a keyframe on frame **20** and insert a keyframe. Put a **stop** code into this keyframe:

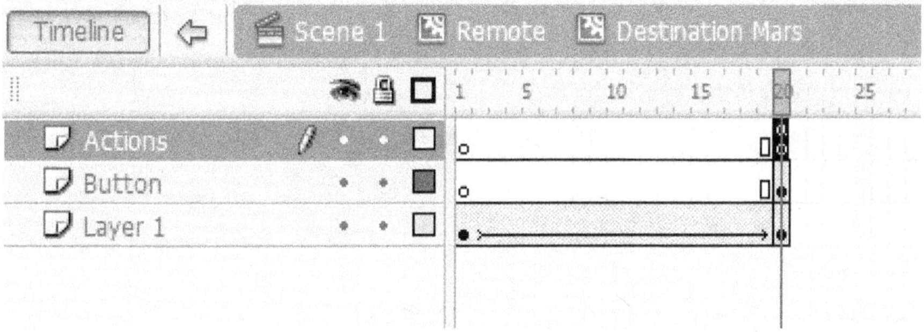

Test your movie. Click the button in the remote. The video should appear and start playing. So now we need to do two things. We need this video to play inside the TV and we also need to control it (stop, play, rewind). Your video probably appeared on the stage at this location:

So we not only need to move the video down and to the right, we also need to shrink it. Go back to Scene 1. Select the **target_tv** Movie clip; when you select it you should see the layer on the timeline become highlighted. Move this Movie clip down and to the right. Test your movie again and check the location. Keep moving the **target_tv** Movie clip until the video is directly over the TV:

Let's make the video smaller so it's a better fit in the TV. Select the **target_tv** Movie clip and go to the Transform panel. Make sure Constrain is checkmarked. Next, type **60** in both percentage windows:

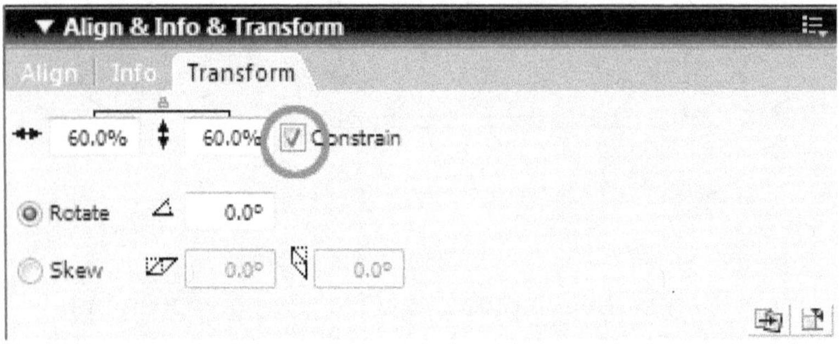

Your Movie clip should be smaller now. Test your movie again. You'll now notice that the video is smaller. This is another advantage of loading movies into Targets instead of Levels.

Since the video is smaller you may have to readjust the location of the video again. Grab the **target_tv** Movie clip again and move it around the stage until your video is right over the TV screen:

So that looks about right. Let's create the mask for this video. Create a new layer above the **Target TV** layer and name it **Mask**:

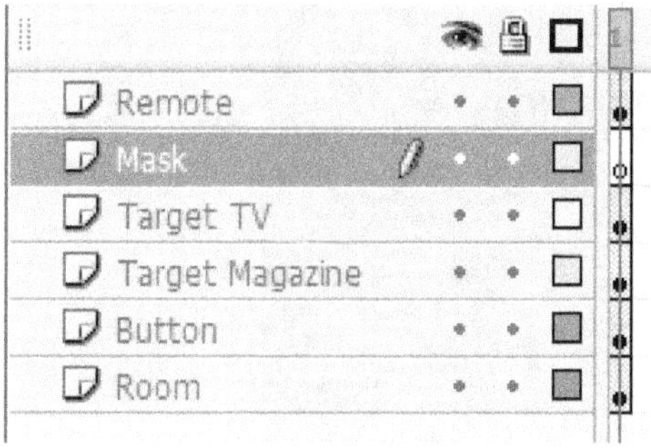

Zoom into the TV 200%. Grab the **Pen Tool**:

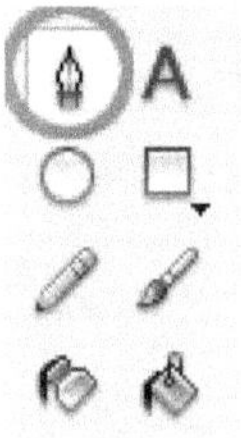

Click at the top middle of the screen:

Next, click on the right part of the screen where it curves; this time, though, don't let go of the mouse button. Click and drag and you should see handles; also, you'll be able to round the line to fit the shape of the screen:

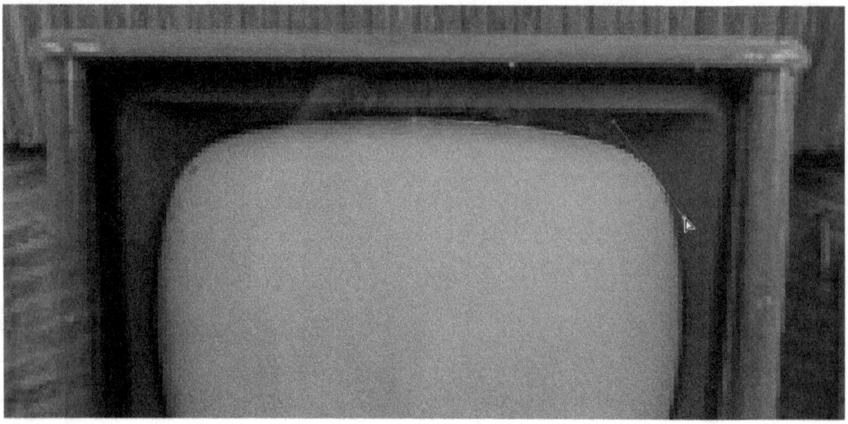

Click on the bottom right of the screen and remember to click-and-drag so you can curve the path:

Click on the bottom left of the screen; click-and-drag to curve the path:

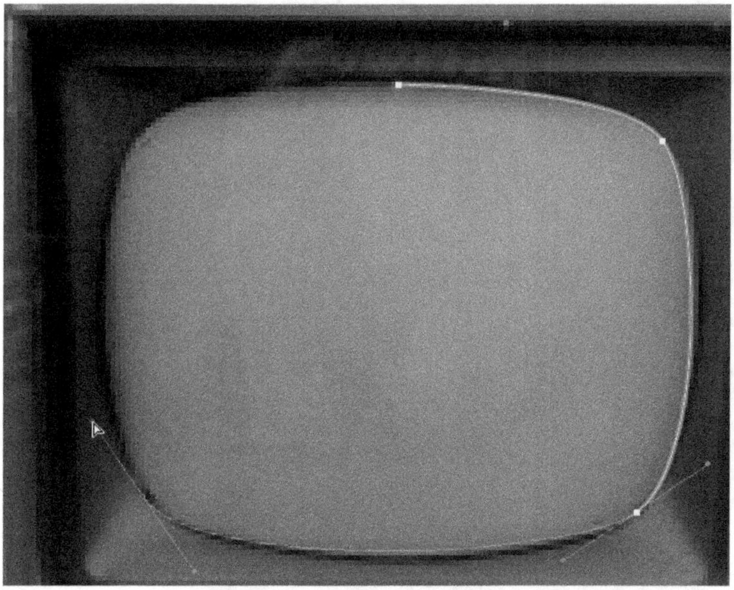

Click at the top left of the screen; click-and-drag to curve the path:

Now, to finish the path, click on the first pen point you created. Click-and-drag to round the corner:

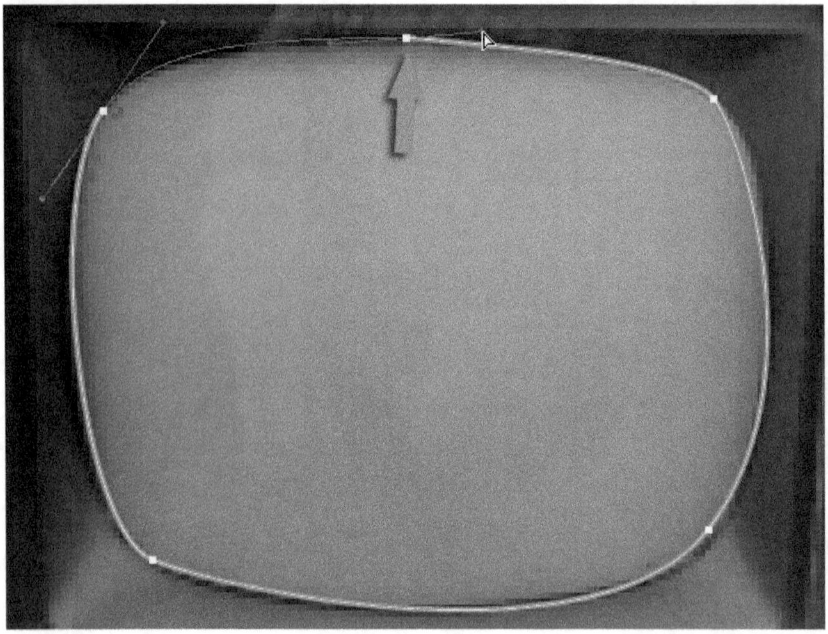

You should now see a red shape over the screen:

My red shape isn't quite perfect so I need to tweak it a bit. Grab the **Subselection Tool**:

Before you start tweaking the mask, lock the **Room** layer so it doesn't accidentally move:

Click on your pen points, specifically the ones that need to be tweaked. On mine, I need to adjust the top left one. Even though you can't see the pen points if you click on the outer edge of the red shape you should see the path once again; the pen points should now be visible. Click on the pen point you would like to adjust:

You can now grab each handle and adjust the curve. If you want to control less of an area with the handle, then *hold down* **Alt** while dragging the handle. Note: if you're having a hard time grabbing the points, zoom in even more into the image. Using the **Pen Tool** takes a little bit of practice as you're probably finding out. Keep playing with it until you get the hang of it.

When you're finished tweaking the mask shape, go to the **Mask** layer and **right click**; select **Mask** from the options:

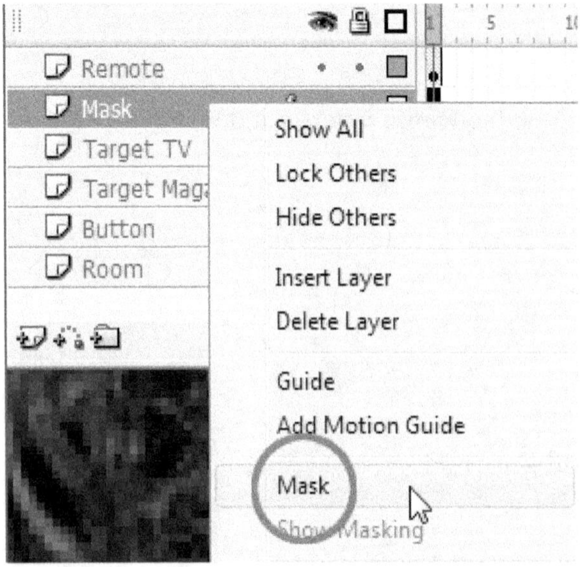

The **Target TV** layer should now be indented under the Mask layer:

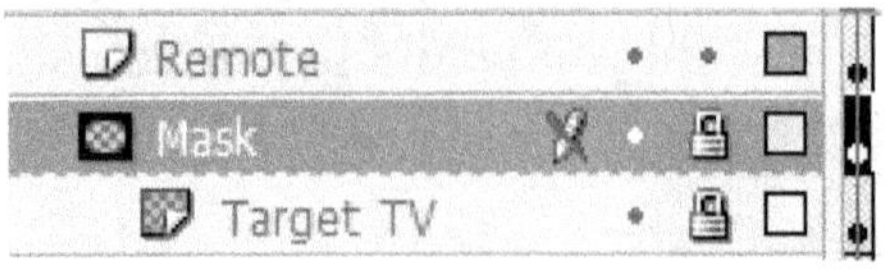

Test your movie. The movie should play nicely within the TV screen. Next, we'll add the video control buttons to the remote. Double-click on the Remote so you can enter its editing stage. Create a new layer and name it **Video Controls**:

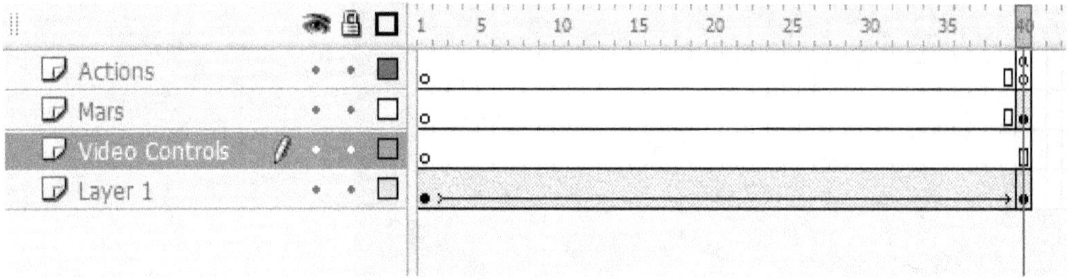

Create a keyframe on frame **40**. Next, go to **File**, **Import**, **Import to Stage**. Select the **VideoButtons.png** from the Pictures folder within the Chapter Four folder. Drag this image over onto the Remote so it's near the bottom of the remote screen:

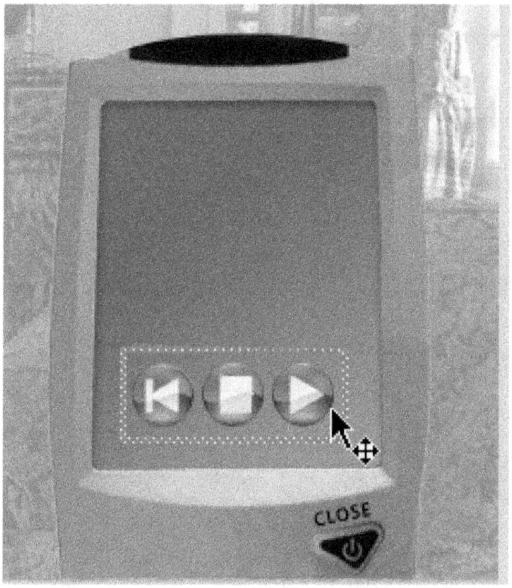

With the buttons still selected go to **Modify**, **Convert to Symbol**. Change the **Type** to Movie clip (we're going to animate the buttons fading in which is why we're choosing Movie clip) and name this symbol **Video Controls**:

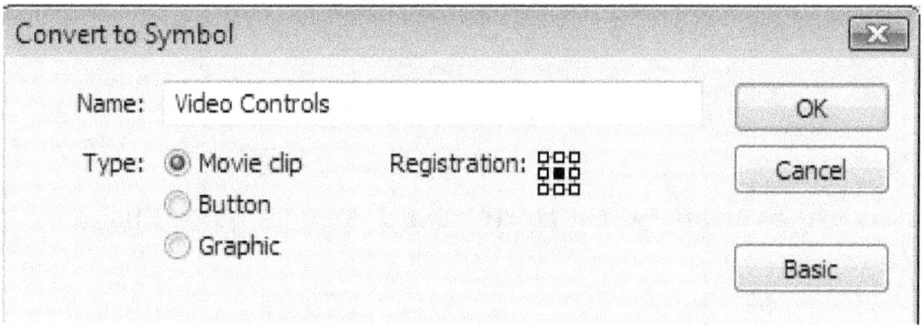

Hit **OK**. Double-click on this new Movie clip to enter its editing stage. We're going to have the buttons fade in just as we did with the text. Go to frame **20** and insert a keyframe. Select any frame between the keyframes and insert a Motion Tween. Click on the first frame and select the video controls symbol on the stage. Open the Properties panel and change the **Color** to **Alpha** and the percentage to **0**.

So now the buttons fade in. Create a new layer and name it **Actions**. Insert a keyframe on frame **20** and enter a **stop** code into this frame; this will prevent this timeline from looping. Next, create another layer and name it **Buttons**. Insert a keyframe on frame **20**:

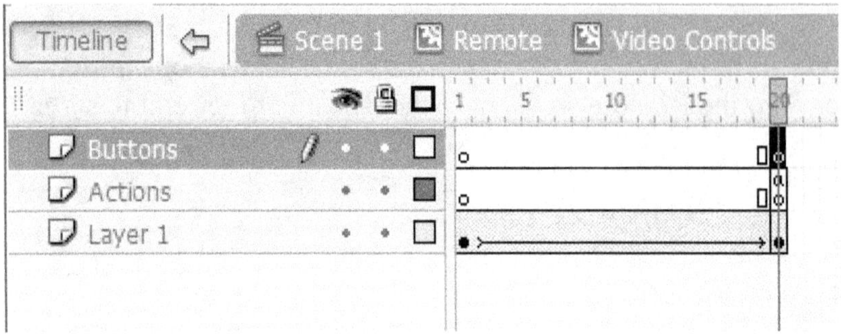

Select the **Rectangle Tool**, turn off **Stroke color** and create a shape over the first button (use any **Fill color**):

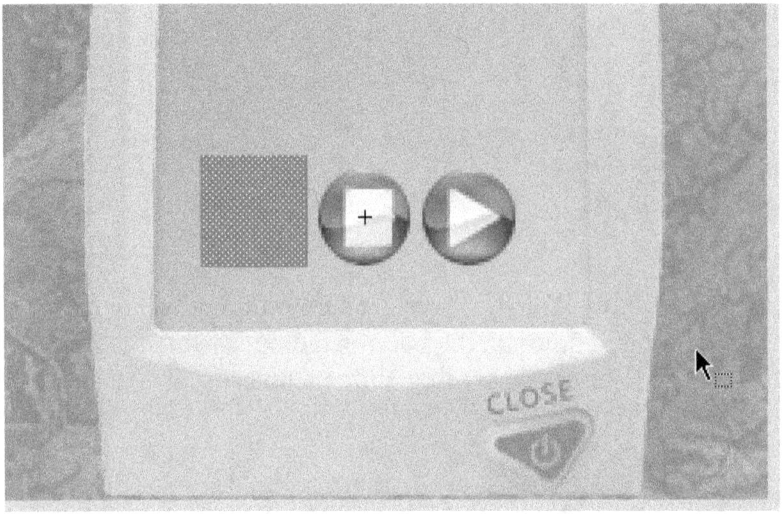

Go to **Modify**, **Convert to Symbol**. Select **Button** for **Type** and name this symbol **Video Button**:

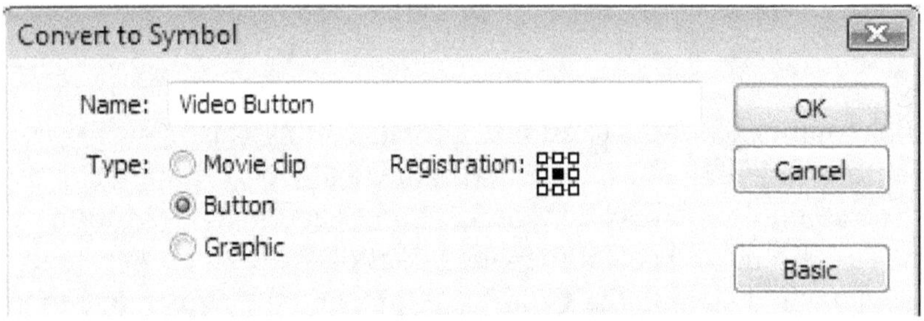

Hit **OK**. Open the Properties panel and change **Color** to **Alpha**, and the percentage to **0**. Your button should now be transparent. Let's add the ActionScript.

Make sure the button is still selected and open the Actions panel. Go to **Deprecated**, **Actions** and double-click **tellTarget**:

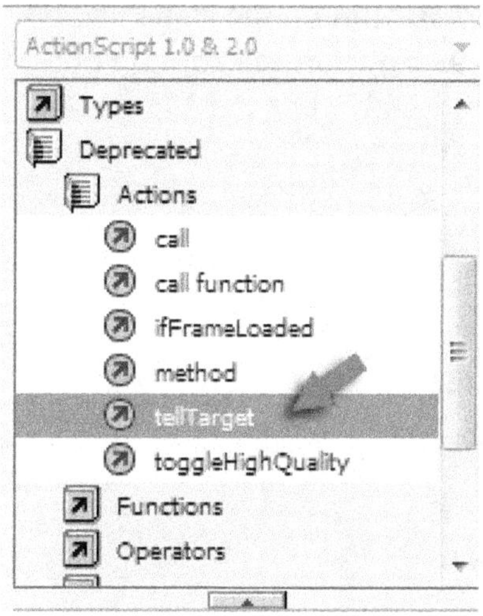

You should now be in the **tellTarget** settings window. Type **/target_tv** in the **Target** window:

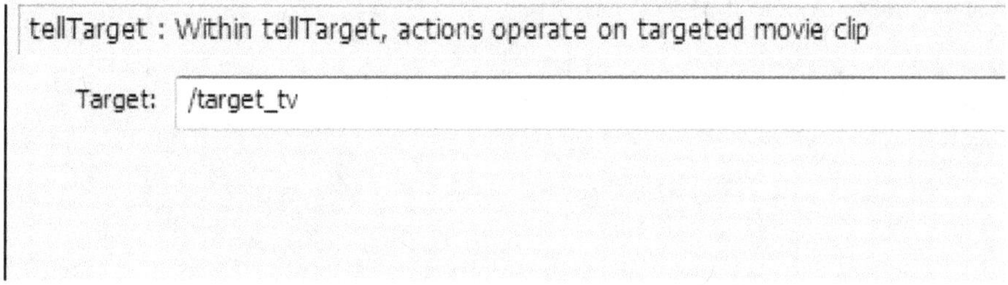

Next, go to **Global Functions**, **Timeline Control** and double-click **goto**. You should now be in the **goto** settings window. You don't need to change anything. The button is telling **target_tv** (the Movie clip that the video loads into) to go to Frame 1 and play:

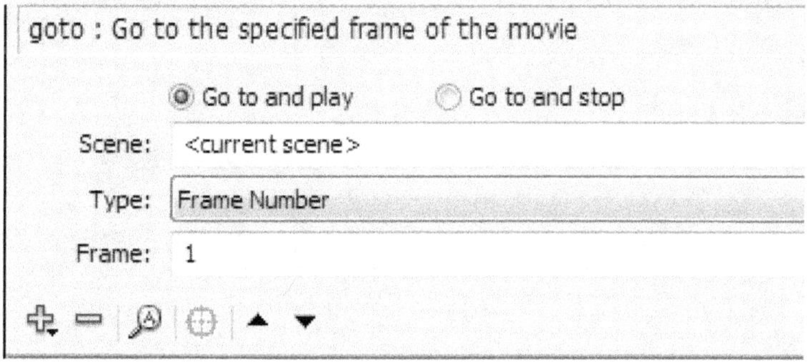

Test your movie. Click the **Destination Mars**! button to load in the video. Test your **Rewind Button**. The video should go back to frame 1 and start playing. Let's create the other two buttons. Select the **Rewind Button** on the stage and go to **Edit**, **Copy**. Next, go to **Edit**, **Paste in Place**. Your new button is on top of the **Rewind Button**. Select it and drag it over the stop button:

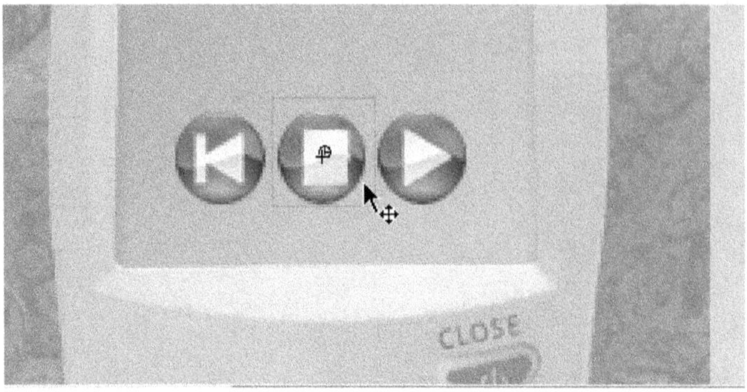

Since this new button is a copy of the Rewind Button it will have the ActionScript that we just created. In the Actions window delete this ActionScript. Go to **Deprecated**, **Actions** and double-click **tellTarget**. In the **tellTarget** settings window type **/target_tv** in the **Target** window:

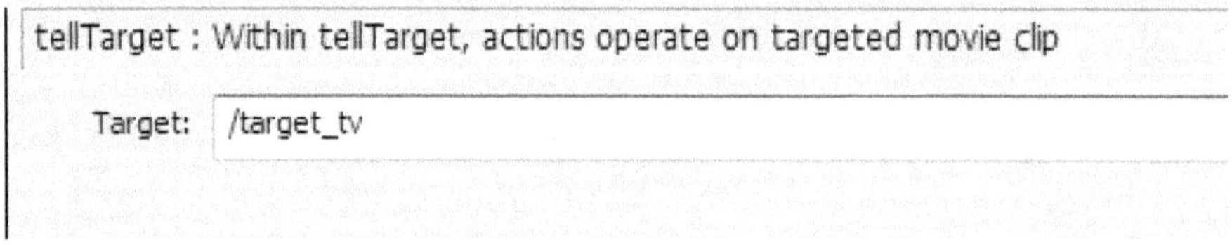

Next, go to **Global Functions**, **Timeline Control** and double-click **stop**.

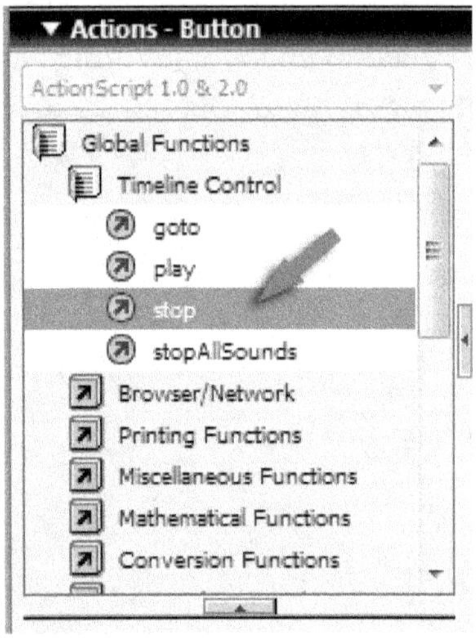

Test your movie. Click on the **Destination Mars!** button and click the **Stop** button. The video should stop playing. Let's add the last button. Select the **Stop** button and go to **Edit**, **Copy**. Next, go to **Edit**, **Paste in Place**. The new button will be directly on top of the **Stop** button; drag it over so it rests over the Play image:

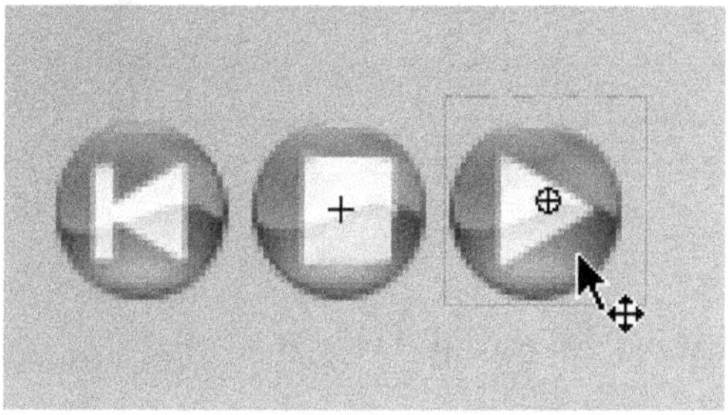

In the Actions panel click on the word **tellTarget**. Next, go to **Global Functions**, **Timeline Control** and double-click **play**. Select the word **stop** in the ActionScript and delete it. The ActionScript should now look like this:

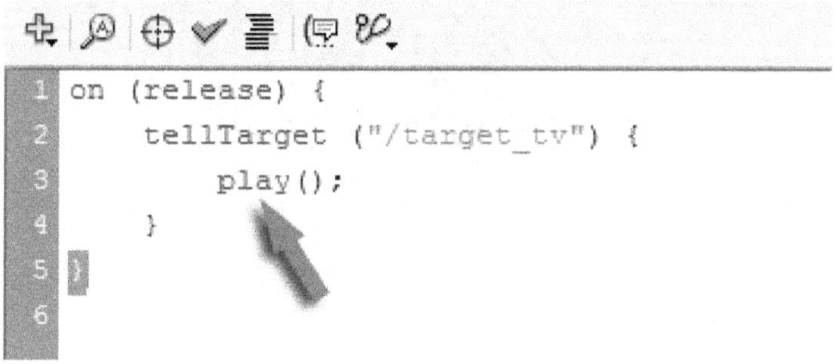

Test your movie. Your video should now rewind, stop and play using your video controls. Let's do a couple cool things. First, you'll notice that there is a **Close** image on the Remote. Let's activate it.

Above the timeline (**CS3-CS4/CS5** - above the stage) click on **Remote**:

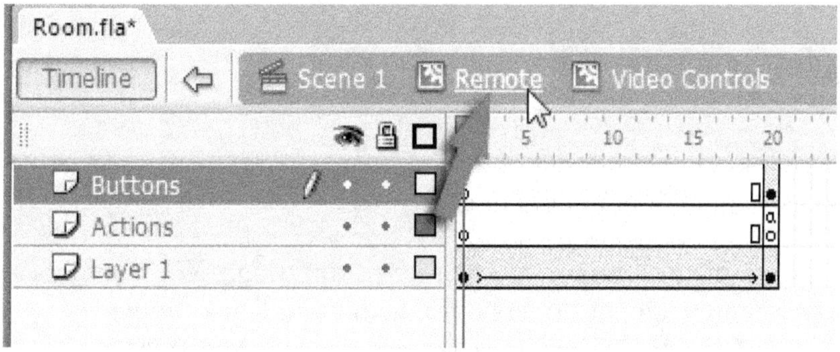

You should now be in the Remote stage. Create a new layer and name it **Close Button**. Create a keyframe on frame **20** of this layer:

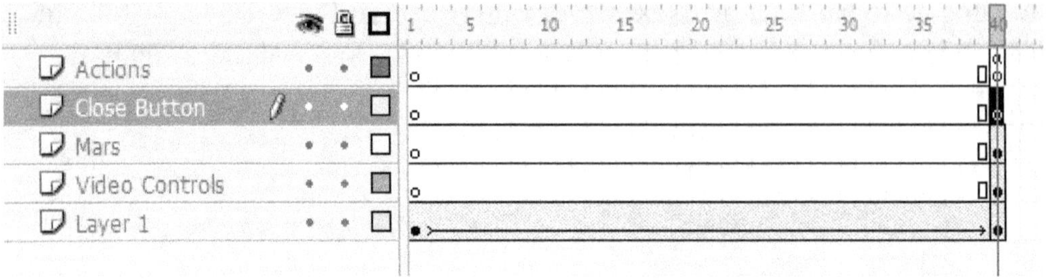

Next, go to **File**, **Import to Stage**. Select **powerDown.png**. Drag it so that it's exactly over the Close image on the Remote:

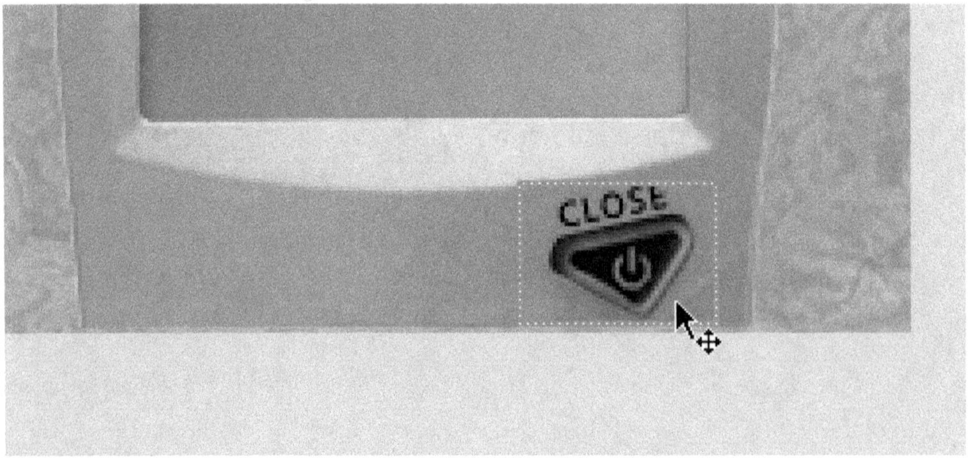

With this image still selected go to **Modify**, **Convert to Symbol**. Change the **Type** to **Button** and the symbol name will be **Close Button**:

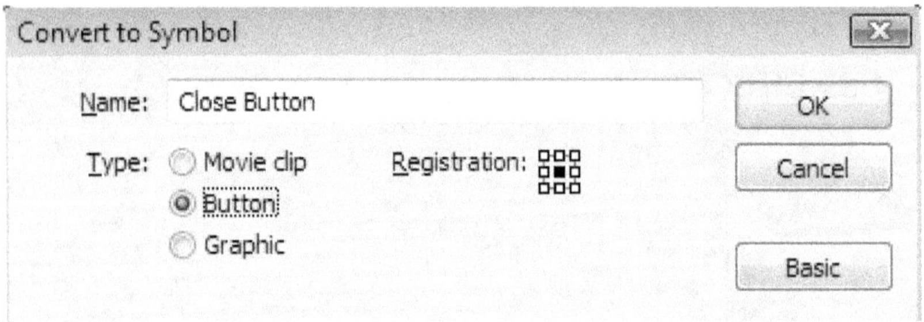

Hit **OK**. Double-click on this new button to enter its editing stage. We want this image to appear only when the cursor hovers over the button. Click on the keyframe under the state **UP**; drag this keyframe so that it's under **OVER**:

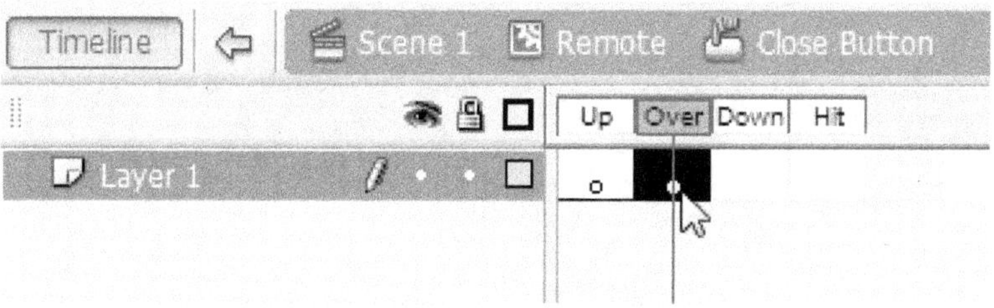

Test your movie. When the Remote finishes its animation, roll over the **Close Button**. You should see a nice little effect. But now we have to activate this button. When we click it we want the Remote to animate back down. Let's do that now.

Go back to the Remote stage. I'm going to show you a little trick that I use all the time. **Hold down the Alt button** and click on the first frame of the **Remote** layer. You should see a tiny little plus symbol:

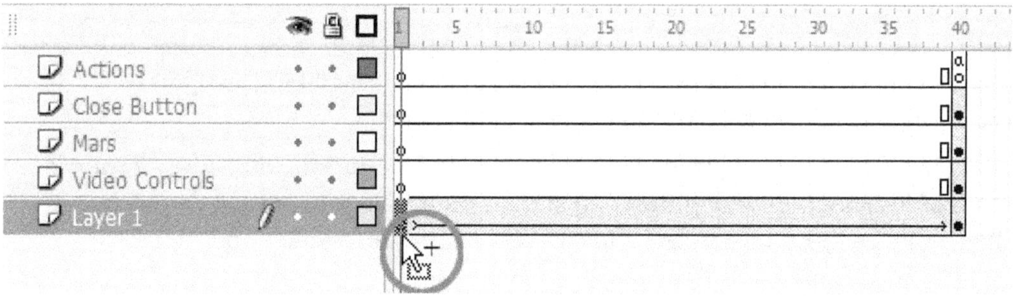

This means that you are about to make a copy of whatever is on this frame. Drag this keyframe to frame **80**. You should have an exact copy of the Remote on frame 80 in the same location as the Remote on frame 1.

Click anywhere between the frames **40** and **80** and insert a Motion Tween:

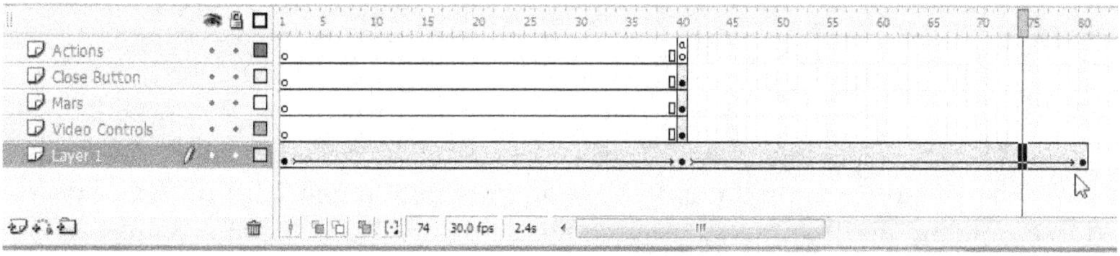

Now we have the Remote image animating up, and then animating back down. We're almost there. Since the **Close** Button is controlling the Remote we need to add Labels. Create a new layer and name it **Labels**. Create a keyframe on frame **2**. Open the Properties panel and type **up** in the **Frame Label** window:

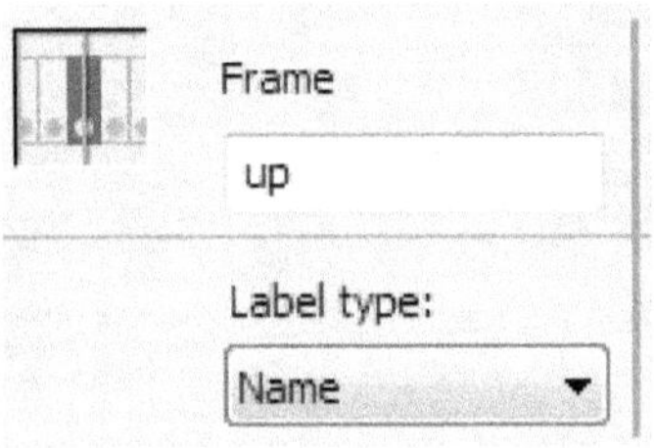

Create a keyframe on frame **41** of the **Labels** layer. Select this keyframe and give it a **Frame Label** name of **Down**. Your timeline should look like this:

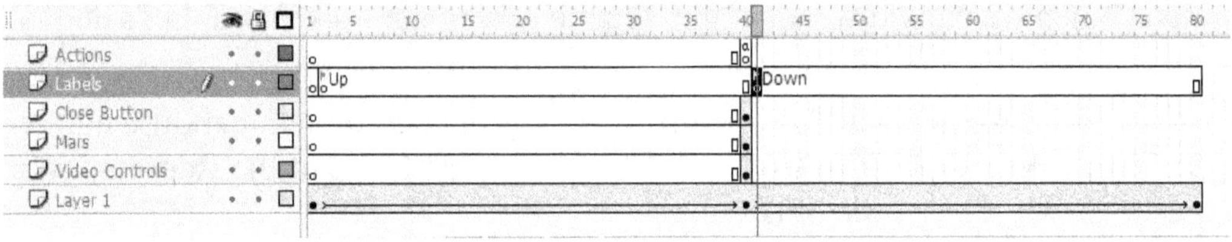

Since we want the animation to stop on frame **80**, we need to put a keyframe on frame **80** of the **Actions** layer and insert a **stop** code.

Select the **Close** button. In the Actions panel go to **Global Functions**, **Timeline Control** and double-click **goto**. You should be in the **goto** settings window. Change **Type** to **Frame Label** and type **Down** in the Frame window:

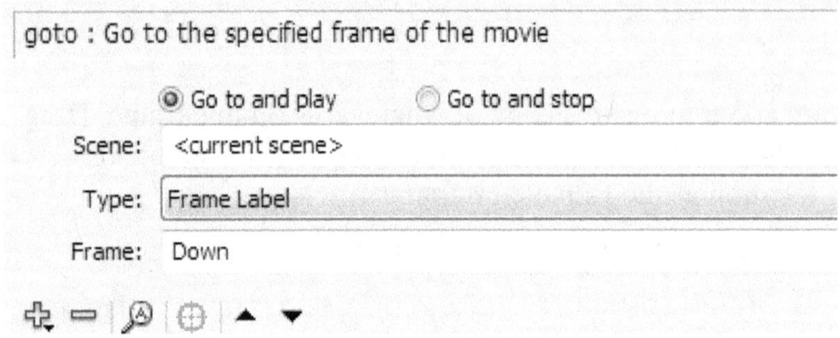

Test your movie. When the remote finishes its initial animation, test the **Close** Button. The Remote should animate back down where it came from. But now we need to command the Remote to animate back up. We'll add that button next. Create a new layer and name it **Remote Button**; next, create a keyframe on frame **80** of this layer:

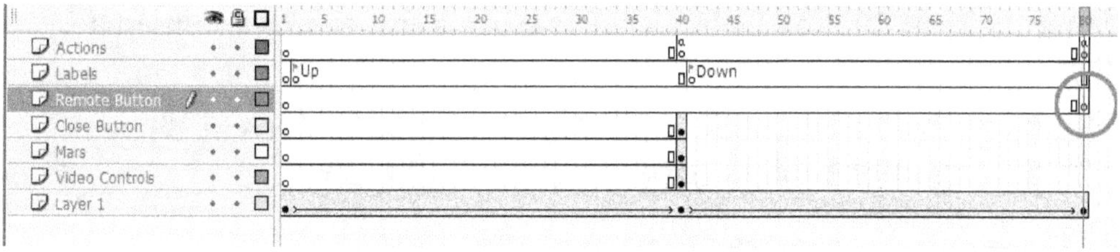

Go to **File**, **Import**, **Import to Stage**. Select **RemoteButton.png** from the Chapter Four Picture folder. You should now see **RemoteButton.png** on your stage. Drag it to the bottom right of the stage; make sure the bottom of the image is flush with the bottom of the stage:

Next, go to **Modify**, **Convert to Symbol**. Change the **Type** to **Movie clip** and name this symbol **Remote** Movie clip:

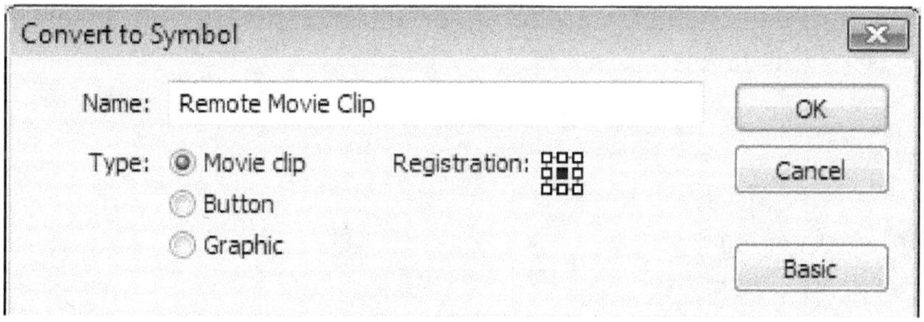

Hit **OK**. We could have made this symbol a Button instead of a Movie clip. But it always looks better when symbols just don't pop onto the stage but instead animate in. So let's do that now with this new symbol. Double-click on the **Remote** Movie clip we just created so we can enter its editing stage. Create a keyframe on frame **20**. Next, select any frame between **1** and **20** and insert a Motion Tween.

Select the first frame and open the Properties panel. Change **Ease** to **100**:

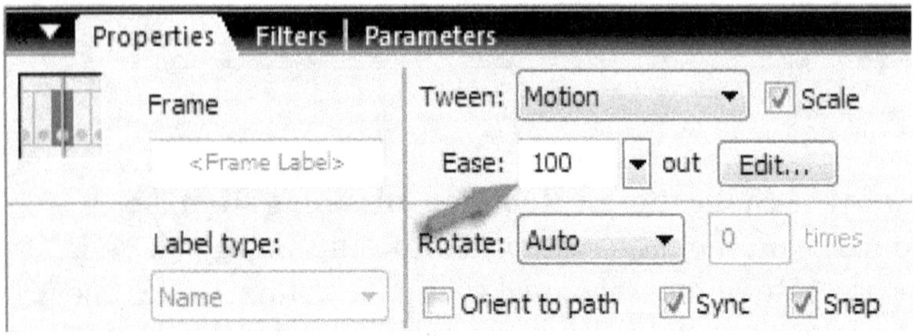

The symbol will now gradually come to a stop. Select the symbol on the stage. Drag it straight down so that it is below the stage:

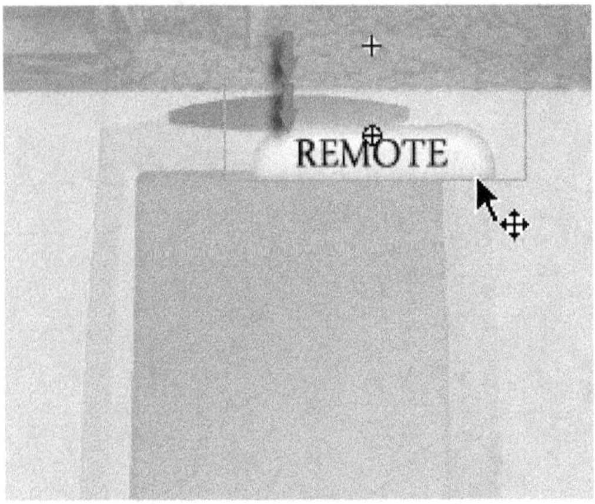

Now we need to put a **stop** code on frame **20** otherwise this animation will loop continuously. Create a new layer and name it **Actions**. Create a keyframe on frame **20** and insert a **stop** code. Create another layer and name it **Button**. Insert a keyframe on frame **20** of this layer:

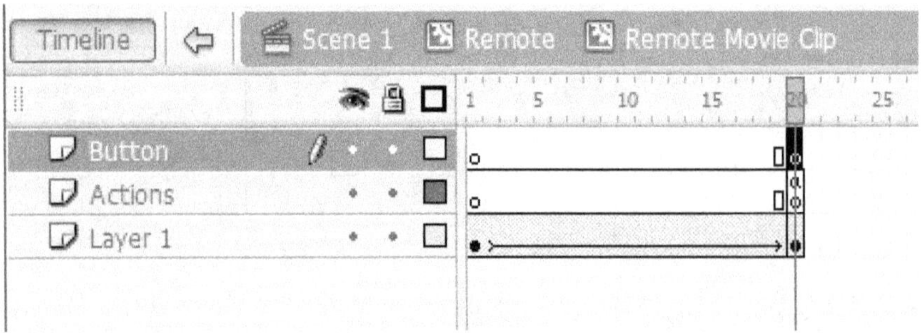

Select the **Rectangle Tool**, turn off **Stroke color**, and create a shape over the remote image:

Select this new shape and go to **Modify**, **Convert to Symbol**. Change the **Type** to **Button** and name this symbol **Remote Invisible Button**:

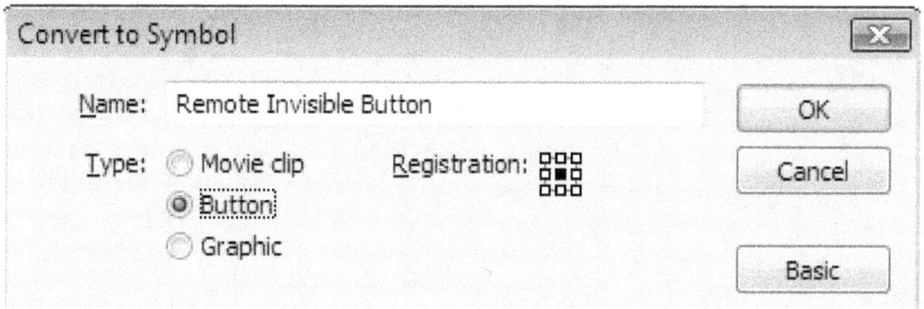

Hit **OK**. Open the Properties panel and change the **Color** to **Alpha**, and the percentage to **0**. You should now be able to see your Remote Movie clip on the stage. Next, open the Actions panel and go to **Deprecated**, **Actions**, and double-click **tellTarget**:

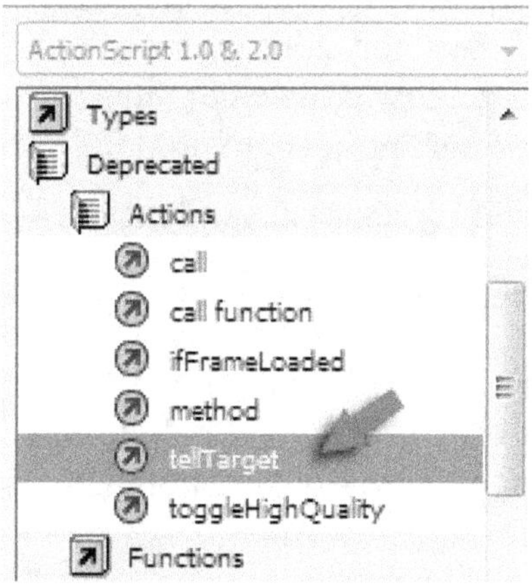

You should now be in the **tellTarget** settings window. Type **/remote** (the Instance Name we gave the Remote Movie clip) in the **Target** window:

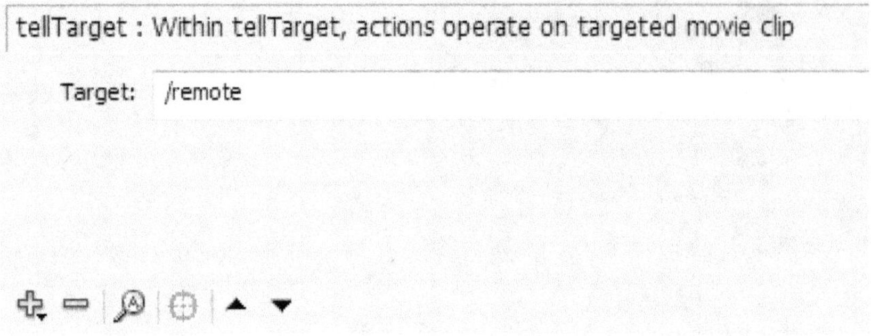

Go to **Global Functions**, **Timeline Control**, and double-click **goto**. You should now be in the **goto** settings window

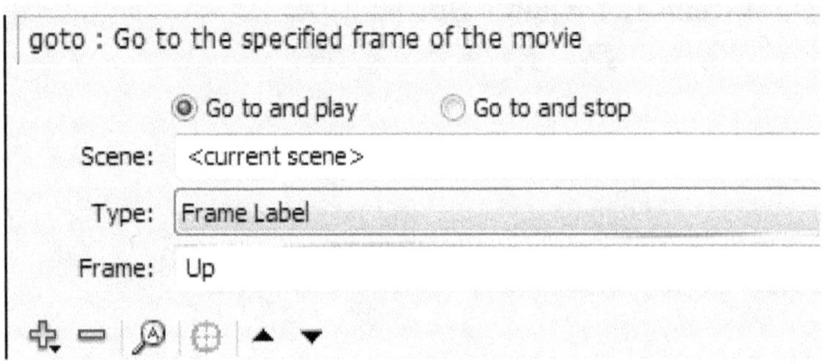

Test your movie. When the Remote finishes animating, hit the **Close** button. You should see the Remote button animate downward. When you click the **Remote** button the remote should animate back up.

Pretty neat huh? You're probably noticing that throughout all of the exercises we've been doing so far, that we're repeating a lot of the same steps over and over again. That's the great thing about Flash. Just by using a few simple commands like **goto** and **tellTarget**, you'll be creating dynamic Flash projects in no time!

Since this TV seems to be an older set, we need to add some static. And maybe have the video roll a couple times when it first comes on; maybe even have the video go out of focus then refocus.

Let's first add the static. We want the static to be within the TV screen mask. Select the **Target TV** layer then select the **New Layer** icon; this will put the new layer above the **Target TV** layer and *within the mask* (this new layer should be indented). Name this new layer **Static**:

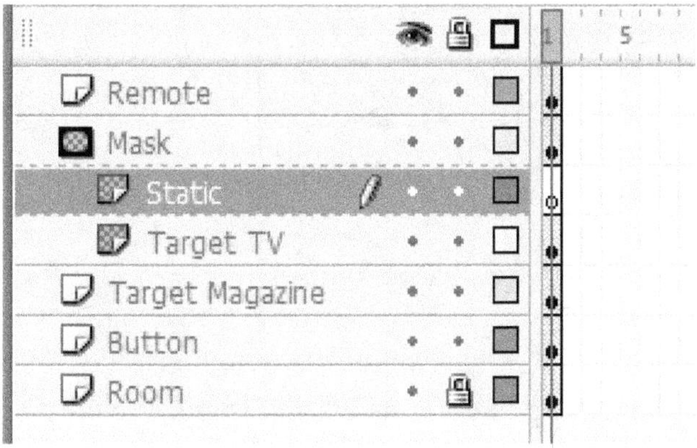

Next, go to **File**, **Import**, **Import to Stage**. We want to import three images at the same time; in the Pictures folder of the Chapter Four folder, select the image **static1.jpg**, then, holding down CTRL, select **static2.jpg**; hold down CTRL again and select **static3.jpg** then select **Open**:

On my stage the Static images are too far right. Select the keyframe of the **Static** layer (this will select all the images on that layer) and click-and-drag the static images to the left so they're over the middle of the Mask.

Go to **Modify**, **Convert to Symbol**. Change **Type** to **Movie clip** and name this symbol **Static**:

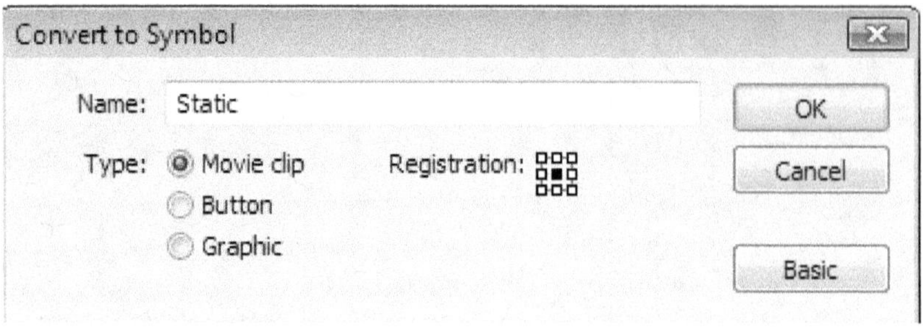

Hit **OK**. Double-click on this new movie clip to enter its editing stage. We now have three static images but they are all on one frame so we can only see one of them. Here's a trick you can do whenever you have more than one image on a frame and you want to put them all on their own individual layers.

Select the keyframe of **Layer 1**; this will select everything on this keyframe. Next, go to **Modify**, **Timeline**, **Distribute to Layers**:

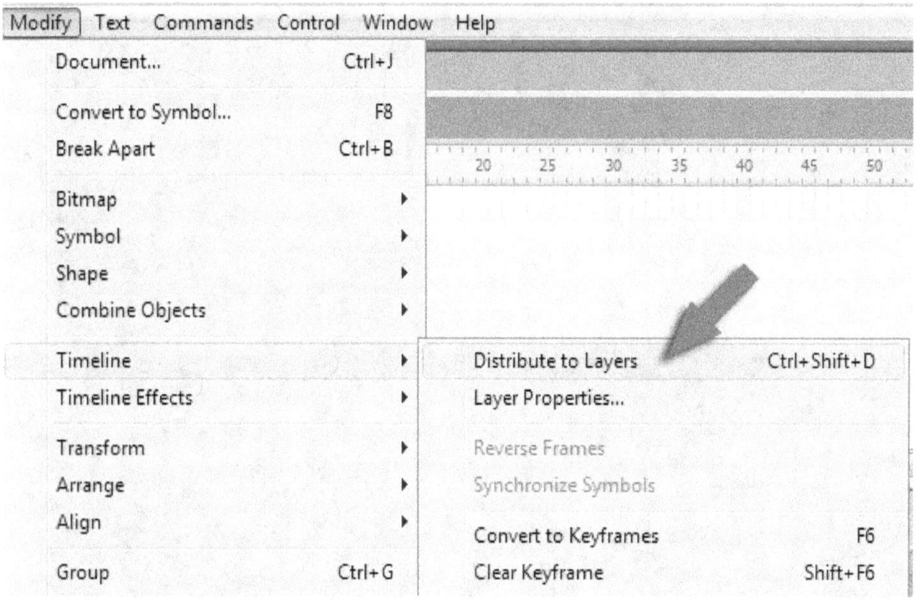

You should now have four layers. Each static image now has its own layer plus your original **Layer 1**:

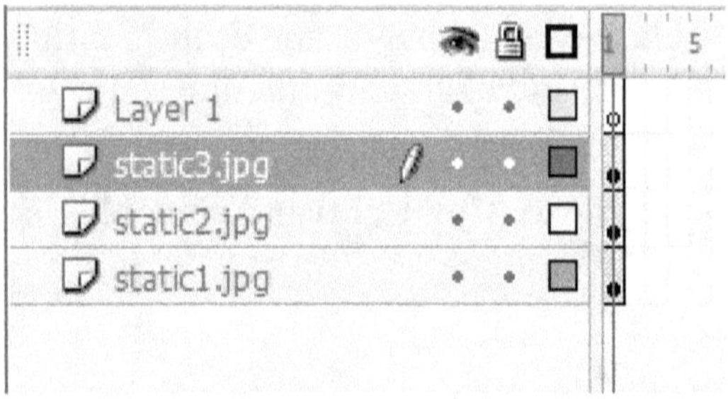

All three of the static images are slightly different. We want to create a animation but we need the images to be on different frames.

Select the keyframe of the layer **static2.jpg** and click-and-drag this keyframe to frame **2**. Then, select the keyframe of **static3.jpg** and click-and-drag this to frame **3**:

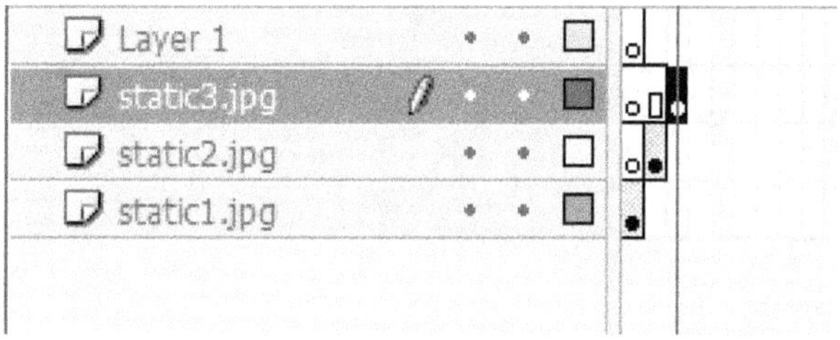

That's it! Since there is no **stop** code in this animation it will loop indefinitely which is what we want. Test your movie. You should see the static animation in the TV screen.

So now when we select the **Destination Mars!** link, we want the static to fade away and the video to appear. Go to back to Scene 1. Go to frame **60** and insert a frame for all the layers:

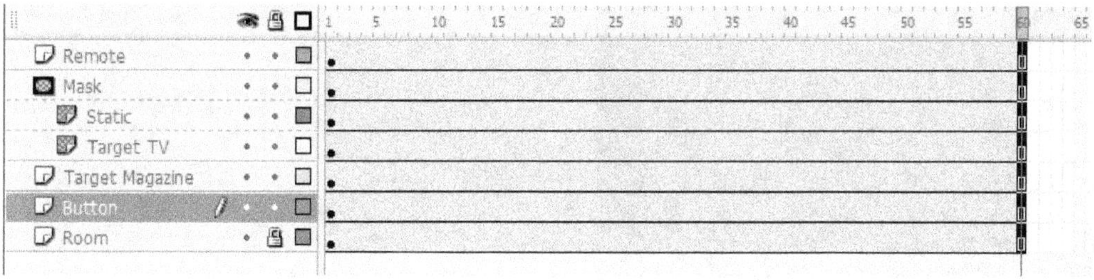

Before we animate the Target we need to put a **stop** code in the first frame. Create a new layer and name it **Actions**. Insert a **stop** code in this layer's keyframe:

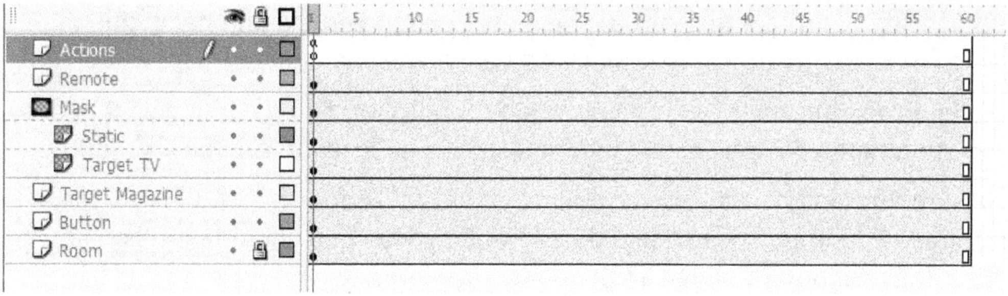

Enter another **stop** code in frame **60** of the **Actions** layer.

When the visitor first enters the site we don't want the static playing since the TV isn't on. Click-and-drag the keyframe on frame **1** of the **Static** layer to frame **2**:

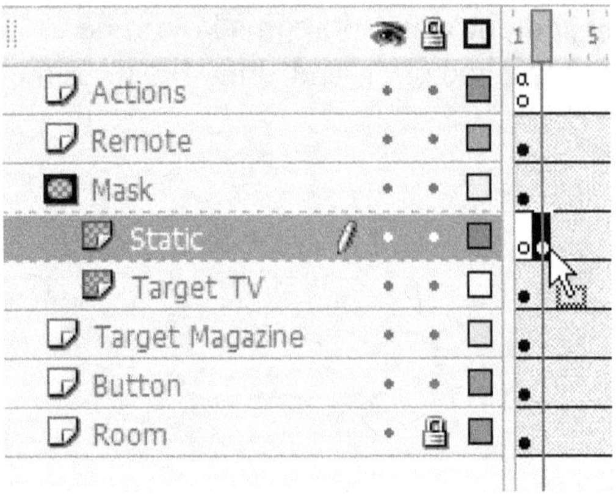

Create a new layer and name it **TV On** Button. Make sure this layer is **above the Mask layer** so it's not masked. Select the **Rectangle Tool** and turn the **Stroke color** off. Create a shape over the right knob of the TV:

Go to **Modify**, **Convert to Symbol**. Change **Type** to **Button** and name this symbol **TV On Button**. Hit **OK** when you are done.

Open the Properties panel and change **Color** to **Alpha** and percentage to **0**. Your button should now be transparent and you should once again see the TV knob.

Make sure this new button is selected and open the Actions panel. Go to **Global Functions**, **Timeline Control** and double-click **goto**. You should now be in the **goto** settings window. Change **Type** to **Next Frame**:

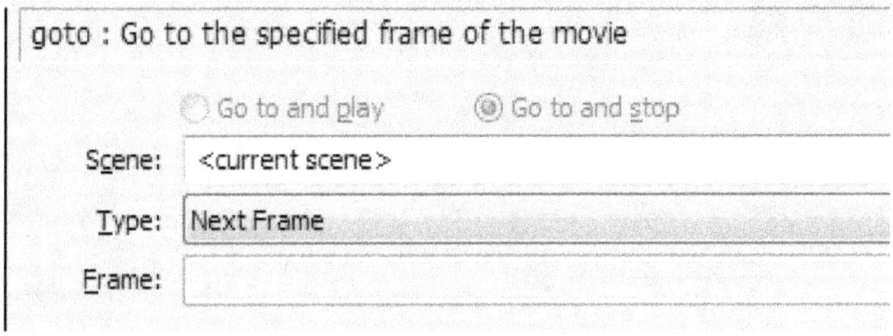

This Action is pretty self-explanatory. When we click the button it will take the user to the next frame (frame 2). Test your movie. Click the **TV On** button to test it. You should now see the Static.

Next, we'll create the animation. First, we want the Static to go in and out then finally disappear altogether. Create a keyframe on frame **45** of the **Static** layer; select any frame between **2** and **45** and insert a Motion Tween. Next, create a keyframe on frames **15** and **30**:

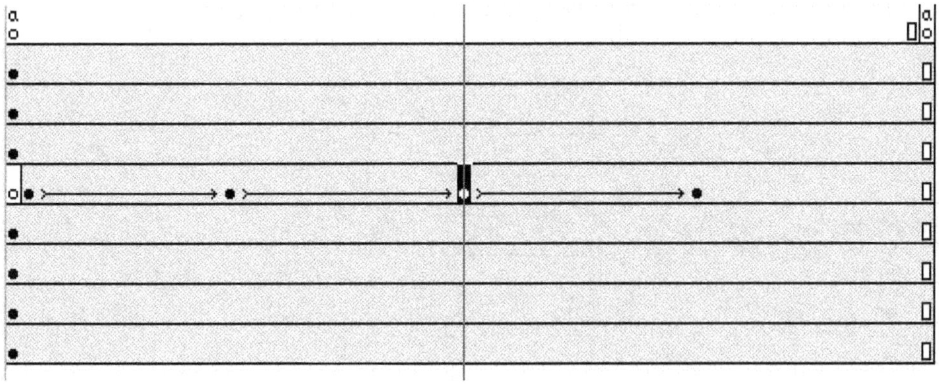

As I mentioned earlier whenever we mask a layer, Flash will lock the layers: both the mask layer and the masked layers. So in order to change the **Static** Movie clip you'll need to turn the lock off this layer. Make sure the lock stays on the **Target TV** layer so we don't accidentally move it:

Now that the lock is off the **Static** layer we can change its properties. Select frame **15** of this layer and then select the **Static** Movie clip on the stage. Open the Properties panel and change the **Color** to **Alpha** and the percentage to **36**:

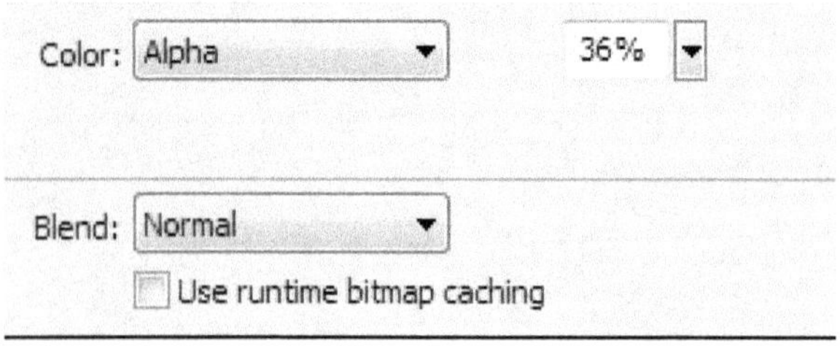

Select frame **45** and select the Static symbol again. Change the Color to **Alpha** and the percentage to **0**.

Now let's animate the video when it first loads in. We'll have it roll. Before we animate the Target symbol, let's unlock this layer and lock the **Static** and **Mask** layer. Also, let's hide both the **Static** and **Mask** layer by turning off the visibility for both layers:

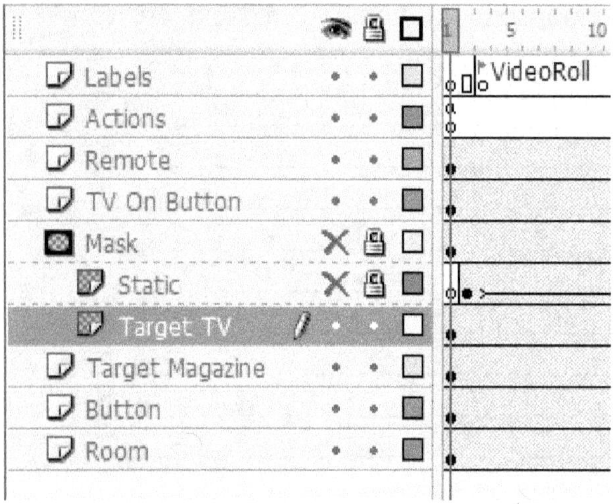

Create a keyframe on frame **60** of the **Target TV** layer. Next, select any frame between 1 and 60 and insert a Motion Tween. Create a keyframe on frame **20**. Select the **Target** symbol on the stage (remember the location of this Target) and drag it upward about an inch or so. Create a keyframe on frame **21** and drag the Target symbol about an inch below its initial position before we moved it upward.

Next, hold down **Alt** and select frame **20**; you should see a little plus sign appear:

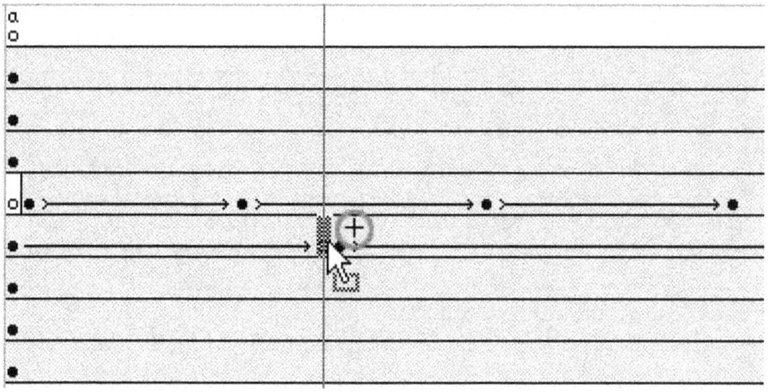

Click-and-drag this keyframe to frame **40**. So you should have a copy of keyframe 20 on frame 40:

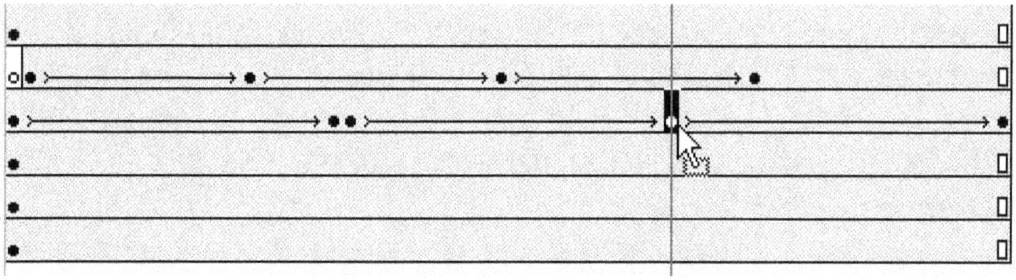

So now the animation is complete. When the video loads into the Target it will begin animating. But now let's load in the video a different way.

Create a new layer and name it **Labels**. On frame **3** insert a keyframe. Select this keyframe and open the Properties panel; type **VideoRoll** in the **Frame Label** window:

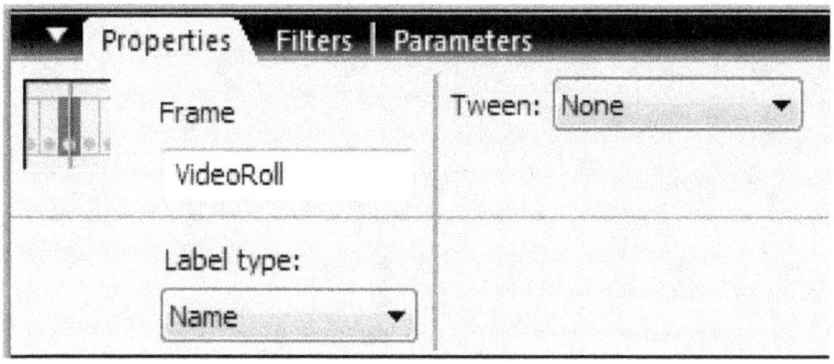

Your timeline should now look like this:

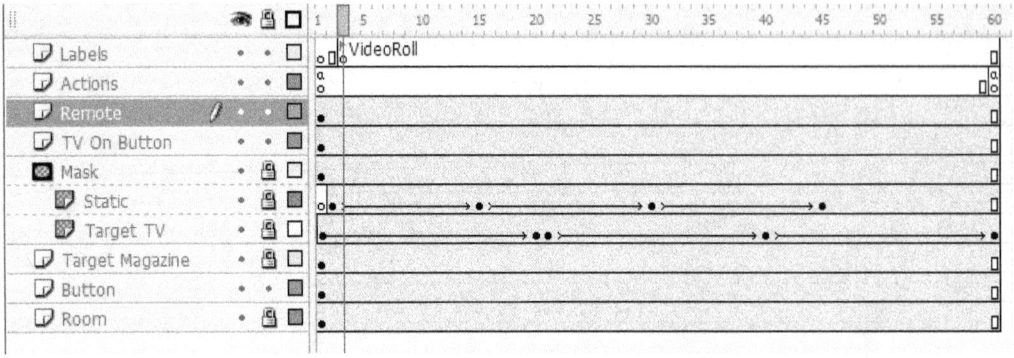

Double-click on the Remote symbol so you can enter its editing stage. Next, select frame **40** of the **Mars** layer. Double-click the Destination Mars symbol on the stage to enter its editing stage. Next, select frame **20** of the **Button** layer then select the **Button** symbol on the stage. Open the Actions panel. You should now see your ActionScript. Go ahead and delete it. We'll create new ActionScript for this button.

Go to **Deprecated**, **Actions** and double-click **tellTarget**. You should now be in the **tellTarget** settings window.

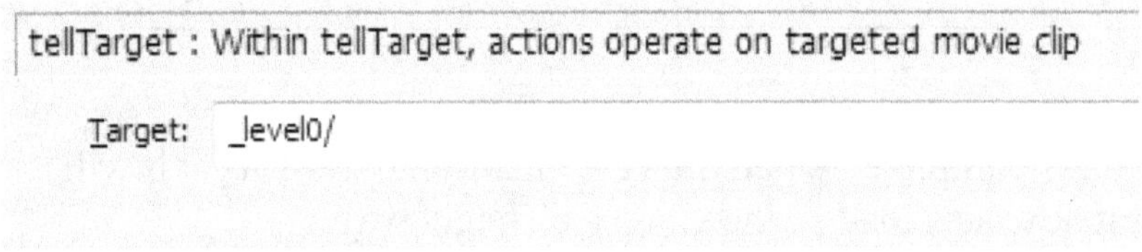

Next, go to **Global Functions**, **Timeline Control** and double-click **goto**. You should now be in the **goto** settings window. Change **Type** to **Frame Label** and type **VideoRoll** in the **Frame** window:

So now when we click the **Destination Mars!** link it will tell Scene 1 to start playing the timeline from the Label 'VideoRoll.'

You may be asking, how does the video load into the **Target** since we deleted that ActionScript from the button symbol? Simple. We can load videos into Targets using Buttons or using ActionScript inside a frame. So all we need to do is put the new ActionScript into frame **3** of the **Actions** Layer of **Scene 1** and everything should play perfectly.

Go back to **Scene 1** and insert a keyframe into frame **3** of the **Actions** layer. Open the Actions panel and make sure Script Assist is turned on. Go to **Global Functions, Browser/Network** and double-click **loadMovie**. In the **URL** window type **mars.swf**. Change **Location** to **Target** and type **target_tv** in the **Location** window:

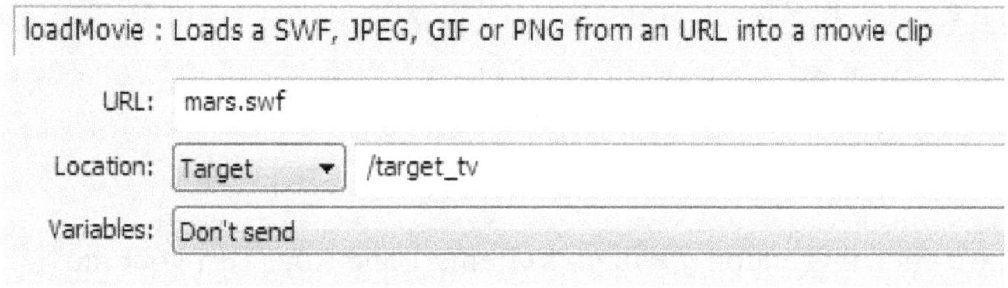

Test your movie. When you click the **Destination Mars!** link it should take you to the Label **VideoRoll** on frame 3 of **Scene 1**. Once Flash gets to this frame on Scene 1 it will also play the ActionScript we just created on frame 3 of the **Actions** layer. This ActionScript will load the video into the Target: **target_tv**.

Ok, so now the video is playing fine. But what if we wanted to turn off the TV? Easy! Select the **TV On** button on the stage. Go to **Edit**, **Copy**. Next, go to **Edit**, **Paste in Place**. Drag this new button so that it is over the other knob:

Open the Actions panel and delete the ActionScript that is there. Next, go to **Global Functions**, **Timeline Control**, and double-click **goto**. You should now be in the **goto** settings window. Keep everything as is except make sure **Go to and stop** is selected:

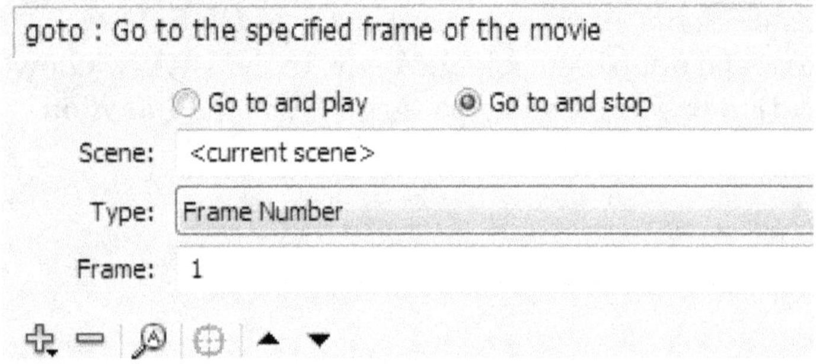

So now when we click this button it will go to frame 1 and stop. Test your movie. Click on the **TV On** button and you should see the static. Click on the **TV Off** button that you just created. The static should turn off. Next, click on the **Destination Mars!** link. The video should start playing. Click the **TV Off** button. Hmmm, the video is still playing. So we need to add one more piece of ActionScript to the **TV Off** button.

With the Action panel still open let's add more code. Go to **Global Functions, Browser/Network**, and double-click **unloadMovie**. You should now be in the **unloadMovie** settings window. Change the **Location** to **Target** and type **/target_tv** in the **Location** window:

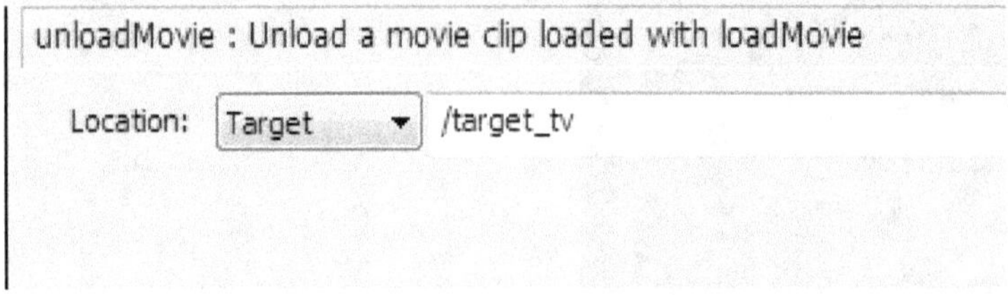

Test your movie again. This time when you play the video and click the **TV Off** button, the video stops playing.

Let's do one more thing using **Targets** and then we'll be wrapped. We're going to create a slideshow that we'll place in the picture frame above the fireplace. We'll load it in using a **Target** and we'll control the slideshow with a separate Movie clip. So let's get started.

Go to **File**, **New**. Select **Flash Document** and hit **OK**. Next, go to **File**, **Save**. Save this file in the Chapter Four folder; name it **Slideshow**.

Select **File**, **Import to Stage**. In the Pictures folder of the Chapter Four folder select **slideshowPic1.jpg**, then **slideshowPic2.jpg**, **slideshowPic3.jpg**,

slideshowPic4.jpg, and **slideshowPic5.jpg** (make sure you hold down the CTRL button so you can select more than one picture).

You should now have all 5 pictures on your stage. The first thing we need to do is separate each picture into their own layer. Select the first frame of **Layer 1** (this selects all the images on the stage). Go to **Modify**, **Timeline**, **Distribute to Layers**:

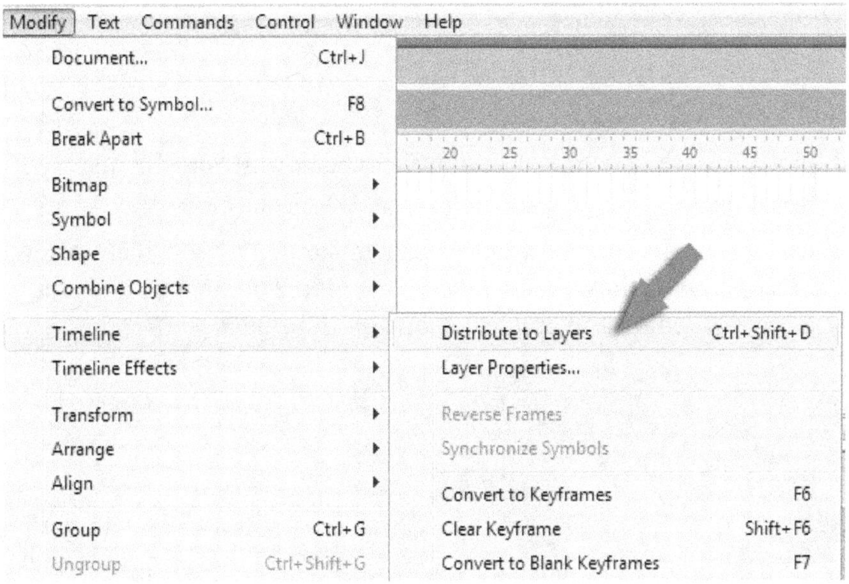

Now the layers should look like this:

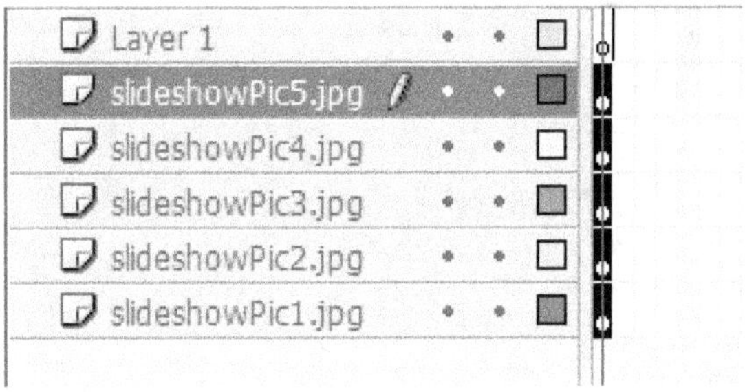

Now each picture is in its own layer. We now need to move each keyframe to a different frame. Click on the keyframe of the layer **slideshowPic2.jpg** so it's highlighted; select this keyframe again and move it to frame **2**. Do the same thing for the **slideshowPic3.jpg** layer, but move this keyframe to frame **3** and so on for the next 2 layers. When you're done, rename Layer 1: **Actions** and put a **stop** code in its frame:

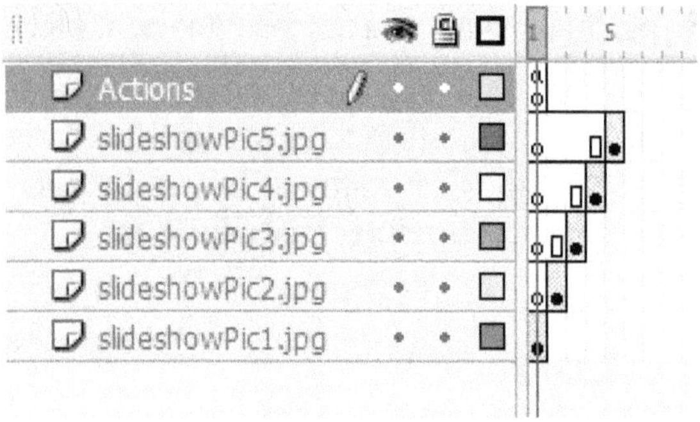

Select **File**, **Publish**. Now we have the slideshow. Go back to **Room.fla** and we'll load in the new slideshow.

We need to load this slideshow into a Target so let's make that now. Create a new layer and name it **Target Slideshow**. Select the **Rectangle Tool** and turn off the **Stroke color**. Use any **Fill color** and create a shape on the stage:

Select this shape and click on the **Fill color** icon. Take the **Alpha** down to **0**:

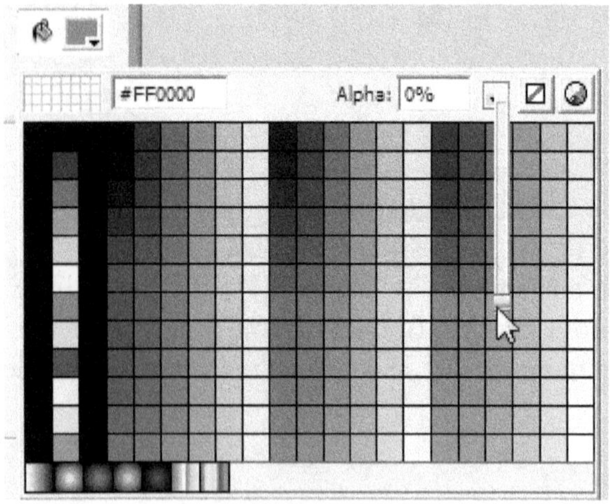

Select this new shape and go to **Modify**, **Convert to Symbol**. Change the **Type** to **Movie clip** and name it **Target Slideshow**:

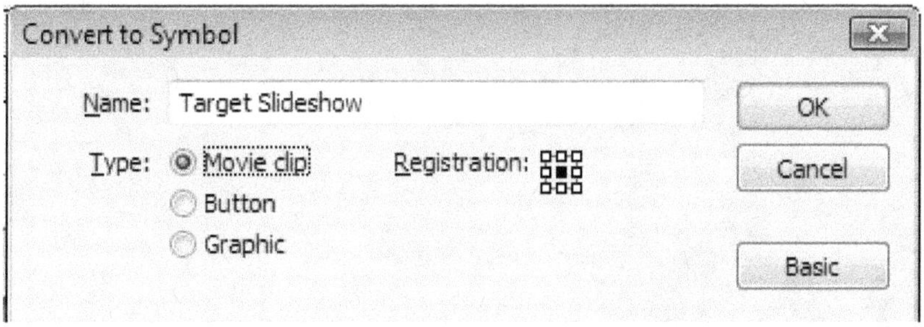

Hit **OK** to close. Open the Properties panel and type **target_slideshow** in the **Instance Name** window:

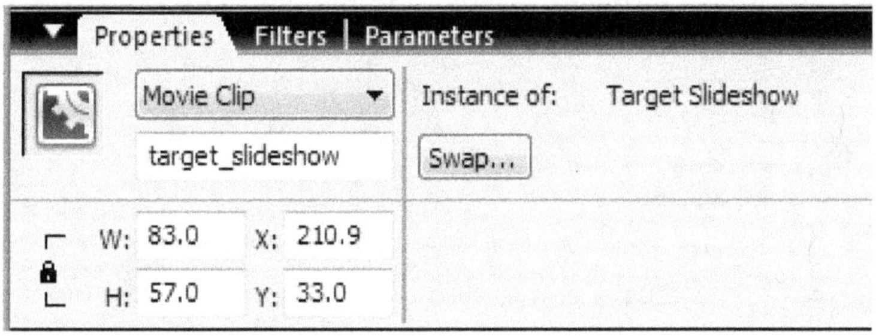

Now we need to add some ActionScript to the **Actions** layer to load in the slideshow. Let's do that now. Select the first frame of the Actions layer and open the Actions panel. Go to **Global Functions, Browser/Network** and double-click **loadMovie**. You should now be in the **loadMovie** settings window. In the **URL** window type **Slideshow.swf**; change **Location** to **Target** and in the **Location** window type **/target_slideshow**:

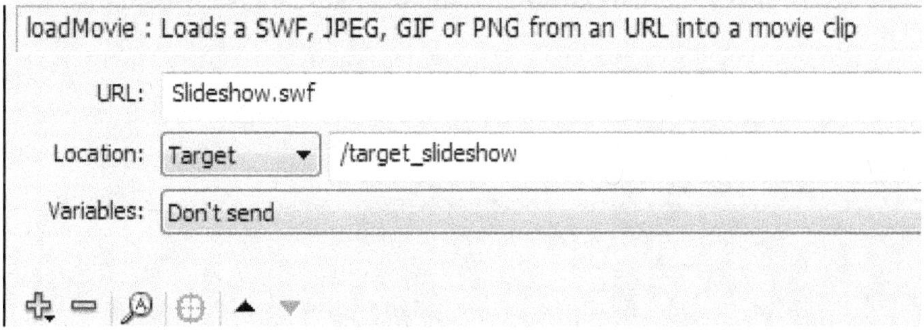

Test your movie. The slideshow should now be visible on the stage. It's probably not positioned where it should be. Go back to your stage and, depending on where the slideshow appeared, *move your Target appropriately* (remember to lock the background layer so you don't accidentally move it). Keep repositioning your Target and testing your movie until the Slideshow is over the picture frame:

Create a new layer above the **Target Slideshow** layer and name it **Mask**:

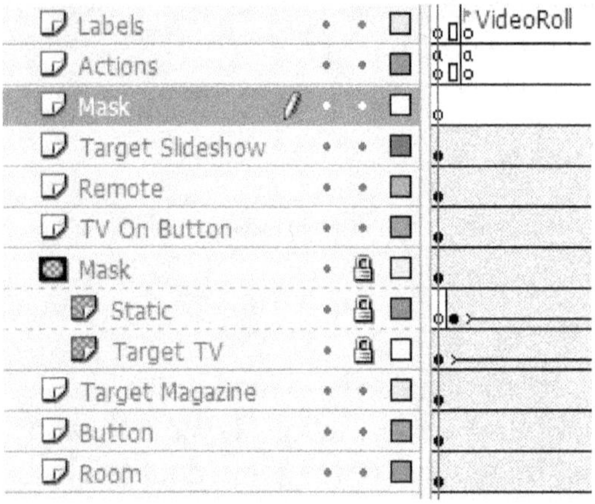

Now we're going to create the mask. Grab the Rectangle **Tool**; turn off **Stroke color** and select any color for the **Fill color**. Create a square shape within the frame:

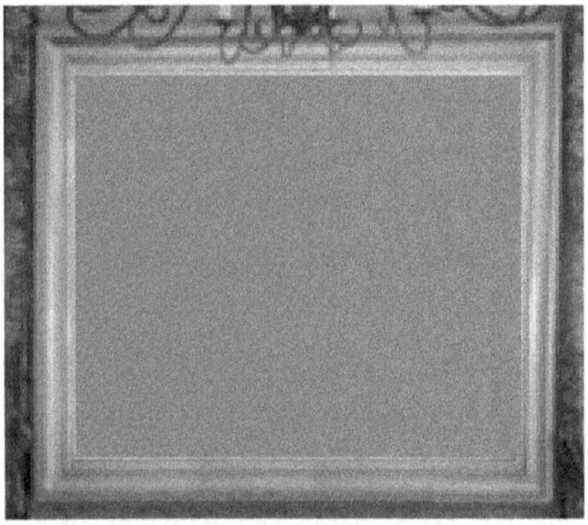

If your square isn't perfectly within the frame you can pull on the edges to correct it. Before you do that select the **Selection Tool** and de-select the shape; then grab the very edge of the shape (you should see a V shape next to the cursor):

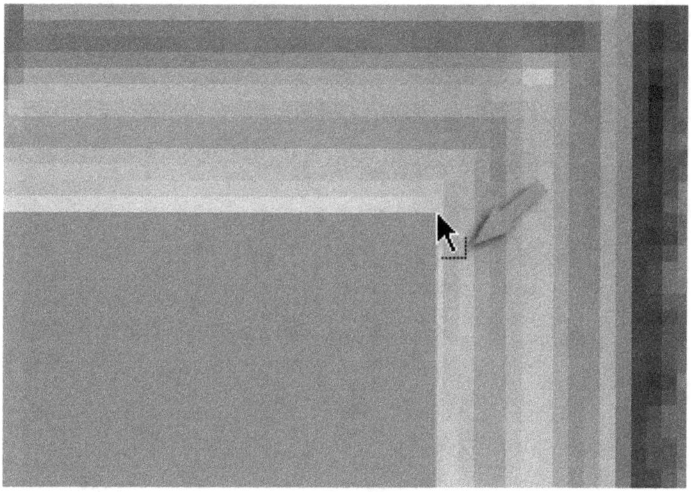

Pull this corner where you want it to go. Do that for all the edges until you have a nice fit. When you finish, right-click on the **Mask** layer and select **Mask**. Your **Target Slideshow** layer should now be masked:

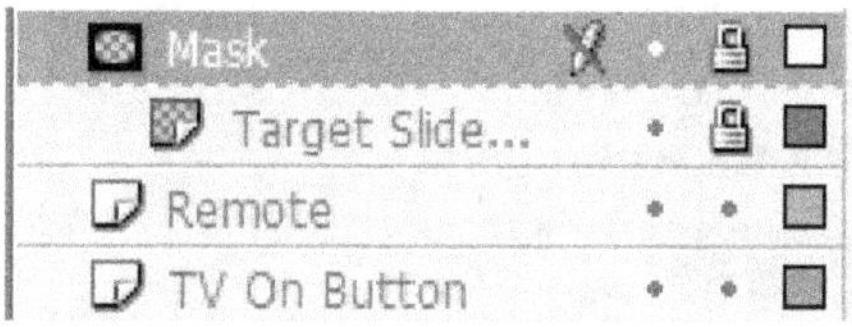

Test your movie again. This time the Slideshow should fit nicely within the picture frame. How do we get the slideshow to play the pictures? You can do it two ways. You can add frames between the pictures in the **Slideshow.fla** file and just have its timeline play. Or, you can create a Movie clip in the **Room.fla** file that controls the slideshow. That's what we're going to do now.

Create a new layer and name it **Slideshow Control**:

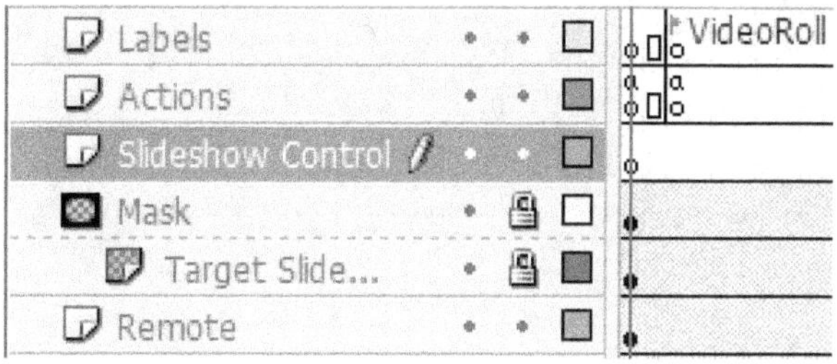

Select the **Rectangle Tool**, turn off **Stroke color**, and select any **Fill color**. Create a shape above the stage:

Using the **Selection Tool**, select this new shape and go to **Modify**, **Convert to Symbol**. Name it **Slideshow Control** and change the **Type** to **Movie clip**. Hit **OK** to close. We don't need to make this Movie clip transparent since we placed it off the stage. With this new Movie clip still selected, open the Properties panel and name it **slideshow_control** in the **Instance Name** window:

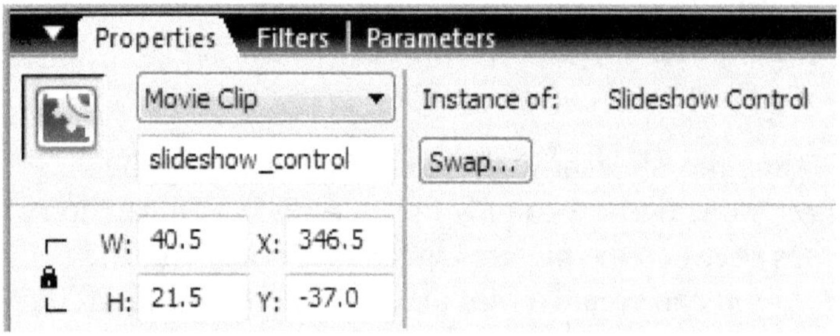

Double-click this new Movie clip to enter its editing stage. Create a new layer and name it **Actions**. Select the keyframe of the **Actions** layer and insert a **stop** code. Next, go to frame **90** of the **Actions** layer and insert another keyframe:

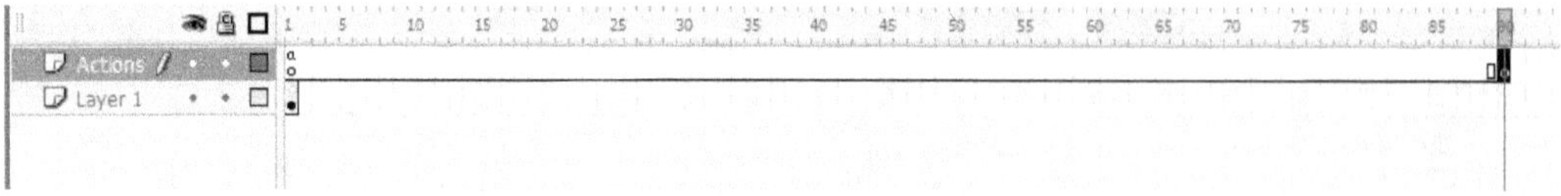

We're now going to add the ActionScript that will communicate with the slideshow. Open the Actions panel. Go to **Deprecated**, **Actions**, and double-click **tellTarget**. You should now be in the **tellTarget** settings window. Type **/target_slideshow** in the **Target** window:

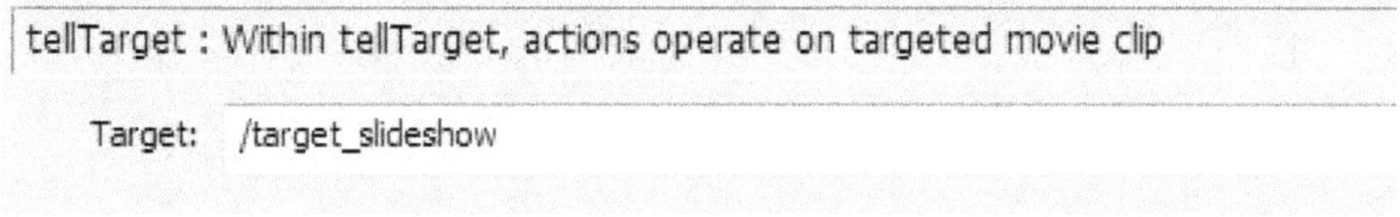

Go to **Global Functions**, **Timeline Control**, and double-click **goto**. You should now be in the **goto** settings window. Change **Type** to **Next Frame**:

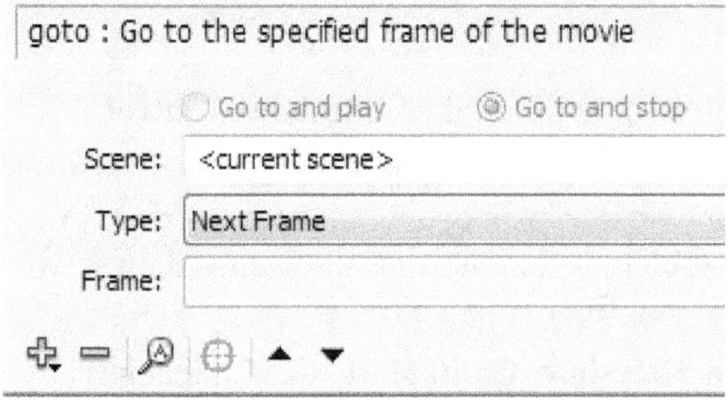

This Movie clip will tell the slideshow to go to the next frame in the slideshow timeline. But you'll notice that there is a **stop** code in the first frame of this Movie clip which means it will never get to frame **90** to communicate with the slideshow. The reason we put a **stop** code in frame 1 is so that this Movie clip doesn't start playing until all the pictures of the slideshow are loaded.

So how does this Movie clip know when the slideshow is loaded into the Target so it can start playing? Simple. We'll put come ActionScript in the slideshow file that will tell this Movie clip to start playing.

Go back to the **Slideshow.fla** file. Select the keyframe of the **Actions** layer. Open the Actions panel and make sure that Script Assist is on. Select **Deprecated**, **Actions** and double-click **tellTarget**. You should now be in the **tellTarget** settings window. Type **/slideshow_control** in the **Target** window:

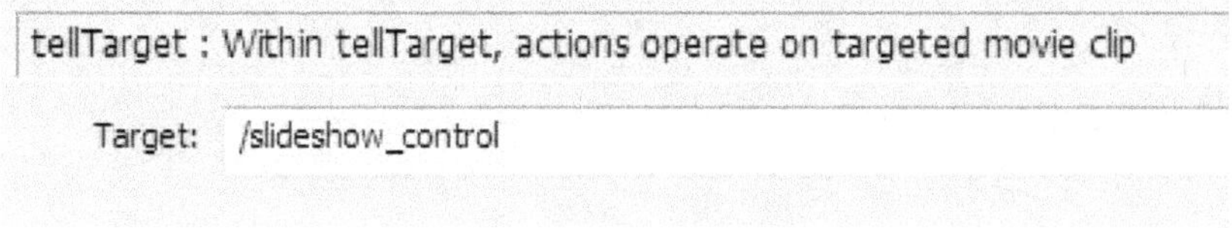

Go to **Global Functions**, **Timeline Control** and double-click **play**:

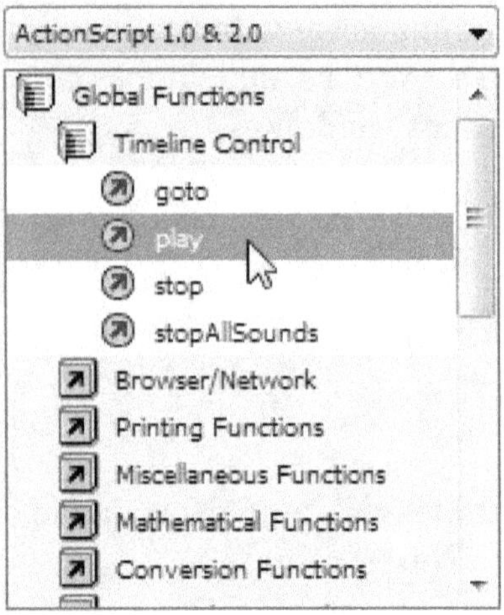

Go to **File**, **Publish**. This new ActionScript will tell the **Slideshow Control** Movie clip to play its timeline.

Go back to **Room.fla** and test your movie. Keep an eye on the picture frame. You should see the picture change. The problem is that the slideshow only shows two pictures and not the rest of them. Can you figure out why?

Here is what's happening. We have a **Slideshow Control** Movie clip that has a **stop** code on frame 1, but when it is told to play by the **Slideshow** file, it plays all the way to frame 90. On frame 90 it then tells the **Slideshow** file to go to the next frame; but the Movie clip doesn't stop at frame 90 since we don't have a **stop** code on frame 90. So this Movie clip returns to frame 1 where it hits the **stop** code.

What we need to do is have the Movie clip *return to frame 2* not frame 1 so it doesn't have to deal with the **stop** code. Let's add that code now. Double click on the **Slideshow Control** Movie clip so you can enter its editing stage. Go to frame **90** of the **Actions** layer and select the keyframe. Open the Actions panel and make sure Script Assist is on. Go to **Global Functions**, **Timeline Control**, and double-click **goto**. You should now be in the **goto** settings window. Change the Frame to 2:

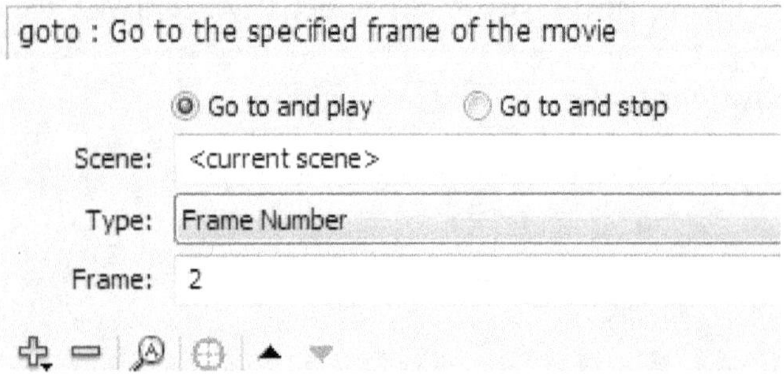

Now when the **Slideshow Control** Movie clip gets to frame **90** it will tell the Slideshow to go to its next frame. Flash will then look at the next line of code we just created which is telling Flash to send the **Slideshow Control** Movie clip to frame 2 and keep playing.

But what happens when the **Slideshow** file gets to frame **5**, its last frame? Since there isn't a next frame to go to, the animation will stop. Go ahead and test your movie to try it out. After 5 pictures the animation ends. How do we keep this slideshow animating indefinitely? One simple line of code.

Open the **Slideshow** file and put a keyframe on frame **6** of the **Actions** layer:

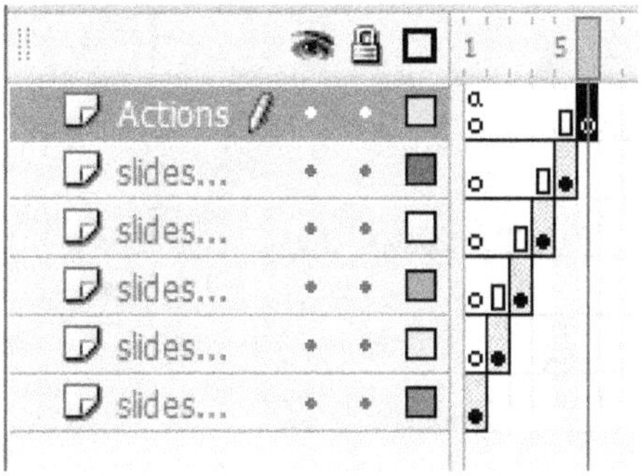

Open the Actions panel and make sure Script Assist is on. Go to **Global Functions**, **Timeline Control**, and double-click **goto**. You should now be in the **goto** settings window. Select **Go to and stop**:

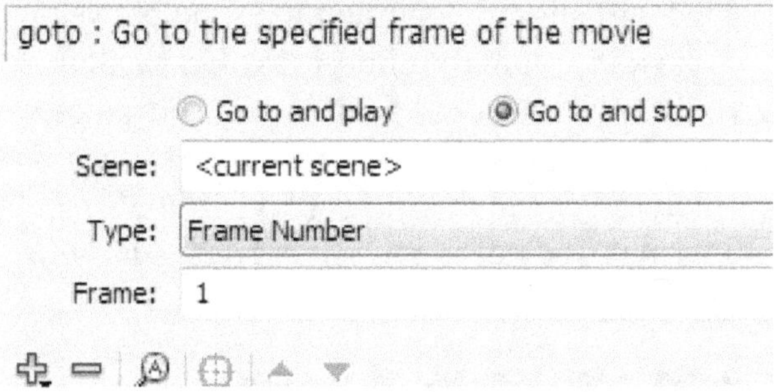

That's it! Go to **File, Publish**. Go back to **Room.fla** and test your movie. Your slideshow doesn't stop at frame 5 but continues to frame 1 and starts all over again.

One advantage of using a Movie clip to control a slideshow is that it's easy to control the amount of time there is between pictures. Let's say that you want to lengthen the time between the showing of pictures. This can be accomplished in a matter of seconds.

Double-click on the **Slideshow Control** Movie clip to enter its editing stage. Click on frame **10** (don't release) and *click-and-drag* across the frames until you reach frame **50**. The frames should darken like this:

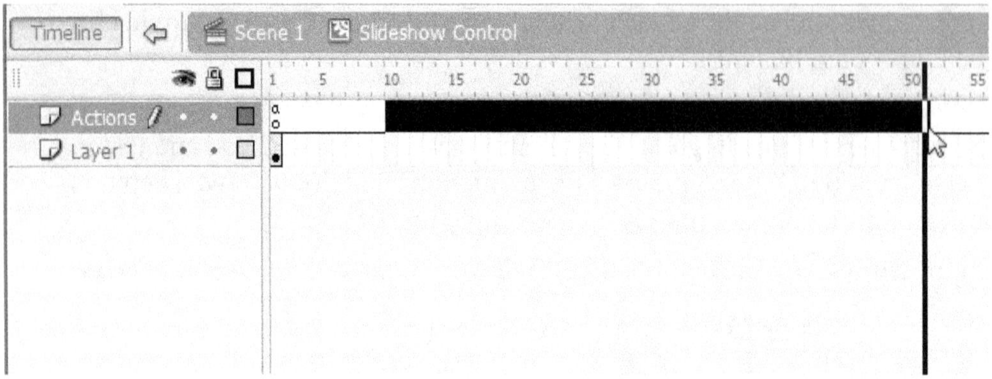

Right-click on these darkened frames and select **Insert Frame**:

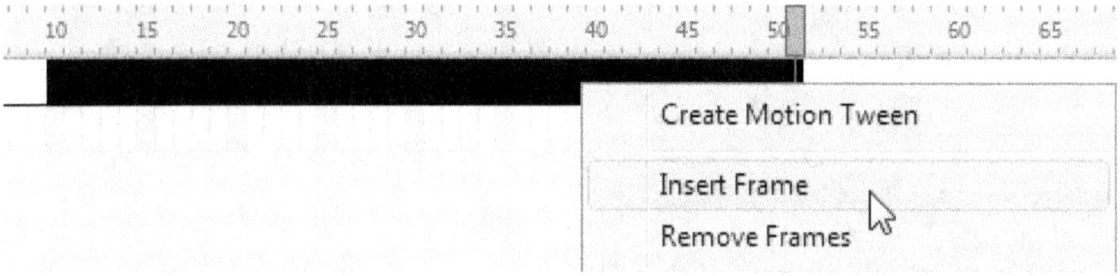

Since you highlighted 40 frames Flash will insert 40 frames in this area extending your overall timeline by 40 frames. This will slightly lengthen the time between the showing of pictures. Test your movie and watch the slideshow. It will show each picture a little longer. So now your timeline should be around 130 frames. What if we want to shorten the amount of time between pictures. Let's say we want only want one second between pictures. Since the file is playing at 30fps, then the timeline needs to be only 30 frames. Select frame 10 and *click-and-drag* across the frames until you get to frame 110:

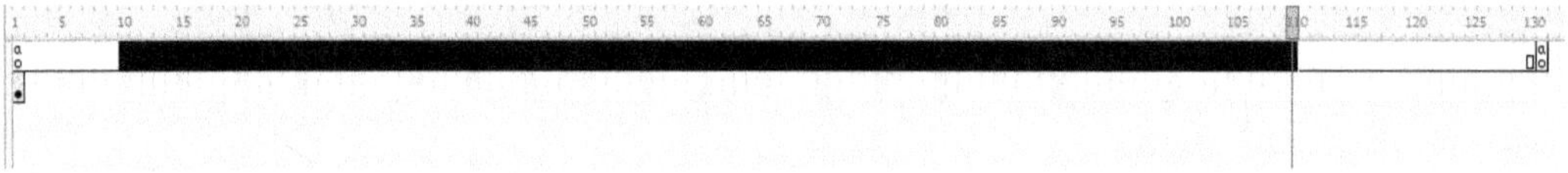

Right-click and select **Remove Frames**:

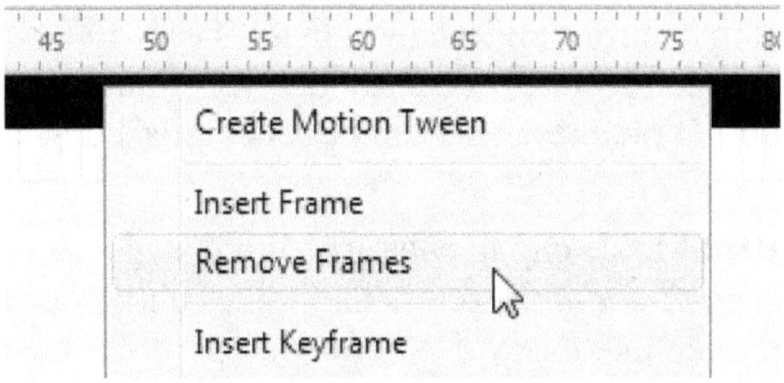

Test your movie. The time between pictures should be 1 second. Ok, I'll show one more thing that is really cool. What if you wanted a nice transition between pictures? Maybe have each picture fade to black then fade in from black. Believe it or not this is pretty simple. And you won't even have to edit your **Slideshow** file. Everything will be done in the **Room.fla** file.

Let's have a four second lapse between pictures in the slideshow. To do this we need to select the last keyframe of the Actions layer (frame 30); then select it again and *click-and-drag* this keyframe to frame **120**:

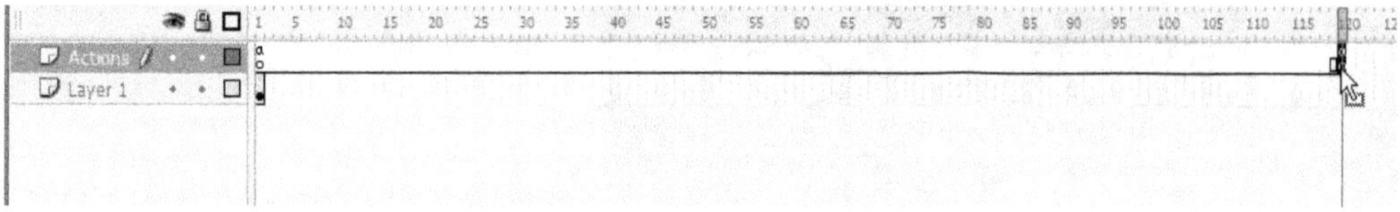

So now if we test the movie there will be a picture duration of 4 seconds. Go back to **Scene 1**. We're now going to create the transition Movie clip. We want this new Movie clip to use the same mask as the **Target Slideshow** layer; so, first select the **Target Slideshow** layer, then click on the **New Layer** icon. Name this new layer **Black Cover**:

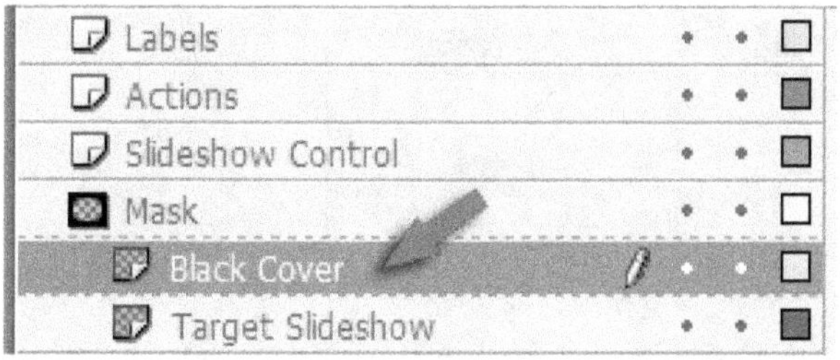

Now your new layer should be masked. With this new layer selected, grab your **Rectangle Tool**. Turn off **Stroke color** and select black for the **Fill color**. Turn off the visibility of the **Mask** layer:

Create a shape over the picture frame. You can make it larger than the frame since this layer will be masked:

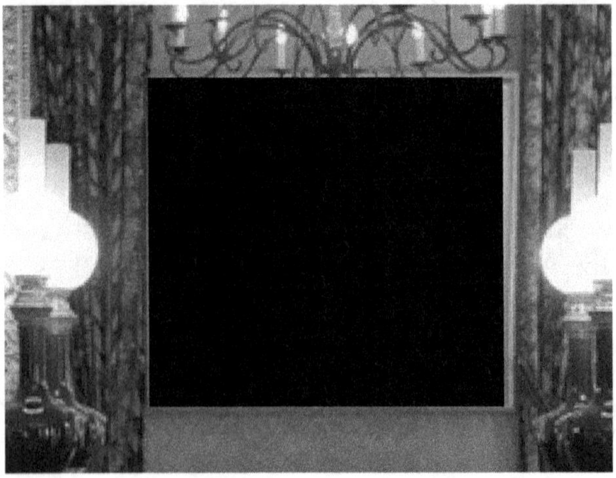

Grab your **Selection Tool** and select this new shape; go to **Modify**, **Convert to Symbol**.

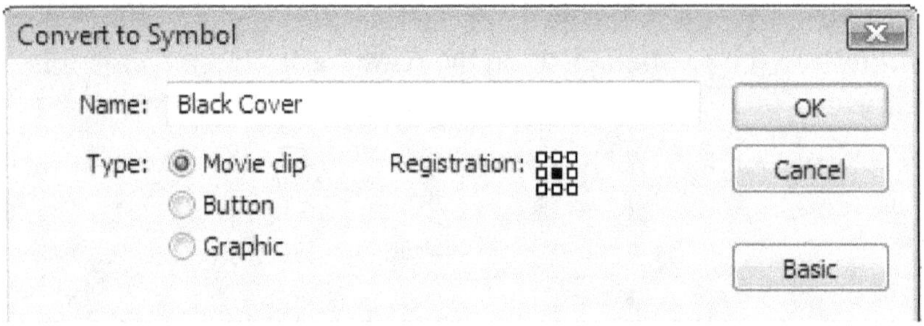

Hit **OK** to close this window. Open the Properties panel and give this new symbol the **Instance Name** of **black_cover**:

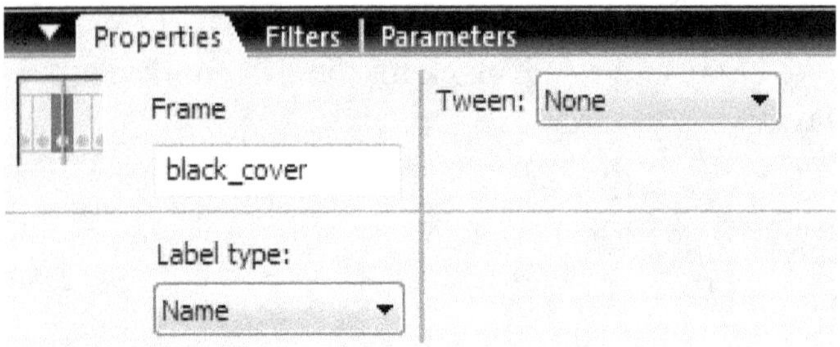

Double-click on this new Movie clip to enter its editing stage. Insert a keyframe on frame **40** of **Layer 1**:

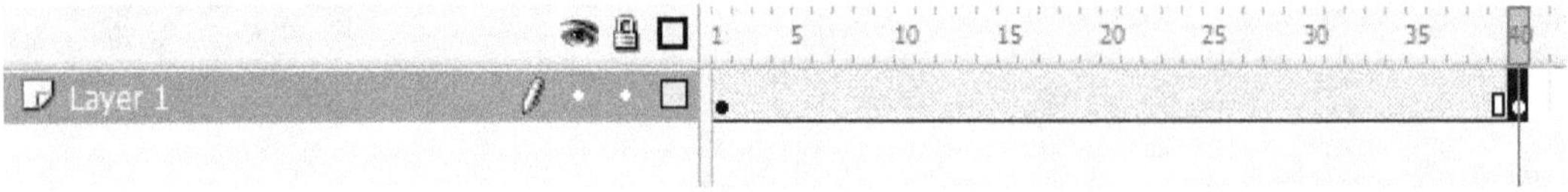

Select any frame between **1** and **40** and insert a Motion Tween. Next, insert a keyframe on frame **20**:

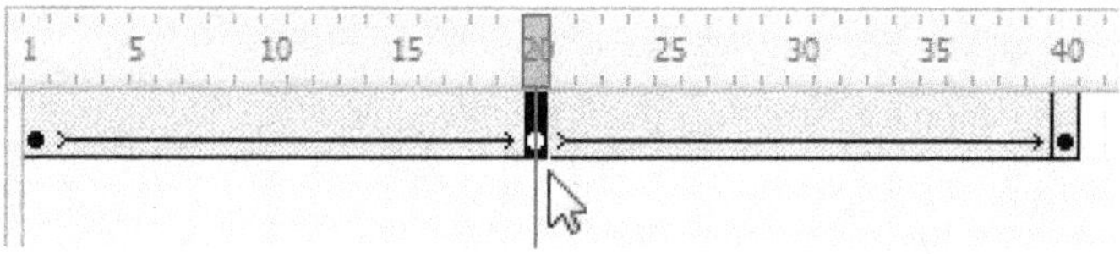

Select frame **1** then select the symbol on the stage; open the Properties panel and change the **Color** to **Alpha** and the percentage to **0**:

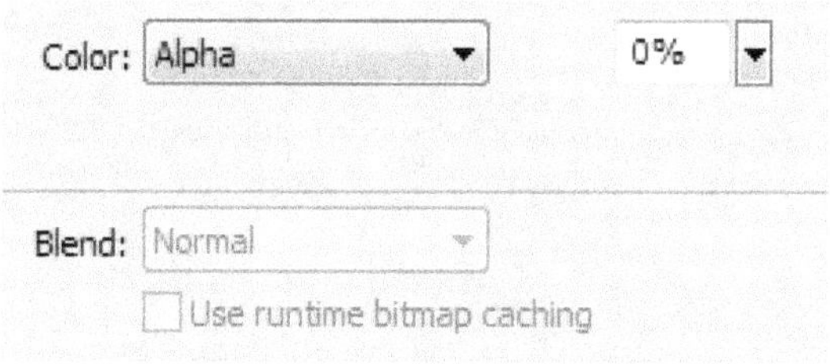

Click on frame **40** of this layer; next, select the symbol on the stage. In the Properties panel change the **Color** to **Alpha** and percentage to **0** just like we just did for the first frame's symbol.

The black shape will fade in then fade out. You can go to **Control**, **Test Scene** to test it out. If we were to test the movie we would not get a very nice effect. The **Black Cover** Movie clip keeps looping. We only want it to play as a transition between pictures.

Create a new layer and name it **Actions**. Select the first frame and open the Actions panel; insert a **stop** code into this keyframe. So now we're done with this Movie clip.

Go back to Scene 1. Double click on the **Slideshow** Control Movie clip to enter its editing stage. Insert a keyframe on frame **100** of the **Actions** layer:

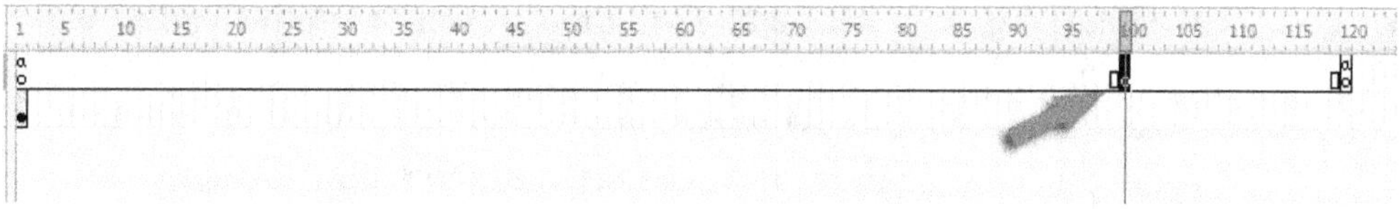

Open the Actions panel and make sure Script Assist is turned on.

We want this frame to tell the **Black Cover** Movie clip to start playing. Go to **Deprecated**, **Actions**, and double-click **tellTarget**. You should now be in **tellTarget** settings window. Type **/black_cover** in the **Target** window:

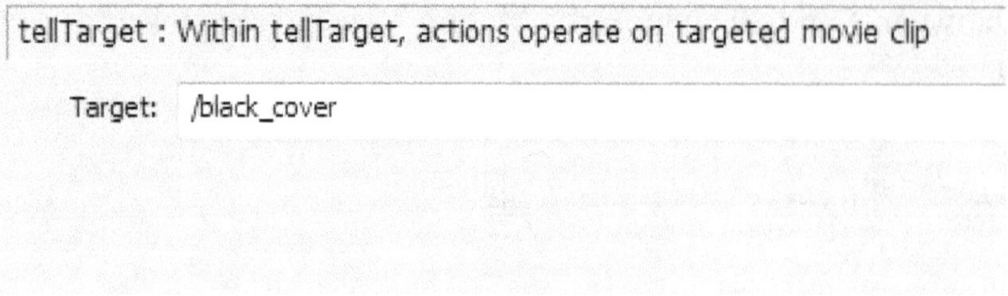

Next, go to **Global Functions**, **Timeline Control** and double-click **play**:

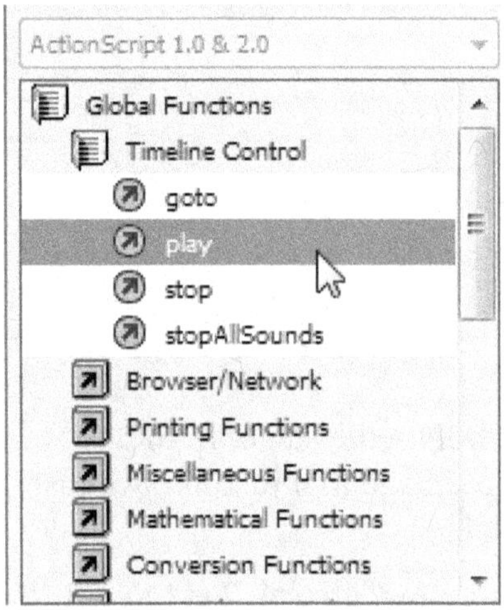

Test your movie. So here is what happens. When the **Slideshow Control** Movie clip gets to frame 100 it tells the **Black Cover** Movie clip to begin playing. When the **Black Cover** Movie clip gets to frame 20 the Black Cover will be at full visibility; at the same time the **Slideshow Control** Movie clip will be at frame 120 which has the ActionScript that tells the slideshow to go to the next frame. So, basically, the Slideshow is switching pictures as the Black Cover is at full visibility.

Pretty cool. But what if we want the pictures fading in from white instead of black? Easy. Go back to **Scene 1** and double-click the **Black Cover** Movie clip to enter its editing stage. Select frame **20**, then select the symbol on the stage. Open the Properties panel and change the **Color** to **Tint**, and the **Color** to **white**:

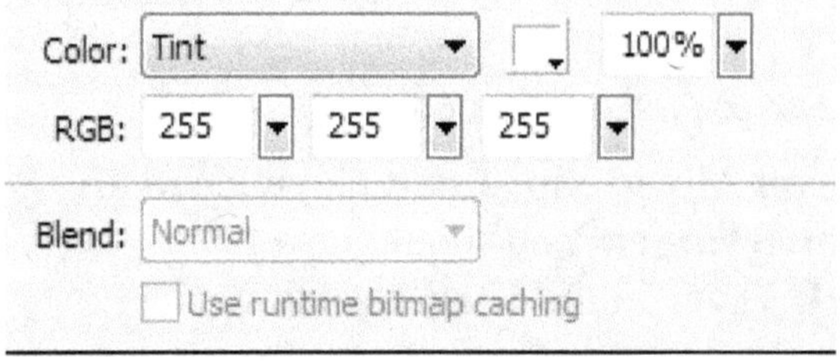

Test your movie again. The pictures now fade in from white. You can actually change the Tint to any color you like.

So you can see the power of Targets! What's really powerful about Targets is that you can control the Movie clips they load into however you like. From colors, to size and location, you're in complete control. You can even have Targets control other Targets, or load in separate Targets. Your imagination is your only limitation.

In the next chapter we'll learn about other commands: startDrag and setProperty. Also, we'll learn about Filters, Anchor Points, Shape Hints, and how to edit multiple frames at once. Let's get started!

Chapter Five:
Odds 'n' Ends

Welcome to the final training chapter! After this chapter you'll be prepared for the Projects chapter. In this chapter one of the things we'll be discussing is startDrag. This is a command that allows a user to click on a object and move it around the stage! Fun stuff. Another command we'll be going over is setProperty. This command allows you to make Movie clips disappear with just a click of a button, or change the location of a Movie clip. You can also make Movie clips smaller or larger with just a click of a button. We'll also be discussing one of the latest features in Flash which is Filters. You can create drop shadows, inner shadows, blurs, and a few other nice effects. This is really exciting, and I'll even show you how to make clouds using the Blur Filter! I also have a few other fun things in this chapter that you'll really enjoy.

setProperty

Before we tackle some of the upcoming sophisticated projects, you'll need to have a fundamental understanding of the setProperty command. Open the file called **setProperty.fla** in the **OddsEnds** folder. You'll see the **Car** Movie clip at the top of the stage that has an Instance Name of **car**; we also have a series of buttons at the bottom:

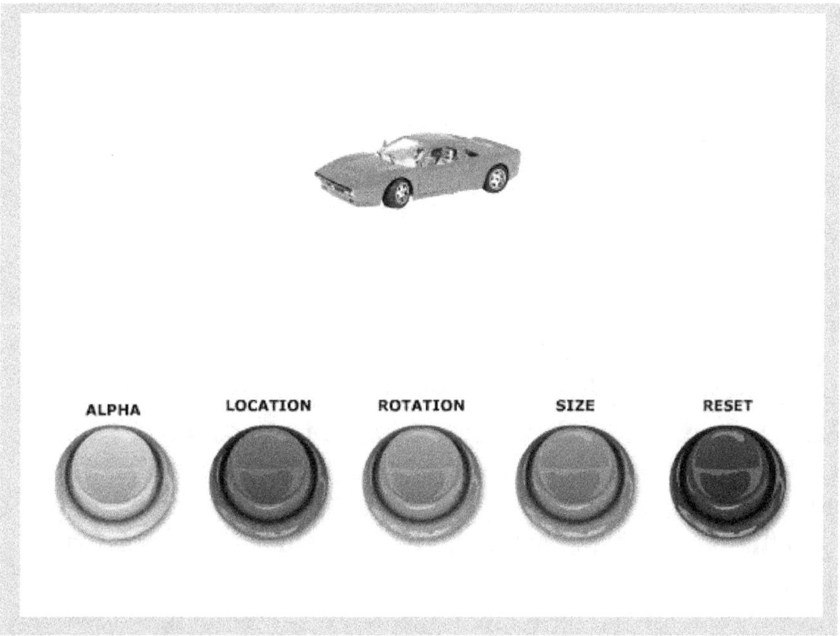

By the way, if you like these buttons they come ready made in Flash! Go to **Window**, **Common Libraries**, and **Buttons**. You have several great selections to choose from! Oh, in **CS4/CS5** you can also select Classes and Sound effects!

In this project we're going to add the **setProperty** code to each button, then, add a **setProperty** code to the RESET button that will take the **Car** Movie clip back to its original state. The first thing we'll do is take the car down to 0 percent Alpha, so the car will become transparent. Let's do that now. Select the **ALPHA** button and open the Actions panel. **Make sure Script Assist is on**. Go to **Global Functions**, **Movie clip Control** and double-click **setProperty**. You should be in the **setProperty** settings window. Next to **Property** select **_alpha**, type **/car** in the **Target** window, and change the **Value** to **50**:

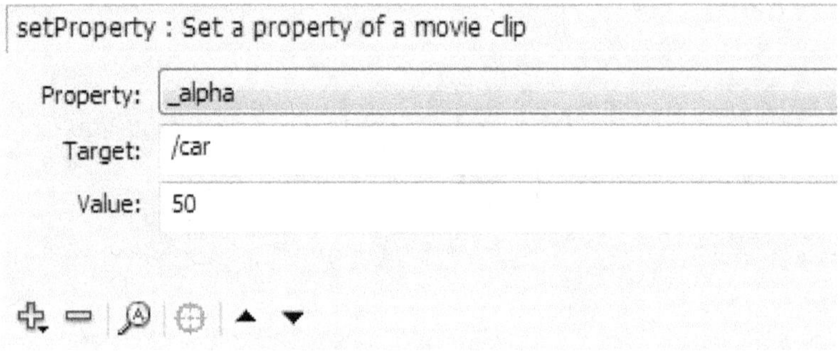

When we click the button it will command the **Car** Movie clip to go to 50% Alpha. Test your movie to try it out. When you click the **ALPHA** button the **Car** Movie clip goes to 50% opacity. This time type **0** in the **Value** window:

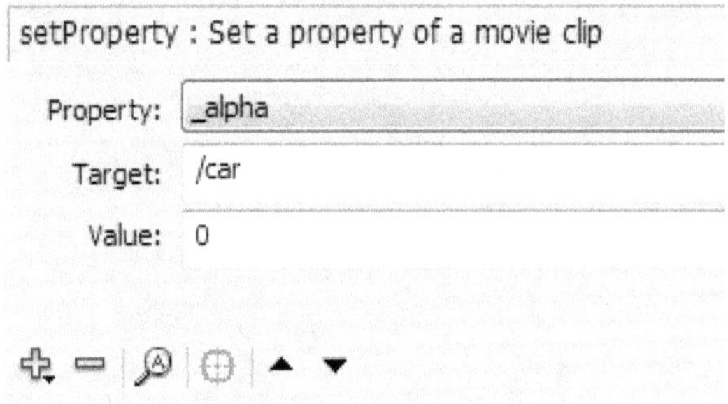

Test your movie. The **Car** Movie clip completely disappears! So how do we bring the **Car** Movie clip back to 100% Alpha? That's where the **RESET** button comes in. Select this button and in the Actions window go to **Global Functions**, **Movie clip Control** and double-click **setProperty**. In the **setProperty** settings window select **_alpha** for the **Property** setting, type **/car** in the **Target** window, and type **100** in the **Value** window:

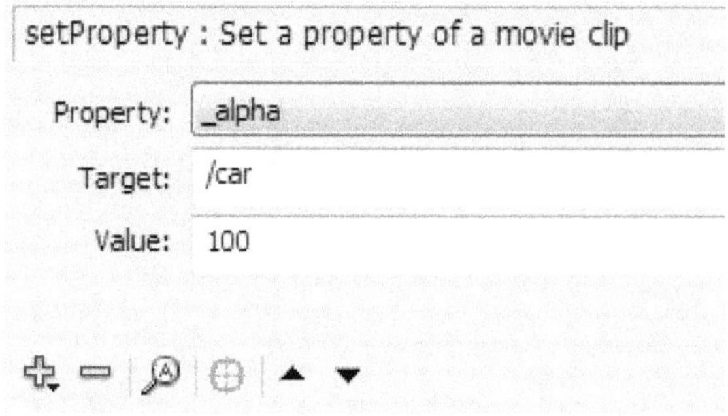

When this button is clicked it tells the **Car** Movie clip to go to 100% Alpha. Test your movie to try it out. Click the **ALPHA** button first which will make the car symbol disappear, then click on the **RESET** button. The car comes back!

Next, we'll change the location of the car. Let's say we want the car to appear above the **LOCATION** button when we click the button. I'll show you a fast way to figure that out. Open the **Info** panel (**Window**, **Info**). Put your cursor over the area above the **LOCATION** button:

Look at the Info panel. The information you need are the X and Y coordinates; they'll give you live feedback depending on where your cursor is:

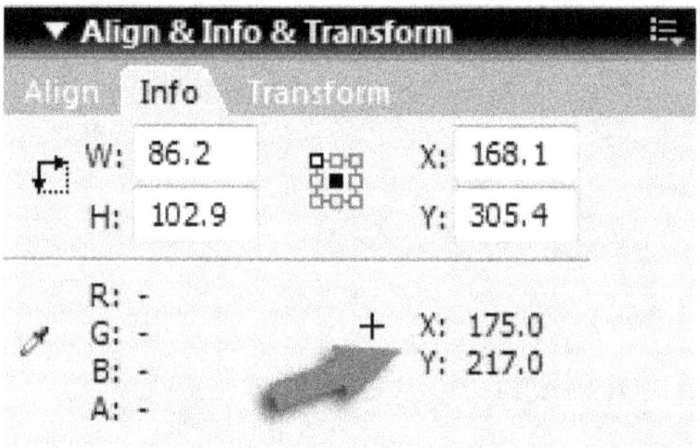

This is the information that you'll be using for the setProperty settings. Let's do that now. Select the **LOCATION** button and in the Actions panel go to **Global Functions**, **Movie clip Control** and double-click **setProperty**:

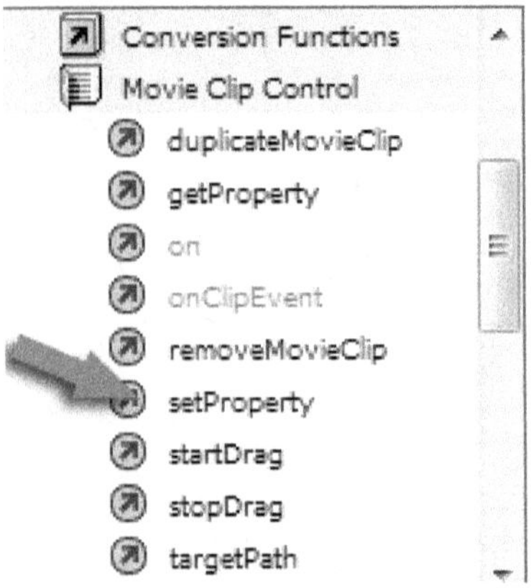

In the **setProperty** settings window select **_y** for the **Property** setting, type **/car** in the **Target** window, and type **217** in the Value window:

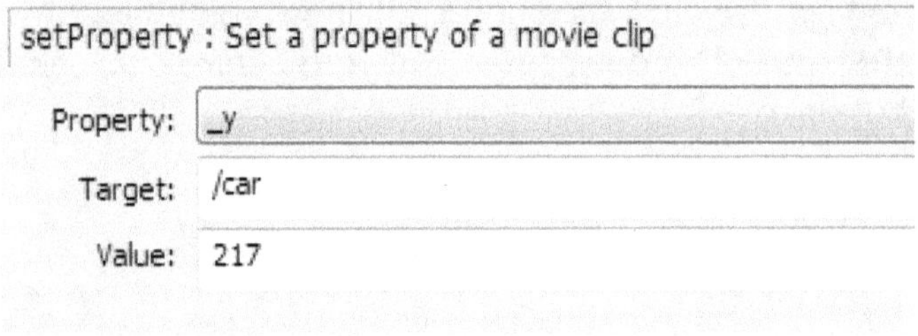

Next, we'll add the code for the X coordinate. Go to **Global Functions**, **Movie clip Control** and double-click **setProperty**. In the **setProperty** settings window select **_x** for the **Property** setting, type **/car** in the **Target** window, and type **175** in the **Value** window:

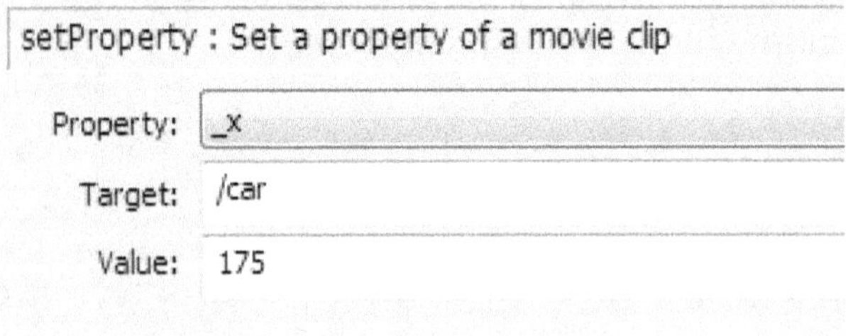

Test your movie. The **Car** Movie clip should now be right above the **LOCATION** button:

Now we'll need to return the car to its original position. Go back to the editing file and click on the car symbol. Open the Properties panel and you'll see the X and Y coordinates of the car:

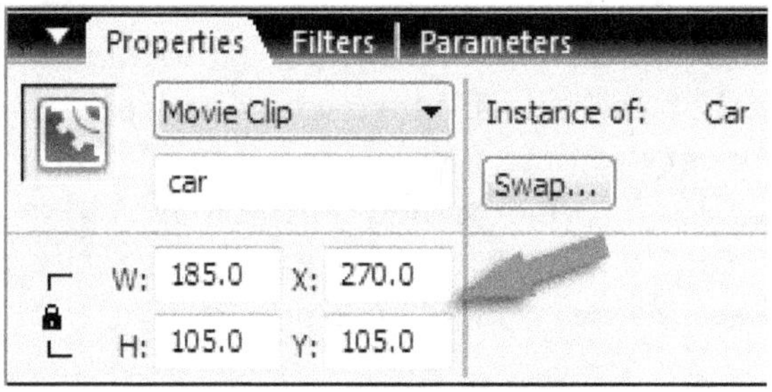

These are the coordinates we'll use for the **RESET** button. Let's add that code now. Select the **RESET** button and open the Actions panel. Go to **Global Functions**, **Movie clip Control** and double-click **setProperty**. In the **setProperty** settings window select **_x** for the Property setting, type **/car** in the **Target** window, and type **270** in the **Value** window. We now need to add the Y code.

Go to **Global Functions**, **Movie clip Control** and double-click **setProperty**. In the **setProperty** settings window select **_y** for the **Property** setting, type **/car** in the Target window, and type **105** in the **Value** window. Test the movie again and click on the **LOCATION** button; the car should now be above the **LOCATION** button. Click on the **RESET** button. The car should go back to its original location.

Next, we'll rotate this Movie clip. Select the **ROTATION** button and open the Actions panel. Go to **Global Functions**, **Movie clip Control** and double-click **setProperty**. In the **setProperty** settings window select **_rotation** for the **Property** setting, type **/car** in the **Target** window, and type **90** in the **Value** window. This will rotate the car 90 degrees. Test your movie and click the

ROTATION button to try it out. The car should rotate 90 degrees. Go back to the editing stage. Next, type **180** in the **Value** window. Test your movie and click the **ROTATION** button. The car should now be upside down:

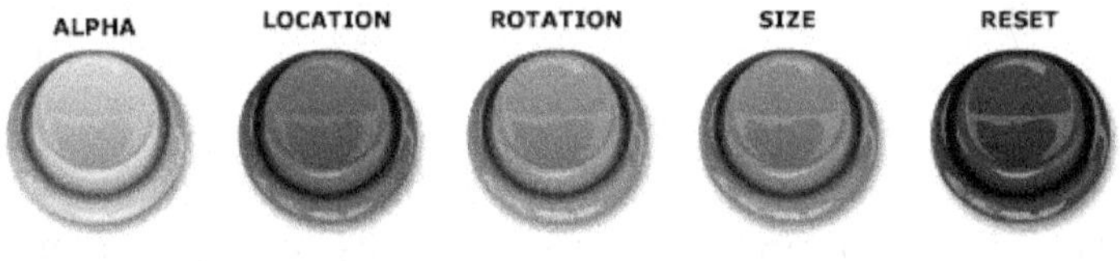

Pretty cool huh? Now we need to add the code that will return this car to normal. Select the **RESET** button and Go to **Global Functions**, **Movie clip Control** and double-click **setProperty**. In the **setProperty** settings window select **_rotation** for the **Property** setting, type **/car** in the Target window, and type **0** in the **Value** window. This will return the car to normal. You'll notice that in the ActionScript for the **RESET** button we have several **setProperty** commands now:

```
on (release) {
    setProperty("/car", _alpha, "100");
    setProperty("/car", _x, "270");
    setProperty("/car", _y, "105");
    setProperty("/car", _rotation, "0");
}
```

Normally when we start a new code for a button we want to make sure that the code is separated from any other code on the button. In this case, however, since they're all setProperty functions and they all use the same mouse event (**Release**), we can get away with having them all grouped together.

The last button is the **SIZE** button. This button, of course, will change the overall size of the car. Select the **SIZE** button. Go to **Global Functions**, **Movie clip Control** and double-click **setProperty**. In the **setProperty** settings window select **_xscale** for the **Property** setting, type **/car** in the **Target** window, and type **150** in the **Value** window:

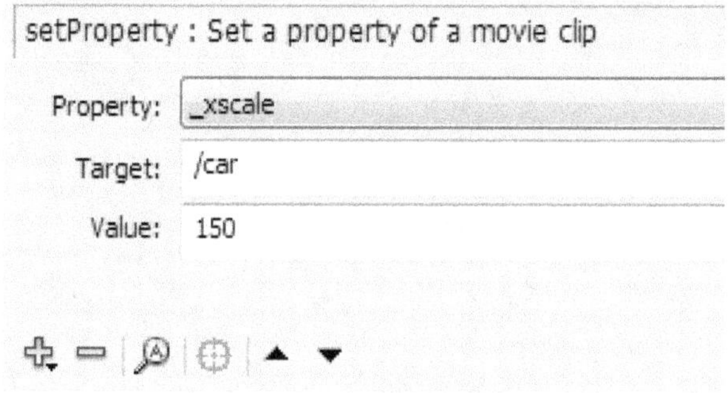

This will increase the **X** (width) of the car by 150%. Test your movie now and you'll see that the width of the car has increased quite a bit. But it looks a bit odd now since it got wider but not taller. Let's fix that now. In the Actions panel go to **Global Functions**, **Movie clip Control** and double-click **setProperty**. In the **setProperty** settings window select **_yscale** for the **Property** setting, type **/car** in the **Target** window, and type **150** in the **Value** window. This will increase the height of the car. Test your movie and the car should now look normal but a lot larger. Can you figure out what we need to do to get it back to normal? See if you can figure out what code you need to put in the **RESET** button before proceeding.

If you guessed putting **100** in the **Value** window then you are correct! When you add the setProperty code to the **RESET** button you simply select **_xscale** with a value of **100**, then **_yscale** with a Value of **100**. Test your movie by clicking on the **SIZE** button then the **RESET** button after adding this code. Now you have a better understanding of the setProperty command. A simple yet powerful command.

startDrag

Have you ever seen those Flash files on the internet that let you drag objects around? They use a function called startDrag. We'll be using this function quite a bit in the Projects chapter so it's important you understand how it works.

Open the file called startDrag.fla in the OddsEnds folder. You'll notice a crayon image in the middle of the stage. If you select it you'll see the Instance Name of **crayon** in the Properties panel. Create a new layer and name it **Actions**. Add a simple **stop** code to its frame. Next, open the Actions panel and go to **Global Functions**, **Movie clip Control** and double-click **startDrag**:

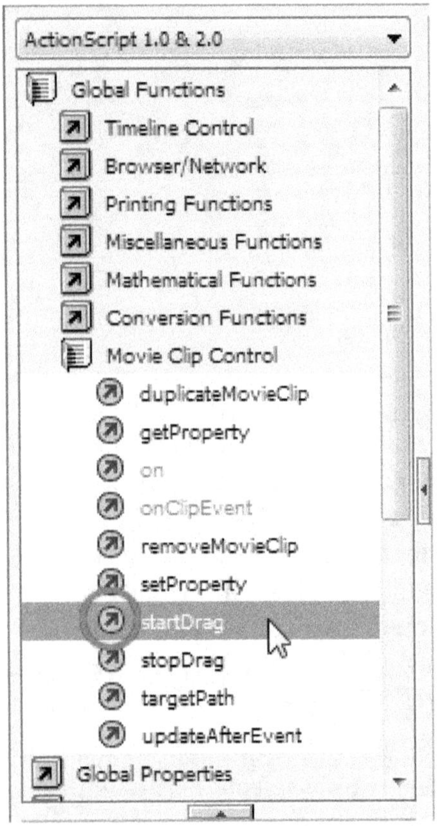

You should now be in the **startDrag** settings window. In the **Target** window type **/crayon** and select **Lock mouse to center**:

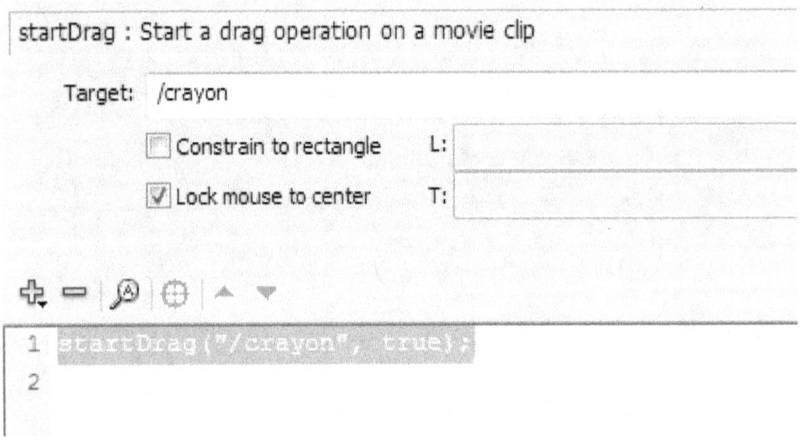

Test your movie. The crayon should follow the cursor around since we selected **Lock mouse to center**. What that means is the center of the crayon image is going to lock onto the cursor. You'll notice that the bottom of the crayon is locked onto the cursor. So how do we determine the center of the crayon image? I'll show that to you now.

Double-click the crayon symbol. You'll see the crayon image and below it you'll see a **little plus symbol**:

This plus symbol indicates the center of the **Crayon** Movie clip. Drag the crayon so that the middle of the crayon image is lined up with the plus symbol:

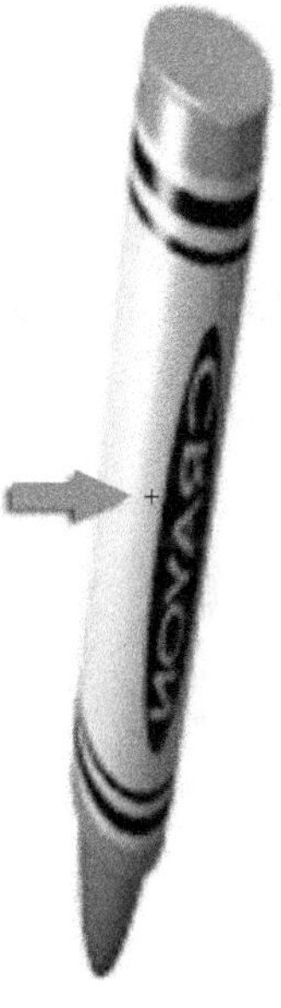

Test the movie. The middle of the crayon is now locked onto the cursor. So when using the startDrag code you can easily change which part of the object gets locked onto the cursor.

This time let's try a different type of startDrag. Open the Scene panel and click on the **Ball Borders** scene. In this scene we have a ball and a black border. We'll be creating a startDrag code to constrain the movement of the ball within this black border.

Select the ball symbol and open the Properties panel. Give this ball symbol an Instance Name of **ball**:

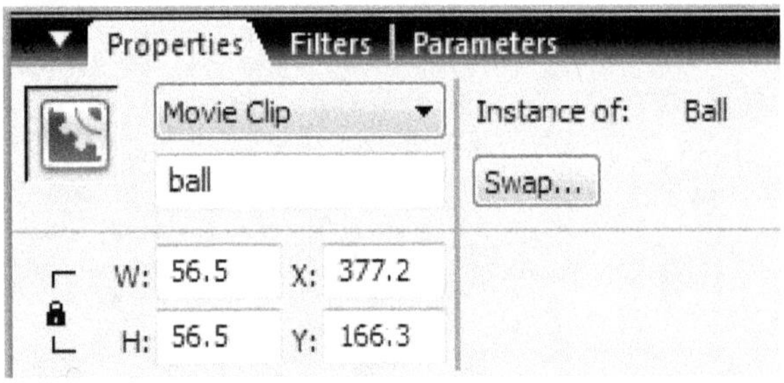

Double-click this Movie clip to enter its editing stage. Select the ball shape on the stage and convert it to a button; name this button **Ball Button**:

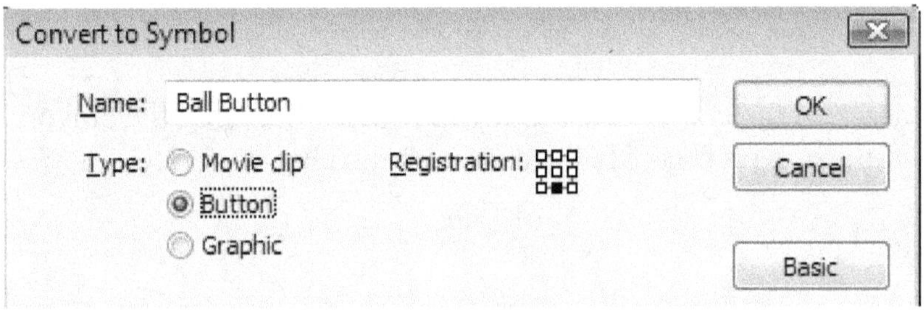

Hit OK when you're finished. Open the Actions panel and go to **Global Functions**, **Movie clip Control**, and double-click **startDrag**:

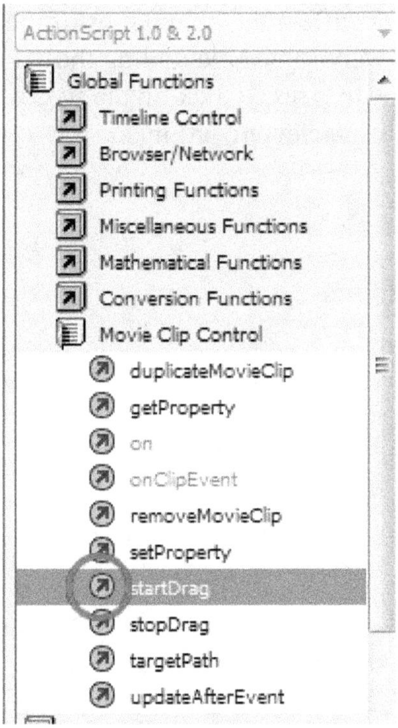

You should now be in the **startDrag** setting window. Since we'll be controlling the ball symbol, then we need to type **/ball** in the **Target** window. We're also going to constrain the movement of the ball within the black border, so we need to select **Constrain to rectangle**. When you select **Constrain to rectangle** you'll see the settings show up on the right. This is where you'll put the coordinate numbers for L (left), T (top), R (right) and B (bottom). Type **120** for **L**, **150** for **T**, **570** for **R**, and **480** for **B**:

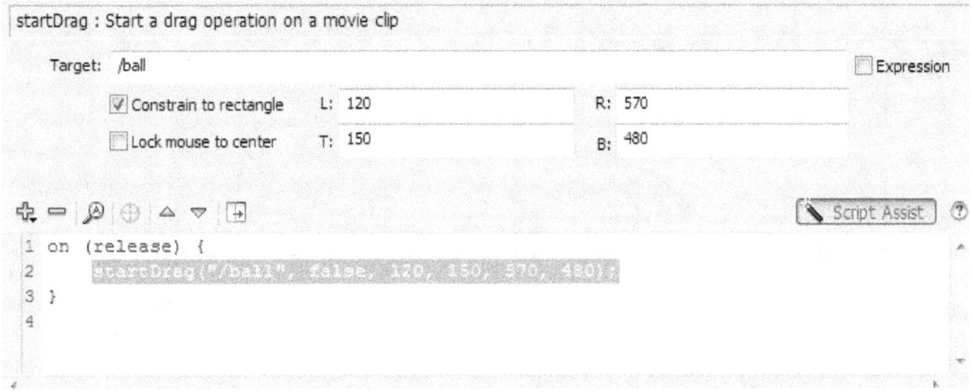

These numbers represent how many pixels from the stage border you want the ball to be constrained within. You can play around with these numbers when we're done so you can get an idea of how the numbers affect the boundaries of the ball. When we press down on the mouse button we want to be able to drag the ball. So we need to change the mouse event: **release**, to **press**. Click on the word **release** in the ActionScript and you should see the **mouse event** settings. Uncheck **Release** and select **Press**:

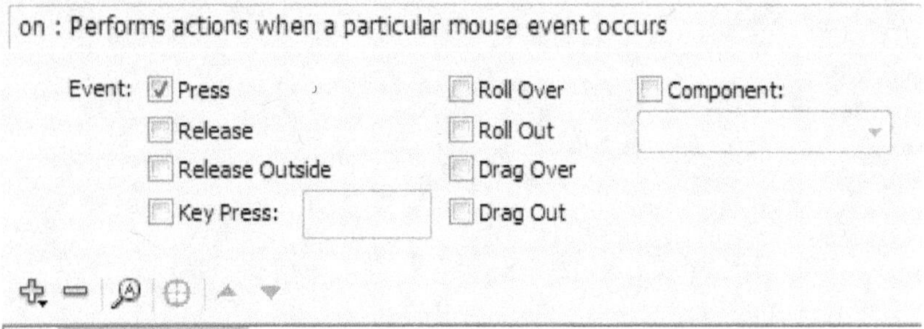


```
on (press) {
    startDrag("/ball", false, 120, 150, 570, 480);
}
```

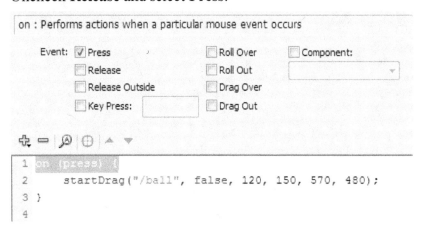

Go back to the **Ball Borders** scene and test your scene by going to **Control**, **Test Scene**. You should be able to drag the ball within the black border. Note, if it's not perfect you can always tweak the numbers in the **startDrag** window. The only problem now is that we can't release the ball. It's stuck like glue to the cursor. When we release the mouse we want the ball to stop being dragged. Let's do that now. Double-click the ball symbol to enter its editing stage. Select the **Ball** Button on the stage and open the Actions panel if it isn't already open. Since we're adding new code we want to make sure it's separate from the first code so select the closing bracket of the last set of code:

```
on (press) {
    startDrag("/ball", false, 120, 150, 570, 480);
}
```

Go to **Global Functions**, **Movie clip Controls** and double-click **stopDrag**:

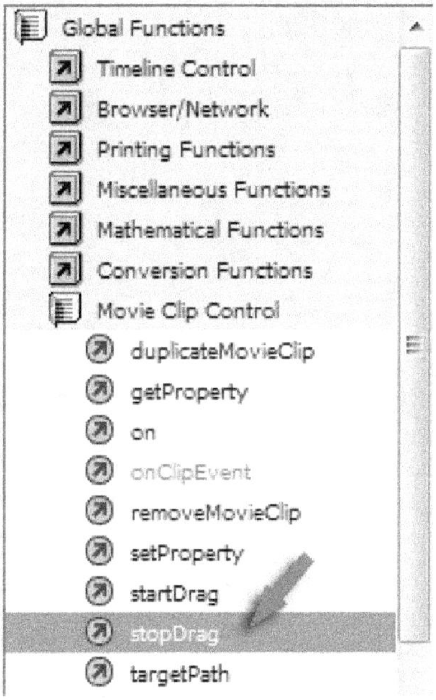

There are no settings to adjust for stopDrag unless you want to change the mouse event (release). Since we want to stop dragging the ball once we release the mouse button, then this is the correct mouse event. Return to the **Ball Borders** scene; go to **Control**, **Test Scene**. Now the ball is confined within the border, and when you release the mouse button the dragging will stop.

Edit Multiple Frames

Before you open the next Flash file, make sure you install the Vladimir font located in the Fonts folder. After you install the font, open the **Edit_Frames.fla** file in the OddsEnds folder. Test this movie so you can see how it works. You'll first see the picture of the woman fade in, then we have her name fade in. Here's the problem. We want her name to appear **above** the line. But if you notice on the timeline we have a layer for each letter in her name; so how do we move the entire name animation above the line without having to move each letter one by one? Easy! The Edit Multiple Frames feature. This feature is great for selecting multiple layers and moving them all at once. A huge timesaver that you'll be using over and over again in your Flash career.

Click on the **Edit Multiple Frames** button below the timeline:

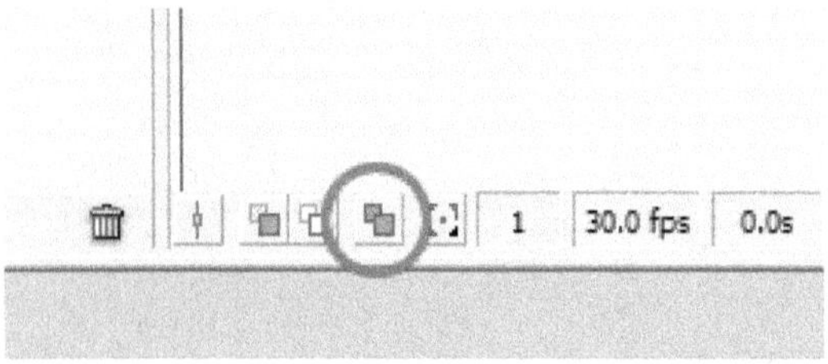

You should now see two bars appear above the timeline. The first one is called **Start Onion Skin** and the second one is called **End Onion Skin**:

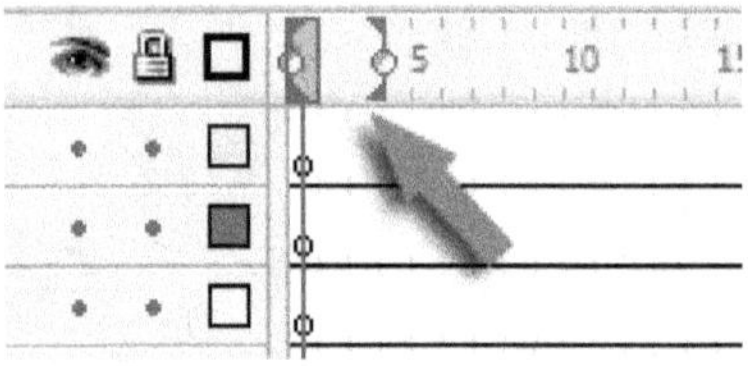

What we need to do is drag the second bar (**End Onion Skin**) to the right on the timeline so that all the frames of the layer we need to move are *within the two bars*. Drag this bar to frame **140**. You may have to use the horizontal scroll to view all the frames. Make sure you grab the bar and not the area between the bars, otherwise you'll end up moving both bars:

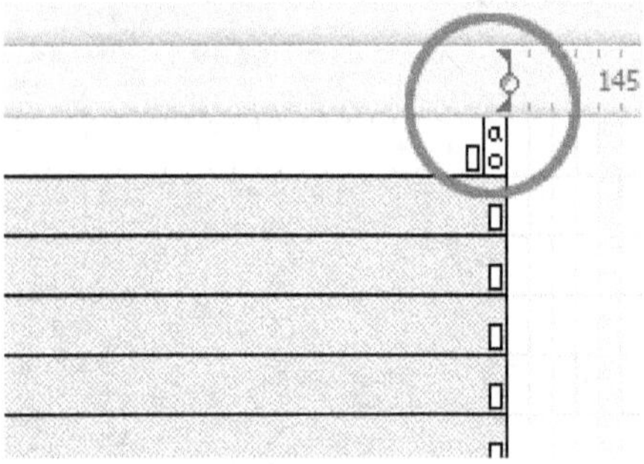

Make sure the first bar is still at frame 1 and didn't get moved:

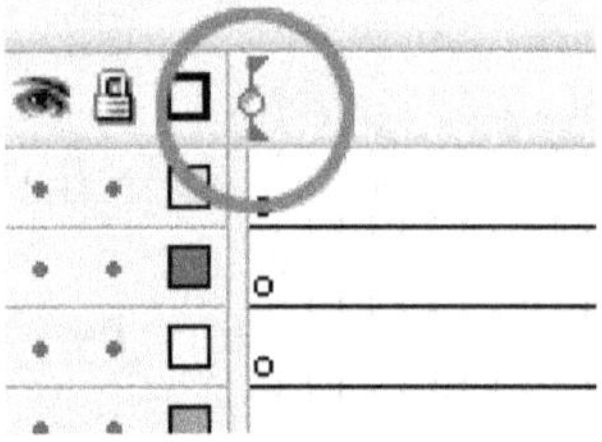

All the objects that are within these two frames will move in unison. Since we don't want the **Picture** and **Line** layer to move, we need to lock these layers:

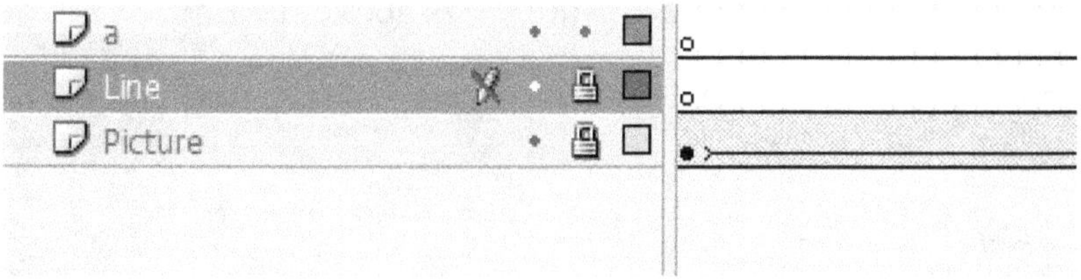

Any layer that is locked won't move. We don't need to lock the **Actions** layer since it holds no objects. Next, select the **V** layer, then hold down the SHIFT button and select the bottommost letter layer: the **a** layer; this should highlight all the letter layers:

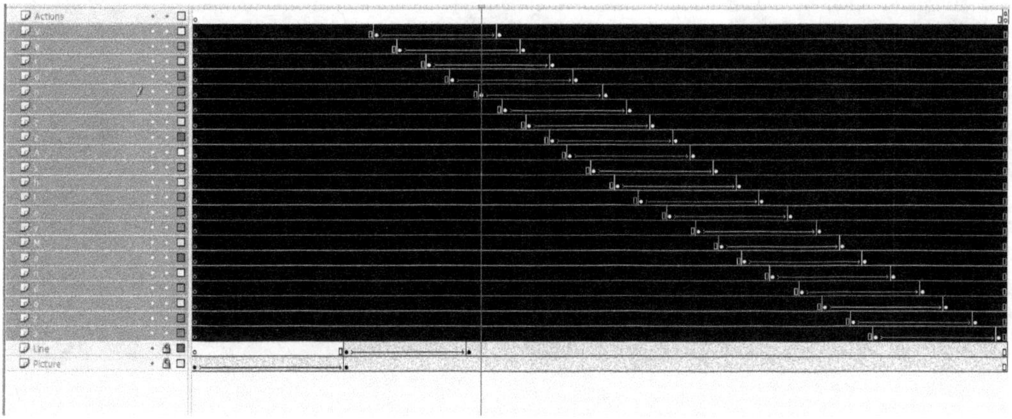

Next, go to **Edit**, **Select All**:

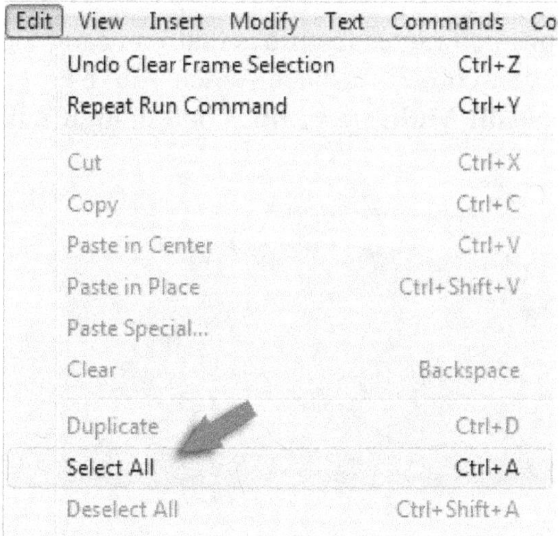

This will highlight all frames within the bars that are unlocked. We can now move all the layers which hold the letters of her name. Grab the **Selection Tool** and select any part of the name; move the name upward so its above the line:

When you're done test the movie. The animation should now be between the line and picture. So now you can see how this will save time! Instead of moving each letter one at a time, we've moved them all as if they were one object.

One other advantage of using the Edit Multiple Frames feature is that you can increase, or decrease the overall size of several objects at once. When you're finished moving your objects, click on the **Edit Multiple Frames** button to turn it off.

Filters

One of the newest features of the past couple years comes in the form of Filters. If you're familiar with Photoshop filters then you'll be comfortable with using the

Flash filters. But even if you're not familiar with Photoshop, they are still easy to learn, and easy to use. So let's get started. Open the file called **Filters.fla** in the OddsEnds folder. You should see two sets of text that both say the same thing. One is against black and the other is against white. So let's add the filters.

Before we can add filters to the text, we have to convert the text to a Movie clip. You can only add filters to Movie clips. Click on the top text and convert it to a Movie clip. Name it **Text 1**:

Hit **OK** when you're done. Now we can add the filter. Open the Filters panel (if you can't find the Filters panel go to **Window**, **Properties**, **Filters**)

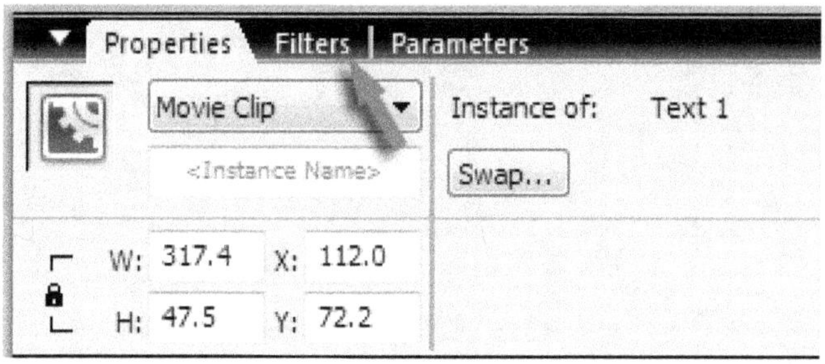

You should now see the Filters panel. Click on the **Add Filter** button:

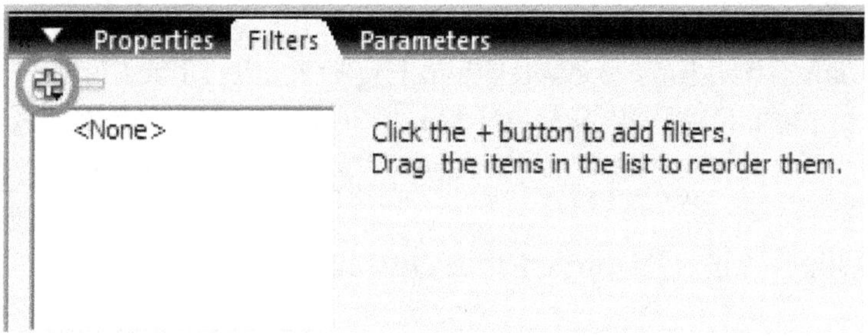

You should now see a list of filters. Select **Glow**:

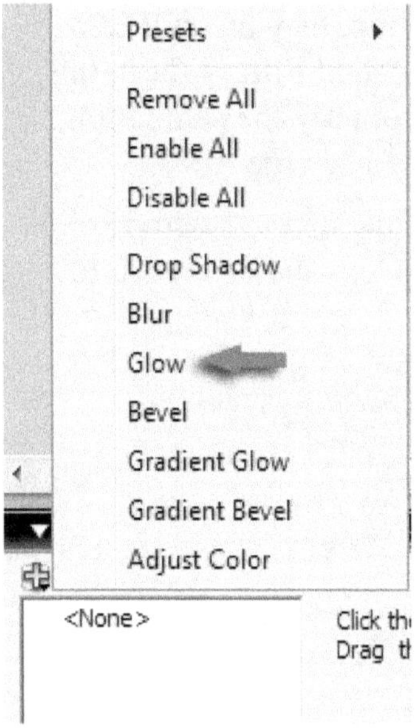

You should now be in the Glow settings window:

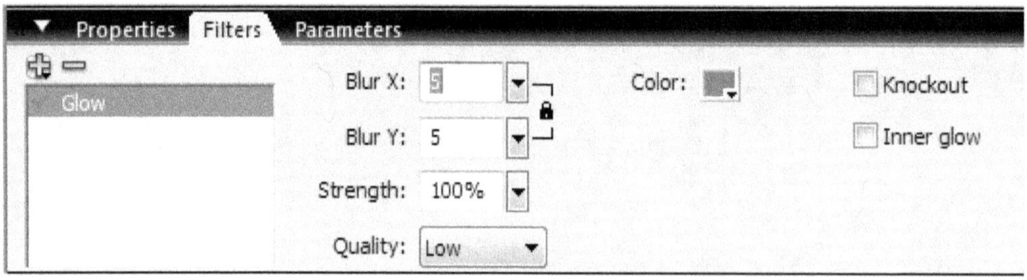

The **Blur X** setting blurs the Glow on the X coordinate. The **Blur Y** setting blurs the Glow on the Y coordinate. I usually use 15 for both settings. The **Strength** setting simply controls how visible you want the Glow. The **Quality** setting is self-explanatory. Low Quality will load up faster than High Quality. The **Color** option changes the color of the Glow. If you select **Knockout**, it will create a stencil of the Text but keep the Glow. **Inner glow** places the Glow inside the Text.

Remove this Filter by clicking on the **Remove Filter button**:

Click on the **Add Filter** button and select **Bevel**:

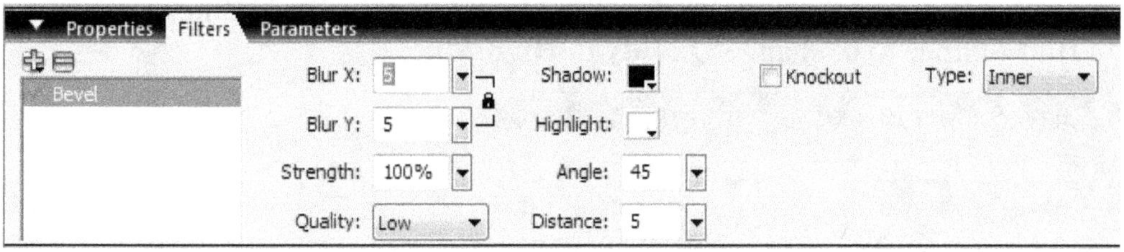

This Filter adds a bevel to your object. The **Blur** functions work the same as the previous Filter; same with Strength. **Quality** also works the same with Low Quality loading up faster than High Quality. The **Shadow** color determines just that: the shadow of the bevel. **Highlight** color determines the highlight of the bevel.

If you click on the **Angle** drop-down arrow you'll see a little circle pop up. Click on the little circle and move it around. This changes the angle of the bevel:

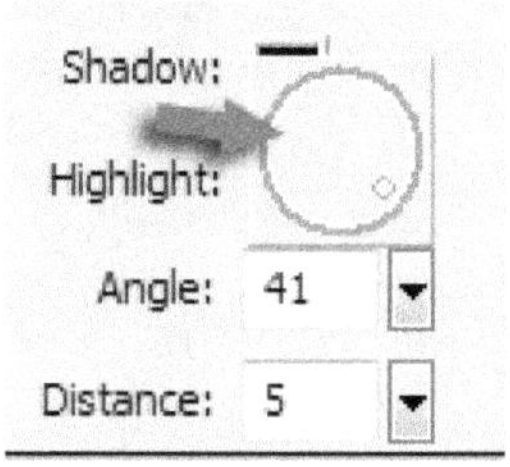

Distance determines how far away the bevel is from the Text. **Knockout** creates a stencil of the Text and just leaves the bevel. And, finally, **Type** determines if you want the bevel on the outside of the Text, the inside of the Text, or both.

Click the **Remove Filter** button. Select the Text that is in the **Text 2** layer. Convert it to a Movie clip; name it **Text 2**. Select this new Movie clip and click on the **Add filter** button. Select **Drop Shadow** from the list of filters. You should now see a slight drop shadow on your text:

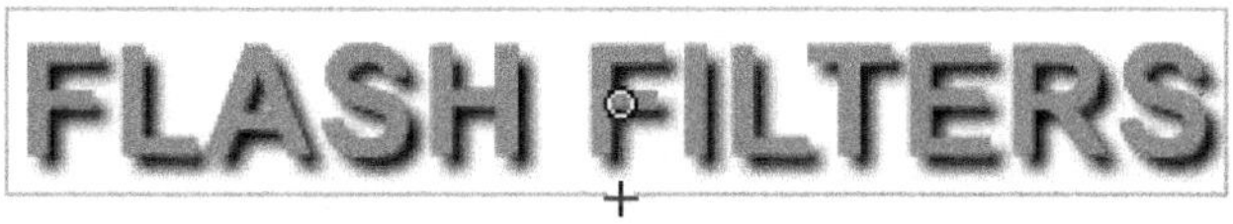

You'll notice that the settings are similar to the other filters. The **Blur** settings will soften the shadow. The **Color** setting will change the color of the shadow. The one setting that is different than the other filters is the **Hide object** setting. This removes the Text altogether and just leaves the shadow.

The Blur filter is my favorite filter. Next, we'll be using the Blur filter to create clouds. Open the Scene panel and click on the **Plane** scene. This scene has a plane that flies in from offstage right to offstage left. Select frame **1** of the **Plane** layer then select the plane symbol on the stage. In the Filters panel click on the **Add filter** button and select **Blur** from the list of filters. In the Blur settings change both Blur settings to **0**; change **Quality** to **High**:

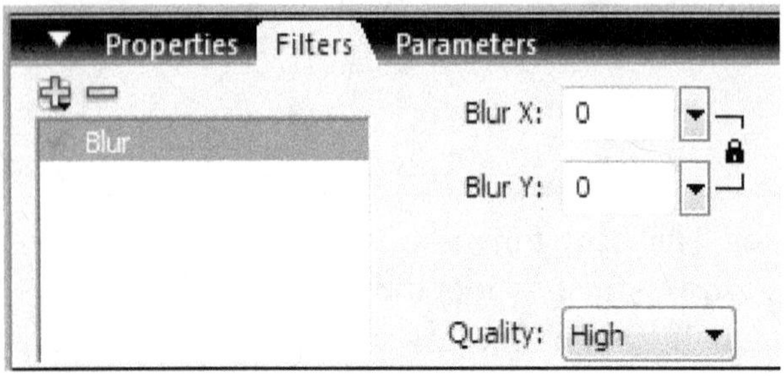

Next, select the keyframe on frame **120** and select the plane symbol on the stage. You should see the **Blur** settings in your Filter panel. Change both Blur settings to **6**:

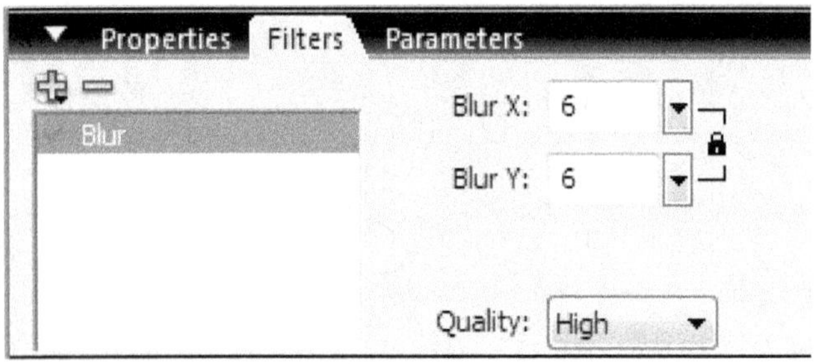

So as the plane gets farther away it becomes a little more blurry. Go to **Control**, **Test Scene**. Pretty cool! Even though this is a simple animation you can imagine what is possible with this Blur filter. You can even make your own clouds. Try this: create a new layer and name it **Cloud 1**. Grab the **Brush Tool**, turn off **Stroke color** and change the **Fill color** to **white**. Draw a cloud shape on the stage like this:

Select this new shape and convert it to a Movie clip. Name it **Cloud**. Select this new Movie clip and click the **Add filter** button in the Filters panel. Select **Blur**. In the Blur settings change the Blur number for X and Y to **63**. Change Quality to **High**:

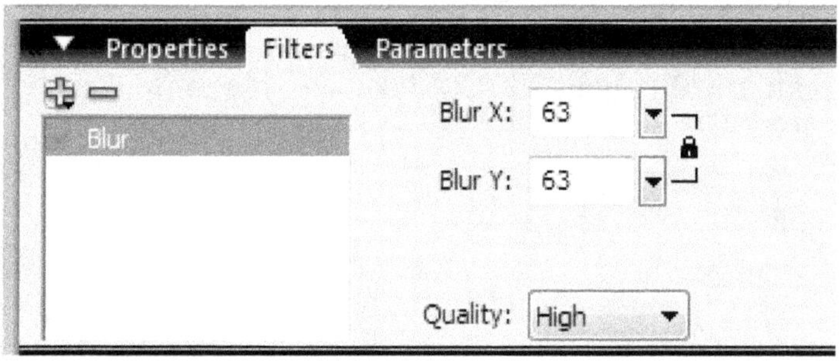

Move this cloud offstage to the left:

Click on frame **30** of the **Cloud** layer and insert a keyframe. Click any frame between the two keyframes and insert a Motion Tween. On frame **30** select the cloud symbol; drag it offstage to the bottom right:

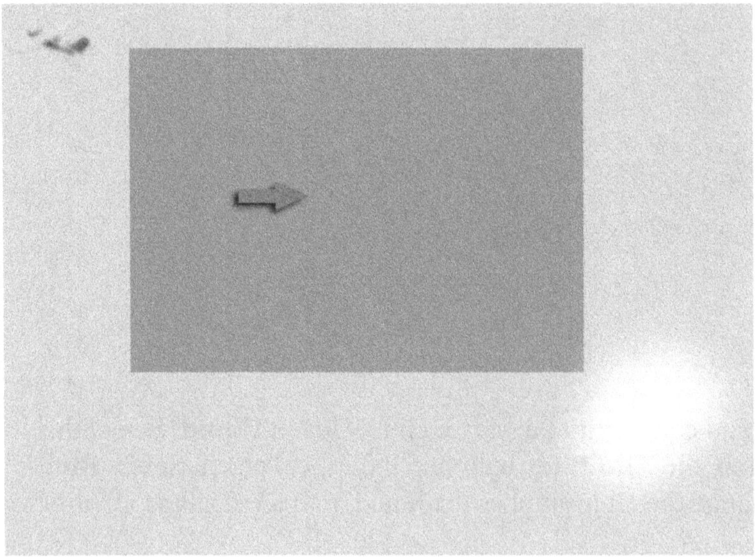

Enlarge this Cloud symbol on frame **30** about 200%. Make sure it's completely off the stage after you enlarge it:

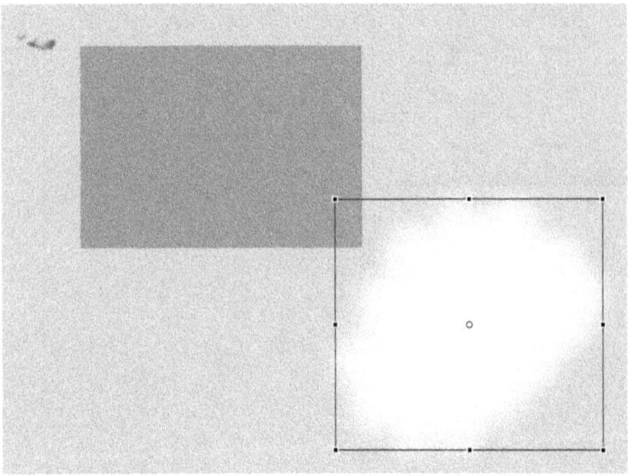

In the Filters panel change the **Blur** for X and Y to **100**:

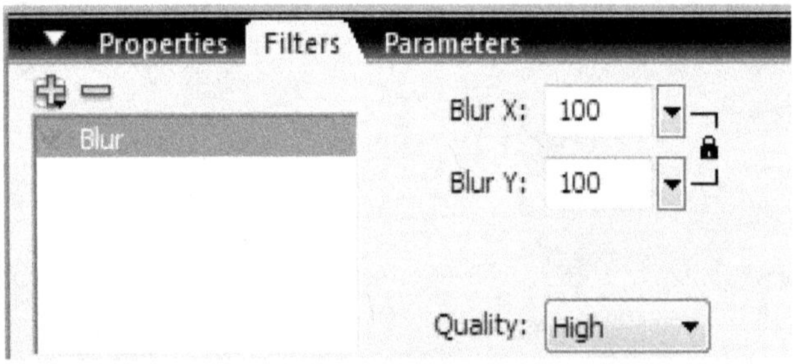

Select the Properties panel. Change **Color** to **Alpha** and the percentage to **0**. Test your scene. As your plane flies it begins to get blurry; the cloud image gradually gets larger and more transparent. So these are two simple examples of using the Blur filter. A powerful filter that I think you'll be using quite often in your Flash career. The other filters, **Gradient Glow** and **Gradient Bevel**, are the same as Bevel and Glow except that you can use gradient colors instead of one single color. It's best to try these filters out and just experiment with the different settings. The last filter, **Adjust Color**, changes the brightness, contrast and color of the symbol. If you were having the plane fly into storm clouds, for example, you can have the plane gradually get darker. You would also be able to change the hue of the plane to match the surrounding sky.

Anchor Point

If you want to rotate a clock hand to spin around a clock in a clockwise motion, you're probably going to have to learn about **Anchors**. Anchors tell the symbol what to rotate around. If you had a wheel, you would want the anchor point in the middle of the wheel; if you had a square and you wanted it to rotate around one of its corners, then you would move the anchor point to that corner. In this example we're going to add a reflector to a bicycle. We're then going to rotate the reflector around the wheels in a realistic motion by moving the anchor point.

On your hard drive go to the **OddsEnds** folder and double-click **Bike.swf** file. Notice how the reflector spins around the wheel. I even added a slight blur to the reflector and a Mask so it appears to be going behind the bars of the wheels. So let's get started. Open the **Bike.fla** file in the **OddsEnds** folder. You'll see a picture of a woman riding her bike against a blurry background. Create a new layer and name it **Reflector**. Zoom into the stage 200%. Drag the graphic **Reflector** from the library onto the stage. Place it over the front wheel:

Convert this graphic to a Movie clip. Name it **Reflector Movie**:

Hit **OK**. Double-click on this new Movie clip to enter its editing stage. Zoom into the stage so you can see the Anchor of the **Reflector** image. It's the little circle in the middle of the image:

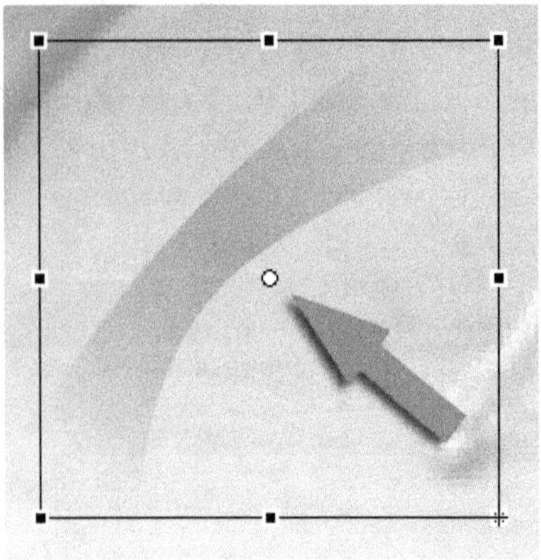

Select frame **60** and insert a keyframe. Select any frame between the keyframes and insert a Motion Tween. Select the first frame and open the Properties panel. Change **Rotate** to **CCW** and type **20** in the **times** window:

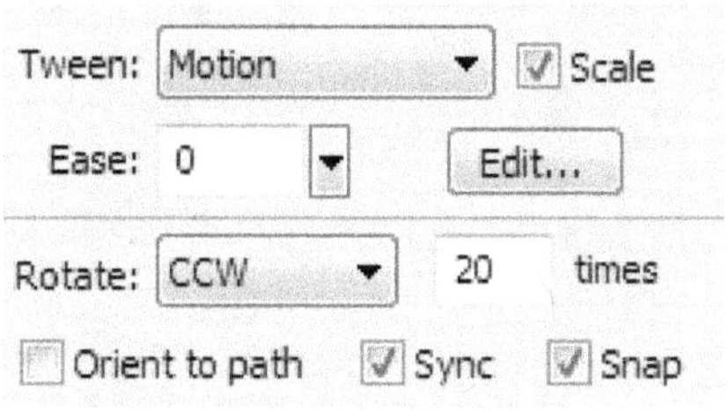

Hit **Enter** to play your animation. You'll notice that the animation isn't quite what we want. That's because the Anchor needs to be moved to the center of the wheel. Let's do that now. Before you can move the Anchor you have to select the **Free Transform Tool**. Next, select the first keyframe. Zoom into the wheel so you can see the Anchor point. Move the Anchor to the center hub of the bicycle wheel like this:

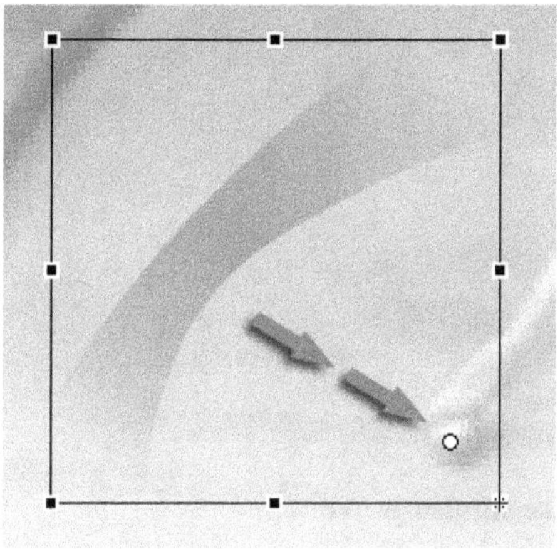

If you play your animation again by hitting **Enter** (or **Control**, **Play**), you'll see that the Reflector rotates correctly at first then slowly moves away from the center. The reason is because we moved the anchor on the first frame but not on the last keyframe. So let's correct that. Select frame **60** and, once again, move the Anchor point of the Reflector to the center hub of the bicycle wheel. If you play your timeline you'll see a nice spinning reflector. But now we need to make it more realistic.

Go back to **Scene 1**. Select the **Reflector** Movie clip on the stage and open the Properties panel. Change **Color** to **Alpha** and change the percentage to **75**. Next, click on the Filters panel and click on the **Add Filter** button; select **Blur** from the list:

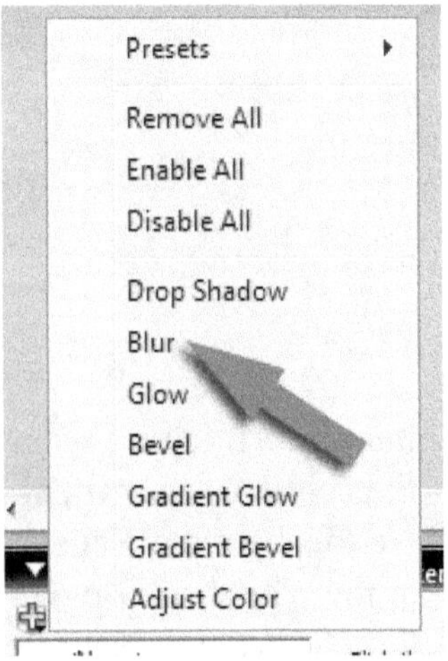

Change **Blur X** and **Blur Y** to **13**. Change the **Quality** to **Medium**:

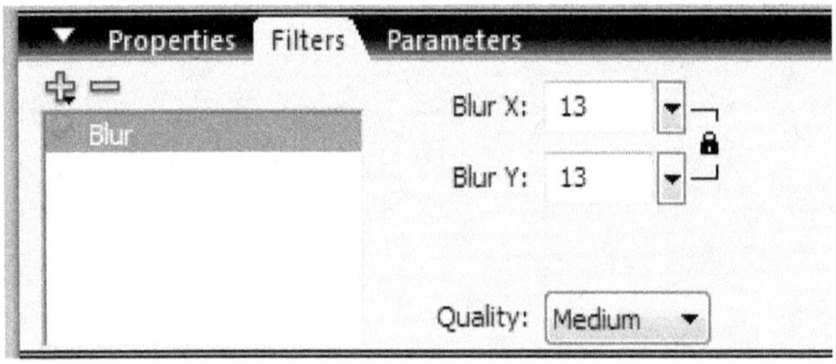

Test your movie. Looks nice. But the reflector is spinning over the bars of the wheel. We need to place this animation behind the bars. Before we do that we need to create a copy of this reflector animation for the back wheel. Select the **Reflector** Movie clip and go to **Edit**, **Copy**. Create a new layer and name it **Back Wheel**. Select the keyframe of this new layer and go to **Edit**, **Paste in Place**. Move this new Movie clip to the right and place it over the back wheel:

Create a new layer and name it **Mask**. Move this layer over the **Reflector** layer:

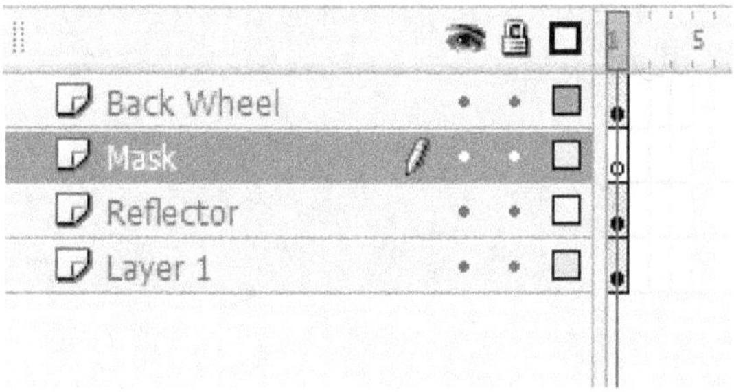

Grab the **Brush Tool** and select **red** for the **Fill color**. Start painting over the wheel. Paint anywhere you think the reflector will be seen. Do not paint over the bar though. The mask shape should look like this:

Right-click on the **Mask** layer and select **Mask** from the list. We'll now create a mask for the back wheel. Select the **Back Wheel** layer and create a new layer. Name this new layer **Mask**. Grab the **Brush Tool**, keep **red** as the **Fill color**. Start painting over the back wheel. Paint over any area where the reflector should be visible. Be careful not to paint over the bars. You may have to change your brush size to get in between the smaller bars:

Right-click on this layer and select **Mask** from the list. Test your movie. You can always tweak the animation if you like. If it doesn't look perfect you can blur the reflector image more, or take down the Alpha.

Shape Hints

There will probably come a time when you'll want to morph a shape into another shape. When this time comes you can either let Flash do the morphing for you or you can use Shape Hints. When Flash morphs shapes it tends to use the path of least resistance; which usually results in a mess. Shape Hints tell Flash which part of the first image will morph into which part of the second shape.

Open **Shape_Hints.fla**. We're going to morph the number 7 into the number 1. Then, the number 1 into the number 5 using Shape Hints. In the middle of the stage you'll see the number 7. Before we start the animation we need to select the first keyframe and open the Properties panel. Next to **Tween** select **Shape**:

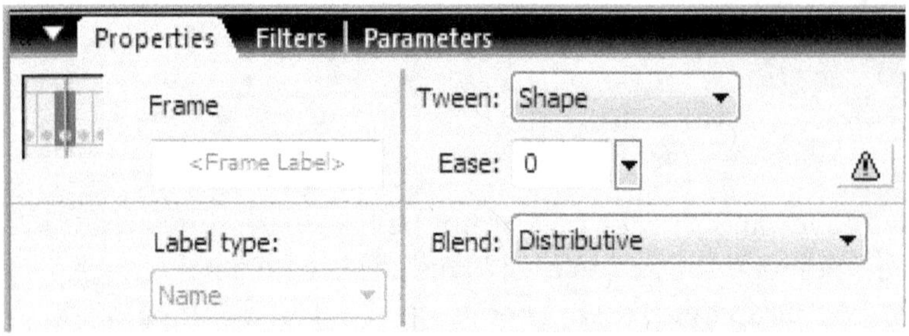

Create a keyframe on frame **30**. Double-click on the number **7** on the stage; highlight the number and change it to number **1**:

The thing about morphing in Flash, is that you can only morph using shapes. So before we morph the number 7 into the number **1**, we need to convert them to shapes. Select the number **1** and go to **Modify**, **Break Apart**:

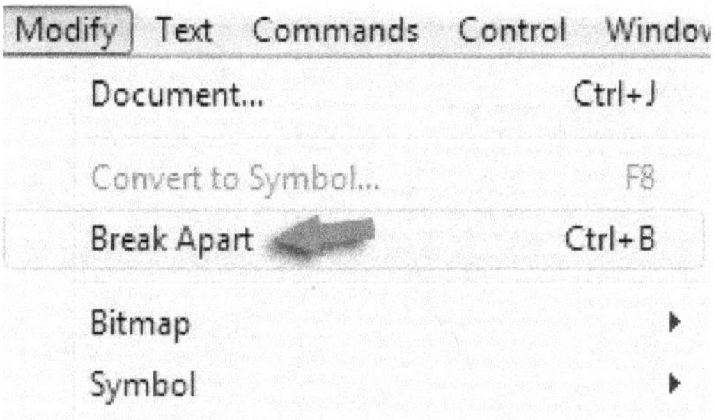

The number **1** should now be a series of tiny dots indicating it's a shape:

Select frame **1** and select the number **7** on the stage. Go to **Modify**, **Break Apart**. On your timeline you should see a green shape tween:

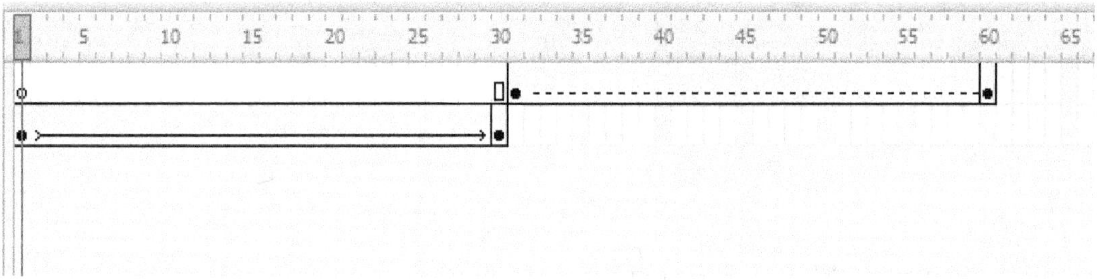

Let's add the Shape Hints. Go to **Modify**, **Shape**, **Add Shape Hint** (**Ctrl Shift H**):

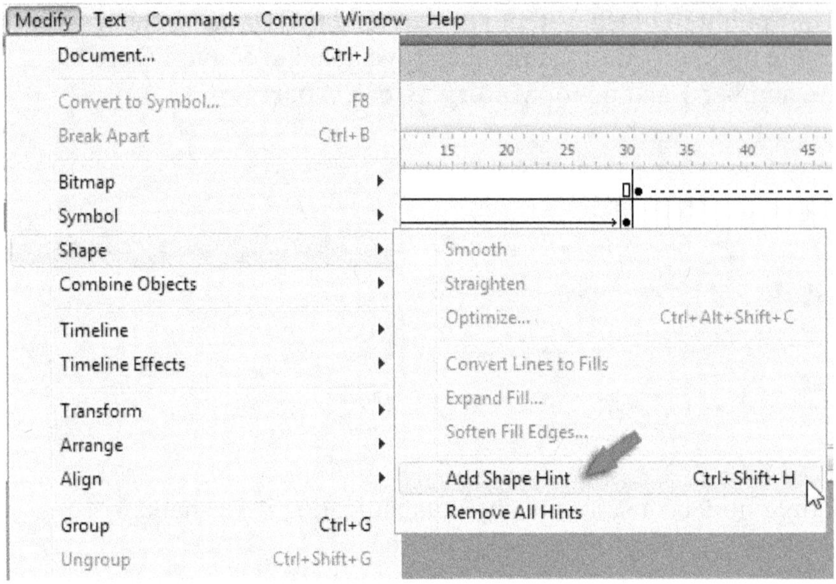

You should see a little circle with the letter **a** inside of it on the number 7:

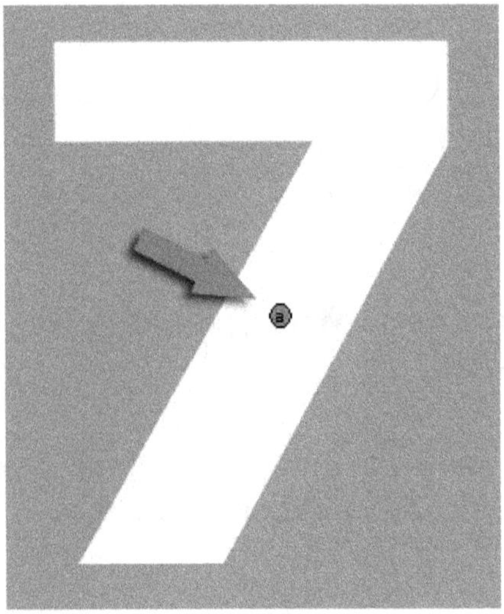

Move this a circle to the top left of the number 7:

Go to frame **30**. You should see the little circle with the **a** in it. Move this to the top left of the number **1**:

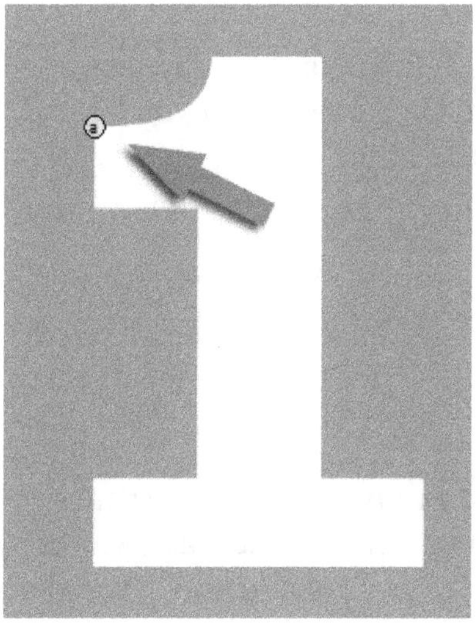

Move the timeline needle from frame **1** to frame **30** and watch the morphing. You'll notice that the corner of number 7 that has the **a** circle, goes directly to the corner of the number 1 that also has the **a** circle. So, let's add a couple more Shape Hints to create a nicer morph. Select frame **1**. Go to **Modify**, **Shape**, **Add Shape Hints**. You'll see a **b** circle appear on the number **7**. Move that to the top right of the number **7**. Add another Shape Hint. Move that to the corner below the **a** circle. Add one more Shape Hint and place it to the right of the **c** circle:

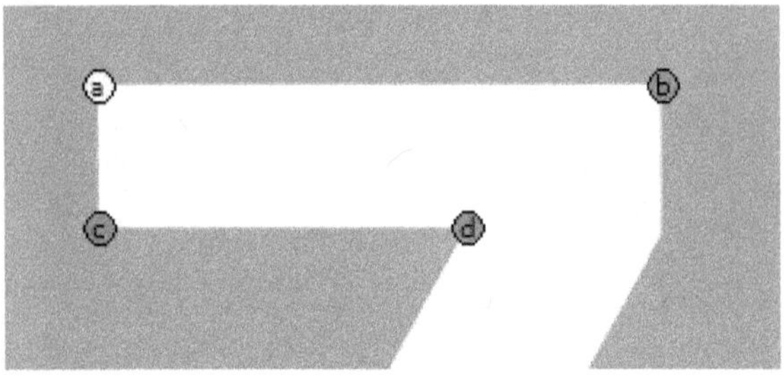

Go to frame **30**. You'll see the **d** circle on the number 1. Move it to the corner diagonally across from the **a** circle. Move the **c** circle below the **a** circle and move the **b** circle to the top right:

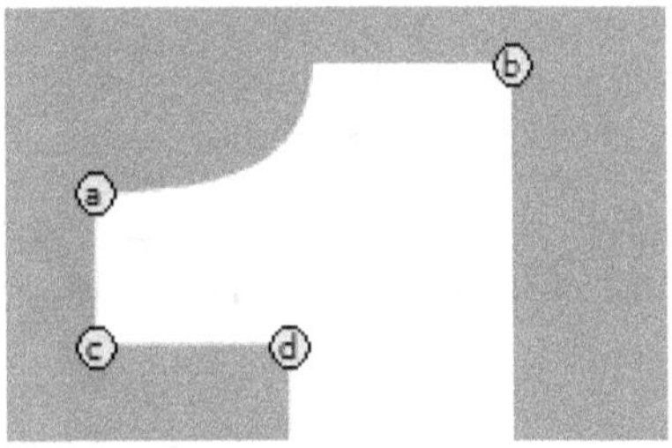

If you play the timeline you'll see how the shape hints help guide Flash when morphing the two shapes. Let's try one more morph. On the layer **1-5** you'll see that the shape tween is broken which is why you see a series of dashes:

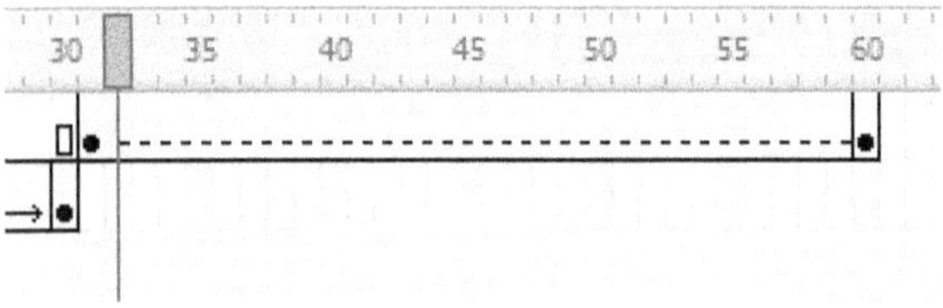

The reason the shape tween is broken is because the two numbers aren't shapes yet. Select frame **31** of the **1-5** layer and select the number **1** on the stage. Go to **Modify**, **Break Apart**. On frame **60** select the number **5**. Select **Modify**, **Break Apart**. So now the numbers are shapes; you should now see an arrow instead of dashes in the shape tween.

If you play the animation from frame 31 to frame 60 you'll notice that the animation looks a little strange. When Flash doesn't have guidance it can sometimes be a disaster. Let's add some Shape Hints and help Flash out. Add four Shape Hints to the number 1. Place the **a** and **b** circles at the top of the **1**, and the **c** and **d** circles to the left corners like this:

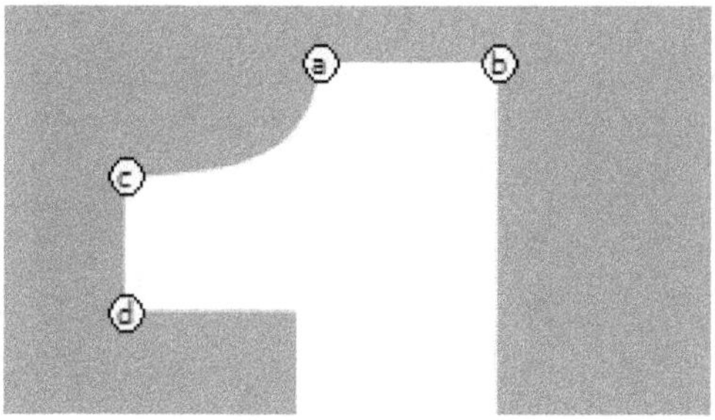

Go to frame **60** and you should see the **d** circle on the **5** number. Move the **d** circle to the bottom left corner, the **c** circle to the top left, the **a** circle to the top right and the **b** circle right below the **a** circle:

Test your movie. Your numbers should morph nicely into each other.

Congratulations! Your training is complete! Next, we'll be creating some great projects including passwords, interactive games, quizzes and much more!

Chapter Six:
Flash Projects

Now that you've completed the training chapters it's time to put what you've learned into practice. In this chapter we'll be creating everything from a simple quiz to a fully functioning roulette game. Each exercise has a difficulty meter so you may want to work your way up to the more complicated projects.

Animated Mask

DIFFICULTY: ●●○○○○

In this exercise we'll create a nice little mask animation that gradually changes the color of an automobile. Also, there is a color palette that allows the user to select which color the car should change to. This is one of those effects that is fast and easy to create, but has a "wow" factor when users first see it. So let's get started!

Open the file called Mask_Reveal.fla. The first thing we're going to do is drag the image **Red Car** from the library over to the stage. We'll now use the Align panel to correctly position it on the stage. Open the Align panel and select **Align left edge**, **Align vertical center**, and make sure **To stage** is selected:

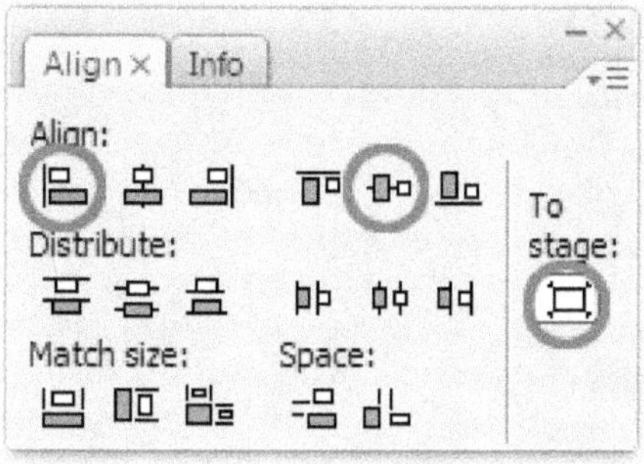

The red car image should now be positioned on the left side of the stage. Rename this layer: **Red Car**. Go to frame **60** and insert a frame.

Create a new layer and name it **Black Car**. Drag the **Black Car** image over to the stage; align this image on the left side of the stage using the Align tools (just as we did with the Red Car). The **Black Car** image should now be directly over the **Red Car** image. We'll now add a mask to the **Black Car** layer. This mask will be used to reveal the red car underneath the black car. Create a new layer and name it **Mask**:

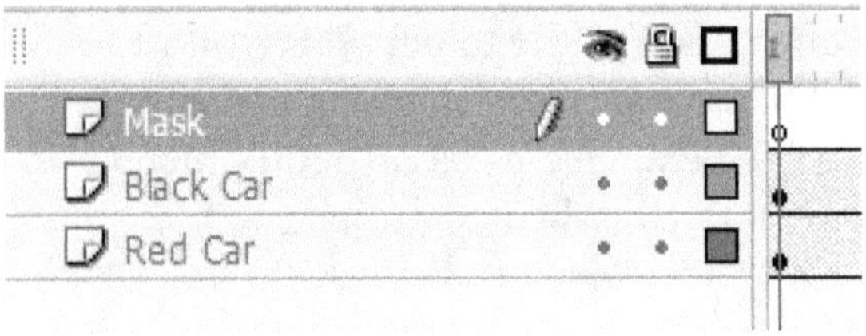

Select the **Rectangle Tool**, turn off the **Stroke color**, and change the **Fill color** to **red**. Zoom out to 50%. Next, create a shape that covers the entire stage. Select the **Free Transform Tool**, select the red shape you just created, and put your cursor over an edge of the red shape; your cursor should change to a rounded arrow:

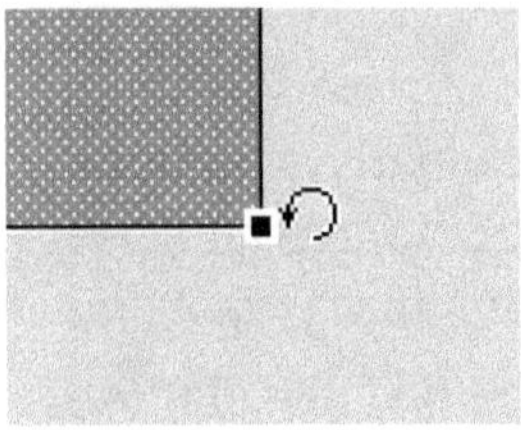

When you see this rounded arrow, drag this corner upward putting your red shape at an angle. Move this shape to the left so that it's directly over the black car:

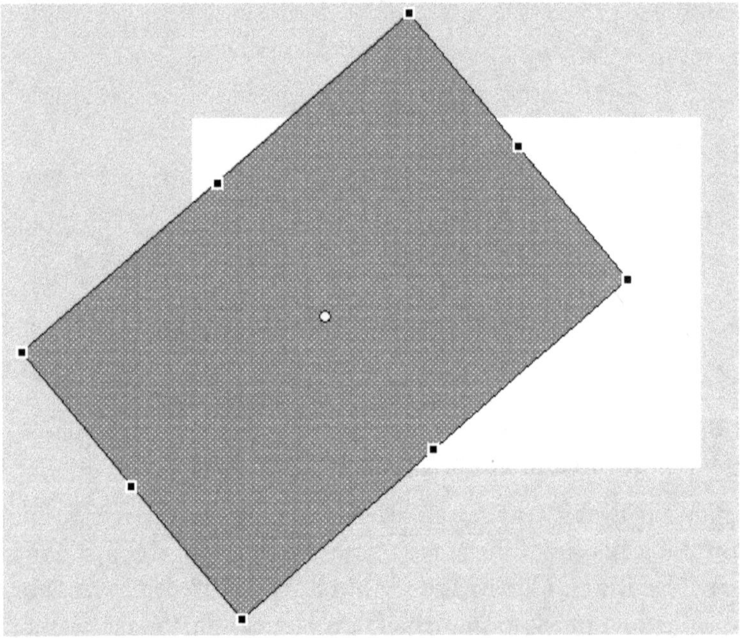

Create a keyframe on frame **60** of the **Mask** layer. Select any frame between **1** and **60** and insert a Motion Tween (CS4/CS5 - **Insert**, **Classic Tween**). Select keyframe **60** then select the red shape on the stage. Drag this shape down and to the left so that it no longer covers any part of the black car:

Right-click on the **Mask** layer and select **Mask**. Test the movie and the car will change from black to red:

This is a nice effect but we'll add one more little touch to it. Create a new layer and name it **Light**:

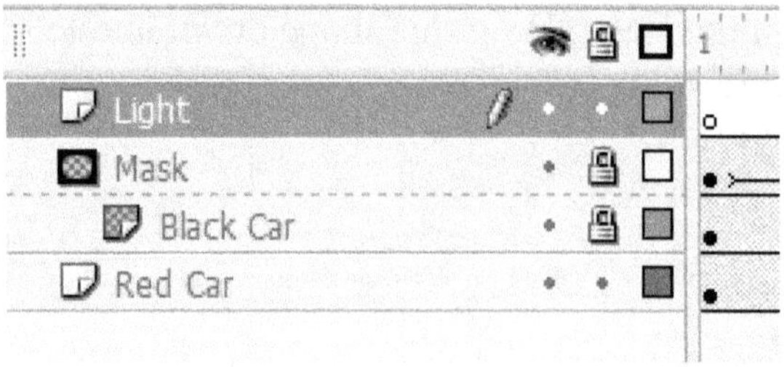

Select the first frame of the **Light** layer then drag the Light graphic from the library over to the stage. We're now going to have this light graphic follow the mask animation creating a nice little effect. We need to see the mask animation so unlock the **Mask** layer and click on the **Outline** icon:

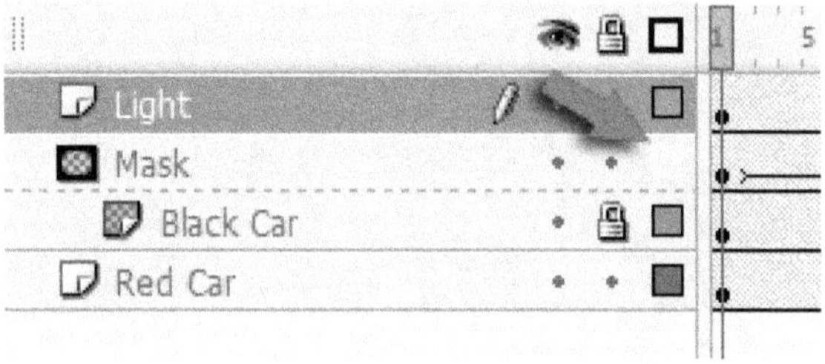

You should now see a colored outline of the **Mask** layer. Next, we're going to line up the Light graphic with the border of the Mask. Select the **Free Transform Tool** and put your cursor over the bottom right corner of the Light graphic; your cursor should change to a rounded arrow:

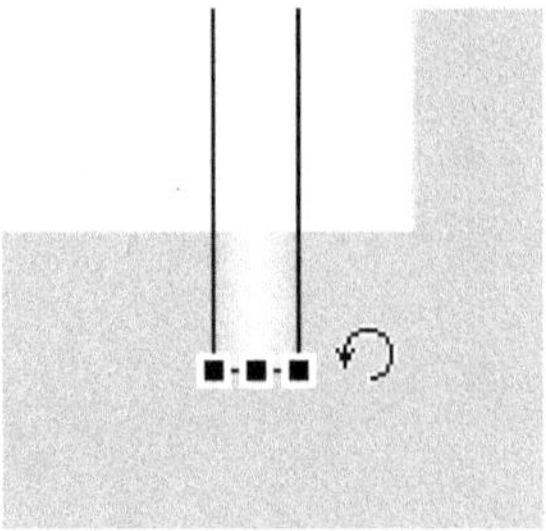

Pull this corner upward putting the Light graphic on the same angle as the Mask border. Drag the Light graphic over so that it rests directly on the Mask edge:

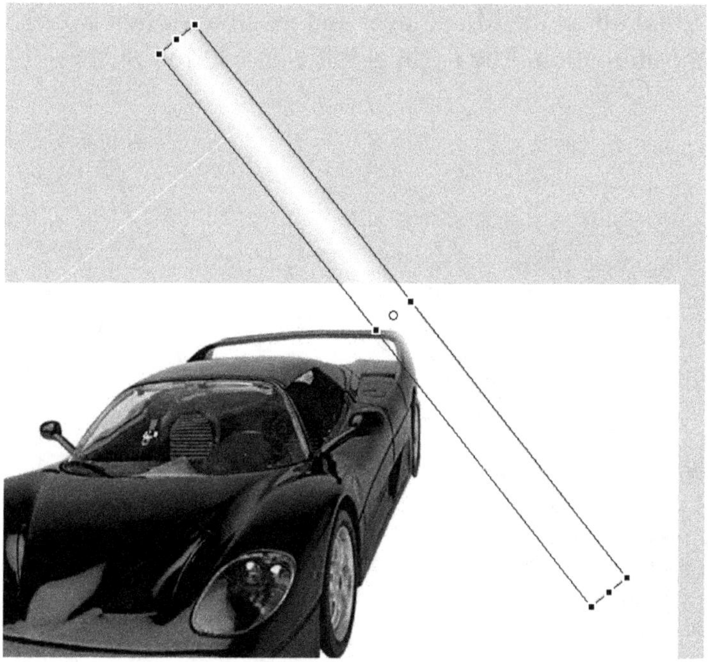

Insert a keyframe on frame **60** of the **Light** layer. Drag this Light graphic so that it follows the direction of the Mask; once again, place the Light graphic directly over the Mask edge:

Select any frame between **1** and **60** on the **Mask** layer and insert a Motion tween. Test your movie to watch the animation. The Light graphic should follow the mask animation perfectly:

Since we don't want the animation to start playing right away we need to add a **stop** code to the first frame. We also want the animation to stop playing when it reaches frame 60 so we'll need to create a Actions layer. Create a new layer and name it **Actions**. Create a keyframe on frame **1** and **60**; insert **stop** codes into both of these keyframes. Next, we'll add a **Labels** layer. Create a new layer and name it **Labels**. Select the second frame of this new layer and insert a keyframe. In the Properties panel type **black_red** into the Instance Name window.

This Flash exercise will be using four different scenes. Each scene will have a different color transition. One trick I like to do when I'm using several scenes in a Flash project, is to have my main buttons load into Level 1. As we learned previously, when items load into Level 1 or higher, they are above the main timeline which means they are unaffected if the user bounces from scene to scene. Even if the project has 50 scenes, as long as we load in the main buttons on Level 1, they'll be visible on every scene. Let's do this now so you have a better understanding of how it works.

Go to **File**, **Open**. Open the file called **Color_Palette.fla** in the Flash Projects folder. You'll see a color palette at the top right of the stage:

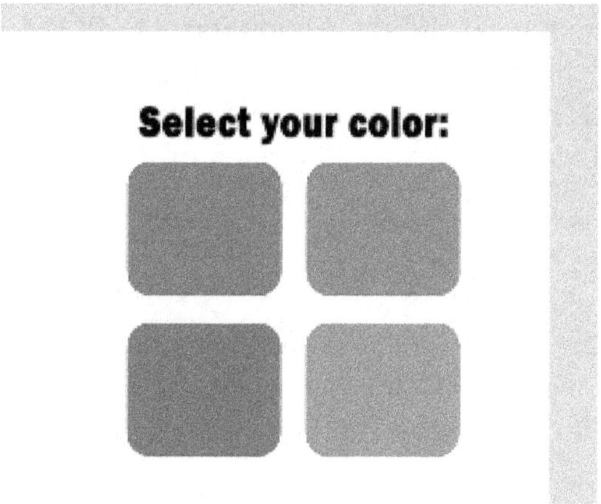

Create a new layer and name it **Buttons**. This is the layer that will hold the transparent buttons that will go over each color swatch. Grab the **Rectangle Tool**, turn **Stroke color** off, and select **red** for the **Fill color**. Create a square shape over the purple swatch:

Select the **Selection Tool** and click on this new shape. Next, convert this shape to a Button and name it **Color Button**:

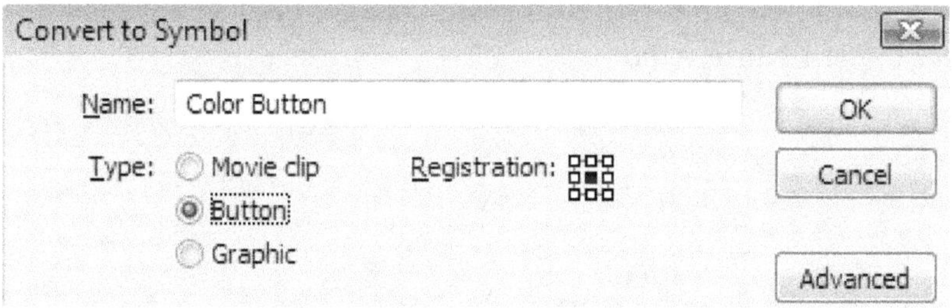

Hit **OK**. In the Properties panel change **Color** to **Alpha**, and the percentage to **0**:

This button should now be transparent. Next, we'll add the ActionScript to this button then we'll duplicate it for the other three swatches. Open the Actions panel and make sure Script Assist is on. Go to **Deprecated**, **Actions**, and double-click **tellTarget**. In the **Target** window type **_level0/**:

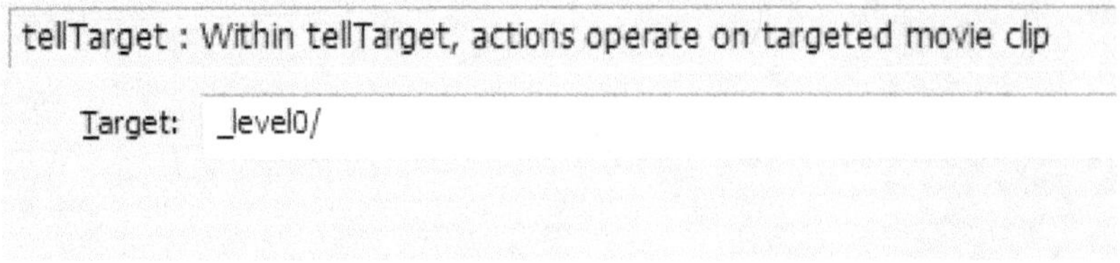

Go to **Global Functions**, **Timeline Control** and double-click **goto**. In the **goto** settings window change **Type** to **Frame Label** and in the **Frame** window type **black_purple**:

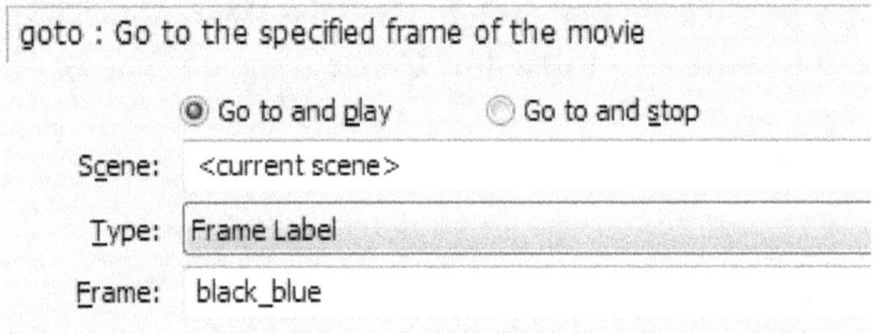

Now when a user clicks on the purple swatch button, it will take them to the black_purple label on the main timeline which has the black car transitioning to the purple car (which we'll create shortly). Once a user clicks a swatch button and watches the animation, we need to have a reset button appear so they can start over if they want. We'll be adding this reset button later along with a Label, but we can still add the ActionScript now. Click on the closing bracket of the first set of code. Next, go to **Global Functions**, **Timeline Control** and double-click **goto**. In the **goto** settings window click on **Go to and stop**, change **Type** to **Frame Label**, and type **reset** in the **Frame** window:

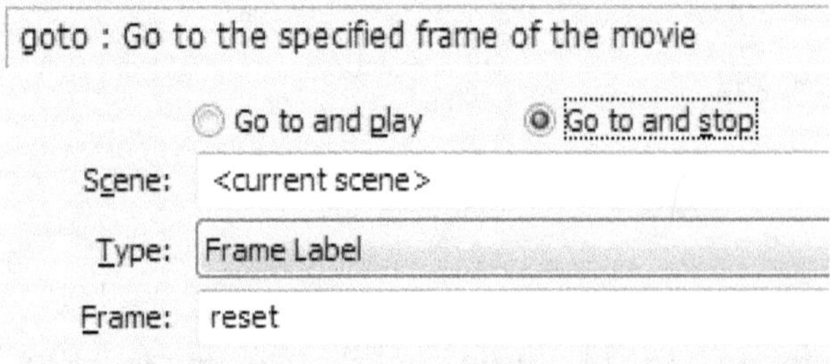

Now when this button is clicked it will take the user to the **reset** Label on this timeline (which we'll add next). Now we'll copy and paste this button on the other swatches. Select this button then go to **Edit**, **Copy**. Then, go to **Edit**, **Paste in Place**. You should now have an exact copy on top of the original button. Drag this new button so that it covers the pink swatch:

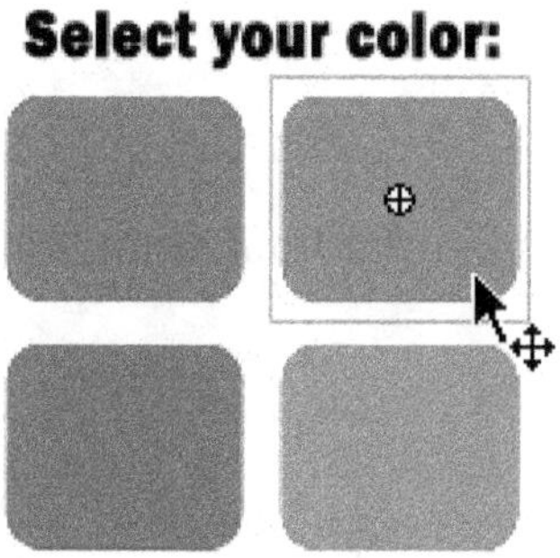

Since this is an exact copy of the original button it will have the same ActionScript. Open the Actions panel and look at the ActionScript. Click on the word **black_purple**. You should now see the **goto** settings window. Change the **Frame** name to **black_pink**:

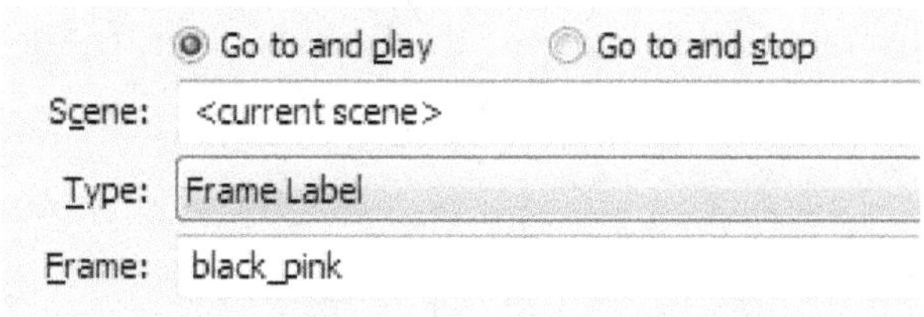

Select this button and go to **Edit**, **Copy**. Next, go to **Edit**, **Paste in Place**. Drag this new button so that it covers the red swatch. So now we'll need to change the ActionScript on this button. In the Actions window click on the word **black_pink**; you should now see the **goto** settings window. Change the **Frame** name to **black_red**:

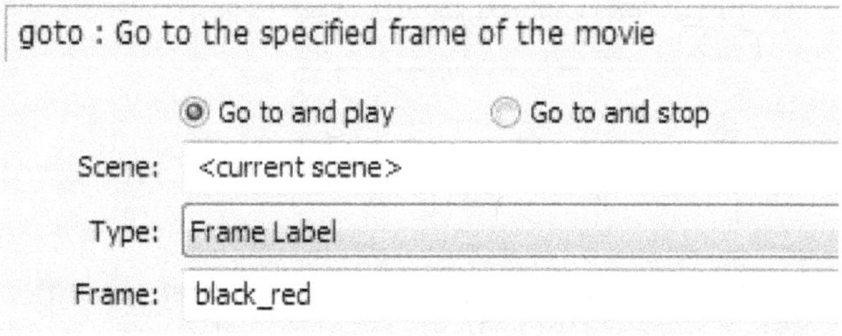

Select this button and once again go to **Edit**, **Copy**. Next, go to **Edit**, **Paste in Place**. Drag this new button so that it covers the green swatch. In the Actions window click on the word **black_red**. You should now see the **goto** settings window. Change the **Frame** name to **black_green**:

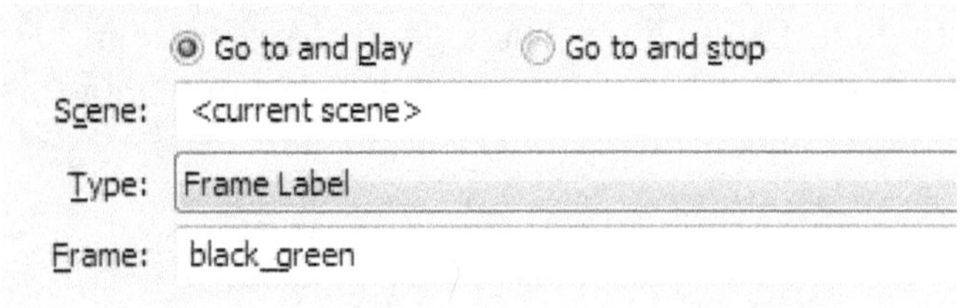

So now we're done with the buttons. Go to frame **20** and insert a frame into both layers. Next, create a new layer and name it **Actions**:

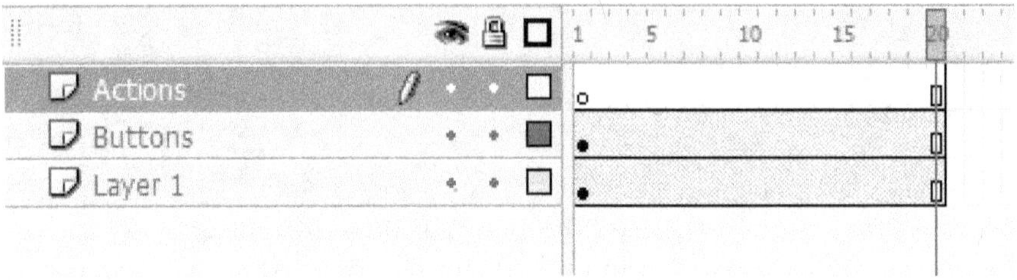

Insert a stop code into the first frame of the **Actions** layer. Next, create a new layer and name it **Labels**. Insert a keyframe on frame **5** of the **Labels** layer. In the Properties panel type **reset** in the **Instance Name** window:

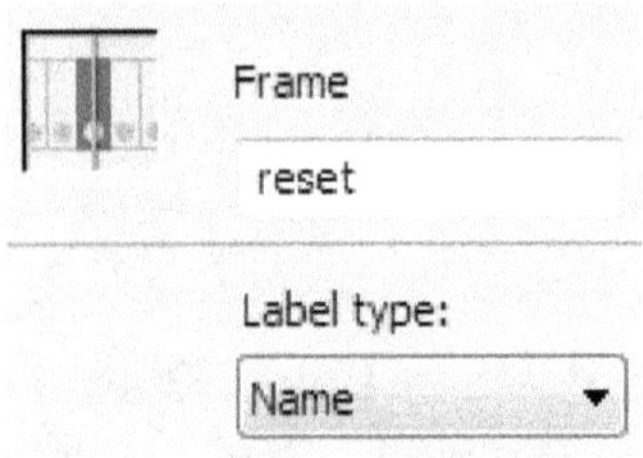

So now the timeline should look like this:

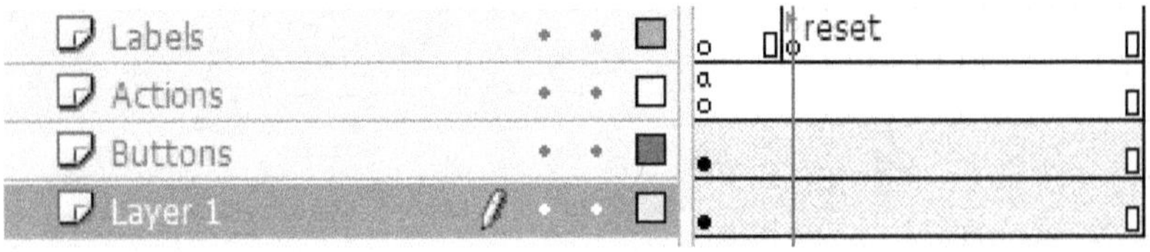

Create a new layer above the **Buttons** layer. Name this new layer: **Reset**. This is where we'll place the reset button that users will click on. Before we can create the reset button, though, we need to remove the color palette and transparent buttons from frame **5**. We do this by inserting a Blank Keyframe into frame **5** of both layers (**Insert**, **Timeline**, and **Blank Keyframe**):

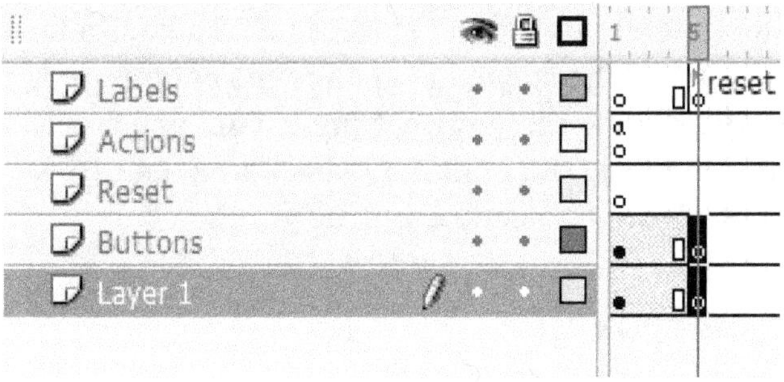

Create a keyframe on frame **5** of the **Reset** layer. Select the **Text Tool**, select **black** for the **Fill color**, **Arial** for the font, size **16**, and **Bold**:

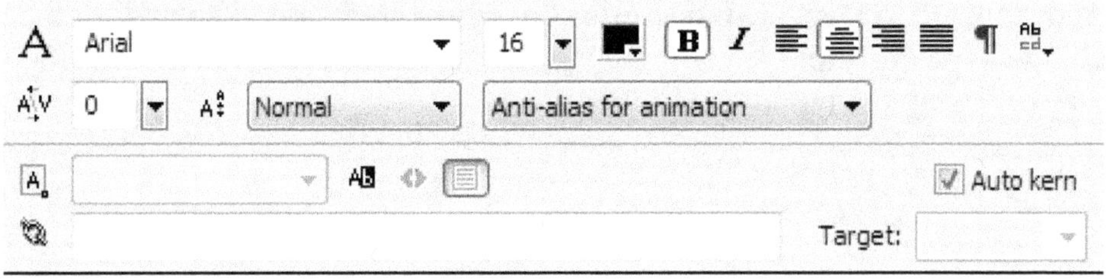

Type the word RESET in the same area as the color palette:

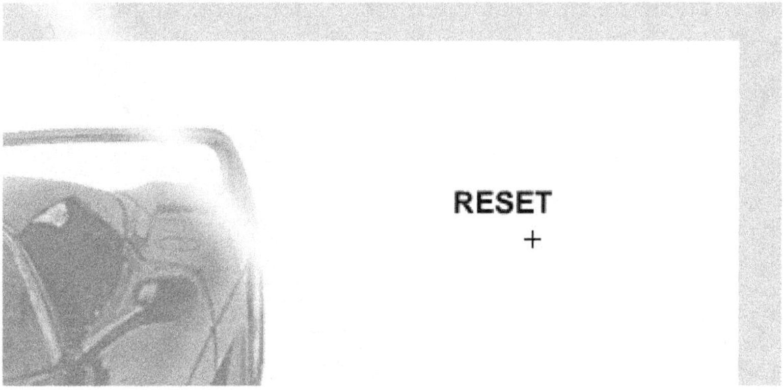

Convert this text to a symbol. Name this new symbol **Reset Button** and change the **Type** to **Button**:

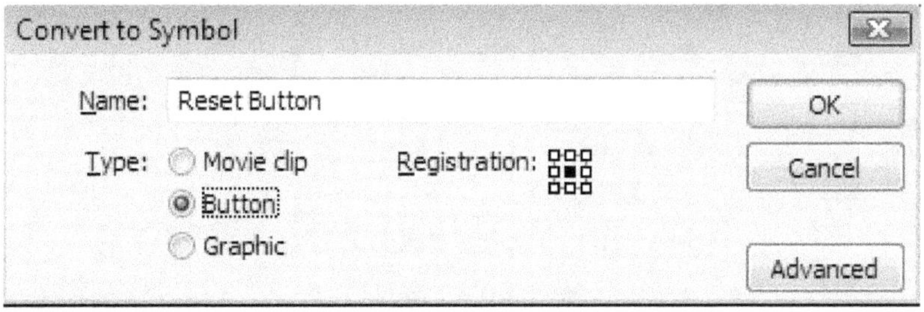

Hit **OK**. Double-click on this button to enter its editing stage. Create a keyframe under the **Over** state. Highlight the text on the stage and change the color to red. Next, create a keyframe under the **Hit** stage; grab the **Rectangle Tool** and create a shape that covers the text. We're done editing the button. Go back to Scene 1 by clicking the **Back** button, or by clicking on the **Scene 1** link above the timeline/stage:

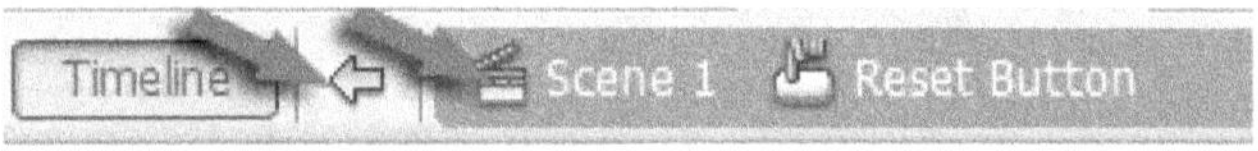

Select the **Reset** button and open the Actions panel. We'll now add the ActionScript to this button. The first code will tell the main timeline to go back to frame 1 and stop. Go to **Deprecated**, **Actions** and double-click **tellTarget**. In the Target window type **_level0/**:

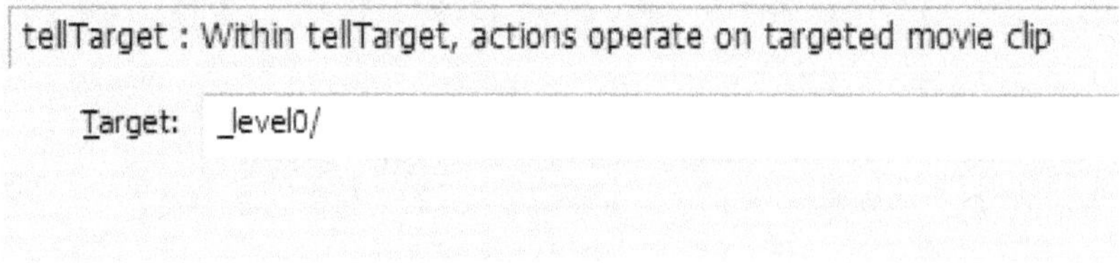

Go to **Global Functions**, **Timeline Control** and double-click **goto**. In the **goto** settings window select **Go to and stop**:

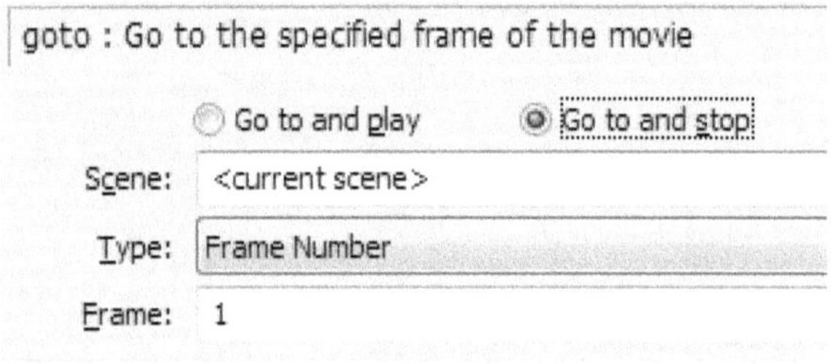

This will tell the main timeline to go to frame 1. Click on the closing bracket of this code in the Actions window. Go to **Global Functions**, **Timeline Control** and double-click **goto**. In the **goto** settings window select **Go to and stop**:

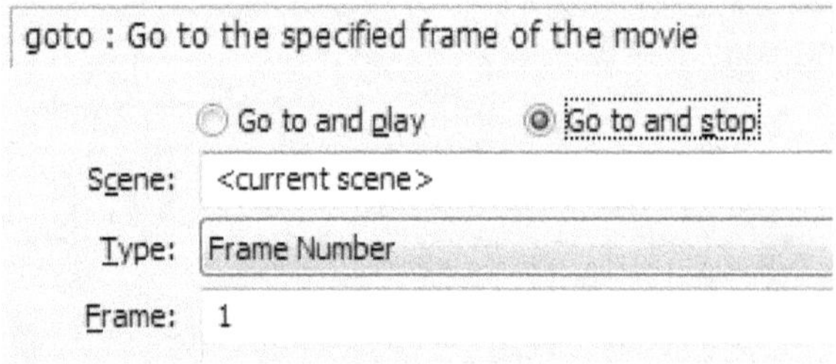

This code will send the current timeline back to frame 1. So now the main buttons are finished. Select **File**, **Publish**.

Go back to the Mask_Reveal file. We'll now quickly create the three other scenes. Open the Scene panel and change the existing scene's name to **Red Car**. Next, click on the **Duplicate scene** button:

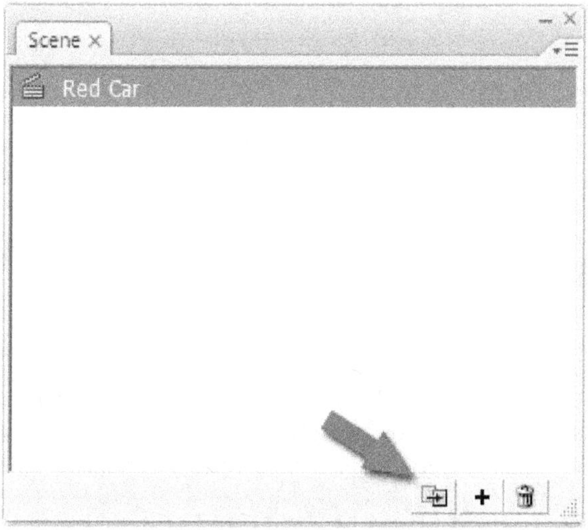

Name this new scene **Green Car**:

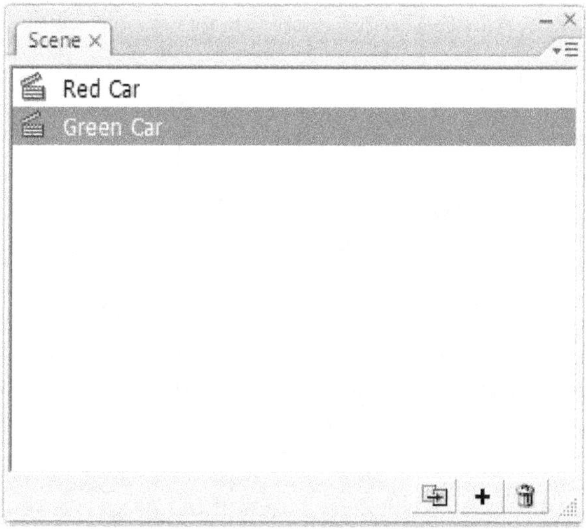

Click on the **Duplicate scene** button two more times to create the last two scenes: **Pink Car** and **Purple Car**:

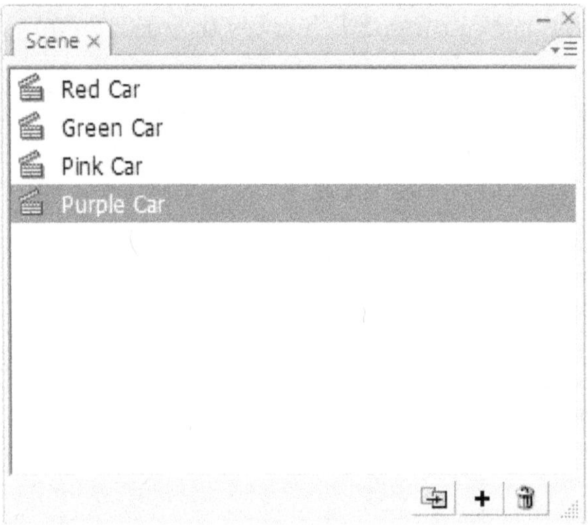

Now we have duplicate animations in each of the scenes. The only thing left to do is to change the Frame Label on each scene, and to swap out the main photo. Let's do that now.

Click on the Green Car scene. Select the second frame of the **Labels** layer and change the **Frame Label** name to **black_green**:

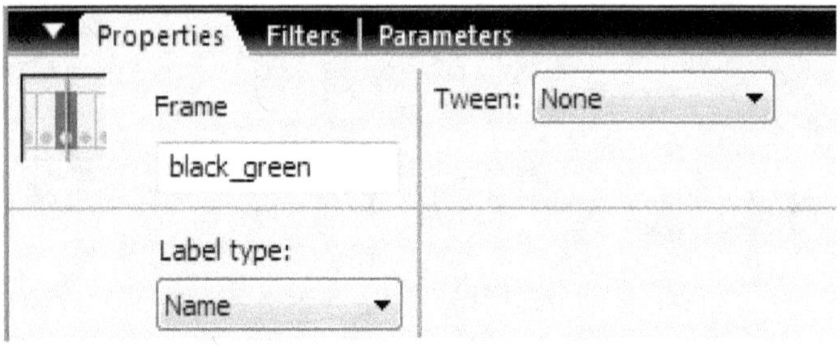

Change the **Red Car** layer's name to **Green Car**. Select the first keyframe and delete the Red Car image. Drag the Green Car image to the stage from the library. Open the Align panel and select **Align left edge**, **Align vertical center**, and make sure **To stage** is selected:

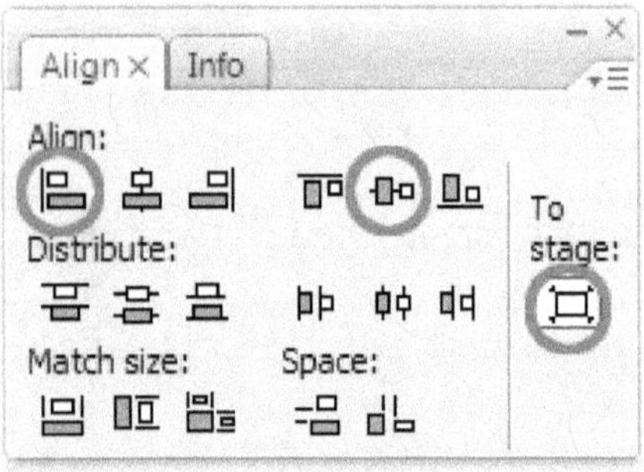

The Green Car image should be positioned on the left side of the stage. Test your movie to see how it works. If you click on the green swatch button the Black Car should transition to the Green Car. You should then see the Reset button appear.

Repeat the above steps for the final two scenes. Remember to change the Frame Label and swap out the pictures. Use the Align tools to position the pictures on the left side of the stage.

Simple Quiz

DIFFICULTY:

Have you ever wanted to put a little quiz on your website but thought it would take complicated coding? I created the following project in a matter of minutes just using Movie clips and a couple different functions. Although this quiz is fairly short and simple, you can make your quiz as long as you want once you understand the principles involved.

Open the Flash Projects folder and double-click on the **Simple_Quiz.swf** file. Go ahead and take the quiz so you can see how it works. Notice that every time you get an answer correct you'll get a point in the **Correct** box at the top; if you get an answer wrong then you'll get a point in the **Negative** box. When you're done you can click to see the answers. To try again there is a **Reset** button. So now I'll show you how easy it is to put together.

Open the file called Simple_Quiz.fla in the Flash Projects folder. Rename Layer 1 **Text**. Drag the file **questions.jpg** from the library over to the stage:

> **Remember!** There are many different ways to create quizzes in Flash! Once you master Movie clips you can create your own variation!

SIMPLE QUIZ

1) Who was the first president?
   A. George Washington
   B. Abraham Lincoln
   C. John Adams

2) Where is the Grand Canyon located?
   A. Arizona
   B. New Mexico
   C. Nevada

3) The Statue of Liberty is in what state?
   A. Maine
   B. New York
   C. Vermont

4) How many states are there?
   A. 42
   B. 50
   C. 52

Lock your **Text layer**. Create a new layer and name it **Red Marker**. Next, grab your **Brush Tool** and select the third size from the top:

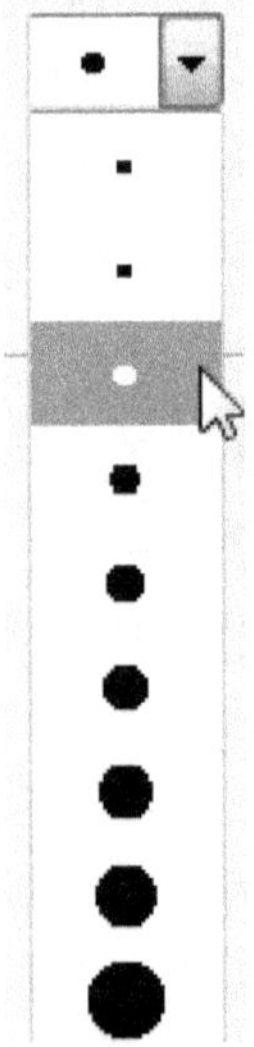

Change the **Fill color** to **red**. Draw a circle around the number **1** in the first question:

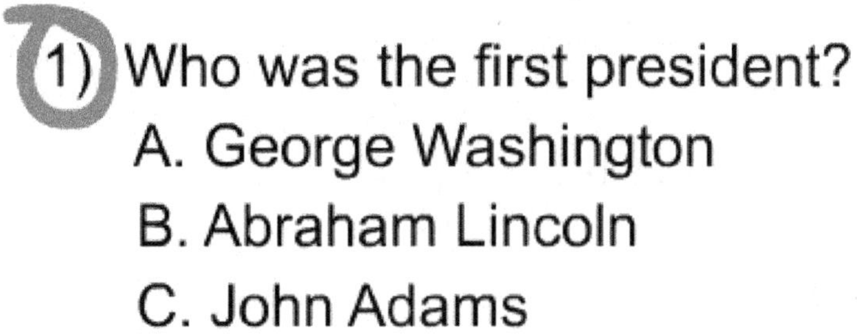
1) Who was the first president?
A. George Washington
B. Abraham Lincoln
C. John Adams

Go to frame **4** and Insert frames for both layers:

1
5
Red Marker
Text

Insert a keyframe on frame **2** of the **Red Marker** layer. You should now see a copy of the red circle you created on the stage. Grab your **Selection Tool** and move this circle so that it covers number **2** of the second question:

2) Where is the Grand Canyon located?
A. Arizona
B. New Mexico
C. Nevada

Insert a keyframe on frame **3** and move this circle so that it covers number **3** of the third question. Next, insert a final keyframe into frame **4** and move the circle so that it covers the number 4 of the fourth question. So on each frame you should have a circle around the question number. Lock this layer since we're done with it.

We'll next create the Score Boxes. Create a new layer and name it **Score Boxes**. Next, grab the **Rectangle Tool**, select the color **blue** for the **Stroke color**, and change the **Fill color** to **white**. Create a square shape at the top of the quiz (remember to hold down Shift when creating your shape to make a perfect square):

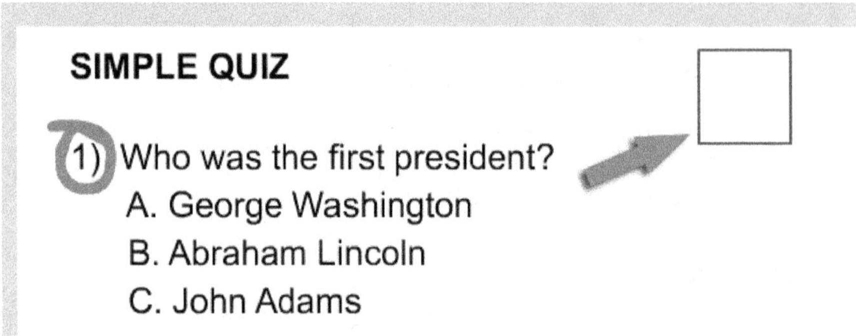

Go to **Modify**, **Convert to Symbol**. Name this new symbol **Right Answers** and change the **Type** to Movie clip. Hit **OK** to close. Open the Properties panel and name this new Movie clip **right_answers**:

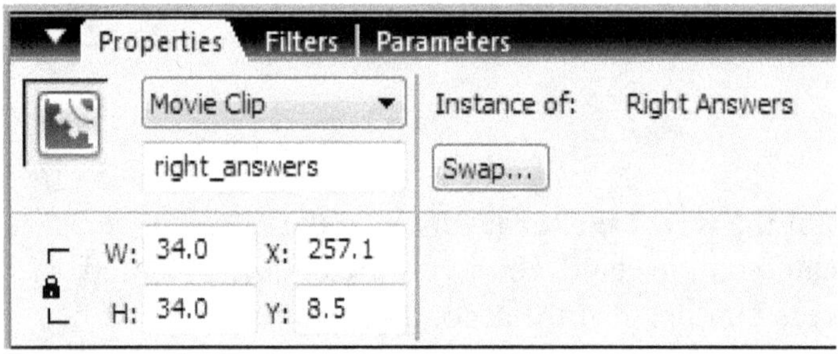

Double-click this new Movie clip to enter its editing stage. Rename Layer 1: **Box**. Create a new layer and name it **Numbers**; create a final layer naming it **Actions**. Go to frame **5** and insert a frame into each layer:

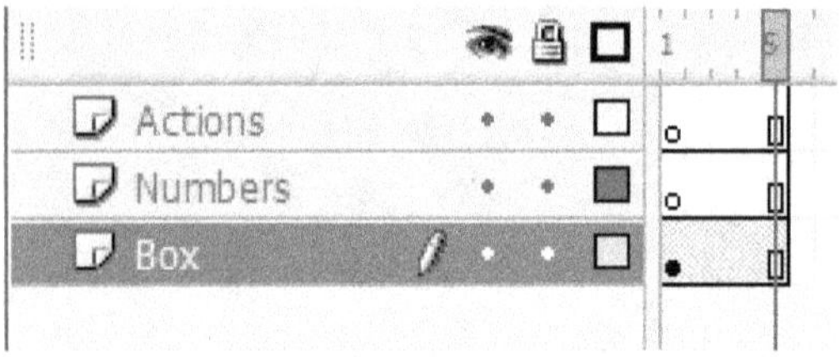

Create a keyframe on frame **2** of the **Numbers** layer. Select the **Text Tool** and open the Properties panel. Change the **Color** to **black**, change **Font** to **Times New Roman**, **Size 12**, and **Bold**:

Type the number **1** in the middle of the box:

Create a new keyframe on frame **3** of the **Numbers layer**. Change the number on the stage to **2**. Create a new keyframe on frame **4** of the **Numbers layer**. Change the number on the stage to **3**. Create a final keyframe on frame **5** of the **Numbers layer** and change the number on the stage to **4**. So on each keyframe you should have a different number.

If you were to test your movie now you would get quite an effect. We haven't put a **stop** code in the timelines so it plays through all the frames without stopping. In the **Actions** keyframe enter a **stop** code. Your final timeline should look like this:

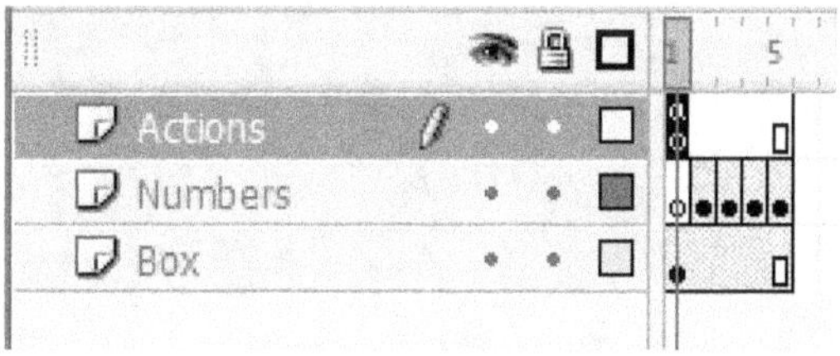

So now we're finished with the **Right Answers** Movie clip. Go back to Scene 1. We'll now create the **Wrong Answers** Movie clip. We'll save time by duplicating the **Right Answers** Movie clip. Select the **Right Answers** Movie clip on the stage and go to **Edit**, **Copy**. Next, go to **Edit**, **Paste in Place**. Drag this copy to the right of the first one:

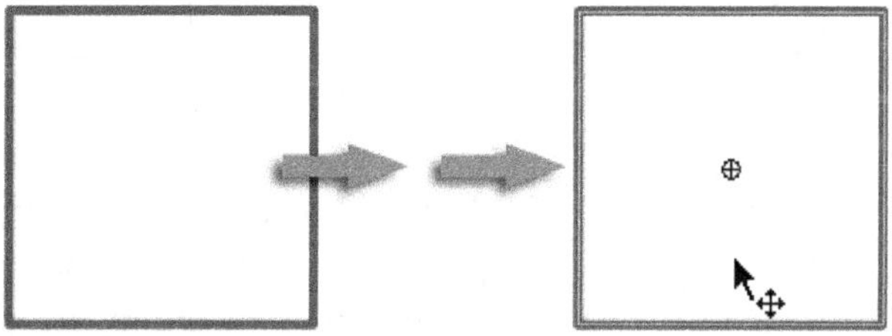

Select this new copy and open the Properties panel. Click on the **Swap** button; now click on the **Duplicate Symbol** button. Type **Wrong Answers** in the **Symbol name** window:

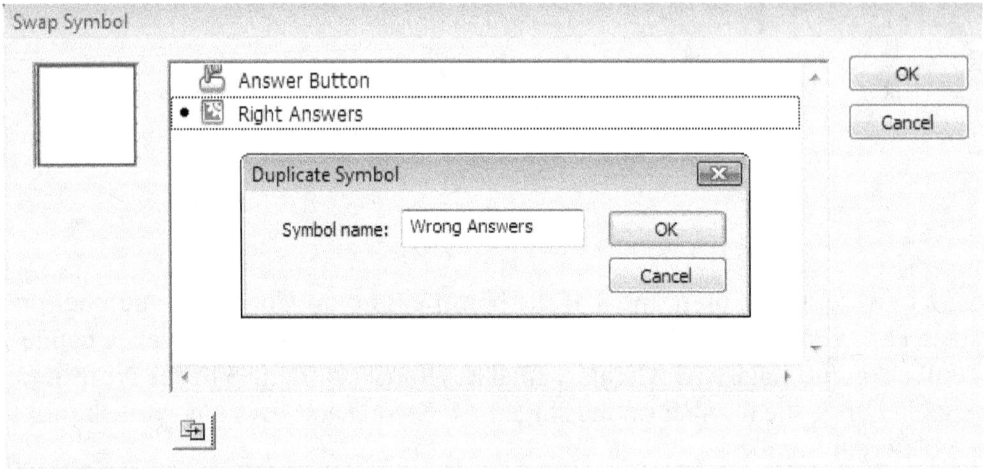

Hit **OK**. Double-click on **Wrong Answers**:

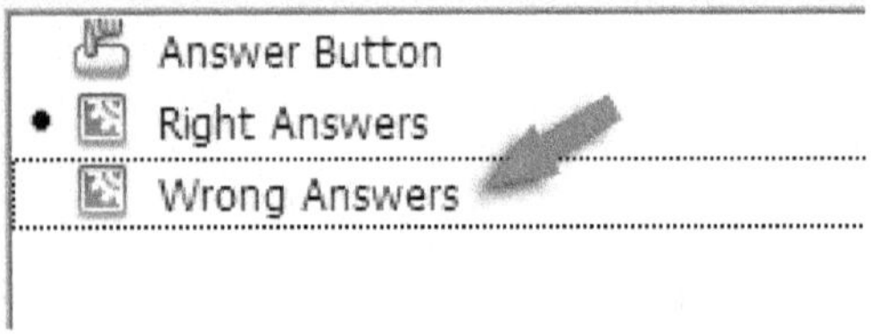

Next, change **the Instance Name** to **wrong_answers**:

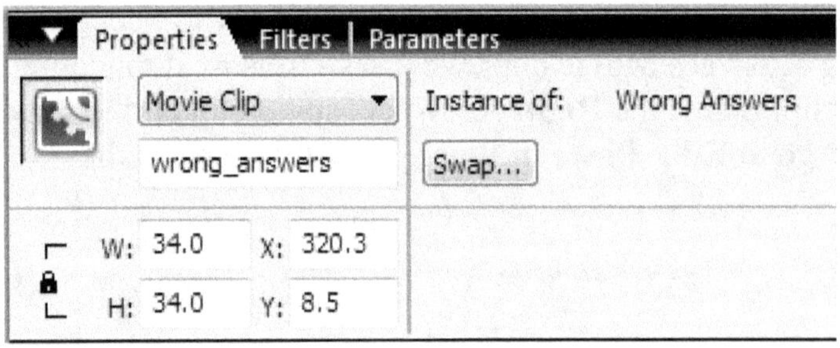

So whenever a user selects the wrong answer it will tell this box to go to the next frame. Let's tweak the color of this new Movie clip. Double-click this new symbol to enter its editing stage. Zoom in to the box (around 400%). Double-click just the Stroke of the box; in the Properties panel change the **Stroke color** to **red**. Next, go to frame **2** of the **Numbers** layer and select the number on the stage; change the color to **red**. Do this for the numbers in all the frames.

Now the Score Boxes are done. All that's left is to add the buttons to the answers. Let's do that now. Go back to Scene 1. Create a new layer and name it **Buttons**. Grab your **Rectangle Tool**, turn off the **Stroke color**, and create a shape over the text **George Washington** in the first question:

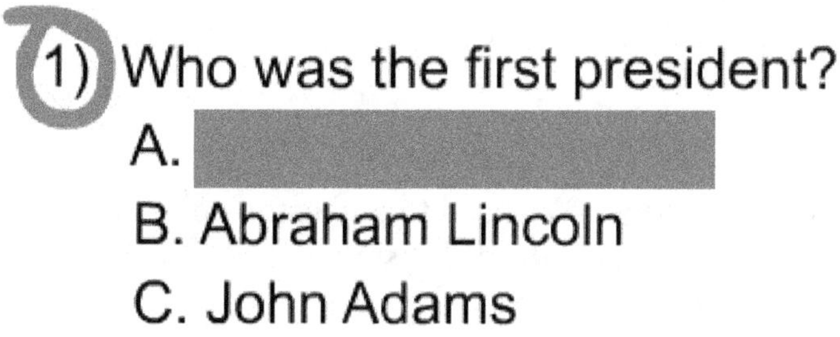

Select this new shape and go to **Modify**, **Convert to Symbol**. Change the **Type** to **Button** and name it **Answer Button**:

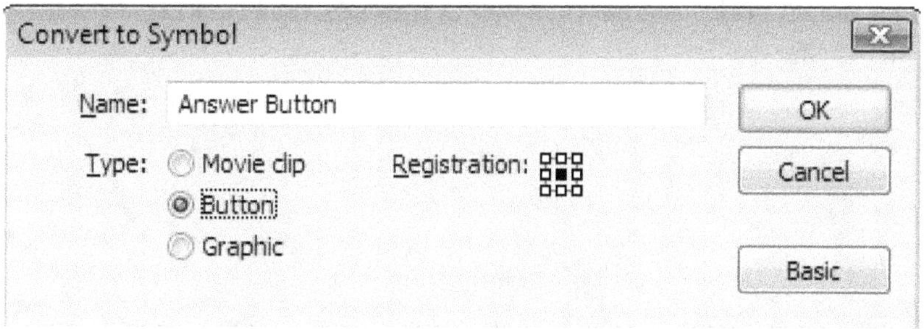

Hit **OK** to close this box. Select this new symbol and open the Properties panel. Change **Color** to **Alpha** and the percentage to **0**. This Button should now be transparent.

Let's add the code now. Since this is the correct answer we want this button to tell the **Right Answers** Movie clip to go to the next frame. With this button still selected open the Actions panel and make sure Script Assist is on. Go to **Deprecated**, **Actions**, and double-click **tellTarget**. In the **Target** window type **/right_answers**:

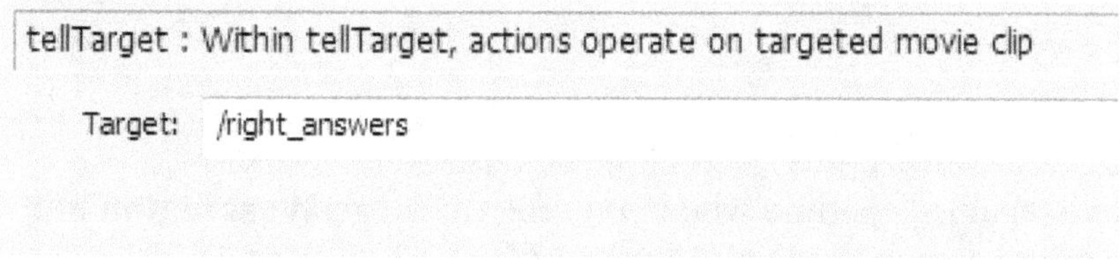

Next, go to **Global Functions**, **Timeline Control** and double-click **goto**. In the **goto** settings window change **Type** to **Next Frame**:

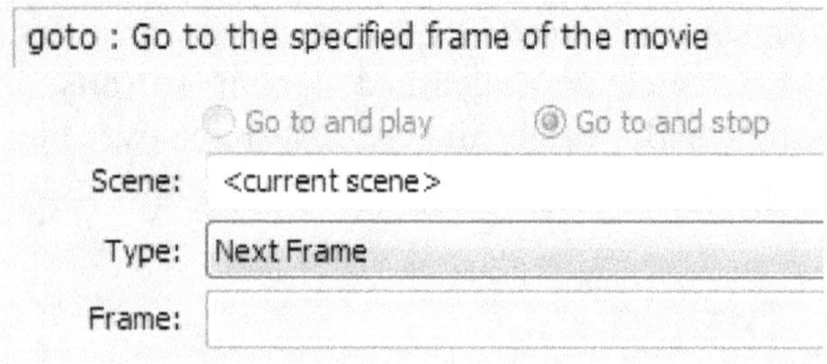

Test your movie to try your code. Whoops! We need to put a stop code in the timeline. Create a new layer and name it **Actions**. Put a stop code in this layer's keyframe. Test your movie again.

When you click the answer **George Washington** you should see the number **1** appear in the **Right Answers** box. But now we need the **Red Marker** circle to be over the number **2** of the second question. That's a simple fix. Select the **George Washington** button. Open the Actions panel. To make sure the new code doesn't end up within the first set of code, we need to select the closing bracket:

```
on (release) {
    tellTarget ("right_answers") {
        nextFrame();
    }
}
```

Go to **Global Functions**, **Timeline Control** and double-click **goto**. In the **goto** settings window change **Type** to **Next Frame**:

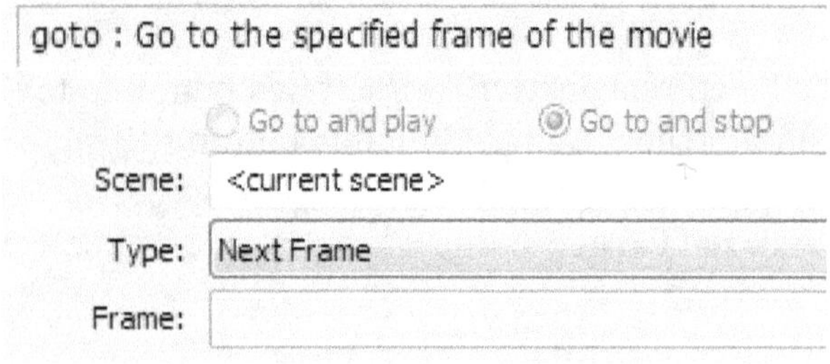

This code tells the main timeline to go to the next frame.

Now test your movie again. This time when you select **George Washington** not only does the number appear in the **Right Answers** box but the Red Marker Circle appears over question 2. Now we just need to add the rest of the buttons. Select the **George Washington** button and copy it; now paste it in place. Drag this new button downward so that it covers the answer **Abraham Lincoln**.

Now, instead of this button telling the **Right Answers** box to go to the next frame, we need this button to tell the **Wrong Answers** box to go to the next frame. Select this new button and open the Actions panel. Find where the code says **right_answers** and click on it; the **tellTarget** settings window should appear. Change **right_answers** to **wrong_answers**:

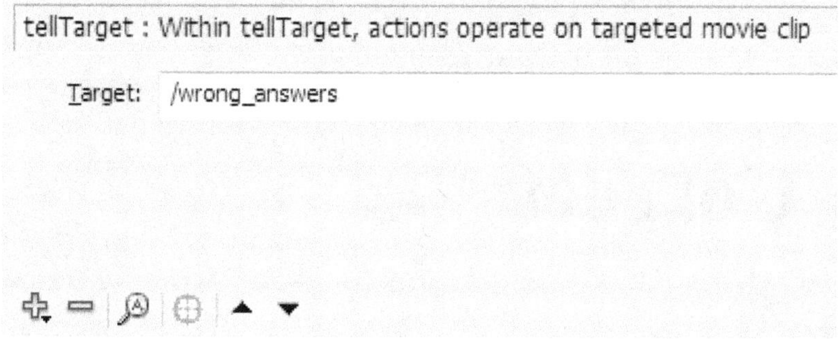

Test your movie. Select the **Abraham Lincoln** button. A number should now appear in the **Wrong Answers** box and the red circle should now cover number 2 of the second question. Copy and paste this new button over the answer **John Adams**. Now we need to add buttons for the second question. Insert a keyframe into the second frame of the **Buttons** layer; this will highlight all the buttons. Drag these buttons so that they cover the answers of the second question.

Since the correct answer of question 2 is Arizona we can keep the same order of buttons. Create a keyframe on frame **3** of the **Buttons** layer. Drag these buttons down to cover the answers of the third question. Since the correct answer is New York then you need to rearrange the buttons; have the first and second button trade places. If you need to double-check if you have the correct buttons over the appropriate answers just open the Actions panel. If the answer is incorrect then the Target in the Actions window will be **/wrong_answers**; if the answer is correct then the Target should be **right_answers**. Create a final keyframe on frame **4** and drag the buttons down over the answers. You can keep the same order.

If you test your movie now you should be able to go through the entire quiz. Even if you make your quiz 100 questions everything would still work perfectly. You would just have to add the appropriate number of frames to the main timeline and also add frames to the **Wrong** and **Right Answers** boxes.

What if when you finish the quiz, you are told what percentage of questions you got right? Believe it or not that's pretty simple.

Create a new layer and name it **Percentage**. Grab your **Text Tool**, change the **Size** to **12**, **Times New Roman**, and **Bold**. Before you start typing lock your **Text layer**; now type **0% Correct** below both score boxes:

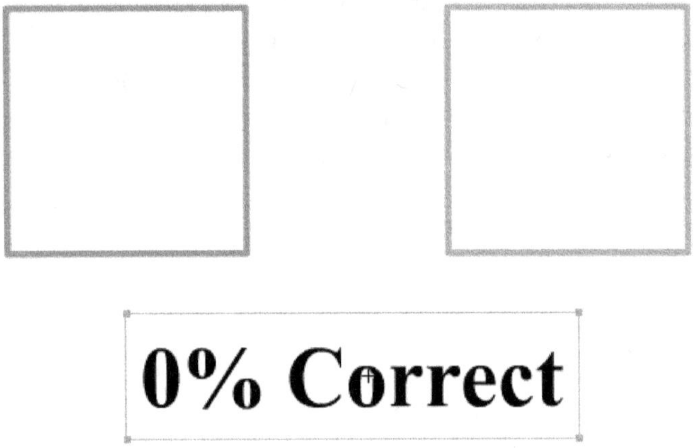

Grab the **Selection Tool** and select this new text. Go to **Modify**, **Convert to Symbol**. Change **Type** to **Movie clip** and name it **Percentage**:

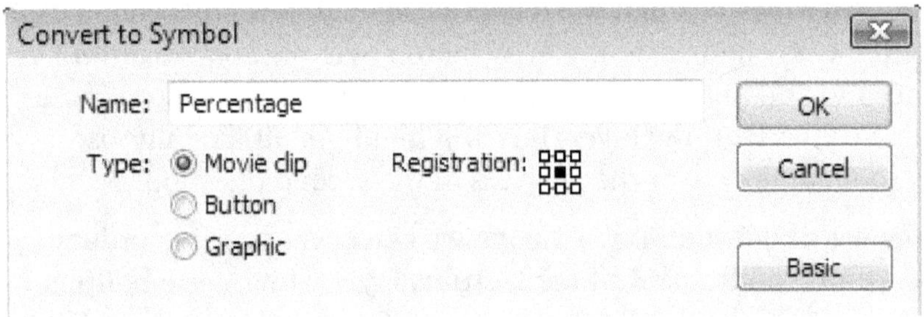

Hit **OK** to close. Before we edit this Movie clip we need to name it since we'll be controlling it. Open the Properties panel and type **percentage** in the **Instance Name** window:

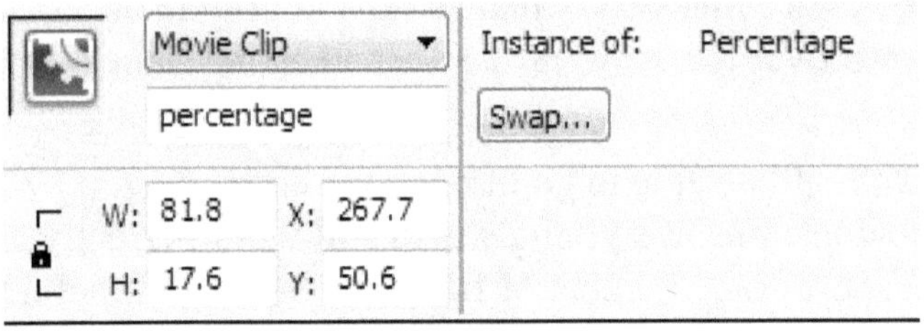

Double-click on this new Movie clip to enter its editing stage. If the user gets none of the answers correct this is the frame that will appear when they are finished. Let's say the user gets one answer correct. Since there are four questions, if the user gets one answer correct then their percentage correct is 25%. So let's add that now. Add a keyframe to frame **2**; change the text to read **25% Correct**. Create a keyframe on frame **3**. Change the text to read **50% Correct**. On frame **4**

insert a keyframe and change the text to **75% Correct**. And, finally, if the user gets all the answers correct, they will see frame **5**; change the text to **100% Congratulations**!.

Since the timeline has more than one frame we need a **stop** code. Create a new layer, name it **Actions**, and insert a **stop** code into the first keyframe. Go back to Scene 1.

Now we're almost done. We just need to add one simple piece of code to all the correct answer buttons. Select the **George Washington** button. In the Actions panel go to **Deprecated**, **Actions**, and double-click **tellTarget**. In the **Target** window type **/percentage**:

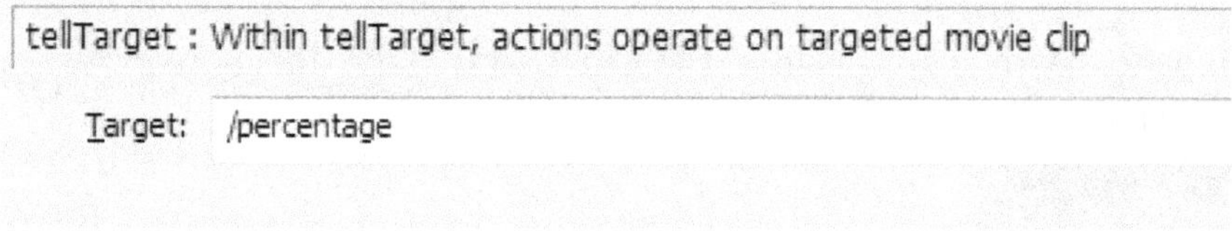

Go to **Global Functions**, **Timeline Control**, and double-click **goto**. In the **goto** settings window change **Type** to **Next Frame**:

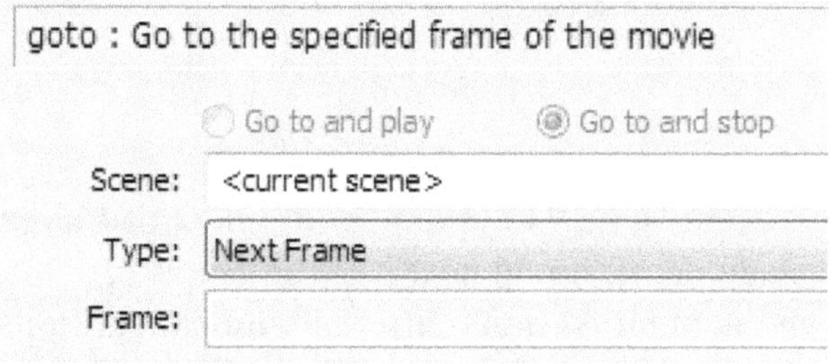

Test your movie. Click on the George Washington button and the percentage should move to **25%**. Add the above code to all the correct answer buttons. If you answer all the questions correctly you should see **100% Congratulations!**. But now we only want to see the percentage text when we're finished with the test. So how do we do that?

Here's a trick I use all the time. Create a new layer and name it **White Cover**; make sure this layer is above the **Percentage** layer. Select the **Rectangle Tool**, turn **Stroke color** off, and change the **Fill color** to **white** (we use the color white since the background is white). Create a shape over the percentage text; make it extra wide so that it covers the congratulations text. Select this new shape:

Convert this shape to a Movie clip. Name it **White Cover**. Give this new movie clip an **Instance Name** of **white_cover**:

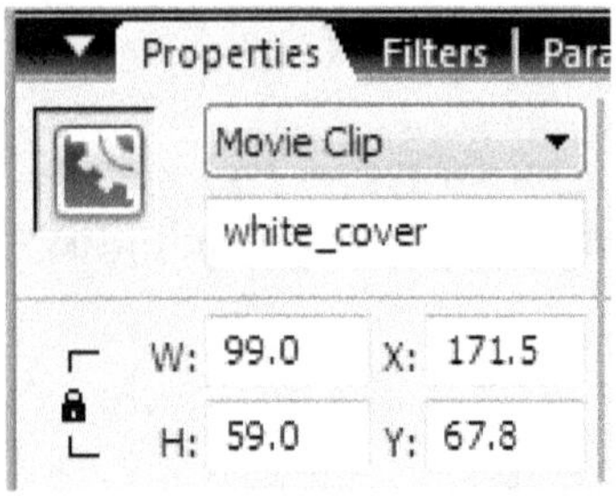

Double-click on this new Movie clip. Create a new keyframe on frame **2** of **Layer 1** and delete the shape that is on the stage. You should now have an empty keyframe. Next, create a new layer and name it **Actions**. Insert a **stop** code into its first frame. Ok, we're done with this Movie clip so go back to Scene 1.

Now we just need to add one last piece of code to the final buttons. Select the button on the answer **42**; click on the closing bracket of the last set of code. Go **to Deprecated**, **Actions**, and double-click **tellTarget**. In the **Target** window type **/white_cover**:

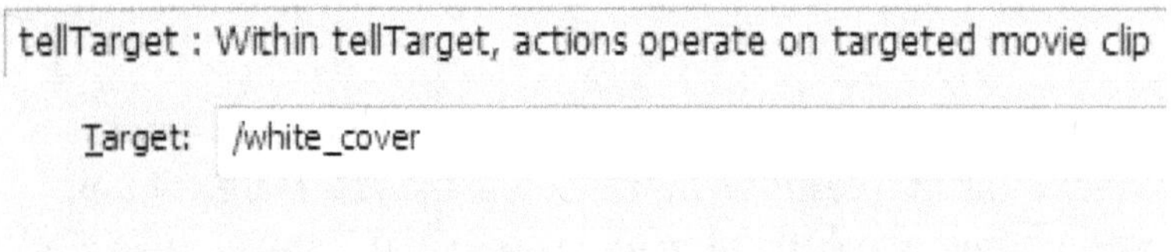

Next, go to **Global Functions**, **Timeline Control** and double-click **goto**; in the **goto** settings window change **Type** to **Next Frame**:

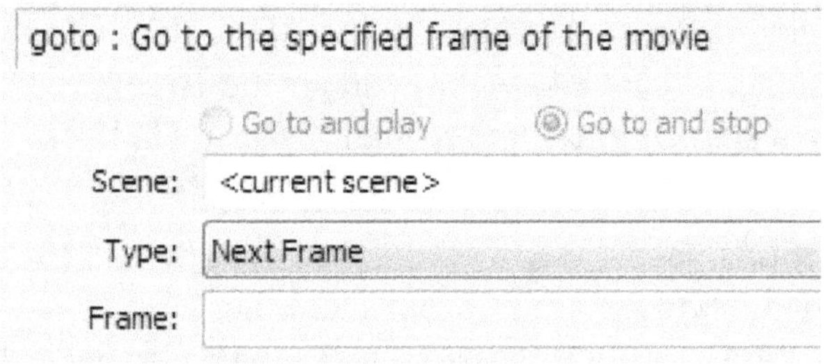

Now when a user clicks on one of the answers of the final question, the **White Cover** Movie clip will go to its second frame which is blank. Select this new code you just created by clicking and dragging across it; it should turn blue when selected:

```
on (release) {
    tellTarget ("/wrong_answers") {
        nextFrame();
    }
}
on (release) {
    tellTarget ("/white cover") {
        nextFrame();
    }
}
```

Right-click on this selected text and choose **Copy**. Select the button over the answer **50**. You should now see its ActionScript in the Actions panel. Click the closing bracket and **right-click**, **paste**. This will paste the above code into the Actions window. Do this for the final button also. Test your movie again. When you finish the quiz the percentage number should be revealed. Finally, let's create a **reset** button.

Create a new layer and name it **Reset**. Next, grab the **Text Tool** and type **Reset** at the top right of the stage:

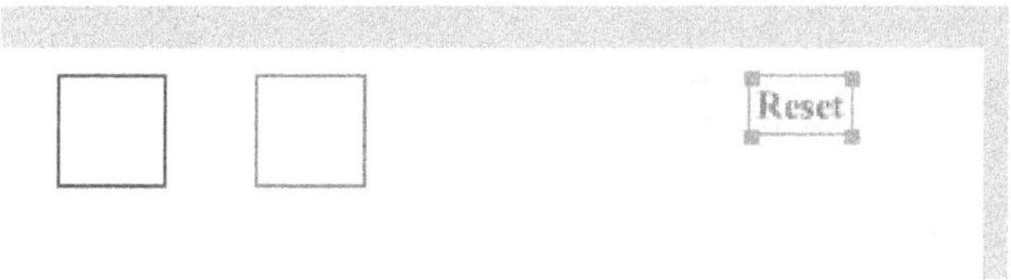

Convert this text to a **Button** and name it **Reset**. Hit **OK** to close. Double-click on this new button to enter its editing stage. Create a keyframe under the **Hit** state. Grab the **Rectangle Tool** and create a shape a little larger than the text. Go back to Scene 1.

Select this new button. Open the Actions panel. We need this button to tell all the Movie clips to go back to their original starting point. So let's add the ActionScript. Go to **Deprecated**, **Actions**, and double-click **tellTarget**. In the **Target** window type **/right_answers**. Next, go to **Global Functions**, **Timeline Control** and double click **goto**. In the **goto** settings window select **Go to and stop**:

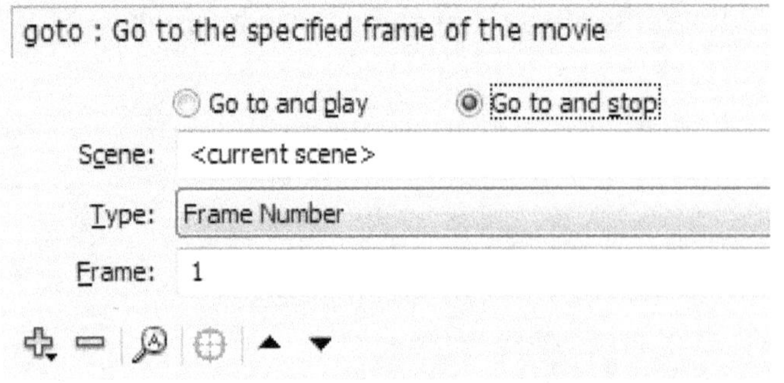

We'll now create the second code. Go to **Deprecated**, **Actions**, and double-click **tellTarget**. Type **wrong_answers** in the **Target** window:

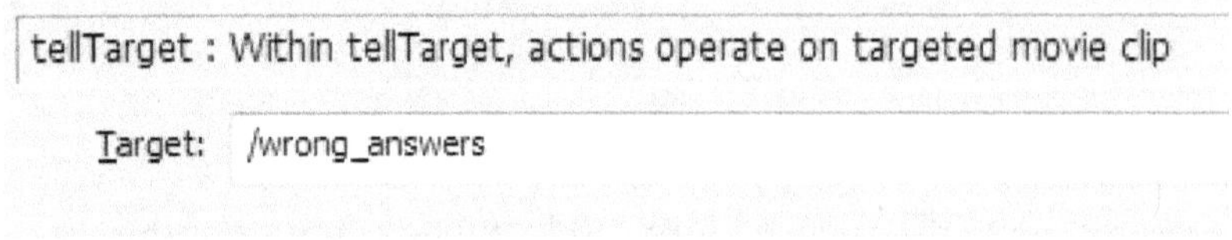

Next, go to **Global Functions**, **Timeline Control** and double-click **goto**. In the **goto** settings window select **Go to and stop**:

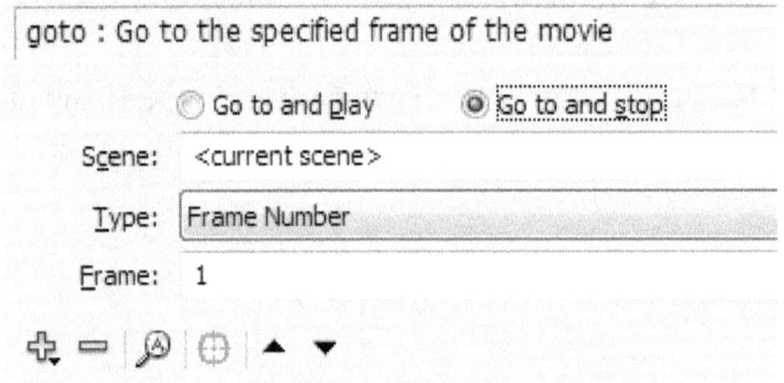

So now when the Reset button is clicked it will take the score boxes back to their original frame. We just need to add code to take the **Percentage** Movie clip, **White Cover**, and the Timeline back to their first frame.

Repeat the same steps you've been doing but in the **Target** window type **/percentage**. Repeat the above steps for the main timeline by typing in **_level0/** in the **Target** window.

Finally, repeat the above steps again, but in the **Target** window type **/white_cover**. Test your movie. Answer all four questions to test it out. When you're done, click on the **Reset** button. All the Movie clips should return to frame 1.

If you become adept at some of the principles involved in creating this simple quiz, you can take these tools that you just learned and create as complicated a quiz as you like.

Draggable Mask

DIFFICULTY: ● ● ○ ○ ○ ○

I was on a website recently that had a great way of showing details on a jacket they were selling. When you placed a magnifier over part of the model, a zoomed in picture would appear on the right. So wherever you moved the little magnifier you would then see a magnified version. Really neat. Of course, I imagine the ActionScript to create such a file would be extensive.

So I started asking myself how I can recreate this file using the commands: **tellTarget** and **startDrag,** along with a **Mask**. After thinking about it for a little bit I came up with the next project. Open the Flash Projects folder on your drive and double-click **Magnify.swf**. You'll see a woman on the left and a magnified version on the right. Wherever you move the cursor across the woman on the left you'll see a magnified version on the right. This is a fun little file that is easy to put together. Open the file called **MagnifyFinal.fla**. On the stage you'll see two pictures; one is the small woman and on the right we have the larger version:

On the timeline you'll see three layers. The **Small Woman** layer which holds the smaller picture. The **Woman** layer which holds the larger version. And a **Actions** layer:

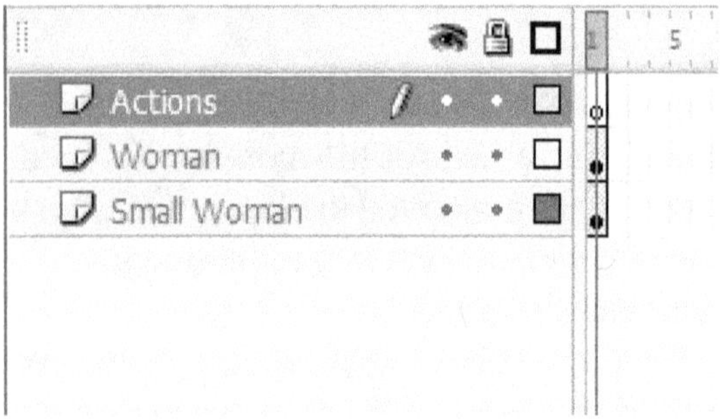

Create a new layer above the **Woman** layer and name it **Magnify**:

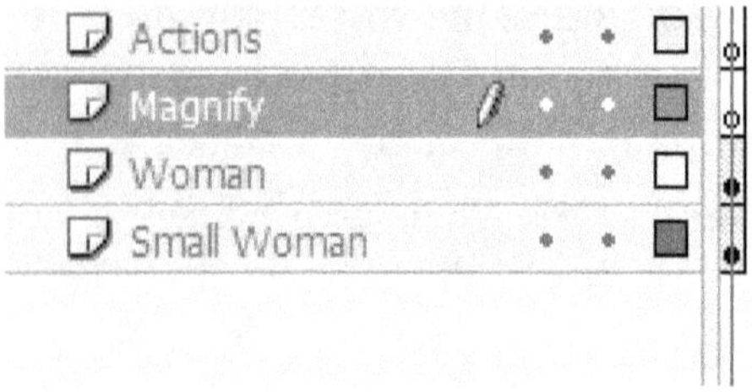

Let's create the **Magnifier** Movie clip. Grab the **Rectangle Tool**, select **black** for the **Stroke color**, and select **white** for the **Fill color;** change the **Alpha** of the white color to **30%**:

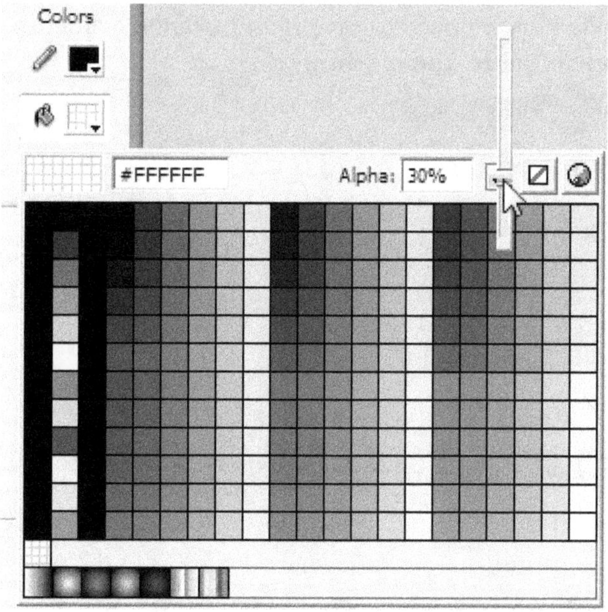

Create a square below the feet of the smaller picture; hold down SHIFT to create a perfect square:

Double-click on this shape to select the shape and the stroke. Go to **Modify**, **Convert to Symbol**. Change the **Type** to **Movie clip** and type **Magnifier** for the **Name**.

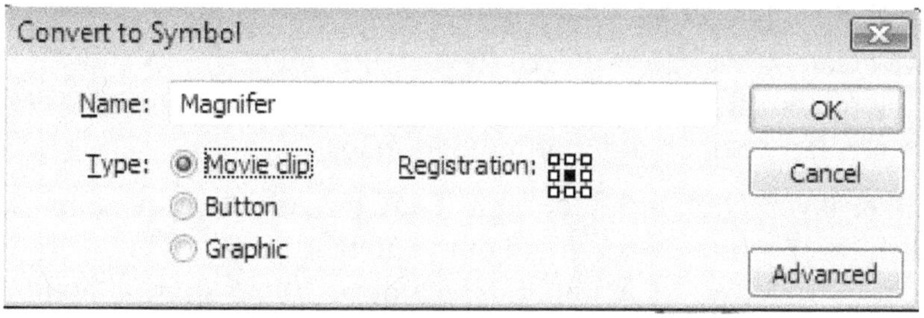

Since we'll be controlling this Movie clip we need to give it an Instance Name. In the Properties panel type **magnifier** in the **Instance Name** window.

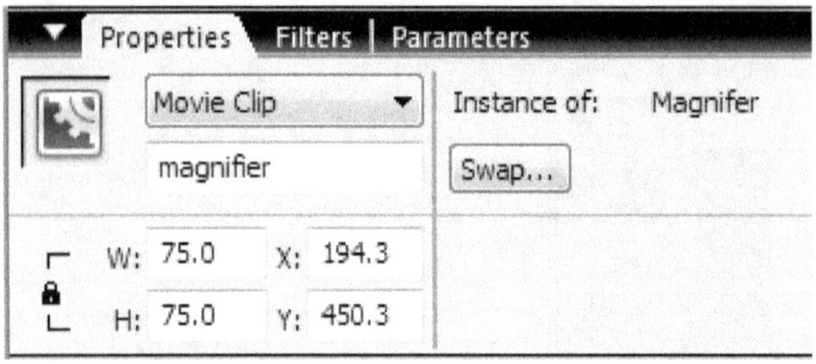

Double-click on this new Movie clip to enter its editing stage. Change the name of **Layer 1** to **Magnifier**. Create a new layer and name it **White Cover**. Next, create another layer and name it **Border**. We're now going to create a large square for the **Border** layer.

Just as we did previously, grab the **Rectangle Tool**, select **black** for the **Stroke color**, and **white** for the **Fill color**. Take the **Fill color** Alpha down to 30%. Create a square that covers the lower part of the legs of the larger image (remember to hold down SHIFT). Make this square about twice as large as the Magnifier square:

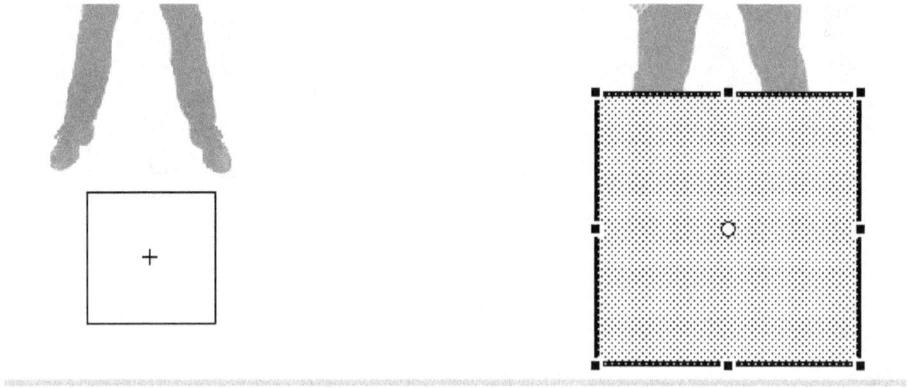

We're now going to create the white cover that will cover up the large image. We'll then cut a hole in the white shape which will reveal the large picture beneath it. Before we create it, though, we need to view the rulers. Go to **View**, **Rulers**. By default the rulers unit of measurement are pixels. Use rulers whenever you want to be more precise when creating or moving shapes.

Select the **White Cover** layer. Grab the **Rectangle Tool**, turn the **Stroke color** off, then make the **Fill color white**. Next, zoom out to **50%**. Create a white shape about twice the height of the stage; the width will be around **700px** starting at the **300px** mark on the top ruler:

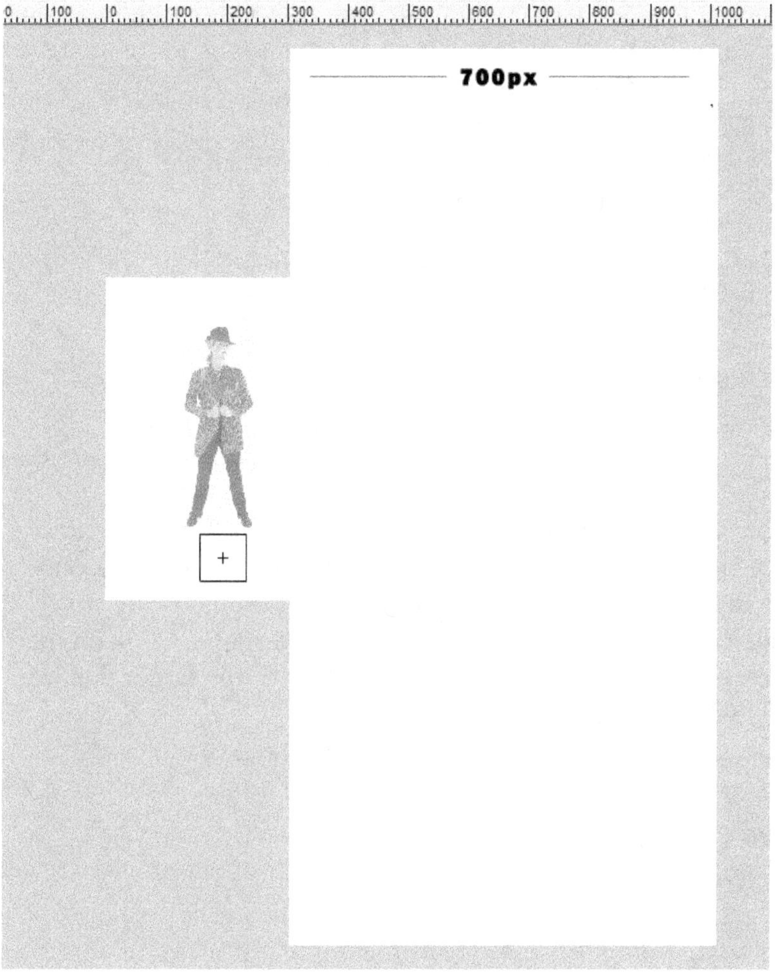

We need to cut a hole in the white shape so we can see the picture below it. I'll show you a neat little trick for cutting holes into shapes. Turn the visibility of the **White Cover** layer off. Click once on the white part of the large square in the **Border** layer; it should be filled with dots after selected:

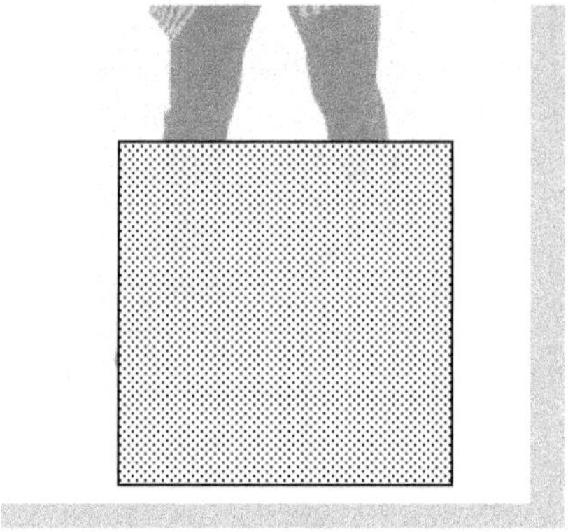

Click on the **Fill color** and change the color to **red**; your highlighted shape should change to a red color:

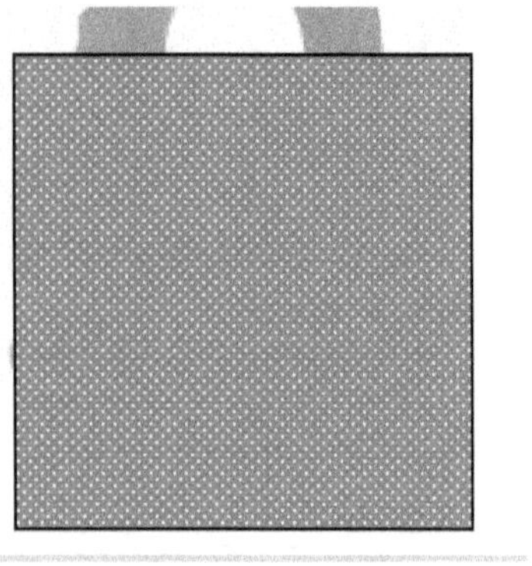

Click on this red shape with your **Selection Tool** and go to **Edit**, **Copy**. Next, delete this red shape. Select the **White Cover** layer, turn the visibility back on, and go to **Edit**, **Paste in Place**. This will place the red shape on the white cover. Click outside the white cover on the stage to deselect the red shape. Click on the red shape and hit delete. You should now be seeing the legs of the larger picture through the hole in the white shape:

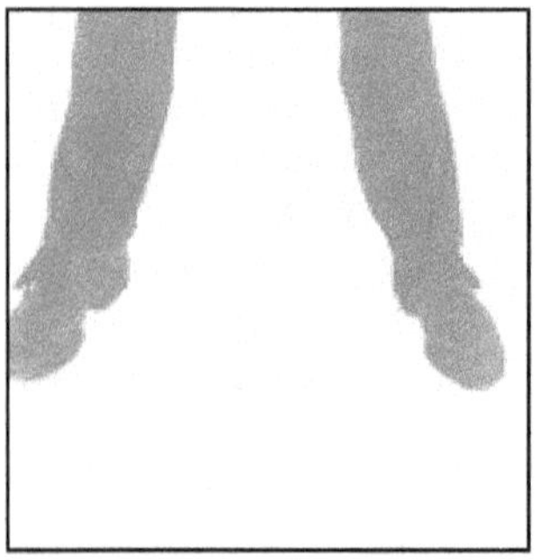

Go back to Scene 1. Select the keyframe of the **Actions** layer and open the Actions panel. We need to add the **startDrag** command to the **Magnifier** Movie clip. Go to **Global Functions, Movie clip Control**, and double-click **startDrag**. In the **startDrag** settings window type **/magnifier** in the **Target** window. Select **Lock mouse to center**:

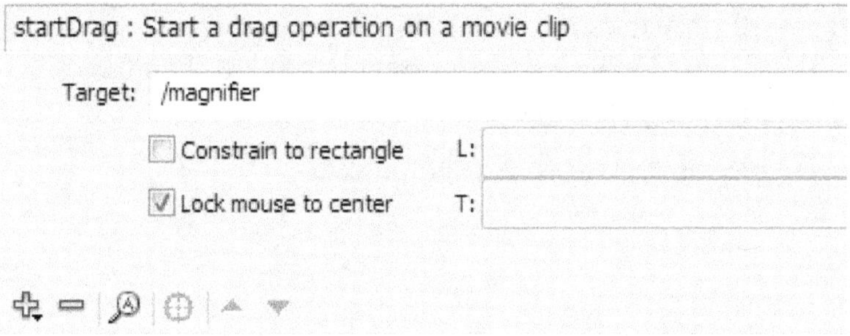

Now the **Magnifier** Movie clip will be draggable. Go ahead and test the movie. You'll notice that when you move the cursor around the stage the mask effect breaks down. We need to constrain the mask to a *specific* area. That's where the **Constrain to rectangle** setting comes into play. In the Actions panel select **Constrain to rectangle**. Once you select it you'll see that the four coordinate windows are now editable. We'll now type coordinates that will constrain the **Magnifier** Movie clip to a specific area. Type **140** in the **L** window, **250** in the **R** window, **100** in the **T** window, and **460** in the **B** window:

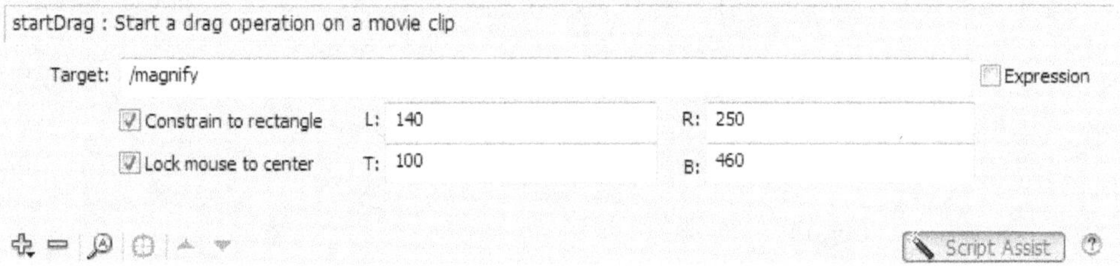

Test your movie again. This time you won't be able to move the magnifier beyond certain boundaries. Everything works perfectly now!

So with just one command, we created a simple yet effective Magnifier.

Creating a Password file in Flash is easy with just a few simple commands. You can create a password box that opens a web page when the correct password is entered, or directs the user to a Label on the timeline. We'll do that now. Open **Password.fla** in the Flash Projects folder. You'll notice that there are two scenes in this file. The first Scene is **Password**, and the second one is **Picture.** We'll create a password box that will only take the user to the Picture Scene if they enter the correct password. If they don't enter the correct password then they'll be asked if they want to try again. So let's get started.

You'll see on the stage we have the Password box graphics:

Create a new layer and name it **Log In**. Next, select your **Text Tool**. Open the Properties panel. Change the **Size** to **12**, **Font** to **Verdana**, **Color** to **black**, and **Bold**. Type **Log In** at the bottom right of the Password box:

Grab the **Selection Tool**. Select this text and convert it to a button. Name it **Log In Button**. Hit **OK** to close the window. Double-click on this new symbol. Insert a keyframe under the **Hit** state; grab the **Rectangle Tool** and create a shape a little larger than the text on this frame.

Go back to **Scene 1**. Now we need to add the text box. Create a new layer and name it **Text Box**. Select the **Text Tool**. **Click-and-drag** the **Text Tool** creating a text area approximately the same size as the text box graphic:

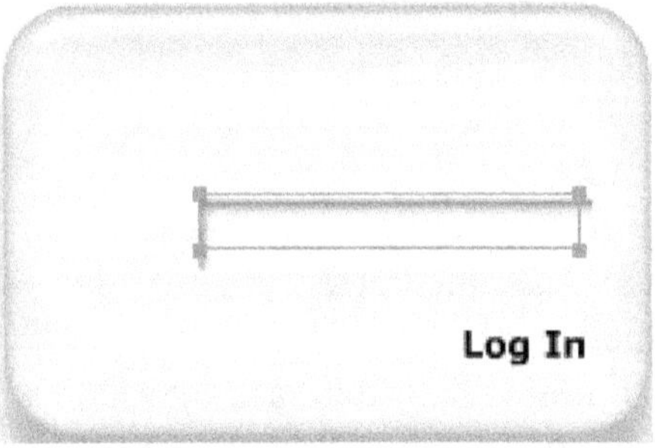

It doesn't have to be perfect. Open the Properties panel and you should see its attributes. Change **Static Text** to **Input Text**, change **Line Type** to **Password**, type **8** in the **Maximum characters** window, and type **password** in the **Variable** window:

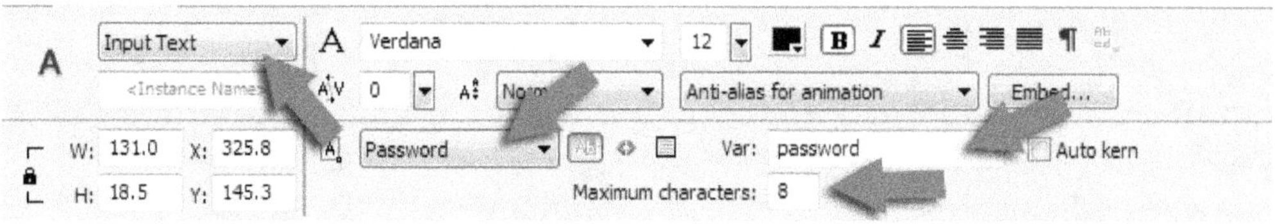

Next, create a new layer and name it **Labels**. Go to frame **20** of this layer and insert a frame; then, insert a keyframe on frame **10**. Give this frame a Label name of **Incorrect**:

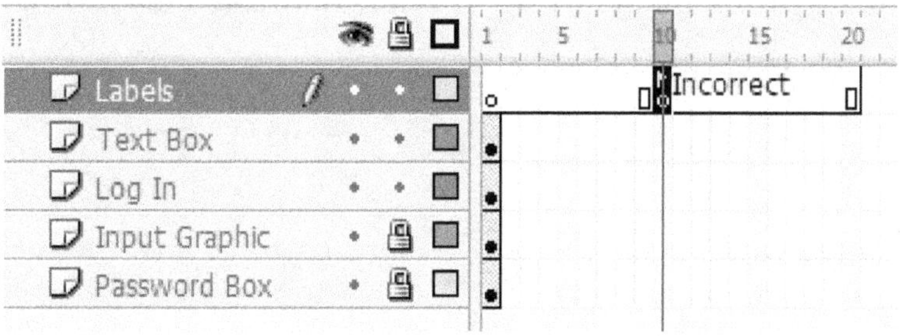

This is the frame users will go to when they have the incorrect password. We need to add the **Try Again?** button to this frame. Create a new layer and name it **Try Again Text**. Insert a keyframe on frame **10** of this layer. Grab your **Text Tool**. Open the Properties panel and select the **Color black**, **Font Verdan**a, **Size 12** and **Bold**. Type **Try Again?** in the middle of the stage:

Grab the **Selection Tool** and select this text. Convert this text to a Button and name it **Try Again Button**. Hit **OK** to close the **Convert to Symbol** box. Double-click this new button to enter its editing stage. Create a keyframe under the **Hit** state. Grab the **Rectangle Tool** and create a shape a little bigger than the text. Go back to the Password scene when you're finished.

This button will simply take the user back to frame 1. So select this button, open the Actions panel and go to **Global Functions**, **Timeline Control** and double-click **goto**. In the **goto** settings window select **Go to and stop**:

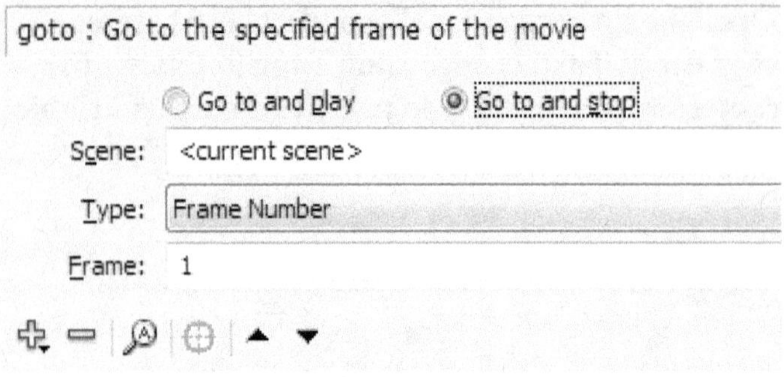

Create a new layer and name it **Actions**. Insert a **stop** code in the Actions layer's first frame and the tenth frame. Insert a keyframe into frame **20** of the **Actions** layer. Open the Actions panel and go to **Global Functions**, **Timeline Control** and double-click **goto**. In the **goto** setttings window select **Go to and stop**:

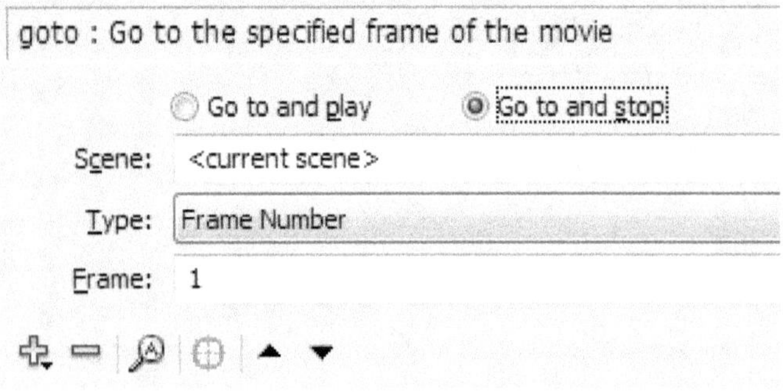

This is to safeguard against the timeline playing past this timeline and ending up in the Picture scene (if a user hits the ENTER key then Flash will play the timeline). Now, if the timeline plays past frame 10, it will reach frame 20 where it will trigger the above command sending the user back to frame 1.

Your layers should look like this:

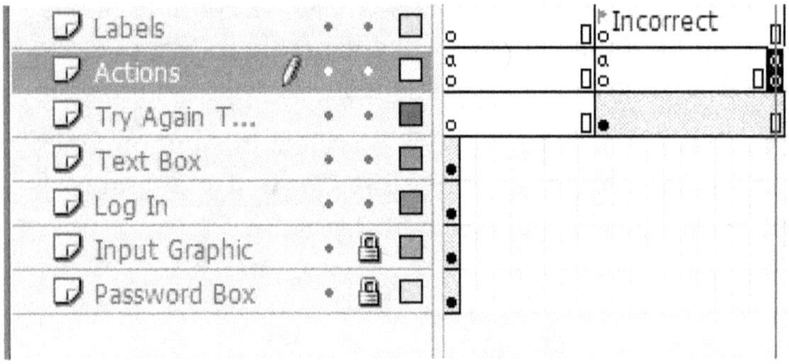

Now we just need to add the ActionScript to the **Log In** button and we're finished. Select the **Log In** button on the stage. Open the Actions panel and go to **Statements**, **Conditions/Loops**, and double-click **if**:

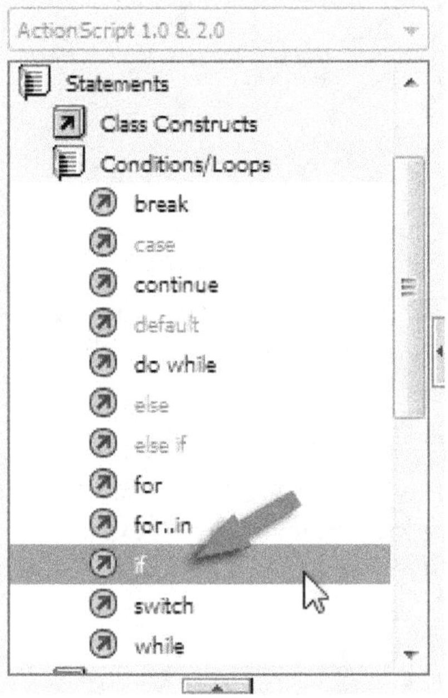

You should now be in the **if** settings window. This is the window where we tell Flash what the password is. For this exercise the password is **lucky**.

In the **Condition** window type **password eq "lucky":**

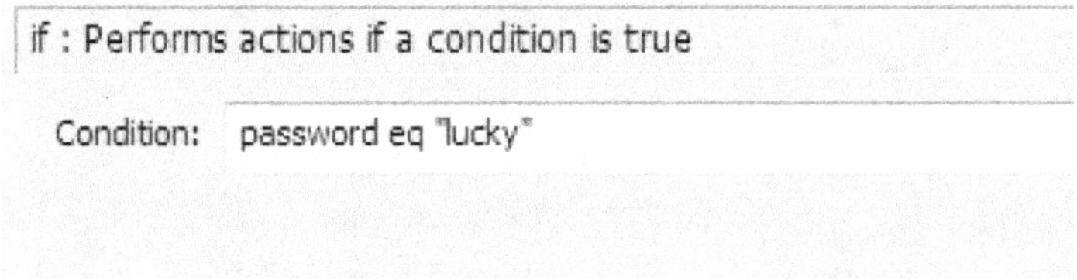

If you remember, **password** is the name we gave the **input text**. So basically what this is telling Flash is: *if the password equals lucky* do this next action...

Now we have to tell Flash what to do if the password equals "lucky". Go to **Global Functions**, **Timeline Control** and double-click on **goto**. In the **goto** settings window change **Scene** to **Picture**, **Type** to **Frame Number**, and number **1** for **Frame**. Also, select **Go to and stop**:

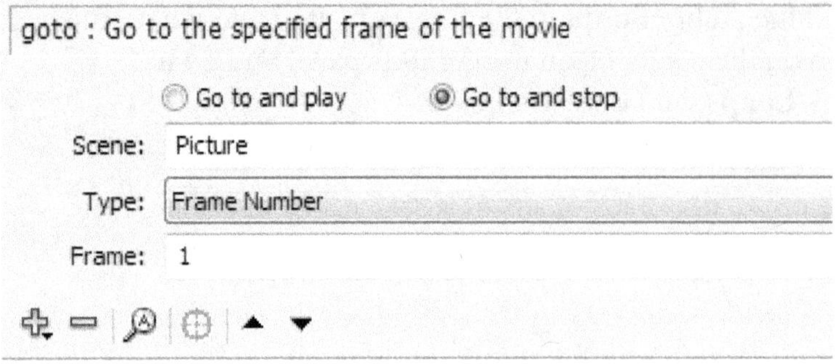

Test your movie. Type **lucky** into the text box. Click on the **Log In** button when you're finished. You should be taken immediately to the Picture scene. With most passwords on the internet you can usually just hit the ENTER key on your keyboard when you're done typing the password. Let's set that up now.

The Actions window should still be open. Click anywhere inside the word **release**. You should now see the **mouse events** window. Select **Key Press** then hit the **Enter** key on your keyboard. You'll see the word **Enter** in the **Key Press** window:

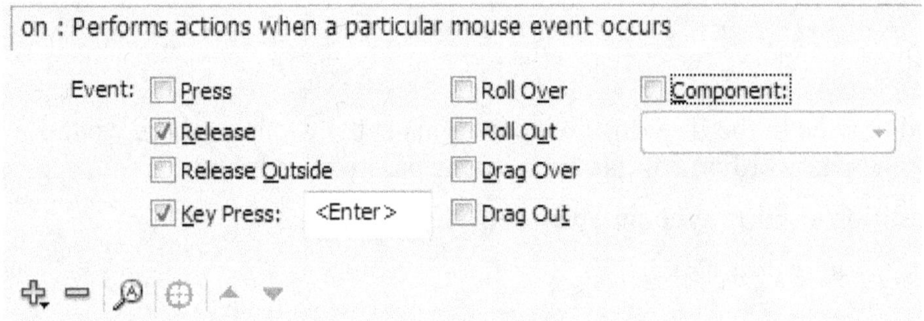

Test the movie again. Type **lucky** into the text box and hit ENTER on your keyboard. You should be taken to the **Picture** scene. The final thing we need to do is put in the ActionScript to tell Flash what to do if the user puts in the wrong password. Let's do that now.

Since we're adding on to the previous code click on the closing bracket of the last set of code. Go to **Statements**, **Conditions/Loops** and double-click **else if**:

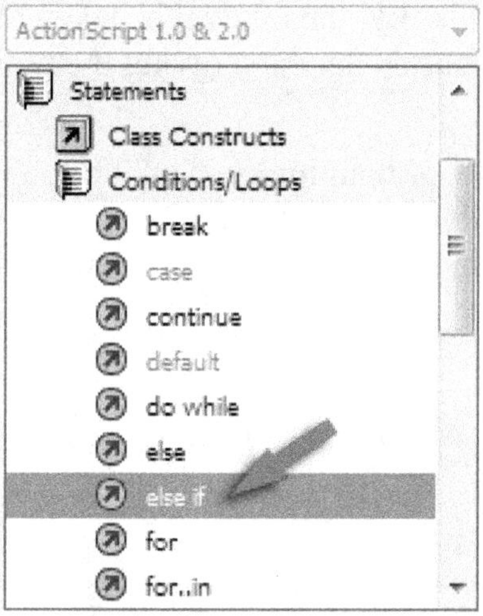

In the **Condition** window type **password ne "lucky"**:

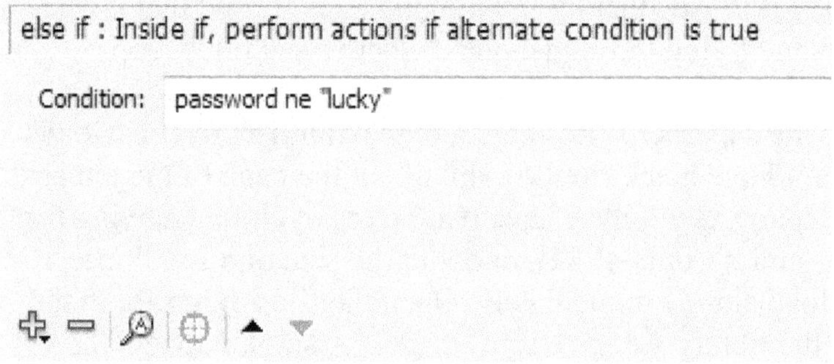

This tells Flash that if the password is ne (not equal) to **"lucky"** do this next action...

We now need to add the code that will tell Flash what to do if the password isn't equal to **lucky**. Go to **Global Functions**, **Timeline Control**, and double-click **goto**. In the **goto** settings window select **Go to and stop**, change **Type** to **Frame Label**, and type **Incorrect** in the **Frame** window:

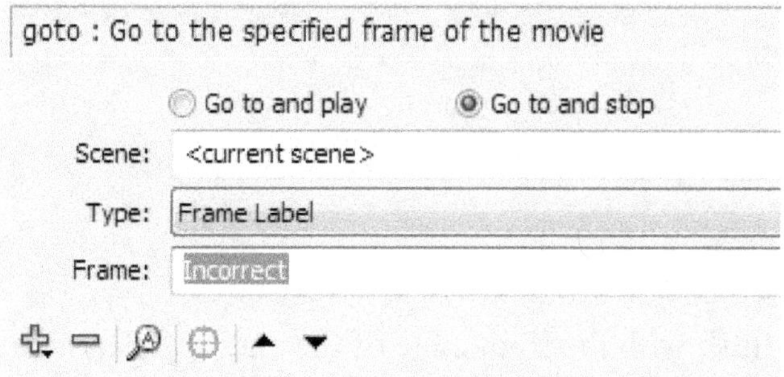

Now if the password the user types in isn't the word **lucky**, then they'll be taken to the Label **Incorrect**. At this frame the **Try Again?** button appears, giving the user a chance to go back and try again.

Go ahead and test your movie. Try a different password than **lucky**. You'll be asked if you want to try again. That's it! If you need to change the password to something else then just change the word **"lucky"** in the ActionScript to whatever word you like.

Looping Background
DIFFICULTY: ●●○○○○

Have you ever seen those Flash Ads that have a moving background that is on a perpetual loop? Like a plane flying through clouds, where the clouds loop continuously making the plane appear to be soaring through the sky. Double-click on **flying.swf**. You'll see the superhero (from the movie **Monarch of the Moon**) flying through the clouds. I have black smoke coming out the back of the jetpack and his little propeller is spinning wildly. I have two layers of clouds moving for added realism. All of this and it's only 43KB, or about the size of a small jpeg! This means it will download almost immediately. Open the file **Flying.fla** in the Flash Projects folder. In the library we have four images. A smoke image, the superhero, and two different cloud images. So the first thing we'll do is create the moving cloud background. Rename **Layer 1: Clouds**. Then, drag **Clouds.jpg** over to the stage. We want the right edge of the Cloud image to be flush with the right edge of the stage. Open the Align panel and select **Align right edge**, **Align top edge** and select **To stage**:

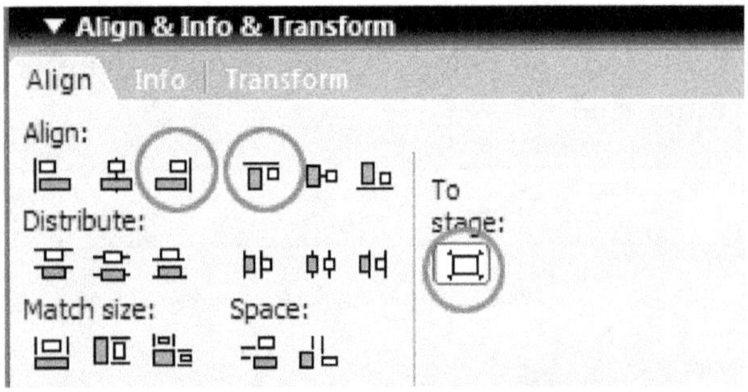

The cloud image should now be flush with the right edge of the stage. Select this image and convert it to a **Movie clip**. Name it **Clouds Movie**:

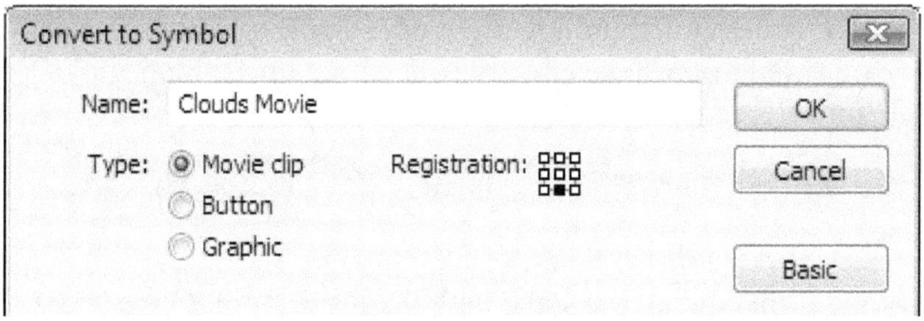

Hit **OK** and close. Double-click on this new Movie clip to enter its editing stage. Now we're going to make two copies of the cloud image for the background animation. Before we copy this cloud image we need to make it a graphic. Select the cloud image on the stage and go to **Modify**, **Convert to Symbol**; in the **Convert to Symbol** box select **Graphic** for **Type** and type **Cloud Symbol** for the **Name**. Hit **OK** when you're done.

The reason you convert images to graphics before you copy them, is because Flash only has to download the cloud graphic once and all of its copies will download instantly and won't add to the overall download size.

Select this cloud graphic and go to **Edit**, **Copy**. Select **Edit**, and **Paste in Place**. Click on this new copy and go to **Modify**, **Transform**, **Flip Horizontal**.

This will flip your picture. Drag this new symbol to the left. You'll want the right side of this copied symbol to *line up with the left side of the original cloud image*. Zoom in if you have to, to make sure all edges line up perfectly:

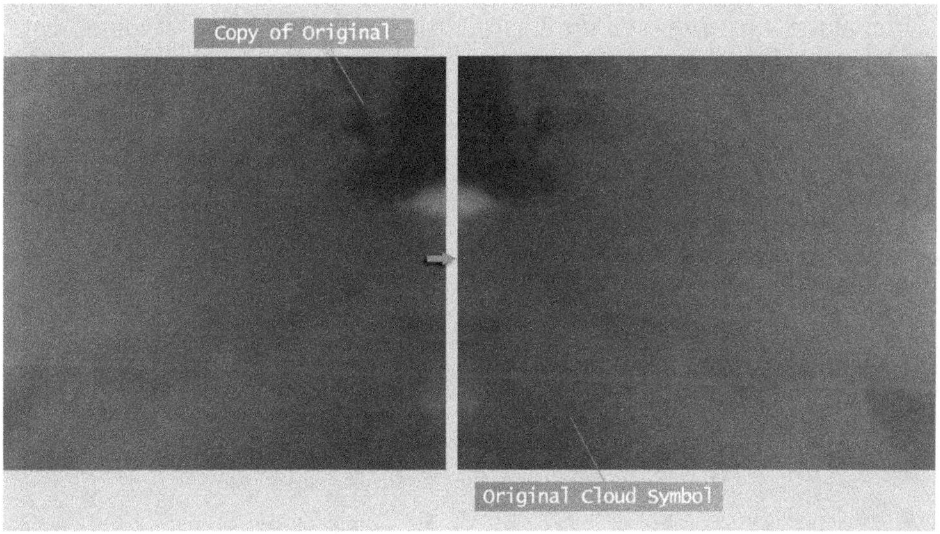

Since we flipped the image horizontally the two symbols now connect seamlessly. Select the original cloud symbol and go to **Edit**, **Copy**. Next, go to **Edit**, **Paste in Place**.

Drag this third symbol all the way left until its right edge lines up with the second symbol's left edge. You should now have a really wide cloud image made up of three copies of the **Cloud Symbol**:

We're going to mark the right edge of the stage with the Ruler Tool. Go to **View**, **Rulers**:

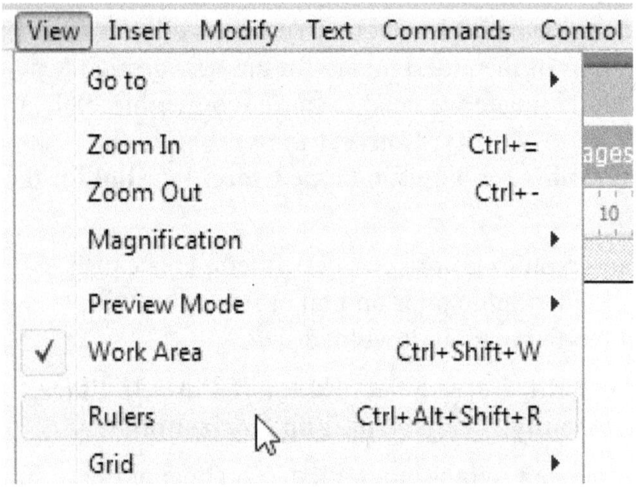

You should now see rulers at the top and to the left of the stage. *Click-and-hold* on the Ruler at the left; *click-and-drag* a Ruler line to the right until it's lined up with the right edge of the stage:

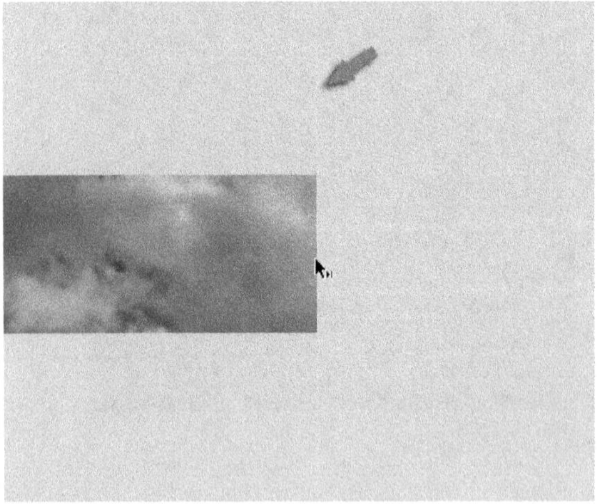

Your line should now be lined up with the right edge of the stage.

Create a new keyframe on frame **140** of **Layer 1**; you should now see the borders of the three images (they'll show up as blue lines):

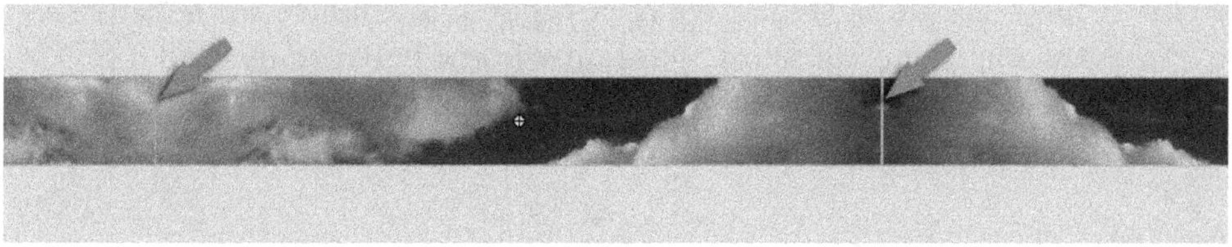

You may have to zoom out to **50%**. Hold SHIFT down and *click-and-hold* on the right edge of the leftmost cloud; drag the entire cloud image to the right so that the right edge of the leftmost cloud image is flush with the ruler line. Your stage should now look like this:

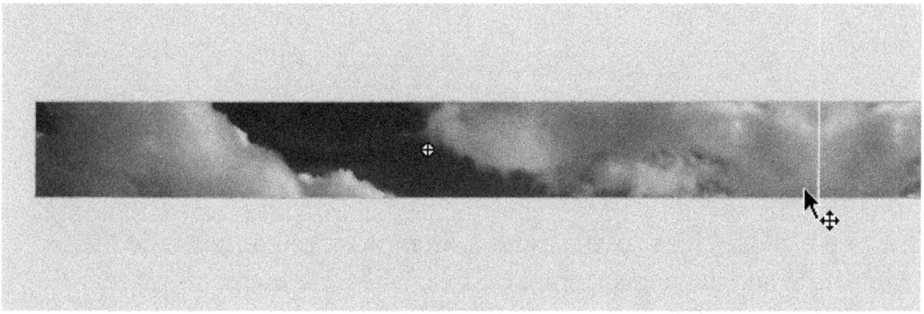

Select any frame between **1** and **140** and insert a Motion Tween. Test your movie. The cloud animation should be seamless as it loops continuously. So now let's add the superhero!

Go back to Scene 1. Create a new layer and name it **Superhero**. Turn off the visibility of **Layer 1** so we can see the stage:

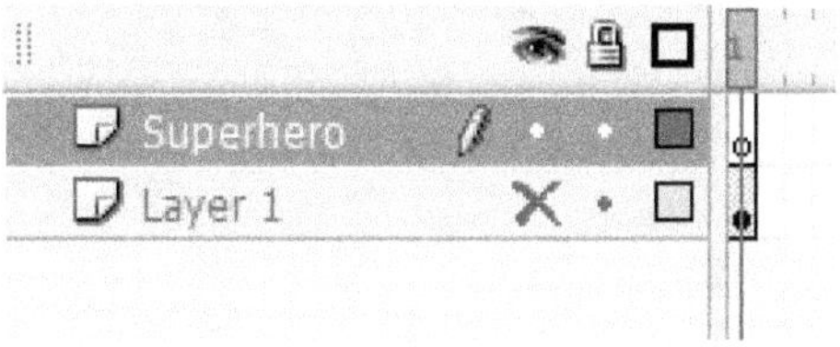

Drag the image **flying.png** to the center of the stage from the library:

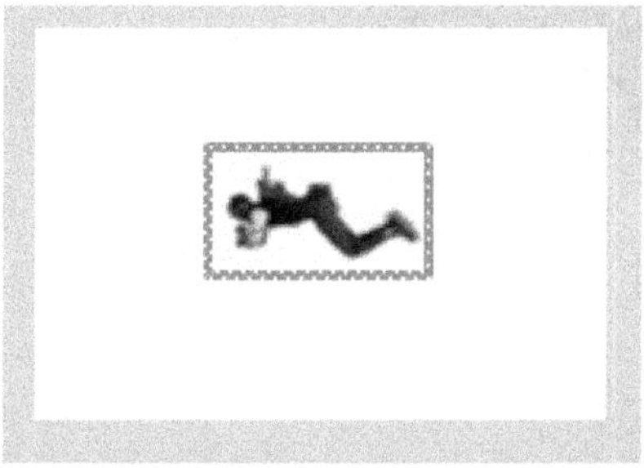

Select this new image and convert it to a Movie clip (**Modify, Convert to Symbol**). Name it **Superhero**. Hit **OK** when you're finished. Double-click on this Movie clip to enter its editing stage. We're now going to animate the superhero. Create a keyframe on frame **200**; now, select any frame between the two keyframes and insert a Motion Tween. Insert a keyframe on frame **100**. Select the superhero on the stage and move him to the left side of the stage:

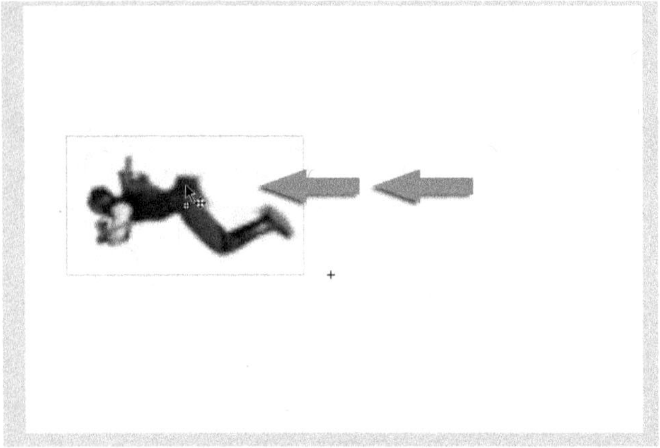

If you want, you can drag him down slightly. So now we're going to add the propeller animation and the jetpack smoke. If we add these elements on this timeline we'll have to animate them so that they follow the superhero, which probably won't work. So the easy way to do it is to put these elements *within the superhero symbol*. Let's do that now. Go to frame **1** and double-click on the superhero symbol on the stage. You should now be in its editing stage.

Create a new layer and name it **Propeller**. Zoom into the stage about 800% or until you have a close view of the superhero's propeller:

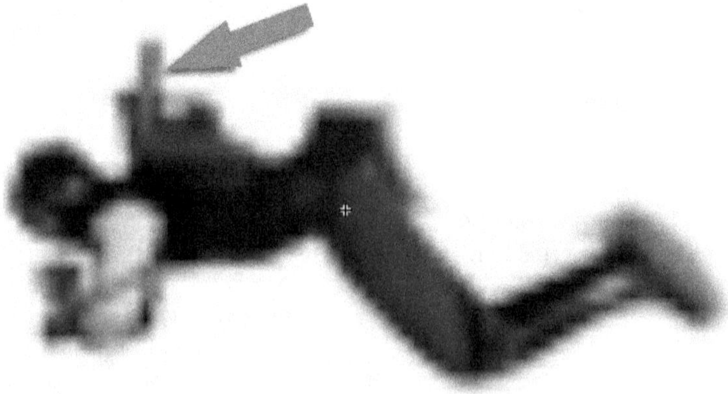

Click on the **Eyedropper Tool**:

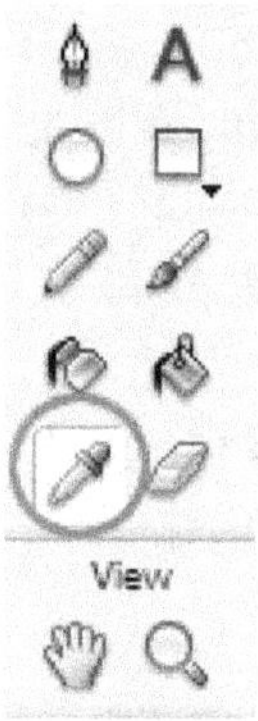

Click on the superhero's propeller:

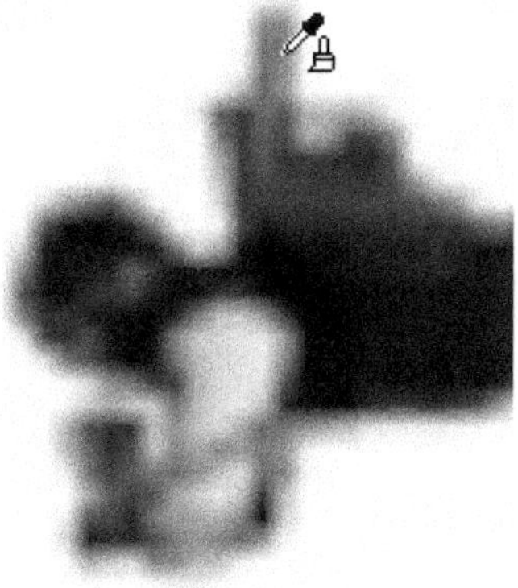

You should now have the propeller's color as the **Fill color**. Select the **Rectangle Tool** and turn off the **Stroke color**. Create a rectangle shape over the superhero's existing propeller:

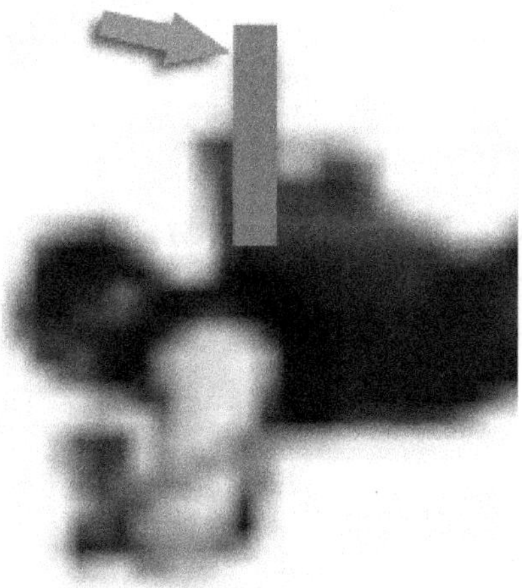

So now we're going to animate this propeller. Select this new shape and convert it to a Movie clip (**Modify, Convert to Symbol**). Name it **Propeller Movie**. When you're done double-click on this new Movie clip to enter its editing stage. Create a keyframe on frame **20**; next, select any frame between the two keyframes and insert a Motion Tween.

Now, select the first keyframe. Open the Properties panel. Change **Rotate** to **CW** and type **6** for **times**:

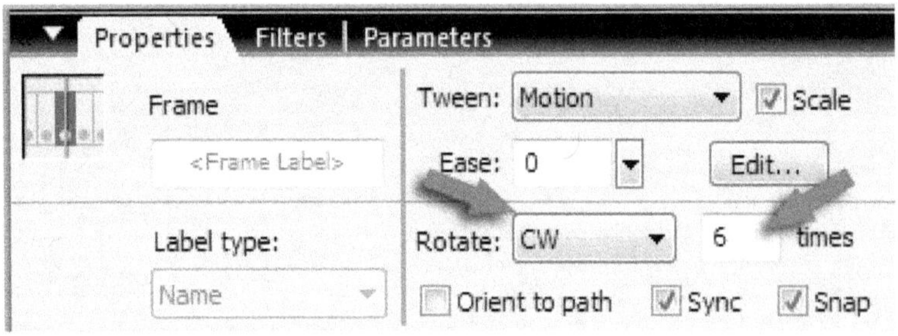

If you grab your timeline needle and scrub the timeline you'll see that your propeller is now spinning. It should do 6 full rotations within the 20 frames. Click on the **Back** button above the timeline/stage:

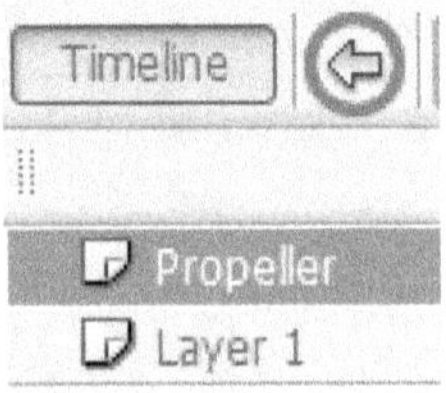

This will take you back to the superhero image stage. We'll now add the smoke to the superhero's jetpack. Create a new layer and name it **Smoke**. Next, drag **smoke.png** over to the stage. Position this image over the superhero's jetpack. Next, convert this image to a Movie clip (**Modify, Convert to Symbol**). Name this new Movie clip **Smoke**. Double-click this Movie clip to enter its editing stage.

Select the smoke image on the stage and convert it to a graphic (**Modify, Convert to Symbol**). Name this new symbol **Smoke Graphic** and hit **OK**. We're converting this image to a graphic so we can add effects to it.

With this new symbol selected, open the Properties panel. Change **Color** to **Brightness** and the **percentage** to **-100%:**

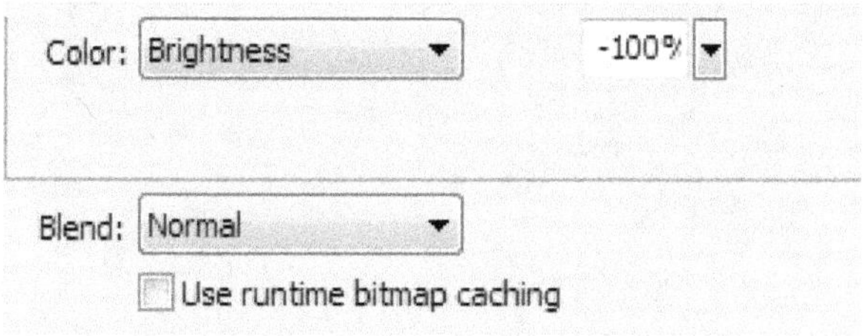

The smoke symbol should now be darker:

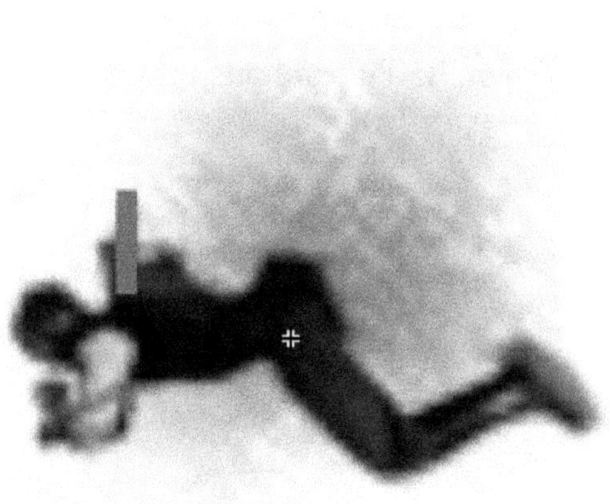

Select the smoke image and grab the **Free Transform Tool**:

You should now see a bounding box surrounding your smoke image:

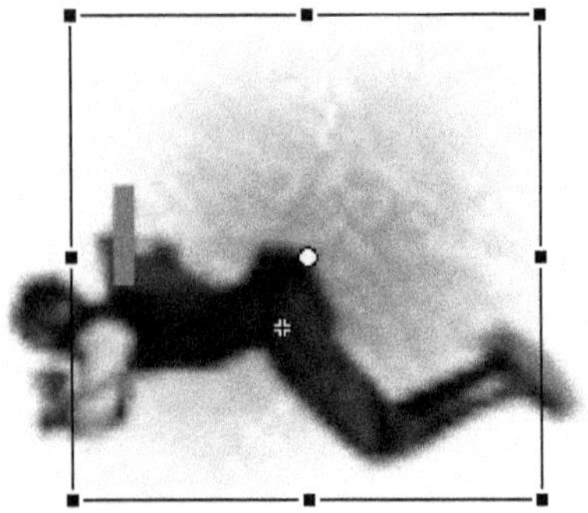

Grab a corner of the bounding box, hold down SHIFT, and push inward until the smoke shrinks to about 30% of its size:

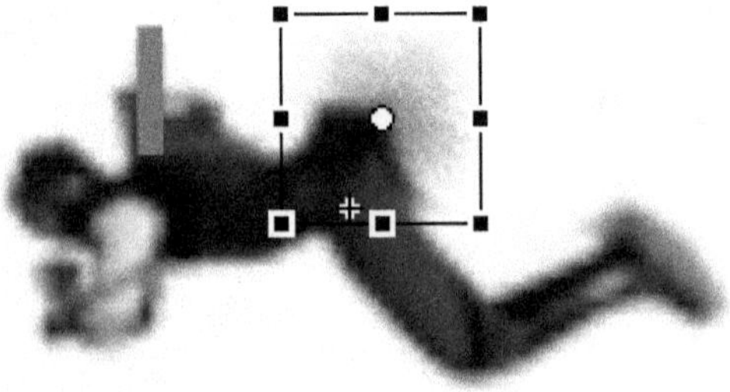

Create a new keyframe on frame **40**. Select any frame between 1 and 40 and insert a Motion Tween. Select frame **40** then select the smoke symbol on the stage. Select the **Free Transform Tool** and enlarge the smoke image about 400%:

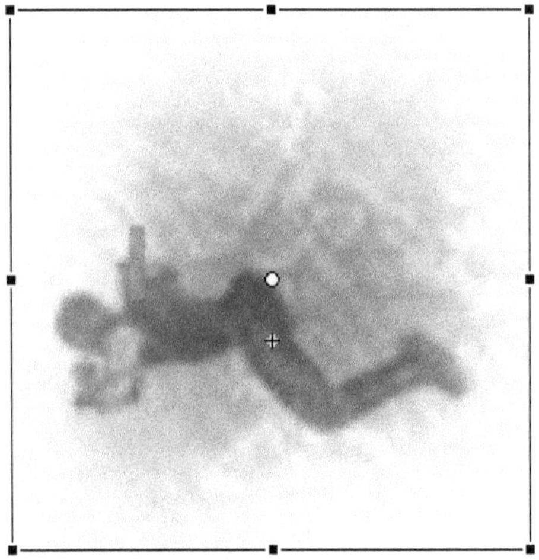

Drag this smoke image so that's completely off the stage on the right side:

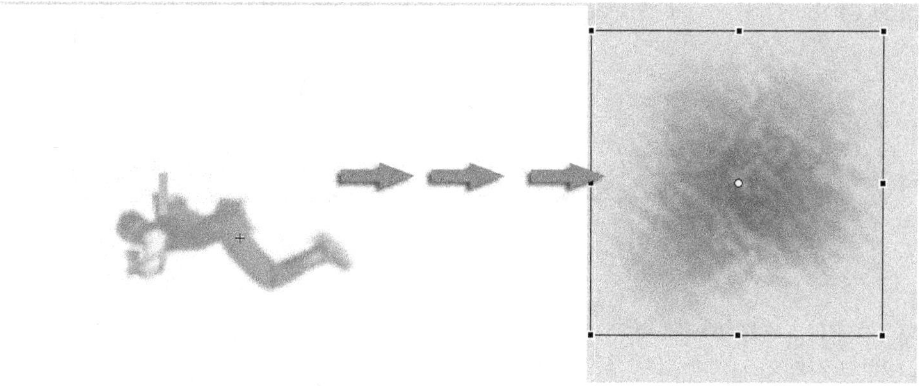

We now need to take down the alpha of this smoke image. Since we already have one effect on this smoke image (Brightness -100) we'll have to use the **Advanced** setting to apply another effect. Change **Color** to **Advanced**. Then, click on the **Settings...** button:

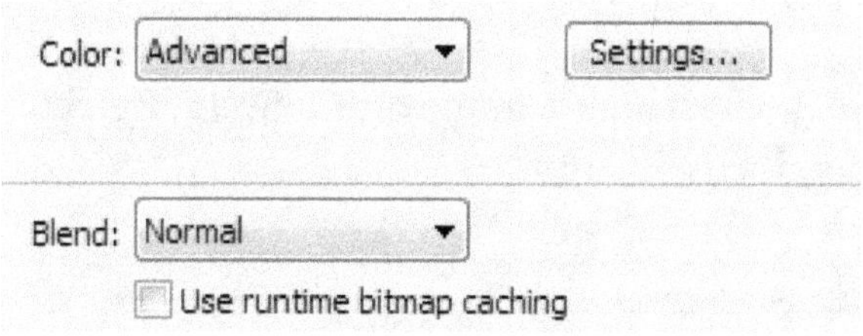

In the **Advanced Effect** box take the **Alpha** down to **0**:

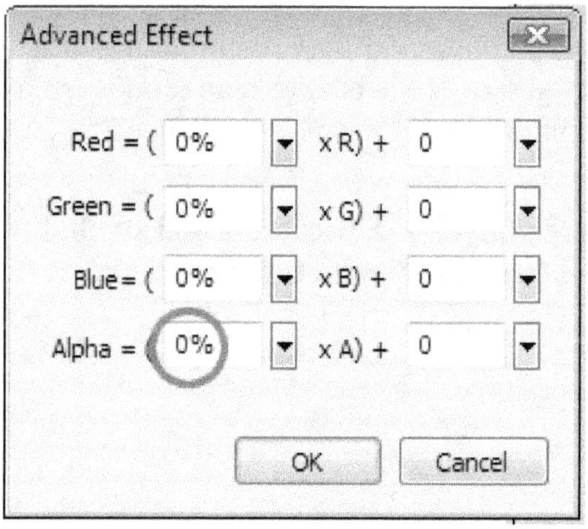

Hit **OK**. Your smoke image should now be transparent. If you play the timeline you'll see the smoke gradually get larger until it fades away.

Create a new layer and name it **Smoke 2**. Create a keyframe on frame **10**. Click on the name of the first layer: **Layer 1**. This will highlight all the frames of this layer:

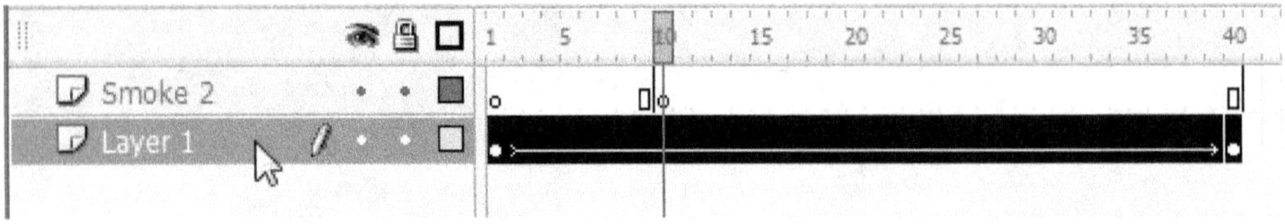

Next, go to **Edit**, **Timeline**, **Copy Frames**. This will copy all the frames of **Layer 1**. Select the keyframe on frame **10** of **Smoke 2**. Go to **Edit**, **Timeline**, **Paste Frames**. You should now have a copy of all the frames of **Layer 1** on the layer **Smoke 2**:

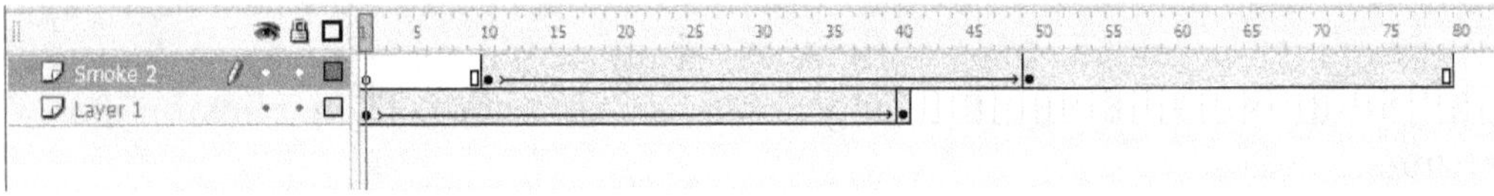

Create a new layer and name it **Smoke 3**. Create a keyframe on frame **15**. Select this keyframe and go to **Edit**, **Timeline**, **Paste Frames**:

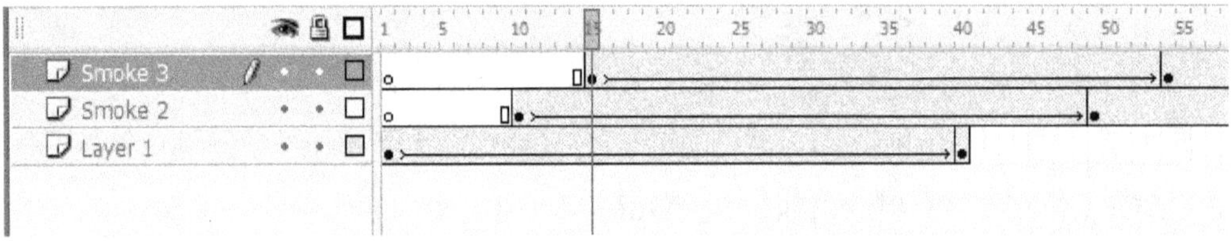

Test the movie. The animation looks pretty good but the background clouds are a bit too dark; it's hard to see the propeller spinning and the smoke. We need to make the clouds less dark.

Go back to Scene 1. Turn on the visibility for **Layer 1**. Select the cloud symbol on the stage. Open the Properties panel and change **Color** to **Brightness** and change the **percentage** to **39**:

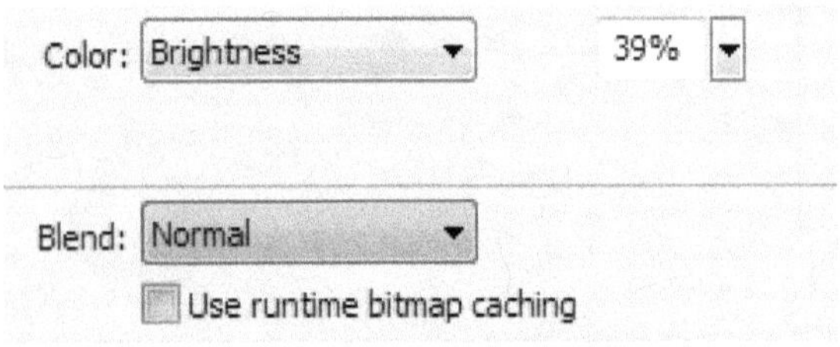

We're now able to see the superhero much better. So we're almost done. We just need to add one more cloud element. Before we do that we need to turn the visibility off for **Layer 1** so we can see the stage.

Create a new layer and name it **Cloud**. Make sure this layer is above the **Superhero** layer:

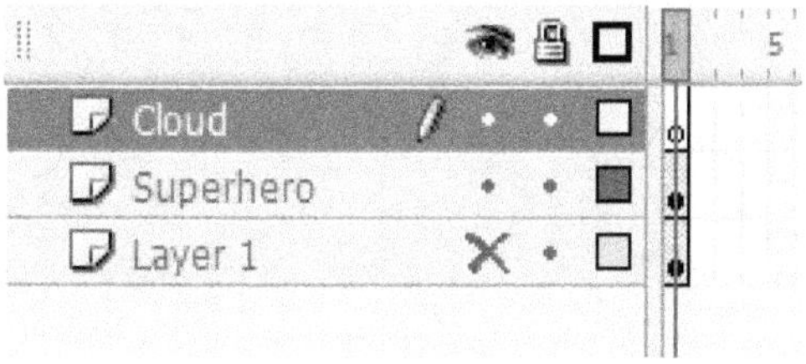

Drag the image **clouds.png** from the library to the left of the stage:

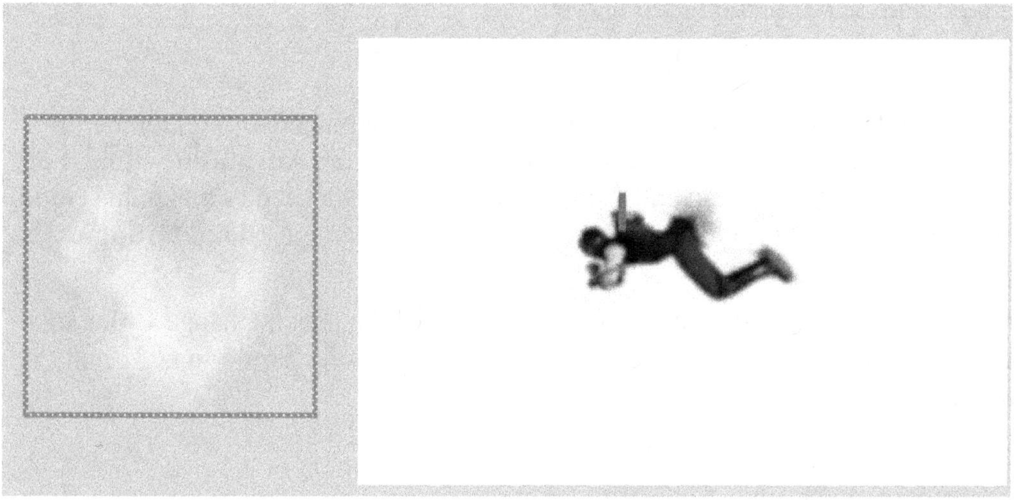

With this image still selected convert it to a Movie clip. Name it **Cloud Foreground**:

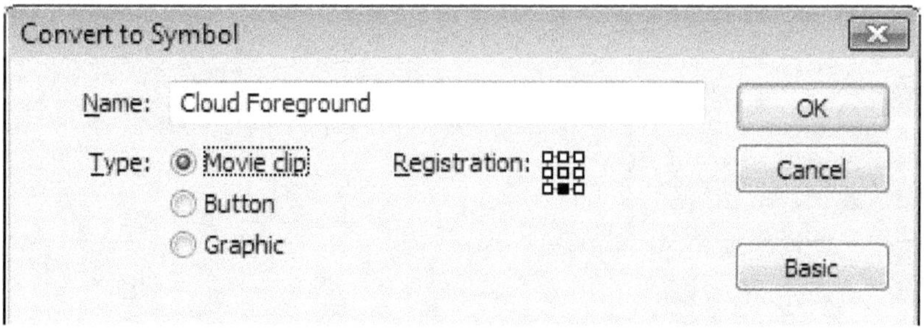

Hit **OK** when you're done. Double-click on this new Movie clip to enter its editing stage. Grab the **Free Transform Tool** and enlarge your cloud about 100%:

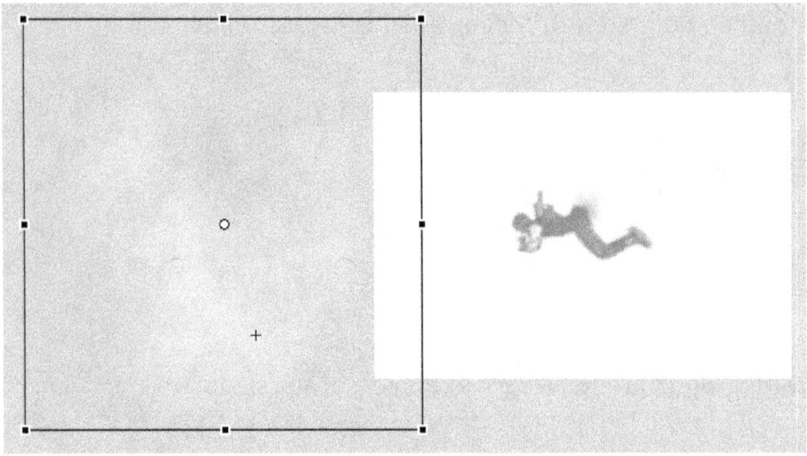

Let's make this cloud a little more blue and take the alpha down. Remember, if you want to add more than one effect you have to use the **Advanced** setting. Let's do that now. Before we can add the effects, however, we need to make this cloud a symbol. Convert this cloud image to a graphic and name it **Cloud Graphic**. Hit **OK** when you're finished.

With the new symbol still selected open the Properties panel. Change **Color** to **Advanced** and click on the **Settings...** button. Change the **Alpha** to **60%** and increase the **Blue** to **122**:

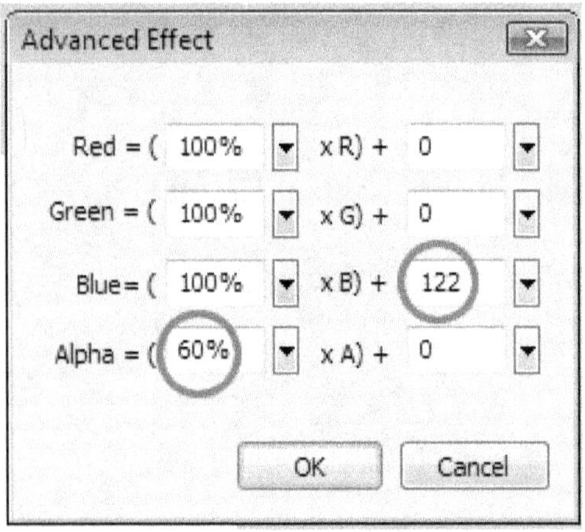

Hit **OK** when you're finished. Now we're ready to animate the cloud. Create a keyframe on frame **30**. Select any frame between the keyframes and insert a Motion Tween. Next, drag the cloud symbol to the right until it's completely off the stage:

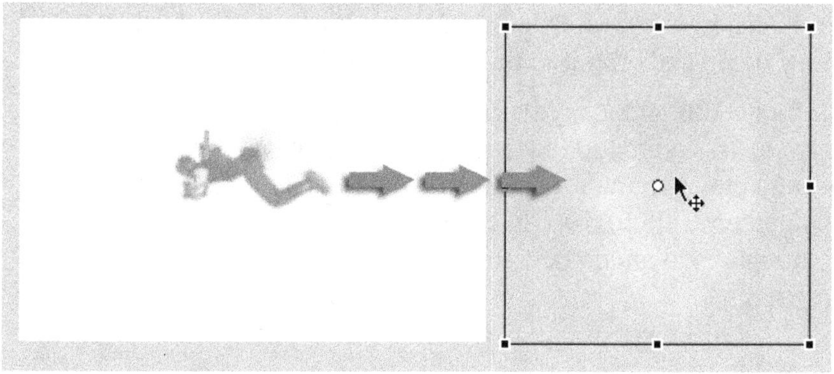

Create a new layer and name it **Cloud Copy**. Create a keyframe on frame **100** of this new layer. Click on the **Layer 1** name to highlight its frames; go to **Edit**, **Timeline**, **Copy Frames**. Select frame **100** of the **Cloud Copy** layer and go to **Edit**, **Timeline**, **Paste Frames**. Since this is a copy then we should try to alter it slightly.

Select the **Free Transform Tool** and enlarge the cloud about 25%. You may have to drag the cloud to the left to make sure that parts of the cloud aren't on the stage

Open the Properties panel and click on the **Settings...** button. Take the **Alpha** down to **40%**:

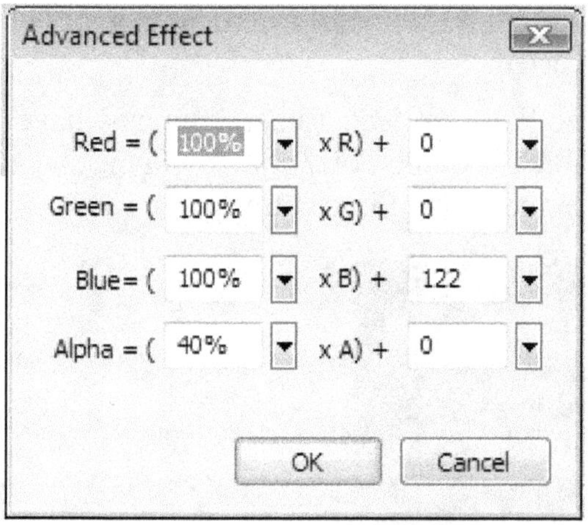

Hit **OK**. Click on the second keyframe of this layer. Select the cloud symbol on the stage. Grab the **Free Transform Tool** and enlarge this symbol also. Drag it slightly right to make sure it's completely off the stage.

With this symbol selected click on the **Settings...** button in the Properties panel and change the **Alpha** to **40%**. Since this cloud is a little larger it should be moving at a slightly different speed. Click the second keyframe of this layer; select this keyframe again and drag it to the right about 10 frames.

Insert a frame on frame **200** of this layer. Test your movie. Looks pretty good! You can always tweak this animation by adding more smoke clouds, slowing down the background cloud animation by lengthening the animation, and playing around with the superhero's flight path. Feel free to get creative! The most important thing, though, is to understand the techniques behind some of the animations we created.

Writing Effect

DIFFICULTY: ● ● ○ ○ ○ ○

Have you ever seen a Flash animation where it looks like an invisible pen is writing out the text? It's a really impressive effect when it's done correctly. And once you learn how it's done you can create a Writing Effect in about **10 minutes**!

I have two examples in this section. The first example is a more traditional type of Writing Effect with a woman's name being written out by an invisible pen. The second example is more of a fun example with a the name of a company being written out by a paint brush! So let's get started.

Open the file called **writingEffect.fla** in the Flash Projects folder. You may have to install the font called Vladimir Script which is in the Fonts folder. On the stage you'll see the picture of a woman and her name below the picture:

Select the **Text** layer and click the **Insert Layer** button. Name the new layer **Mask**:

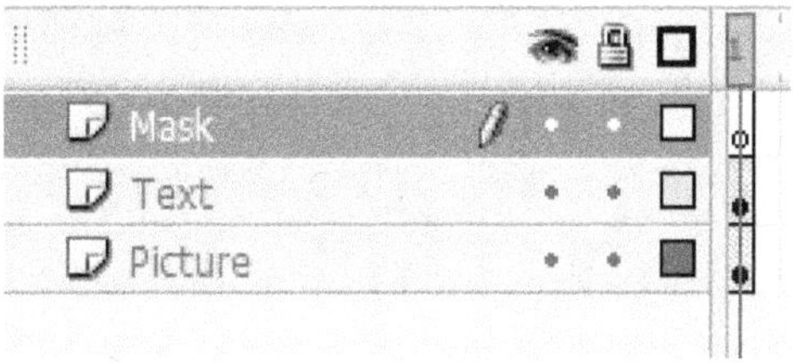

Zoom into the stage 400%. Use your **Hand Tool** to move the stage around until you can see the **V** in **Veronica**. Next, grab the **Brush Tool**. Select **red** for the **Fill color** and choose the third from the largest brush size:

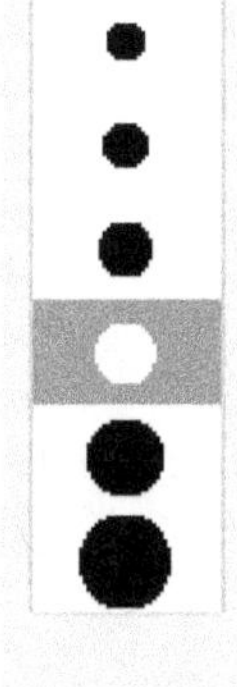

We're going to start painting the mask frame by frame. Click the **Brush Tool** on the first swirl of the letter **V**:

Next, go to **Insert**, **Timeline**, **Keyframe** (**F6**). Flash will automatically create a second keyframe on the timeline. Paint away more of the swirl:

Hit **F6** to create a new keyframe. Paint away more of the swirl:

Hit **F6**. Once again, paint away more of the swirl:

If you look at the timeline you should have four frames in each of the layers:

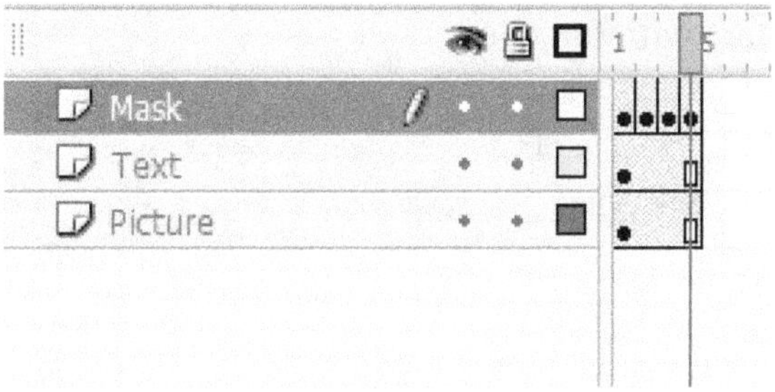

Hit **F6** again and paint away more of the swirl:

By now you should be seeing a pattern develop. Each time you paint away part of the letter hit **F6** to create a new keyframe and keep going. By frame 25 you should be finished with the letter **V**:

When creating a writing effect remember that the more keyframes it takes you to paint away a letter the more realistic the animation will appear. Also, whenever I do the writing effect I keep one finger on **F6** while I'm working, then I just click it after each brush stroke.

When you finish the **V** letter hit **F6** to start with the **e** letter:

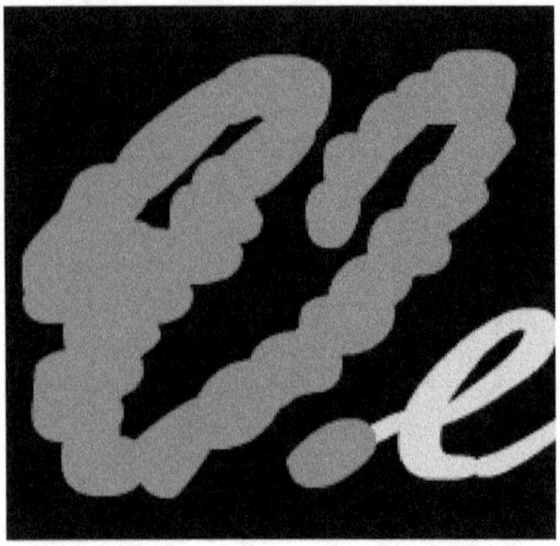

Hit **F6** then paint away more of the letter:

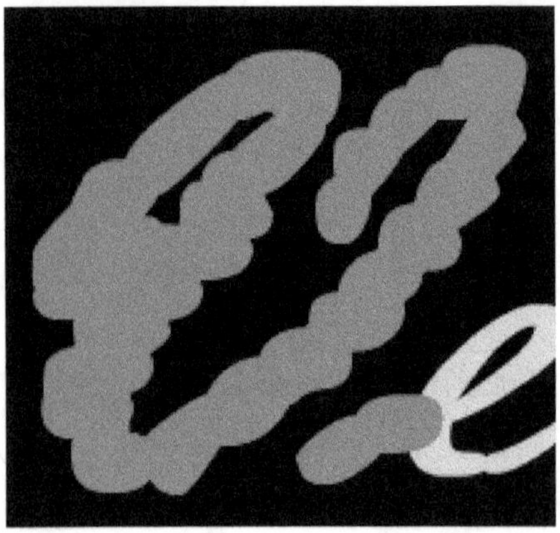

One rule to remember when doing the writing effect is to try and simulate how the name would be written out. For instance, in the letter **e** in the example, we should follow the path of the stroke as it swirls around:

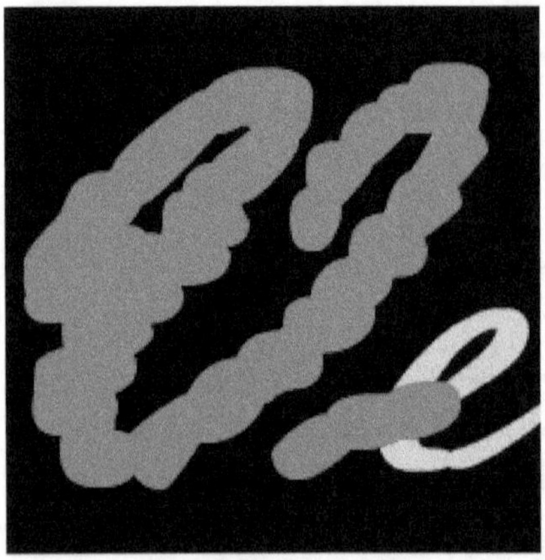

Keep following the stroke of the letter around the loop to create a natural stroke:

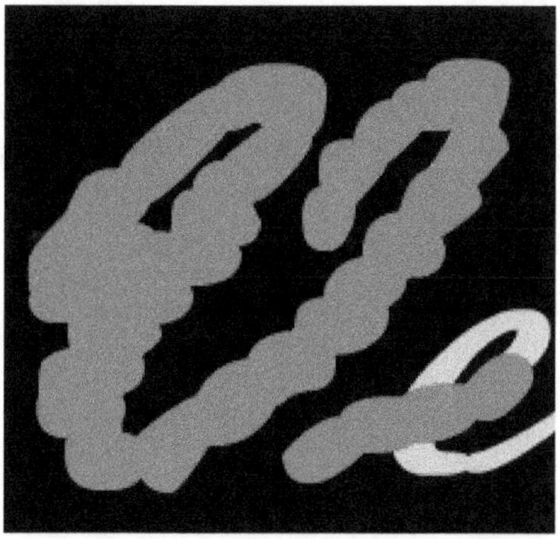

Don't worry if your mask looks a little messy. When we're finished the **Mask** layer will be invisible. Hit **F6** and keep painting:

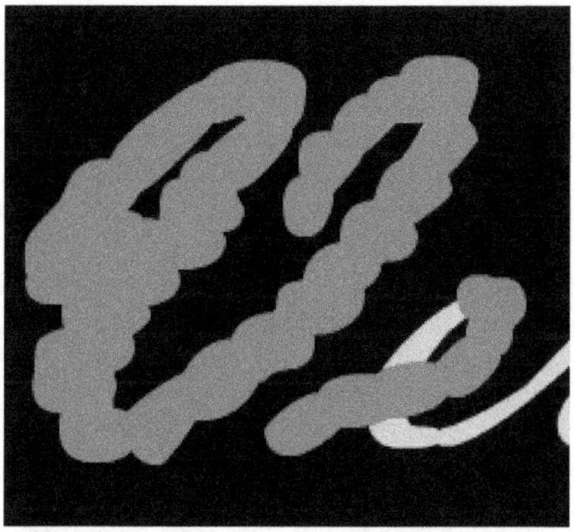

Keep creating keyframes and painting. When you get to the **i** in **Veronica** your mask should look similar to this:

The number of keyframes may be different from mine which is 59 at this point. You may have more or less but not a big deal. Keep painting until you finish the first name. Don't paint over the dot above the **i** just yet:

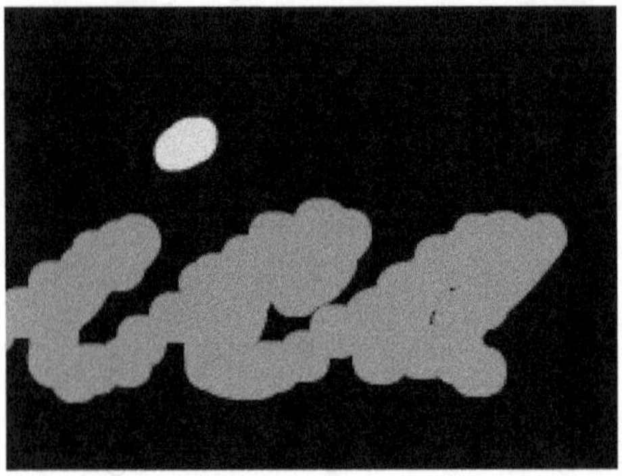

Most people dot their **i's** after they finish writing their entire name. After you finish the **a** in **Veronica** go ahead and paint over the dot in the **i:**

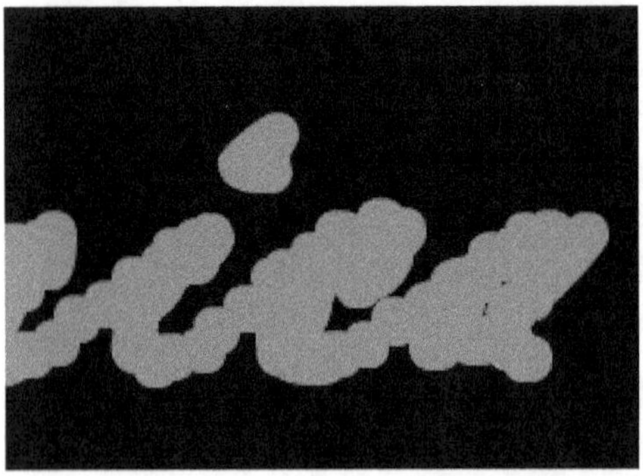

Whenever you create a writing effect try to figure out the most natural way for the letters to be revealed. For example, in the **A** letter of **Ashley** we want to reveal the line that goes through this letter last:

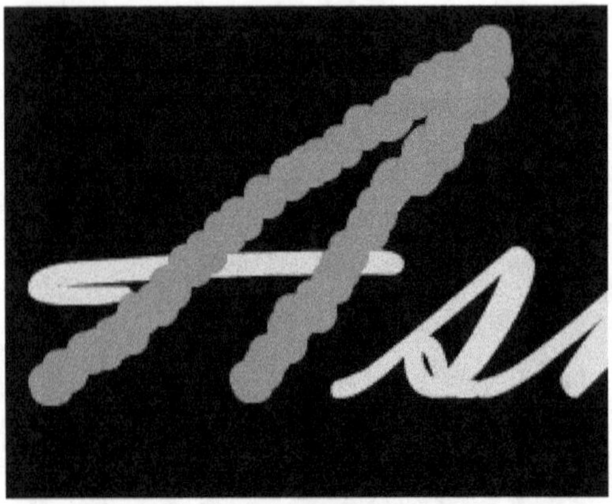

Also, remember that the more frames you take to create your final mask the more realistic the animation, but it will take more time to play out.

Keep painting and creating new keyframes. When you finish painting, the final mask should look something like this:

On my timeline the number of keyframes is 330. Yours may be higher or lower. Right-click on the **Mask** layer and select **Mask** from the drop-down list. Test your movie. Cool huh? That's all there is to it! You'll now have to insert a **stop** code in the final frame if you don't want the animation to loop. In the next exercise we'll be creating a different type of writing effect.

In this project that I created for a Pottery Studio, I had their company name write out but I also had a paintbrush float across the graphic as if it were painting the title. I also created a little fire animation for their logo using a Shape tween along with a few other bells and whistles. To see the completed header click on **Write_Target_Mask.swf** in the Flash Projects folder. I'll walk you through the steps to create this nice little header.

Open the file **Party_Header.fla**. You'll see a few of the images in the library. Select the **Header Background** and drag it over to the stage. Use the Align panel to center this image on the stage:

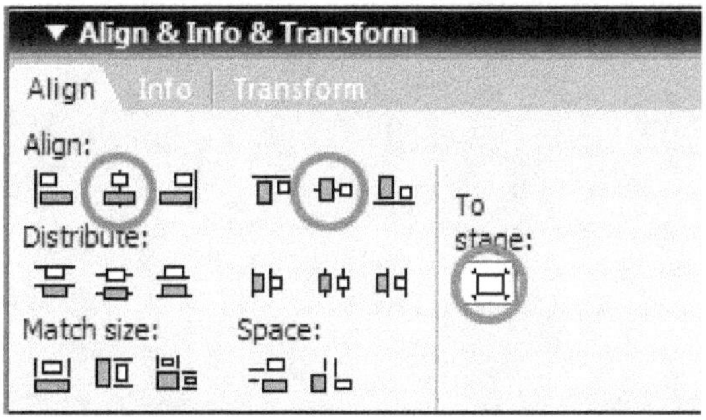

Since we won't be moving this background image anymore, we'll lock the layer. Create a new layer and name it **Kid**:

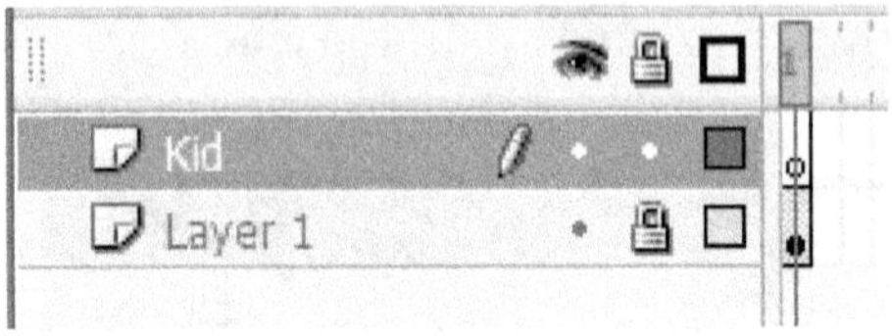

Drag the **Kid.png** file from the library. Position it in the window of the background similar to this:

We'll create a mask so we can bring back some of the flowers that have been covered up by the Kid image.

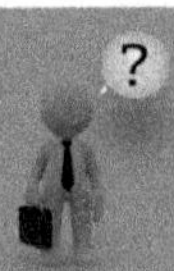

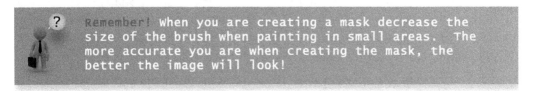

Remember! When you are creating a mask decrease the size of the brush when painting in small areas. The more accurate you are when creating the mask, the better the image will look!

Create a new layer and name it **Mask**. Grab the **Brush Tool**, select **red** for the **Fill color**, and select the fourth largest brush size:

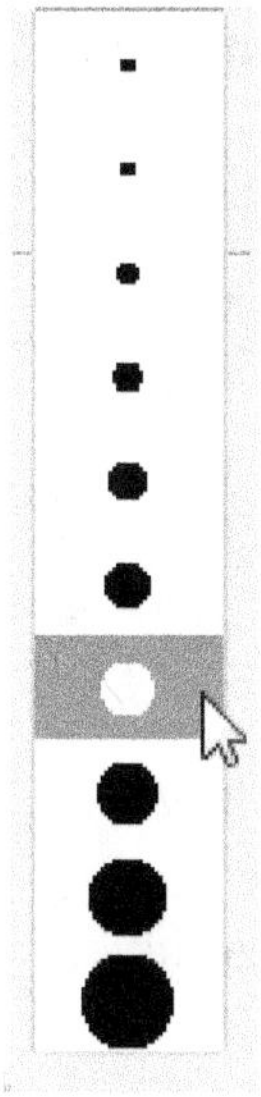

Paint a mask over the kid image. It doesn't have to be perfect just make sure the red paint covers the kid image. Stop when you get down to just above the flowers:

Zoom into the image 400%. Turn the visibility off for the **Kid** layer:

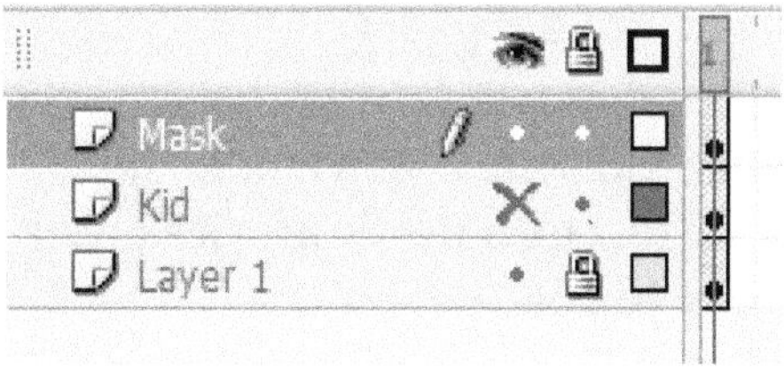

Continue painting the Mask. Paint in-between the flowers being careful not to paint over them:

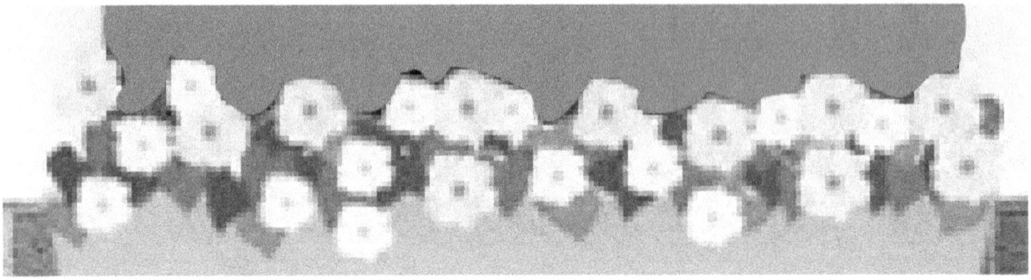

When you finish right-click on the **Mask** layer and select **Mask** from the drop-down list. Zoom back out to 100%. Turn the visibility back on for the **Kid** layer and he should now be nicely masked behind the flowers.

We'll be adding some animations to this timeline so let's add extra frames. Select frame **120** and add frames to all three layers.

We want the kid image to fade in from white. Turn the visibility off for the **Mask** layer and unlock the **Kid** Layer:

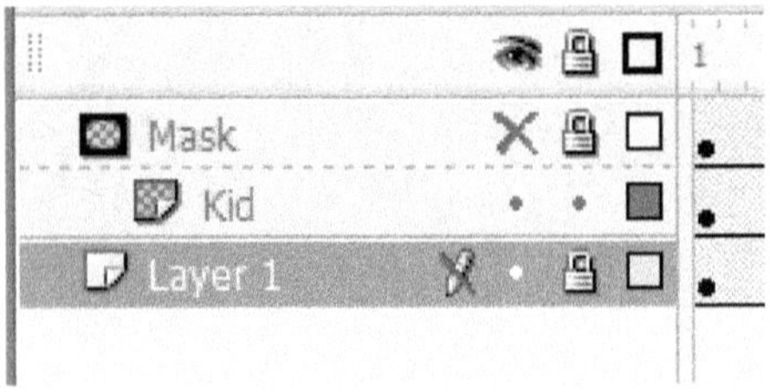

We don't want the kid symbol coming in right away. We'll have the symbol come in at 2 seconds. To do this select the keyframe of the **Kid** layer; now, select it again and drag it to frame **60**. Place another keyframe at frame **90**. Select any frame between these two keyframes and insert a Motion Tween:

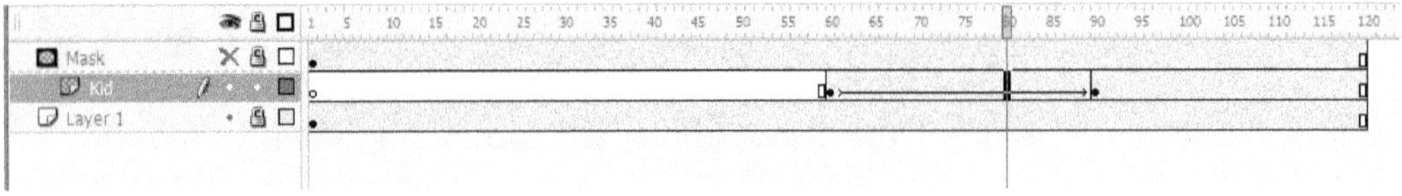

Select the keyframe on frame **60** and then select the kid symbol (switch to the **Selection Tool** before selecting symbols) on the stage. Open the Properties panel and change **Color** to **Brightness** and the percentage to **100**:

The kid symbol should now be bright white. It will fade from white to normal. We'll now add the paint splotches. Create four new layers above the **Mask** layer. Name them: **Blue Splotch**, **Red Splotch**, **Green Splotch**, and **Orange Splotch**:

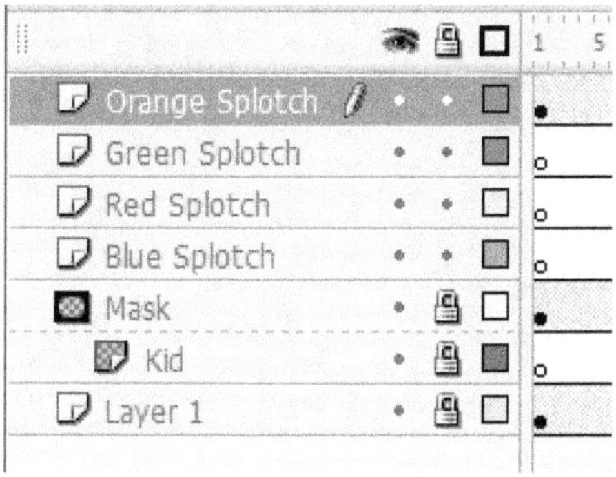

Select the **Orange Splotch** layer and drag **the orange_splotch.png** image from the library over to the stage. Put it at the bottom right of the window shutters:

Select the **Green Splotch** layer and drag the **green_splotch.png** file from the library. Place this splotch at the top right of the shutters:

Select the **Red Splotch** layer and drag the **red_splotch.png** file from the library. Place this splotch at the top left of the window shutters:

Finally, select the **Blue Splotch** layer and drag the **blue_splotch.png** file from the library. Place it at the bottom left of the window shutters:

Select this **Blue Splotch** and convert it to a Movie clip. Name it **Blue Splotch**. Double-click on this new Movie clip to enter its editing stage. Create a keyframe on frame **10** and insert a Motion Tween. Select the first frame then select the splotch image on the stage. Select the **Free Transform Tool** and enlarge the Splotch image:

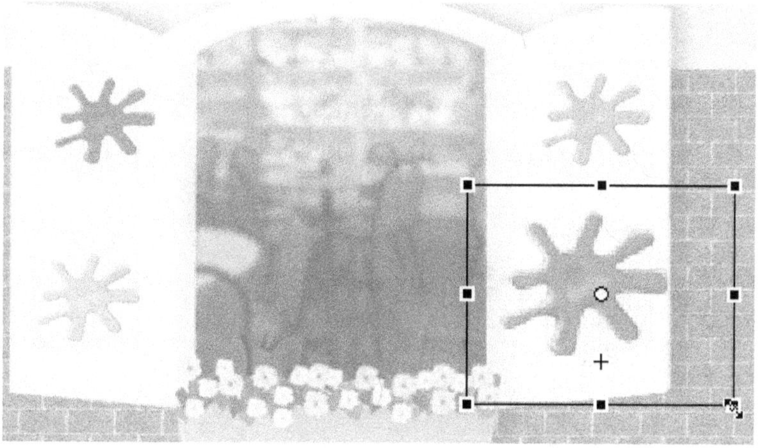

Select the first frame and open the Properties panel. Change **Ease** to **100**, **Rotate** to **CW** and **times** to **1**:

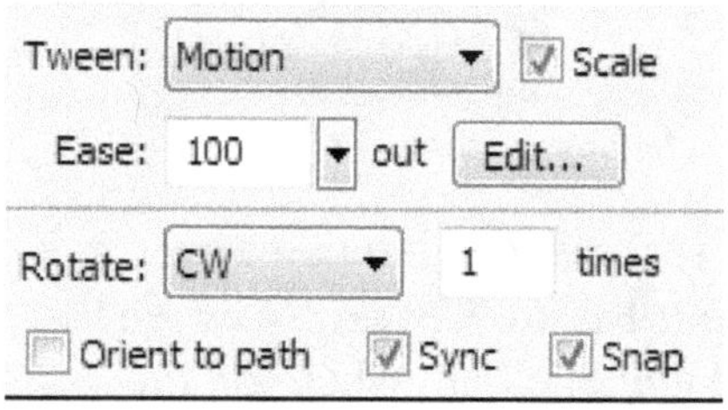

The Splotch will rotate once as it gets smaller. Since we don't want this animation to loop forever let's put a **stop** code on frame **10**. Create a new layer and name it **Actions**. Create a keyframe on frame **10** and insert a **stop** code. Now we're done with this splotch. Go back to Scene 1.

Repeat the previous steps for the rest of the splotches. Convert them all to Movie clips then add the animation. When you're done return to Scene 1. We don't want these splotches to appear until the Kid symbol appears. So click on the **Orange Splotch** keyframe; then, select it again and drag it to frame **60**. Drag the **Green Splotch** keyframe to frame **70**, **Red Splotch** keyframe to frame 80 and the **Blue Splotch** keyframe to frame **90**:

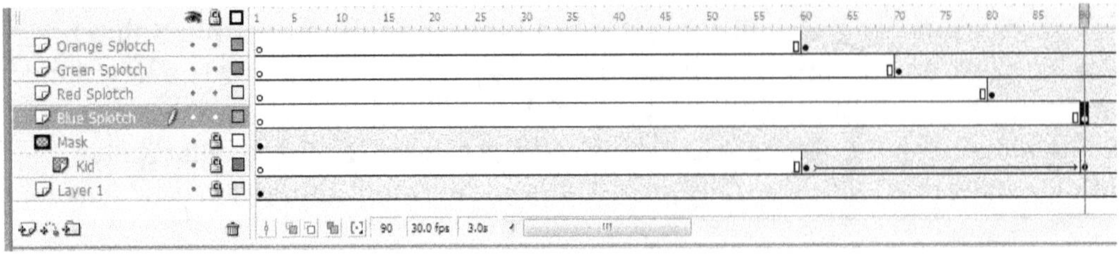

Now let's create the writing effect! Create a new layer and name it **Title**. Drag the image **Company Name** from the library to the stage. Position it above the wall and center it:

We're going to be animating the flame (above the **i**) so we need to paint over it. Create a new layer above the **Title** layer and name it **Flame Cover**. Now we'll paint over the flame. Select the **Eyedropper Tool** and click anywhere on the yellow of the background image:

The **Fill color** should automatically change to this yellow color. Select the **Brush Tool** and make sure that **Object Drawing** isn't selected:

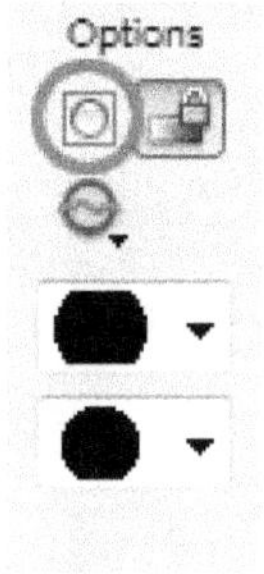

Zoom into the stage 400%, and paint over the flame:

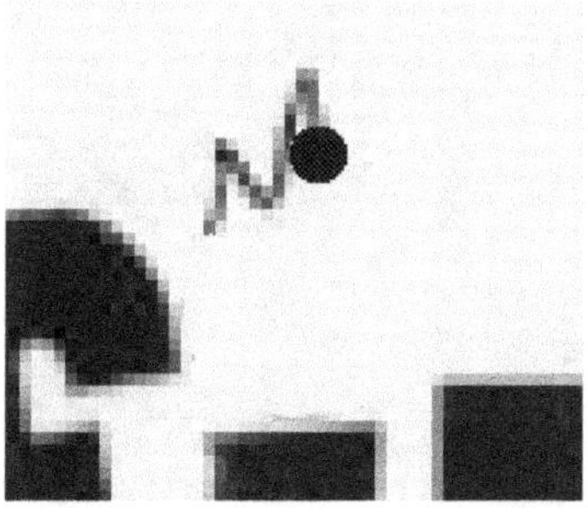

Once you finish, create a new layer above the **Title** layer. Name this layer **Mask** and then select the first frame of this layer. Make sure you're still zoomed in at 400%. Grab the **Brush Tool**, select **red** for the **Fill color**, and then select the large brush size:

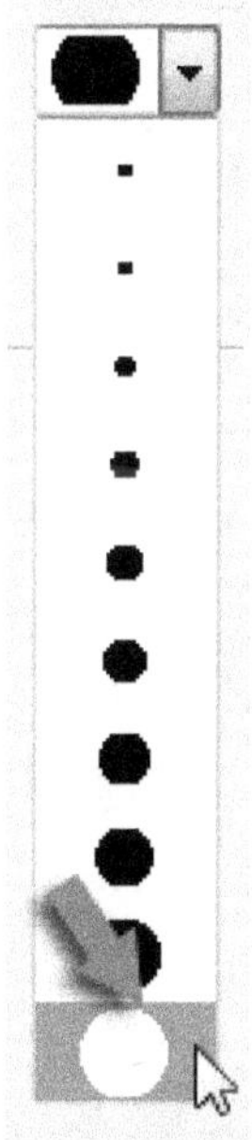

Just like we did in the previous exercise we're going to start painting the mask over the letters. Paint over a small part of the **B** letter in the title:

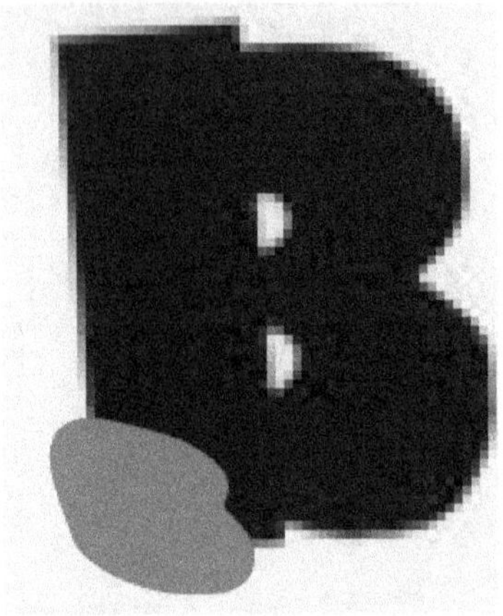

Go to **Insert**, **Timeline**, **Keyframe** (**F6**). Flash will create a keyframe on frame 2. Paint over more of the **B** letter:

Create a new keyframe and paint over more of the **B** letter:

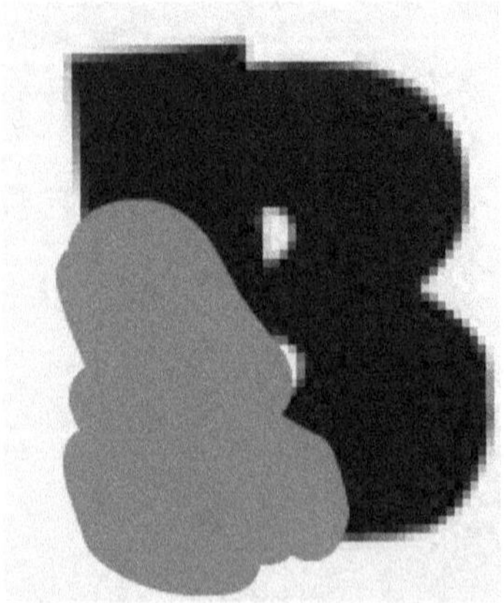

Create a new keyframe and paint over more of the **B** letter. Continue this pattern of painting over the **B** letter, creating a new keyframe, painting over more of the **B** letter, creating a new keyframe, and so on. Continue this until the **B** letter is completely painted over. The paint effect should take **20** keyframes for the **B** letter to be completely covered.

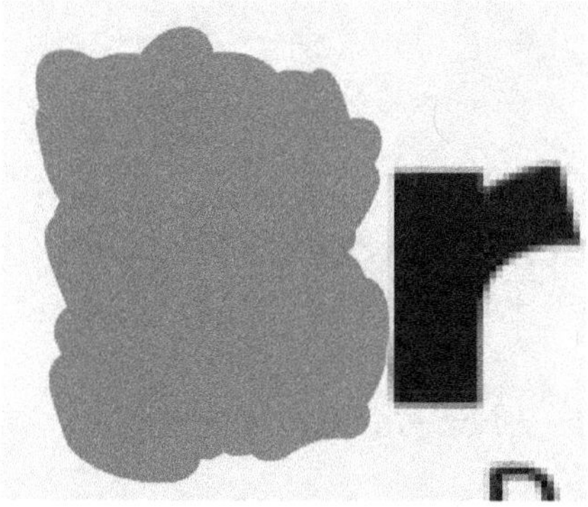

Create a new keyframe. Paint over part of the **r** letter:

Create a new keyframe and paint over more of the **r** letter:

So, as with the **B** letter, keep creating new keyframes and painting over more and more of the **r** letter. It should take about seven or eight keyframes to completely cover the **r**.

> **Remember!** The more keyframes you use when creating a writing effect, the more realistic the animation will be!

So you'll continue this pattern of painting, creating keyframes, painting, etc. until you have painted over all the letters. I usually keep one finger on the **F6** button; I'll paint a little over a letter then I'll press **F6**, paint some more, then hit **F6**, and so on.

It may take about 100 or more keyframes to finish. When you're done the mask should look similar to this:

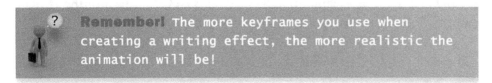

Right-click on the **Mask** layer and select **Mask**. You can test your movie. You'll see a nice little writing effect revealing the title. But now we need to add the paintbrush to finish the animation.

Create a new layer above the **Flame Cover** layer. Name this new layer **Paint Brush**. Drag the **brush.png** file from the library over to the stage. Position the brush over the small part of the **B** letter that is showing on frame **1**:

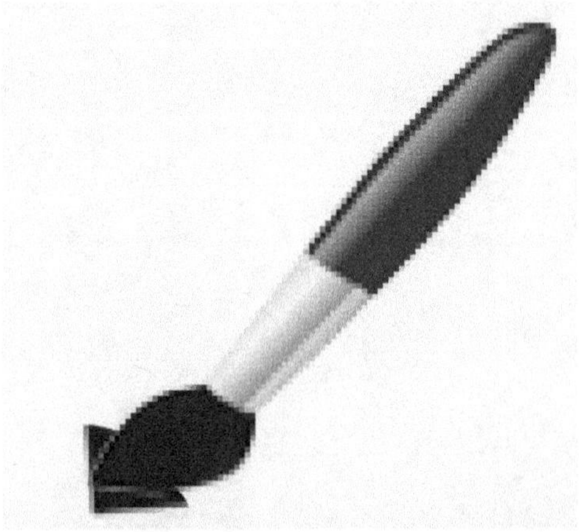

If the red paint is still visible on the **Mask** layer, lock the **Mask** and **Title** layers:

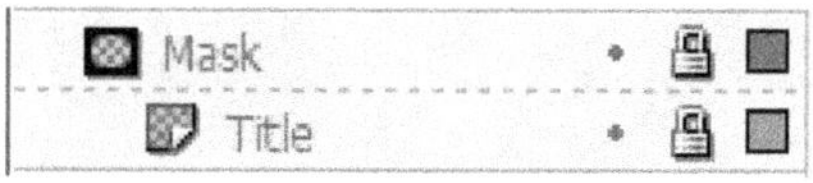

Also, lock **Layer 1** so we don't accidentally move the background image. Next, select the first frame of the **Paint Brush** layer and open the Properties panel. Change **Tween** to **Motion**:

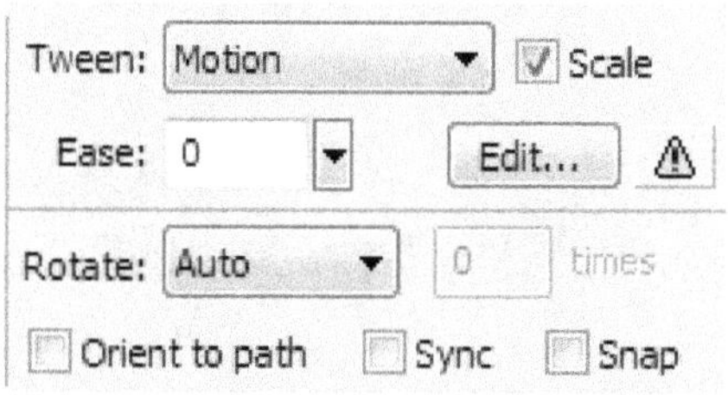

Insert a keyframe on frame **5** of the **Paint Brush** layer. Move the Brush symbol on the stage so that it follows the flow of the painting effect:

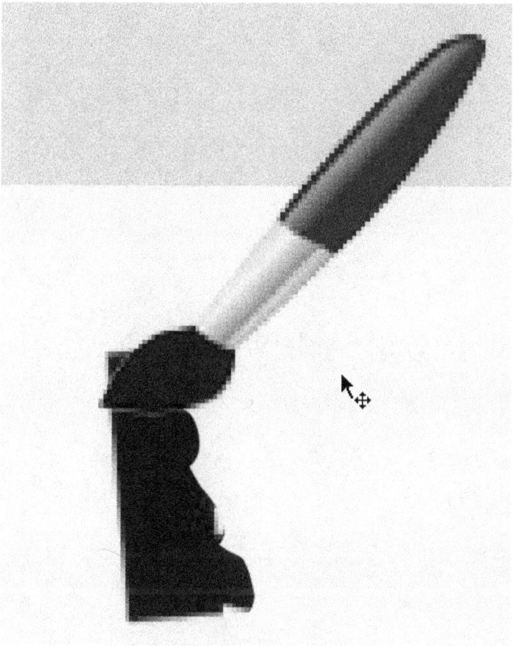

Create a keyframe on frame **10** and move the Brush symbol so that it continues to follow the flow of the paint effect:

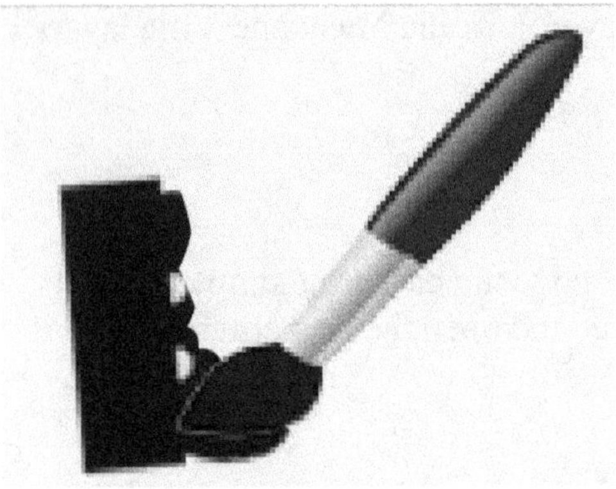

Create a keyframe on frame **15** and move the brush symbol on the stage so that it continues to follow the flow of the paint effect:

Finally, create a keyframe on frame **20** and move the brush symbol on the stage so that it follows the paint effect:

Find which frame on the timeline that the letter **r** first appears. On my timeline it's on frame **22**:

Create a keyframe on this frame. Move the brush symbol so that it covers this area:

Create a keyframe five frames from this keyframe, and once again move the brush symbol so that it follows the flow of the effect. Keep doing this until you finish the **r** letter.

Just as before, find out which frame the **u** letter first appears and create a keyframe on this frame. Move the brush symbol so that it covers this area. When moving the brush symbol across the letters you'll create a keyframe about every five frames. When a new letter begins just create a keyframe on that frame and move the brush appropriately. This will be the technique you'll use for the remainder of the letters.

When you're finished, test the movie. The brush should animate across the letters giving the impression that it's painting the letters. There may be a couple spots where the effect isn't synced up with the brush symbol. Find out what frame this happens on and move the brush. Keep tweaking the animation until everything is in sync.

Now, to finish this animation we'll create the flame above the **i** letter. Create a new layer and name it **Flame**. Place this new layer above the **Flame Cover** layer. Turn the visibility off for the **Flame Cover** layer and the **Mask** layer so you can see the logo flame:

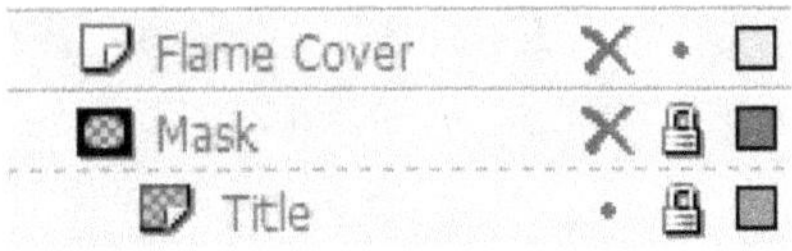

You should now see the flame from the logo:

Create a keyframe on frame **120** of the **Flame** layer. Select the **Pencil Tool**:

Open the Properties panel and select **black** for the **Color** and **1** for the **Size**:

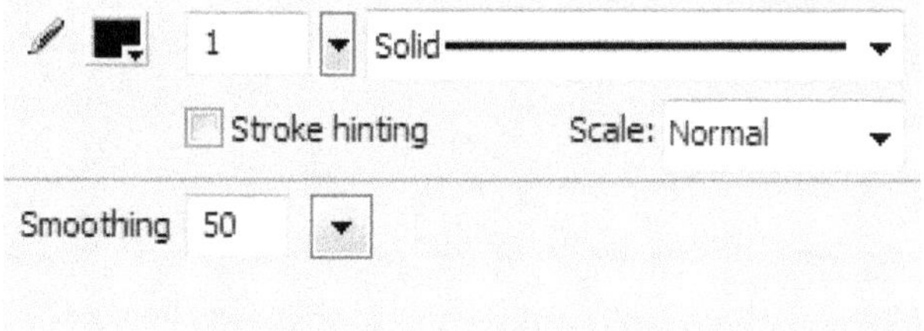

Trace the outside of the logo flame with the **Pencil Tool**:

We need to fill this with yellow. Select the **Paint Bucket Tool** and change the **Fill color** to **yellow**:

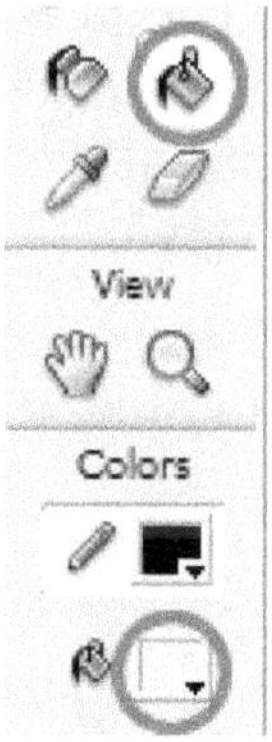

Next, click on the **Gap Size** button and select **Close Small Gaps**:

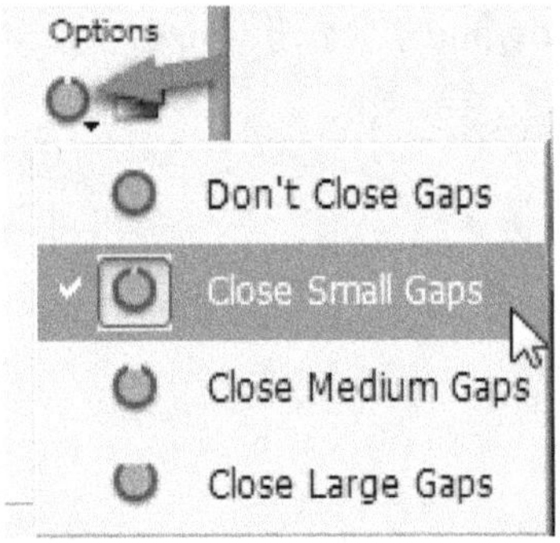

This will fill the pencil outline with yellow. Click anywhere inside the pencil outline:

The flame should now be filled with yellow. Grab the **Selection Tool** and double-click on this new shape. Make sure both the yellow fill and the pencil outline are highlighted. Convert this shape to a Movie clip (**Modify**, **Convert to Symbol**). Name it **Flame Movie**. When you're finished, double-click on this new Movie clip to enter its editing stage.

Select the first frame and open the Properties panel. Change the **Tween** to **Shape**:

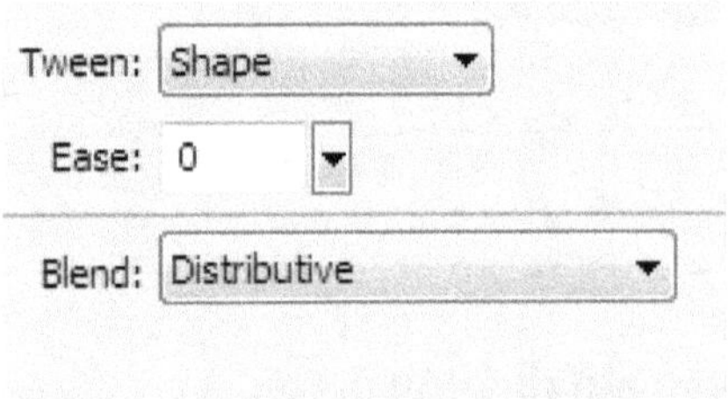

Create a keyframe on frame **15** and frame **30**:

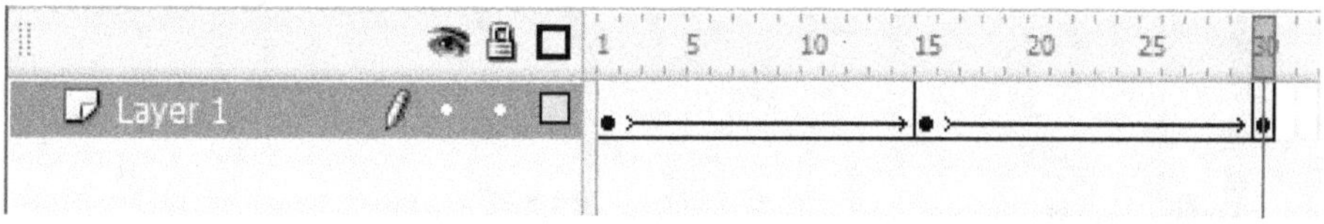

Click on frame **15** and click anywhere on the stage to deselect the flame shape. Put your cursor over the first point of the flame; you should see two little lines when it's directly over the point:

Pull down on this point

Next, pull down on all the points. When you're done the flame should look something like this:

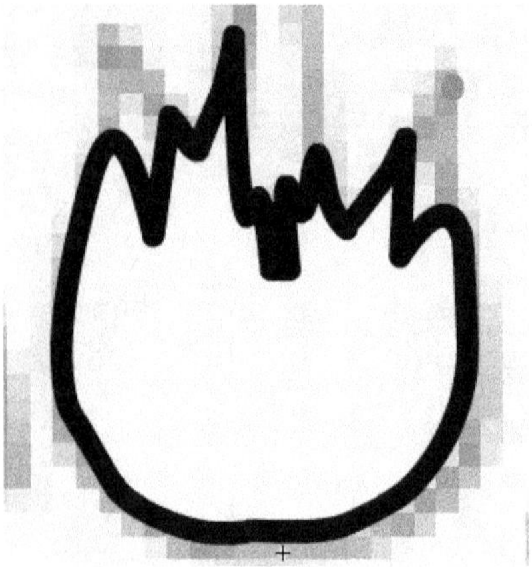

We need to create the internal flame. Create a new layer and name it **Flame Small**. Grab the **Pencil Tool** and open the Properties panel. Select **red** for the **Color** and the **Size** should be **1**:

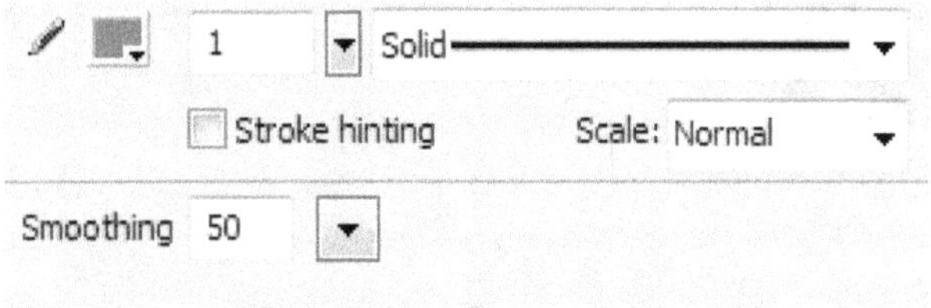

Draw a smaller flame within the larger flame:

Select the **Paint Bucket Tool**, change the **Fill color** to **red** and click inside the small flame. It should now be completely red:

Select the first frame of the **Small Flame** layer and change the **Tween** to **Shape**:

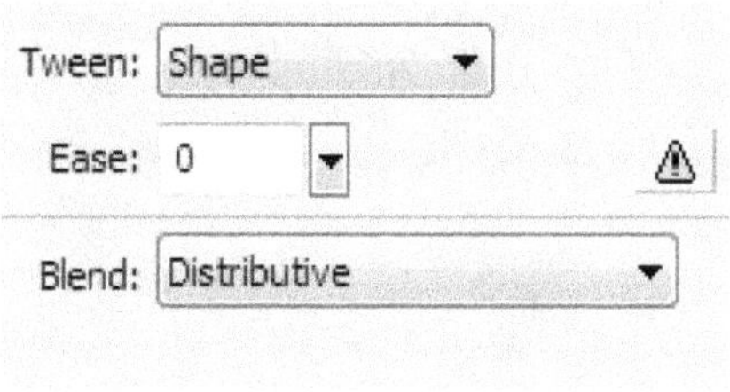

Create a keyframe on frame **15** and **30**. Select frame **15** then click anywhere on the stage to deselect the small flame shape. Grab each point of the flame and pull down:

Go back to Scene 1. Create a new layer and name it **Actions**. Create a keyframe on frame **120** and insert a **stop** code. Test your movie. You should now have a nice flame effect above the i letter.

Create a new layer and name it **Pottery Studio**. Create a new keyframe on frame **90** of this layer. Drag the image **studio.jpg** from the library over to the stage. Center it below the main title:

Let's have the Pottery Studio graphic fade in. Create a keyframe on frame **110** of the **Pottery Studio** layer. Select any frame between the two keyframes and insert a Motion Tween. Select frame **90** then select the pottery studio graphic on the stage. Open the Properties panel and change the **Color** to **Alpha** and the percentage to **0**. If you test your movie Pottery Studio should fade in nicely.

Let's add the balloons. Create a new layer and name it **Balloons**. Drag the **Balloon 1 graphic** and the **Balloon 2 graphic** from the library. Position them on the left side of the wall:

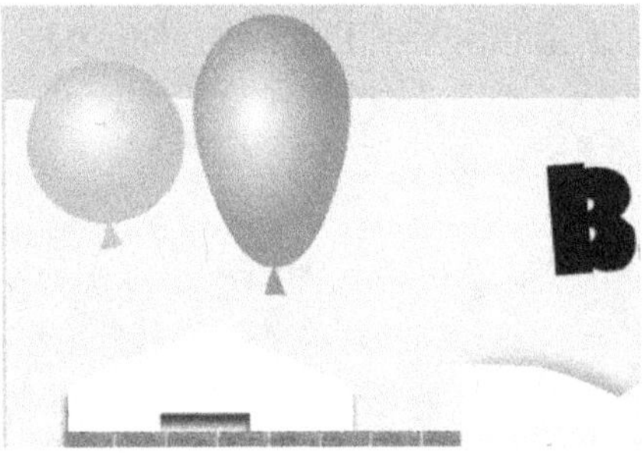

Select the green balloon and convert it to a Movie clip. Name it **Green Balloon.** Double-click this new Movie clip to enter its editing stage. Drag the balloon graphic so that it's below the top of the wall:

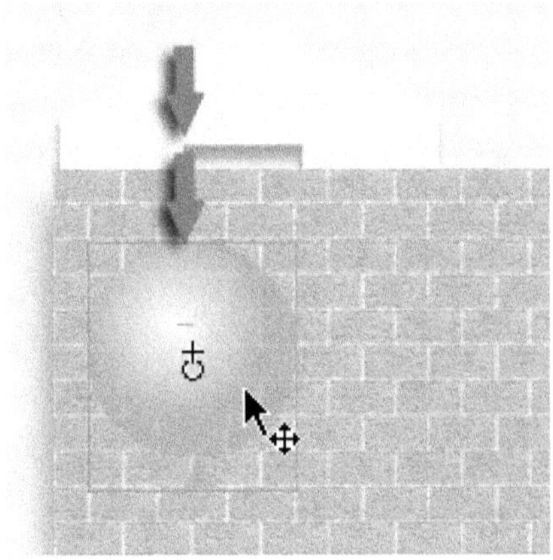

Next, click on the **Add Motion Guide** button (**CS4/CS5 -** right-click and select **Classic Motion Guide**):

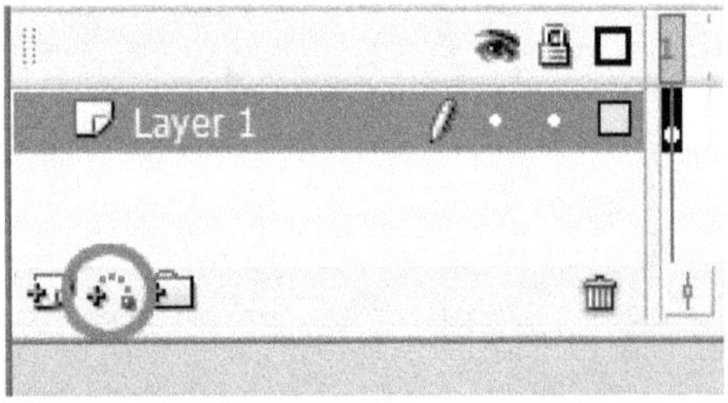

Click on the first frame of this new layer and select the **Pencil Tool**. Select **black** for the **Color** and the **Size** should be **1**. Draw a curvy line that goes from the green balloon to the top of the stage:

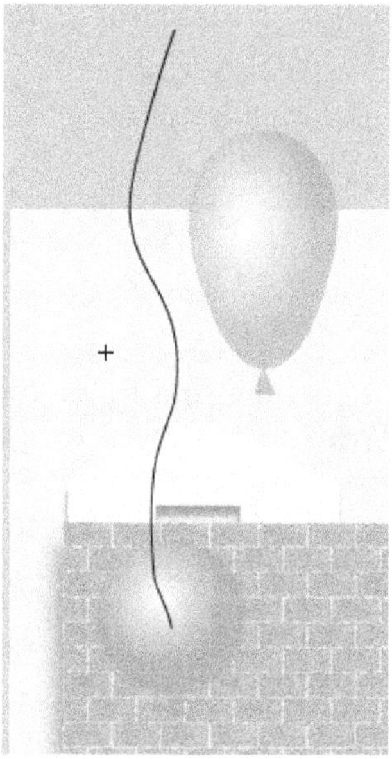

Go to frame **80** and insert a frame. On frame **80** of **Layer 1** insert a keyframe. Select any frame between the two keyframes and insert a Motion Tween. Select the first frame then select the balloon graphic on the stage. Position the anchor point (little circle) with the beginning of the line:

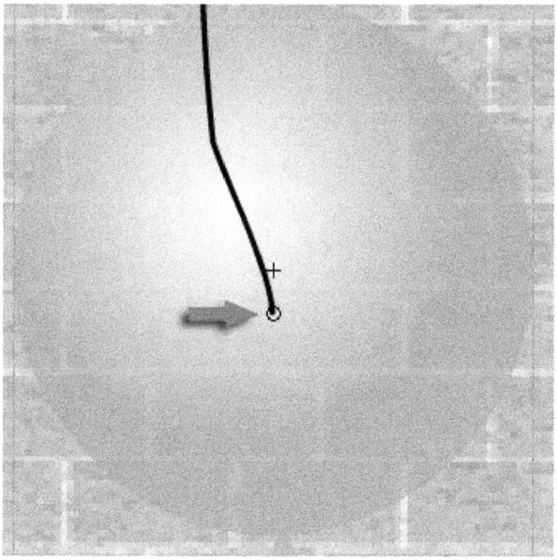

Click on frame **80** then select the balloon graphic on the stage. Position the anchor point with the end of the line:

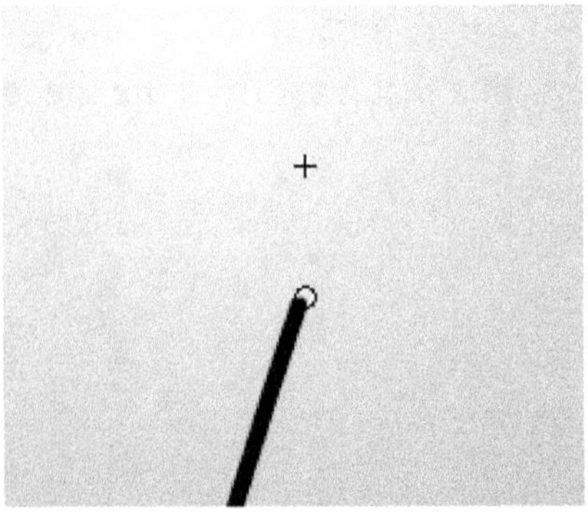

We want the balloon to sway a bit as it travels up the line. Select the first frame of **Layer 1**. Open the Properties panel and select **Orient to Path**:

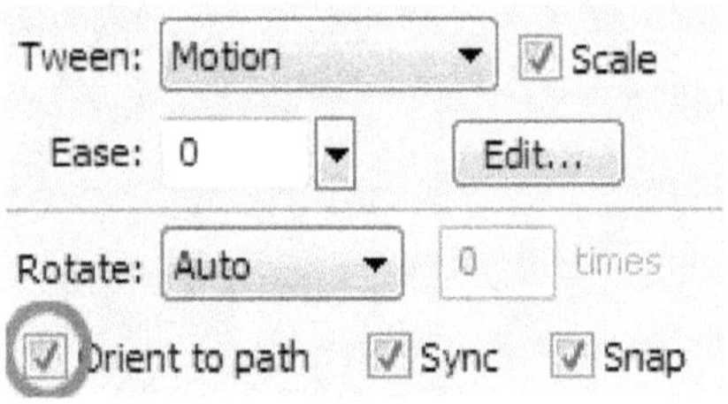

This causes the balloon to more realistically follow the line. Create a new layer and name it **Actions**. Create a keyframe on frame **80** and insert a **stop** code. You can test the movie to see the balloon's animation. Looks nice. But now we have to place it behind the wall. Go to Scene 1 and create a new layer above the **Balloons** layer; name this new layer **Balloon Mask**. Select the **Pen Tool**. Create your first point where the wall meets the shutter:

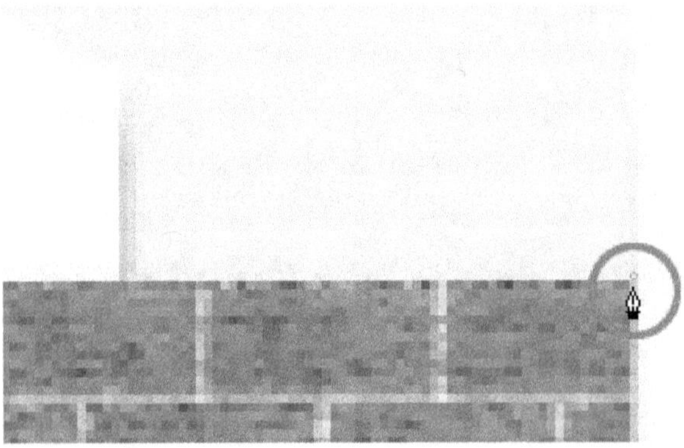

Add a point where the white roof meets the wall:

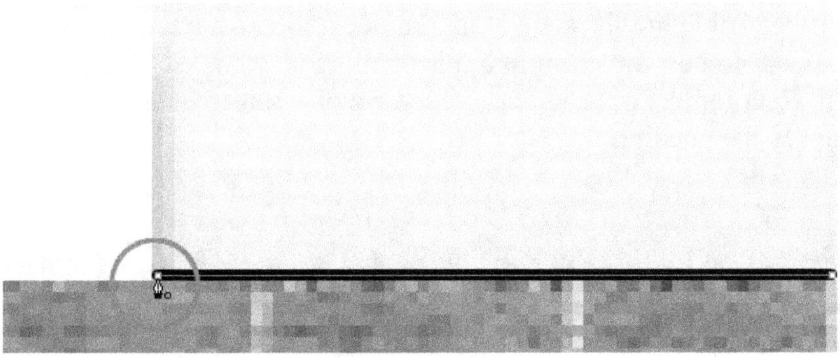

Create points around the top of the roof:

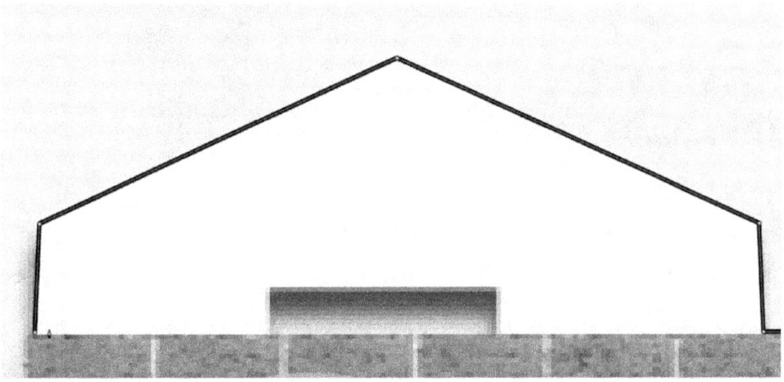

Next, create a point off the stage on the left. Create another point off stage at the top left. Create another point offstage above the shutters, then the final point will be at the same location as the first point. Your path should now look like this:

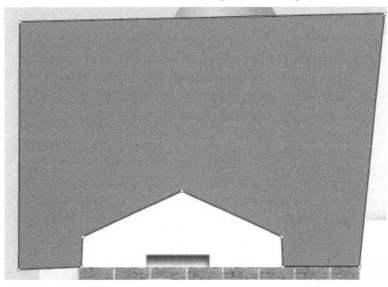

So the balloon will be visible in this area. You'll notice a there's a opening in the roof. The balloon needs to be visible through this opening so we need to add to the mask. Grab the **Rectangle Tool** and turn off the **Stroke color**. Create a shape about the same size as the opening:

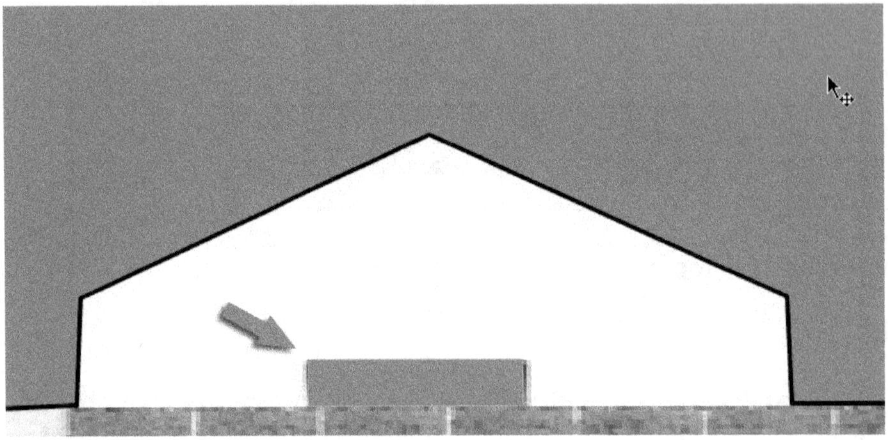

Right-click on the layer and select **Mask**. Test your movie. Your balloon should now appear is if it's coming up from behind the wall. Turn off the visibility of the **Balloons Mask** layer:

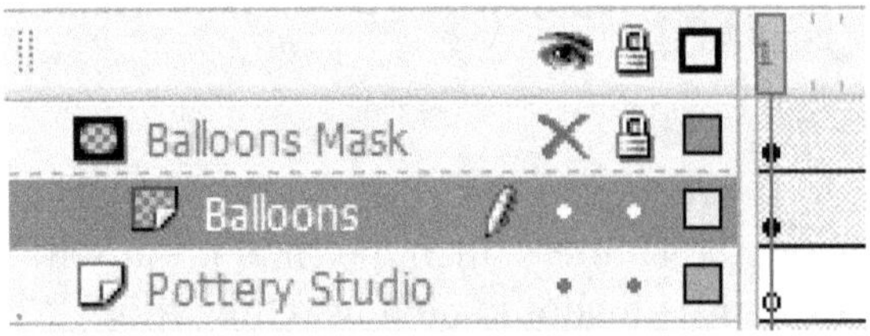

Select the **balloon 2 symbol**. Convert his symbol to a Movie clip and name it **Orange Balloon**. Just as we did with the first balloon we need to add a Motion Guide and create the animation similar to the first balloon. Try to be more creative with the Motion Guide line; maybe have it go more left to right (remember not to go too far right since the Mask ends at the shutters):

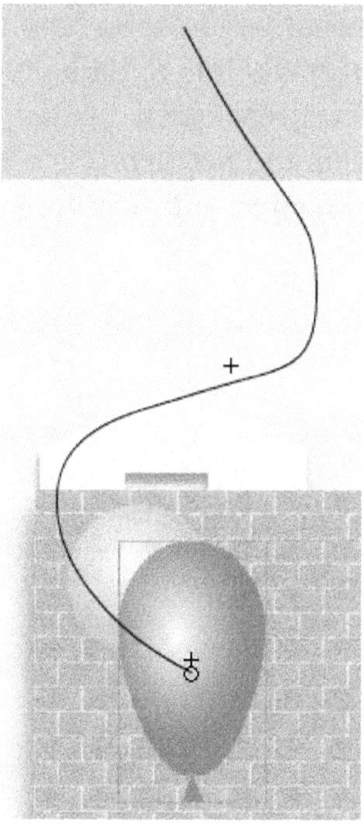

When you're done creating the balloon's animation, return to Scene 1. If you want to add more balloons you'll need to create a copy of one of the balloons. I'll quickly show the steps and how to make the new balloon a little different.

Select the Orange Balloon and go to **Edit**, **Copy**. Go to **Edit**, **Paste in Place**. Drag this Orange Balloon copy away from the original.

Open the Properties panel and select **Swap**. The **Swap Symbol** box will open; click on the **Duplicate Symbol** button and type **Yellow Balloon** in the **Symbol name** window:

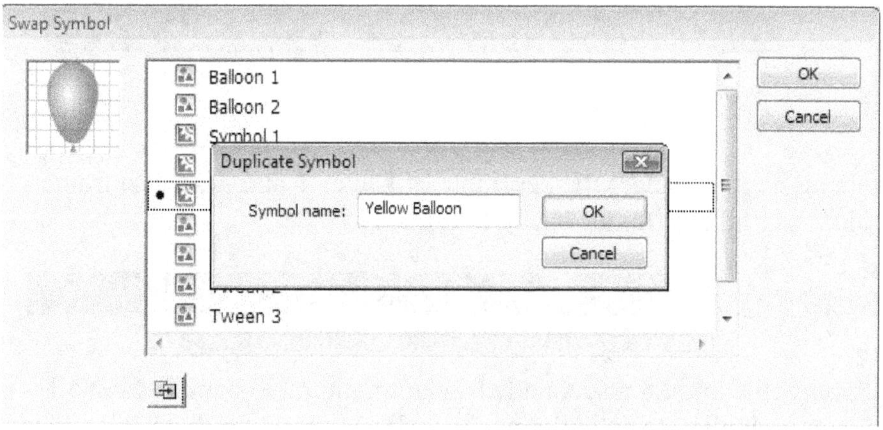

Hit **OK**. Double-click on this new symbol in the **Swap Symbol** window. So now your **Yellow Balloon** can be edited without affecting the original Orange Balloon. Let's change the color of this new balloon. With this balloon still selected, open the Properties panel. Change **Color** to **Advanced** and click on the **Settings...** button. In the settings window type **18%** for **Blue**, **81** for **Green +**, and **-255** for **Blue +**:

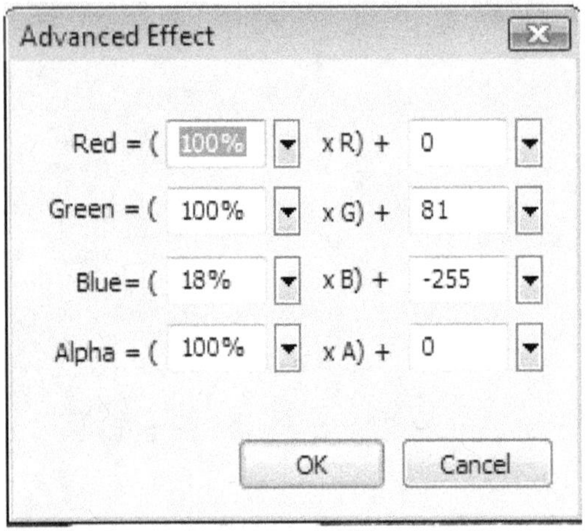

Hit **OK** when you're finished. Select the **Free Transform Tool** and slightly alter the shape. Make it a little smaller.

Double-click on this new Movie clip to enter its editing stage. Click on the first keyframe of the **Motion Guide** layer and delete the line path. Grab the **Pencil Tool** and create a new path. You can get as creative as you like. When you're done remember to align the balloon image to the beginning and end of the path. When you're done select both layers so they are both highlighted:

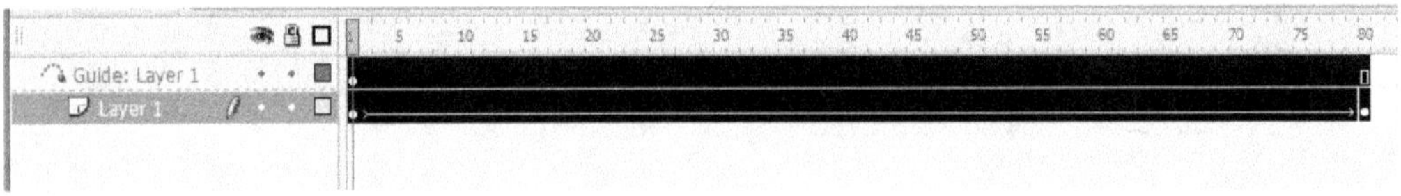

With the layers highlighted select the keyframe of **Layer 1** and drag it to frame **15**. This should move all the frames back 15 frames:

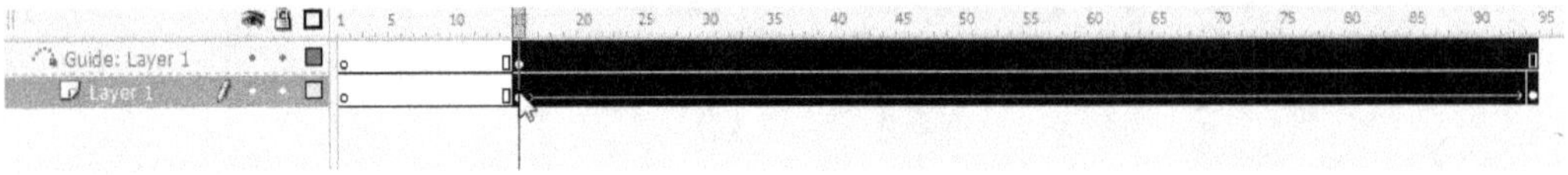

Now this balloon will wait half a second before animating. Go back to Scene 1. You can continue to duplicate the balloons if you like, changing their color, size and animation path.

So now to wrap up the header we just need to add ActionScript that loads in the **specials.swf** file. Create a new layer and name it **Target**. Create a keyframe on frame **120** of this layer. Grab the **Rectangle Tool**, turn off **Stroke color** and change the **Fill color** to **red**. Draw a shape off stage, at the top left:

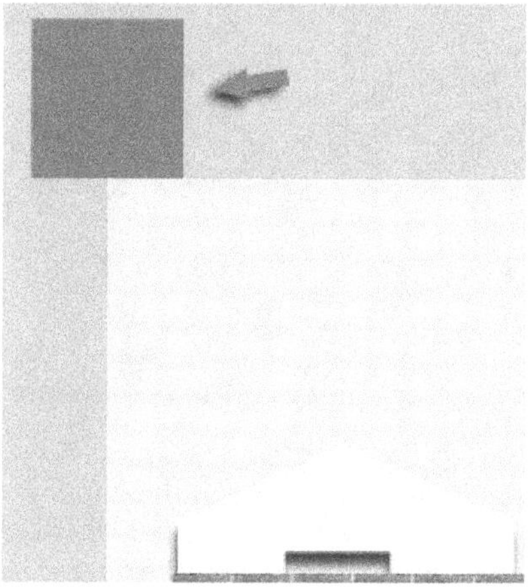

Select this new shape. Click on the **Fill color** button and take the **Alpha** down to **0**. Convert this shape to a Movie clip and name it **Target**. Next, with this Movie clip still selected, open the Properties panel and type **target** in the **Instance Name** window:

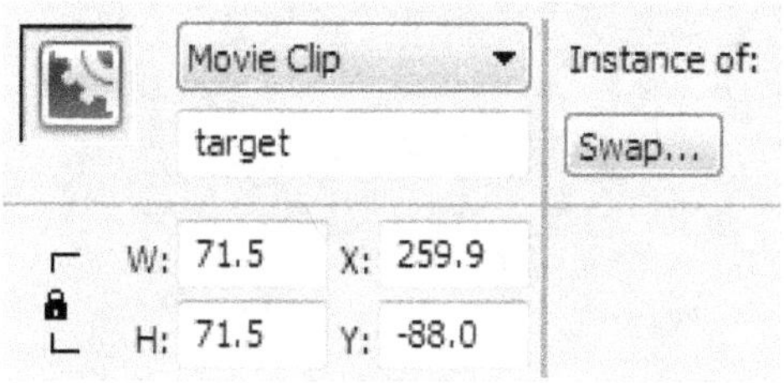

Create a new layer and name it **Actions**. On frame **120** of this layer create a keyframe. Open the Actions panel and turn on Script Assist. Go to **Global Functions**, **Browser/Network**, and double-click **loadMovie**. You should now see the **loadMovie** settings window. In the **URL** window type **specials.swf**. Change **Location** to **Target** and type **/target** in the **Location** window:

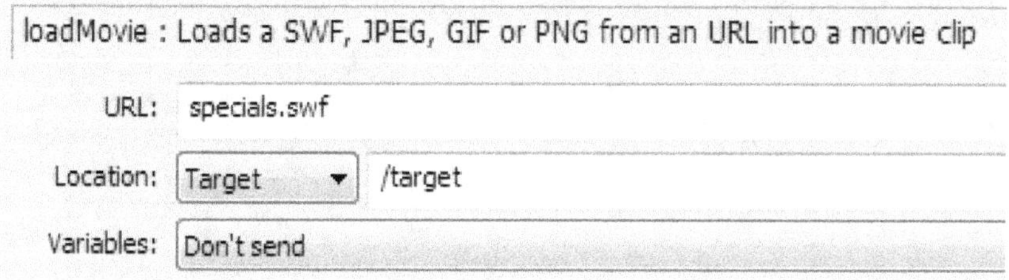

Next, we just need to add the **stop** code. Go to **Global Functions**, **Timeline Control** and double-click **stop**. Test your movie. When the movie gets to frame **120** it should load in the boy and girl. This file already has a mask on it and is designed to load in-between the roof and the shutter on the right:

If they're not positioned correctly, move the **Target** Movie clip slightly on the stage and keep testing your movie until you get it exactly right.

Congratulations on creating your first Flash header! In the next exercise I'll teach how to create a animated preloader.

Have you ever seen those animated preloaders that tell you what percentage of the website has been loaded? Normally you would have to write ActionScript to create your own percentage loader but I'll show a way you can do it without writing one line of code. Double-click the file called **Animated_Loader.swf** in the Flash Projects folder. You'll see a glass slipper fill with a blue color as the slideshow loads up. When the glass slipper is done filling with the blue color it fades away and the slideshow begins playing. Open the file called **Animated_Loader.fla** in the Flash Projects folder. You'll see five layers:

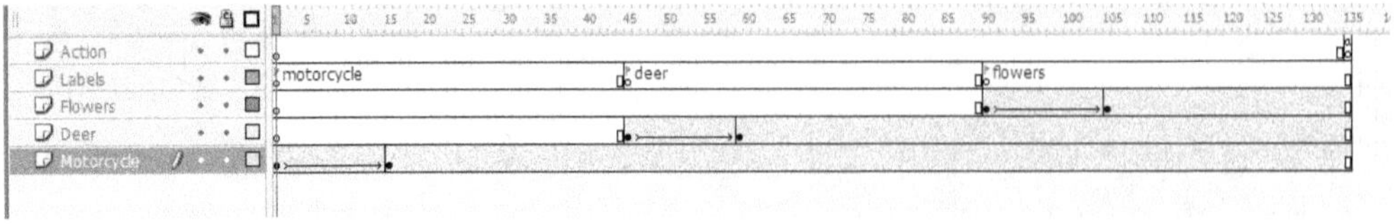

This is a simple slideshow with each picture fading in. The **Actions** layer has a simple **stop** code on frame **135** which stops the slideshow. Let's make the preloader. Open the Scene panel. If it's not visible go to **Windows**, **Other panels**, **Scenes**. Click the **Add scene** button and name the new scene **Preloader**:

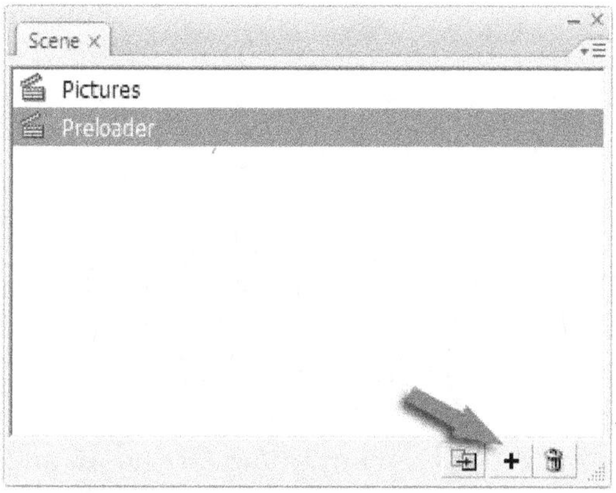

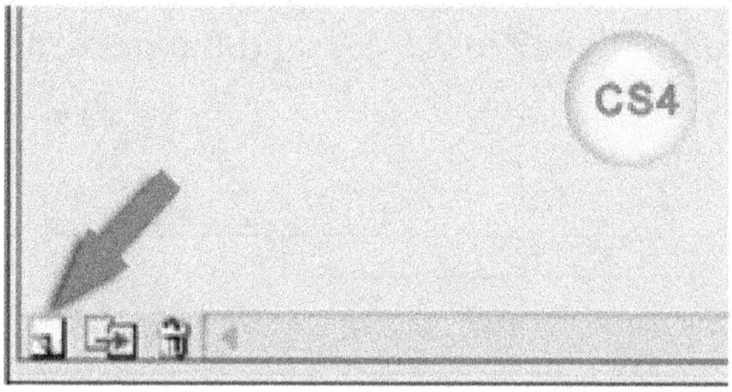

Move the Preloader scene so it's above the Pictures scene:

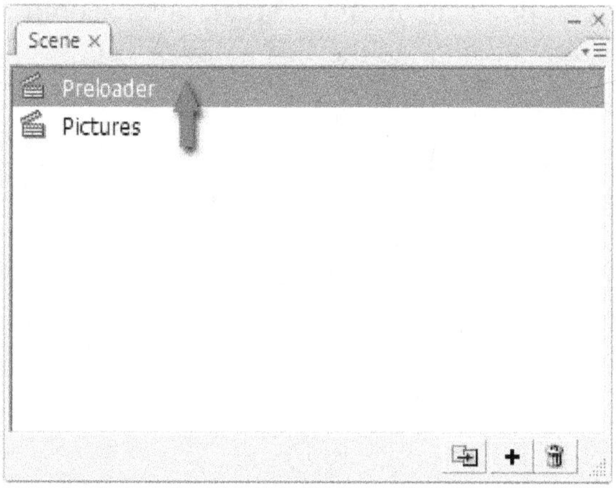

The first scene that will now load in, will be the Preloader scene. Let's begin creating the loader animation. Rename **Layer 1: White Slipper**. Select the keyframe of this layer and drag the image **loaderpic1.jpg** from the library over to the stage. Use your **Align** panel to center it in the stage:

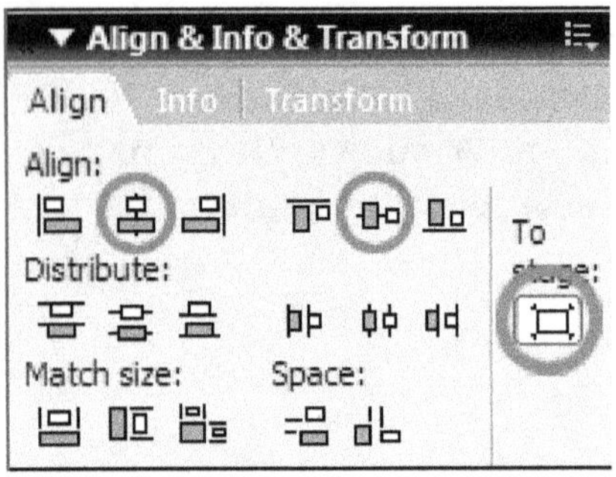

Next, insert a frame on frame **60** of this layer. Create a new layer and name it **Blue Slipper**. Create a keyframe on frame **3** of this layer. Drag the image **loaderpic2.jpg** from the library over to the stage. Use the **Align** panel to center this image on the stage. Create a keyframe on frame **60** of this layer. Create another keyframe on frame **80**. Select any frame between keyframe **60** and **80** and insert a Motion Tween. Select keyframe **80** and select the slipper image on the stage. Open the Properties panel and change **Color** to **Alpha**, and the **percentage** to **0**. Your timeline should now look like this:

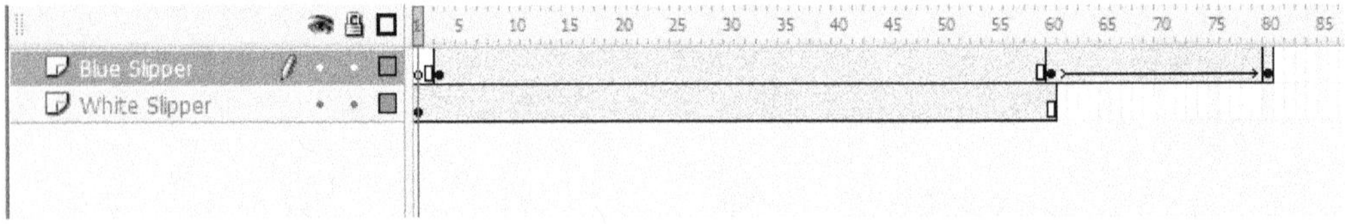

Go ahead and lock these two layers since we're done with them. Create a new layer and name it **Mask**. Create a keyframe on frame **3** of the **Mask** layer. Zoom into the stage 200%. Select the **Brush Tool** and change the **Fill color** to **red**. Select the **Round Brush Shape** and the largest Brush Size:

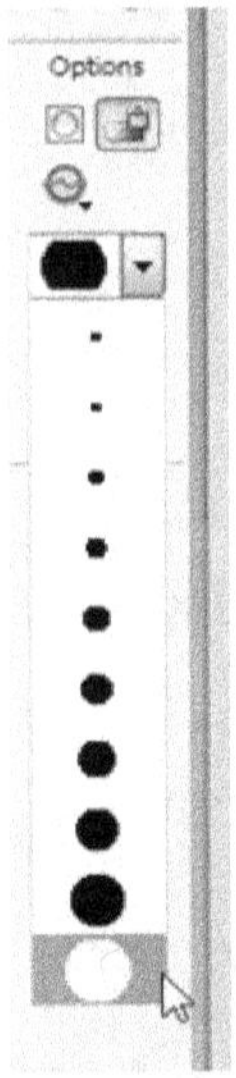

Now we're going to gradually paint a mask over the Blue Slipper. Paint over the very tip of the slipper:

Create a new keyframe (**F6**) and paint over a little more of the slipper:

Create another keyframe and paint over a little more of the slipper. By frame **20** about half of the slipper should be painted:

Skip frame 21 and create a keyframe on frame **22**. Begin painting over the slipper again. Keep painting and creating keyframes. By frame **40** you should be to this point:

Skip frame 41 and create a keyframe on frame **42**. Continue painting and adding keyframes. Always remember to add keyframes after every brush stroke, otherwise you'll just be adding onto your last paint shape. By frame **60** you should be finished painting over the slipper:

Right-click on the **Mask** layer and select **Mask** from the drop-down list. Move the timeline needle across the timeline so you can see your animation. The slipper should fade away at the end of the animation.

Create a new layer and name it **Actions**. Select the first frame and open the Actions panel. Make sure Script Assist is turned on. So now we're going to create ActionScript to see if the Motorcycle picture is loaded (the first picture of the slideshow). In the Actions panel go to **Deprecated**, **Actions**, and double-click **ifFrameLoaded**:

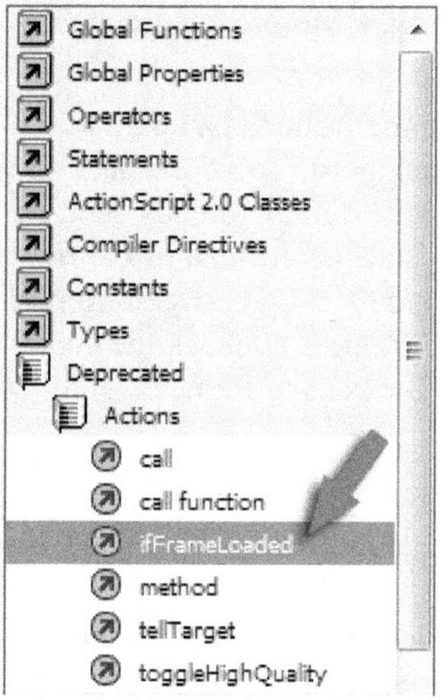

You should now be in the **ifFrameLoaded** settings window. Change the **Scene** to **Pictures**, the **Type** to **Frame Number**, and the **Frame** to **1**:

Next, go to **Global Functions**, **Timeline Control**, and double-click **goto**. In the **goto** settings window change the Frame to **3**:

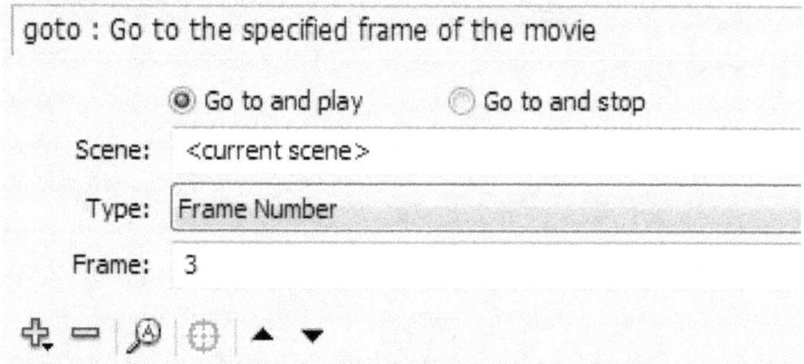

Now if the Motorcycle image is loaded, the Preloader timeline will go to frame **3** and start playing. But what if the Motorcycle image isn't loaded? We don't want the Mask animation playing until the Motorcycle image has fully loaded. So we need to create a code on frame **2** of the **Actions** layer that sends the timeline back to frame **1** to repeat the command of checking whether the Motorcycle image has loaded.

Create a keyframe on frame **2** of the **Actions** layer. In the Actions panel go to **Global Functions**, **Timeline Control**, and double-click **goto**. You don't need to change any settings in the **goto** settings window since the default already sends it back to frame **1**. Notice that we want **Go to and play** selected instead of **Go to and stop**. The reason is that we want to create a continuous loop between frame **1** and **2**. Frame **2** will keep sending the timeline back to frame **1** to check the code. Once the Motorcycle image has loaded then the timeline goes to frame **3** bypassing the **goto** code on frame **2**.

If we had selected **Go to and stop** then there would be no loop. The timeline would go to frame **1**, check the code, then stop without continuing back to frame **2**.

We need to create a keyframe on frame **20** of the **Actions** layer. We're going to create another code, but this time we want it to check whether or not the Deer image has loaded (the second image in the slideshow). In the **Actions** panel go to **Deprecated**, **Actions** and double-click **ifFrameLoaded**. In the **ifFrameLoaded** settings window change the **Scene** to **Pictures**, the **Type** to **Frame Number**, and the **Frame** to **45**:

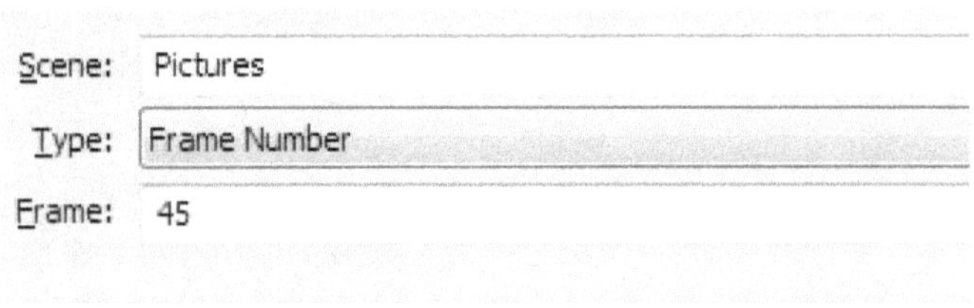

Next, go to **Global Functions**, **Timeline Control** and double-click **goto**. In the **goto** settings window change the Frame to **22**:

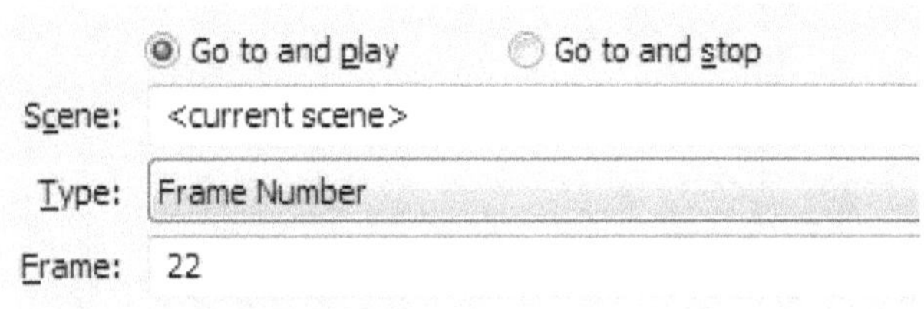

If the Deer image is loaded the Preloader timeline will go to frame **22** and play. Just as with the first frame we need to create a continuous loop to keep checking this code. So create a keyframe on frame **21** of the **Actions** layer. Select this keyframe and go to **Global Functions**, **Timeline Control** and double-click **goto**. In the **goto** settings window change the Frame to **20**:

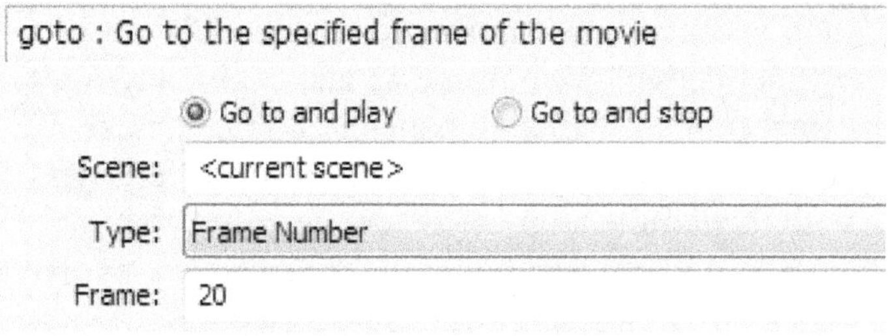

So now if the Deer image isn't loaded the timeline will continue to frame **21** where it will read this code sending it back to frame **20** to check the **ifFrameLoaded** code again.

We need to create the final ActionScript to see if the Flowers image has loaded. Create a keyframe on frame **40** of the **Actions** layer. In the Actions panel go to **Deprecated**, **Actions**, and double-click **ifFrameLoaded**. In the **ifFrameLoaded** settings window change the **Scene** to **Pictures**, the **Type** to **Frame Number**, and the **Frame** to **90**:

Next, go to **Global Functions**, **Timeline Control**, and double-click **goto**. In the **goto** settings window change the **Frame** to **42**:

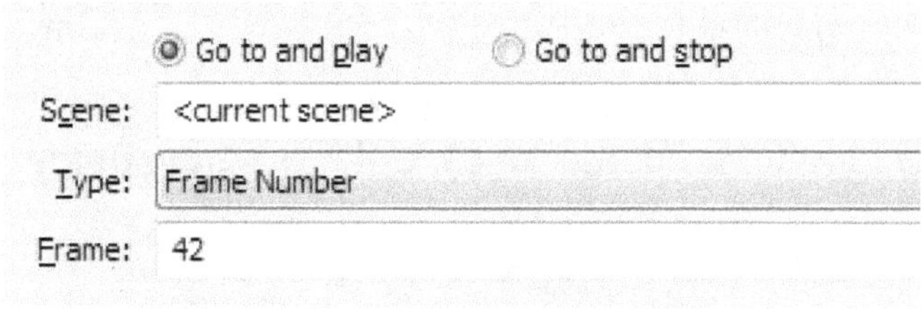

On frame **41** of the **Actions** layer create a keyframe. In the **Action**s panel go to **Global Functions**, **Timeline Control**, and double-click **goto**. In the **goto** settings window change the **Frame** to **40**:

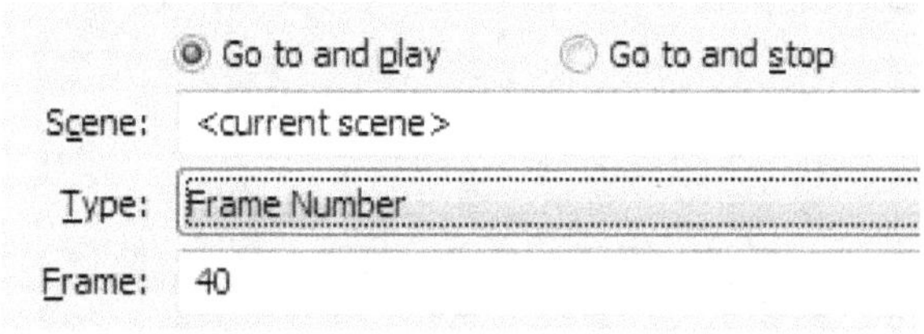

Now we have the continuous loop between both frames. So once the Flowers image is loaded, the **Preloader** timeline will go to frame **42** and begin playing. When the timeline reaches the final frame it will automatically go to the next scene which is the Pictures scene. It's important to learn exactly how Preloaders work since you'll be working with them quite a bit as you create your Flash projects. You can be as creative as you like once you learn the principles involved in creating a preloader.

In the next section we'll be creating some really nice scrolling text files. These come in handy when you're limited on space.

One problem you may run into when working in Flash is text that exceeds the allotted space. That's where a scroller comes in handy. You've probably seen these little scrollers in your favorite websites. In this project we'll create scroll buttons for text, a horizontal scroll box, and a scrolling Text box that has text buttons embedded in it. So let's get started! Open the file called **Scroll.fla** in the Flash Projects folder.

You'll see the picture of flowers on the stage. Now we need to add the text we'll be using in the scroller. In the Flash Projects folder you'll see a text file called **Scroll.txt**. Open that file and copy the text.

Create a new layer and name it **Text**. Next, select the **Text Tool**. Open the Properties panel and change the **Font** to **Arial**, **Size** to **13**, **Color** is **white**, **Bold**, and **Line Space** to **2**:

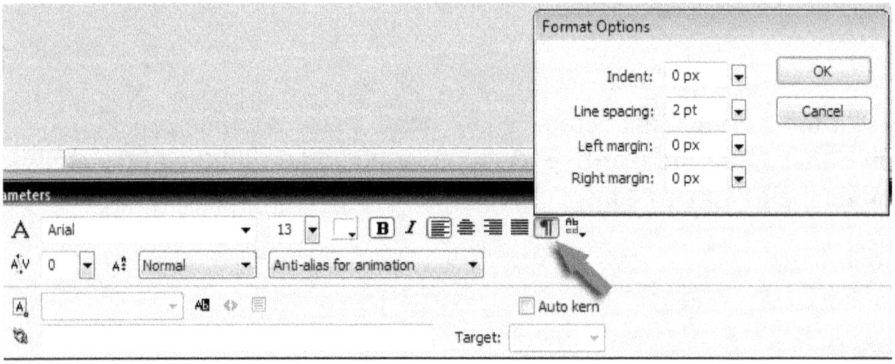

Click-and-drag across the right side of the picture like this:

When you click-and-drag with the **Text Tool**, it creates a defined width for the text. We need to add the text. Go to **Edit**, **Paste**. The text you copied from the Scroll.txt file should now be inside the text area:

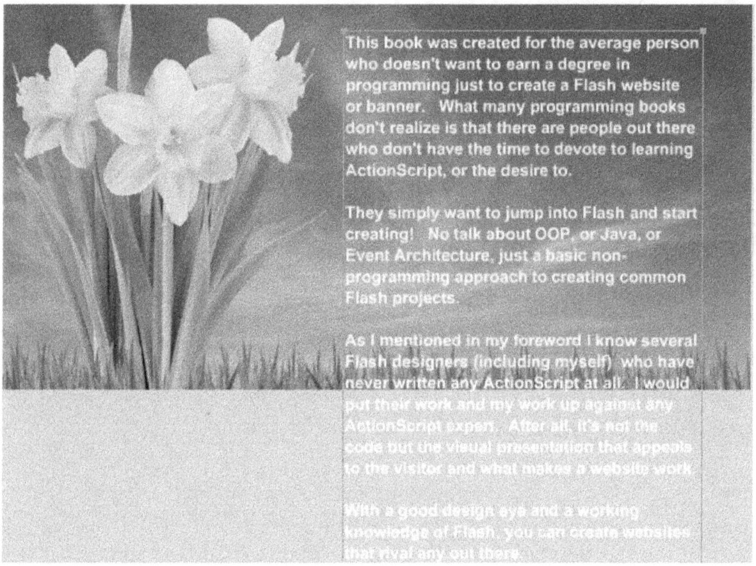

Go to **Modify**, **Convert to Symbol**. Change the **Type** to **Movie clip** and name it **Text**:

Hit **OK**. In the Properties panel give this Movie clip an **Instance Name** of **text**:

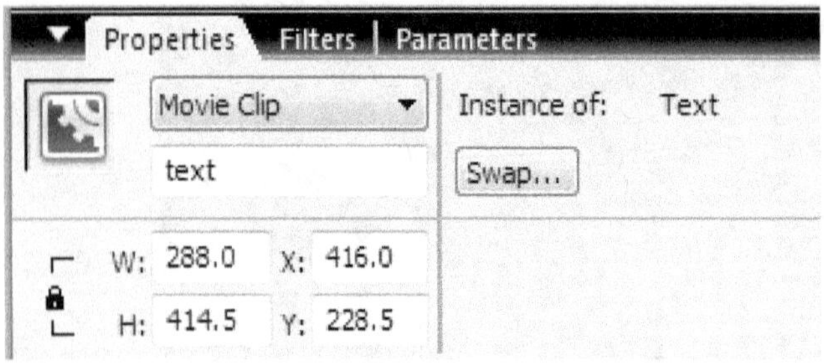

We'll next add the Mask to the **Text** layer. Create a new layer and name it **Mask**. Grab the **Rectangle Tool**, turn off the **Stroke color**, change the **Fill color** to **red**, and create a Mask shape over the text; this will be the area that will be visible when we see the text:

Right-click on the layer and choose **Mask**:

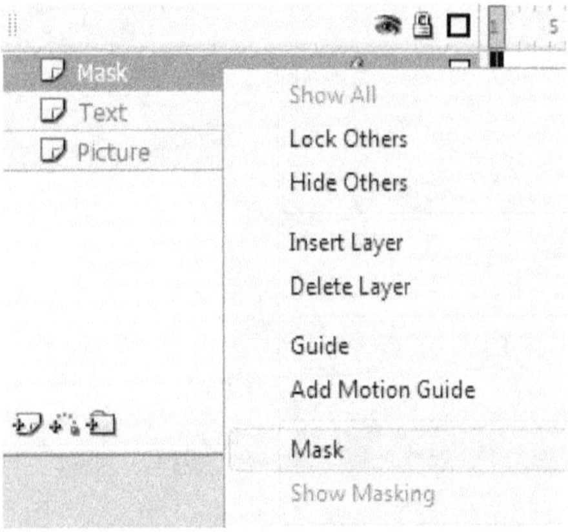

Now the text should be masked:

When you mask layers, Flash locks both the Mask layer and the masked layers. Unlock the **Text** layer and turn on the Outline for the **Mask** layer:

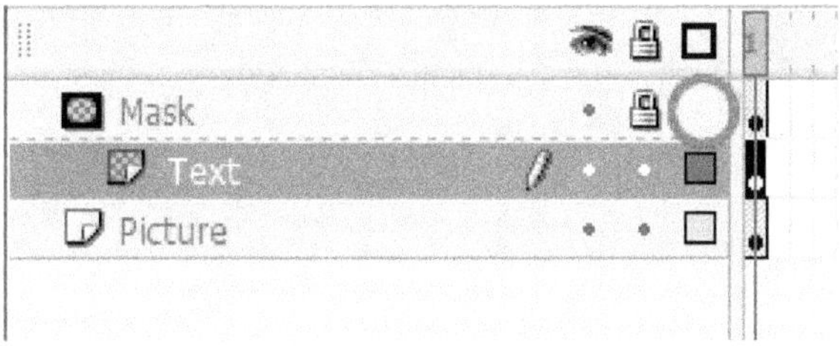

The Outline allows you to see the edges of the mask while making the mask transparent. Double-click the **Text** Movie clip to enter its editing stage. Create a keyframe on frame **40** and insert a keyframe. Select any frame between the keyframes and insert a Motion Tween. Select frame **40** and click on the text symbol on the stage. Drag it upward until the bottom of the text is within the mask:

Create a new layer and name it **Actions**. Insert a **stop** code into the frame of this layer (**Global Functions**, **Timeline Control**, double-click **stop**). So now we have the text animation. If we test the movie we'll see that the text is nicely masked. Now we just need to add the buttons to make the text move.

Go back to Scene 1. Create a new layer above the **Mask** layer and name it **Buttons**. Drag **Scroll Button** from the library over to the stage. Place it to the right of the text:

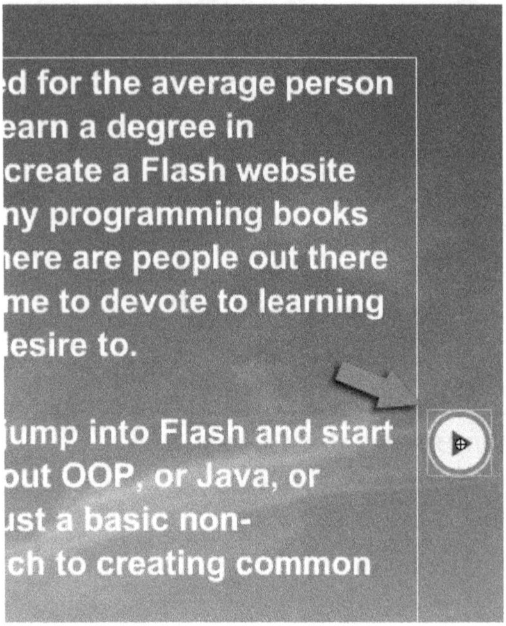

Select the **Free Transform Tool**. Move your cursor over a corner of the bounding box surrounding the button; the cursor will change to a curled icon:

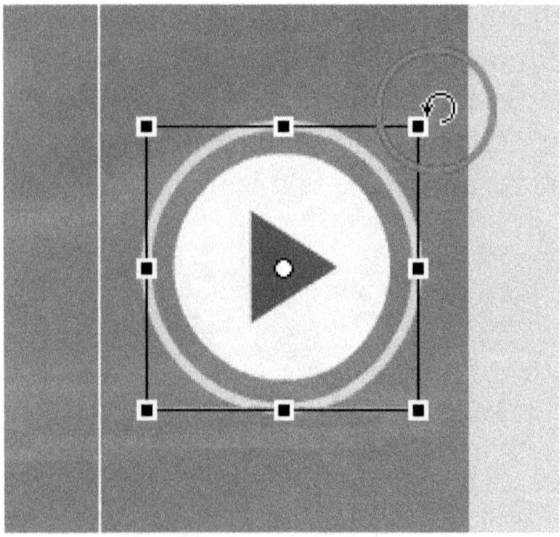

Hold down **SHIFT** and drag this corner down until the arrow of the button is pointing downward:

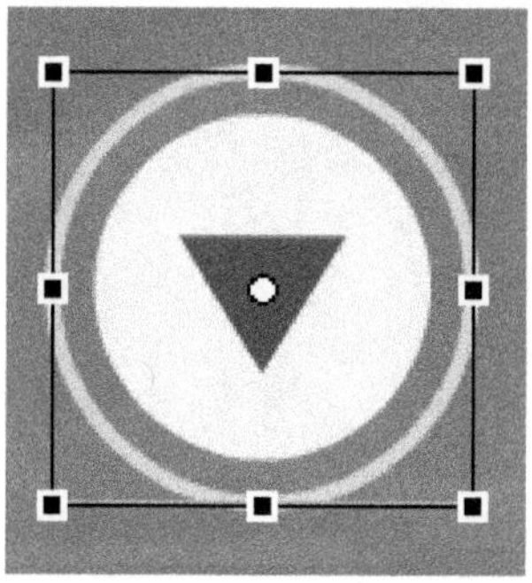

> **Remember!** The latest Flash programs come with several pre-built buttons that are ready to use! They are located under Window, Common Libraries.

Create a new layer and name it **Text Control**. Grab the **Rectangle Tool**, select the color **red**, and create a shape offstage to the right of the button:

Convert this shape to a Movie clip. Name it **Text Down**:

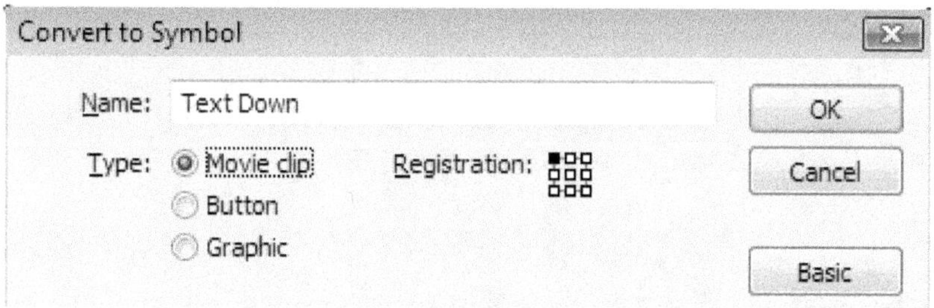

Hit **OK**. In the Properties panel type **text_down** in the **Instance Name** window:

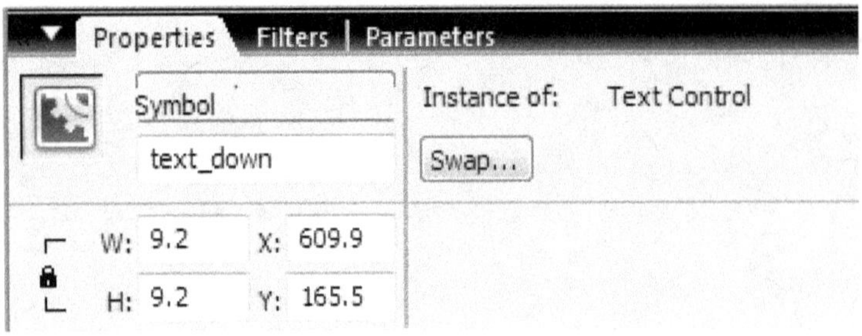

Double-click on this Movie clip to enter its editing stage. Create a new layer and name it **Actions**. Insert a **stop** code in the first keyframe of this layer. Create a keyframe in the second frame. In the Actions panel make sure Script Assist is on. Go to **Deprecated**, **Actions**, and double-click **tellTarget**. In the **Target** window type **/text**:

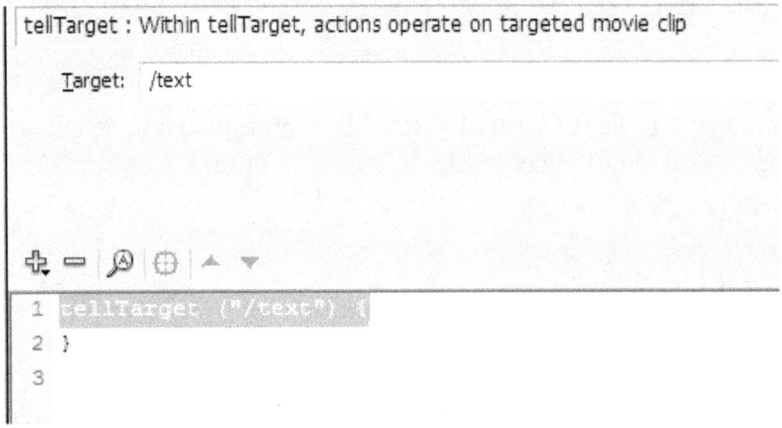

Now, go to **Global Functions**, **Timeline Control**, and double-click **goto**. Change **Type** to **Next Frame**:

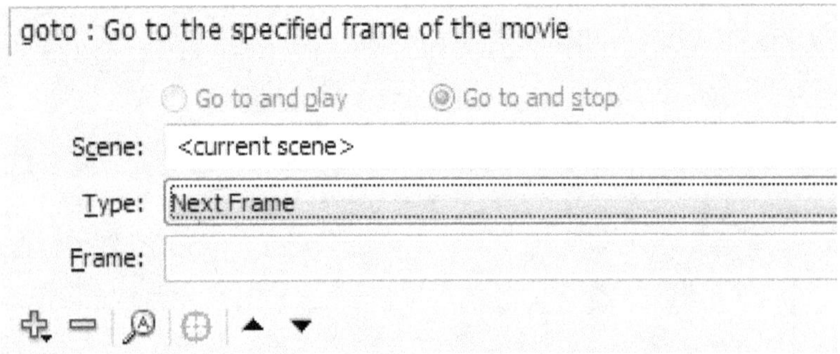

Insert a keyframe in frame **3** of this layer. In the Actions panel go to **Global Functions**, **Timeline Control**, and double-click **goto**. In the **goto** settings window change the Frame to **2**:

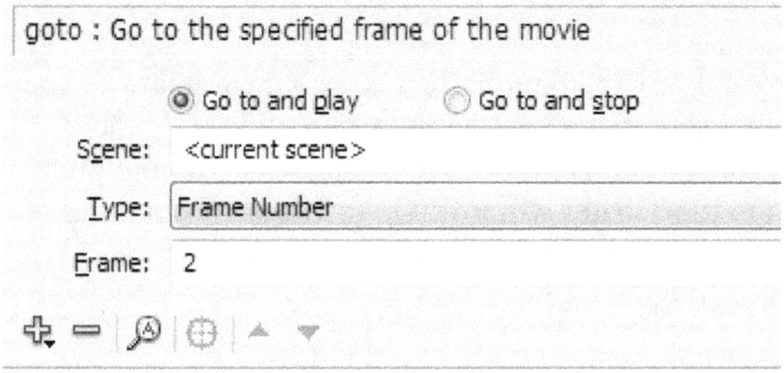

So the code on frame **3** tells Flash to go back to frame **2** and repeats the tellTarget code. It is a continuous loop that repeatedly tells the **Text** Movie clip to go to the next frame which will animate the Text. Let's add the ActionScript to the text button so you get a better idea of how it works.

Go back to Scene 1. Select the **Text Down** button and open the Actions panel. Go to **Deprecated**, **Actions**, and double-click **tellTarget**. Type **/text_down** in the **Target** window:

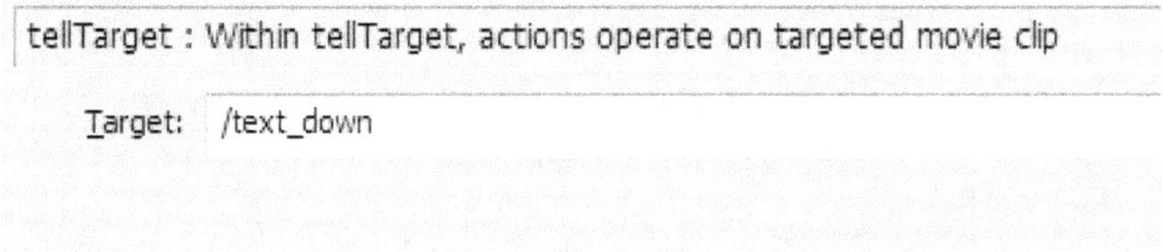

Go to **Global Functions**, **Timeline Control**, and double-click **play**. When we press the button it will tell the **text_down** Movie clip to play; the **text_down** Movie clip will then play its timeline going to frame **2**, which will tell the **Text** timeline to go to the next frame; the **text_down** Movie clip will continue to play its timeline until it gets to frame **3** which will send it back to frame **2** and, once again, tell the **Text** Movie clip to go to the next frame.

Since we want the text to move down when the mouse button is pressed, we need to change the **mouse event**. Click on the word **release** in the ActionScript. You should now see the **mouse event** window. De-select **Release** and select **Press**:

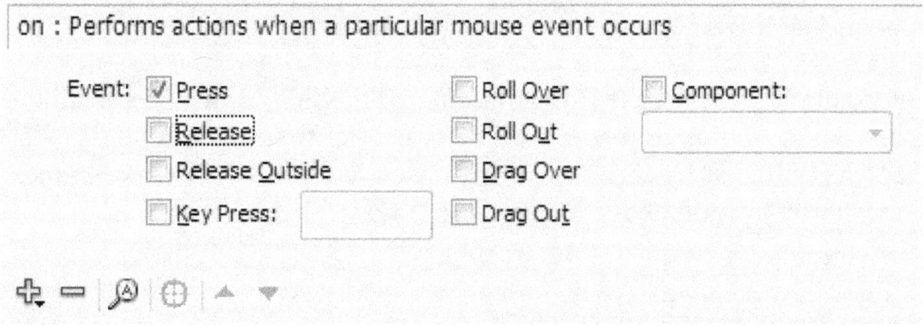

Test your movie. Now when you press the button, the text should animate down. The only problem is that the text should stop animating when we release the mouse button. In the Actions panel go to **Deprecated**, **Actions** and double-click **tellTarget**. Type **/text_down** in the **Target** window. Go to **Global Functions**, **Timeline Control**, and double-click **goto**. In the **goto** settings window select **Go to and stop** and the **Frame** should be **1**:

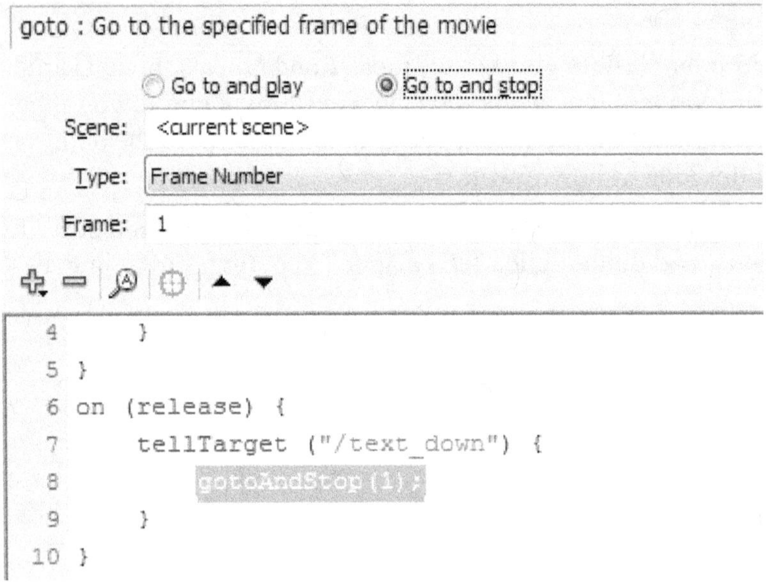

Test the movie. Press down on the button and the text should start animating down. When you release the button the text will stop animating. So can you figure out how to get the Text to animate back up? See if you can figure that out before reading the answer.

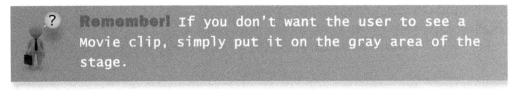

Remember! If you don't want the user to see a Movie clip, simply put it on the gray area of the stage.

We just have to duplicate the **Text Down** button and the **text_down** Movie clip. Then we'll tweak the ActionScript and we'll be done. So, first, we'll duplicate the button. Select the button and go to **Edit**, **Copy**. Then, go to **Edit**, **Paste in Place**. Drag this new button upward above the original button:

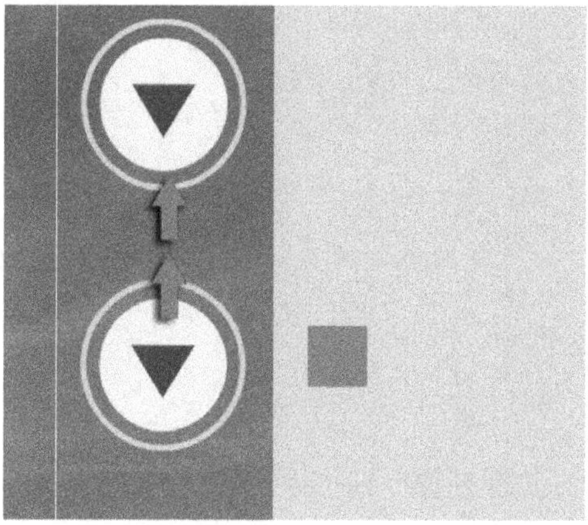

With this new button still selected, go to **Modify**, **Transform**, **Flip Vertical**:

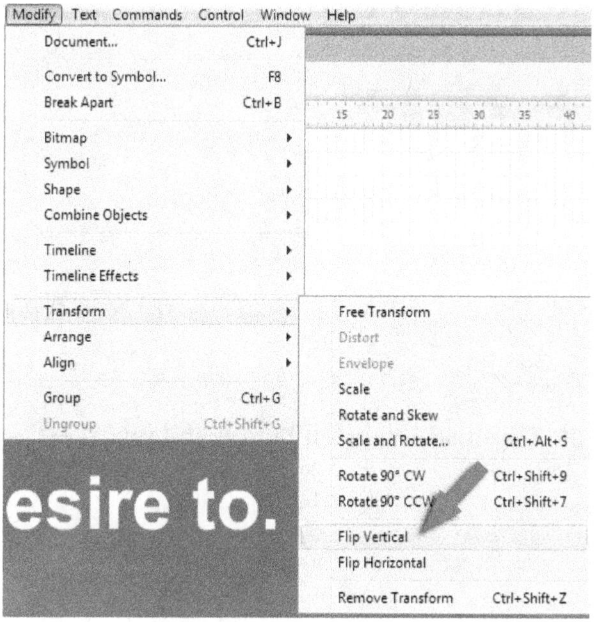

This new button should now be flipped, with the arrow pointing upward. Next, duplicate the **text_down** Movie clip. Select the **text_down** Movie clip and copy it. Then go to **Edit**, **Paste in Place**. Drag this new symbol upward above the original Movie clip:

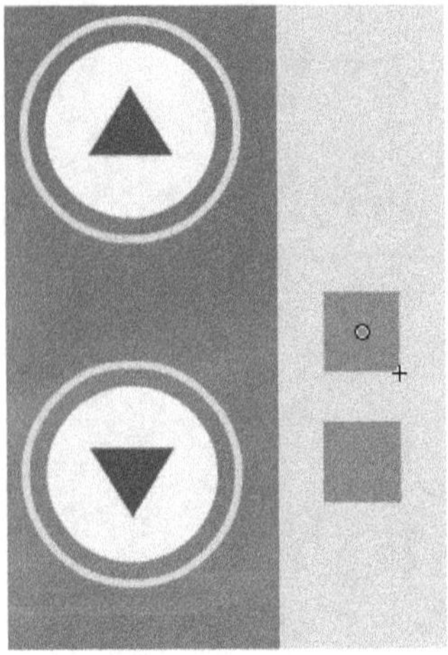

Open the Properties panel and change the **Instance Name** from **text_down** to **text_up**:

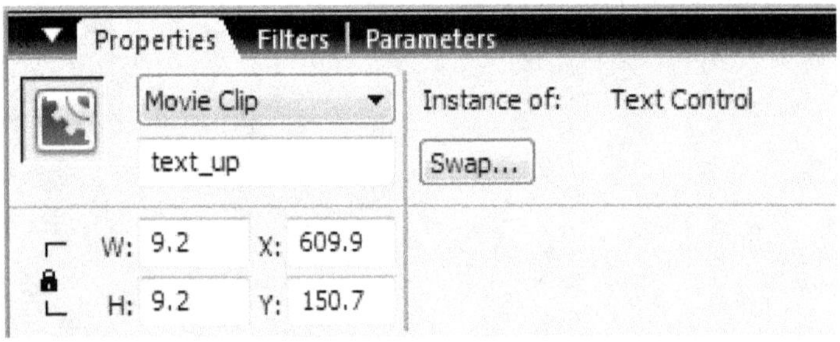

Click on the **Swap...** button. Select the **Duplicate Symbol** button and type **Text Control 2** in the **Symbol name** window:

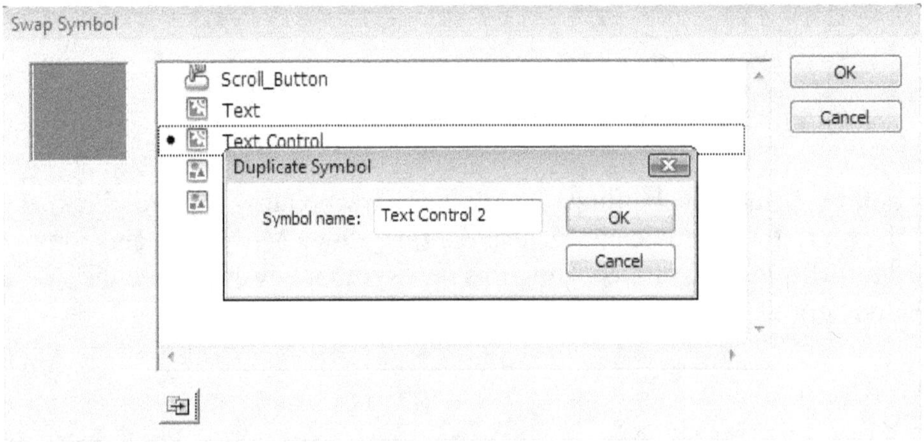

Hit **OK**. Double-click **Text Control 2** in the **Swap Symbol** window:

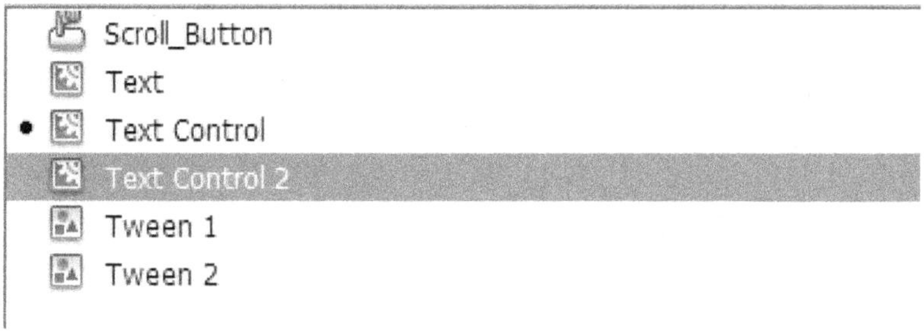

You should now have a copy of the original that you can safely edit. Double-click on this new Movie clip and select the second keyframe of the **Actions** layer. Open the Actions panel and make sure Script Assist is still on. Find the text: **nextFrame** and click on it. You should now see the **goto** settings window. Change **nextFrame** to **previousFrame**:

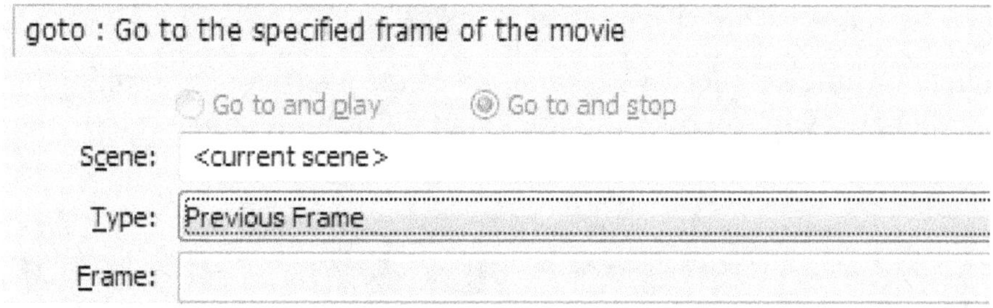

So this is the same principle. The timeline will continuously loop from frame **3** to frame **2**. Frame **2** will tell the **Text** Movie clip to go to the previous frame, over and over again. Go back to Scene 1 and select the new button. Open the Actions panel. Find the text: **text_down** next to the two **tellTarget** codes. Click on **text_down** which will bring up the **Target** window. Type **text_up** in the **Target** window:

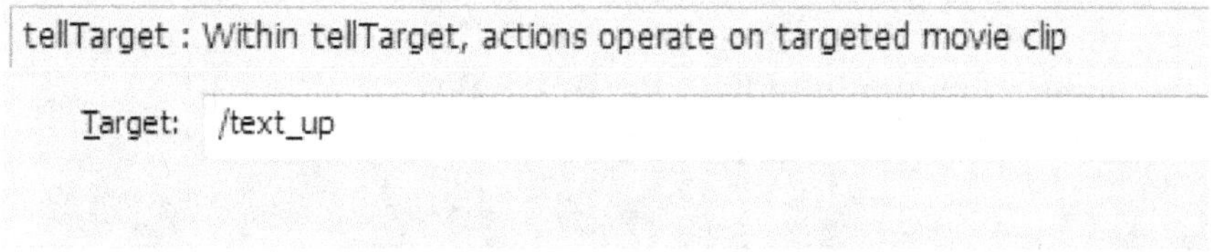

Repeat this step for the second **text_down** code. Your final code should look like this:

```
on (press) {
    tellTarget ("/text_up") {
        play();
    }
}
on (release) {
    tellTarget ("/text_up") {
        gotoAndStop(1);
    }
}
```

Test your movie. Your buttons should now work properly. If you want to tweak it any further you can double-click the **Text** Movie clip, select the first frame, and change the **Ease** to **100**. Now the Text will slow down when it gets to the end.

The next scroller is a little simpler. We're going to create a horizontal scrolling text that stops whenever you roll over it. When you roll off it, it continues its animation. Let's get started.

Go to the Scene panel and select the Horizontal Scroll scene. You'll see three layers. We have the **Gray background** layer, **Bar** layer, and the **Title** layer. Create a new layer and name it **Text**. Drag the symbol **Horizontal Text** over to the stage from the library. Position it to the right of the **Bar**:

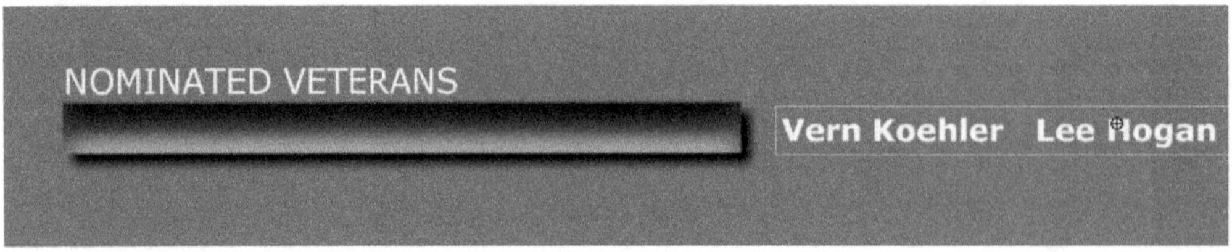

Convert this text to a Movie clip. Name the Movie clip **Text**:

Hit **OK**. In the Properties panel type **text** in the **Instance Name** window:

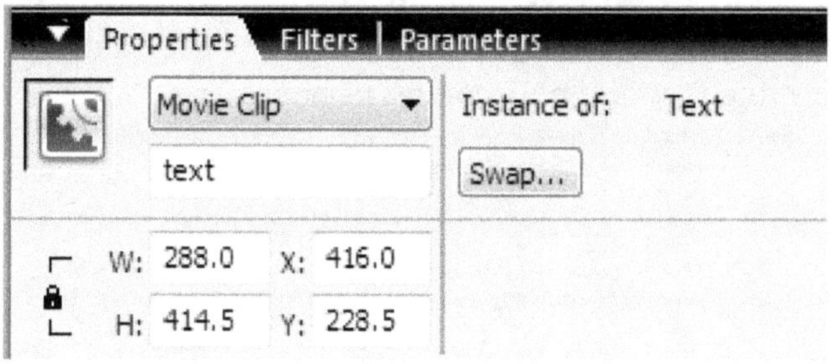

Double-click on this new Movie clip to enter its editing stage. Since we want the scroll to stop when we roll over it, then we need to make the text a button. Select the text and convert it to a button. Name it **Text Button** and hit **OK** when you're done. Before we create the animation we'll add the ActionScript to this button. Open the Actions panel and make sure Script Assist is turned on. Go to **Deprecated**, **Actions** and double-click **tellTarget**. In the **Target** window type **/text**:

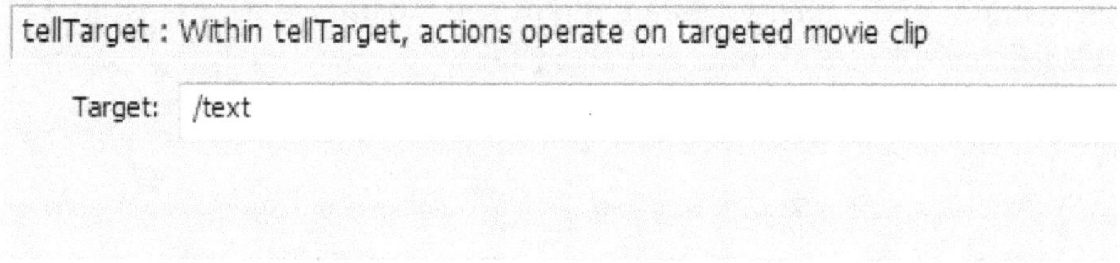

Next, go to **Global Functions**, **Timeline Control** and double-click **stop**. Since we want the text to stop when we roll over it we need to change the **mouse event** from **Release** to **Roll Over**. In the ActionScript window click on the word **release**. You should now see the **mouse event** window. Uncheck **Release** and select **Roll Over** and **Drag Over**:

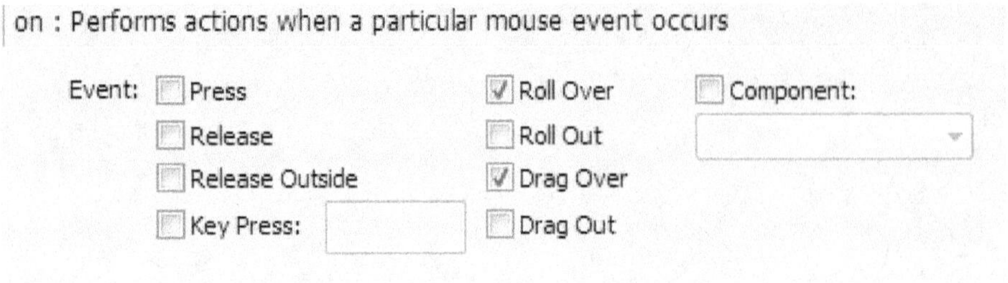

Drag Over is where the user clicks his mouse button first, then rolls over the text. I always check **Drag Over** when I select **Roll Over**. The next code will tell Flash to continue the Text animation when the cursor rolls off the text. Let's do that now. Select the closing bracket on line **5** so the new code will be separate from the first set of code:

```
1 on (rollOver, dragOver) {
2     tellTarget ("/text") {
3         stop();
4     }
5 }
6
```

Go to **Deprecated**, **Actions**, and double-click **tellTarget**. Type **/text** in the **Target** window. Go to **Global Functions**, **Timeline Control** and double-click **play**. This code will tell Flash to continue the Text animation when the cursor rolls off the text. We need to change the mouse event before we finish. Select **release** in the second set of code; you should now see the **mouse events** window. Uncheck **Release** and select **Roll Out** and **Drag Out**:

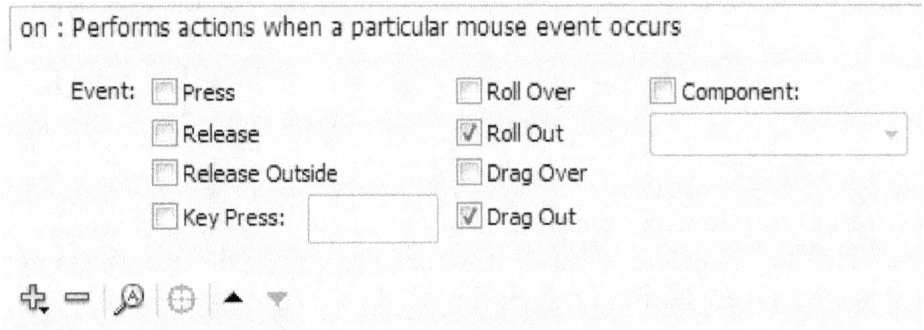

Drag Out is when the user clicks his mouse and rolls off the text before releasing the button. So we're almost done! Next, create a keyframe on frame **600**. Drag the text straight left (hold down SHIFT while dragging to keep it straight) until the right side of the text symbol is to the left of the bar:

Select any frame between the two keyframes and insert a Motion Tween. Next, create a new layer and name it **Mask**. Grab the **Rectangle Tool**, turn off **Stroke color** and select **red** for the **Fill color**. Create a shape across the bar image like this:

Right-click on the **Mask** layer and select **Mask**. Your text should now be masked. Go back to the scene: Horizontal Scroll. Test this scene. Your text should scroll from right to left. When you roll over the text it should stop; when you roll off the text it should start to play again.

The final scroller is a scroller that you've probably seen a few times on various websites. The text animates vertically and when you roll over one of the text buttons on the scroller the animation stops and you can click the button to go to the link's website.

Go to the scene Vertical Scroller. You'll see three layers; the first layer is the **Gray Background**, the second layer has the darker gray text background, and the third layer has the text. Since we'll be animating this text we need to convert it to a Movie clip. Select the text and convert it to a Movie clip; name this new Movie clip **Scroll**. With this new Movie clip selected, give it an **Instance Name** of **text**. Double-click this Movie clip to enter its editing stage.

We now need to add the buttons. Your first thought might be to add the buttons to this timeline. But, since we'll be animating the text on this timeline, we'll be adding the buttons within the actual text symbol. Select the text on the stage and convert it to a **Graphic**. Name it **Text Buttons**:

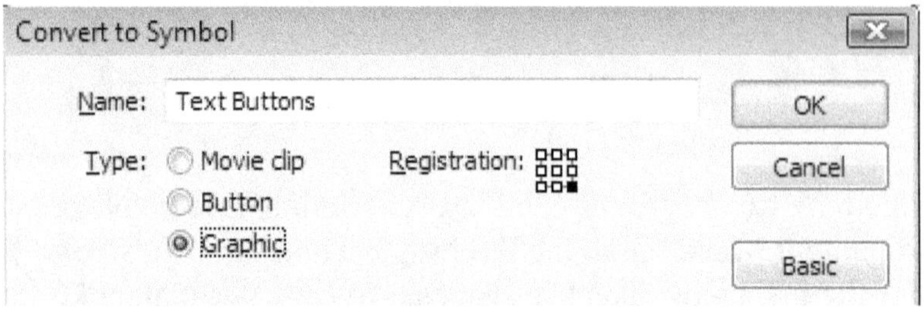

Hit **OK**. Double-click on this new graphic to enter its editing stage. Create a new layer and name it **Buttons**. Drag the item **Invis Button** from the library and place it over the word **GOOGLE**:

In the Properties panel change **Color** to **Alpha** and the **percentage** to **0**. This button should now be transparent. Now we just need to add the ActionScript. Open the Actions panel and go to **Global Functions**, **Browser/Network** and double-click **getURL**.

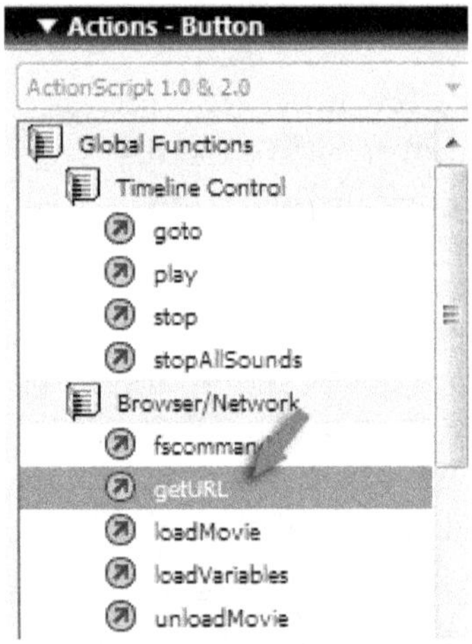

In the **getURL** settings window type **http://www.google.com** in the **URL** window and select **_blank** in the **Window** field:

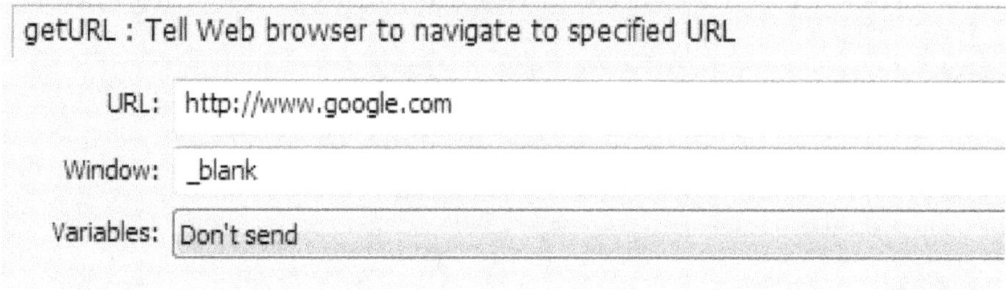

When using the **getURL** function always put the complete web address including the **http://** part. I almost always choose **_blank** for the Window setting. **_blank** means the website will open in a separate browser window.

Next, go to **Deprecated**, **Actions** and double-click **tellTarget**. In the **tellTarget** settings window type **/text** in the **Target** window. Next, go to **Global Functions**, **Timeline Control** and double-click **stop**. Select the word **release** in the last bit of code. You should now be in the **mouse events** window. Uncheck **Release** and select **Roll Over** and **Drag Over**. When the user rolls over this button it will tell the text file to stop. We'll now create the final code. Make sure you select the closing bracket of the last bit of code:

```
on (release) {
    getURL("http://www.google.com", "_blank");
}
on (rollOver, dragOver) {
    tellTarget ("/text") {
        stop();
    }
}
```

Go to **Deprecated**, **Actions** and double-click **tellTarget**. Type **/text** in the **Target** window. Next, go to **Global Functions**, **Timeline Control** and double-click **play**. Select the word **release** in this new code; in the **mouse events** window uncheck **Release** and select **Roll Out** and **Drag Out**.

Select the button on the stage. Go to **Edit**, **Copy**. Next, select **Edit**, **Paste in Place**. Drag this new button over the word YAHOO. Go to **Edit**, **Paste in Place** again. Drag this new button over the word CNN. Keep repeating these steps until you have a button over every link. You should end up with eight buttons. When you're done the only code you'll have to change on each button is the **getURL** info. Select the YAHOO button. In the Actions window click anywhere within the text **http://www.google.com**. You should now be in the **URL** settings window. Change the **URL** to **http://www.yahoo.com**:

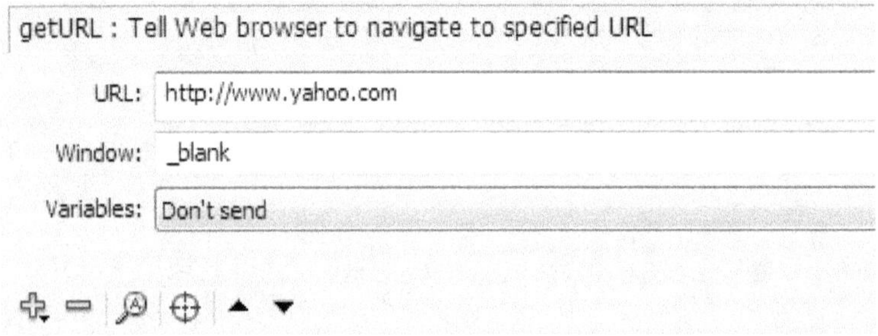

Select the button on CNN and do the same thing. Change the **URL** to **http://www.cnn.com**. Do this for every button. When you're finished go back to the Scroll timeline by clicking on the Scroll link or hitting the **Back** button above the timeline/stage:

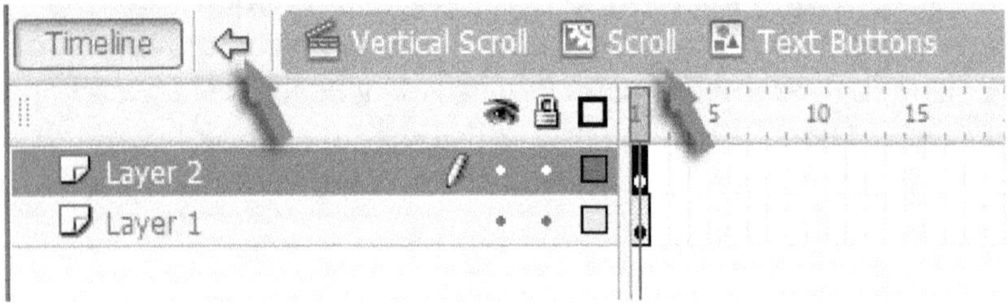

In the Scroll timeline drag the **Text** Movie clip below the gray area:

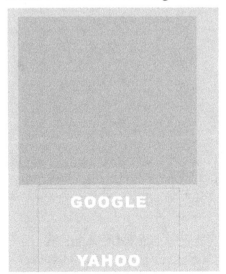

Next, create a keyframe on frame **300**. Drag the **Text** Movie clip so that the text **FACEBOOK** is above the top of the gray area:

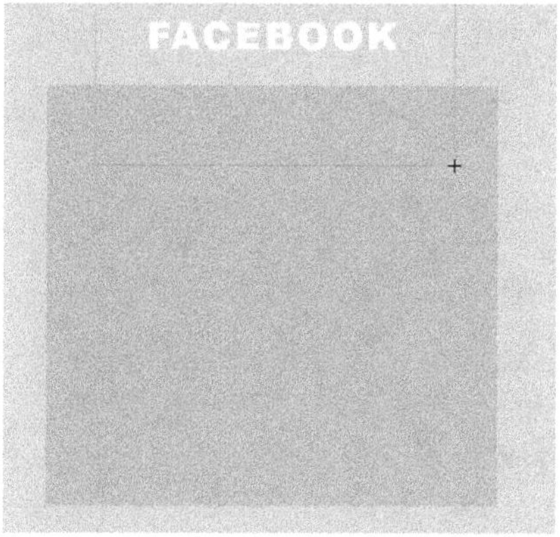

Select any frame between **1** and **300** and insert a Motion Tween. Now we just have one last thing to do. Go to the **Vertical Scroll** scene and create a new layer; name this new layer **Mask**. Select the **Rectangle Tool**, turn off **Stroke color**, change the **Fill color** to **red**, and create a shape within the **Gray text** background:

Right-click on this layer and choose **Mask**:

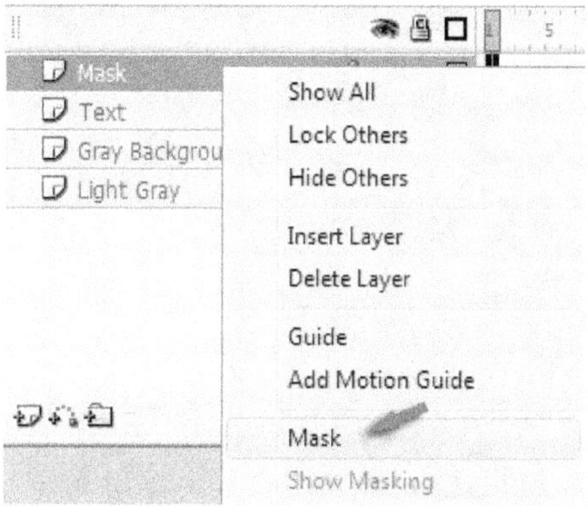

Test this scene. Your text should scroll upward. If you roll over one of the buttons the text should stop. If you roll off one of these buttons the text will continue its animation. If you click one of these buttons the website should appear in a browser window.

Drag 'n' Drop

DIFFICULTY:

In this exercise we're going to create a Drag 'n' Drop game using mainly the **tellTarget** command. When you learn the principles behind the creation of this game you'll be able to create all sorts of interactive, exciting projects! The Drag 'n' Drop game rewards you when you successfully drop the symbols in their proper destination and returns the symbols to their original location if you miss the correct destination. The game also knows when you've finished and gives you the option to reset the symbols.

In the Flash Projects folder double-click the **dragdrop.swf** file. Drag the symbols over to their appropriate destinations. After every successful drop you'll receive a **successful!** animation. When you're finished, the **Finished!** animation appears along with a **RESET** button. This **RESET** button will return all the symbols to their original position. Let's learn how this projects works. Open the file called **DragnDrop.fla**. You'll see the symbols along with their destination cutouts:

You'll then see that we have two layers. The **Stage** layer and also the **Symbols** layer. Lock the **Stage** layer so you don't accidentally move the stage image. Next, we're going to create the diamond symbol. Select the diamond image and go to **Modify**, **Convert to Symbol**. Select **Movie clip** for **Type** and name this Movie clip: **Diamond**:

Hi **OK**. Before we edit this new Movie clip we need to give it an **Instance Name**. In the Properties panel type **diamond** in the **Instance Name** window:

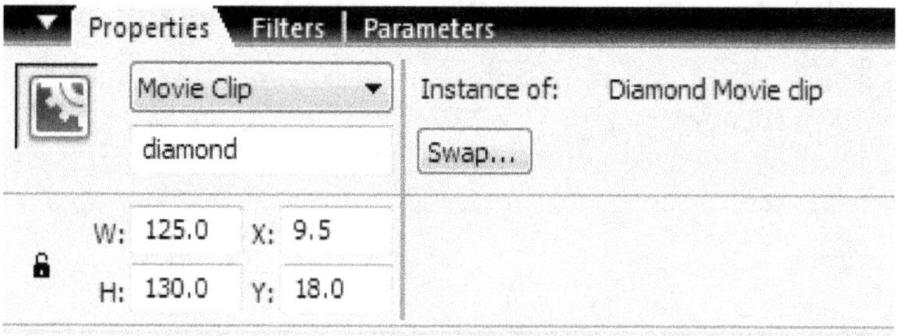

Double-click this Movie clip to enter its editing stage. This timeline will have two frames, one frame will have the button and the second frame will have just the raw graphic. You'll learn why we're doing this in a moment.

Name the existing layer (Layer 1): **Button**. Create a new layer and name it **Actions**:

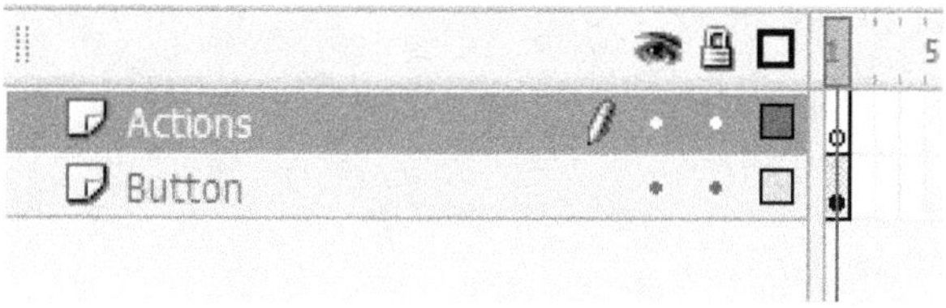

Since we'll be adding two frames to this timeline we'll need a **stop** code in the first frame. Select the first frame of the **Actions** layer and open the Actions panel. Go to **Global Functions**, **Timeline Control**, and double-click **stop**.

Next, select the diamond image on the stage and convert it to a button. Name it **Button Diamond**:

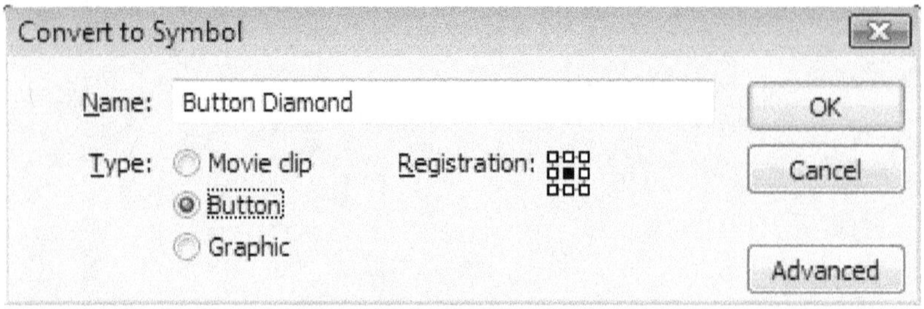

Hit **OK**. Now we'll add the ActionScript to this button. In the Actions panel make sure Script Assist is on. Go to **Global Functions**, **Movie clip Control**, and double-click **startDrag**. In the **startDrag** settings window, type **/diamond** in the **Target** window:

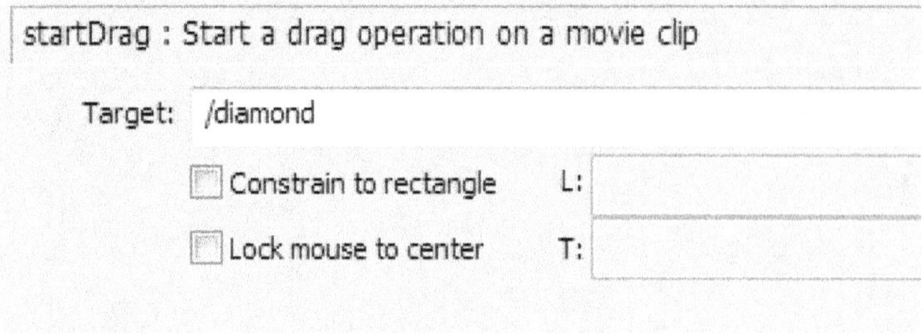

If you look at the ActionScript you'll see that the **startDrag** action will be triggered by the mouse event **release**. We want the **startDrag** command to work when we *press down* on the mouse button. So let's change that now. Click on the word **release** in the ActionScript. You should now be in the **mouse event** settings window. Uncheck **Release** and select **Press**:

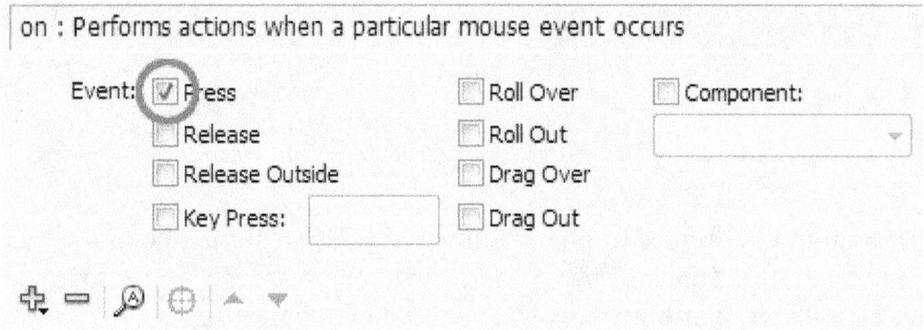

If you test the movie you'll be able to drag the **Diamond** Movie clip around the stage. We now need to add code that will stop the drag command when we *release* the mouse button. Before we do that, however, we need to make sure this code is separate from the first set of code. Click on the closing bracket of the first set of code:

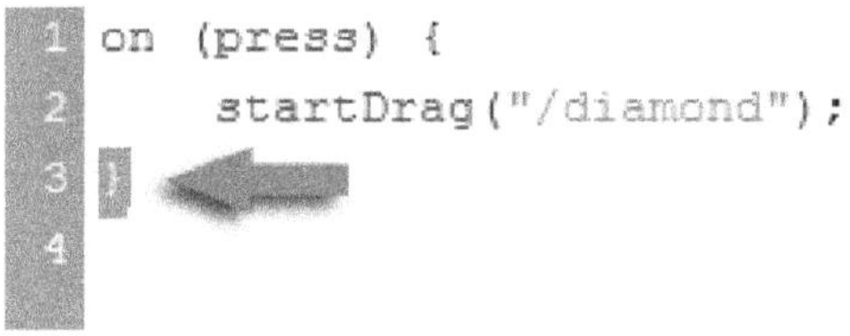

The new code will now be separate. In the Actions panel go to **Global Functions**, **Movie clip Control**, and double-click **stopDrag**. Test your movie and try dragging the **Diamond** Movie clip around the stage. When you release your mouse button the dragging will stop. So each time you press down on your mouse button it triggers the startDrag command. Every time you release your mouse button, it triggers the stopDrag command.

Next, create a keyframe on frame **2** of this timeline:

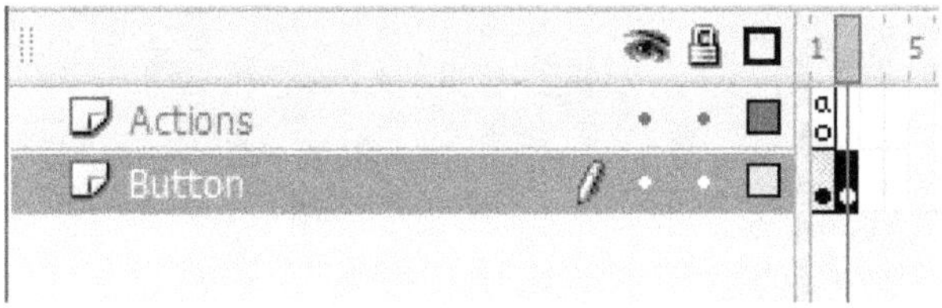

This will create a copy of the button that was on the first frame. You should see the copy on the stage. So what we need to do is make this symbol a raw image and *not a button*. Select the copied button on the stage and go to **Modify**, **Break Apart**:

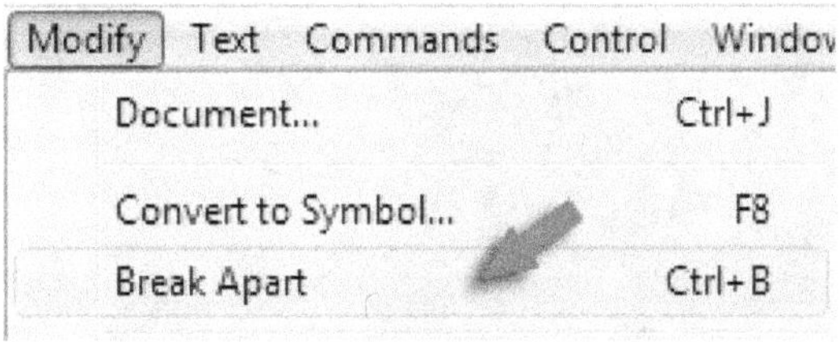

If you look at the Properties panel it should say **Bitmap**:

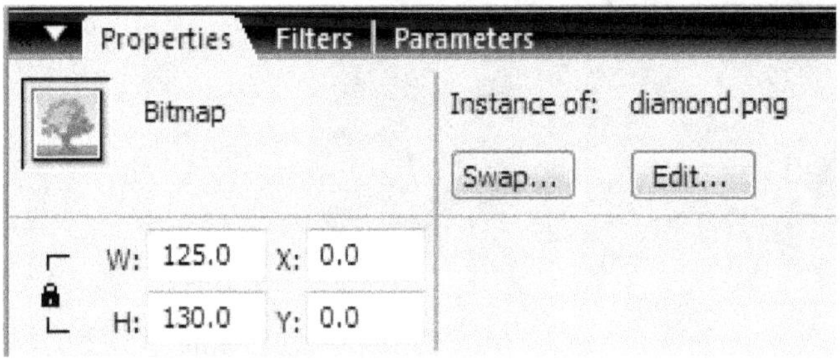

Now we have the raw image on the second frame. When this timeline gets to frame **2** the diamond symbol is no longer a button but a bitmap. You'll learn why we did this in a moment.

Now, go back to Scene 1. We're going to create a transparent button over the stage image. This button will sense when the **Diamond** Movie clip is over it. This will be the button that sends the diamond symbol back to its original starting position when the symbol is released over the incorrect destination.

Note: there is a diagram at the end of this exercise that will help you understand how all the Movie clips communicate with each other. You may have to go through this exercise a few times before you fully understand the techniques involved.

Create a new layer and name it **Invisible Stage Button**. We need this layer to be *below* the **Symbols** layer:

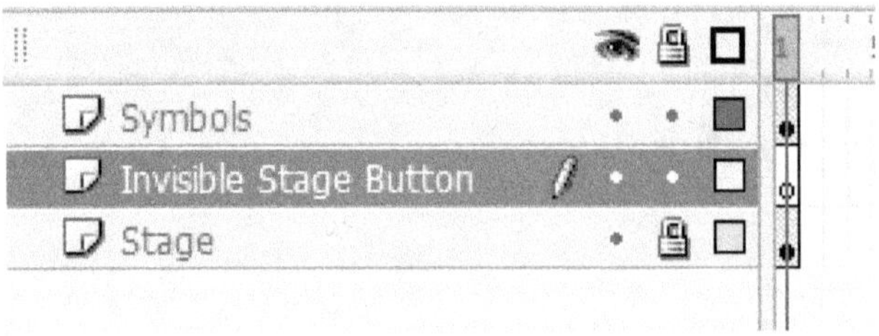

Next, grab the **Rectangle Tool**, turn off **Stroke color**, and select **red** for the **Fill color**. Create a shape that covers the entire right side of the canvas where the cutouts are:

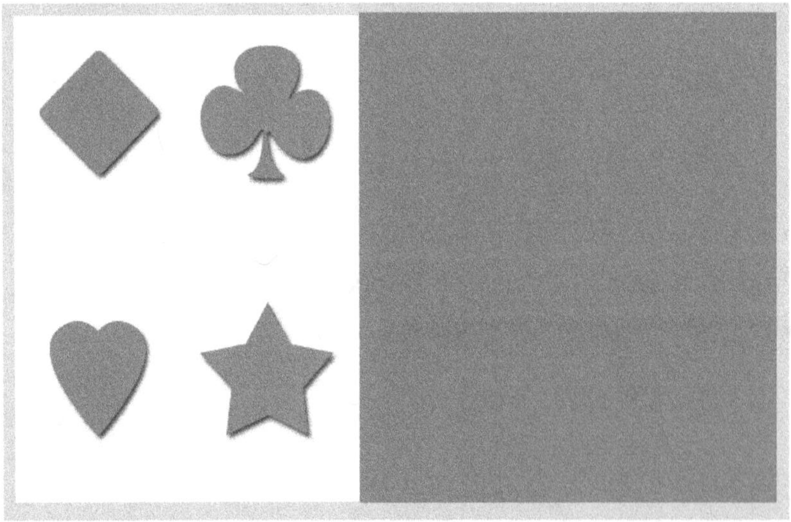

Select this new shape and convert it to a button. Name this button **Invisible Stage Button**:

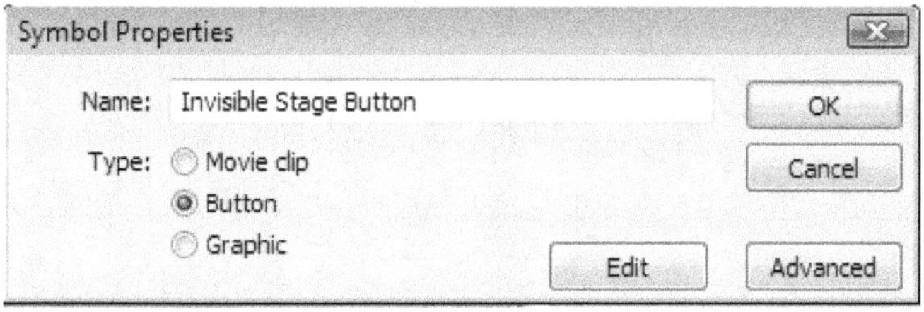

Hit **OK** when you're finished. With this new image selected, go to the Properties panel and change **Color** to **Alpha** and take the percentage down to **0**:

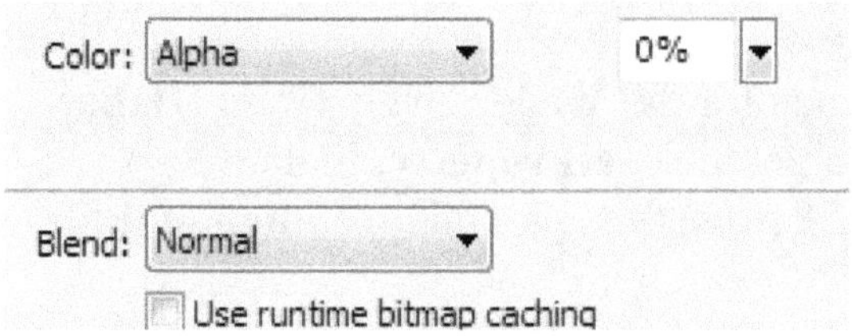

You should now be able to see the stage image again. Next, we're going to add the code which will return the **Diamond** Movie clip back to its original starting position. Select this button and in the Actions panel go to **Global Functions**, **Movie clip Control**, and double-click **setProperty**. In the **setProperty** settings window select **_x** for **Property** and type **/diamond** for the **Target**:

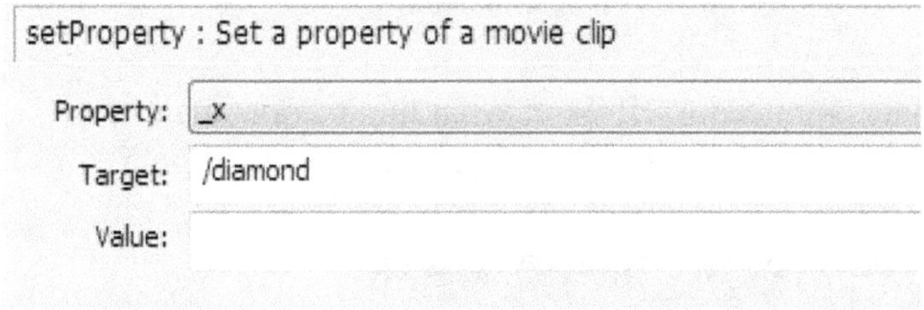

Before we can enter the Value**,** we have to find out what the _x value is of the diamond symbol. Select the **Diamond** Movie clip on the stage; in the Properties panel look at the **X** coordinate:

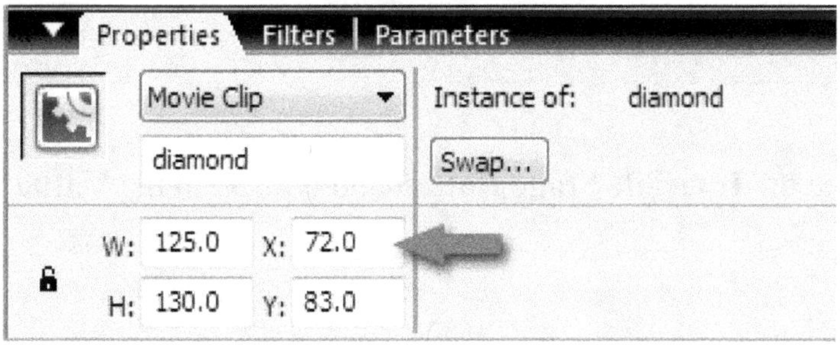

The **X** coordinate is **72**. This will be the number we need to type into the **Value** window:

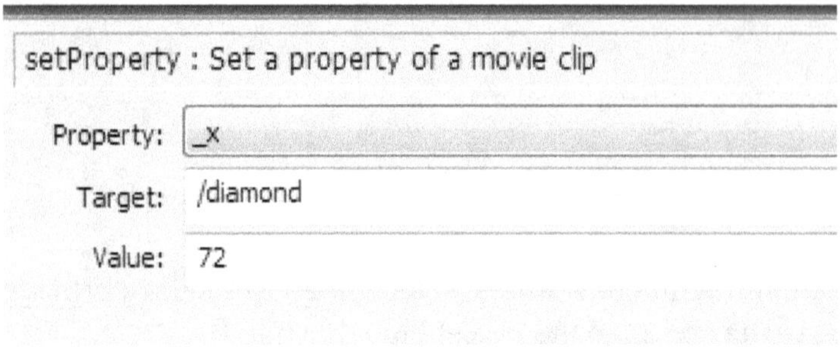

Now we need to create the **setPropety** code for the **Y** coordinate. Go to **Global Functions**, **Movie clip Control**, and double-click **setProperty**. In the **setProperty** settings window change the **Property** to **_y** and type **/diamond** for the **Target**:

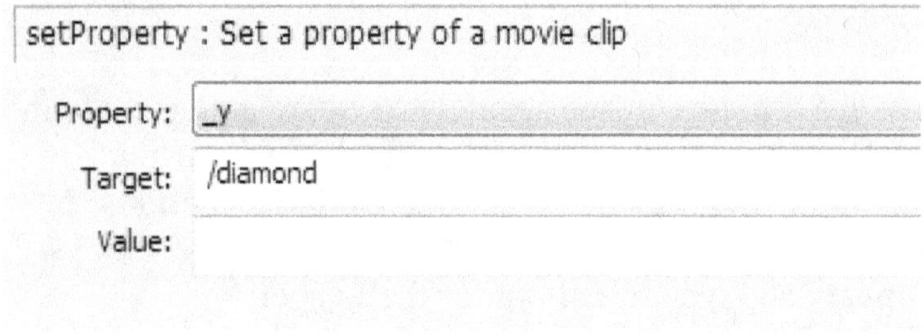

Just like with the **X** coordinate, we need to find out what the **Y** coordinate is of the **Diamond** Movie clip. Select the **Diamond** Movie clip and look at the **Y** coordinate in the Properties panel:

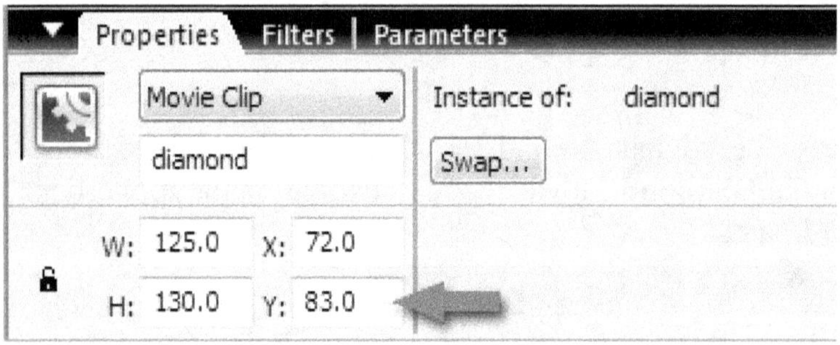

It should say **83**. Go back to the **Invisible Stage Button** and type **83** in the **Value** window:

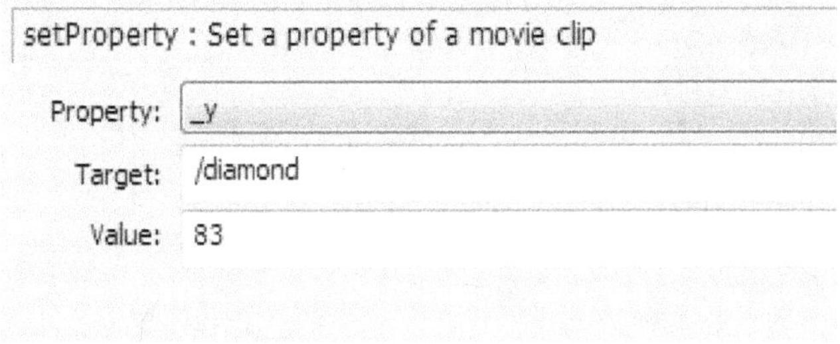

Also, if you look at the ActionScript you'll notice that Flash inserted the second **setProperty** command within the first **setProperty** code:

```
on (release) {
    setProperty("/diamond", _x, "72");
    setProperty("/diamond", _y, "83");
}
```

Since we want both of these **setProperty** actions to happen at the same time, and they're both using the same mouse event, it won't hurt to have them combined in the same code. Normally, though, you'll want to be safe and click on the closing bracket of the last set of code before beginning a new set of commands.

Next, we need to change the **mouse event** for these two commands. Click on the word **release** in the Actions window. You should now see the **mouse event** settings. Uncheck **Release** and select **Roll Over** and **Drag Over**:

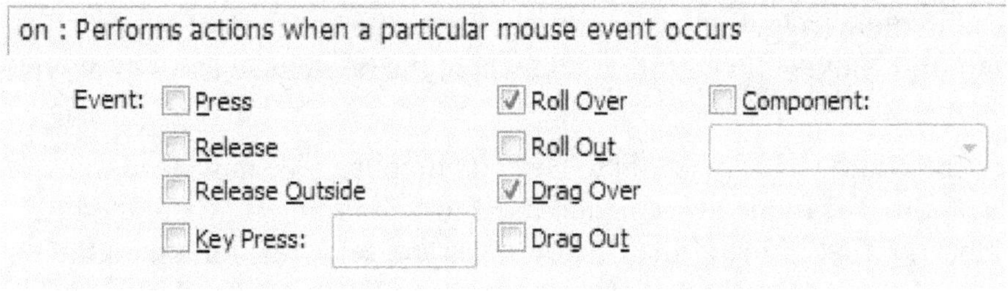

When the user drags the **Diamond** Movie clip over this button, the actions are triggered and the **Diamond** Movie clip will return to its original position.

Go ahead and test the movie. Drag the **Diamond** Movie clip over the **Invisible Stage Button**; if you release your mouse button you'll notice that the **Diamond** Movie clip doesn't return to its original starting position. So why isn't the code on the **Invisible Stage Button** working?

Drag the **Diamond** Movie clip over the **Invisible Stage Button** again:

This time release your button, then drag your cursor anywhere over the stage area *away from the **Diamond** Movie clip*. You'll notice that once we move the cursor over the stage area away from the diamond symbol, the code is triggered and the diamond symbol is sent back to its original starting position.

If you remember, we have a button on the first frame of the **Diamond** Movie clip. This is what triggers the **startDrag** command. Since the cursor is over this button, it can't read any other buttons below it. So, to correct this, we need to tell the **Diamond** Movie clip's timeline to go to frame 2 where there isn't a button. Once that happens, the cursor will automatically trigger the **Invisible Stage Button**.

What we need to do to trigger the actions in the **Invisible Stage Button**, is to have the **Diamond** Movie clip go to frame 2 where the raw image is. Let's do that now.

Double-click the **Diamond** Movie clip to enter its timeline. We now need the button that's on the first frame to command itself to go to frame 2 where the raw image is. Select the first frame of the **Button** layer and select the button on the stage. Open the Actions panel and click on the closing bracket of the last set of code:

```
on (press) {
    startDrag("/diamond");
}
on (release) {
    stopDrag();
}

```

Next, go to **Global Functions**, **Timeline Control**, and double-click **goto**. In the **goto** settings window change **Type** to **Next Frame**:

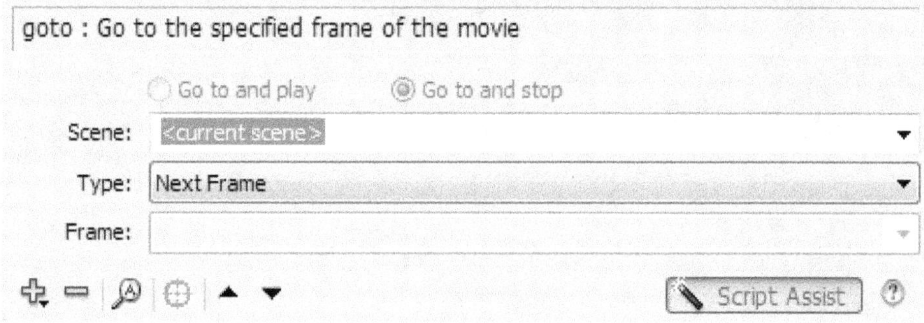

Test your movie again. This time when you drag the **Diamond** Movie clip over the stage area and release, the symbol goes back to its original starting position. So do you understand what happened? Once we released the mouse button it triggered the *above code* which sent the timeline to frame 2 where the raw image is. Since the diamond symbol was no longer a button, it triggered the commands of the **Invisible Stage Button**.

But now we have another problem. When we release the diamond symbol over any part of the stage, it returns to its original starting position but it no longer let's us click and drag it. So how do we tell the **Diamond** Movie clip to go back to frame 1 of its timeline where the button is? That's where the second invisible button comes into play.

Create a new layer and name it **Invisible Button**. Make sure this layer is *below the Symbols layer*:

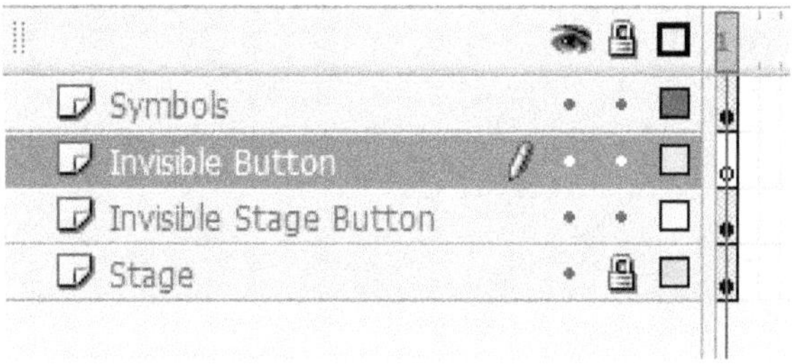

Now we'll create a large transparent button that surrounds the symbols on the left side of the stage. We'll add actions to this button so that when the user rolls over it, it will tell the diamond symbol to go to frame 1 of its timeline where the button is. Before we make this new button, turn on **Outline** for the **Invisible Stage Button** layer. You should see now see a outline of this button. Your new button will cover the area not covered by this button.

Select the **Rectangle Tool**, turn **Stroke color** off and select **red** for the **Fill color**. Select the **Invisible Button** layer and create a shape that covers the left side of the stage:

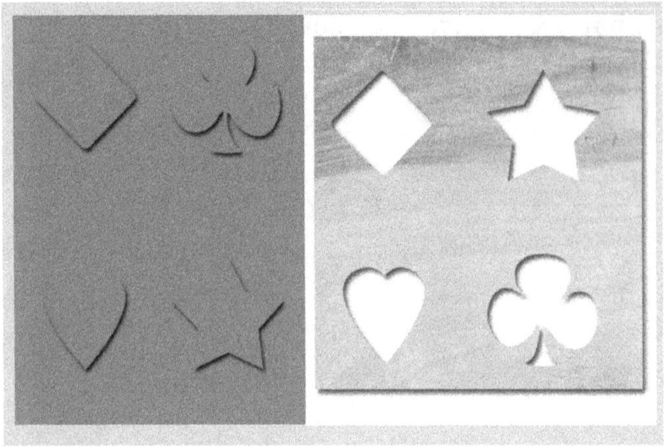

Convert this new shape into a button. Name it **Invisible Button**:

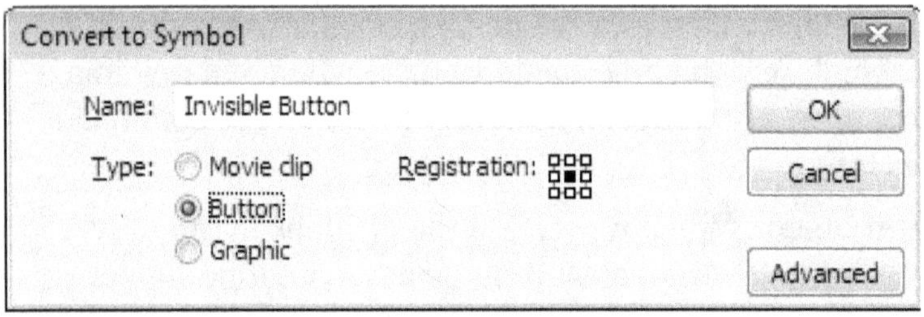

Hit **OK**. Next, we'll need to make this button transparent. In the Properties panel change **Color** to **Alpha** and change the percentage to **0**:

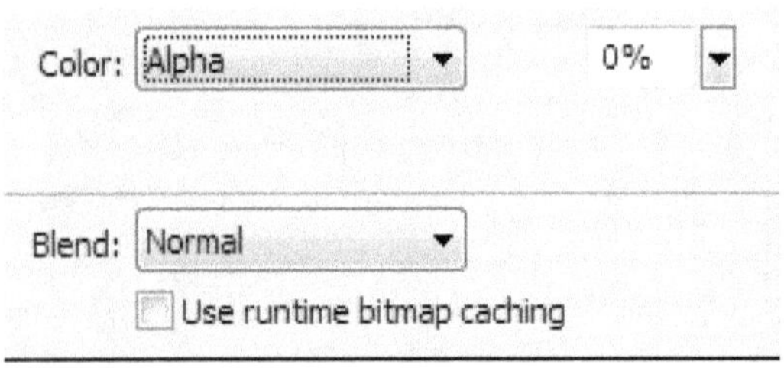

So now your button is transparent. Let's add the ActionScript to this button. In the Actions panel go to **Deprecated**, **Actions**, and double-click **tellTarget**. In the **tellTarget** settings window type **/diamond**:

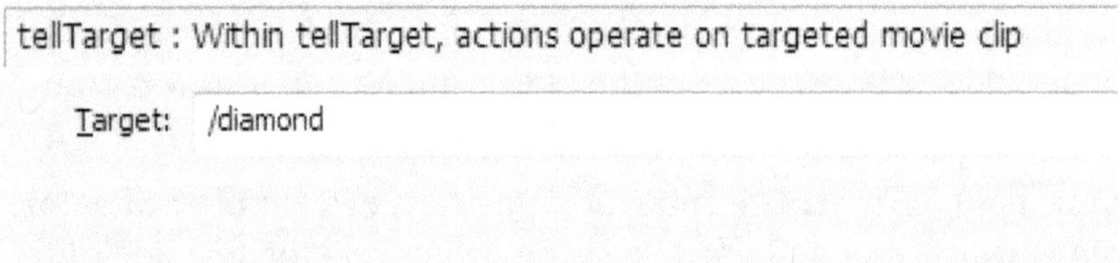

Next, go to **Global Functions**, **Timeline Control**, and double-click **goto**. In the **goto** settings window type **1** in the **Frame** window and select **Go to and stop**:

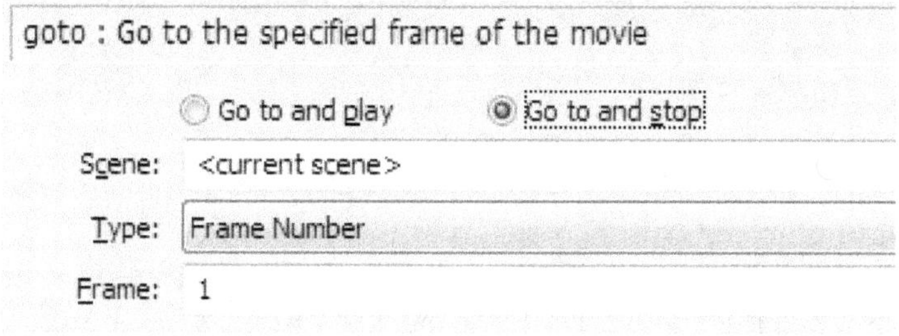

Next, we need to change the mouse event. We want this code to be triggered when the user rolls over it. Click on the word **release** in the Actions window to view the **mouse event** window. Uncheck **Release** and select **Roll Over** and **Drag Over**:

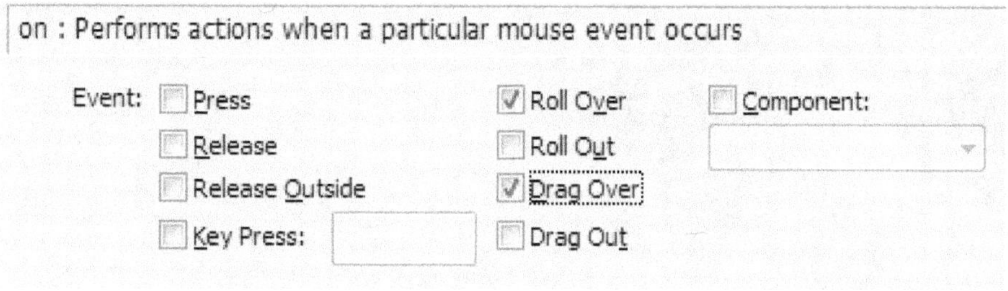

Now when the user rolls over this button it tells the **Diamond** Movie clip to go to frame 1 where the button is. Go ahead and test your movie. Release the diamond symbol on the left side of the stage. Notice that when you release it, you're instantly able to click and drag the symbol again. So even though the **Diamond** Movie clip is telling its timeline to go to frame 2, the **Invisible Button** is sending it right back to frame 1 where the button is. Drag the diamond symbol over the stage where the stage image is. Release the mouse button. The diamond symbol goes back to its original starting position. When you roll off the stage image and roll over the **Invisible Button** it tells the **Diamond** Movie clip to, once again, go to frame 1 where the button is.

If you get confused at any time I've included a diagram at the end of this exercise.

If the user places the diamond symbol over the correct destination (diamond cutout), we want the diamond symbol to remain on the stage and not return to its starting position. Plus, once it's placed on its correct destination it should no longer be clickable. So how do we do this? Try to figure this out before proceeding.

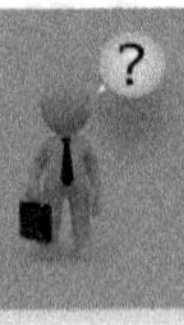

Remember! It's a good idea to first put your Flash Project on paper. Create a diagram that illustrates how all the Movie clips will communicate with each other.

The first thing we'll need to do is tweak the **Invisible Stage Button**. Double-click the **Invisible Stage Button** to enter its editing stage. Turn the visibility off for **Layer 1**. Create a new layer; you don't need to name it since we'll be deleting it in a moment. Select the **Brush Tool** then select **blue** for the **Fill color**. You should be able to see the symbol cutouts from the stage image. Take your **Brush Tool** and paint over these cutouts; don't worry about being perfect. Your shapes can be a little rough. When you're done the shapes should look like this:

Click on the keyframe of this layer to select all the shapes you just painted. Go to **Edit, Copy**. Next, go ahead and delete this layer by clicking on the garbage can icon. Turn the visibility back on for **Layer 1** and go to **Edit**, **Paste in Place**. Your blue shapes should now be part of the large red shape:

Select the **Selection Tool** and click on the gray area outside the stage to deselect the blue shapes. Next, click on each blue shape and hit **delete** on your keyboard:

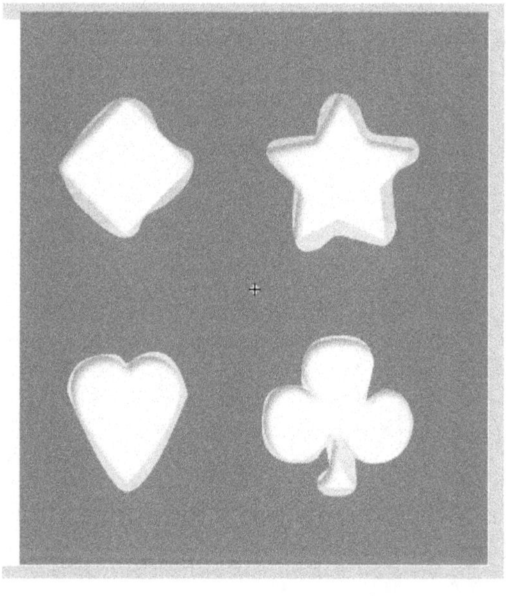

You should now have symbol cutouts in your red shape. Go ahead and test the movie. Place the diamond symbol over the diamond cutout on the stage image. You'll notice that when you release the mouse button the diamond symbol doesn't go back to its original starting position. Since we created a diamond cutout in this area the **Invisible Stage Button** won't be activated if you roll over this part of the button. But, once you roll off the diamond symbol, the **Invisible Stage Button**

once again gets activated and sends the diamond symbol back to its starting position.

So how do we keep the diamond symbol in place after we drop it into its correct destination? That's where a little slight of hand takes place! When we place the diamond symbol on the correct cutout we're going to have it trigger a button that will make it transparent; then, we'll replace the diamond symbol with a raw image of the diamond picture. Let's do that now so you understand how it works.

Create a new layer and name it **Symbol Button**. Place this layer below the **Symbols** layer:

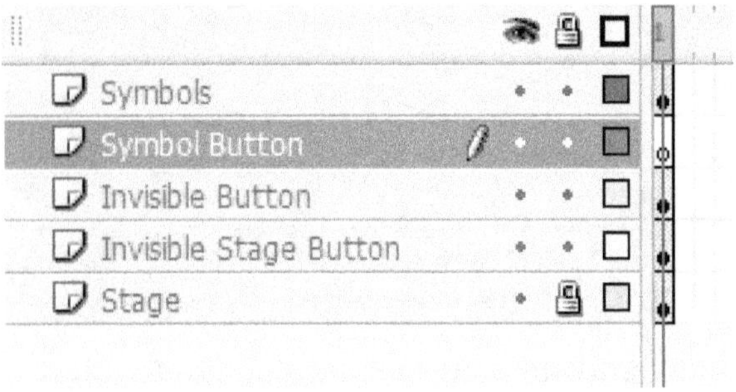

Grab the **Brush Tool** and select **red** for the **Fill color**. Paint over the diamond cutout of the stage image:

Now we have the diamond shape. Select this shape and convert it to a Movie clip. Name this new Movie clip **Diamond Button**:

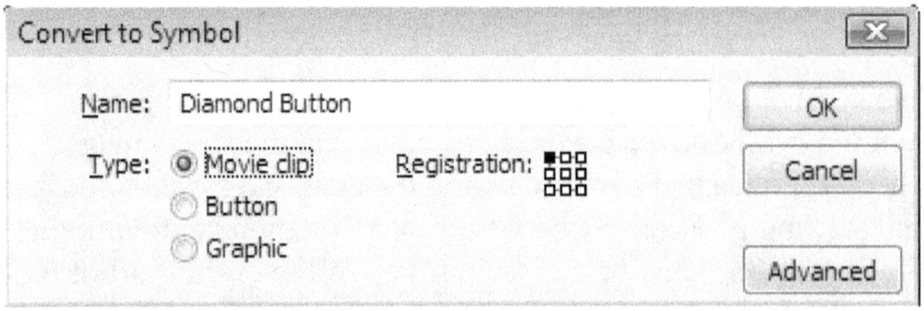

Hit **OK**. Since we'll be controlling this Movie clip we'll need to give it an **Instance Name**. In the **Instance Name** window type **diamond_button**:

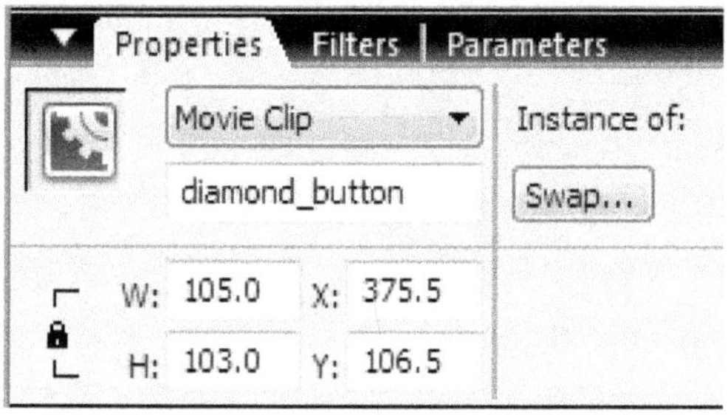

Double-click on this new Movie clip to enter its editing stage. Create a keyframe on frame **2** of **Layer 1**. Select the shape on the stage and go to **Modify**, **Convert to Symbol**. Select **Button** for **Type** and name it **Diamond Button 2**:

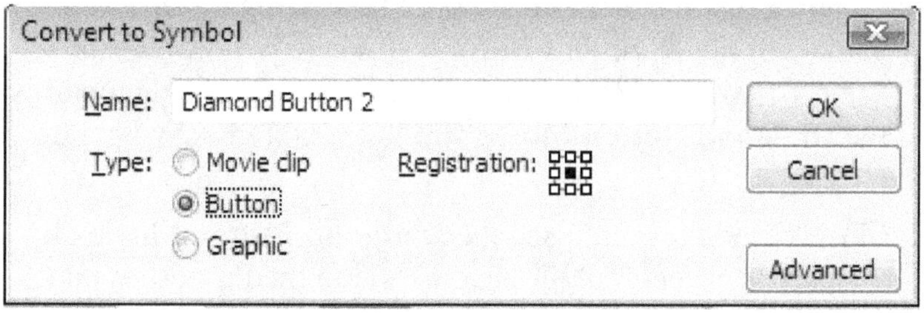

Hit **OK**. So on the first frame we have just the red shape, and on the second frame we have a button. Since we have more than one frame in this timeline we'll need to add a **stop** code. Create a new layer and name it **Actions**. Put a **stop** code in the first frame of this layer.

So here is what's going to happen. When the user drags the diamond symbol over the diamond cutout, we'll have it tell the **Diamond Button** Movie clip to go to frame 2 where the button is. On this button we'll add code which will make the diamond symbol transparent. Let's do that now. On the second frame of **Layer 1** select the button on the stage. In the Actions panel go to **Global Functions**, **Movie clip Control**, and double-click **setProperty**. In the **setProperty** settings window, change **Property** to **_alpha**, **Target** will be **/diamond**, and the **Value** will be **0**:

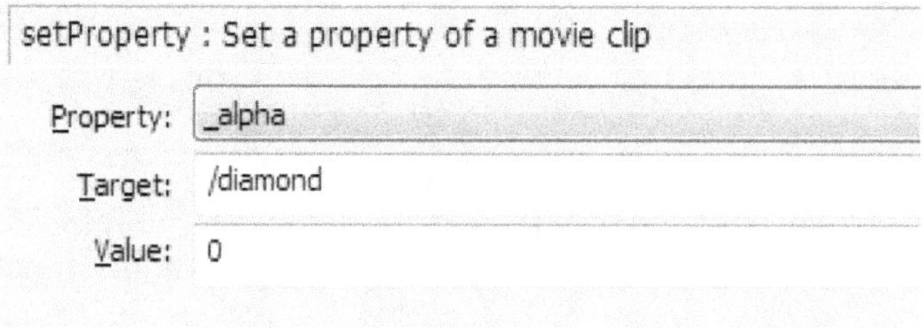

Since we want this action triggered when the user *rolls over* this button, we need to change the mouse event. Click on the word **release** in the Actions window to view the **mouse event** settings window. Uncheck **Release** and select **Roll Over** and **Drag Over**:

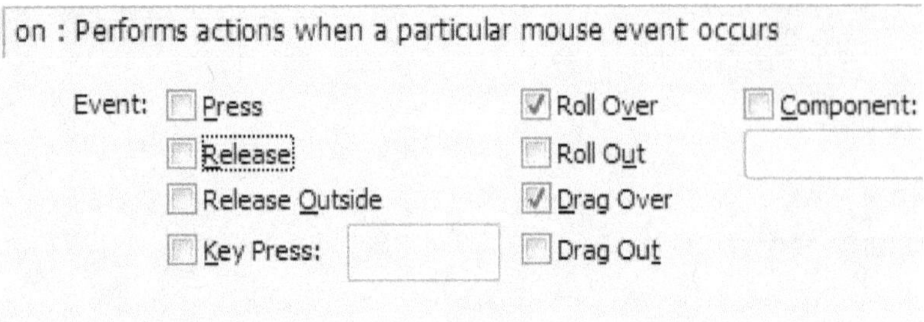

Now when the user rolls over the **Diamond Button** Movie clip, the above code will be triggered which will make the diamond symbol transparent. But, since these actions are on frame 2 of the **Diamond Button** Movie clip, how does this Movie clip go from frame 1 to frame 2? We'll need to add code to the diamond symbol that will tell the **Diamond Button** Movie clip to go to frame 2 where the above actions will be triggered.

Go back to Scene 1. Since we don't want to see the **Diamond Button** Movie clip we need to make it transparent. Select this Movie clip and in the Properties panel change **Color** to **Alpha** and change the percentage to **0**. This Movie clip should now be transparent. Now, let's add the code on the diamond symbol that will tell the **Diamond Button** Movie clip to go to frame 2.

Double-click the **Diamond** Movie clip to enter its editing stage. Select the button on the stage and open the Actions panel. Click on the closing bracket of the last set of code:

```
on (press) {
    startDrag("/diamond");
}
on (release) {
    stopDrag();
}
on (release) {
    nextFrame();
}
```

Go to **Deprecated**, **Actions**, and double-click **tellTarget**. In the **Target** window enter **/diamond_button**:

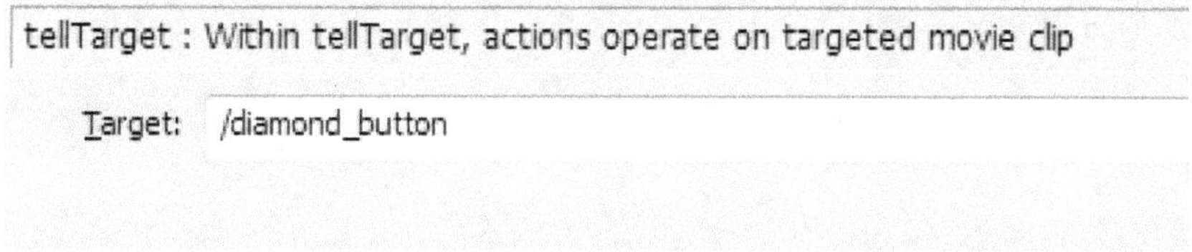

Next, go to **Global Functions**, **Timeline Control** and double-click **goto**. In the **goto** settings window type **2** in the **Frame** window and select **Go to and stop**:

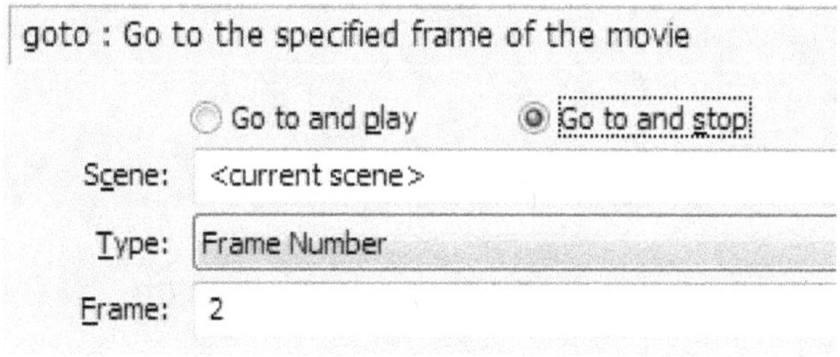

Now when we release the **Diamond** Movie clip it will tell the **Diamond Button** Movie clip to go to frame 2 where its button is; the **setProperty** action on this button is then triggered making the **Diamond** Movie clip transparent. Go ahead and test your movie. When you drag the diamond symbol over the diamond cutout of the stage and release the mouse button, the diamond symbol should become transparent.

Next, we'll need to create one more Movie clip that contains a diamond image which shows up when the **Diamond** Movie clip disappears (you may want to write down the different Movie clips and what they do, to avoid confusion). Create a new layer and name it **Symbol Image**. Place this layer below the **Symbols** layer:

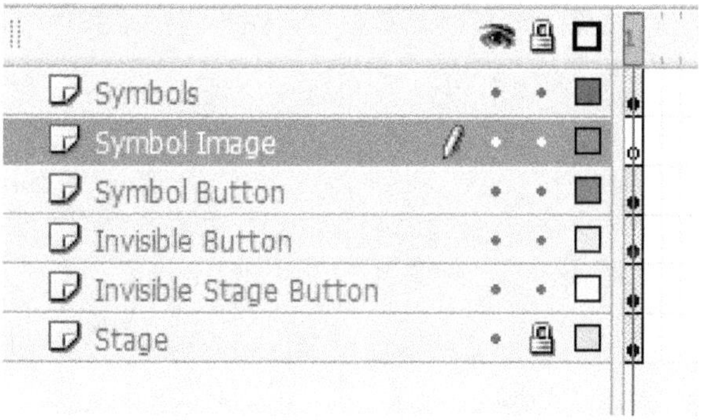

Grab the **Rectangle Tool**. Turn off the **Stroke color** and select **red** for the **Fill color**. Create a shape over the diamond cutout:

Select this shape and convert it to a Movie clip. Name this new Movie clip **Diamond Image**:

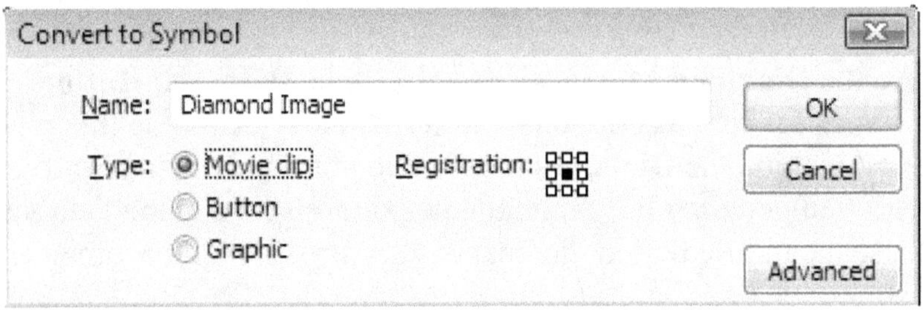

Hit **OK**. Since we'll be controlling this Movie clip we need to give it an **Instance Name**. In the Properties panel type **diamond_image** in the **Instance Name** window:

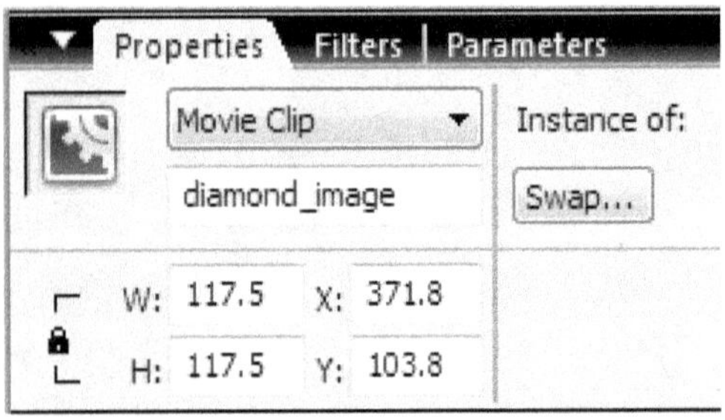

Remember! You only need to give your Movie clip an Instance Name if you plan on controlling it with a frame or button.

This will be the Movie clip that holds the diamond image that appears once the **Diamond** Movie clip becomes transparent. Double-click on this new Movie clip to enter its editing stage. Since this timeline will have two frames we'll need to create a **stop** code. Create a new layer and name it **Actions**. Insert a **stop** code into frame **1** of this layer. Create a second keyframe on the **Layer 1** layer. You should now have a copy of the red shape in this frame. Select this red shape and delete it. Drag **diamond.png** from the library over to the stage. Place it directly over the diamond cutout:

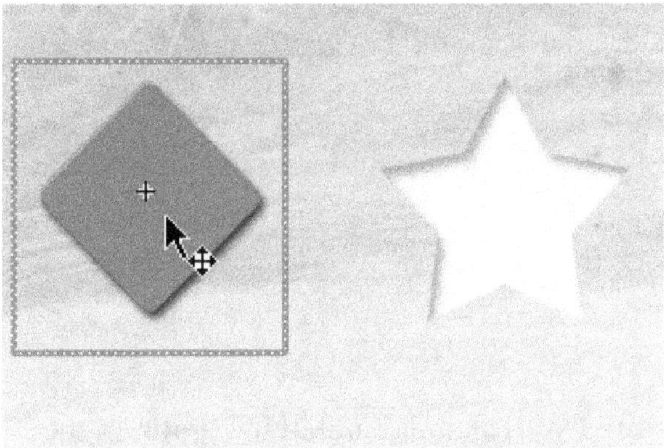

This is the image that appears when the diamond symbol becomes transparent. Go back to frame **1** of **Layer 1**. If you test your movie you'll see the new **Diamond Image** Movie clip. The problem is that the red shape is appearing over the diamond cutout. We need to make this transparent. Select this red shape in the first frame of **Layer 1**. Click on **Fill color** and take the **Alpha** down to **0**:

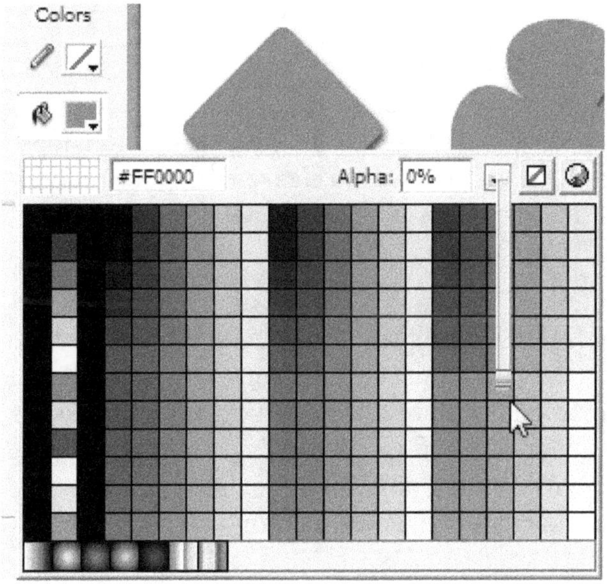

This shape will now be transparent. Now when we drop the diamond symbol on the diamond cutout we need to tell the **Diamond Image** Movie clip to go to frame 2 where the diamond image is.

Let's add that code to the **Diamond Button** Movie clip. Go back to Scene 1. Lock the **Symbol Image** layer. Double-click the **Diamond Button** Movie clip to enter its editing stage. Select the button on the second frame of **Layer 1**. If you open the Actions panel you'll see the ActionScript. Click on the closing bracket of the first set of code.

Next, go to **Deprecated**, **Actions** and double-click **tellTarget**. In the **Target** window type **/diamond_image**:

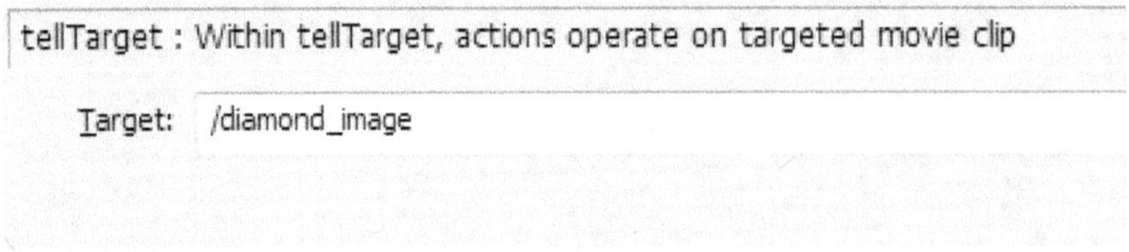

Next, go to **Global Functions**, **Timeline Control** and double-click **goto**. In the **goto** settings window change the **Frame** to **2** and select **Go to and stop**:

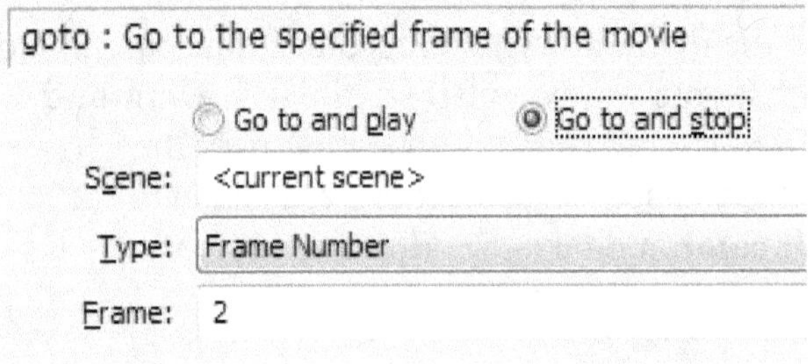

Since we need this command to happen when the user rolls over this button, then we need to change the mouse event. Click on the word **release** in the ActionScript. You should now see the **mouse event** settings window. Uncheck **Release** and select **Roll Over** and **Drag Over**.

Test your movie. If you drag the diamond symbol over to the diamond cutout and release, the diamond symbol becomes transparent and the diamond image from the **Diamond Image** Movie clip appears inside the cutout. But we have a little glitch. Can you find it? Drag the diamond symbol over to the stage and release it (not over the diamond cutout). The diamond symbol returns to its original starting position but now roll your cursor over the diamond cutout. You should now see the diamond image inside the diamond cutout; also, the diamond symbol has disappeared.

So that's a problem. But why is that happening? Well, remember when we release the diamond symbol it triggers the **Diamond Button** Movie clip to go to its second frame where the button is. So now when we roll over the diamond cutout with the cursor, it triggers the ActionScript of this button. That ActionScript then triggers the **Diamond Image** Movie clip to go to frame 2 where the diamond image is.

In Flash you'll be running up against problems like this all the time. Part of the fun, though, is figuring out a way to solve these problems. And in Flash, there is *always a way to fix a problem*! So think about this one and see if you can figure out a solution.

I have a diagram at the end of the exercise which will help you better understand how all the Movie clips are communicating with each other. But try to figure out a solution on your own before peeking at the diagram.

When I run across a problem like this I try to think to myself: how can I tell my **Diamond Button** Movie clip to go back to frame 1 when the diamond symbol is released in an area not over this Movie clip? Since whenever we release the diamond symbol it tells the **Diamond Button** Movie clip to go to frame 2.

What if we add code to the **Invisible Stage Button** that not only sends the diamond symbol back to its original starting position, but also has code that will send the **Diamond Button** Movie clip back to frame 1? Let's see if this will work. Select the **Invisible Stage Button** and open the Actions panel. Click on the closing bracket of the last set of code. Go to **Deprecated**, **Actions** and double-click **tellTarget**. In the Target window enter **diamond_button**:

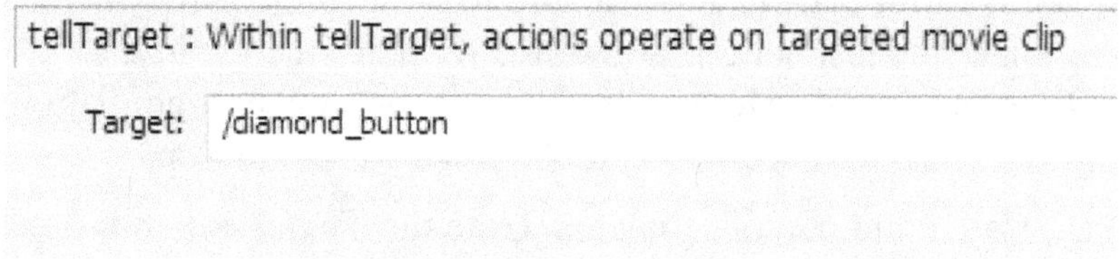

Next, go to **Global Functions**, **Timeline Control** and double-click **goto**. In the **goto** settings window select **Go to and stop**:

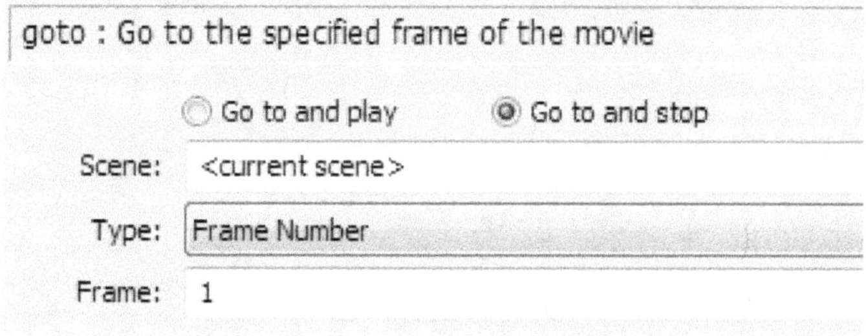

We now need to change the mouse event for this command. Click on the word **release**. In the **mouse event** settings window uncheck **Release** and select **Roll Over** and **Drag Over**:

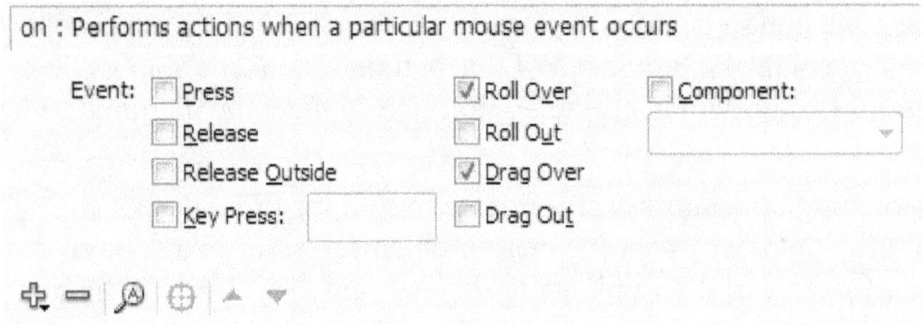

Test your movie again. This time release the diamond symbol anywhere on the stage away from the diamond cutout. The diamond symbol should go back to its starting position. If you roll over the diamond cutout the little glitch is gone! If you have a problem at any time following these steps, refer to the diagram at the end of this exercise. Getting Movie clips and frames to communicate with each other is the key to unlocking the power of Flash! Learn these principles and you'll soon be creating all sorts of dynamic interactive projects.

Now, how do we get the **Success!** animation to play? And how does Flash know when we've completed the game to display the **Finished**! animation?

The way to figure this out is to look at the final action that happens when we place the diamond symbol on the diamond cutout. This triggers the **Diamond Button** Movie clip to go to frame 2 where its button is; then, this button's actions are triggered sending the **Diamond Image** Movie clip to its second frame where the diamond image is. That's the last action. So what if we place a code in the second frame of the **Diamond Image** Movie clip that tells the **Success!** animation to play? Let's try that. But first, we need to create the **Success!** animation.

On Scene 1 create a new layer and name it **Success**. Grab the **Text Tool** and select **red** for the **Fill color**. Type the word **Success!** in all caps over the middle of the stage image:

Grab the **Selection Tool** and click on this word. Convert it to a Movie clip and name it **Success Animation**:

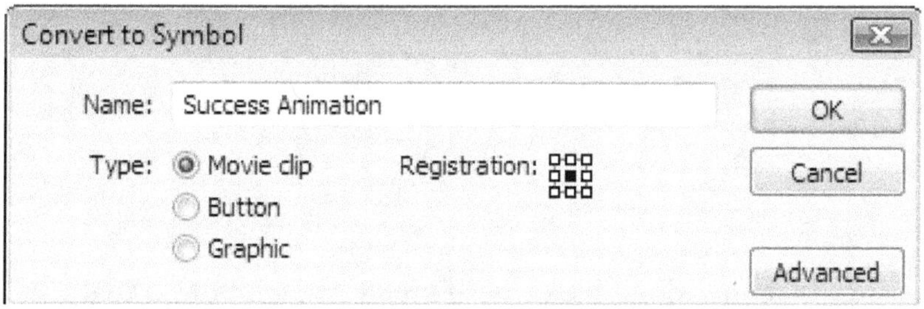

Hit **OK**. Since we'll be controlling this Movie clip we need to give it an Instance Name. In the Properties panel type **success** in the **Instance Name** window:

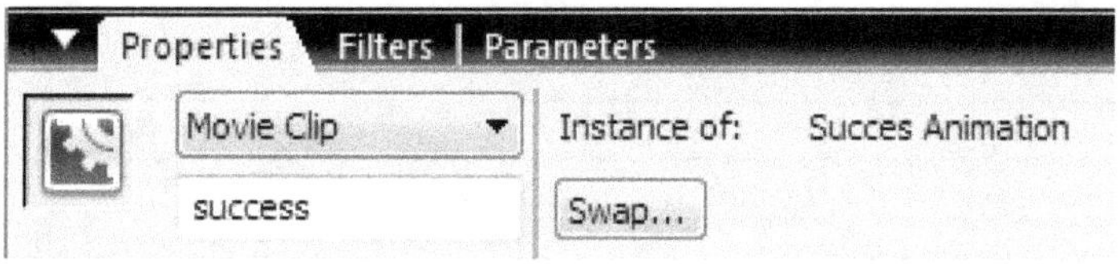

Double-click on this Movie clip to enter its editing stage. Rename Layer 1: **Success**. Create a keyframe on frame **45**. Next, select any frame between the two keyframes and insert a motion tween:

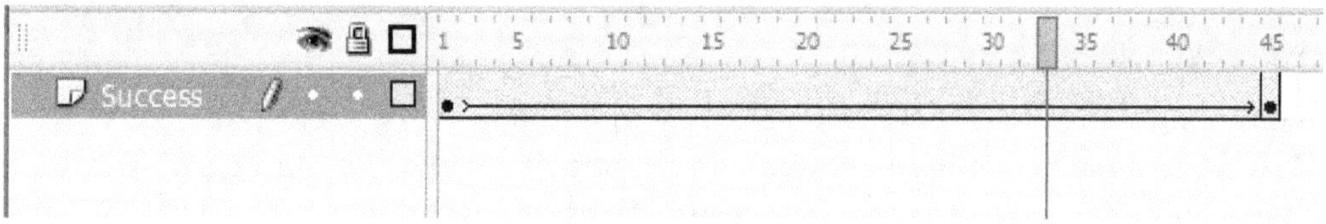

Select the first frame then select the text symbol on the stage. In the Properties panel change **Color** to **Alpha** and take the percentage down to **0**. Insert a keyframe on frame **15**. Select the text symbol on frame **15** and change **Color** to **Alpha** and take the percentage back up to **100**. Create a keyframe on frame **30**. Select the text symbol on the stage and take the **Alpha** of this symbol down to **0**. If you move the timeline needle back and forth across the timeline you should see the success symbol appear and disappear a couple times. Create a new layer and name it **Actions**. Insert a **stop** code into the first frame of the **Actions** layer. Next, create a new layer and name it **Labels**. In the second frame of the **Labels** layer insert a Frame Label: **success**:

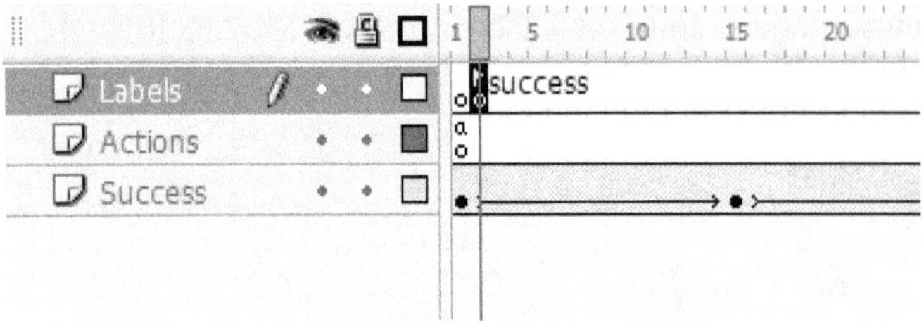

So now we have the success animation. Next, we'll create the animation that occurs when a user finishes the game. Create a new layer above the **Success** layer and name it **Finished**:

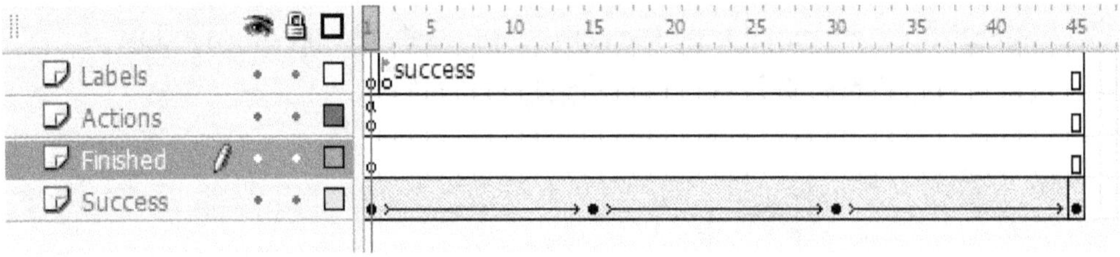

Next, insert a frame into frame **92** for each layer. Select the **Success!** text symbol on the stage and go to **Edit**, **Copy**. Create a keyframe on frame **47** of the **Finished** layer. Select this new keyframe and go to **Edit**, **Paste in Place**. You should now have a copy of the **SUCCESS!** text on your **Finished** layer. Select this text symbol and go to **Modify**, **Break Apart**. This will now make this symbol editable so we can change the text.

Change the text to: **FINISHED!.** You may notice that we're seeing the **SUCCESS!** underneath the new text. To fix this problem click on frame **46** of the **Success** layer and go to **Insert**, **Timeline**, **Blank Keyframe**. This will remove the **SUCCESS!** text from all frames beyond frame **45**.

Insert a keyframe on frame **92** of the **Finished** layer; next, select any frame between the two keyframes and insert a Motion Tween:

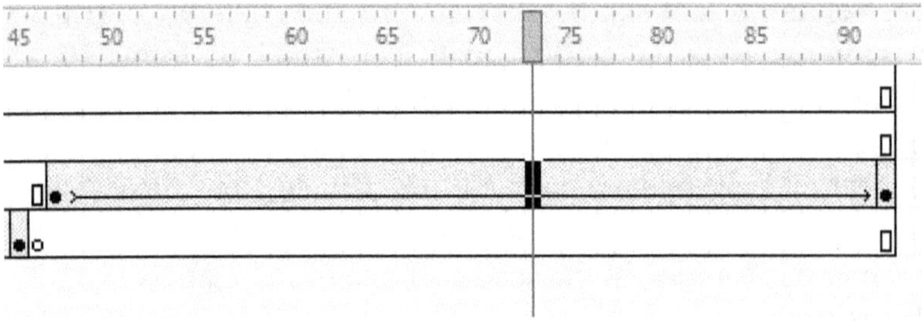

Select a keyframe on frame **68** of the **Finished** layer. Select the **FINISHED!** text symbol on the stage and open the Properties panel; change **Color** to **Alpha** and take the percentage down to **0**. Now the **FINISHED!** animation will fade out then back in by the final frame. Since we want this animation to stop when it gets to the final frame we need to add a **stop** code to frame **92**. Create a keyframe on frame **92** of the **Actions** layer and insert a **stop** code. Next, we'll add the code to the **Diamond Image** Movie clip that will control this timeline.

Go back to Scene 1 and double-click on the **Diamond Image** Movie clip to enter its editing stage. Create a keyframe on frame **2** of the **Actions** layer. Select this keyframe and open the Actions panel. Go to **Deprecated**, **Actions** and double-click **tellTarget**. In the **Target** window type **/success**:

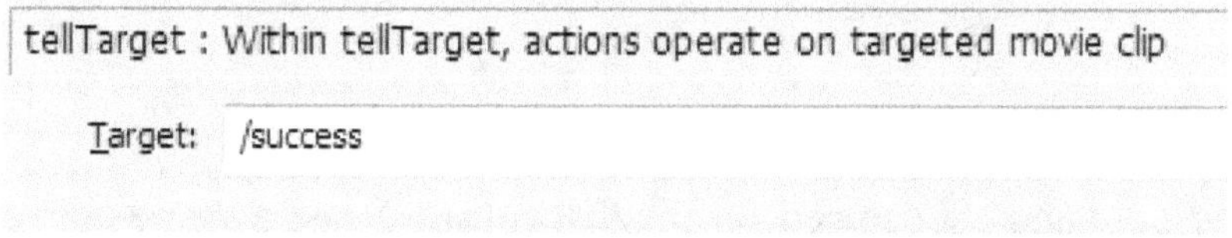

Next, go to **Global Functions**, **Timeline Control** and double-click **goto**. In the **goto** settings window change **Type** to **Frame Label** and enter **success** in for the **Frame**:

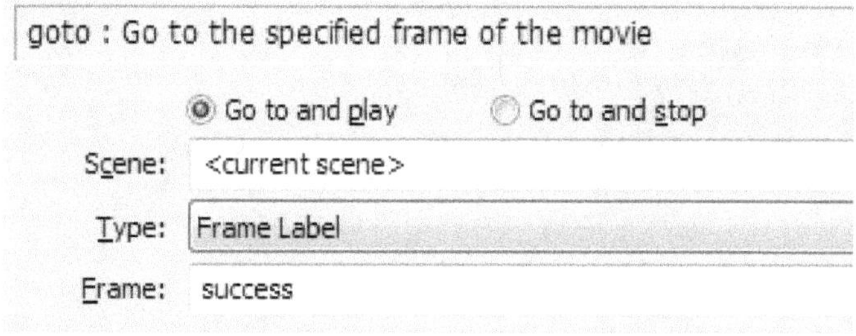

Now when this timeline is told by the **Diamond Button** Movie clip to go to frame 2, the ActionScript we just created will be activated. Test your movie. Drop the diamond symbol in the diamond cutout. You should now see the **SUCCESS!** and the **FINISHED!** animations. We'll add a **stop** code in a moment to this timeline to prevent the **FINISHED!** animation from playing too soon.

Before we wrap on this symbol we need to add one more Movie clip. If you remember, when you drag all four symbols over to their correct destinations, you'll get a **FINISHED!** animation then a **RESET** button appears (we'll add the **RESET** button later). So let's create the Movie clip which controls this animation.

Create a new layer on Scene 1 and name it **Finish**:

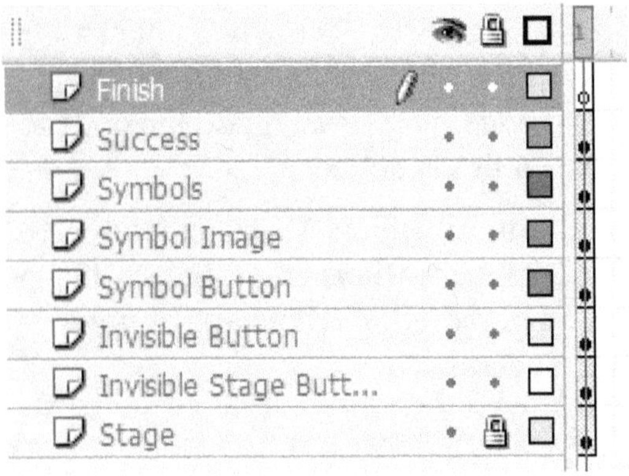

Select the **Rectangle Tool** and choose **red** for the **Fill color**. Create a shape above the stage in the gray area:

Since this Movie clip is in the gray area it won't be seen by the user. Select this red shape and convert it to a Movie clip. Name this new Movie clip **Finish**:

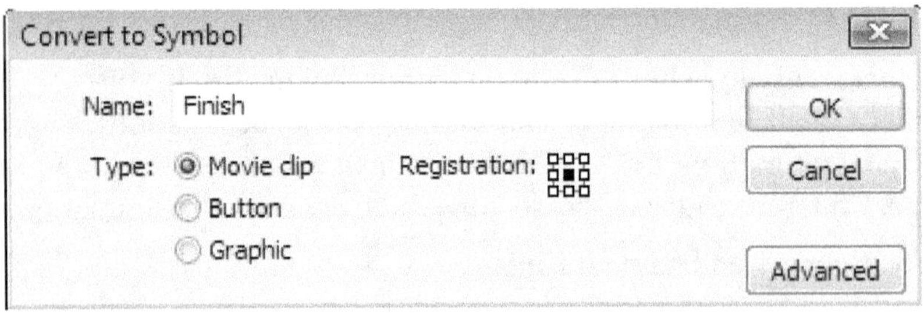

Hit **OK** when finished. Since we'll be controlling this Movie clip we need to give it an Instance Name. In the Properties panel type **finish** in the **Instance Name** window:

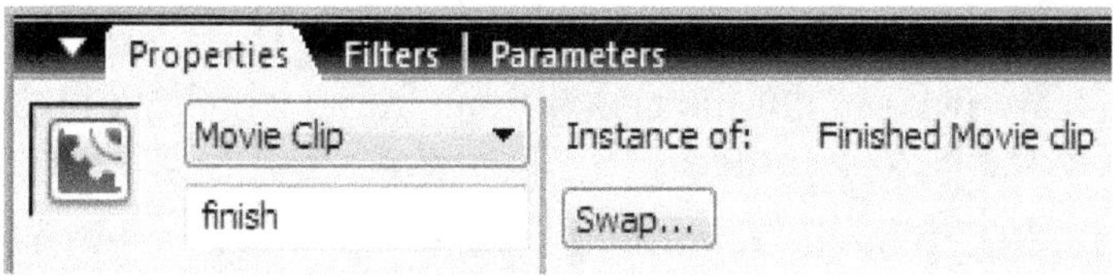

Double-click on this new Movie clip to enter its editing stage. So here is what's going to happen. Every time we place one of the symbols in the correct cutout, a code will tell the **Finish** Movie clip to go to the next frame. So after the fourth symbol gets placed on the correct destination, this Movie clip will be told to go the **Next Frame** four times. Which means it will end up on frame 5. On frame 5 we'll have a code that triggers the animation on the **Success Animation** Movie clip.

Create a new layer and name it **Actions**. Put a **stop** code in the first frame of this layer. Create a keyframe on frame **5**. Select this keyframe and in the Actions panel go to **Deprecated**, **Actions**, and double-click **tellTarget**. In the **Target** window type **/success**:

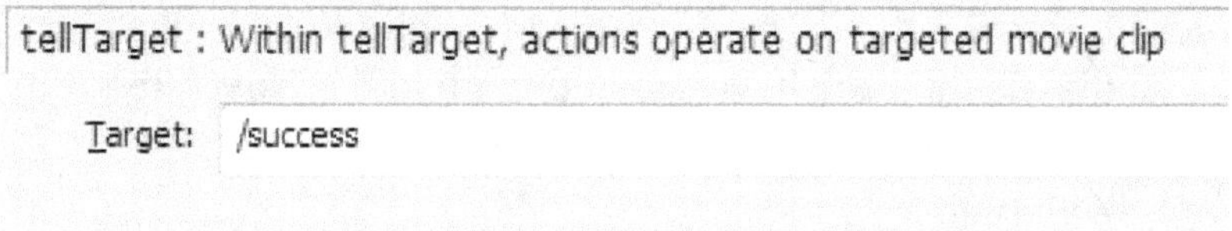

Next, go to **Global Functions**, **Timeline Control** and double-click **goto**. In the **goto** settings window change the **Type** to **Frame Label**, select **Go to and play**, and type **finish** in the **Frame** window:

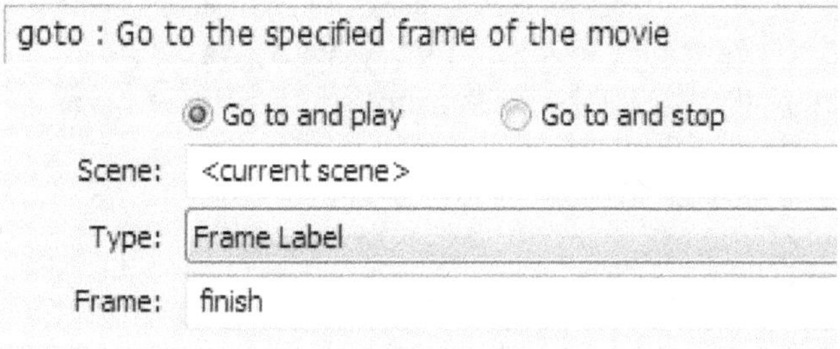

So when the timeline gets to this keyframe it will tell the **Success Animation** Movie clip to go to the Label: **finish** and play. So to recap, after we place each symbol in their correct destination it will tell this Movie clip to go to the **Next Frame**. After all four symbols are placed correctly, this timeline will have moved forward four times ending up on frame 5 where the above code is. Next, we need to add the code to the **Diamond Image** Movie clip that commands this Movie clip to go to the next frame. Let's do that now.

Since the last step in the process involves a command that takes the **Diamond Image** Movie clip to frame **2**, we need to put the code in this frame which will tell the **Finish** Movie clip to go to the **Next Frame**.

Go back to **Scene 1** and double-click on the **Diamond Image** Movie clip to enter its editing stage. Next, select the second keyframe of the **Actions** layer and open the Actions panel. Click on the closing bracket of the last set of code and go to **Deprecated**, **Actions**, and double-click **tellTarget**. In the **Target** window type **/finish**. Go to **Global Functions**, **Timeline Control** and double-click **goto**. In the **goto** settings window change **Type** to **Next Frame**:

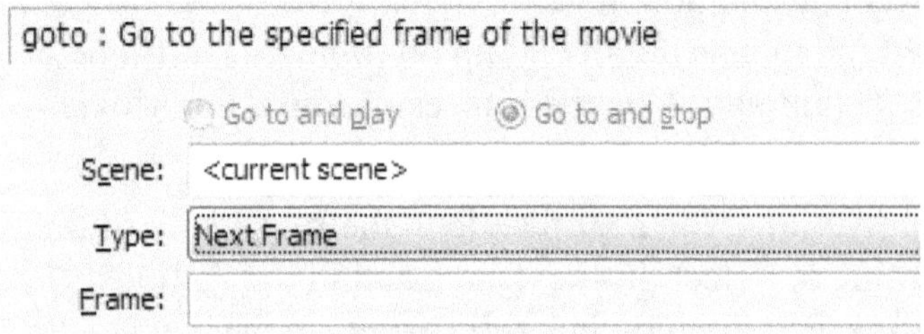

When this timeline gets to frame **2** it tells the **Finish** Movie clip to go to the **Next Frame**. After each symbol tells the **Finish** Movie clip to go to the **Next Frame** the **Finish** Movie clip will end up on frame **5** which holds the ActionScript triggering the **FINISH!** animation.

Next, let's create the **RESET** button. Go back to Scene 1 and double-click the **Success Animation** Movie clip (if you can't find this Movie clip, select its layer and the Movie clip will now be highlighted). Create a new layer and name it **Reset**. Create a keyframe on frame **92** of this layer and insert a keyframe. Select the **FINISHED!** text symbol and go to **Edit**, **Copy**.

Select the keyframe on frame **92** of the **Reset** layer and go to **Edit**, **Paste in Place**. We now have a copy of the **FINISHED!** text symbol on the **Reset** layer. Slide this text to the left so it's on the left half of the stage:

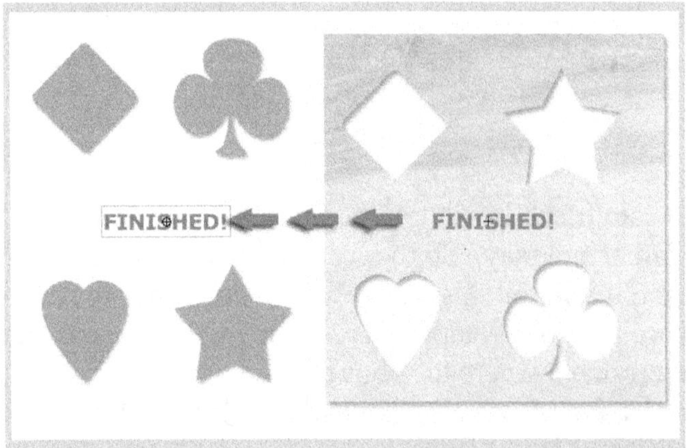

With this text symbol still selected go to **Modify**, **Break Apart**. You should now be able to edit the text. Change the text to **RESET**.

When you're done grab the **Selection Tool** and select the text. Convert this text to a button; name it **Reset Button**:

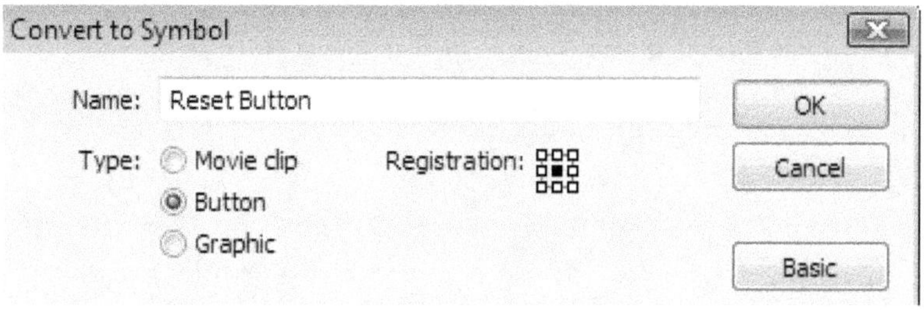

Hit **OK**. One rule to remember when converting a text file to a button is that you should always add a shape to the Hit stage. Double-click on this new button to enter its editing stage. Create a keyframe under the **Hit** stage. Grab your **Rectangle Tool**, use any color, and create a shape that covers the entire text:

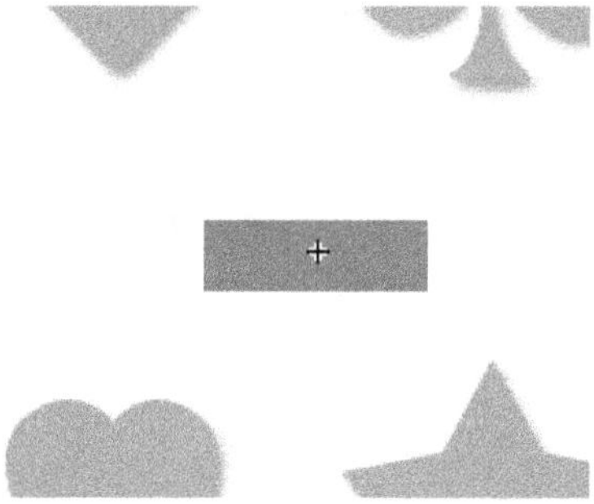

The reason you have to do this, is because if text is converted to a button the space between the letters won't be active. If the user clicks on your text button in the space between the letters the button may not work. If we add a shape to the **Hit** stage, then that is no longer a problem.

Let's add the ActionScript to this button. Open the Actions panel. This button is going to send all of the Movie clips back to frame **1**. A quick way to do this is to create one tellTarget code and copy and paste it for every Movie clip. Let's do that now.

In the Actions panel go to **Deprecated**, **Actions** and double-click **tellTarget**. In the **Target** window type **/finish** in the **Target** window:

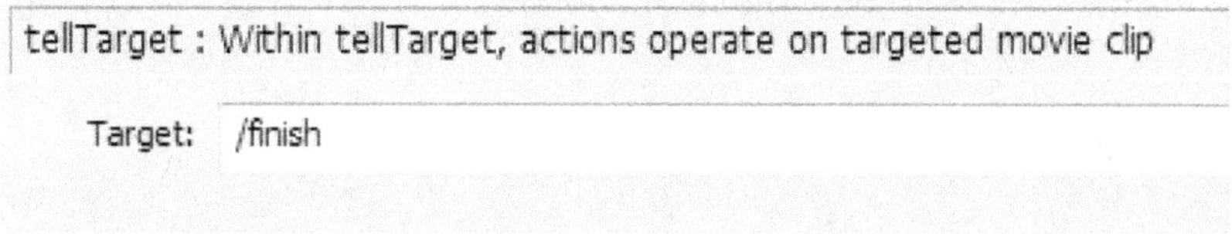

Go to **Global Functions**, **Timeline Control** and double-click **goto**. In the **goto** settings window select **Go to and stop**, **Frame Number** for **Type**, and enter **1** for the **Frame**:

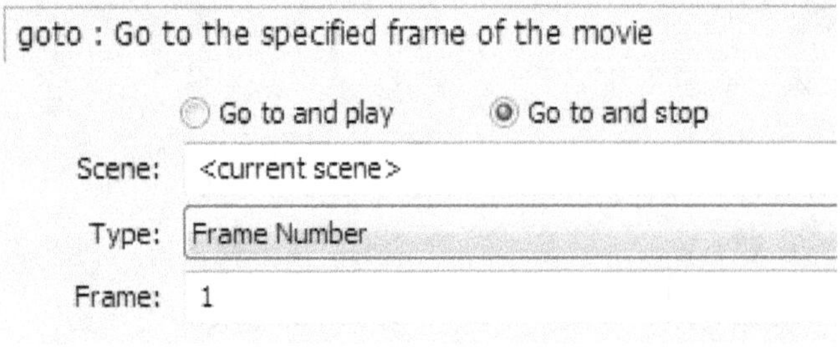

Since this command will be triggered when the button is released then we don't need to change the mouse event. We'll now copy and paste this code below itself. Select the entire set of code by clicking-and-dragging over it until it's entirely highlighted. Go to **Edit**, **Copy**. Click on the closing bracket and go to **Edit, Paste in Center**. You should now have an exact copy of the code below the first set of code:

```
on (release) {
    tellTarget ("/finish") {
        gotoAndStop(1);
    }
}
on (release) {
    tellTarget ("/finish") {
        gotoAndStop(1);
    }
}
```

Click on the word **/finish** in the second set of code. In the **Target** window change the name to **/success**:

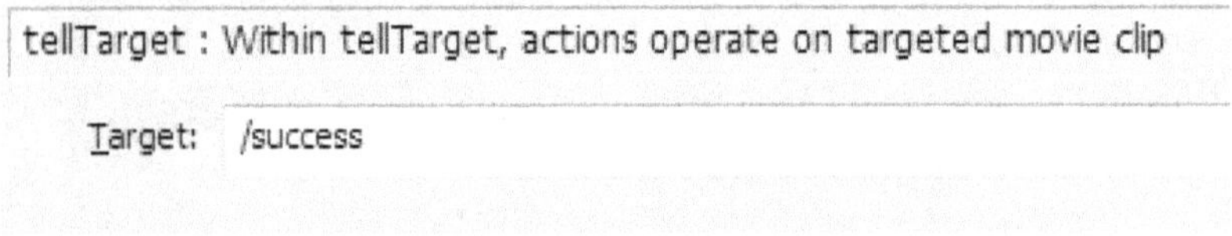

The new ActionScript should look like this:

```
on (release) {
    tellTarget ("/finish") {
        gotoAndStop(1);
    }
}
on (release) {
    tellTarget ("/success") {
        gotoAndStop(1);
    }
}
```

Highlight the second set of code and go to **Edit**, **Copy**. Select the closing bracket of the second set of code and go to **Edit**, **Paste in Center**. So now we have a copy of the second set of code. Click on the word **/success** and the **Target** window should come up. Change the Target name to **/diamond_image**:

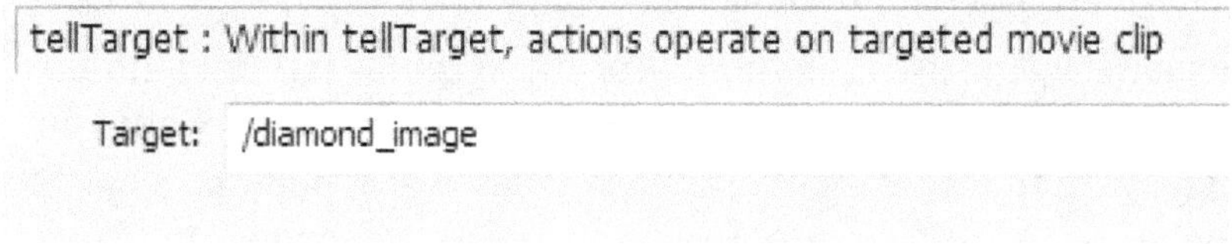

We now have three of the Movie clips going back to frame **1**. We have one more Movie clip to send back to frame **1**, and that is the **Diamond** Movie clip. Highlight the last set of code and go to **Edit**, **Copy**. Click on the closing bracket and go to **Edit**, **Paste in Center**. You should now have a copy of the third set of code. Select the word **/diamond_image** and you should see the **Target** window. Change the name to **/diamond**:

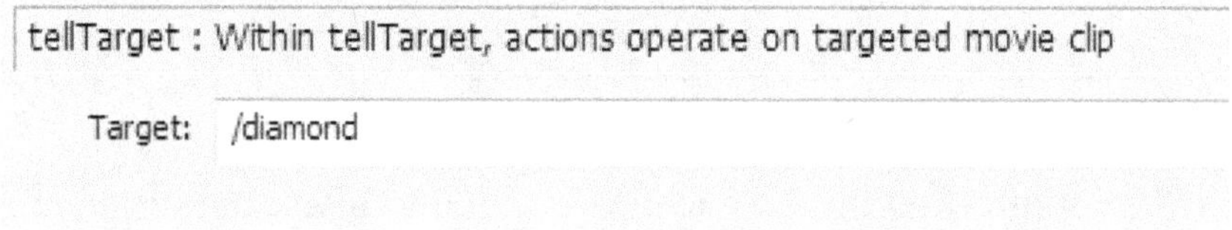

So now we have all of the Movie clips returning to frame **1** except for the **Diamond Button** Movie clip. This Movie clip gets sent back to frame **1** when the user rolls over the **Invisible Stage Button** so we don't need to add it.

Next, we need to add a setProperty code. Remember when we added the setProperty code to the **Diamond Button** Movie clip that changed the **Alpha** of the diamond symbol to **0**? Until we change this Alpha back to 100 the diamond symbol will remain transparent. So let's add that code now.

Click on the closing bracket of the last set of code. Go to **Global Functions**, **Movie clip Control**, and double-click on **setProperty**. In the **setProperty** settings window change the Property to **_alpha**, type **/diamond** in the **Target** window, and make the Value **100**:

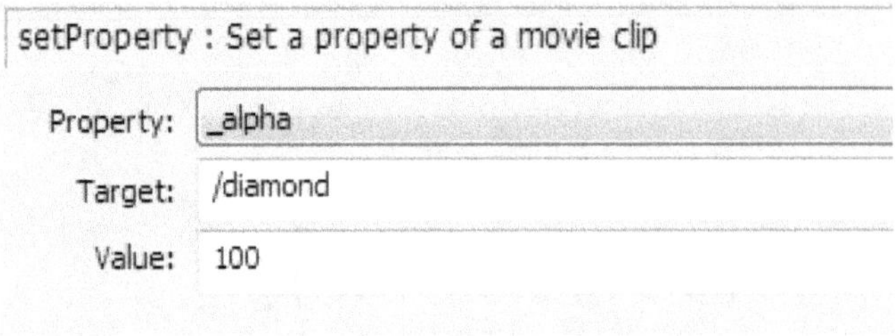

Go ahead and test your movie. Drop the diamond symbol onto the diamond cutout. You should get a **SUCCESS!** message then we'll see the **FINISHED!** animation. The **RESET** button will then appear. Click on this button and everything should return to their original positions.

Now that we've finished the first symbol, the rest of the symbols will be a little easier. We'll just have to copy and paste the code into their buttons. I'll walk you through how to do this with the Club symbol then you can just repeat the steps for the rest of the symbols.

Select the Club image and convert it to a Movie clip. Name this Movie clip **Club** Movie clip:

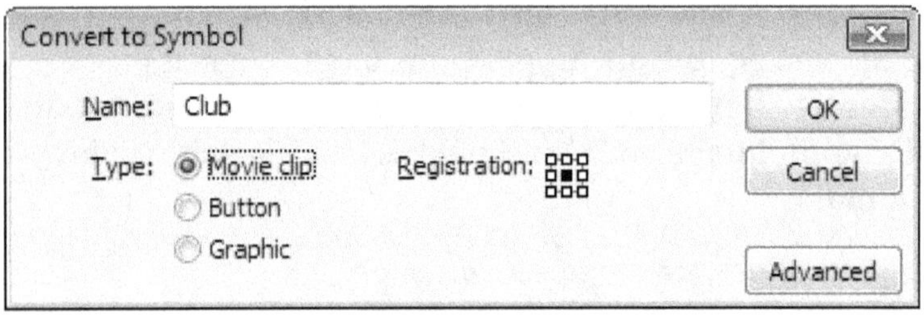

Hit **OK**. Since we'll be controlling this Movie clip we need to give it an Instance Name. Name this Movie clip **club**:

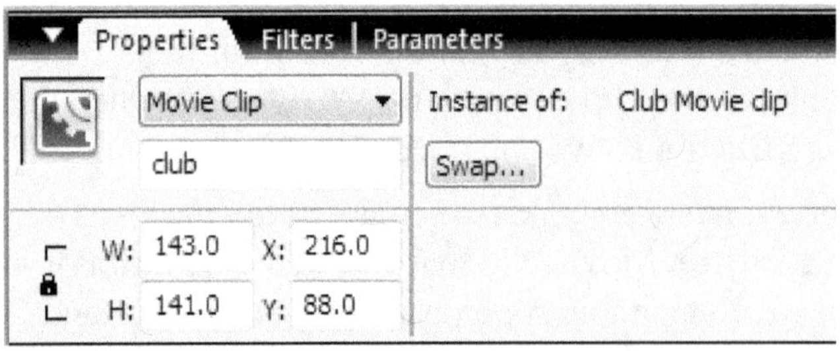

Double-click on this Movie clip to enter its editing stage. Create a keyframe on frame **2** of **Layer 1**. Create a new layer and name it **Actions**. Put a **stop** code into frame **1** of this layer. Select the club image on frame **1** of **Layer 1** and convert it to a button. Name this button **Club Button**:

Hit **OK**. Instead of going through all the steps to create code for this button we'll simply copy and paste the code from the **Diamond Button**. Let's do that now. Go back to Scene 1. Double-click on the **Diamond** Movie clip to enter its editing stage. Select the button on the stage and open the Actions panel. Highlight all the ActionScript and go to **Edit**, **Copy**.

Go back to Scene 1. Double-click on the **Club** Movie clip to enter its editing stage. Select the **Club Button** and click anywhere inside the Actions window and go to **Edit**, **Paste in Center**. You should now have a copy of the **Diamond Button** code in your window:

```
on (press) {
    startDrag("/diamond");
}
on (release) {
    stopDrag();
}
on (release) {
    nextFrame();
}
on (release) {
    tellTarget ("/diamond_button") {
        gotoAndStop(2);
    }
}
```

We need to change the word **/diamond** to say **/club**. Click on **/diamond** in the first set of code. In the **Target** window change the name to **/club**. Click on the word **/diamond_button** in the last set of code. In the **Target** window change the name to **/club_button**. The code should now look like this:

```
on (press) {
    startDrag("/club");
}
on (release) {
    stopDrag();
}
on (release) {
    nextFrame();
}
on (release) {
    tellTarget ("/club_button") {
        gotoAndStop(2);
    }
}
```

We'll now add the code to the two large invisible buttons. Go back to Scene 1. Select the **Invisible Button**. In the Actions panel you should see this code:

```
on (rollOver, dragOver) {
    tellTarget ("/diamond") {
        gotoAndStop(1);
    }
}
```

Highlight this code and go to **Edit, Copy**. Click on the closing bracket and select **Edit, Paste in Center**. In this new code change **/diamond** to **/club**:

```
on (rollOver, dragOver) {
    tellTarget ("/diamond") {
        gotoAndStop(1);
    }
}
on (rollOver, dragOver) {
    tellTarget ("/club") {
        gotoAndStop(1);
    }
}
```

Next, lock the **Invisible Button** layer. Select the **Invisible Stage Button**. Highlight all the code in the Actions window and copy it. Click on the last closing bracket and Paste this code back in the Actions window:

```
on (rollOver, dragOver) {
    setProperty("/diamond", _x, "9.5");
    setProperty("/diamond", _y, "18");
}
on (release) {
    tellTarget ("/diamond_button") {
        gotoAndStop(1);
    }
}
on (rollOver, dragOver) {
    setProperty("/diamond", _x, "9.5");
    setProperty("/diamond", _y, "18");
}
on (release) {
    tellTarget ("/diamond_button") {
        gotoAndStop(1);
    }
}
```

In the copied code we just pasted into the window, click on the word **/diamond** in the **setProperty** code. Here is where we need to put the **X** and **Y** coordinates of the **Club** Movie clip. Select the **Club** Movie clip on the stage and open the Properties panel. In the **X** coordinate window we se **216**, and the **Y** coordinate is **88**:

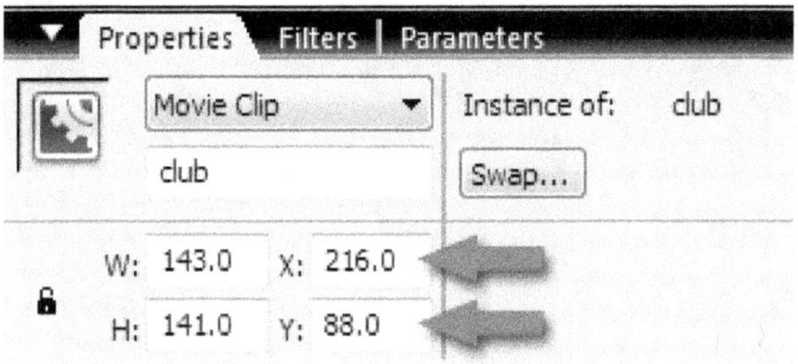

Select the **Invisible Stage Button** again. In the Actions window click on the _x coordinate within the copied setProperty code. Type **216** in the **Value** window and change the **Target** to **/club**:

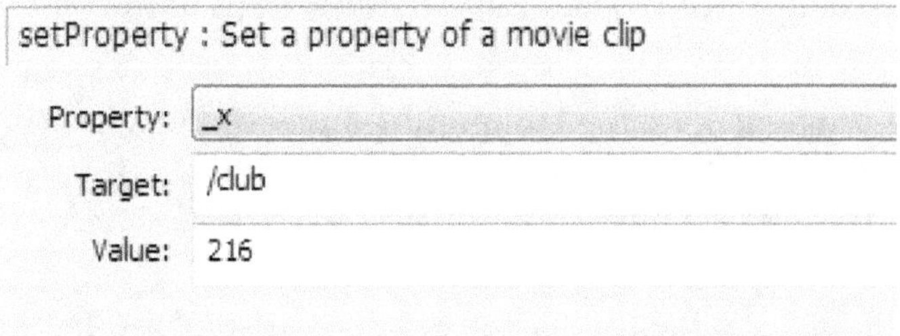

Next, select the **_y** coordinate below the previous code. Change the **Value** to **88** and type **/club** in the **Target** window:

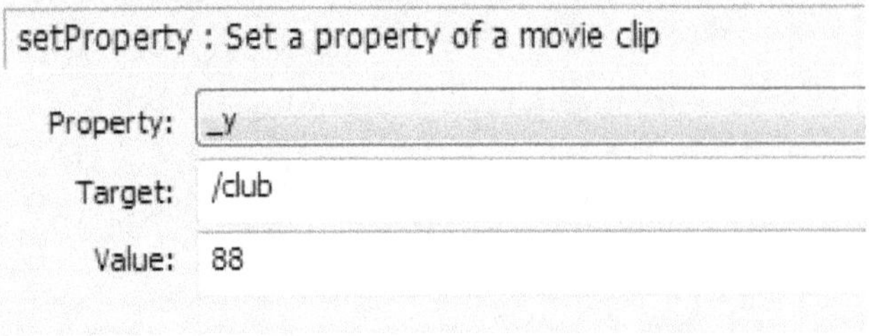

In the last set of code change **/diamond_button** to **/club_button**. Your final code should look like this:

```
on (rollOver, dragOver) {
	setProperty("/diamond", _x, "72");
	setProperty("/diamond", _y, "83");
}
on (rollOver, dragOver) {
	tellTarget ("/diamond_button") {
		gotoAndStop(1);
	}
}
on (rollOver, dragOver) {
	setProperty("/club", _x, "216");
	setProperty("/club", _y, "88");
}
on (rollOver, dragOver) {
	tellTarget ("/club_button") {
		gotoAndStop(1);
	}
}
```

If you test your movie you should now be able to drag the club symbol around the stage. If you drag it over the stage image and release the mouse button, it should return to its starting position. We now need to add the symbol buttons to the club cutout and we'll be done.

Select the layer **Symbol Image** and click on the **Diamond Image** Movie clip over the diamond cutout. Go to **Edit**, **Copy**. Next, go to **Edit**, **Paste in Place**. Move this copied Movie clip so that it's over the club cutout:

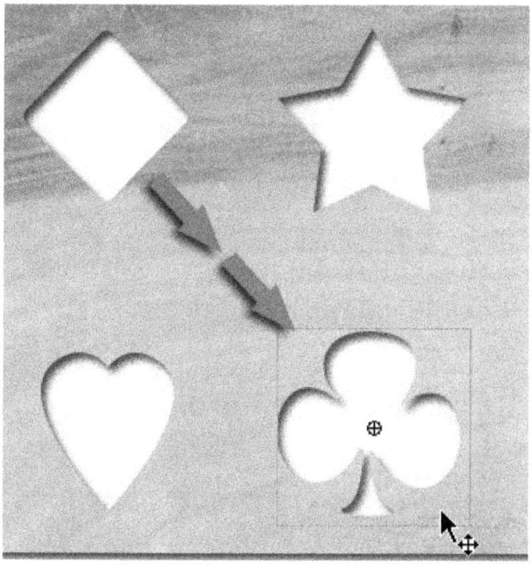

Since this is a copy of the **Diamond Image** Movie clip we need to duplicate it before we can edit it. In the Properties panel click on the **Swap...** button:

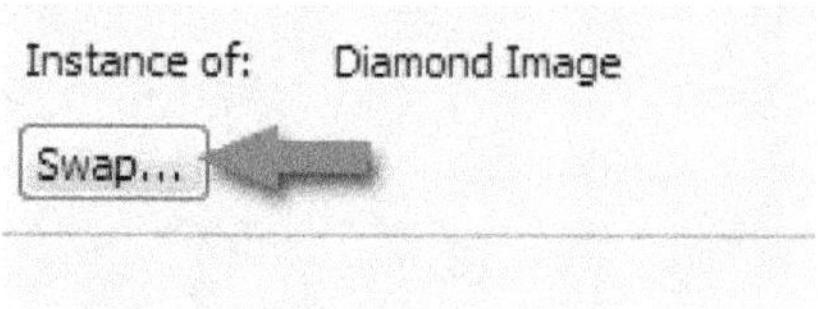

Click on the **Duplicate Symbol** button and type **Club Image** in the **Symbol name** window:

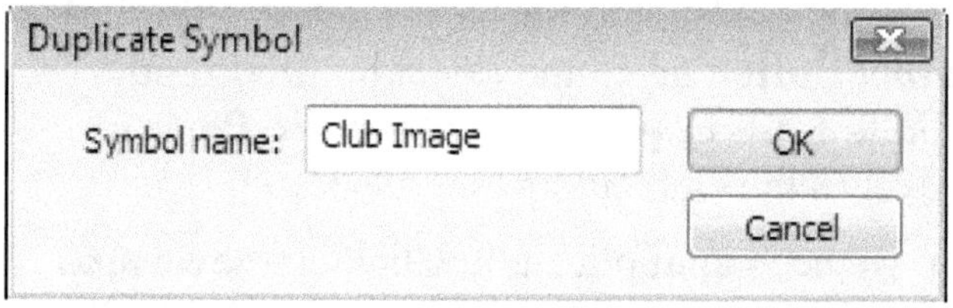

Hit **OK**. In the **Swap Symbol** window double-click on this new Movie clip. Your **Swap Symbol** box should close automatically. With this symbol still selected you'll see its Instance Name in the Properties panel. Delete this Instance Name and type **club_image**:

Double-click on this new Movie clip to enter its editing stage. Above the timeline (above the stage in **CS3/CS4/CS5**) make sure you see **Club Image**:

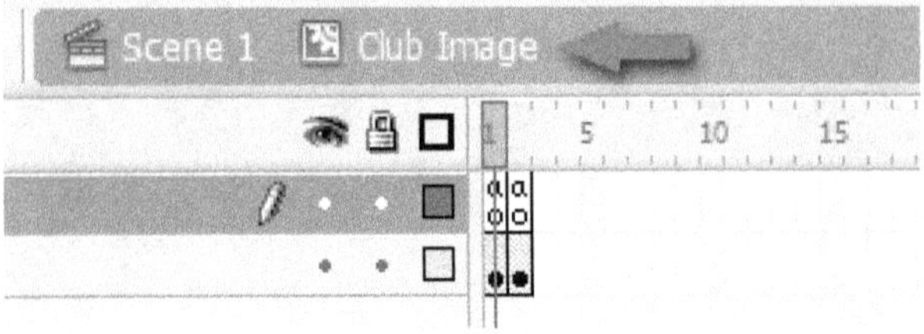

Whenever you duplicate a symbol always check the stage name to make sure you aren't accidentally editing the original symbol.

In this symbol we don't need to change any ActionScript. The only thing we need to do is delete the diamond image on frame 2 and replace it with the club image. Select the second frame of **Layer 1**. Delete this image. Next, drag the **clubCard.png** file from the library over to the stage. Place this image directly over the club cutout of the stage image:

So now we're done with this Movie clip. Go back to Scene 1. Lock the **Symbol Image** layer. Next, select the **Symbol Button** layer and select the **Diamond Button** Movie clip on the stage. Go to **Edit**, **Copy**. Next, go to **Edit**, **Paste in Place**. Drag this new Movie clip over to the club cutout.

Before we can edit this Movie clip we need to duplicate it. Click on the **Swap...** button in the Properties panel. In the **Swap Symbol** box click on the **Duplicate Symbol** button. Change the name to **Club Button** and hit **OK**. Double-click on this new Movie clip in the **Swap Symbol** box and it should close automatically. In the Properties panel change the Instance Name to **club_button**:

Double-click on this new Movie clip to enter its editing stage. Select the button on the second frame of **Layer 1**. Click on the **Swap...** button in the Properties panel and select the **Duplicate Symbol** button. Name this button **Club Button 2** and hit **OK**. Double-click on this new button symbol in the **Swap Symbol** window. Next, double-click on this button and delete the red shape. Grab the **Brush Tool** and select **red** for the **Fill color**. Paint over the club cutout of the stage image:

You don't have to make it perfect. Click on the **Back** button to go back to the **Club Button** Movie clip timeline:

Select the button on frame **2** of **Layer 1** and open the Actions panel. In the ActionScript wherever it says **/diamond** change that to **/club**:

```
on (rollOver, dragOver) {
    setProperty("/club", _alpha, "0");
}
on (rollOver, dragOver) {
    tellTarget ("/club_image") {
        gotoAndStop(2);
    }
}
```

When you're done, select this button symbol and go to **Edit**, **Copy**. Select the first frame of **Layer 1** and delete the red shape on the stage. Go to **Edit**, **Paste in Place**. We should now have a copy of the button in frame **1**.

Next, go to **Modify**, **Break Apart**. The button is now a red club shape. Go ahead and test your movie. Everything should work. Place both symbols in their correct destinations and you'll see the **FINISHED!** animation. You should then see the **RESET** button. Click on the **RESET** button. The club symbol isn't showing up in its original position so we need to fix that.

Double-click on the **Success Animation** Movie clip to enter its editing stage. Go to frame **92** and select the **RESET** button on the stage. Open the Actions panel. Highlight the last three sets of code:

```
on (release) {
      tellTarget ("/diamond_image") {
            gotoAndStop(1);
      }
}
on (release) {
      tellTarget ("/diamond") {
            gotoAndStop(1);
      }
}
on (release) {
      setProperty("/diamond", _alpha, "100");
}
```

Go to **Edit, Copy**. Next, click on the closing bracket of the last set of code and go to **Edit, Paste in Center**. You should now have copies of the last three sets of code. Wherever you find **/diamond** in the last three sets of code change that to **/club**:

```
on (release) {
      tellTarget ("/club_image") {
            gotoAndStop(1);
      }
}
on (release) {
      tellTarget ("/club") {
            gotoAndStop(1);
      }
}
on (release) {
      setProperty("/club", _alpha, "100");
}
```

Test your movie again. Place both symbols on their cutouts and wait for the **RESET** button to appear. Click on the **RESET** button. Both symbols should return to their original positions. One last thing before we finish. We don't want the **FINISHED**! animation to appear until all four symbols have been placed on their proper cutouts. In the **Success Animation** timeline place a keyframe on frame **46** of the **Actions** layer. Next, place a **stop** code into this keyframe. Now when you place a symbol on their proper cutout the **SUCCESS!** animation will animate then disappear. Once all four symbols have been placed on their proper cutouts then that triggers the **FINISHED!** animation and **RESET** button to appear.

So now all that's left is to finish the last two symbols. Just use the same steps we used in creating the club symbol. Review the following diagram to help you better understand the chain of events:

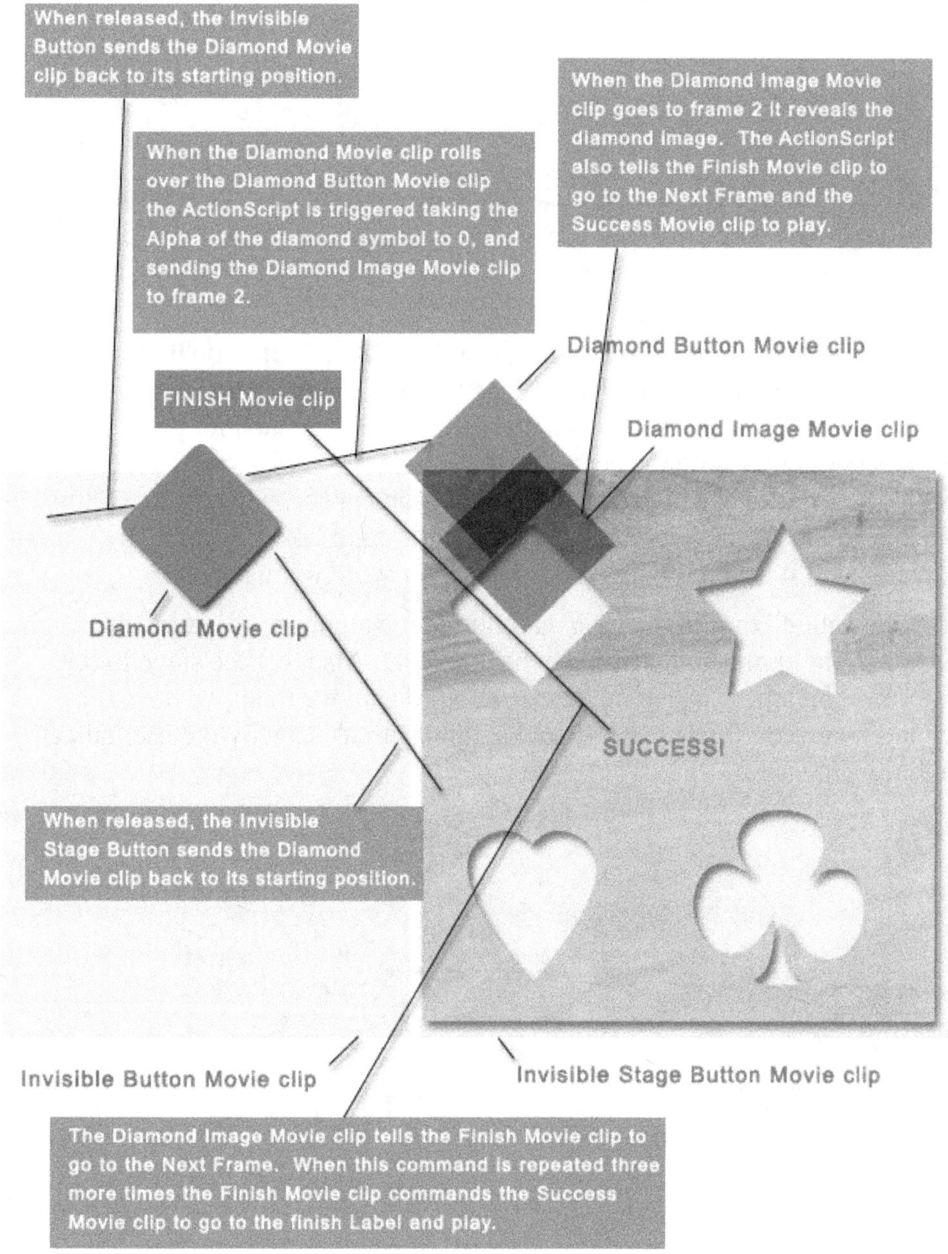
When released, the Invisible Button sends the Diamond Movie clip back to its starting position.
When the Diamond Image Movie clip goes to frame 2 it reveals the diamond image. The ActionScript also tells the Finish Movie clip to go to the Next Frame and the Success Movie clip to play.
When the Diamond Movie clip rolls over the Diamond Button Movie clip the ActionScript is triggered taking the Alpha of the diamond symbol to 0, and sending the Diamond Image Movie clip to frame 2.
Diamond Button Movie clip
FINISH Movie clip
Diamond Image Movie clip
Diamond Movie clip
SUCCESS!
When released, the Invisible Stage Button sends the Diamond Movie clip back to its starting position.
Invisible Button Movie clip
Invisible Stage Button Movie clip
The Diamond Image Movie clip tells the Finish Movie clip to go to the Next Frame. When this command is repeated three more times the Finish Movie clip commands the Success Movie clip to go to the finish Label and play.

You may have to go through this exercise more than once so you can fully understand the chain of events that occur when a symbol is released on the stage or on their proper cutout. Once you understand how frames and Movie clips communicate with each other you'll be able to create all sorts of exciting interactive games and other projects.

The next example is a simple Hangman game. I created this game to show how just using the **tellTarget** command you can create an interactive game.

Play the file called **Hangman.swf** in the Flash Projects folder. You'll see that it operates like a normal Hangman game. If you have 5 incorrect answers the propeller blades of the Non-Geek character stop, then the character plummets to earth. If you guess the word correctly then the character flies away and you'll get a congratulations message. The **Next** button will then appear; when pressed, this button takes you to the next game. I'll walk you through how the game is constructed then I'll have you add your own secret word to this game.

Open the file called **Hangman.fla**. You'll notice the alphabet of letters, the character with the flying suit, and a sky background. Also, off the stage to the right, we have the letters which make up the words; above them we have the Correct and Incorrect Movie clips. These symbols aren't seen by the user since they're in the gray area:

The first thing we'll look at is one of the letters on the stage. Double-click on the **A** Movie clip:

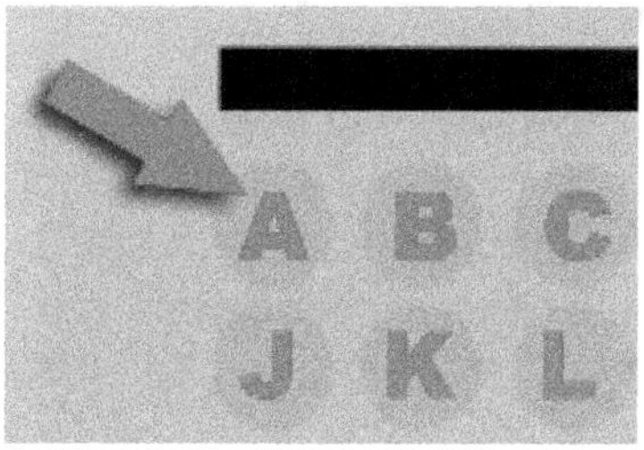

You should now be in the **A** Movie clip's editing stage.

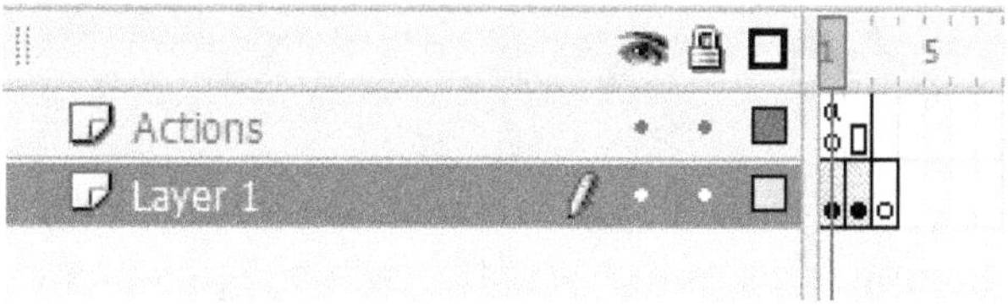

The **Actions** layer has a simple **stop** code in it. The layer that we need to examine is **Layer 1**. Click on the first frame of **Layer 1** then select the transparent button on the stage:

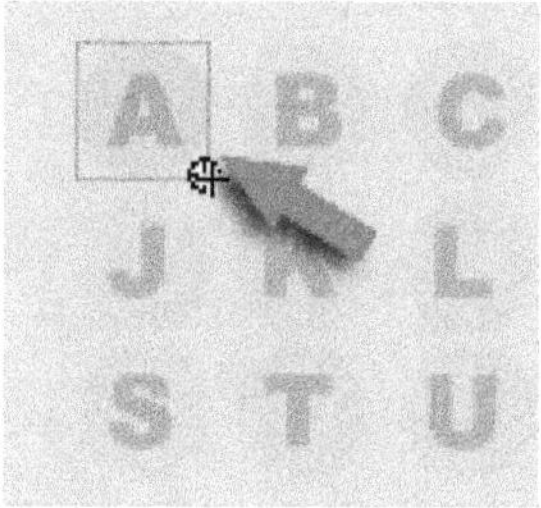

Next, open the Actions panel so you can see the ActionScript of this button:

```
on (release) {
    tellTarget ("/incorrect") {
        nextFrame();
    }
}
on (release) {
    gotoAndStop(3);
}
```

The first set of code tells the **Incorrect** Movie clip to go to the next frame. The next set of code tells this timeline to go to frame **3** (you'll notice there is a blank keyframe on frame 3).

So here is what happens when the game first starts. Every letter will have the above ActionScript in their first frame. So if the secret word is Flash and the user clicks on the **Y** button, then the **Incorrect** Movie clip will go to the next frame in its timeline. We'll examine the **Incorrect** Movie clip in a moment but here is a quick look at its timeline:

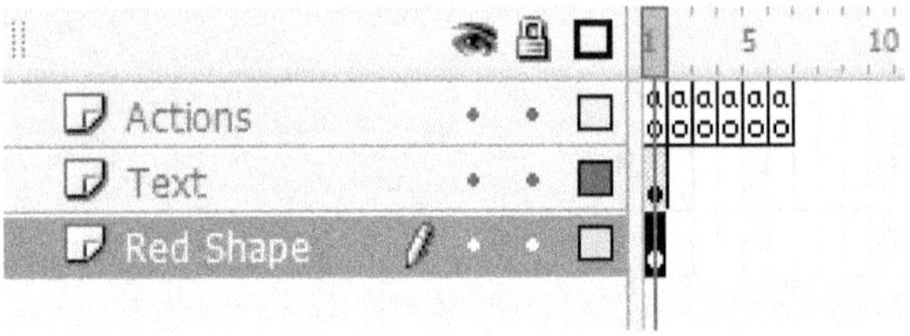

When the **Incorrect** Movie clip's timeline goes to the next frame it triggers a new set of Actions that control the Character. We'll study this timeline more in a moment, but for now we'll keep examining the **A** Movie clip.

The last set of code in the **A** Movie clip's transparent button, sends the letter's timeline to frame **3** where there is a blank keyframe. When the timeline gets to frame **3** where the blank keyframe is, this letter is no longer clickable.

Click on frame **2** of **Layer 1** and select the transparent button on the stage. In the Actions window you'll see this ActionScript:

```
on (release) {
    tellTarget ("/correct") {
        nextFrame();
    }
}
on (release) {
    tellTarget ("/words/a_letter") {
        gotoAndStop(2);
    }
}
on (release) {
    tellTarget ("/words/a_letter2") {
        gotoAndStop(2);
    }
}
on (release) {
    gotoAndStop(3);
}
```

The first set of code tells the **Correct** Movie clip to go to the next frame. The next set of code tells the **A Letter** Movie clip to go to frame **2** of its timeline. When the **A Letter** Movie clip gets to frame **2** the letter A then becomes visible indicating that the user guessed correctly (we'll examine the **A Letter** Movie clip in a moment). So what happens if a secret word has more than one **A** letter? That's where the next set of code comes into play. This code tells the second A letter (**a_letter2**) to go to frame 2 revealing the A letter. The last set of code simply tells this timeline to go to frame 3 where the blank keyframe is.

Go back to Scene 1. Double-click on the **Words** Movie clip:

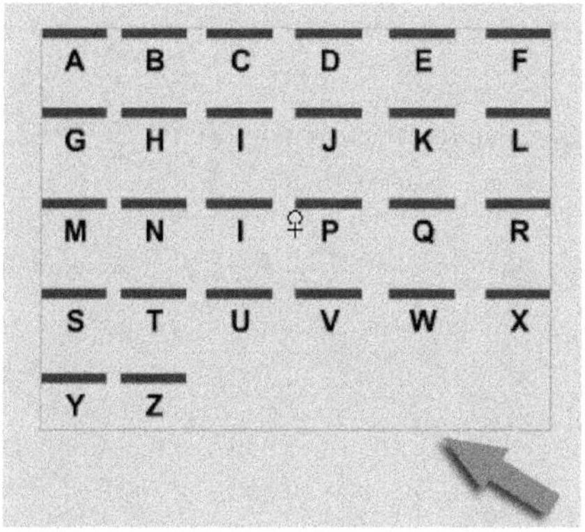

You should now be in the **Words** Movie clip editing stage. The timeline should look like this:

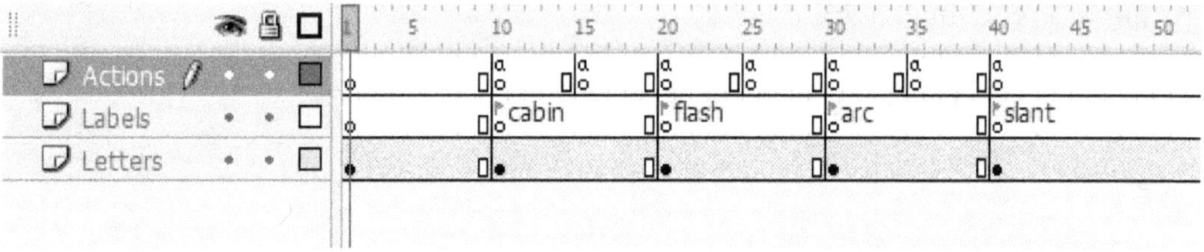

In the **Labels** layer you'll see the secret words: **Cabin**, **Flash**, **Arc**, and **Slant**. This is the timeline where you can add as many secret words as you like. Later, we'll have you add your own secret word to this timeline.

Go to frame **10** of the **Actions** layer and look at the ActionScript:

```
stop();
tellTarget ("/c") {
	gotoAndStop(2);
}
tellTarget ("/a") {
	gotoAndStop(2);
}
tellTarget ("/b") {
	gotoAndStop(2);
}
tellTarget ("/i") {
	gotoAndStop(2);
}
tellTarget ("/n") {
	gotoAndStop(2);
}
tellTarget ("/correct") {
	gotoAndStop(15);
}
```

If you study the ActionScript of the frames **20**, **30** and **40** of the **Actions** layer you'll see they all contain similar code. For instance, the code on frame **30** of the **Actions** layer contains this code:

```
stop();
tellTarget ("/a") {
	gotoAndStop(2);
}
tellTarget ("/r") {
	gotoAndStop(2);
}
tellTarget ("/c") {
	gotoAndStop(2);
}
tellTarget ("/correct") {
	gotoAndStop(17);
}
```

You'll see that this frame has similar code. It tells the letter Movie clips associated with the secret word to go to frame **2**. You'll also notice that the last set of code tells the **Correct** Movie clip to go to frame **17** (we'll study the **Correct** Movie clip in a moment). First, though, go back to frame **10** of the **Actions** layer. Let's examine the code on this frame more closely.

The first code is a simple stop command. The next five sets of code tell the letter Movie clips: **C**, **A**, **B**, **I**, and **N** to go to frame **2**. For example, look at the second set of code:

```
tellTarget ("/a") {
    gotoAndStop(2);
}
```

This code tells the **A** Movie clip (the one we examined in the beginning of this exercise) to go to frame **2**. As we learned earlier, on frame **2** of the **A** Movie clip it has code which tells the **Correct** Movie clip to go to the next frame; it also had code that tells the corresponding letter in the secret word to go to frame **2**. So when the game first starts, this timeline stops on frame 10 which then performs the above code. Only the letter Movie clips that are in the secret word are told to go to frame 2. When these letter Movie clips are clicked, they tell the corresponding secret letter to go to frame 2 revealing their letter.

The last set of code tells the **Correct** Movie clip to go to frame 15. We'll be examining the **Correct** Movie clip shortly.

Next, select frame **10** of the **Letters** layer. You'll see the letters of the secret word **Cabin** positioned over the black bar:

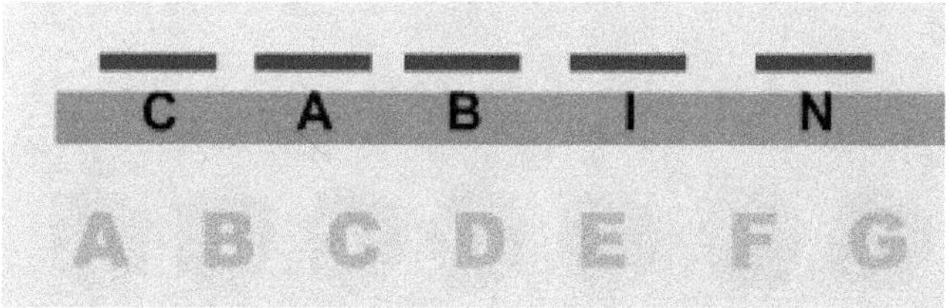

If you test the movie you won't be able to see these letters since they're over the black bar. These letters are primarily used to help the Flash creator know which letter is which . Double-click on the **A Letter** Movie clip:

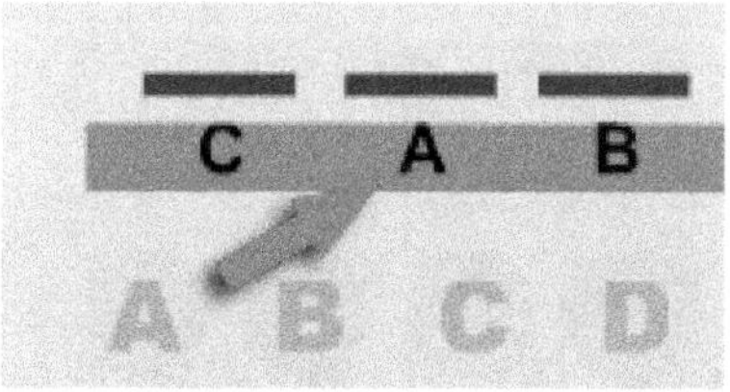

You should now be in the **A Letter** Movie clip's editing stage. This Movie clip has four layers:

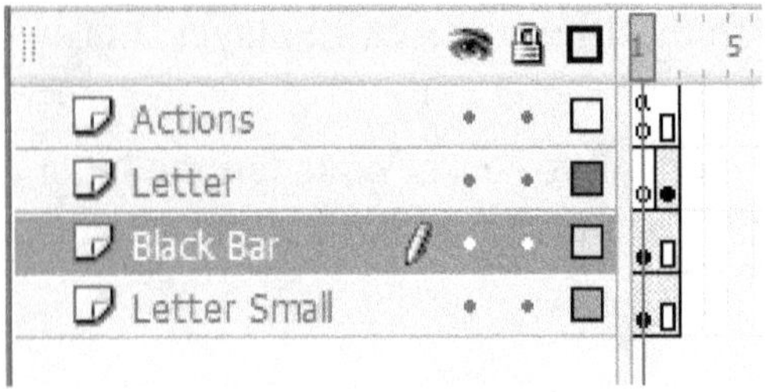

The layer, **Actions**, has a simple **stop** code in its first frame. Next, if you click on the second frame of the **Letter** layer, you'll see a red **A** appear above the black bar. The **Black Bar** layer simply holds the black bar that appears under the letter. The **Letter Small** layer holds the hidden letter.

When a user clicks on the **A** Movie clip, it tells this Movie clip to go to frame **2** revealing to the user the red **A**. Go back to the **Words** Movie clip stage by clicking its link:

Next, we'll look at the frames **15**, **25** and **35** of the **Actions** layer. Select frame **15** of the **Actions** layer and look at the ActionScript:

```
tellTarget ("/a") {
    gotoAndStop(1);
}
tellTarget ("/b") {
    gotoAndStop(1);
}
tellTarget ("/c") {
    gotoAndStop(1);
}
tellTarget ("/d") {
    gotoAndStop(1);
}
tellTarget ("/e") {
    gotoAndStop(1);
}
```

You'll see similar code for all of the Letter Movie clips. What this code does is reset all the Letter Movie clips to frame **1**. So here is what happens. When a game is finished, a **Next** button appears. When this button is clicked it tells the **Words** Movie clip to *play*. This timeline will play from frame **10** to frame **20** where it stops due to the **stop** code on frame 20. As the timeline travels to frame **20** it performs the above ActionScript on frame **15** which sends all the Letter Movie clips back to frame **1**.

For instance, the first set of code:

```
tellTarget ("/a") {
    gotoAndStop(1);
}
```

Tells the **A** Movie clip:

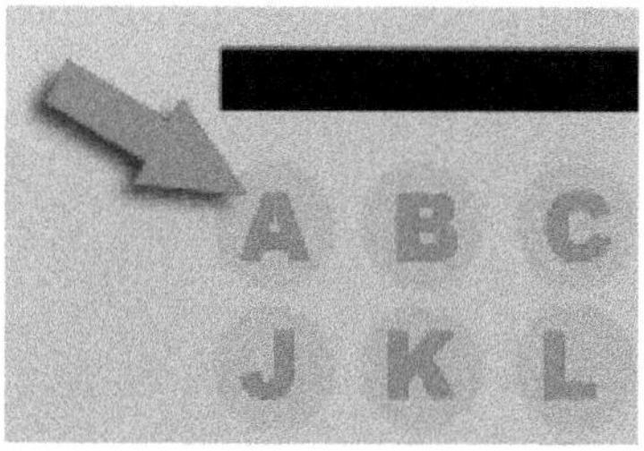

To go to frame **1** and **stop**. Scroll down in the Actions window so you can see the second type of code on this frame:

```
tellTarget ("/words/a_letter") {
    gotoAndStop(1);
}
tellTarget ("/words/b_letter") {
    gotoAndStop(1);
}
tellTarget ("/words/c_letter") {
    gotoAndStop(1);
}
tellTarget ("/words/d_letter") {
    gotoAndStop(1);
}
tellTarget ("/words/e_letter") {
    gotoAndStop(1);
}
```

These sets of codes tell the Secret Word letter Movie clips to go to frame **1**. For instance, the first set of code:

```
tellTarget ("/words/a_letter") {
    gotoAndStop(1);
}
```

Tells the **A Letter** Movie clip:

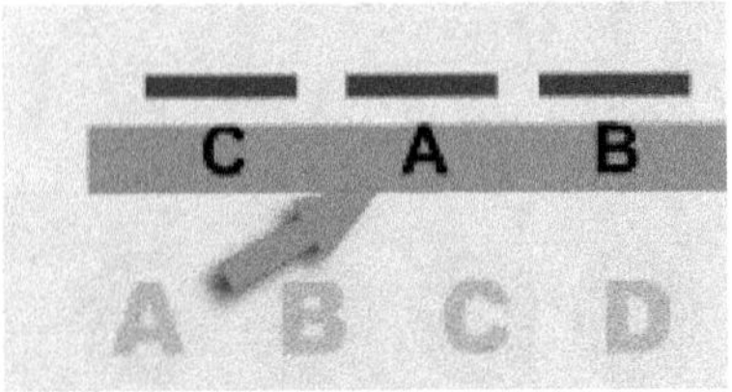

To go to frame **1** and **stop**. The ActionScript of frame **15** is the same for frames **25** and **35** of the **Actions** layer. So after each game all of the letter Movie clips are reset. Go back to Scene 1. Double-click on the **Incorrect** Movie clip:

You should now be in the editing stage of the **Incorrect** Movie clip. You'll see three layers in the timeline:

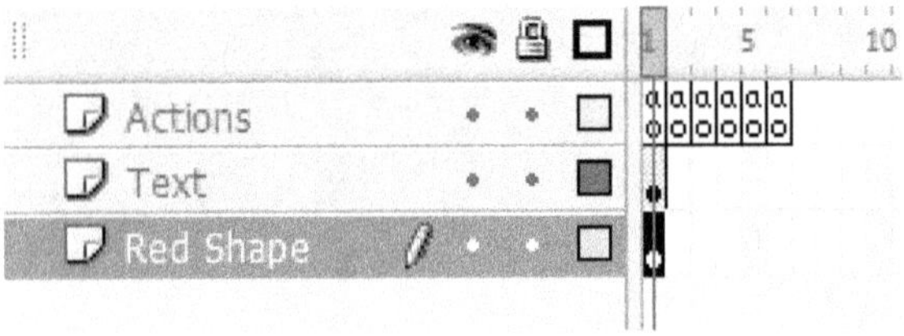

The **Red Shape** layer simply holds a red shape. The Text layer holds the word **Incorrect**. Both the Text and the red shape are never seen by the user. This is strictly done as identification purposes for the Flash creator. Select the first frame of the **Actions** layer and look at the ActionScript:

```
stop();
tellTarget ("/character/character_flying/blades") {
    gotoAndPlay("blade1");
}

```

Since this is the first frame of the **Incorrect** Movie clip, these actions will be performed when the game first begins. The first set of code is a simple **stop** code. The next set of code tells the **Blades** Movie clip of the **Character** Movie clip to go to the Label **blade1** and *play*. Click on the second frame of the Actions layer so you can see its ActionScript:

```
tellTarget ("/character/character_flying/blades") {
    gotoAndPlay("blade2");
}

```

This code is similar to the code on frame 1, except that this code tells the **Blades** Movie clip to go to the Label **blade2** and *play*. If you select frames **3**, **4** and **5** of the **Actions** layer you'll notice they all have similar codes. Each subsequent frame tells the **Blades** Movie clip to go to a higher number Label. Select frame **6** of the Actions layer and look at the ActionScript:

```
tellTarget ("/character/character_flying/blades") {
    gotoAndPlay("blade6");
}
tellTarget ("/a") {
    gotoAndStop(3);
}
tellTarget ("/b") {
    gotoAndStop(3);
}
tellTarget ("/c") {
    gotoAndStop(3);
}
tellTarget ("/d") {
    gotoAndStop(3);
}
```

The first code tells the **Blades** Movie clip to go to the Label **blade6** and *play*. The next sets of code tell all of the Letter Movie clips to go to frame 3 of their timelines (where the blank keyframes are).

So here is what happens. Let's say the secret word is *Cabin*. If the user selects the T letter (**T** Movie clip) it will tell the **Incorrect** Movie clip to go to the next frame. As we've seen, each frame in the **Incorrect** Movie clip tells the **Blades** Movie clip to go to a higher number Label. When we examine the **Blades** Movie clip you'll see that each time the timeline goes to a higher number Label the blade rotations decrease slightly. On the Label **blade6** the blade rotations stop altogether which causes the character to plummet to earth. So after five incorrect answers the **Incorrect** Movie clip will end up on frame 6 which triggers all of the above actions.

Go back to Scene 1. Double-click the **Correct** Movie clip:

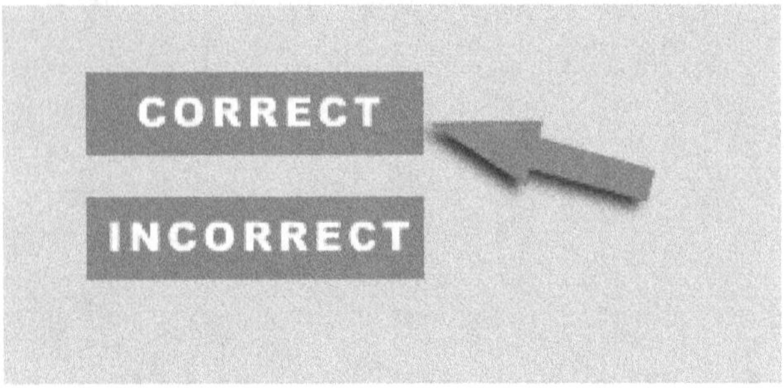

You should now be in the **Correct** Movie clip's editing stage. You'll see four layers:

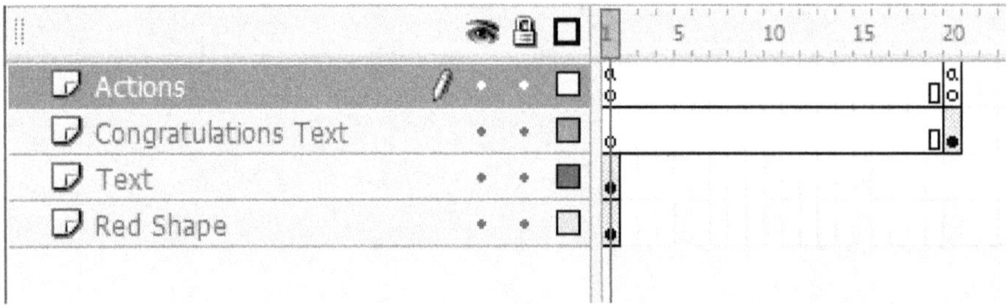

The Red Shape layer simply holds a red shape. The Text layer holds the word **Correct**. Both the Text and the red shape are never seen by the user. This is strictly done as identification purposes for the Flash creator. The **Congratulations Text** layer holds the CONGRATULATIONS! text on frame 20. In the Actions layer we have a simple **stop** code in the first frame. Select frame **20** of the **Actions** layer and open the Actions panel so you can see the ActionScript:

```
tellTarget ("/character/character_flying") {
    gotoAndPlay("success");
}
```

When a user clicks on a correct letter, it sends this **Correct** Movie clip timeline to the next frame. When this timeline gets to frame **20** it triggers the above code which sends the character flying upward off the stage. For instance, let's say the secret word is **Arc**. The **Words** Movie clip timeline will be on frame **30**, so the Actions on frame **30** will be performed:

```
stop();
tellTarget ("/a") {
    gotoAndStop(2);
}
tellTarget ("/r") {
    gotoAndStop(2);
}
tellTarget ("/c") {
    gotoAndStop(2);
}
tellTarget ("/correct") {
    gotoAndStop(17);
}
```

If you look at the last set of code it tells the **Correct** Movie clip to go to frame 17. Once the user selects all three correct answers it will send the **Correct** Movie clip to the next frame three times ending up on frame **20**. If you look at the code on frame **10** where the **Cabin** Label is, you'll see the same code sending the **Correct** Movie clip to frame **15** (since the word Cabin has 5 letters). You'll understand this better when we create a new secret word later in this exercise. For now, let's examine the flying character.

Go back to **Scene 1**. Double-click the **Character** Movie clip. You should now be in the **character** editing stage. You'll notice that it's a long Motion Tween of the character moving around the stage. On frame **1** double-click the character symbol on the stage. You should now be in the **Character Flying** editing stage. Drag the timeline needle across the timeline. You'll see that once the character arrives at the label: **drop**, it falls straight down off the stage. When the **Incorrect** Movie clip gets to the final frame it tells the **Character** Movie clip to go to label **drop** and *play*. Select frame **32** of the Actions layer. Open the Actions panel so you can see the ActionScript:

```
stop();
tellTarget ("/next") {
    gotoAndStop(2);
}

```

The **stop** code simply stops the timeline. The next set of code tells the **Next** Movie clip to go to frame **2** where its button will become active. This is the **Next Button** that appears when the game is over.

If you look at frame **57** of this timeline, after the **success** label, you'll see the exact same code. Let's look at a couple of the embedded Movie clips. First, select the first frame of the **Tie Animation** layer. Then, double-click on the tie symbol on the stage:

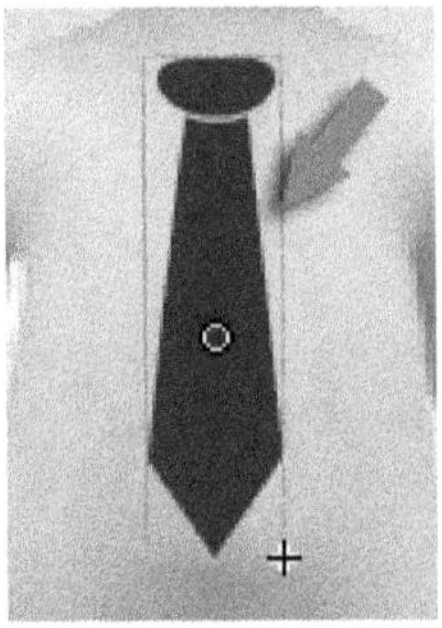

You should now be in the editing stage of the **Tie Animation** Movie clip. You'll see three layers, the **Tie** layer, the **Tie Reverse** layer and the **Top of Tie** layer:

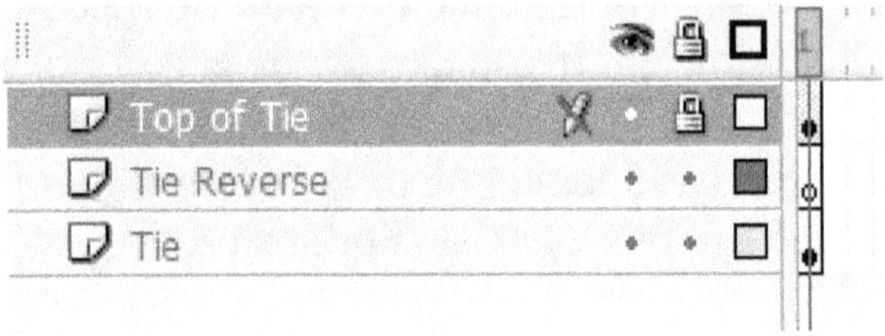

So we want the tie to blow in the wind. To get the most realistic type of animation we'll use frame by frame animation. This is similar to cell animation in that on each frame we're going to move the tie just a little bit to give the appearance of movement. So let's get started. Zoom into the stage about 800% or whatever works for you; you need to have a nice close view of the tie. Create a keyframe on frame **2** of the **Tie** layer. Click on the stage away from the tie shape to deselect it. Move your cursor over the bottom of the tie; you should see a little arrow show up:

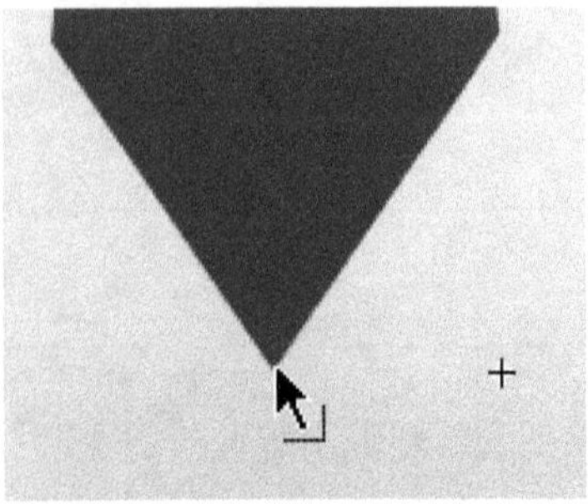

Move the tie to the left slightly:

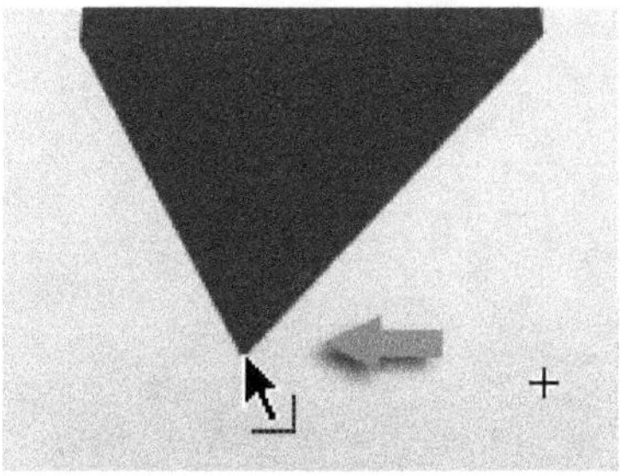

Create a keyframe on frame **3** of the **Tie** layer. Whenever you create a new keyframe you'll need to click on the stage away from the tie to deselect the tie (if the tie is selected, then you'll end up moving the entire tie). Next, select the bottom of the time and move it to the left even more; grab the right corner of the tie and move it to the left slightly:

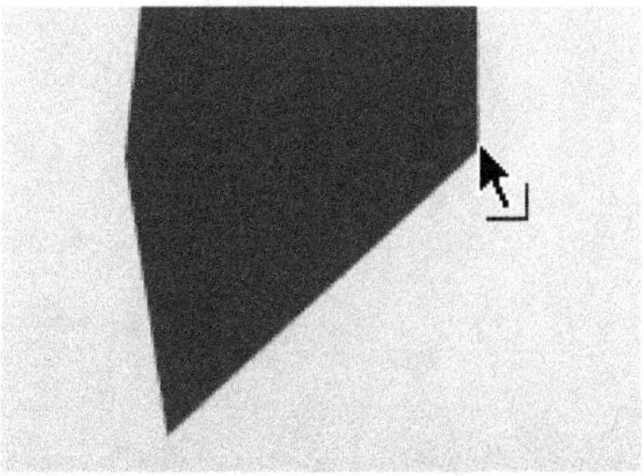

Remember to only move the corners of the tie when you see that little arrow next to the cursor. Create another keyframe on frame **4**. Deselect the tie. This time drag the bottom of the tie upward and to the left slightly. Move the left corner upward also:

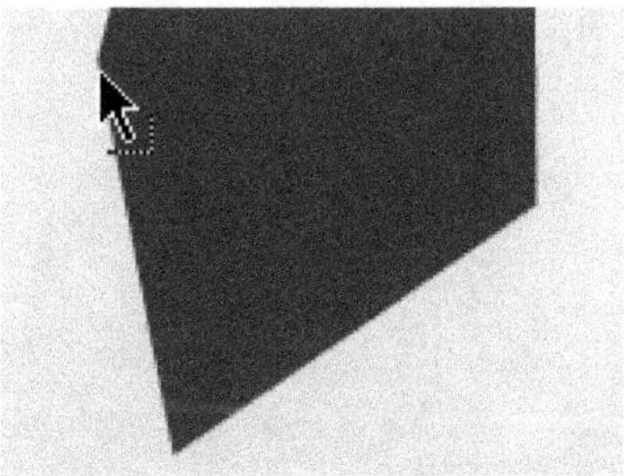

Create another keyframe and deselect the tie. This time we're going to curl the tie slightly. Put your cursor over the left side of the tie; you should see a slight curl line next to the cursor:

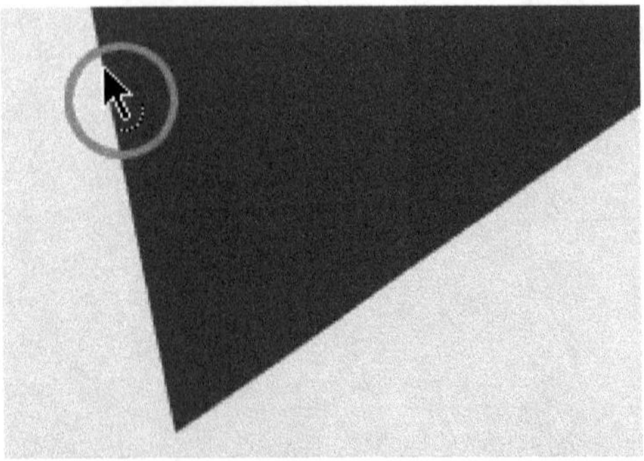

Pull this line inward creating a curved line. Next, pull the bottom of the tie up and to the left:

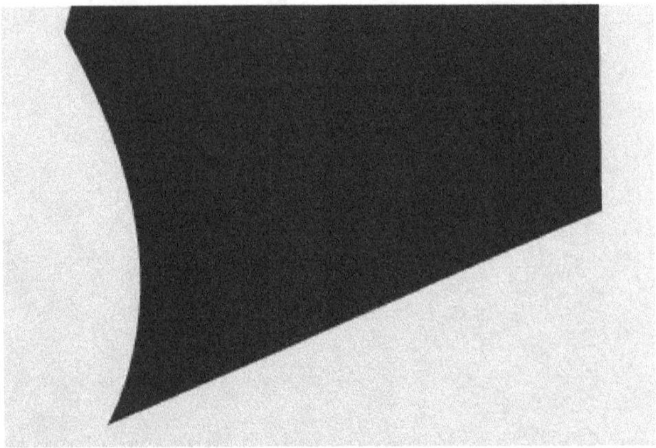

So now you should be getting the idea of how this frame by frame animation works. Keep creating your frame by frame animation until you get to frame 20. At the end of the animation your tie should look similar to this:

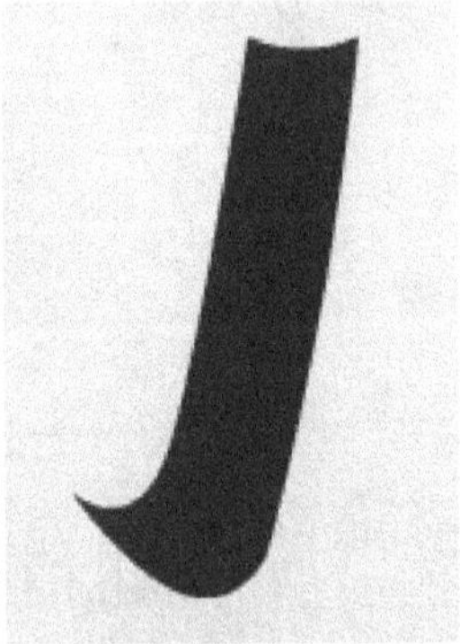

Don't worry if it doesn't exactly look like this. In fact, if you want to create your own type of animation go ahead. Just always keep in mind that we want the appearance of a tie blowing in the wind. We now want the animation to reverse to the first frame. Here's how to do this. First, we need to select all the frames of the **Tie** layer. We do this by clicking on the **name** part of the layer:

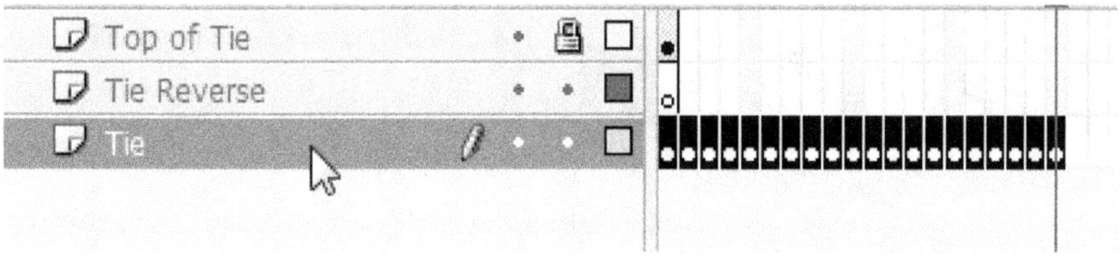

Go to **Edit**, **Timeline**, **Copy Frames**. Next, click on the first frame of the **Tie Reverse** layer; go to **Edit**, **Timeline**, **Paste Frames**. Your timeline should now look like this:

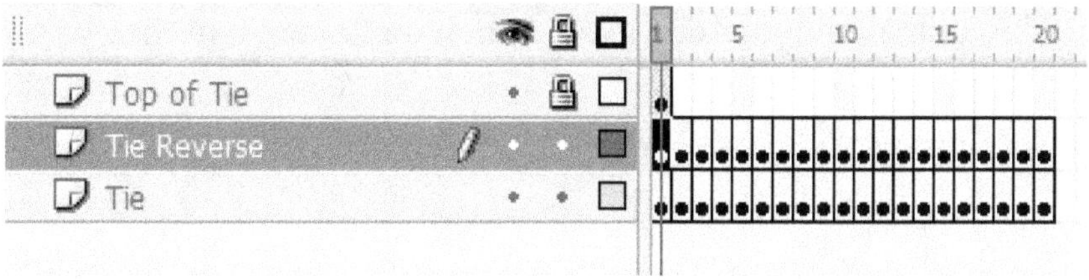

Select the name part of the **Tie Reverse** layer to select all the frames. Go to **Modify**, **Timeline**, **Reverse Frames**. With these reversed frames still selected, drag them to the right until the first frame is on frame **21**:

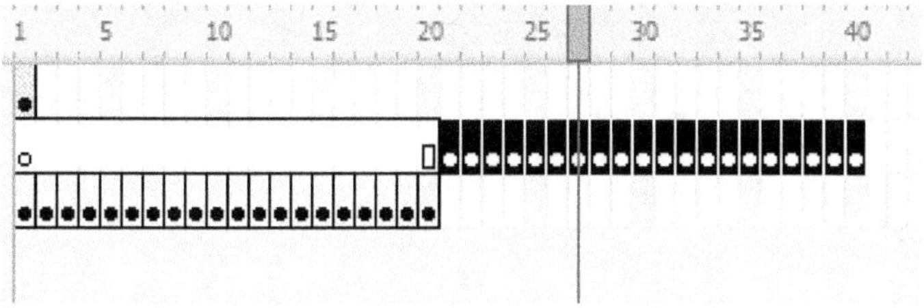

So now when the animation gets to frame 21 it will play the initial animation in reverse to end up back at the original tie. It will then loop over and over again. Before we wrap on this animation, insert a frame on frame **40** of the **Top of Tie** layer. You can test the movie to see how the animation looks. The tie should now be blowing in the wind. Go back to the **Character Flying** stage:

Double-click the **Blades** Movie clip:

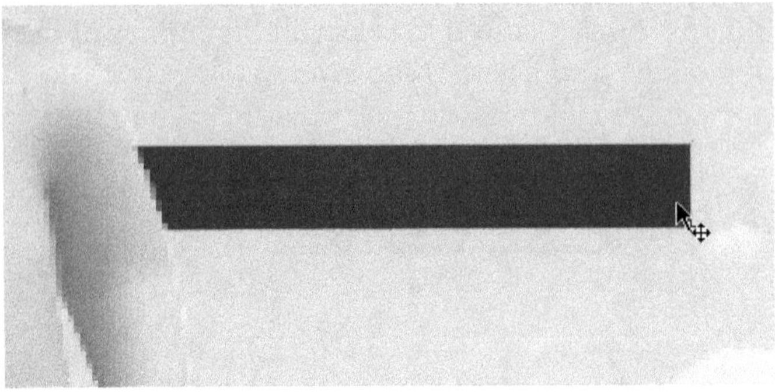

Now we're in the editing stage of the **Blades** Movie clip. You'll see that the timeline has six different labels. The **blade1** animation is what we first see when the game begins. This animation loops due to an Action on frame 50 of the **Actions** layer:

```
gotoAndPlay("blade1");
```

Select the first frame of the **Blades** layer. Open the Properties panel; next to **Rotate** you'll see **CCW** and **10 times**.

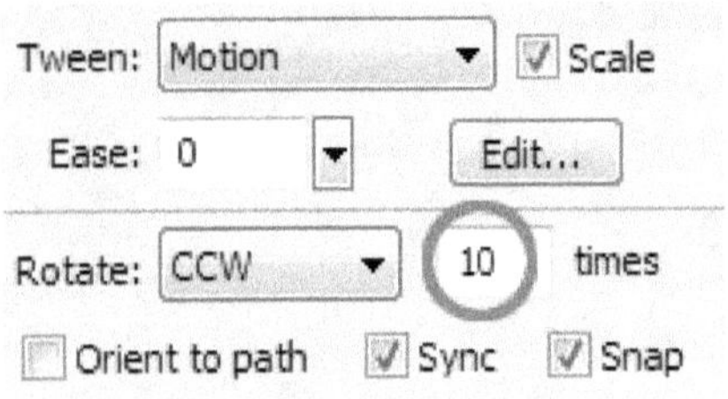

This means the blade graphic will rotate 10 times by the time it gets to frame 50. Click on keyframe **55** of the **Blades** layer. Next to **Rotate** you'll now see that it says **8** for **times**, which means the blades will only rotate 8 times by the time it gets to frame 105. If you select the keyframe on frame 105 of the **Actions** layer you'll see the looping code in the Actions window:

```
gotoAndPlay("blade2");
```

Select frame **220** of the **Blades** layer under the **blade5** Label. In the Properties panel you'll see **2** for times:

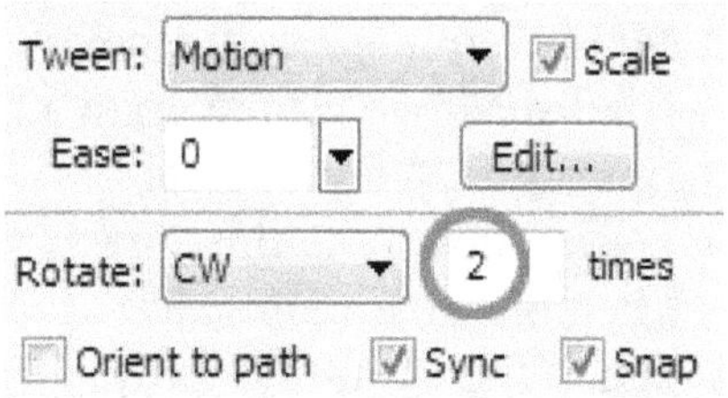

So each Label animation has fewer and fewer blade rotations. If you remember, the frames in the **Incorrect** Movie clip timeline each have a code controlling the **Blades** Movie clip. For instance, on frame **5** of the **Incorrect** Movie clip we have this code:

```
tellTarget ("/character/character_flying/blades") {
    gotoAndPlay("blade5");
}

```

So this code tells the **Blades** Movie clip timeline to go to Label **blade5** and *play*. The blades will then slow down to only 2 rotations. If the user gets another incorrect answer it will tell the **Incorrect** Movie clip to go to the next frame, frame **6**. The code on this frame commands the **Blades** Movie clip timeline to go to the Label **blade6** and *play*. Go to frame **325** of the **Actions** layer. In the Actions window you'll see the code that gets triggered when a user gets to this frame:

```
stop();
tellTarget ("/character/character_flying") {
    gotoAndPlay("drop");
}

```

The first code is the **stop** code. This stops the timeline from going back to frame **1** of this timeline. The next set of code tells the **character_flying** timeline to go to the **drop** label and **play**. If you remember, when the animation reaches the Label **drop**, the character falls downward off the stage.

So here is what happens. When the user selects an incorrect letter, the letter button then tells the **Incorrect** Movie clip to go to the next frame. So the first incorrect answer will take the **Incorrect** Movie clip to the next frame, which is frame **2** of its timeline. On frame **2** of this timeline, the ActionScript tells the **Blades** Movie clip to go to **blade2** where the rotation is only **8 times**. If the user selects another incorrect letter, that letter button tells the **Incorrect** Movie clip to go to the next frame which would be frame **3**. That frame tells the **Blades** Movie clip to go to **blade3** and *play*. On **blade3** the animation is down to **6 times**. After several incorrect answers, the **Blades** Movie clip will keep moving down the timeline until it finally reaches the **blade6** animation. That's when the final animation reaches the above ActionScript on frame **325**. This Action then commands the **Character Flying** timeline to go to the Label **drop** and *play*; the Actions at the end of this animation tell the **Next Button** to go to frame **2**.

The last symbol we'll examine is the **Next Game** Movie clip. Go back to Scene 1. Click on the first frame of the **Next Game** layer. You should now see the **Next Game** Movie clip below the alphabet of letters. Double-click on this symbol to enter its editing stage:

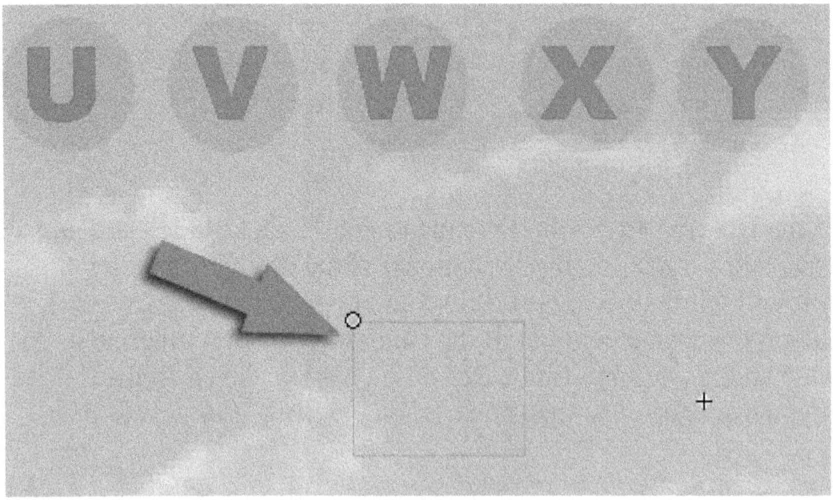

You should now see the timeline of this Movie clip:

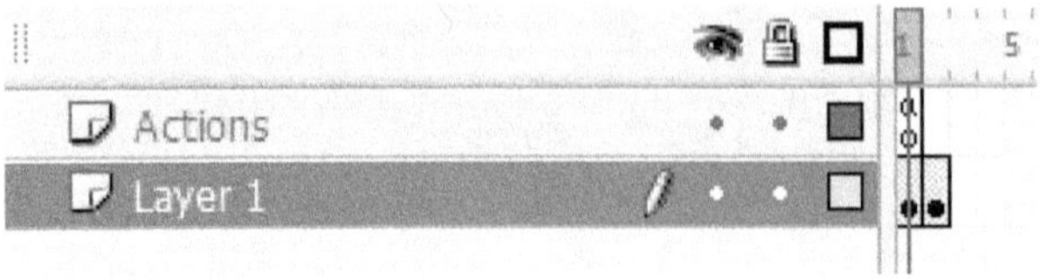

The first frame of the **Actions** layer simply holds a **stop** code. The first frame of **Layer 1** holds the transparent shape. This is used to make it easier for the Flash creator to double-click on this symbol.

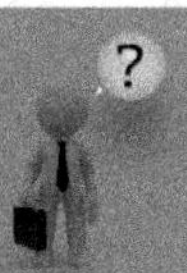

Remember! When you're creating Movie clips that don't need to be seen by the user, use the gray area surrounding the stage.

The second frame of **Layer 1** holds the Next Game button:

Select this button and open the Actions window. You'll see this code:

```
on (release) {
     tellTarget ("/words") {
          play();
     }
}
on (release) {
     tellTarget ("/character/character_flying") {
          gotoAndStop(1);
     }
}
on (release) {
     tellTarget ("/correct") {
          gotoAndStop(1);
     }
}
on (release) {
     tellTarget ("/incorrect") {
          gotoAndStop(1);
     }
}
on (release) {
     gotoAndStop(1);
}
```

The first set of code tells the **Words** Movie clip to play. So if the user finishes the first game (Cabin) and clicks on the **Next Game** button, this code tells the

Words Movie clip timeline to play until it gets to frame 20 where a **stop** code is. The user can then try to guess the second secret word (Flash).

The next set of code tells the **Character Flying** Movie clip to go back to frame 1 and *stop*. The next two sets of code reset the Correct and Incorrect Movie clips to frame 1. The last set of code sends the **Next Game** Movie clip back to frame 1.

Now that you have a better understanding of how the Hangman game works, let's add another secret word to this game. Go back to Scene 1. Double-click on the **Words** Movie clip to enter its editing stage. Create a keyframe on frame **50** of the **Labels** layer and add the word **highland** in the **Instance Name** window:

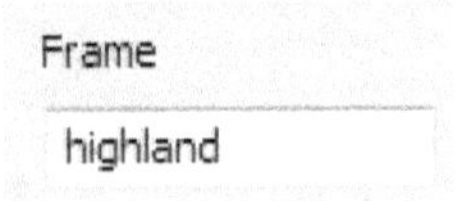

Next, we need to add the letters to frame **50** of the **Letters** layer. On frame **1** of the **Letters** layer we have the complete alphabet. We'll copy these over to frame 50. Hold down **ALT** on your keyboard, then click on the first frame of the **Letters** layer:

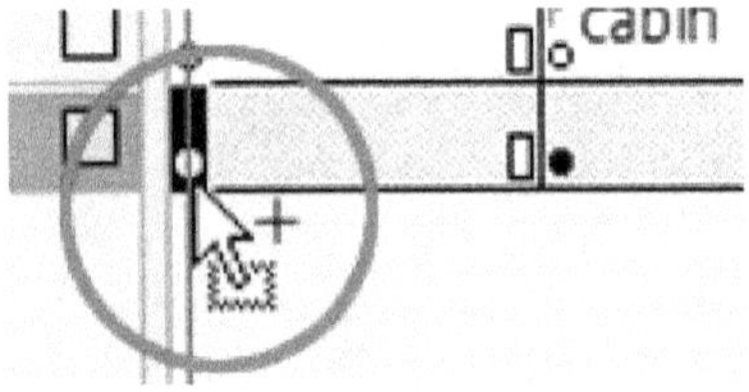

You should see a little plus symbol. Without letting go of your mouse button, drag this keyframe to frame **50**:

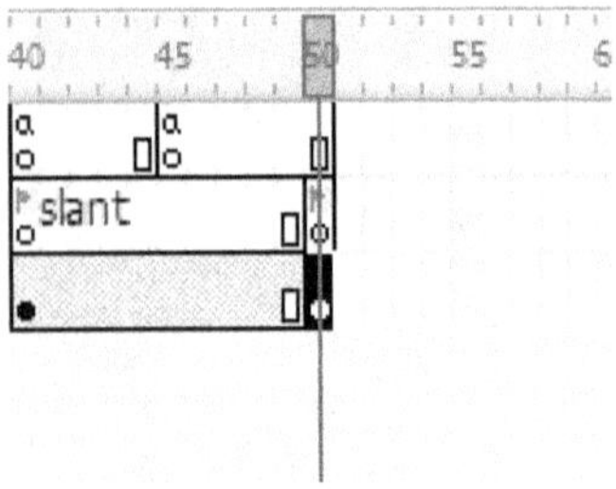

You should now have all the alphabet letters on the right side of the stage:

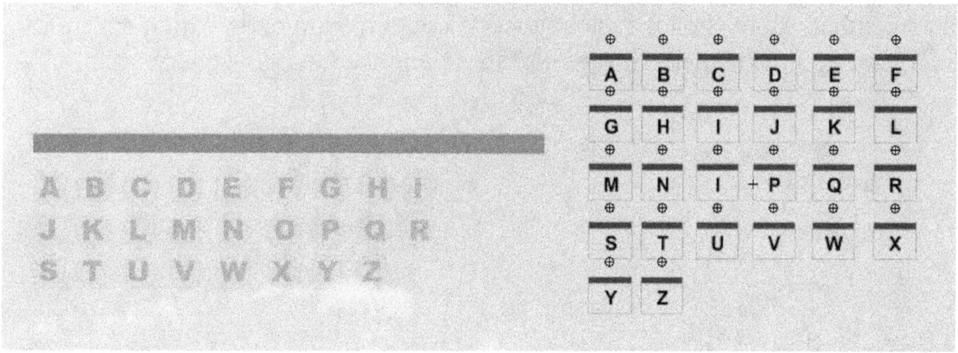

Since the secret word is *Highland*, we need to drag these letters over to the stage. Let's do that now. Select the **H**, **I**, **G**, **H**, **L**, **A**, **N**, and **D** letters and place them over the bar area:

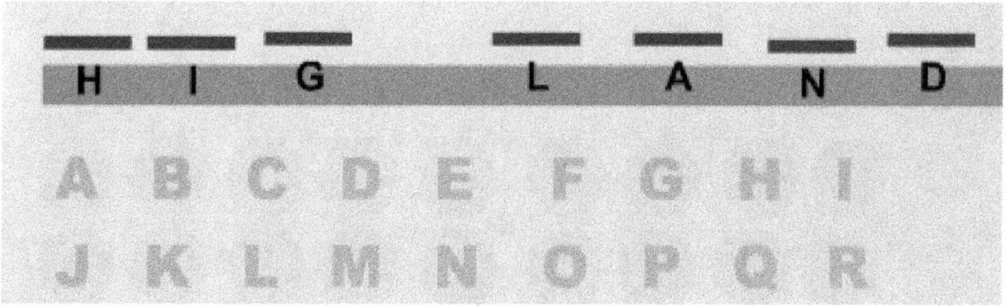

You'll see that we have only one **H** Movie clip. Also, the letters may not be aligned perfectly. Before we align the letters let's add the second H. Select the **H Letter** Movie clip then go to **Edit**, **Copy**. Next, go to **Edit**, **Paste in Place**. This will place an exact copy of the **H Letter** Movie clip on top of itself. Drag this new Movie clip to the right between the **G** and **L**:

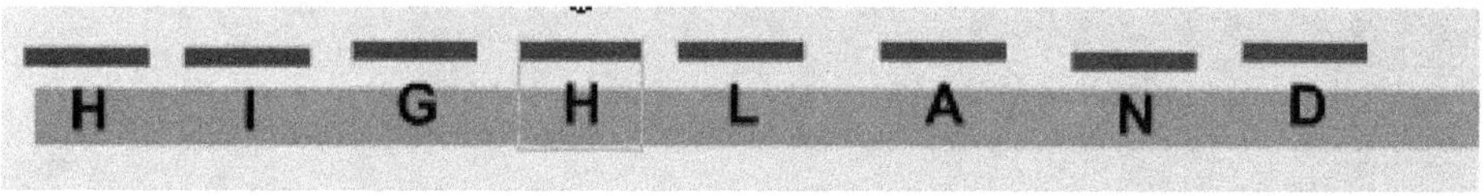

With this new H letter still selected, open the Properties panel. In the **Instance Name** window change the name to **h_letter2**:

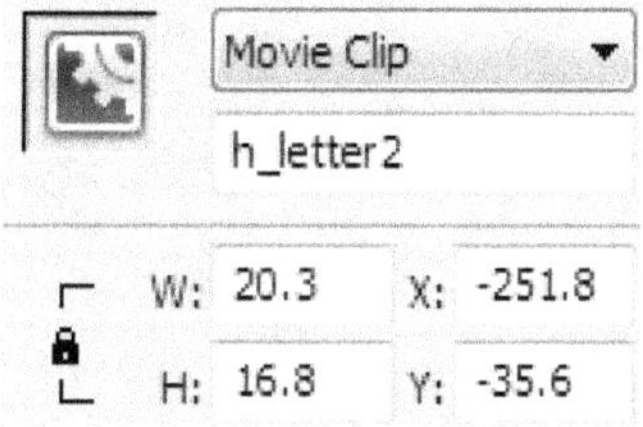

If you remember, all of the letter Movie clips contain extra code which controls duplicate letters. For instance, on the **H** Movie clip we have this code:

```
on (release) {
     tellTarget ("/words/h_letter") {
          gotoAndStop(2);
     }
}
on (release) {
     tellTarget ("/words/h_letter2") {
          gotoAndStop(2);
     }
}
```

The second set of code controls the second **H Letter** Movie clip. What if the word has three H's? You would simply add one more piece of code to the **H** Movie clip that controls h_letter3:

```
on (release) {
     tellTarget ("/words/h_letter3") {
          gotoAndStop(2);
     }
}
```

Let's align these letters so they look better. Click on the first **H Letter** Movie clip, hold down SHIFT, and select the rest of the letters in the word. They should now all be highlighted:

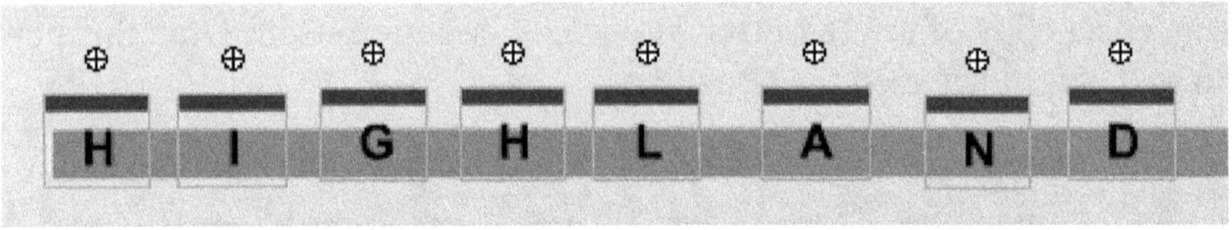

Open the Align panel. Select **Align top edge** and **Distribute horizontal center**. Make sure **To stage** is not selected:

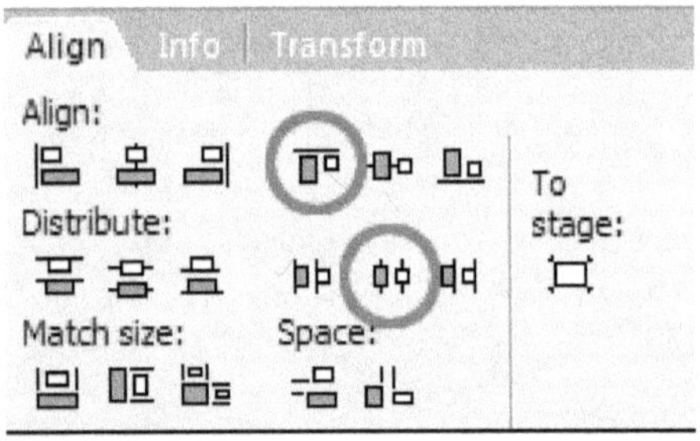

The letters of your secret word should now be properly aligned. Before you deselect them, use the arrow keys on your keyboard to nudge the letters so they are all in the black bar area:

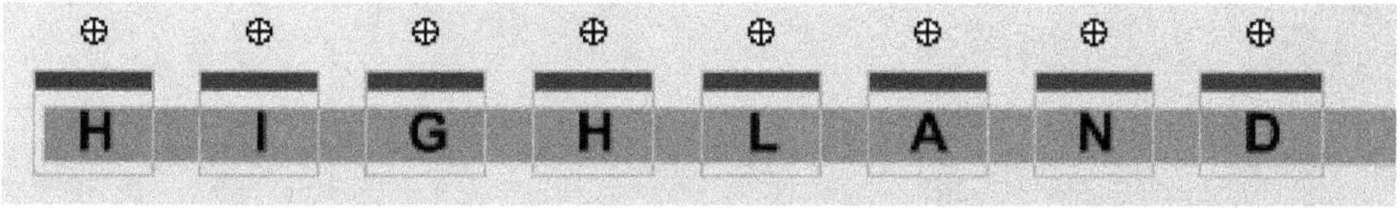

So now we'll add the secret code which will control which letter Movie clips are sent to frame 2. Create a keyframe on frame **50** of the **Actions** layer. Open the Actions panel. The first thing we'll do is add a **stop** code. Go to **Global Functions**, **Timeline Control** and double-click **stop**. Next, we'll add the code that will command the letters of the secret word to go to frame 2. Go to **Deprecated**, **Actions** and double-click **tellTarget**. In the **Target** window type **/h**:

Go to **Global Functions**, **Timeline Control** and double-click **goto**. In the **goto** settings window change the **Frame** to **2** and select **Go to and stop**:

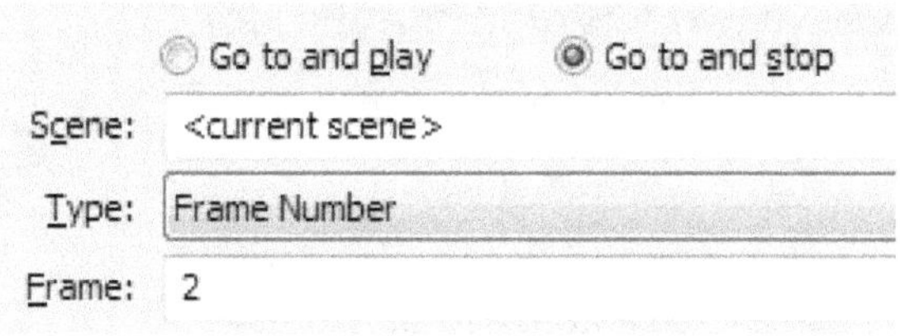

Now the H letter will go to frame 2. Since we need to repeat this code for the rest of the letters, we'll copy and paste it for every letter. Highlight the tellTarget code you just created:

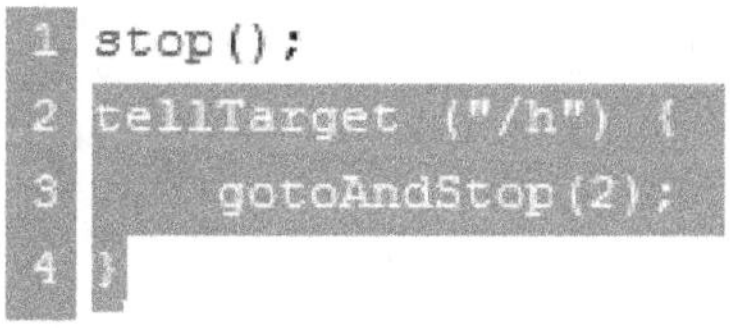

Go to **Edit**, **Copy**. Click on the closing bracket of this code and go to **Edit**, **Paste in Center**. You should now have a copy of the tellTarget code. Click on the tellTarget word of the copied code; the **Target** window should now be visible. Change **/h** to **/i**. The new code should look like this:

```
stop();
tellTarget ("/h") {
    gotoAndStop(2);
}
tellTarget ("/i") {
    gotoAndStop(2);
}
```

This time highlight both sets of code:

```
stop();
tellTarget ("/h") {
    gotoAndStop(2);
}
tellTarget ("/i") {
    gotoAndStop(2);
}
```

Go to **Edit**, **Copy**. Click on the closing bracket of the last set of code and go to **Edit**, **Paste in Center**. You should now have two sets of identical codes:

```
stop();
tellTarget ("/h") {
    gotoAndStop(2);
}
tellTarget ("/i") {
    gotoAndStop(2);
}
tellTarget ("/h") {
    gotoAndStop(2);
}
tellTarget ("/i") {
    gotoAndStop(2);
}
```

In the second **/h** code, click on the word tellTarget. In the Target window, change **/h** to **/g**. Next, in the second **i/** code click on the word tellTarget. In the Target window change **/i** to **/l**. Since we already have code telling **/h** to go to the second frame we don't need to repeat that code. Continue to copy and past the code until you have code for all the letters of the secret word: H, I, G, L, A, N and D:

```
tellTarget ("/h") {
    gotoAndStop(2);
}
tellTarget ("/i") {
    gotoAndStop(2);
}
tellTarget ("/g") {
    gotoAndStop(2);
}
tellTarget ("/l") {
    gotoAndStop(2);
}
tellTarget ("/a") {
    gotoAndStop(2);
}
tellTarget ("/n") {
    gotoAndStop(2);
}
tellTarget ("/d") {
    gotoAndStop(2);

```

The last code we'll create is the action that tells the **Correct** Movie clip what frame to go to. Click on the closing bracket of the last set of code. Go to **Deprecated**, **Actions** and double-click **tellTarget**. In the Target window type **/correct**:

Next, go to **Global Functions**, **Timeline Control** and double-click **goto**. In the **goto** settings window type **13** in the **Frame** window and select **Go to and stop**:

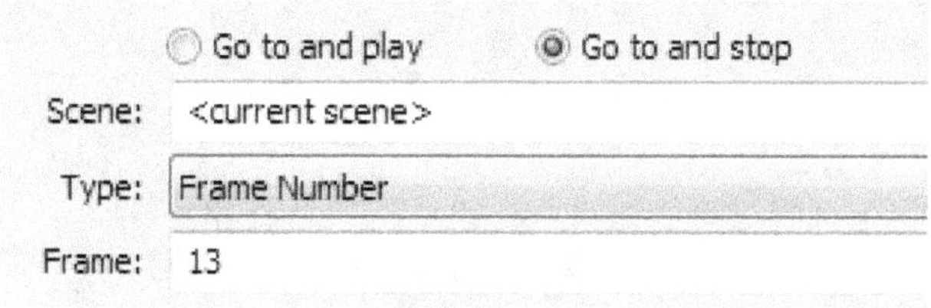

The reason we send the **Correct** Movie clip to frame 13 is because the secret word (highland) has 8 letters in it, but since one of the letters (H) gets repeated, we count the word as having 7 letters. The **Correct** Movie clip has 20 frames so 20 - 7 is 13.

The code is now finished for the secret word. Before we can test it we need to add the reset code to frames 45 and 55. A fast way to do that is to hold down ALT, then click on frame **35** of the **Actions** layer. Once you see that little plus sign drag this keyframe to frame **45**. Do this one more time, but this time drag the keyframe to frame **55**. Select frame 55 of the Labels and Letters layers and insert frames. The timeline should look like this now:

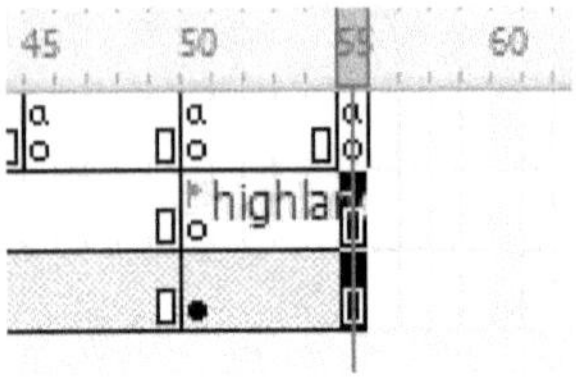

If you're done adding secret words add one more code to the **Actions** layer. Create a keyframe on frame **60** of the **Actions** layer. In the Actions window go to **Global Functions**, **Timeline Control** and double-click **goto**. In the goto settings window change **Type** to **Frame Label**, type **cabin** in the **Frame** window and select **Go to and stop**:

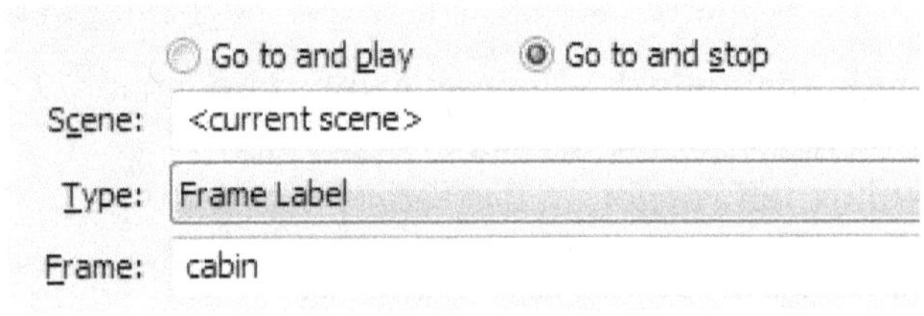

Test your movie to try it out. This Hangman game is a great example of how powerful Flash is with only using a few simple commands. Next, we'll examine how to build a classic Concentration game using mainly the tellTarget command.

A friend recently sent a Christmas E-card that was pretty interesting. Similar to the card game Concentration, you had to flip over shapes until you correctly flipped over matching pairs of pictures. When you succeeded in matching all the pictures, there was a nice animation that began playing. I began thinking about how to recreate this game by just using one or two commands, mainly the tellTarget command. That's when I came up with this next game that we'll be examining. I've added a few extra touches though. You are only given 5 incorrect guesses. After the fifth incorrect guess the game is over and you are asked if you want to try again. If you click on the **Try Again** button you're taken to a new game where the images are now in a different location. If you happen to succeed in matching all the pairs of pictures, you are given a cool animation of hot air balloons rising into the air. This balloon animation is really a Flash video (I'll explain how to create this video at the end of this exercise).

I'll walk you through how this game is created then I'll have you create different versions of this game. So let's get started!!

In the Flash Projects folder double-click the Concentration.swf file. Play the game a few times until you complete it. You should see a nice little animation when you're finished. So let's examine how this game works. Open the file called Concentration.fla. You'll see the main stage which has the puzzle:

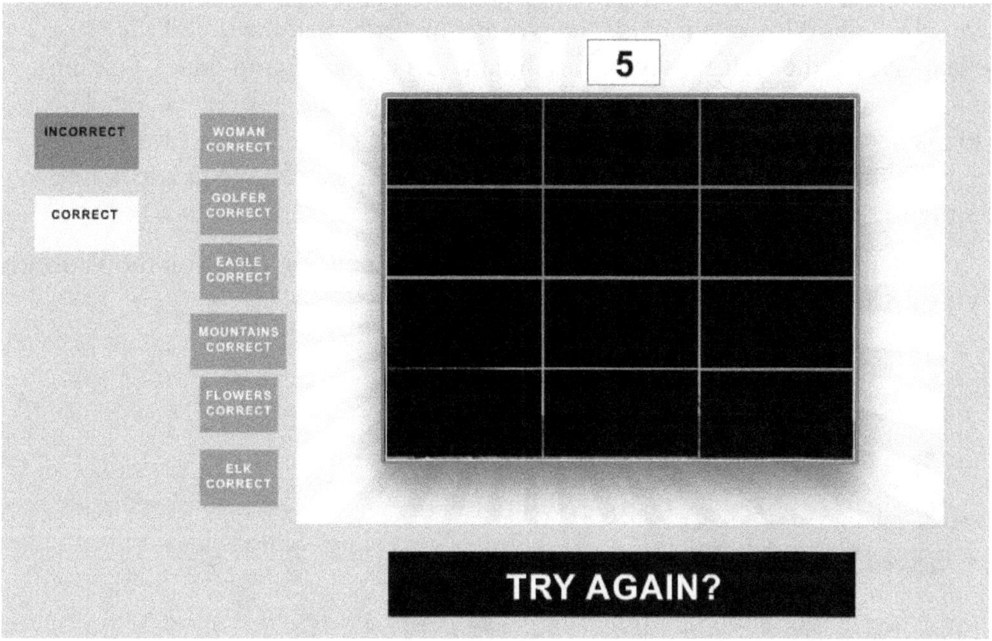

In the gray area to the left of the stage, you'll see the Movie clips which control correct and incorrect answers (these Movie clips aren't seen by the user since they're in the gray area). When users incorrectly guess on a picture match, the **Incorrect** Movie clip is triggered, which triggers the **Wrong Answer** Movie clip at the top of the stage. When a user correctly guesses on a picture match, the **Correct** Movie clip is triggered. We'll learn more about how these Movie clips work in a moment.

Let's take a look at the timeline. You'll see six layers:

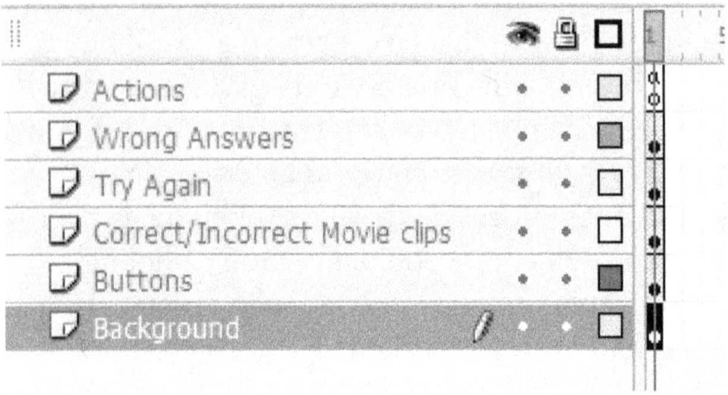

The first layer, the **Background** layer, holds the hidden picture. The **Buttons** layer holds all of the picture buttons. The third layer is the **Correct/Incorrect** Movie clip**s** layer, which contains the correct and incorrect Movie clips which are on the gray area of the canvas. The fourth layer is the **Try Again** button which appears after five wrong answers. The fifth layer holds the **Wrong Answers** Movie clip. This Movie clip holds the wrong answer box at the top of the stage. The last layer is the Actions layer, which contains a simple **stop** code. You may be asking why we need a **stop** code since the timeline only has one frame. The reason is because we'll be adding more scenes to this project, and as we learned earlier, if you have more than one scene in your project you have to add a **stop** code to the first scene.

So the first thing we'll examine is one of the picture buttons. Click on the **Woman** Movie clip located at the top left of the stage:

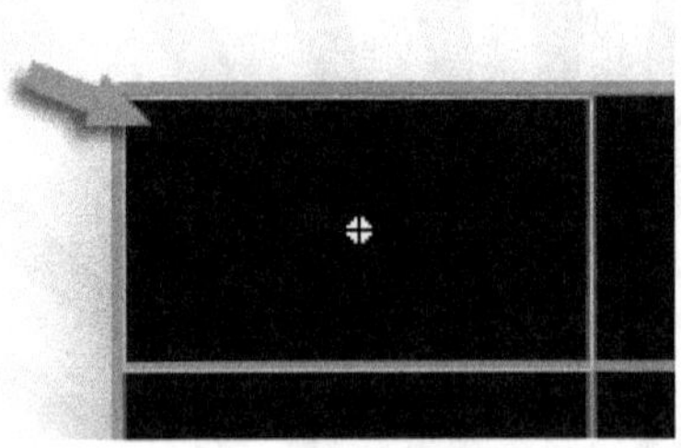

You'll notice that in the Properties panel the Instance Name for this Movie clip is **woman**. Double-click on this Movie clip to enter its editing stage. In the timeline you'll see five layers:

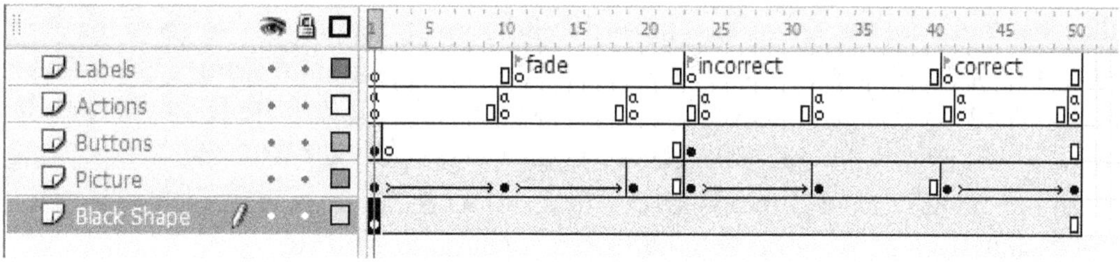

The **Black Shape** layer simply holds the black shape. The next layer, **Picture**, is the picture of the woman. Scrub the timeline back and forth with the timeline needle so you can see how the picture fades in and out. The next layer is the **Buttons** layer. Select the first frame of the **Buttons** layer and select the button on the stage; you should now see the ActionScript in the Actions window:

```
on (release) {
    play();
}
on (release) {
    tellTarget ("/woman2") {
        gotoAndStop("correct");
    }
}
on (release) {
    tellTarget ("/golfer") {
        gotoAndStop("incorrect");
    }
}
on (release) {
    tellTarget ("/golfer2") {
        gotoAndStop("incorrect");
    }
}
on (release) {
    tellTarget ("/eagle") {
        gotoAndStop("incorrect");
    }
}
```

The first set of code is a simple **play** action. When this button is clicked it tells this timeline to play. The timeline then plays until it gets to frame **10** where a **stop** code is. The next code tells the matching picture (**woman2**) to go to the label **correct** in its timeline. If you scroll down the rest of the ActionScript you'll notice that the codes are very similar. They all tell the incorrect pictures to go to the label **incorrect** of their timelines. So all of the buttons contain similar code. The eagle button would tell its matching picture (eagle2) to go to the label **correct**; it would then tell all the incorrect pictures to go to their label **incorrect**.

Select frame **23** of the **Buttons** layer. Next, select the button on the stage. You'll notice that it's a Movie clip with an Instance Name of **button**:

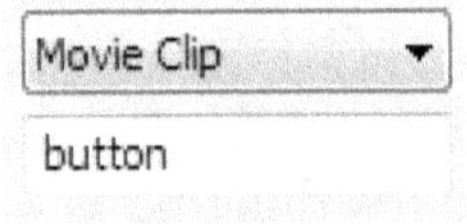

Double-click on this Movie clip to enter its editing stage. You'll see two layers:

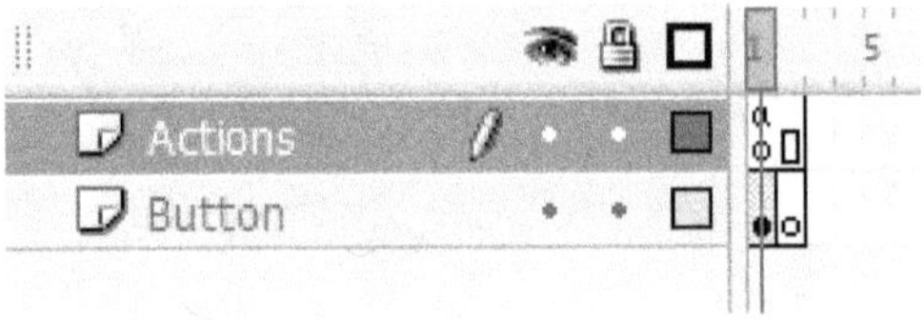

The **Actions** layer contains a simple **stop** code in frame **1**. Select the first frame of the **Button** layer and select the button on the stage. In the Actions window you should see this code:

```
on (release) {
    tellTarget ("/woman") {
        play();
    }
}
```

This code tells the timeline of the **Woman** Movie clip (the timeline we were just in) to **play**. You'll notice that on frame 2 of this layer is a blank keyframe. This is important. When a user is playing the game and clicks on the second picture selection, we need to disable all of the buttons on the stage. If we don't disable all the buttons the user can quickly click on a third or fourth button. So when a user clicks on his second selection it tells all of the Button Movie clips to go to frame 2 where the blank keyframe is. Go back to the Woman stage:

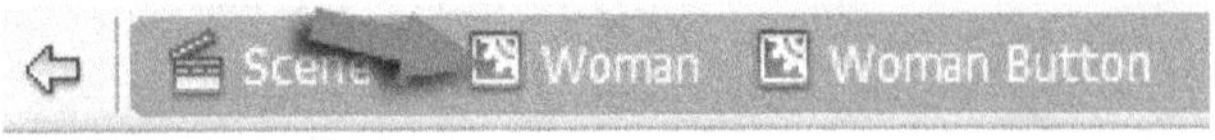

Let's examine the **Actions** layer. The 1st frame of this layer contains a simple **stop** code. Click on frame **10** of the **Actions** layer and look at the ActionScript in the Actions window:

```
stop();
tellTarget ("/correct_woman") {
    nextFrame();
}
```

The first code is a simple **stop** action. The next set of code tells the **Woman Correct** Movie clip to go to the next frame. So when a user first clicks any of the picture buttons they go to this frame where the above action is performed. For instance, if the user first clicks the Elk Picture button, it would send its timeline to frame **10** where the above code is (except instead of **/correct_woman** it would say **/correct_elk**). Once the above action is performed the **Woman Correct** Movie clip is sent to its next frame. We'll be looking at the **Woman Correct** Movie clip in a moment, but for now here is a quick look at its timeline:

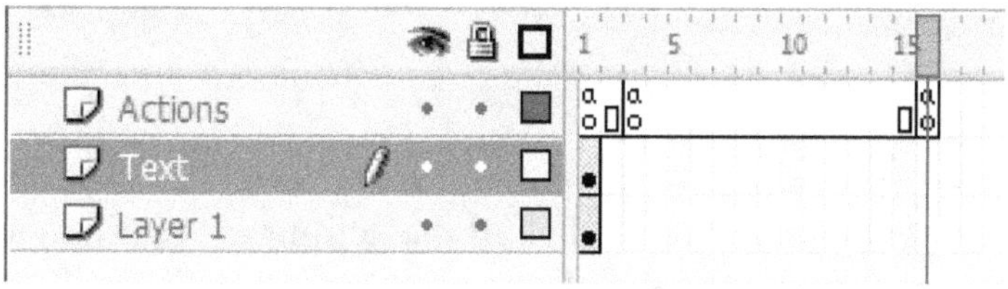

When this timeline is sent to the next frame as commanded by the previous code, it will end up on frame 2. If this timeline gets to frame 3 it initiates a **play** action which sends this timeline to frame **16** where more actions are performed. The actions in frame **16** cause both Woman Movie clips to go to the label **fade** in their timelines and **play** causing them both to disappear.

Note: the reason for the number of frames between 3 and 16 is so that the pictures will remain visible for a few moments before they disappear.

Back to the **Woman** timeline. Let's see what happens when the **Woman** Movie clip is told to go to the label **fade** and *play*. Click on frame **19** of the **Actions** layer and look at the ActionScript:

```
stop();
setProperty("/woman", _x, "-100");
```

This is code that is performed at the end of the **fade** animation. The first code is a simple **stop** command. The second code is a setProperty code that positions the **Woman** Movie clip offstage using the x coordinate; this is the action that removes the woman picture. So here is what happens. When the user first clicks on this **Woman** Movie clip it performs the actions that are on the Button in the first frame. These actions command all incorrect pictures to go to their label **incorrect** and **stop**. It also tells the matching picture, **woman2**, to go to the label **correct**. So now if the user correctly clicks on the **Woman 2** Movie clip it plays the timeline from the **correct** label forward. When it reaches frame **42** it performs all the actions in that frame:

```
tellTarget ("/golfer2/button") {
    gotoAndStop(2);
}
tellTarget ("/golfer/button") {
    gotoAndStop(2);
}
tellTarget ("/woman/button") {
    gotoAndStop(2);
}
tellTarget ("/woman2/button") {
    gotoAndStop(2);
}
```

If you scroll down the Actions window you'll see that all the actions are similar. These are the reset codes that send the buttons of all the Movie clips to frame **2**. If you remember, on frame **2** of the Movie clip buttons we have a blank keyframe:

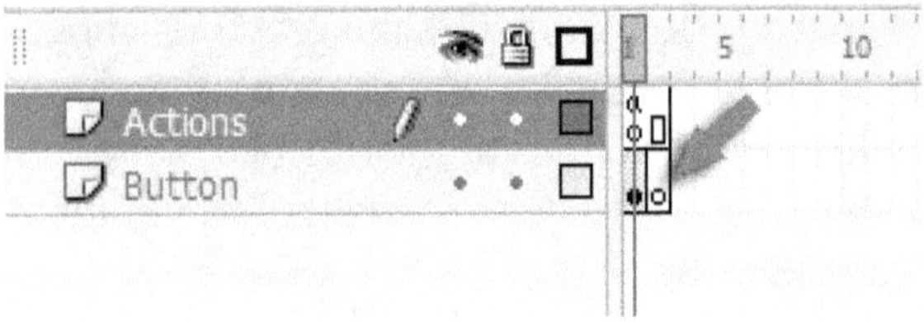

Once Flash performs these reset codes the timeline continues playing until it gets to the final frame:

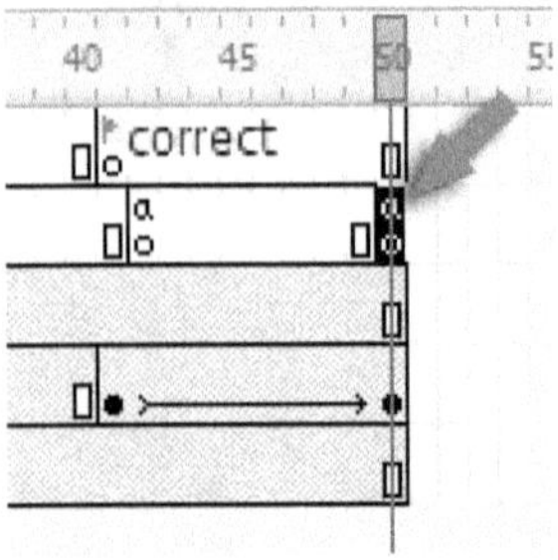

The code in this frame tells the **Woman Correct** Movie clip to go to the next frame which has the *play* code:

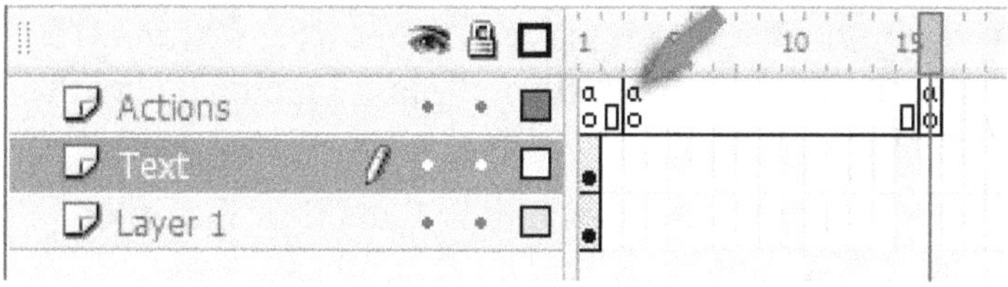

When the *play* code is triggered, the timeline continues playing until it reaches frame **16** which contains these two codes:

```
tellTarget ("/woman") {
    gotoAndPlay("fade");
}
tellTarget ("/woman2") {
    gotoAndPlay("fade");
}
```

These two actions tell both Woman Movie clips to go to the label **fad**e and **play**. As we learned earlier, when the timeline plays the fade animation it triggers the ActionScript in frame **19**:

```
stop();
setProperty("/woman", _x, "-100");
```

This ActionScript moves the position of the Woman Movie clips offstage. If you want to test it, go to **Control**, **Test Movie** and click on both Woman Movie clips:

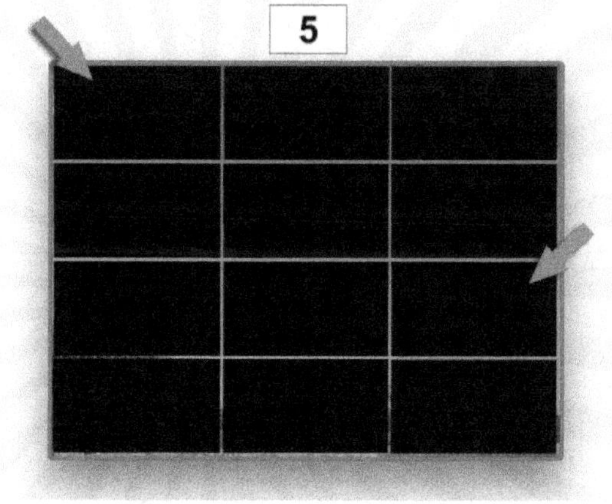

When you click on the first Woman Movie clip it sends the matching Woman Movie clip to the label **correct**. When the second button is clicked it sends the

Woman Correct Movie clip to frame **3** where it plays to frame **16**. At frame **16** it tells both Woman Movie clips to go to the label **fade** and **play** which triggers the setProperty code sending them both offstage.

You'll also notice that after you click on the second button that all of the other buttons are disabled. This is due to the button reset code on frames 24 and 42.

So what happens when a user selects an incorrect match? Let's say a user selects the elk picture first:

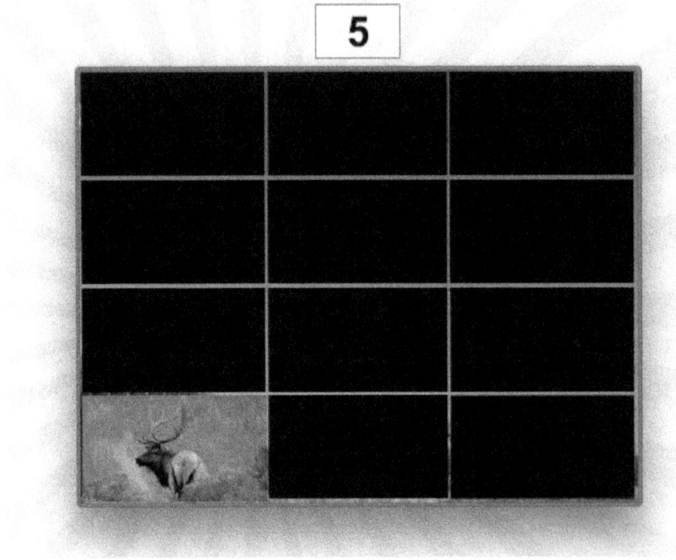

Once they click the elk button, it tells all the incorrect picture Movie clips to go to their label **incorrect**. Go back to the **Woman** Movie clip's timeline and look at the timeline where the **incorrect** label is:

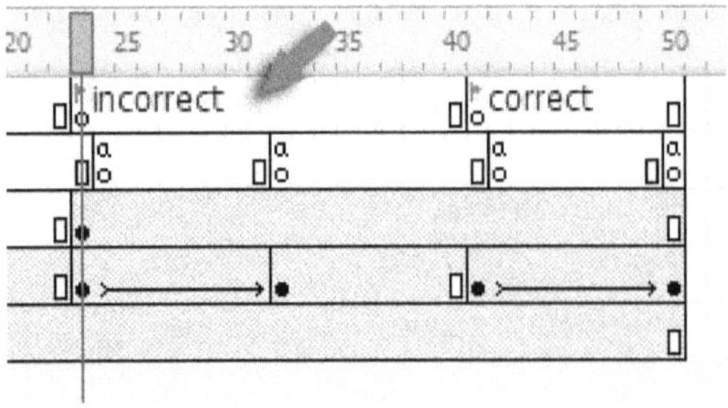

So now the **Woman** Movie clip's timeline is at the label **incorrect**. If the user clicks on the **Woman** Movie clip now it will trigger any actions that are on the frames from **23** to **32** as the picture fades in:

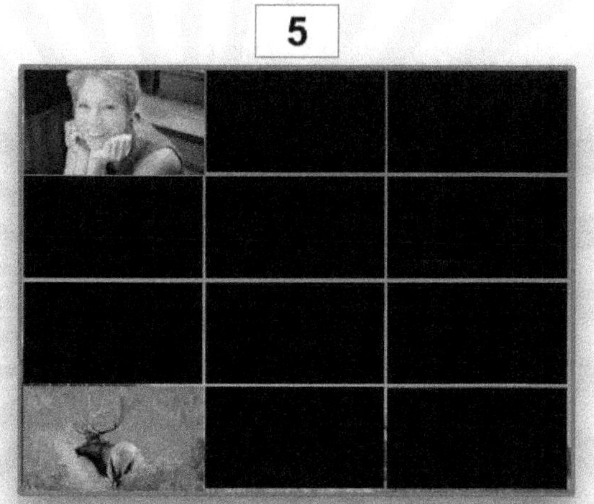

As the timeline plays it gets to frame **24** where the button reset code is we just examined. Flash then performs all of these actions which reset all the Movie clip buttons disabling them. The timeline then continues playing until it gets to frame **32**. If you click on frame **32** of the **Actions** layer you'll see its ActionScript:

```
stop();
tellTarget ("/incorrect") {
    gotoAndPlay("close");
}
```

The first code is a simple **stop** code. The next set of code tells the **Incorrect** Movie clip to go to the label **close** and play. We'll be examining the **Incorrect** Movie clip in a moment, but for now here is a quick look at its timeline:

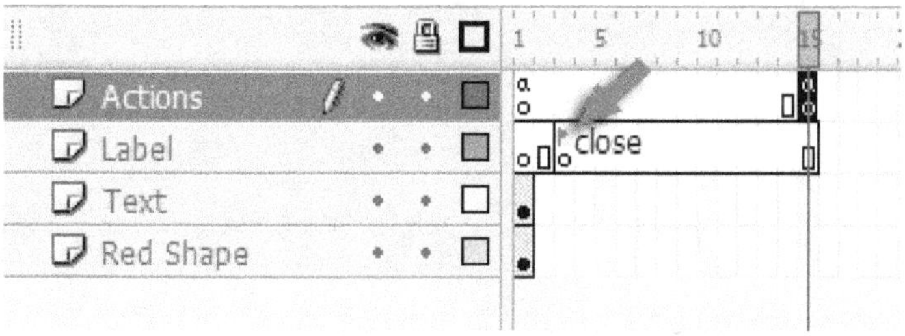

When this timeline goes to the Label **close** and plays, it continues until it reaches frame **15**. The code in this frame resets all the picture Movie clips. The reason for the number of frames between the label close and the final frame, is so the pictures are visible for a few moments before disappearing.

Let's take a closer look at the **Incorrect** Movie clip. Go back to Scene 1. Next, double-click on the **Incorrect** Movie clip:

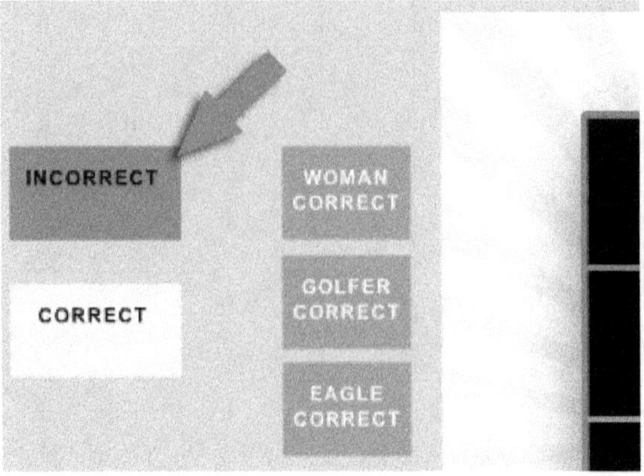

You should now be in the **Incorrect** Movie clip**'s** editing stage. Click on frame **15** of the **Actions** layer:

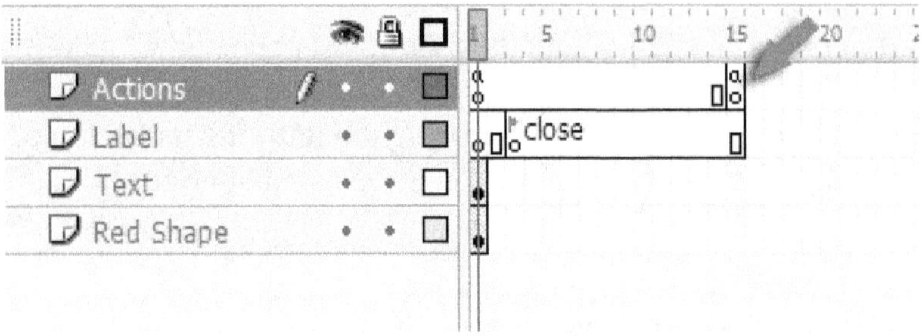

You should now see the ActionScript of this frame:

```
tellTarget ("/wrong_answers") {
    nextFrame();
}
tellTarget ("/elk") {
    gotoAndStop(1);
}
tellTarget ("/elk2") {
    gotoAndStop(1);
}
```

The first set of code tells the **Wrong Answer** Movie clip to go to the next frame. This is the Movie clip that controls how many wrong answers we have left:

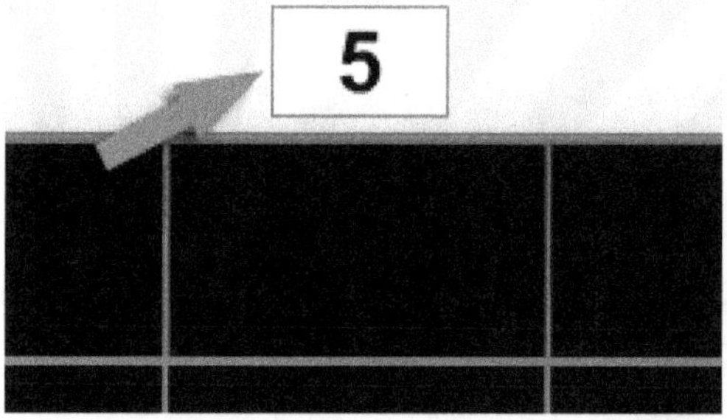

The next series of commands tell all of the picture Movie clips to go back to frame **1**. Basically, this code resets them. Scroll down in the Actions window until you see this code:

```
tellTarget ("/correct_woman") {
    gotoAndStop(1);
}
tellTarget ("/correct_golfer") {
    gotoAndStop(1);
}
tellTarget ("/correct_eagle") {
    gotoAndStop(1);
}
tellTarget ("/correct_mountains") {
    gotoAndStop(1);
}
tellTarget ("/correct_elk") {
    gotoAndStop(1);
}
tellTarget ("/correct_flowers") {
    gotoAndStop(1);
}
```

This code sends all of the Correct Movie clips back to frame **1**. If you remember, when a user selects, for instance, the **Woman** Movie clip, it sends the **Woman Correct** Movie clip to frame **2**. If the user selects an incorrect match then the above code sends the **Woman Correct** Movie clip back to frame **1**. Let's take a look at one of these correct Movie clips. Go back to Scene 1.

Double-click on the **Woman Correct** Movie clip:

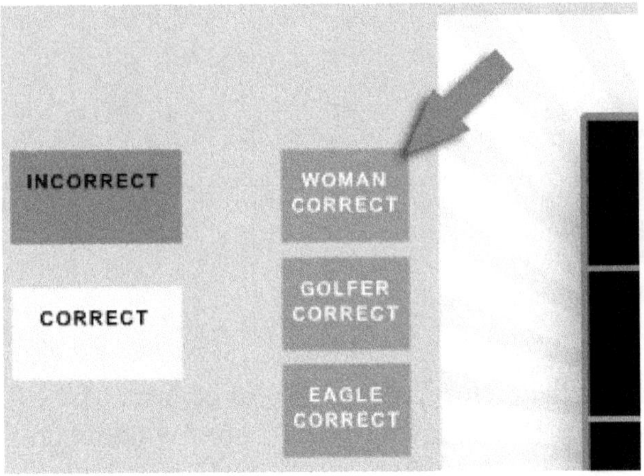

You'll see the three layers:

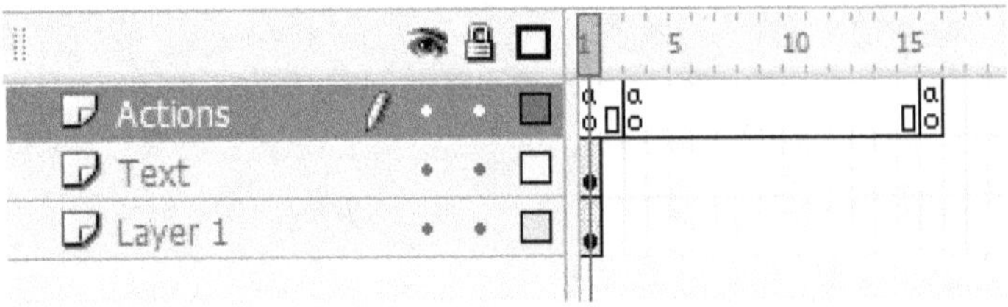

The first two layers hold the background color and the text. Let's examine the **Actions** layer. The first frame of the **Actions** layer holds a simple **stop** code. If the user selects one of the woman pictures of the puzzle it tells this timeline to go to the next frame, or frame **2**. If the user selects the matching woman picture, it tells this timeline to go to the next frame which would send it to frame **3**. On frame **3** you'll see a **play** code:

```
play();
```

This play code plays the timeline until it gets to frame **16**. The reason the next set of actions are on frame **16** is so that the pictures will remain visible for a few moments before disappearing. Click on frame **16** and look at the ActionScript:

```
tellTarget ("/woman") {
    gotoAndPlay("fade");
}
tellTarget ("/woman2") {
    gotoAndPlay("fade");
}
tellTarget ("/flowers") {
    gotoAndStop(1);
}
tellTarget ("/flowers2") {
    gotoAndStop(1);
}
```

As we learned earlier, the first two sets of code send both matching pictures to the label **fade**. Once both pictures timelines play the **fade** animation it triggers the setProperty code that sends them both offstage. The next series of codes reset the rest of the Movie clips back to frame **1**. Scroll down until you see the next set of codes:

```
tellTarget ("/incorrect") {
    gotoAndStop(1);
}
tellTarget ("/correct") {
    nextFrame();
}
tellTarget ("/correct_woman") {
    gotoAndStop(1);
}
```

The first code resets the **Incorrect** Movie clip back to frame **1**. The next set of code tells the **Correct** Movie clip to go to the next frame. This is how Flash knows when you've successfully finished the puzzle. When the **Correct** Movie clip reaches frame **7** it triggers the balloon animation. We'll study this Movie clip more closely in a moment.

The next set of codes reset all of the correct Movie clips. If you scroll down you'll see that there is code for resetting all of the correct Movie clips back to frame 1.

Go back to Scene 1. Double-click on the **Correct** Movie clip:

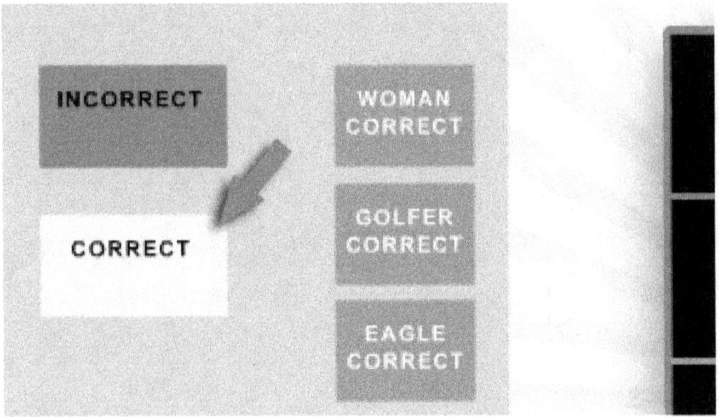

You should now be in its editing stage. You'll see three layers:

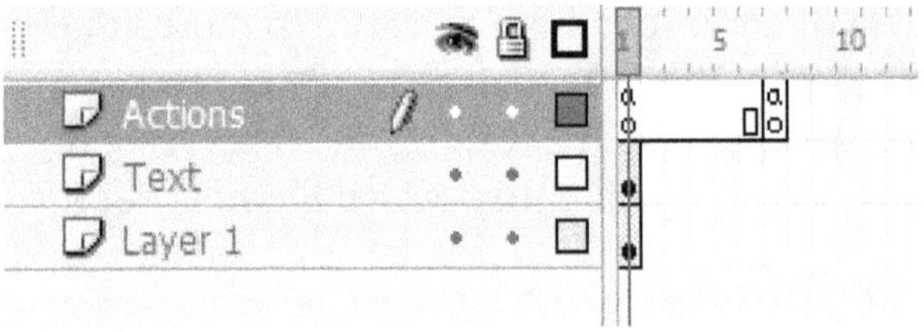

The first two layers hold the background color and text. In the first frame of the **Actions** layer is a simple **stop** code. Click on frame **7** and look at the ActionScript:

```
loadMovieNum("balloonvideo.swf", 1);
tellTarget ("/wrong_answers") {
    gotoAndStop("congratulations");


```

The first code loads in the balloon video into Level 1. The next set of code tells the **Wrong Answer** Movie clip to go to the label **congratulations**. This is the frame that has the text CONGRATULATIONS!. So each time a user successfully matches two pictures, it tells their respective correct Movie clip to play the Actions on frame **16**; in this frame there is code that tells the **Correct** Movie clip to go to the next frame. After six successful matches, the **Correct** Movie clip will end up on frame **7** where the above code is.

Let's look at the **Wrong Answers** Movie clip. Go back to Scene 1 and double click on the **Wrong Answers** Movie clip:

You should now be in the editing stage of this Movie clip. Let's examine the timeline:

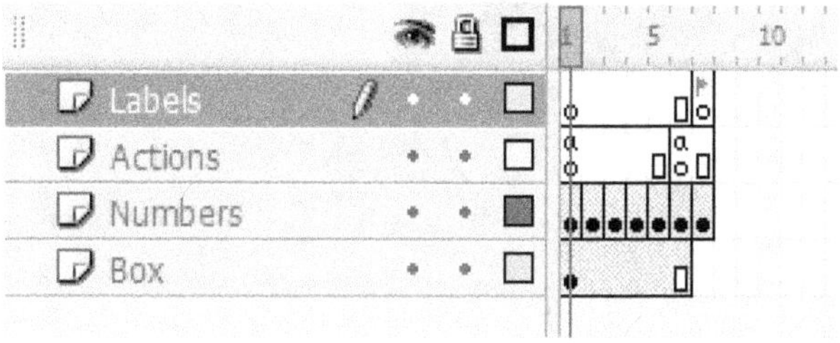

The **Box** layer holds the box shape for the text. The **Numbers** layer holds all of the text numbers. If you scrub the timeline you'll see that the numbers go from **5** to **0**. In frame **7** of the **Numbers** layer you'll see the CONGRATULATIONS! text. In the first frame of the **Actions** layer we have a simple **stop** code. Click on frame **6** of the **Actions** layer so you can see its ActionScript:

```
stop();
tellTarget ("/try_again") {
    gotoAndStop(2);
}
```

The first code is a simple **stop** code. The next set of code tells the **Try Again** Movie clip to go to frame **2** and stop. On frame **2** of the **Try Again** Movie clip we have the **Try Again** button. So here is what happens. Each time a user selects an incorrect match it triggers the **Incorrect** Movie clip to go to its final frame and perform the Actions. One of the Actions tells this **Wrong Answers** Movie clip to go to the next frame. So each time the user incorrectly guesses on a match the **Wrong Answers** Movie clip moves forward one frame. After five unsuccessful attempts the Wrong Answers timeline will end up on frame **6** which tells the **Try Again** button to appear.

Select frame **7** of the **Labels** layer. In the Properties panel you'll see that this Label has an Instance Name of **congratulations**. If you remember, when the **Correct** Movie clip gets to its final frame it tells the **Wrong Answers** Movie clip to go to the label **congratulations**.

Before you learn how to make variations of this game I'll show you the **Try Again** button. Go back to Scene 1 and double-click on the **Try Again** Movie clip:

You should now be in its editing stage. Now, let's look at the layers:

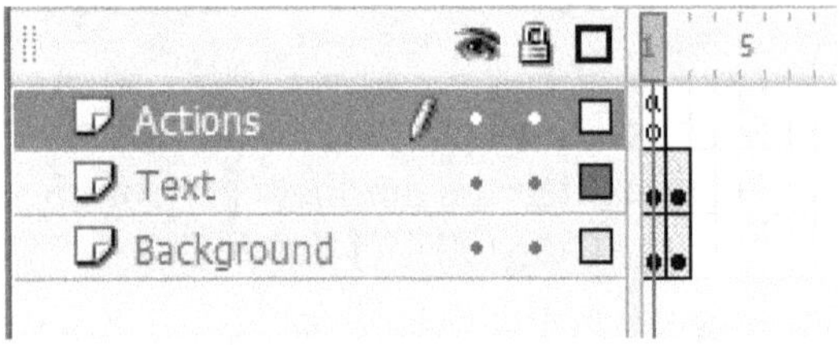

The **Background** layer has a transparent solid in the first frame. The first frame of the **Text** layer has the **Try Again?** text. This text isn't seen by the user; its primary use is to help the Flash creator find this Movie clip on the stage. The first frame of the **Actions** layer holds a simple **stop** code. Go to frame **2** and you'll see the **Try Again** button. Right now this button doesn't link to anything. We'll be adding a link to it shortly.

Also, in the second frame of the **Background** layer we have a large transparent button. Even though this large button doesn't click to anywhere, the reason it's a button is so that the user is unable to click any of the picture buttons below it.

We'll now add another variation of this game. Open the Scenes panel. Click on the **Duplicate scene** button. Name this new scene **Game 2**:

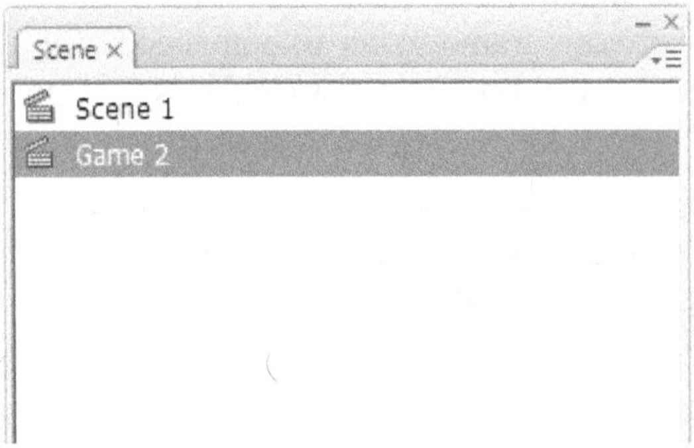

You should now be in the Game 2 stage. Now we're going to rearrange the picture Movie clips. I'll show you a quick and easy way to do this. Grab one of the picture Movie clips and drag it to the right offstage:

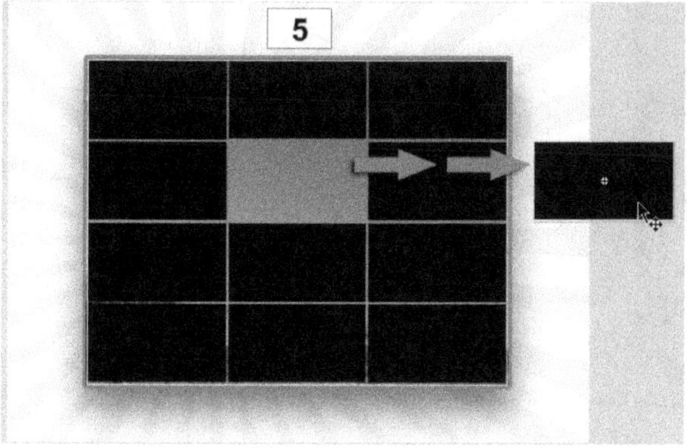

Next, place one of the other picture Movie clips into the empty space:

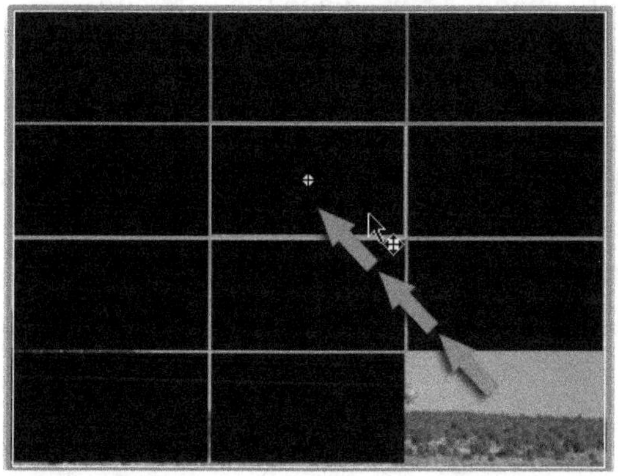

Use the dotted lines to help align the Movie clips:

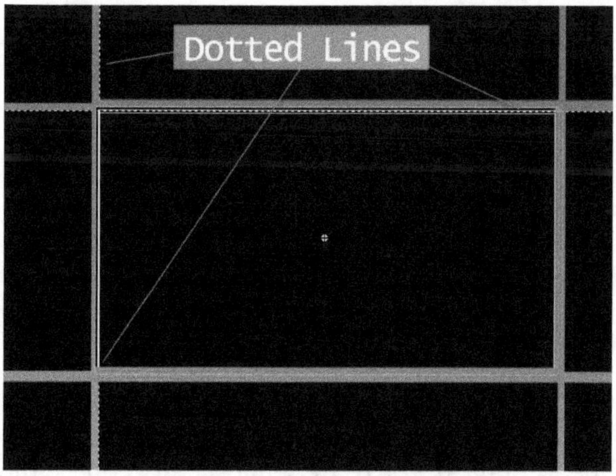

Drop the first Movie clip into the empty space

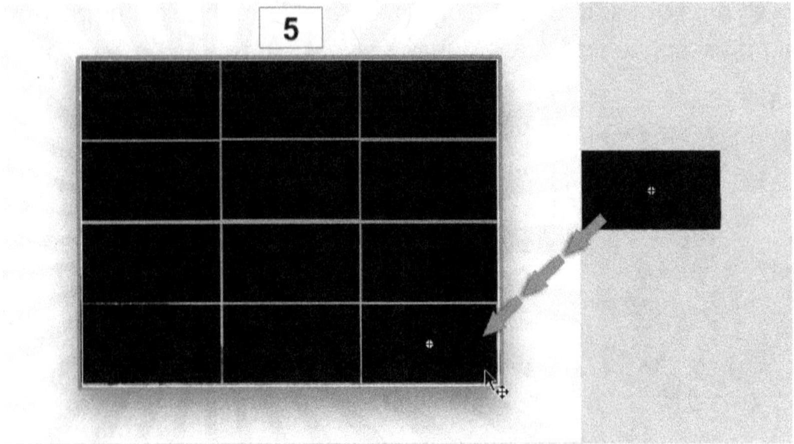

Do these steps for the rest of the Movie clips. Drag one Movie clip offstage then reposition another Movie clip into the empty space. Then, place the offstage Movie clip into the new empty area. When you're finished you'll have an all new puzzle. Let's try it out. Before we can test it, however, we need to add the code to the **Try Again** button that will send the user to the next game. Double-click on the **Try Again** Movie clip. On the second frame of the **Text** layer select the **Try Again** button on the stage. Open the Actions panel. So we need this button to tell the timeline to play to the next scene. So go to **Deprecated**, **Actions**, and double-click **tellTarget**. In the **Target** window type **_level0/**:

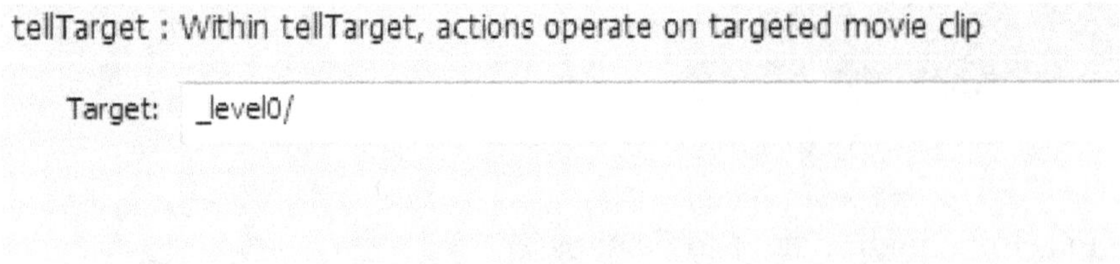

Go to **Global Functions**, **Timeline Control** and double-click **play**. Your final code should look like this:

```
on (release) {
    tellTarget ("_level0/") {
        play();
    }
}
```

So this code will tell the main timeline to play. If you're in Scene 1, this code will tell the main timeline to play, which will take it to the Game 2 scene. If you're in the Game 2 scene, this code will send the main timeline back to Scene 1, or to the next new scene you create.

That's it! So even if you add 10 more scenes with new puzzles, this button will always take the user to the next scene. Go ahead and test your movie. Try selecting incorrect matches to bring up the **Try Again** button. Once it appears, click it and you should now be in the new puzzle. You now know how easy it is to create variations of this puzzle. Create as many scenes as you like. Also, you can make the games harder by reducing the number of misses to 4.

Before we wrap on this project I'll briefly explain how I created the Balloons video that appears when you successfully complete the puzzle. The balloons that appear in the video are actual balloons that were in the background picture. In Photoshop I cut them out and put them on their own layers, I deleted the main background picture. In Photoshop I had all of these balloons against a transparent background. This file was then opened in After Effects. Each individual balloon was animated using keyframes. When I had completed the animation I went to **File**, **Export**, **Flash Video (FLV)...** In the FLV settings window I selected **Encode alpha channel**:

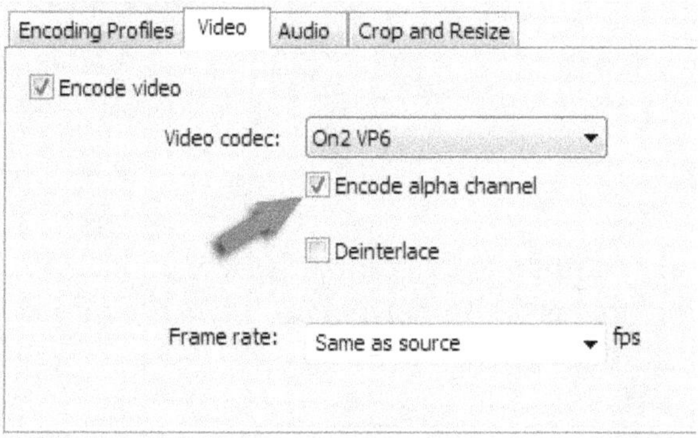

This will export a FLV that has no background. Next, in Flash I select **File**, **Import**, and **Import Video**. In the **Import Video** settings window I use the **Browse** button to find the FLV file:

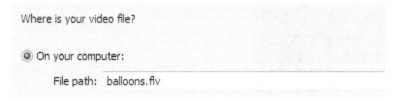

I then hit the Next button to go to the Deployment window. This is where I choose **Progressive download from a web server**:

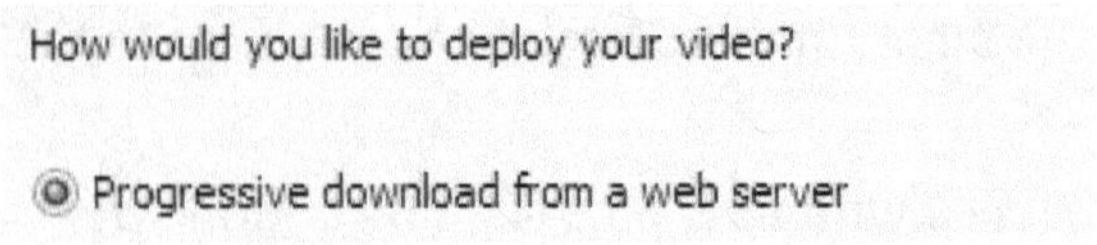

The next screen is the **Skinning** window. This is where you can select the type of menu bar. I chose **none** for this video:

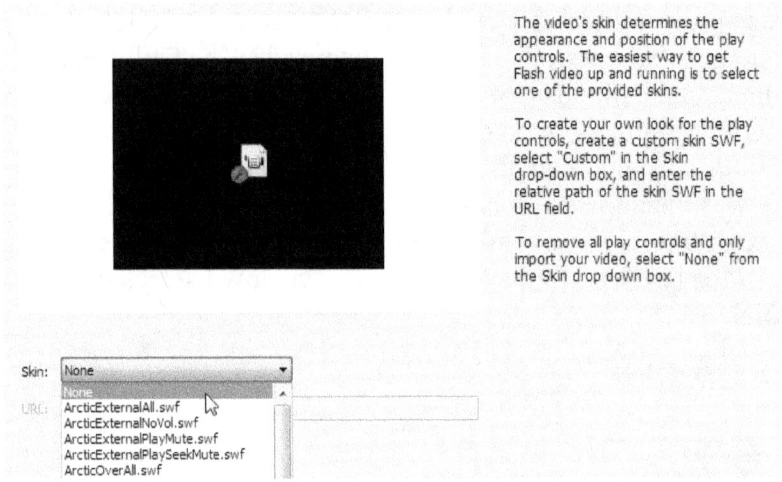

The next window just informs you that you're done customizing the video. Hitting the button **Finish** will begin the process of importing the FLV file into your Flash file. When it's done you'll see the video on the stage:

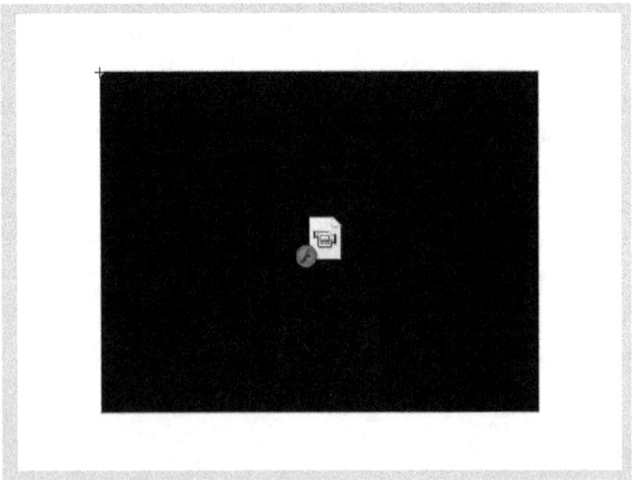

Once you publish this file you'll create a SWF file that you'll have to load into your project. For instance, in the Concentration game the file that gets loaded in is balloonvideo.swf. Which means the FLV file was loaded into the **balloonvideo.fla** editing file.

In the next exercise we'll be studying a roulette game that randomly selects the winning object and keeps track of your winnings!

Random Roulette

DIFFICULTY: ●●●●●●

A few years ago I was asked by a large company to create a roulette game that used pictures of automobiles as wheel symbols. The user could place a chip on any of the symbols and spin the wheel. If the user reached $50 then they won a prize that they could pick up at a dealership. The problem is that this company needed the game in the next couple days to meet a deadline. The Flash designer they had originally hired needed a week to write all the ActionScript. I told them I would have a working roulette game done in one day! Not only did I finish the game the next day, it was better than they had ever imagined. Oh, when their Flash designer realized I had created this game in one day without writing ActionScript he didn't believe it! The speed at which you can work in Flash when you're not writing code cannot be understated. In the end it's all about satisfied clients.

In this exercise I'll go through how I constructed the roulette game. I've altered the game slightly in that I've replaced the car pictures with animal pictures. Other than that, the game is exactly the same. When the game first starts the user gets a dollar chip that they can place on any image of an animal; once they place the chip on one of the animal images their money total goes down by 1 dollar. Then, they click a button which spins the roulette wheel. If the wheel doesn't land on the animal they chose then they lose a dollar. If the wheel does land on the animal they chose, then they win 7 dollars and get a little win message. The game continues until they either go bankrupt or get to 50 dollars. In either case the game is over and the user will be asked if they want to play again.

So how do you create a game that keeps track of the user's money total, randomly selects animals on the roulette wheel, and automatically increases the person's total if they win, without writing one line of ActionScript? Believe it or not this game was created using just a few simple commands like tellTarget and setProperty.

Open the Flash Projects folder and double-click the **Random_Roulette.swf** file. Play the game for a while to understand it better. Keep playing the game until you either go bankrupt or you get to 50 dollars and win the game. Notice how the roulette wheel randomly stops on animal pictures, and how Flash keeps track of the money total. And if you win, Flash automatically does the math and adds seven dollars to your total. When you're done playing, open the editing file called **Random_Roulette.fla**. Click on the **Edit Scene** button and you'll notice that there is a scene for every animal:

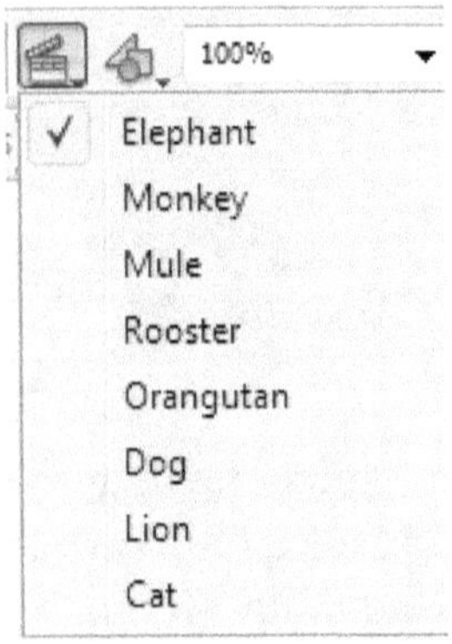

The scenes have identical layers except for a couple minor differences. One of the difference is that on every scene if you go to frame **77**, you'll notice that the picture of the animal at the top of the wheel is different. For instance, on the **Elephant** scene if you go to frame **77** you'll see that the elephant picture is at the top of the wheel; in the **Cat** scene the cat image is at the top of the wheel on frame **77** and so on.

In the **Elephant** scene go to frame 1 and hit Enter on your keyboard. You'll see the animation and how it slowly stops at the elephant image:

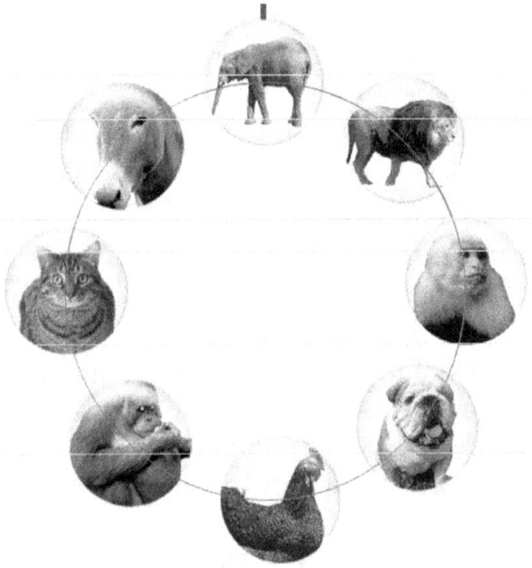

Each scene is divided into three sections. The first section is the flipper animation. Go to frame **1** and move the timeline needle slowly across the timeline. You'll see how the flipper animates back and forth as the animal pictures hit it. This layer uses a shape tween to animate the flipper. Below the **flipper** layer is the **Sound** layer which has a small roulette wheel sound effect.

The next section is the blurry picture layers. If you select frame **2** of the **Blur 1** layer you'll see the blurry picture on the stage. This is just a radial blur of the wheel with the animal pictures. If you go to the **Blur 2** layer and click on frame **9**, you'll see that we have another blurry image of the wheel, but this image isn't quite as blurry. You'll notice that there is a Motion Tween on both Blur layers. Both blur pictures gradually fade to 0 Alpha. When they are played together they give the appearance of a fast spinning wheel.

The next section are all the layers with the animal pictures. To better understand how the animation works we'll look at the **Mule** layer and **guide** layer. First, *turn off the visibility for all the layers below the mule layer*. Zoom into the stage 400%. Move the stage until you have a close view of the Mule picture.

You'll see that there is a small break in the guide circle. The center of the mule picture is attached to the guide above the break:

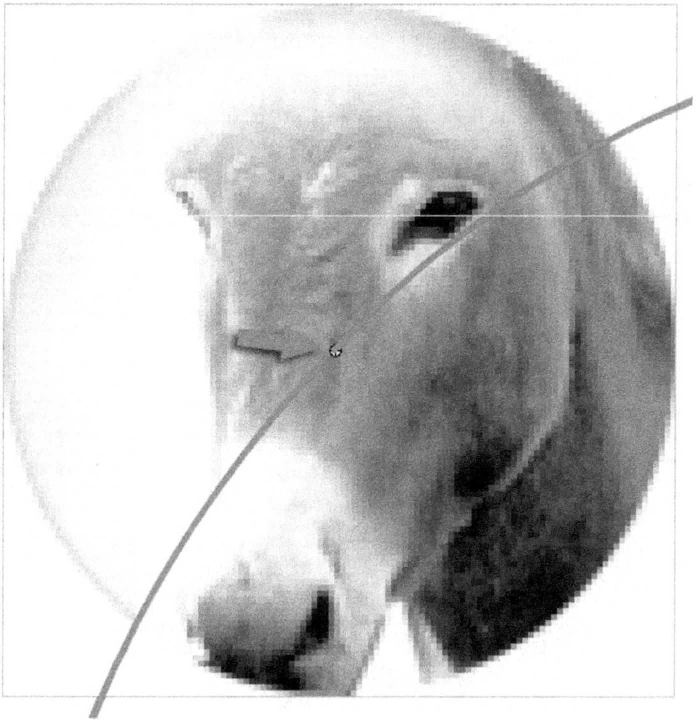

Go to frame **77**. Select the mule image on the stage. You'll see that the mule picture is attached to the guide circle right below the break:

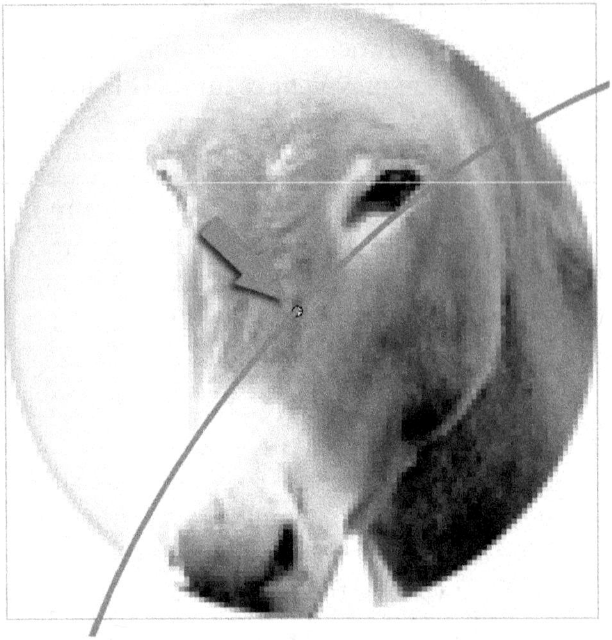

Move the timeline needle slowly over the timeline so you can see how the mule image follows the guide layer. Let's look at one more animal layer. Turn off the visibility for all the animal and guide layers except for the **Elephant** layer and its **guide** layer. Make sure you're still zoomed in at 400% and look at the elephant image. Go to frame **77**; you'll see that the elephant guide circle is a complete circle except for the break at the top of the circle. The elephant image is attached to the left of this break:

On frame **1** the elephant image is attached to the right of the break. So every animal image has their own guide circle. The break in each of these guide circles determines where the image will end up in the roulette wheel. Look at some of the other animals and their guide layers (*make sure all other guide layers have their visibility turned off*). So each animal has the same guide circle with a break in different locations.

Let's look at frame **1** of the **Actions** layer in the **Elephant** scene:

```
stop();
loadMovieNum("Button.swf", 1);
loadMovieNum("RouletteTable.swf", 2);
```

The first command is a simple **stop** code. This prevents the wheel from spinning before we click on the spin button. The next two pieces of code load in separate Flash files. The first one: **Button.swf**, loads into **level 1**. The second file: **RouletteTable.swf** loads into **level 2**.

So let's open both of these files. Go to **File**, **Open** and open the **Button.fla** file in the Flash Projects folder. Next, open **RouletteTable.fla** in the same folder. The first one we'll look at is the **RouletteTable.fla** file:

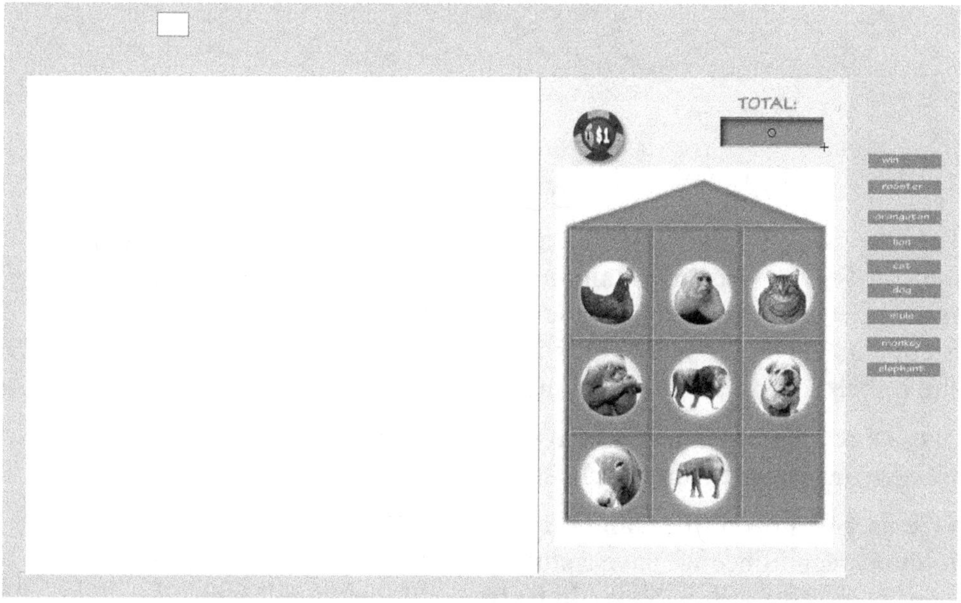

On the right of the stage is the roulette betting table. It's simply a JPEG image. On each of the animal pictures on the table we have transparent buttons. Surrounding this JPEG is a large transparent button. Turn the visibility on and off for the **Invis Button** layer so you can see where it is. We'll get back to this button in a moment.

At the top right we have the **Total** window. This is the Movie clip that holds the dollar figures. To the right of the stage we have the **Win** Movie clip; this is the Movie clip that gets triggered when the user guesses the correct animal. Below this Movie clip we have all of the animal Movie clips. These Movie clips get triggered when the user puts the chip down on one of the animal pictures. Since these Movie clips are off the stage they won't be seen by the user. And, at the top left of the table we have the dollar chip. This is a Movie clip with a **startDrag** command. This exercise uses the same technique as the *Drag-and-Drop* method we discussed earlier, which is why we need the large transparent button.

At the very top above the stage we have the **Bankrupt** Movie clip. This is the Movie clip that gets triggered when the money gets down to 0 dollars.

In a bit I'll go through how everything works. But first, open the **Button.fla** file and look at its stage:

You'll see the Click Me button in the middle of the stage. If you look at the timeline you'll see the **Buttons Random** layer, which controls how the animal images are selected. You then have the **Pictures** layer which holds the large pictures of animals that appear over the Click Me button. Above this layer we have the **Labels** layer. We'll be breaking down these layers in a bit.

Keep these three files open in Flash so you can easily go back and forth. Let's go through how the roulette game works step by step.

When the user first opens the **Random_Roulette** game, they'll stop at frame **1** of the **Elephant** scene since we have a **stop** code in the **Actions** layer. The ActionScript in this frame will load in **Button.swf** into **level 1** and **RouletteTable.swf** into level **2**:

```
stop();
loadMovieNum("Button.swf", 1);
loadMovieNum("RouletteTable.swf", 2);
```

The first thing the user will do is select the one dollar chip. This is a chip that the user can click-and-drag. Go to **RouletteTable.fla** and select the chip on the table:

In the Properties panel you'll see the Instance Name of **chip**. Double-click on this chip symbol so we can see how it works. In the chip editing stage you'll see two layers. The **chip** layer and the **Actions** layer which has a **stop** code. In the **chip** layer we have the chip button in the first frame and in the second frame of the **chip** layer we have just the raw image of the chip picture. Select the chip button on the first frame and open the Actions panel so you can see the ActionScript:

```
on (press) {
    startDrag("/chip", true, 600, 60, 900, 500);
}
on (release, rollOut, dragOut) {
    stopDrag();
}
on (release) {
    tellTarget ("_level2/rooster_button") {
        gotoAndStop(2);
    }
```

The first two sets of code control the Drag commands. When we press down on the chip symbol we start the **startDrag** command. When we release the mouse the Drag stops.

The next sets of code control the transparent Movie clips that are over the animal pictures on the roulette table. Each one of these Movie clips contain a button on the second frame. So when the user releases the mouse button it tells all of the transparent Movie clips on the roulette table to go to the second frame where their buttons are. This ActionScript is repeated several times for every animal Movie clip.

Scroll down the panel until you see the last piece of ActionScript:

```
on (release) {
    tellTarget ("_level2/chip") {
        gotoAndStop(2);
    }
}
```

This ActionScript tells the **Chip** Movie clip to go to the second frame where there is no button, just the chip picture. Once the chip is on frame **2** of its timeline (where there is no button) it can then control whatever button is below it (either the large invisible button or one of the animal buttons).

Go back to Scene 1. Let's look at some of the layers. The first layer holds the large invisible button. If you remember the Drag-and-Drop exercise we did earlier, this large invisible button will look familiar. Select this **invisible** button and look at its ActionScript:

```
on (rollOver, dragOver) {
    tellTarget ("/chip") {
        gotoAndStop(1);
    }
}
```

Let's say the user releases the chip above the table away from all the animal Movie clips. When the user releases the mouse button it tells the **Chip** Movie clip to go to frame **2** of its timeline *where there is no button.* The chip can then control whatever button is below it, which in this case would be the **Invisible** button. So if you look at the code in the **Invisible** button you'll see that if the user rolls over this button it will tell the chip to go back to frame **1** of its timeline; since the chip's button is on frame **1** of its timeline then the user will once again be able to drag the **chip** symbol again.

Let's look at one of the animal Movie clips so we can see what happens when the user drags the chip over one of them. Select the transparent Movie clip over the rooster image:

In the Properties panel you'll see that this Movie clip has an Instance Name of **rooster_button**. If you go back to the **Chip** Movie clip ActionScript, you'll see that it commands the **rooster_button** to go to frame **2** once we release the chip:

```
on (release) {
    tellTarget ("_level2/rooster_button") {
        gotoAndStop(2);
    }
```

Double-click the **Rooster** Movie clip to enter its editing stage. You'll see two layers. **Layer 1** and the **Actions** layer. The **Actions** layer simply has a **stop** code. Select the first frame of **Layer 1**. You'll see a red shape appear on the shape. This is simply a shape with the transparency taken down to **0**. Next, select frame **2** of this layer and select the button on the stage. Open the Actions panel so you can see the ActionScript:

```
on (rollOver, dragOver) {
    tellTarget ("_level2/rooster_total") {
        nextFrame();
    }
}
on (rollOver, dragOver) {
    tellTarget ("_level2/total") {
        prevFrame();
    }
}
on (rollOver, dragOver) {
    tellTarget ("_level2/dog_button") {
        gotoAndStop(1);
    }
}
```

If the user drags the chip over the rooster image and releases the mouse button, the chip button will disappear since the chip timeline will go to frame **2**. Since the chip button is gone the **Rooster** Movie clip will become active.

Note: At the end of this exercise is a diagram that should help you better understand how all of the Movie clips communicate with each other if you get confused. You may have to review this exercise a few times until you understand it completely.

Let's go through the above code. The first set of code tells the **Rooster Total** Movie clip to go to the next frame. We'll look at this Movie clip in a moment. The second set of code tells the **Total** Movie clip to go backward one frame. Since the user's dollar amount starts at 20 this code will tell the total to go back one frame to 19. The third set of code tells the **Dog** Movie clip to go to frame 1. If you scroll down you'll notice that this code is repeated for every animal button. What this does is send all of the animal Movie clips back to frame 1 where they once again become inactive since there is no button on frame **1** of their timelines.

If the user drags the chip over the rooster image and releases his mouse button, this triggers the Actions we just discussed. Now, we'll look at the **Rooster Total** Movie clip. Go back to Scene 1 and double-click on the **Rooster Total** Movie clip:

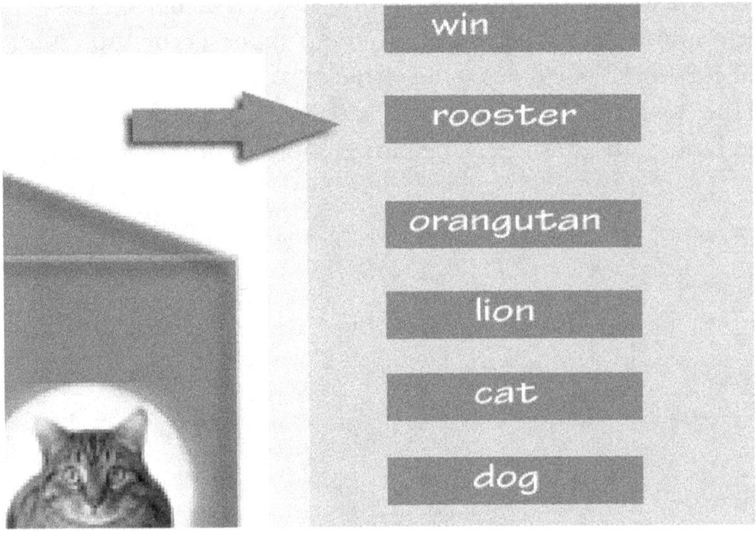

You should now be in its editing stage. The first layer has the red shape and text. This really serves no purpose, it just makes it easier to find the Movie clip when you're on Scene 1. The second layer is the **Actions** layer. Make sure the Actions panel is open and select the first frame of the **Actions** layer. You'll see a simple **stop** code. Click on the second frame. You will see another **stop** code. So when the **Rooster** Movie clip goes to frame 2 and its ActionScript is triggered, it tells the **Rooster Total** Movie clip to go to the next frame. After the user places the chip on the rooster image the **Rooster Total** Movie clip will go to frame 2 where it stops. Select frame **3** and look at the ActionScript:

```
stop();
tellTarget ("_level2/win") {
    play();
}
gotoAndStop(1);
```

The first one is a **stop** code. The next set of code tells the **Win** Movie clip to play; we'll get to this Movie clip in a moment. The third set of code tells this timeline to go back to frame **1** and stop. So if the user puts his chip on the rooster image, this triggers the **Rooster Total** Movie clip to go to frame **2**. But what triggers this Movie clip to go to frame **3**? Go back to the file **Random_Roulette.fla**, and go to the **Rooster** scene. Select frame **77** of the **Actions** layer and look at the ActionScript:

```
stop();
tellTarget ("_level1/") {
    gotoAndStop("rooster");
}
tellTarget ("_level2/rooster_total") {
    nextFrame();
}
```

We'll discuss the rest of the ActionScript later but for now look at the third set of code. This is the action that tells the **Rooster Total** Movie clip *to go to the third frame* where it triggers the **Win** Movie clip. So if we had never placed the chip on the rooster image then the **Rooster Total** Movie clip's timeline would never had gone to frame 2, it would have remained on frame 1.

Once the user places the chip on any of the animal Movie clips it triggers a domino type effect as several Movie clips begin communicating with one another. So how does the roulette wheel know where to stop? Go back to the **Button.fla** file. Let's focus on the **Buttons Random** layer. This is the area that controls where the roulette wheel stops. Select the first frame and then select the **Click Me** button on the stage. Open the Actions panel and look at the ActionScript:

```
on (rollOver, dragOver) {
    tellTarget ("_level1/") {
        stop();
    }
}
on (release) {
    tellTarget ("_level0/") {
        gotoAndPlay("lion");
    }
}
```

The first set of code tells **level 1** to **stop**. Since the file that we are on loads into **level 1**, this ActionScript is telling the current timeline to stop. The next set of code tells the main timeline, where the roulette wheels are, to go to the Label: **lion** and play. If you quickly look at the **Random_Roulette.fla** file and go to the **Lion** scene, you'll see the label: **lion** on frame **2** of the **Labels** layer.

Go back to the **Button.fla** file and select the second frame of the **Buttons Random** layer; select the **Click Me** button on the stage. You'll see it has code similar to the first button:

```
on (rollOver, dragOver) {
     tellTarget ("_level1/") {
          stop();
     }
}
on (release) {
     tellTarget ("_level0/") {
          gotoAndPlay("cat");
     }
}
```

The first code is the same as the first button; it stops the **Button** timeline. The next set of code tells the main timeline to go to the Label: **cat** and *play*. So each **Click Me** Button on the first 8 frames send the main timeline to a different label on the main timeline. Select frame **9** of this layer. You'll see that it's an empty frame except for some ActionScript:

```
gotoAndPlay(1);
```

This tells the timeline to go back to frame 1 and continue playing. This creates a continuous loop. So here is what happens. When the user first begins the roulette game, the **Button.swf** file loads into **level 1** of the main stage where the roulette wheels are. As soon as the **Button.swf** file is loaded, it begins playing its first 8 frames one after the other. When it gets to frame 9 it reads the code that sends it back to frame **1** to start over again. So you have a better understanding of this, test your movie. Turn on your **Bandwidth Profiler**. You should see the timeline marker go back and forth at a fast pace:

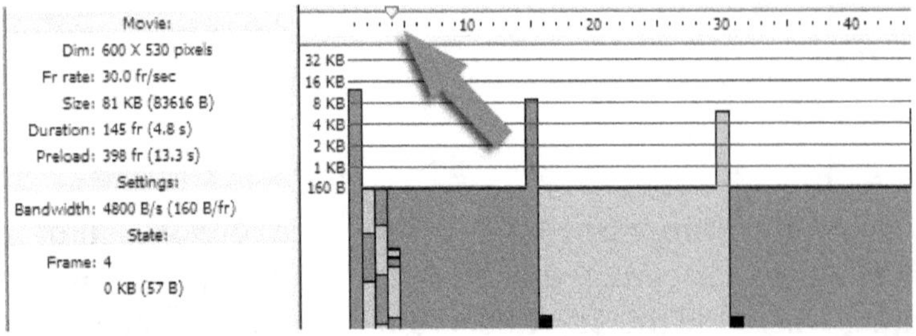

When the user clicks the **Click Me** button, the timeline instantly stops on one of the buttons. Flash then performs the next set of code which sends the main timeline to a specific Label.

So now let's look at the rest of the timeline in the **Button.fla** file. You'll see that there is a label for every animal:

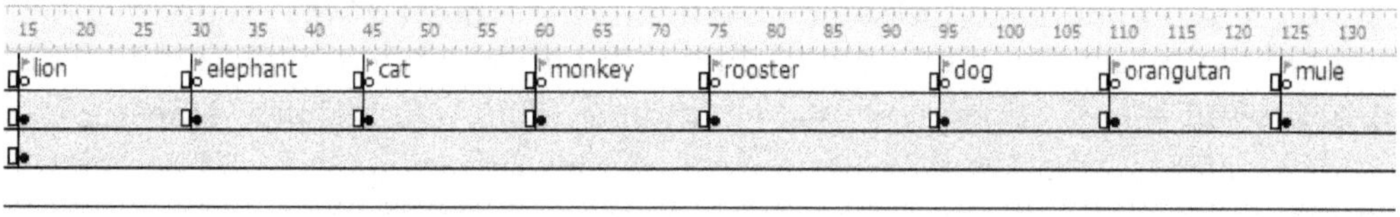

When the wheel stops on an animal, a large picture of that animal appears where the **Click Me** button is. That's where this part of the timeline comes into play. Select frame **15** of the **Pictures** layer. Double-click the **Lion** Movie clip on the stage (it will be above the **Spin Again** text):

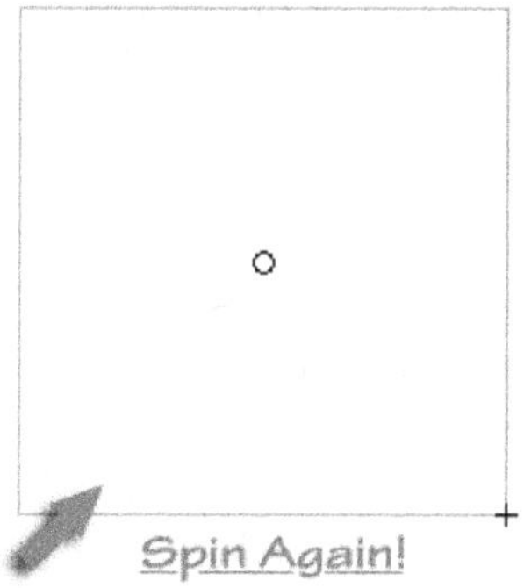

You should now be in the **Lion** Movie clip editing stage. Move the timeline needle back and forth across the **Lion** Movie clip timeline. You'll see that the lion picture gradually fades in. Let's examine the ActionScript that tells the Button timeline to go to the Label: **lion**.

Open the **Random_Roulette.fla** file and go to the **Lion** scene. Go to frame **77** of the **Actions** layer and look at the ActionScript. The second code of this ActionScript is the one that tells the **Button** file to go to the label: **lion**:

```
stop();
tellTarget ("_level1/") {
    gotoAndStop("lion");
}
tellTarget ("_level2[illegible]n_total") {
    nextFrame();
}
setProperty("_level2/chip", _x, "900");
setProperty("_level2/chip", _y, "-100");
tellTarget ("_level2/rooster_button") {
```

We'll go through the rest of the code in a moment. So here is what happens when the game first begins:

As soon as the user opens the game, the first 8 frames of the **Button.swf** file begin playing. The user drags the chip over the rooster image. When the user releases the mouse button it tells the **Chip** Movie clip to go to frame **2** of its timeline where there is no button; at the same time it tells the **Rooster** Movie clip to go to frame **2** where a button is. This will trigger the next set of actions which tell the **Rooster Total** Movie clip to go to the next frame. The Actions in the **Rooster** Movie clip also tell the **Total** Movie clip to go back one frame taking a dollar away from the total.

When the user rolls over the **Click Me** button it stops the animation in the first 8 frames of the **Buttons Random** layer. So let's say the user rolls over the **Click Me** button stopping the timeline on frame **7**. On that frame is the **Click Me** button that tells the main timeline to go to the Label: **rooster**. When the main timeline goes to the label: **rooster**, it plays the wheel animation on that timeline. The wheel will then stop at frame **77** with the rooster image at the top of the wheel. The ActionScript in the **Actions** layer of that frame then tell **level 1** (or the **Button.swf** file) to go to the Label: **rooster** where the large rooster image fades into view.

So how does the Flash file know when the **chip** has been placed on the winning animal? When we place the chip on, say, the **Rooster** Movie clip, it tells the **Rooster Total** Movie clip to go to frame 2. If we spin the wheel and it lands on the Rooster image, then, on frame **77** of the roulette timeline, it will command the **Rooster Total** Movie clip to go to the next frame which would be frame 3 (since it's already on frame 2). This triggers the **Win** Movie clip. So if we put the **chip** on the **Rooster** Movie clip and the wheel stopped on the elephant image, the **Rooster Total** Movie clip would never get to frame 3 to trigger the **Win** Movie clip.

Let's take a look at how the **Total** Movie clip works. Go back to the **RouletteTable.fla** file. Double-click the **Total** Movie clip:

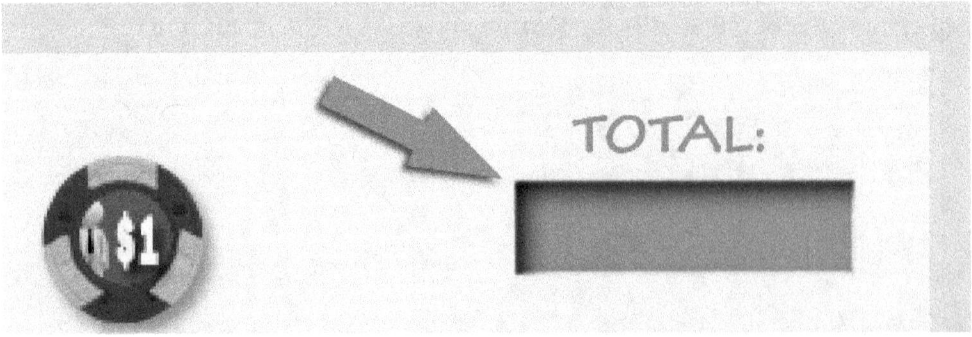

You should now be in the **Total** Movie clip editing stage. You'll see four layers. The first layer is just the Total graphic. The next layer, **Total**, has the money total. Use the timeline needle and scrub the timeline going all the way up to frame **53**. You'll first see the word **Bankrupt**, then the money count goes from **$0** to **$49**. It ends on the **WIN** frame.

The next layer is the **Actions** layer. Let's go over some of the ActionScript. Select frame **1** of the **Actions** layer and open the Actions panel. You'll see a **gotoAndPlay** code:

```
gotoAndPlay(4);
```

This code tells Flash to *bypass the first three frames* and go directly to the fourth frame where the **$1** total is; since it's a **gotoAndPlay** action, it tells the timeline to go to frame **4** and *continue playing* until it reaches a **stop** code. Select frame **3** of the **Actions** layer. You should see the ActionScript in the Actions panel:

```
tellTarget ("_level2/bankrupt") {
    gotoAndStop("bankrupt");
}
```

On this frame you'll see that the total in the window is **$0**. So if the user is down to **$1** and they place the chip on one of the animal Movie clips, the Movie clip will tell the **Total** Movie clip to go to the previous frame which will subtract $1 from the user's total money. So this places the **Total** timeline at **$0**. If the user doesn't win after spinning the wheel, then the **Total** timeline needs to go to the **Bankrupt** frame. So what triggers the **Total** timeline to go from the **$0** frame to the **Bankrupt** frame? Look at the above code. When the user reaches the **$0** frame it tells the **Bankrupt** Movie clip to go to the Label: **bankrupt**. Let's look at the **Bankrupt** Movie clip so you can see how it works.

Go back to Scene 1. The **Bankrupt** Movie clip is above the stage at the top left:

Double-click this Movie clip to enter its editing stage. You'll see three layers on the timeline:

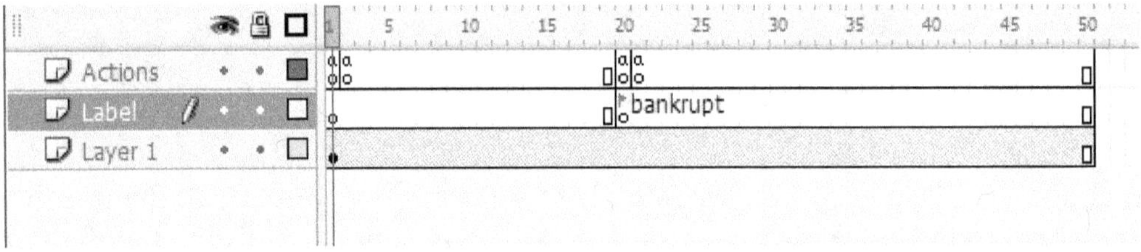

The first layer contains the graphic. The next layer is the **Label** layer. You'll see one Label on this layer called **bankrupt**. The top layer is the **Actions** layer. The first frame of this layer has a **stop** code and the second frame simply tells the timeline to return to frame **1** and stop.

If you remember the frame in the **Total** Movie clip tells the **Bankrupt** Movie clip to go to the label **bankrupt**. Go to frame **20** where the Label **bankrupt** is. In frame **20** of the **Actions** layer we have a **stop** code.

So when the user is down to **$1** and they place a bet, that tells the **Total** Movie clip timeline to go back one frame. On the **$0** frame there is a action that tells the **Bankrupt** Movie clip to go to the **bankrupt** Label (frame 20), which is where we are right now. So nothing happens on this frame but if we go to the next frame we'll see this ActionScript in the **Actions** frame:

```
stop();
tellTarget ("_level1/spin") {
    gotoAndStop("playagain");
}
tellTarget ("_level2/total") {
    gotoAndStop(2);
}
```

The first code is the **stop** code. The next set of code tells the **Spin Again!** Movie clip to go to the Label: **playagain** where the text **Play Again?** is.

The third set of code tells the **Total** Movie clip to go to frame **2** where the text **Bankrupt!** is. But what triggers the **Bankrupt** Movie clip timeline to go from frame **20** to frame **21** where the ActionScript is?

If you look at the beginning of the timeline of this Movie clip you'll see that there are two Actions in frame **1** and **2**. A **stop** code in frame **1** and a **gotoAndStop** code in frame **2**. When the user first goes on the Roulette game this timeline is on frame **1**. After the wheel is done spinning there is a code on frame **77** of each animal scene that tells the **Bankrupt** Movie clip to go to the next frame (go to the **Random_Roulette** file and look at frame **77** of the **Actions** layer in one of the animal scenes).

The next frame (frame 2) on the bankrupt timeline has the **gotoAndStop** code in it. This sends the timeline back to frame **1**.

If the user is down to **$1** when they place their bet, it tells the **Total** Movie clip to go to the previous frame which is the **$0** frame. On this frame there is ActionScript that tells the **Bankrupt** Movie clip to go to the label **bankrupt**. So, when the wheel gets done spinning and lands on a losing animal symbol, the code on frame **77** tells the **Bankrupt** Movie clip to go to the next frame; the next frame would then be frame 21 which would trigger the above ActionScript on that frame.

But now what happens if the user wins? Let's go step by step to see how the Movie clips communicate with each other when the user selects the winning animal.

Let's say the user drags the chip over the lion picture on the roulette table. The **Lion** Movie clip becomes active and performs its actions. One of the Actions is to tell the **Lion Total** Movie clip to go to the next frame, or frame **2**.

The user then clicks the **Click Me** button which spins the wheel. If the wheel goes to the **Lion** scene it will stop on frame **77** where it performs this action:

```
tellTarget ("_level2/lion_total") {
    nextFrame();
}
```

So this will send the **Lion Total** Movie clip to the next frame which would be frame **3**. On frame **3** of the **Lion Total** Movie clip we have this Action:

```
tellTarget ("_level2/win") {
    play();
```

So when the **Lion Total** Movie clip gets to frame **3**, it tells the **Win** Movie clip on **level 2** to play its timeline. Let's take a look at the **Win** Movie clip. Go back to Scene 1 and double-click on the **Win** Movie clip:

You'll see three layers. The first layer is the graphic layer. The second layer is the **Actions** layer and the third layer has the sound effect. Open the **Actions** panel and select the first frame of the **Actions** layer. You'll see a simple **stop** code. Now, when the **Lion Total** Movie clip performs the above action, the **Win** timeline will start to play. When it gets to the second frame it will perform the action in that frame:

```
tellTarget ("_level1/spin") {
    gotoAndStop(1);
}
```

This tells the **Spin** button on **level 1** to go back to frame **1**. This code ensures that the button says Spin Again? and not Play Again?. Next, the **Win** timeline will go to frame **3** where it will perform this code:

```
tellTarget ("_level2/total") {
    nextFrame();
}
tellTarget ("_level2/win_text") {
    play();
}
```

The first set of code tells the **Total** Movie clip to go to the next frame which will add **$1** to the total. The next set of code tells the **Win!** text to begin to animate (we'll examine this animation in a moment). Select the other frames in the **Actions** layer that have ActionScript. You'll see that they all have the same ActionScript:

```
tellTarget ("_level2/total") {
    nextFrame();
}

```

So as the timeline plays it will perform each of these Actions one by one. Every time it reaches one of these frames it tells the **Total** Movie clip to go to the next frame which forces the total money to go up by $1. Altogether there are 8 frames that hold this ActionScript which will move the **Total** Movie clip up by 8 dollars. Go to frame **18** of the **Actions** layer and you'll see this code:

```
gotoAndStop(1);
tellTarget ("_level2/bankrupt") {
    gotoAndStop(1);
}

```

The first code sends this timeline back to frame **1** where it stops playing. The second code tells the **bankrupt** Movie clip to go to frame **1**. If the user is down to $0 and they win, this code ensures that the **Bankrupt!** text doesn't appear; it also makes sure that the game continues and doesn't end.

Go back to Scene 1 and double-click on the **Total** Movie clip. When the user first starts the game the timeline reads the code on the first frame which tells the timeline to go to frame **4** and begin playing. The timeline plays the timeline until it gets to frame **23** which has a **stop** code. The dollar amount it stops at is **$20**.

So when a code tells this Movie clip to go to the previous frame, the dollar count goes down by $1. When the user selects the correct animal it triggers the **Win** Movie clip; the **Win** timeline has 8 frames which tell the total timeline to go to the next frame 8 times.

Go to frame **53** of the **Total** Movie clip timeline. If the user arrives at this frame then he has won the game. You'll see this code:

```
setProperty("_level2/chip", _x, "900");
setProperty("_level2/chip", _y, "-100");
tellTarget ("_level1/spin") {
    gotoAndStop("playagain");
}
```

The two setProperty codes tell the chip to go to the **x** coordinate **900** and the **y** coordinate **-100**. What this does is completely remove the chip from the stage. The next set of code tells the **Spin Again?** button to go to the label: **playagain** which has the text **Play Again?**.

In a upcoming page I have a diagram that will help illustrate the series of events that occur when a bet is placed. It should help you better understand how the Movie clips are communicating with one another.

Now let's look at one final set of commands. Open the **Random_Roulette.fla** file and go to the **Lion** scene. Select frame **77** of the **Actions** layer. You should see this code:

```
stop();
tellTarget ("_level1/") {
    gotoAndStop("lion");
}
tellTarget ("_level2/lion_total") {
    nextFrame();
}
tellTarget ("_level2/bankrupt") {
    nextFrame();
}
setProperty("_level2/chip", _x, "900");
setProperty("_level2/chip", _y, "-100");
}
tellTarget ("_level2/rooster_button") {
    gotoAndStop(1);
```

The first code is a simple **stop** action. The next set of code tells the **Button** file (level 1) to go to the Label: **lion** where the large picture of the lion is. The next piece of code tells the **Lion Total** Movie clip to go to the next frame, which would be frame 3 since the chip that was placed on the **Lion** Movie clip, commanded the **Lion Total** Movie clip to go to the next frame (**2**).

The next set of code tells the **Bankrupt** Movie clip to go to the next frame. If the user is down to $0 then the **Bankrupt** Movie clip will be on the Label: **bankrupt** since the code on the **$0** frame (in the **Total** Movie clip timeline) tells the **Bankrupt** timeline to go to the Label: **bankrupt**. When Flash reads this action it tells the **Bankrupt** Movie clip to go to the next frame which will trigger the Actions on that frame which end the game. But, since the user won, before the **Bankrupt** code can be triggered Flash will perform the action in the third piece of code. This tells the **Lion Total** Movie clip to go to the next frame (**3**) which will trigger the **Win** Movie clip, which begins playing. On frame **18** of this timeline there is ActionScript that tells the **Bankrupt** Movie clip to go back to frame **1** where it won't trigger the end of game actions.

The next two sets of code are **setProperty** functions. These commands completely remove the chip off the stage since the wheel is done spinning. The next bit of code, and the code that follows, tell the animal buttons to return to frame **1**. When all of these animal buttons return to frame 1 they become inactive (since there is no button on frame 1 of their timelines).

Go through this exercise a few times until you can fully understand how the mechanics behind it work. On the next page is a diagram that should help you better understand how all the Movie clips communicate with each other:

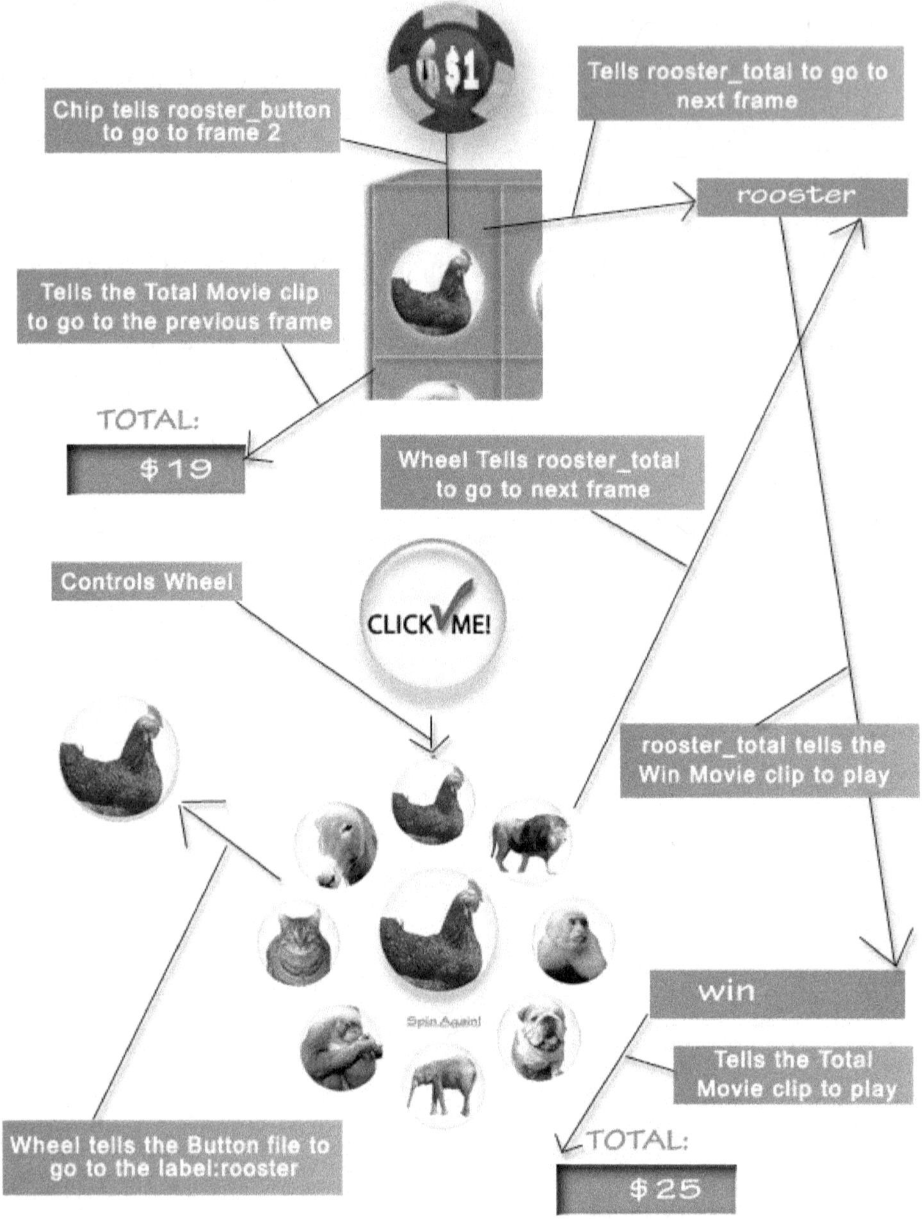
Chip tells rooster_button to go to frame 2
Tells rooster_total to go to next frame
rooster
Tells the Total Movie clip to go to the previous frame
TOTAL:
$19
Wheel Tells rooster_total to go to next frame
Controls Wheel
CLICK ME!
rooster_total tells the Win Movie clip to play
win
Tells the Total Movie clip to play
Wheel tells the Button file to go to the label:rooster
TOTAL:
$25

Understanding how Movie clips communicate with each other is the secret to unlocking the power within Flash without writing ActionScript.

In the next example we'll examine a floating button Flash file. A recreation of the sophisticated animation that was part of the Sony website.

Floating Buttons

DIFFICULTY: ●●●●○○

A film distributor approached me a few years ago and asked to recreate the animation that was on the Sony website at that time. It was a great animation with menu buttons floating over the map of the world. When you rolled over one of the buttons, its animation would stop and the button would change color. The other buttons would continue their animation but their transparency went down to 50%. The entire color of the animation also changed to match the button that was being activated. So I thought about the best way to do this and I came up with the following file. Open the file called **Floating_Boxes.swf** in the Flash Projects folder. You'll see the buttons floating around the screen, but when you roll over one of the buttons, the background color changes and the other buttons change their transparency. So let's take this file apart so you can better understand it. Open the file called **Floating_Boxes.fla**. You'll see nine layers:

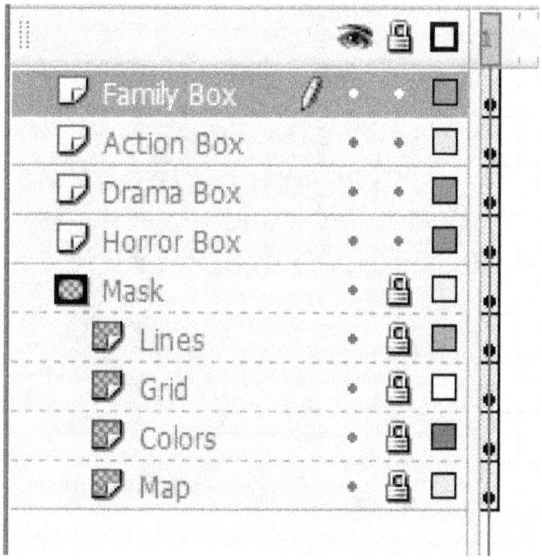

The first layer is the Map graphic. The next layer is the **Colors** layer which changes the color of the entire map. We'll look at this layer more closely in a bit. The next layer is the **Grid** layer. This layer holds the **Grid** Movie clip. The next layer is **Lines** which is just a layer that has some line shapes. The next layer, **Mask**, holds the grid shape which masks all the layers below it. The top four layers each hold the Button boxes. So let's see how this file works. Select the **Family** Movie clip on the stage:

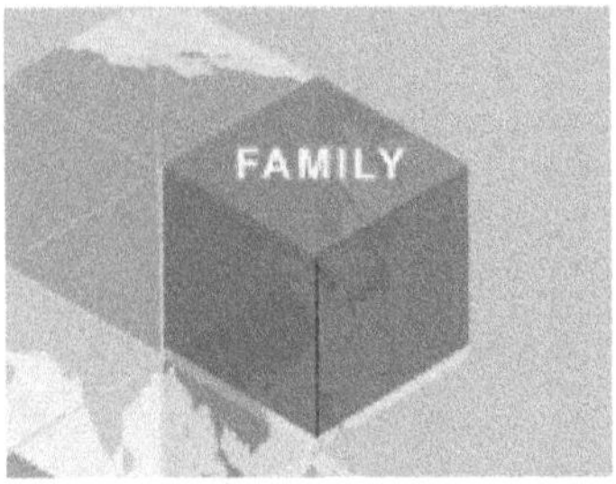

In the Properties panel you'll see that the Instance Name is **family_box**. Double-click on this Movie clip to enter its editing stage. In this stage you'll see the Motion Tween that moves this box around the stage. Select the first frame, then select the box on the stage. In the Properties panel you'll see that the Instance Name is **family_box2**. Double-click the box on the stage to enter its editing stage. You'll see three layers:

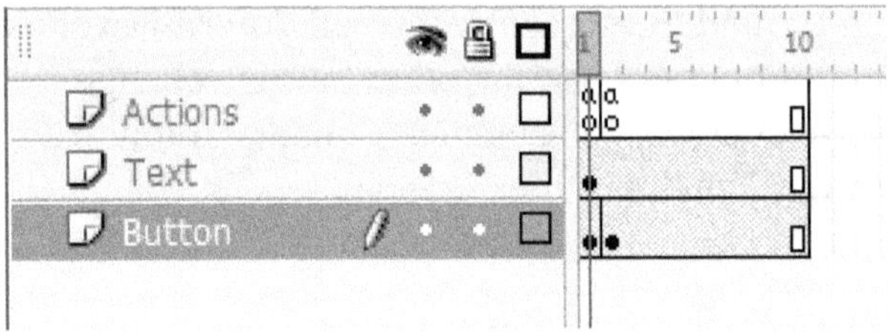

The **Button** layer contains the **Family Button**. The **Actions** layer has two frames each with **stop** codes. Select the first frame of the **Button** layer and select the **Box** button on the stage. Open the Actions panel so you can see the ActionScript:

```
on (rollOver, dragOver) {
    tellTarget ("/family_box") {
        stop();
    }
}
on (rollOut, dragOut) {
    tellTarget ("/family_box") {
        play();
    }
}
on (rollOver, dragOver) {
    tellTarget ("/colors") {
        gotoAndStop("blue");
    }
}
on (rollOut, dragOut) {
    tellTarget ("/colors") {
        gotoAndStop(1);
    }
}
on (rollOver, dragOver) {
    setProperty("/drama_box", _alpha, "20");
}
on (rollOut, dragOut) {
    setProperty("/drama_box", _alpha, "100");
```

I'll briefly go through each piece of code then afterward we'll spend more time on each one and how they work.

The first piece of code tells the **Family Box** Movie clip to stop when we roll over the **Family Box** Movie clip. The next set of code tells the **Family Box** Movie clip to continue playing when we roll off the Movie clip. The next set of code tells the **Colors** Movie clip to go to the Label: **blue**. This changes the entire background to a blue color.

The next set of code tells the **Colors** Movie clip to go back to frame **1** where it's no longer a color when the user rolls off the Movie clip. The next set of code takes the alpha of the **Drama Box** Movie clip down to 20% when the user rolls over the **Family Box** Movie clip. The next piece of code takes the alpha back up to 100% when the user rolls off the **Family Box** Movie clip. This code is repeated for the **Action Box** and the **Horror Box** Movie clips.

After this code we have the following code:

```
on (rollOver, dragOver) {
    tellTarget ("/action_box/action_box2") {
        gotoAndStop(2);
    }
}
on (rollOut, dragOut) {
    tellTarget ("/action_box/action_box2") {
        gotoAndPlay(3);
    }
}
on (rollOver, dragOver) {
    tellTarget ("/drama_box/drama_box2") {
        gotoAndStop(2);
    }
}
on (rollOut, dragOut) {
    tellTarget ("/drama_box/drama_box2") {
        gotoAndPlay(3);
    }
}
on (rollOver, dragOver) {
    tellTarget ("/horror_box/horror_box2") {
        gotoAndStop(2);
    }
}
on (rollOut, dragOut) {
    tellTarget ("/horror_box/horror_box2") {
        gotoAndPlay(3);
    }
}
```

The first set of code tells the **Action Box2** Movie clip, which is within the **Action Box** Movie clip to go to frame **2**. On frame **2** of the **Action Box2** Movie clip's timeline there is no button. So if we roll over the **Family Box** Movie clip we don't want the other Movie clips to have their buttons active in case they travel by the **Family Box** Movie clip.

The next set of code tells the **Action Box2** Movie clip to return to frame **1** where its button is active.

So let's break down the entire ActionScript code by code.

The first code:

```
on (rollOver, dragOver) {
    tellTarget ("/family_box") {
        stop();
    }
}
```

This code simply tells the animation to stop. If you go to Scene 1 and double-click on the **Family Box** Movie clip you'll see the animation timeline. This is the timeline that sends the **Family Box** Movie clip around the stage. When the user rolls over the **Family Box** Movie clip it tells this timeline to stop. To resume the animation we need the next set of code in the ActionScript:

```
on (rollOut, dragOut) {
    tellTarget ("/family_box") {
        play();
    }
}
```

When the user rolls off the **Family Box** Movie clip the animation plays again. Now, let's look at the next two sets of code:

```
on (rollOver, dragOver) {
    tellTarget ("/colors") {
        gotoAndStop("blue");
    }
}
on (rollOut, dragOut) {
    tellTarget ("/colors") {
        gotoAndStop(1);
    }
}
```

When the user rolls over the **Family Box** Movie clip it tells the **Colors** Movie clip to go to the Label: **blue**. When the user rolls off the **Family Box** Movie clip, the **Colors** Movie clip goes back to frame **1**.

Let's look at the **Colors** Movie clip. Go to Scene **1** and lock all the layers except for the **Colors** layer; turn off the visibility for the **Mask** layer and select the first frame of the **Colors** layer. Double-click the **Colors** Movie clip on the stage to enter its editing stage. You'll see five layers:

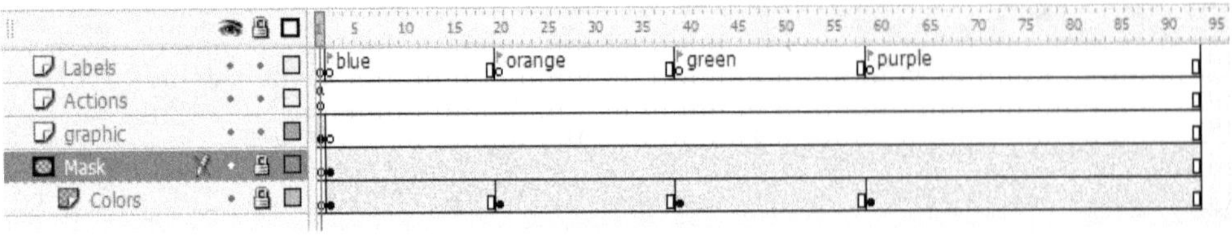

The first layer is **Colors**. This is the layer that holds the colored grid shapes. Unlock both the **Colors** layer and the **Mask** layer. Go to frame **2** where the label: **blue** is. You can now see the blue shape and the mask shape:

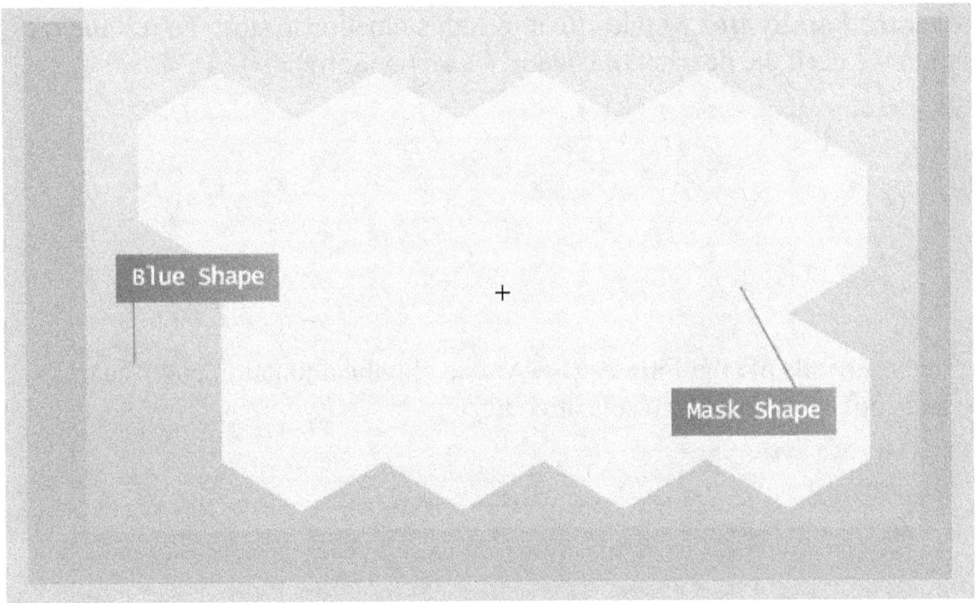

Drag the timeline needle across the timeline so you can see the other colored shapes in the **Colors** layer. The next layer is a simple transparent graphic. I sometimes use these when the first frames of a Movie clip are empty; it makes it easier for me to select the Movie clip from Scene 1. The next layer is the **Actions** layer; this layer simply has a **stop** code in the first frame. The last layer is the **Labels** layer which has all the labels for each color.

Let's go back to the ActionScript. The next set of code is the **setProperty** code:

```
on (rollOver, dragOver) {
    setProperty("/drama_box", _alpha, "20");
}
on (rollOut, dragOut) {
    setProperty("/drama_box", _alpha, "100");
}
on (rollOver, dragOver) {
    setProperty("/horror_box", _alpha, "20");
}
on (rollOut, dragOut) {
    setProperty("/horror_box", _alpha, "100");
}
on (rollOver, dragOver) {
    setProperty("/action_box", _alpha, "20");
}
on (rollOut, dragOut) {
    setProperty("/action_box", _alpha, "100");
}
```

The *rollOver, dragOver* codes tell all of the other boxes to become transparent while the user's cursor is over the **Family Box** Movie clip. The *rollOut, dragOut* codes tell all of the other boxes to become opaque when the user rolls off the **Family Box** Movie clip. The last sets of code control the Movie clip that is embedded in each of the other boxes:

```
on (rollOver, dragOver) {
    tellTarget ("/action_box/action_box2") {
        gotoAndStop(2);
    }
}
on (rollOut, dragOut) {
    tellTarget ("/action_box/action_box2") {
        gotoAndPlay(3);
    }
}
on (rollOver, dragOver) {
    tellTarget ("/drama_box/drama_box2") {
        gotoAndStop(2);
    }
}
on (rollOut, dragOut) {
    tellTarget ("/drama_box/drama_box2") {
        gotoAndPlay(3);
    }
}
on (rollOver, dragOver) {
    tellTarget ("/horror_box/horror_box2") {
        gotoAndStop(2);
    }
}
on (rollOut, dragOut) {
    tellTarget ("/horror_box/horror_box2") {
        gotoAndPlay(3);
    }
}
```

If we examine the first code, when the user rolls over the **Family Box** Movie clip it tells the Movie clip **Action Box2**, which is inside the **Action Box** Movie clip, to go to frame 2. Let's take a closer look at the **Action Box2** Movie clip. Go back to Scene 1 and double-click on the **Action Box** Movie clip. Select the first frame, then select the box on the stage. If you look at the Properties panel you'll see that this box has an **Instance Name** of **action_box2**. Double-click this Movie clip to enter its editing stage. You should see three layers:

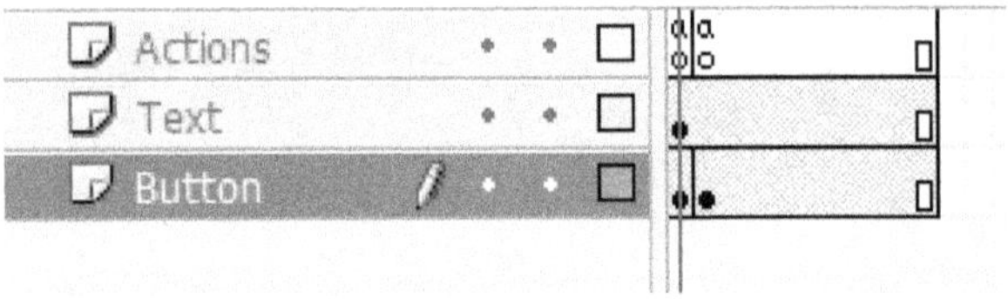

In the first layer we have the **Button** layer. Just like in the **Family Box2** Movie clip and the other Movie clips, we have a button in the first frame and a normal symbol in the second frame. If we select the box symbol on the stage and open the Actions panel, you'll see that this ActionScript is nearly identical to the family button ActionScript except for a few minor changes. For instance, when we roll over the **Action Box** Movie clip it tells the **Action Box** Movie clip to stop its timeline (instead of **family_box**). The other differences is that now the **Family Box** Movie clip is getting controlled by the **setProperty** function. So when we roll over the **Action Box** Movie clip the **Family Box** Movie clip becomes transparent. Now lets see what happens when the ActionScript tells the **Action Box2** Movie clip to go to frame **2**. Select frame **2** then select the symbol on the stage; you'll see that it's neither a Movie clip or a button, but rather a graphic. So when a user rolls over the **Family Box** Movie clip it tells the **Action Box2** Movie clip (as well as the **Horror Box2** and **Drama Box2** Movie clips) to go to frame **2** where this Graphic is; this is to deactivate their buttons. When the user rolls off the **Family Box** Movie clip it tells the **Action Box2** Movie clip (as well as the **Horror Box2** and **Drama Box2** Movie clips) to go to frame **3** and play. Here is the reason for this ActionScript. When the user rolls off the button there needs to be a few moments of buffer time before the other Movie clips are once again active. So when the timeline goes to frame **3** and plays it gives the user a chance to move his cursor off the stage without triggering any of the other Movie clips. When the timeline gets to frame **10** it automatically goes back to frame **1** and stops. Go through this exercise a few times until you completely understand it. Hopefully by now you're starting to see how powerful Movie clips are!

Psychic Test

DIFFICULTY:

I was asked a few years ago to put together a psychic test for a psychic website. They wanted users to test their psychic ability but in a fun type of way. So I thought about how to do this for a little while and came up with the following psychic test. In studying how programmers had put together similar projects they had used hundreds of lines of code and took several days to weeks to complete the project. I knew that just by using the simple **tellTarget** command I could create an interactive test that would also give feedback when completed; plus, I could complete it in about one day. The end result was highly popular by users of the psychic website. In the Flash Projects folder double-click the file named PsychicTest.swf. Play a couple rounds to test your psychic ability. Notice that when you finish a round you get a nice scroll animation which gives you a quick analysis of your progress.

Before we open the editing file, install the Asrafel font located in the Fonts folder. Next, open the **PsychicTest.fla** file in the Flash Projects folder. I'll very quickly give you an overview of what happens, then I'll have you create your own test! If you play the main timeline you'll see a animation of the cards separating and going to their final positions. On the final frame of this animation you'll see the scroll. It's part of a Movie clip called **Cards**. Double-click on this Movie clip and you'll see several keyframes. They are all divided by the Labels: **test 1**, **test 2**, **test 3** and **test 4**. If you scrub the timeline next to **test 1**, you'll see the answers to the first test. On the **Cards** layer we have the card buttons. If you open the Actions panel you'll be able to see the ActionScript for each button. Select the star button on the first frame of the **Cards** layer:

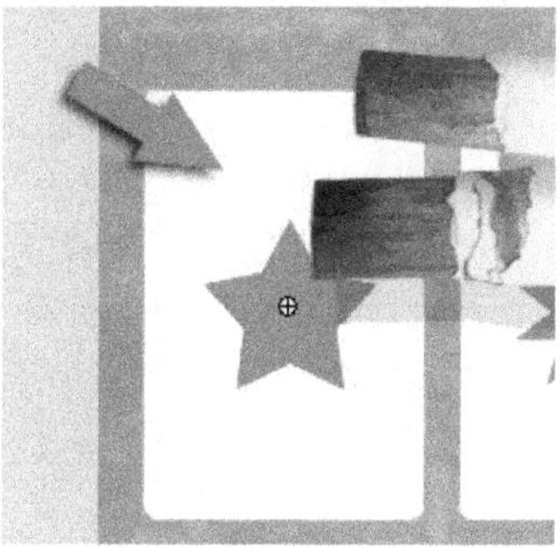

In the Actions window you'll see the ActionScript:

```
on (release) {
    tellTarget ("/correct") {
        nextFrame ();
    }
}
on (release) {
    nextFrame ();
}
```

So here is what happens. Since the **Star** is the correct answer, if the user selects this button it will tell the **Correct** Movie clip to go to the next frame. Select another card button on frame 1 of the **Cards** Layer, and you'll see that they are controlling the **Incorrect** Movie clip:

```
on (release) {
    tellTarget ("/incorrect") {
        nextFrame ();
    }
}
on (release) {
    nextFrame ();
}
```

All the buttons contain the second set of code:

```
on (release) {
    nextFrame ();
}
```

This code tells the **Cards** Movie clip timeline to go to the next frame on the timeline. So, in a nutshell, if the user picks the correct card, that button will tell the **Correct** Movie clip to go to the next frame. Also, when the button is clicked it takes the user to the next frame of the **Card** Movie clip where they have to, once again, guess the next card. Go through this timeline until you get a full understanding of how it works. You'll notice that there is minimal ActionScript in each button; it's basically Movie clips controlling other Movie clips.

Go back to Scene 1 and double-click the **Correct** Movie clip:

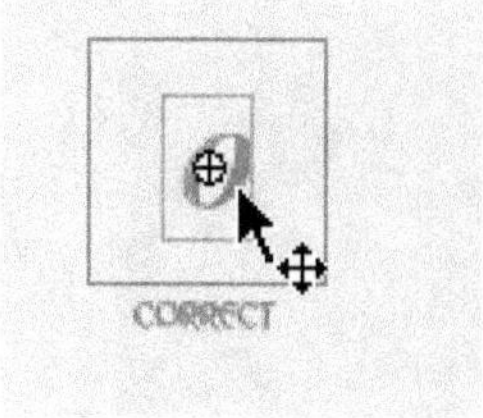

In the **Correct** Movie clip timeline you'll see that the number changes in each frame, from 0 to 10. When a user selects the correct card button, it will tell this timeline to go to the next frame. Open the Actions panel so you can see the code. Scrub the timeline with the timeline needle and you'll see the ActionScript of each frame. You'll notice that on each frame there is a ActionScript that controls the **Scroll 2** Movie clip (**/cards/scroll/scroll2**):

```
stop();
tellTarget ("/cards/scroll/scroll2") {
    gotoAndStop("9");
}

```

The **Scroll 2** Movie clip is the Movie clip that controls the red outline on the Scroll that highlights your score:

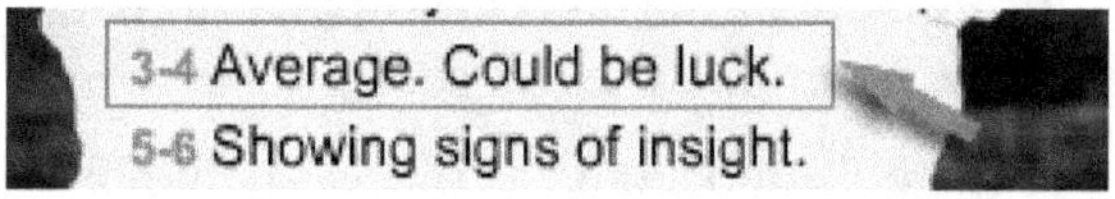

So here is what happens. Every time the user selects a correct card, that button tells the **Correct** Movie clip timeline to go to the next frame. So if the user gets eight predictions correct, then the **Correct** Movie clip will have been sent to the next frame eight times. The **Correct** Movie clip will end up on frame **9**. On frame **9** you'll see that it tells the **Scroll 2** Movie clip (red outline) to go to Label **9**. So let's go to the **Scroll 2** Movie clip so you can better understand this.

Go back to Scene 1 and double-click on the **Cards** Movie clip (the big scroll):

The **Scroll 2** Movie clip is located within the **Scroll** Movie clip which is within the **Cards** Movie clip. Double-click on the **Scroll** Movie clip. You should now be in the **Scroll** timeline. Go to frame **50** and double-click the **Scroll 2** Movie clip on the stage (the large scroll on the **Scroll Animation** layer).

You should now be in the **Scroll 2** timeline. This is the timeline that is controlled by the **Correct** Movie clip. So the more questions the user gets correct the higher the frame they end up on in the **Correct** timeline; if they end up on frame **9** of the **Correct** Movie clip the ActionScript on that frame will tell the **Scroll 2** timeline to go to Label **9**. The frames under Label **9** have the red outline around the 9-10 score. If the user only gets 1 or 2 cards correct, then the **Correct** Movie clip will send the user to Label **1** where the red outline is around the 0-2 score.

One thing you may have noticed is that in the editing file the Scroll is visible on the first frame, but when you test your movie the Scroll disappears. This is due to a setProperty code in the first Actions frame of every test. For instance, in the **Cards** timeline, select frame **27** of the **Actions** layer. This is the first frame of **Test 2**. In the Actions window you should see this ActionScript:

```
stop();
setProperty("/cards/scroll", _visible, "0");
tellTarget ("/cards/scroll") {
    gotoAndStop(1);
}
```

The first code is a simple stop code. The next set of code tells the alpha of the **Scroll** Movie clip to go to 0, making it transparent. The last set of code resets the Scroll timeline back to frame 1. Whenever you change the alpha of a symbol you'll have to use a setProperty command to *bring back* the visibility of this symbol. Click on frame **37** (the final frame of **Test 2**) of the **Actions** layer. In the Actions window you'll see this ActionScript:

```
setProperty("/cards/scroll", _visible, "100");
tellTarget ("/cards/scroll") {
    gotoAndPlay(1);
}

```

At the end of **Test 2** we need to make the Scroll visible again. That's what the first line of code does. The next set of code tells the Scroll timeline to go to frame 1 and play. This will begin the Scroll animation. The last thing we'll look at is the **Reset** button code. Click on the **Reset** button on the stage:

You should now see its ActionScript in the Actions window:

```
on (release) {
    play();
}
on (release) {
    tellTarget ("/incorrect") {
        gotoAndStop(1);
    }
}
on (release) {
    tellTarget ("/correct") {
        gotoAndStop(1);
    }
}
```

The first set of code tells the timeline to play. If the user just finished **Test 2**, then the timeline will play until it hits the **stop** code on frame **54**, the first frame of **Test 3**. The next set of code tells the **Incorrect** Movie clip to go to frame **1** and **stop**. The last set of code tells the **Correct** Movie clip to go to frame **1** and **stop**. These two codes basically reset both Movie clips.

So that's how this psychic test works. You can add as many tests as you like. I'll walk you through how to add your own test to show you how easy it is!

The first thing we'll do is create a copy of the **Test 4** frames. Then we'll tweak the frames for the new test. Click on frame **84** of the **Labels** layer (don't let go of the mouse button). Drag across all the frames of **Test 4** highlighting them:

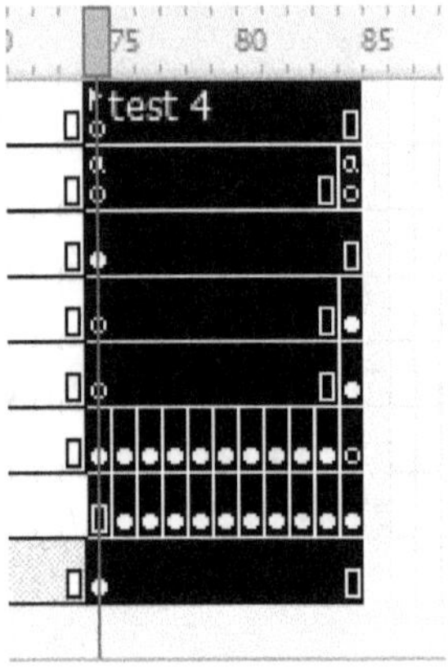

Once the frames are highlighted you can let go of the mouse button. Next, hold down the ALT key and click on frame **74** of the **White Card layer**; without letting go of the mouse button or the ALT key, drag these highlighted frames to frame **95**:

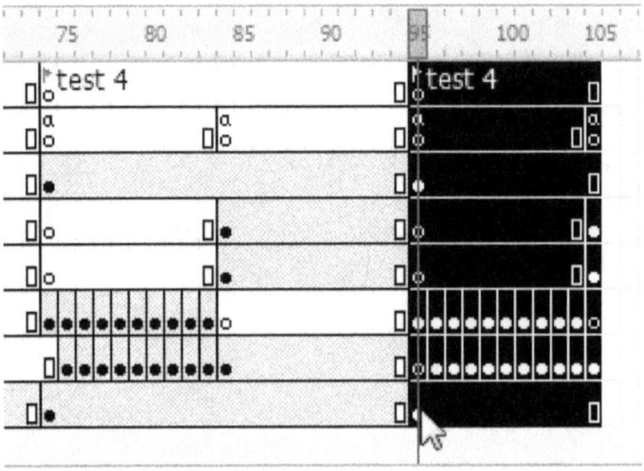

So now we have copies of all the frames from **Test 4**. The first thing we'll do is change the Label name. Click on frame **95** of the **Labels** layer and change the Frame Label name to **test 5**:

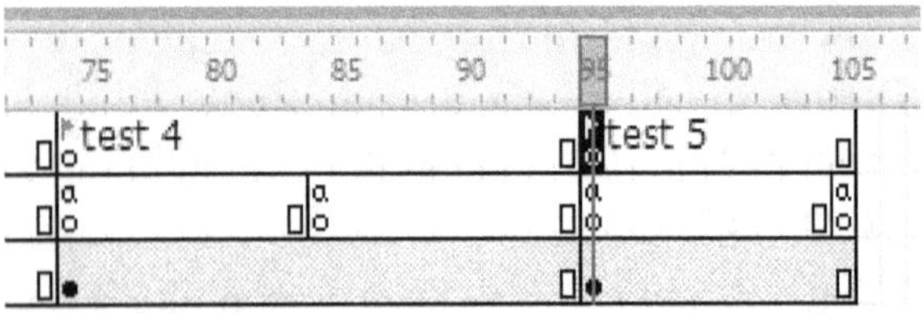

The next thing we need to do is rearrange the order of the symbols. Click on frame **100** of the **Symbols** layer; click on this frame again and drag it to frame **105**.

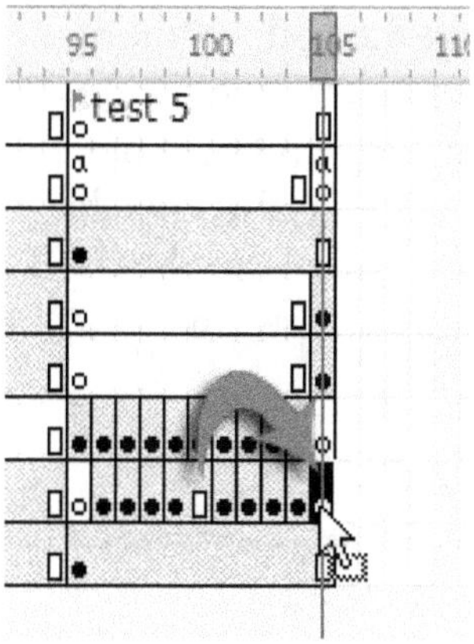

Drag one of the other symbols into the vacated frame of **100**:

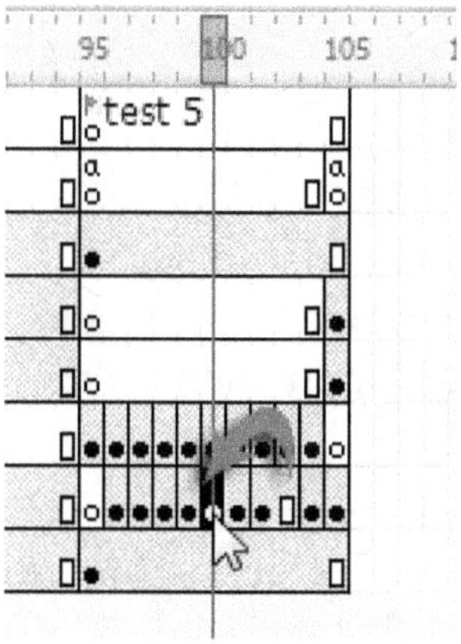

Move another symbol into the vacated frame:

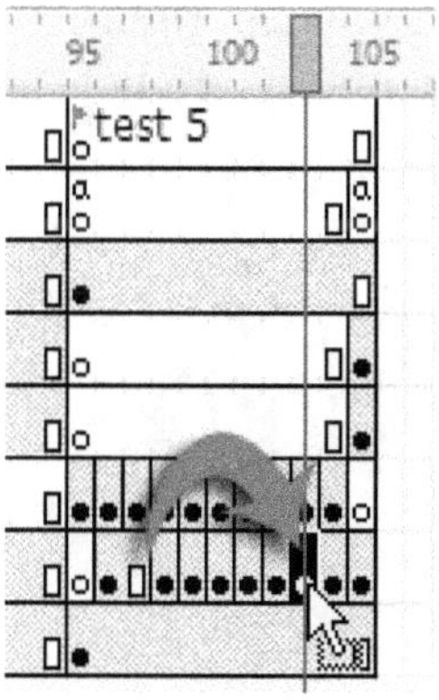

Keep swapping the symbols until you're happy with the new order. If you finish with the order and you have a vacant spot, hold down the ALT key and copy one of the other keyframes to fill the spot.

Now that you have a new order of symbols we need to tweak the code of the buttons. Select frame **96** of the **Symbols** layer and either memorize or write down what symbol card you see. For instance, let's say that the Square symbol is on frame **96**. Move the timeline needle to frame **95** and select the **Star Button** (the code on the Card buttons will refer to the symbols on the *next frame*. So the Card buttons on frame 95 will refer to the symbols on frame 96, and so on). In the Actions window you should see this ActionScript:

```
on (release) {
    tellTarget ("/incorrect") {
        nextFrame();
    }
}
on (release) {
    nextFrame();
}
```

Since this is the **Star Button** then this code is correct. All of the Card buttons should have this code, except for the **Square Button** which will control the **Correct** Movie clip. So, you first find out what symbol is on frame 96, and then you change the code of the Card buttons so that the matching Card button is the only one that controls the **Correct** Movie clip.

Next, find out what symbol is on frame 97. You then tweak the codes of the Card buttons on frame 96 so that only the matching button controls the **Correct** Movie clip. Do the same steps for the rest of the frames. Remember that the Card buttons will refer to the symbols on the next frame.

So that's it! Using only a few lines of ActionScript you now have a interactive psychic test! You can add as many tests as you like. Also, see if you can figure out how to make a **Correct!** message appear every time a user properly predicts a card.

Space Attack!

DIFFICULTY:

The next exercise came about when I tried to figure out a way to create a shooting game using Movie clips. I wanted to create a game that incorporates many of the elements found in similar games: a timer, levels, a scoreboard, and a final screen that displays your score. I also wanted to create the game in 3 or 4 hours to show how quickly even sophisticated projects can be developed once you master Movie clips.

The main obstacle in creating a shooting game, of course, is the collision detection. How does Flash know when you've hit your target? And once you hit your target how do we tell the score to update? The secret to making it all work is using a variation of the drag-and-drop technique we used earlier. Before we examine how it works, try out the game! Go to the Flash Projects folder and double-click on the file called SpaceAttack.swf.

You get 10 points for the slow moving ship and 20 points for the fast moving ship. You need 100 points to get to the second level. You have 30 seconds to complete the level.

In the second level you have to shoot the bombs before they self-destruct and cost you 20 points. The small ship is worth 10 points. You need 100 points to win the game. You have 25 seconds to complete the second level:

It may take a few tries to get the hang of firing. The weapon uses a click-and-drag function; when you release the click-and-drag function it fires.

Open the file called Attack.fla in the Flash Projects folder. You should see the space picture, the cannon weapon, a ship, and a scoreboard at the top:

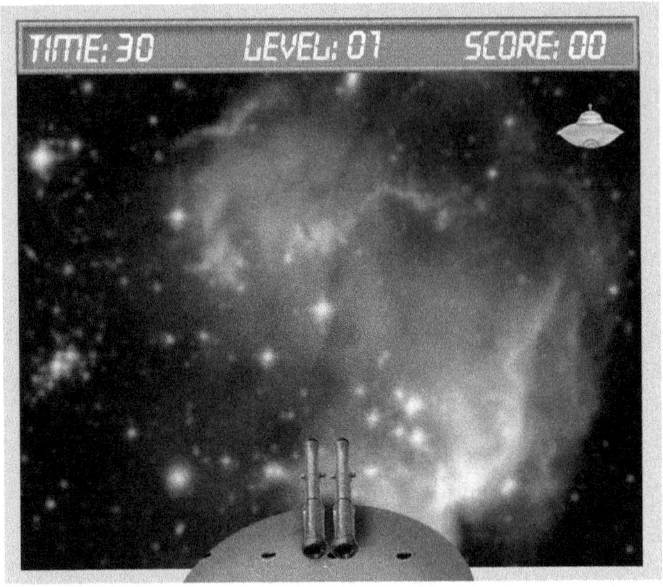

Also, you'll notice that the **Start Screen** layer has the visibility turned off. This is the layer that has the introduction screen, and the final screen that tells us how well we did. We'll go through this Movie clip later so you can understand how it works.

The first thing we'll do is look at how the **Timer** Movie clip works. Double-click the **Timer** Movie clip to enter its editing stage:

Take a look at the timeline of the **Timer** Movie clip. You'll notice that every 30 frames the text file changes by one number. For instance, go to frame 30 and the text now says 29:

So every 30 frames the text file changes by one number. The reason it changed every 30 frames is because the frame rate is 30 frames per second. So the time between the text changes is exactly one second. Altogether the timeline has 900 frames (30 X 30). Go to frame **900** and you'll see that the timer now says 00:

Select the first frame of the **Actions** layer. Open the Actions panel and you'll see that we have a **stop** code in this frame. This prevents the timer from starting before we've hit the start button. Go to frame **900** of the **Actions** layer and you'll see its ActionScript:.

```
tellTarget ("/ship1") {
    stop();
}
tellTarget ("/ship2") {
    stop();
}
tellTarget ("/cannon") {
    gotoAndStop(30);
}
stop();
setProperty("/start", _alpha, "100");

```

When the timer reaches 00 these actions are triggered. The first two commands tell the ships to stop playing. The third code instructs the **Cannon** Movie clip to go to frame **30** and **stop** (on frame 30 of the **Cannon** Movie clip its button is deactivated). The next command, **stop**, stops the timeline on this frame.

The last code, the setProperty command, tells the Alpha of the **Start** Movie clip to go to 100 making it visible. We'll discuss the **Start** Movie clip in a moment. Go back to Scene 1. Double-click on the **Score** Movie clip:

You should see three layers: **Actions**, **Score** and **Sound**:

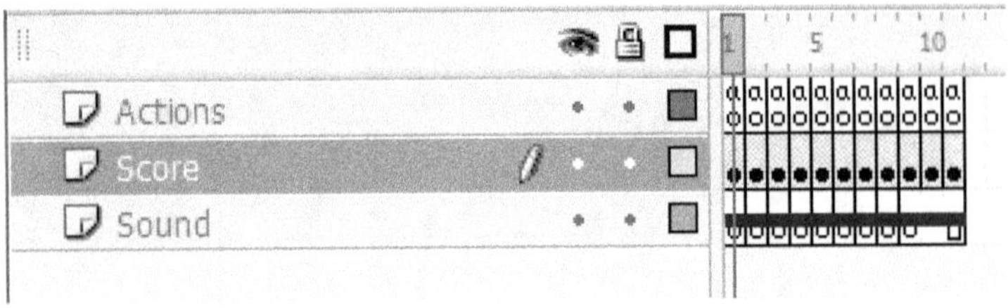

Grab the Timeline Needle and move it across all the frames. You'll see the text on the **Score** layer goes from 00 to 100. Select the first frame of the **Sound** layer. Open the Properties panel and you'll see that we have a audio file attached to this frame, and to all the Sound frames:

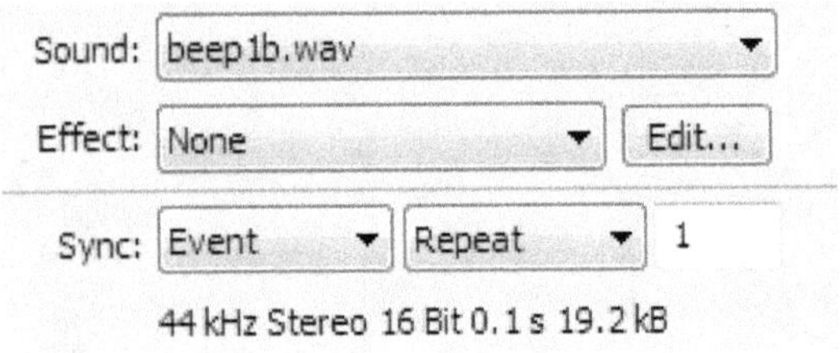

Every time the score goes up we hear a beep noise. Select the first frame of the **Actions** layer and open the Actions panel. You'll see that we have a **stop** code in this frame. Without the **stop** code the score would play through all its frames over and over again. Select the second frame of the **Actions** layer and you'll see this code:

```
tellTarget ("/start") {
      gotoAndStop(3);
}

```

This command tells the **Start** Movie clip to go to frame **3**. If you click on the other frames you'll see that they all tell the **Start** Movie clip to go to a certain frame. This is how the **Start** Movie clip knows what your score is when the game is over. So if your score is 10 points it tells the **Start** Movie clip to go to frame **3**; on frame **3** of the **Start** Movie clip we have the text file that says 10.

Click on frame **11** of the **Actions** layer and look at the ActionScript:

```
tellTarget ("/start") {
    gotoAndStop(12);
}
tellTarget ("/timer") {
    gotoAndStop(900);
}
```

This is the code that will be triggered if the user reaches 100 points. The first code sends the **Start** Movie clip to frame 12 of its timeline, where the number 100 is. The next set of code tells the timer to go to frame 900 (its last frame). By telling the **Timer** Movie clip to go to its last frame, this essentially stops the game.

We'll go through the **Start** Movie clip next. Go back to Scene 1. Turn the visibility on for the **Start** layer. You should now see the welcome screen:

Double-click on this Movie clip to enter its editing stage. You'll see several layers:

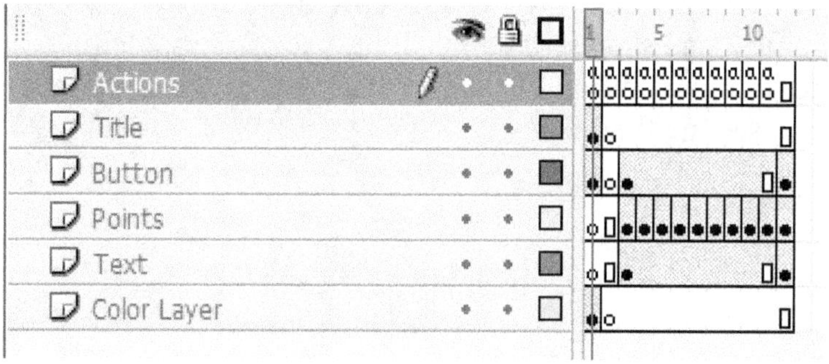

The **Color** Layer is simply a white shape that is slightly transparent. The **Text** layer contains the score text. Turn off the visibility of the **Points** layer. Select frame **3** of the Text layer:

This is the text you'll see if you don't have enough points to continue to the next level. You'll see that we have a space in the text which will display the points. Turn the visibility on again for the **Points** layer. You should now see 10 in the text space:

If you remember, when we were looking at the **Score** Movie clip, it has ActionScript telling the **Start** Movie clip to go to a specific frame. When the **Score** Movie clip is on frame **2** and shows 10 points, it has ActionScript telling the **Start** Movie clip to go to frame **3** which displays the above text. Select frame **12** of the **Text layer**. You'll see the final text:

The final frame of the **Score** Movie clip has ActionScript that will take us to this frame. This is the screen you'll see if you manage to score 100 points. Select the transparent button on frame **12** of the **Button** layer and open the Actions panel. This is the ActionScript that will take you to level 2:

```
on (release) {
    tellTarget ("_level0/") {
        gotoAndStop("level2");
    }
}
```

What this code does is it takes the user to the Frame Label: **level2**. This Frame Label is on the second scene. So when they click this button it takes them to the first frame of the scene **Level 2**. We'll be creating Level 2 in a moment, but for now, select the third frame of the **Button** layer. Select the transparent button on the stage and you'll see this ActionScript:

```
on (release) {
    gotoAndStop(2);
}
```

This is the button the user will click when they don't get 100 points. This code tells this timeline to go to frame **2** and **stop**.

Next, select frame **1** of the **Button** layer. You'll see the start text on the stage. Select the transparent button of the **Button** layer and you'll see its ActionScript:

```
on (release) {
    nextFrame();
}

```

When the user is ready to play they click this button. This button then takes the timeline to frame **2**. So we have two buttons that will take the user to frame 2. Let's examine what happens when the user gets to frame 2 by examining the **Actions** layer.

In the first frame of the **Actions** layer you'll see a **stop** code. This prevents the **Start** Movie clip from playing through all of its frames. Select frame **2** of the **Actions** layer and in the Actions panel to view the ActionScript:

```
tellTarget ("/ship1") {
    play();
}
tellTarget ("/ship2") {
    play();
}
tellTarget ("/timer") {
    gotoAndPlay(2);
}
tellTarget ("/score") {
    gotoAndStop(1);
}
tellTarget ("/cannon") {
    gotoAndStop(1);
}
setProperty("/start", _alpha, "0");
```

The first two tellTarget commands tell the ships to start playing. If you remember, when we reach the end of the **Timer** Movie clip it tells these Movie clips to stop playing.

The next command tells the **Timer** Movie clip to go to frame **2** and start playing. This begins the timer countdown. The next code tells the **Score** Movie clip to go to frame **1** and **stop**. This resets the **Score** Movie clip back to 00. The next code tells the **Cannon** Movie clip to go to frame **1** and **stop**.

The last code is a setProperty command that tells the **Start** Movie clip to go to 0 Alpha making it transparent. If you remember that on the last frame of the **Timer** Movie clip we have a setProperty command that tells the **Start** Movie clip to go to 100 Alpha, making it visible. Once the game first starts the **Start** Movie clip is visible. Once they click the start button that takes them to frame 2 of the **Start** Movie clip timeline; the code on this frame tells all the Movie clips to start playing and at the same time takes the Alpha of the **Start** Movie clip down to 0 making it transparent.

Turn the visibility of the **Start** Movie clip layer off. Let's see how the weapon works. Double-click on the **Cannon** Movie clip to enter its editing stage:

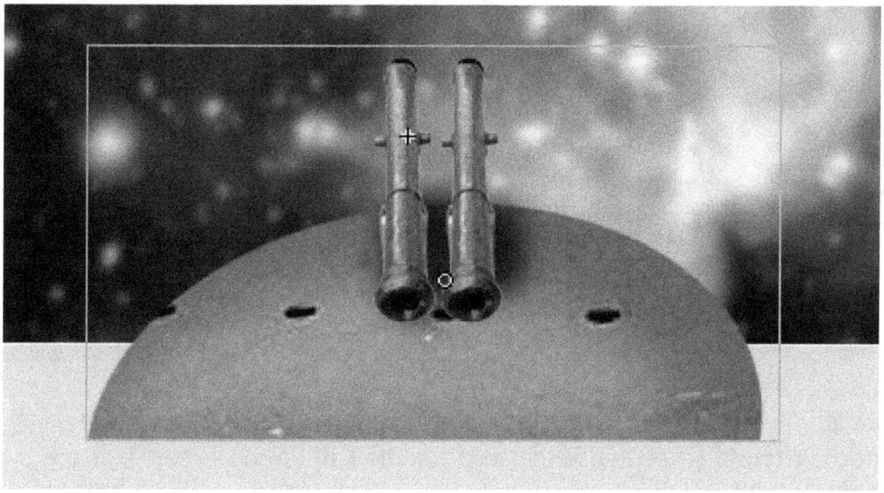

Once inside the **Cannon** Movie clip you'll see several layers:

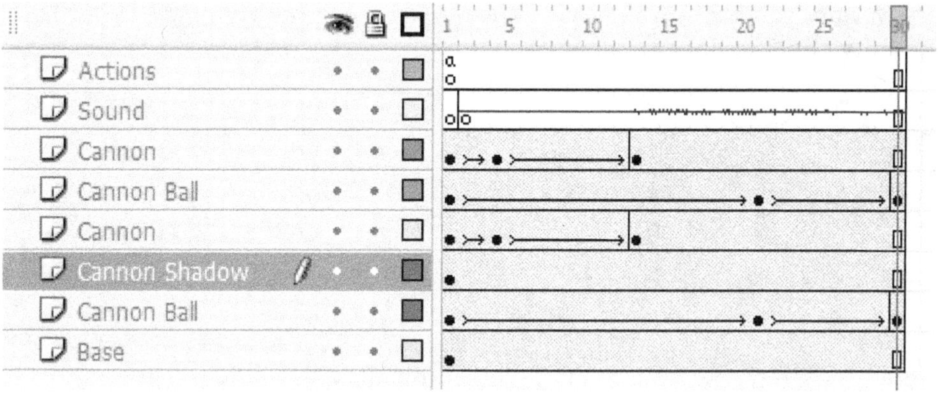

The **Base** layer is simply the layer that has the weapon base graphic. The next layer has the cannon ball animation. If you hit ENTER you can watch the cannon balls fly upward then disappear. Both Cannon Ball layers do the same animation. The next layer is the **Cannon Shadow** layer; this is simply a shadow symbol below the cannons. The next layer is the **Cannon** layer which has the cannon graphic. This layer has an animation that will move the cannon back and forth when fired. Both Cannon layers have the same animation.

The **Sound** layer has the firing sound effect. The **Actions** layer has a **stop** code on frame **1**. Next, I'll walk you through on how to make the weapon destroy the ships. We'll create the code for the weapon first, then we'll create the ship animation. Fun stuff! Create a new layer and name it **Button**; place this layer below the **Sound** layer:

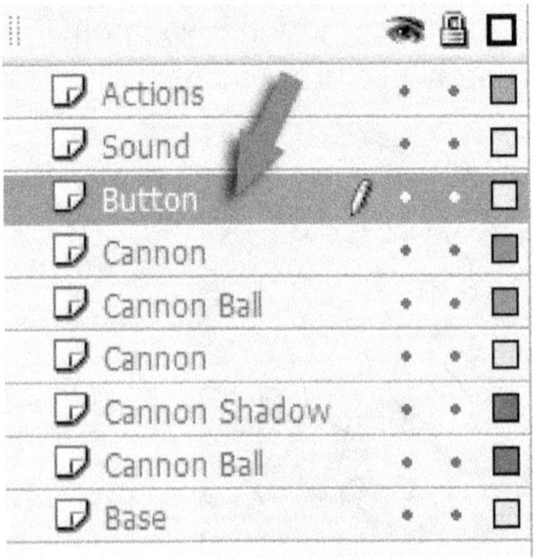

Next, we'll create the button that will trigger the weapon. Grab the **Rectangle Tool**, turn off the **Stroke color** and select **red** for the **Fill color**. Create a shape that covers the cannons:

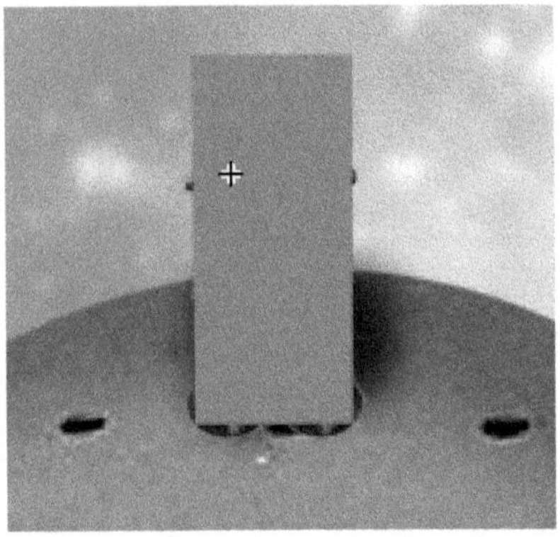

Change your tool to the **Selection Tool**. Select this new shape. Next, go to **Modify**, **Convert to Symbol**. Name this new button **Cannon Button** and change the **Type** to **Button**:

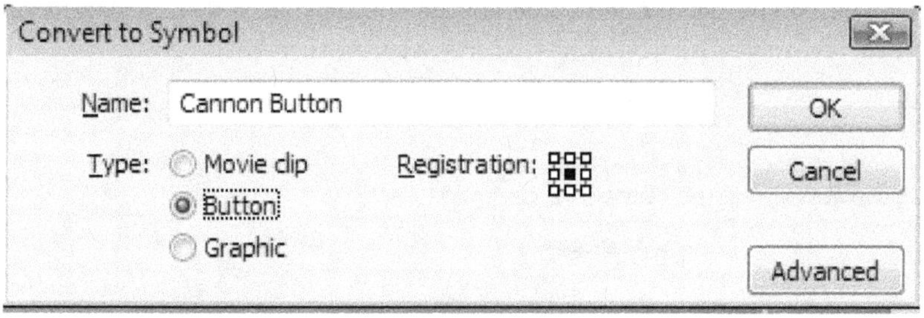

Hit **OK** when you are finished. Next, open the Properties panel and change **Color** to **Alpha** and the percentage to **0**:

So now the **Cannon Button** is transparent. Next, we'll add the ActionScript. With this button still selected open the Actions panel. The first code will enter is the startDrag code. Make sure Script Assist is on. Next, go to **Global Functions**, Movie clip **Control**, and double-click **startDrag**. In the **startDrag** settings window type **/cannon** in the **Target** window. So now the **Cannon** Movie clip will be draggable.

Since we only want to drag the **Cannon** Movie clip along the bottom of the screen, we need to select **Constrain to rectangle**. We want the **Cannon** Movie clip to move all the way to the left of the stage so we'll add **20** in the **L** window. This means that the Movie clip will stop at 20px from the left side of the screen. Next, type **640** in the **R** window. This will allow the Movie clip to move 640px from the left side of the stage. Next, type **500** in the **T** window. This means that the limit on movement is 500px from the top of the screen. Lastly, we'll add **600** to the **B** window. Your settings window should look like this:

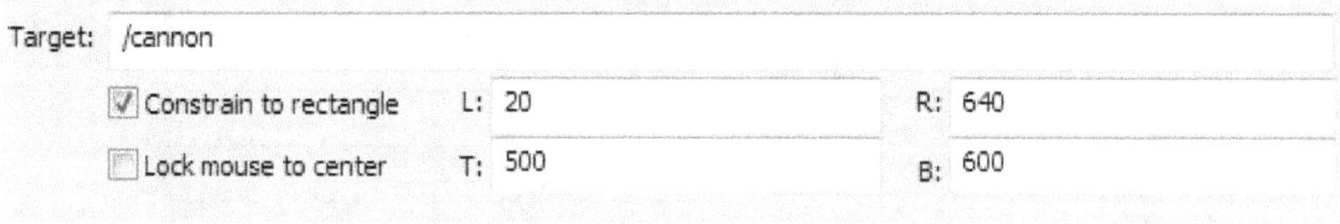

Next, we only want to drag the cannon when we press down on the mouse button. So we need to change the mouse event for this command. In the Actions window select the word release. Uncheck **Release** and select **Press**:

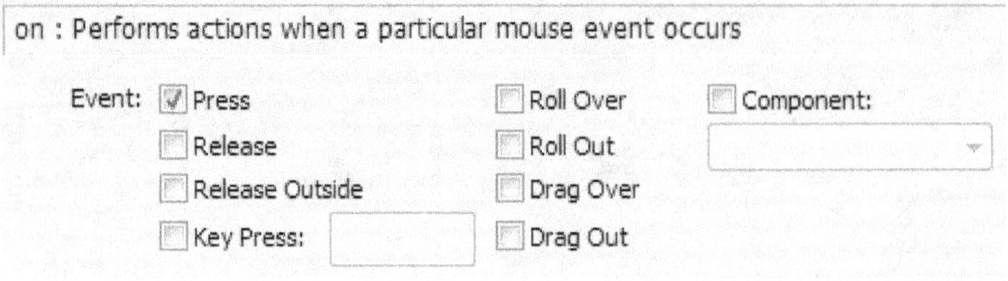

So now we need to add the stopDrag command. First, select the closing bracket of the first set of code:

```
on (press) {
     startDrag("/cannon", false, 20, 500, 640, 600);
}
```

Next, go to **Global Functions**, Movie clip **Control**, and double-click **stopDrag**. This will stop the dragging command once we release the mouse button.

The next piece of code we'll add will tell the Cannon timeline to go to frame 2 and start playing. Go to **Global Functions**, **Timeline Control** and double-click **play**. Now when we release the mouse button, the timeline will begin playing which then plays the cannon ball animations. But this command does one more thing. In order for the Ship's button to be triggered, we need to remove the button from the **Cannon** Movie clip (just like in the Drag 'n' Drop game). Once this button is gone the weapon will *trigger any button that is below it*. So if the ship's button is below the cannon it will be triggered and the explosion animation will begin. So how do we remove the button from the **Cannon** Movie clip? Select frame **2** of the **Button** layer then go to **Insert**, **Timeline**, and **Blank Keyframe**:

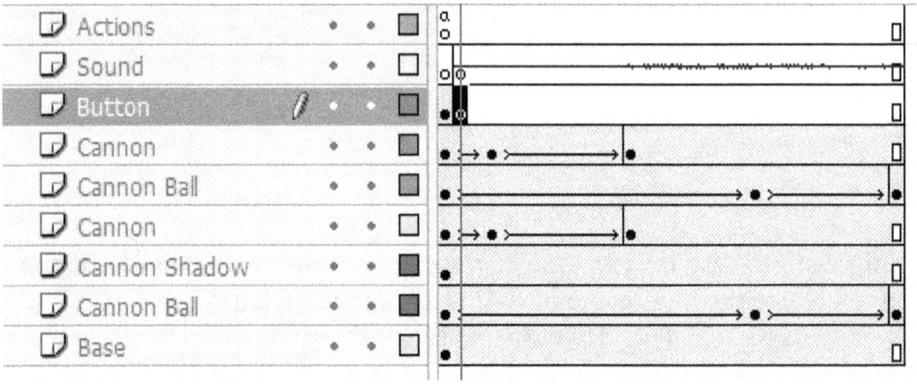

Now when we release the mouse button it tells this timeline to play. Once the timeline gets to frame 2 the button is gone which means any button that falls below the weapon will be triggered. We don't want the button to be gone for the whole timeline though, since without a button we can't drag the weapon. Create a keyframe on frame **5** of the **Button** layer. Select frame 1 of this layer and go to **Edit**, **Copy**. Next, select the keyframe on frame **5** and go to **Edit**, **Paste in Place**. You should now have a copy of the button on frame **5**. Finally, select frame **30** of the **Button** layer and go to **Insert**, **Timeline** and **Blank Keyframe** :

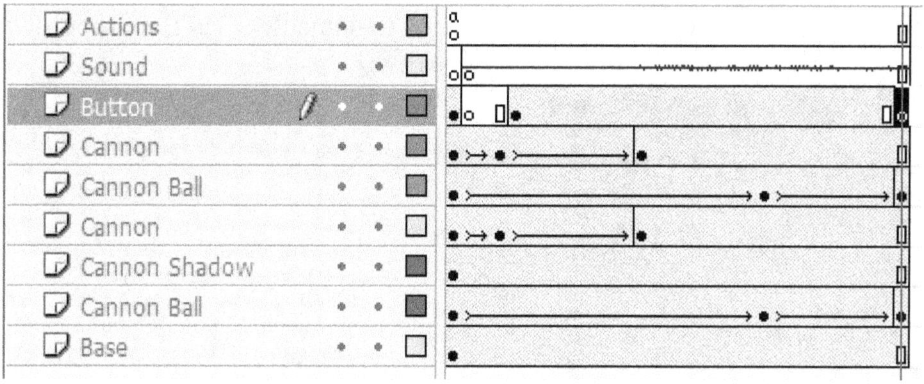

The reason we place a blank keyframe on frame 30 is because this is the frame the **Cannon** Movie clip is sent to when the game is over. This will disable the weapon from firing.

Let's create the ship's animation now. Go back to Scene 1 and select the ship at the top right of the screen:

After you select it, go to **Modify**, **Convert to Symbol**. Select **Movie clip** and name this new symbol: **Ship 1**:

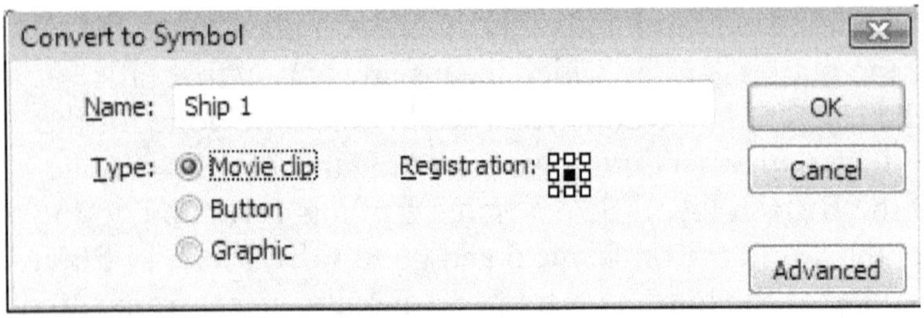

Since we'll be controlling this Movie clip we need to name it. Open the Properties panel and type **ship1** in the **Instance Name** window:

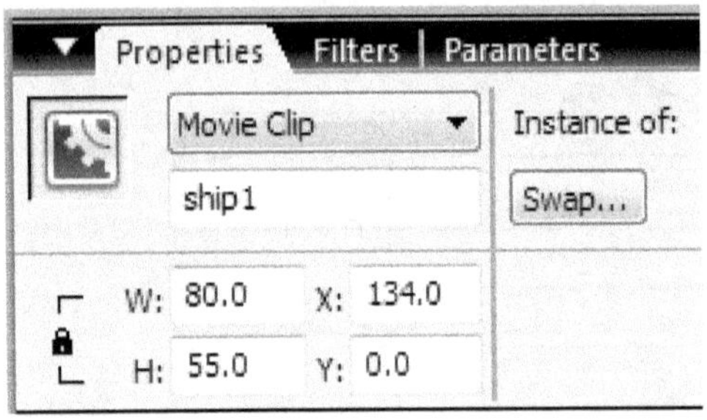

Double-click on this new symbol to enter its editing stage. We'll convert this symbol to another Movie clip. The reason we do this is because the ship is going to contain an explosion animation.

Select the symbol on the stage and go to **Modify**, **Convert to Symbol**. Select **Movie clip** and name it **Ship 1 Explosion**:

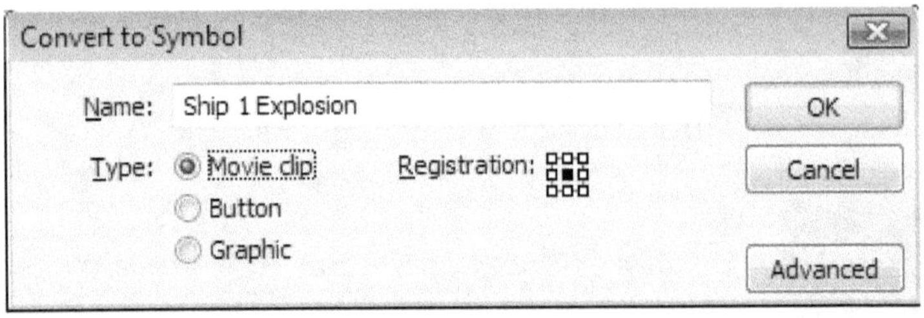

Hit OK when finished. With this new symbol still selected open the Properties panel and type **ship1** in the **Instance Name** window:

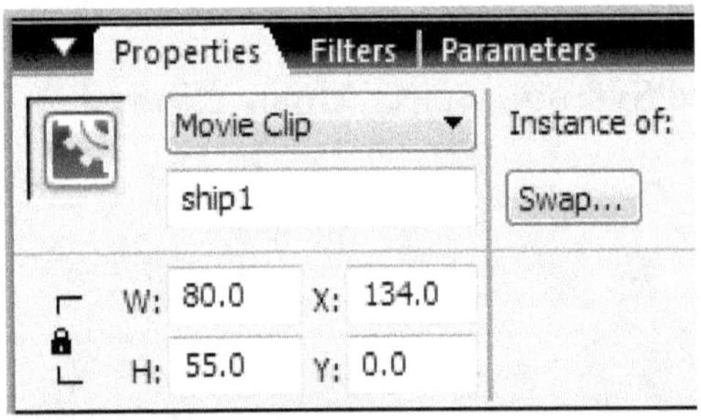

We'll create the explosion timeline in a moment. First, we'll animate the ship across the stage.

Create a keyframe on frame **90** of **Layer 1**; next, select any frame between **1** and **90** and go to **Insert**, **Timeline**, **Create Motion Tween** (**CS4/CS5** Users: Select **Classic Tween**). You should now have a Motion Tween on **Layer 1**.

Click on frame **90** then select the ship symbol on the stage; drag this ship symbol straight left until its off the stage:

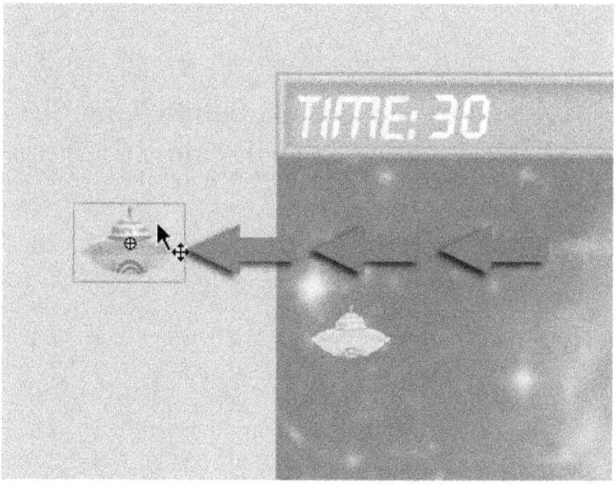

Select frame **1**. Drag the ship straight right until it's off the stage:

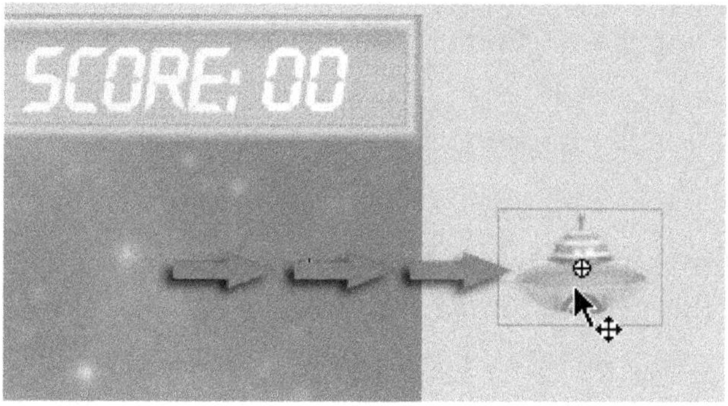

The ship will now animate from right to left. Next, we're going to add a few more frames to the end of this animation. Select frame **170** of **Layer 1** and insert a frame.

Next we'll create the explosion animation. Select frame **1** of **Layer 1**, then double-click the ship symbol on the stage to enter its editing stage. Select frame **125** of **Layer 1** and insert a frame. Create four new layers: **Labels**, **Actions**, **Button** and **Explosion**:

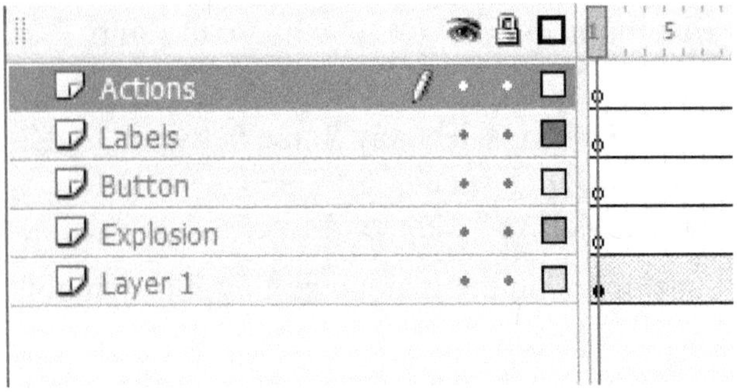

We'll now create the button that will be triggered by the weapon button. Grab the **Rectangle Tool**. Turn off **Stroke color** and select **red** for the **Fill color**. Create a rectangle shape to the right of the cannon:

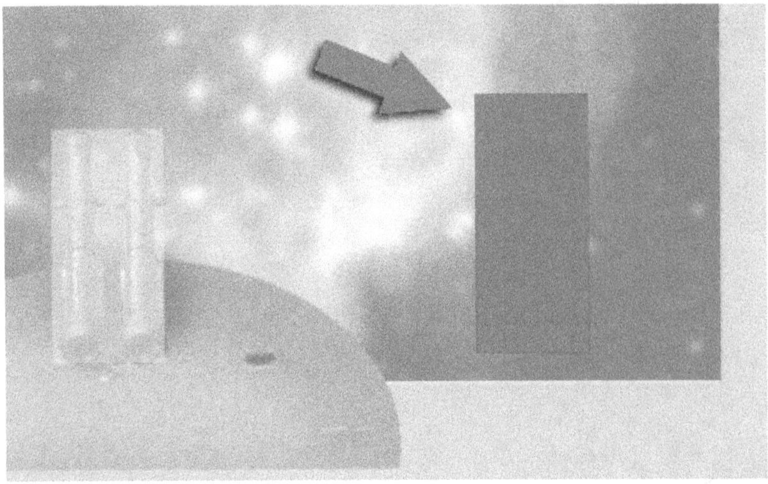

Using the **Selection Tool** select this shape and go to **Modify**, **Convert to Symbol**. Select **Button** and name this symbol **Ship 1 Button**:

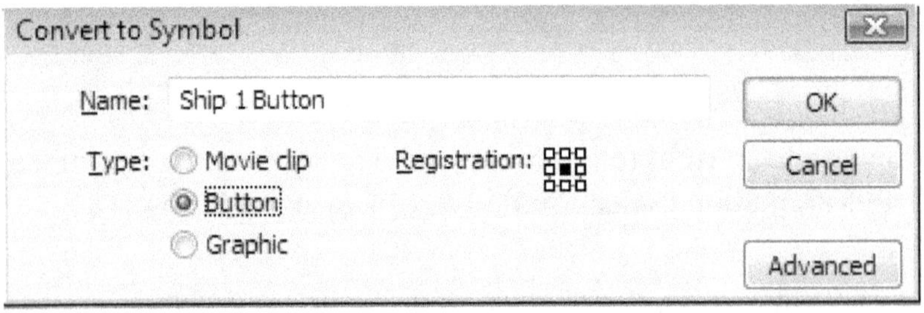

Hit **OK** when finished. We'll next add the ActionScript to this button. Go to **Deprecated**, **Actions** and double-click **tellTarget**. In the **Target** window enter **/ship1/ship1**:

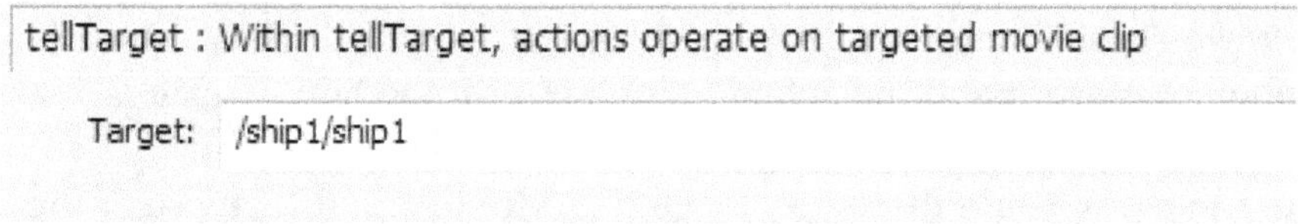

Next, go to **Global Functions**, **Timeline Control** and double-click **goto**. In the **goto** settings window change **Type** to **Frame Label** and type **explosion** in the **Frame** window:

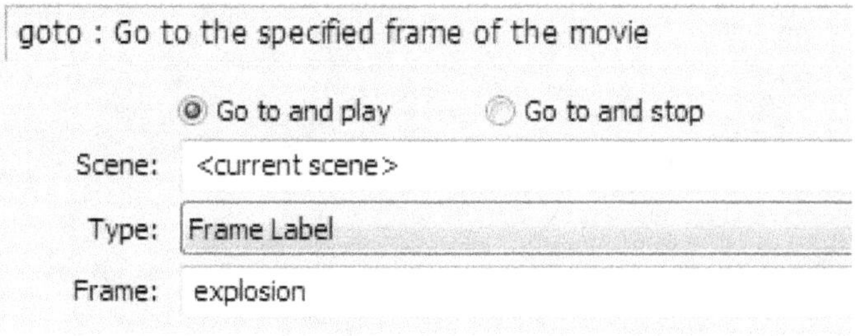

This is the code that is triggered when this button is under the weapon button. Since this code is triggered when the user rolls over it we need to change the mouse event. In the code window click on the word **release**. You should now see the mouse event settings window. Uncheck **Release** and select **Roll Over** and **Drag Over**:

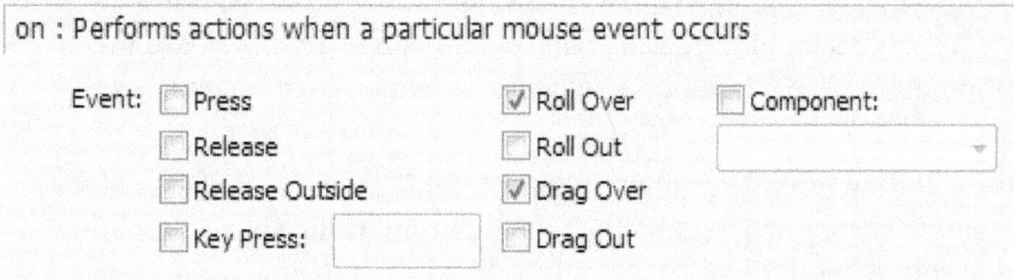

Put a **stop** code in the first frame of the **Actions** layer. Next, create a keyframe on frame **5** of the **Labels** layer. Select this keyframe and open the Properties panel; give this keyframe a Frame Label name of **explosion**:

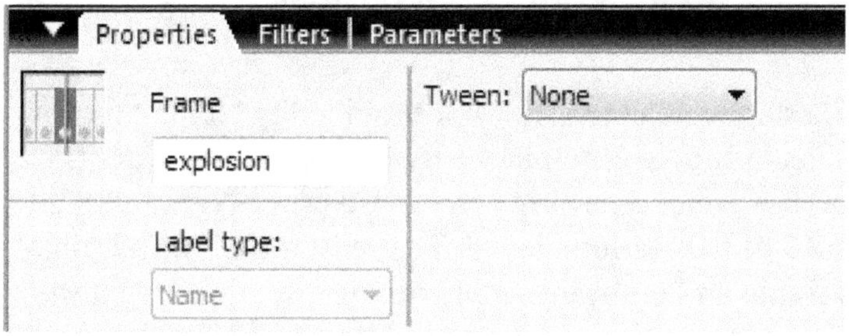

Since the bullets won't reach the ship for a few moments we need a few frames between the Label: **explosion** and the actual **Explosion** Movie clip. Create a keyframe on frame **35** of the **Explosion** layer. Next, drag the Movie clip **Explosion** from the library onto the stage. Place this Movie clip directly over the ship symbol:

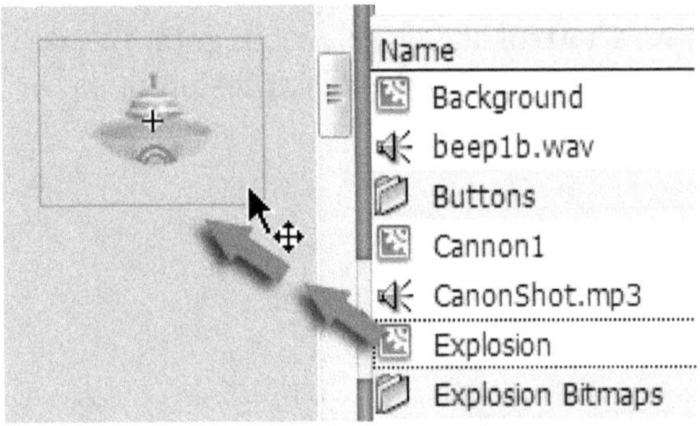

So now when the user rolls over the **Ship 1 Button** it will tell this timeline to go to the Label: **explosion** and play. 30 frames later the explosion takes place which should give the bullets enough time to reach the top of the screen.

Let's try it out! Test your Movie. Press and drag the weapon around the bottom of the screen. Notice that when you release your mouse button the weapon fires. When the ship is traveling across the stage you should be able to see the red button travel with it. Try to release the weapon button over this red button. If you time it out correctly, it should trigger the ship's explosion. If you release the weapon's button before the red button reaches the weapon then no explosion happens.

If the ship is exploding after the bullets fly past it, or if the ship explodes before the bullets reach it, then you need to adjust the position of the ship button. For instance, if the ship explodes before the bullets reach it, then you need to move the **Ship 1 Button** to the right. If the ship explodes after the bullets have already finished their animation then move this button to the left.

You may also notice that when the explosion happens you can still see the ship below the explosion. So we need to make the ship transparent when the explosion happens. We'll do that by creating a setProperty code that tells the ship's Alpha to go to 0. Let's do that now

Select the ship symbol on the stage and convert it to a Movie clip. Name this new Movie clip **Ship**. Since this is the Movie clip that we'll be making transparent, we need to name it. In the Properties panel type **ship1** in the **Instance Name** window. Create a keyframe on frame **45** of the **Actions** layer. The reason we'll be adding the setProperty code to this frame and not frame 35 is because we don't want the ship disappearing right away. In the **Actions** layer go to **Deprecated**, **Actions** and double-click **tellTarget**. In the **Target** window type **/ship1/ship1/ship1**:

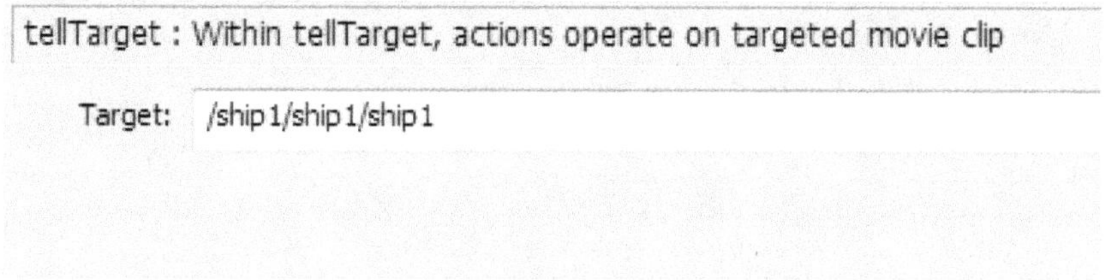

Next, go to **Global Functions**, Movie clip **Control** and double-click **setProperty**. In the **setProperty** settings window make the **Property _alpha**, type **/ship1/ship1/ship1** in the **Target** window and make the Value **0**:

You'll notice that the Target name is **/ship1/ship1/ship1**. This means the setProperty code is controlling **ship1** which is inside two other Movie clips. To get a better idea on how this works go to Scene 1 and select the ship symbol. You'll see that it has an **Instance Name** of **ship1**. Double-click on this symbol to enter its editing stage, and select the ship symbol. This ship also has an Instance Name of **ship1**. Double-click on this symbol to enter its editing stage and select the ship symbol. You'll see that this ship also has an Instance Name of s**hip1**.

Test your movie. When the ship explodes it should disappear about 10 frames into the explosion making the explosion more realistic.

Next, we'll add a simple code that will trigger the score to go up. Create a keyframe on frame **35** of the **Actions** layer. In the **Actions** panel go to **Deprecated**, **Actions** and double-click **tellTarget**. In the **Target** window type **/score**:

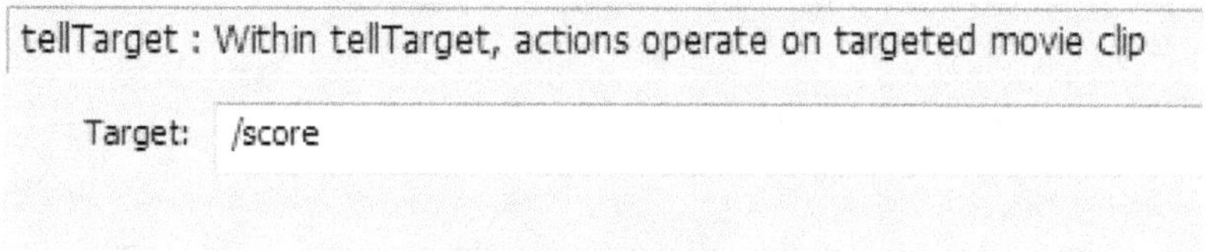

Next go to **Global Functions**, **Timeline Control** and double-click **goto**. In the **goto** settings window change **Type** to **Next Frame**:

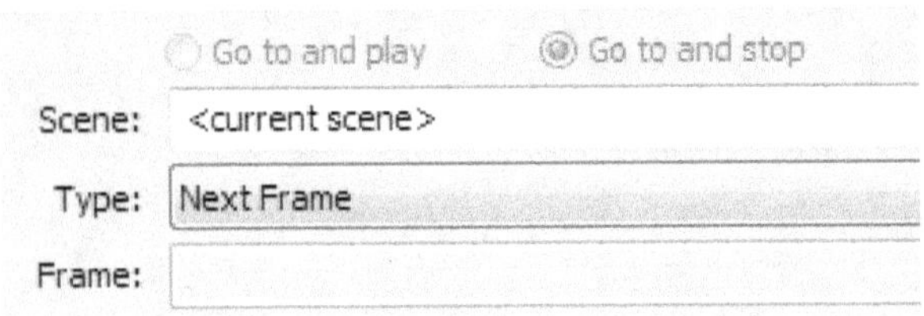

So now when the timeline gets to this frame it will trigger the **Score** Movie clip to go to the next frame. Go ahead and test the movie. Now when the ship explodes the score goes up by ten points. But you'll notice that after the ship explodes the ship remains transparent for the remainder of the game. This is because we used a setProperty command to take down its Alpha. We can fix this by adding a simple code to the **Ship Animation** timeline. Click your **Back** button or select the **Ship 1** button to go back to the previous timeline:

You should now be in the **Ship 1** animation timeline. Create a new layer and name it **Actions**:

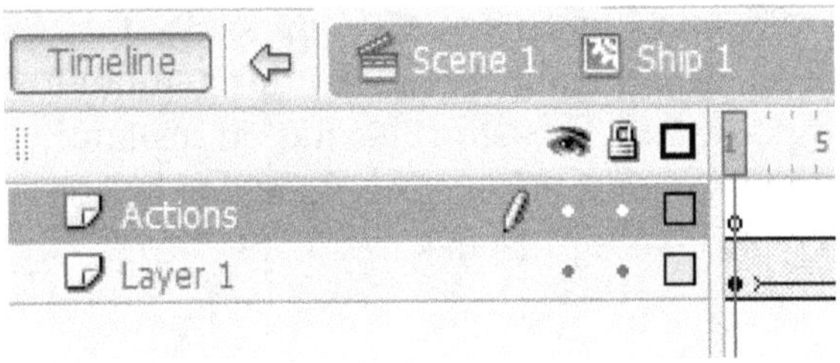

Select the first frame of the **Actions** layer and open the Actions panel. Go to **Global Functions**, **Movie clip Control** and double-click **setProperty**. In the **setProperty** settings window the **Property** should be **_alpha**, type **/ship1/ship1/ship1** in the **Target** window and make the **Value 100**:

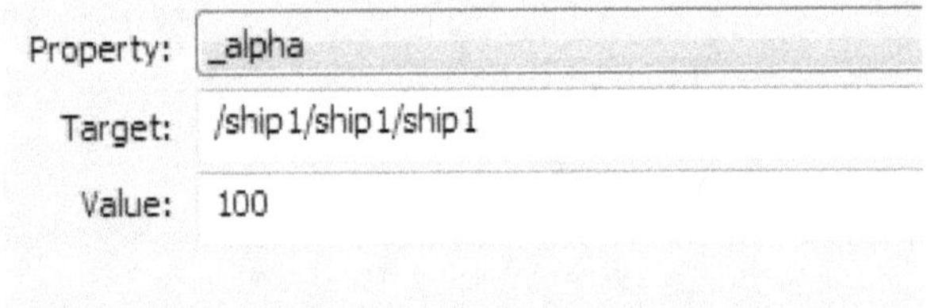

When the ship begins its animation again, it's alpha will reset to 100. Test your movie again and try it out. You'll see that after the ship explodes it's alpha goes back to 100.

The next thing we need to do is take the Alpha of the ship button down to 0 since we don't want it to be visible. Double-click on the ship symbol to enter its editing stage. Select the button on the stage:

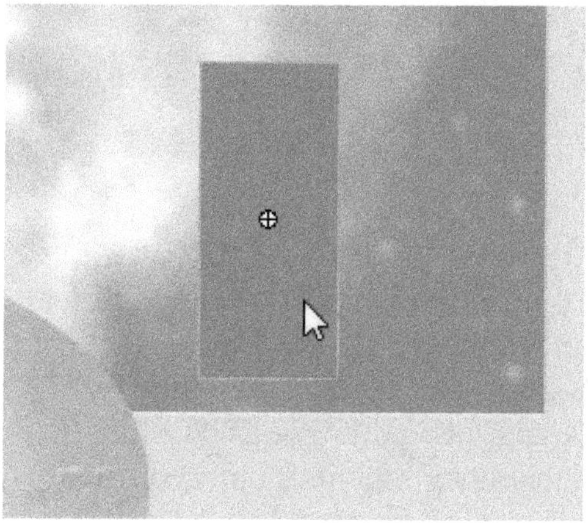

In the Properties panel change **Color** to **Alpha** and take the percentage down to **0**. Test your movie again and now the ship button should be transparent.

I'll quickly show you how to add another ship. Go back to **Scene 1**. Next, double-click on the ship symbol to enter its editing stage. We're going to copy the ship animation and paste it into another layer. We do this by first clicking on **Layer 1** which will highlight the entire layer's timeline:

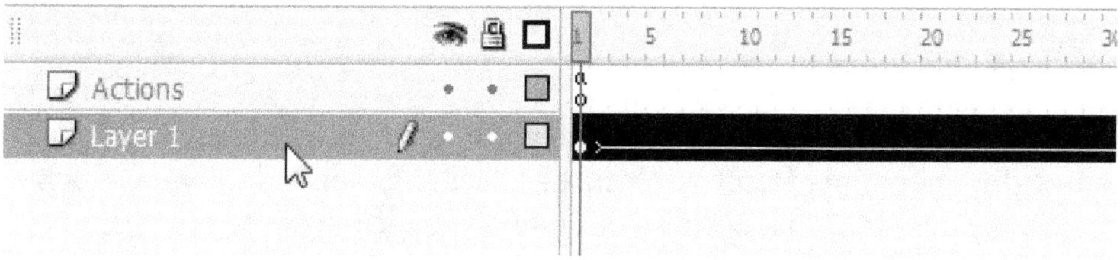

Go to **Edit**, **Timeline**, **Copy Frames**. Create a new layer and name it **Ship 2**. Create a keyframe on frame **171** of this layer:

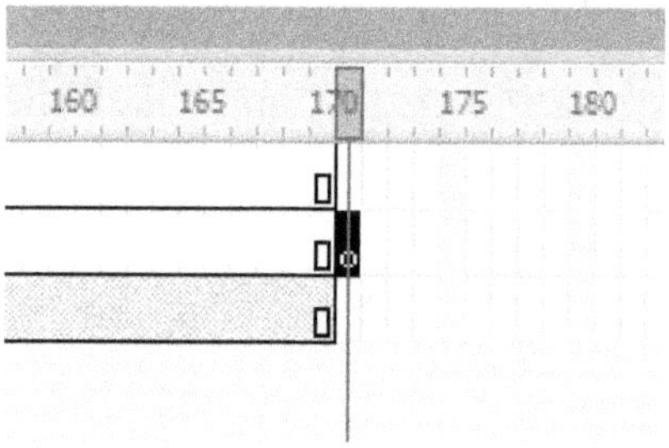

Next go to **Edit**, **Timeline**, **Paste Frames**. You should now have a copy of the first ship's animation on this layer:

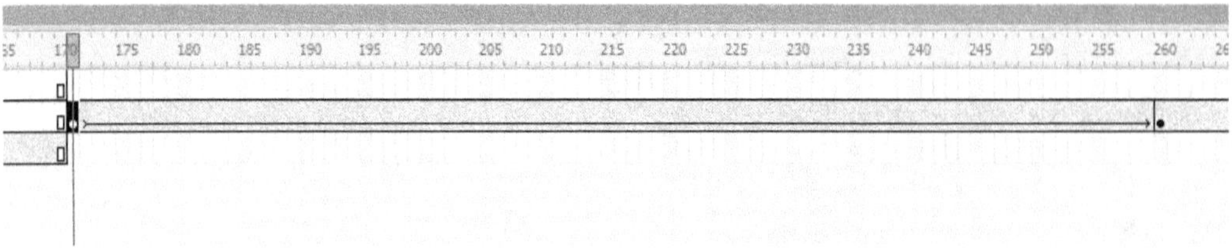

If you test your movie you should have two ships play one after the other. Since both animations are identical we need to change it up a bit. Let's make the second animation much quicker and worth 20 points instead of 10. To make the animation quicker we need to remove some frames. Select frame **200** of the **Actions** layer and click-and-drag across all three layer timelines until you get to frame **220**:

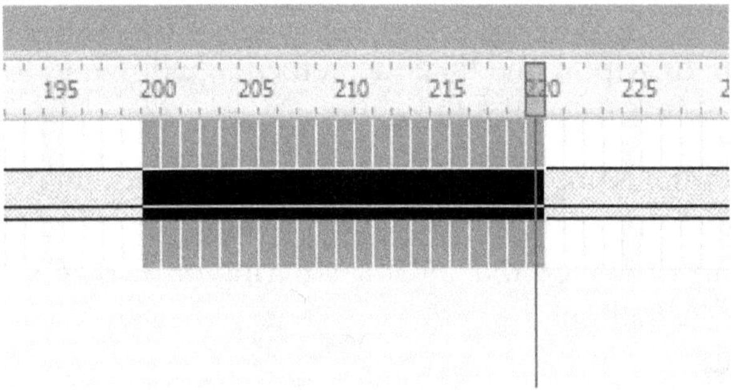

The frames of all three layers should now be highlighted between frames 200 and 220. Go to **Edit**, **Timeline**, **Remove Frames**. The animation will now be much quicker. Test the movie. You'll notice a definite difference in speed between the two ships. Since the second ship is a lot faster, the ship's button needs to be adjusted. Before we can do that, however, we need to make a duplicate of this ship symbol so we don't affect the original ship.

Select frame **171** of the **Ship 2** layer and select the ship symbol on the stage. In the Properties panel click the **Swap...** button. In the **Swap Symbol** box click the **Duplicate Symbol** button. Go ahead and keep the default name that appears in the Symbol name window:

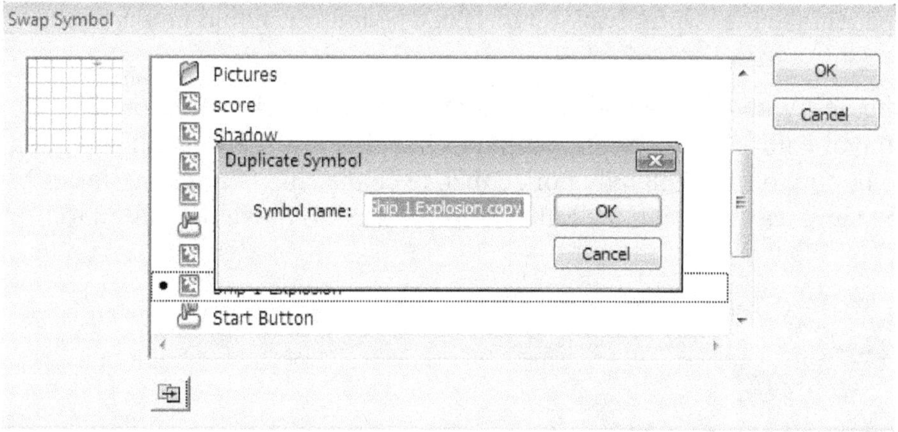

Hit **OK**. Double click on this new Move clip to select it:

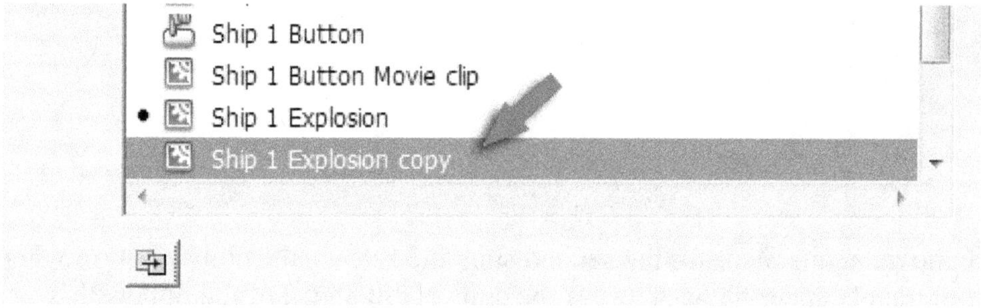

The window should close by itself. Before we continue we need to change the Movie clip on the second keyframe also. Select the second keyframe of the **Ship 2** layer:

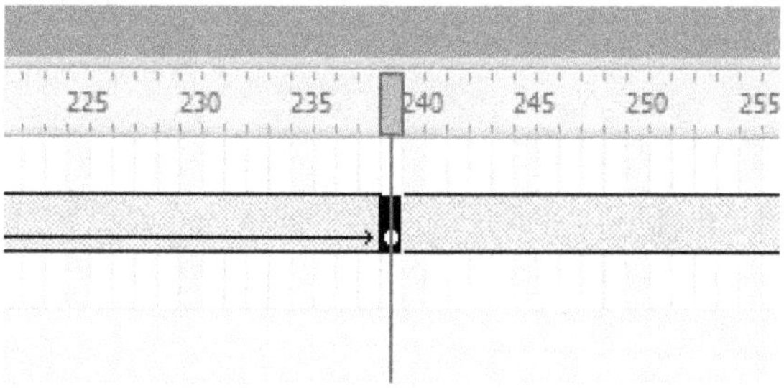

Select the ship symbol on the stage. In the Properties panel click on the **Swap...** button and in the **Swap Symbol box** double-click the new Movie clip we just created: **Ship 1 explosion copy**.

Double-click on this new Movie clip to enter its editing stage. Next we'll adjust the button. Before we adjust it we need to make it visible again. Select frame 1 of the **Button** layer so you can see where the button is. Select this button and in the

Properties panel take the **Alpha** back up to **100**. The button should now be red again.

Test your movie. When the second ship enters from stage right you should see the button travel with it. Wait for this button to travel below the weapon and click your mouse button to fire. You may notice that since the ship is traveling faster than the first ship, it's outpacing the bullets. So we need to move the button to the left slightly:

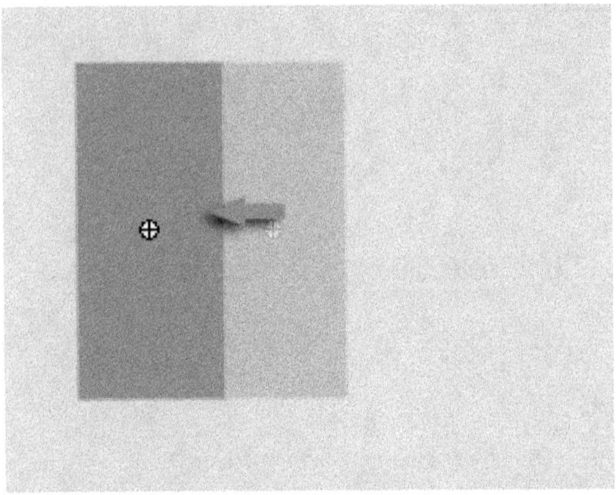

Test the movie again. Wait for the second ship and release the mouse button when the button travels under the weapon. If the ship is still ahead of the bullets then move the button more to the left. Keep adjusting this button until the timing of the explosion is perfect. Once you have the button adjusted correctly, take its Alpha back up to 100. Since this ship is harder to hit we need to make it worth 20 points.

Select frame **35** of the **Actions** layer. In the Actions window highlight the code and copy it (CTRL + C). Click on the closing bracket and paste in the copied code (CTRL + V):

```
tellTarget ("/score") {
    nextFrame();
}
tellTarget ("/score") {
    nextFrame();
}
```

If you test your movie and hit the second ship you should get 20 points added to your score.

The last thing we'll do is create the ship that comes from the other side of the screen. Go back to **Scene 1**. Select the ship symbol and go to **Edit**, **Copy**. Create a new layer and name it **Ship 2**. Select the first frame of this layer and go to **Edit**, **Past in Center**. You should now have a copy of the ship Movie clip in the center of the stage. Drag this Movie clip offstage to the left:

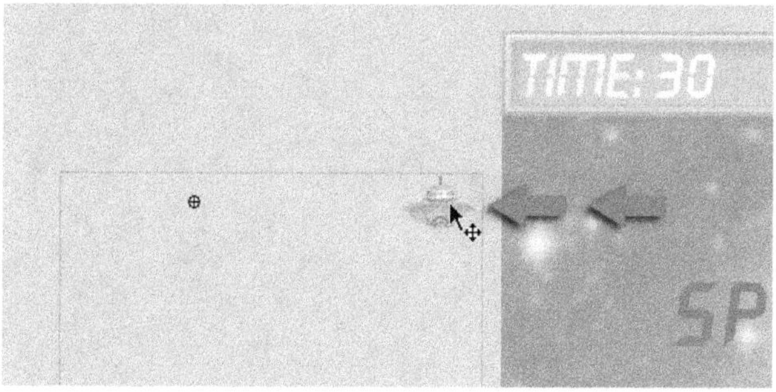

Since this ship travels right to left we need to flip it horizontally so it travels in the opposite direction. With this Movie clip still selected, go to **Modify**, **Transform**, **Flip Horizontally**. The Movie clip should now be facing the other direction. If it's too far from the left edge of the screen move it to the right. Also, drag it down slightly so it's not at the same level as the other ship:

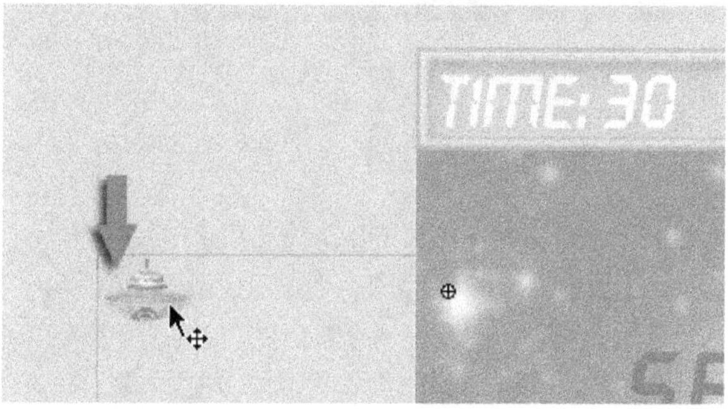

Before we edit this ship Movie clip we need to duplicate it first. In the Properties panel click on the **Swap...** button. Next, click on the **Duplicate Symbol** button and name this new ship **Ship 2**. Hit **OK** and double-click on this new Movie clip name in the **Swap Symbol** window. In the **Instance Name** window name this new ship: **ship2**:

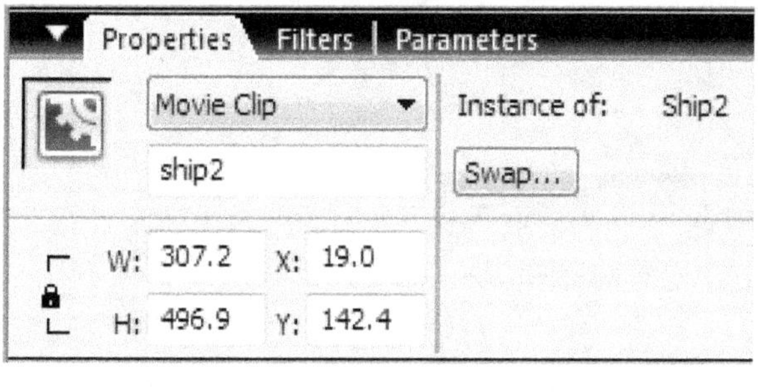

Double-click on this new Movie clip. We need to change the timing of these ships. We want the fast ship to start first then the slow ship. We do this by first clicking on **Layer 1** to highlight all its frames:

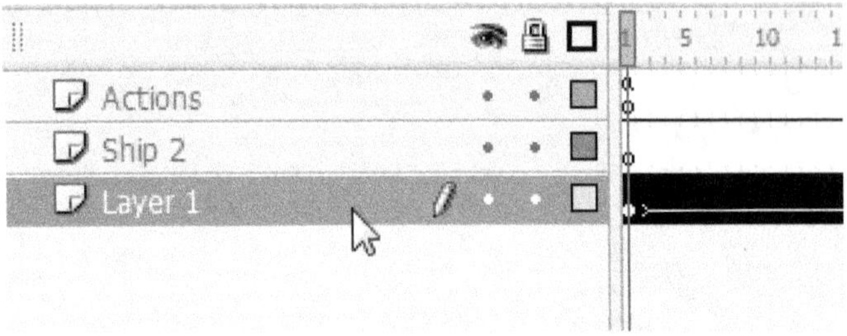

Click on the first frame of **Layer 1** and drag it to frame **150**:

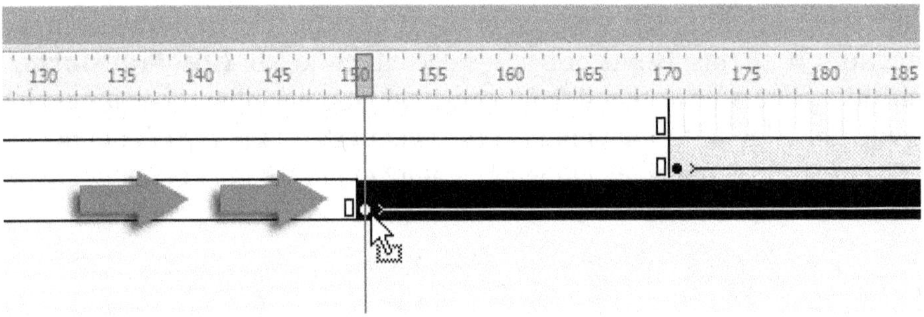

Select the last keyframe of the **Ship 2** layer and, without releasing the mouse button, drag across all the frames until you get to the first keyframe highlighting all the frames:

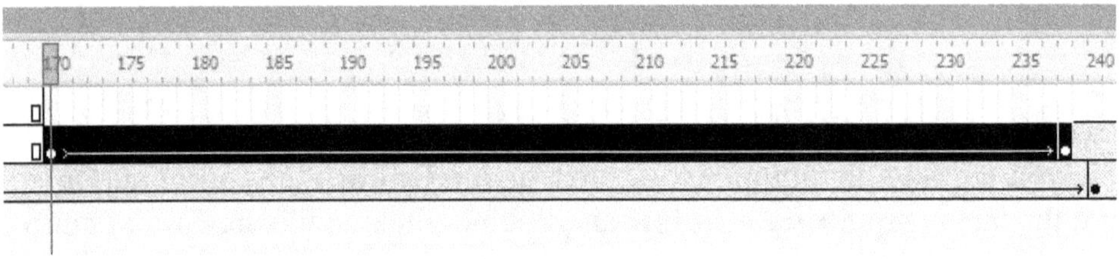

Next, click on the first keyframe and drag that to frame **1**:

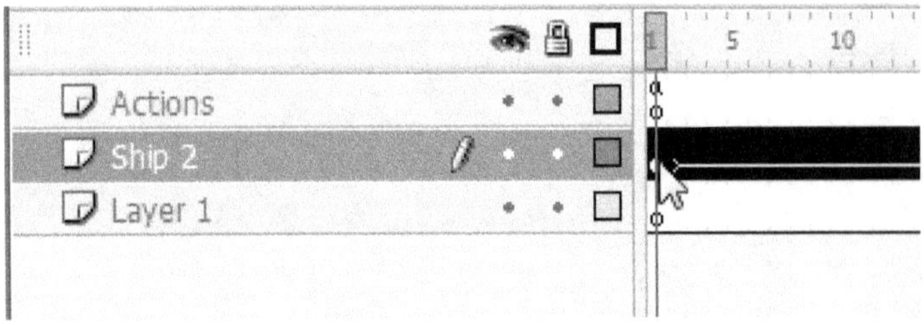

Next, let's delete some frames between the first and second ship. First, highlight all the frames between **80** and **140** for all the layers:

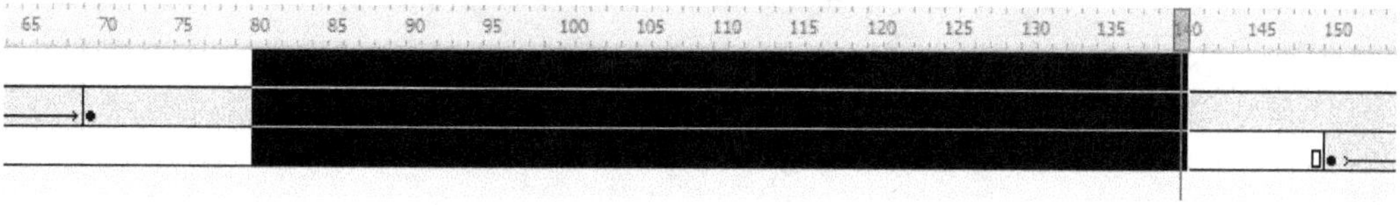

Go to **Edit**, **Timeline**, **Remove Frames**. The animation for the second ship should come in much quicker now:

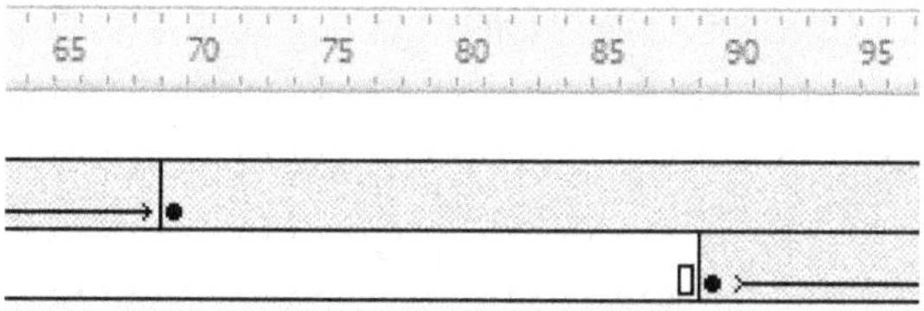

Next, select the first keyframe of **Layer 1**, then select the ship symbol on the stage. Change the **Instance Name** of this ship to **ship2**. Next, hit the **Swap...** button. Click the **Duplicate Symbol** button and name this new Movie clip: **Ship 2 Explosion**:

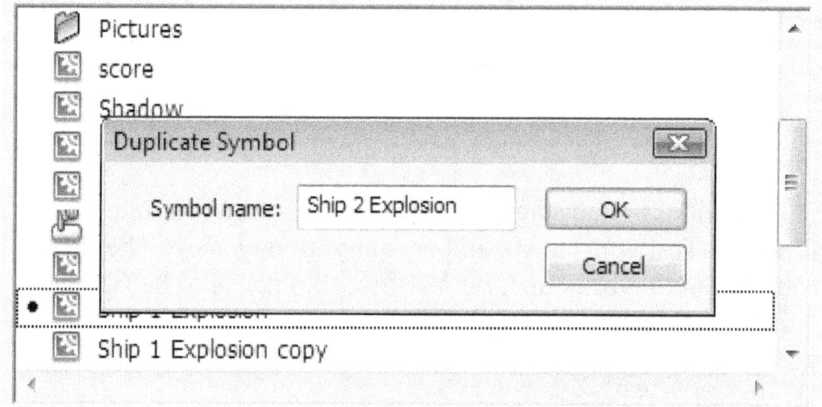

Hit **OK**. Double-click on this new Movie clip in the **Swap Symbol** window. Since we have another keyframe on this timeline we need to repeat the above steps for the Movie clip on the other keyframe. Select the second keyframe of **Layer 1**. Select the ship on the stage and change the **Instance Name** to **ship2**. Click on the **Swap...** button and double-click on the **Ship 2 Explosion** Movie clip.

So now we can edit this Movie clip without affecting the original. Double-click the ship symbol to enter its editing stage. Select the first frame of the **Button** layer; this will highlight the button symbol so you can see where it is. Click on this button symbol then open the Actions panel. Make sure Script Assist is on and click on the part of the code that has **/ship1/ship1**:

```
on (rollOver, dragOver) {
    tellTarget ("/ship1/ship1") {
        gotoAndPlay("explosion");
    }
```

You should now see the **Target** window. Change **/ship1/ship1** to **/ship2/ship2**:

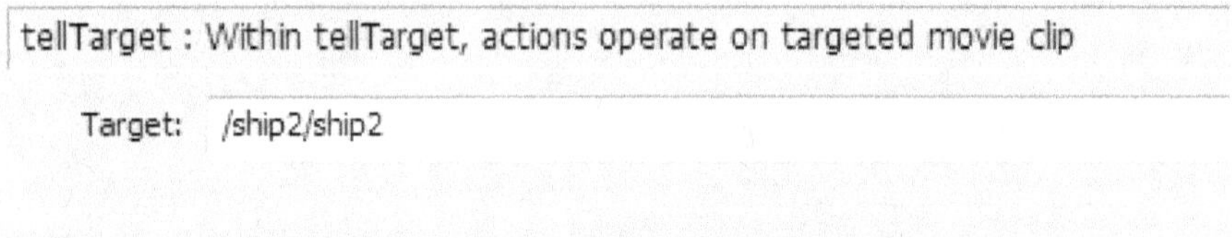

Next, we just need to tweak the code on frame **45** of the **Actions** layer. Change **/ship1/ship1/ship1** to **/ship2/ship2/ship2**:

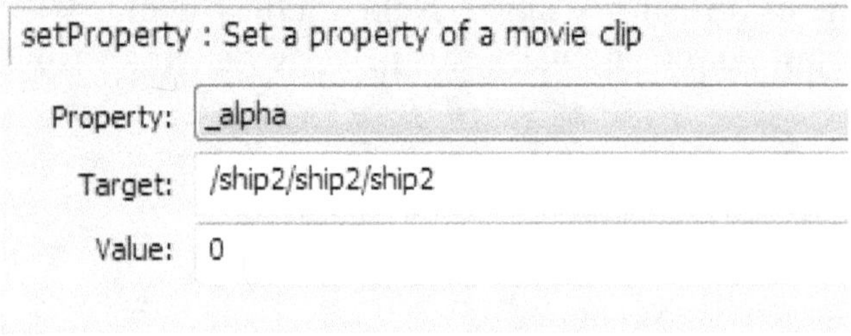

Lastly, select the ship symbol on the stage. In the Properties panel change the **Instance Name** to **ship2**. Test your movie and try out your new ship. The second ship that enters from stage left works fine, but the first ship needs to be tweaked. Click on the **Back** button or select the **Ship2** button:

Select the first keyframe of the **Ship 2** layer then select the ship symbol on the stage. Click the **Swap...** button in the Properties panel. In the **Swap Symbol** window double-click the **Duplicate Symbol** button and type **Ship 2 Explosion copy**:

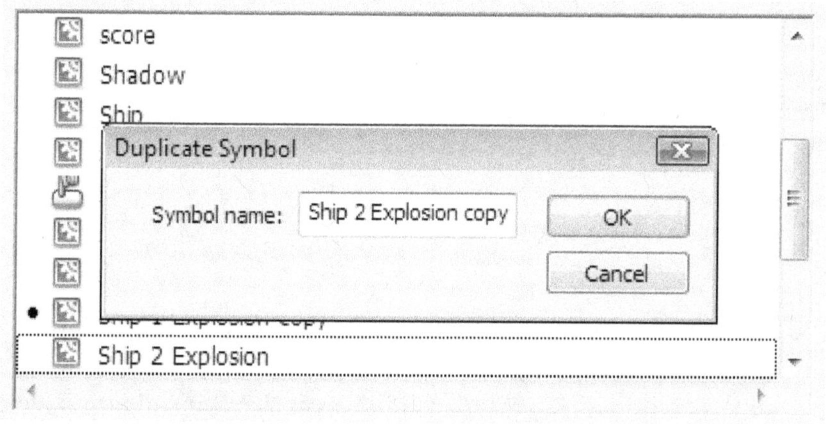

Hit **OK**. Double-click on this new Movie clip in the **Swap Symbol** window. Next, with this new Movie clip still selected, change its **Instance Name** to **ship2**. Select the second keyframe of the **Ship 2** layer; select the ship symbol on the stage and change its **Instance Name** to **ship2**. Next, click the **Swap...** button and double-click the **Ship 2 Explosion copy** Movie clip.

Double-click this Movie clip to enter its editing stage. Just as we did with the other ship, we'll need to change the ActionScript of the button. Click the first frame of the Button layer so you can see the button outline. Select the button and open the Actions panel. Click on the part of the code that has **/ship1/ship1**:

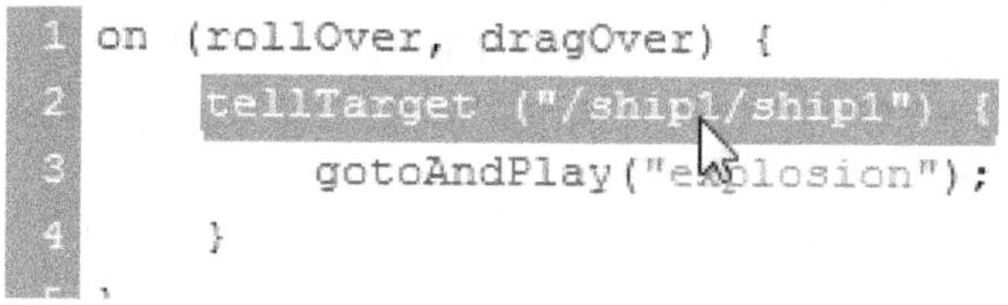

You should now see the **Target** window. Change the **Target** to **/ship2/ship2**:

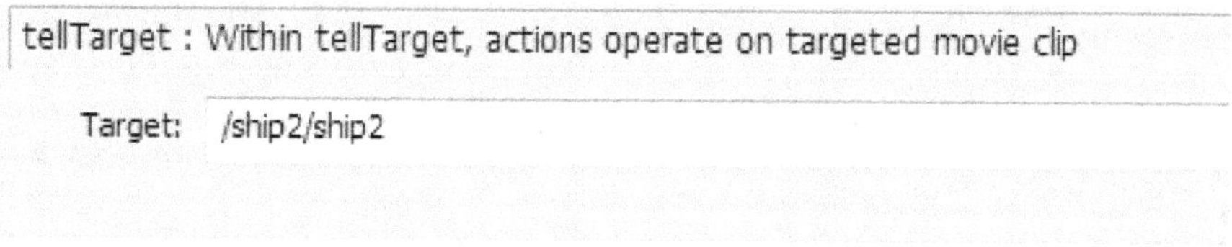

Next, we just need to tweak the code on frame **45** of the **Actions** layer. Select frame **45** of the **Actions** layer and change **/ship1/ship1/ship1** to **/ship2/ship2/ship2**:

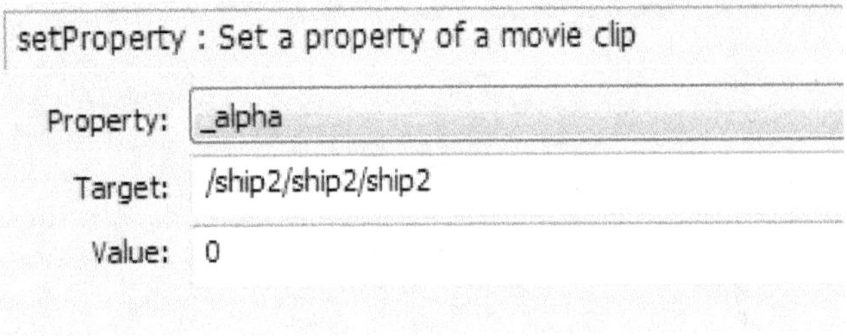

Lastly, select the ship symbol on the stage. In the Properties panel change the **Instance Name** to **ship2**. Test your movie and try out your new ship. Next, we're going to create the game's next level. In this level, however, we'll be adding a new element to the game.

Open the Scene panel. Change the name of **Scene 1** to **Level 1**:

Even though Level 2 will look different than Level 1, there are still several elements that are the same as Level 1. So the quickest way to create Level 2 is to duplicate Level 1. Click on the **Duplicate Scene** button:

Name this new layer **Level 2**:

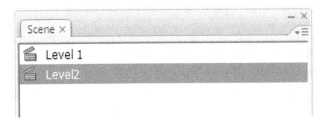

You should now have a copy of the first scene. We'll quickly tweak this new scene to create Level 2. The first thing we'll do change the background picture. Click on the keyframe of the **Background** layer. Hit DELETE on your keyboard to remove this picture. Drag ShipBackground from the library over to the stage. Open the Align panel and select **Align bottom edge**, **Align horizontal center** and **To stage**:

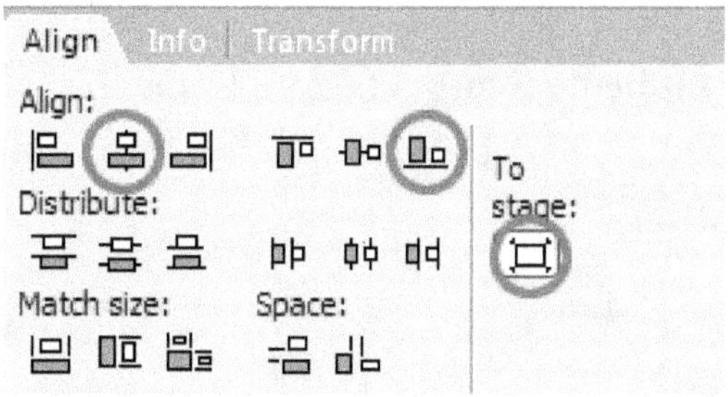

The background picture should now be properly positioned under the Score bar:

Let's change the amount of time the user has to play Level 2. Before we can change the **Timer** Movie clip, we need to make a copy of it. Select the **Timer** Movie clip:

In the Properties panel click on the Swap... button.

In the Swap Symbol window click on the **Duplicate Symbol** button. Name this new symbol **Timer 2**:

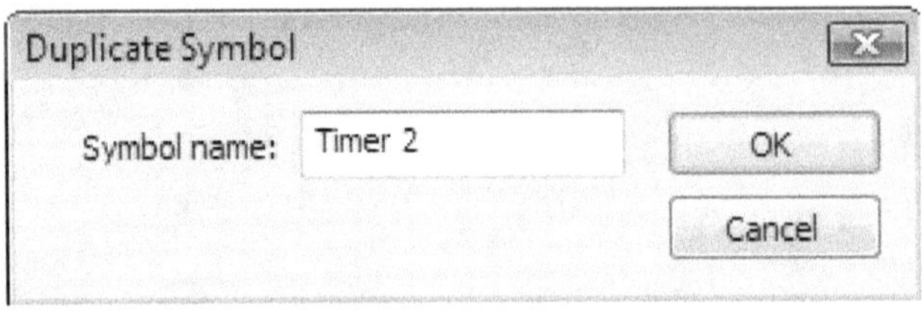

Hit OK when finished. Double-click on this new symbol in the Swap Symbol window. You can now edit this Movie clip without affecting the original. Double-click this new Movie clip to enter its editing stage. Since we only want this Level to have 25 seconds we need to remove some frames from the Text layer. Select frame **149** and, without letting go of your mouse button, drag across all the frames between **149** and **1**:

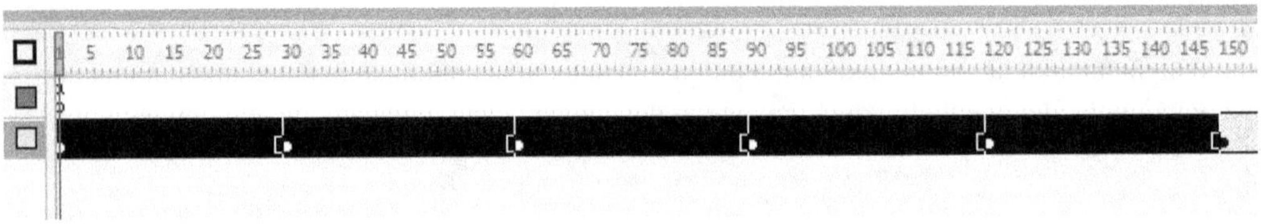

Next, go to **Edit**, **Timeline**, **Remove Frames**. You should now have the text **25** on the first frame. Since we removed frames from the **Text** layer and not the **Actions** layer, we need to move the final frame of the **Actions** layer so it's in sync with the final frame of the **Text** layer. Click on frame **900** of the **Actions** layer. Select this frame again and drag it to frame **750**:

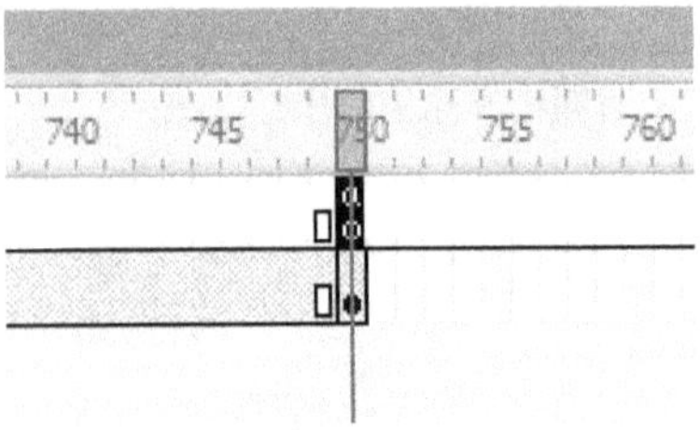

So now we're done with this Movie clip. Go back to Level 2. In the **Start** Movie clip there is a button that takes the user to the Label **level2** if they score 100 points. Let's add that label now. Create a new layer and name it **Labels**. Select the first frame of this layer and type **level2** in the Frame Label window:

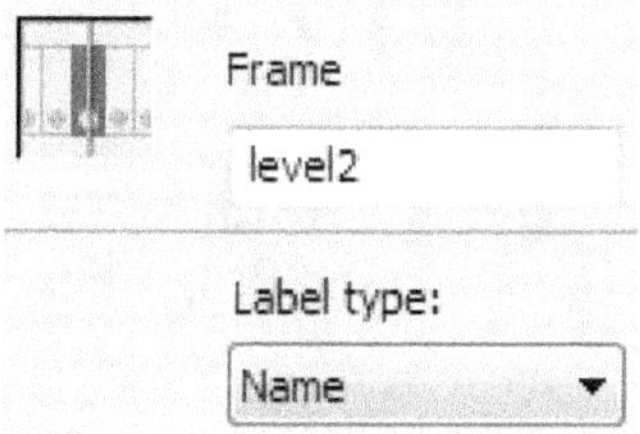

We now need to change the name of the Level. Double-click on the level text and change the number **01** to **02**:

We'll now add the Bomb animation. Click on the **Ship2** Movie clip:

We'll be adding the Bomb animation to this Movie clip but the first thing we need to do is make a copy of it. In the Properties panel click on the **Swap...** button. In the **Swap Symbol** window select the **Duplicate Symbol** button and name this new symbol **Bomb Animation**:

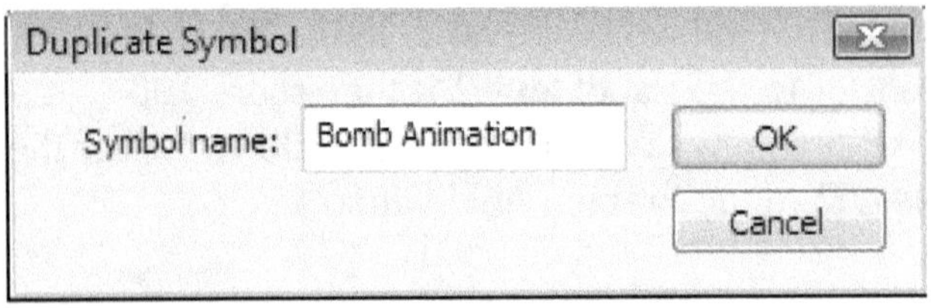

Hit OK then double-click on this new Movie clip in the Swap Symbol window. You can now edit this Movie clip without affecting the original. In the Properties panel change the **Instance Name** to **bomb1**:

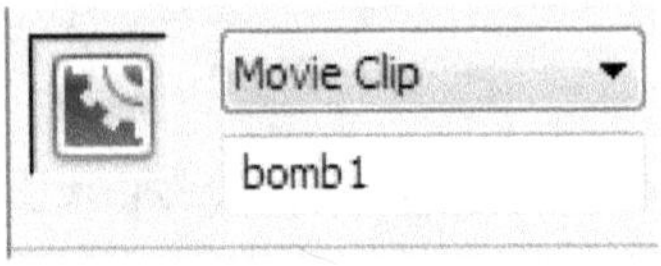

Double-click on this new Movie clip to enter its editing stage. We'll change the second animation on this timeline to a bomb animation. Click on the first frame of **Layer 1**:

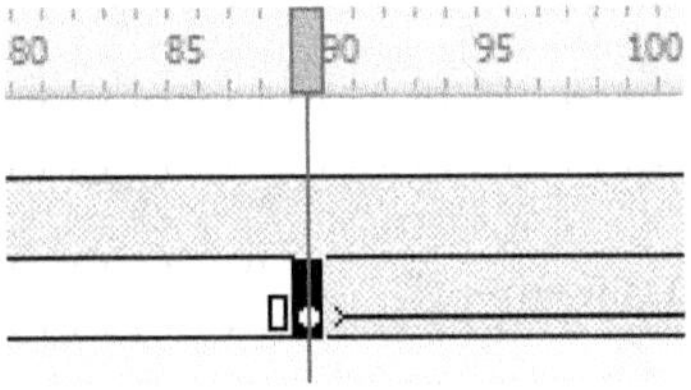

Next, select the ship symbol on the stage. In the Instance Name window change the name to **bomb1**:

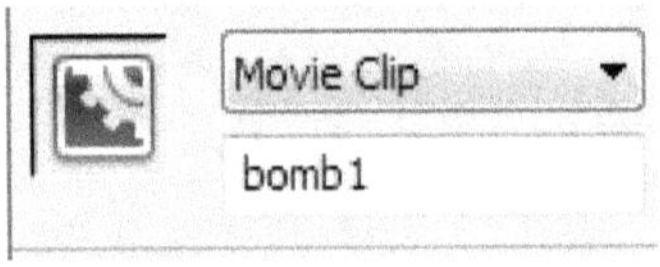

Before we can edit this Movie clip we need to duplicate it. Click on the **Swap...** button. In the Swap Symbol window click on the **Duplicate Symbol** button; name this new Movie clip **Bomb 1 Explosion**:

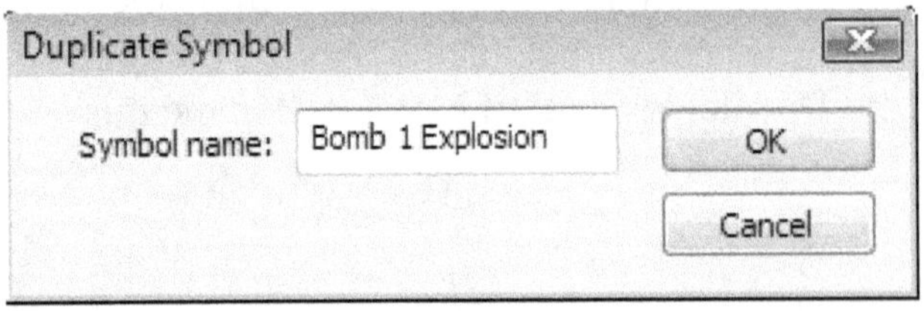

Hit OK. Double-click on this new Movie clip to select it. As we learned before, since this Movie clip is part of an animation we need to change the Movie clip on all the keyframes. Select the second keyframe of Layer 1. Select the ship symbol on the stage and change the **Instance Name** to **bomb1**.

Next, click on the **Swap...** button. In the Swap Symbol window double-click on the Movie clip **Bomb 1 Explosion**. The window should close automatically after you select the Movie clip. Double-click on this new Movie clip to enter its editing stage. The first thing we'll do is change the ship to a bomb. Click on the ship symbol:

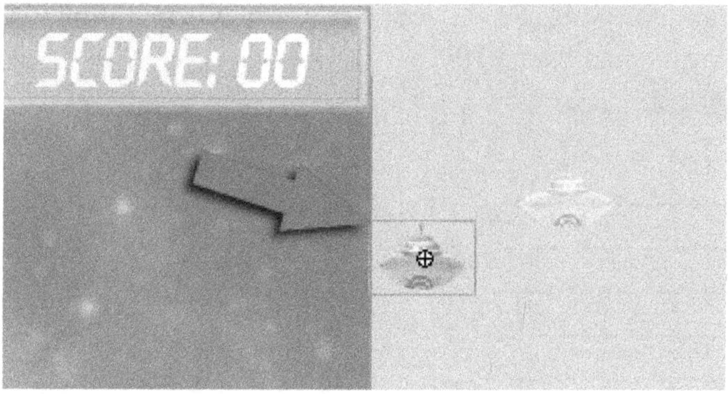

Hit DELETE on your keyboard to remove the ship from the stage. Drag the Movie clip **Bomb** from the library over to the stage. Place this Movie clip around the same area that the ship Movie clip occupied:

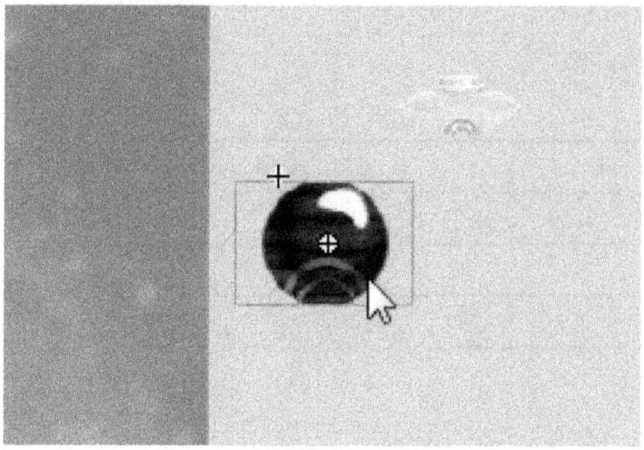

In the **Instance Name** window, name this Movie clip **bomb1**. Next, we'll add some more frames to this timeline. Highlight the frames from frame **2** to the frame right before the Label **explosion**:

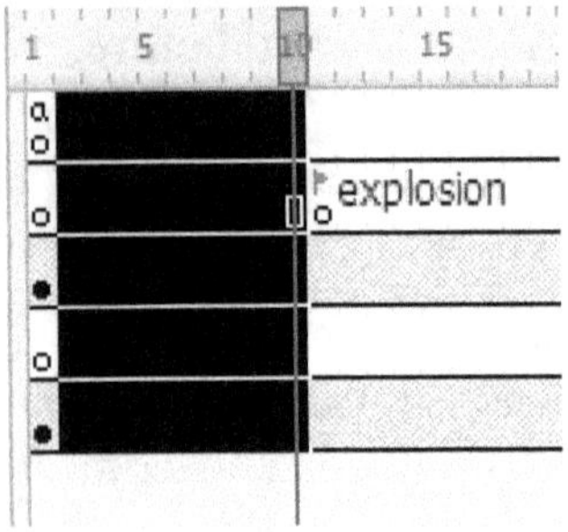

Go to Insert, Timeline, and Frame or Click **F5** on your keyboard. Keep adding frames until the Label **explosion** is past frame **100**:

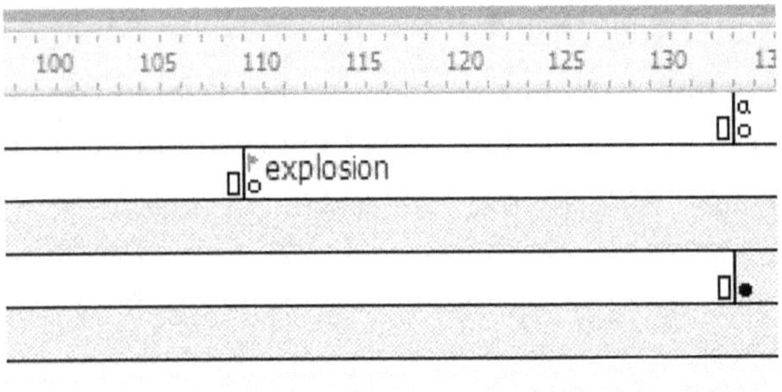

We're now going to add another Label. Select frame **10** of the **Labels** layer and insert a keyframe. In the Properties panel add the Frame Label: **self_destruct**. The timeline should now look like this:

Here is the reason why we need two Labels. If the user fires their weapon and strikes the Bomb, then this timeline is instructed to go to the Label **explosion** and *play*. If the user doesn't strike the Bomb, and the Bomb self-destructs, then this timeline goes to the Label **self_destruct** and *plays*.

So now we need to add the **Explosion** Movie clip to frame **10** of the **Explosion** layer. Create a keyframe on frame **10** of the **Explosion** layer. Drag the **Explosion** Movie clip from the library over to the stage; place this Movie clip directly over the bomb symbol.

Let's add the ActionScript now. Insert a keyframe on frame **25** of the **Actions** layer. Open the Actions panel. Go to **Global Functions**, **Movie clip Control**, and double-click **setProperty**. Change Property to **_alpha**, in the **Target** window type **/bomb1/bomb1/bomb1**, and make the Value 0:

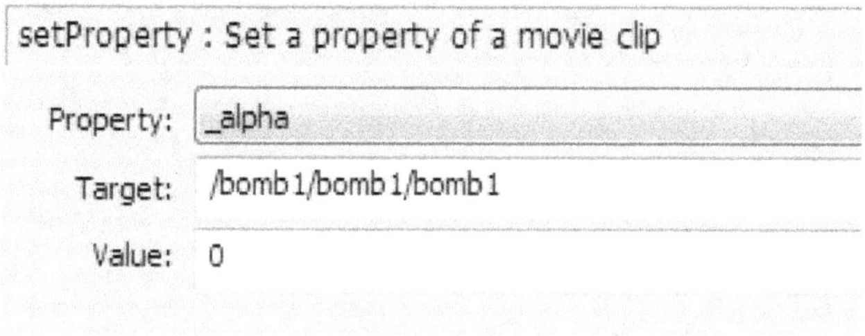

So here is what's going to happen. This Bomb will self-destruct when it nears the end of its animation. There will be code on this animation (we'll add this shortly) that will tell this current timeline to go to the Label **self_destruct** and *play*.

The next code we'll add is the code that subtracts points from the user's score. Since a self-destruction costs the user 20 points, we'll need two separate codes. Let's add those now. Go to **Deprecated**, **Actions**, and double-click **tellTarget**. In the Target window type **/score**:

Go to **Global Functions**, **Timeline Control** and double-click **goto**. In the **goto** settings window change the **Type** to **Previous Frame**:

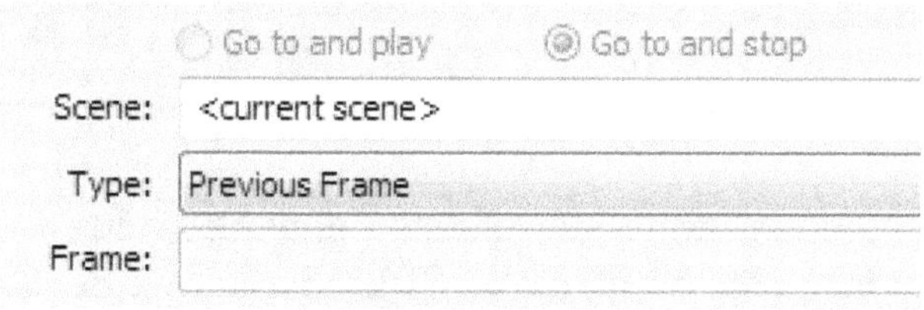

So now the **Score** Movie clip will go back one frame which will take the score down by 10 points. Since a self-destruction costs the user 20 points, we need to repeat the above code. Highlight the above code:

```
setProperty("/bomb1/bomb1/bomb1", _alpha, "0");
tellTarget ("/score") {
    prevFrame();
}
```

Go to **Edit**, **Copy**. Next, click on the closing bracket of this code and go to **Edit**, **Paste in Center**. You should now have two sets of this code:

```
setProperty("/bomb1/bomb1/bomb1", _alpha, "0");
tellTarget ("/score") {
    prevFrame();
}
tellTarget ("/score") {
    prevFrame();
}
```

Next, we need to add some ActionScript to frame **100** of the **Actions** layer. Create a keyframe on frame **100** of the **Actions** layer. Select this keyframe and open the Actions panel. Go to **Deprecated**, **Actions** and double-click **tellTarget**. In the Target window type **/bomb1**:

Go to **Global Functions**, **Timeline Control** and double-click **goto**. In the **goto** settings window change the **Type** to **Frame Number**, and type **300** in the **Frame** window:

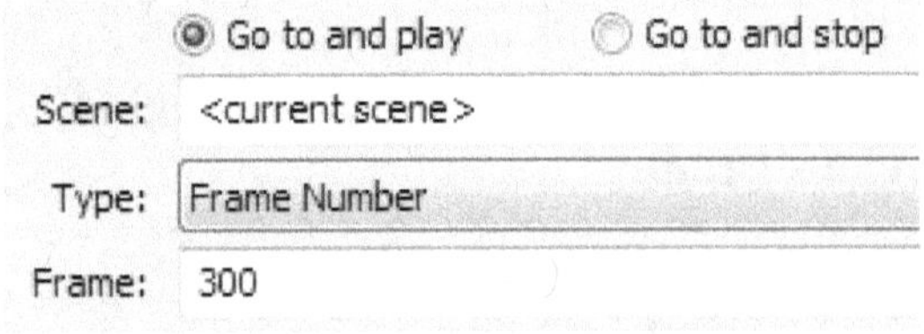

This code tells the bomb animation to go to frame 300 and start playing again. Since we used a setProperty code to make the bomb symbol transparent, we need to add another setProperty code to make it visible again. Click on the closing bracket of the last set of code. Next, go to **Global Functions**, **Movie clip Control** and double-click **setProperty**. In the **setProperty** settings window select **_alpha** for the Property, type **/bomb1/bomb1/bomb1** in the Target window, and type **100** in the **Value** window:

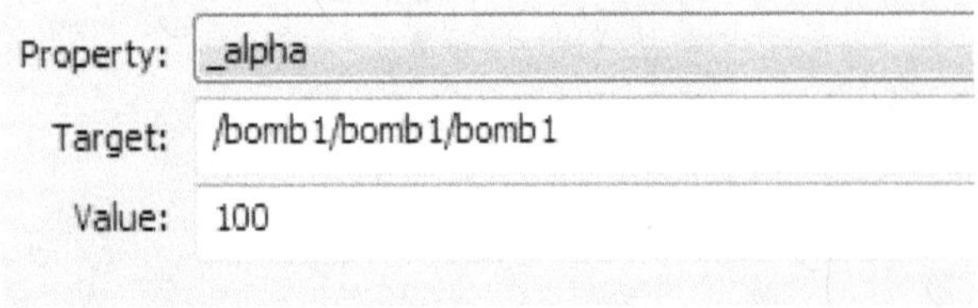

Select the closing bracket of this code. Go to **Global Functions**, **Timeline Control** and double-click **goto**. In the **goto** settings window select **Go to and stop**:

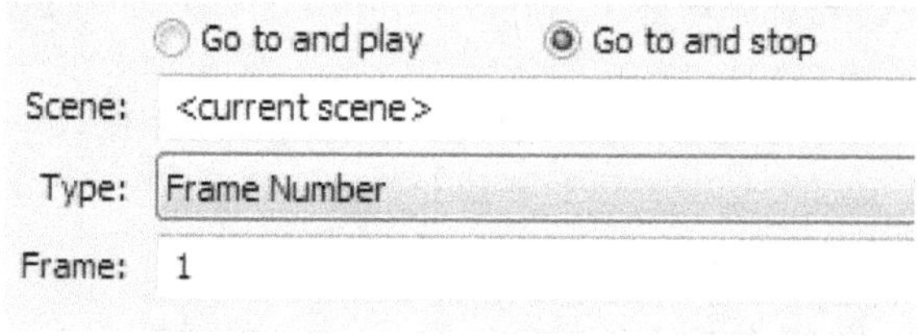

This sends the timeline back to frame 1 before it can reach the second Label. Next, we need to add a Blank Keyframe into frame **100** of the **Explosion** layer:

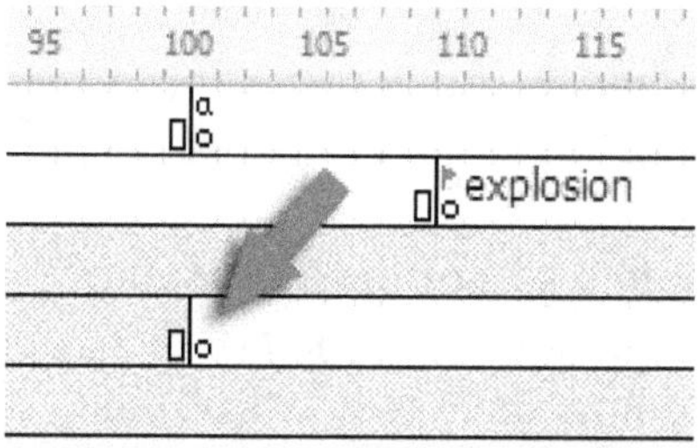

Here is why we do this. If the user correctly fires the weapon at the right time it will send this timeline to the Label **explosion** and *play*. If the **Explosion** Movie clip extends past frame 110 then when the timeline gets to the Label **explosion** the **Explosion** Movie clip will begin playing immediately which is what we don't want. There needs to be a delay before the explosion happens to give the bullets time to hit their target.

I'll explain how all this works in a moment, but first we need to change the code of the button. Select frame **1** of the **Button** layer and select the transparent Button symbol on the stage. You should now see the ActionScript of this button in the Actions window. Click on the word **tellTarget**; you should now see the **Target** window. Change **/ship2/ship2** to **/bomb1/bomb1**:

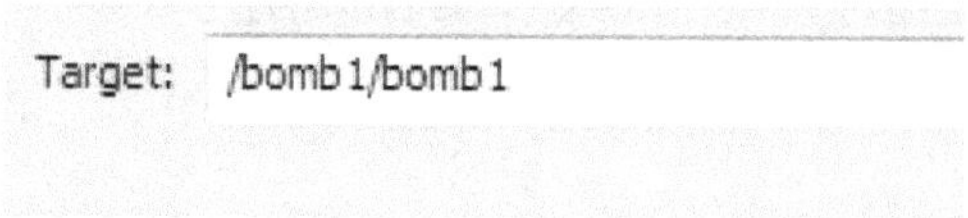

Next, find the first ActionScript frame after the Label **explosion**:

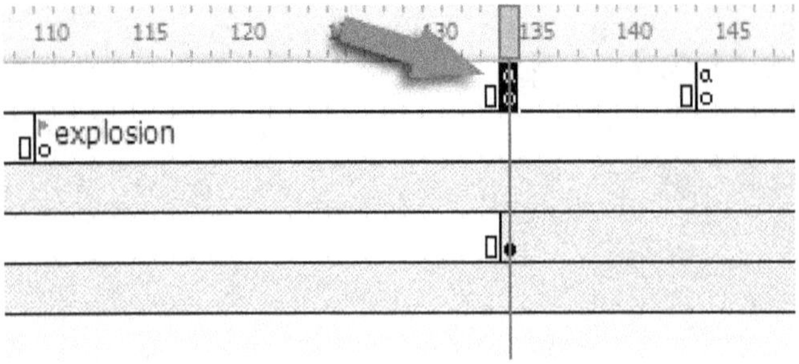

Click on this frame so you can see the ActionScript:

```
tellTarget ("/score") {
      nextFrame();
}
```

Since this Bomb is worth 20 points we need to have two sets of the above code. Highlight this code and go to **Edit**, **Copy**. Click on the closing bracket of this code; next, go to **Edit**, **Paste in Center**. You should now have two sets of this code:

```
tellTarget ("/score") {
      nextFrame();
}
tellTarget ("/score") {
      nextFrame();
}
```

Once the Bomb reaches this frame the explosion will occur. As soon as the explosion happens we want the bomb animation to stop. Let's add that code now. Click on the closing bracket of the last set of code. Next, go to **Deprecated**, **Actions** and double-click **tellTarget**. In the **Target** window type **/bomb1**:

Target: /bomb1

Next, go to **Global Functions**, **Timeline Control** and double-click **stop**.

Select the second frame with ActionScript:

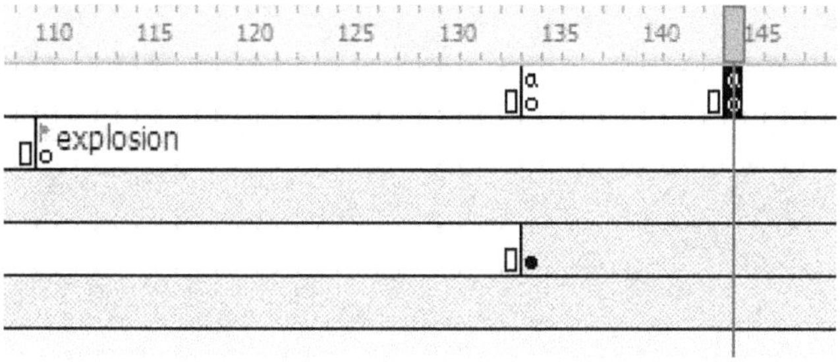

The ActionScript of this frame should look like this:

```
setProperty("/ship2/ship2/ship2", _alpha, "0");
```

This is the code that makes the ship transparent after the explosion happens. In the **setProperty** settings, change the **Target** to **/bomb1/bomb1/bomb1**:

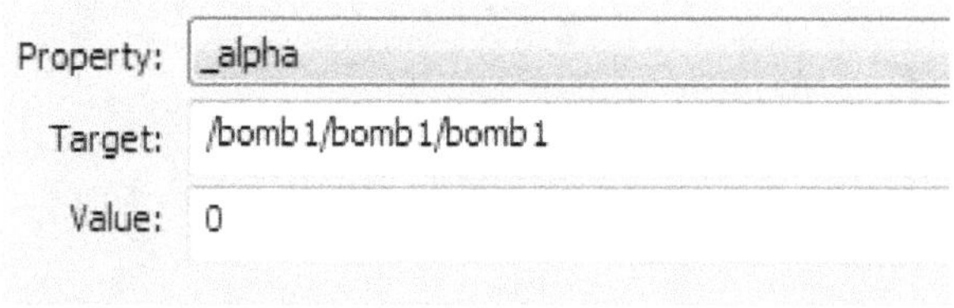

We'll now add the final ActionScript for this timeline. Select frame **215** of the **Actions** layer and insert a keyframe. Select this keyframe and open the Actions panel. We need to add two sets of code. The first set of code will bring the alpha of the bomb symbol back to 100, and the second set will tell the bomb animation to continue playing. Go to **Global Functions**, **Movie clip Control** and double-click **setProperty**. In the **setProperty** settings window select **_alpha** for the Property, type **/bomb1/bomb1/bomb1** in the **Target** window, and type **100** in the **Value** window:

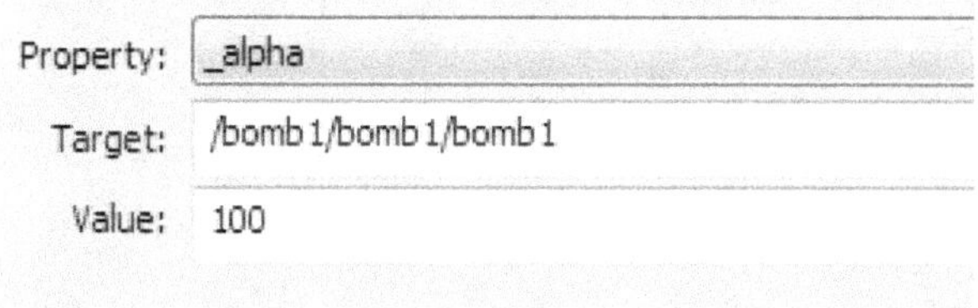

The bomb symbol will be visible again. Go to **Global Functions**, **Timeline Control** and double-click **goto**. In the **goto** settings window change the **Type** to **Frame Number**, and type **300** in the **Frame** window:

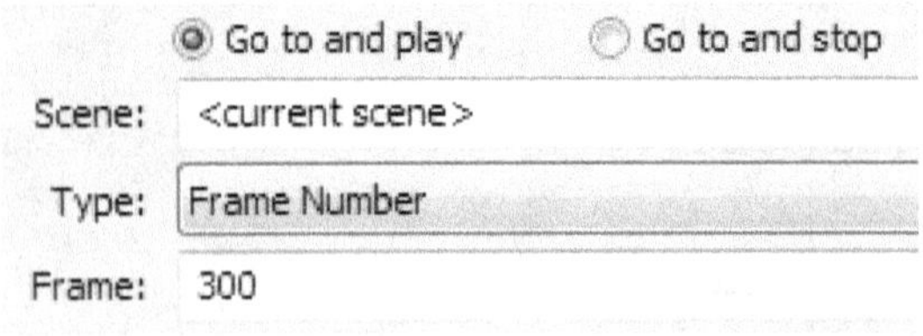

This will start the bomb animation again. That's it for this timeline. Let's add the self destruct code to the bomb1 animation. Click the Bomb Animation link above the timeline/stage:

Move the timeline needle across the bomb animation until the bomb gets near stage right. Create a keyframe in the **Actions** layer at this point and insert a **stop** code:

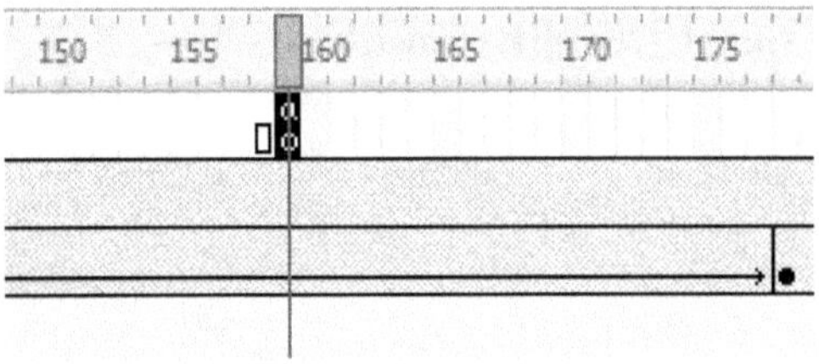

Next, we'll add the self destruct code to this keyframe. Go to **Deprecated**, **Actions** and double-click **tellTarget**. In the **Target** window type **/bomb1/bomb1**:

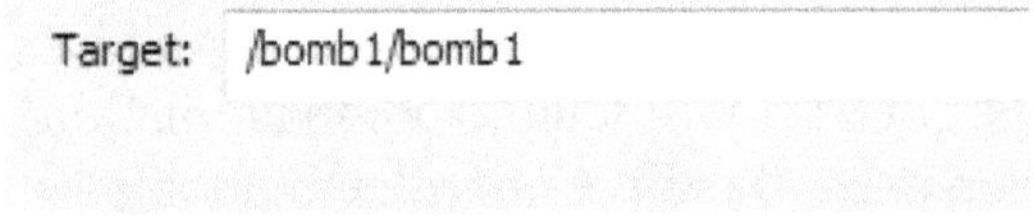

Go to **Global Functions**, **Timeline Control** and double-click **goto**. In the **goto** settings window change **Type** to **Frame Label** and enter **self_destruct** in the **Frame** window:

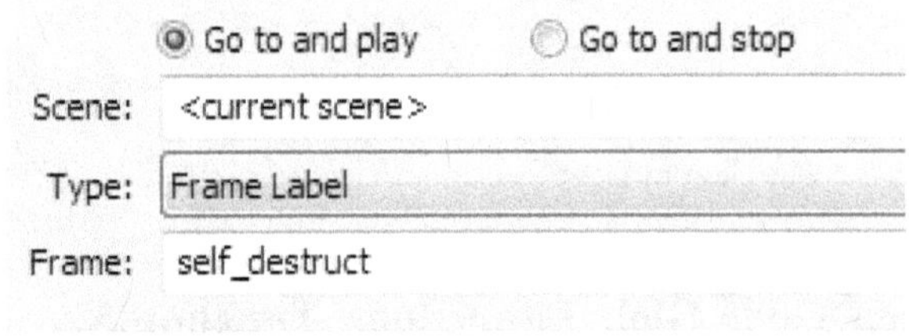

So now when the timeline reaches this frame it will send the Bomb 1 Explosion timeline to the Label **self-destruct**.

The last thing we'll tweak is the **Start** Movie clip. In this game you can add as many Levels as you like. For this exercise, however, we'll say that Level 2 will be the final Level. Let's change the **Start** Movie clip so that the game ends when you finish Level 2. Go back to the Level 2 stage.

Turn the visibility back on for the **Start** Movie clip layer, then select the **Start** Movie clip on the stage. In the Properties panel click on the **Swap...** button. In the **Swap Symbol** window click on the **Duplicate Symbol** button. Name this new symbol **Start Movie clip 2** and hit **OK**. Double-click on this new symbol in the **Swap Symbol** window:

You can now edit this Movie clip without affecting the original Movie clip. Double-click this Movie clip to enter its editing stage. Select the second frame of the **Actions** layer so you can see the ActionScript in the Actions window. Select the second code in the window:

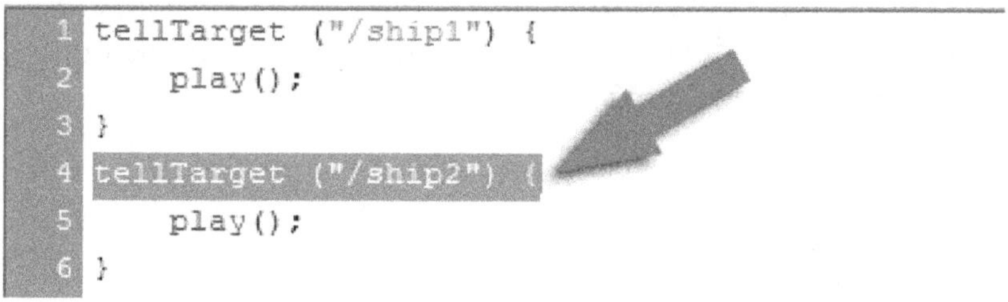

Change **/ship2** to **/bomb1**:

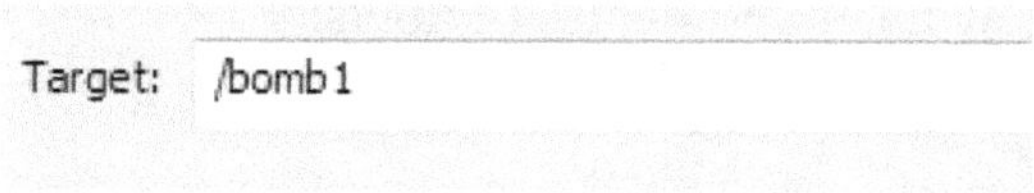

Next, go to frame **12** of the **Button** layer and delete the transparent button:

Next, select frame **12** of the **Points** layer and delete the text:

Double-click on the CONGRATULATIONS... text. Change the text to CONGRATULATIONS! YOU COMPLETED THE GAME!:

Go back to the Level 2 stage. Select the **Actions** layer frame and you should see the ActionScript in the Actions window. Select the word **tellTarget** in the third set of code. Change the **Target** from **/ship2** to **/bomb1**:

The last thing we need to do is add a Label to this timeline. When a user finishes Level 1 they click on the button that takes them to the Label **level2**. So we need to add this Label to this timeline. Create a new layer and name it Labels:

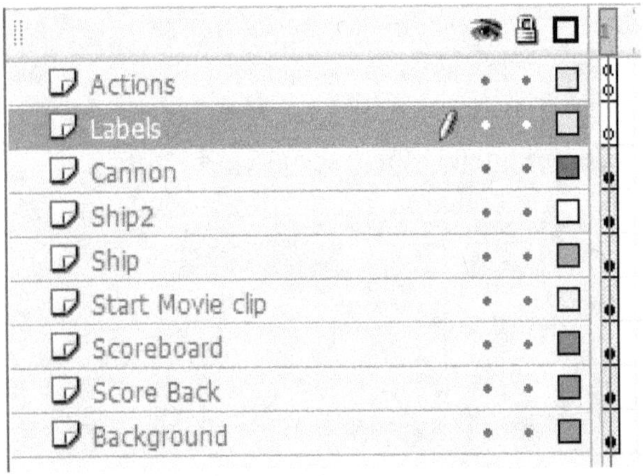

Select the first frame of this layer; in the Properties panel type **level2** in the **Frame Label** window:

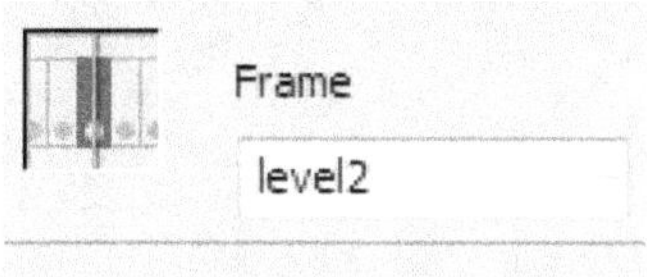

Test the movie. Congrats! You now have a working video game! You can add more levels or add different types of ships. You can also change the amount of time. When you get more proficient at using the command tellTarget, you'll be able to have a dynamic list of the high scores; or, allow the user to win extra time by hitting a certain ship. Anything is possible in Flash, once you master a few simple commands!

Chapter Seven:
Publish Movies

Optimize Images/Sounds

Before you publish your project to the internet you'll need to make sure that all your images are optimized correctly. If you're proficient at Photoshop then you can optimize the images before you import them into Flash. If you're not familiar with Photoshop then you can still optimize your images in the Flash program.

Open the file called **Publish_Settings.fla** in the Publish Movies folder.

On the stage you'll see a deer picture. To find out how large a file this is going to be when it's on the web, go to **Control**, **Test Scene**. If you don't see the Bandwidth Profiler then go to **View**, **Bandwidth Profiler**:

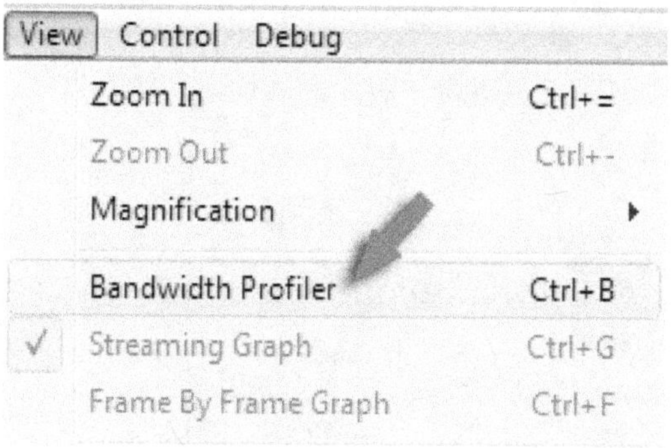

At the bottom of the **Bandwidth Profiler** you'll see the size of the image, which is **77KB**:

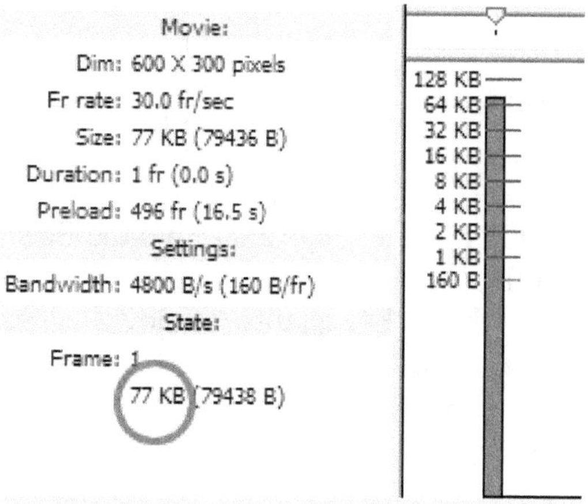

Let's see if we can lower the file size of this picture. Go back to the **JPEG** scene. In the library select **Deer.jpg**, then click on the **Properties...** button:

You should now see the **Bitmap Properties** box. You'll see an option named **Use Imported JPEG data** which is checked:

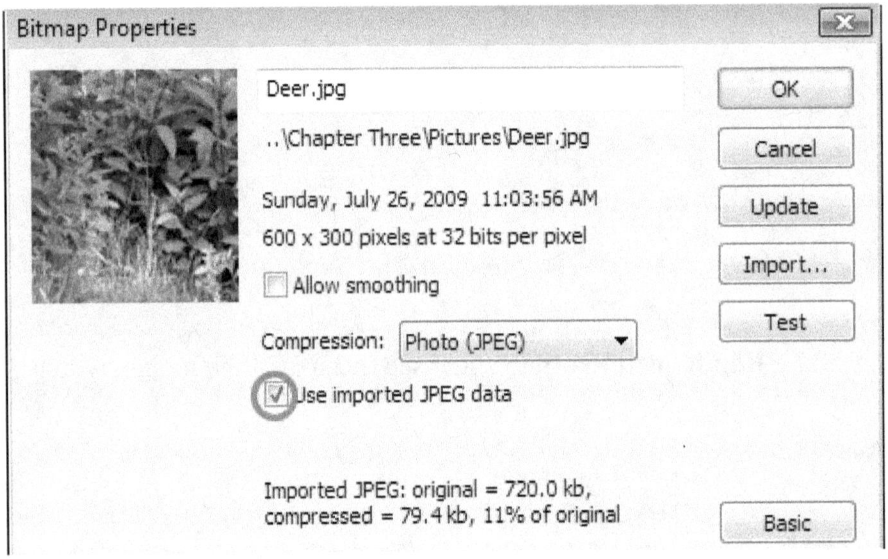

This simply means that whatever size the JPEG is when you bring it into the Flash project, is the size it will be in the final Flash file. To decrease the size of the JPEG uncheck this option. You should now see the **JPEG** quality window:

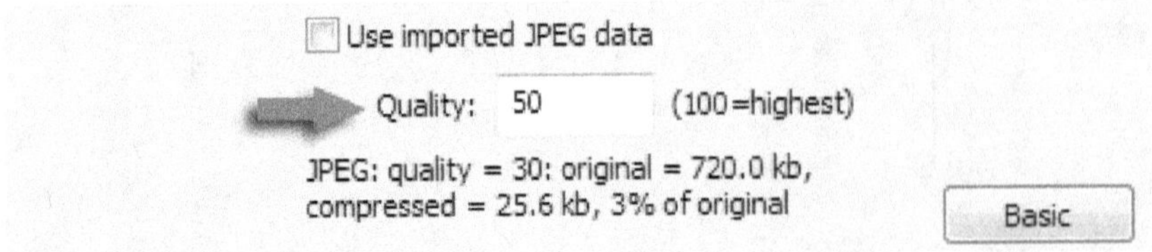

You should see **50** in the **Quality** window; if it's not in there type it in now. This means that the **JPEG** will be about **50%** of it's original size. Hit **OK**. Go to **Control**, **Test Scene**. In the **Bandwidth Profiler** you'll see that the **JPEG** size is much smaller:

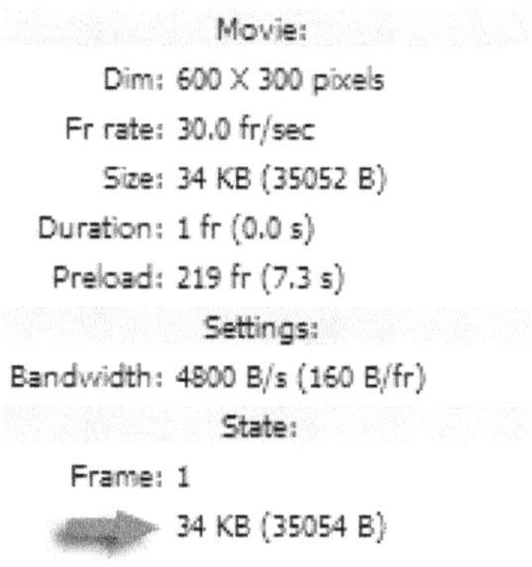

Just remember that the lower the number you put in the **Quality** window, the more pixilated your picture will become.

Go to the **Sound** scene. You'll see an empty stage. But if you look at the first frame of the **Sound** layer you'll notice that it has a line through it indicating it contains a sound file. In the library select the **lion growls.wav** file, then click on the **Properties...** button:

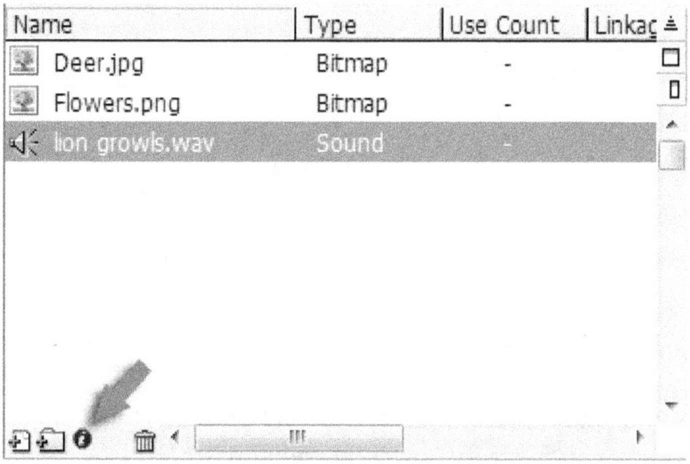

You should now see the **Sound Properties** box. The setting that we need to adjust is the **Compression** setting:

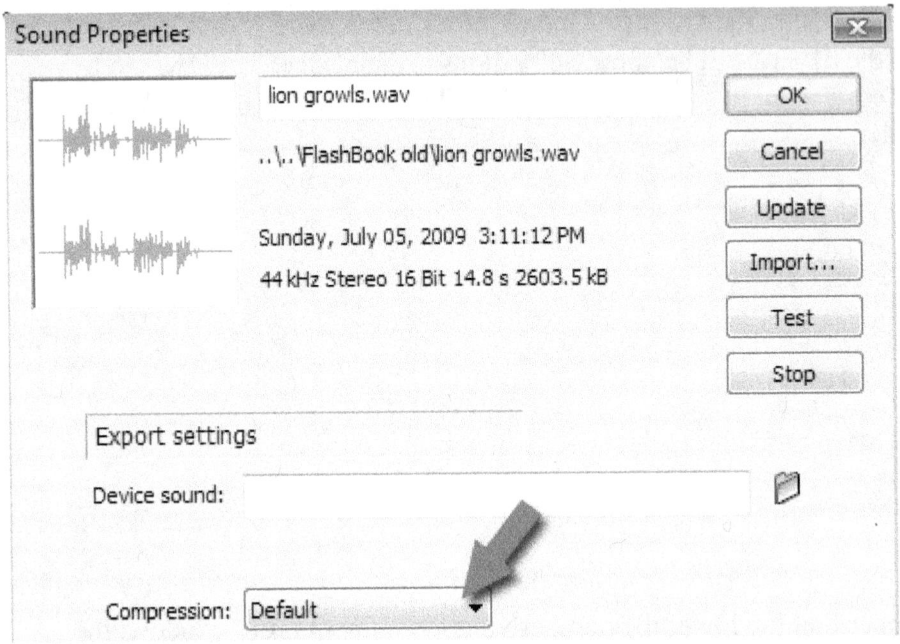

It should be set at **Default**. Click on the drop-down arrow next to **Compression** and choose **MP3**. You should now see the **MP3** settings:

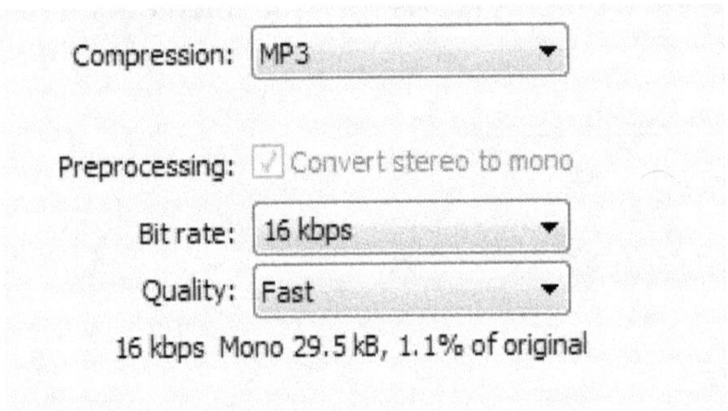

You have two settings that you'll have to tweak. The first one, **Bit rate**, is the sound quality of the audio file. If you click the drop-down arrow next to **16 kbps** you'll see Bit rates from **8 kbps** to **160 kbps**. A good rule of thumb to remember, is that if you have a mono file, like a sound effect, you can keep the Bit rate small, around **32 kbps**. If you have a music file, then you'll want to make it around **64 kbps** or higher. The **Quality** setting controls the overall files size of the audio file. For this sound effect let's change **Bit rate** to **32 kbps** and **Quality** to **Medium**:

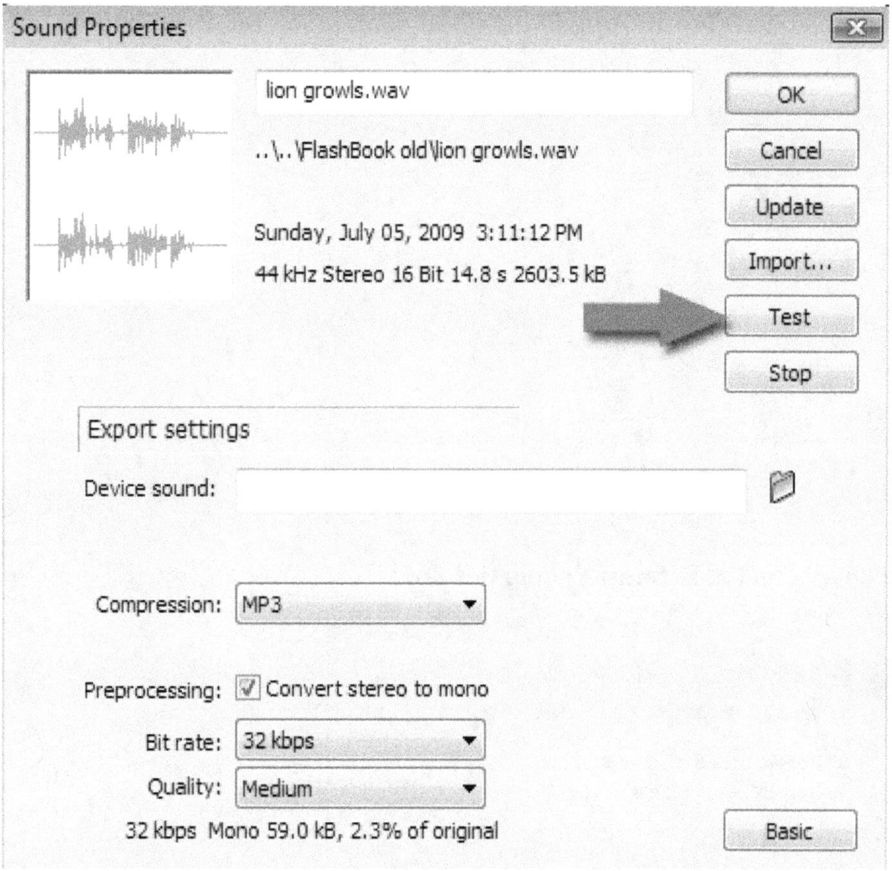

You'll notice that when you select a size larger than 16 kbps you'll be able to convert the audio file from mono to stereo. I usually like my sound effects in stereo, and you'll definitely want any music files in stereo. So uncheck this selection. Click on the **Test** button to hear your audio file. If it sounds good then you're all set. Hit **OK** whenc you're done.

Select the PNG scene. The only time I use PNG files is when I need a picture with a transparent background. On the PNG scene you'll see the picture of the flowers. Go ahead and test this scene. In the **Bandwidth Profiler** you'll notice that the file is **95 KB**:

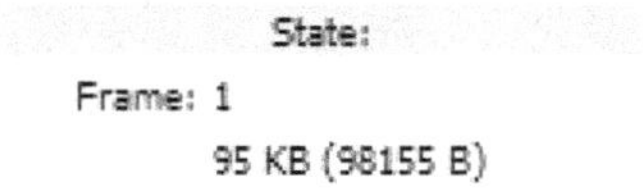

When you use PNG files, Flash will convert them to a JPEG to reduce their overall file size. This is fine but sometimes you don't want your PNG files converted since it does lower their quality a bit. To keep your PNG file from being converted, go to **Flowers.png** in the library and select the **Properties...** button:

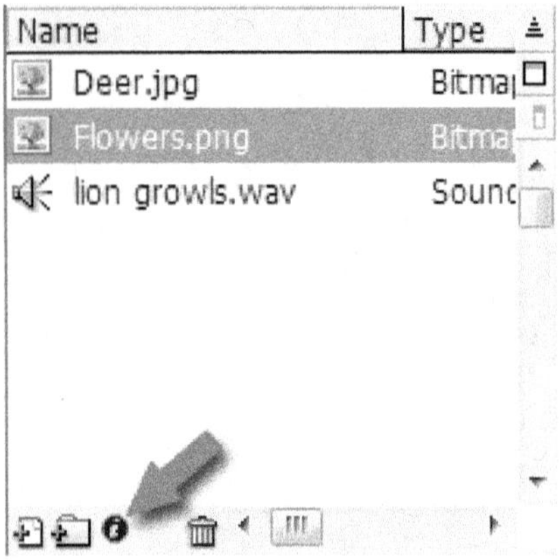

You should now be in the **Bitmap Properties** box:

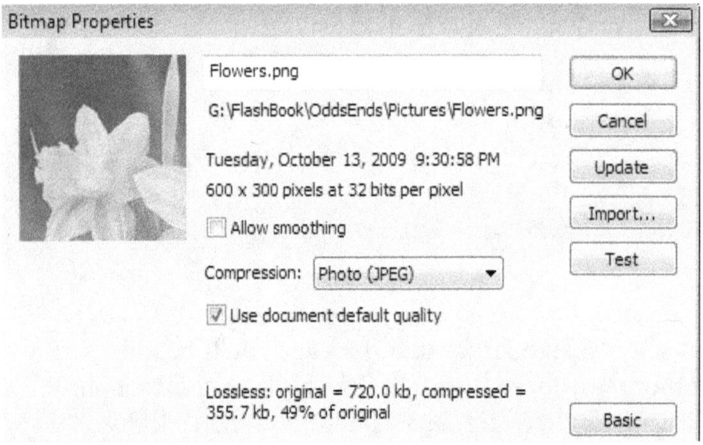

Next to **Compression** you'll see **Photo (JPEG)**. When you import a PNG file, Flash will convert it to a JPEG. To avoid this, change **Compression** to **Lossless (PNG/GIF)**:

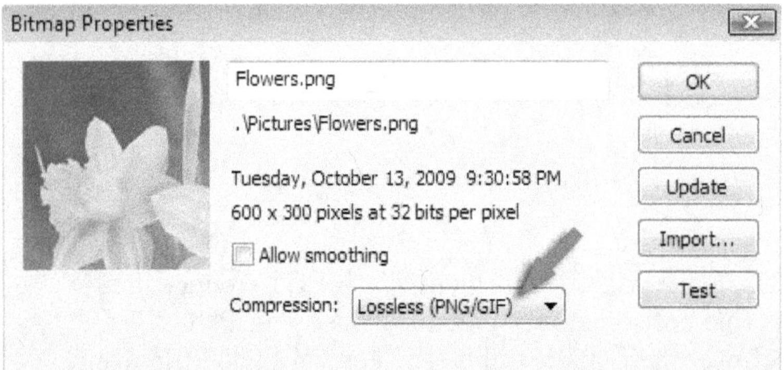

This will retain the image's original quality. Hit **OK**. Test your scene again. This time you'll notice a much larger file size of **347 KB**:

A much larger file but the picture will be a little sharper. Usually I only use PNG files when I absolutely have to. Recently, I was asked to convert a Musical poster into a Flash animation. In Photoshop I cut out the characters of the poster and saved them as PNG files since I wanted them cut-out with no background. A JPEG image will always have a default background.

Publish Settings

So you've created a great banner, or website, and you're ready to publish it to the internet! This is where Publish Settings comes into play. With Publish Settings you'll be able to optimize your flash file, rename it, change the version (as we learned earlier), and a few other things.

Let's go through a few of the settings so you have a better idea of how to use them. In the Publish_Settings.fla file, go to **File**, **Publish Settings**:

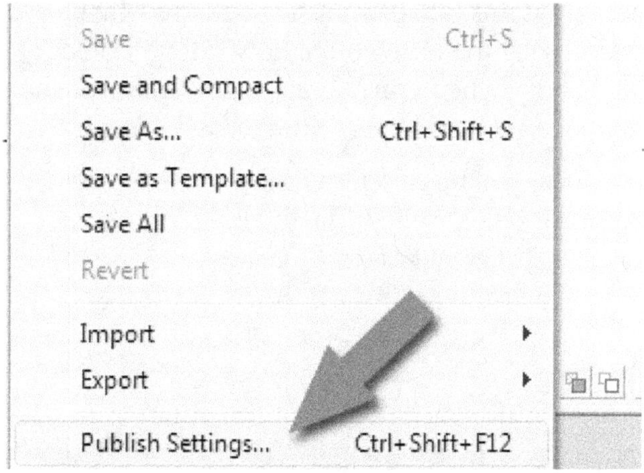

You should now see the **Publish Settings** window:

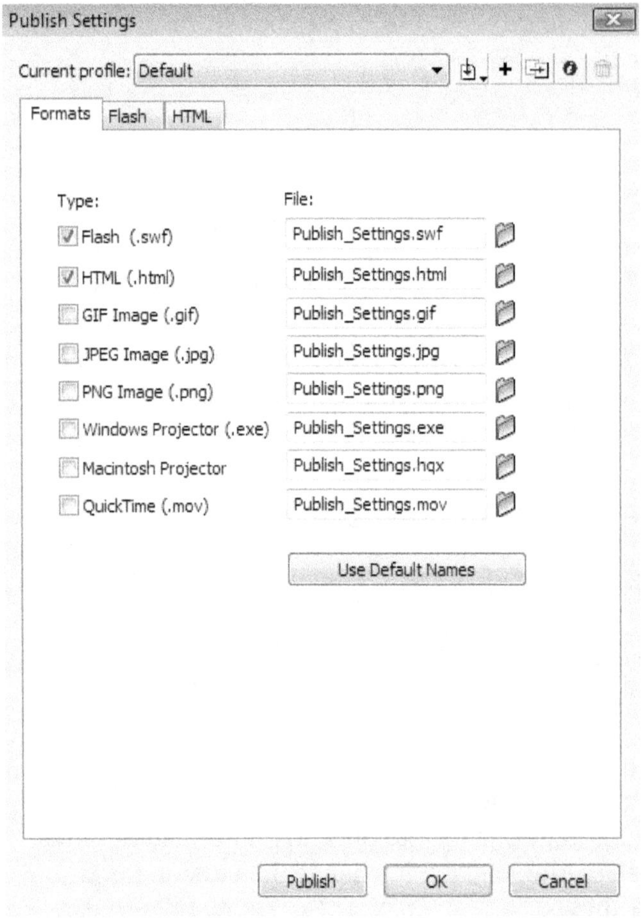

You'll notice on the left there is a list of different files you can create with your Flash project. Usually, though, the only items you'll want selected are **Flash (.swf)** and **HTML (.html)**. The majority of the time you're only going to need **Flash (.swf)** selected. **HTML** is used only when you're creating a Flash website. It will automatically create the web page for you along with the **.swf** file.

To the right of the selections, under **File**, you'll see text windows where you can change the name of the **.swf** or the **html**. Click on the **Flash** tab:

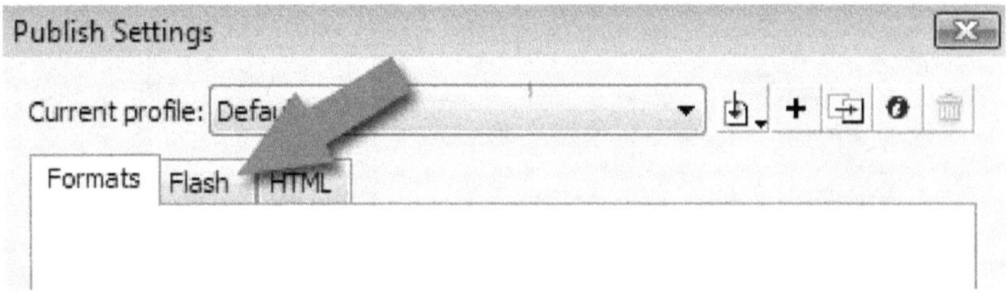

You should now be in the Flash settings:

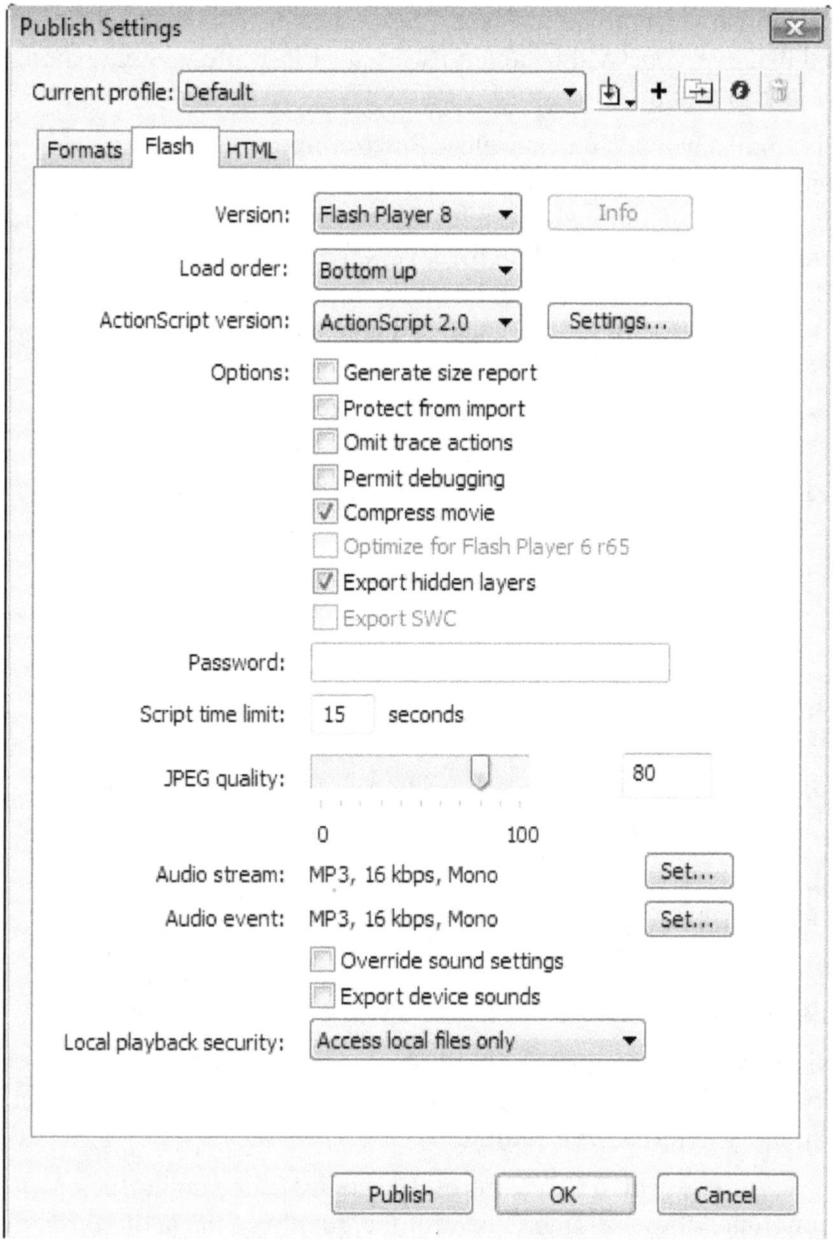

I won't go through all the settings since many of them you may never use. I rarely change the default settings. I'll go through a few of the more common settings.

Starting at the top you'll see **Version**. If you select the drop-down arrow next to **Flash Player 9** you'll see several selections. If you choose **Flash Player 4**, for instance, then any user that has the **Flash 4 plugin** will be able to see your Flash file on the internet. If you keep the **Version** at **Flash Player 9** then the user will have to have the latest Flash plugin to view your Flash file. A good rule of thumb is if you're doing a Flash file that isn't using the latest bells & whistles (filters, 3D objects, etc.) then publish your movie in **Flash Player 4 or 5**. This makes it almost guaranteed that everyone will be able to see your Flash file without having to upgrade their Flash plugin.

The next option is **Load Order**. You can select **Bottom up**, or **Top down**. This refers to how Flash loads up the layers of your timeline. **Bottom up** means Flash will load whatever objects are on the bottom layer first, then the second layer, and so on. **Top down** means Flash will load up the layers from the top down. Usually with my Flash files my heaviest image will be on the bottom layer. So I'll choose **Top down** so at least the user can see the smaller images loading up before the large image loads.

ActionScript version. If you are using ActionScript that is based on the new ActionScript 3.0 then you will have to choose **ActionScript 3.0** from the drop-down selections. If you're not using ActionScript 3.0 then you can keep the ActionScript at **2.0** or **1.0**.

Generate size report will create a size report when you publish your movie. It will break down each frame and let you know how large the objects are in those frames.

Protect from import will prevent people from downloading and opening your flash file in Flash.

Omit trace actions will ignore any trace actions you've added to your movie.

Permit debugging will check the Flash file for ActionScript errors.

Compress movie. This only works on Flash Player 6 and higher. This will compress your Flash movie so the download time is shorter.

Export hidden layers will export any layers that are hidden in your Flash file. This is only available in later versions of Flash. I always leave this selected.

JPEG quality will control the quality of the JPEGs in your Flash file. I usually control the quality of the JPEGs through the steps outlined in the previous project. I leave the JPEG quality at the default setting.

Audio stream and Audio event. These control the quality of the audio files. Once again, I rarely touch these settings. I control the quality of the audio through the steps outlined in the previous project.

Export device sounds. This makes the audio suitable for mobile devices.

Local playback security allows the published SWF file access to local files or files over a network.

Select the HTML tab:

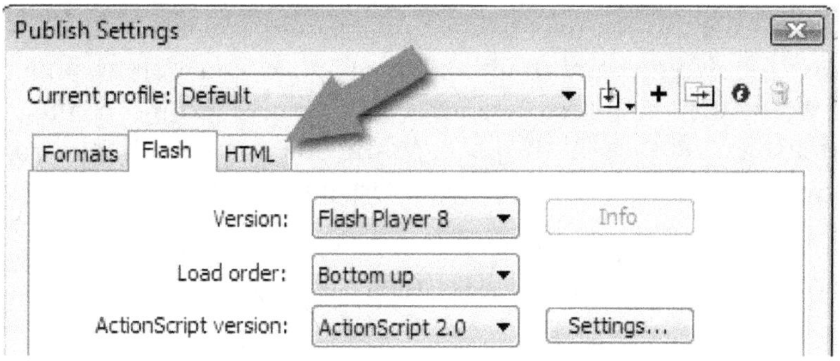

You should now be in the HTML settings:

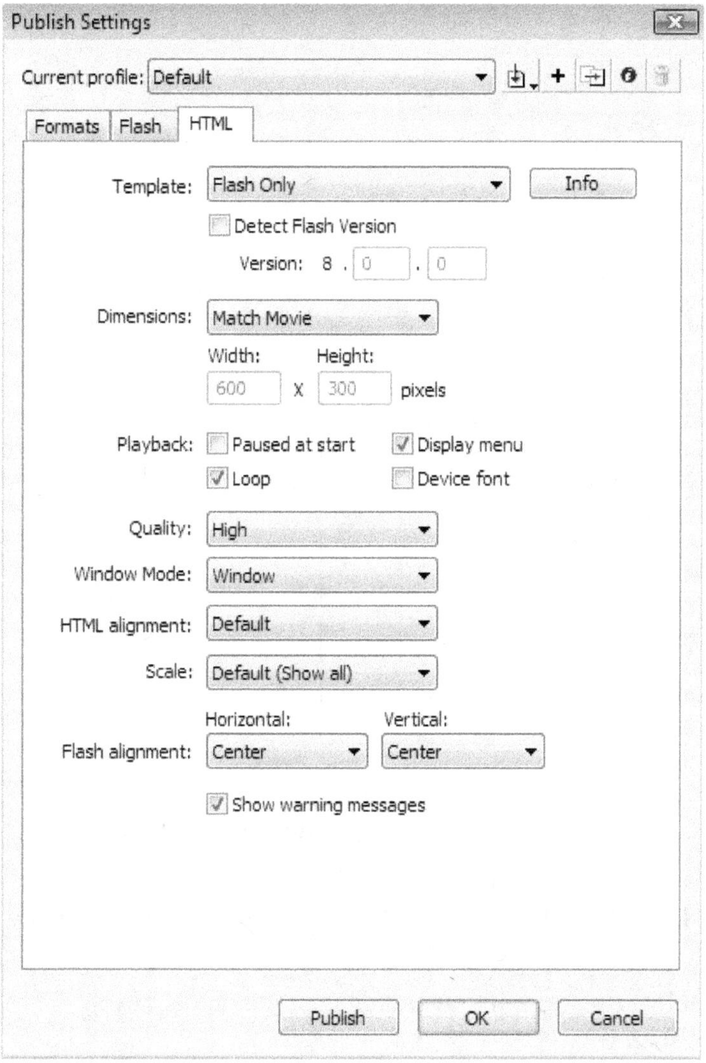

If you have **HTML** selected in the Formats tab, then Flash will create a HTML page along with the .swf file. If you were to upload this page to your server along with the .swf file you would then be able to see your Flash project online. Some people prefer having Flash create the HTML page. While others, myself included, prefer dropping the .swf file into a web program like Dreamweaver.

Template: This lets you choose from templates that enable or support the Flash player. Click on the drop-down arrow next to **Flash Only**. Select **Flash Only - Allow Full Screen:**

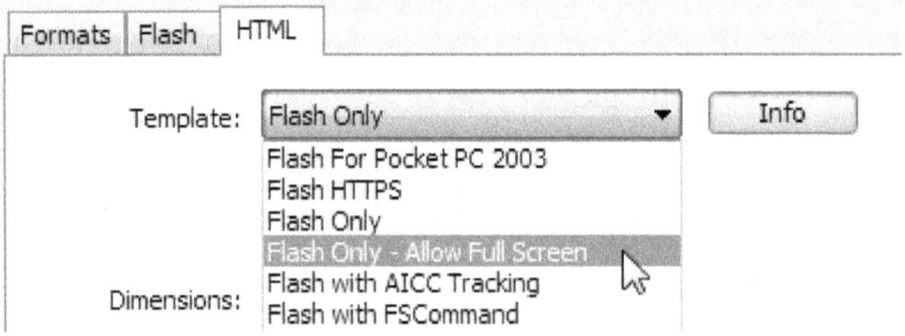

Select the **Info** button. A box will pop up and give you the information on the selection you chose:

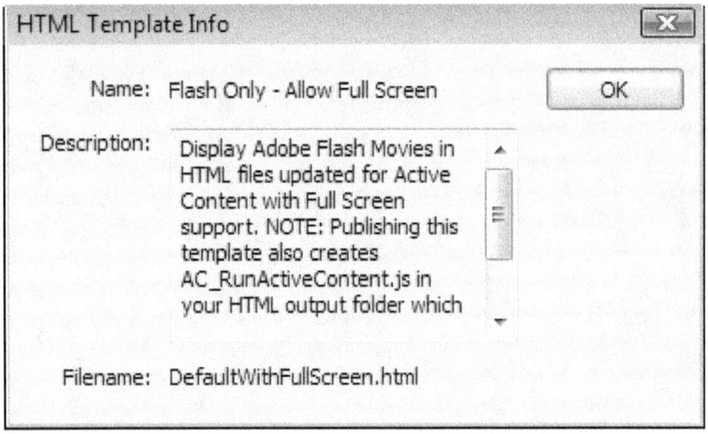

Dimensions: This lets you choose the size of the Flash file. You'll see three different selections:

Match Movie: This matches the dimensions of the Flash project you just created.

Pixels: When you select this option you can change the actual pixel dimensions of the published file.

Percent: This will make the dimensions of your Flash project a percentage of the available area in the HTML file.

Playback: This controls how the Flash file is displayed. You can have a context menu displayed which allows the user to rewind or zoom into the Flash file. You can also allow the user to substitute a font.

Quality: This setting controls the quality and how the Flash file is displayed for the user. A higher quality setting comes at a performance cost. A setting such as Auto High will start the Flash file off in high quality mode, but switch it to a lower quality if the computer can't handle it. Auto Low does the opposite starting the Flash file off in low quality and increasing the quality depending on the computer's performance.

Window Mode: This allows control over how the Flash file interacts with the surrounding HTML file. You'll see three different settings:

Window: This mode makes the background opaque and uses the stage background color as the background color for the .html file.

Opaque Windowless: This mode allows the HTML file to stack content above the Flash file.

Transparent Windowless: This makes the background of the Flash file transparent.

HTML alignment: This mode controls how the .swf file is positioned within the .html file.

Scale: If you choose percentage in the Dimensions setting then Scale controls how the .swf file is sized within the HTML page.

Flash alignment: This is different than HTML alignment in that this setting aligns the .swf file within its own display area.

Show warning messages: This will display a warning message if you have a conflict with any of the settings you have chosen. It's a good idea to keep this selected.

Chapter Eight:
Flash Code Diagram

The following diagram will help you if you run into any problems with your coding. If, for some reason, your code isn't working study this diagram and double-check your code against a similar code in the diagram.

If you study the diagram you'll notice that we have a button (**A** Button) on the Scene 1 timeline along with a Movie clip with an Instance Name of **picture**. Within this Movie clip we have another Movie clip which has an Instance Name of **deer**. On the **Picture** Movie clip timeline we also have a button (**B** Button).

Within the **Deer** Movie clip we have another Movie clip with an Instance Name of **lake**. Below the diagram there is a breakdown of the code needed for each button to control all the Movie clips along with the main timeline and **Level 1**. Also, we have one more scene: **Scene 2** with a Label: **flower** on its timeline (Scene 2 not pictured):

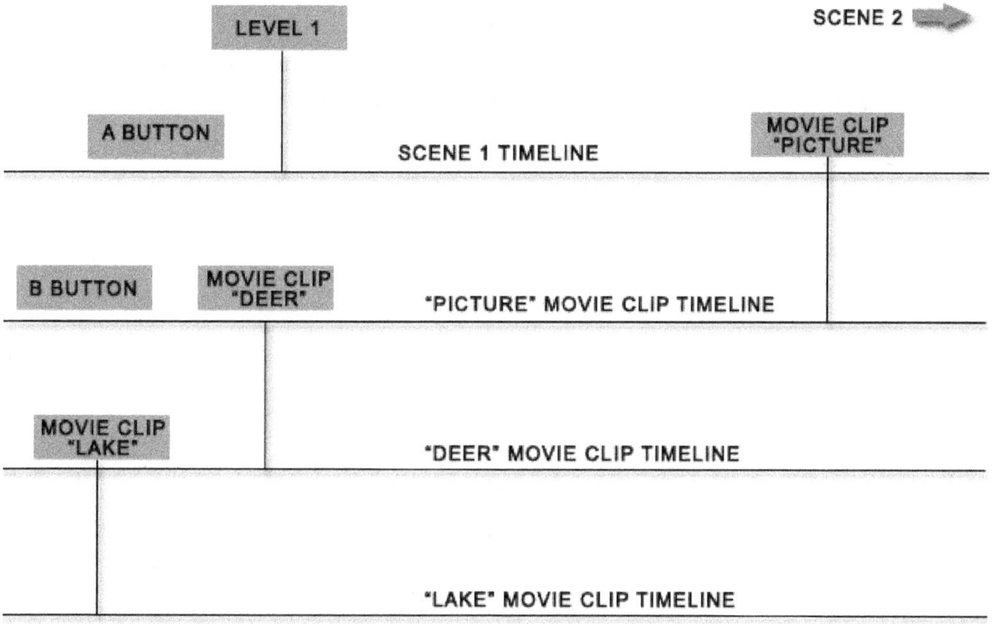

A Button - **Scene 1**: The A Button is commanding **Scene 1** to go to frame **10** and play. Since the A Button is on the Scene 1 timeline, then we don't need to use the tellTarget command.

Go to **Global Functions**, **Timeline Control** and double-click **goto**. In the **goto** settings window, type **10** in the **Frame** window. Your final code should look like this:

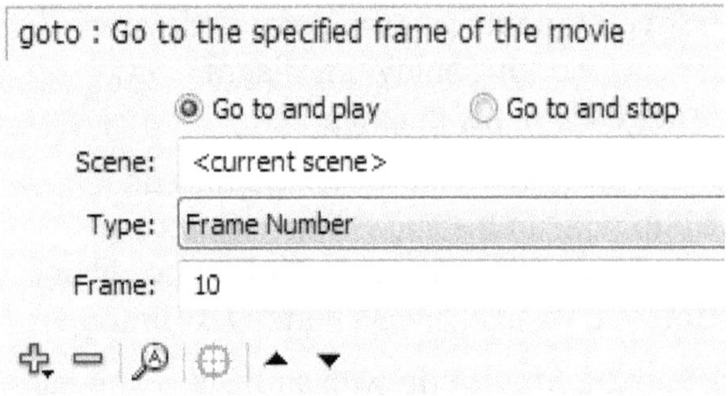

A Button - Picture Movie clip: The **A** Button tells the timeline of the **Picture** Movie clip to go to frame **10** and play. Since the **A Button** is controlling a timeline that it isn't on, then we need to use the tellTarget command.

Go to **Deprecated**, **Actions** and double-click **tellTarget**. In the **Target** window, type **/picture**. Next, go to **Global Functions**, **Timeline Control** and double-click **goto**. In the **goto** settings window type **10** in the **Frame** window:

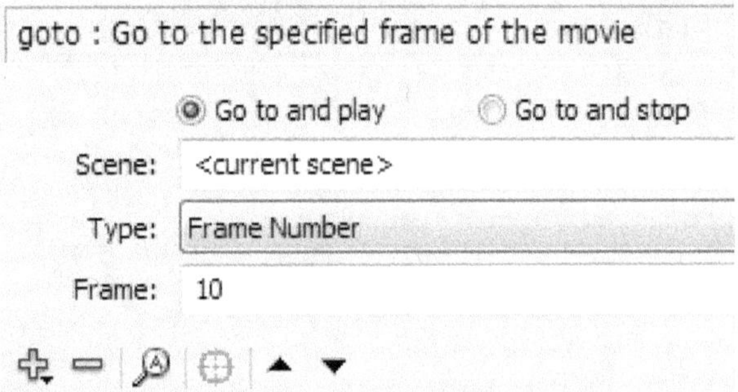


```
on (release) {
    tellTarget ("/picture") {
        gotoAndPlay(10);
    }
}
```

A Button - **Deer** Movie clip: The **A** Button tells the timeline of the Deer Movie clip to go to frame 10 and play. Since the Deer Movie clip is within the Picture Movie clip the Target name is: **/picture/deer**.

Go to **Deprecated**, **Actions** and double-click **tellTarget**. In the **Target** window, type **/picture/deer**. Next, go to **Global Functions**, **Timeline Control** and double-click **goto**. In the **goto** settings window type **10** in the **Frame** window:

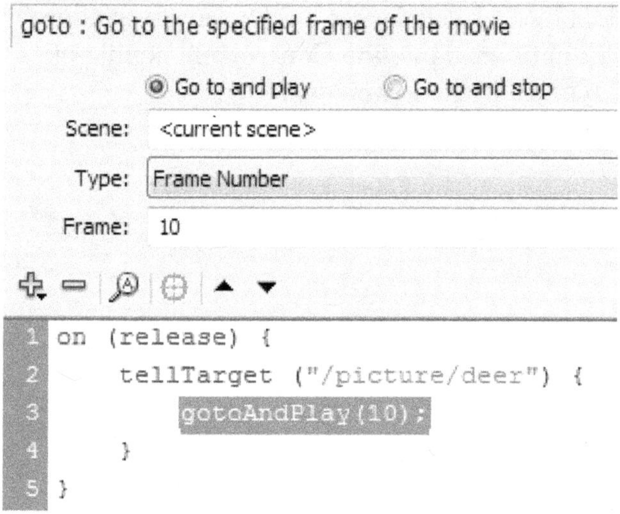

A Button **- Lake** Movie clip: The **A** Button tells the timeline of the **Lake** Movie clip to go to frame 10 and play. The **Lake** Movie clip is within the **Deer** Movie clip which is within the **Picture** Movie clip. The Target name is: **/picture/deer/lake**.

Go to **Deprecated**, **Actions** and double-click **tellTarget**. In the **Target** window, type **/picture/deer/lake**. Next, go to **Global Functions**, **Timeline Control** and double-click **goto**. In the **goto** settings window type **10** in the **Frame** window:

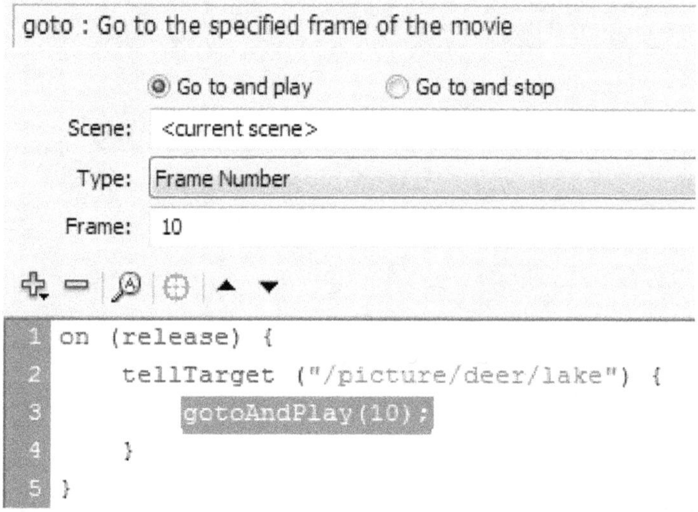

A Button **- Level 1**: The **A Button** tells the timeline of **Level 1** to go to frame **10** and play.

Go to **Deprecated**, **Actions** and double-click **tellTarget**. In the **Target** window type **_level1/.** Next, go to **Global Functions**, **Timeline Control** and double-click **goto**. In the **goto** settings window type **10** in the **Frame** window:

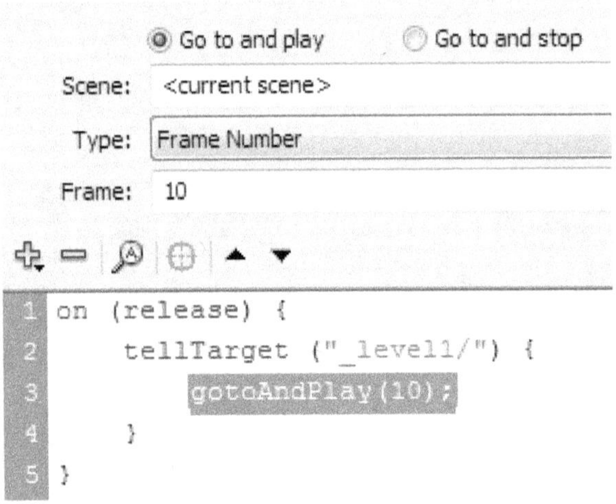

A Button - **Scene 2**: The **A Button** tells the timeline of **Scene 2** to go to the Label: **flower** and play. Since the button is on a timeline of a scene (**Scene 1**) then we don't need to use the tellTarget command.

Go to **Global Functions**, **Timeline Control** and double-click **goto**. Change **Scene** to **Scene 2**, **Type** to **Frame Label**, and type **flower** in the **Frame** window:

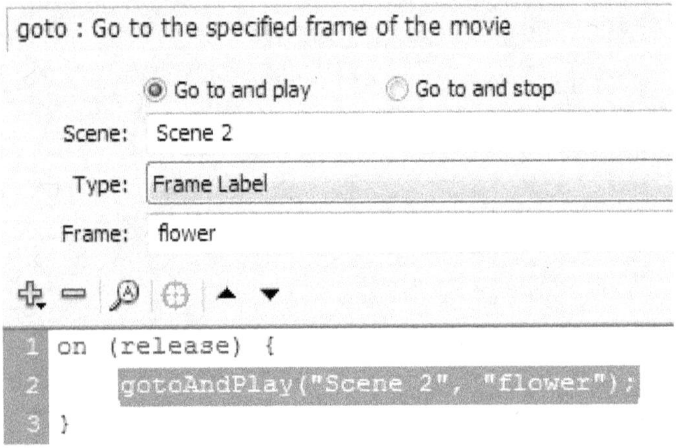

B Button - **Scene 1**: The **B Button** tells the timeline of **Scene 1** to go to frame **10** and play. Since the **B Button** isn't on this timeline we need to use the tellTarget command.

Go to **Deprecated**, **Actions** and double-click **tellTarget**. In the **Target** window type **_level0/.** Next, go to **Global Functions**, **Timeline Control** and double-click **goto**. In the **goto** settings window type **10** in the **Frame** window:

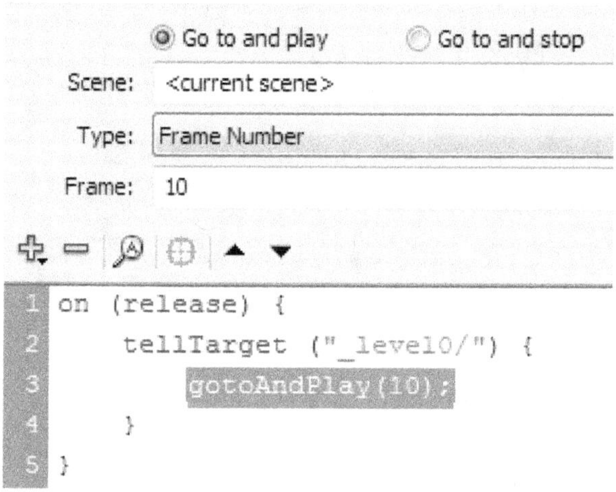

B Button - **Picture** Movie clip: The **B Button** tells the timeline of the **Picture Movie c**lip to go to frame **10** and play. Since the **B Button** is on the same timeline as this Movie clip we don't need the **tellTarget** command.

Go to **Global Functions**, **Timeline Control** and double-click **goto**. In the **goto** settings window type **10** in the **Frame** window:

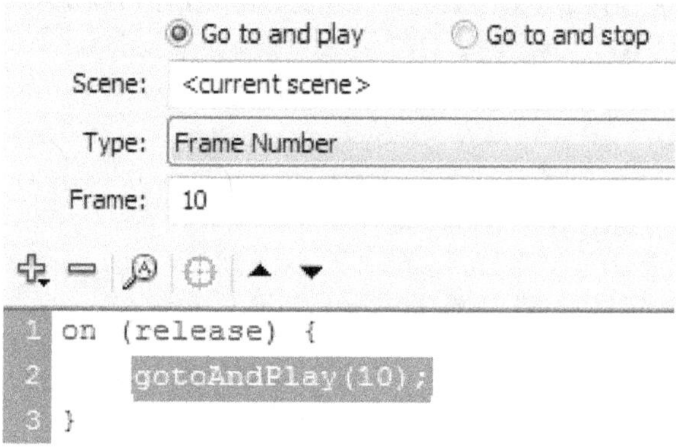

B Button **- Deer** Movie clip: The **B** Button tells the timeline of the **Deer** Movie clip to go to frame **10** and play. Since the **Deer** Movie clip is within the **Picture** Movie clip the **Target** name is: **/picture/deer**.

Go to **Deprecated**, **Actions** and double-click **tellTarget**. In the **Target** window, type **/picture/deer**. Next, go to **Global Functions**, **Timeline Control** and double-click **goto**. In the **goto** settings window type **10** in the **Frame** window:

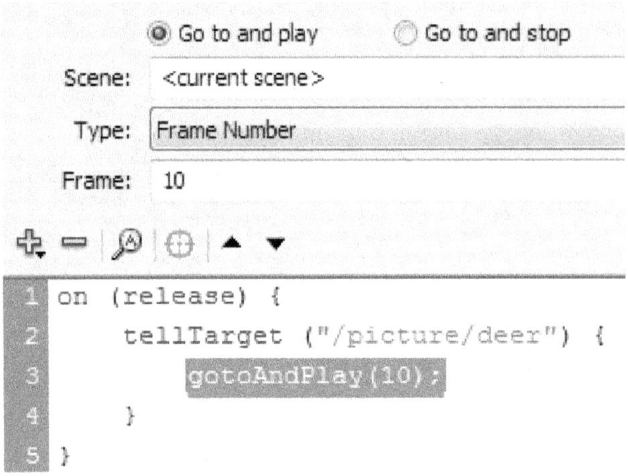

B Button - **Lake** Movie clip: The **B Button** tells the timeline of the **Lake** Movie clip to go to frame **10** and play. The **Lake** Movie clip is within the **Deer** Movie clip which is within the **Picture** Movie clip. So the **Target** name is: **/picture/deer/lake**.

Go to **Deprecated**, **Actions** and double-click **tellTarget**. In the **Target** window enter **/picture/deer/deer**. Next, go to **Global Functions**, **Timeline Control** and double-click **goto**. In the **goto** settings window type **10** in the **Frame** window:

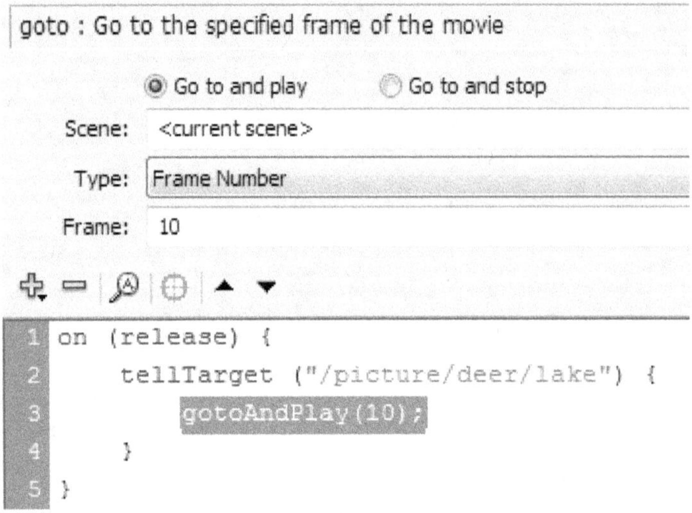

B Button - **Level 1**: The **B** Button tells the timeline of **Level 1** to go to frame **10** and play.

Go to **Deprecated**, **Actions** and double-click **tellTarget**. In the **Target** window type **_level1/.** Next, go to **Global Functions**, **Timeline Control** and double-click **goto**. In the **goto** settings window type **10** in the **Frame** window:

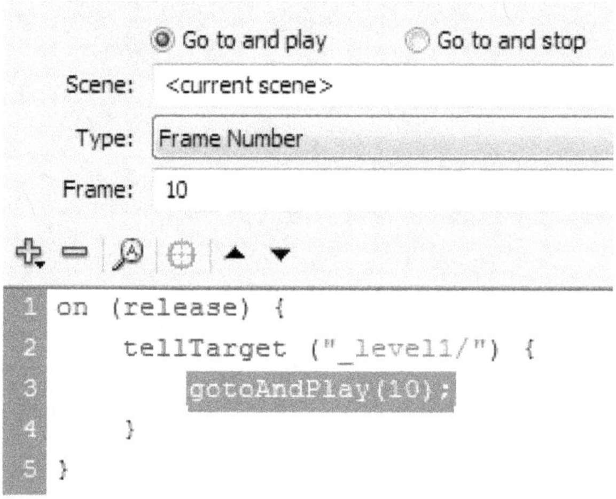

B Button - **Scene 2**: The **B** Button tells the timeline of **Scene 2** to go to the Label: **flower** and play. Since the **B** Button is in a Movie clip timeline and not a main timeline like the **A** Button, then we have to use the tellTarget command along with a Label.

Go to **Deprecated**, **Actions** and double-click **tellTarget**. In the **Target** window type **_level0/.** Next, go to **Global Functions**, **Timeline Control** and double-click **goto**. In the **goto** settings window change **Type** to **Frame Label** and type **flower** in the **Frame** window:

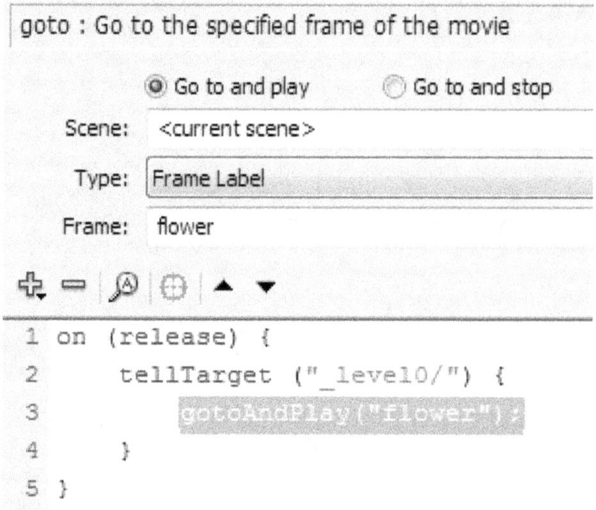

Chapter Nine: Quick Flash

Quick Banner

So you need to create a quick banner for yourself or a client and you don't have time to read this book! And let's say your client wants a nice animation with a button that links to a website. Maybe even have some text flash in. And he wants it this afternoon! Well, you can either panic or follow the step-by-step directions that follow. It's really not as hard as you might think. So let's get started!

So what size is your banner? Many banners for websites are around 468 pixels wide and 60 pixels for the height. For the purposes of this exercise we'll use the above dimensions.

Open up Flash. In the welcome screen, select **Flash File** (**ActionScript 2.0**):

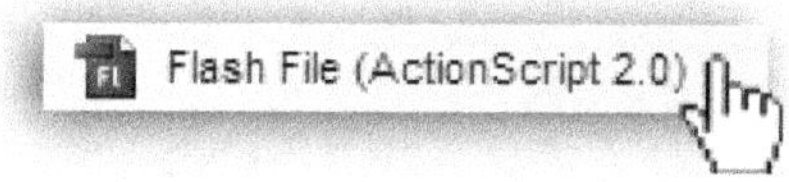

Next, we need to change the Flash Player for **CS4/CS3** users. Go to **File**, **Publish Settings**:

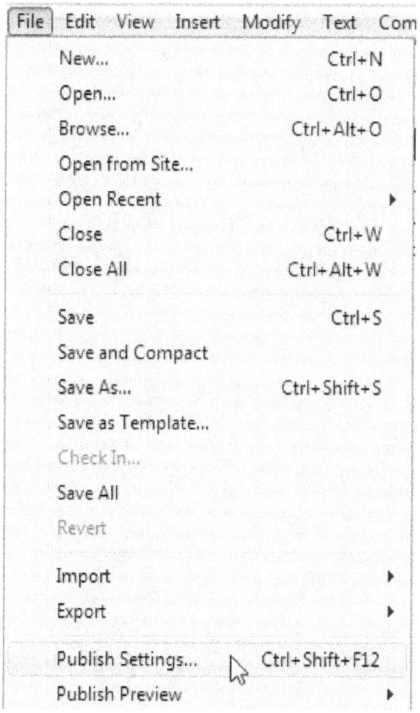

You should now see the **Publish Settings** window. Select the **Flash** tab.

In order to add ActionScript to buttons you have to make sure you are not working in Flash 10. Flash 10 uses a different approach to adding ActionScript to buttons. To change the setting click on the drop-down arrow next to **Player**; select **Flash Player 8** from the list. Next to **Script** select **ActionScript 2.0**:

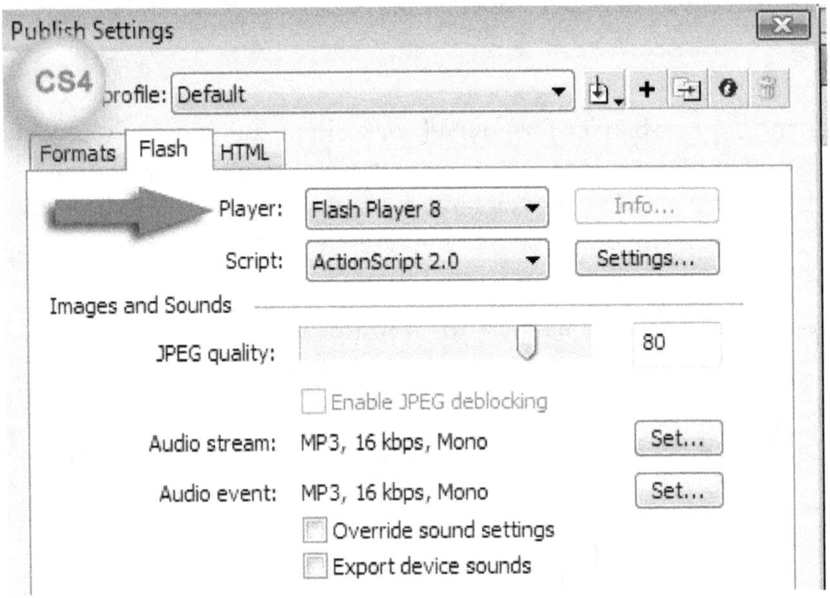

Next, we need to tell Flash what dimensions are Banner is. Go to **Modify**, **Document**:

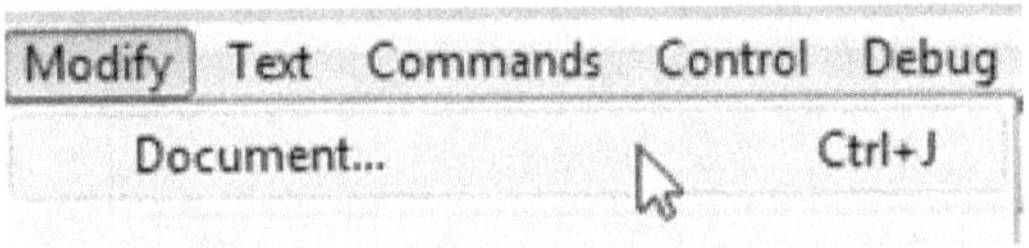

You should see a box pop up. This is the Document Properties box. Next to **Dimensions** change the width and height to **468** and **60**. Next, change the **Frame rate** to **30**:

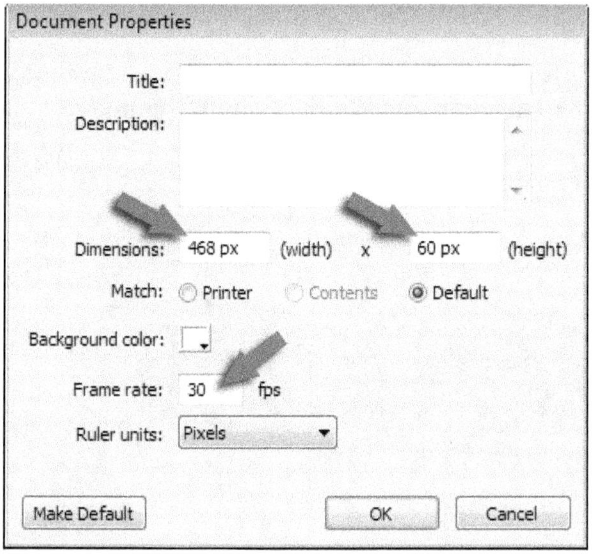

Hit the button **OK** when you are finished. This will close out the box. Your stage should now be much smaller. Most banners have some sort of picture for the background so we'll add ours now. Go to **File**, **Import**, **Import to Stage**:

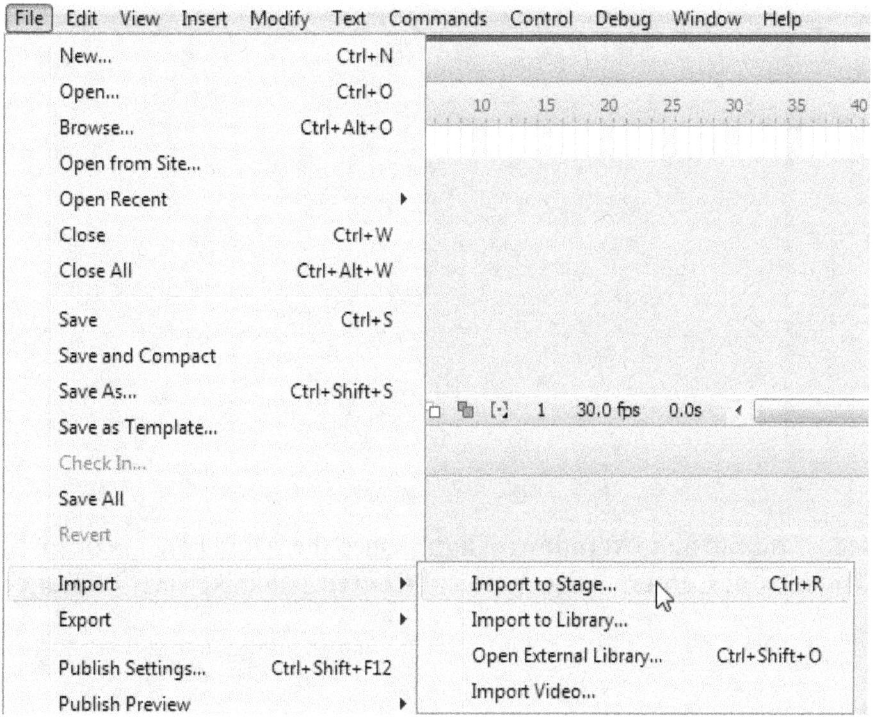

The **Import** window should now appear and you can browse your computer for whatever picture you want to use as the background. If you need a sample picture to use for this exercise, import the fishing.jpg file located in the Pictures folder within the Quick Flash folder.

Select the picture then hit **Open** in the **Import** window; the fishing.jpg image should now be on the stage:

So now we need to make sure this picture is placed perfectly within the stage. Select the fishing.jpg image and open the Align panel. It's usually located at the right of the Flash screen:

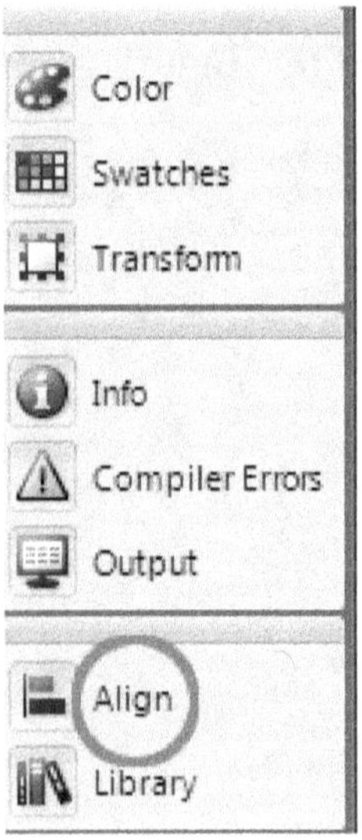

If you don't see it you can go to **Window**, **Align**. Once the Align panel is open, select **Align Horizontal Center**, **Align Vertical Center** and make sure **To stage** is pressed:

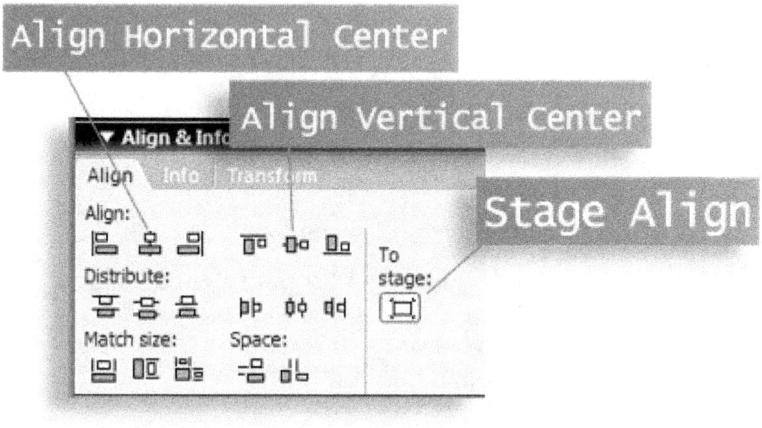

This will perfectly place the fishing.jpg image on the stage. Let's have the picture fade in. Click on frame **30** of the timeline:

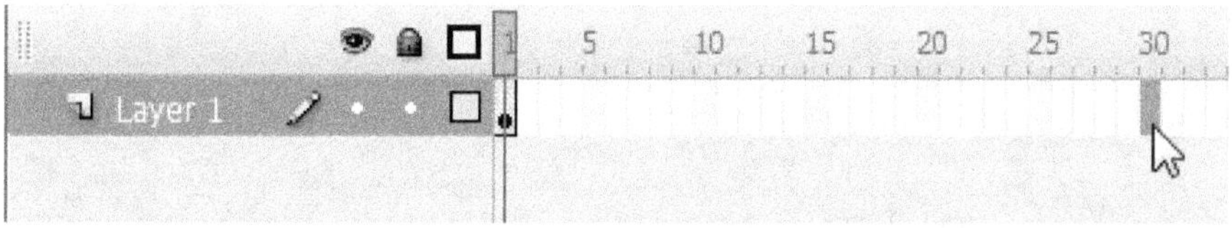

Next, go to **Insert**, **Timeline**, **Keyframe**:

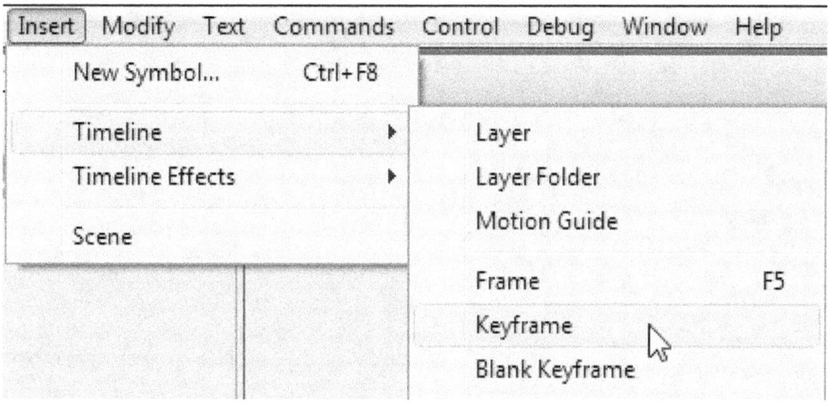

Your timeline should now have a keyframe on frame **30**:

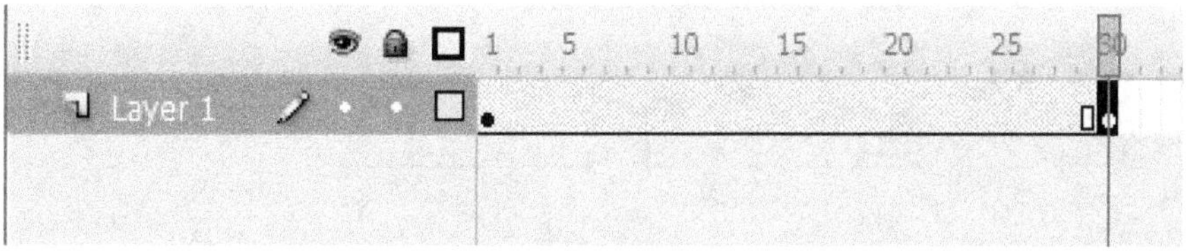

Next, select frame **15**:

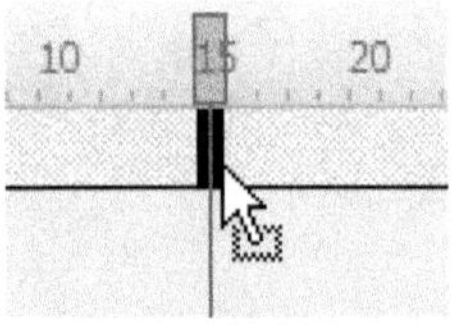

Go to **Insert**, **Timeline**, **Create Motion Tween** (**CS4** users - refer to the next instruction):

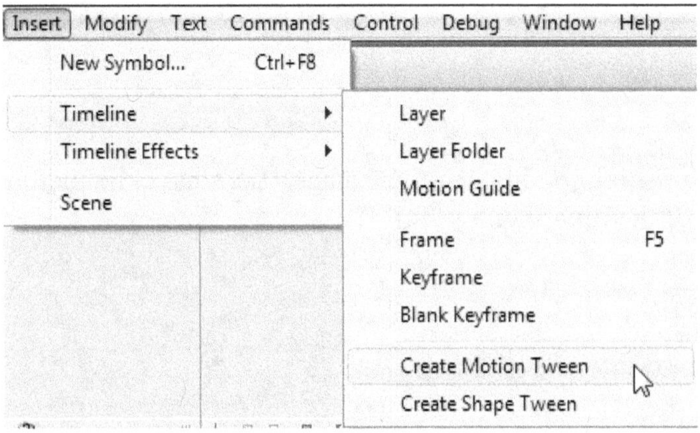

CS4 Users: Select **Classic Tween**:

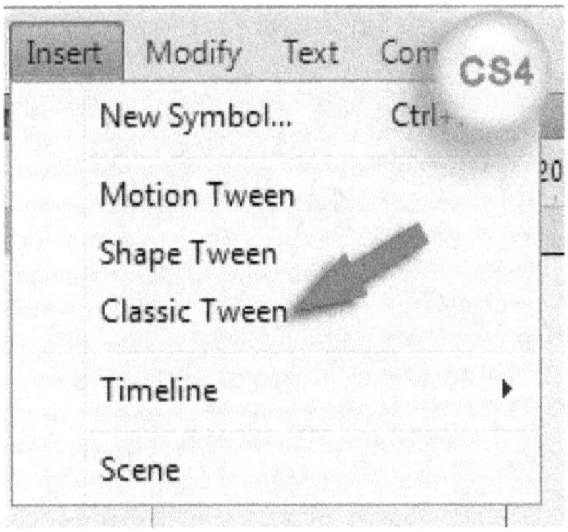

You should now have a blue line across the timeline:

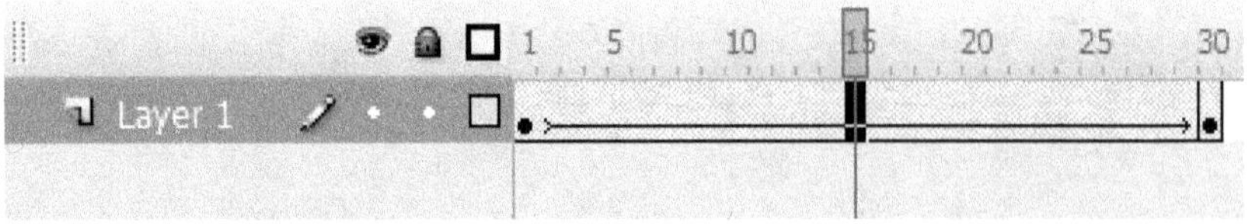

Select the first keyframe:

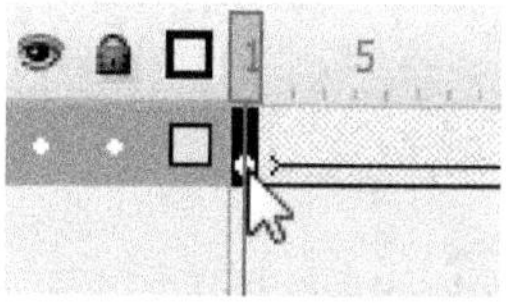

Next, select the fishing.jpg image on the stage. Open the Properties panel. It should be on the bottom of the Flash screen. In **CS4** it may be located on the right side of the screen. If you don't see the panel, go to **Window**, **Properties**, **Properties**:

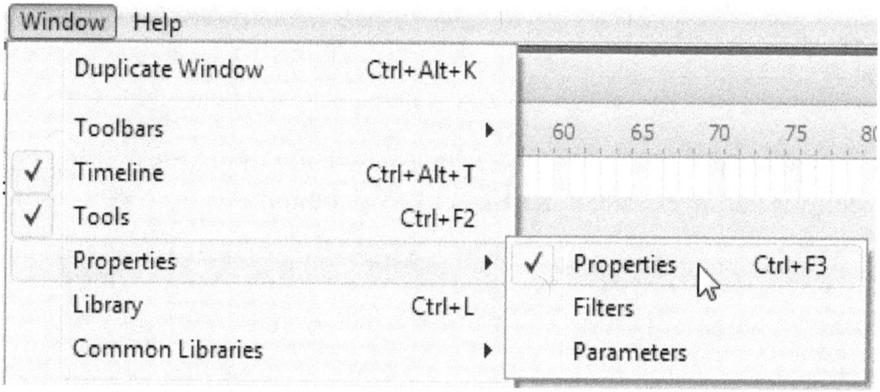

In the Properties panel you'll see a **Color** setting:

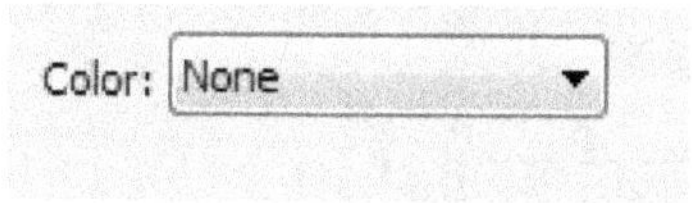

Click on the drop-down arrow next to **Color** and select **Alpha**. You'll see a percentage window appear to the right of **Alpha**. Take this percentage down to **0**:

So now your fishing.jpg image should be transparent. If you hit ENTER on your keyboard you'll see your picture slowly fade in. Let's add the text. Select the **Text Tool**:

In the Properties panel change the **Font** to **Arial**, **Size** to **16**, and select **Bold**. Choose white for the color:

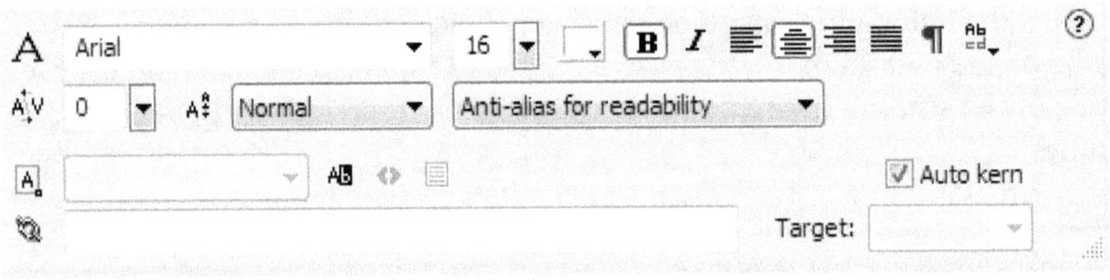

Before we start typing the text we need to create a new layer to put his text in. On the timeline, below your layer, select the **Insert Layer** button:

This will create a new layer:

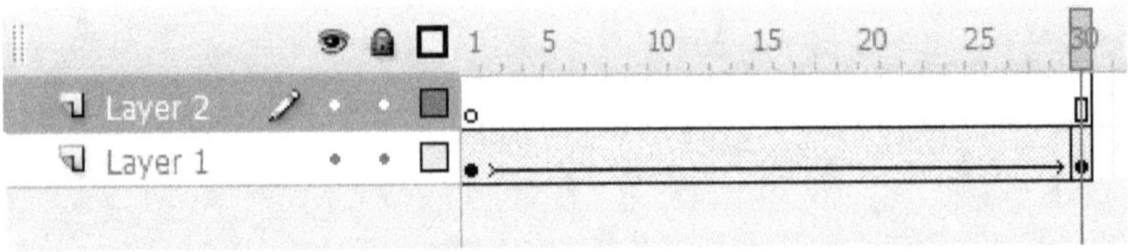

You can now type your text onto the stage. For the purposes of this exercise I'll use the text: **Sam's Fishing House**:

Select the **Selection Tool:**

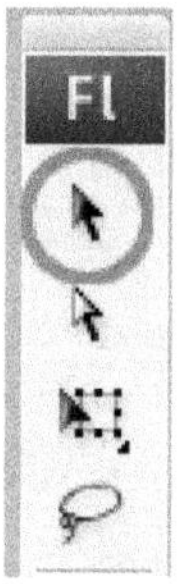

Using this tool select the Text you just created. Next, go to **Modify**, **Convert to Symbol**:

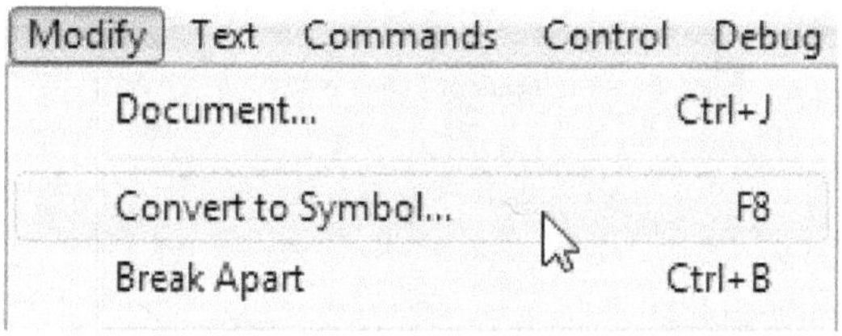

You should now see the **Convert to Symbol** box. Type in **Text** in the **Name** window and select Movie clip:

Hit **OK** when you are finished. The Text is now a Movie clip. Double-click on the Text symbol on the stage. You should now be in the Text editing stage. If you look above the stage you'll see Scene 1, which is where the picture is, and to the right of that you'll see **Text**:

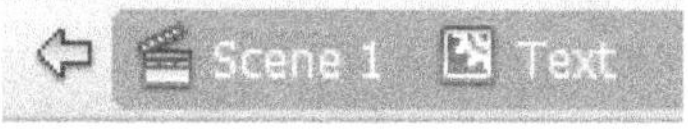

This indicated that you are now in the **Text** editing stage. Next, create a keyframe on frame **60** of the timeline:

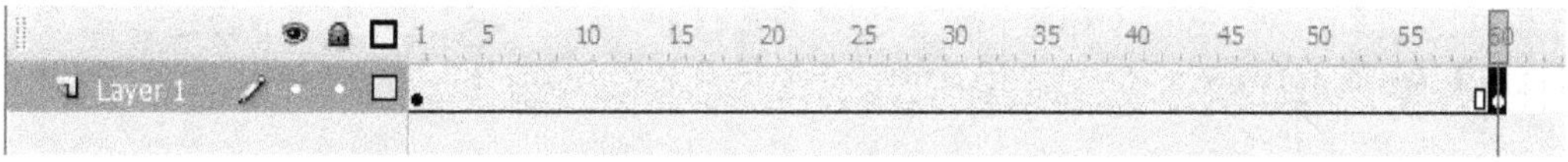

Select frame **30**:

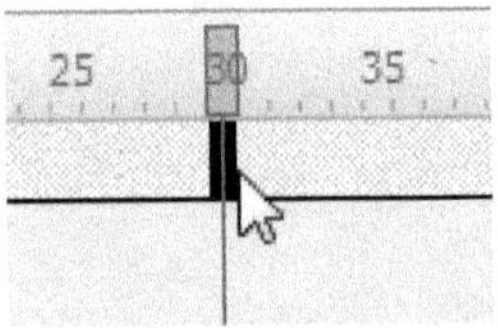

Go to **Insert**, **Timeline**, **Create Motion Tween** (**CS4** users - refer to the next instruction):

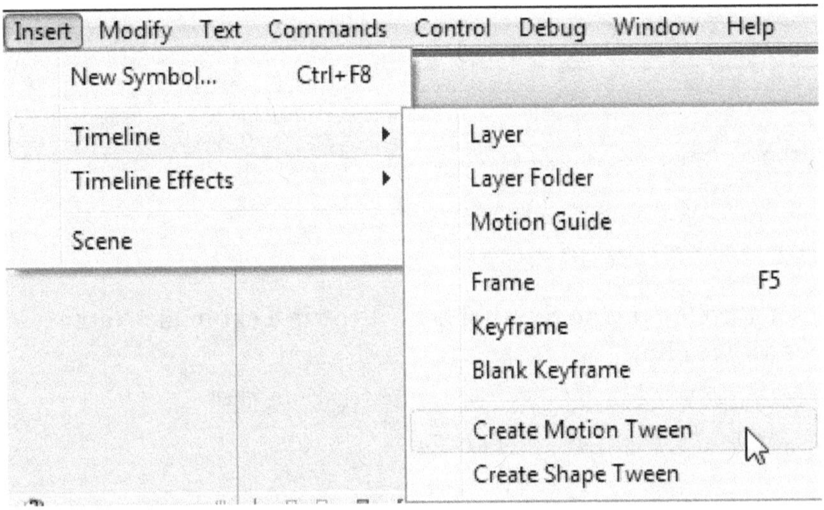

CS4 Users: Select **Classic Tween**:

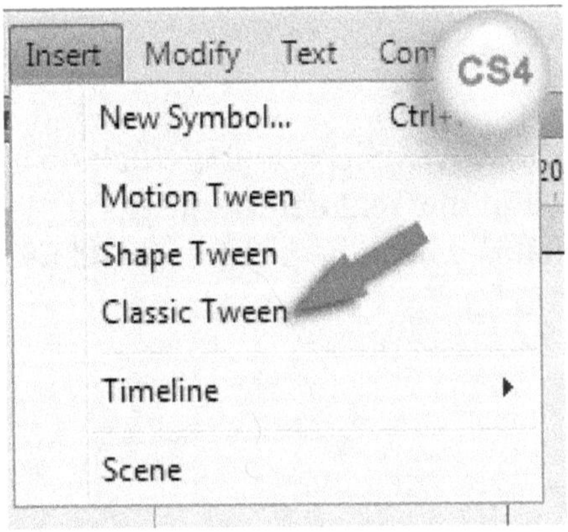

You should now see the blue line across the timeline. Next, go to **Insert**, **Timeline**, **Keyframe**:

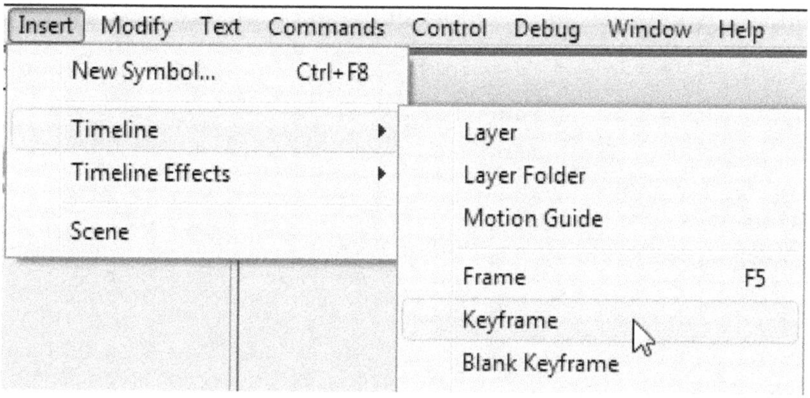

So now your timeline should look like this:

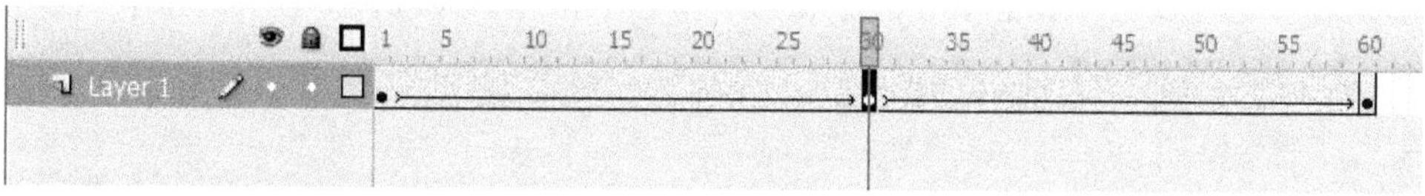

Select the Text symbol on the stage. In the Properties panel change **Color** to **Tint**. You should then see the **Color Selector**:

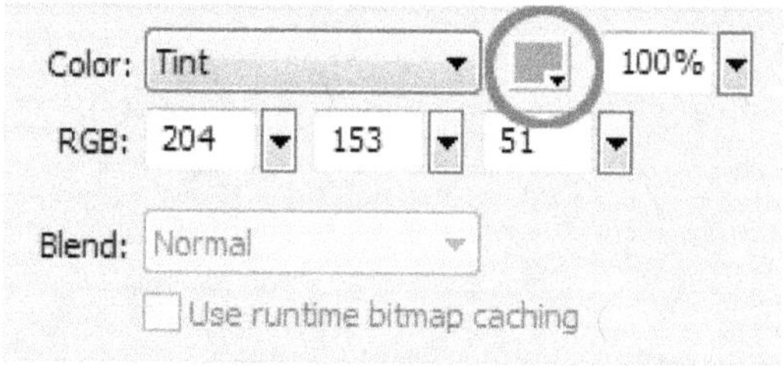

Click on the **Color Selector** and pick a color. Any color will work as long as it's different than the normal color of the Text symbol. Hit ENTER on your keyboard and you'll see the Text symbol change colors. Go back to Scene 1 by clicking on its name:

Now it's time to test the movie! Go to **Control**, **Test Movie**:

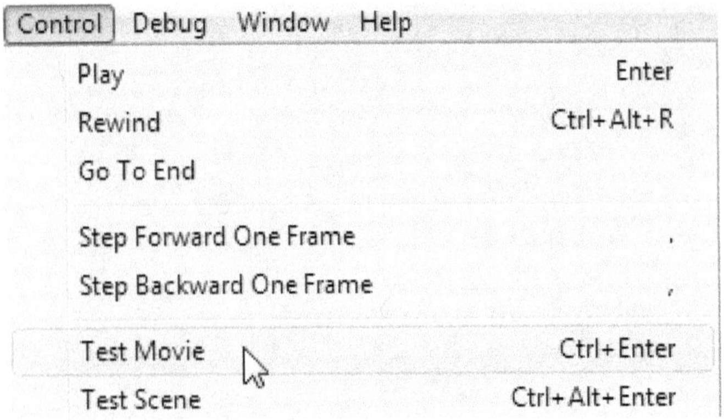

You should now see your animation in a pop-up box. It's not quite ready though, since it keeps looping. Close the pop-up box. Create a new layer by clicking on the **Insert Layer** button:

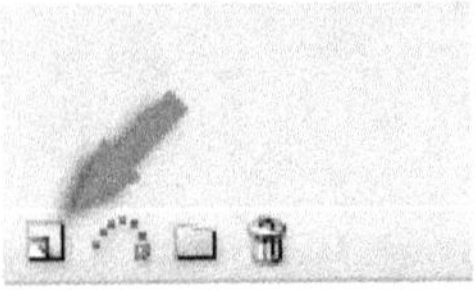

Select frame **30** of this new layer:

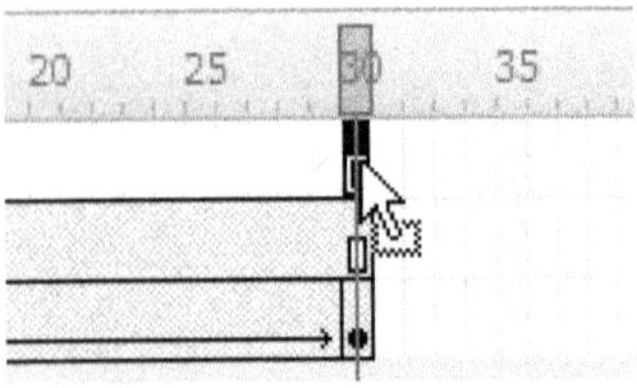

Next, we'll add a keyframe. Go to **Insert**, **Timeline**, **Keyframe**:

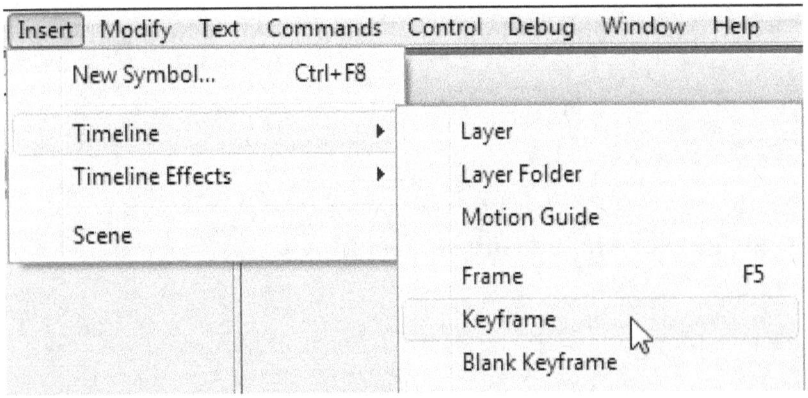

You should now have a keyframe on this frame:

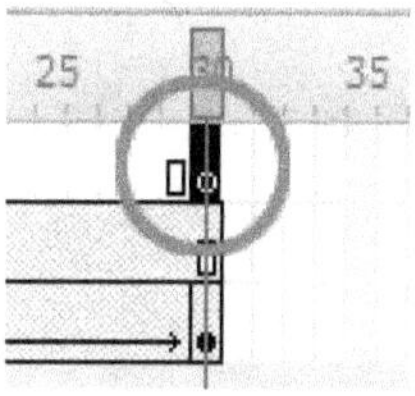

Next, open the Actions panel. If you don't see the Actions panel, go to **Window**, **Actions**. We're now going to add a **stop** code into this keyframe so the animation stops looping. In your Actions panel go to **Global Functions**, **Timeline Control** and double-click on **stop**:

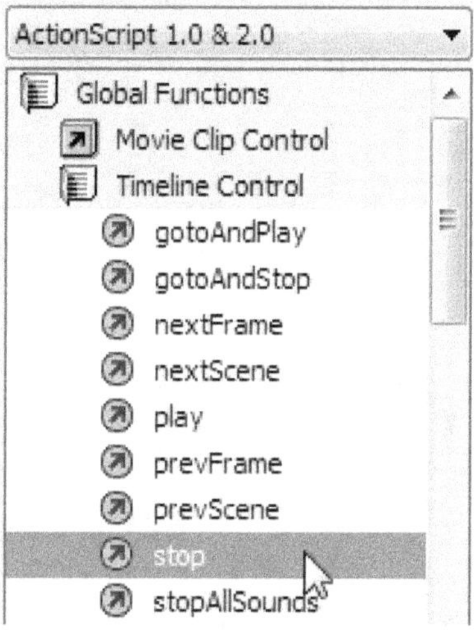

The keyframe should now have a little a letter inside of it. This means that you have code on this keyframe:

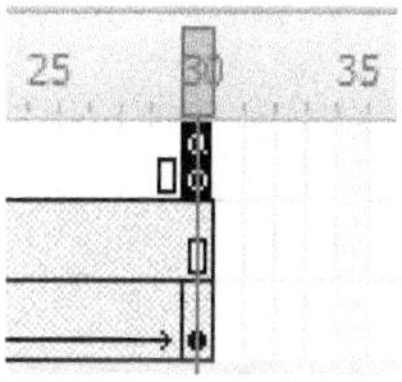

Test your movie again by going to **Control**, **Test Movie**. Your animation should play without looping. Your text animation should change colors. The last thing we'll do is add the button that will take the user to a website.

Create a new layer by clicking on the **Insert Layer** button:

Next, grab the **Rectangle Tool**:

Select the color **red** by clicking on the **Fill color**:

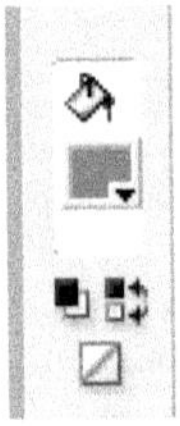

Click and drag this shape so that it covers the entire stage:

Select the **Selection Tool**:

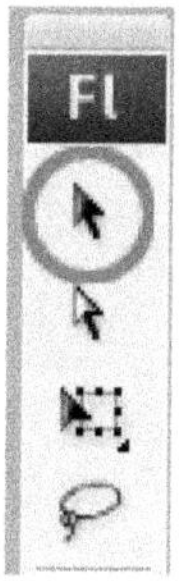

Double-click on the red shape you just created. After you select it go to **Modify**, **Convert to Symbol**. Name this new symbol **Button** and change the **Type** to **Button**:

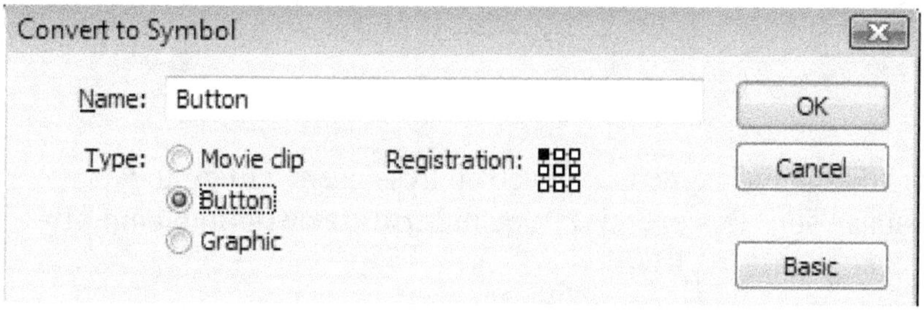

Hit **OK** when you're finished. Select this new button and open the Properties panel if it isn't already open. Change **Color** to **Alpha** and the percentage to **0**:

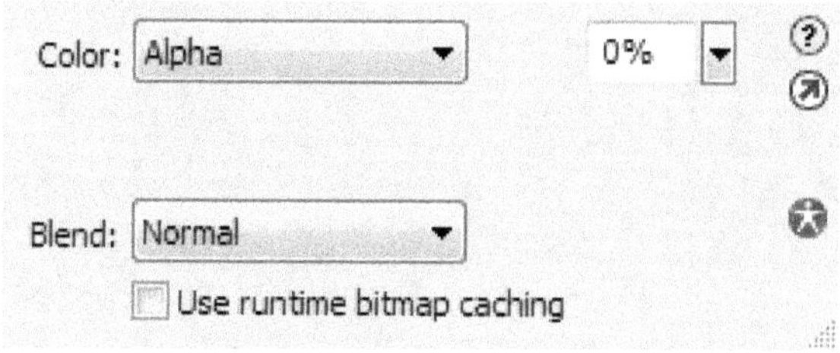

Your button should now be transparent. Next, open the Actions panel. We're going to add code which will take the user to a website. In the Actions panel we'll first turn on Script Assist:

Next, go to **Global Functions**, **Browser/Network** and double-click **getURL**:

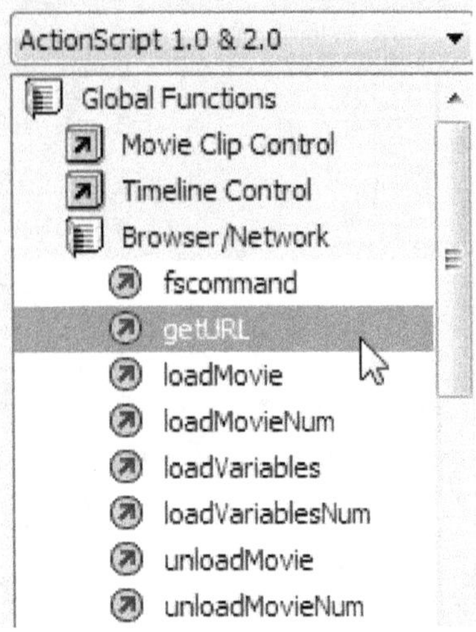

This is the window where you'll type in the web address users will go to when they click on the banner. For this exercise type in **http://www.yahoo.com**. In the **Window** field change that to **_blank**:

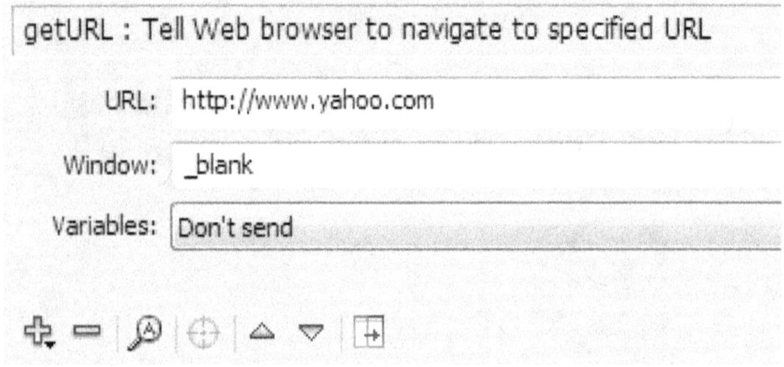

_blank means that the browser window will open in a separate window.

Test your movie by going to **Control**, **Test Movie**. Your banner should play perfectly. If you click on your banner it should bring up the yahoo home page.

The last step is saving the file. Go to **File**, **Save**:

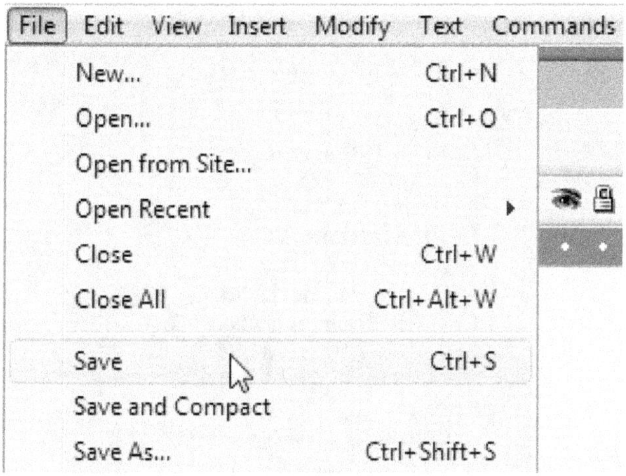

Name your project **banner** and save it in a folder. When you're finished saving, find this folder on your computer and open it. You'll find two files inside: banner.swf and banner.html. The file you'll need to upload is banner.swf.

www.ingramcontent.com/pod-product-compliance
Lightning Source LLC
LaVergne TN
LVHW062258060326
832902LV00013B/1936
* 9 7 8 1 4 5 3 7 4 5 1 3 7 *